Laëtitia HAMON

2000

didn't cover
ch.
18, 19

ENTREPRENEURSHIP
AND
SMALL BUSINESS
MANAGEMENT
Text, Readings and Cases
Third Edition

A. Bakr Ibrahim

Concordia University

Willard H. Ellis

McGill University (Ret'd)

KENDALL/HUNT PUBLISHING COMPANY
4050 Westmark Drive   Dubuque, Iowa 52002

To:
Sarah & Eva Ibrahim
Jean M. Ellis

CONTENTS

PART THREE: MANAGING GROWTH 229

CHAPTER 20   Letting Go: The Transition from Entrepreneurial to Professional Management   263

PART FOUR: THE FIELD   299

CHAPTER 21   Research Methodology   301

PART FIVE: READINGS 309

△ CHAPTER 1 △
THE ERA OF
ENTREPRENEURSHIP

INTRODUCTION

The small business sector is the fastest growing segment of the North American economy and is emerging as a strategic sector. Approximately 97 percent of all businesses in the United States and Canada are categorized as "small." Indeed, small businesses play a crucial role in both the stability and the health of the national economy in terms of employment, taxes, global competition and support to their local communities. As a group, small businesses employ nearly 60 percent of the work force and produce 45 percent of the gross national product and approximately two thirds of the new jobs. In addition, recent trends in the new economy have helped to spark the belief that small business will play a dominant role in the national economy. These trends include the move toward knowledge based economy, the sectoral shift from manufacturing to services, the growing trend towards home based businesses, globalization as a result of international trade agreements such as the GATT, NAFTA and FTA, and the emergence of the niche marketing concept. Further, massive layoffs, down-sizing, restructuring and outsourcing in large organizations have shaken people's confidence in "big" business and have helped spur interest in small business and entrepreneurship.

SMALL BUSINESS DEFINED

There is no generally accepted definition of a small business. From the literature, the criteria that delineate a small business include size, number of employees, sales volume, type of customers, assets and capital requirement.

The U.S. was the first country to define a small business in 1948, through the Selective Service Act. According to the definition contained in this legislation, an enterprise is "small" if three specific criteria are met. First, the business's position in the industry is not dominant. Second, the business employs fewer than 500 people. Third, the business is independently owned and operated.

This chapter is based on published work by Professor A. B. Ibrahim.

In Canada, the legal definition drawn by the government followed the U.S. criteria. However, in most Canadian government organizations, the U.S. definition has been modified to qualify a small business as having fewer than 100 employees. The province of Quebec uses 200 employees or less in its definition of a small business. Industry Canada defines small businesses according to their size. Thus any firm with fewer than 100 paid employees in the manufacturing sector and fewer than 50 paid employees in all other sectors, is considered small. In certain cases having annual revenues of less than $5 million is taken into account in defining small business.

THE CHANGING ENVIRONMENT: THE NEW ECONOMY

This century has witnessed a number of strategic changes in the business environment. Each strategic change has its own characteristics, dominant industries and driving forces as shown in Figure 1.1. In the early part of this century, the resource endowment era, the business environment was dominated by industries such as the mining, ship building, railroad and textile industries. These industries relied on endowment resources such as coal, wood products and cotton. Successful entrepreneurs and captains of industry were those who were able to follow economic indicators, such as production and consumption levels, and secure coal for railroads and textile and steel mills. By the middle of the twentieth century, these industries were dying and they were replaced by industries such as the automobile, oil and machining industries. Today we are witnessing the dramatic change from a manufacturing economy to a technology driven economy. The dominant industries—the computer, telecommunications and biomedical industries—are knowledge-based. Micro-chips have replaced coal and oil. Knowledge and highly skilled workers have replaced equipment and assembly line workers.[1] These changes have had a profound impact on the business environment and in particular on the growth of entrepreneurial activities.

Indeed, technology entrepreneurs hold the key to the commercial future of knowledge based industries in the new economy. In the explosive world of the computer, telecommunications and biotechnology industries, small niche firms, many of which are still in an embryonic stage, may well shape these industries. Joseph Shumpeter coined the term "creative destruction" to describe the process by which small firms force large firms to respond to innovation and changing technology. Steven Jobs, founder of Apple Computer, literally changed the computer industry by introducing the personal computer, or PC, from his garage, forcing the giant IBM corporation to change its strategy in response to the changing environment.

In the new economy, small businesses have claimed a more substantial share of innovations than larger firms for several reasons. First, they are more flexible and can adapt rapidly and with less cost to technological changes in the new economy. Second, they are more likely to attract innovators and act as incubators than large firms. Small businesses have always attracted entrepreneurs who are excited by their innovation and the opportunity to make a significant impact on a growing venture and industry.

	The Resource Endowment Era	The Industrial Era	The Knowledge-Based Era
Dominant Industries	Mining, ship building, textiles and steel	Automobile, machining and oil	Computers, telecommunications, bio-medical and service
Characteristics			
Business Cycle	Long	Medium-long	Short
Key Assets	Hard assets: mills and shipyards	Hard assets: equipment	Knowledge and knowledge workers
Degree of Flexibility	Low	Low	High
Driving Technology	Coal Railroads and ships	Oil Mass production Telegram and telephone	Micro-chips Knowledge Satellites, fiber-optics and microwave
Style	Autocratic	Bureaucratic	Entrepreneurial
Degree of Innovation	Low	Low	High
Size	Large	Large	Small independent business units

Figure 1.1. The Changing Business Environment.

The Fallacy of Large Organization

For years, national economic policies in general, and regional development policies in particular, have focused on large businesses. Universities were no exception, reflecting a traditional view that large businesses hold the key to economic growth. This view is based on the notion that these businesses, through mass production, can achieve economies of scale, a key competitive advantage. However, in today's knowledge-based economy, with flexible manufacturing and management techniques and the tumbling cost of computing, economies of scale can be realized by ever-smaller businesses.

The Emergence of the Strategic Alliance Concept

The new technology driven economy is characterized by rapid technological change and customer demand for variety, quality, customization and convenience. These changes have forced many large companies to downsize and form strategic alliances with small firms. The size and flat structure of small firms offers the flexibility to adapt quickly to changes in the macro-environment. As a result, big businesses have been outsourcing services or the production of parts to small businesses. In many cases, large businesses have helped to provide not only the markets for small businesses, but also the start-up financing. For example, the big three automobile manufacturers funded a number of small businesses in the

Windsor/Detroit area. Now these big automobile makers concentrate their business on auto design and assembly, leaving the intermediate steps to subcontractors, who are typically small businesses.[2]

The Shift from Manufacturing to Services

A major trend that has been emerging is the shift from the manufacturing sector to the service sector. This trend is having a profound impact on small business. The service sector tends to be dominated by small firms for several reasons. First, service based industries require very little capital, inventory or fixed assets, and thus offer many opportunities to small firms. Second, the new technology driven economy has made it possible for many entrepreneurs to pursue opportunities in this sector. Advances in information technology, such as the Internet, allow today's entrepreneur to have access to valuable information about the market, the competition, the industry as well as general economic and social trends.

The Emerging Trend Toward Home-Based Businesses

Recent studies have revealed a growing trend toward home-based businesses in North America.[3] The emergence of this cocooning trend is attributed to several factors. First, advances in computer and telecommunications technology have made it possible for many entrepreneurs to operate their businesses from their homes. Second, massive layoffs in large companies as a result of downsizing have forced many talented professionals to start their own businesses armed with experience, skills and a reasonable amount of capital. Third, many large companies are now encouraging their employees to work at home. Fourth, the trend to combine career and family is enhanced by the flexibility inherent in a home-based business. Finally, the overhead costs of operating a business from home are low. The trend toward home-based business has been a major factor in the upsurge of self-employment and entrepreneurship.[3]

The Move Toward the Global Economy Globalization

International trade continues to grow at a phenomenal rate as a result of advances in information technologies such as the Internet, and trade agreements such as the GATT, NAFTA and FTA. We are becoming a global village with no distinction between local and foreign markets. The globalization of trade has created many opportunities for small businesses and offered entrepreneurs access to a large market.

The Concept of Niche Marketing

With globalization and increased competition, the concept of niche marketing is emerging as a critical ingredient in a successful business. Exploiting gaps and small niches and responding rapidly to windows of opportunity can only be achieved by small businesses.

The Trend Toward Clustering

The trend among many small firms to cluster in protective group-enclaves may have a profound effect on the growth of the small business sector. The ability of small firms to form a cluster allows them to achieve a critical mass and bargaining power similar to those achieved by large firms. The clustering phenomenon has been observed in high tech industries such as the Silicon Valley and New England in the U.S., and the Kitchener-Waterloo, Ottawa and Montreal regions in Canada.

The Trend Toward Virtual Corporations

Advances in information technology have been the driving force for a new form of company—the virtual corporation. In this form of organization there are no offices, managers, employees or hierarchies. The entrepreneur working from a small office in his or her home forms temporary strategic alliances with other entrepreneurs through computer communications to exploit an opportunity in the market place.

SUMMARY

In the new economy a number of major trends are emerging that will have a profound effect on the growth of the small business sector in particular and entrepreneurial activities in general. These trends include the move toward the knowledge based economy, the sectoral shift from manufacturing to services, the growing trend toward home-based business, globalization and the emergence of the niche-market concept. Further, massive layoffs and downsizing in large companies and their move toward outsourcing some of their activities to entrepreneurs and small firms indicate that this decade is the era of entrepreneurship.

NOTES

1. See for example: N. Beck, "Shifting Gears: Thriving in the New Economy," Toronto: HarperCollins Publishing, 1992; A. P. Carnevale, "America and the New Economy: How New Competitive Standards are Radically Changing the American Work Place," San Francisco: Jossey-Bass Publishers, 1991.
2. A. Morgan, "Small Business, Canada's Strategic Sector for the 1990s," *Canadian Business Review,* Spring 1994, p. 14.
3. *Home Enterprise—Canadian and Home-Based Work,* Toronto: Barbary Orser and Mary Foster, February 1992.

THE ENTREPRENEUR

Bill Gates
The Master Entrepreneur

Bill Gates, founder of Microsoft—one of the most valued companies in the U.S.—has been described as a master entrepreneur. He began working with computers in seventh grade and earned money designing schedule software for his school. At age 14 he formed a company with Paul Allen and made a profit. Later, he worked briefly as a programmer at TRW and enrolled at Harvard. However, Allen persuaded Gates to work with him again, and they both moved to Albuquerque and formed Microsoft. In 1975 Bill Gates's vision was to develop an inexpensive software that would be used by every personal computer user. Sales and profits of Microsoft soared, and in 1986 the company went public. The company was described by *Business Week* magazine as one of the most valuable companies in the U.S.

Source: *Business Week*, November 1989; June 1990; Also see: K. Vesper, *New Venture Strategies*, Prentice Hall, 1990, Revised Edition.

△ CHAPTER 2 △
THE SUCCESSFUL ENTREPRENEUR

Each year, thousands of new businesses start in the United States and Canada. The fate of these ventures is highly variable and in general is a chronology of the economic growth. Some of these small firms have evolved into corporate giants, others have failed. It is estimated that approximately 80 percent of all start-ups fail within the first five years of operation. What does it take to succeed in venture creation? What are the characteristics of successful entrepreneurs? This chapter is devoted to exploring the critical success factors as well as causes of small business failures. Subsequent chapters will deal with these factors in more depth.

Studies have shown that entrepreneurial behavior and management skills and competence are key ingredients in operating a successful small business. Entrepreneurial behavior includes those psychological characteristics and behavioral traits associated with successful ventures. Management skills and competence include critical business skills necessary to operate a business effectively. Let us explore these two critical factors.

THE ENTREPRENEURIAL FACTOR

One of the first truly objective studies that examined the characteristics of successful entrepreneurs was conducted by John Hornaday and John Aboud, and was published in Personal Psychology in 1971. The study added much to the then popular view that entrepreneurs are driven purely by a need for achievement, and pointed to a need for a psychological profile of successful entrepreneurs, if only to give investors some tool for gauging the likely success for an enterprise. Objectivity, from the authors' point of view, is important for two reasons. In the first instance, it allows researchers, other than highly trained psychologists, to administer the test; in the second, it permits factors other than the achievement need (n. Ach) to be identified as success components. The authors employed three methods of measurement that met their needs: The Kuder Occupational Interest Survey (OIS), Gordon's Survey of Interpersonal Values (SIV), and an adaptation of Edward's Personal Preference Scale (EPP's). The target was a group of forty entrepreneurs who met Hornaday and Aboud's criteria for success: the subjects had started an enterprise

---

Box 2.1. Successful Entrepreneurs.

1. Male entrepreneurs do indeed show a greater need for achievement, independence and effectiveness in leadership when compared with the male population as a whole.
2. The educational and occupational interests of entrepreneurs do tend to lead them into their businesses. However, while all entrepreneurs showed above average scholastic perform-ance, significant differences between black and white respondents were evident. Fewer blacks (32%) had graduated from college, for example, against whites (82%). The interests of blacks proved to be more broadly based and diffused than whites, who showed a greater degree of specialization. Whites were generally to be found in roles that required higher educational levels: manufacturing, for instance, which places a premium on technical education. Whether or not these results reflect disparate educational opportunities open to blacks at the time, or poorer economic standing (the proportion of blacks who financed their own education was nearly double that of whites) is acknowledged as an issue by the authors.
3. The question of family background is not explicitly considered by the authors in their discussion of results. They note, however, that divorce and separation rates for the entre-preneurs is lower than that of the general population (16% vs. 33%). In this regard there were once again differences between white and black: 6% of whites had separated compared with 32% of blacks. The authors attribute this to cultural differences, although no meaningful comparative data were presented for separation/divorce rates on the basis of race, or (a more likely explanation perhaps) on the basis of economic and educational standing.
4. Entrepreneurs saw themselves much as the observers did, with a higher than average need for achievement, competitiveness, confidence and innovation. Hornaday and Aboud dismiss these results as "so highly subjective that they are of little value," and suggest that the test be administered to a standardized group for comparison.
5. Apart from those differences between white and black respondents recorded above, the authors found no significant disparities between the two groups. Both pointed to a need for hard work, perseverance and a facility for managing people as ingredients in their success.

 Hornaday and Aboud are careful to point out that although the testing methods that they have used have the virtue of being easy to administer by comparatively inexperienced technicians (in comparison with tests used by earlier researchers), and the results are an objective measure of entrepreneurship, they are not a reliable predictor of entrepreneurial success, as no attempt was made to sample entrepreneurs who had failed in their endeavours. This, and much further investigation, is left to others.

Source: John Hornaday and John Aboud, "Characteristics of Successful Entrepreneurs," *Personnel Psychology* 24, 1971, pp. 141–153.

---

from scratch, employed a minimum of eight persons and had operated the business for at least five years. The authors' definition excluded management buy-outs, franchise opera-tors and turnarounds, all of which make up a very significant proportion of entrepreneurial activity today. Box 2.1 summarizes some of the study findings.

 To explore further the question of whether there are unique and measurable behavioral traits that separate successful entrepreneurs from average entrepreneurs let us turn to David McClelland's work. Professor McClelland studied two samples of entrepreneurs, classified as "successful" and as "average" business people, in a number of countries. He found nine traits that distinguish a "successful" entrepreneur from an "average" entrepreneur. The findings can be grouped in the following three broad categories:

1. "Pro-active traits." Successful entrepreneurs are pro-active. They address problems before they occur and take action.
2. "Achievement orientation." Successful entrepreneurs ensure that their work and their employees' work is of the highest quality. They also ensure that they use feedback to improve the quality of their work at all times. They seize opportunity when and where it is found.
3. "Commitment to others." Successful entrepreneurs are extremely concerned with customer needs and wants. They try hard to build solid customer relationships.

Interestingly, McClelland also tested whether external variables such as parents' occupation, and education are more important in predicting entrepreneurs' success than personality traits. Surprisingly McClelland found that these external variables and an entrepreneur's success are not correlated. The entrepreneur succeeded because of internal competencies.[1]

Recent research indicates that entrepreneurial traits such as high need for achievement, moderate risk taking, innovation, locus of control and independence are associated with successful entrepreneurs.[2] Indeed, according to Charles Hofer and William Sandberg, successful entrepreneurs exhibit particular traits. They are perceptive, disciplined observers of their environment who rarely fall victim to self delusion and usually learn from their own experience. They feel compelled to act on their observations, usually with an urgency born of a need for achievement or control. Lastly, they are adept at provoking empathy and inducing others to follow them.[3]

MANAGEMENT SKILLS AND COMPETENCE

The second critical success factor can be grouped under management skills and competence. These skills and competencies include management of cash flow, systematic accounting and record keeping systems, niche strategy, strategic planning, networking, delegation and marketing skills (see Figure 2.1). Studies have shown that lack of these skills and competencies result in business failure. Let us discuss each of these factors briefly. Later chapters will explore these critical factors in more depth.

Management of Cash Flow

Effective management of cash flow is crucial to the entrepreneur's success. Indeed, profits do not guarantee a healthy cash flow situation especially if the firm is growing rapidly without prior financial planning.

Financial planning is critical in all stages of the operation but more important in the infancy and rapid growth stages. In the infancy stage, the firm is usually struggling to establish a name for itself and *attempting* to get a favorable line of credit from suppliers

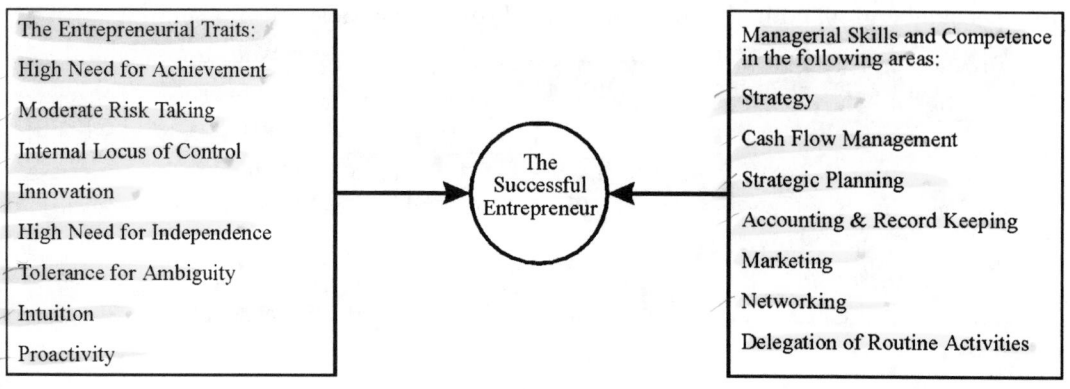

Figure 2.1. The successful entrepreneur.

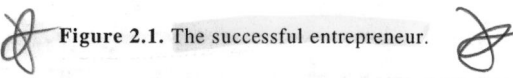

who have no prior dealing with the firm. In the meantime, it has to extend credit to its customers to carve a market niche and to establish good customer relations. In the growth stage, the firm is struggling to maintain a proper balance between the funds generated and business growth. Efficient management of accounts payable and receivable allows the firm to operate during difficult stages with little operating capital. If a proper balance is maintained between payment (90-day) and collection (30-day), the small firm can finance its needs of working capital internally.[4]

Monitoring the Inventory Level

Monitoring the inventory level is crucial to the effective management of the new venture. Inventory level affects operation, scheduling, manufacturing cost and the overall profit picture of the firm. Maintaining a level of inventory higher or lower than needed may result in higher manufacturing cost, deterioration of stored materials and/or loss of customers and credibility. Designing a proper inventory policy requires knowledge of the market (peak periods), suppliers' dependability and the cost system.

Networking

The ability to build and maintain a network of contacts is critical to the entrepreneur's success. Networking is a process that may take years before the entrepreneur can reap its benefits. Two types of contacts form the entrepreneur's network. The first is the formal type such as those contacts established with bankers, Provincial and Federal government officials, legal and financial experts. The second type is the informal type of contacts such as family members, colleagues and friends. Both types are important in providing the entrepreneur with a pool of information and advice.[5]

Strategic Planning

An effective but simple strategic planning system is crucial to successful entrepreneurs. A strategic planning system helps the firm identify its objectives, mission, assess its internal capacity and its external environment. Internal assessment of the strengths and weaknesses and external evaluation of windows of opportunity as well as constraints give an indication of the firm's real capacity to carry out the intended mission successfully, and may suggest a more attractive and less competitive niche. Studies of successful ventures have shown that the strategic planning process should be simple and inexpensive, and focus on short and medium range planning. Box 2.2 examines the perceptual difference between loan officers and small business owners.

Box 2.2. Perception of Success.

In a study of perception of entrepreneurial success characteristics, Montagne, Kuratko and Scarcella examined the differences between loan officers and small business owners on their perception of success. Loan officers were found to perceive successful entrepreneurs in terms of managerial objectives such as goal setting, planning, organizing and problem analysis, while owners perceive success in terms of traits such as confidence, initiative, innovation, caring and encouragement.

Source: R. V. Montagne, D. F. Kuratko and J. H. Scarcella, "Perception of Entrepreneurial Success Characteristics," *American Journal of Small Business,* Winter 1986, pp. 25–32.

Strategy—Carving a Niche

Perhaps the most critical success factor in business is the formulation of an appropriate strategy. Earlier studies have shown that carving a niche is the most effective type of strategy for small business. The entrepreneur must tailor the firm's product or service to meet a specific customer. The niche need not necessarily emphasize high quality. To understand the essence of strategy in small business let us discuss briefly two essential concepts: distinctive competence and industry structure.

Distinctive Competence

In a highly competitive business environment only those firms that have established distinctive competence will succeed. Distinctive competence refers to the unique skills, activities and operation that the businesses have, compared with rivals. Distinct competence in a specific area such as product, cost efficiency, marketing and management skills allows the firm to build a competitive advantage.

Industry Structure

Industry structure and attractiveness dictate the type of strategy the venture should pursue. Industry structure can be described in terms of the following:

1. stages of industry growth be it aggressive growth, maturity or decline
2. types of competition (fragmented, competitive, oligopoly)
3. industry concepts, such as entry/exit barriers, economy of scale and capital investment.

Charles Hofer and William Sandberg examined critical success factors in new ventures. They concluded that industry structure, business strategy and behavioral characteristics of the founder (in that order), are the principal determinants of success.[6]

Record Keeping System

A large percentage of small business failure has been attributed to the lack of a proper record keeping system. Indeed systematic recording of business transactions is the prime factor in any decision making process. Basically an efficient record keeping system provides management with two types of information on past and present performance. The first type is accounting information such as sales volume, inventory turnover, accounts receivable, bad debts, overhead cost, long and short term debts and the overall profitability and financial picture of the business. The second type is general information such as employees' record and performance, information about the firm's suppliers and customers, contacts and legal information related to partnership agreement, franchising agreements, and federal, provincial and municipal regulations of importance to the operation of the business.

Accounting Skills

A systematic record keeping system is of little use unless the entrepreneur has a good knowledge and understanding of accounting and finance techniques. Studies have shown that accounting skill is critical to small business success. Accounting techniques such as break-even analysis, depreciation and inventory methods, ratio analysis, cash flow projection, and sensitivity analysis are crucial to the small firm. Let us take for example two major decisions. The first is the decision to price the product or service. Here the entrepreneur or manager has to have a basic understanding of the manufacturing cost, variable or fixed, contribution margin, overhead cost, break-even level and the safety margin. He or she will then be able to set the price competitively in light of other internal and external factors.

The second decision is to determine the economic viability of an opportunity. Here again the entrepreneur or manager is expected to have a thorough knowledge of accounting techniques such as ratio analysis to determine the expected rate of return on investment (ROI) or on equity (ROE). Cash flow projection will also give an indication to when the business opportunity is expected to achieve a positive cash flow and thus, decide on the appropriate financing vehicle (short term/long term). A business opportunity that will be able to generate a positive cash flow in 3 or 4 months, for example, does not need long term financing. The entrepreneur may also employ sensitivity analysis techniques in his or her evaluation of the economic viability of the opportunity. Sensitivity analysis provides the entrepreneur or manager with different scenarios, best guess, worst and possible scenarios and thus the ability to make a proper decision. Box 2.3 examines the application of some of these accounting techniques in small business.

Box 2.3.

Why do once prosperous small companies suddenly seem to come upon hard times? Herbert N. Woodward, in his article, applies the lessons he has learned from reviving ailing firms to explore the reasons that seemingly sudden problems can develop in small businesses. His analysis is intended to help entrepreneurs improve their management skills and to steer clear of major problems before they occur.

The author's first argument is that growth in sales is seen as the cure-all solution. Accounting methods seem to associate profitability with sales volume.

The first accounting practice that the author considers is Marginal Income Accounting. Managers believe that they can add extra sales to normal sales levels for a short time period even when the new product prices do not cover a suitable percentage of fixed cost. Because new business is responsible for fixed cost just as the old one, managers must therefore develop a pricing strategy that covers all overhead costs. The next accounting practice that leads managers to make errors in judgement is break-even analysis. Entrepreneurs and small business managers believe that total cost is a static figure and that the small firm must have a larger sales volume to cover this figure. The author argues that with the exception of early stage, very little fixed costs are incurred by the small firm.

The author then turns his attention to problems of poor cost analysis. For example, he points to the fact that new product lines incur more overhead because of extra start-up costs than older product lines, yet usually the same proportionate amounts of overhead are charged to each line. The result is that managers are not fully aware of which product lines are most profitable. The author recommends that all product lines be reviewed to determine the amount to be charged to each and whether low-margin product lines should be dropped. Funds are then freed up for investments elsewhere.

The final point that the author discusses, for the entrepreneur to consider, is that the balance sheet can be a source of capital in good and bad times, and entrepreneurs should not only be concerned with the sales figures and profits on the income statement. Cash flow can be generated by collecting on late accounts receivable, by taking a loss and reducing taxes on inventory no longer worth full value, and by re-examining the fixed asset account. For example, funds may be freed up if some subcontracting is undertaken and other resources of the company can be more profitably used. Other fixed assets could be thought of as sources of capital on the balance sheet.

The author concludes by recommending that entrepreneurs should try to improve Return On Investment. If assets employed can be reduced, the Return On Investment will go up, especially if assets were previously employed inefficiently.

Source: Herbert N. Woodward, *Management Strategies for Small Companies,* in David Gumpert edition, *Growing Concerns—Building and Managing the Smaller Business,* Harvard Business Review Executive Book Series, John Wiley & Sons, 1984, pp. 131–141.

Marketing Skills

Management competencies include marketing skills. The flow of goods and offering of services to fulfill the needs and desires of customers are fundamental to the successful operation of the venture. Indeed, today's entrepreneur is expected to have a good understanding of the marketing functions. In a highly competitive business environment, an effective marketing strategy is the key to a successful business. Marketing skills include the ability to position the product or service competitively, to set an effective pricing and promotional strategy. They also include market research and marketing planning.

Delegation

Many entrepreneurs attribute success to their ability to divorce themselves from the day-to-day routine activity of the business and focus on strategic type decisions. Yet studies have shown that a large number of entrepreneurs and small business managers are usually reluctant to let go of many small details that would have otherwise been handled by their staff. As a result many small firms are unable to attract competent people. Indeed many young M.B.A. graduates who may be attracted to small business because of the informal structure and personal contacts, are unwilling to join small firms because of their perception that they will never be able to further their career. The dominance and single-handed attitude of many entrepreneurs stand as an obstacle. Box 2.4 summarizes some research findings.

Box 2.4. Growing Pains.

  According to G. Parks, entrepreneurs have to overcome the following problems in order to grow and succeed.
1. The start-up problem. This refers to firms that experience difficulties in the launching up phase. The author suggests that entrepreneurs should have 80% of the necessary skills before launching new ventures. In addition, entrepreneurs must carefully design their accounting systems, assess the time and initial capital needed at this early stage.
2. The cash-flow problem. The author suggests that entrepreneurs pay particular attention to inventory control, accounts receivable collection and sales projections. This allows entrepreneurs to minimize funds being tied unnecessarily in inventories and receivables.
3. The delegation problem. The author contends that entrepreneurs should have a good team of qualified people that they can trust. Entrepreneurs must delegate to team members and allow them to make mistakes.
4. The idea problem. New ideas are always needed in order for the venture to grow. The author suggests that entrepreneurs should be able to solicit new ideas, listen to internal and external advice and be open minded.
5. The leadership problem. Finally Parks asserts that entrepreneurs should devote more time to manage the growth process in terms of planning, organizing and controlling.

Source: G. Parks, "How to Climb a Growth Curve: Eleven Hurdles for the Entrepreneur-Manager," *Journal of Small Business Management,* 15, 1, 1977, pp. 25–29.

THE VENTURE SUCCESS MODEL

A. B. Ibrahim suggests four critical elements for a successful venture: the market acceptance of the product/service's innovation; the industry attractiveness; the new venture
capabilities; and the entrepreneur's traits, skills and competence as shown in Figure 2.2.
These elements will be examined throughout the book.

PREDICTION AND DEVELOPMENT

A critical question that follows is, can we predict who will become a successful entrepreneur? And how to develop these success traits? McClelland noted that early research in the
field of entrepreneurship had only uncovered lists of characteristics that entrepreneurs and
experts had felt are the key personality traits for success in small business. These observations prompted Professor McClelland to attempt to develop a test that would predict which
persons show a greater or lesser probability of succeeding as an entrepreneur. He found
that those who score highly on the need to achieve have a high probability of success, and
are more likely to benefit from business training courses than those whose scores are lower.
Box 2.5 summarizes McClelland's findings.

It is interesting to know that certain entrepreneurial traits can be predicted early. In a
study by M. Kourilsky, traits such as creativity and persistence were identified in a sample
of elementary school children.[7]

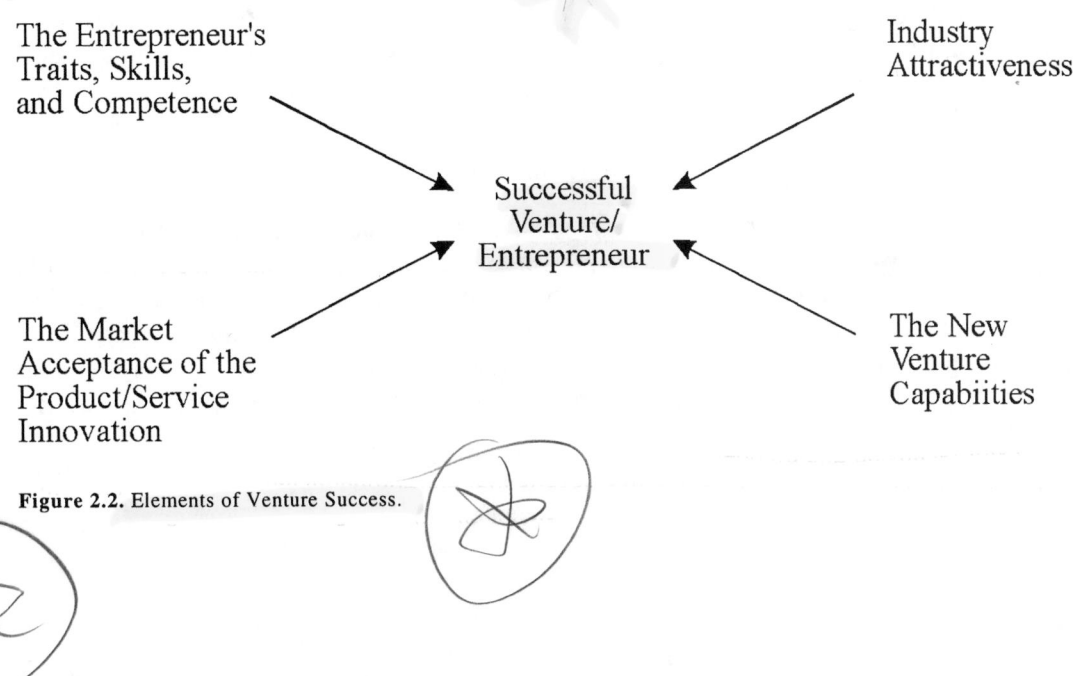

Figure 2.2. Elements of Venture Success.

Box 2.5. Can We Predict Successful Entrepreneurs?

The first important steps in this direction were the early studies McClelland conducted that discovered that the need to achieve plays a dominant role in creating a successful entrepreneur. In a study conducted in India by the author and his associates, it was discovered that those who score highly on a measure of the need to achieve also have a higher probability of going into small business and succeeding. Another useful finding from the study was that those who score highly on the need to achieve, benefit from business training courses more than those whose scores are lower. The persons tested were potential entrepreneurs enrolled in a small business training course. An important outcome of these results is that it may be possible to predict who will become a successful entrepreneur by measuring the need to achieve of potential entrepreneurs and enrolling those with a high need to achieve in a business training course to further enhance their chances of success in small business.

Source: David McClelland, "Characteristics of Successful Entrepreneurs," *The Journal of Creative Behavior* 21, 3, 1987, pp. 219–33.

Studies have also shown that experiential learning is critical in developing entrepreneurial behavior and skills. Experience based education was found to increase entrepreneurial aspiration and behavior as well as teaching decision making skills. A. B. Ibrahim and J. R. Goodwin suggested that entrepreneurial courses should be designed to meet the psychological characteristics of budding entrepreneurs.[8] Indeed universities are excellent training grounds for budding entrepreneurs not only for learning theories and concepts but also skills development. Individual case analysis and unstructured type courses were found to enhance entrepreneurial and managerial skills. In fact, new ventures that were started by students participating in these courses seem to live up to "prior measure of success."[9]

SUMMARY

We have attempted to describe the factors contributing to successful small business. Two critical factors were described in this chapter, entrepreneurial traits and management skills and competence. Entrepreneurial traits include psychological characteristics such as high need for achievement. Managerial skills and competence include management of cash flow, monitoring the inventory level, networking, strategic planning, niche strategy, systematic record keeping system, accounting skills, marketing skills and delegation of routine activities.

NOTES

1. David McClelland, "Characteristics of Successful Entrepreneurs," *The Journal of Creative Behavior* 21, 3, 1987, pp. 219–33.
2. A. B. Ibrahim and J. R. Goodwin, "Perceived Causes of Success in Small Business," *American Journal of Small Business* 11, 2, 1986, pp. 41–50.
3. Charles Hofer and W. Sandberg, "Improving New Venture Performance: Some Guidelines for Success," *American Journal of Small Business* 12, 1 (Summer 1987), pp. 11–25.
4. K. Said and K. Hughey, "Managerial Problems of the Small Firm," *Journal of Small Business Management,* January 1977, pp. 37–43.
5. Sue Birley, "The Role of Networking in the Entrepreneurial Process," *Journal of Business Venturing* 1, 1985, pp. 107–117.
6. Charles W. Hofer and William Sandberg, "Improving New Venture Performance: Some Guidelines for Success," *American Journal of Small Business* 12, 1 (Summer 1987), pp. 11–25.
7. M. Kourilsky, "The Kinder-Economy: A Case Study of Kindergarten Pupils' Acquisition of Economic Concepts," The *Elementary School Journal* 3, 1977, pp. 39–50.
8. A. B. Ibrahim and J. R. Goodwin, "Perceived Causes of Success in Small Business," *American Journal of Small Business* 11, 2, 1986, pp. 41–50.
9. B. Clark, C. Davis and V. Harnish, "Do Courses in Entrepreneurship Aid in New Venture Creation?" *Journal of Small Business Management* 22, 1984, pp. 26–31.

THE ENTREPRENEUR

Tom Monaghan—The Successful Entrepreneur
Domino's Pizza Inc.

Considered by many as the entrepreneurial hero of the 1980s, heading up a billion dollar a year company in Domino's Pizza Inc., and owner of the Detroit Tigers baseball team, Tom Monaghan started in the humblest of ways.

Born in 1937, Tom spent a number of years in an orphanage after the death of his father in 1941. He later saw service in the United States Marine Corps, and had an abbreviated college career at the University of Michigan. This diverse background was prior to his purchase of a pizza parlor with a $500 loan in 1960.

All was still not smooth sailing, for a co-owner kept on extracting a disproportionate amount of their modest funds.

In 1969, Monaghan lost control over Domino's growth and in the late 1970s almost lost his trademark to Amstar Corporation, makers of Domino sugar.

With the loyal support of his family, his wife and four daughters, he was able to weather yet another storm, so much so that in the spring of 1989 the company had opened more than 5,000 pizza parlors.

The Company is split into three main divisions—distribution, franchises and the home offices of Domino's Pizza International Inc.

THE ENTREPRENEUR
(continued)

The company and its management grow ever more decentralized as the empire expands. Monaghan remains a powerful force throughout the organization, right down to monthly call-in sessions with employees. References to his growth and development seem to suggest that it really took off when he bought the Detroit Tigers baseball club, in 1983. He is reported to have said, "Even if baseball meant nothing to me—and owning the Tigers is the highest material thing that I ever aspired to—it would've made sense from a free-publicity point of view."

The company has seen the scars of many management trials and tribulations, difficulty with lenders and creditors, and lawsuits with franchisees. By the time that he took over the Tigers in late 1983 at a price of $53 million, he was considered "a successful entrepreneur." With a personal fortune estimated at $250 million, he did have control over one of the fast-food industry's most spectacular growth companies.

Second in total sales only to Pizza Hut Inc. among the national chains, Domino's excelled at doing something that nobody else did: getting orders to customers in 30 minutes or less, or the pizza came free.

In the beginning of 1984, there were 900 units, of which 300 were company-owned and two-thirds being franchised, with virtually no outstanding debt and extensive expansion plans for the forthcoming years. By the Fall of 1989 there were 5,100 units, with the saying that every 24 hours, somewhere in the world, three more Domino's delivery outlets are launched. Having risen out of obscurity, he says that "what matters is not simply the overcoming of obstacles, it is the opportunities created once those obstacles are left behind."

His frequent references to Frank Lloyd Wright, the noted architect, suggest that in many ways, he might have found a "role model."

Reports say the "Even though he never met him, Tom Monaghan obviously has a great interest, a reverence, really, for Mr. Wright's work. It may be less intellectual than instinctive, but that's the best situation to have, because [Wright] didn't necessarily create his designs for people of great wealth or intellectual accomplishment. His architecture spoke directly to the people, and obviously it spoke to Tom Monaghan a long time ago. He has a great dream and we hope that he sticks to it."

Like his fascination with Frank Lloyd Wright, his ownership of the Tigers is a hobby, not a business.

"I know more about Domino's than I ever will about running a baseball team," he says. "In fact, there aren't too many people—if any—who operate a company this size and understand it as well as I do. It's an emotional involvement, not just an intellectual one. That's why I could never be involved the same way with another company. My life is plenty exciting right now, but you know, nothing will ever compare to the years when I was in the back of my own store, making pizza, beating the rush, building something I believed in."

Source: *Forbes*, October 23, 1989, pp. 30, 220; *Inc.*, February 1986, pp. 61–65.

△ CHAPTER 3 △
THE MAKING OF AN ENTREPRENEUR

The entrepreneur is currently a fashionable animal, so much so that entrepreneurs and "entrepreneurship" have become synonymous in the public mind with corporate success, and the epithet has become a stock in trade solution of popular writers for a variety of North America's economic woes. But what exactly IS entrepreneurship? This chapter is devoted to exploring the complex phenomenon of entrepreneurship.

DEFINING THE ENTREPRENEUR

Defining who is an entrepreneur is a difficult process. Reviewing the literature reveals that there is no generic definition of the entrepreneur. As Kets de Vries noted, there is a lack of "conceptual clarity." The term entrepreneur has never been precisely defined. Many scholars from different schools of thought have tried over the years to define this complex phenomenon. For example, economists such as Jean Baptist and J. Schumpeter view the entrepreneur as the fourth factor of production who is rewarded by profit for his innovation and risk taking activity. Sociologists on the other hand regard the entrepreneur as a deviant individual who is driven by a number of factors, such as personality, family and society, towards a particular pattern of behavior. Psychologists have turned their attention to the personal characteristics of the entrepreneur.

Kets de Vries draws a broad profile of an individual with a high need for achievements and autonomy, as might be expected. Interestingly, these qualities are frequently coupled with higher than average anxiety, a developed aesthetic sense and lower than average interpersonal skills.[1]

There may indeed be more than one entrepreneurial archetype. Howard Stevenson and David Gumpert have shown that the popular view of the entrepreneur as a bold architect of new high technology enterprises differs from the managerial picture of a flexible, risk-taking innovator. Neither stereotype is entirely false, but entrepreneurship can be more aptly defined as a mode of behavior, a cast of mind (Box 3.1 outlines Stevenson and Gumpert's observations).

Box 3.1. Two Types of Entrepreneurs.

Howard Stevenson and David Gumpert believe that the entrepreneur (or "promoter") simply occupies one extreme end of a spectrum of managerial behaviour, at the opposite end is the administrator (or "trustee"). The former is concerned with locating and exploiting opportunity, the latter with exploiting the organization to its best advantage. Where the individual's self interest is concerned, the authors contend, there is an instinctive tendency toward the promoter's role, a bias that must somehow be aligned with the objectives of the corporation if both are to flourish.

The characteristics of either extreme of the spectrum are described to illustrate their point. Driven on by diminishing opportunities or an environment that is in a state of flux the entrepreneurial organization has a strategic focus on opportunity. The administrative organization is preoccupied with maintaining social contracts and an outward appearance of equilibrium, and must therefore adopt a strategic posture that is cautious, formal and oriented to a much longer planning horizon than the promoter. It is this cast of thinking that leads the trustee to overcommit resources to its enterprises, to "go first class." As the authors correctly point out however, the size of the resource commitment is of secondary importance when compared with the nature of their deployment. The promoter is forced by necessity to squeeze the most from limited resources and therefore must employ them to their best advantage. Modern history abounds with examples of the success of such Davids over corporate Goliaths.

It follows therefore that the administrator's predilection for control and longer planning horizons instills a preference for outright ownership of assets (the better to exercise control), whereas the promoter prefers to rent and thereby dispose of them easily when they are not required. For the same reasons, the trustee chooses a formal, predictable managerial structure, whereas the promoter, given the necessity of quick adaptation to changing circumstances and rapid dissemination of information, operates a fluid, informal organization.

Source: H. H. Stevenson and D. E. Gumpert, "The Heart of Entrepreneurship," *Harvard Business Review* (March–April 1985), pp. 85–94.

From our perspective, an entrepreneur is defined as an individual who sees an opportunity that others do not and marshals the resources to exploit it. According to this definition, an entrepreneur is someone who introduces new products or processes, identifies new markets or sources of supply or creates a new type of organization. In addition, he or she raises the necessary capital, creates the new venture and assumes the control and risk of the operation. The independent undertaking is emphasized throughout the process.

We see two possible roles for the entrepreneur in the corporate world: those of the innovator/risk taker and the manager/coordinator.

Innovator and Risk Taker

The entrepreneur is the creative wellspring for the enterprise; he/she understands its purpose and can best devise methods that are untried or unconventional. Innovation and risk taking are traits which distinguish entrepreneurs from managers.

Manager/Coordinator

Marshalling and controlling the resources needed for the venture to survive, the entrepreneur formulates the organization's strategy and selects the appropriate structure and management process to exploit the window of opportunity. The critical question is: why do some individuals see opportunities while others do not? This question has intrigued academics and practitioners. To answer it, let us examine some schools of thought.

THE MAKING OF AN ENTREPRENEUR

Because of the difficulty in defining an entrepreneur, many scholars have turned their attention to the entrepreneurial process to provide an explanation. A number of research studies have focused on the factors that shape and influence entrepreneurs, such as individual traits, culture, family background, functions and a host of other psychological and sociological factors. As shown in Figure 3.1, these factors are grouped under four schools of thought: the traits, the environment, the behavioral, and the contingency approach.

The Traits Approach—Who Is an Entrepreneur?

The internal (traits) model assumes that entrepreneurs possess certain personality traits that drive them to the choice of an entrepreneurship career. Entrepreneurial characteristics and personality traits have been the subject of many research studies. Figure 3.2 lists some of the characteristics found to be associated with many entrepreneurs. Chapter 4 discusses the entrepreneurial traits.

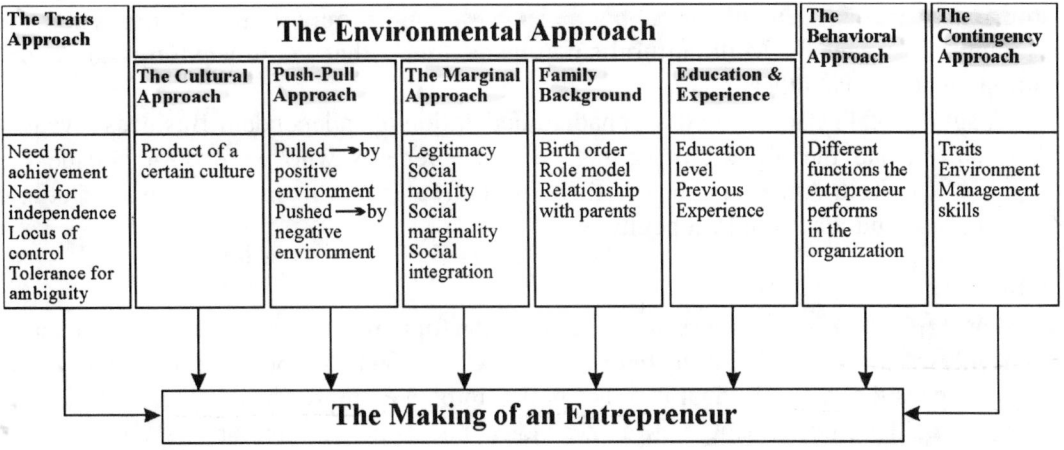

Figure 3.1.

Characteristics—Traits Associated with Entrepreneurs
1. High Need for Achievement
2. Risk Taking Propensity
3. Tolerance for Ambiguity
4. Innovation
5. Intuition
6. High Need for Independence and Autonomy
7. Internal Locus of Control
8. Low Need for Conformity

Figure 3.2.

The Environmental Approach

The environmental approach argues that the choice of entrepreneurship is related to external factors beyond the individual's control. In the following section, we discuss the critical role the environment plays in shaping an entrepreneur.

The Role of the Culture

Why is it that some groups demonstrate more entrepreneurial characteristics than others? One obvious explanation is that entrepreneurs are products of their culture. Some cultural groups see entrepreneurship as a more desirable career opportunity than others. For example, a survey by Multiculturalism Canada found that certain cultures are more entrepreneurial than others.[2]

A survey of 11 nations by the Canadian Federation of Independent Business revealed that Canada had the highest percentage of entrepreneurs who were born outside the country.[3] In North American society there are entrepreneurs from a multitude of ethnic backgrounds and identifiable subcultures.

The "Push-Pull" Theory

The "push-pull" theory proposes that the motivation for new venture creation is not so much the result of entrepreneurial traits but rather of external factors—positive or negative. The theory argues that an individual is either pulled into an entrepreneurial career by positive elements in the environment such as new ideas and opportunities, or pushed into it by negative elements such as job dissatisfaction or being laid off.[4]

Some industries are more likely to act as incubators for entrepreneurs than others. They simply pull or attract entrepreneurs to create their own ventures. The computer, garment and restaurant industries are good examples. Many entrepreneurs worked in these industries before starting their own businesses. For example, Steve Jobs, founder of the Apple Computer Company, worked at Atari while his partner, Steve Wozniak worked at Hewlett-Packard. Ken Olson, founder of Digital, worked at IBM. Push entrepreneurs, on the other hand, are driven by negative elements in the environment. For example, there is evidence of a strong relationship between a rising level of unemployment and an increased number of start-ups.[5]

The Marginal/Displacement Approach

Closely associated with the negative environment is the marginal entrepreneur. Why are entrepreneurs frequently from outside "mainstream" society? Some researchers suggest that marginal individuals are most likely to become entrepreneurs. On an individual level, it has been suggested that entrepreneurs are marginal individuals who are spurred on by a diverse experience in early childhood; they have become "misfits," in Kets de Vries words, who are unable to accept the authority of other individuals and to "fit into" an organization.[6]

On a social level, various theories about marginal individuals have been suggested to explain the entrepreneurship phenomenon. These theories are based on the concepts of social marginality, mobility, legitimacy and the social integration of individuals and groups. Entrepreneurs' perceptions that they are not part of the mainstream group drive them into an entrepreneurial career. Examples of this are women who face a "glass ceiling" in their organization, or minorities who may feel they are being discriminated against. These individuals may be driven to start their own business more out of necessity than by choice. Thus the marginal approach may explain the disproportionately large percentage of entrepreneurs who belong to ethnic or religious minorities.[7]

Family Background

Family background has been espoused to explain the making of an entrepreneur. Research has traditionally focused on three aspects: birth order, role models and the experience of rejection in childhood.

First Born. It has been argued that entrepreneurs are often first born. The basis for this argument is simple. The first born often receives more special care and attention from his or her parents than her siblings do. This contributes to the development of traits such as self-confidence, independence and locus of control.

The Role Model. Some research suggests that individuals who come from entrepreneurial environments are more likely to start their own business. Research suggests that two thirds of entrepreneurs come from families where the father or mother is self-employed. The entrepreneurial environment and parental guidance and support appear to be conducive to fostering entrepreneurial traits such as risk-taking, independence, creativity and achievement. The self-employed parent becomes a role model and a mentor to the budding entrepreneur and is usually inclined to encourage entrepreneurial behavior. The role model provides the potential entrepreneur with the aspiration to follow the same career choice. He or she usually identifies with the role model or mentor's life style and attitude. Mancuso wrote "Even when he is in his thirties and his dad is retired, the approval and praise of his father still provides a basis for his drive."[8] For example, Edgar Bronfman Jr., the CEO of Seagram Company, followed his father and mentor, Edgar Sr., and his uncle Charles's footsteps. Both were role models for Edgar Jr.

The Experience of Rejection. According to this approach, entrepreneurs might have experienced parental rejection early in their childhood. Kets de Vries, a noted management scholar, contends that poor and troubled family relations may explain the weak compliance motive and thus the need to be independent in order to avoid authority figures, be they parents or managers.[9] Box 3.2 provides some interesting notes on the making of an entrepreneur.

EDUCATION AND EXPERIENCE

Education

Entrepreneurs' educational levels have been explored. The myth of the uneducated entrepreneur has been challenged by many research studies. Today, according to U.S. census data, the typical entrepreneur is more educated than the person who is not self-employed.[10] Research studies suggest that the majority of entrepreneurs have university degrees.[11]

Experience

Research has revealed that the entrepreneur's previous experience increases the likelihood of success in the new venture. Both managerial and industry specific experience are critical in new venture creation. Thus it is no surprise that a large percentage of entrepreneurs start businesses in industries with which they are familiar. Indeed, certain industries are more likely to act as incubators than others. For example, Dan Lasater, founder of Ponderosa Restaurants, learned the restaurant business by working for McDonald's. Similarly, Bill Gates, founder of Microsoft, had worked in the computer industry since he was 14 years old. Sam Walton, founder of Wal-Mart, learned the retail business while working at J. C. Penny.

The Behavioral Approach—What the Entrepreneur Does

This approach views the entrepreneur as part of the venture creation process. Karl Vesper noted that entrepreneurship is the creation of new organizations. The emphasis in this approach is placed on the organization and the different functions that the entrepreneur performs. Thus the research question shifted from who is an entrepreneur to what the entrepreneur does.

Howard Stevenson, Michael Roberts and Irving Grousbeck argue that it is not helpful to focus on certain personality traits or sociological issues, rather they view entrepreneur-

Box 3.2. The Making of an Entrepreneur.

What makes an entrepreneur tick? Writing in the Journal of Management Studies, M. F. R. Kets de Vries has attempted to answer the question. His exploration into the roots of entrepreneurship is not so much intended to plumb the depths of the entrepreneurial psyche, but to understand the forces that propel successful entrepreneurs, and the implications for the organizations that they build.

Kets de Vries joins with others before him in noting that entrepreneurs frequently emerge from an ethnic or minority background. The reasons for this are complex, as the author acknowledges. However, it is easy to appreciate that in the face of discrimination, with established avenues for achievement closed to him, the ethnic entrepreneur frequently has no choice but to follow paths that are unconventional. Although Kets de Vries provides no specific examples, it is worthwhile remembering that many of the most important figures of the industrial revolution came from backgrounds well outside the British establishment of the day—Wedgewood, Tate, Lloyd, etc. Many were drawn from the ranks of the Puritans or Presbyterians.

A second common factor is that of a father self-employed. The author suggests that turbulence associated with such an environment serves to condition the child and provide a role model for risk taking. Neither of the foregoing factors should be taken as to guarantee to produce an entrepreneur, however, only to ensure a propensity for such a career.

Family background shapes the entrepreneur in a second way. Kets de Vries notes that many report having experienced hardship during their childhood, some in the form of rejection or withdrawal of a father figure, some merely the victim of poverty (with its attendant strains on family life). Whether or not the hardship was real is irrelevant as a source of motivation, it need only be perceived. As a result, the youth passes into adulthood harbouring feelings of insecurity and possibly antipathy towards authority.

Typically the entrepreneur-to-be then passes through a period of restlessness, indecision and rejection during early adulthood. He or she fails to find a "fit" with any organization that presents itself and may appear non-conformist or inconsistent. In fact, he or she is displaying all the signs of uncertainty and lack of self-direction that a more conventional upbringing might obviate.

As the entrepreneur matures, the insecurities of childhood are manifested in the form of driving ambition and restless energy. These symptoms Kets de Vries terms a "reaction" against the stresses of childhood; where the child feels rejected, the adult removes himself from the parents' shadow. A search for quick gratification, impulsiveness and a disinclination toward analytical thinking are concomitant traits. Paradoxically success, when it arrives, serves only to heighten the entrepreneur's insecurities. The persistent belief in his or her inferiority intercedes to persuade (through guilt) that the success is undeserved, that it must be "paid for" at a later date. From the same roots spring the need for ostentatious trappings of luxury or power so often sported by successful entrepreneurs: they are physical reassurance against the anxieties harboured within, tangible evidence of accomplishment and identity.

Source: M. Kets de Vries, "The Entrepreneurial Personality," pp. 34–57

ship as "an approach to management." Thus entrepreneurship is a way of handling key managerial functions, that is, the organization strategy, structure and management process.[12] In other words, the entrepreneur is viewed by the behavioral approach as a person who can effectively marshal resources, pursue an appropriate strategy, structure, reward, and control systems to exploit a window of opportunity.

Indeed the behavioral approach or way of managing is gaining more credibility. Recent research suggests that industry structure, organization strategy and behavioral characteristics of the entrepreneur (in that order) are the key success factors in new venture creation.[13]

The Contingency Approach

A. B. Ibrahim suggests that entrepreneurship is a complex phenomenon that involves two critical elements. The first is sensing an opportunity which is usually influenced by traits and environmental factors such as culture, family background, early experience of rejection, education and work experience. The second element is the exploitation of the opportunity which requires the effective management of the venture resources and capabilities to ensure success.[14] Figure 3.3 depicts the contingency approach.

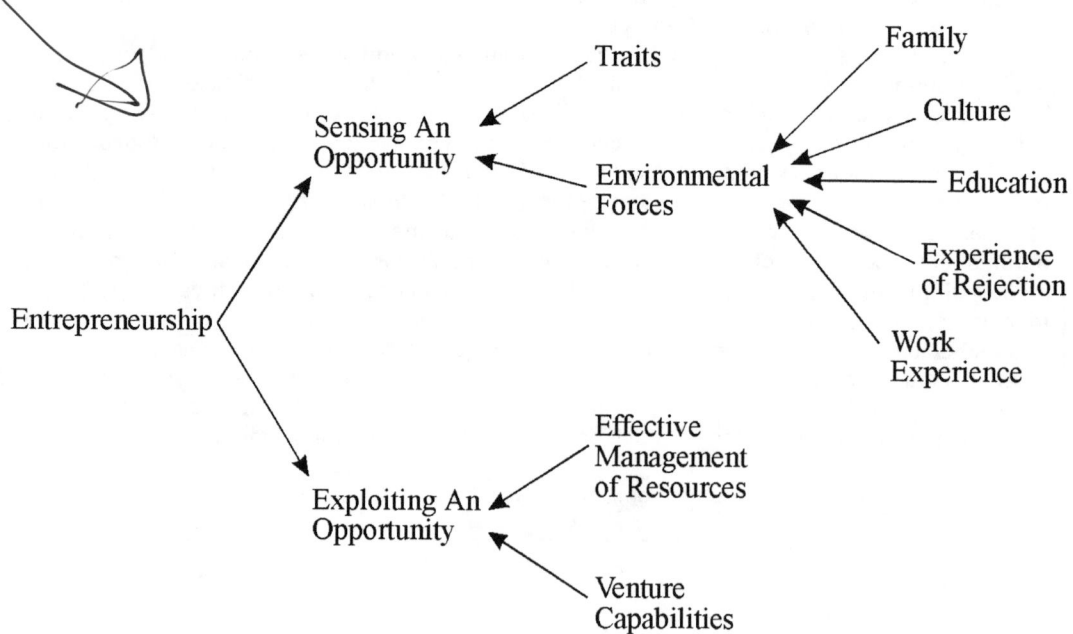

Figure 3.3. The Contingency Approach to Entrepreneurship.

SUMMARY

We have attempted in this chapter to focus on the entrepreneurial process and the making of an entrepreneur. Three different approaches were discussed, the traits approach, the environmental approach and the behavioral approach. The traits approach emphasizes the different traits associated with entrepreneurs such as high need for achievement, risk taking propensity, tolerance for ambiguity, innovation, high need for independence, low need for conformity and internal locus of control. The environmental approach views the entrepreneur as a cultural phenomenon and that the choice of an entrepreneurial career is related to external factors beyond the individual's control. The behavioral approach focuses on what the entrepreneur does, and the different functions he or she performs in the venture creation process. Finally, the contingency approach focuses on sensing and exploiting an opportunity.

NOTES

1. M. Kets de Vries, "The Entrepreneurial Personality: A Person at the Cross Roads, *Journal of Management Studies* XIV, 1977, pp. 34–57.
2. L. Dana, "An inquiry into Culture and Entrepreneurship: Case Studies of Business Creation Among Immigrants in Montreal." *Journal of Small Business and Entrepreneurship.* Sept. 1993, pp. 16–27. Also see: Albert Shapiro, "The Displaced Uncomfortable Entrepreneur," *Psychology Today*, Nov. 1975.
3. J. Bulloch. "Entrepreneurship and Development." *Journal of Small Business & Entrepreneurship* (1988), pp. 3–7.
4. Albert Shapiro, 1975; B. Bird, Entrepreneurial Behavior, Scott, Foresman and Company, 1989, pp. 35–112. Also see: F. Fry, *Entrepreneurship: A Planning Approach.* (Minneapolis: West Publishing Company, 1993), p. 62.
5. F. Fry, 1993.
6. M. Kets de Vries, "The Entrepreneurial Personality: A Person at the Cross Roads," *Journal of Management Studies* XIV, 1977, pp. 34–57.
7. P. Wilkin, Entrepreneurship. *A Comparative and Historical Study.* (New Jersey: Ablex, 1979). Also see: M. Kets de Vries, 1977.
8. J. Mancuso, "What It Takes To Be an Entrepreneur: A Questionnaire Approach," *Journal of Small Business Management,* 12, 4, 1974.
9. M. Kets de Vries, 1977.
10. J. Katz. "Entry Strategies of the Self-employed: Individual Level Characteristics and Organizational Outcomes." *Frontiers of Entrepreneurship Research,* 1984, pp. 396–399.
11. Ibid.
12. H. Stevenson, M. Roberts and H. I. Grousbeck, *New Business Ventures and The Entrepreneur,* 3rd ed. (Homewood, Ill.: Richard D. Irwin, 1989), pp. 6–19.
13. C. Hofer and W. Sandberg, "Improving New Venture Performance: Some Guidelines for Success," *American Journal of Small Business,* 12, 1 (Summer 1987), pp. 11–25. Also see: Rein Peterson and Kimble Ainslie, *Understanding Entrepreneurship.* (Dubuque, Iowa: Kendall/Hunt Publishing Company, 1988).
14. A. Bakr Ibrahim and Ron McTavish, *Risk Evaluation of SMEs*, The Institute of Bankers, 1997.

THE ENTREPRENEUR

A. K. Velan—The Successful Immigrant

At the age of 79, A. K. Velan, president and CEO of Velan Inc., has shown no sign of slowing down. He was recently named "Entrepreneur of the Year" for 1996 by Canadian Business Magazine. He has added this title to a long list of other awards for outstanding business performance.

A. K. Velan fled his native Czechoslovakia in 1949 when the Communist government took power. He came to Canada armed with his engineering know-how and a belief in his entrepreneurial drive and innovation. To him, Canada was a land of opportunity and freedom. In 1950, A. K. started a business from his house in Montreal based on his development and patenting of a device that would eliminate condensation from steam piping, the bimetallic stream trap. The company was incorporated in 1952 under the name of Velan Inc.

In the early years A. K. struggled to make his business a success. He made prototypes of his invention, and tested and modified them in his house. His first big break came when the U.S. Navy ordered the Velan bimetallic steam trap for seven of its new destroyers. These were the challenging times. He can remember working late into the night in his garage with his wife to pack the steam traps destined for the U.S. Navy. A. K. thrived on his new found success and greeted the challenges with great enthusiasm and hard work. With the development of other innovations, his business became too big for his house so he moved it to a manufacturing plant.

In the late 1950s, A. K. saw a window of opportunity developing with the birth of nuclear power. He began developing valves to be used specifically in the nuclear power industry. His products were used by the U.S. Navy and NATO for ships, nuclear submarines and aircraft carriers. Newly established nuclear power plants were also using his products.

Velan Inc. started as a small business and grew under the leadership of its founder into a multinational corporation with eight manufacturing plants in six countries and over 1,100 employees.

Velan Inc. prides itself on being a family business that is run by family members. Velan also tries to provide employment opportunities for other immigrants to North America, and has offered hundreds their all important first job.

Source: Excerpt from a case study by Ingrid Sinclair, M.B.A. under the direction of Professor A. B. Ibrahim. Copyright A. B. Ibrahim, 1997.

△ CHAPTER 4 △
THE ENTREPRENEURIAL TRAITS AND MOTIVATION

INTRODUCTION

What motivates entrepreneurs? What makes them tick?

William Hewlett and David Packard started Hewlett-Packard (HP), one of the largest computer companies. Bill Gates founded one of the most successful companies in this century—Microsoft. In thinking back to all the entrepreneurs you have known, does it strike you that they share common characteristics?

THE ENTREPRENEURIAL TRAITS

Entrepreneurial traits have been the object of much study. It has been suggested that certain traits are the driving force and motivation underlying the choice of an entrepreneurship career. Research has identified a number of entrepreneurial traits such as a high need for achievement and independence, a moderate risk-taking propensity, an internal locus of control, and tolerance for ambiguity and innovation. Figure 4.1 lists some of the traits associated with successful entrepreneurs. Understanding these traits provides some insight into entrepreneurship that could serve as a benchmark to measure potential entrepreneurs' chances of success.

Need for Achievement
Need for Independence
Moderate risk-taking propensity
Internal locus of control
Tolerance for Ambiguity
Innovation
Proactivity

Figure 4.1. Traits Associated with Entrepreneurs.

This chapter is based on published work by Professor A. B. Ibrahim.

Need for Achievement

David McClelland's "need for achievement," first proposed in the *Achieving Society* (1961) is the best-known research associated with the traits approach. Need for achievement or n. Ach. motive seems to influence the individual to select an entrepreneurial career. A strong desire to set one's own goals and objectives and carry them out has been documented as a driving force for many entrepreneurs. The need for achievement is seldom satisfied by the traditional career path. Entrepreneurs want to take responsibility for their actions, do well in competitive situations, are result driven, take moderate risks and dislike routine activities.

The achievement motive of entrepreneurs predisposes them to perform different activities exceptionally well as a measure of their achievements. Among these is an intense preoccupation with producing high quality products or services and a desire to satisfy customer needs and wants. Bill Gates, founder of Microsoft and one of the most successful entrepreneurs of this century, is known for his long working hours, his constant demand for innovation and quality and his ability to take calculated risks.

McClelland's theory of the need for achievement identified three traits that are associated with entrepreneurs:[1]

- the desire to solve problems and gain satisfaction from attaining goals that they have set and prioritized themselves;
- the ability to take moderate risks after assessing the alternatives; and
- the need for feedback as a measure of their success.

According to MacClelland, those who score highly on n. Ach were found to have a higher probability of going into business and succeeding. They also have a higher probability of benefiting from business training courses than those whose scores are lower.[2] It is interesting to note that according to research, there is a strong relation between the need for achievement in a given country and the level of economic growth in that country: the higher the need for achievement, the higher the level of the country's economic growth.

Need for Independence and Autonomy

One of the strongest motivating factors underlying the choice of an entrepreneurial career is the need for independence. Many entrepreneurs have left successful executive careers to start their own businesses because of the strong need to work independently and be their "own boss." Jim Treybig left a well-paid position as marketing manager at Hewlett-Packard to start his own company, Tandem Computers, to satisfy his need for independence. Research has revealed that entrepreneurs tend not to seek assistance from other people and thus tend to score low on the need for support.[3]

However, the need for independence might impede the firm's growth, as few entrepreneurs are willing to delegate, be it out of a perceived or real lack of competent employees or out of an inherent unwillingness to let go. Entrepreneurs' tendency to do everything themselves can prove detrimental to the company's long term survival.

Research has suggested that as the level of influence of other individuals, such as creditors or bankers, increases in relation to that of the entrepreneur, the latter begins to experience a loss of self-esteem and autonomy, which reduces the ability to manage the business effectively.[4] It has been suggested that the entrepreneur's need for independence and autonomy could be the result of his or her resentment of authority figures, be it a parent or a bank manager.[5]

Moderate Risk-Taking Propensity

Folklore has produced a belief that entrepreneurs are high risk takers. In the popular press, the entrepreneur is generally depicted as a dare-devil who thrives on risk and enjoys the challenge of the unknown. While this portrait may be true of some high-profile entrepreneurs, in general they have been found to be calculated risk takers. They do not deliberately seek out high-risk situations, nor do they strive to avoid risk altogether. In essence, they are willing to accept the risk and uncertainty inherent in new opportunities. A moderate risk-taking propensity is typical of entrepreneurs with a high need to achieve. Furthermore, they take care to research problems and consider several alternative solutions before reaching a decision. This notion of "controlled boldness" is a key characteristic of many successful entrepreneurs. For example, in their study of an entrepreneurial firm, Henry Mintzberg and James Waters noted: "Sam Steinberg pursued what can be called a 'test-the-water' approach, always sensing an environment with minor probes before plunging in. In the earlier years at least, Steinberg never undertook a bold move until he had a pretty good idea what the consequences would be."[6]

While it may appear to outsiders that an entrepreneur is engaging in a risky venture, the new business may in fact be considered less risky by the entrepreneur than any other available alternative. The perceived risk of losing autonomy and independence by working for someone else may outweigh the risk of being self-employed. For example, Ted Turner, founder of Turner Broadcasting System, is known for his risk-taking ability. He bought the virtually bankrupt Metro-Goldwyn-Mayer and turned it around.

Internal Locus of Control

Of all the traits generally ascribed to entrepreneurs, internal locus of control is perhaps the one that is most consistently positively related to the entrepreneurial personality. In fact, locus of control has been found to distinguish entrepreneurs from corporate executives as well as successful from less successful entrepreneurs.[7] Locus of control refers to entrepreneurs' perception that all the events in their lives are under their control and thus they are able to influence events and determine the outcome of their own actions. Internal locus of control individuals are confident that they can make things happen. They believe that they control and influence their own accomplishments and failures. They seek initiative and take responsibility for their actions. Entrepreneurs therefore feel that the results of their efforts and actions are attributable to themselves and not to such intangibles as "fate" and "luck." This trait has a direct link to the need for achievement trait, as entrepreneurs would not typically feel that they had achieved something if an outcome were not the result of their own endeavors. They therefore take responsibility for their own actions and do not blame their success or failure on the external environment. In contrast, external locus of control individuals believe that the outcome of their actions is influenced by events beyond their control, including other individuals, luck or fate.

Research has revealed that internal locus of control persons are alert, discover opportunities and scan their environment for the information needed to ensure effective exploitation of those opportunities.[8] Further, it has also been shown that a higher level of perceptual awareness—defined as the ability to discover new opportunities—is associated with internal locus of control. The results of a recent study suggest that internal locus of control entrepreneurs are more inclined to plan for expansion of their businesses despite an unfavourable environment such as a high interest rate and inflation. The confidence in their own ability to achieve the desired performance and to recognize new opportunities enables them to be relatively undaunted by unfavourable external events.[9] For example, Walt Disney had to overcome many obstacles and unfavourable events before he was able to achieve profits with the introduction of *Snow White and the Seven Dwarfs* in 1937.

Tolerance for Ambiguity

David McClelland identified tolerance for ambiguity as one of the traits associated with most entrepreneurs. This trait refers to the ability of the entrepreneur to perceive ambiguous situations in a positive and challenging way. Ambiguity in this sense is defined as a lack of complete and definitive information. Tolerance for ambiguity is a definite asset to entrepreneurs, it allows them to organize their thoughts and make decisions under conditions of uncertainty. Being an entrepreneur means that one is irresistibly drawn to a great deal of uncertainty, for many reasons. First, many start ups involve innovation and unproven concepts. Second, small businesses have very limited resources to scan the environment and to gather all relevant information. Entrepreneurs must therefore rely on their intuition and fragments of information in making decisions. Further, the lack of human resources with functional expertise dictate that entrepreneurs must make decisions in every aspect of the business. Entrepreneurs find this ambiguous and uncertain environment stimulating and challenging and usually reject the monotony and highly structured environment of routine job. While other individuals may suffer anxiety and stress in this type of environment, entrepreneurs thrive on ambiguity and are able to identify and pursue opportunities. J. Scheré tested a sample of entrepreneurs and managers and found entrepreneurs to be more tolerant of ambiguity than managers.[10] For example, William Hewlett and David Packard, founders of Hewlett-Packard, endured long periods of uncertainty while working in Packard's garage. They liked the challenge, and their efforts became a success story.

Innovation

In Peter Drucker's eyes, innovation, the mechanism by which entrepreneurs create or increase wealth, is an essential quality of entrepreneurship. He says it "is the effort to create purposeful, focused change in an enterprise's economic or social potential." It arises from a powerful search for opportunity in situations that may be both inside and outside the corporation. Unexpected occurrences, incongruities, process needs and industry or market changes may provoke innovation inside the firm or industry. Demographic changes, changes in perception and new knowledge may act as catalysts outside the firm. Drucker asserts that innovation is a skill that can be acquired and taught.[11]

Joseph Shumpeter, the great economist, identified innovation as a key characteristic of the entrepreneur. In most industries, significant innovations originate from the garages and basements of entrepreneurs. Most of the Silicon Valley high-tech firms were founded by entrepreneurs such as Steve Jobs, founder of Apple computer, William Hewlett and David Packard, founders of Hewlett-Packard, and Ken Olson, founder of Digital. David McClelland's research confirmed the entrepreneur's predisposition to innovate,[12] suggesting a strong relationship between a high need to achieve and innovation.

Proactivity

Proactivity is another prevalent trait associated with entrepreneurs; it is closely related to locus of control. Entrepreneurs have an ability to take control of events and take initiative in solving problems that arise. Further, they are able to set objectives and implement solutions effectively. Sam Walton, founder of Wal-Mart, was known for his proactive style of management.

OTHER ENTREPRENEURIAL CHARACTERISTICS

Intuition

Much has been written about entrepreneurs' intuitive behavior. Research has revealed that the entrepreneur's intuition plays a critical role in the decision making process in small firms. In many of these firms, strategic decisions are based not on facts or complete information, but on the entrepreneur's experience, business sense and "gut feeling." Indeed, Alfred P. Sloan noted that the final act of judgement is intuitive.[13] Pierre Péladeau, founder of Quebecor—the largest printing company in the world—was known for his intuitive behavior.

Vision

The starting point of a new venture is the entrepreneur's vision. In many respects, it is a dream of what the entrepreneur wants to achieve in the long term. This dream allows the entrepreneur to persevere. Short term failure is seen only as an obstacle that must be overcome in order to achieve the dream. Vision is a driving force behind the entrepreneur's success. Author Jeffrey Timmons noted that most entrepreneurs do not speak of their failures with regret, but are able to look at them as good learning experiences.[14] Microsoft was founded in 1975 by two technology entrepreneurs, Bill Gates and Paul Allen, with a dream to develop inexpensive software that can be used by every PC user.

THE ENTREPRENEURIAL QUIZ[*]

The following quiz is meant to stimulate your thinking about who is an entrepreneur. It is not meant to give conclusive evidence. No statistical reliability or validity is claimed.

Answer the following questions by marking the appropriate box provided.

Yes No

☐ ☑ 1. I like to go to work at a regular time.

☑ ☐ 2. I often find myself telling people what to do.

☐ ☑ 3. Taking small risks makes me nervous.

☐ ☑ 4. I do not like surprises.

☑ ☐ 5. I like to solve problems.

☐ ☑ 6. I believe you are either lucky or unlucky in this world.

☑ ☐ 7. I am the first child in the family.

☐ ☑ 8. I am the youngest child in the family.

☐ ☑ 9. I immigrated to North America some years ago.

☑ ☐ 10. My parents immigrated to North America many years ago.

☑ ☐ 11. My family has deep roots in this country.

☐ ☑ 12. My parents are/were self-employed.

☐ ☑ 13. One of my parents are/were self-employed.

☑ ☐ 14. I come from a family that always had a steady career in government or a large corporation.

15. When my boss assigns me a job, I prefer the details of the assignment to be:

☑   a. specifically spelled out

☐   b. left for me to exercise some imagination

☐   c. clear as to the objectives.

16. When my office is cluttered I feel:

☐   a. at ease and have no problem with it

☐   b. lazy and tired

☑   c. something needs to be done right away.

17. When I start a new project, I usually:

☑   a. set goals and priorities and seek feedback

* © 1982 Dr. A. B. Ibrahim

☐   b.   set a deadline for completion

☐   c.   delegate to other people.

18. In the different jobs I have had, I:

☑   a.   always introduced something different

☐   b.   always followed company policy and procedure

☐   c.   never deviated from what I was asked to do.

19. If I were asked to toss a coin into a bowl I would:

☐   a.   stand not too far away where, with focus and persistence, I would score high.

☑   b.   stand very close to score every time

☐   c.   stand far away and test my chances.

20. In my job I have always liked to work:

☐   a.   under close supervision

☑   b.   with very little supervision

☐   c.   alone so I can do things my own way.

Answers

1. Yes: 2, 5, 7, 9, 10, 12, 13

No: 1, 3, 4, 6, 8, 11, 14

2. 15 (b); 16 (a); 17(a); 18 (a); 19 (a); 20 (c).

SUMMARY

Entrepreneurial traits have been the object of much study. A high need for achievement and independence, a moderate risk-taking propensity, internal locus of control, and tolerance for ambiguity and innovation are traits associated with entrepreneurs. These traits have been found to be the driving force and motivation for the choice of entrepreneurship as a career. Other traits described in this chapter such as proactivity, intuition and vision are also critical for a successful entrepreneur and for venture creation.

NOTES

1. D. McClelland, Human Motivation, Glenview, Il.: Scott Foresman, 1985, p. 250. Also see B. Bird, Entrepreneurial Behavior, Glenview, IL.: Foresman, 1989, p. 78
2. D. McClelland, "Characteristics of Successful Entrepreneurs," The Journal of Creative Behavior 21, 3, 1987, p. 219–233.
3. J. Hornaday and J. Aboud, "Characteristics of Successful Entrepreneurs," *Personnel Psychology*, Summer 1971, p. 141–153.
4. S. Brennan and M. McHugh, "Coping with Recession: the Impact upon the Entrepreneur," *International Small Business Journal*, October–December 1993, p. 71–75.
5. O. Collins, D. Moore and D. Unwalla, *The Enterprising Man*, Michigan State University: East Lansily Bureau of Business & Economic Research, 1964.
6. Henry Mintzberg and James Waters, "Tracking Strategy in an Entrepreneurial Firm," Academy of Management Journal 25, 3, 1982, p. 465–499.
7. E. Ward, "Motivation of Expansion Plans of Entrepreneurs and Small Business Managers," Journal of Small Business Management, January 1993, p. 33.
8. E. Ward, 1993.
9. E. Ward, 1993.
10. J. Scheré, "Tolerance of Ambiguity as a Discriminating Variable Between Entrepreneurs and Managers," Academy of Management Proceedings, 1982, p. 406.
11. Based on an interview with Peter Drucker by Tom Richman, "The Entrepreneurial Mystique," *INC*. (October 1985).
12. D. McClelland, 1985.
13. D. Dean et al., *Executive ESP*, Englewood Cliff, N.J.: Prentice-Hall, 1974.
14. J. Timmons, "The Entrepreneurial Mind," *Success*, April 1994, p. 50.

THE ENTREPRENEUR

William Hewlett & David Packard
University As Incubator

William Hewlett and David Packard founded one of the most successful electronics companies in North America. The initial idea was incubated at Stanford University under the guidance and mentorship of Professor Frederick Terman. As a result of Professor Terman's encouragement, the two entrepreneurs created their company in 1939, in Packard's garage and with very little money, after they designed a unique and inexpensive type of audio oscillator. The product was an instant success and the two entrepreneurs embarked on developing a series of products that used the same design principles. They located the company in Stanford Research Park, close to their mentor Professor Terman. Their entrepreneurial efforts led to the formation of the Silicon Valley. Many of the Silicon Valley entrepreneurs worked at Hewlett-Packard before venturing out on their own. The two entrepreneurs are known for their innovation and for encouraging their employees to be creative and innovative.

Source: E. Roberts, *Entrepreneurs in High Technology,* New York: Oxford University Press, 1991.

△ CHAPTER 5 △
WOMEN, MINORITY & ABORIGINAL ENTREPRENEURS

THE ERA OF WOMEN ENTREPRENEURS

Women entrepreneurs represent a large and growing segment of the business population in North America. About 30 percent of all small businesses in North America are run by women, according to the Small Business Association. The post-war world has witnessed a dramatically different role for women in the workforce as a result of the change in social values. Not only have women moved out of the traditional roles of housewife, secretary and teacher, but they also emerged as an economic force. Indeed, this decade represents the era of women entrepreneurs.

The woman entrepreneur is defined as "the female head of a business who has taken the initiative of launching a new venture, accepting the associated risks, the financial, administrative and social responsibility and who is effectively in charge of its day-to-day management."[1]

THE ENTREPRENEURIAL TRAITS

As we discussed in an earlier chapter, the traits approach assumes that certain traits are common among entrepreneurs and are the driving force underlying the choice of an entrepreneurship career. These include a high need for achievement, risk taking, a high need for independence and autonomy, internal locus of control and a low need for conformity. Research studies have found that there are more similarities between male and female entrepreneurs than between female entrepreneurs and females in general. According to Saxton and Bowman, both male and female entrepreneurs score low on the need to conform and high on risk-taking and autonomy compared with women in general.[2] Another study by De Carlo and Lyons found similarities between male and female entrepreneurs on achievement, independence, autonomy, leadership and conformity. However, De Carlo and Lyons found significant differences between female entrepreneurs and females in general.[3]

This chapter is based on published research by Professor A. B. Ibrahim.

Box 5.1. The High Achiever & Risk Taker.

Elizabeth Arden (original name Florence Nightingale Graham) left a nursing career to start her own beauty salon. With the help of a chemist friend, she began to develop her own cosmetics. Elizabeth Arden endured hardship before her brand of cosmetics became known.

Chaganti found no significant difference between male and female entrepreneurs on internal locus of control, achievement, autonomy and nonconformity.[4]

ENVIRONMENTAL FACTORS

The environmental approach argues that the choice of an entrepreneurship career is related to environmental factors such as family background, early experience of rejection, prior business experience and education.

Family Background

According to Hisrich and Brush, male and female entrepreneurs have similar family backgrounds. They tend to be first born; come from middle to upper class families with a self-employed parent, usually the father.[5] This type of background provides women entrepreneurs with role models and makes the choice of an entrepreneurship career more attractive.

Early Experience of Rejection

Both male and female entrepreneurs reported rejection by their fathers or an authority figure.[6]

The Incubator Business

Prior business experience in a particular industry tends to drive entrepreneurs to start their own business. According to Stevenson, male entrepreneurs tend to have more relevant experience prior to launching their business, while female entrepreneurs tend to gain their

---

Box 5.2. The Entrepreneurial Family.

Mary Kay Ash, founder of Mary Kay Cosmetics, grew up in an entrepreneurial environment. Her parents owned and operated a hotel and restaurant near Houston. When she was seven, her father fell sick and she helped her mother to run the business. She developed her successful door-to-door selling concept after working as a saleswoman for Stanley Home Products. Now her son is helping her run the huge family business.

---

experience after starting their own business.[7] Hirsch and Peters suggest that female entrepreneurs' level of experience tends to be limited compared to male entrepreneurs. Female entrepreneurs' experience tends to be more service and retail oriented, while that of males tends to be technical and management oriented.[8] This profile is rapidly changing as more science and business oriented female entrepreneurs enter the market.

Education

Both male and female entrepreneurs are college educated. However, early research reported that male entrepreneurs tend to have science and business related education, while female entrepreneurs tend to have a liberal arts education.[9] Women's education background implied that they lack the relevant training necessary to start and operate a business. Recent research has found no significant differences between the types and levels of education of male and female entrepreneurs.[10]

Motivation

Both female and male entrepreneurs cite a desire for autonomy, independence and achievement as primary motives for starting their own businesses. However, among women, according to Hirsch and Peters, these needs arise out of a frustration with their current employment. When women feel they can't reach their full potential as a result of the glass ceiling encountered in large corporations, they start their own businesses,[11] A second explanation is that entrepreneurship offers female entrepreneurs greater flexibility to fulfill their household obligations. Box 5.3 describes some research findings.

Box 5.3. Women Entrepreneurs.

  Carole E. Scott studied 154 women entrepreneurs to investigate why more women are becoming entrepreneurs. She found that, essentially, women become entrepreneurs for the same reasons as men: to be independent, to be their own boss, to earn more money and to achieve personal goals. In addition, some women entrepreneurs indicated that a lack of opportunities for women, the glass ceiling effect they encountered in large corporations, as well as the flexibility offered by independent business in terms of working hours were among the reasons for becoming entrepreneurs.

Source: Carole E. Scott, "Why More Women Are Becoming Entrepreneurs," *Journal of Small Business Management*, October 1986, pp. 37–44.

TYPE AND CHARACTERISTICS OF BUSINESS

As we discussed earlier, research suggests that female entrepreneurs tend to be concentrated in service and retail business, while male entrepreneurs tend to be concentrated in manufacturing, construction and high-tech business.[12] In addition, female entrepreneurs tend to operate smaller firms in terms of number of employees and net earnings compared to male

---

Box 5.4. The Successful Entrepreneur.

Debbie Fields, founder of Mrs. Fields Cookies, exemplifies today's successful woman entrepreneur. Her innovative approach, management skills and high need for achievement have contributed to her success. She began selling cookies when she was nineteen in a modest store. She would ask passersby to sample her product. At the end of her first year, she had sold $200,000 worth of cookies, and after ten years she had opened two hundred stores with total sales of over $100 million. She had also designed a highly elaborate and centralized control system to monitor service and quality in all her stores.

---

entrepreneurs.[13] Further, they employ fewer family members, have more female customers, employ more workers, and launch their ventures more slowly.[14] With the dramatic increase in the number of female entrepreneurs, many are now venturing into "nontraditional" fields such as the high tech and manufacturing sectors.[15]

MANAGEMENT STYLE

Women's upbringing allows them to acquire certain traits and skills that make them successful entrepreneurs. Female entrepreneurs seem to focus on sharing rather than on winning, and winning and losing do not mean the same thing to males and females. Females tend to share ideas and information and demonstrate more of a team approach than male entrepreneurs. Female entrepreneurs have a strong sense of practicality and are often frugal with resources. They do not feel uncomfortable asking questions, and most recognize their weaknesses and are not afraid to seek advice. They are detail oriented and devote more time developing relationships with customers. As a result, they have a better knowledge of customer needs and wants than their male counterparts.[16]

Female entrepreneurs develop much larger and more formal networks than male entrepreneurs. Consequently, they have better access to information than their male counterparts. A key person in the female entrepreneur's network is her husband. That may not necessarily be true for male entrepreneurs, who usually turn to outside advisors. Further, female entrepreneurs more often seek outside advice than male entrepreneurs.[17]

Female entrepreneurs place greater emphasis on idea generation, innovation, human resources and interpersonal skills.[18]

Box 5.5. The Motivator.

Anita Roddick, founder of The Body Shop, has constantly been cited for her ability to build and motivate her employees. She has achieved an almost cult-like following. Their respect for her and her innovative approach to marketing and management has enabled The Body Shop to achieve tremendous success.

COMMON PROBLEMS ENCOUNTERED BY WOMEN ENTREPRENEURS

Financing

Research studies have reported that female entrepreneurs encounter greater difficulties obtaining financing and securing credit for their businesses compared with male entrepreneurs.[19] This problem may be due to sex stereotyping as well as the types of business that women entrepreneurs have traditionally ventured into, which tend to be service oriented. This type of business has very few hard skills for a bank to use as collateral. Today, however, many financial institutions have changed their traditional lending approach and place more emphasis on the potential of the business, the industry and the entrepreneur. In addition, financial institutions are intensifying their training programs for account managers to ensure more objective assessment of the business. The success stories of female entrepreneurs such as Anita Roddick, founder of The Body Shop, has contributed to creating a more positive and supportive environment for women entrepreneurs.[20]

Limited Access to Networks

Networks provide valuable information to entrepreneurs. Female entrepreneurs have less access to the networks that male entrepreneurs usually form as a result of prior business experience and school ties, "the old boys network." It is only recently that women entrepreneurs have started forming networks.

Lack of Managerial Experience

Research studies reported that female entrepreneurs lack the management experience and training necessary to start a business, skills that their male counterparts usually acquire from previous work.[21]

The problems discussed in the previous section call for collaborative efforts from universities, financial institutions and government agencies to ensure that adequate attention is paid to overcoming these problems.

MINORITY ENTREPRENEURS

Minority entrepreneurs represent a large and rapidly growing segment of the business population. Today it is common to see entrepreneurs from a multitude of ethnic backgrounds and identifiable subcultures. According to the Canadian Federation of Independent Business, Canada has the highest percentage of ethnic entrepreneurs in the industrialized world.[22] Indeed, the success of minority entrepreneurs has proved vital to regional development and the national economic health.

Emergence of Minority Entrepreneurs—The Marginal/Displacement and the Cultural Approaches

The postwar era brought waves of immigrants from a multitude of ethnic backgrounds to Canada and the U.S. Ethnic minority groups are communities who settle in a host country and are differentiated from the indigenous population by skin color and/or subscription to noticeably different cultural and religious norms or values. They are usually drawn to the host country by the prospect of a higher standard of living, the prospect of employment and, for some, a necessary move from the repressive conditions of their homeland.

One of the predominant explanations of minority entrepreneurship is the marginal/displacement theory, discussed in an earlier chapter. The theory argues that social marginality, or a lack of mobility, legitimacy and social integration, "pushes" ethnic and religious minorities into self-employment. Shapero suggests that ethnic groups become entrepreneurs as a result of displacement and social marginality.[23] Many minority entrepreneurs are "pushed" into self-employment as a result of negative factors such as a lack of upward mobility in large organizations.

A second explanation for the rapid growth of minority entrepreneurs is the cultural approach discussed in an earlier chapter. Some ethnic groups see entrepreneurship as an opportunity and a desirable career.

The Entrepreneurial Traits

As with female entrepreneurs, there are more trait similarities between minority and mainstream entrepreneurs than between minority entrepreneurs and minorities in general. De Carlo and Lyons found no significant differences between minority and non-minority entrepreneurs on achievement, independence, autonomy, nonconformity and leadership.[24] Earlier research by Hornaday and Aboud reported some differences, which were attributed to socio-economic rather than racial factors.

Box 5.6. Sensing an Opportunity, Naya.

Sensing a worldwide demand for bottled water, Ahmed Hbauss, a Lebanese immigrant, began scouting for a place to build a water business. The entrepreneur selected a place in the Laurentians, close to Montreal, Canada, and formed Nora Beverages Inc. in the mid 1980s. The company's well-known Naya bottled water has been a hit in the market. Today the company holds over 35 percent of the Canadian market of bottled water and exports Naya water to the U.S., Europe and the Middle and Far East.

Naya's success is attributed to the ability of the entrepreneur to sense and exploit the growing demand for bottled water and position the product competitively.

Source: *The Gazette*, Montreal May 30, 1994 and Oct 31, 1994.

Motivation

Like mainstream entrepreneurs, minority entrepreneurs cited achievement, autonomy and job satisfaction as motives for the decision to become entrepreneurs. However, like female entrepreneurs, a lack of upward mobility in large organizations was reported as a primary motive for self-employment among minority entrepreneurs.[25]

Family Background and Education

According to a nationwide study, minority entrepreneurs tend to be first born. Their fathers are usually blue-collar workers or self-employed, while their mothers are generally home makers. However, unlike female and mainstream entrepreneurs, minority entrepreneurs tend to describe their personalities as being more like those of their mothers, with whom they had closer relationships during childhood.

Education and Prior Business Experience

Minority entrepreneurs have consistently been found to be well educated, often with college degrees.[26] Like their mainstream counterparts, minority entrepreneurs tend to start businesses in industries in which they have prior business experience.

Types and Characteristics of Minority Businesses

Like female entrepreneurs, minority entrepreneurs tend to be concentrated in the service sector. Their businesses tend to be smaller than those of mainstream entrepreneurs. The typical minority entrepreneur starts a new business rather than buying an existing one.[27] A study of minority and non-minority entrepreneurs found no significant differences with regard to profitability, indebtedness and liquidity.[28] In fact, minority firms in sectors other than retailing achieved a higher return on investment than non-minority firms.[29] Further, minority entrepreneurs were found to be less likely to default on their loans.[30]

Management Style

Research studies have found that minority entrepreneurs tend to subscribe to value systems that more closely resemble those of their key customers. This approach allows minority entrepreneurs to narrow the gap between themselves and their customers, who are predominantly from the mainstream culture. By espousing similar values, they build trust and legitimize their business to their customers.[31]

Like female entrepreneurs, minority entrepreneurs develop formal types of networks, including university small business centres, government agencies and entrepreneurial associations. They also place greater emphasis on idea generation, innovation and interpersonal skills.[32]

The Minority Business Pattern of Growth

Minority businesses seem to follow a certain pattern of growth, in which the ethnic stage is followed by the local market stage.

The Ethnic Stage

Minority businesses are initially launched to serve ethnic communities' needs and wants. These businesses tend to be concentrated in minority residential areas. The minority entrepreneurs' knowledge of their community's needs, tastes and preferences allow them to build a competitive advantage and carve a market niche.

The Local Market Stage

Once minority entrepreneurs have gained the skills, experience and confidence, they expand their businesses to serve mainstream customers as well as other ethnic communities. To succeed, ethnic entrepreneurs place greater emphasis on their unique ethnic products and their highly committed workers, who are usually family members or from the same ethnic community. Figure 5.1 depicts the minority business pattern of growth.

Problems Encountered by Minority Entrepreneurs

The pioneering research study of both female and minority entrepreneurs conducted in 1975 by the U.S. Commission on Civil Rights revealed a number of major problems often encountered by these two groups. These include obtaining financing, securing credit and obtaining information about available opportunities. Further, the study reported a negative perception about the effectiveness of both female and minority entrepreneurs.[33] Ronstadt found that both female and minority entrepreneurs encounter difficulties obtaining financing. This is despite the evidence discussed earlier in the chapter that minority firms have similar financial performances to those of mainstream entrepreneurs and are less likely to default on their loans.[34] Hisrich and Brush recommend that aspiring entrepreneurs establish a credit record early in their careers to help them obtain financing later on and to familiarize them with the credit policies.[35]

As is the case with female entrepreneurs, finance and general management are areas of concern to minority entrepreneurs.[36] This is due to a lack of managerial training. Hisrich and Brush suggest that minority entrepreneurs could benefit from training in areas such as finance, marketing and planning. They recommend that minority entrepreneurs cultivate networks that would provide them with much needed support. Further, they must find mentors to guide and encourage them.[37] Box 5.7 describes one such effort to help minority entrepreneurs.

Pattern of Growth	Market	Characteristics
The ethnic stage	serve ethnic customers	small, niche market, ethnic areas
Local market stage	ethnic, mainstream and other ethnic customers	Large, unique ethnic products, highly committed work force, ethnic and non-ethnic areas

Figure 5.1. Minority Business Pattern of Growth.

Box 5.7. In Partnership.

The Mathieu da Costa Business Development Corp. is a Black business group that manages millions of dollars in Quebec government grants. The objective of the organization is to help finance Black entrepreneurs. The organization evaluates business plans in collaboration with the Consulting Bureau of the Concordia University Centre for Small Business and Entrepreneurial Studies before granting funds. Armed with a good business plan and initial funding, Black entrepreneurs can then apply to banks for working capital loans.

The problems encountered by minority entrepreneurs call for collaborative efforts from universities, government agencies, financial institutions and leaders of ethnic communities to help this important segment of the business population. Government and financial institutions could provide startup seed financing, and universities and community leaders could provide training, support and mentorship. Box 5.8 describes some of these efforts.

ABORIGINAL ENTREPRENEURS

Aboriginal entrepreneurs share many characteristics with mainstream entrepreneurs. A study of the performance of Aboriginal small firms found no significant differences between the performance of these firms and that of small businesses in general. Further, the study found that Aboriginal small businesses have contributed to the economic development of remote regions.[38] Author Wanda Wuttunee even suggests that promoting entrepreneurial activities is critical for sustaining regional economic development.[39] Research on Aboriginal entrepreneurs has found a strong correlation between entrepreneurs' success and the political sovereignty of the band. The more control the band has over its resources and decision making, the higher the success rate of its members' entrepreneurial activities.

Box 5.8. Concordia Minority Institute.

The Minority Institute of the Concordia University Centre for Small Business and Entrepreneurial Studies was established to provide much needed training for minority entrepreneurs in Montreal. The Institute has forged ties with the Black, East and West Indian and Cree communities.

Problems Facing Aboriginal Entrepreneurs

Lack of Business Training

Aboriginal entrepreneurs lack managerial and entrepreneurial training. The problem has intensified as a result of the move towards self-government and the increased demand for Aboriginal managers. However, many universities in the U.S. and Canada are currently offering business programs for Aboriginals aimed at enhancing their business skills. For example, the Concordia University Centre for Small Business and Entrepreneurial Studies provides business training for the Cree.

The Indian Act.*

Section 89 of the Indian Act represents a major impediment to entrepreneurial activities on reserves. This section prevents any non-Indian entity from having the power to seize the personal property of an Indian. Obviously, when the Act was written this was seen as a way of preventing Aboriginals from losing what little land was left to them. In today's business world, this section works against Aboriginal entrepreneurs by limiting their ability to raise capital. Furthermore, the act discourages venture growth by limiting tax exemptions to two legal forms, the sole proprietorship and partnership. Thus a corporation is not considered to be Indian even if it is owned by Aboriginal entrepreneurs. Modification of the act has been considered to allow Aboriginal people to use the various forms of financing available to other entrepreneurs.

Traditional values

Although Aboriginals have always been traders, traditional values of sharing go against the entrepreneurial spirit and encourage more cooperative forms of business. However, today more and more Aboriginal entrepreneurs are venturing successfully into business.

Institutional Efforts

Different programs at the provincial, state and federal levels in the U.S. and Canada were created to enhance Aboriginal entrepreneurs' capabilities and provide much needed funds to Aboriginal ventures. For example, Aboriginal Business Canada (ABC) was created as a division of Industry Canada to assist Aboriginal entrepreneurs in various activities, including export, management and financing. Further, Aboriginal Capital Corporations (ACC) was created by Industry Canada to provide loans to Aboriginal entrepreneurs across Canada.

Economic Development Corporations, located in different regions, assist Aboriginal entrepreneurs in developing business plans and obtaining funds from various sources such as bands and settlements.

---

* The words Indian and Aboriginal refer to status Indians as defined by Indian and Northern Affairs Canada.

SUMMARY

Women and minority entrepreneurs represent a large and growing segment of the business population. Both groups have been found to have similar traits, family and education backgrounds to those of mainstream entrepreneurs. A negative experience such as a lack of upward mobility tends to "push" minority and female entrepreneurs to an entrepreneurship career. Minority and female entrepreneurs encounter similar problems including lack of financing, networking, lack of management training and experience. Aboriginal entrepreneurs were also discussed and the problems they encountered were examined.

NOTES

1. D. Lavoie, "A New Era for Female Entrepreneurship in the 80s," *Journal of Small Business*, Winter 1984–85, pp. 34–43.
2. D. L. Saxton, and N. B. Bowman. "The Validation of Personality Index: Comparative Psychological Characteristics Analysis of Female Entrepreneurs, Managers, Entrepreneurship Students and Business Students." In R. Ronstadt, J. Hornady, R. Peterson, and K. Vesper (eds.) *Frontier of Entrepreneurship Research,* Wellesley, MA: Babson College, 1986.
3. J. De Carlo and Paul R. Lyons, "A Comparison of Selected Personal Characteristics of Minority and Non-Minority Female Entrepreneurs," *Journal of Small Business Management* (December 1979), pp. 22–29.
4. R. Chaganti, "Management in Women-Owned Enterprises," *Journal of Small Business Management,* (October 1986), pp. 18–29.
5. R. D. Hisrich and C. Brush, "The Woman Entrepreneur: Management Skills and Business Problems," Journal of Small Business Management, January 1984, pp. 30–37.
6. Kets de Vries, "The Entrepreneurial Personality: A Person at the Crossroads," *The Journal of Management Studies,* February 1977.
7. L. Stevenson, "Against All Odds: The Entrepreneurship of Women," Journal of Small Business Management, Oct., 1986.
8. R. Ronstadt, *Entrepreneurship: Text, Cases and Notes,* Dover, MA: Lord, 1984.
9. R. D. Hisrich and M. Peters, *Entrepreneurship: Starting, Developing and Managing a New Enterprise,* Second Edition, Homewood, ILL.: Irwin, 1989, pp. 66–68.
10. E. Fisher, "Sex Differences and Small Business Performance Among Canadian Retailers and Services Providers," *Journal of Small Business and Entrepreneurship,* July–September 1992, pp. 2–13.
11. R. D. Hisrich and M. Peters, Entrepreneurship: *Starting, Developing and Managing a New Enterprise,* Second Edition, Homewood, ILL.: Irwin, 1989, pp. 66–68.
12. R. Ronstadt, 1984. Also see: D. Hisrich and M. Peters, 1989.
13. Ibid.
14. S. Birley, C. Moss, and P. Saunders, "The Difference Between Small Firms Started by Male and Female Entrepreneurs Who Attended Small Business Courses" in R. Ronstadt, J. Hornaday, R. Peterson, and K. Vesper (eds.), *Frontiers of the Entrepreneurship Research,* Wellesley, MA: Babson College, 1986.
15. D. Lavoie, 1984–85.
16. A. Reznik, "Just Like a Woman," *Your Money,* July–August 1987, pp. 44–47. Also see G. Forsyth, J. Mount and J. T. Ziner, *Entrepreneurship and Small Business Development: Text and Cases,* Scarborough, Ontario: Prentice-Hall Inc., 1991, pp. 333–334.
17. S. Birley, C. Moss, and P. Saunders, 1986.
18. R. D. Hisrich and C. Brush, 1984, pp. 30–37.
19. Ibid.
20. A. B. Ibrahim, *Canadian Entrepreneurial Studies,* Institute of Bankers, 1994.
21. R. D. Hisrich and C. Brush, 1984. Also see D. Lavoie, 1984.
22. J. Bulloch, "Entrepreneurship and Development," *Journal of Small Business & Entrepreneurship* (1988), pp. 3–7.

23. A. Shapero, "The Displaced Uncomfortable Entrepreneur," *Psychology Today*, 133 (November 1975), pp. 83–88. Also see A. Shapero, and L. Sokal, "The Social Dimensions of Entrepreneurship," in C. Kent, D. Sexton and K. Vesper (eds.), *Encyclopaedia of Entrepreneurs,* Prentice-Hall, N.J., 1982.
24. J. De Carlo and P. Lyons, 1979.
25. R. D. Hisrich, C. Brush, "Characteristics of the Minority Entrepreneur," *Journal of Small Business Management*, Vol. 24, No. 4, October 1986, pp. 1–9.
26. E. Gomolka, "Characteristics of Minority Entrepreneurs and Small/Business Enterprises," *American Journal of Small Business*, Vol. 2, 1977–1978, pp. 174–184. Also see: R. D. Hisrich & C. Brush, 1986.
27. C. Enz, M. Dollinger, and C. Daily, "The Value Orientations of Minority and Non-Minority Small Business Owners," *Entrepreneurship: Theory and Practice*, Vol. 15. No. 1, Fall 1990, pp. 23–25.
28. W. Scott, "Financial Performance of Minority- Versus Non-Minority-Owned Business," *Journal of Small Business Management*, 21, 1, January 1983, pp. 43–48.
29. T. Bates and A. Furino, "A New Nationwide Data Base for Minority Business," *The Journal of Small Business Management* (April 1985), pp. 41–52.
30. W. Scott, 1983.
31. E. Gomolka, 1977–78. Also see: C. Enz, M. Dollinger, and C. Daily, 1970.
32. R. D. Hisrich and C. Brush, 1986. Also see: A. Triana, H. Welsh and E. Young, "Information Search Pattern Among Hispanic Entrepreneurs," *Journal of Small Business Management*, 14 (October 1984), pp. 39–48.
33. "Minorities and Women as Government Contractors," Report of the United States Commission on Civil Rights (May 1975).
34. W. Scott, 1983.
35. R. D. Hisrich and C. Brush, 1986.
36. Ibid.
37. Ibid.
38. Industry Canada, 1994. Also see: K. Thomas, Canadian Business Review, Summer 1994, p. 12.
39. A. Simmons, Windspeaker, Canada's National Aboriginal News Publication, 9 November 1992, p. 8.

THE ENTREPRENEUR

Micheline Charest
The Cinema Entrepreneur

Cinema czar Micheline Charest represents one of the most successful stories of women entrepreneurs. Charest is the chairman and CEO of Cinar Films Inc., a leading Canadian company involved in the development, production, post production and international distribution of non-violent, non-sexist children's programming.

Charest studied at the London Film School and worked at the National Film Board before starting her own company—Cinar Films—with her husband in 1976. Under her leadership Cinar became a leading firm in the children's entertainment industry. The company has grown rapidly, with 1997 revenues of over $67 million. Its animated and live-action programs have been seen in 110 countries and dubbed into 30 languages.

Charest is the producer of all its company's programs including highly acclaimed series such as *Arthur, Are you Afraid of the Dark?* and *The Busy World of Richard Scarry.*

Charest is also the founder of Teletoon, a Canadian, all-animated cable network. Cinar recently acquired an educational publishing house in North Carolina in order to expand its activities into the educational field.

Charest was named Canadian Entrepreneur of the year by the Association of Canadian Venture Capital Companies for her entrepreneurial activities and innovation. She was ranked among the "50 Most Powerful Women in Entertainment" by Hollywood Reporter and among the 50 top people in animation by Animation Magazine. Further, Charest has received over 20 corporate and 100 industry awards for her innovation and excellence.

Fifty percent of Cinar's work force are women and fifty percent of these women are senior managers. In a recent interview in the Montreal Gazette, Charest admits that her biggest achievement is that she founded a successful company in a predominantly male industry. She says "don't believe any woman who tells you she didn't have to work harder to counteract the prejudices."

Charest's venture start up was not without problems. Her first release, The Wicker Man, was poorly marketed. However, Charest was able to overcome the start up problems. She has demonstrated her keen financial acumen both in building the company and serving as a key negotiator in many of Cinar's deals. Cinar is a publicly traded company with listings on Montreal stock exchange as well as on the Nasdaq.

Source: *Women in Management*, Richard Ivey School of Business, The University of Western Ontario, Vol. 5, 4, June 1995; *The Gazette*, Monday January 5, 1998; Monday Oct 3, 1994.

△ CHAPTER 6 △
THE ENTREPRENEUR—
THE INNOVATOR

Steve Jobs of Apple Company created the personal computer from his own garage and changed the entire computer industry. Michael Dell of Dell Computer introduced mail order to the computer industry. Fred Smith of Fedex introduced the concept of overnight delivery. What do these entrepreneurs have in common? They are all innovators, a primary trait of entrepreneurship.

ENTREPRENEURSHIP AND INNOVATION

Joseph Schumpeter,[1] the well-known economist, regarded innovation as a key activity that most successful entrepreneurs must perform and a critical factor in determining who is an entrepreneur. Entrepreneurship in this sense is the ability to bring together consumers and innovation in order to satisfy a need. Thus innovation implies newness, a new product in the case of product innovation, faster delivery in the case of service innovation or an efficient production facility in the case of process innovation. According to Schumpeter, innovation within industries destroys the established order, rendering old products obsolete in a short period of time.[2] For example, think of how entrepreneurs such as Steve Jobs and Bill Gates changed the computer industry.

TYPES OF INNOVATION

A popular perception is that innovation is born out of a flash of genius. However, according to Peter Drucker, innovation arises more often from a deliberate and voluntary effort by the entrepreneur to satisfy customer needs and wants.[3] The most important motivation for innovation is the opportunity for higher growth resulting from increased value added of a product or service. Innovation involves two broad categories: breakthrough and incremental innovation.

This chapter was developed by Professor A. B. Ibrahim based on published research.

Breakthrough Innovation

This is radical change leading to completely new product/service process. Examples of breakthrough entrepreneurs include Thomas Edison, who introduced electricity, Alexander Graham Bell, who introduced the telephone, and Edwin Land—founder of Polaroid company—who introduced the instant camera. Breakthrough innovation is characterized by large initial investments in R&D and by an all-or-nothing outcome. The entrepreneur may sustain heavy losses in R&D or enjoy a successful leadership position and a lucrative market. For example, Edison lived through many failures and had to raise funds from private sources before his efforts were brought to fruition. Edwin Land raised funds from investors to conduct research on polarizing and photographic technology before he unveiled the first instant camera.

Incremental Innovation

This type of innovation involves the improvement and enhancement of an existing product/service/process. Typically, the entrepreneur uses past experience or a proven process and applies it to new opportunities.[4] Most entrepreneurs fall into this category. The R&D investment in incremental type innovation tend to be moderate compared with breakthrough type innovation as the former tends to evolve from the existing, proven technology. Further, the market has already been developed and the potential for higher growth and profitability can be projected. For example, entrepreneurs Bill Gates and Paul Allen founded Microsoft with a dream to develop an affordable software that can be used by every personal computer user. It has been suggested that the entrepreneur must know the firm's "core competence" in order to use incremental innovation to the firm's advantage.[5]

Product, Service and Process Innovation

Innovation can involve a physical product or a service. It may also result in applying an existing product or service to new markets, in cost cutting or in increasing distribution effectiveness.[6]

Product Innovation

Product innovation involves developing a new product with known or unknown needs or enhancing and refining existing products. For example, entrepreneur Edwin Land created the need for the instant camera; Max Braun, founder of Braun AG, introduced the electric razor; and Dr. Michael Cowpland, founder of Corel Systems Corporation (a Canadian company) introduced a new version of WordPerfect.

The Product Development Stages. To understand product innovation we will discuss briefly the product development stages.

1. The idea generation stage. Innovation is the result of a creative process. The entrepreneur may have a new idea or tinker in his or her garage with a problem in search of a solution. The motivation to innovate is often to satisfy customer needs and wants. A. K. Velan, founder of Velan Valve, a Montreal-based

company, started his business from his garage with an idea that would solve the problem of condensation from steam piping.[7] The entrepreneur's idea may become an obsession, driving the entrepreneur to find a solution. For example, Edwin Land's obsession with the idea of polarizing light led to the development of the instant camera.

2. The development and incubation stage. In this stage the entrepreneur tries to develop his/her idea further. He or she may gather information, conduct tests and then design a crude model or sketch to see if the idea is workable and worth pursuing. For example, A. K. Velan was on the road a great deal of the time trying to gather information about the market. When he was not travelling, he was at the drawing board designing his steam trap valve. He constructed a prototype of his invention and tested and modified it in his house. Based on the design and/or the prototype, the entrepreneur may develop a proposal to raise seed money from government, friends and wealthy individuals. For example, after his initial research on polarizing light technology, Edwin Land raised over $375,000 from wealthy individuals in order to continue his research work on photographic technology. At this stage, the entrepreneur may conduct brainstorming or focus group sessions to get feedback from customers and experts and to ensure that the product satisfies customer needs. Feedback is essential in order to refine the product and identify the unique features of the product innovation. For example, Peter McAuslan, founder of McAuslan Brewing Company, a Montreal based micro brewery, conducted focus group sessions. Feedback indicated that the taste and flavor of his beers were unique.[8]

3. The incubation stage. At this stage the entrepreneur has solved most of the technical problems, designed and refined the idea/concept and constructed a prototype. The entrepreneur's major concern in this stage is to test the idea/concept/design or prototype for feasibility. Steve Jobs, founder of Apple Computer, recalls:

> "We bought one microprocessorchip between the two of us and designed a microcomputer. Woz (Steve Wozniak) designed about 75 percent of it, and with some of Hewlett-Packard and Atari parts, we built one. Our first computer, The Apple I, looked like a mess, but it worked."[9]

The incubation stage also includes market testing. This involves identifying the customer group or target, the customer profile, the competition and substitute products. Limited production may be required at this stage for samples to test the market. For example, Peter McAuslan of McAuslan Brewing Co. provided free samples of beer to pubs in the Montreal area and noted that "beer drinkers welcomed this new microbrew which tasted like an imported ale but at a cheaper price."[10]

As a result of the market testing, the entrepreneur may choose not to proceed further. However, if the market testing results in positive feedback, the entrepreneur begins to develop the business plan, including the idea, the product, the concept, the market, the management team, the financial projections and required funds, the deal structure and the risk involved in the new venture. Again, the entrepreneur may discover, based on the business plan, that the venture is not viable because of resource constraints. At this stage the entrepreneur may also consider securing legal protection for his new product, such as a patent or a trademark.

4. The Commercial Stage. This stage involves producing the product on a limited or large scale, deciding on the appropriate promotion and venture strategies and designing the appropriate structure and management process. The customer response to the new product is the real test. Indeed, passing the threshold of commercial viability is the ultimate objective of the entrepreneur. After all, the entrepreneur is driven to innovate by the opportunity for higher growth and return on investment. For example, A. K. Velan's first big break came when the U.S. Navy ordered the Velan bimetallic steam trap for its new destroyer. He can remember the late nights in his garage working with his wife to pack them.[11] Sometimes customers' responses are not encouraging and the entrepreneur may be forced to discontinue the new product. For example, after leaving Apple Computer, Steve Jobs started another company and introduced a new personal computer called Next. The market response was negative and Next turned out to be a flop.

Service Innovation

The small business service sector has been growing at a phenomenal rate in the last decade as a result of the technological revolution in the telecommunication and computer industries. However, low entry barriers have intensified the level of competition as many players jockey for market position. Innovation in the service industry is critically important as it allows the entrepreneur to build areas of distinctive competence that are hard to erode. Innovation in the service industry involves introducing a new concept or enhancing an existing service concept. The objective is to satisfy customer needs and wants. For example, Fred Smith, founder of Fedex, introduced the concept of overnight delivery. Smith realized that customers would pay a significant premium for this service. Innovation in the service industry involves the different features that make the business concept unique such as a new design and/or faster delivery. For example, Tom Monaghan, founder of Domino's Pizza, introduced 30-minute delivery guarantee, an innovative marketing approach that yielded an advantage to Domino's. A creative idea is a key ingredient in an innovative concept. Think of how Walt Disney built his company based on the introduction of his successful cartoon in 1937—*Snow White and the Seven Dwarfs*. An innovative concept may also include a new marketing approach. For example, Sam Walton, founder of Wal-Mart, introduced the discounting concept to the retail business.

Process Innovation

Process innovation involves introducing a new process or enhancing an existing one. The objectives of process innovation are to cut cost and improve quality and efficiency in the manufacturing of a product or a service offered. Process innovation in manufacturing may include a new method to improve productivity. For example, Henry Ford introduced the concept of assembly lines, which enabled Ford Company to mass-produce his model-T car and thus reduce manufacturing costs. Process innovation may include a new management or marketing approach. For example, Sam Walton, founder of Wal-Mart, introduced an innovative distribution approach that enabled the company to reduce delivery costs.

SOURCES OF INNOVATION

Sources of innovation may include incubators, prior work experience, R&D activities, customer needs and feedback, and competitors.

Incubators

Universities, research institutes, or other entrepreneurs may provide the mentorship and the positive environment necessary for idea generation and innovation. For example, Stanford professor Frederick Terman provided mentorship to many entrepreneurs in Stanford Research Park, which is now known as the Silicon Valley. He encouraged and guided two of his students, William Hewlett and David Packard, to start their own company, Hewlett-Packard. The initial idea for HB was incubated at Stanford University.

Prior Work Experience

Most entrepreneurs generate their ideas while working for someone else in the same industry. Some industries, such as the computer and retail industries, seem to serve as incubators for new products or service ideas. For example, Ken Olson, founder of Digital Equipment Corporation (DEC), worked at IBM before he decided to start his own business.

Research and Development

The entrepreneur's research efforts contribute significantly to new product and service ideas. For example, Andy Grove, Bob Noyce and Gordon Moore, founders of Intel, conducted their own research in solid state electronics. Most often these research activities are conducted under crude conditions such as a lab or workshop in a basement or garage. In many cases primitive tools are used. For example, Nolan Bushnel, founder of Atari, used scrapped electronic parts and his daughter's old toys to develop his first electronic product.

Consumers

As discussed earlier, customer needs and wants are the primary motive for innovation. Max Braun, founder of Braun AG, was known for introducing new products that are based on real customer needs, such as the electric razor and other household products.

Competitors

A competitor's product or service may provide the entrepreneur with the initial idea. For example, Philip Knight and Bill Bowermann developed Nike based on existing athletic shoes on the market.

THE TECHNOLOGY LIFE-CYCLE—TLC

In the new knowledge-based economy, technology plays a key role in the innovation process. Innovation in this sense is the application of the technology to a particular product, service or process. An example is the application of fiber optics technology to voice, data and video communication.

Technology follows a life-cycle similar to the product life-cycle concept. Figure 6.1 depicts the technology life-cycle and the different stages of development: development, application, growth, maturity and decline (degraded).[12]

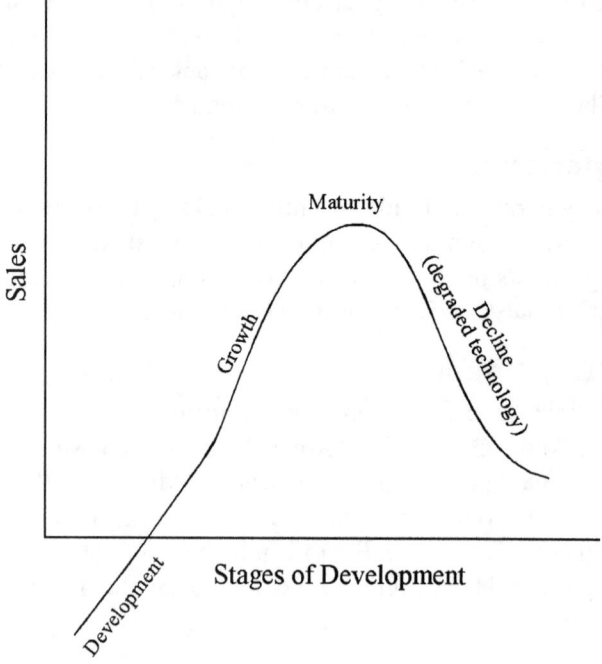

Figure 6.1. The Technology life-cycle.

1. The Technology Development Stage. In this stage the entrepreneur tries to answer a fundamental question: Is the technology worth pursuing? The entrepreneur must assess the possible application of the technology, the cost associated with developing it and the expected return. This stage requires moderate investment in R&D and market research. Cash flow is usually negative and credit terms are difficult to obtain from suppliers.

2. The Technology Application Stage. This stage involves applying the technology to a particular product. A major concern is the cost of applying the technology. The entrepreneur might find that the cost of applying the new technology, including the investment in R&D, to be prohibitive. In addition, the firm may not have the resources or the capabilities to continue further development. In these situations the entrepreneur may decide to abandon the new product or license the technology to a large firm.

3. The Growth Stage. Once the entrepreneur has established the economic viability of applying the technology to a particular product/service or process, the new product is launched. According to Abernathy and Utterback, the entrepreneur at this stage tries to maximize the sales of the new product as the customer demand reaches its peak and the firm enjoys a competitive market position.[13]

4. Maturity Stage. Customer demand for the new product is levelling off and the entrepreneur usually tries to find new market niches for the product.

5. The Decline/Degraded Stage. Demand at this stage is declining as the technology becomes degraded and customers shift to a new technology.

INNOVATING TO COMPETE

In the new economy, product, service and process innovation allow the entrepreneur to build a formidable competitive advantage. The success of the entrepreneur's innovation efforts depends a great deal on the following critical factors.

1. Timing of entry. Early entry into the market is critical to the success of the new product or service as it allows the entrepreneur to gain a substantial advantage and formidable barriers to entry being the first mover. This includes large market share, customer loyalty and cost leadership. Further barriers may include high switching cost. Late entrance, by contrast, may motivate competitors to leap-frog the entrepreneur's efforts.

2. Uniqueness. The new product or service must offer unique features, such as superior functional performance, ease of use, quality and reliability.

3. Customer needs and wants. The new product or service must be based on real customer needs.

Box 6.1. Effective Innovation.

Peter Drucker suggests some guiding principles to effective innovation. These include:

1. Purposeful, systemic innovation begins with the analysis of the innovative opportunities. All the sources of innovative opportunity should be analyzed and studied systematically.
2. The innovation has to be based on market needs.
3. To be effective, an innovation has to be simple and focused. It should do only one thing, otherwise it confuses the consumer.
4. Effective innovation starts small. It is not grandiose. It tries to do one specific thing.
5. A successful innovation aims at leadership. That is, it should focus on being the pioneer.

Source: Peter Drucker, *Innovation and Entrepreneurship*, New York: Harper & Row, 1985.

SUMMARY

Innovation is a primary trait of entrepreneurship. It involves a creative change to a product, service or process. Innovation consists of two broad categories, breakthrough, which implies radical change, and incremental, which involves the enhancement and refinement of an existing product. Innovation must be based on customer needs and wants. Thus the litmus test for the entrepreneur's innovation is the market response. After all, the objective of innovation is to achieve growth and profitability. To compete effectively, the entrepreneur must take into consideration three key factors: timing of entry, uniqueness of the innovation and customer needs and wants.

NOTES

1. Joseph Schumpeter, *The Theory of Economic Development* (Cambridge, MA: Harvard University Press, 1934).
2. Ibid.
3. Peter Drucker. "The Discipline of Innovation." *Harvard Business Review*, May–June 1985, pp. 67–72.
4. C. Prahalad and G. Hamel. "The Core Competence of the Corporation." *Harvard Business Review*, May–June 1990, pp. 79–91.
5. C. Lengic-Hall, "Innovation and Competitive Advantage: What We Know and What We Need to Learn," *Journal of Management*, vol. 18, 1992, pp. 399–427.
6. M. Starr, "Accelerating Innovation." *Business Horizons*, July/August 1992, pp. 44–51.
7. Velan Valve, A case study developed by Ingrid Sinclair (M.B.A.) under the direction of Professor A. B. Ibrahim, 1997.
8. McAuslan Brewing Co., A case study developed by Jose Lam (M.B.A.) and Ludo Sergers (M.B.A.) under the direction of Professor A. B. Ibrahim, 1997.
9. J. S. Gable, S. Tylka, and M. A. Maidique, *Apple Computer,* Stanford School of Business, 1983.
10. McAuslan Brewing Co., 1997.
11. Velan Valve, 1997.
12. David Ford and Chris Ryan, "Taking Technology to Market," *Harvard Business Review*, March–April 1981, vol. 59, no 2.
13. William J. Abernathy and J. M. Utterback, "A Dynamic Model of Process and Product Innovation," *Omega* 3, no. 6, 1975.

THE ENTREPRENEUR

Dr. Francesco Bellini
The Scientist Entrepreneur

Dr. Francesco Bellini is a typical entrepreneur: he is a high achiever, has a strong sense of perseverance and simply refuses to take no for an answer. Dr. Bellini is president and CEO of Biochem Pharma Inc., a multimillion dollar international drug company based in Montreal, Canada.

Dr. Bellini immigrated from Italy in 1967, armed with an engineering degree. However, like many immigrants he found upon arrival that his degree meant very little in North America, so he enrolled at Concordia and attended classes at night. In 1972 he obtained a bachelor of science and in 1977 he received a doctorate in organic chemistry from the University of New Brunswick.

After a successful career as a researcher at the Montreal-based subsidiary of a multinational firm and later as the head of the Biochemicals Division of the Institut Armand-Frappier at the Université du Québec, Dr. Bellini decided to achieve his dream of forming an international biopharmaceutical company in Montreal. Dr. Bellini approached the federal government with his idea; he recalls "they said I was crazy, a dreamer, and that it could not be done because the Canadian market could not support the high cost of such an enterprise. At one point they didn't even want to talk to me any more. But when people tell me something is impossible that is when I try even harder."

In 1986, Dr. Bellini co-founded Biochem Pharma Inc. with only five employees. Under his leadership the company's growth has been exceptional. It now has 1000 employees and annual revenues of over $160 million. Its products are marketed around the globe. One of Dr. Bellini's greatest achievements was the discovery of a new drug for treating complications associated with diabetes. In addition, he has over twenty patents to his credit.

Dr. Bellini and Biochem have received several honorary distinctions including, most notably, 1996 Prix Galien Canada for excellence in pharmaceutical research in the discovery of 3TC[P] for the treatment of the HIV/AIDS virus.

Today Biochem is a leading Canadian biopharmaceutical company, one of the few firms active in prevention (vaccines), diagnosis (diagnostic) and treatment (pharmaceutical).

Source: *The Montreal Gazette*, January 9, 1996; a case study by A. B. Ibrahim, 1997.

△ CHAPTER 7 △
INTRAPRENEURSHIP

INTRAPRENEURSHIP IN THE NEW ECONOMY

The new knowledge-based economy is characterized by rapid technological change and consumer demand for variety, quality, customization and convenience.[1] Further, the new technology-driven economy is characterized by short business cycles and a gradual shift from physical to intellectual assets. Indeed, recent trends indicate that the new economy has changed the way a firm operates, sparking the belief that corporate entrepreneurship will play a key role in the growth and success of corporate America. These trends include massive layoffs and downsizing in many large firms, and the growing trends toward outsourcing and the development of strategic alliances with smaller entrepreneurial ventures.

RECIPE FOR SUCCESS: A MODEL OF CORPORATE ENTREPRENEURSHIP

Today many large organizations recognize that the only way to avoid the corporate death trap is by marrying entrepreneurial traits such as innovation, risk-taking, independence and a high need for achievement with the management and resource capabilities of large organizations. In the following sections we offer a model of corporate intrapreneurship. As shown in Figure 7.1, the model focuses on five elements: creating intrapreneurial culture, the manager as a champion of innovation, corporate venturing, venture capital support and sponsoring independent entrepreneurs.

Creating the Intrapreneurial culture

Large organizations are usually characterized by layers of organizational hierarchies, rigid process technology, inflexible structures, a low level of employee participation in the decision making process and a high level of political activity. This type of environment does not foster innovation and creativity among organizational members. An intrapreneurial culture, on the other hand, provides a high degree of flexibility and inde-

This chapter is based on a research model developed by Professor A. B. Ibrahim.

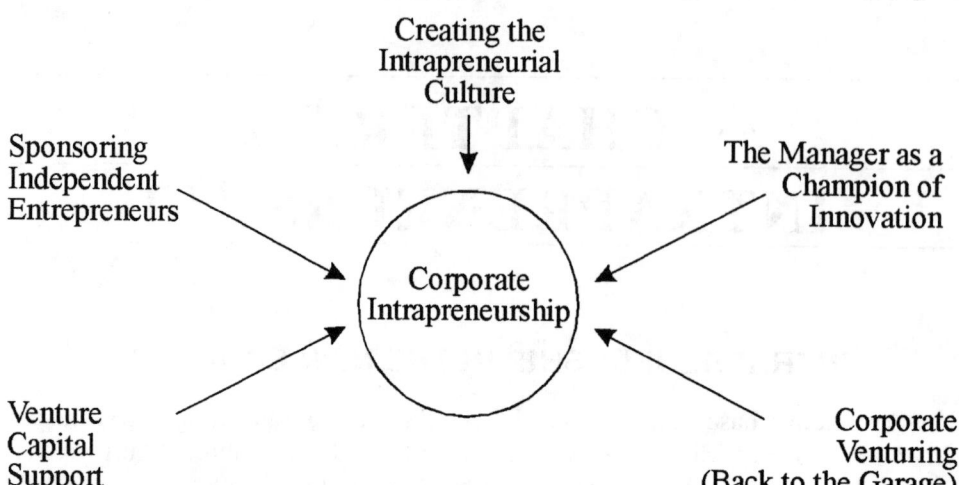

Figure 7.1. A Model of Corporate Intrapreneurship.

pendence and encourages innovation and risk-taking. In the following sections we discuss some elements that contribute to enhancing an intrapreneurial culture.

The Organizational Structure

The organizational structure plays a critical role in the development of the intrapreneurial culture. An entrepreneurial structure has fewer layers of hierarchies, is flexible and allows employees to communicate and participate in the decision making process more frequently. Let us briefly discuss two structural forms that enhance entrepreneurial activities.

The Flat Structure. A flatter structure allows organizational members to communicate effectively, take initiative, respond quickly to customer needs, and participate in decision making. It also provides a feeling of intimacy among organization members.

Small Autonomous Units. Creating small autonomous units allows the large organization to benefit from the capabilities of the large established firm and the flexibility and innovation typical of the small entrepreneurial firm. IBM developed the concept of independent business units to encourage intrapreneurial activities. The unit can take strategic decisions as an autonomous company. Many of the new product innovations at IBM, such as the IBM personal computer, are credited to these independent business units. A similar concept was introduced by Jack Welch, chairman of General Electric. GE was restructured around a group of small firms.[2]

Perhaps 3M's experience in creating such small entrepreneurial business units is unmatched. Lew Lehr, 3M's chairman, was quoted as saying:

"For many years the corporate structure has been designed specifically to encourage young entrepreneurs to take an idea and run with it. If they succeed, they can and do find themselves running their own business under the 3M umbrella. The entrepreneurial approach is not a sideline at 3M. It is the heart of our design for growth."[3]

Promoting Intrapreneurial Behavior

Empowerment. Empowering employees is critical to an intrapreneurial culture. Intrapreneurs must have the freedom to make decisions and take initiative. Hewlett-Packard decentralized the organization to ensure that intrapreneurs were involved in the decision making process. The result was a phenomenal increase in product innovation.

Risk Taking. An intrapreneurial culture must encourage its members to try new ideas and to take initiative. The organization must be able to commit resources to these ideas and provide time to intrapreneurs to try them. The organization must also be able to accept mistakes and failures and consider them as temporary setbacks. Intrapreneur Arthur Fry developed Post-it Notes at 3M as a result of a strong intrapreneurial culture that encourages risk taking.

Innovation as a Continuous Process

To avoid the death trap that is often associated with rapid technological change, innovation must be seen as a continuous process. This can only happen if the organizational climate encourages innovation efforts. Here are some examples:

- Trial and Error. Innovation is an evolving process in most cases and thus trial and error in the development of new ideas must be accepted and encouraged.
- The Innovation "Hot Box." This concept encourages intrapreneurs to suggest new ideas without having to go through the formal organizational channels. Ideas are examined on a regular basis by senior management, and those that merit further examination are pursued and their developers encouraged.
- Routine Brainstorming Sessions. Today it is not unusual for many large organizations to conduct brainstorming sessions to generate or refine new ideas.
- Company Retreats. Retreats such as those conducted by Steve Jobs of Apple Computer allow organizational members to generate ideas in a less formal manner and encourage them to be more creative.

Career Development and Reward System

The career paths of intrapreneurs must be carefully designed to encourage this particular breed of people to be innovative and to stay with the organization. Many intrapreneurs tend to start their own ventures once they realize that their dreams are difficult to achieve in a large bureaucracy. Companies such as 3M, IBM, American Express, Xerox, and Nortel have designed effective career development systems for intrapreneurs. The objective is to foster intrapreneurs' creativity and innovation and to recognize their achievements. The reward system includes both monetary and intrinsic rewards.

Monetary Rewards include

- equity position in the new venture
- stock options
- cash gifts
- bonuses
- slush funds

Intrinsic Rewards include

- special promotion
- free time and sabbatical
- fellowship
- recognition
- access to funds and resources

For example, both IBM and 3M offer free time to encourage intrapreneurs to try new ideas. The IBM fellow's program recognizes outstanding achievement.

The Sponsor/Manager as Champion of Innovation

New ideas and innovation may never see the light in the organizational maze unless there are corporate champions behind them. Champions in large organizations are usually visionary managers who see innovation as the best way to avoid the corporate death trap. The manager/sponsor usually takes an active role in championing the idea by committing resources and protecting and sheltering the intrapreneur from the organization's bureaucratic and political machine.

To ensure the venture's success, the sponsor must have the qualities of power, prestige and vision.

- Power. The sponsor must have enough power in the formal organizational hierarchy to commit organizational resources to the new venture, offer time off to the intrapreneur to pursue the idea, and enhance the career path of the intrapreneur. Lehr of 3M sponsored surgeons from a Cleveland Clinic who developed an adhesive surgical drape. He protected the project from 3M's bureaucracy and provided the necessary resources. Lehr went on to develop an entire division of health care products.[4]
- Prestige. The sponsor/manager must be highly respected in the organization to protect the new venture from being killed as a result of organizational politics. For example, Dick Drew protected the profab lap project at 3M from being killed. Drew is highly respected by management and the organization at large for his own entrepreneurial track record (Scotch tape).[5]

- **Visionary.** The sponsor must be a visionary who sees the long term benefits of the innovation rather than the short term effects on the budget. For example, Bob Malenda's vision kept Art Fry's Post-it Notes project at 3M from being killed at the last moment.[6]

Corporate Venturing—Back to the Garage

Most of today's large organizations started in the garages or basements of their founders, most of whom would attribute their early success to the innovative and creative environment. This includes closeness, intimacy, rationed resources, modest facilities, a high degree of freedom and a high level of motivation to succeed. The stakes are usually high if the desired results are not achieved—life savings, assets and marriages could be threatened. Obviously, intrapreneurs in large organizations may not have the same urge and motivation to innovate. Thus it has been argued that the recreation of the garage or leaky roof[*] environment may allow intrapreneurs to be creative and innovative and insulate them from the bureaucracy and politics of large organizations.[7]

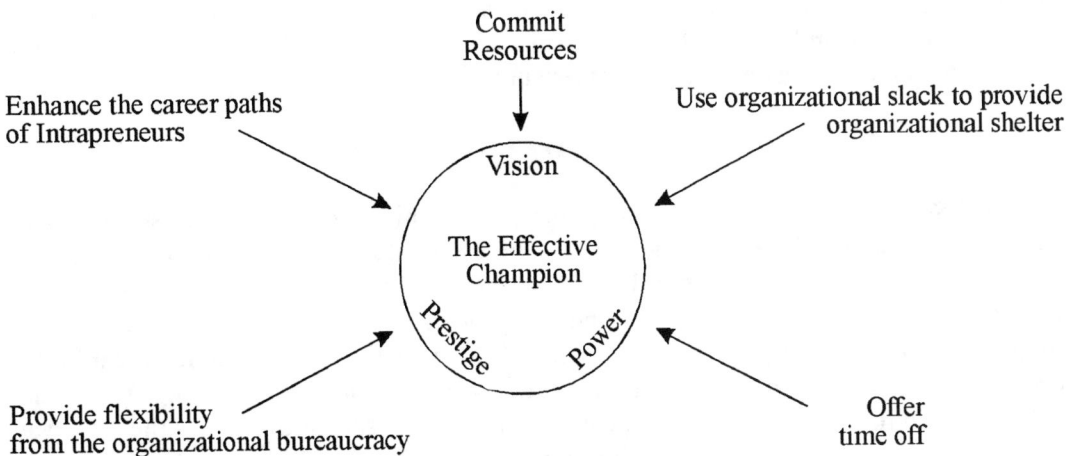

Figure 7.2. The Effective Sponsor-Champion.

* Sometimes referred to as skunk work.

Venture Capital Support

To ensure continued support to entrepreneurial activities, be they from inside (intrapreneur) or outside (entrepreneur), large organizations must allocate a separate budget to fund them. This budget must be an integral part of the corporate budget and the formal strategic planning process. The reason for such formality is to ensure long term commitment and to avoid the politics involved in the resource allocation process.

Some organizations, such as 3M, Xerox, AT&T, IBM and Nortel, have recognized the need to encourage innovation and intrapreneurial activities by establishing venture capital capabilities. The objective of these venture capital units is to provide funds and support to both intrapreneurs and independent entrepreneurs. For example, Xerox established Xerox Technology Ventures (XTV) to provide funds and support to new ventures. Similarly, Texas Instruments established the IDEA grant to fund innovation and intrapreneurial activities.[8]

Sponsoring Independent Entrepreneurs

To maintain an innovative environment, large organizations must scan the environment for entrepreneurs with new ideas. 3M is an excellent example of a large organization that maintains a strong intrapreneurial culture through sponsoring independent entrepreneurs. The entire 3M structure is designed to encourage successful entrepreneurs to run their own businesses under the 3M corporate umbrella. Dupont also sponsors independent entrepreneurs who have the ability to build on the firm's existing products.[9] Figure 7.3 summarizes the critical elements of a corporate intrapreneurship.

SUMMARY

In today's technology driven economy, entrepreneurship is critical to the survival and growth of corporate America. The success of corporate intrapreneurship depends on creating the intrapreneurial culture that encourage innovation, creativity and risk-taking, and provides a high level of flexibility and independence. This chapter offered a model of corporate intrapreneurship. The key elements of this model include: establishing a flatter structure, empowering employees, and encouraging innovation and risk-taking. The model also discussed the role of top managers as champions who see innovation as the only way to ensure organizational survival and growth. Further, the model discussed other critical elements including establishing corporate venturing, designing career development and reward systems, developing venture capital capabilities and encouraging independent entrepreneurs.

i.	The Intrapreneurial Culture	• the organizational structure
		  Flat
		  Autonomous units
		• promoting intrapreneurial behavior
		  Empowerment
		  Risk-taking
		  Innovation
		• career development & reward system

ii.	The Sponsor/Manager Qualities: power prestige vision	• commit resources • use organizational slack • provide protection and shelter • offer time off • provide flexibility from the organizational bureaucracy • enhance the career paths of intrapreneurs
iii.	Corporate Venturing Back to the Garage	• closeness • intimacy • rationed resources • modest facilities • freedom • risk • motivation
iv.	Venture Capital Support	• separate budget
v.	Sponsoring Independent Entrepreneurs	• scanning the environment

Figure 7.3. The Five Elements of Corporate Intrapreneurship.

NOTES

1. A. P. Carneval, "America and the New Economy: How New Competitive Standards are Radically Changing the American Work-Place," San Francisco: Jossey-Bass Publishers, 1991.
2. "GE's Wizards Turning from the Bottom Line to Share the Market," *Wall Street Journal*, July 12, 1982, p. 1.
3. Lew Lehr, "Dreaming in Color: The Engineer as Entrepreneur," Speech given at University of Nebraska, April 2, 1983.
4. G. Pinchot 3rd, *Intrapreneuring,* New York: Harper & Row, 1985, p. 159.
5. Ibid, p. 150.
6. Ibid, p. 150. For further discussion see R. Peterson & D. Berger, "Entrepreneurship in Organizations," *Administrative Science Quarterly* 16 (August 1971). pp. 97–106.
7. See, for example: John Kao, *Entrepreneurship, Creativity & Organization,* Englewood Cliffs, New Jersey: Prentice-Hall, 1989, p. 401; and D. Miller and P. Friesen, "Innovation in Conservative and Entrepreneurial Firms: Two Models of Strategic Momentum," *Strategic Management Journal 3* (May 1982), pp. 1–25.
8. G. Pinchot 3rd, 1985, p. 215.
9. Ibid, p. 158.

THE INTRAPRENEUR

Art Fry
Post-it Notes

Intrapreneur Art Fry developed one of the most successful products at 3M—Post-it Notes. 3M is best known for its intrapreneurial activities. Fry conceived the idea while singing in a church choir. Frustrated with paper markers constantly falling out from his hymnal, he thought of a special type of adhesive which had been recently discovered by another intrapreneur, Spence Silver. The adhesive is easy to remove without damaging the surface and not as sticky as other adhesives. Fry decided to apply the adhesive to the edge of the paper and use it as a book marker. Taking advantage of a 3M policy instituted by Bill McKnight (the champion behind Dick Drew's scotch tape) which allows intrapreneurs to work up to 15 percent of their time on ideas of their own, Fry began tinkering with this new type of adhesive. Finally he refined his original idea and developed those popular yellow note pads known as Post-it Notes.

To create awareness and to gain support Fry distributed samples of the Post-it Notes to executive offices at 3M. The early market test of the product was not encouraging. However, with the support and encouragement of Bob Molenda, his manager, Post-it Notes became a success. In short, free time, strong intrapreneurial culture, visionary managers and a reward system that encourages innovation are critical elements for the success of intrapreneurs such as Art Fry.

Source: G. Pinchot 3rd, Intrapreneuring, New York: Harper & Row, 1985; A. B. Ibrahim, Case Histories, 1987.

△ CHAPTER 8 △
THE BUSINESS PLAN

Paperwork is anathema to the vast majority of entrepreneurs who very frequently have chosen their calling as a refuge from it. Yet one piece of paperwork is absolutely indispensable: the business plan. At its best, it is the cornerstone of a new enterprise, at its worst, an exercise in self delusion and very likely the nemesis of its authors. Indeed, nothing could be more damaging than an ill-conceived idea and a poorly prepared business plan.

NINE GOOD REASONS FOR PREPARING A BUSINESS PLAN

The business plan is probably the most important document the entrepreneur will ever prepare for the following reasons:

1. A well thought-out, carefully prepared business plan is a valuable vehicle to introduce the entrepreneur and the small business management to different sources of financing, such as venture capital firms, bankers and investors.
2. It provides the entrepreneur and the small business management with a tool for assessing the window(s) of opportunity and its own economic viability.
3. It allows the entrepreneur and the small business management to conduct an in-depth analysis of the venture's internal and external capabilities.
4. It allows the entrepreneur and the small business management a means of assessing the opportunity in light of the venture's capabilities. (See Figure 8.1).
5. The business plan is an excellent vehicle for self-assessment. It enables entrepreneurs to assess their strengths and weaknesses.
6. It forces the entrepreneur or the small business management to formulate its objectives in a more realistic fashion.
7. It forces the entrepreneur and the small business management to get involved in strategic thinking at an early stage of operation.
8. It is an essential document for going public and approaching underwriters.
9. It provides direction in the early days of operation.

This chapter is based on research work for the banking industry conducted by professor A. B. Ibrahim.

Figure 8.1. The Opportunity-Capabilities-Fit.

PREPARING THE BUSINESS PLAN*

Many entrepreneurs don't know where to begin and how to prepare this important document in a systematic fashion. We discuss in the following section a number of critical elements of an effective business plan followed by a detailed outline of a business plan.

The Business Concept and Objectives

An effective business plan should explain clearly the idea/product/service and the window of opportunity that motivated the entrepreneur to start the business. The forces creating the opportunity such as technological forces, shift in demand, government regulations, social and economic trends, should be outlined. For example, technological change in the computer and telecommunication industries has created windows of opportunities for many entrepreneurs. Meeting the needs of the baby boomers has created a demand for services and products.

The objectives and goals of the new venture should be clearly stated in the plan to give the target audience a sense of where the new venture is heading. The personal objectives of going into business should also be included. While the economic viability of the business concept is crucial, personal satisfaction of the entrepreneur could be equally important. For example, becoming independent or building a legacy.

The Entrepreneur and the Management Team

The business plan is an excellent medium to introduce the entrepreneur and the management team to the target audience. After all, the venture success is a function of the entrepreneur's ability to exploit the window of opportunity and carry out the intended mission. The entrepreneur should describe his/her education, qualification, skills and prior experience and that of the management team to demonstrate their ability to manage the venture successfully. Indeed, the business plan provides entrepreneurs with an excellent opportunity to perform a self-assessment of their strengths and weaknesses. Weaknesses should not be left out of the plan. Today's investor expects the entrepreneurs to provide a realistic assessment of their capabilities. However, entrepreneurs should be able to demonstrate how they intend to complement their skills. For example, a technical entrepreneur may choose to have a partner with strong managerial skills.

The roles and responsibility of the entrepreneur and the management team should be spelled out in the business plan. An organizational chart may be provided to show the reporting relationship of each member. Further, the salary and compensation of the

*© Dr. A.B. Ibrahim, 1994

management team should be clearly stated in the plan to avoid future problems with investors. The entrepreneur must demonstrate commitment. For example, an entrepreneur who left a high salaried position to start a new venture with a low or no salary during the start up period is perceived by investors as a highly committed individual who could be trusted.

Demonstrating the Viability of the New Venture

The entrepreneur must be able to demonstrate in the business plan the economic viability of the new venture and identify its competitive advantage. The target audience must perceive the venture as a viable concern.

- Demonstrating the economic viability of the venture. The entrepreneur must establish the economic viability of the idea/opportunity. Accounting techniques such as break-even analysis, sensitivity analysis, cash flow projections, ı ratio analysis and pro-forma income and balance sheet statements may be utilized to demonstrate to the target audience the soundness of the venture. These techniques are discussed in Chapter 13 of this book.
- Assumptions and projections. The financial and market analysis in the plan are based on projections. Therefore, the entrepreneur must provide and explain the assumptions behind these projections. This allows the reader to appreciate the analysis and conclusion reached. The assumptions must be sound and realistic. It should be based on objective assessment of the venture external environment and internal capabilities.
- The venture capabilities and its competitive advantage. To demonstrate the viability of the new venture, the business plan should include an objective assessment of the external environment and the internal capabilities of the venture. Indeed the business plan allows the entrepreneur to evaluate the opportunities and threats facing the venture from the external environment as well as the venture strengths and weaknesses. This type of analysis allows the entrepreneur to identify the venture's distinctive competencies and its competitive advantage. After all, the target audience needs to know what the new venture can do best in comparison to rivals.
- The external analysis include assessing the market and the demand for new product/service as well as the industry and competition. The internal analysis includes the functional plans which reflect the venture's activities such as the marketing, the product, and the operational plan as well as the organizational structure. These activities are discussed in later chapters of this book.

Risk Assessment

Risk assessment is an integral part of an effective business plan. Presenting only the positive elements in the plan while ignoring the downside provides the target audience with an unrealistic picture of the new venture. Sophisticated investors, such as venture capital

firms, may form a negative impression about the new venture. Therefore, a well prepared plan should include a section of potential risk elements and contingency plans to manage these elements. For example:

potential risk: supplier is unable to deliver on time.

contingency plan: a) explore possibility of having multiple suppliers, b) working a second shift.

The Legal Form

The business plan should inform the targeted audience of the legal form of the new venture - sole proprietorship, partnership or corporation. Box 8.1 examines the different legal forms and key factors to consider before making a decision.

Box 8.1. Selecting the Legal Form.

There are two key factors to consider before deciding the appropriate legal form of organization, be it single/sole proprietorship, partnership or corporation. First, is the degree of liability (limited or unlimited). Second, who is going to manage the organization, that is, the owner or outside professional manager.

1. The single or sole proprietorship assumes that the firm is owned and managed by one person. The sole proprietorship form is easy to create and terminate, and requires less formality. It allows the owner to control all aspects of the operation and to enjoy all the fruits of his business. However the liability in the sole proprietorship form is unlimited and the owner is personally liable if the business is unable to meet its obligations. The sole proprietorship discontinues upon the death or removal of the owner.

2. The partnership assumes two or more persons agree to carry on as co-owners of a business for profit. This legal form of organization allows the owners or partners to pool their talents and resources. It also allows the organization to obtain more capital to manage growth. However, the partnership form has a limited life. The partnership will cease to exist upon the death, disagreement, removal and/or addition of partners. Also, the liability in this legal form, as in the sole proprietorship, is unlimited.

3. The corporation is a legal entity, a "creation" of the law. Its ownership is divided into shares. The liability in this legal form of organization is limited to the amount invested in shares. The shares are transferable to other individuals. This legal form allows the organization to expand and grow as a result of its ability to sell additional shares. On the negative side, incorporating requires a lot of paper work as a result of government regulations, in addition to the cost involved in incorporating.

Funds Required

The business plan is an essential document for approaching investors. Financial analysis and projections serve to determine the amount and type of financing required. For example, a venture that will be able to achieve positive cash flow in three months may not need equity financing, a short term loan (debt financing) is more appropriate and less costly. On the other hand, equity financing is more desirable when large investment is required and timing of return is difficult to predict as in many knowledge based firms. Therefore, the entrepreneur should match the sources of funds to the use of funds.

The Deal Structure

The deal structure is an essential part of the business plan as it provides investors with the terms of financing. In order to craft a deal that maximizes the entrepreneur's return, he or she must understand and explain to the target audience in the plan the venture's financing characteristics including:

- amounts of funds required,
- timing - when these funds are needed,
- the risk level,
- and timing of return.

These characteristics vary from venture to venture. For example, a genetic engineering firm may require a large investment at the onset and may take 3-5 years before a large return is achieved. Other ventures may generate positive cash flow in a shorter period of time - 6 months. The entrepreneur's task should be to match the venture's financing characteristics with the investor's own needs and select those investors that are willing to accept the lowest return. This leaves the entrepreneur with the largest economic return.

Therefore the business plan should spell out the terms of the deal to attract the proper investor. These include:

- control: how much equity the entrepreneur is willing to relinquish in return for the needed financing. Investors provide funds in exchange for one or more of the following:
  - shares
  - profit
  - warranties
  - guarantees
  - rights
  - royalty
  - collateral
- Exit route available to investors. This includes buy-back or put provisions which basically force the owner to buy the stock back at a multiple of earnings.
- License including terms and royalty.

In some situations the deal structure is provided to interested investors in a separate memorandum.

Other Critical Factors in Preparing the Business Plan

Only a well thought out, carefully prepared and written business plan can gain the confidence of investors. Entrepreneurs must pay particular attention to the following issues.

- A business plan should be well documented; the more detailed a business plan the more comfortable the potential investor will feel. It also gives an indication that the entrepreneur is serious and has done his/her homework and can be trusted. Further details allow the entrepreneur to assess the venture in a more systematic fashion.
- Different types of investors require different levels of details. A business plan prepared to acquire funds from venture capital firms and or financial institutions requires more details than a plan targeted at wealthy individuals.
- A business plan should look and read professionally; sloppiness in writing and calculations of the financial analysis carry a very negative image to potential investors.
- Ambiguity should be avoided. It may be an indication that the entrepreneur is trying to deceive potential investors.
- A large contribution of the entrepreneur's own fund, or resigning his job to work full time for the venture demonstrate commitment.

Box 8.3 summarizes a number of critical issues most budding entrepreneurs are likely to raise.

Box 8.3. Starting a Business.

Based on interviews with a number of entrepreneurs, Joshua Hyatt outlines five basic issues:

1. Acceptability of the idea. According to Hyatt, it doesn't matter how many hours you spend preparing your business plan. What really counts is if customers are willing to spend money to buy your product or service. Therefore, market research is critical.
2. Management skills. The author contends that self assessment is critical. It allows would be entrepreneurs to know their strengths and weaknesses and thus find the right people to complement their skills. Mentors, board members and advisers could provide the needed skills.
3. Money. The author contends that money is not the only reason for starting your own business. Other objectives such as managing your own business or going public could be equally satisfactory. In essence you have to identify clearly your objectives of going into business.
4. Risk. Successful entrepreneurs are risk averse. Many entrepreneurs feel that working for an employer was riskier than starting a business. A good example is the recent layoff of many middle and upper level executives in large organizations.
5. Family. Starting up a business may be stressful to many entrepreneurs as they have to spend less time with their families, in addition to the possibility of risking the family income. Thus the author suggests that would be entrepreneurs should have a frank discussion with their families.

Source: Joshua Hyatt, "Should You Start a Business," *INC.*, February 1992, pp. 48–58.

Figure 8-2 provides a detailed outline of business plan.

Outline of the Business Plan*

1.	Executive Summary	• Highlights key issues in the business plan.
2.	Table of Content	
3.	The Business Concept	• The idea, the product/service, the opportunity
		• Forces creating the opportunity
		• Uniqueness and competitive advantage
4.	Goals and Objectives	• Including personal objectives of starting the business
5.	The Management Team	• Education, qualification, skills and prior business experience
		• Self assessment: strengths and weaknesses
		• Responsibilities of each member
		• Salary and compensation
6.	Market Analysis	• Market size
		• Market condition
		• Market trends
		• Level of demand
		• Customer buying behavior
		• Target market
		• Expected market share
7.	Industry Analysis	• Industry characteristics (economies of scale, entry and exit barriers, product differentiation and degree of concentration)
		• The Industry's phase in the life-cycle (emerging, growth, mature and declining)
		• The industry key success factors
		• The different strategic groups operating in the industry
		• Types of competition and relative size
		• Competitive forces: suppliers, bargaining power, risk of new entrants, customers bargaining power, the intensity of competition.
		• Forces operating in the industry: technological and governmental regulations
8.	The Marketing Plan	• Market research
		• The intended niche (segment)
		• The product mix (all the benefits the customer will receive)
		• Pricing strategy (cost-based, competition based and value based)
		• Promotion strategy (advertising media and budget)
		• Distribution channels
		• Market positioning strategy
		• Sales force
9.	The Product/Service Plan	• Benefits to customers
		• Unique characteristics
		• Competitive advantage

Figure 8.2. Outline of the business plan.

* © Dr. A. B. Ibrahim, 1996

		• Product development stage (idea, prototype, or commercial stage)
		• Stage in the product life-cycle
		• R&D activities
		• R&D budget in comparison with industry norms or an industry leader
		• Legal protection (copyright, patent)
10.	The Production/Operation Plan	• Scheduling
		• Capacity utilization
		• Facilities (leased/purchased)
		• Quality control
		• The optimal inventory level
11.	The Human Resources Plan	• Skills, experience and education required
		• Career development
		• Responsibilities
		• Training
		• Compensation
12.	The Financial Plan	• Financial Analysis
		• Ratio analysis
		• Trend Analysis
		• Sensitivity Analysis
		• Break-even analysis
		• Pro-forma financial statements
		• Proforma income statement
		• Proforma balance-sheet statement
		• Cash flow projections
		• Assumptions
13.	The Organizational Structure	• Tasks, roles, reporting relationship
14.	The Legal Form	• Sole proprietorship/partnership/corporation
15.	Risk Assessment	• Anticipated risk
		• Assessment
		• Contingency plans
16.	Funds required	• Amount
		• Type
		• Equity
		• Debt
		• Timing of return
		• Intended Use
		• When the funds are needed
		• Risk level
17.	The Deal Structure	• Ownership
		• Control
		• Exit Route
		• License
18.	Appendices	• Resumes of the management team
		• The organizational chart
		• Illustrations of the new product, service concept
		• Market Research Conducted

Figure 8.2. (Continued)

The Effective Plan

Stanley Rich and David Gumpert, both seasoned veterans of entrepreneurship, argue that too many would-be entrepreneurs ignore other, implicit partners in the venture when drafting their plans: the investors and the clients. No company can exist by paying only lip service to its customers or financiers. It is an essential quality for success, that the architects of the business plan be able to place themselves in the shoes of other interested parties as Box 8.2 shows.

SUMMARY

The business plan is the most important document the entrepreneur will ever prepare. The plan serves many purposes such as introducing the entrepreneur to potential investors, customers, suppliers and employees. The plan can also be used as a self-assessment exercise. Indeed, the business plan allows the entrepreneur to assess the economic viability of the opportunity, his or her strengths and weaknesses, the intended strategy and business concept, the risk factors and contingencies, and the appropriate financing vehicle.

Box 8.2.

According to Stanley Rich and David Gumpert, the best written business plan is the one that concisely addresses its "key constituents": investors, customers and owners.

First and foremost in importance is the market. Why should the customer buy the product or service? What benefit will it confer? Why should buyers choose it over existing market offerings? All of these must be addressed in the business plan. Testing market interest is a corollary problem, as the venture may not have reached a stage where production or supply has begun, and customer acceptance gauged. The authors suggest offering the product to select customers at a discount, or in prototype form, to elicit detailed evaluations and demonstrate market potential. This, coupled with scrupulously honest evaluation of test results, provides the entrepreneur with a much more realistic picture of the product's profit potential and therefore, from the investor's point of view, reduces risk.

As the investor's most fundamental concerns are with the basic viability of the enterprise, it follows that by addressing the marketing issues the entrepreneur has begun to build a case for investment. But these are not the only worries that investors are likely to have. In order to assuage those remaining, the entrepreneur must first categorize the investors. Are they to be bankers, venture capitalists, wealthy sponsors or small shareholders? As the authors point out, the founders themselves are investors of no little significance; if not from the point of view of financial capital, then at least on the basis of time and energy. A cold hearted assessment from their own vantage point is every bit as necessary, but likely to be even more difficult in the face of personal bias.

All likely investors are apt to have some concerns in common, irrespective of their legal standing. Chief among these is the manner in which the investment will be harvested ultimately. Rich and Gumpert note that new ventures rarely possess the means to begin dividend payments in their early years (and such a policy would divert funds from growth); therefore investors are compelled to seek rewards in the form of capital appreciation. A well written business plan then, must specify how this is to be accomplished: via a public offering, sale to another corporation, or investor buy-out.

Investor confidence is further buoyed by financial projections that are comprehensive and realistic. Two extremes of failure are possible here: estimates of costs and sales that have no foundation in actual conditions (or are not provided at all), and a surfeit of projections and detailed forecasts that are patently beyond the bounds of accuracy (a "smog of numbers"). The authors remark that new ventures rarely achieve their forecasted return, a fact usually taken into account by professional investors when making their evaluations.

The final issue is the amount of the investment, and the return expected. Rich and Gumpert suggest that investors frequently require a compound annual return of between 35% (for highly developed products offered by proven management) to 60% (for ventures deficient in either category). The investors' earnings expectations together with the entrepreneur's financial projections and own expectations are used to arrive at an anticipated valuation of the company some years (usually five) hence. From this, relative shareholdings at the present day are imputed.

Source: Stanely R. Rich and David E. Gumpert, "How to Write a Winning Business Plan," *Harvard Business Review* (May–June 1985), pp. 156–166.

THE ENTREPRENEUR

**Ben Cohen and Jerry Greenfield
The Entrepreneurial Spirit
Ben & Jerry's Homemade Inc.**

In 1977, two ex-hippies, Ben Cohen and Jerry Greenfield, both 26 years of age, bought an abandoned gas station in Burlington, Vermont, and started making ice cream using old fashioned, rock-salt freezers of the type featured in many of the articles and cartoons on the early settlers. Neither had any particular knowledge about making ice cream, but were helped immeasurably by sending away to Pennsylvania State University for a $5 correspondence course on ice cream making.

So taking $8,000 and a product described as a "super premium brand," containing a 15% butterfat content and less air than the standard ice cream, with no chemicals, preservatives or artificial colours added, the 34 flavours have grown to an estimated sales of $50 million in 1988. In mid-1989, the company had five franchised outlets in Canada compared with 90 franchised outlets and six stores in the United States. Plans were underway to open an ice cream parlor in Moscow.

In addition to having products that obviously have consumer acceptance, the success of Ben & Jerry's in a very competitive market has been due to their unorthodox business style. They aspire to promote social change while still satisfying indulgent customers. In the United States, the company gave 7.5% of its pre-tax income to charities and hands out free ice cream at school sports days and hospitals. It is also part of the company's philosophy that it "would rather give our money and use it for causes like these than spend it on advertising. It's just something we feel is part of the Ben & Jerry approach to doing business." This is also a philosophy that the company expects its franchisees and employees to share to a large degree.

Another aspect of the company's philosophy of doing business is a firm rule—intended to insure that all its 350 employees share relatively equally in the success of the company— that no employee will make more than five times what any other employee makes. In 1989, the lowest paid worker is an entry-level administrative person who gets about $16,400, with the highest salary of approximately $75,000 going to the president, Ben Cohen. The co-founder is reported to receive about the same amount.

Source: *Globe & Mail* (January 1, 1988), p. B1; *The New York Times* (Sunday, March 26, 1989), p. F4; *This Week in Business* (April 15, 1989), p. 17.

CASES FOR DISCUSSION

—————————————— **CASE 1** ——————————————

Richard Branson and The Virgin Group

> I see Virgin becoming the largest entertainment group based outside the U.S. Getting to where we are now was quite difficult. Getting from here to a billion-pound company will be much easier. I sometimes wonder what type of company we'll be then.

So spoke Richard Branson, the youthful chairman of the Virgin Group of companies, following the presentation in 1985 of the Confederation of British Industry's Business Enterprise Award in recognition of "the enterprise shown in the design, manufacture and marketing of Virgin's goods and services." Virgin had grown from a small alternative mailorder record company to a diverse entertainment and leisure Group in only fifteen years.

The award was another milestone in the career of the young man who started his first business venture while still at school and who has never been in anyone's employ. To receive the award, Branson purchased a formal suit, an infrequent happening in his life.

THE BEGINNINGS

Richard Branson was born in 1950 and enjoyed a comfortable childhood. His grandfather was a High Court judge and his father was a barrister. He grew up in awe of his grandfather, Sir George Branson, whose involvement in condemning murderers portrayed in Madame Tussaud's wax-works had made a great impression on him. As a child he wanted to be an explorer like Scott of the Antarctic, a cousin of the same Sir George.

Branson went to Stowe, an exclusive private boarding school for boys. His entry to Stowe had not been assured, however, following his previous lackluster academic performance (as opposed to his interest in sports), but his parents, anxious for him to have a traditional education, had sent him to a preparatory school specializing in intensive tutoring. His mother, in particular, was ambitious for her only son ("One day Richard will be Prime Minister"). She had always encouraged her children to be self-reliant and active like she herself had been in a wide variety of endeavors (and still is today).

Branson's first entrepreneurial venture took place when he was about 12 years old. He planted a thousand seedlings expecting to make a killing selling Christmas trees. But,

This case was prepared by Robert Dick Research Associate, under the direction of Manfred F. R. Kets de Vries, professor at INSEAD. It is intended to be used as a basis for class discussion rather than to illustrate either effective or ineffective handling of an administrative situation. Copyright © 1989 by INSEAD-CEDEF. All rights reserved.

unfortunately, rabbits ate the trees. A venture in breeding budgerigars—a type of parrot—came to a similar sad ending.

At the age of 16, while still at Stowe, Branson started *Student* magazine for British students, with the aim of "putting the world to rights." The venture was subsequently discontinued but not before Branson claimed a circulation of above 100,000. He had solicited articles from the likes of Jean-Paul Sartre, Vanessa Redgrave and Norman Mailer. The magazine was sold from the telephone kiosk that Branson used as his office. Speaking of that time he commented: "All I wanted to do was to edit the magazine, be a journalist. I like the idea of meeting people, getting out and finding out about things. It's a very varied life not perhaps too dissimilar to the life I lead now."

Branson left school in the late 60s. His indifference to school-work manifested itself in only average results that would not permit a legal or other professional career. His disappointed parents were initially opposed to his leaving school, but eventually his father, himself a reluctant lawyer, took a more relaxed view of his son's predicament and agreed to let him pursue his magazine business. Branson left few close friends behind. While not unpopular, his energetic and single-minded pursuit of that which pleased him left little room for others. His friends were usually those inveigled into his many projects.

Commenting on the end of his schooldays, Branson said, "Having left school without going on to university, I decided to make money . . . I never really considered failure." His headmaster's last words to him were: "Richard, you will end up either in prison or a millionaire." These words have proved to be prophetic. Not only has Branson become a millionaire many times over but a recent straw poll of young British people voted him third most popular after Prince Charles and Pope John Paul II.

THE FOUNDING OF VIRGIN

Student magazine did not develop into the financial success that Branson had hoped for. Casting around for a new project, he thought he saw potential in the record business. Like many of his contemporaries, Branson enjoyed popular music, although his tastes were relatively conservative. Prices were high, however, and not all retail outlets stocked records that appealed to young people. This gave him the idea of starting a mail-order business aimed at young people like himself which would offer cut-price records usually only available in specialist London shops. At someone's suggestion he jokingly called his business "Virgin" to demonstrate his commercial innocence, but also to be in tune with the antiestablishment mood of the time. The first advertisement was placed in *Student* magazine.

Since the business was undercapitalized, Branson and his minority partner, Nik Powell, a school friend, would wait until sufficient orders and cash were received before buying the records wholesale for shipment to customers. When record companies became suspicious of their intentions and refused to supply them direct, a small record shop was used as the purchasing agent. Through this minor subterfuge and the timely abolition of retail price maintenance (government retail price controls on certain items were discontinued), the mail-order business prospered. However, a long postal strike in the early '70s threatened the existence of the company. Branson recognized his vulnerability and the need for diversification. This led to the opening in 1971 of the first Virgin retail store in Oxford Street, London's main shopping thoroughfare.

VIRGIN THROUGH THE '70S: EARLY SUCCESS

The company's erratic progress and profits through the '70s were always centered on the core business of popular music. The retail side of the business expanded slowly as new outlets were found. The first major profits (and a loan from an aunt of Branson's) financed recording studios in a country mansion. "We were doing what the business schools apparently call vertical integration," says Branson. "I call it common sense."

In 1971 Simon Draper, a relative from South Africa, joined Virgin as a record buyer after graduating from university. Intensely interested in rock music, with left-of-center political views, Draper fitted in well with the Virgin cooperative ethos. At that time everyone received the same wage, although, as he later recalled, "There was never any doubt who owned Virgin; that was Richard, and I could recognize a true blue capitalist when I saw one." With time Draper gained experience in all aspects of the music business. His success in spotting and developing bands earned him the epithet of "golden ears," the industry accolade to successful producers.

In 1973 a little-known composer called Mike Oldfield walked into the company's offices unannounced and offered a series of tapes made when he was 15 years old. Branson became his manager and later his close friend and confidant. Oldfield's first LP record sold over 7 million copies, giving a considerable fillip to Virgin. Nik Powell, commenting on the signing of Mike Oldfield, said: "Mike's success probably stopped the company going under. Overnight our cash flow became really positive and instead of a few thousand £'s a month coming in, we had tens, even hundreds, of thousands. It was a turning point for the company in every way—profits, visibility, everything."

By 1981 Oldfield was suing for damages arising from "the imposition of unfair contracts," a tactic frequently used by rock bands once success has been achieved in an attempt to renegotiate contract conditions. Draper, commenting on this and other cases of alleged hard bargaining, said, "The bands come in and see the informality and the casual dress and they think . . . well you know what I mean . . . our contract terms are no more onerous than anywhere else. They just expect more." Oldfield has remained with Virgin to this day. Branson ascribes this to his approach to business:

> The world is very small and in a business sense we are dealing with the same people time and again. In sixteen years of running a record company we have never had a major artist leave us. Dealing with people fairly and properly makes for good business sense as well as a pleasant way of living.

In 1977 the notorious punk rock band, the Sex Pistols, was signed by Branson despite Draper's doubts. Their considerable commercial success once again boosted flagging profits. During this period Branson demonstrated his sympathy for radical and humanitarian causes. He set up more sex counseling clinics, having founded the original clinic in London at the age of 17 when his girlfriend became pregnant and they had nobody to advise them. He refused to advertise in a magazine that turned down advertising (by others) in favor of legalizing marijuana. Branson himself reputedly dislikes drugs after his first and only experiment with LSD, the hallucinatory drug, went badly wrong. A former girlfriend commented, "Richard could not stand to be out of control."

It was also in the '70s that Branson learned that saving "a few pennies of tax" by making false export declarations could lead to humiliating consequences. A police interrogation followed by a night in the cells could later be laughingly dismissed. The embarrassment caused to his father and his mother's anger and sadness at having to arrange an out-of-court financial settlement were harder to bear. Branson resolved to "avoid sleepless nights and pay the taxes."

VIRGIN IN THE '80s: DIVERSIFICATION

In 1980 the record industry hit a bad patch. Growth, which had been averaging 20 percent a year during the '70s, came to a halt. For Virgin this general problem coincided with both the lack of a major star to follow the Sex Pistols and major cash outflows to finance a nightclub, the Venue. Moreover, the record label founded in the U.S. in 1978 had not been successful and was forced to cease trading. The 16 retail outlets, under shaky management, were unprofitable. Moreover, they were gaining the reputation of being the meeting place for pot-smoking music freaks. The year ended with a £400,000 loss.

A management review carried out by consultants recommended the development of complementary activities, managed on a divisional basis, to reduce dependence on the music business. Non-profit-making bands were removed from the company roster.

Diversification plans were introduced in the early '80s, not always with success. In summer 1981, *Time Out*, the main London magazine for cinema and theater listings, had been off the street for some time. Branson, seeing an opportunity, rapidly founded a new magazine called *Event*. Within a short time, however, *Time Out* was back and another rival, *City Limits,* had been founded by former *Time Out* staff. The market was not big enough to support so many magazines. Within a year *Event* had folded with a loss acknowledged by Branson to be "around £300,000."

Robert Devereaux, now Managing Director of Virgin Communications and married to one of Branson's sisters, was put in charge of the *Event* closure. "It was traumatic because it was Virgin's first major public failure and involved so many sackings, quite apart from the financial disaster." Branson's management style of promoting from within and developing the most unlikely people for positions of responsibility had created strong loyalty and staff acceptance of modest financial rewards. The unexpected redundancies put this to the test. The ill feeling that had been generated led to talk of union representation. A shocked Branson, who felt he knew what was best for his staff ("I believe in benevolent dictatorships"), ordered an immediate salary review.

Nik Powell left the company in 1981. One senior Virgin executive commented that "Nik wanted to do his own thing in videos. I suppose there was a bit of an ego thing about it although everyone is still friends. Anyway he sold his shareholding to Richard and moved on." With these additional shares, Branson held 85 percent of Virgin and Simon Draper the balance. Looking back on his departure, Nik Powell remarked that he ". . . always wanted to be Number One in a Company and there was never any chance of that at Virgin. My time with Richard was very enjoyable but we always had a hot-blooded relationship—perhaps we were too close." Simon Draper thinks the problem started ". . . in 1980 when the recession hit the company. The accountants and Nik became very powerful and he brought in the consultants."

In 1984 Don Cruickshank, a Scottish accountant with an M.B.A. from Manchester Business School, joined the company as Group Managing Director. His career had spanned consultancy at McKinsey and general management in newspapers, publishing, and film production. He commented, "I found it very refreshing when I got here since I expected to find a lot of dead wood but I found that the managing directors of the various companies are almost excellent to any man or woman. Because Richard keeps things small, the right people have got into the right job."

By 1985 the Virgin Group was attracting City interest. It had come to be recognized as one of the fastest growing private companies, ranking 15th in the U.K., with a turnover of £153 million, and was seen as having changed from a purely entrepreneurial company to a professionally led Group. No formal design on a flotation was made, but for the first time Branson raised £25 million for "acquisitions" from a dozen City institutions in the form of convertible preference stock.

Some social causes were still supported by Branson. He co-invested £10,000 in a new magazine sympathetic to the fledgling U.K. Social Democratic Party. He also became involved in the issue of freedom of information in purchasing a banned TV documentary on M15, the British intelligence service. Virgin retailed video copies. Publicly and privately Branson also aided charitable schemes.

VIRGIN ATLANTIC

In early 1984, Branson got a call from Randolph Fields, a 31-year-old California lawyer who had founded British Atlantic, a cut-price transatlantic airline. Fields was seeking additional financing to get his airline airborne. There was considerable reluctance among Virgin's senior managers to consider a move so different from the company's main business. Branson, however, was eager, sensing that perhaps the timing was right. None of the major carriers would risk squeezing out a small operator after the Laker airline debacle, he felt. Within less than a month, Branson had raised more than £1.5 million from internal funds to buy a 75 percent shareholding and changed the name of the new airline to Virgin Atlantic. (Jokers at the time referred to Virgin Atlantic as "the airline that Boy George built," a reference to the latest highly successful Virgin rock band, Boy George's Culture Club, led by a transvestite singer). Simon Draper professed considerable doubts about the move. "When he told me he was going to do it, it was the first time I thought 'Well . . . I'm not sure I want to go with this.'"

Protracted bargaining with Boeing led initially to the purchase of a refurbished 747 for £18 million with options to sell it back after one, two, or three years. (Within three months of purchase, the same 747 was valued at £26 million due to currency fluctuations). Lloyds of London, after long negotiations, provided special insurance to cover losses arising from mechanical failure. Branson subsequently did a sale and leaseback deal with a major U.K. bank. He remarked, "We're always prepared to walk away from a deal. There's no psychological pre-commitment. That put us in a position to do a good deal on the airline—unlike, say, British Airways who've got to buy aircraft."

Virgin Atlantic started operating in the summer of 1984 on the London/New York route. The London/Miami and London/Tokyo route was added later. London/Los Angeles operation is planned, as are flights from London to Singapore and to New York's Kennedy airport. The airline operated at a loss until 1987 when profits before taxation were £4.96 million on a revenue of £59.99 million. The financial year to July 1988 saw revenue increased by 25 percent to £75.4 million and profits leaped to £10.1 million. Problems have arisen, however, because the company has so few planes, causing delays and cancellations in case of mechanical difficulties.

The move into the airline business forced Branson to adopt a far more public profile, a role with which he was not always comfortable (since his preferred method of communication is the telephone). The airline was launched with a great deal of fanfare. The inaugural flight saw Branson dressed up in World War I flying gear posing for the cameras. Later he was filmed on the flight deck of his 747 for an American Express Card advertisement. However, his first major publicity stunt was his attempt to win the Blue Riband, the award presented for the fastest transatlantic sea crossing. Branson financed the building of the Virgin Atlantic Challenger, a high-powered speed boat, at an estimated cost of £1.5 million. The boat with Branson aboard sank just a few miles short and was lost on its first attempted crossing. Branson immediately announced that a new boat would be built, which later went on to break the record.

In 1987 another exploit turned into a world media event. Branson and Per Lindstrand, an experienced balloonist, attempted the fastest transatlantic balloon crossing. They achieved their aim but only after just escaping with their lives when the balloon made a forced landing in the Irish Sea. A chastened Branson resolved to stick to his business interests and leave record breaking to others, although he was well pleased with the publicity. "To get that much exposure would have cost ten times as much in the normal way."

Meanwhile, Fields, who had been dissatisfied with the airline's proposed slow rate of expansion, left the company. Rumors of a boardroom conflict were discounted by Branson publicly. Roy Gardner was promoted to Managing Director of Virgin Atlantic in February 1985. An aviation man all his working life, he had joined the airline when it was founded as Technical Director. Speaking early in 1986 of his promotion and of Branson, Gardner said:

I knew that a replacement had to be found but was astonished when Richard rang up to say, "Roy, I want you to be MD, do you think you can do it?" Apparently he had quietly sounded out all the senior managers here as to who should be next MD. I got the vote and the job. He offered me a year's trial and my old job back if it didn't work out. Well, I'm still here.

That way of doing things is typical of Richard. He listens a lot before finally deciding. He's always asking questions and even now, I still get several calls a day about all kinds of operational details. With respect to his way of operating when a decision's made, never say "It can't be done." He hates that—that and people who complain. He'll listen to arguments and can be persuaded but he wants his senior people to be like him—never take no for an answer.

VIRGIN RETAIL

The retail outlets are primarily located in the U.K., but also elsewhere in Europe, selling records, cassettes, and a range of other related products. From industry estimates in early 1988 Virgin had just over 8 percent of the U.K. music market. The Retail division also exports records, cassettes, videos and compact discs to wholesalers and retailers around the world, principally in the U.S. and Japan.

However, a strategic review highlighted for Don Cruickshank the differences in company cultures that existed between, say, retail and music or communications and the airline. He commented:

> The music culture at Virgin is based around 550 people worldwide in about 20 countries. By a quick calculation you can see that that's relatively few people with a high intellectual level given a lot of artistic and business freedom. So you can go into any office worldwide and you get the same Virgin "feel." This is maintained by the small numbers of new recruits mostly in the same mould and on top of that you have Richard and his visits and attitude which remains even when he's not there. But when you look at Retail it is very different. A large number of employees in the U.K. with only a few at the top are required to apply a lot of business creativity to get the right retail environment. Most of the employees are young females of whom a third leave every year and they are told what to sell, how to sell it, at what price. The retail culture is one of control or "count the paper clips" and that struggles to be effective in Virgin.

After concentrating on both big and small outlets, in 1988 Virgin sold seventy-four of the smaller record shops for £23 million to "Our Price" a rival chain. The sale was intended to reduce debt and release resources to develop the Megastores, particularly overseas. Each Megastore has over 500 square meters of selling space and offers the widest range of goods. The Oxford Street Megastore has a turnover of £15 million and is the biggest music store in Europe. New Megastores have been opened in Paris, Dublin, Sydney and Melbourne and others are planned.

VIRGIN MUSIC

Virgin Music is led by Chairman Simon Draper and Managing Director Ken Berry, who joined the company as an accountant. Draper states:

> What Richard saw in me was that I knew a lot about music whereas he didn't—he ended up in music more by accident than design. Even today my first interest is music, not business, and although I'm a director of the Group I have very little to do with the running of the other companies. I'm with the core business which is Music.

Draper became Managing Director of Virgin Records in 1978 as Branson moved out of the day-to-day running of the record company. The music division has three principal areas of activity—the record label, music publishing and recording studios.

The record label has a roster of over 100 artists and bands and is placed among the top 6 recording companies in the U.K. Most of the staff are engaged in the search for, development, marketing and promotion of artists and their products. The company does not have manufacturing or distribution facilities, preferring to subcontract this work out to avoid high overheads but retaining control in terms of production quality, pricing and discounting. In return for a royalty paid to the artist, the record label has the right to commercially exploit the recording copyright and associated videos. Often large advance royalties are paid. The company retains the right to terminate the contract if an artist is considered to be unsuccessful.

The Virgin label was created in 1972. In 1983 and 1984 the company acquired majority interests in three other labels. The rationale was that rapid expansion was best pursued through new businesses, since the smaller size allows management to serve the artist better. The record label has some 15 overseas subsidiaries which mostly distribute recordings by U.K. artists. France, Germany and Italy are countries where a significant roster of local artists has been developed. Recently, Virgin entered the U.S. market once more. Draper's comments about that move were as follows:

> When we went to the U.S. the first time we did it wrong. We thought we could expand our own record companies using U.K. people and artists. But we didn't have enough funds, the right artists and so on and in the end we pulled out with a million pound loss and went back to licensing. In Europe we did it differently. We identified key management locally and built around them, using established U.K. acts first and developing local artists if possible. Since we already had sales in Europe we could use that as the beginning. The experience we gained in Europe taught us a lot of things that we are applying in the U.S. now. It took time but we have identified key local people in the U.S. We were looking for people poised to make the next move, someone of our own age who was energetic and ambitious, not someone who was already at the top. We were also looking for A & R (Artistes & Repertoire) people to develop new acts. That's different from Europe where most of our people have a marketing background to market the U.K. artists.

The people we have hired in the States are both experienced in the music business and about our age. They have an attractive financial package plus a 10 percent stake each in VRAI—Virgin Records America Inc.

Given the fashion element in popular music, one band or artist can dominate in terms of profit and contribution. For this reason, management at Music is constantly seeking to acquire a broad range of talent to ensure stability of earnings.

Music publishing is involved with the exploitation of songwriters' compositions through the generation of royalty income. Contracted songwriters are independent or come from either Virgin's roster of artists or those of other record companies. The company seeks to maximize its return by seeking outlets for composers in films, videos, TV programs and advertising, as well as record production. Group profits benefit significantly from this activity.

As for the recording studios, Virgin has seven which offer facilities to its own artists as well as those from other recording companies.

Commenting on the management of the Music division, Simon Draper has said:

> It is a very self-contained business. Ken and I run it between us. My first interest is developing the bands, the creative side. Ken provides the business back up and at that he is a real star. We have a good balancing act and I wouldn't want to underestimate his contributions. He's one of the best in the business. He has no pretensions about or deep interest in music and A & R but knows the music business from top to bottom, not just in the U.K. but worldwide.

VIRGIN COMMUNICATIONS

Robert Devereaux, a history graduate, joined Virgin Books in 1979 from another publisher. In 1982 he became MD of Virgin Vision (later named Communications). The division has four main activities: distribution of filmed entertainment, services to TV and video industries, broadcasting and publishing. Film and video distribution accounts for 75 percent of its turnover, television and video services another 10 percent. Broadcasting and publishing take care of the rest. Virgin has also taken over W. H. Allen, the publishers, acquired a minority stake in Mastertronic, a leader in computer software games, and has bought Rushes, makers of TV commercials. Virgin Communications' 45 percent holding in Super Channel, a British satellite television station, has been losing money since it began operations last year. Communications, however, is seen as a division with major growth potential. Devereaux stated:

> I think Virgin is successful because it's a people-led company. People here know that if they come up with a good idea they'll get a hearing, and the resources if it looks good—then they've got to make it work. That makes choosing people very important so Richard always looks for personal fit as well as experience, people who will fit in with him and the company.
>   But I think expansion plans should fit into the current set-up and that is why I was against the move into the airline, although I am now prepared to admit I was wrong

on that one and Richard was right, he'd covered the risk. Risk is something Richard likes to control.

VIRGIN ENTERPRISES

Until the flotation, Virgin Enterprises contained those activities not comfortably fitting into any of the other divisions. It included, for example, hotels, a tour operation (Virgin Holidays), theme pubs and nightclubs, property development and venture capital.

Rod Vickery has been with Virgin almost continuously since the *Student* magazine days. A graphic designer by training, he has held a number of positions in the company. In 1985 he was assigned the management of pubs and clubs reporting to Don Cruickshank. He has two pubs and two nightclubs under his control. A third club, the very profitable "Heaven," catering to homosexuals, is managed separately. Talking of the early days, Vickery remarked that "Richard hasn't changed much. He's still inventive and opportunistic which you needed to be in those days because you were never sure if you would have a job tomorrow. You had to put your hand to everything. You couldn't say 'that's not my job.'"

THE HOUSEBOAT

Virgin operates out of a variety of modest, even sometimes dilapidated, offices spread throughout northwest London. Virgin Communications, for example, is located in a converted canal building and Virgin Music in a large refurbished Victorian house. All the offices have the same air of bustle and clutter. Popular music can usually be heard in some parts of the building, and there is a constant stream of visitors ranging from motorcycle messengers to Rastafarians bearing instruments. Only the airline offices are in a modern high-rise office complex, located near Gatwick Airport.

Large numbers of small companies (about a hundred and twenty in twenty-three different countries at the latest count), delegation of authority, and promoting of loyalty are three aspects of the indelibly "Branson" management touch. Branson has said that he wants to create the right environment for the staff to work in. To use his words:

> We didn't go for a big deluxe office block in central London but have about 10 different buildings with no more than, say, 180 people in each. Therefore our people can identify with a particular manager and not get lost in corridors and feel they are working for something impersonal. One thing that we have with Virgin over other companies is that the people have literally grown up with the company over the years. We began so young, and I think that it has had a tremendous binding effect on everybody—it's not people who come from outside who have just come in as a job. As a leader it is very important to accept people's weaknesses as well as their strengths. I think it is important that they respect you, so that if you say "well done" to them, it means something to them and that you can motivate them. You've got to motivate them through your own example. What we try to do is create a situation where they are really running their own companies, so that they can make their own

mistakes and their own success. If there are people with the company who are capable of becoming millionaires we want them to stick with the company to do it.

Branson himself works alone, apart from two secretaries, in a houseboat moored on a canal in a pleasant part of west London. The boat was previously his home. He has now moved to a house nearby with his Scottish girlfriend and two young children, since his daughter "was starting to answer the phones and run the office." There is a constant stream of visitors who approach the boat through the gardens of adjoining houseboats to reach him. Once inside they find a comfortable, but not luxurious, home setting with one bedroom acting as an office for the two secretaries. On occasions, as friends recall, the bathroom has served as a boardroom with Branson conducting meetings from his bath. Photographs of Branson's family, and his Caribbean island and other mementos line the walls. The two telephones ring constantly and Branson is rarely off the phone, scribbling in a notebook that he uses to jot down ideas:

> I always know what went on at a meeting, even one held 4 or 5 years ago; I simply get out my old notebook and look it up. The nice thing about the boat is that it attracts people to come here like City people and bankers, especially when the weather's nice. Also I can get more done here. My secretaries can fob people off and make sure my desk is clear to do the important issues. I get wodges and wodges of paperwork, which is probably the thing I dislike most about my work. Not that I think it's productive to dislike things. My attitude towards life is to enjoy it to the full. What I dislike now as the business grows is the lack of time I have for any one person or issue or company. It means I have to rush people which I don't like to do.

FROM THE ROCK MARKET TO THE STOCK MARKET

During October and November 1986, a series of press and TV advertisements appeared in the U.K. under the title "From the Rock Market to the Stock Market." The advertisements invited the public to buy shares in the Virgin Group, which was to be quoted on the London Stock Exchange after its flotation at the end of November.

Prior to the flotation, Richard Branson, Ken Berry and Simon Draper had purchased certain of the Group's assets, at a cost of £5.1 million, in order to form a new private company called "Voyager." These assets included the Virgin Atlantic Airline, and Virgin's travel and nightclub interests. The new company was to be owned and managed separately from the publicly quoted company under an agreement designed to avoid a conflict of interest. It was expected that only Branson would give any of his time to manage the private company and he would limit this to about "three days a month." A managing director was to be sought. In 1987 David Benson, an M.B.A. with wide experience in the travel business, was appointed to that position.

The new private company made an operating loss before tax of £5.7 million (of which £2.8 million was attributable to the airline) on a turnover of £55 million in the year to July 31, 1986. The trading year ending July 1987 saw a turnover of £78 million and a net profit before taxation of £4.2 million.

The flotation was carried out successfully using the rather unusual method of offer-by-tender whereby investors nominate a price which is then accepted or rejected. The striking price of 140p per share valued the public company at approximately £240 million. City institutions holding convertible preference stock took up their option to convert their holding to ordinary shares. Other institutions acquired part of the new issue through subscription and trading in the after-market created by profit-taking among smaller shareholders, who initially numbered 85,000. Virgin artists and employees acquired 7 percent of the new issue under the terms of the offer, which gave them priority access to up to 10 percent. After the flotation Richard Branson, Simon Draper, and Ken Berry controlled 63 percent of the issued share capital. Exhibits 1–3 give statistical information on continuing activities.

OWNING A PUBLIC COMPANY

In the spring of 1988 the senior management of Virgin took stock of the U.K. company's development following its flotation. The previous 18 months had seen the move to re-enter the U.S. music market requiring heavy investment; Branson's balloon exploit, which had caused unease among financial analysts unused to the idea of the Chairman of a public company deliberately risking life and limb; and rapid growth in the activities of Virgin Communications. Some senior managers were having to adapt to the public scrutiny that comes with public ownership. Simon Draper, for example, found it difficult to explain the popular music business to investors:

> I have found it particularly onerous dealing with the City, although it is getting easier now. Contact with the City is mainly Don's role but of course the analysts want to meet me and Ken. Ken finds it easier than I do; he doesn't resent the time it takes and we both realize it is necessary. I don't think we'll ever be fully appreciated by the City and they seem to undervalue Virgin. It is seen as a one-man company which makes us appear vulnerable if anything should happen to Richard and I have also heard from a number of quarters that Richard is not much liked in the City. Maybe he is too young, too successful. I don't understand why this should be but it goes back to the time of the flotation and the tender offer. Last year the knives were out in the business press and not even our stunningly good results could make things better.
>
>   The company has become more disciplined as I expected it would, I mean it is totally oriented towards the bottom line, delivering profits. That is probably a good thing. Another good thing about the discipline is that it has kept us in the main Virgin business, not flying in several directions because that's Richard's style. Voyager is doing that and I'm really relieved that it is all over there, to the extent that I'm going to sell some of my shares in it and spend some money on something else.

Draper mentioned that the public flotation almost coincided with the launch of the U.S. company, although the two events were not directly related. He felt that it would have been better to have done them at different times because the U.S. investment would need a while to produce profits and would not necessarily live up to expectations in the short-term.

Looking to future growth in the Music Division, Draper saw two distinct themes:

Firstly we will go for organic growth. The U.S. will play a big part in that because we'll have American products selling in the U.S. and the rest of the world. But also we are developing other types of music. For example, we now have a classical music label, another label called Earthworks that covers Third World music and a folk label. We are expanding our range of music. Secondly, if the opportunity comes up we may think about making a big acquisition of an existing music company like EMI. With their huge back catalogue of thirty or forty years they generate an enormous amount of income. The problem is that there would be big competition for such a company particularly from the Japanese like Sony who would want it for other strategic reasons.

Robert Devereaux, looking back over the previous 18 months, noted that:

Virgin Communications is still doing mostly the same thing, albeit in a more structured way, in the same places. Perhaps the U.S. is more important where we've gone from six to forty people and we are more committed to print publishing. Otherwise everything is just much bigger. We certainly look more closely at profit potential. In the past we may have said: "If it makes a pound profit, let's do it." Now we might say, "It can only be spread so far." We don't have vast management resources and they have to be concentrated on the really valuable businesses.

One of the real challenges is to continue to grow and to maintain the creativity. We do that by pushing decision making down the line and letting young managers have their heads. I spend my time listening to people and playing the devil's advocate, but at the end, depending on the financial risk, I will say, "Go ahead and do it." Those who don't will go. Perhaps we have wonderful managers because nobody ever goes. In any event it is still the same company, its heart is the same, its spirit the same. Its outer clothing might have changed and may change again but it is still the same company and I hope still will be.

It was a "test of strategy" that made Cruickshank half-jokingly remark that:

The houseboat may be moored in mid-Atlantic in the not too distant future. If you add up what we are doing, the nature of the business, the people we employ and so on you see that the centre of our world market is in the U.S. The U.K. is only 6 percent of that market. If everything we do is successful you will be looking at an organisation with influential individuals in Los Angeles with Hollywood nearby and all that means in cinema, music, TV. The U.S. market will produce a big percentage of the profit. That creates a very interesting situation.

Outside the company, Branson has invested £5 million in the Virgin Health Care Foundation, a charity run on business lines with its main product being condoms sold under the "Mates" label. All profit goes toward AIDS research.

Branson chaired U.K. 2000, a youth-directed job development organization that the Thatcher government asked him to be involved in. He has also become a director of Russia's Intourist in the U.K.

ANNOUNCEMENTS

In 1988 two major announcements came from Virgin. The first announcement was made following the release of Virgin's half-yearly financial result. An article in the *Daily Telegraph* was typical of those commenting on the results.

> Richard Branson needed all his communication skills to explain how investing for the future has led to a 22 percent fall in Virgin's first-half profits. Virgin's shares fell 8p to 92p as some of Virgin's dwindling band of institutional investors decided they did not have enough patience to hold on. Mr. Branson left it to Don Cruickshank to detail the £100 million investment the group has made, mainly in developing the communications and music businesses in America. Virgin's record label in America lost between £2 million and £3 million in the first half on a turnover of £16 million and may lose up to £10 million in the first year. Mr. Branson said the figures were encouraging and that profits were expected in two years.

But in July 1988 Branson made his second, most startling announcement, which created considerable furor in the business press. One article in the *Financial Times,* under the headline "The Honeymoon is over for Virgin," described the latest development that surprised even seasoned Virgin watchers.

> Almost all members of Virgin management will be buying back 37 percent of the company's shares, making it effectively a private company once again. Richard Branson has expressed concern for the 40,000 small investors who have not benefited from purchasing Virgin shares. However, he remains faithful to his long-term investment strategy and, if the two cannot be compatible, prefers to stick with a management formula which has worked for him in the past. The buy-out, Britain's largest to date, is expected to be completed by January 1989.
>
>   As usual, Richard Branson has the last word: "The buy-out is like the ideal marriage, or the ideal divorce. I don't know of any managing director who does not want to do the same thing."

Exhibit 1. Virgin Group—Continuing activities only, turnover/operating profit (loss) by division. (£'000).

| | Year ended January 31 | | | Year ended July 31 | | | |
	1983	1984	1985	1986*	1986	1987	1988 (6 mths)
1. *Music*							
Turnover	32,353	71,527	82,439	152,813	118,410	143,338	84,208
Profit	3,797	14,203	14,608	22,158	20,158	20,298	11,528
2. *Retail & Property*							
Turnover	16,150	22,658	34,308	74,488	55,925	98,438	74,333
Profit	484	319	1,411	291	285	4,588	4,295
3. *Communications*							
Turnover	700	2,957	4,872	19,298	16,333	43,008	39,711
Profit	(244)	(916)	(190)	1,046	1,294	6,409	3,574
4. *Group*							
Turnover	n/a	n/a	n/a	3,445	2,150	1,461	324
Profit	—	—	—	(3,447)	(2,329)	(2,386)	(1,693)
Less Intra-group							
Turnover	—	—	—	(9,583)	(5,036)	(7,133)	(3,368)
5. *Total*							
Turnover	49,203	97,142	121,619	243,632	188,597	279,112	195,208
Profit	4,037	13,606	16,209	19,905	19,342	28,909	17,704

*18 months to July 31, 1986, following change in year end.
**Retail only for years 1983 to 1985.

Exhibit 2. Virgin Group—Continuing activities only, turnover by region (£'000).

| | Year ended January 31 | | | Year ended July 31 | | |
	1983	1984	1985	1986'	1986	1987
U.K.	34,477	44,638	48,970	119,697	91,791	141,029
Rest of Europe	11,390	33,037	37,630	83,951	66,850	96,113
North America	2,748	10,409	23,670	25,863	19,131	28,647
Asia & Australia	—	5,541	7,663	12,665	9,603	12,696
Rest of World	—	387	756	1,456	1,222	627
Total	**48,615**	**94,012**	**118,689**	**243,632**	**188,597**	**279,112**

*18 months to July 31, 1986, following change in year end.

Exhibit 3. Virgin Group—Continuing activities only.

Division Name	Senior Executives Position	Age	Years of Service
Group			
Don Cruickshank	Group Managing Director	46	4
Music			
Simon Draper	Chairman	38	17
Ken Berry	Managing Director	37	15
Torrens Lyster	Finance Director	42	3
John Webster	Director—International	33	12
Patrick Zelnik	Managing Director—France	40	7
Udo Lange	Managing Director—Germany	36	5
Shelagh Macleod	Director—Legal & Business Affairs	35	3
Steve Lewis	Managing Director—Music Publishing	34	10
Barbara Jefferies	Managing Director—Recording Studios	38	14
Charlie Dimont	Managing Director—Merchandising	35	5
Jeff Ayeroff	Joint Managing Director—USA	40	—
Jordon Harris	Joint Managing Director—USA	34	—
Retail			
Maggie Garrett	General Manager	32	9
Jonathan Gilbride	Managing Director—Export	37	11
Communications			
Robert Devereaux	Managing Director	32	9
Stephen Navin	Director—Legal & Business Affairs	37	8
Julian Portman	Finance Director	37	2
Mike Watts	Managing Director—Film & Video	40	3
Nick Alexander	Managing Director—Computer	32	5

Videocab

Ron Spiller worked for the Aceview videostore for 3 years. He was a real movie buff and adored speaking with customers and giving his insight into the latest video rentals. Over the years, Ron had been asked by a number of customers if the store delivered movies. Although the store did not offer this service, Ron couldn't help thinking what a wonderful business opportunity this was.

Ron, with the advice of the owner of Aceview, learned all there was to know about running a video rental shop. Although many of the video stores had gone out of business in the local area, Ron believed that his store would have a distinctive difference. He would deliver movies to older people, young mothers and handicapped people who had trouble getting out of the house to visit a traditional video shop. The customers would call in and request a movie; if he had it in stock, Ron would deliver it directly to their homes. He would be a one man shop. He would carry the movies and a cellular phone in his vehicle and could therefore take orders from home or even when he was on the road. Although Ron would not charge a delivery fee to his clients, he intended to charge a premium of about $1.50 more per movie than traditional video stores.

Ron just got a new credit card when he turned 19, and bought $2000 worth of movies; the limit of credit on the card. He also leased a van which would act like his "store on wheels." Ron was pretty excited. He named his business "VIDEOCAB," and advertised with flyers placed on windshields in car parking lots.

After about a week he began to get customers calling for movies. Along the way, however, Ron came into some problems. He realized that his revenue from the movies was not sufficient to cover the gas expense and maintenance on his vehicle. He also came into problems in the winter when it began to snow and his van was not prepared to travel on the icy roads. Ron also started getting nasty calls from the bank when 6 months had passed without him making a minimum payment on his credit card. Ron was in trouble.

There were basically three options from which he could choose, although none seemed particularly appealing to him. He could either abandon the whole business and cut his losses; or he could try to go to friends and family to raise additional money. He assumed that the bank would not lend him the money because he was in debt and had no collateral. He also had the option of returning to Aceview, which was prepared to offer a delivery service under Ron's management. Aceview also offered to pay all the movie and vehicle expenses in return for 80% of the revenues Ron made in his deliveries.

This case was developed by a participant in the Entrepreneurship graduate seminar under the direction of Professor A. B. Ibrahim.

It is obvious that Ron failed quite badly in his small business startup. What do you think were his mistakes, and what do you suggest that he do?

Speedflow Inc.

Peter Noonan, a senior account manager with the Henley Bank, glanced with some concern at the business plan lying on his desk. Just minutes earlier he had completed a meeting with Susan Drucker who was requesting a substantial loan for her new company, SpeedFlow Inc. But as she explained her idea and highlighted the financial statements, Peter grew increasingly hesitant about authorizing such a loan. Several issues concerned him. First, Susan's proposal consisted of marketing a new product which was technologically sophisticated but had never been market tested. Peter did not trust his own capabilities to evaluate her product. He also believed that Susan's idea could benefit from the advice and evaluation of a technical specialist. Secondly, in examining Susan's business plan Peter had become aware of her lack of experience in marketing and general management. The plan was missing a detailed marketing strategy and Susan seemed to be overly optimistic about the ease with which she could generate the sales required to break even. Thirdly, SpeedFlow Inc. owned very few assets that could be used as collateral.

Despite these trepidations Peter believed that, with some guidance, Susan's venture could be successful. Susan had been taking care of her personal banking needs with this branch of the Henley Bank since 1984 and could, in the future, also prove to be a valuable commercial client. In the past two years the Henley Bank had encouraged all account managers to use a broader approach in servicing their business clientele. Such a strategy implied providing advice and suggestions on managerial or financial issues. But it also meant, for start-up ventures that were considered too risky by the bank, suggesting alternate sources of capital. As he reflected on their meeting, Peter wondered what course of action he should recommend to Susan to enable her to test the commercial application and economic viability of her product and improve the marketing strength of her organization.

Susan graduated in 1986 with a bachelors degree from the local university, a highly recognized institution in computer science. In the past few years, its computer science department had played an important role in several government funded research projects. Susan, having worked at ICN for several summers, was immediately recruited to their product development department on a full-time basis. Although Susan had been approached by other companies, accepting ICN's offer enabled her to remain in the city she considered home and to plan for the optimal time to start her own business. Over the next six years Susan received several promotions at ICN. By 1993 she had reached the position of Senior

This case was prepared by D. Balas, M.B.A., under the direction of Professor A. B. Ibrahim, as a basis for class discussion rather than to illustrate either effective or ineffective handling of an administrative situation. © Dr. A.B. Ibrahim, 1994.

Project Manager. Her rise within the company was based as much on her ability to recognize and champion new ideas as on her technical capabilities. When Susan believed in a new product or process she was very tenacious in convincing her superiors to have faith in her judgement. Susan enjoyed the challenge of developing new ideas and found it highly rewarding when the projects she managed led to an increase in her department's revenues or a reduction in its costs. In general, an above average number of projects under her supervision had been adopted by ICN. As part of her strategy of identifying and developing new products, Susan had relied heavily on the company's technical support staff and R&D and marketing departments. Unlike some of the other project managers in her department, Susan was not in the habit of championing ideas that were too far removed from ICN's core product areas. Her hard work and commitment to the company had placed her on the "fast track" within ICN's product development department.

In early 1992 Susan became increasingly convinced that a need existed for sophisticated Queuing software. Anxious to develop and test her idea, she submitted a proposal to the head of her department. However, at the time ICN, faced with an eroding market share and diminishing profitability, was streamlining the development of new products. This meant that only the most promising new products or process developments would receive budget approval. The development of all other ideas—the Queuing software being one of them—was indefinitely frozen. It was the first time in her career at ICN that Susan was at odds with her superiors. Not only was she unable to pursue a project that, according to her, showed great potential, but she was also increasingly expected to coordinate her work more closely with that of other project managers. Consequently, Susan felt the quality of her work was being compromised since she performed best independently of others.

Susan was so convinced of her idea that she began experimenting and developing the software on her own time. ICN marketed Queuing software for mainframe computers but had no such program available for small PCs and work stations. In 1992 very rudimentary Queuing software was available from smaller high-tech companies that specialized in software. It was, however, not user-friendly and not versatile enough to handle a large number of work stations. As Susan progressed in designing her version of the software and as it became increasingly evident that ICN was not interested in developing and marketing it, she began to consider leaving ICN to create her own company. Finally, in the spring of 1994, with the encouragement of her husband, Susan resigned and created SpeedFlow Inc. By this time the Queuing software was sufficiently advanced to allow Susan to create a prototype. It was the first time that she was entirely responsible for the creation of a new product—that is without the help of a technical support team to test the technical viability and market team to price and promote the product.

Having earned just over $100,000 in her last years at ICN, Susan was able to save a portion of the money required to develop a prototype of her product. She still had some equity in the company but it was neither sufficient to fully test and promote the product, nor sufficient to buy additional computer equipment. Because of the shortage of funds, Susan also strove to keep operating expenses to a minimum. She had reluctantly hired a technical assistant but did not want to hire someone with marketing expertise until sales reached a sufficiently high level.

CASE 4

The Time-2ZX

It had been a long time since Marie Taylor had seen such an impressive business plan. All of the necessary information was there; complete market analysis, cost estimates and projected financial statements for the next three years. This young entrepreneur, who sat eagerly across from her at her huge oak desk, had even performed a comprehensive SWOT analysis—a rather sophisticated approach that Marie had rarely seen from an aspiring businessman during her long career as an account manager with Citizen's Bank.

Marty Abdul was a 35-year old Canadian of Indian descent. His parents had moved here from New Delhi and started up their own business in the manufacturing of high-tech circuit boards to be used in mass telecommunications systems. Like his father before him, Marty graduated first in his class with a Bachelor's of Science in Engineering. Marty had always done exceptionally well in academics and was also a very gifted athlete and had excellent interpersonal skills. Marty was no stranger to success and Marie Taylor could determine this by the air of confidence and professionalism that he exuded.

This thriving entrepreneur had developed an innovative little gadget that could be used to automate a labour-intensive function performed on his father's factory floor. The device, which Marty named the Time-2ZX used a computer aided design package which Marty developed. With the use of a robotic arm, the mechanism could tighten the tiny screws that were used in the electronic components that the factory produced. The device could fit into small spaces easily and eliminated the need for manual labour to complete the operation.

Marty felt that the potential for this device was infinite as it could be applied and integrated to a variety of manufacturing functions. He knew that it could be a raving success. Marty even tested the product in the factory for a full two months to assure its durability and reliability. The Time-2ZX did not disappoint him. Not only did the device eliminate the need to have manual labour perform the screw-tightening function, but the device was also directly responsible for a 30 percent increase in the rate of production.

Marty had even sent the logistics of the device to a major technological institute in Boston for analysis. A study was returned with very positive results saying that the Time-2ZX was a superior and functional electronic device with many possible applications. These facts, as well as comprehensive written documentation of the tests performed on the Time-2ZX, were included in Marty's business plan. This was especially impressive to Marie Taylor as she scrutinized Marty's dossier. Marty would need a large amount of funds

This case was prepared by L. McWhinnie, M.B.A., and D. Balas, M.B.A. under the direction of Professor A. B. Ibrahim, as a basis for class discussion rather than to illustrate effective or ineffective handling of an administrative situation.
© Dr. A.B. Ibrahim, 1994.

to acquire the production capacity and personnel to manufacture and market the Time-2ZX on a large scale. He estimated this capital requirement at about $100,000.

Everything seemed perfect to Mrs. Taylor except for one detail—Marty had absolutely no collateral to put up against the loan. This was a major prerequisite at Citizen's Bank where collateral of at least 20 percent of the value of the loan was required. Marty had no real estate, no personal savings or any other assets with which to gain a loan. It appeared that Marty was stopped dead in his tracks and he didn't know exactly how to persuade Mrs. Taylor to grant him the loan. Mrs. Taylor was equally frustrated as she too was confident that the product had a very big potential in the high-tech industry.

Questions

1. Evaluate the product innovation.
2. Evaluate the entrepreneur.
3. What would you recommend Marty to do?

CASE 5
Home-Aid

Jack Keller finished shooting his nine holes of golf by noon and dreaded going into the office that day. A true-blue company man, Jack had been in his account management position with First National Bank for over 25 years. In that time he had lent to many small businesses and had also seen many of them ultimately fall to their demise. At 2:00 o'clock he was meeting a young man named Eddie Carlyle, who had visited the bank on several occasions trying to obtain a $50,000 loan in seed capital to start a business. On his first visit, Eddie didn't have a business plan; but after several consultations with Jack Keller he was finally prepared to make a serious effort to obtain his loan. Jack Keller was tied up in knots over this particular lending decision. He undeniably liked Eddie and his enthusiasm, but he had some very serious concerns over his ability to create a viable business. Nonetheless, Jack felt that Eddie had a fabulous product to bring to the marketplace.

Eddie was without a doubt a computer wizard. He had earned his bachelor's degree in computer science when he was 22 and had landed a computer programmer's job with a large computer company immediately after he graduated. Eddie was a very creative individual and it did not take long for him to resent the strict rules and regulations enforced upon employees. Eddie like to make his own rules. Although his job paid the bills, it was Eddie's hobby that consumed most of his attention. Eddie would stay up until all hours of the night writing software programs on his PC. He especially liked to write programs that he envisioned the average person, largely illiterate in computers, would find useful. Eddie created a fully functional word processing package, a spreadsheet package, a day-time organizer and a personal budgeting tool; all in a very easy menu-driven interface. Eddie recognized very early in the PC revolution that personal computers were quickly making inroads into people's homes. Eddie felt that if he could fully integrate the four software programs that he had written, he could create a system that would meet all of the needs of businessmen, homemakers and students in the home. It took six months of painstaking trial and error before Eddie finally perfected the product. He called it Home-Aid, the first fully integrated software package for PCs. Eddie proceeded to give the software to a few of his friends and some colleagues to try out an their PCs at home. Without exception, everybody adored the functionality, features and flexibility of Home-Aid. Eddie was ecstatic and without giving it a second thought, quit his job and began to promote his software. He was willing to take a risk for something he had the utmost confidence in.

This case was prepared by L. McWhinnie, M.B.A., D. Balas, M.B.A. under the direction of Professor A. B. Ibrahim as a basis for class discussion rather than to illustrate effective handling of an administrative situation. © Dr. A.B. Ibrahim, 1994.

Eddie had only $6,500 in his savings account. He used the funds to buy computer supplies and a portable computer with which he could make demonstrations to potential clients. He soon discovered, however, that customers were not ready to take him seriously as he peddled his diskettes around town. He had no packaging, service contracts or formal promotional material with which to attract clients. The answer was to try to obtain financing from a bank so that he could give Home-Aid the kick-off a product of such high calibre deserved.

Here it was 2:00 p.m. and Eddie was at Jack Keller's office once again. He had done what Mr. Keller had instructed; written a formal business plan complete with pro-forma balance sheets, budgets, forecasts and all the other bells and whistles that didn't mean much to Eddie. This lack of business sense was what caused the most concern for Jack. Although he had confidence in Home-Aid and had seen the excellence in product quality first hand, he had doubts in Eddie's management abilities. In many ways, Eddie was rather impulsive. Although Jack Keller felt that Eddie had many entrepreneurial traits, he needed guidance when it came to making practical decisions about the company's future.

Questions

1. Evaluate the product innovation.
2. What would you advise Eddie to do?
3. What would you recommend if you were Mr. Keller?

PART TWO

SMALL BUSINESS MANAGEMENT

△ CHAPTER 9 △
MANAGING THE SMALL BUSINESS

Managing small business is simply sequencing activities and events so that things turn out the way the entrepreneur or manager wants them to be. To achieve this, entrepreneurs and managers of small firms must know what the management process is all about. Every organization, regardless of its size, requires good management to survive and prosper. Managing involves objective-setting, planning, organizing and controlling.

OBJECTIVE SETTING AND THE SMALL BUSINESS

Formulating objectives and goals is the first step in the management process. Organizations exist to accomplish a purposeful action or objective. Indeed, formulating objectives is essential for any organization, for it determines the future course of action. Entrepreneurs may have multiple objectives. These include making profits, extending their share of the market, and improving their social standing. Peter Drucker suggests that the organization needs to set objectives in all of its key activities:

> A business must first be able to create a customer. Therefore, it needs a marketing objective. Business must be able to innovate or else their competitor will make them obsolete. There is need for an innovation objective. All businesses depend on the three factors of production of the economist, that is, on the human resources, the capital resources, and physical resources. There must be objectives for their supply, their employment, and their development. The resources must be employed productively and their productivity has to grow if the business is to survive. There is need, therefore, for productivity objectives. Business exists in society and in the community and, therefore, has to discharge social responsibilities at least to the point where it takes responsibility for its impact upon the environment. Therefore, objectives in respect to the social dimensions of business are needed.
>   Finally, there is a need for profit, otherwise none of the objectives can be attained. They all require effort, that is, cost. And they can be financed only out of the profits of a business. They all entail risks; they all, therefore, require a profit to cover the risk of potential losses.[1]

To achieve organizational objectives, the entrepreneur or the small business manager must get all the employees involved. Management by objectives (MBO) is a widely known method for doing just that.

MBO and the Small Business

Management by objectives emphasizes participation in goal setting. The program essentially involves translating the small firm's overall objectives into specific objectives for different units and/or team members in the small firm. In essence, establishing a link between organization needs and individual needs. Thus, if organization members achieve their goals then their unit goals will be achieved and the firm's overall objectives are also attained.

For MBO system to work effectively in a smaller firm it has to have a specific objective, a time frame, and provide continuous feedback. But above all, it must allow for total participation of organization members in objectives-setting. Let us discuss each of these elements.

First, objectives-setting should be a team effort. The small firm staff should participate jointly with the entrepreneur or manager in identifying the overall corporate objectives, the unit objectives and the individual objectives. Second, objectives have to be spelled out clearly with no ambiguity and should be quantifiable and tangible. To increase market share by 4 percent, to increase ROI by 2 percent, or to cut overhead costs by 3 percent are all examples of measurable objectives. Third, objectives should have a specific time frame in which they are to be accomplished such as end of the first quarter or end of the year. Fourth, it is essential for an effective MBO program to provide continuous feedback on performance and how the firm is progressing toward achieving the objectives formulated earlier.

PLANNING AND THE SMALL BUSINESS

Planning is basically the activities involved in choosing courses of action to achieve the small firm's objectives. Plans spell out objectives, mission and strategy. Planning is essentially concerned with the future, because it anticipates and precedes action. But predicting the future in small firms involves risk. To minimize such risk entrepreneurs and managers of small firms perform situation audits to assess the strengths, weaknesses, opportunities and risks and to establish a network of reliable information about the future.

Planning is essential to small business because it reduces uncertainty about the future, minimizes waste, makes effective use of the limited resources of the smaller organization and facilitates the monitoring process. Studies have shown that small businesses which are involved in planning are more successful than their non-planning counterparts. Box 9.1 describes different organization stages and management capabilities to match each stage.

Box 9.1. The Life Cycle.

It is generally accepted that a successful firm passes through several distinct phases as it grows; a "life cycle." As each phase makes differing demands on an organization, it requires differing capabilities and characteristics of its management. Carroll Kroeger summarizes each as:

1. Originator/Inventor—at the firm's inception its founders must be creative, independent, perceptive and risk-takers. As Kroeger points out, these are perceptual/conceptual skills that are imperative if the enterprise is to surmount the 75% failure rate typical of this stage.
2. Planner/Organizer—as the corporation progresses through its development stage it begins to take on a more definite form and structure. Relationships with other organizations, particularly for finance, are cemented. Analytical and interpersonal skills must be brought to the fore, to aid in planning and to generate confidence among bankers, suppliers and the like.
3. Developer/Implementer—as the enterprise enters its stage of most rapid growth and the complexity of its interrelationships increases proportionately, it demands professional competence in planning, supervision, cost control, and marketing. Managers must work within increasingly formalized limits.
4. Administrator/Operator—when the firm reaches maturity and further growth is unsustainable, it must exploit or "harvest" its position to its best advantage, and therefore needs management geared to efficiency and coordination: bureaucratic administration.
5. Successor/Reorganizer—lack of growth and direction bring about decline; dramatic changes are necessary to arrest it. Management must therefore set a new course with new technology, or products (requiring vision and most of the other qualities of stage 1) or must bring about a revival with disciplined cost cutting, control and retrenchment (requiring doggedness, self-assurance and a facility for outside relations).

As the author notes, large multi-product firms can afford the luxury of rotating managers with each of the above capabilities among product divisions as they pass through each successive stage. A small firm obviously cannot. Managers require a career-long learning process, Kroeger argues, and in the small firm that dictates a reliance on outside education. Business schools have begun to provide for the educational needs of the mature manager, but further innovation, he feels, is necessary.

Source: Carroll V. Kroeger, "Managerial Development in Small Firms," *California Management Review* 17, 1, 1976, pp. 41–47.

ORGANIZING AND THE SMALL BUSINESS

Organizing specifies the structure of the small firm; it sets out the lines of authority and communication among people and determines what information must flow along these lines.

T. Burns and G. M. Stalker in The Management of Innovation identified two types of structure, Mechanistic and Organic.[2] The mechanistic, which is appropriate to a relatively stable environment, employs traditional pyramidal structures that are made up of units, and roles that are tightly defined. People communicate through the proper channels and decision-making is centralized at the top. The organic structure on the other hand is more appropriate to innovative, dynamic and changing type environments. Thus the organic structure is flexible and it can rapidly respond to new opportunities.

Size, Technology, Environment and Structure

An organization's size, type of technology, and environment have a significant influence on structure. Studies have shown that increased organization size leads to increased complexity, which in turn makes it more difficult for the entrepreneur or manager to get involved in different aspects of the business. Therefore formalization of the management process as well as decentralization of the decision-making process replace the entrepreneur or manager.[3]

Studies on technology-structure relationship have shown that the degree of routineness is a determinant factor in organization structure. That is, the more routine the technology, the more mechanistic or standardized the structure, and the more non-routine the technology, the more organic the structure.

In a study of 100 small manufacturing firms, J. Woodward found that organization structures adapt to the degree of technology and that organization effectiveness is a function of the fit between technology and organization structure.[4]

Studies have also shown a strong relationship between environment and the type of structure. In the Casual Texture of Organizational Environment, Emery and Trist[5] identified four types of business environment according to the degree of complexity: placid randomized, placid clustered, disturbed reactive and turbulent type environment. While the placid environment on the one end is relatively stable, the turbulent environment on the other end is highly unstable. Indeed, research work by Lawrence and Lorsch[6] demonstrated that environmental-structure fit is critical to organization success. Figure 9.1 depicts the small business environment.

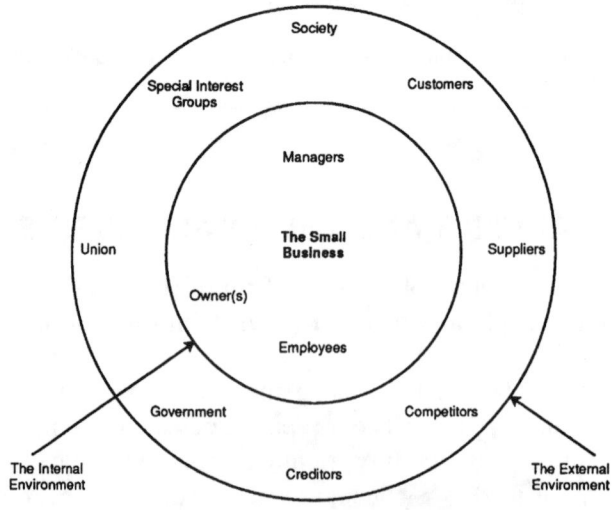

Figure 9.1. The small firm's environment.

Structural Forms and the Small Business

There are essentially four types of structure: simple, functional, divisional and matrix. Let us discuss each briefly.

The Simple Structure

The simple structure is the most common type of organizational structure in small business. It is characterized by low degree of complexity and formalization, and high degree of centralization. The simple structure can be described as "flat," with the owner or manager on the top of the hierarchy.[7] It is most effective when the organization is in the start-up phase and the environment is simple but dynamic with few employees.[8] Most small business firms adapt this structure in their early stage because of the following advantages: simplicity, flexibility, reporting and accountability are clear, less formalization, and fits well with simple and dynamic environment of many small firms. In the new technology driven economy, a flat structure is desirable as it offers the needed flexibility.

However, as can be seen from Figure 9.2, all aspects of the business depend on the owner or manager. If anything happens to him or her the business suffers. In addition, the simple structure is inadequate to handle organizational growth and expansion because of the high degree of centralization and low degree of formalization.

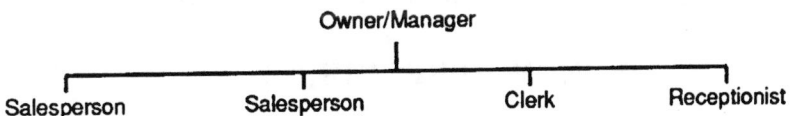

Figure 9.2. The simple structure.

The Functional Structure

The functional structure refers to grouping of related activities under one function, be it accounting, marketing or production as shown in Figure 9.3. The functional structure is more applicable to organizations with single product line or service. Some small firms have adopted this type of structure because of the following advantages: (1) economy of scale,

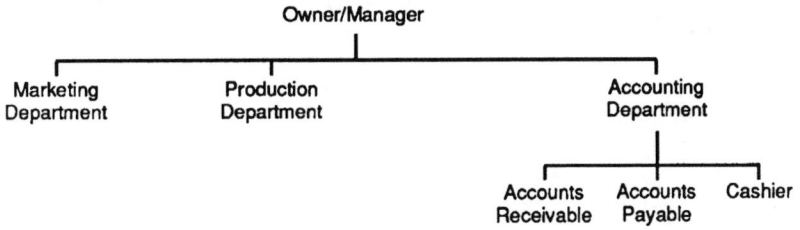

Figure 9.3. The functional structure.

as a result of the grouping of similar activities in specialized units. (2) It is well suited for developing a functional-based distinctive competence and thus allows the small firm to build competitive advantage. (3) It also enhances operating efficiency and permits the entrepreneur or small business management to exercise tighter control over major activities.

The Divisional Structure

The divisional structure is basically designed to achieve a high degree of decentralization. Each division or strategic business unit (SBU) is autonomous. Thus the divisional manager is responsible for the division's performance. The corporate level integrates the activities of the different divisions to ensure the implementation of the overall corporate strategy. The divisional structure is seldom used in small business. However, as the organization grows and expands, this structure form becomes more suitable.

The Matrix Structure

The matrix structure achieves the advantages of both the functional structure, in terms of specialization, and the divisional structure, in terms of decentralization, while avoiding the disadvantages of both. The structure simply allows multiple projects or programs that rely on functional support. Thus the matrix structure creates a dual reporting system. This form allows the firm to respond rapidly to technological and environmental changes. The matrix structure is often used in small knowledge-based and service firms.

HUMAN RESOURCES

Getting the right person into the right job is part of the managerial process. The process of managing human resources in small business begins with human resource planning in which owners and managers assess their future needs in light of the overall objectives. Second, is the recruitment and selection of potential job applicants utilizing different selection devices such as interview, background information and/or tests. Finally career development is achieved by means of training and job rotation to enhance employees performance.

The owner/manager of the small firm is expected to direct his or her staff or team members in a way that helps the firm both achieve its objectives and give its employees a sense of growth and development. Indeed, the owner or manager of the small firm has to provide leadership to his or her team. This includes motivating and directing team members as well as resolving conflicts among members. Human resources are key assets of small knowledge-based firms in the new economy.

DELEGATION

Entrepreneurs and managers of small firms are often guilty of not delegating enough of their routine activities to their staff. Studies on causes of failure in small business have cited the reluctance of owners and managers to delegate as a contributing factor to small business failure.[9]

Delegation may be defined as the assignment of responsibility by the owner or manager to his or her staff. Indeed, management can be defined as getting things done through people. Owners and managers of small business cannot oversee all aspects of business, therefore they have to delegate some of their authority to team members. Many owners and managers might find it difficult to let go of small details and routine activities. There is always the fear that something may go wrong or his or her staff will make mistakes. However, for delegation to be effective, the owner or manager has to learn to trust his or her team members, support their actions and allow them to make mistakes. Without such supportive environment, team members of the small firm may have difficulty assuming their responsibilities.

CONTROL

No matter how you planned and organized your small business, there is the possibility that something may go wrong. Control is essentially concerned with measuring the degree of the small firm's success. It allows the owner or manager to monitor the actual performance and to ensure that it is going as planned and correct deviations when necessary.

Budgeting

Budgeting is the most well known financial control device. Budgetary control for small business consists of two steps. The first step involves setting goals for the next twelve months based on: the overall objectives of the firm, assessment of the firm's capabilities, forecasts and future expectations. The second step includes monitoring and comparing actual data against planned figures. Analyses of variance (favorable or unfavorable) are essential to determine the course of action and/or corrective measures to be taken. Continuous feedback is necessary for budgetary control to be effective in small firms.

Financial Statement Analysis

Financial statement analysis uses balance sheet and income statement data to assess the financial position of the business. The use of ratio analysis to assess the financial statements provides entrepreneurs and small business managers with an overall picture of their financial position. Ratio tests such as liquidity, profitability, leverage and general operating ratios are excellent tools in financial analysis and control in small firms.

THE STRATEGIC DECISION

Strategic decisions are concerned with the direction the small business wishes to pursue in order to achieve its mission and to reach its objectives.

Entrepreneurs should focus their attention on strategic type decisions as opposed to routine decisions. In a highly competitive environment such as ours, entrepreneurs and managers of small business cannot afford getting involved in the day-to-day operation of their businesses. Strategic decisions such as buying or leasing, expansion, capital investment, dealing with rivals, market positioning and going public are critical decisions that require the entrepreneur's attention.

SUMMARY

In this chapter we have attempted to describe the different elements of the managerial process including objective setting, planning, organizing and controlling. Entrepreneurs may have different objectives for starting a business such as making profits, building long-term security, building a legacy for their families or even acting out a fantasy. Organizing is an important element in the managerial process. It includes selecting the proper structure, the lines of authority and communication, and the information flow. Critical factors such as size, technology and environment determine the type of structural forms the organization should implement. The simple structure is the most common type of structure in small business. Delegation of routine activities is important to small business survival. Delegation is the assignment of responsibility by the entrepreneur to his or her staff. Finally, control is concerned with monitoring performance to ensure that it is going according to plan.

NOTES

1.   Peter F. Drucker, *Management: Tasks, Responsibilities, Practices* (New York: Harper & Row, Publishers), 1973, p. 100.
2.   Tom Burns and G. Stalker, *The Management of Innovation* (London: Tavistock Publications Ltd., 1961).
3.   Peter M. Blau and Richard A. Schoenherr, *The Structure of Organizations* (New York: Basic Books, 1971).
4.   Joan Woodward, *Industrial Organization: Theory and Practice* (London: Oxford University Press, 1965).
5.   E. Emery and E. Trist, "The Casual Texture of Organizational Environment," *Human Relations* 18 (February 1965), pp. 21–32.
6.   Paul Lawrence and Jay Lorsch, *Organization and Environment: Managing Differentiation and Integration,* Boston: Harvard Business School, Division of Research, 1967.
7.   Henry Mintzberg, "Structure in 5's: A Synthesis of the Research on Organization Design," *Management Science* (March 1980), p. 331.
8.   Henry Mintzberg, *Structuring of Organizations* (Englewood Cliffs, N.J.: Prentice-Hall, 1979), p. 308.
9.   A. B. Ibrahim and W. H. Ellis, "An Empirical Investigation of Causes of Failure in Small Business and Strategies to Reduce It." *Journal of Small Business and Entrepreneurship* 4, 4 (Spring 1987), pp. 18–24.

THE ENTREPRENEUR

Sam Moore Walton—The Manager
Wal-Mart Stores, Inc.

Born in 1918 and growing up during the depression years, the son of a farm-mortgage banker, Sam Walton delivered newspapers and worked on the farm in order to help support the family.

He graduated from the University of Missouri in 1940 with an economics degree and began working at J. C. Penney for $85 per month. This undoubtedly gave him his initial experience into the realities of the retail world. Further trial and error experiences, amongst which was the discount store concept for small towns, lead to the opening of the first Wal-Mart store in 1962 near the current headquarters in Bentonville, Arkansas.

Now reputed to be among America's billionaires, the enormous success has resulted in the operation of more than 1,300 discount stores and 110 Sam's Wholesale Club warehouse outlets in 27 mid-western, eastern and southern states.

Wal-Mart's sales in 1989 were estimated at nearly $26 billion with net profits in the order of $1 billion. The Company's sales have had an annual compound growth rate of 36% for the last ten years with earnings of 39%. Much of this activity stemmed from the basic fundamentals initiated by Sam Walton: efficient distribution, sharp buying, clean stores and aggressive customer service making for profitable stores. It has been well recommended by Wall Street analysts with expressions such as, "Wal-Mart is my highest recommendation," "Wal-Mart is the finest managed company we have ever followed," and "We do not expect to find another Wal-Mart in our lifetime."

It has also been said that a $1,000 investment in Wal-Mart's 1970 initial offering would be worth a half a million dollars in 1989. The president and chief financial officer, Mr. David Glass, believes that the principles and the basic values that Mr. Sam used in founding the company were so sound and so universally accepted that they will prevail in the future, where "there is more opportunity ahead of us than behind us—we'll be fine as long as we never lose our responsiveness to the customer."

Source: *Fortune* (January 30, 1989), pp. 52–61; *Forbes* (October 23, 1989), pp. 162–164; *Forbes* (October 30, 1989), pp. 130–134.

△ CHAPTER 10 △
STRATEGIC PLANNING

PLANNING

The business climate of this decade can best be described as turbulent and uncertain. Customer demand for superior technology, quality, customization has dramtically altered the conditions under which small business will operate. Alvin Toffler coined the term "future shock" to describe the enormous and unpredictable change in technology, economics, politics and social forces. Because of these massive changes, entrepreneurs and small business firms will be forced to use effective, inexpensive planning tools. This chapter is devoted to exploring the concept and process of strategic planning in small business.

What Is Planning?

Planning can be described as a process by which the entrepreneur systematically evaluates the internal and external capabilities of his/her business and formulate a strategy to carry out the firm's intended mission successfully to carry out the intended mission successfully.

A plan is crucial because it allows assessment of past, present and future issues related to the business, and guides the entrepreneur throughout the entire operation.

Small Business Failure and Lack of Planning

Lack of planning coupled with optimism has been cited by many researchers as a major cause of small business failure. It has been suggested that a formal, systematic planning activity is conspicuously absent in small firms. Small business planning has been characterized as unstructured, sporadic, incremental, informal, reactive and incomprehensive.[1] Studies have also suggested that owners and managers of small businesses engage in "strategic thinking" but without taking action.[2]

The critical problems of initiating planning in small business can be described as getting started, allocating time, setting goals, and lack of planning knowledge.

THE STRATEGIC PLANNING PROCESS

Before describing the different steps in the strategic planning process, it is useful to set forth a conceptual frame of reference for our discussion. Figure 10.1 depicts the different premises and steps involved in the strategic planning process.

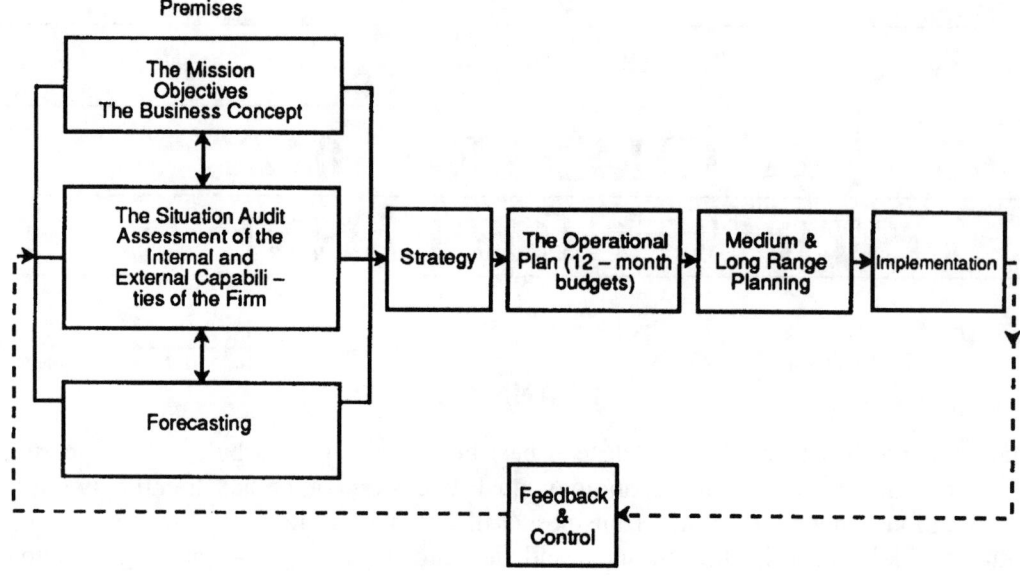

Figure 10.1. The small business strategic planning process.

1. The Mission Statement

The first step in the strategic planning process involves identifying what business you are in. A small firm cannot be all things to all people. Defining the small firm's mission helps to identify the scope of the business, and hence, focuses the search for opportunities. According to Peter Drucker,[3] management must be able to ask and answer some fundamental questions such as: What is our business? What should our business be? Who is our customer? To do that, the small business management must identify its expectations, its competitive advantages and its domain or scope of operation, be it a specific industry, market segment or geographical scope.

2. Objectives

Objective setting consists of the targets the owner/manager wants to achieve. A simple approach might be to record 5 or 10 primary objectives for operating your business, then eliminate those that are unrealistic and rank the rest in order of their importance to you. This simple approach may help you identify your real and achievable objectives. It is not unusual for a small firm to pursue multiple objectives, such as profitability, market share, and/or going public. However, to effectively implement these objectives, they must be hierarchically ranked from the most to the least important.

3. Strategy

Once you have identified your objectives for operating the business, then your next step is to identify the strategy to achieve these objectives. Today small firms survive by carving niches in the market and exploiting windows of opportunities; that is, by introducing products or services that have some unique appeal. There are many strategies that entrepreneurs can adopt, such as focus or niche strategy, market differentiation and cost leadership.[4] The strategy chapter of this text discusses the different strategic directions that are available to the small business in more depth.

4. Strategic Mapping

Strategic mapping provides the small firm with a powerful tool to assess competition in a particular segment. The concept allows the owner/manager to examine competitors' behaviour under different scenarios. Strategic mapping allows the small firm to anticipate competitors' strategic moves. The firm can then change its strategic direction to avoid head-on collision or to move to a more attractive niche.

5. The Situation Audit

The small business management should be able to assess the internal and external capabilities of its business. Figure 10.2 lists a number of areas to be examined in the situation audit. Internal assessment is simply an evaluation of the firm's strengths and weaknesses in different functional areas such as finance, accounting and record-keeping, marketing, production, and management. For example, assessing strengths and weaknesses in marketing could simply be done by asking and being able to answer questions such as: What customers am I serving? Is the promotion and advertising campaign effective (relative to sales volume)? Do I need more market research? Are the marketing research efforts effective? In assessing the production area the owner/manager could evaluate the following: capacity (over/under), quality of product. Assessing the management function is probably the most difficult but crucial to the success of the entire venture. It entails self-assessment. Entrepreneurs should be able to assess their own skills and their own strengths and weaknesses For example, research has shown that entrepreneurs who delegate their routine activities tend to be more successful than those who do not. The entrepreneur could also evaluate the skills of the management team or partners in terms of what they could do best.

The situation audit includes an assessment of the external environment, to explore windows of opportunity and prepare contingencies for external threats. The external assessment involves evaluation of the micro and macro environmental forces. Assessing the micro-environment includes evaluation of the economic, governmental, technological and societal forces. Assessing the macro-environment includes evaluation of the industry, competition, customers and suppliers. For example, to assess the industry in which the firm operates, management must be able to ask and answer fundamental questions such as: Is the industry in a growth/mature stage? What is the current rate of growth? To assess the competition, the small firm may look at types (monopoly, oligopoly, fragmented), size and

Areas to Be Assessed	Internal Assessment		
	Strengths (S) (Major/Minor)	Weaknesses (W) (Major/Minor)	Comments

Marketing
  Customer wants, needs
  Market research
  Market share
  Sales force
  Distribution channels
  Advertising & promotion
  Sales volume
  Pricing strategy			

Production
  Capacity (over/under)
  Production facilities (condition)
  Product quality
  Product features
  Research and development			

Human Resources
  Skills and knowledge
  Relationship
  Absenteeism and turnover
  Hiring/firing policies
  Adaptability to change
  Attitude
  Training
  Compensation			

Finance
  Rate of return on investment or equity (ROI/ROE)
  Cash flow management
  Capital structure
  Leverage
  Tax shelters
  Cost control
  Accounting and record-keeping system			

Management
  Leadership succession
  Delegation
  Skills			

Areas to Be Assessed	External Assessment		
	Opportunities (Attractive: high/low)	Threats (Major/Minor)	Comments
Market (regional/national) Competition (cut-throat-gentleman) Government (provincial/federal) Technology Economy			

Figure 10.2. The situation audit.

The Situation Audit Questionnaire (To be answered in light of the firm's strengths, weaknesses, opportunity and threats.)

What business am I in?
What business do I want to be in in the next 3–5 years?
What is/are the product(s) or service(s) for which customers come to us?
What added value do we provide?
What are our plans for developing new product(s) or services(s)?
Do we own the production facilities or are they leased?
What is our place in the industry?
What customers am I serving?
What new markets should we serve? Local/National/International?
What is our image? How do our customers perceive us?
How do we compare with competitors?
How are our prices set?
How do they compare competitively?
What sources of funds are available? What sources should we use?
What type of monitoring do we have over cash, receivables, inventories and other assets?
How effective is our accounting system?
What key questions are critical to our business?
What are our sources of information?
What is our rate of return? How do we compare with competitors of the same size and type of business?
What is the cost structure in our business? How do we compare with the industry?
What is our greatest strength? What is our greatest weakness? How can we overcome our weaknesses?

Figure 10.3. Situation audit questionnaire. (To be answered in light of the firm's strengths, weaknesses, opportunity and threats.)

capacity of competitors. For example: Do competitors enjoy a unique position? Why? The small business management should be able to devise an information gathering mechanism that allows them to collect as much information as possible about their competitors. It could be as simple as asking customers or employees questions about competitors, or by visiting competitor's sites. You might discover that a major competitor is retiring or selling his/her business and/or you might be able to find other niches to exploit which your competitors have neglected. Figure 10.3 lists a number of questions to be asked and answered in light of the internal and external assessment.

Assessment of opportunities and threats includes evaluation of government and political actions; for example, subsidies or loans to small business from provincial or federal agencies, tax shelters and/or grants for small high technology firms. Assessment of the economic situation is equally important, in particular general economic trends concerning interest rates, inflation and recession.

In general, the situation audit should be performed periodically and should be based on past and present performance, as well as future expectations. Comparative data from the industry, competition and general economic trends should be utilized to assess performance. Figure 10.4 is a Situation Audit Matrix based on the firm's internal assessment (strengths and weaknesses) and external assessment (opportunities and threats).

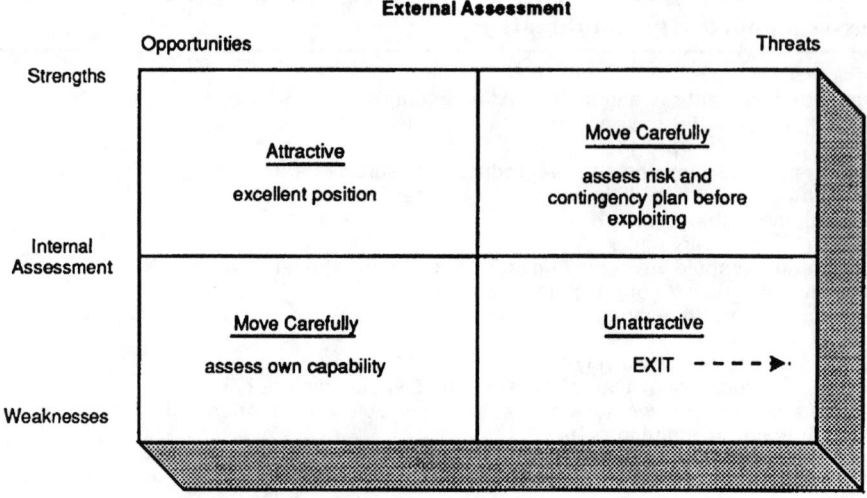

Figure 10.4. The situation audit matrix.

6. Planning

Once the entrepreneur has identified the objectives, formed his/her strategy and assessed the firm's capabilities, he/she should be able to determine a sensible planning horizon. It is suggested that small firms should only focus on short (operational) and medium range planning rather than long range planning, for the simple fact that they have little control over many of the external factors, due to the size of their operations.

The operational plan reflects the business direction for the next 3, 6, and 12-month periods. It covers monthly cash flow projections, production scheduling, material purchase and shipment schedules, as well as expected sales and profit margin. Because of the short span of time, every effort should be made to quantify the operational plan and integrate it with the financial plan (budget).

The medium range plan reflects the business direction for the next 2 to 4 years of operation and includes targets that are critical to the survival of the firm. While it is difficult to quantify the medium range plans, entrepreneurs should try to formulate some figures and adjust them periodically every 3 to 6 months based on the operational plan and the actual performance of the firm.

7. Forecasting—The Big Business Syndrome

Because of the size of the business, smaller firms should be able to utilize inexpensive techniques in forecasting their future course of action. Industry and general economic trends are published regularly by government and private sources. Elaborate statistical and econometric models of forecasting could be expensive, and, in many cases, of little use to small firms since many factors are beyond their control.

8. Monitoring

A plan without a monitoring process is of no use to today's entrepreneur. There are many variables beyond the control of the small business firm. Therefore it is advisable to set up clear milestones or targets against which to assess performance on a regular basis. Deviation from plans should be studied carefully to identify potential problem areas and contingency plans (see Figure 10.5). In case of major deviation ((+) or (−) 15 percent), resource implications should be investigated. Figure 10.6 provides a comprehensive planning checklist for the small business.

Area	Target Quarterly				Actual Quarterly				Analysis	Contingencies
	1st	2nd	3rd	4th	1st	2nd	3rd	4th		
Marketing Production R & D Human Resources Financing Profit Margin Sales Cost of Goods Sold										

Figure 10.5. Small business planning and control form.

Process	Critical Issues	Basis and Sources of Judgment
1. Objectives	Profitability, market share and/or a life style	Historical data, competitors, industry average and self assessment.
2. Strategy	Windows of opportunity, niches, the unique appeal of the product/service	Objectives, mission, strengths, weaknesses and comparative advantages
3. Situation Audit *Internal Factors:*	Identify strengths/weaknesses and comparative advantages	
Product or Service	Product quality, product techniques, product scope (full-scope/limited), position (leader/follower), innovation, technical skills, new product ideas, facilities, experience	Historical data, customers, similar product(s) on the market
Marketing	Sales-force skills, distribution network, customer service, readiness, knowledge of customer needs, promotion, pricing, segment(s)	Historical data, customers, consultants, market research
Human Resources	Skills, training, employee attitudes, compensation, delegation	Historical data, owner/manager opinion
Financial	ROI, ROE, cash flow, growth pattern	Accounting records, Industry average (i.e., Dunn and Bradstreet)
External Forces: Customer	Identify opportunities and risks Market segment, potential gap (niche), customer needs	Customer contacts, trends and economic indicators, market research, trade magazines and publications
Competitor Intelligence	Size up competitors in terms of: product quality, dealers and distribution channels, marketing and selling capabilities, and financial capabilities	Trade magazines, personal observation, competitor's staff, bankers, consultants, and customers
Economic, Social and Political	Social changes: life styles, women, minorities, political and economic changes: consumer policies, environmental policies and provincial policies	Published documents, statistics, journals, magazines, media
4. Strategic Alternatives	Select strategic alternatives; market segments that are not feasible to large competitors, identify a niche early and act quickly	Situation audit, objectives, and mission
5. Planning Operational Plan	3, 6, 12-month quantify if possible, link with budget	All of the above
Short-term plan	Less details, maximum two years	Operational plan and objectives
6. Control System	Deviations from planned	Budget analysis
7. Contingency Plan	If major deviation (± 15%) a contingency plan should be designed	Strategic alternatives

Figure 10.6. Planning checklist for small business.

SUMMARY

Strategic planning is critically important for small business in today's environment. The strategic planning process includes defining the business mission, setting objectives, identifying the strategic direction to achieve the objectives, assessing the internal and external capabilities of the small firm, selecting the planning horizon, forecasting future course of action and finally, monitoring performance. Strategic planning for small business need not be expensive or formal to be effective. The small firm should avoid big business concepts. Econometric models, for example, may be necessary for a large corporation in order to forecast future demand but may be misleading as well as expensive for a small business. Simple and inexpensive techniques are essential in designing a strategic planning model for a small business.

NOTES

1. R. Crawford and A. B. Ibrahim, "A Strategic Planning Model for Small Business," *Journal of Small Business and Entrepreneurship* 3, 1 (Summer 1985), pp. 45–52.
2. D. Sexton and P. Van Auken, "Prevalence of Strategic Planning in Small Business," *Journal of Small Business Management* 20, 1982, pp. 20–26.
3. Peter Drucker, *Management: Tasks, Responsibilities, Practices* (New York: Harper & Row, 1973).
4. Michael Porter, *Competitive Strategy: Techniques for Analyzing Industries and Competitors* (New York: Free Press, 1980).

THE ENTREPRENEUR

Steven Jobs
The Visionary

Steven Jobs' driving belief that "computers are the metaphor of our time," and that the computer is the "most remarkable tool we've ever built" as humans, has created Jobs' vision of a world where the personal computer is accessible to the majority of people in their homes and at work.

As one of the leading entrepreneurs in the computer industry, he attracted the best and brightest young talent to help him develop the Apple, then the MacIntosh. He brought to his projects a zeal and a sense of destiny. "At Apple," he said, "we want to make computers that change the world."

Steven Jobs is a man who has continuously risked failure in order to act on his vision. In the 1970s Jobs saw a window of opportunity in the market for personal computers that were easy to use by those who had no experience in computer programming and scientific applications. He created the Apple to meet the needs of these people and in doing so created a new market niche.

Jobs quickly developed a leadership style that motivated his employees to build Apple into a multi-million dollar company. Jobs promoted a strong corporate culture and channelled his employees' efforts into building the best products he felt could be made.

Steven Jobs left Apple when his entrepreneurial style could no longer fit with the structure required of the company that he had created. At the time he left, it was felt that Apple could no longer be run as if the impassioned ideas of its founder were all that mattered. Apple was no longer the only personal computer company in the market and was in need of the structure that would enable it to survive in the competitive environment. Jobs' entrepreneurial leadership and the style of Jobs' chief advisor, John Scully, could no longer be harmonized within one company.

After his unsuccessful efforts to build a new company, Next Inc., Jobs returned to Apple in order to turn the company around.

Source: Steve Jobs: Byting Back at Apple, *The Gazette* (Sunday, August 13, 1989); *Inc.* (April 16, 1989), pp. 116, A. B. Ibrahim, 1996.

△ CHAPTER 11 △
STRATEGY

There are many sophisticated concepts of strategy formulation that are offered in the strategy literature. However, the large majority hold little promise for small firms. This chapter is devoted to exploring the concept of strategy in small business. Different strategic directions that are relevant to the small firm are discussed.

THE CONCEPT OF STRATEGY

There are a number of factors which shape the formulation of strategy in small business. The firm's external environment, including economic trends, industry structure and competition, is important in deciding what course of action the organization should pursue. The internal capacity of the organization is an equally important factor in shaping the strategic decision, including the small firm's resources, skills, strengths and weaknesses and in general, areas of distinctive competence.

However, the internal and external capacity of the small firm are just ingredients in the strategic decision making process. Entrepreneurs in most cases are heavily influenced by what they personally want to achieve. In other words, the strategic decision is a choice of the entrepreneur or the manager of the small firm.[1] The relationship could be described by the following model (see Figure 11.1). Therefore one way to study strategy in small business is to study the entrepreneur, his personality, values and motivation. The values, beliefs and attitudes of the entrepreneur set the tone for the organization in all aspects, be it dealing with an employee, or customer, or deciding on such issues as product quality, market niche, pricing, or even sources of financing. Indeed, Alfred P. Sloan has noted that the final act of judgment is intuitive.[2]

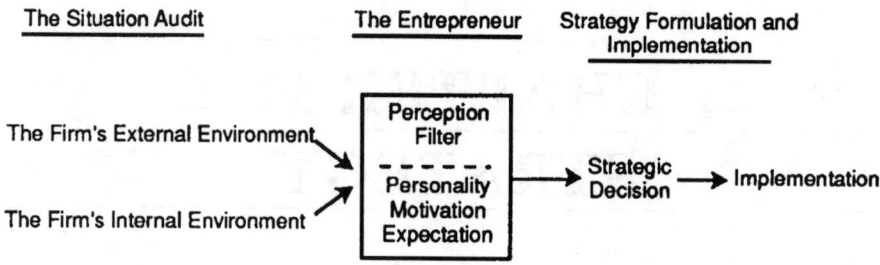

Figure 11.1. Strategy formulation in small firms.

WHAT IS STRATEGY?

Hofer and Schendel define strategy as a pattern of objectives, purposes or goals defining what type of business we are in, or should be in.[3] Michael Porter of Harvard distinguishes between two types of strategy: competitive and corporate strategy. Competitive or business strategy refers to the distinctive competence of the firm. Corporate strategy on the other hand refers to the firm's mission and what business the firm should be in.[4]

Strategy Formulation in the Entrepreneurial Firm

Henry Mintzberg of McGill University tracked the strategy formation of Steinberg Inc., a retail chain, over a period of 60 years. He found that strategy in the entrepreneurial mode tends to be more intuitive, based on the entrepreneur's judgment, wisdom and vision:

> yet the entrepreneur protects himself in his bold action, controls it, for successful entrepreneurship is not equivalent to foolhardiness. As noted, earlier periods of sprinting were used to ensure that the organization remained viable. In addition, with a few exceptions that were to prove significant, Sam Steinberg pursued what can be called a "test-the-water" approach, always sensing an environment with minor probes before plunging in.[5]

However, as organizations grow, a formal and systematic process emerges and a planning mode takes place.

DISTINCTIVE COMPETENCE AND COMPETITIVE ADVANTAGE

Closely associated with strategy are the concepts of distinctive competence and competitive advantage. Distinctive competence refers to the skills or activities that a firm can do best in comparison with rival firms. Indeed, developing distinctive competence is the corner stone for establishing competitive advantage and effective strategy for small firms. A firm builds competitive advantage by such different means as cost leadership, superior product and technology, quality and reliability of service. Studies have shown that small firms must build competitive advantages to compete effectively in the market place. C. R. Stoner studied areas of distinctive competence for small firms, and the extent to which they form a competitive advantage. The common areas of distinctive competence identified in the study include experience and knowledge, uniqueness of the product or service, better than average service, location, low cost and price, quality and variety of products, friendly atmosphere, reputation and a unique method of marketing.[6]

COMPETITIVE FORCES

The five competitive forces identified by Michael Porter of the Harvard Business School are perhaps the best single analytical tool available for understanding how competition works. These five forces shape and influence the strategic direction the small firm is intending to pursue, be it defensive or offensive. These forces are: rivalry among firms, few large suppliers and customers, potential entry of new firms and availability of substitute product.[7] Let us examine each briefly.

1. *Availability of substitutes.* The availability of a substitute creates a ceiling on prices and thus the firm is unable to set the price it wants for its product or service.
2. *Threats from suppliers.* Few large suppliers could become a bargaining power pushing for higher prices of their products which means an increased cost and a low profit margin for the firm.
3. *Threats from customers.* Few large customers could also bargain for a lower price and thus lower the profit margin of the firm.
4. *Rivalry among firms.* If industry demand is falling and existing barriers are high, cut throat competition becomes reality.
5. *Potential entry of new firms.* In the absence of entry barriers such as cost advantages, as a result of economy of scale or learning curve, potential entry of new firms could be a real threat, especially if the firm is in a high growth industry.

INDUSTRY STRUCTURE

The way an industry is structured influences the type of strategy a firm may want to pursue. Therefore, industry structure analysis is an essential component of the strategy formulation process. It allows the small business management to map its competitive environment (see Figure 11.2). Industry structure involves assessing the following elements:

- Stages of industry growth (growth, maturity, decline).
- Types of competition and relative size (fragmented, competitive, oligopoly).
- Industry leaders and different strategic groups.
- Industry concepts (entry/exit barriers, economy of scale, capital investment).
- Types of business (retail, wholesale and service).

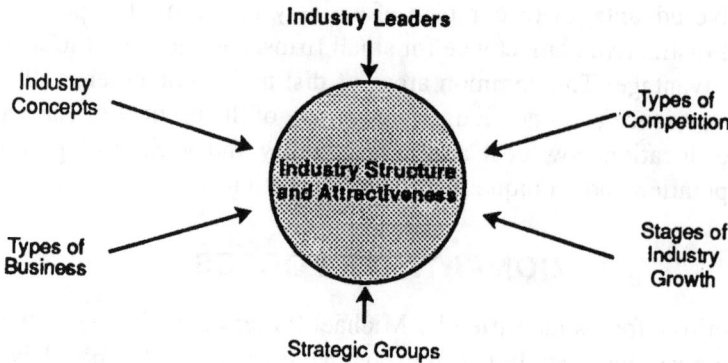

Figure 11.2. Industry structure.

PORTER GENERIC STRATEGY

In his classic work-Competitive Strategy[8], Michael Porter identified three types of generic strategies that can be pursued by almost any organization. These strategies help the firm achieve, build, defend and sustain its competitive advantage. The three generic strategies are: Focus (niche), differentiation, and cost leadership. Let us examine each of these strategies:

1. Focus (Niche) Strategy

A focus strategy involves concentrating on a specific market, group of customers, product or service. The firm pursuing this strategy creates a competitive advantage in a narrow and well defined niche to avoid head-on collision with large competitors. To build competitive advantage, the firm must be able to identify, develop and sustain its distinctive competence or what it can do best. The firm must also be able to erect barriers to entry and to defend its niche aggressively. But above all, the niche must be of sufficient size to generate an acceptable rate of return.

Studies have shown that focus strategy is very effective for small firms. Small firms could pursue two types of focus, cost focus and differentiation focus.[9]

2. Cost Leadership Strategy

This strategy implies that the firm intends to be a low-cost producer. Therefore the strategy emphasizes cost efficiency throughout the whole operation. This requires an in-depth study of the firm's cost structure, and an efficient cost control system. Cost efficiency is a strong competitive advantage if the small firm is able to sustain it over a long period of time. Cost advantages can be achieved by:

- **Economies of scale:** As production volume increases, the cost per unit is reduced.
- **Capacity utilization:** Increasing capacity utilization reduces fixed cost per unit. A study of small business strategies found that the use of process technologies

(improvement in the manufacturing process rather than research on new product development) is of low risk for small firms and results in reducing cost and thus builds a strong competitive advantage.[10]

- **The Experience Curve:** Lasting cost advantage can be obtained as a result of the learning and experience gained over time. Bruce Henderson, the founder of the Boston Consulting Group (BCG) found that the unit cost of production, marketing, and distribution will decrease by 20 to 30 percent each time total output doubles. This decrease in cost is the result of learning and experience gained from repetitive performance, product design, know-how and step-by-step improvement in operation.[11]

3. Differentiation Strategy

This generic strategy involves offering a unique product or service that allows the firm to charge a higher price for its product. There are different ways to differentiate the small firm's product such as improved product design, features, appearance, reliability, durability, quality, faster or free maintenance and repair service, warranty, and/or providing sufficient information to its customers

A recent study has shown that while niche strategy may be appropriate for many small firms, other generic strategies such as differentiation, low cost, or both, could be equally important and could complement other strategies.[12] Indeed, in a study of 17 new ventures, differentiation-type strategy was found to be more effective than focus-type strategy.[13]

Miles and Snow Typology

Raymond Miles and Charles Snow developed a typology of strategic directions. The typology is derived from first hand study and research in corporate strategy. The study identified four types of organizations or strategies based on their response to the environment. These four types are: the Defender, the Prospector, the Analyzer and the Reactor. Let us examine each organization/strategy briefly.[14]

Defenders. The Defender firm carves a narrow product/market domain and tries to protect it heavily by building strong competitive advantages. Defenders do not scan the environment for new opportunities outside their domain. They plan intensively, have centralized control systems and are functionally structured with a high degree of formalization and cost efficiency.

Prospectors. These firms scan the environment continuously looking for windows of opportunity such as a new market, product or service. As a result, prospectors tend to be highly decentralized, flexible, less formalized and structured on a divisional, or product basis. Prospectors emphasize R & D activities and use flexible-type technologies.

Analyzers. Analyzer firms combine some characteristics of both defenders and prospectors. Analyzers maintain their traditional lines of business or domains while scanning for new opportunities. Therefore an analyzer has a characteristic of a mixed strategy. That is, the traditional domain is highly centralized, formalized and cost efficient, while the scanner part is highly decentralized, flexible and less formalized. A matrix-type structure is well suited for this strategy.

Reactors. These are firms that were found to be consistently poor performers as a result of the lack of proper strategy. Reactors are unable to respond effectively to the environment.

IMPLICATIONS FOR SMALL BUSINESS

A recent study of 60 small businesses found that firms pursuing defender and prospector strategies achieve better results in terms of profitability, followed by firms pursuing analyzer-type strategy. Reactor-type was by far the worst strategy to follow. The authors concluded that prospector and defender strategies are more effective for small firms in fragmented industries.[15] A. Bakr Ibrahim examined strategy types in 220 small firms and identified a number of strategic directions and competitive devices that are associated with a high level of performance (profitability). The study identified four prevalent strategy types pursued by profitable small firms. These are niche, defender, prospector and differentiation type strategies. In addition, the study identified a number of competitive devices that contribute positively to the profitability of the small business. These are uniqueness of the product or the service, quality, location, know-how and pricing.[16]

LIFE CYCLE—INDUSTRY GROWTH

Small business strategies may differ under different stages of growth (life cycle). Stages of growth include: growth, maturity and decline (Figure 11.3). A recent study of small business strategies under different stages of growth found those industries in a growth stage to be more attractive for small firms because the learning curve presents an opportunity for the small firm to build a competitive advantage. The study also suggests that during maturity and decline stages of an industry, a differentiation strategy (market segmentation or product differentiation) is more appropriate for the small firm.[17]

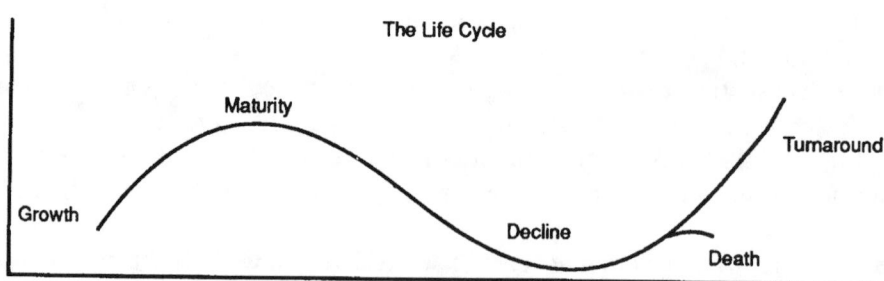

Figure 11.3. The life cycle.

STRATEGIC GROUPS

A strategic group consists of firms that have similar competitive strategy and market position. Firms in a strategic group may have similar products, types of customers and/or similar distribution channels. A strategic group map can be easily constructed by plotting different firms in the industry on a two-dimensional map utilizing competitive variables that differentiate firms in the industry (i.e., price, quality, product, etc.)

STRATEGIC ALLIANCES

With increased global competition and rapid change in technology the concept of strategic alliances (SA) is emerging as an alternative strategy for many small firms. Strategic alliances involve long term relationships between firms to achieve a strategic goal. Strategic alliances may take different forms of agreement depending on the objective sought, the type of industry and the rate of change. Alliances may involve different levels of cooperation, which may take the form of partnership, joint venture, license, or simply collaborative efforts between firms.

THE TROIKA OF SUCCESS

Recent research studies refute the belief common to many in academe and industry that the factors critical to the success of a new enterprise center around the entrepreneur himself (personality, education, experience, etc.). Charles Hofer and William Sandberg examined critical success factors in new ventures and found that an industry structure, the firm's strategy, and the behavioral characteristics of the founder (in that order) are the principal determinants of success as shown in Figure 11.4. Box 11.1 summarizes Hofer and Sandberg's findings.

The Troika of Success

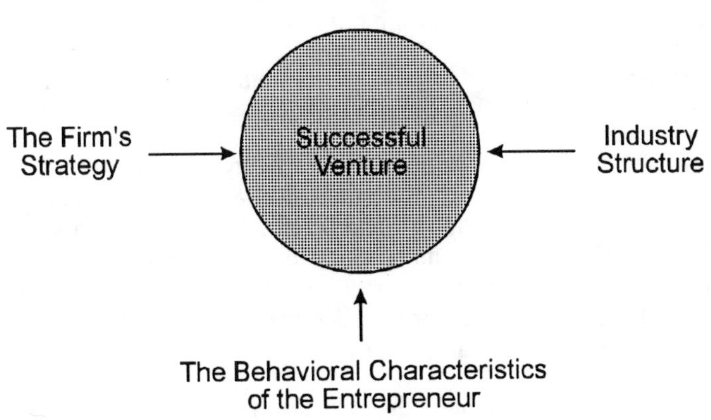

Figure 11.4. The Troika of Success.

Box 11.1. Success—A Function of Industry Structure and Strategy.

The Structure of an Industry, say Hofer and Sandberg, may be characterized in five different ways:

1. Stability. Industries that are undergoing change and are fragmented, are far more fertile for small ventures. The withdrawal of a major competitor, regulatory changes, and changes in fundamental technology can all push an industry into disequilibrium, opening opportunities that an adroit entrepreneur can exploit.
2. Market Structure. Drawing on previous empirical research, the authors conclude that the industry most favourable to a new entrant has a single dominant competitor with a 49% market share or greater. A single market dominator, as they note, implies that other competitors are far weaker and therefore less able to resist entry by a new competitor (who rarely competes with the market leader). "Compete where the competition is weakest" they recommend.
3. Market Development. From the same philosophy, the authors cite studies that demonstrate that success is more likely in industries that exhibit the early, high growth of maturity. Obviously, such an environment should prove more amicable to the new entrant as growth for established players can be achieved through growth of the industry as a whole, rather than at the expense of other, smaller, players.
4. Entry Barriers. Success is also more likely where barriers to market entry are low and where the new entrant can erect barriers to deter other entrants from following; for example, development of customer loyalty, and exclusive distribution.
5. Product Characteristics. The problem of product differentiation and selection of a market niche (a key ingredient to success) is made much easier in a market of heterogeneous products rather than homogeneous.

Business Strategy, the factor listed as second-most in importance by Hofer and Sandberg, is also considered to have several parameters:

1 There is a strong link between product differentiation and success. The authors echo other researchers in recommending that the differentiation be based on high quality, price and service. For, as they remark, a new entrant can seldom draw upon economies of scale or accumulated experience to reduce internal costs and is therefore at an inherent cost disadvantage.
2. Differentiation should be coupled with an overall objective of dominating the firm's particular market segment. Domination in turn allows the firm "quasi-monopoly profits" necessary to fuel above average growth.
3. Differentiation should be created and maintained through a policy of innovation, particularly in the enterprise's early years, at a level higher than that of competitors. A barrier to entry is therefore fostered.
4. Success is more likely if growth is pursued in markets that are a logical, natural extension of the firm's established area of expertise and capabilities, not by attacking larger but unknown market opportunities.

Even more important than business strategy and industry structure alone, are the two acting in concert. Strategies that were broadly defined and based on differentiation are far more appropriate when executed in industries in their youth. The shifting market characteristics of such an industry allow the firm to adjust its strategy to meet conditions and the growth inherent in young markets leaves more room for error. In contrast, a mature market implies that competition has usually reduced overall profitability to such a level as to dictate a strategy that focuses exclusively on a particular market niche.

Source: Charles W. Hofer and W. Sandberg, "Improving New Venture Performance: Some Guidelines for Success," *American Journal of Small Business*, 12, 1 (Summer 1987), pp. 11–25.

HOW TO DEVELOP A STRATEGY FOR A SMALL FIRM

In order to develop an appropriate strategy for the small firm, management must be able to assess the following steps.

1. The Small Firm's Mission—What Business Are You In?

The first step in the strategic process is the definition of organizational purpose or mission. Mission statement is concerned with the kind of business the firm should be in. It is an awareness of the capabilities of the business and what it can do best.

2. Objective Setting

Objective setting defines clearly the firm's objectives in terms of profit, market share and/or in terms of the entrepreneur's personal objectives and goals.

3. The Situation Audit

The situation audit involves an assessment of both the internal and external capabilities of the small firm. The internal assessment includes assessment of the strengths and weaknesses in different functional areas such as marketing, accounting and control, finance, human resources, production, operation and general management skills such as delegation of routine activities. It also includes a self assessment of the entrepreneur's strengths and weaknesses.

The external assessment includes assessment of opportunities and threats that affect the business from the external environment including competitive, technological, social, economic and political forces.

4. Developing Alternative Strategies

Once you have identified and assessed your objectives. mission and the internal and external environment, you should be able to identify different alternative strategies that are available to you (Figure 11.5).

This step involves evaluating each alternative in light of your objectives, mission, strengths, weaknesses, opportunities and threats. Richard Rumelt suggested the following criteria in assessing the firm's alternative strategies. The strategy:

a. Must be internally consistent.
b. Must provide a fit between the firm and its environment, and
c. Must be feasible in light of the firm's resources.[18]

5. The Strategic Choice

Once you have assessed the different alternative strategies available to you, it becomes an easy task to select the appropriate strategy for your small firm. However, the success or failure of the selected strategy will depend on your in-depth assessment of your capabilities and competitive advantage. In addition, the selected strategy should fit with your expectations and lifestyle. Figure 11.6 provides a check list of strategy formulation issues in small business.

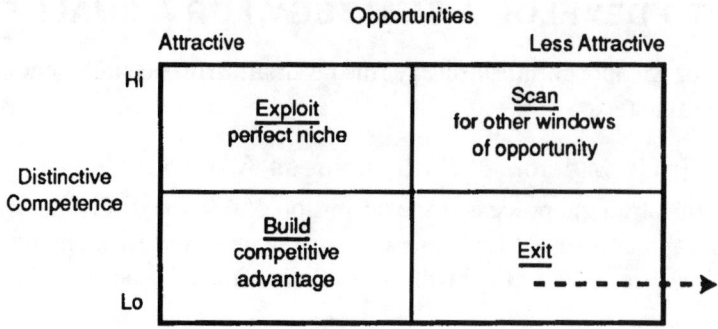

Figure 11.5. Strategic alternatives matrix.

1.	What are your objectives?	Rank your objectives (with 1 the most important, 5 the least important).
2.	What business are you in?	Define your mission statement.
3.	What are the firm's strengths and weaknesses?	List all your business strengths and weaknesses in different areas such as: finance, marketing skills, production and operational facilities, location and general management skills.
4.	What are your own strengths and weaknesses?	Do a self assessment of your own skills, and what you can do best taking into consideration your life style.
5.	What are the industry trends?	Technological, economic and social.
6.	What are the windows of opportunities?	A strong competitor is retiring, a new market segment, government assistance, a new technology, and favorable economic trends.
7.	What are the major threats?	Cut-throat competition, new entrants, change in technology, higher taxes, high interest rates.
8.	What are your competitive advantages?	Rank your distinctive competence: What you can do best compared with your rivals (1 the best, 5 the least). For example: Product or service Cost advantage Location Distribution Warranty Free service Product features
9.	What are the alternative strategies available to you?	Identify and evaluate each possible strategy in light of the above.
10.	Select the appropriate strategy.	Identify the different steps to implement your strategy.

Figure 11.6. Strategic analysis-checklist for small business.

SUMMARY

We have attempted to describe in this chapter the fundamental concepts of strategy formulation in small business. To develop a strategy for a small firm, the entrepreneur must be able to identify and evaluate the firm's objectives, mission, the internal and external capabilities, distinctive competence, and alternative strategies available. Distinctive competence refers to the skills or activities the small firm can do best in comparison with rival firms. It allows the small firm to erect competitive advantage and pursue an effective long term strategy. There are five forces that shape and influence the strategic direction the small firm is intending to pursue. These forces are: rivalry among firms, few large suppliers and customers, potential entry of new firms and availability of substitute product. There are three types of generic strategies that can be pursued by almost any organization. These are: focus, differentiation and cost leadership. These strategies allow the firm to erect and sustain its competitive advantage. Finally, the small firm can also pursue the following strategies: defender, prospector and analyzer.

NOTES

1. A. B. Ibrahim and J. Kelly, "Leadership Style at the Policy Level," *Journal of General Management* 11, 3 (Spring 1986), pp. 36–45.
2. D. Dean, J. Mihalasky, S. Ostrander and L. Schroeder, *Executive ESP* (Englewood Cliffs, NJ.: Prentice-Hall, 1974).
3. C. W. Hofer and D. Schendel, *Strategy Formulation: Analytical Concepts* (St. Paul, MN, West Publishing, 1978).
4. M. Porter, "From Competitive Advantage to Corporate Strategy," *Harvard Business Review* (May–June 1989), pp. 43–59.
5. Henry Mintzberg and James Waters, "Tracking Strategy in an Entrepreneurial Firm," *Academy of Management Journal* 25, 3, 1982, pp. 465–499.
6. C. R. Stoner, "Distinctive Competence and Competitive Advantage," *Journal of Small Business Management* (April 1987), pp. 33–39.
7. Michael E. Porter, "How Competitive Forces Shape Strategy," *Harvard Business Review* 57, 2 (March–April 1979), p. 141.
8. M. E. Porter, *Competitive Strategy.*
9. D. Watkin, "Toward a Competitive Advantage: A Focus Strategy for Small Retailers," *Journal of Small Business Management* (January 1986), pp. 9–15.
10. E. Hughes, "Responding to Changes in Process Technology: Strategies for the Small Business," *Journal of Small Business Management* (January 1984), pp. 9–15.
11. Bruce D. Henderson, "On Corporate Strategy," in R. B. Lamb, ed., *Competitive Strategic Management* (Englewood Cliffs, N.J.: Prentice-Hall 1984), pp. 1–34.
12. A. Cooper, W. Gary and C. Woo, "Strategies of High Performing New and Small Firms: A Re-examination of the Niche Concept," *Journal of Business Venturing* (January 1986), pp. 247–260.
13. W. Sandberg and C. Hofer, "Improving New Venture Performance: The Role of Strategy, Industry Structure and the Entrepreneur," *Journal of Business Venturing* (May 1987), pp. 5–28.
14. Raymond Miles and Charles Snow, *Organizational Structure and Process* (New York: McGraw Hill 1978).
15. W. Davig, "Business in Smaller Manufacturing Firms," *Journal of Small Business Management* (January 1986), pp 39–47.
16. A. Bakr Ibrahim, "Strategy Types and Small Firms' Performance: An Empirical Investigation," *Journal of Small Business Strategy,* 5, 1 (Spring 1993).
17. R. Chaganti, "Small Business Strategies in Different Industry Growth Environments," *Journal of Small Business Management* 25, 3 (July 1987), pp. 52–59.
18. Richard Rumelt, "Evaluation of Strategy: Theory and Models," in Dan Schendel and Charles Hofer (eds.), *Strategic Management: A New View of Business Policy and Planning* (Boston: Little Brown 1979).

THE ENTREPRENEUR

Frederick W. Smith—The Strategist
Federal Express Corp.

The determination that seems to be a universal characteristic of an entrepreneur is borne out in the frequently repeated anecdote of Frederick Smith's experience while a student at Yale. In an economics class term paper, Smith spelled out an idea for a nationwide overnight parcel delivery system. Whatever the reason or rationale, he received a "C" grade for his thoughts and efforts, which undoubtedly were perceived as being too far-out by many. The fact that he was not deterred is now history.

Unlike many entrepreneurs, Fred Smith, born in 1945, came from a wealthy family—his father had built Greyhound's bus system in the South. In 1969, after a stint as a Marine pilot in Vietnam, Smith began selling corporate jets. Still not deterred by the "C" grade of a few years earlier, he started to develop his parcel delivery plan. In two years, with the help of his family, he was able to raise $80 million from venture capitalists. At the time, it was the largest venture capital package assembled.

With this backing, in 1973, Federal Express began its delivery service based on a single concept of reliability. It was Fred Smith's conviction that people would pay a premium if they could be assured that their parcels would arrive at the designated destination the next day.

The focal point of the operation was the terminal in Memphis, Tennessee, selected because of its central location in the United States and also because of the generally favourable weather which could cause the least amount of delay.

Again, as is the fate of many start-up situations, it was not all smooth flying, for the company suffered substantial losses in its early stages. Now, however, one million items is an average night of accepting and sorting for Federal Express. The company flies some 255 planes, with 24,000 computerized delivery vans and a workforce numbering 57,000 individuals, sales in the neighbourhood of $4.6 billion, and a marketshare thought to be about 45%.

Although many factors can be cited for the success of Federal Express, Fred Smith passes credit on to his employees. By the same token, the employees say the top management is a strong proponent of what Tom Peters and Robert Waterman described as "management by walking around." It has been said that the average Federal Express employee deeply appreciated that kind of personal attention.

Federal Express' unique "guaranteed fair treatment program" and recorded no lay-offs over the life of the company has helped to explain its rapid growth.

"They talk of a sense of adventure associated with a company that is changing so rapidly. People work hard at Federal Express and they're proud of it."

Source: *Wall Street Journal*, (June 6, 1989); M. John Sterey, *Inside America's Fastest Growing Companies* (John Wiley & Sons, 1989), pp. 39–138.

△ CHAPTER 12 △
FINANCING

There were a few lines in a recent publication that perhaps say as much as anything about the financial aspects of small business operations: "Therein lies a warning to all young, and not-so-young entrepreneurs (and their backers) who think they can rub some assets and debt together and produce commercial magic."[1]

For most entrepreneurs and owner/managers, the one prime difficulty they face, and the area with which they tend to be the least familiar, is finance. No matter what type of business one is involved with, or is contemplating, whether it is buying into a franchise or starting up, it is necessary to have funding to get it off the ground. But before doing so, entrepreneurs must know exactly what it is they are going to do or are planning to do. So where do you start? As mentioned in an earlier chapter, this is one area in which the business plan comes into prominent play.

THE BUSINESS PLAN

The business plan is essential in the initial stages of a small business operation since it can act both as a management tool, and in this particular context, as a vehicle for determining the finances required and the form in which they might be obtained.

The plan assists the entrepreneur in defining objectives, and provides a means of ensuring that the business stays on target as it grows and develops. For those potential investors, the plan tells them who you are, what your business intends to do and the rationale behind your request for funding. The business plan, therefore, has to demonstrate the viability of your undertaking and the risks involved, as well as your knowledge and understanding of what it is that is required to ensure the successful operation of the enterprise. With this as the basis, potential investors can evaluate the people who will be running the company and the expected return on their investment. The importance of the "people" aspect of the business and the business plan is emphasized in the findings of the study done by Ian C. MacMillan of Columbia University when he states that in a business plan there is generally little to indicate the characteristics of the entrepreneur—it is generally devoted to a detailed discussion of the product/service, the market, and the

Portions of this chapter is based on published work for the banking industry by Professor A. B. Ibrahim.

competition. The business plan should also show as clearly as possible that the "jockey is fit to ride;" namely, it should indicate by whatever feasible and credible means possible that the entrepreneur has staying power, has a track record, can react to risk well, and has familiarity with the target market.[2]

FUNDING

The size of the business determines the amount of financing that will be required and the sources from which it might be obtained. The most common source of initial funding is from personal funds—through savings, a home mortgage or relatives. According to a survey by the National Federation of Independent Business, start-up money was obtained from the following sources:[3]

Savings	48%
Banks, other institutional lenders	29%
Friends	13%
Individual investors	4%
Venture capital firms	less than 1%
Government	less than 1%
Other sources	5%

While so-called "love money" represents the single largest source of funds for the start-up and small business operation, it can also be a possible source of friction within the family. Any agreement involving love money should be on a strictly business basis, with stipulated rates of interest and repayment schedules.

As the business grows, the financing requirements will probably come in one or both of two forms: debt financing, where the investors do not receive ownership in the business and/or equity funding in which the investors receive representative ownership, through shares in the company.

DEBT FINANCING

Debt financing for the small business is similar to the debt incurred by an individual. The money has to be repaid, principal and interest, over a specified period of time. Any interest paid on the debt is tax-deductible to the business and is considered as a normal business expense.

Debt can be expensive in terms of dollars, but may be partly underwritten by the government through the tax structure or loan agreements. It does not divide ownership, nor does it involve loss of control, unless there is a default, but it is structured in regard to terms and covenants that will be imposed by the agreements.

Debt financing can be obtained from two principal sources: private and public. Private sources would consist of personal loans, bank loans, and to some extent, loans by venture capitalists. Public sources include government programs of various sorts and agencies, both federal and state, or provincial bodies.

Private Sources

There are three types of private sources of financing: banks, factoring and leasing.

Banks

While personal sources tend to be the largest single source of funding, bank loans are the most common form of outside financial assistance, and usually, the least expensive.

Generally speaking, banks do not lend money to launch a new business, and if they do, it would have to be accompanied by a well-prepared business plan. In addition, banks are more interested in offering funds for operating capital to a business with some history of successful operations behind it.

In a new venture, the bank would probably require a personal guarantee supported by mortgages on personal property and other personal assets as well as having one's spouse, parents or partners co-sign the loan agreement.

A company that cannot get funding from the so-called regular banks may have to turn to commercial finance companies for short-term funds by offering inventories, receivables, and similar assets as collateral. However, the cost of such funding will tend to put an added burden on what could undoubtedly be an already difficult task. Relationships with the bank are, therefore, very important and every effort should be made to foster them.

Because funds are needed for different purposes, the types of loans and services that the banks offer vary according to the need. The most common types of loans for small business are:

1. Operating or working capital loans. These may include lines of credit and are provided by the banks for day-to-date operations. They may be used to purchase raw materials, merchandise for resale or supplies, to pay employees, and to liquidate obligations. In other words, these are the funds required to keep operating until the company shows a profit. The amount and conditions are negotiated with the bank, who, in turn, will insist on adherence to the covenants of the loans agreement.
2. Term loans. Term loans are made by chartered banks for plant expansion, renovation, machinery, equipment, land and buildings. Granted for a period of up to five years, they require repayment at regular intervals, at the negotiated rate of interest and conditions.
3. Equipment financing. Machinery or equipment will serve as collateral for loans made for the purchase of these assets.
4. Letters of credit. These are essential to small businesses operating on the international scene. They are issued by the bank on behalf of its clients and guarantee payment for merchandise under terms and conditions that are universal in scope.

Factoring

This is another type of private financing available to small business, focusing on borrowing with accounts receivable serving as collateral. In factoring, the receivables are actually purchased by the factor without recourse. This non-recourse arrangement is normally limited, however, to the credit risk, and the factor is protected against circumstances which would invalidate sales. Traditionally, factors are used in industries where they have better firsthand knowledge of customers and their credit-worthiness than do the sellers and where as a consequence, they can be more effective in converting the accounts receivable into cash.

Essentially, in factoring, you get paid cash on delivery of your product or service while your customers receive credit on terms that they require. The factor actually purchases your accounts receivable for their full value, usually for up to 80% of their worth, at the time goods are shipped. The remainder of their worth is paid to you when your customers pay. The factor checks the credit of each of your customer's accounts and purchases these receivables from you without recourse, which means that the factor absorbs any bad debt losses. To compensate for these risks, factors typically charge a 1% to 2% fee for each invoice, plus interest, on the advance that they make to you. The total amount is usually greater than bank and commercial finance company rates for comparable loans. Also, obtaining money from a factor can be fast, possibly within 24 hours.

Leasing

Leasing is a useful method of conserving capital and is an alternative to purchasing. Small businesses are leasing all types of equipment, including motor vehicles, computers, office furniture, manufacturing machinery and a wide variety of other fixtures.

Basically, leasing is a long-term agreement to rent equipment, land, buildings and fixtures. Such an arrangement may have possible tax advantages besides releasing funds which would otherwise be tied up in ownership of the equipment. Payments cover the original cost of the equipment or facility to the lessor and provide the lessor with a profit for this service. The period of the lease frequently approximates the depreciated life of the equipment that is leased.

Leverage Buy Out—LBO

Leverage buy out is simply the use of assets of an acquired company as collateral for a loan. The loan usually covers all or part of the purchase price of the acquired company. Thus the relation between assets, cash flow, and the purchase price is a determinant factor in the decision to lend money. James McNeill Stancil recommends the following guidelines for an effective LBO deal:

1. The assets must be enough to cover the loan. The entrepreneur must ensure that the cash flow from operation can cover the loan and other regular expenses.
2. All "hockable assets" such as land, equipment, accounts receivable and inventory must be evaluated carefully to ensure that they are acceptable and sufficient to service the loan.[4]

Public Sources

Public sources of funds consist of government guaranteed loans to assist potential small business owners with start-up costs. These loans can come in a variety of forms and differ from country to country and locale to locale but have the same basic objective—to assist the small entrepreneur.

In the United States, the best known programs are those that are offered under the Small Business Administration (SBA). It was designed to help small businesses improve their managerial skills and to assist them in borrowing money. The SBA can make a loan directly or guarantee a bank loan, usually on more generous terms than can be obtained on a conventional loan, and it is this function that comprises the major part of the SBA's financial assistance program.

Small businesses operating in Canada have much the same government financial sources available to them through programs such as the Small Businesses Loans Act (SBLA), for new (or additions) to fixed equipment or buildings or leasehold improvements. The Business Development Bank of Canada (BDC) functions very much like the SBA in the United States with programs to help finance small and medium-sized businesses.

It is a good idea for small businesses seeking assistance from government programs to first discuss them with their banker, who should be familiar with what is available. Not only are there many types of programs available but they tend to vary considerably in different regions and also with the amount of actual funds that may be on hand at any particular time in a government's mandate.

EQUITY

Equity is the second of the two types of funding available for small businesses and differs from debt in that it does not have to be paid back. It represents ownership in the business and means selling off a portion of your holdings to another investor in return for funding. A very important decision that faces the entrepreneur is exactly how much to give up since one of the basic reasons that he has started or bought a business is to be "his own boss." The dividing up of control and correspondingly, profits, may well be the tradeoff in order to get the necessary funding.

"Going public" may appear to be a ready source of equity funding but small businesses may not have that opportunity, and are not able to meet the requirements of the various exchanges in which they might wish to be listed. In addition, investment dealers and underwriters have to be convinced of the marketability of the offering, and timing can be an important factor in this decision. The cut of placing a small issue of, say, less than $10 million, is usually disproportionate to the net yield to it in equity funding. The new business venture seeking outside funds wanting to grow through the influx of outside resources will probably look first to private sources of equity capital—friends, relatives, wealthy individuals—or second, to the external market provided by venture capital.

VENTURE CAPITAL

Venture capital has been defined as "the early-stage financing of relatively small rapidly growing companies."[5] This may be further expanded to indicate that venture capitalists may provide seed, start-up, and early-stage development and expansion financing to on-going companies that may not have access to public or credit-oriented institutional funding.[6]

According to the Association of Canadian Venture Capital Corporations, 1997 statistics, venture capital investment in Canada has grown considerably in the last few years. In 1998 the venture capital pool of funds are expected to reach close to $6 billion up by $2 billion from 1993. These funds are invested in just about every industry imaginable. Investment in new ventures accounted for almost 35% of the total amount invested and technology based companies took more than half of this amount. In the United States, the capital stock in venture capital firms for 1998 is expected to reach over $50 billion, considerably greater than the traditional tenfold differential frequently used for comparative statistics.

VENTURE CAPITAL AND RISK

By its very nature, venture capital is risk financing, because the funds are generally unsecured by a pledge of assets. Venture capital investors are prepared to take this higher risk in anticipation of higher returns. In return for assuming the risk of financing start-ups, venture capitalists usually demand a stake or level of control in the business in which they invest. While they may not be interested in the day-to-day operations of the firm, they will undoubtedly demand a seat on the board of directors and an equity position so that they can be reasonably assured of eventual financial return.

Venture capitalists moderate their risk in several ways. They diversify across industries, geographical lines and size of deal. As it is their objective to ultimately realize a return on their investment, they will likely invest in ventures that will provide the most flexibility from a financial and taxation viewpoint.

Venture capitalists follow a strategy of buying a minority equity position in the private company. They then follow this with restrictions, obligations and strong controls to safeguard this minority position. Such controls may include the right of approval of large capital expenditures, remuneration of senior management, long term lease commitments, disposal of assets, payment of dividends, borrowing from other sources and any other financial decisions that could have a long term effect on the company.

They evaluate the quality of the entrepreneur and take many precautions before committing their funds. Venture firms consider it a lack of confidence and commitment if entrepreneurs do not invest personal savings. In addition, they expect the company's management to combine technical expertise with management skills. The venture capital company can be involved in supplying management to the small business, researching and implementing the business plan or supplying guarantees.

Investors look for significant potential growth in earnings. Sometimes the company management's opinion of the future financial results of the venture may differ from that of the investors. Besides the marketability of the product, investors will analyze factors such as anticipated growth rate, future liquidity, the degree of risk associated with the investment, and pricing of similar companies.

Venture capital firms usually tend to liquidate their investments in three to five years so as to generate funds for investment in other ventures. The professional investor wants to cash out with a large capital appreciation, in the order of 25% to 50% per annum.

Venture Capital and Stages of Development

While it is typically thought that the venture capital infusion of funds occurs at the start-up stage, in fact it may be needed at different stages in a company's life cycle. In addition to the start-up stage, there are five other stages that attract different types of venture capital such as seed financing, development, expansion, turn-around and buy out. For example, the entrepreneur may use venture capital to acquire an existing firm, or to acquire an attractive division of a larger company. It is estimated that leveraged buy outs (LBOs) and other acquisition type financing make-up about 40 percent of the venture capital activity in Canada and the U.S.

A study conducted in 1993 examined the investment preferences of 69 venture capital firms and at which stage of development they preferred to invest. The study revealed that the venture capital firms that chose to invest in the earlier stages of a firm's development were more actively involved, more willing to devote time to analyzing the company's projects, and to provide management expertise.[7] These "early-bird" venture capitalists are less concerned with managing the risk of a project. They usually turn to a public offering of their equity as a means of exit, as there is the highest potential upside return with this option. Later stage investors, on the other hand, demonstrate a less active role in the routine operations of the small business. As a means of exiting the firm, these late stage venture capitalists usually choose to be bought out by the firm or by another investor. These investors are typically more risk averse. Box 12.1 summarizes some interesting findings with respect to start up financing.

Sources of Venture Capital

The most prominent sources of venture capital are: private sector venture capital firms, corporate venture investment (i.e. investments from other companies), large financial institutions, and government. Each of these will be examined in turn.

Private Sector Venture Capital Activity

Private sector capital firms exist for the sole purpose of seeking out market opportunities. These firms usually develop expertise in a particular type of funding and a particular industrial sector. A large proportion are involved in investing in high-technology industries, for example. However, many of these firms also find it in their best interest to diversify into several sectors in order to hedge their risk. Typically, these firms have a significant

---

Box 12.1. Bootstrapping or Venture Capital.

What is the best approach to finance start-up ventures? Amar Bhide of Harvard Business School interviewed entrepreneurs from the INC. 500 fast growing privately held companies. His study revealed some interesting findings with respect to start-up financing. The majority of entrepreneurs interviewed financed their start-up phase from personal savings and credit cards. He asserts that start-up ventures usually pursue market niches that are too small to attract investors. Venture capital firms are more likely to invest in a large scale operations. In addition venture capital firms set criteria that are difficult to meet in the start-up phase such as a well written business plan, technological advantage offered by the new venture and reputation of the entrepreneur. The author contends that having large sums of money at the start-up phase may result in loss of perspective as to the hidden problem in the company. The real challenge is to successfully manage without large sums of money. Thus Bhide suggests bootstrap financing (financing with entrepreneur's modest savings) as a realistic strategy for start-ups. He offers the following advice for effective bootstrapping:

1. Move from the idea generation to the actual implementation without delay
2. Select ventures that allows you to generate cash and break-even in a very short time
3. Maintain some kind of competitive advantage by offering a premium product
4. Avoid premature growth
5. Pay attention to cash flow not high return or market share
6. Establish good relations with bankers as early as possible
7. Do not waste your time forming a team of expensive professionals at this early stage

Source: Amar Bhide, "Bootstrap Finance: The Art of Start-ups," *Harvard Business Review*, December 1992, pp. 109–117.

---

involvement in the operations of the firm. The secret for successful venture capital companies is their in-depth knowledge of the industry. In essence, they target industries they are familiar with.

Corporate Venture Capital Activity

Corporate venture investors' motivation for investing in small businesses is not commonly financial gain but could be derived from trying to develop new markets, aiding its traditional clients, acquiring entrepreneurial talent, or to strategically keep a product out of the hands of its competitor. For example, the auto industry and the telecommunication industry have invested equity money in many small knowledge based companies in Canada and the U.S. These corporate venture capitalists are looking increasingly to their own employee pension funds to finance their venture activities. (See Box 12.2)

Large Financial Institutions—Venture Capital Activity

Large financial institutions have access to huge pools of capital, and typically reserve a portion of it for investment in small businesses. These investors include among others, Royal Bank Capital Corporation, Roy Nat, and Canadian Imperial Bank of Commerce Wood Gundy.

Box 12.2. Competing for High-Tech Financing.

Technocap is one of the recent venture capital firms in Canada. The company currently runs a $40 million fund which comes from the Caisse de dépôt et placement which manages the Quebec Pension Plan, the pension funds of the Desjardins caisse populaire group, Hydro-Québec, Bombardier and the Quebec Federation of labour.

The company specializes in start-up high-tech companies that have innovative products which could generate huge sales and profits in 3 to 5 years.

Source: *The Montreal Gazette,* October 11, 1994.

Government Venture Capital

In the United States, probably the best known source of venture capital from government is through the small business investment companies, or SBICs, and minority enterprise small business investment companies, or MESBICs, both of which are regulated by the Small Business Administration (SBA). The SBIC's equity capital is generally supplied by one or more commercial banks, wealthy individuals, and the investing public. There are reportedly about 450 SBICs in the United States, of which about 137 have active venture capital rather than just loan programs and some of these 137 are affiliates of venture capital firms. SBICs are limited by law to take minority shareholder positions and to invest no more than 20% of their equity capital in any one situation. SBICs tend not to finance start-ups and early stage companies but rather to make investments in more mature companies. A typical financing is in the $100,000-$300,000 range.

Small business development companies (SBDCs) operate in the same fashion as the SBICs except that they are capitalized entirely by private sources, including banks, large manufacturing firms, utility companies and other private sources. They too make loans on a long-term basis or purchase stock in the venture. Many states have their own particular development corporations and programs which are capitalized through funds from the various states.

The Business Development Bank of Canada (BDC) is the equivalent organization to the SBA in the United states, and is a major factor in government related venture capital markets. Operating through branch offices in the provinces, it had committed to 66 investments for a total of $73 million in 1997. A large portion of these investments is in high-tech and exporting firms. Further, the BDC provides term loans financing as well as a complete range of management services such as counselling and mentoring services. As with the SBA sponsors programs, the BDC may take an equity position in the companies. Box 12.3 describes two successful investment stories.

The provinces have various venture capital programs to assist the small business manager such as the Small Business Development Corporation of Ontario (SBDC), Alberta Opportunity Co., B.C.'s Discovery Enterprise and AQVIR in Quebec. The Quebec government also sponsores two venture capital activities aimed at knowledge based businesses: Innovatech Grand Montreal and recently Innovatech Quebec-Chaudière/Appalaches. Many

---

Box 12.3. Two Successful Investment Stories.

The BDC helped a number of well known Canadian companies get started. For example, Ted Rogers of Rogers Communications started with a small loan from the bank for his first venture—Toronto radio station CHFI. Rogers Communications is currently one of the largest Canadian companies in the telecommunications industry.

Andrés Wines is another success story. A number of years ago the bank provided a working capital loan to help the company overcome its initial loss. The company is presently one of the largest and most profitable in the industry.

Source: Profits, Summer 1994.

---

of these funds are aimed at filling the shortfall in private sector venture capital and mainly focus on start-ups and high-technology firms.

Venture Capitalists Sponsored by Labour Funds

Labour funds have contributed significantly to the establishment of a number of venture capital corporations. They control approximately 30% of the institutional venture capital market in Canada and the U.S. For example, the Quebec Federation of Labour—QLF's Solidarity Fund is one of the largest venture capitalists' sponsored Labour Funds in North America with a pool of over $1 billion invested in small firms. It is expected that venture capital corporations sponsored by Labour Funds will grow significantly in the next 5 years. This large pool of equity funds may represent some relief to the capital needs of small businesses.

Informal Venture Capital—Angels

Relatively few venture capital firms invest less than $500,000. They are usually attracted to investment of $1 million or more leaving a gap at the low end of the equity financing market ($50,000–$500,000). However, government programs as well as the recent phenomenon known as angels are expecting to fill this void in the equity market.

Angel investors range from professionals such as doctors, lawyers and accountants to wealthy individuals. According to a recent study, the average investment is $110,000 and the desired rate of return is 50 percent. Angel investors do not usually play an active role in management. However, their accountants and lawyers may scrutinize their investment projects.[8]

GOVERNMENT FINANCING

In Canada one of the major government initiatives to-date which attempts to address the needs of small business is the Small Business Loans Act (SBLA). The SBLA promotes lending to small companies with sales of less than $5 million. Through this legislation, the Industry Canada's Entrepreneurship and Small Business Office registers loans made by authorized lenders, such as banks, to entrepreneurs. These loans are guaranteed up to 90 percent, with a maximum loan ceiling set at $250,000. The purpose of the SBLA is to provide financing to start-ups and existing businesses for the acquisition of fixed assets. Small business in manufacturing, retail, service, wholesale, construction, communication and transportation qualify under the act. However, the act does not provide financing for the purchase of inventory or working capital. On the other hand, the SBLA has been criticized for it allows lenders such as banks to reduce their risk on loans that would have been made without the guarantee, such as using SBLA, to finance fixed assets.

In the U.S. the Small Business Administration (SBA) through its Eximbank, guarantees 90% of working capital loans to small business. Figure 12.1 outlines the different sources of financing available for small business.

Sources	Critical Issues	Basis and Sources of Judgment
Equity Financing		
1. Savings	Possible source of friction with spouse	Trust
2. Friends & relatives	Possible source of friction May be the end of friendship	Trust, their perception of the entrepreneur's skills and competence
3. Wealthy individuals	Less expensive May end up dealing with their accountants and lawyers	The business plan
4. Venture capital and Angels	Start-up and expansion Liquidate their investment in 3–5 years Demand an equity position and board representation	The business plan Potential The economic viability of the opportunity
Debt Financing		

Banks	Least expensive
	Not for launching a new business
	Types: operating working capital loans
	      equipment financing
	      letter of credit
		The business plan
		Proven track record
		Personal guarantee
		Collateral

Factoring	Borrowing with accounts receivable serving as collateral, up to 80% of accounts receivable value	Knowledge of customers and their creditworthiness
Leasing	Alternative to purchasing Tax advantages	Knowledge of customers and their creditworthiness
Government guaranteed loans	Start-up Improvement of current operation	The business plan

Figure 12.1. Sources of financing.

FINANCIAL PLANNING

The financial plan is logically an integral part of the business plan, but many small business owners have not prepared a business plan, and consequently, do not have a financial plan.

With their businesses underway, owners tend to direct their efforts to those functions with which they are most familiar and like doing the best. Be that as it may, it is still a fact that without financing, no business can exist. A fundamental reason for financial planning is to force the small business owner to think about the future in very practical terms, and to develop solutions to potential problems before having to face crisis situations.

Before it is possible for owners to make an estimate of the growth and future direction of their company, they must determine the nature of their goals and objectives and the strategy required to achieve them. With these having been formulated in broad terms, they can then be brought more clearly into focus by looking at sales, production, and manpower together with the financial resources needed to bring them to fruition. These will be reflected in the basic components of financial planning which are the income statement, the balance sheet, the cash flow projection, and the capital budget. The emphasis placed on each of these as with all other facets will depend upon the particular type of business; for example, a service industry may require little or no capital or expenditures for manufacturing processes, but manpower needs will be greater.

Financial planning is essential to the future survival of the business. For the small business, the financial plan should cover a minimum of one year and a maximum of three years. For the small businessman to think beyond this time frame is not realistic. It is, of course, not only necessary to anticipate the growth and development of the company and the means of achieving the goals and objectives, but management must have the mechanism for providing continuous feedback in order to assess its progress in reaching those objectives. Therefore, while details on the operational aspects of the small business explain actions to be taken during the planning stages in an effort to reach the company's goals, it is the financial plan that indicates the ultimate profits resulting from the operations.

Fortunately, with the computer technology available today in the form of spreadsheets and programs, the financial planning operation and the measurement procedures are readily available and enable the small businessman to assess his operations on an on-going basis.

SUMMARY

Financing is the single most difficult problem facing entrepreneurs and small business management. They are generally more intent on the operational aspects of a particular product or service with which they are familiar than on obtaining the necessary funding or learning how to deal with the financial side of the business. Successful entrepreneurs will take steps to ensure that every advantage works in their favour.

Starting with a business plan that clearly outlines the goals and objectives and the means for achieving them leads to the desired sources of financial assistance, be it friends, relatives, banks, venture capitalists or government programs. The business plan, therefore, provides the road map for investors, as well as forcing the small business to focus on the parameters of the operation.

NOTES

1. *Forbes Inc.* (New York, May 29, 1989), p. 1.
2. Ian C. MacMillan, "Criteria Used by Venture Capitalists to Evaluate New Venture Proposals," *Journal of Business Venturing* 1, 1985, pp. 119–128.
3. *Wall Street Journal* (November 24, 1980).
4. James McNeill Stancill, "LBOs for Smaller Companies," *Harvard Business Review* (January–February, 1988), pp. 18–24. Also see: A. B. Ibrahim, *Financial Management for Small Business* (University Press, 1978), Chapter 4.
5. Stanley E. Pratt, *Guide to Venture Capital Sources,* 6th ed. (Prentice Hall, 1982), p. 7.
6. Cynthia C. Ryans, *Managing the Small Business* (Englewood Cliffs, New Jersey: Prentice Hall 1989), p. 106.
7. J. Carter and H. Van Auken, "Venture Capital Firm's Preferences for Projects in Particular Stages of Development," *Journal of Small Business Management*, January 1994, p. 61.
8. *Report on Business Magazine*, June 1993.
9. A. B. Ibrahim, *Canadian Entrepreneurial Studies*, Institute of Bankers, 1994.

THE ENTREPRENEUR

Richard Branson—The Risk Taker
Virgin Group PLC

Reportedly trailing only Prince Charles and the Pope in British popularity, and as a rambunctiously adventuresome entrepreneur, Richard Branson has been a headliner ever since he started into business ventures.

Born in 1950, he grew up in a relatively comfortable, legal environment: his grandfather (Sir George Branson) and his father both being barristers and judges. At the age of 15, while still at school, Branson started a magazine called "Student," which, as the name suggests, was basically for students with the aim of "putting the world to rights." The first issue sold 50,000 copies and two years later, he left school to run "Student" full-time, remarking that "having left school without going on to university, I decided to make money . . . I never really considered failure."

Soon afterward he started a mail-order company selling records at discounted prices. Like many British youth of the period, he enjoyed popular music, but when, in 1971, a postal strike played havoc with mail-order, he opened a discount record shop over a shoe store on Oxford Street. Other stores quickly followed. Branson called his business "Virgin" simply because he had had no experience running a business and also to be in tune with the prevailing anti-establishment mood that was prevalent in Britain at the time. The company's progress and profits through the 1970s were erratic but always centered on the core business of popular music, encompassing retailing, production, publishing and recording. In Branson's words, "We were doing what the business schools apparently called vertical integration. I call it common sense."

THE ENTREPRENEUR
(continued)

The 1970s and the 1980s saw the company's fortunes ebb and flow, but in 1984, Don Cruickshank, an accountant with an M.B.A., joined the company and proceeded to formulate company strategy which was described as "to become a major international entertainment company with interests beyond that in leisure areas." This, undoubtedly, was a factor leading to the formation of Virgin Atlantic Airways in 1984. Going public in 1986, The Virgin group now operates in 19 other countries including the United States and consists of three main divisions: music, retail and video. In addition, Branson also owns Voyager Group Limited, a private company that operates night clubs, provides holiday tours, and air-freight services.

As if all this activity wasn't enough, he crossed the Atlantic in a speedboat in 1985 to break the trans-Atlantic speed record and while failing in his first attempt, succeeded on his second try. In 1986, Branson crossed the Atlantic in a hot-air balloon. The balloon made the crossing in about one and a half days, but unable to land the craft, Branson and his companion had to leap into the Irish Sea. The balloon project was on the front page of most newspapers in the world for a couple of days and ran on most television stations. Branson say that he believes that he received in the order of $40 million of free advertising. As a result, Branson is now turning the experience into a company which will include a ballooning school, balloon manufacturer and balloon holiday services.

Branson's world headquarters are in a houseboat moored on a canal. He say that working here avoids interruptions and at the same time gives his officers a greater sense of autonomy. He says that people always want to deal with the top person in a building, and with his companies so spread out, the ranking executive in each structure becomes the power centre and takes complete responsibility. He then, can be left to concentrate on more forward planning and look into growth areas. Branson says that his attitude towards life "is to enjoy it to the full. Another thing I dislike now as the business grows is the lack of time I have for any one person, issue, or company. It means I have to rush people, which I don't like to do."

Source: *Inc.* (November 1987) pp. 84–96; Macleans (June 12, 1989), p. 11; *Forbes* (June 12, 1989), p. 21.

△ CHAPTER 13 △
FINANCIAL MANAGEMENT

Small business owners usually have knowledge and experience in the production or selling of their goods and services, but are less likely to have as much interest or familiarity with the "numbers" part of the operation. Failure to understand fundamental operating procedures and their financial relationships have frequently put companies into great difficulties, creating situations which should have been recognized and solved earlier. Thus, understanding financial and accounting concepts and techniques is essential to the small business' survival. Indeed, the small firm is heavily dependent on accurate financial information provided by the accounting system. In this chapter we will discuss some of the concepts and techniques that are needed to effectively launch a new venture as well as managing the small business.

FINANCIAL PLANNING

Financial planning allows the entrepreneur to quantify the small business objectives and hence, assess the economic viability of the business. It also allows the small business management to effectively monitor the performance, and correct undesirable deviations from the plan. As can be shown in Figure 13.1, the financial planning process must be based on three essential elements. These are 1) the small firm's objectives; 2) the internal and external capabilities of the firm including its financial position; and 3) assumptions based on forecasts of markets, sales and economic trends.

COST-VOLUME-PROFIT RELATIONSHIPS

Break-even analysis is a very powerful tool for today's entrepreneur and small business management. It explains the relationship between three critical elements: cost, volume and profit. The break-even point as can be shown in Figure 13.2 and the equation below refers to the sales volume point in which the total revenues and cost are equal. In other words, there is no profit or loss from the operation.

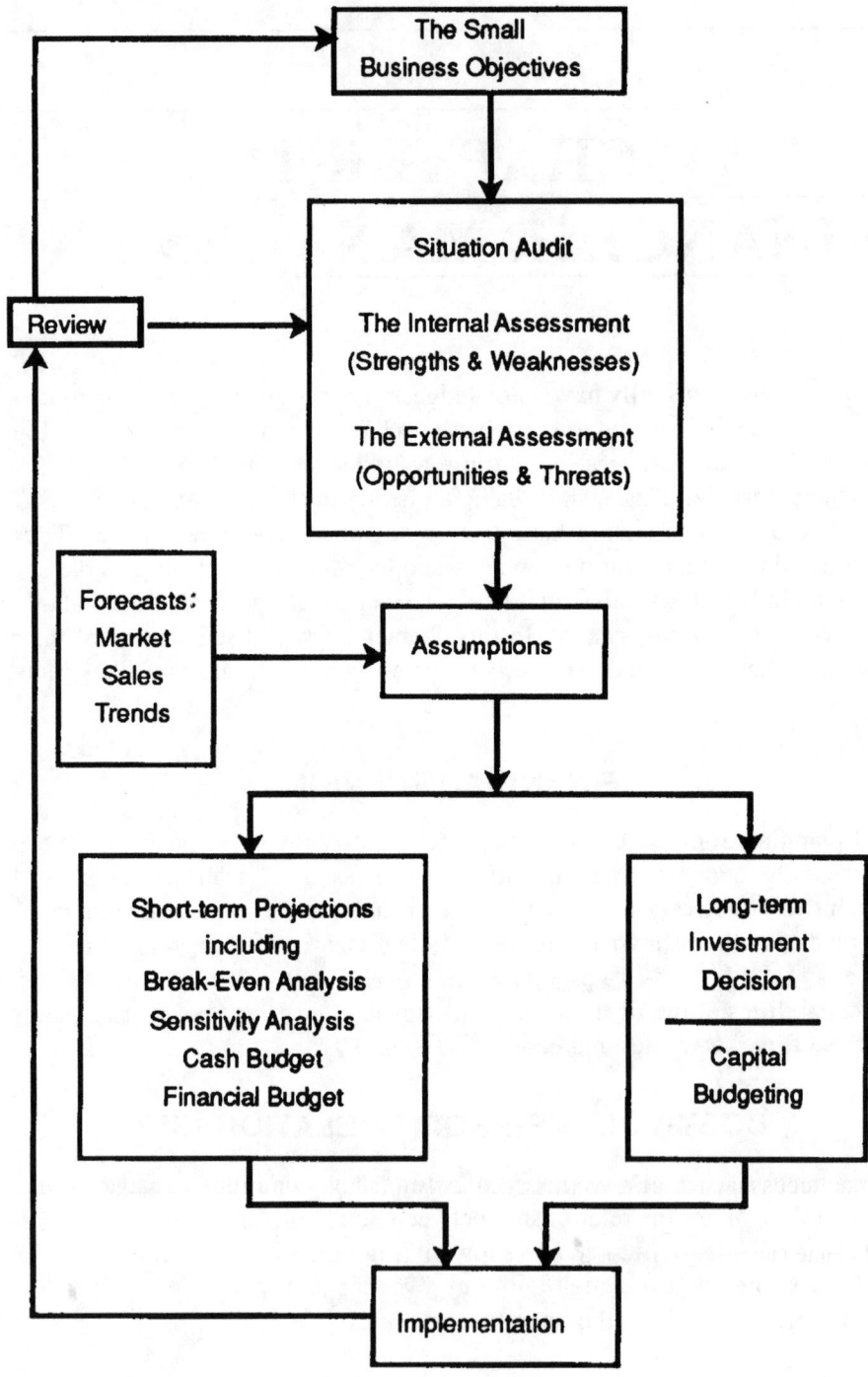

Figure 13.1. The financial planning process.

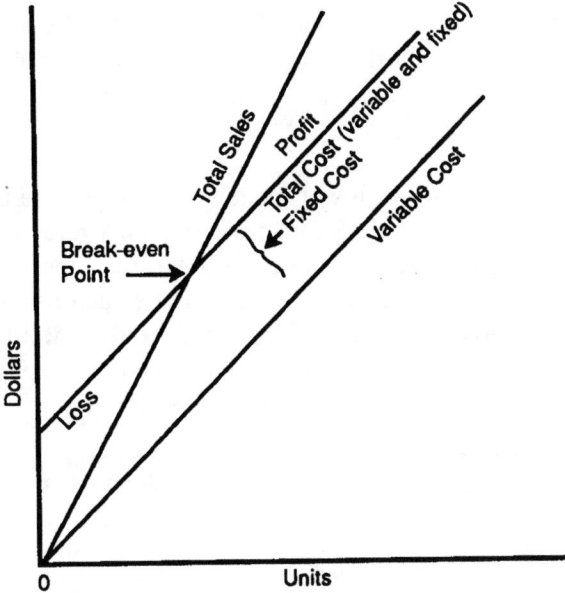

Figure 13.2. The break-even chart.

TOTAL SALES = VARIABLE COSTS + FIXED COSTS + NET PROFIT

A more appropriate approach for small firms is to calculate the contribution margin first and then the break-even point as shown below:

Contribution margin per unit = sales price per unit - variable cost per unit

$$\text{Break-even point} = \frac{\text{total fixed cost}}{\text{contribution margin per unit}}$$

$$\text{or} \qquad = \frac{\text{fixed cost}}{1 - \dfrac{\text{variable cost}}{\text{sales}}}$$

It is also possible for the small business management to set the desired profit and calculate the revenue necessary to achieve this goal as can be shown in the equation below:

$$\text{Sales Revenue (necessary to achieve the desired profit)} = \frac{\text{fixed cost + desired profit}}{\text{contribution margin}}$$

Indeed break-even analysis allows the small business management to make critical decisions about the economic viability of the opportunity and the different strategic alternatives available to the firm. However, break-even analysis is based on projections of cost, fixed and variable, expected sales volume, and an anticipated price. These projections are based on one assumption or scenario. In other words, break-even analysis assumes a condition of certainty. To minimize the risk involved in the certainty model, sensitivity analysis is often utilized.

Sensitivity Analysis

In sensitivity analysis, different scenarios or models may be built to incorporate different assumptions with regard to cost, sales volume, price and other relevant factors. Therefore, sensitivity analysis is more realistic than the one-scenario certainty model. It allows the small business management to assume different scenarios such as: best estimates, worst guess and optimistic scenarios as shown in Figure 13.3. Indeed it allows management to see how the expected value will be affected by changes in assumptions and/or errors in prediction and thus make more realistic decisions.

	Scenarios		
	1	2	3
Sales Volume (units)	500,000	300,000	50,000
Sales Revenue ($10 per unit)	$5,000,000	$3,000,000	$500,000
Variable Cost ($2 per unit)	1,000,000	600,000	100,000
Contribution Margin	$4,000,000	$2,400,000	$400,000

Figure 13.3. Sensitivity analysis.

Financial Performance Analysis

Detailed discussion of financial statements is beyond the scope of this particular chapter, but properly arranged and considered, relatively few numbers can tell the small businessman what is going on in the company, point out the likely future path of the company, and flag and highlight existing or future problems. In addition, the comparison of financial ratio data across companies is a well accepted technique, and is the reason that companies and industry associations produce the industry average ratio data. Care must be taken, however, to compare similar data since firms in different industries are likely to have differing ratio profiles.

What Ratios Can Do

The primary purpose in computing ratios is to highlight important relationships within the business that will help the small businessman determine the state of health of various financial aspects of the business. They will serve as indicators as to the strengths and weaknesses of the financial operation, as well as providing clues as to where and how to develop better financial results.

As with many other purely mathematical calculations, there are limitations to the use of ratio analysis that should be borne in mind. First and foremost, they represent past performance. One must therefore balance what has taken place with what is expected to occur in the future.

	Ratio	Significance
	Liquidity Ratio	
1.	$\text{Current} = \dfrac{\text{Current Assets}}{\text{Current Liabilities}}$	Ability to meet short-term obligations, i.e., the ease of being able to turn assets into cash
2.	Quick or "Acid Test" = $\dfrac{\text{Current Assets} - \text{Inventory}}{\text{CurrentLiabilities}}$	By excluding inventories, the ratio concentrates on the really liquid assets, with values that are fairly certain
	Profitability Ratio	
3.	$\dfrac{\text{Gross Profit (or Margin)}}{\text{Sales}}$	Profitability after cost of manufacturing and/or inventory expenses
4.	$\text{Profit margin} = \dfrac{\text{Net Profit}}{\text{Sales}}$	Useful when comparing company figures with other comparable businesses
5.	$\text{Return on Net Worth} = \dfrac{\text{Net Profit}}{\text{Net Worth}}$	Determines the percentage return on funds invested in the business by its owners
	Leverage Ratio	
6.	$\text{Total Debt to Total Assets} = \dfrac{\text{Total Debt}}{\text{Total Assets}}$	Measures the percentage of total funds in the business provided by its creditors
7.	$\text{Times Interest Earned} = \dfrac{\text{Earnings before Interest and Taxes (EBIT)}}{\text{Interest Expense}}$	Provides an indication of the firm's ability to meet its interest requirements
8.	$\text{Debt to Net Worth} = \dfrac{\text{Total Debt}}{\text{Net Worth}}$	Expresses the relationship between the capital contributions from creditors and owners
	Activity Ratio	
9.	$\text{Average Collection Period} = \dfrac{\text{Accounts Receivable}}{\text{Sales}/365}$	Tells the average number of days it takes to collect accounts receivable; thus how well the credit department is collecting these accounts
10.	$\text{Inventory Turnover} = \dfrac{\text{Cost of Goods Sold}}{\text{Inventory (or average inventory)}}$	Shows how fast merchandise is moving and the amount of capital tied up in inventory to support the company's operations
11.	$\text{Total Asset Turnover} = \dfrac{\text{Sales}}{\text{Total Assets}}$	Provides an indication of the firm's ability to generate sales in relation to its asset base

Figure 13.4. Key financial ratios.

Since ratios are based on the financial statements, they represent the status as of a particular date that the statements represent.

In the third instance, comparisons between companies and industries must be taken with caution, to ensure that the users recognize what is actually being compared. There are numerous ratios that might be used but those appearing in Figure 13.4 are key, and are basic to the financial analysis of most company operations.

Ratio Analysis For Knowledge-Based Small Firms

In the new knowledge-based economy, technological capability is critical to the firm's survival and ability to sustain its competitive advantage. We offer a number of ratios that are more relevant in assessing the financial performance of knowledge-based small firms.

The Technological Capabilities Ratios[*]

- R&D capability ratios

  R&D capability ratios measure the firm's investment in R&D and knowledge workers.

$$\text{R\&D expenditure to total expenditure} = \frac{\text{R\&D expenditure}}{\text{total expenditure}}$$

This ratio measures the firm's commitment to R&D. The ratio of an industry leader or industry average may be used as a benchmark. Spending less than the industry average on R&D is a sure sign that a firm's competitive advantage is eroding.

$$\text{knowledge workers to total employees} = \frac{\text{total number of knowledge workers}}{\text{total number of employees}}$$

This ratio measures the firm's commitment to innovation. The ratio of an industry leader or industry average may be used as a benchmark.

A ratio higher than the industry leader or industry norm indicates a high level of technological capabilities.

- R&D efficiency ratio

  This ratio measures the efficient use of R&D resources, including knowledge workers. The ratio is calculated as follows:

$$= \frac{\text{number of patents/new products developed}}{\text{R\&D expenditure}}$$

or

$$= \frac{\text{number of patents/new products developed}}{\text{total investment in knowledge workers}}$$

A ratio higher than the industry leader or industry norm indicates efficient use of both R&D expenditure and knowledge workers.

---

* Copyright © 1997 Dr. A. B. Ibrahim.

- Innovation ratio

    This ratio measures the firm's commitment not only to developing and improving its existing products, but also to developing new products. The ratio is calculated as follows:

    $$\text{innovation ratio} = \frac{\text{total investment in research expenditure}}{\text{total investment in development expenditure}}$$

    A balanced ratio indicates that the firm is committed to innovation.

- Return on technology investment

    This ratio is a powerful indicator of the knowledge-based firm's ability to earn a decent return on its investment on R&D and knowledge workers. The ratio could be calculated as follows:

    $$\text{return on technology investment} = \frac{\text{net income}}{\substack{\text{R\&D expenditure \& investment} \\ \text{in knowledge workers}}}$$

Cash Management

In order for a business to stay "alive," the most important item that is needed is cash. Without adequate working capital, the day-to-day expenses of running a business cannot be met. Not only is it important to obtain the necessary cash, but it is essential that the operators develop the mechanism to keep the necessary cash available as problems arise with the growth and development of the business. The job of managing cash is always a part of small business management, because cash flow or the lack of it can cause the failure of a small business.

An understanding of the components of the balance sheet is essential, together with an understanding of the relationship between them. The manner in which they affect working capital is fundamental. This requires, at a minimum, the ability of the small business management to prepare a monthly cash flow statement and also a projection of cash requirements. This means that if there is a likelihood of cash shortage, the small business owner can take steps to remedy the situation. By the same token, if it appears that there will be a cash surplus, the owner can put the excess funds to work through short-term investments, thus generating additional funds, such as short-term securities. Indeed, if a proper balance is maintained between payment (90-day) and collection (30-day), the small business can finance its needs of working capital internally.[1] Box 13.1 suggests some steps for implementing an effective cash management system.

There are currently a wide range of electronic spreadsheet programs, both computer and non-computer based, readily available that make the cash handling procedures relatively simple and easily adaptable to the smallest of businesses.

Box 13.1. Steps for Effective Management of Cash Flow.

---

1. Responsibility of handling cash should be assigned to a specific individual(s).
2. Cash disbursements and receipts should be balanced on a daily basis.
3. Maintain a cash reserve for emergencies. The reserve should be established based on prior experience. Cash reserves have literally saved many small firms from bankruptcy.
4. Maintain a proper balance between suppliers' credit term and customer collection period; ninety/thirty days is suggested.
5. Maintain a record (invoice, receipt) for all your transactions.
6. Monitor your credit sales policy and accounts receivable collection to avoid too many bad debts.
7. Negotiate favorable credit terms with suppliers. Suppliers are good sources of inexpensive funds.
8. Maintain a proper balance between your sources, and use of funds. Unplanned growth should be avoided.

Controlling Credit, Collections and Inventory

In today's economy, operating with credit is taken to be a matter of course for most businesses. The fundamental problem therefore, is not whether or not to grant credit, but how much and to whom. In essence, the management of credit requires consideration of such items as:

- minimizing the amount of money tied up in accounts receivable
- minimizing bad debt losses
- maximizing profit through credit loss reduction

These items require that the small business have a policy program to control credit procedures. These will include a statement as to whom credit will be extended, the terms of the credit, and the conditions and procedures under which collections will be made.

Most small businesses have started without being concerned with credit collection or inventory problems, but before too long they realize that there is a need for control and rigidity of details related to operational procedures. Excessive losses in accounts that could eventually become worthless and tie up badly needed capital could cause immeasurable harm and difficulty for the small business.

Sound credit policies begin with a thorough knowledge of the customer's financial position. This should be followed by a systematic accounting of all dealings with customers. Procedures must be implemented which can quickly establish standards of the terms and conditions of sales and collections.

By the same token, inventory control and purchasing procedures must receive equal attention. Not only must the small business owner employ proper purchasing methods, but must utilize methods and procedures that will minimize the dollar outlay for material.

For many small companies, the investment in inventory may be their largest outlay and so steps must be taken to protect this investment. The accuracy of the buying decisions, quantity and timing are dependent upon inventory control.

Fortunately, there are a number of techniques available which can assist the small businessman, among which are ordering the economic quantities (EOQ), the establishment of optimal re-ordering points and the now popular Just-in-Time (JIT) technique.

Under the JIT system, materials and inventory arrive at the appropriate location "just in time" instead of well beforehand, which could mean a costly inventory stockpile and corresponding tie-up of funds. JIT is a manufacturing technique that purports to improve a company's efficiency. The key measure of manufacturing efficiency is the level of inventory maintained; the lower the level of inventory, the more efficient the production system.

Thus, sound purchasing, credit and collection procedures are essential to the profitable operation of the small business.

Budgeting

Budgeting is another equally important tool for managing the small business effectively. Budgeting is not only a planning technique but also a powerful control device. The budget quantifies the small business plans and expectations regarding future revenue, cost, cash flow and profit. It indicates how goals are to be achieved and how resources are to be acquired and utilized. Indeed, the budget rations the small business' scarce resources and forces the organization to assess the situation in a more realistic way, and to maintain proper records. However the small business budgeting system need not be as elaborate and complex as in large organizations. An inexpensive and simple system is the name of the game.

There are many forms of budgets, such as cash, capital and operating budgets, as shown in Figure 13.5. The operating budget simply translates the short-term plan into quantifiable measures. It includes expected sales, production, cost of goods sold, administrative cost and expected net profit from the operation.

The cash budget is a very useful technique for assessing the small business' needs for short-term funds. It is a forecast of cash receipts and disbursements against which actual cash flow can be measured, and represents a very important tool for business control. Monthly cash budget is essential to the small business survival. A yearly cash flow projection may be deceiving. It may show a positive cash flow at the end of the year while any particular month may indicate a large negative cash flow, enough to wipe out the entire firm.

In addition, the control of cash calls for a constant planning process, because if changes are needed, they can be made relatively quickly. A revised budget might be called for at this stage and a cash report drawn up to determine whether or not the cash control procedures are really working.

Budgeting is also a powerful control device for small businesses. It allows the small firm to monitor performance by comparing actual performance against planned (budgeted) performance. Management then can take the necessary steps to correct undesirable deviations and/or revise the plans. Figure 13.6 illustrates the use of budget as a control device.

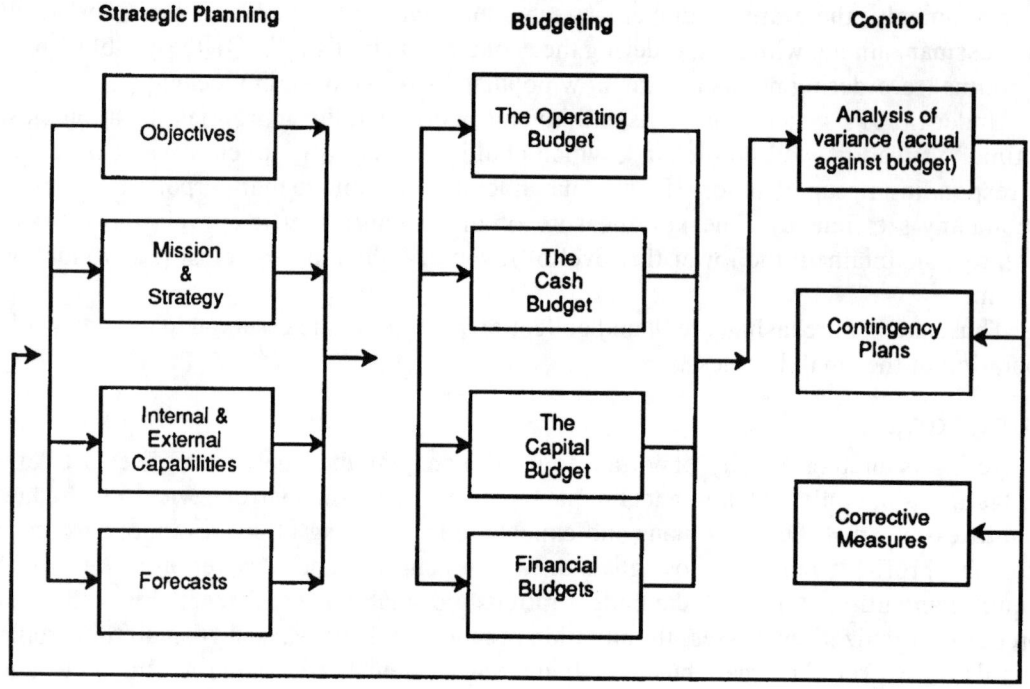

Figure 13.5. The budgeting process-planning and control.

	Budget	Actual	Deviation* ± from Budget	Action/ Contingency Plan
Sales				
Cost of Goods Sold				
Gross Profit				
Operating Expenses:				
Selling expenses				
- Advertising expenses				
- Sales commissions				
Total Selling Expenses				
General Expenses				
- Office salaries				
- General office expenses				
Total General Expenses				
Total Operating Expenses				
Net Profit Before Income Tax				

*+ Desirable deviation from budget
 – Undesirable deviation from budget

Figure 13.6. Budget analysis income statement. (Budget compared with actual performance.)

The Capital Budget—The Investment Decision

The capital budget is essentially concerned with assessing the long-range economic viability of an opportunity or investment proposal. This may include launching a new product, construction of a new site for the business operation and replacement of machines or vehicles. The technique assumes that small business capital is limited and scarce and therefore should be utilized in the most effective way possible in order to provide the greatest return. Thus before any investment decision is made a number of critical factors must be assessed. These are: (1) the small business objectives, (2) the amount invested, and (3) the expected rate of return from the investment. Indeed investment proposals are assessed based on the expected future returns. Therefore, future returns must be discounted to a present value. Different approaches are available to evaluate investment proposals such as the payback and the discounted cash flow methods. Let us discuss each method briefly (see Figure 13.7).

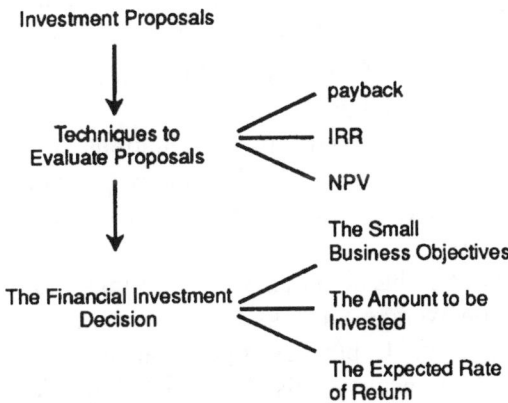

Figure 13.7. The investment decision.

The payback method simply indicates the time period it takes to recover the initial amount invested from annual net cash flows. The investment proposal with the shortest payback period is the most desirable.

The Discounted Cash Flow (DCF) method involves two approaches, the Internal Rate of Return (IRR) and the Net Present Value (NPV). Both methods are reliable since they depend on the time value of the funds. Table 13.1 shows the present value of $1 to be received at "n" year and discounted at rate "r."

The Internal Rate of Return (IRR) simply compares the amount invested with a stream of net cash flows discounted at a demanded rate of interest. The Net Present Value—NPV method is similar to the IRR method. It involves comparing the initial amount invested with the net present value of the cash flow discounted at an appropriate rate of discount.[2]

Table 13.1. Present Value of $1.

Years Hence	4%	8%	10%	12%	16%	20%	24%
1	0.962	0.926	0.909	0.893	0.862	0.833	0.806
2	0.925	0.857	0.826	0.797	0.743	0.694	0.650
3	0.889	0.794	0.751	0.712	0.641	0.579	0.524
4	0.855	0.735	0.683	0.636	0.552	0.482	0.423
5	0.822	0.681	0.621	0.567	0.467	0.402	0.341
6	0.790	0.631	0.564	0.507	0.410	0.335	0.275
7	0.760	0.583	0.513	0.452	0.354	0.279	0.222
8	0.731	0.540	0.467	0.404	0.305	0.233	0.179

Valuation Techniques

Determining the value of the firm is a real challenge to the entrepreneur and the small business management. Valuation techniques can help the entrepreneur make a better decision not only in the early stage of purchasing a business, but also in the harvesting stage when he or she finally decides to sell the business. There are at least two useful techniques with which to value a business: asset and earning valuations.

Asset valuations may be based on the book value as stated in the balance sheet. The book value may also be adjusted to reflect the actual market or replacement cost and thus give a more realistic estimate.

Earning valuations could be based on previous earnings (not necessarily recent earnings), and could be based on average earnings over a period of five years. They could also be adjusted to reflect a reasonable business operation by omitting unusual expense or revenue items. Earning valuations could also be adjusted to reflect future earnings under the new management.[3] Figure 13.8 summarizes different valuation techniques.

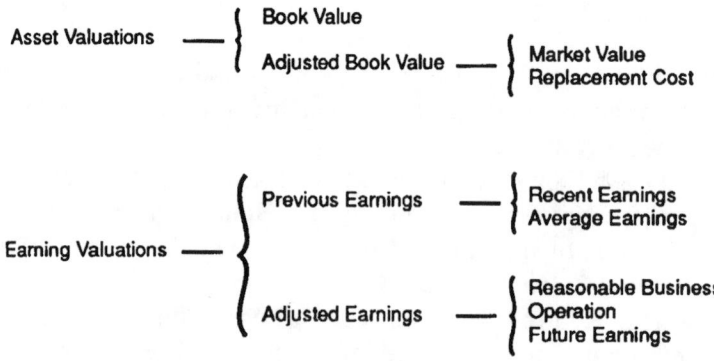

Figure 13.8. Valuation techniques.

SUMMARY

The lack of financial skills has been cited as a major contributing factor to the high failure rate of small businesses. This chapter emphasized a number of financial and accounting concepts and techniques. An understanding of these concepts and techniques is essential not only in the launching of the new venture, but also in managing the small business effectively. Breakeven analysis, sensitivity analysis, financial performance analysis, and budgeting are important tools for today's entrepreneur.

NOTES

1. K. Said and K. Hughey, "Managerial Problems of the Small Firm," *Journal of Small Business Management* (January 1977), pp. 37–43.
2. A. B. Ibrahim, *Financial Management for Small Business* (University Press 1978), Chapter 5.
3. H. Stevenson, M. Roberts and H. Grousbeck, *New Business Ventures and the Entrepreneur*, 1994, pp. 39–48.

THE ENTREPRENEUR

Victor Kiam
"Shaves as Close as a Blade or Your Money Back"

Victor Kiam is perhaps one of the most popular entrepreneurs in this decade. Kiam bought the Remington Company and turned it into a success story. In his book *Live to Win: Achieving Success in Life and Business,* Kiam summarizes his entrepreneurial philosophy. He advises budding entrepreneurs to be more focused and approach their target with full force. "The entrepreneur can't be half-pregnant," says Kiam.

Entrepreneurship, according to Kiam, is a way of life. "The entrepreneurial spirit should enliven every waking minute," he tells us.

Entrepreneurs are high achievers. "These are people in love with what they are doing. Their ladder reaches up to the heavens and beyond. There is always another ladder to climb . . . they are pleased with success but always hungry for more." Indeed the Kiam School of Entrepreneurship advocates that today's entrepreneur "cannot stand still. If he does, those laurels he chooses to sit on will attach themselves to his backside."

Kiam is a happily married man. "You can make your lifestyle fit your business and vice versa," says Kiam. He and his wife and daughter launched their business from home. "My friends, you can have it all," say Kiam.

Source: V. Kiam, *Live to Win: Achieving Success in Life and Business* (Harper & Collins, 1989).

△ CHAPTER 14 △
HUMAN RESOURCE MANAGEMENT

No matter how well an entrepreneur has planned and obtained the necessary funding, in the final analysis, it is the human aspects of the operation that will decide whether or not it will succeed or fail. The entrepreneur can manage the business, but it can only grow and develop as the people side of the business grows and develops. Indeed, the success of the small business is heavily dependent upon the contribution made by its human resources. The management of people is the heart of small business management.

In the beginning, entrepreneurs generally start with the minimum of assistance, probably with only members of the immediate family, so as to keep overhead to its lowest level. When it does become necessary to add additional help, in many cases the immediate decision is to hire part-time help. This can, of course, be only a temporary step and the long-term solution would call for a proper strategy for managing the human resources, including selection, hiring and training of personnel who will be the means for the company's ultimate success.

Human Resource Management (HRM) is an important activity regardless of the organization size. It is required whenever people are employed. It involves all management decisions that affect the nature of the relationship between the organization and employee— its human resources.

Indeed the ultimate success of the organization will depend on the skills of the entrepreneur in managing his human resources. This includes planning, staffing, training and development, wage and salary administration, employee welfare and record keeping. A basic review of the modern human resource function in a small business is portrayed in Figure 14.1.

HUMAN RESOURCE PLANNING

The human resource function must be the responsibility of the owner-manager or one of his more senior managers, since they are the ones who must articulate the policies and philosophy critical to the design and administration of the human resource systems.

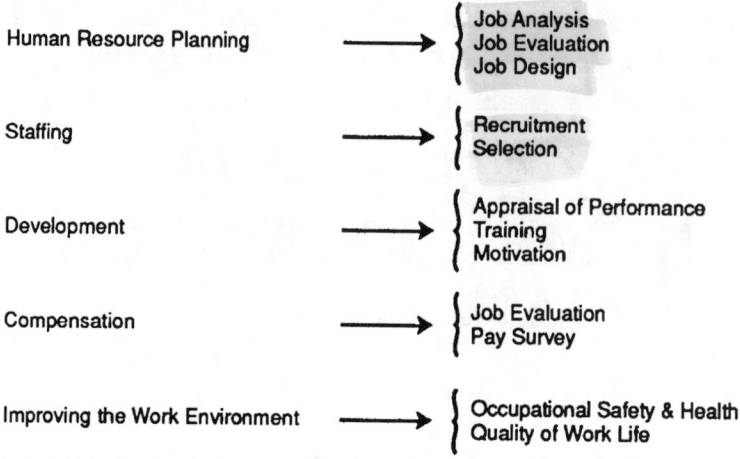

Figure 14.1. The human resource function.

Any business, whether profit-making or non-profit, operates to supply products or services of one kind or another. The expansion of the business requires the proper hiring of new personnel and of satisfying the needs of the personnel—the human resources. Planning, therefore, is critical if the right type of personnel are to be brought into the business, because smallness creates a unique situation in the selection. It creates distinctive opportunities, but it also has some very severe limitations and problems in the development of good human relations amongst its members. There is very little room for error and few possibilities for correcting an error by providing alternative job opportunities.

The degree of formalization of human resource management is a function of the size and type of organization. In the small enterprise, there may not be as clear-cut a structure because a closeness usually exists between the owner and his employees, and many functions may be performed on an informal basis. However, as the organization grows, this informality becomes, of necessity, less informal, and contact between the management and employees requires a more structured format.

Human resource planning involves four essential activities. These are job analysis, job design, job description and job specification. Job analysis involves collecting and recording information about the task to be performed including skills and abilities. Job design includes characteristics of the different activities to be performed. Job description involves key tasks to be performed, duties and responsibilities. Job specification includes the qualifications, and skills necessary to accomplish the task.

Many small companies function without formal or written job descriptions, with the employees doing just whatever the owners decide they should do. Some operations are unpredictable and do not lend themselves to any clear description, with whatever work that has to be done performed by the nearest worker—a flexibility function of many small businesses. As a company tends to grow it usually takes on a more structured form and whether or not it is actually written down, each employee must know:

- what his duties and responsibilities are
- what authority the job carries
- what the performance standards or objectives of the job are.

A job analysis should be a clear evaluation of all the facts about a job which in turn could be used to analyze the owner's needs pertaining to that function.

STAFFING

Staffing needs are tied in with the overall planning of the organization. This requires answers to questions such as: the expansion of the business, adding new products or services, changing the nature of the business, how many persons will be needed to meet the objectives of the organization this year, next year? The staffing process, looking at it from the broad perspective, includes any activities pertinent to the recruitment and selection of employees required to meet the objectives of the company. Recruitment could be from within the company or from outside sources such as colleges and professional associations. Selection in small firms is usually based on interviews, tests and references. While relatively little planning, policy and procedure may be necessary initially, the sooner they are developed and implemented with details and procedures that are understood by all employees, the less likely it is that errors and misunderstanding will ensue, leading to trouble and expense at a later date. Box 14.1 suggests a three-step personnel selection process.

EMPLOYEE DEVELOPMENT

Employee development includes appraisal of performance, training and motivation.

Appraisal of Performance

Appraisal of performance is important in order to determine the degree of effectiveness. Performance appraisal may serve several purposes such as:

1. Establishing a basis for compensation
2. Assisting training and development
3. Providing feedback

Training

In a new small enterprise, most training occurs on the job with the immediate supervisor undertaking the training process. However, as the business grows, the need for more thorough and advanced training becomes a necessity. This means that plans for better training procedures should be in place early to fill the vacancies as the company grows. In

---

Box 14.1. The Personnel Selection Process.

The personnel selection process currently employed by small business owners consists overwhelmingly of the general application form and follow-up interview. Often, the result of such a process is an inaccurate and costly hiring decision. In their concise article, Gatewood and Feild propose a three-step selection process to improve the hiring decisions made by small business owners, and to reduce personnel costs.

Gatewood and Feild's main contention is that present selection procedures used by small business owners collect information that is too general to help owners select the most qualified candidate for a job. Instead, the selection process should determine which specific tasks performed on the job are the most important, then collect information from the candidate to measure the extent to which he or she has performed such tasks in the past. The authors go on to say that an explicit scoring procedure should be used to rank each candidate.

The authors list and describe three steps in the selection process for choosing an appropriate candidate. They are:

1. "Job analysis" requires the collection of specific job-related tasks, and then ranking each task in order of importance and on the time it takes to complete each task.
2. "Identifying worker characteristics" involves determining as exactly as possible the skills and knowledge needed to perform the key job-related tasks.
3. "The development of the selection instruments" focusses on collecting information about the job applicant's past education and job experience directly related to the critical tasks. The authors recommend that the small business owner administer a three level procedure for each hiring situation. The procedure consists of: a) "a training and experience form," b) a formal interview, and c) a simulated work situation. Each successive level is administered only to the highest scorers of the preceding level.

In summary, the authors contend that small business owners can be helped to make less costly and more accurate hiring decisions if they incorporate their personnel selection program in selection procedures.

Source: Robert Gatewood and Herbert S. Feild, "A personnel selection program for small business," *Journal of Small Business Management* 25, 4 (October 1987), pp. 16–24.

---

the long run, growing from within will be less costly than bringing in supervisors and managers from the outside.

Present employees might have to be upgraded also, to prevent obsolescence when job requirements change, or when they are transferred or promoted to new jobs as the organization expands. Present employees might also have to learn skills of more than one job because the organization has a variety of outputs which require a flexible staff who can switch from one job to another, or because the survivors of layoffs have to learn the jobs of those who are laid off.

Training makes good business sense too, because an employee who has shown promise by virtue of productivity, attendance, interpersonal skills, responsibility—is worth retraining and encouraging. The alternative may be the loss of a valuable employee or the costly

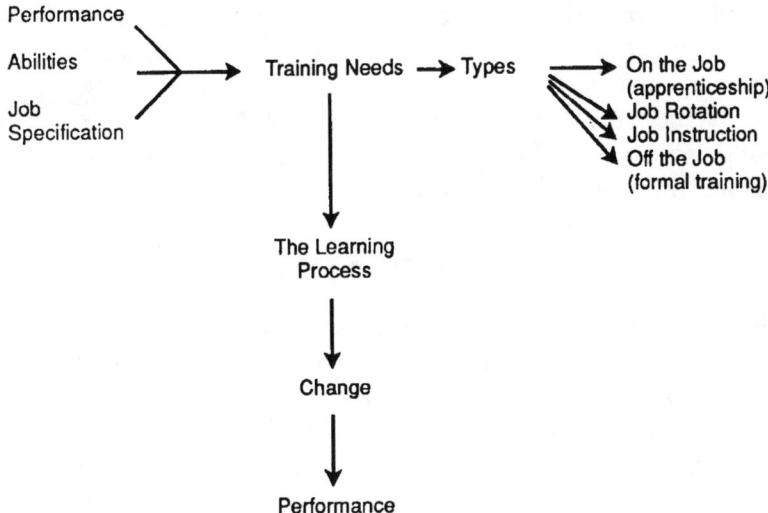

Figure 14.2. The training process.

process of hiring another person and going through the whole retraining process without wholly predictable results. Figure 14.2 depicts the training process.

Employee Motivation

The ability to perform on the job is not sufficient enough to achieve high performance. Employees must also have the desire and the will to achieve the desired performance. Therefore, ability and motivation are key ingredients for high employee performance. There are different instruments for managing motivation in the small firm; money, competition, job design and participation in goal setting are all motivators. However, the critical element here is to identify the motivator which will stimulate the employee to act and perform highly on the job. The entrepreneur must realize that differences among employees in the way they respond to various stimuli do exist. These responses are a function of the way they perceive the motivator or reward.

Management by Objectives

MBO is an excellent approach to employee motivation. Participation in goal setting and appraisal of performance according to these goals leads to improved employee performance.

Motivating Knowledge-Based Employees

While training allows the employees to enhance their skills, it does not necessarily lead to innovation, enhanced performance and decreased production costs. In the new economy, the small or medium-sized firm must be able to provide a positive environment that encourages creativity and innovation, which are the building blocks for erecting lasting competitive advantage. A positive environment includes a culture that allows for innovation and participation in the decision-making process, a career development program, a healthy and safe working environment, an effective compensation system and a leadership style that encourages innovation and values consensus.

COMPENSATION

To retain good key employees, the small or medium-sized firm must design a competitive compensation package that takes into consideration the labour market demand, seniority, knowledge and experience. The entrepreneur can not simply decide on the compensation without regard to the labour market. Wage and salary surveys allow the firm to maintain a competitive compensation system. The alternative may be the loss of a valuable employee to a competitor and the costly process of rehiring and training or—even worse—the loss of valuable knowledge.

A number of compensation methods are commonly used by small and medium-sized firms. These include

- **Payment for time worked.** This is the most common compensation method for small and medium-sized firms. It requires maintaining records of the work hours of each employee.
- **Incentive plans.** This method ties pay to performance. Employees compensation are based on their output, such as the number of units produced or sold.
- **Stock option plans in knowledge-based companies.** To retain its key people, most knowledge-based firms offer stock option plans. These plans are designed to encourage scientists and skilled workers to remain in the firm.

In general, the pay level is determined by a number of factors:

- supply and demand for workers in the area
- pay practices in the area/region
- pay practices in the industry
- union negotiation
- type of work performed

Knowledge Workers as Assets

In the knowledge-based economy, knowledge and knowledge-based workers have become the firm's real assets, replacing equipment in the old economy. The entrepreneur must ensure that knowledge workers are utilized properly in order to sustain the firm's technological capabilities. We suggest that the entrepreneur measure the percentage of knowledge-based workers to total workers and the return investment in knowledge workers. A ratio higher than the industry leader or industry norm indicates competitive innovation capabilities.

1. Knowledge-based workers ratio is calculated as follows:

$$\frac{\text{Total Number of Knowledge–Based Workers}}{\text{Total Number of Employees in the Firm}}$$

2. The return on investment on knowledge-based workers can be calculated as follows:

$$\frac{\text{Net Profit}}{\text{Total Investment in Knowledge–Based Workers}}$$

Protecting Knowledge[*]

Knowledge is the firm's assets in the new economy. In knowledge-based firms, key employees often control the firm's knowledge. Risk of death or of leaving the company to start their own business or to join a competitor is extremely high. The firm must take measures to protect these valuable assets. These include

- Confidentiality clause to ensure that employees or former employees will not reveal the knowledge acquired during their work in the firm.
- Information is stored electronically in a safe place. In one company that the author was associated with, the key scientist knew the entire design but no records were kept in the firm.
- The firm is insured against the death of its key employee or the possibility of the employee accepting a better offer from a competitor.

⑥ Employee Welfare

Most countries have laws similar to that of the Occupational Safety and Health Act in the United States and Canada to ensure safe and healthy working conditions, and to preserve our human resources. Figure 14.3 depicts The Occupational Safety and Health Process.

If the small business management followed the basic principle of maintaining safe and healthy working conditions, communication within the company between management and workers would likely be such that employees would be able to relay any difficulties to management. Failure to do so will inevitably lead eventually to some form of unionized activity. There is an old saying that "if you have a union, you deserve it."

Many small business owners look at unionization with suspicion and resent employees who seek union affiliation. One of the main reasons for this reaction is the feeling that it will encroach upon his or her control over the business, particularly if the union is an outside organization, national or international, and may be more powerful than the organization the entrepreneur currently operates.

In most jurisdictions, employees have the legal right to organize and if they actually do, it may be that by joining together and bargaining collectively, they hope to bring more effective pressure on management to protect what may be perceived as having to be improved.

Most employees join unions because of the actions or inactions of management, be it in relation to wages, safety standards, working conditions, benefits or purely the communication process with management.

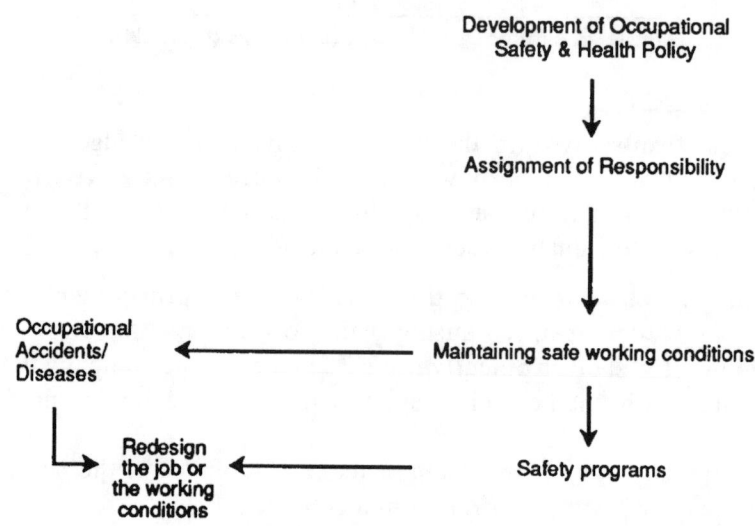

Figure 14.3. The occupational safety and health process.

Record Keeping

Some records are required for business reasons and some for legal reasons. Whatever the reason, the system should be devised so that it works for the organization and in particular for those responsible for the human resource activities.

All information must be accurate, up to date and readily accessible to authorized persons. With computer facilities available to most small businesses in this day and age, the task can be made considerably easier and can be used to advantage. Software programs containing standard record data would be readily available with probably only minor modifications necessary for any particular company's needs.

Figure 14.4 is a checklist of the human resource function.

Critical Issues	Sources/Types	Bases of Judgment
1. Formulating the Human Resource Plan	The small business objectives Need analysis	The strategic plan Number of jobs, job analysis, design and specifications
2. Sources of Recruitment	From within Outside: colleges, co-op program and internship, referrals from professional associations	Past performance in the firm Recommendations, Interviews and tests
3. Selection	Application forms Interviews References Tests	Background information, skills, qualifications, and ability to perform
4. Training and Development	On the job Formal training	Training needs, analysis, performance appraisal
5. Performance Appraisal	Quantitative Qualitative	Productivity Critical incidents
6. Compensation	Salary Commission Profit sharing Fringe benefits	Salary survey Job evaluation
7. Motivation	Extrinsic: pay, job security Intrinsic: Job design, Rotation and Involvement	Job satisfaction, performance

Figure 14.4. The human resource function checklist.

TOTAL QUALITY MANAGEMENT—TQM

As global competition intensifies, quality emerges as a key competitive advantage. Total Quality Management (TQM) is emerging as a critical issue in today's business. Box 14.2 describes TQM in the context of small business.

Box 14.2. TQM in Small Business.

Randall S. Schuler and Drew L. Harris examined Deming's approach to TQM in the context of a small company. The authors summarized Deming's approach to TQM in three key principles: (1) The organization as a system, (2) variance within the system, and (3) the relationship between productivity and costs. The first principle is to approach the organization as a system with different functions each has inputs from suppliers and outputs to customers. Regardless of whether those suppliers and customers are internal or external, quality must be achieved. The second principal focuses on reducing variation in order to improve quality. Deming distinguishes between two types of variance: single (i.e., caused by an operator) and common-system related (i.e., flaw in design or in a communication system). Common variance is management responsibility and must not be dealt with as a single variance. The third principal suggests that high quality leads to higher productivity and lower costs. According to Deming this can be achieved by having a well trained work force and the use of effective tools.

The authors examined a small firm's application of TQM and implications for human resource management and noted the following interesting findings:

1. The company eliminated the link between compensation and appraisal of performance. Performance appraisal was no longer based on qualitative measures; but rather on qualities such as communication skills and adaptability.
2. The company increased on-the-job training and applied a job rotation program.
3. Employees dismissal and discipline became the responsibility of peers and not management (management only sets the rules).
4. Quality issues communicated to the shop floor workers reached them quicker and clearer in the small firm.
5. Management-employee trust proved to be critical for a successful implementation of TQM.

Source: R. S. Schuler and P. L. Harris, "Deming Quality Improvement: Implications in a Small Company," *Human Resource Planning,* Volume 14, Number 3, 1991.

FUTURE ISSUES

Recent research in human resources management in the context of small business, clearly indicates that personnel practices are much more complex than originally assumed. Historically human resources management in small business has been a neglected area by scholars. This, despite empirical data that rank human resources management as the second critical task in managing the small business. Box 14.3 outlines current practices and future trends.

> **Box 14.3. Future Issues in Human Resource Management.**
>
> Jeffrey S. Hornsby and Donald F. Kuratko, surveyed 247 small businesses to gain insight into current personnel practices and to explore future trends. Concerning current personnel practices they found that organization size seems to influence the type of methodology employed. The larger firms tend to employ more sophisticated personnel techniques in such areas as job analysis, job description, personnel selection, wages and compensation. Concerning future trends in personnel practices a number of issues were identified by owners /managers as critical in the 1990s. These include: Availability of quality workers, wages, benefits, government policies, training and development and job security.
>
> Source: Jeffrey S. Hornsby and Donald F. Kuratko, "Human Resource Management in Small Business: Critical Issues for the 1990s, *Journal of Small Business Management,* July 1990, pp. 9–17.

SUMMARY

Human resources are key ingredients in a successful venture. Human resource management involves planning, staffing, training and development, compensation, policies and record keeping. Staffing includes developing personnel sources, recruiting potential employees, the selection process and orientation. Training and development involves training needs analysis, on-the-job or off-the-job training. Compensation includes job evaluation, wages and salary survey, and wages and salary administration. Employees' welfare includes preparing employee handbooks, instituting health and safety standards and handling of employee grievances. Record keeping involves maintaining employees' files, records, reports and appraisals.

NOTES

1.   N. Beck; *Shifting Gears: Thriving in the New Economy,* Harper Collins, 1992.

THE ENTREPRENEUR

Isadore Sharp—The Popular Employer
Four Seasons Inc.

Based on the belief that there was indeed a niche in the highly competitive hotel industry, Isadore Sharp, chairman and president of Four Seasons, Inc., heads up what is reputed to be the world's largest luxury hotel chain.

Born in 1931, the son of a Polish father who emigrated from Palestine in 1925, and became involved in residential construction in Toronto, Ontario, Issy Sharp studied architecture at Ryerson Institute of Technology before joining his father's construction team.

In 1959, believing that there was room for an upscale hotel in a less than prestigious area of Toronto, Sharp was able to convince some of his boyhood friends to assist in the financing of the venture, since none of the conventional money sources were willing to become involved. The hotel quickly became an overwhelming success and Mr. Sharp commented that it gave the company the insight that it needed and "that going for the top end of the market was possible without compromising quality. From there, it was a matter of refining the idea."

Included in the Financial Post's 1988 list of the 100 best companies to work for in Canada, Mr. Sharp's policy towards the employees of Four Seasons is indicated by the statement that skills can be taught "but it is people and personalities which guests notice. All business, sooner or later, is show business."

This philosophy has obviously paid off in that Four Seasons, by mid-June 1989, owned or operated some 22 hotels in Canada, the United States and the United Kingdom, recording a profit of $13.1 million, with profits expected to be in the order of $14 million in 1989. Plans call for further expansion and developments leading to Europe, the Far East and Mexico. Charles Suddaby, Laventhol & Howarth, an expert for the hotel industry, is reported to have said that "Four Seasons hotels are consistently among the best in the industry. They have managed to raise the standards of the entire hotel business."

Undoubtedly another reason for this company's growth has been its human relations management, having been cited as one of the 100 best companies to work for in Canada. "The company wants its people to advance and grow, and encourages job enrichment wherever possible. It fully reimburses all employees for courses to broaden their work horizons. One employee remarked, 'It's nice to earn good money, but if you earn okay money and are happy, that counts a lot.'"

Source: "The Financial Post selects the 100 Best Companies to Work for in Canada," Eva Innes, Robert L. Perry and Jim Lyon (Collins Publishers, Don Mills, Ont. 1986), pp. 307–351.

$\triangle$ CHAPTER 15 $\triangle$
MARKETING

MARKETING AND SMALL BUSINESS

There is an old adage which says that, "Nothing happens until somebody sells something." In its simplest form, this is what marketing is all about. But behind all things that seem to be so simple and obvious, there is a great deal that has to take place for it to happen, and the answers provided to an equal number of questions. Some of these are: to whom are you selling your product or service, for how much, how do you make it available, and when?

The marketing scene is one of constant change, so that even if you have considered some of the above questions, you will have to cope with shifting demographic and social trends—aging populations, double-income families, single parents, and even more discerning customers. New technologies are constantly coming onto the marketing scene, such as telemarketing and marketing with videos and computers. Thus, the whole marketing scene is a sea of ebb and flow—a feature that is of concern and interest to the entrepreneur, particularly since he or she is in a position, as a small business person, to be able to adapt in a changing environment so much more than his or her larger counterpart. Small businesses—explicitly or implicitly—recognize that their marketing strategy enables them to survive and adapt in a dynamic arena.

While there are a multitude of definitions, marketing is the process whereby needed goods and/or services are delivered to target customers at the right place, at the right time, and at the right price. It demands that all of these activities go towards winning and keeping customers.

Successful marketing implies a clear statement of what business you are in, or are going to be in, the market niche or target market at which you will aim, the critical factors which you expect will be crucial to your decisions leading to your success or failure, and a marketing plan which will provide the focus for the marketing concept. The marketing concept, in turn, dictates that your business sells what customers want, and at prices that produce profits. It is a way to focus your attention on what is fundamental to your operation—serving your customers profitably. The marketing concept, therefore, serves the purpose of forcing the entrepreneur to look at his or her business with the customer predominately in mind, because without the customer, there is no business.

The focal point of every business undertaking, every aspect of the business in fact, must concentrate on putting the customer first in planning and subsequent actions. In building this orientation, four objectives of the small company's marketing plan should be to:

1. determine customer needs and wants through market research
2. pinpoint the company's specific niche and target markets
3. develop a marketing strategy utilizing the company's competitive advantages
4. assess the components of the marketing mix that will service the needs and demands of the company's customers as defined by its marketing strategy.

MARKET RESEARCH

Having established what you want to do, and how you want to do it, you must now determine to whom it is that you must actually sell your product or service. You need to define more closely your particular market segment—those people who are to buy whatever it is you are thinking of offering.

Market research is simply the systematic collection and analysis of data that is relevant to your company and your products or services in such a manner that you will be able to apply them in a useful and intelligent way. What is crucial in market research is the precise definition of what it is that you need to know, so that when the research is finished, you will have information that will form the basis for decision making. The planning and design of any survey and research process is very important.

The key to market research then, lies in knowing what it is that you are trying to obtain, doing it systematically and analyzing the data in such a manner that it is meaningful. As has been said, "You have to know the direction in which you want to go, have some sense of what the destination will look like, and understand what you need to get there. When you get the answers, you must be able to fit them into some pattern that makes sense in terms of your business."[1]

Since market research serves as the foundation for the marketing plan, it should be designed to answer such questions as:

Who are my customers and potential customers?
What kind of people are they?
Where do they live?
What are their purchasing habits?
What do they know about my business?
Through which advertising media can I most effectively reach them?

In marketing its goods and services, a small company does not have much room for error, with funds generally in fairly tight supply. By the same token, it may be that market research, in addition to merely confirming some preconceived concepts of the market, could uncover needs in the market place that the entrepreneur was unaware of and can now turn to his or her advantage.

While finances may be somewhat of a restriction, small companies often have an advantage over larger ones, in that they tend to be closer to their customers and know what they like and dislike. And market research can be reassuring and confirmatory.

Despite all that may be positive to undertaking market research, common reasons for failure to do so include lack of time, lack of knowledge as to how it might be done, concern about the cost and what the findings might be.

Types of Market Research

There are three types of market research important to any small business: internal information, secondary research and primary research.

Internal information is particularly useful because it is close at hand and costs little or nothing to obtain as it is located within the company's own records. The data is contained in the sales record, salesmen's reports, complaints and anything else that shows and tells who the customers are, what they have bought and where they live.

Secondary research concerns information that is readily available from outside sources and has already been compiled by someone else. It includes census data, government agencies, trade associations, chambers of commerce, newspapers, and many other sources. This information has already been collected by someone else, hence the name "secondary research."

Primary research will be undertaken because none of the two other types of research provide the information that you feel is still lacking. It requires a special approach, specifically tailored to the company's needs and probably conducted by an outside organization.

In most cases, careful study of the research results, regardless of the type utilized, will enable the entrepreneur to make strategic decisions. The market research process is by no means complete until it is acted upon and incorporated into the operation of the business. Box 15.1 summarizes small firms' attitude toward market research and offers some recommendations.

Market Research in Knowledge-Based Small Firms

Market research must start at the initial idea generation phase and continue during the product technology development phase. Market research allows the small or medium-sized firm to determine customer needs and wants more objectively. Ineffective market research in the product's technology development phase could lead to a disastrous situation, as a large investment in R&D expenditure is turned into losses overnight. If early market research indicates that there is no real need for the technology, then there is no point in investing in R&D to develop the technology further. Too often, scientists are motivated by the technology concept and pay little attention to the commercial application of the technology and the end user's needs and wants. Further, in order to cut the cost of hiring marketing professionals, the technical people are often involved in the marketing activities of the small or medium-sized firm regardless of their qualifications.

Box 15.1. Market Research.

Market research is critical to today's entrepreneur in terms of understanding customer needs and wants. S. McDaniel and A. Parasuraman surveyed 160 small firms on the attitude towards marketing research. The authors found a number of interesting findings such as: (1) only 40% of the sample conducted market research; (2) internal market research conducted by small firms is more popular than externally conducted research; (3) external market research is perceived to be much more expensive than internal research; and (4) owner/managers who conducted marketing research felt that it was worth the money.

The authors also suggested the following guidelines for conducting marketing research: First, define the scope and reason for conducting the study (i.e., customers, competitors, promotion, etc.); Second, identify the sources of data, primary or secondary. Primary sources include personal interviews, telephone or mail survey. Secondary sources include published documents; Third, design the data collection method, (i.e., to learn more about customers' preference, competitors or to plan a promotion strategy) questionnaire is the most commonly used method; Fourth, select the sample and ensure that it represents the subjects under study; Fifth, data collection; and Finally, data analysis and the final report.

Source: S. W. McDaniel and A. Parasuraman, "Practical Guidelines for Small Business Marketing Research," *Journal of Small Business Management,* January 1986, pp. 1–8.

In general, market research must be tied to R&D activities to avoid costly error and to ensure effective design of the market research and of the product's technology itself. Indeed, while the R&D team must understand customer needs and wants to ensure market acceptance of the technology, the marketer must also have a sound knowledge of the technology and its commercial applications. Lack of coordination between R&D and marketing has contributed to many product failures in the marketplace.

The Target Market

Having defined the type of business you are in, you will have to define more closely the particular target market at which you wish to aim—those people who are to buy the specific goods or services that you are selling. There must be a match between what you have to offer and the target, and this is one of the primary objectives of the market research that you will have undertaken.

An effective marketing program depends on having the company's customers clearly targeted. The most successful businesses have well-defined pictures of the customers they are seeking to attract. It is important to emphasize that target marketing does not necessarily suggest small market segments—only ones that are homogeneous. A large market may well be fairly homogeneous and the target marketer will deliberately focus his or her selling efforts on it.

The principal reason for this focus on specific target customers is to gain a competitive advantage in knowing what particular variables should receive the most weight in order to achieve the most profitable results to the firm.

MARKETING STRATEGY

Marketing strategy may be described basically as those actions that a company must take in order to be competitive. As an entrepreneur, the special benefits that you can sell to customers are advantages that you hold over your competition—your competitive edge or competitive advantage. A competitive advantage is nice to have because it gives you some flexibility in differentiating your product and/or service and permits you to look at a broader range of competitive marketing strategies. It allows you to sell the customer something that nobody else has or can sell.

Indeed, whatever it is that you have defined as the benefits of your product or service, must be perceived by the customer as real and as a special benefit in order for it to provide you with a competitive advantage. Regardless of how outstanding this advantage may be in your opinion, unless it is communicated and shared by your customers, the advantages, real or not, will be of no avail. You will not be permitted the flexibility that comes with product or service differentiation.[2]

However, according to Theodore Levitt, any product or service can be differentiated, even the commodity that seems to differ from competitors' offerings only in price. He adds that:[3]

> . . . the management of the marketing process can itself be a powerful differentiating device. This device is constantly and assiduously employed in the better-managed branded, packaged consumer goods companies. It is a matter of staying aware of exactly what's going on in the market, of how people use, misuse, or modify their products, of how and where they buy, of who makes buying decisions and how these get modified, and the like. It is a matter of looking continuously for gaps in market coverage that the company can fill, of looking continuously at new ways of influencing buyers to choose one's product instead of a competitor's. In this unceasing effort of the manager, the way in which he operates becomes an extension of the idea of product differentiation itself.
>
> While differentiation is most readily apparent in branded, packaged consumer goods, in the design operating character, or composition of industrial goods, or in the features or 'service' intensity of intangible products, differentiation consists as powerfully in how one operates the business. In the way the marketing process is managed may reside the opportunity for many companies, especially those that offer generically undifferentiated products and services, to escape the commodity trap.

Since every entrepreneur must make a conscious strategic decision about how he or she hopes to create this differentiation and competitive edge, the entire organization must be geared to a commitment of producing products or providing services consistent with a predetermined marketing strategy. Successful businesses do not operate on the premise that it will simply happen; they create the strategy that will enhance their chances.

There are many marketing strategies that have been proposed for small businesses in order to assist them with achieving their objectives which in essence include market penetration, market development and product development.

A strategy of *market penetration* aims to increase the sale of goods or increase the revenue of service goods in present markets through greater sales or advertising efforts. Since the small businessman is usually closer to his customers than his larger counterpart, this should be quite feasible for most small businesses.

A *market development strategy* attempts to increase sales by introducing existing products or services into new markets. This does require, however, that the small businessman remains cognizant of what he or she has determined is the target market and that this market development aspect remains within the parameters he or she has already defined.[4]

A *product development strategy* calls for an increase in sales efforts through the in-products or services or the addition of entirely new ones.

Market segmentation is yet another strategy that may be used in developing markets. In this operation, the small businessman reduces the size of some of his or her larger targets into smaller, more homogeneous segments within the market in order to select and develop the appropriate marketing mixes. Market segmentation is concerned with a more clearly defined portion of the overall market to which a marketing strategy might be directed.

The whole idea behind market segmentation is that any market will, most likely, consist of activities that will require separate marketing mixes to produce better overall results.

Target marketers segregate the large markets into smaller, more homogeneous targets which they may be able to satisfy more precisely than if they tried to treat all aspects the same.

To segment a market the small business must:

1. differentiate among its customers on the basis of their traits, personalities, or other identifiable characteristics
2. establish that the segments are large enough and have enough purchasing power to be profitable for the company
3. ensure that the segment is accessible.

In the same vein, and associated with market segmentation, is the "niche" concept, which indicates a focus on a single or limited number of market segments. The niche strategy allows a small company to maximize the advantages of its size, and compete effectively in an area that may be dominated by larger firms. One of the main characteristics of the small firm is that it tends to be much more flexible than its larger counterpart and therefore can be quicker to take advantage of a situation, and more so, if it is able to identify a particular market niche.

The other side of the niche strategy, which involves an element of risk, lies in the size of the niche. The danger may be that the niche would be too small to be profitable, or if profitable and of sufficient size as to attract the larger companies, its life span might be of short duration.

In essence, the marketing strategy must be the result of determining the features and advantages of the company's product or service which will differentiate the entrepreneur from his or her competitors and to identify, in turn, what will be of benefit to its customers.

These must be readily understood by them for the basic marketing strategy of the company must be built around these benefits.

Marketing Mix

The key elements of a marketing strategy are the traditional four "P's" of marketing—product, place (distribution), price, and promotion. Small business managers must be able to determine the weighing or mix of these four elements that will meet the needs of their particular market segments, and at the same time, constitute a profitable undertaking.

The key notion in the use of the marketing "mix" is the notion of fit, i.e., having the right combination of the ingredients such that they will induce your customers to buy your products, or take your services over those of your competitors.

An important aspect of the marketing mix structure concerns that of the product life-cycle (see Figure 15.1). All products and services—as do consumers—have life cycles. So the particular stage at which the product or service is, has a direct bearing on the emphasis that must be placed on the other mix components, and since the purpose of the life-cycle is to measure the various stages of growth, the measurements enable the company's management to make decisions about whether to continue selling a product or offering a particular service.

Promotion

Developing a good quality product is not a guarantee that it will sell well in the market. Effective promotion is essential in today's competitive environment. It allows the small firm to communicate with potential consumers. In a small business, promotion could be handled by the owner/manager or a sales person. This may include setting the promotion strategy, the budget, displays and other media such as direct mail advertising.

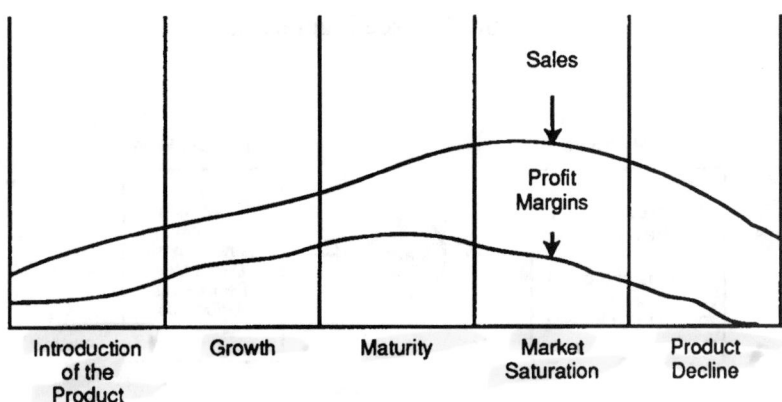

Figure 15.1. The product life cycle.

Advertising strategy is based on the target market and the marketing strategy. In general, the advertising strategy is intended to Inform, Remind or Persuade the consumer to buy the product.

Media Selection

Deciding which media the small business should select is essential to the effective implementation of the advertising strategy. The following critical factors must be considered in media selection:

1. The target market to be reached.
2. The type of product and media suitability.
3. The cost and advertising budget.

For example, television advertising is more expensive for the small business compared with other media such as the newspaper or direct mail. Also, certain types of products may not be suitable for television advertising, while others require demonstration. In other words, matching the target market and the media is crucial for an effective advertising strategy. Figure 15.2 summarizes the critical factors and types of media available to the small business.

Pricing Strategies

The pricing strategy is essential to the small business' survival and growth. In setting the pricing strategy the small business must consider the internal and external environment. The internal environment includes the company's objectives and strategy, the marketing mix and above all the cost. The external factors include the demand, the competition and the socioeconomic factors.[5]

The small business can pursue different pricing strategies such as cost-plus, market skimming, market penetration, complementary (razor and blades), and flexible pricing strategy. Let us discuss each strategy briefly (see Figure 15.3).

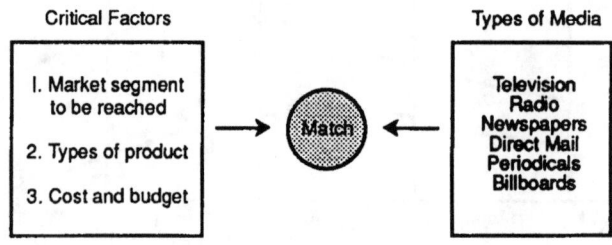

Figure 15.2. Media selection.

Pricing Strategies	When to Use
Cost-plus (full, or variable)	Mass merchandising, in-bidding, cut-throat competition
Market skimming	New product or technology
Market penetration	New product or technology; to capture large market share
Flexible pricing	To fit different customer needs
Prestige pricing	Psychological satisfaction

Figure 15.3. Alternative pricing strategies.

The Cost-Plus Strategy

This involves basically adding a percentage mark-up to the full cost, or variable cost. The strategy is simple and very popular among small business.

Market Skimming Strategy

Small firms introducing a new product or technology in the market may pursue this strategy. It involves charging a premium and setting a high initial price for the product to allow the firm to skim the market. The price is then lowered in later stages to capture a larger segment of the market.

Market Penetration Strategy

This strategy involves setting a relatively low price for the new product or technology and thus captures a large market share.

Complementary Product Strategy

Better known as razor and blades strategy, this involves setting a low price on one item and making profit from the other item such as blades (razor) or films (camera).

Flexible Pricing

The small business may choose to set different pricing systems to fit different customers. This strategy allows the firm to adjust the price to customer needs, location, early payment, and large volume purchase.

Prestige Pricing

This involves setting a higher price to attract a certain segment of the market. This strategy implies that the buyer sees some differences in the product, or may get certain satisfaction associated with a high priced prestigious item.

Marketing Planning

The basic purpose of the marketing plan is to bring all facets of the company's marketing strategy into perspective such that it will enable the entrepreneur to meet his or her objectives in getting his/her products and/or services to satisfied customers at a profit to the organization. This means that the small businessman has made an assessment of the market, examined the market segments, whether they are classified as targets or niches, analyzed competition and environmental forces, culminating in a forecast of total market potential and an assessment of the current market share. With the company's objectives clearly in mind, the market strategy that is most likely to achieve these objectives has been set. There now remains the development of the marketing plan, the vehicle which incorporates all these elements, including those of the marketing mix.

In essence, a marketing plan is a detailed, written plan that lays out the steps that a company must take to create customers, and in so doing achieve its sales and marketing objectives.

There are many forms and types of marketing plans and each organization may well have specific needs and individual requirements. The following will, however, serve as a suggested outline of a marketing plan that could be used as a guide for any small business.

1. Mission statement—What business are you in?
2. The small business' objectives.
3. Marketing objectives for the next three years—these could be quite specific for the first year and somewhat more general for the subsequent ones.
4. The products/services concept—brief description by product/service lines, including proposed changes and any recent changes that would affect marketing goals.
5. Target markets—description of market/segments/niches that have been defined.
6. Strategic directions:
    A. Overall strategy
    B. Competitive strategies
    C. Promotion strategies
    D. Pricing strategy
7. The marketing budget.
8. Implementation and measurement of timetables and benchmarks.
9. Review and evaluation schedule—to ensure follow-up by responsible individuals and continuity of action to the plan. Figure 15.4 provides some guidelines for effective marketing in small business.

SUMMARY

Marketing represents the truly dynamic aspect of a successful business operation. We have described a number of marketing tools such as; the marketing research required to obtain information that identifies the target market or niche; and the formulation and implementation of the marketing strategy that would permit the company to concentrate on the most

Critical Issues	Sources and Basis of Judgement
Market Research	
1. Scope	Define your market segment
	Define precisely what you need to know
2. The Survey	Design the survey to answer the following questions:
	Who are my customers?
	What kind of people are they?
	Where do they live?
	What are their purchasing habits?
	What do they know about my business?
	Through which advertising media can I most effectively reach them?
3. Types of market research	Internal information
	Secondary research
	Primary research
Marketing Strategy	Market penetration
	Market development
	Product development
	Market segmentation
Marketing Mix	The four "P's"—product, place, price and promotion
Pricing Strategy	Cost-plus
	Market skimming
	Market penetration
	Flexible pricing
	Prestige pricing
Advertising Strategy	The target market
	The type of product
	The cost and budget allocated

Figure 15.4. Guidelines for effective marketing in small business.

effective use of the 4 P elements. These data will form the basis for the marketing plan which, in turn, will be a key ingredient to the success of the enterprise.

NOTES

1. W. M. Greenfield, *Developing New Ventures* (New York: Harper & Row, Publishers 1989), p. 69.
2. W. M. Greenfield, *Developing New Ventures,* p. 89.
3. Theodore Levitt, "Marketing Success Through Differentiation of Anything," *Harvard Business Review* (February 1980), p. 83.
4. N. Scarborough and T. Zimmerer, *Effective Small Business Management,* 2. ed (Ohio: Merrill Publishing Co., 1988).
5. Philip Kotler, *Marketing* (Englewood Cliffs, New Jersey: Prentice-Hall Inc., 1987).

THE ENTREPRENEUR

H. Ross Perot—The Leader
Perot Systems Corp.

Hailed by the publication *Inc* as "The Hottest Entrepreneur in America in 1988," H. Ross Perot, the Chief Executive Officer of the company that bears his name, was born in 1930 in the depths of the great depression. The son of a Texas cotton broker, his introduction to business began at the early age of 11, delivering newspapers. A four year stint in the navy lead to a sales position with IBM. In his first year as an IBM salesman, he made so much money that a promotion would have resulted in a pay cut. He filled an entire year's sales quota three weeks into the year. While still at IBM, he came up with the idea of selling customers computer services along with their hardware. Unable to get a favourable reaction from the company, Perot formed EDS in June, 1962, with $1,000 of his wife's savings. Over the next 19 years, EDS grew to $947 million in revenue and 14,000 employees. In 1984, he sold EDS to General Motors for $2.5 billion, but two years later, in 1986, a parting of the ways took place whereby GM board members voted to pay Perot approximately $750 million to move his interest farther afield. Limited by a clause in the separation agreement that forbade him to hire away EDS employees before June, 1988, Perot diverted his energies into other interests—$20 million to assist Steven Jobs with his NEXT program; helped finance I. M. Pei's Morton H. Meyerson Symphony Center in Dallas, and his son's facilties for "global manufacturing" near Dallas. Honouring the agreement with GM to the letter, on June 1, 1988, Perot announced that eight EDS managers were joining him to form Perot Systems and that the first project that the company would undertake was to help the U.S. Postal Service get its costs under control—to bring it into the twenty-first century.

While Perot's confrontations with General Motors are legendary and received widespread coverage, he also received extensive publicity as a result of the book *Leadership Secrets of Attila the Hun*. He commented that "Attila reminds you that a leader lives in the field with his troops. In a classless society, you can't afford to separate yourself from the Huns; you've got to be the first guy to take the bullet; and you can't lead anybody unless your people trust and respect you. The main thing is to treat other people the way you'd like to be treated. There's something in each person that screams out, 'I'm special.' And it's part of your job as a leader to deal with each person as a special individual."

Perot says that he has never had a problem delegating responsibility and authority and that his experience was that people who are really, really, bright find it difficult to delegate, because they literally can do the job better themselves. Claiming to be average himself, Perot says, "I know I need help, so I go and get the very best people."

Source: *Success* (March, 1989), p. 53; *Inc.* (January 1989), pp. 54–69; *Forbes* (October 23, 1989), p. 156; Jay A. Conger, *The Charismatic Leader* (Jossey-Bass Publishers 1989), p. 95.

_____ **CASE 1** _____

Blue Sky Travel Limited

In March 1987, Jim Elliott, President of Blue Sky Travel Limited, Mississauga, Ontario, was reviewing the operations of his agency and plans for the years ahead. Mr. Elliott anticipated a substantial increase in the volume of business his agency would generate next year and hoped it would continue the growth experienced in recent years.

The lease for his present office space was due to expire in May 1987, and Mr. Elliott believed he was faced with four possible courses of action. He could renegotiate his present lease to include additional space; move to another location; buy a small office building and locate his agency in it; or stay in his present space and open a branch office nearby.

Mr. Elliott knew that there were many factors to be considered in each case. One thing he felt certain of was that more capital would be required than he could finance out of retained earnings. Therefore, he would be required to develop some plan for outside funding.

As a first step, Mr. Elliott decided to take a copy of his financial statements for 1985 and 1986 (Exhibits 1, 2, 3, and 4) to his banker, Mr. MacPherson, and discuss the matter with him. After studying the financial data, Mr. MacPherson asked Mr. Elliott to prepare projected monthly statements for the year ending December 1987 listing earnings, cash flow, and a balance sheet.

Acting on the advice of Mr. MacPherson, Mr. Elliott set down what he thought might be points that would have a bearing on his company's activities in the year ahead.

OBJECTIVES OF THE COMPANY

1. Continue increase of market penetration.
2. Expand physical plant in keeping with the image of industry and service functions.
3. Continue to improve quality of service while maintaining operation costs at an appropriate level.

ASSUMPTIONS UPON WHICH THE STATEMENTS FOR THE YEAR 1987 WOULD BE BASED

1. Twenty-five percent sales increase over 1986 on an annual basis.
2. Same gross profit margin (percentage) in 1987 as in 1986.

3. Ten percent increase in administration and selling expenses over 1986.
4. Collection of accounts receivable within thirty days.
5. Current liabilities consisting of accounts payable, taxes deducted at source, deposits received in advance and provision for corporate taxes would be held to $94,680 month by month (see the projected monthly balance sheets in the following exhibits).
6. Labour costs and any interest expenses paid as incurred.
7. Set aside $600 a month for estimated income tax payments.
8. Sales period categorized as:
   peak months: December, January, February, June, July and August
   shoulder months: March, September, November
   low months: April, May, October
9. Any consideration of the purchase of fixed assets would be deferred to a later date.
10. Cash sales account for twenty-five percent of total sales.
11. Capital stock remains at $10,000 (see the projected monthly balance sheets in the following exhibits).
12. Reserve for doubtful accounts, $620 per month.
13. Accumulated depreciation at the rate of $260 per month.

Exhibit 1. Blue Sky Travel Limited Balance Sheet (as at December 31).

Assets	1985	1986
Current Assets		
Cash	$ 6,428	$ (1,213)
Time deposits	18,000	19,500
Accounts receivable	95,683	134,951
Prepaid expenses	524	603
Total Current Assets	$120,635	$153,841
Fixed Assets		
Office equipment, leasehold improvements, automobiles at cost	$ 15,347	$ 28,136
Less: accumulated depreciation	9,540	13,663
Total Fixed Assets	$ 5,807	$ 14,473
Total Assets	$126,442	$168,314

Liabilities		
Current Liabilities		
Accounts payable	$ 65,489	$ 89,222
Taxes deducted at source	1,143	1,271
Deposits received in advance	2,749	1,596
Provision for corporation taxes	2,543	2,591
Total Current Liabilities	$ 71,924	$ 94,680

Shareholders' Equity		
Capital Stock		
Authorized: 3,000 preferred shares, 6 percent non-cumulative, redeemable of a par value of $10 each		
Issued and fully paid: 1,000 common shares	$ 10,000	$ 10,000
Retained earnings	44,518	63,634
Total Capital	$ 54,518	$ 73,634
Total Liabilities and Equity	$126,442	$168,314

Exhibit 2.   Blue Sky Travel Limited. Statement of Earnings (for the year ending December 31).

	1985	1986
Revenue		
Net sales	$1,820,447	$2,124,706
Purchases	1,675,273	1,943,155
Gross Earnings	$ 145,174	$ 181,551
Expenses		
Selling expenses (Schedule A)	$ 103,862	$ 122,810
Administrative expenses (Schedule B)	21,849	32,921
	$ 125,711	$ 155,731
Earnings from operations	19,463	25,820
Other income (Schedule C)	2,340	4,887
Earnings before income taxes	$ 21,803	$ 30,707
Income Taxes	5,823	8,291
Net earnings for the year	$ 15,980	$ 22,416

Exhibit 3. Blue Sky Travel Limited. Schedules to Statement of Earnings (for the year ended December 31).

	1985	1986
Schedule A—Selling, Expenses		
Wages	$ 79,860	$ 95,436
Advertising	2,092	1,153
Sales promotion	4,216	5,191
Travelling expenses	3,173	2,624
Delivery expenses	395	969
Telephone telegraph	8,012	8,356
Subscriptions/donations	1,696	2,568
Commissions	1,059	1,249
Automobiles—expenses	2,522	2,581
—depreciation	837	2,683
	$103,862	$122,810
Schedule B—Administrative Expenses		
Printing and stationery	$ 3,400	$ 4,789
General and office expenses	1,713	2,716
Postage	1,461	1,520
Interest and bank charges	580	753
Professional services	1,675	2,050
Rent	3,600	5,250
Electricity	314	282
Repairs and maintenance	577	614
Taxes	424	643
Unemployment insurance	763	1,337
Provincial pension fund	848	997
Insurance	994	1,466
Health insurance	608	645
Minimum wage commission	59	72
Workmen's compensation insurance	69	94
Bad debts	3,147	6,768
Depreciation:		
Office equipment	745	1,604
Leasehold improvements	872	1,321
	$ 21,849	$ 32,921
Schedule C—Other Income		
Investments and exchange	$ 2,340	$ 4,887

Exhibit 4. Blue Sky Travel Limited. Statement of Source and Application of Funds (for the year ended December 31).

	1985	1986
Source of Funds		
Net earnings for the year	$15,980	$22,416
Add: Expenses requiring no cash outlay; Depreciation of fixed assets	2,454	5,608
Funds provided by operations	$18,434	$28,024
Proceeds from disposition of automobiles	—	2,700
	$18,434	$30,724
Application of Funds		
Purchase of rolling stock	—	$ 9,690
Addition to leasehold improvements	—	2,244
Purchase of office furniture	1,924	5,640
Dividends paid	2,400	3,300
	$ 4,324	$20,874
Increase in working capital	$14,110	$ 9,850
Working capital at beginning of the year	35,201	49,311
Working capital at end of the year	$49,311	$59,161

Exhibit 5. Blue Sky Travel Limited. Projected statement of monthly earnings (for the year ending December 31, 1987).

	Jan.	Feb.	Mar.	Apr.	May	June	July	Aug.	Sept.	Oct.	Nov.	Dec.	Total
Net Sales													
Less: purchases													
Gross Earnings													
Selling Expenses													
Wages and commissions													
Advertising and sales prom.													
Telephone and telegraph													
Travel and delivery expenses													
Subscriptions and donations													
Automobiles—exp. and depre.													
Total Selling Expenses													
Administrative Expenses													
Printing and stationery													
Professional services													
Rent													
Administrative and fin. exp.*													
Fringe benefits**													
Provision for bad debts													
Depreciation													
Total Administrative Expenses													
Total Selling and Admin. Exp.													
Income before income taxes													
Income taxes													
Net income													

*Administrative and financial expenses include: postage, general and office expenses, electricity and maintenance, taxes, interest and bank charges.
**Fringe benefits include: unemployment insurance, pension fund, insurance, health insurance, minimum wage commission, workmen's compensation.

Exhibit 6. Blue Sky Travel Limited. Projected statement of monthly cash flow (for the year ending December 31, 1987).

	Jan.	Feb.	Mar.	Apr.	May	June	July	Aug.	Sept.	Oct.	Nov.	Dec.	Total
Cash Receipts													
1. Accounts receivable													
2. Cash sales													
3. Time deposits													
4. Total cash receipts													
Cash Disbursements													
5. Purchases													
6. Total selling expenses													
7. Total administrative exp.													
8. Income taxes													
9. Total cash disbursements													
10. Cash over (under)—lines 1 to 4 minus line 9													
11. Cash balance—beginning													
12. Cash Balance—end—lines 10 and 11													

Exhibit 7. Blue Sky Travel Limited. Projected statement of monthly balance sheets (for the year ending December 31, 1987).

	Opening Balance Sheet	Jan.	Feb.	Mar.	Apr.	May	June	July	Aug.	Sept.	Oct.	Nov.	Dec.
Current Assets													
Cash	$ (1,213)												
Time deposits	19,500												
Accounts receivable	147,305												
Less: reserve for doubtful accounts	(12,354)												
Prepaid expenses	603												
Total current assets	153,841												
Fixed assets													
Office equipment, leasehold improvements, automobiles at cost	28,136												
Less: accumulated deprec.	13,663												
Total fixed assets	14,473												
Total assets	168,314												
Liabilities													
Total current liabilities	94,680	$94,680											$94,680
Shareholders' Equity													
Capital stock	10,000												
Retained earnings	63,534												
Total shareholders' equity	73,634												
Total liabilities and shareholders' equity	$168,314												

Required: calculate the following ratios for the years 1985 and 1986.

Ratio | *Meaning*

1. Liquidity

a) Current Ratio

$$\frac{C.A.}{C.L.}$$

Ability to meet short-term obligations

b) Quick Ratio $\dfrac{C.A.-Inventory}{C.L.}$

Acid Test Ratio

Ability to meet short-term obligations without liquidating its inventories

2. *Profitability*

a) $\dfrac{Gross\ Profit\ (margin)}{Sales}$

Profitability after cost of manufacturing & inventory expenses

b) $\dfrac{Net\ Profit}{Sales}$

Return on $ of sales

c) Return on Net Worth

Return on what is invested in the company (R.O.I.)

$$\frac{Net\ Profit\ A.T.}{Net\ Worth}$$

3. *Leverage*

a) $\dfrac{Total\ Debt}{Total\ Assets}$

% of funds provided by creditors

b) Times Interest Earned

$$\frac{Income\ B.T.\ +\ Interest}{Interest\ Charges}$$

Ability to meet interest payments

c) Debt/Net Worth

$$\frac{Total\ Debt}{Net\ Worth}$$

Relationship of what is owed to creditors to what owners have in the company

4.   *Activity*

    a) Average Collection Period

$$\frac{\text{Accounts Receivable}}{\text{Sales}/365}$$ Ability to recover cash from receivables

    b) Inventory Turnover

$$\frac{\text{C. of G. Sold}}{\text{Inventory}} \text{ or } \frac{\text{Sales}}{\text{Inventory}}$$ Ability to generate sales on inventory

    c) Total Assets Turnover

$$\frac{\text{Sales}}{\text{Total Assets}}$$ Company's turnover of all assets

Paisley Sportswear Ltd.

Paisley Sportswear Ltd. is a women's garment firm located in the North End of Montreal. The assets are held entirely by members of the founding family, the McLeods. Angus McLeod, the grandson of the founder, is the current CEO. Paisley has a full-time work force of 42 people, which they supplement in peak periods with seasonal and part-time employees. They produce several types of better-quality items such as shirts, skirts and blouses in relatively conservative styles and materials. Their focus is clearly the upper-middle and upper-class woman, whose fashion statement is not merely that she has arrived: the Paisley customer's grandmother may have arrived, but today's Paisley woman regards arrivists as gauche. Paisley fashions are marketed in "better" stores across North America under their own label, but a growing portion of their output is contract work for resale as house brands in specialty shops and top department stores. Accepting those contracts was a painful decision for the McLeod family, who regarded it as the first step toward becoming yet another mass producer. However, the current generation was able to force the decision past the family on the condition that no compromise of quality be accepted. A similar crisis occurred a generation earlier when the firm took the daring step of experimenting with colors beyond white and pastels, and when it became evident that permanent press fabric was inevitable.

Angus McLeod was unresponsive when asked about corporate strategy, saying in effect that he does not think in those terms. He stated that his objective was to produce an honest, lasting value at a fair price, and that his sales and profitability had been taking good care of themselves without any explicit planning. His brother, Keith McLeod, presently the director of operations, voiced essentially the same sentiments. He commented that everyone in the firm has been running at near full capacity for years without achieving more than keeping up with increases in orders. Angus' son-in-law Luc Bergeron, a recent marketing graduate, is nominally in charge of that function. However, he describes his real role as one of recording, expediting, and following up orders from established customers. Luc's comment about strategy was particularly pointed. "Mr. McLeod's corporate strategy is clear. He is a portfolio manager with a one-item portfolio: If we have a business strategy, it is to keep doing what has worked for us in the past." Porter would describe this as a niche strategy.

The work process at Paisley is extremely labor-intensive. The plant was last modernized about six years ago, and is bright, clean, and a pleasant environment by industry standards. Like many small firms modernization has come as new generations make their impressions

This case was prepared by Professor Ron Crawford. Revised by Professor A. B. Ibrahim, 1990.

on the traditional ways of doing things. The business side of the enterprise is now converted to the use of personal computers, although hard copies of all important documents are kept in parallel. Patterns are now stored for most regular items in their line, and that capacity is linked to a computer controlled cutting operation. Other items are still cut by skilled cutters from hard patterns. All other steps in the production process are carried out by handwork. The sewing, pressing, finishing, and packing operations utilize modern, well maintained machines, equipped with a variety of jigs and fixtures that aid proper feeding and alignment. However, the machines are all manually fed, actuated, and off-loaded. In outline, the process looks much like any other large batch or mass production process, with each work station contributing a limited cluster of sewing or finished operations. The only way in which a visitor might distinguish Paisley's production from those of comparable firms would be in the time allotted per garment.

The production work force at Paisley, with the exception of the few highly skilled employees who work with designs, patterns, and cutting, is composed almost exclusively of semi-skilled machine operators. There was general agreement among the managers interviewed that the supply of production workers is the critical problem with which Paisley will have to deal in the future, and that labor costs would become an issue as well. Historically Paisley, along with most similar manufacturers, was able to staff positions as needed from a seemingly inexhaustible supply of previously trained and highly motivated immigrants. Their countries of origin varied over the years as one wave of immigrants succeeded the next, but the fundamental ingredients of basic sewing skills, a strong work ethic, and high standards of work quality were already in place.

The influx of trained garment workers to North America began to decrease in the 1960s and has slowed to a trickle. The principal reason has been improved opportunity and stability in countries with established garment industries, coupled with more stringent regulation of overseas recruiting. This has left Paisley in a precarious position. The current production employees represent a rapidly aging resource. The average age is now 52. Simultaneously their prospects for re-recruiting suitable candidates are greatly diminished. Luc Bergeron stated the situation most succinctly.

> "In today's labor market we are finding two kinds of people, the ones who understand the need for quality and have a strong work ethic to see our jobs as low-paid, monotonous, and dead-ended. Those people are out to entrench themselves in the high-tech and service sectors, and we would do the same if we were in their position. The other kind of person we encounter we frankly don't want to hire. It really isn't that hard for us to train an unskilled person to do most of our jobs—if they have the eye/hand coordination needed, the tasks can be learned in a matter of weeks. What we cannot do successfully is to teach them to recognize when a job is performed well enough and to care about it."

The firm has been able to maintain its work force in recent years only by having a policy of trying large numbers of applicants and letting them go if they cannot perform to Paisley standards. The supply issue is a major barrier to growth already, and is projected to become critical even for current volumes within the next several years.

The McLeod family, as noted, do not characteristically think in strategic terms. It is clear to them, however, that a crisis is imminent, and they know how many of their contemporaries in the trade are facing the same issue. The family feels a strong obligation to maintaining the firm and its traditions, to remaining in Montreal, and to their many loyal employees. As experts in human resource management and its relationship to corporate action, what can we offer the McLeods in evolving a corporate strategy and a human resource program that support one another?

Porteous Manufacturing Company Limited

In March 1976, Mr. David Porteous, President of the Porteous Manufacturing Company Limited of Lachute, Quebec had just returned from two weeks of skiing at Vail, Colorado. The company, a family-owned business, had manufactured steel display cabinets and component parts for many years, employing 45 people.

On reaching his desk after his vacation, the first thing Mr. Porteous found was the following memo from Paul Belanger, his plant manager:

> While you were away, we received a Petition for Certification from the Amalgamated Steel Workers of the World which asked for collective bargaining representation rights for the following group of our employees:
>
>> "All employees within the meaning of the Quebec Labour Code in the plant and office, and including salesmen, quality assurance technicians, plant guards and working foremen."
>
> Initially, I was disappointed that our employees, many of whom have been with us for twenty years, would do such a thing because we have always got along with all of them and have done many special things for them, such as the turkeys we distributed last Christmas.
>
> My immediate reaction was to try to get to the bottom of this and find out who are the instigators. I identified three employees in the Finishing and Coating Department named Lavalléé, Lamontagne and Lariviére who I fired immediately. They have since filed a complaint claiming that we should reinstate them because they were fired for Union activities. A copy of the Petition for Certification and of each of the complaints is attached hereto, and I am presently working on a write-up in each of the three cases of the fired employees to accumulate reasons which we can use to justify their dismissal. I will forward these to you when they are completed.
>
> On the day after the Petition was received, I had a visit from one Joe Desjardins who claimed to be the Union organizer. I told him that we would have no truck or trade with the Union, that if they came in we would probably go out of business and that we are certain that our own employees didn't want this but had been intimidated or misled by the Union which had instigated everything from the outside. He didn't answer anything I said, but merely smiled. He left me a copy of the Union's demands, which are also attached and, as you will see, they are ridiculous because they want increases of over a dollar an hour and, if we give in to this, we are certainly priced out of the market and might as well close our doors. I have not contacted the Labour

Department or the company lawyer since I did not know whether you would want to involve the lawyers at this stage, and it seems to me we can handle this by ourselves.

One other thing should be mentioned: my assistant, Andre Robert, tells me that his brother-in-law knows of a chap whose name is John Ostiguy who is in the business of helping companies fight unions. Apparently, what he does is to plant a few key people on the floor posing as employees and to try to organize a little shop association to defeat the International Union. He would want $5,000 from us on the side before commencing work and pretty well guarantees success. It seems that his people are tough guys and pretty hard to say no to. A number of employees have also come to me privately to say that they didn't know what the Union card was when they were asked to sign it, that they thought it was some kind of raffle ticket, that they personally never paid any Union dues or initiation fees. Also, as you know, the plant guards are not our employees, but come from the Rourke Security Agency.

I would recommend that you write to the Labour Department demanding a vote by secret ballot as the only way of finding out the true intentions of our employees.

If you were Mr. Porteous, what would you do?

ALFA Electronics, Inc.

ALFA Electronics Inc. was founded in Boston in 1975 by J. R. Gordon, a computer engineer. Mr. Gordon had developed a successful design for a new type of electronic security alarm system and under his leadership ALFA emerged as a major force in the electronic security alarm market. However, since 1988 the company has been experiencing a decline in profit and market share. The decline was said to have been a result of generally poor economic conditions in the New England and Quebec areas and higher overall costs of doing business.

However, Mr. Gordon was concerned with the growth and strategic position of his company in the next decade. In May 1983, Gordon hired John Hunt, a recent M.B.A. graduate from a leading business school, as a corporate planner and instructed him to prepare a strategic plan for ALFA as soon as possible.

John Hunt, 33, had worked in corporate planning for over 5 years with a leading American electronics firm in New York before taking his M.B.A., and was well qualified for his new position.

John worked assiduously during July, reading ALFA reports and its Mission Statement. The Mission Statement described the company as "a highly innovative firm in the electronic alarm field. . . ." The statement went on to outline ALFA's goals: "to grow and earn at a rate commensurate with the best in the industry." Throughout the corporation there existed a strong emphasis on growth and return on equity.

John also set out to gather information about the internal capabilities of ALFA in different functional areas such as production, finance and marketing. Functional managers were invited to write a brief report assessing their area's strengths and weaknesses. The following is a summary of their report.

PRODUCTION

ALFA produces electronic security alarm systems and has recently introduced a new line of fire protection equipment. The electronic security alarm system is of superior quality and technically advanced. However, ALFA has very little experience in fire protection equipment. The company has recently modernized its production facilities, but production lines are working at only 80 percent capacity.

This case was prepared for class discussion rather than to illustrate either effective or ineffective handling of an administrative situation. Copyright © 1985 by A. B. Ibrahim, Revised edition, 1989.

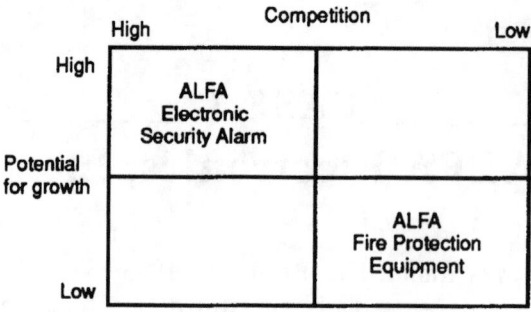

Figure 1. Market share.

FINANCE

The company has a strong financial position. ALFA has a very high liquidity ratio and its debt ratio is below average in this type of business. However, the inventory turnover for fire protection equipment is very low.

MARKETING

The company employs three energetic sales people who travel extensively to Toronto, Montréal and Vancouver on a salary commission base. Lately, however, the sales people have been complaining that ALFA's fire protection equipment is not doing well in the market.

ALFA has 55 percent of the New England and Quebec security alarm market, mostly in Boston and Montreal. Its main competitors are small Swedish and Dutch firms. However ALFA is facing stiff competition in the fire protection equipment line, with three large American and Canadian firms competing for 86 percent of the market and more than 30 small firms competing for the remaining 14 percent.

Demand analysis indicated customers prefer ALFA electronic alarm systems because of their high quality and advanced technology. Demand analysis also indicates an increase in demand for alarm systems in Quebec because of provincial regulations regarding security in public buildings. However, demand for ALFA's fire protection is expected to decline because of stiff competition (large competitors depend on mass production, low price, high quality and a large dealer network).

External analysis revealed that Vermont state has started a 5 year tax exemption program for small business in the high technology industry.

Based on the above data John utilized the matrix in Figure 1 to identify the business growth rate and market share for the electronic fire alarm and fire protection equipment that ALFA produces.

John decided that there was a need for selecting alternative strategies for ALFA and making a strategic choice after assessing each alternative. John had come up with two alternatives available to ALFA: (1) to drop the fire protection equipment line and to focus on ALFA Electronic Fire Alarm systems, (2) to pursue an aggressive growth strategy in both fire alarm and fire protection. John had to assess each alternative before reporting his final recommendations.

Francis Hankin & Co., Limited (A)

In the spring of 1970, Mr. E. A. Hankin, President of Francis Hankin & Co. Limited, Montreal, Canada sat down in his office to reflect on an important decision he had just made. For some years he had been studying the effect of family control of the Company on the future of its business. Now the time had come for action to be taken regarding a major change of control from the Hankin family to Company employees. After several meetings with his two vice-presidents, Mr. M. L. Tucker and Mr. E. R. Fox, to review this important subject, Mr. Hankin decided to offer a substantial part of the family's stock for sale and thus relinquish control of the Company.

However, the price at which the family's interest would be sold was crucial as well as the actual format that would be involved in making the transfer. These two points were of fundamental concern not only to Mr. Hankin but also to Mr. Tucker, Mr. Fox and the other employees of the Company.

HISTORY

The Company was founded in 1905 by Francis Hankin, who had immigrated to Canada from England and began operations as a representative of U.K. manufacturers of steel and iron products. Mr. Hankin soon started buying and selling on his own and found a ready market for products in the municipal waterworks field, such as watermeters and valves. At that time, few, if any, of these products were being manufactured in Canada, while U.S. firms were too busy catering to their own market. Thus, by importing from England, Mr. Hankin could meet demands and establish a relationship with municipalities which to-date had been an important aspect in the Company's growth and nature of business.

The Company started to grow, was incorporated in 1916 and specialized more and more in the expanding waterworks field. When Canadian manufacturers, attracted by the growth of this field, began producing these products in the early twenties, many of them decided to sell to municipalities through the established distribution network of the Francis Hankin Company.

Up to the early twenties, the Company's activities were confined to sales of predominantly waterworks products. Then as a market began to develop in the water filtration field, Francis Hankin obtained the selling rights for pressure filters made by two U.S. firms. Design and installation was included in their contracts, thus necessitating a greater amount

This case was prepared by Fred D. Wiersema under the direction of Professor W. H. Ellis of McGill University as a basis for class discussion rather than to illustrate either effective or ineffective handling of an administrative situation. Copyright © 1978 by W. H. Ellis.

of technical and engineering know-how of Company employees. Unfortunately, one of these U.S. firms went out of business shortly thereafter, while the other decided to set up its own Canadian selling and installation division.

These drawbacks did not stop the Company from developing its business with municipalities. The treatment of sewage was beginning to increase, which led Mr. Hankin to set up a distribution agreement for the U.S. and Canadian markets with a U.K. equipment manufacturer. After about five years, the depression hit North America and municipalities were no longer allowed to buy imported equipment. This, together with patent problems that came up, caused the end of this market for the Company.

Another developing municipal activity was refuse incineration and the Company went into this field by acting as agents for a Cleveland company that made incinerators. This firm provided the engineering know-how while Francis Hankin & Co. took care of the construction aspects of incinerator installation. Construction aspects like chimney building were sub-contracted by the Company and all this led to a take-off in the field of incinerators and chimneys for industrial purposes. The Company's staff had now acquired the know-how to design and build their own incinerators and chimneys and started to sell these under the Hankin name.

Throughout the Company's history, a step-by-step approach had been followed by entering a new field on a sales agent basis, until enough knowledge had been acquired to operate independently. Over the years the Company's focus had shifted gradually from a sales agent merchandising role to technical, engineering activities and since the fifties considerable growth had been realized in the latter area.

While merchandising activities had been very profitable initially, growth in this field started to slow down in the late sixties. This was due to two factors: first, manufacturers were in some instances entering the market directly and second, top management of the Company now consisted of engineers more interested in this part of the business and not fully trained for straight merchandise selling.

Shortly after the second world war, Mr. Francis Hankin turned over control of the business to his son, E. A. Hankin, who became the Company's second president.

OPERATIONS

In its Montreal head-office and branch offices in Toronto and Ottawa, the Company employed approximately 93 people in 1970. Its operations extended to all parts of the country, either through personnel working out of its offices, or through outside agents.

The Company's business centered on the control and mitigation of air and water pollutants. It had four operating divisions, as follows:

- The Municipal Merchandise Division was involved in the distribution of water-works products and services across Canada. It also distributed a variety of other products to municipalities, including sewer collector maintenance products and water flow measurement products.

- The Water Pollution Control Division provided a broad range of services to municipal and industrial markets. These services included the supply and installation of process equipment and systems for water, sewage and waste treatment plants.
- The Solid Wastes Disposal Systems & Stacks Division was active in both the areas of municipal refuse/garbage disposal and concrete chimney construction for industry. The division designed, purchased, installed and constructed units that are used in these fields.
- The Pipeline Contract Services Division was a new division that was started in 1969. It offered a contract service to clean sewage collection and plant drainage systems. Only available in Ontario, this service catered to both municipalities and industry.

The operating divisions showed steady growth over the years with the result that sales in 1970 had reached over $7.5 million and net profits after taxes, $67,000. Projections for the year 1971 were nearly $10 million and $110,000 respectively. (Financial information is contained in Exhibits 1, 2 and 3).

SHAREHOLDING AND OWNERSHIP

The Francis Hankin Company had remained as a private company controlled by the Hankin family ever since its foundation in 1905. During the 1950s, senior management and other employees, former employees and their children had been given the opportunity to buy stock in the Company, which had resulted in the following shareholding structure at the beginning of 1970:

Table 1. List of Shareholders as of January 1970.

Hankin Family Holdings		9,660
Management & Key Employee Group		
G. Decaqueray	500	
E. R Fox	700	
S. Stocker	600	
M. L. Tucker	500	
	2,300	2,300
Other		
A total of 12 shareholders holding as many as 1,500 and as few as 50 shares		5,600
Total Shares Outstanding		17,560

Each share certificate contained the proviso that except for transfer to relatives, shares had to be offered to employees before being made available to the open market.

SHAREHOLDERS' INTEREST

It was Mr. E. A. Hankin's intention to sell a total of 6,500 of his and his sister's shares, so that control of the Company would change from the family to a group of key employee shareholders.

In assessing the options that were open to him, he realised that such a change would have implications for the Hankin family, as well as for the senior management and minority shareholders. In fact, while the interests of these groups were to some extent overlapping, he believed that it would be difficult to devise a plan for stock transfer which would completely satisfy all concerned.

Starting with his own interests, Mr. Hankin explained why he wanted to offer a portion of his shares for sale:

> From a strictly personal point of view, with the rate of taxation and my own rate of expenditure for the standard of living that I have maintained, I have not been able to accumulate sufficient savings to cover succession duties on the majority holding of the stock that I own. The Company's policy, over which I have had considerable control, has been to retain earnings in the Company. This has had the dual effect of reducing the amount of savings that I might have accumulated and increasing the value of my shares for succession duty, thereby the need for other liquid assets in my estate.

Mr. Hankin further mentioned that he had considered selling the majority interest to outsiders, who were constantly approaching him to sell out. From the standpoint of realising the maximum value for his shares, this would be the best method, yet, he turned down all approaches, because he preferred to continue his participation in the affairs of the Company for as long as he would be one of the major shareholders.

Besides this, he stated that:

> I am of the firm opinion that the success of the Company both in the past and in the future is dependent upon the initiative and flexibility of its management. Any sale to outsiders would restrict these requirements and both I and present management personnel are of the opinion that we wish to protect and continue our current method of operation. Also, while it may sound altruistic, I feel that I owe something to the existing management because of their efforts in building the Company to its present position. In actual fact, this is not completely altruistic in light of a possible sale because any purchaser would take into consideration in setting the price, the availability of the existing personnel.

With retirement facing him, Mr. Hankin believed that his inclination to take a more conservative point of view in order to protect his financial position might hinder the development of the Company. In his words:

> I am inclined to agree with the younger management that greater risks may be the correct decision for greater gains in the future and don't want to stand in the way of such a policy.

He summarized his point of view as follows:

> The Company has become too large to remain a family company yet is not large enough to go public. I wish to continue my association with the Company for some time and my primary objective is to develop a plan which will ensure the continuation of the management philosophy of the business, that is to say, to maintain a reasonable return on invested capital, a satisfactory living for the employees and of equal or more importance, the provision of a working environment and atmosphere satisfactory to all employees and of a nature where initiative and flexibility can flourish.

From the standpoint of non-family shareholders, Mr. Hankin's decision not to sell out to outsiders had several implications. It meant that they would not get a chance to sell their shares to an outsider at a handsome profit. On the other hand, they would not face the risk of outsiders buying a controlling share of the Company, instead of 100% of the stock, and cutting dividend payments. While Mr. Hankin's decision would mean that employees would be offered the advantage of a fair return on investment coupled with a continuation of the working environment they currently enjoyed, Mr. Hankin warned them that investment in shares would not guarantee employment nor would it give the owner of shares the right to take part in day-to-day management decisions.

Nevertheless, he was firmly convinced that the Company would be in good hands if Mr. Tucker and Mr. Fox were allowed the opportunity to become the principal shareholders of the Company. At the same time, Mr. Hankin did want to be sure that the price at which the stock changed hands was not only just and equitable to the new people, but represented an equally just and fair return to the existing members of the Hankin family.

CORPORATE STRUCTURE

The Board of Directors consisted of six members, divided between four employees and two outside personnel. The officers were all employee directors, consisting of a president and two vice presidents. The position of treasurer was combined with that of the president, while one of the vice presidents also acted as the secretary.

Mr. M. L. Tucker, vice president, operated out of the Montreal office and held 500 shares. Mr. E. R. Fox was the vice president in charge of the Ontario region and held 700 shares. These two men, as senior members of the Company, took a leading position in the Key Employee Group, formed to look into the purchase of shares from the Hankin family. (See Exhibit 4 for background data on Mr. Tucker and Mr. Fox.)

The management and Key Employee Group felt that it lacked the expertise to prepare an offer of purchase and also the precise details for making a transaction that would not only be feasible, but acceptable to both sides. Specifically, the advice and expertise sought covered the following points:

1. The value of Francis Hankin and Co. Limited in the market place if a controlling block of shares was available to prospective purchasers. The purchaser would have to undertake, however, to offer to all Company shareholders the same price per share offered for the controlling block of shares.
2. An estimate of the value which would be set by the Federal and Provincial Governments for Estate Tax purposes on the Hankin family controlled block of shares.
3. A range of "share price" that the management group could consider offering the Hankin family and rationale to back up that position.
4. An opinion on the group control concept and the practical problems that may arise. Specifically, advice was desired on whether this concept would be practical and if not, why not? Furthermore, could the concept be self-perpetuating?

5. Sources from which the Company might obtain additional working capital once the purchase negotiation had been completed. The sources of capital would have to keep in mind that the management and Key Employee Group would be retaining control. Any equity capital, therefore, would have to be content with a minority position.
6. The purchase transaction should keep in mind that the Hankin family wished to realize as much cash as possible and on the other hand, the Management group was equally anxious to put up as little cash as possible. Advice would also be sought on liquidity problems and possible solutions to them.
7. Expert opinion was needed on the legal and/or moral obligation towards minority shareholders who might very well be interested in selling their shares at the price negotiated between the Hankin family and the Management group.
8. Advice would be sought on the future of a company of this size, particularly with reference to the limitations imposed upon it by the Management Control Concept and its ability to finance expansion. Was such a concept practical?

Once the Key Employee Group had obtained the answers to these questions, they would feel more confident about being able to come to an agreement that would be acceptable to all concerned.

Exhibit 1. Francis Hankin & Co., Limited Select operating statistics 1953–1971.

	1953	1954	1955	1956	1957	1958
Sales Total	2,548,316	2,550,133	3,256,828	3,627,435	3,806,803	2,917,372
Gross Profit on Operations	465,660	522,738	614,780	574,381	636,871	628,536
% of Sales	18.25	20.50	18.88	15.83	16.73	21.54
Operating Expenses includ. depreciation	348,141	387,833	477,781	474,091	532,698	525,685
% of Sales	13.66	15.21	14.67	13.07	13.99	18.02
Net Profit before Taxes	117,518	134,904	136,998	100,289	104,172	102,851
% of Sales	4.58	5.29	4.21	2.76	2.74	3.53
% of Net Worth	41.39	40.58	36.81	24.82	23.68	21.68
Reserve for Income Taxes	60,628	60,000	61,000	42,000	42,000	41,000
Net Profit after Taxes	56,890	74,904	75,998	58,289	62,172	61,851
% of Sales	2.23	2.94	2.33	1.61	1.63	2.12
% of Net Worth	20.04	22.53	20.42	14.42	14.13	13.04
Dividends	26,340	26,340	26,340	26,340	26,340	26,340
Surplus	30,550	48,564	49,658	31,949	35,832	35,511
Earned Surplus Cumulative	108,313	156,877	196,536	228,486	264,319	299,830
Net Worth	283,913	332,477	372,136	404,086	439,919	474,430
Working Capital	258,581	303,538	306,868	339,219	231,778	324,974

Exhibit 1. (continued)

	1959	1960	1961	1962	1963	1964
Sales Total	3,824,627	3,267,296	3,104,806	3,523,300	3,752,886	4,971,874
Gross Profit on Operations	697,207	662,637	602,656	668,290	647,789	703,131
% of Sales	18.23	20.28	19.41	18.97	17.26	14.14
Operating Expenses includ. depreciation	547,624	564,464	521,226	569,908	582,628	639,962
% of Sales	14.32	17.28	16.79	16.18	15.52	12.87
Net Profit before Taxes	149,583	98,173	81,329	98,382	65,121	63,168
% of Sales	3.91	3.00	2.62	2.79	1.74	1.27
% of Net Worth	27.85	17.61	14.06	16.35	10.60	10.04
Reserve for Income Taxes	61,500	42,750	34,000	40,000	26,000	22,500
Net Profit after Taxes	88,083	55,423	47,329	58,382	39,121	40,668
% of Sales	2.30	1.70	1.52	1.66	1.04	.82
% of Net Worth	16.40	9.94	8.18	9.70	6.37	6.47
Dividends	26,340	35,120	26,340	35,120	26,340	26,340
Surplus	61,743	20,303	21,039	23,262	12,761	14,328
Earned Surplus Cumulative	361,573	381,877	402,916	426,179	438,960	453,289
Net Worth	537,173	557,477	578,516	601,779	614,560	628,889
Working Capital	387,022	415,192	441,847	458,618	473,866	483,520

						Projected
	1965	1966	1967	1968	1969	1970	1971
Sales Total	4,659,728	6,150,044	6,562,008	6,272,671	6,903,161	7,592,035	9,870,000
Gross Profit on Operations	881,171	1,069,897	1,078,351	1,101,750	1,127,731	1,383,190	1,668,120
% of Sales	18.91	17.40	16.43	17.56	16.34	18.22	16.90
Operating Expenses includ. depreciation	746,426	864,490	949,898	982,338	981,475	1,266,004	1,329,977
% of Sales	16.02	14.06	14.48	15.66	14.22	16.68	13.47
Net Profit before Taxes	134,745	205,407	128,453	119,412	146,256	117,186	201,643
% of Sales	2.89	3.34	1.96	1.90	2.12	1.54	2.04
% of Net Worth	19.87	27.37	16.22	14.51	16.74	16.05	25.60
Reserve for Income Taxes	59,000	98,000	52,200	53,000	60,500	50,000	91,500
Net Profit after Taxes	75,745	107,407	76,253	66,412	85,756	67,186	110,143
% of Sales	1.63	1.75	1.16	1.06	1.24	.88	1.13
% of Net Worth	11.17	14.31	9.63	8.07	9.82	9.43	11.44
Dividends	26,340	35,120	35,120	35,120	35,120	35,120	52,680
Surplus	49,405	72,287	41,133	31,292	50,636	32,066	57,463
Earned Surplus Cumulative	502,694	574,981	616,114	647,406	698,042	730,108	787,571
Net Worth	678,294	750,581	791,714	823,006	873,642	905,708	963,171
Working Capital	509,290	563,498	599,820	625,330	692,178		

Exhibit 2. Francis Hankin & Co., Limited Balance sheet as at February 28.

Assets	1965	1966	1967	1968	1969	1970
Current Assets						
Cash	$117,797	$ 15,202	$ 37,494	$ 321,544	$ 230,209	$ 1,370
Accounts receivable	847,431	1,784,001	1,356,448	1,351,316	1,782,943	2,500,613
Deposits on Tenders and Plans	24,107	51,637	11,289	23,619	46,184	102,826
Prepaid Expenses	4,890	6,925	9,157	13,332	11,141	23,194
Inventories						
Stock on hand	217,310	208,545	249,987	254,934	192,055	465,000
Work in progress	231,631	131,732	130,390	239,287	70,373	286,363
	448,941	340,277	380,377	494,221	262,428	751,363
Less Progress billings	286,669	159,407	201,699	422,940	—	—
	162,272	180,870	178,678	71,281	262,428	751,363
Total Current Assets	1,156,497	2,038,635	1,593,066	1,781,092	2,339,547	3,382,687
Other refundable income tax	—	—	3,413	3,321	3,321	—
Fixed Assets						
Land	27,000	27,000	27,000	27,000	13,500	13,500
Buildings	97,922	98,560	94,363	90,823	73,070	69,416
Furniture & fixtures	14,403	17,429	15,309	22,044	25,411	31,869
Automobiles and trucks	41,588	45,172	45,780	35,876	34,413	20,258
Equipment	8,201	11,997	20,979	28,612	27,532	50,879
Total net depreciated value	189,114	200,158	203,431	204,355	173,926	185,922
Leasehold improvements, at						
unamortized cost	—	—	—	—	16,038	14,034
					189,964	199,956
	$1,345,611	$2,238,793	$1,799,910	$2,411,708	$2,526,190	$3,582,643

Liabilities						
Current Liabilities						
Bank Loan	$ —	$43,000	$ —	$ —	$ —	$28,931
Accounts Payable and Accrued						
charges						
Trade	475,862	1,186,760	830,616	1,108,602	1,335,170	2,328,513
Other	105,151	137,672	143,979	422,940	281,016	248,757
Sales taxes payable	7,092	28,928	11,934	24,186	13,365	10,530
Income taxes payable	49,212	66,852	1,667	17,974	14,497	52,704
Current Installment on mortgage	5,000	5,000	5,000	5,000	—	—
Total Current Liabilities	642,317	1,468,212	993,196	1,578,702	1,644,048	2,669,435
Mortgage—$30,000 at 6½%						
due 1st May, 1969, less						
current installment of $5,000	25,000	20,000	15,000	10,000	—	—
Deferred income taxes	—	—	—	—	8,500	7,500
Shareholders' Equity						
Capital Stock						
Authorized—25,000 shares of						
$10.00 each issued and						
fully paid—17,560 shares						
of $10.00 each	175,600	175,600	175,600	175,600	175,600	175,600
Earned Surplus						
Balance at beginning of year	453,289	502,694	574,981	616,114	647,406	698,042
Profit for the year	75,748	107,407	76,253	66,412	85,756	67,186
	529,034	610,101	651,234	682,526	733,162	765,228
Less: Dividends paid during						
the year	26,340	35,120	35,120	35,120	35,120	35,120
	502,694	574,981	616,114	647,406	698,042	730,108
	$1,345,611	$2,238,793	$1,799,910	$2,411,708	$2,526,190	$3,582,643

Source: Company Records

Exhibit 3. Francis Hankin & Co. Ltd. Source and application of funds for the year ended February 28.

	1968	1969	1970
Source of Funds	$	$	$
Operations			
Net earnings	66,412	85,756	67,186
Charges not requiring outlay of funds			
Depreciation and Amortization	38,133	37,574	43,703
Loss (Gain) on disposal of fixed assets	17	(29,728)	3,561
Deferred income taxes	—	8,500	(1,000)
Funds from operations	104,562	102,102	113,450
Proceeds from disposal of fixed assets	12,194	77,803	10,476
Deferred income taxes	92	3,321	—
Application of Funds	116,848	183,226	123,926
Dividends	35,120	35,120	35,120
Expenditure on: Fixed assets	51,268	53,215	67,732
Leasehold improvements	—	18,043	—
Reduction in long-term debt	5,000	10,000	—
	91,388	116,378	102,852
Increase in Working Capital	25,460	66,848	21,074
Working Capital at beginning of year	599,870	625,330	692,178
Working Capital at end of year	625,330	692,178	713,252

Source: Company Records

Exhibit 4. Francis Hankin & Co. Limited background of the principal individuals in this case.

Mr. E. A. Hankin

Mr. Hankin was born on April 29, 1912 and joined the Company in July 1934. Since December 30th, 1935 he has been a Company Director. He was elected Vice-President and Treasurer on May 23rd, 1951. On May 19th, 1953 Mr. Hankin was elected President and on April 5th, 1966 became both President and Treasurer.

Mr. E. R. Fox

Mr. Fox was born on September 10th, 1919 and graduated in Chemical Engineering from the University of Toronto in 1949. He served in the Royal Canadian Navy from December 1940 until September 1945. Mr. Fox joined Francis Hankin & Co. Ltd. on April 15th, 1950 as a Project Engineer in the Company's Toronto Office. He was appointed Manager of this office in 1955. On May 28th, 1958 he was appointed a Company Director and on May 25th, 1966 Mr. Fox was appointed Vice-President.

Mr. M. L. Tucker

Mr. Tucker was born on October 21st, 1930 and graduated in Civil Engineering from McGill University in 1953. After graduation he worked for a general contractor for 3 years and then for a large industrial company for 2 years. Mr. Tucker joined Francis Hankin & Co. Ltd. on July 8th, 1957 and was appointed a Company Director on May 28th, 1969. On May 28th, 1970 he was elected Vice-President and Secretary.

Francis Hankin & Co. Limited (B)

In the spring of 1970, Mr. E. A. Hankin, president of Francis Hankin & Co. Limited, Montreal, Canada, had decided to offer a substantial portion of the family's holdings in the Company for sale to a key group of employees led by Mr. M. L. Tucker and Mr. E. R. Fox. (Case A)

Acting on behalf of the Key Employee Group, Mr. Tucker stated:

> We decided that we would require expert counsel to advise us during the preparation of our offer to purchase. One major question was that of the value of the shares. After all, it was not a clear-cut issue as the value of a controlling block of shares in the market place could very well be different from the book value per share or the value of the stock for estate tax purposes. We were further faced with the question of control of the company by a group of key employees and were wondering if this would be a practical set-up. And, of course, some other questions, for example with regard to future sources of new capital, would require answers. Finally, our own financial resources played a role in deciding on the specifics of our offer.

Accordingly, both parties agreed to have independent appraisals made and reports prepared as the basis for determining an appropriate price and method for achieving the transfer of control.

Mr. Hankin engaged a firm of chartered accountants to prepare an evaluation and plan for him (Exhibit 1) while Mr. Tucker, on behalf of the employees, opted for the services of a firm of investment consultants (Exhibit 2). The findings and recommendations of these firms are reproduced as submitted to the respective parties.

A meeting was scheduled for the first week of August 1970, at which time it was hoped the negotiations would reach a final stage, a price agreed upon and the ownership of the company completed.

Exhibit 1. Francis Hankin & Co. Ltd. Evaluation report prepared by a firm of chartered accountants for Mr. Hankin.

In accordance with your instructions I have studied the affairs of Francis Hankin & Company, Limited primarily from the point of view of determining an appropriate price for the shares of the Company on the predicate that control would be sold to existing associates in the business.

I should say at the outset that after review of the Company's operating history for the last twenty years, and making an assessment of its present position, I have come to the conclusion that a sale of shares presently belonging to yourself and Mrs. Collins, either in total or in sufficient numbers so as to confer control, would not yield a price commensurate with the full inherent potentialities.

This case was prepared by Fred D. Wiersema under the direction of Professor W. H. Ellis of McGill University as a basis for class discussion rather than to illustrate either effective or ineffective handling of an administrative situation. Copyright © 1978 by W. H. Ellis.

Exhibit 1. (continued)

The Company is not of sufficient size in total volume or in holdings, nor are the earnings of the magnitude, that would lend itself to a public financing at this time. The earnings, despite the quite remarkable stability considering the nature of the business, are not of the order that would make a public issue, even of a limited placement character, a feasible proposition. The other features that would also render such a course impractical are the small number involved in the management team and the basic characteristics of the contracting business itself.

The record of Francis Hankin & Company, Limited over the last twenty years is a truly remarkable one in the evenness of its performance. Throughout this period of time a reasonable return has been earned by way of profit in every year averaging better than ten per cent after income taxes on the net investment. In any consideration of the quantum of profit there must be taken into account the fact that substantial bonuses have been earned by the directing personnel of the Company throughout the period. The Company has also paid dividends without a break and at a remarkably consistent rate, either $1.70 or $2.00 a share, over the last nineteen years.

In any consideration of the real value of this Company at this time, cognizance must be taken not only of the exceptional record of the past, but much more so, the possibilities of the future. The past policies have not been directed so as to attain a rapid enhancement in the share values. The policies referred to are those of even, regular earnings, the provision of above average personal incomes for all members of the management team, steady dividends and controlled growth, coupled with the development of a high degree of expertise and an outstanding reputation.

These policies, whilst they did not operate to bring about a rapid enhancement of share values, and particularly those values subject to formula approaches, nevertheless set the stage for future realization. The Company is entering a stage where the market for its sales and services would be limited only by the availability of capital and the fleshing out of its management contracting and sales force. This is a classic situation for purchase by another company with larger cash and credit resources and the ability to expand the Company's management forces. Having regard to all these factors, the Company would represent an attractive buy to another corporation advantageously situated, at a figure in a vicinity of $1,500,000 or even appreciably higher.

The other alternative for disposal of the Company at anything close to its proper value to its present owners would be to a younger group to be directly engaged in the business themselves. The Company would be a highly attractive proposition for a small group of young men with an expectation of at least twenty years' active business life in front of them. The Company could be carried by them through the stage of being both at one and the same time too large and too small, to the point where both their own efforts and the real potentialities of the Company could be capitalized upon. The opportunity is there for the right group with the capital available both to buy the existing control and finance the expansion offered by present opportunities. A price of $75.00 a share would be the appropriate figure around which any such discussions should revolve. This price is not arrived at on the application of a precise formula but rather by my own assessment of the minimum figure it would command in the corporate market and yet low enough to represent a most attractive business opportunity for those with the vision, the capacities and the resources to tackle the proposition.

I made mention earlier in this letter of the fact that in my view it would be difficult to secure anything close to the right price for a controlling interest in the shares from present senior associates. The reasons for the foregoing conclusion are several, and must be viewed against the background of their association with the Company. They would be aware, of course, that recent transfers have been made at a price of $27.50 per share. This price in turn rested upon a theoretical valuation made in September 1966 primarily for the purpose of sustaining the lowest possible values for estate duty purposes. The situation insofar as the Company is concerned, in terms of both value and profits, is much the same today as it was at the time this valuation was made, and it would be hard for these associates to appreciate the basic underlying economic conditions that warranted such a much higher value today. The answer is, of course, the combination of a very low value determined for the aforementioned reason, coupled with the tremendous potentialities of a company geared to serve one of the most expansive fields in today's industrial scene, namely the control or mitigation of air and water pollutants.

This overall assessment of the Company's present-day value would not be complete without a discussion of formula approaches, having particular regard to present realization values. The approach of a capitalization of either earnings or dividends has little application in the present circumstance owing to the permeating effect of the substantial bonus policy of the Company in the first instance and the high degree of individual control exercised in the second, although the ability to pay dividends over a lengthy period is an impressive demonstration of inherent strength.

Exhibit 1. (continued)

The book value of the shares based on the interim balance sheet as at February 28, 1970 amounts to $51.50 per share. The realization value on break-up is not too far short of this figure when considering the tax implications of winding up. The whole is greatly strengthened by the fact that dividends have been paid back to and including the year ending February 28, 1952 totalling $561,920. This would make available a like sum for withdrawal by election at a 15% tax rate paid by the Company. This would amount to the payment of taxes in the amount of $84,288, and even after allowing for a 50% tax rate on the remainder of the retained earnings, there is a realizable value in the order of $45.00 per share. The foregoing assumes that the appreciation on disposal of the Company's properties and business would at least offset the expenses of winding up—in my view a most conservative assumption. The earnings and dividend record at least support the value of $45.00 per share. The foregoing represents in my judgement the absolute minimum at which any transaction or valuation could be contemplated.

Before closing I might make mention of the fact that the reason why election to tax at the corporate rate of 15%, an amount equal to the qualifying dividends, has not been pursued heretofore is because of the Company's need for the funds in the business. However, if immediate disposal is not to be proceeded with, it may well be the course of prudence to make such an election at this time, even though the funds would have to be by agreement reloaned to the Company by the shareholders, for with the whole subject of tax reform very much to the forefront, this privilege could disappear.

Exhibit 2. Francis Hankin & Co. Limited Evaluation report prepared by a firm of investment consultants for Mr. M. L. Tucker and Mr. E. R. Fox.

Under most circumstances, the value per share of a block of shares representing control of a company would be transferred to a new group at a price in excess of the market for occasional lots of shares in the same company. Obviously, there is a value to being able to "call the shots." In the case of the Hankin Company, however, the family was selling a total of 6,500 shares, which represented about 37 percent of the company, and it is only because the prospective purchasers already own 13 percent that the block comes to represent control. Furthermore, since restrictions exist which prohibit the sale of shares to other than employees, directors, and immediate family, then the range of prospective purchasers is considerably reduced. Only if Mr. Hankin wishes to sell substantially all of his shares and those of Mrs. Collins, and has sufficient voting control to arrange for revisions to the by-laws, could control actually be priced in a competitive market situation.

In view of the foregoing, and particularly in view of the expressed spirit of any transaction, little attention will be paid to the premium aspect to which control might be entitled, nor to what a prospective third party, either a competitor or someone to whom the Hankin activities would be complementary, would pay. In the latter case, it should be acknowledged, such a range of prices would involve a premium, depending on the particular intentions of the buyer.

(a) Book Value

The book value as shown in the financial statements of the company at February 28, 1970, is approximately $51.50 per share prior to any adjustments. Without further intimate knowledge of the specific fixed asset items, no adjustments are possible. However, a cursory inspection of the items and review with key employees indicate that no adjustments are warranted. The working capital position at balance sheet date is approaching some strain, as considerable inventory has been built up, and accounts receivable have risen by over $800,000 from the previous year. Offsetting these increases has been a roughly $1 million increase in accounts payable. Thus, while the balance sheet is clean, there does not appear to be any redundant or excess working capital around. In fact, an important consideration for any buyer is the amount of additional working capital that might have to be introduced to finance a rate of growth which makes the acquisition attractive in the first instance. Based on book value, the stock, which has been paying a $2.00 dividend rather consistently, yields slightly under 4%, somewhat under average in today's market environment. The prospective purchaser should be aware that in the event the company were eventually liquidated, some tax would be payable on the accumulated earned surplus in the company, so that in effect, paying book value is really over-paying on a purely liquidating basis.

Exhibit 2. (continued)

(b) Time-adjusted Return

This method of value calculation is perhaps the most elastic, since the determination of a reasonable rate of future earnings capitalization (or price to earnings multiple) is a function of many considerations, among which are the desired rates of return and the historic and projected growth of the company.

An examination of the sales trends of the Hankin Company over 12 years, i.e., from 1959 through projected 1971 inclusive, shows an average annual sales growth of 9.35%. The same figure for the actual latest five-year period, 1965 through 1970 inclusive, shows an 11% rate. (All references are to fiscal years ending February 28.) Historically the company has exhibited spurts where sales would grow as much as 30% plus in a year, and then extended periods of no growth and in fact occasional declines. It should be pointed out that in order to double sales as projected in the five-year period beginning 1971, an average annual rate of growth in sales of approximately 14% will be required.

I would consider it equitable for an investor in Hankin to be looking for a minimum 15% return on his money.

Using a five-year horizon as a reasonable one in which to prepare a profit plan, as well as a reasonable one over which to discount the future (with anything beyond too far out to even bother forecasting), then if the company averages a 10% return on its investment (defined as book value at February 28, 1970) over the five years through 1975, the book value per share, assuming no dividends, will have increased by 61% to $83 per share. Discounting an $83 book value five years hence at a 15% rate of return would yield a present value of roughly $41.50 per share.

(c) Price Earnings Ratios

This popular approach to evaluate marketable securities is really a simplified version of the preceding paragraph's attempt to discount the future. For the record, the earnings per share of the Hankin Company in recent years has been

F/Y Feb 28	e.p.s.
1966	$6.12
1967	4.35
1968	3.78
1969	4.88
1970	3.83
1971 projected	6.27
5 year average 1966–1970	$4.59
6 year average 1966–1971	$4.87

The choice of a multiplier is the critical factor, with the market typically ascribing a higher multiplier (or price-earning ratio) to a situation of "high growth with confidence" and a lower multiplier where the situation is static or cyclical.

At 10 times—or a 10% return on market price—the shares would be worth from $45.90–$48.70 on the previously derived averages. At 8 times—or a 12½% return—the corresponding range is $37.80–$39.00. A higher multiplier might be justified if growth in earnings could be projected with a high degree of confidence, and a lower multiplier if the more recent record were a truer indication of the situation except that in the latter case the higher assumed liquidating value would come into play. This rate is higher, on average, than either the most recent five years or 12 a year/period ending with the current fiscal year. While it is true that the basic for future growth was built into the company these past number of years, the purchasers should examine closely whether the projection is achievable in light of history, and if so, should a premium multiple be established for growth still to be produced, perhaps as a result of the new ownership influence. The selling shareholder through his retention of 3,500 shares, will still be in a position to benefit, if only partially, should the forecasts be achieved or surpassed.

Exhibit 2. (continued)

As sales have fluctuated so have net profits after taxes, and these not necessarily directly with sales. For instance, on a large sales increase of over 30% in 1964 over 1963, pre-tax profit actually declined by a small margin and after-tax profits as a per cent of sales declined from 1.04% to .82%, the lowest return on sales during the entire period for which statistics were made available. An examination of the profits statistics discloses years in which increases in sales resulted in declines in profits and particularly in declines of net profits after taxes as a per cent of sales. It also discloses periods in which increases in sales resulted in proportionately higher profits, as one might have expected. In all, the trend of profits after taxes as a per cent of sales has been at best stable and, depending on the period examined, has exhibited a small decline. Again, emphasis on a different product or customer mix in the future could conceivably bring about a return to a higher level of profitability and profits.

For the period of 1959 to 1971 inclusive (which includes the projections for 1971), the average net profits after taxes as a per cent of the ending net worth of the company was 10.11%. The actual experience for the five-year period 1966 through 1970 inclusive was 9.85%. The average results belie, however, considerable fluctuations year to year.

In the objectives of the five-year plan through 1975, management is looking to improve the return on investment internally to 10% after taxes as a minimum standard. This return is related to the investment defined as book value. Thus, if 10% is a minimum standard for the company, should not 10% be a minimum standard for the investors in the company? It might be argued by a seller that over the next few years the return on investment in the company will increase above the 10% level. Let us assume, for purposes of illustration only, that the return averages 14% for the next five years, in other words, that the book value of the company doubles in the next five years. Thus we would have a situation in which sales doubled and the net worth did likewise. Assuming that in five years the company could be sold at the then current book value, then in order for the purchasers to realize a 10% return on their funds, they would be willing to pay approximately 1.25 times the present book value, or $64 per share.

Even though no competitive bid is being sought which the prospective key employee purchasers are being asked to match, the purchasers should look at the size of the commitment they are making and what other alternative uses and returns they might secure for that kind of money in today's money market. A very important part of the consideration however, rests with the terms that the purchasers might secure.

Triple "A" mortgage rates are in excess of 10%; Government of Canada bonds yield close to 8%; and while the income on both these instruments is taxable, they do to varying degrees eliminate most risks and bother of supervision. On the other hand, the purchase of equity shares in a private business involves a long-term commitment in a smaller company which is subject to all of the usual competitive forces in the economy, and to the pressures exerted by larger and financially more secure factors within an industry. Most importantly, private companies involve a degree of *illiquidity* which is hard to match. Therefore, the return must take these factors into consideration. As well, the position of the firm within its industry, its reputation, life, strength of balance sheet, and depth of management personnel are all important factors in determining the probabilities for its future success. With the prospect that a revision to Canada's tax laws will make taxable part or all of the appreciation which might be expected through the compounding of retained earnings in the future, equity investment loses some attraction. Thus, those people committing their funds at this stage should be asking for greater potential return.

(d) Liquidation Value

As previously indicated, the proceeds of liquidation would yield approximately $44.50 per share, assuming realization of book values, after a 15% tax cut before any expenses involved. Since no such procedure is intended, the value is included herein only for the sake of completeness.

Exhibit 2. (continued)

(e) Other Benchmark Transactions

In November 1966, certain shares were transferred intra-family as well as to the key management group at $27.50 each. To the extent that this transaction represented a reasonable evaluation consistent with the spirit now prevailing, it is an interesting basis for extrapolation. Since the 1966 fiscal year through February 28, 1970, the company has increased its retained earnings (i.e. has made profits less paid out dividends) of $8.80 per share. Thus, adding the incremental earnings to the 1966 transaction basis yields a price of $36.30 today.

(f) Summary of Evaluations

Book value	$51.50
Time adjusted return	$41.50
Price-earnings basis	$38.40 av.–$46.80 av.
Liquidation value	$44.50
Benchmark transaction	$36.30

In our view a reasonable range would be the time adjusted return of $41.50 on the lower side and the theoretical liquidating value of $44.50 on the higher end.

Some flexibility in the price should be involved since the terms of payment are almost as important a consideration as the price itself.

Susan James—The Framing Store

Susan James sat at the back of her framing store and pondered her future. Her store was 7 years old, she had built it from scratch, and now had a staff of 4, including 2 part-time employees. As a businesswoman who had trained as an accountant and then seen an opportunity to open in the downtown Montreal area, she had survived the recent recession in spite of the fact that her sales had dropped by about 25% over 2 years, and had remained stagnant since the year ended April 30, 1992. She had slashed costs, especially salaries, and was in a reasonably strong position to begin to gradually rebuild. She needed ideas that would fuel this process, and had just hired one part-time employee to continuously rearrange the retail space in the store and another one who could actively solicit corporate accounts. Sales in the present location could double without having to expand physically.

The channels of distribution are loosely defined in the framing business, since there are a number of wholesalers who compete with the retailers for the larger corporate accounts. Accessibility is of prime importance, whether through location or ease of service, and Ms. James felt that she had excelled because she was very conscious of both these factors. She had maintained her extremely high margins throughout the recession when all competitors around her were slashing theirs, and the client had obviously perceived value in her product. Recently a few more competitors had gone bankrupt and although her sales were flat she knew that her results could have been even more dismal.

The store had a well-known name, and clients were well treated—in terms of choice and the knowledge and courtesy of the staff. The store accepted rush orders, and offered pick-up and delivery to save customers the inconvenience of looking after such details. Do-it-yourselfers could also order frame components, another innovation which was very popular.

Ms. James had printed several thousand copies of a promotional brochure which she and her staff distributed to customers and prospects when they either came into the store or were solicited by telephone. The only customers who were approached by telephone and mail were corporate clients since they had the most interesting volume potential, although she did spend quite a lot on window display to attract walk-in traffic. Based on a continuing survey in the store, thus far the yellow pages, the decor of the store, and word-of-mouth were the points customers mentioned when asked what induced them to come in and buy the first time. From experience Ms. James knew that the likelihood of repeat business was

This case was prepared by Angela Burlton, CA under the direction of Professor A. B. Ibrahim as a basis for class discussion rather than to illustrate effective or ineffective handling of an administrative situation, May 1993.

extremely high—and that all she expected her promotion to achieve was that crucial first visit and subsequent purchase.

The store's moulding samples were very up-to-date, and in fact custom framing accounted for roughly 60% of total sales. Ms. James could not decide whether to continue selling posters and reproductions in the store, since she was undecided whether their slow volume was a function of poor display, assortment, or the saturation of the product.

There are no barriers to entry in framing, although rudimentary knowledge is helpful. Ms. James was trying to discover what other promotional tools were open to her, and what were her prospects for expansion. She had approached other businesses to discuss buying them, but was frustrated by their high asking prices. She knew nothing about choosing appropriate retail space other than some idea that traffic should be constant.

PART THREE

MANAGING GROWTH

△ **Family Business**
△ **Going International**
△ **Franchising**
△ **Going Public**
△ **Letting Go**

△ CHAPTER 16 △
FAMILY BUSINESS

Family business represent the most prevalent type of business in the U.S. and Canada. It is estimated that 90 percent of all the business in the U.S. and Canada are family owned and operated. Although family businesses are usually thought of as being small businesses, they are reported to represent over one-third of the Fortune 500 list of large firms.[1] Think of such names as the Rockefellers, the Fields of Chicago, the DuPonts, the Forbes, the Fords, the Molsons, the Eatons, the Bronfmans, the Birks and the Desmarais.

According to A. B. Ibrahim and W. Ellis, family business is defined as one in which 51 percent of the business is owned by a single family, and at least two family members are involved in the management activities, in addition to which transfer of leadership to next generation is anticipated.[2] Thus the criteria delineate a family business include degree of ownership, management by family members, extent of family involvement and the potential for generational transfer of power.

ADVANTAGES OF FAMILY BUSINESS

Family firms offer many advantages including:

- Shared values, beliefs and vision
- Strong sense of mission
- The confidence that customers have in a family name
- Long-term commitment to the business
- Economic independence for family members

DISADVANTAGES OF FAMILY BUSINESS

- Family infighting
- Lack of objectivity
- Nepotism
- Inward looking

This chapter is written by Professor A. B. Ibrahim based on earlier research on the topic and the book: Family Business Management—Concepts and Practice by A. Bakr Ibrahim & W. Ellis, Published by Kendall/Hunt Publishing, 1994.

THE DUAL RELATIONSHIP

Family businesses are characterized by the dual relationship of two naturally separate functions, the social (family) function and the business function. The family in its social function satisfies different social and emotional needs such as the need for belonging. The decision-making process in the social function is not necessarily based on a rational model, but rather, on an emotional and biological imperative. On the other hand, the business function is result-oriented. The decision making process and behavioral pattern must be based on an objective, economic model in order for the family business to compete effectively.

Much of the blame for the family firm's woes rests on the overlap between the social and business functions. We discuss in the following sections some of the issues related to the overlap between these two functions.

The Problem of Carry-Over

Research has found that tension and conflict in one function are usually carried over to the other function. The quarrels and ill feelings among relatives have a way of spreading out to include other family and non family members. It is often difficult to separate the roles and rules of one function from the other. For example, a husband may find it difficult to distinguish between the wife's role at home and her role as the financial officer in the family firm. A classic example is the family infighting that erupts between family members— wives, mothers and other members during the succession process.

Forming One's Own Identity

It is difficult for the offspring to develop their own identity separate from the family. The perception of family members of the next generation may hinder the process of integrating the offspring into the family business. The son may be perceived as "junior" and the daughter as "daddy's little girl" regardless of their qualification and position in the family firm. The offspring usually craves autonomy and tries to emerge from the founder's shadow. However in many cases, the presence of a strong dominant father may hinder the offspring's ability to form their own identity and work independently. In his book, "Father, Son and Co,"[3] Tom Watson of IBM tells about a dominant, strong-willed father—Tom Watson, Sr. Pierre Peladeau, founder of Quebecor Inc., the largest printing and publishing company in the world was labelled a tyrant entrepreneur. It is not known yet how his two sons Erik and Pierre-Karl will manage the printing empire after his death early this year.

Zone of Comfort

Establishing well-defined interpersonal boundaries—zone of comfort is critical in family firms. Too often family members complain of a lack of privacy. Being together for many hours at home and in business creates a lot of pressure and tension among family members. It is not unusual for family members who are working together to distance themselves in order to avoid tension and conflict situation.

Nepotism

The advancement of family members on the basis of their relationship in the social function rather than their qualifications is a direct result of the overlap between the family and the business functions.

DECOUPLING THE TWO FUNCTIONS—
THE FAMILY AND THE BUSINESS

Successful management of the family business requires decoupling the business function from the social-family function. We offer a number of guidelines:

- Clear organizational goals and objectives should be established.
- Policy and procedure guidelines should be formulated.
- A code of conduct should be developed.
- Clear policies concerning career development including compensation, promotion and performance appraisal should be established.
- An organization chart should be designed and communicated to family and nonfamily members.
- A succession plan should be developed.

CONFLICT IN FAMILY FIRMS

Ill feelings between the older and younger generations, and the rivalries between the offspring can lead to tension and create conflict that involves other family members such as wives, daughters, mothers and other relatives. Conflict can paralyze the family firm unless it is managed effectively. Increasingly, family firms are learning conflict resolution mechanisms and ways to manage conflict.

Common Sources of Conflict in Family Firms

Conflict in family firms arises as a result of the overlap between the social-family function and the business function. Common sources of conflict in family firms include:

- Ambiguity of roles and rules in the family business
- Differences in power and status among family members and among family and non family employees
- A hasty and/or unfair succession process
- Rivalries among family members—in particular the offspring
- The favorite son/daughter syndrome
- Lack of clear boundaries between family members
- Lack of clear career development policies regarding hiring, promotion, compensation and performance appraisal

Father—Son/Daughter Rivalry

Conflict between the founder and his son or daughter may arise as a result of the founder's psychological make-up including his strong sense of attachment to the business and his reluctance to let go of the business to the successor. Conflict may also arise as a result of value difference between generation's and the son or daughter's drive to equal or outdo the father.

Rivalries between the Offspring

Conflict may arise and intensifies leading to a bitter family feud as a result of:

- A father playing off the sons against one another
- An emotional involvement with a son or a daughter—the favorite son/daughter syndrome
- An unfair succession process
- An older son not being selected as a successor.

Conflict between Family and Non-Family Members

This type of conflict may arise as a result of nepotism, lack of clear policies governing hiring, compensation and promotion. The Son of Boss (SOB) syndrome is a classic example of how non-family executives feel toward an incompetent son. In addition the decision-making process in some family firms may be a source of conflict. Non-family employees may feel frustrated as a result of not being consulted. For example, the family Supper is often a weekly activity in many family firms in which important business decisions are made in the absence of non-family executives.

MANAGING CONFLICT IN FAMILY FIRMS

Family members must learn conflict resolution techniques and develop strategies to resolve conflict. We offer a number of strategies to resolve conflict:

1. Setting Clear Guidelines concerning different aspects of managing the family business including career advancement, hiring and compensation. Further a code of conduct must be established and adhered to.
2. Face to Face Confrontation is an effective approach to resolve conflict. The issues, consequences, and remedies are explored and commitment to a specific course of action is obtained. Confrontation may take different forms such as one-to-one or group confrontation.
3. The CEO—The Chief Arbiter plays a key role in resolving conflict and therefore must avoid enlisting allies or taking sides in conflict situations.
4. The Peacemaker is often an elder relative who emerges as the wiseman/woman. This person may help reconcile different points of view among family members which at the beginning may seem irreconcilable. Non family third party such as

family friends, lawyers, bankers and accountants can also provide mediation and help to defuse tension between family members.

5. Communication is a common problem in family business; "we don't talk enough in our family" is a common complaint that is often heard. However the Weekly Family Supper or the Family Council provide a better environment for family members to communicate their points of view, express their feelings, resolve disputes and defuse tension and conflict before they bleed into other relationships.

6. Introducing Professional Management to the family business provides more objectivity and allows the family to develop a more professional attitude in their relationships. Levinson suggests that the only solution to conflict in family business is to bring in professional management.[4]

THE SUCCESSION PROCESS

Succession is a central issue in family business. However many family businesses pay scant attention to planning for succession. Lack of a succession plan has led to the death of many family firms or, as Danco termed it "corporeuthanasia."[5] Indeed succession is a major source of family disputes as shown in Box 16.1.

Box 16.1. Family Feuds.

Canadian Tire Corp. Ltd. After the death of the company's co-founder A.J. Billes, his offspring engaged in a bitter fight about how to manage the business. Alfred, the eldest son, had always assumed that he is the natural successor. However, his sister Martha disputed his claim. Finally they managed to resolve the dispute.

McCain Food Ltd. Harrison and Wallace McCain fought bitterly over who should succeed them at the helm of their frozen food empire.

The Trapp Family Lodge. The Von Trapp family whose courage was documented in the classic film—The Sound of Music is fighting over who should run the Trapp Family Lodge in Stowe, Vermont.

Henry Birks & Sons. The Birks third generation family members Jonathan, Barrie and Thomas fought bitterly over who should run the well known Jewelry chain founded by their grandfather Henry Birks. As a result of the dispute among the three brothers the business was sold in 1993.

Steinberg. The Steinberg family fought bitterly over control of the well-known grocery chain founded by Sam Steinberg.

Campbell Soup. The Dorrante family fought over the estate of the grandfather John T. Dorrante—founder of Campbell Soup. They decided to sell the company.

Planning for Succession

A healthy succession process is one that is well planned and in which family and non family members contribute to the process of selecting a successor.[6] Levinson[7] and, later Schein[8], found that proper planning is critical to an effective succession process. However, recent studies suggest that a very small percentage of family firms plan adequately for succession.[9] Research attributes the lack of planning for succession in family firms to the entrepreneur's unwillingness to engage in a succession plan for a number of reasons, such as fear of retirement or death, lack of other interests and a reluctance to let go and relinquish power (thus precipitating a loss of self esteem).[10] Therefore, before any planning process takes place, the entrepreneur must understand that succession is a biological necessity and that he or she must accept his or her limitations. Further succession is not a business transaction, it is a non-market transfer of power.[11] Box 16.2 provides examples of successful successions in a number of family firms.

Box 16.2. The Successful Succession.

Seagram Company & The Bronfman Family. One of the best planned succession process has recently taken place at the Seagram Company. At the Company's annual shareholders' meeting at the Sheraton Centre in Montreal, Edgar Bronfman Sr. handed over the reins to his son Edgar. Edgar Jr. is now heading the company founded by his grandfather 75 years ago with total assets of over $12 billion. The third generation Bronfman has been mentored by his father Edgar Sr. and his uncle Charles, now cochairman of the company.

The Forbes Empire. Steve Forbes took over the Forbes empire from his father Malcolm Forbes and managed the company successfully.

Estée Lauder, Inc. Leonard Lauder took over the Estée Lauder empire from his mother and was able to expand the business successfully.

Molson Brewery Company succession process from generation to generation has been exemplary. Eric Molson is currently the head of the family business.

Passing The Baton—Some Guidelines

An effective succession plan must take in consideration the following critical elements:

- Early inclusion of the offspring in the family business. This step includes proper mentoring and training to prepare the next generation for its future leadership role.
- The gradual transfer of power. This allows both the departing CEO and the successor to adjust to their new roles. For example, Henry Block built H & R Block into the largest tax preparation service in North America. Tom, his son, is now managing the entire business while the father is content doing the T.V. commercials.
- Adjusting the job to fit the successor's skills and competence. This involves a restructuring at the top level of the organization hierarchy. The objective of such restructuring is to make the job more suitable to the successor's capacity to lead and function effectively.

- Providing a zone of comfort. The restructuring process must provide a zone of comfort for siblings in order to avoid conflict and tension during the transition. Garfield Weston, founder of George Weston Ltd. divided the company between his two sons with Galen running the Weston food conglomerate, owner of Lablaw supermarkets in North America, and Garry handling the company's food operation everywhere else.
- Family and non family members must be encouraged to participate in the succession plan.
- Next generation family members' careers, seniority, ages and needs must be considered in the succession plan.
- An inheritance plan must be developed and discussed with family members.

SUMMARY

Family businesses represent a large and important sector of the business population. Family business is characterized by the dual relationships of two different systems: the social, family system and the business system. This chapter examined the problems and issues that arise as a result of this dual relationship including the problem of carry over; the difficulties the offspring face in forming their own identity; nepotism and the importance of establishing boundaries or zone of comforts in the family firm. Sources of conflict in family firms were also discussed and a number of strategies to resolve conflict were offered. Finally the succession process in family firms were examined and a number of guidelines for an effective succession plan were offered.

NOTES

1. I. Lansberg, "Managing Human Resources in Family Firms: The Problem of Institutional Overlap," Organization Dynamics (Summer 1983), pp. 71–80.
2. A. Bakr Ibrahim & W. Ellis, Family Business Management—Concepts and Practice, Iowa: Kendall/Hunt publishing, 1994.
3. T. Watson, Father, Son and Co., Bantam Books
4. H. Levinson. "Conflicts that Plague the Family Business," *Harvard Business Review* (March/April 1971), pp. 71–80.
5. L. Danco, Inside the *Family Business* (Cleveland: The Centre for Family Business, The University Press, Inc., 1992), pp. 23–236. Also see: Leo Danco, *Beyond Survival: A Business Owner's Guide for Success* (Cleveland, The Centre for Family Business, The University Press, Inc., 1992).
6. L. B. Barnes and S.A. Hershon, "Transferring Power in the Family Business," *Harvard Business Review* (July/August 1976), pp. 105–114.
7. H. Levinson, "Conflicts that Plague the Family Business" *Harvard Business Review* (March/April 1971), pp. 71–80.
8. E. Schein, "The Role of the Founder in Creating Organizational Cultures," *Organizational Dynamics,* 12, 1, 1983, pp. 13–28.
9. W. C. Handler, "Succession in Family Firms: A Mutual Role Adjustment between Entrepreneurs and Next-Generation Family Members," *Entrepreneurship: Theory and Practice* 15, 1, 1990, pp. 37–51.
10. N.C. Churchill and K. J. Hatten, "Non-Market-Based Transfers of Wealth and Power: A Research Framework for Family Business," *American Journal of Small Business* 11, 3,1987, pp. 51–63.
11. N. C. Churchill and K. J. Hatten, 1987.

THE ENTREPRENEUR

Paul Desmarais—Second
Generation Takes Over

Recently Paul Desmarais founder of Montreal-based Power Corporation retired as Chief Executive Officer of the company. His two sons Paul Jr. and André will share the chief executive job. However Paul Sr. will remain chairman of the board to ensure a smooth transition of power to the second generation. Both sons have been working their way up the ladder gradually under the mentorship of Paul Sr.

Paul Desmarais grew up in Sudbury, Ontario where he inherited his ailing family bus company. He convinced a family friend and an Inco executive to lend him money and in a few years he was able to turn the company around. He then sold the company and moved to Montreal where he mastered his strategy of buying ailing companies and turning them around. Paul Desmarais went on to diversify his holdings using a technique that became his trademark—reverse takeover. He then formed Power Corp., a conglomerate.

Desmarais' success is attributed to his networking skills and his strong sense of observation. Paul Jr., a quiet and conservative type, has focused on the financial aspects of the business. André on the other hand is more of a risk taker with excellent managerial skills.

Source: P. C. Newman, The Canadian Establishment, McClelland and Stewart, 1983; The Montreal Gazette April 6, 1996.

△ CHAPTER 17 △
GOING INTERNATIONAL

As the domestic market becomes highly competitive and/or mature, going international is increasingly seen as an opportunity for small business growth. Indeed, today's entrepreneur must become more active in the international arena. The explosive growth in international business is phenomenal. International trade has increased from approximately $200 billion in the early 70s to $2 trillion per year, and the number of countries participating in international business have also increased. We are becoming a global village with global markets and global products. Consumers are changing in many ways; life style, education and habits reflect these changes.

REASONS FOR GOING INTERNATIONAL

Small business may pursue an international strategy for many reasons. Here are some:

1. Open up new markets or windows of opportunity. As the market in the home country intensifies, matures or faces slow growth, looking for new opportunities abroad becomes crucial to the small firm's survival.
2. Increase the profitability picture of the small firm. By increasing sales volume, and/or setting desirable pricing strategy with lesser competition, the small firm is able to improve its overall financial picture.
3. Enjoy cheaper resources such as materials and skilled labour.
4. Enjoy benefits offered by foreign countries such as grants, tax exemptions and interest-free loans.
5. The desire to expand and grow. Foreign markets offer greater opportunity to pursue a growth strategy.
6. Acquire products or services for the domestic market. Appeals for foreign products may offer an opportunity in the home market.

MARKET RESEARCH AND ASSESSMENT

Before selecting a foreign market the small firm must undertake market research and prepare an assessment. Market assessment includes initial screening of foreign markets to

---

Critical Factors in Selecting a Foreign Market

1. Market size
2. Potential for growth
3. Intensity of the competition
4. Political stability of the foreign market
5. Economic forces such as inflation, interest rates and economic policies
6. Currency exchange rate and restrictions
7. Tariffs and quotas imposed by the foreign country
8. Tax system complexity
9. Entry barriers to protect domestic products
10. Benefits offered by the foreign country such as tax exemptions, grants, subsidies and interest-free loans
11. Life style and dominant beliefs
12. The foreign country's national plans and priorities

Figure 17.1. Critical factors in selecting a foreign market.

determine first of all if there is a potential need for the product or service. It would be a waste of resources to consider foreign markets where the need is lacking. After the initial screening the small firm may consider other factors in selecting a foreign market such as those outlined in Figure 17.1 above.

ENTRY MODES

There are two modes of entry available to small business: (1) exporting, which consists of direct and indirect exporting; and, (2) foreign manufacturing which may take the form of a direct investment, joint venture, licensing and franchising.

Exporting

Small businesses can export their products to foreign markets. The exporting mode of entry does not require much investment, and is of little risk. The small firm manufactures all its products in the home country with very little, if any, change or modification. There are two types of exporting: direct and indirect. Direct exporting means that the small business is handling the export operation entirely by itself. The entrepreneur or a sales person may select the foreign market, and assume responsibility for the operation which may include paying visits to the foreign market on a regular basis. This requires knowledge of the foreign market, greater investment, and hence, greater risk.

Indirect exporting on the other hand involves a third party, usually an export company or an overseas agent commissioned by foreign customers. The agent handles the export operation with very little involvement from the small business, thus indirect exporting involves little investment and risk. The small firm does not need to have a sales office in the foreign country nor the expertise and contacts in that market.

Manufacturing in the Foreign Market

The small business may choose to establish a manufacturing base in a foreign market for reasons that we have outlined before such as cheap materials, and labour and/or government incentives, such as tax advantages or grants. There are different types of entry modes to establishing a foreign manufacturing base or operation. These include: wholly owned manufacturing facilities, joint venture, licensing, and franchising. Let us discuss each briefly.

Wholly Owned Manufacturing Facilities

The entrepreneur may wish to own his or her own foreign company and build or acquire operation facilities. This mode of entry allows the small business direct access to foreign markets without having to share either profit or control of the operation with another party. However, this type involves a great deal of risk. Entrepreneurs and small firms should collect as much information as possible on the foreign market before embarking on such an operation. Trade missions, universities and non-profit organizations are excellent sources of information. Knowledge of laws and regulations governing foreign investments and transfer of profit is a must before pursing this mode of entry.

Joint Venture

While many multinational companies (MNC's) may not favour the idea of a joint venture because of the inherent partnerships and sharing of control and profit, mixing western technology and know-how with foreign resources is probably the best mode of entry for entrepreneurs and small business. In a joint venture, two firms agree to share responsibility of critical functions such as management, marketing and/or production. In other words, the small firm joins a foreign company to set up production and marketing facilities. This mode of entry allows the small business to get first-hand knowledge of the foreign market, and access to the foreign partner's skills and distribution system, as well as markets otherwise forbidden to foreign companies. In many cases, the host country requires that the foreign company have a local partner. The host country may encourage joint venture agreements with local partners by granting favourable treatment, such as protection against foreign competition or tax advantages.

Licensing

Under licensing agreement, one firm sells to another trademarks, trade secrets, know-how or the right to its patents for a royalty, usually a percentage of profit or sales. This entry mode is recommended for small firms that lack the resources, skills and/or experience to negotiate and manage a foreign venture. However, a small firm following this entry mode may stand to lose control over its operation in the long run.

Franchising

With the phenomenal increase in franchising systems worldwide, this mode of entry allows the franchisor to minimize his or her risk in the foreign market. The franchising agreement grants the franchisee, usually a local company, the right to sell the product or service in the foreign market. In return the franchisor gets a royalty.

STRATEGIC ALTERNATIVES FOR THE SMALL BUSINESS

The real challenge facing entrepreneurs and small business in the new global economy is to stretch their own technology and resources beyond the North American boundaries, and to attack problems facing developing countries. It is no secret that many developing countries are eager to acquire technology from the industrial world. This offers many windows of opportunity to entrepreneurs and small business. Let us explore three types of strategy: the innovation, the adaptive and the "not so recent" type strategies.[1]

1. *The Innovation Strategy.* The small firm could pursue a strategy of fundamental research and development and focus on transfer of new technologies in vital areas such as agriculture, forestry and energy. Two approaches could be pursued here. The first is the *pre-solution technology* in which entrepreneurs and small firms could introduce and apply recent technology to the developing countries' markets with no modification. This approach involves no additional cost, and is of little risk. The second approach is the *after solution technology* which requires a study of the particular needs of the foreign market and finding a suitable solution. This second approach requires small firms to study the foreign environment and do some research before reaching a suitable solution to the problem. Longer lead time and greater investment are usually required.
2. *The Adaptive Strategy.* Entrepreneurs and small firms could simply adapt a technology used by large western companies to the needs and special requirements of the foreign market. This strategy requires some research and a longer lead time, as modification usually entails a thorough knowledge of the foreign environment. The investment and risk are somewhat greater, but so is the potential return.
3. *The "Not So Recent" Technology.* Entrepreneurs could enter foreign markets by focusing on abandoned technologies, which large firms are no longer applying. This strategy could be ideal in some foreign markets where inexpensive technology is desired.

UNDERSTANDING FOREIGN CULTURE

Culture sums up the values and beliefs of a certain group of people. It is shaped by different elements such as religion, language, values, beliefs, education and socio-political forces. Learning about the foreign culture is critical to success in the foreign market. Culture influences the different aspects of the business such as product appeal and customer acceptance, marketing and promotional techniques employed and relations with foreign workers.

How do entrepreneur and small business managers learn to deal with other cultures? The answer is simply an awareness that cultural differences do exist and that to succeed internationally, the small firm must learn the characteristics of the foreign culture and respect them.

CRITICAL FACTORS

Small businesses have limited resources, thus to pursue an international strategy they have to plan and prioritize the different aspects of going international. Studies have shown that the following factors are critical to success in the international market.[2]

1. Market research
2. Identifying distribution channels or foreign agents
3. Quality of product or services
4. Establishing good customer relations in the foreign market
5. Pricing strategy in the foreign market
6. Understanding cultural differences
7. Risk assessment of political and economic factors in the foreign market

SOURCES OF INFORMATION

One of the problems frequently cited in going international is insufficient knowledge about the foreign market.[3] Market research, entry mode, strategic direction, pricing strategy, risk assessment and knowledge of the foreign culture all depend on collecting accurate information about the foreign market. Here are some sources of information:

1. Visits to the foreign market
2. Trade fairs
3. Trade missions
4. Board of Trade and Chamber of Commerce
5. Export management companies and export agents
6. International accounting firms
7. Banks (international banks)
8. Foreign export/import agents
9. Market research consultants

Some of these sources provide detailed assessment of the foreign market and could be helpful to many entrepreneurs who lack the experience in assessing foreign markets.

THE IMPACT OF TRADE AGREEMENTS ON SMALL BUSINESS*

The General Agreement on Tariffs and Trade (GATT) and the North American Free Trade Agreement (NAFTA) will push businesses to build a sustainable competitive advantage in order to compete domestically and in the international arena. In a global economy, much of the contribution will come from small companies that are flexible and can adapt to new markets and changing technology. To understand the implications of trade liberalization on small businesses, let us briefly consider both the Free Trade Agreement (FTA) and the North American Free Trade Agreement (NAFTA).

The Free Trade Agreement

The Canada-U.S. Free Trade Agreement of 1989, legislating the eventual removal of all tariffs on trade in goods and services by the year 1998 is a natural progression of globalization. This agreement is unprecedented in terms of trade liberalization and broader in scope than any other trade agreement ever signed.

For small business, the implications of free trade are significant. First, it eliminates the problem of trading within the domestic economy which limits the potential for growth. The FTA provides wide access to the huge North American market, and gives opportunities for increased efficiencies and economies of scale. During the debate over free trade, a study by the Canadian Federation of Independent Business showed that, in general, there was a high level of support for the FTA.[4] Small and medium sized companies supported the deal as a way to gain a competitive advantage and reduce administrative and procedural red tape. Interestingly, it was the wholesale sector that demonstrated the strongest backing of the FTA, followed by the manufacturing, construction and primary industries.[5]

The FTA provides trade advantages for the small business sector in a number of ways. The most advantageous clause relates to temporary access. Traditionally, small Canadian businesses exporting abroad were met with problems when they attempted to send their personnel across the border to service or set-up the products they sold in the U.S. market.

This issue was addressed in the Free Trade Agreement through Annex 1502.1. This clause allows entry of Canadian employees supplying products into the neighbouring country without employment authorization. This clause applies to entrepreneurs involved in research and development, marketing, manufacturing, production, sales, distribution or service activities. Likewise, Americans are granted the right to enter the Canadian market-place under the same conditions. This removes much of the bureaucracy that hinders trade, and is an obstacle to small businesses entering the two neighbouring countries.

---

* This section is based on published research work by Professor A. B. Ibrahim.

Another provision of the agreement stipulates that the remaining tariffs on inputs to Canadian products imported from the United States would be eliminated. In some cases, these tariffs were very high and provided a heavy cost burden to small business. Their removal has allowed small enterprises to be more competitive in both domestic and foreign markets.

Chapter 13 of the Free Trade Agreement deals with government procurement policies in both countries. This section of the deal increased the number of government contracts open to competition by both Canadian and American firms in each country. Specifically, the procurement threshold amounts were reduced from $179,000 (U.S.) to $25,000 (U.S.). This amendment to government procurement policies allows for tremendous opportunities to small businesses in both Canada and the U.S. to bid on lucrative government contracts.

Also of great relevance to small businesses are the more liberal trade policies provided for the service sector under the FTA. Chapter 14 of the deal allows for new rules in service trade similar to those that apply in the trade of goods. This more liberal trade arrangement is an especially positive feature of FTA because of the importance of the service sector to small businesses.

Overall, the FTA provides a trade environment conducive to entrepreneurship and allows entry into new and limitless markets for many small businesses. In addition to the Free Trade Agreement, the North American Free Trade Agreement (NAFTA) of 1993 provides an even larger market potential for small business by adding Mexico as a trade partner. This trade deal encompasses over 360 million people and an output of more than $6 trillion dollars (U.S.). NAFTA has made trade between the three countries simpler and has abolished many of the conflicting and complicated trade regulations at the borders. It also provides for less stringent rules for customs documentation and accounting requirements for businesses and eliminates tariffs and non-tariff barriers. Much like the FTA, NAFTA also includes binding trade liberalization in services. Further, NAFTA addresses the issue of intellectual property to a larger extent than does the Free Trade Agreement. Specifically, intellectual property rights and patent protection are strengthened, quelling the fear of loss of control that many small businesses have. This is of particular concern to the many small, knowledge-based businesses. Figure 17.2 presents a checklist for going international.

SUMMARY

Going international is increasingly seen as a window of opportunity for a growing small business. We have attempted in this chapter to explore a number of issues affecting the decision to go international such as the reasons for taking such an initiative, critical factors in selecting a foreign market, entry modes, and strategic alternatives. There are a number of reasons for going international, such as new market opportunities, increasing the profitability picture, cheaper sources and benefits offered by the foreign market. To select a foreign market a number of critical factors have to be considered such as market size,

Critical Issues	Basis and Sources of Judgement
Why	1. Open up new markets or windows of opportunities 2. Increase the overall profit picture of the small firm 3. Enjoy cheaper resources 4. Enjoy benefits offered by foreign countries
Market Research and Assessment	Size Potential for growth Competition Socio-political factors Benefits

Entry Modes	*Exporting:*
	  direct, indirect
	Foreign manufacturing:
	  wholly owned
	  joint venture
	  licensing
	  franchising

Strategic Alternatives	Generic type strategy Transfer of technology
Understanding Foreign Culture	Values and beliefs Awareness
Sources of Information	Visits to foreign markets Trade fairs Trade missions Board of Trade & Chamber of Commerce Export companies International accounting firms International banks Consultants

Figure 17.2. Going international—a checklist for entrepreneurs.

growth potential, competition, economic and political forces and benefits offered by the foreign country. There are two modes of entry available to the small firm: exporting and foreign manufacturing.

NOTES

1.   A. B. Ibrahim, "International Strategic Directions For Canadian Entrepreneurs," *Export Digest* (December 1988), p. 3.
2.   R. Seely and H. IgLarsh, International Marketing in the Context of the Small Business, *American Journal of Small Business,* VI (October–December 1981), pp. 33–37. Also see: E. Kaynak, P. Ghauri and T. Olofsson-Bredenlöw, "Export Behavior of Small Swedish Firms," *Journal of Small Business Management* (April 1987), pp. 26–32.
3.   Rein Peterson, *Encouraging Entrepreneurship Internationally,* (Dubuque, Iowa: Kendall/Hunt Publishing Company 1988).
4.   Swift, Catherine, "Small Business and the Canada-United States Free Trade Agreement," *Journal of Small Business and Entrepreneurship*, V5(5), Summer 1988, p.6.
5.   Swift, p.7.

THE ENTREPRENEUR

Kenneth Rupert Murdock–The International Entrepreneur
The News Corporation Limited

Born in Australia in 1941, it might have been a natural course of destiny that in somewhat less than forty years, he has built a giant corporation in the communications world, on four continents, embracing virtually every conceivable facet of the media including books, TV, movies, magazines and newspapers. At the age of 23, after the death of his father, who was the managing director of the *Melbourne Herald*, he took over the *Adelaide News*, now the biggest newspaper and magazine publisher in Australia.

In addition, his empire in the United States alone consists of Twentieth Century Fox Film and the Fox TV Network, six television stations, the *Boston Herald* and the Daily Racing Form newspapers, *TV Guide* and *New York* magazines, and a 50% interest in Harper and Row, the book publishing firm. He owns the *South China Morning Post* in Hong Kong, while in the United Kingdom, he is also the biggest newspaper publisher, with five national papers, including the *Times* in London, together with publishing a number of magazines and owning the satellite TV broadcaster Sky Television. Overall, his assets are believed to be worth approximately $1.7 billion.

When asked to comment on his strategy for building his media empire, Mr. Murdock stated that he simply made use of opportunities as they came up and that he had been quite skillful in making use of them—as his results show. He also remarked that if, ten years or so ago, he had attempted to chart on paper the destiny of his company, he would never have anticipated the 30 very diverse acquisitions he has made on four continents, almost all of which arose from unique and unanticipated events. Business situations and business opportunities simply changed too quickly for him to become loaded down with piles of strategic speculation. He nevertheless feels that there is a strategy emerging which is building up an international company of record that is able to adapt to new technologies.

Being well-established on four continents makes Mr. Murdock an international entrepreneur.

Source: *Forbes* (November 27, 1989), pp. 98–104; *Forbes* (October 23, 1989), p. 168.

△ CHAPTER 18 △
FRANCHISING

One of the biggest problems facing today's entrepreneur is the high failure rate in small business. It is estimated that about two thirds of the new businesses that will start up in the United States and Canada this year will fail by the fifth year. Franchising may offer a solution and an alternative strategy for many budding entrepreneurs.

THE FRANCHISE PHENOMENON

The notion that if it is eatable, drinkable, wearable, or thinkable, it is franchisable, may have some validity today. Franchising has become a popular strategy in the nineties among many entrepreneurs who may not have the skills to start a business on their own. Today franchising strategy accounts for approximately one third of all retail sales in North America and is expected to grow at an increasing rate. A study by the International Franchise Association indicated that sales of goods and services from franchised outlets in North America totalled over $600 billion in 1988 and are expected to grow to over $1 trillion by the year 2000. Indeed, franchising is not a fad but a long term strategy and a revolution in marketing. Most people recognize such successful marketing stories as McDonalds, Kentucky Fried Chicken and Holiday Inn.

WHAT IS FRANCHISING?

Franchising is a marketing system for distributing products or services. From a legal standpoint, it is a two-party legal agreement in which one party (the franchisor) provides product, service, trademarks and expertise in return for consideration from the second party (the franchisee).

THE ADVANTAGES OF FRANCHISING STRATEGY

Lack of management skills and competence are the most frequently cited cause of failure in small independent businesses.[1] Advocates of franchising have pointed out the important role the franchisor plays as a consultant, training institution and changing agent for budding entrepreneurs. The management ability of the entrepreneur or franchisee is greatly enhanced by the franchisor's skills and experience. Strategic planning, a systematic accounting and record system, effective marketing and cash flow management are all advantages of franchising strategy over independent small businesses.[2] Franchising could also provide an excellent opportunity to entrepreneurs by merging local resources with national and/or brand names and established products or services. In addition, many financial institutions have accepted the fact that the franchising option has a better survival rate than the independent business, and thus, is a low risk business. This perception has helped many entrepreneurs obtain financing with better terms.

On the negative side, the franchise contractual obligations could be quite cumbersome to many franchisees. For example, profit sharing or royalty clauses, obligations to purchase from the franchisor only, restrictions on expansion, or provisions allowing the franchisor to buy back the franchise may restrict the franchisee's freedom to operate his or her business. Indeed the most frequently cited disadvantage of the franchising strategy is the loss of independence, a trait many entrepreneurs value. Figure 18.1 lists some advantages and disadvantages of franchising to franchisor and franchisee.

TYPES OF FRANCHISES

Today the franchising system is in every business sector. We can differentiate, however, between three different types of franchises:

1. *Traditional—Product and Trade Name.* This is the oldest and most conventional type of franchising. The system is characterized by the franchisors supplying the franchisees with their products. Gasoline service stations and automobile dealers are typical of this traditional type.
2. *Non-Traditional—System Format.* This type of franchising system is more recent. It is usually identified by the name of the franchisor, as well as the unified system including outlay and design of the store, operating procedures, training, marketing, promotion, quality and financial control. Over 2000 franchisors are currently operating system format type franchising. Fast food restaurants, motels and real estate agents are good examples of this type.
3. *Collective-Type Franchise.* The recent spread of this type is phenomenal enough to allow us to discuss it under a separate category. In this type a group of small business owners/managers form a "cooperative group" to be able to make a bulk purchase on behalf of their members, thereby obtaining volume discount as well as bargaining power.

GUIDELINES FOR A SUCCESSFUL FRANCHISING STRATEGY

Having discussed types and advantages of the franchising system, let us now discuss some guidelines for a successful franchising strategy. In general, the success of the franchising strategy depends on two key elements: first, is the commitment from both the franchisor and the franchisee, and second, is a well thought out plan and support system.

Advantages	
To the Franchisor	**To the Franchisee**
1. Ability to expand and grow in a short span of time with minimal resources. Little capital investment and human resources are required.	1. The support system offered by the franchisor including: financial, training, marketing, selection of location, design of layout, national promotion and general guidance in management.
2. Shared cost. Many cost items are transferred or shared with franchisees.	2. The proven and tested business concept—product or service is a built-in protection to many budding entrepreneurs against the risk involved in the start-up phase.
3. Having a local franchise is an assurance of consumer acceptance in different locations and regions.	3. Economies of scale as a result of bulk purchases and thus volume discount.
4. Ability to maintain control. The franchise agreement allows the franchisor to exercise control over certain critical aspects of the business such as quality control.	4. A massive national and local promotion campaign provided by the franchisor.
	5. Ability to start with limited skills and experience compared with independent business. The franchisee gets free advice on the different aspects of the business from the day-to-day operation to management policies.

Disadvantages	
Franchisor	**Franchisee**
1. Difficulties of maintaining control over large number of franchisees in different locations.	1. Partial loss of independence, a trait many entrepreneurs value.
2. Risk of losing image and credibility as a result of poor selection of franchisees.	2. Contractual obligations may restrict the franchisee's freedom. For example, royalty clause, profit-sharing plan, restriction on expansion and/or buying back provisions.

Figure 18.1. Advantages and disadvantages of franchising strategy.

STARTING A FRANCHISE: WHAT FRANCHISORS SHOULD LOOK FOR

To start a franchise, potential franchisors should assess three essential elements:

1. *The window of opportunity and the business concept.* A sound business concept and a product or service with a long life cycle (not a fad) are basic ingredients for success.
2. *Transferability of the business concept to different areas.* A business concept that is only attractive to a specific area or region is unfranchisable.

3. *Adequate resources including financial and management resources.* Franchising is an expansion strategy, and while it is pursued with others' money (franchisees) it nevertheless requires resources to support the national promotion program, training and development of franchisees, and standardization of key elements such as product or service, accounting system, design and layout.

SELECTING A FRANCHISE: WHAT FRANCHISEES SHOULD LOOK FOR

To select a franchise, potential franchisees should evaluate three key issues:

1. *Objectives and life style.* Potential franchisees should identify clearly their objectives keeping their own life styles in mind. Self assessment is an excellent exercise whereby potential franchisees assess their strengths and weaknesses.
2. *Time span of the opportunity.* To insure that the opportunity is not a fad with a short life cycle, market research is essential.
3. *Soundness of the business concept.* Assessment of the market acceptance of the product includes a thorough assessment of the franchise prospectus as well as undertaking market research.
4. *Proven track record and support system including financial, training and development support as well as local and national advertising campaign.* Assessment of the financial statement provided by the franchisor, as well as information gathered from other sources such as franchise associations, Dun & Bradstreet and trade journals. Employees working in a franchised outlet could be an excellent source of information and may give a clear indication of the positive and negative aspects of the franchise. Figure 18.2 provides a detailed checklist for buying a franchise.

THE AGREEMENT

Before signing the franchise agreement, the potential franchisee must carefully review this legal document. The obligations and the relationship between both parties (the franchisor and the franchisee) must be clearly defined. The potential franchisee should give particular attention to different provisions that may restrict his or her freedom of choice, such as the freedom to sell the franchise and/or buy-back clauses. Lack of clear understanding of such legal obligations could lead to legal nightmares that will only drain the franchisee's resources.

DISCLOSURE

Because of the inherent problems in the franchise agreement, many states and provinces in the United States and Canada require the franchisor to prepare a detailed disclosure document, including financial statements to be given to potential franchisees.

Process	Critical Issues	Basis and Sources of Judgement
1. Objectives	Life style Expected rate of return Strength and weakness (self assessment)	Self assessment
2. Business concept	Windows of opportunity, niches, unique appeal of product or service and time span (life cycle)	Market research The franchise prospectus Trade journals
3. Proven track record	Rate of return, product quality and appeal, market position and share, innovation	Financial statement provided by the franchisor Dun and Bradstreet The International Franchising Association
4. Franchise support system	Training and financial support, local and national promotion campaign, standard management policies, and accounting system	Visits to different outlets Employees working in franchised outlets Other franchisees The franchisor's prospectus

Figure 18.2. Checklist for buying a franchise.

Potential franchisees could also do some research on their own before buying a franchise; this research would include visiting existing outlets and talking to other franchisees or owners of these outlets. Credit officers, franchise associations and customers can provide the potential franchisee with an overall picture before signing the legal agreement.

In general, the potential franchisee is advised to look for franchisors that are well-reputed and have been in business for a number of years with a proven track record and competent management teams. The existence of a trade secret, know-how and a unique product/service may indicate that the franchise has potential for growth.

In addition, potential franchisees should look for a franchisor that could assist in the selection of a site, and outlay, provide training and effective standardized cost control and cash management systems, as well as an effective national promotional campaign.

Potential franchisees are also advised to read The Franchise Opportunities Handbook published by the U.S. Department of Commerce, which provides helpful tips on franchising. The Uniform Franchise Offering Circular—UFOC—by the Federal Trade Commission (FTC) provides information about disclosure.

The Franchising Associations in the U.S. and Canada which are part of the International Franchise Association (IFA) provide their members with valuable information.

Finally, Small Business Centres and student consulting activities in a number of universities across the U.S. and Canada are excellent sources of information for potential franchisees.

SUMMARY

The spread of franchising in North America and worldwide in the last decade has been phenomenal. We have attempted to describe different aspects of franchising including advantages and disadvantages for both the franchisor and the franchisee, types of franchises, guidelines for a successful franchising strategy, the agreement and disclosure. Advocates of franchising have stressed the important role the franchisor plays in training and assisting budding entrepreneurs in the early stage of operation. However, the franchise contractual obligations may restrict the entrepreneur's freedom to operate his or her business. There are three types of franchises: traditional, non-traditional and collective-type. To select a franchise, potential franchisees must assess their objectives, life style, time span of the opportunity, soundness of the business concept and the franchisor's track record. Thus the franchisor must prepare a detailed disclosure document to assist the potential franchisee in the evaluation process before signing the franchise agreement.

NOTES

1.   A. Bakr Ibrahim and W. H. Ellis "An Empirical Investigation of Causes of Failure in Small Business and Strategies to Reduce It," *Journal of Small Business and Entrepreneurship* 4, 2 (Spring 1987), pp. 18–24.
2.   A. Bakr Ibrahim, "Is Franchising the Answer to Small Business Failure Rate? An Empirical Study," *Journal of Small Business and Entrepreneurship* 3, 2, 1986, pp. 48–54.

THE ENTREPRENEUR

Anita Roddick–The Woman Entrepreneur
Body Shop International PLC

In the United Kingdom, the latter part of the 1970s saw a profound change in the economic and cultural environment from that in which the very word "entrepreneur" was pejorative and an entrepreneur was regarded as being socially suspect, greedy and downright un-British. All this to say nothing of being a woman entrepreneur.

Anita Roddick appeared on the scene at the right time and exemplifies not only the breed of the new entrepreneurs, but also takes her place amongst the many, many women who have been so successful as entrepreneurs in their own right, not only in the United Kingdom, but in Canada and the United States as well, over the past two or three decades.

Mrs. Roddick was born in 1942 into an Italian immigrant family in England. After working at various jobs, taking a trip around the world, getting married, and having two children, she opened the first Body Shop in Brighton, England in 1976. It sold products made from natural recipes that she had picked up on her travels.

In 1989, there were some 400 franchised Body Shop outlets in 27 countries, with sales reaching £55.4 million, pre-tax profits expanded by 56% to £11.2 million and earnings per share up 38%. Plans call for expansion across the United States, Japan and Europe to boost the number of outlets to 1,000 within five years.

Body Shop products are manufactured from raw materials that largely come from Third World countries or economically disadvantaged areas of developed countries. This is part of Mrs. Roddick's "trade, not aid philosophy." Searching for raw material has taken her all over the world: foot rollers are found in southern India, textiles in Nepal, aloe vera gel in southern Texas, seeds and plants for aromatic oils in Brazil.

Body Shop outlets do not advertise in the normal sense. Instead, they try to build a community profile by supporting various causes, and word-of-mouth. With environmental groups such as Green Peace, Body Shop runs joint campaigns that cover issues on acid rain, recycling, the vanishing countryside, and the depleted ozone layer. Body Shop pays employees to give at least four hours a week to community programs "because what you take from the community, you should give back."

Anita Roddick feels exasperated by the inertia of big business to take up social causes and sees herself as a conduit for campaigning and as a part of a group of concerned citizens out to change corporate values.

Source: *The Economist* (September 9, 1989), p. 82; *Wall Street Journal* (March 15, 1989, p. 34; *Financial Post* (December 29, 1989), p. 14.

△ CHAPTER 19 △
GOING PUBLIC

THE DECISION TO GO PUBLIC

The decision to go public is perhaps the most important decision facing a small, growing firm. For some entrepreneurs, prestige is the primary reason for going public. But for the majority, the need for capital to fund growth is the deciding factor.

Going public is an attractive financing strategy for many entrepreneurs and small business owners who may have an established, successful venture and a good growth record of earnings. Going public provides them with an appropriate financial vehicle to expand with little cash and without having to relinquish control to a venture capital firm. Indeed, a large number of small businesses are attracted to the public market because of the advantages that accrue to the business and the owner(s). However, many small businesses that went public too soon and unprepared have also suffered crises in management, plunging market shares and ultimately failure.

ADVANTAGES OF GOING PUBLIC

Going public has many advantages including:

1. Public offering allows the business to raise equity capital to fund its planned growth without having to resort to debt financing and the huge cost of interest.
2. Public offering increases the net worth of the business, and thus the potential borrowing power as debt to equity ratio improves.
3. If the initial public offering (IPO) is successful and the company continues to grow, it is easier to raise additional funds through different debt financing instruments such as debentures.
4. As the market value of the company's shares appreciates, banks and lenders may be encouraged to lend the company more money.
5. Personal gain for the owner. If the firm continues to do well after the initial public offering, the stock prices will appreciate and the owner(s) may be able to realize a handsome profit.
6. Going public enhances the founder's image and prestige. It is an indication of the entrepreneur's success.

DISADVANTAGES OF GOING PUBLIC

Going public has disadvantages as well. These include:

1. The cost of going public is prohibitive for many entrepreneurs and small business owners. Underwriter's commission (around 8 percent), prospectus cost, registration fees and the like, can run to several hundred thousand dollars. In addition, there is the added accounting cost as a result of increased disclosure required from a public company. Usually a smaller company with a smaller initial public offering (IPO) pays relatively more to go public. Of course, there is always the risk of not being able to sell the stocks in the market and the company ends up with a huge bill to pay.
2. Unless the founder retains at least 51 percent of the shares, he or she may lose control of their company. The potential for loss of control exists through subsequent public offerings.
3. A public company must disclose all its business transactions and activities in the business plan, the prospectus and later on in the annual reports. The public company is scrutinized by regulators, shareholders and the financial press. Information about the company in general and officers' salaries not ordinarily disclosed by privately owned companies must be made available to the public, be it competitors, customers or suppliers.

CRITERIA FOR GOING PUBLIC

When to go public? Studies of successful initial public offerings (IPO's) have shown that the following factors are critical:

1. *Management Capability.* A strong capable management with a proven track record is a key factor in a successful public offering. Investors and analysts must perceive that the management team will be able to handle the added responsibilities and pressure of going public.
2. *Proven Track Record.* The small business must have a proven track record, in many cases, of at least two years. The past and present performance of the firm must indicate a consistently high growth rate and an outstanding performance. Such performance provides an incentive in attracting investors and underwriters.
3. *Potential For Growth.* A strong management team and an outstanding performance doesn't carry much weight unless the investors perceive that there is potential for growth. The firm must demonstrate that the existing product, service and/or opportunity have potential for growth.

THE BUSINESS PLAN

As discussed in earlier chapters, the business plan is the most important document the entrepreneur will ever prepare. Regardless of the financing strategy, be it bank loans, venture capital or public offering, a well-prepared and documented business plan is the first step in pursuing the financial strategy. It allows the underwriter to evaluate the business, its potential for growth, and the management team, and hence, to decide if the initial public offering would be successful.

THE PROSPECTUS

The prospectus is an important document for the initial public offering. It is the principal source of information about the company's health. It contains information about the company, its strengths, weaknesses and financial position, and plans, in particular, the following:

- Assessment of the business: strengths, weaknesses and opportunities.
- The management team: investors pay particular attention to management salaries.
- Risk assessment and contingencies.
- Details of the offering.
- How the company intends to use the proceeds of the initial public offering.
- The capital structure.

SEEKING ADVICE

The decision to go public is one of the most important decisions the entrepreneur will ever make. Therefore, it has to be well planned and researched. The entrepreneur should seek the advice of his or her lawyer, accountant and banker. Talking to these experts should be the initial step to ensure that the company is prepared for this transition, and that the entrepreneur understands the reason for going public along with the advantages and disadvantages of such a major decision.

The Accountant

Entrepreneurs intending to go public must rely heavily on their accountant for the following reasons. First, going public requires a complete audit of all financial transactions, internal control mechanism, and asset verification as to inventory and accounts receivable. Second, advice and assistance are needed in preparing the financial part of the prospectus. Third, other services related to the initial public offering (IPO) are required before and after the offering.

The Lawyer

Legal advice is crucial in executing the offering. Your lawyer has to ensure that all laws and regulations are adhered to before and after the offering.

The Underwriter

The Underwriter's Role

The role of the underwriter is simply to sell the firm's stock for a commission. Underwriters are usually familiar with the market conditions, prices of stock of similar companies and have access to investors (buyers).

Selecting an Underwriter

Selecting an underwriter for an initial public offering (IPO) is critical. Shopping for a brokerage house will give the entrepreneur an idea of different prices, products and services offered. Most small firms go public through small dealers as large brokerage houses may not deal with issues less than $10 million.

The Underwriter's Commission

The commission paid to the underwriter is usually the difference between the price the brokerage house pays for the firm's share and the market price.

Criteria for Selecting an Underwriter

The following criteria are suggested in selecting an underwriter:

a. Reputation of the underwriter among the investors and quality of his or her deals. The underwriter is part of the deal, and his or her name will appear on the prospectus of the initial public offering (IPO).
b. Support offered by the underwriter, including advice and market research before and after the offering. The after-offering support is important in order to maintain interest in the company's shares.
c. The price the underwriter is willing to pay for the company's shares.
d. Experience in underwriting securities of companies in the same industry.

PRICING THE STOCK

Usually the underwriter provides an estimate of the value of the stock. This estimate, while relying on projection, is in many cases arbitrary. Indeed the initial public offering (IPO) price is subject to the ups and downs of the market, making valuation more of an art and more arbitrary than an exact science. The brokerage firm bases the IPO price on similar firms (in terms of size, type and earning) that are publicly traded. However, IPO prices are usually adjusted to reflect the stock market just before the proposed IPO date approaches. A sudden downturn in the market may lower the IPO price. Timing therefore is crucial; the best time to go public is when there is a high demand for stocks. But it is difficult to know when that will happen. The stock prices of many public companies rarely meet the early expectations of their owners. Research studies have shown that initial public offerings are usually underpriced to hedge against risk and the legal liability facing the brokerage firm.

Another deciding factor in IPO pricing is its appeal to investors. Certain kinds of issues are more appealing and therefore easier to sell. For example, high technology issues are in great demand in the 1990s.

The result of all these factors is a price-earning multiple, which indicates the worth of the firm. Figure 19.1 is a checklist for going public.

Critical Issue	Basis and Sources of Judgement
1. When to go public? Is your company ready?	1. Strong management team 2. Proven track record: The firm's past and present performance 3. Potential for growth
2. The business plan	1. Executive summary
	2. The business concept 3. Objectives and strategy 4. The management team 5. The products or services 6. The competition 7. The market 8. Financial plans: projections 9. Risk assessment
3. Seeking advice	1. Banker
	2. Lawyer 3. Accountant
4. Selecting an underwriter	1. Reputation 2. Experience 3. Support
5. The prospectus	1. Summary: overview 2. The business concept 3. Assessment of the firm's strengths, weaknesses and opportunities 4. Risk assessment 5. The management team 6. Details of the offering 7. Use of IPO proceeds
6. Pricing the Initial Public Offering—IPO (the price earning multiple)	1. Similar firms currently trading (in terms of size, type and earning) 2. Appeal to investors 3. Ups and downs of the stock market

Figure 19.1. Checklist for going public.

SUMMARY

To many successful entrepreneurs, going public is an attractive financing strategy. There are many advantages for going public, such as increasing the net worth of the business and thus the potential borrowing power, the ability to expand with little cash and without having to relinquish control, and the prestige and enhanced corporate image. However, going public is costly and may entail loss of control and privacy as a result of disclosure and periodic reporting requirements. There are a number of factors to be assessed in order to determine if the time is ripe to go public. These include management capability, track record and potential for growth. Once a decision is made to go public, a number of steps must be undertaken such as selecting an underwriter, preparing the prospectus, and pricing the stock.

THE ENTREPRENEUR

Peter McAuslan
The College Administrator Turned Successful Entrepreneur

In 1987, Peter McAuslan and his wife, Ellen Bounsall, gave up their jobs as administrators at Dawson College in Montreal and sold their house to raise money to achieve their dream of starting a microbrewery. In January of 1989, McAuslan began brewing operations and launched St. Ambroise Pale Ale, a draft beer named after the street where the brewery is located. "We'd go to sleep with the hissing sounds of the brewery and I'd think that's the independence of your own business, right?" says Peter. The company's brand of beers became a success with the younger, well-educated crowd. McAuslan's beers won four medals at the World Beer Championship held in Chicago. McAuslan has remained a family-oriented business, Peter and Ellen were basically responsible for almost all the functions in the company. As the operations of the brewery became more complex professional managers were hired. Peter feels that it is important to maintain the family atmosphere amongst the employees. Ellen is the brewmaster in the family business. Under her leadership, the company has focused on producing quality beer and St. Ambroise beers are now recognized as some of the best beer in the world.

Source: Excerpts from a case study developed by Jose Lam (M.B.A.) and Ludo Segers (M.B.A.) under the direction of Professor A. B. Ibrahim.

△ CHAPTER 20 △

LETTING GO: THE TRANSITION FROM ENTREPRENEURIAL TO PROFESSIONAL MANAGEMENT

When do entrepreneurs let go of their businesses? This chapter is devoted to exploring the transition from entrepreneurial to professional management.

STAGES OF GROWTH

Organizations pass through different distinct phases as they grow; a life-cycle. Indeed, the study of organization life-cycle is useful and holds more than just academic interest; it may also serve as a prescriptive tool. Both managers and consultants can better anticipate the difficulties that an organization may face from a study of the problems common to many as they reach an equivalent size or level of earnings. The different phases of the organization life-cycle can be described as: start-up (birth), growth, maturity, decline and death or turn-around as shown in Figure 20.1. In the start-up phase the entrepreneur's vision is critical to the success of the new-born venture. The entrepreneurial skills, the highly centralized decision making process and the informal laissez-faire management style are all necessary ingredients to move and nourish the organization.

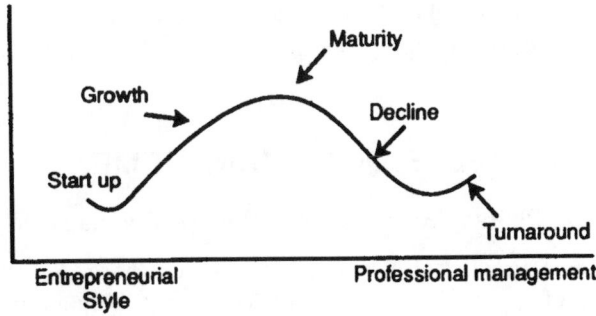

Figure 20.1. Phases of growth.

Box 20.1. The Entrepreneurial Style of Management.

In the face of the entrepreneur's conviction (and demonstration) that he or she is quite unable to adapt to an organization controlled by others, and for psychological reasons, his or her inclination to impulsive decision-making and predilection for direct control, the organizational structure of the enterprise is likely to be centered entirely around the entrepreneur. In Kets de Vries' terms, it is a "spider's web" with the entrepreneur in the middle, orchestrating and controlling every action. Boldness and autocracy are hallmarks of the leader at the centre; characteristics that are frequently essential for success in the enterprise's formative stages. In fact, the organization is simply an organic extension of the entrepreneur. The implications of such a structure for growth are two-fold:

1. Further growth must eventually over-power the entrepreneur's capacity to control and coordinate every aspect of the firm's operation. Delegation and subordination will inevitably be necessary, but these require trust and the reliance on others' judgement, qualities that do not come easily to the entrepreneur, if at all.
2. Mistrust, and the political infighting that inevitably accompanies such an egocentric organizational structure, dictates that the problem of succession will be difficult to resolve. The entrepreneur's compulsion to assert his authority further exacerbates the problem by making it difficult for him to give up the reins of power if and when a sufficiently competent replacement can be found. The old adage "nothing grows in the shadow of an oak" seems appropriate here.

Kets de Vries argues that the very qualities that make an entrepreneur successful are likely to make it difficult, or perhaps impossible for the organization that he creates to grow beyond the size of a personal fiefdom.

Source: M. F. R. Kets de Vries, "The Entrepreneurial Personality: A Person at the Crossroads," *Journal of Management Studies* XIV, 1977, pp. 34–57.

Entrepreneurial traits such as high need for achievement, risk taking propensity, tolerance for ambiguity, creativity, intuitiveness and self confidence are essential in the start-up stage. However, research has demonstrated that those attributes that accounted for early success were among the very things that had to be changed to ensure long-run success.[1] Box 20.1 describes the entrepreneur's style of management.

If a conscious decision has been made to pursue a growth strategy, then formalization of the different activities has to take place. This includes the formalization of the planning and decision-making process, changing the organizational structure and hiring of professional management.

PROFESSIONAL MANAGEMENT

Charles Hofer and Ram Charan described the professionally managed firm as:

> one . . . which has a functional organization structure based on its current needs, permits delegation of appropriate day-to-day decision-making authority to its subordinate managers, utilizes formal information analysis and the intra-firm consultative

process to make administrative decisions, reflects in its routine operations stable corporate and business strategies that recognize both the long and short-term needs and goals of the organization, is free from excessive dependence on any particular individual or individuals for their skills and talents, and displays a certain degree of interchangeability among its components.[2]

The professional style of management exhibits the following characteristics: the ability to be a team player who delegates decision-making responsibility to middle level managers, to be formal with more emphasis on planning, and to be conformist, systematic, calm, cautious and conservative (see Figure 20.2).

The Entrepreneurial Style	The Professional Style
Vision	Planning
Intuitive	Systematic
High centralized decision-making	Delegation of decision-making responsibility
One-man show	Team player
Informal laissez-faire	Formal
Creative	Conformist
Risk taker	Cautious

Figure 20.2. A comparison of the entrepreneurial and professional management styles.

DETECTING THE SYMPTOMS

There are a number of symptoms to indicate that the entrepreneurial firm is ready to move to the professional management phase. The first symptom is the entrepreneur's feeling that he or she is over-extended and over-burdened with many management activities as a result of expansion and business growth. The second symptom is the entrepreneur's feeling that he or she lacks the skills and experience to handle the management of growth, in particular, financial, marketing and human resources issues that emerge as a result of pursuing a growth strategy. Third, there may be a period of decline of the overall financial performance. In many cases, such a decline may be mistaken for economic downturn. However, the longevity of such poor financial performance is a clear manifestation that the organization is no longer capable of managing growth. Fourth, there are usually problems with communication, co-ordination and motivation of personnel. As the organization continues to grow, the informal style and lack of proper structure and management process become a burden. Fifth, there are usually problems with customers and suppliers due to a backlog of orders. Quality of products or services may also suffer. Finally, more mistakes are made in every aspect of the business which cause the overall performance of the organization to deteriorate.

THE TRANSITION TO PROFESSIONAL MANAGEMENT

Entrepreneurs and small firms pursuing a growth strategy have to plan a smooth transition from entrepreneurial to professional management. Indeed, the success of the growth strategy will depend on the effective management of change. Studies have shown that many small businesses experience problems during transition. Unless a high "priority" and attention are given to solve these problems, failure may be the end result. Indeed, the transition from entrepreneurial to professional management is responsible for the extremely high casualty rate in small businesses. Let us briefly discuss two critical problems, the entrepreneur's reluctance to let go and the entrepreneurial culture.

PROBLEMS DURING TRANSITION

1. *Reluctance to Let Go.* A major problem encountered during the transition to professional management is the entrepreneur's reluctance to let go of his or her business. This resistance may be attributed to a number of factors. The first is the entrepreneur's emotional attachment to the business and the difficulties in letting go of it. Research studies have reported that many entrepreneurs experience negative feelings during transition due to decreased responsibility. The second factor is the entrepreneur's lack of trust of the professional manager's skills and abilities to handle his or her business, the business he or she started from scratch and nourished over the years. The third is the entrepreneur's perception that the cost of hiring professional managers will be too high for a small firm.[3] Finally, retirement reminds the entrepreneurs of death.

2. *The Entrepreneurial Culture.* A second major problem is the entrepreneur's values and the organization culture, which are built around a highly centralized decision-making process, with an over-dependence on the entrepreneur for managing the business, and a very informal structure and style of management. Employees who have been working in this type of culture for many years will likely resist the change to a formal, planning, systematic and professional-type culture. Such resistance is due to three factors. First, there is the feeling that formalization may inhibit the firm's ability to respond to a changing environment, thereby stifling growth. They become torn between following the new policy and procedure and taking personal initiative. Second, those employees who have been working with the entrepreneur for many years are not used to making decisions, hence they may lack the skills, competence and experience to take action. Third, resistance may arise as a result of inaccurate perception about the nature and implication of change.

Box 20.2. Managing Change.

R. Charan, C. Hofer and J. Mahon suggest the following guidelines to manage the change from entrepreneurial to professional management.

Step 1. An assessment of the business concept, strategy, structure and decision making of the small firm. This situation audit allows the firm to assess its strengths and weaknesses before introducing any change.

Step 2. The small firm should then try to formalize the decision-making process and information flow. The entrepreneur in this stage should try to rationalize and bureaucratize the process.

Step 3. The entrepreneur must prepare a human resource strategy including hiring and developing key personnel and managers. The entrepreneur must be able to deal with resistance to change. He or she must be able to retain the newly hired professionals through an attractive compensation package and other means.

Step 4. Finally, the process must be monitored to ensure effective management of change.

Source: R. Charan, C. Hofer and J. Mahon, "From Entrepreneurial to Professional Management," p. 3.

MANAGING THE TRANSITION

Studies have shown that certain critical tasks must be implemented for an effective transition to take place. The first task is setting organization policies and procedures that will guide the organization. The second task is to delegate more activities to organization members. The third task is an understanding that managing the change from entrepreneurial to professional management requires not only change in the structure and process, but also in attitudes, behavior and ultimately the organization's culture.[4]

Changing attitude is perhaps the most difficult task during the transition. Employees who have been with the firm since its inception have become used to the entrepreneur's informal style of management. As a result, resistance to a formal-professional style of management is expected.

One way to deal with employees' resistance to change is to have them participate in the change process. This could be accomplished by simply keeping them informed about the change and the underlying rationale. Box 20.2 describes a set of guidelines for managing the change from entrepreneurial to professional management.

Budgeting could be the key to the small business' formalization process. The budget process allows the small firm to: (1) plan its activities ahead of time, (2) assign responsibilities to middle level management, (3) define key tasks and the flow of information, and (4) allows employees at all levels to participate in the process.

ATTRACTING PROFESSIONAL MANAGEMENT

Human resource planning is the key to an effective change of management to take place. The first step in human resource planning at this stage is to attract professional managers. Entrepreneurs and small firms have often complained of their inability to attract young professional managers who prefer large corporations. This may be due to a number of reasons. For example, entrepreneurs do not delegate enough and thus inhibit the development of decision-making skills in their subordinates. As a result, the small firm is not a good training ground for many aspiring young managers. Thus, entrepreneurs must show continuous support and enthusiasm from the first moment they make the decision to hire a young professional manager. Training and career development plans must be clearly stated. A compensation package must also be part of the plan in order to attract desirable talents.

THE CHANGING AGENT

Often the move from entrepreneurial to professional management requires the assistance of a changing agent. The agent could be a consultant, a friend, a relative of the entrepreneur or a member of the board or quasi-board of the small firm. In any case, to effectively induce and manage the change process, the agent must have prestige, power, experience and above all patience. Indeed, convincing a reluctant entrepreneur to let go is not an easy task. Equally difficult is the task of convincing employees of the need to change. Thus, formalizing the system requires proper planning and commitment on the part of the agent.[4]

Figure 20.3 summarizes critical issues during the transition from entrepreneurial to professional management.

Critical Issue	Basis of Judgement
1. Symptoms	• Entrepreneur is over-extended • Inability to handle growth issues and problems (i.e. finance, marketing and human resources issues) • A long period of decline is reflected in the overall financial performance • Problems with communication, coordination and integration • Problems with customers and suppliers (i.e. backlog of orders) • Product quality suffers

2. The Transition
   —Problems
 	
   —Managing the Transition
 	
   —Attracting Professional Managers
   —The Changing Agent
   • Who
   • Qualification
	• The entrepreneur's reluctance to let go
	• The entrepreneurial culture
	• Setting organizational policies and rules
	• More delegation
	• Changing employees' attitude
	• Attractive compensation scheme
	• Involvement in the decision-making process
	
	Consultant/relative/friend
	Power/prestige and experience

Figure 20.3. The transition from entrepreneurial to professional management.

SUMMARY

We have attempted to explore the transition from entrepreneurial to professional management. A number of critical issues were discussed, such as: when to let go, detecting the symptoms, problems during transition, managing transition, attracting professional management and the changing agent. Symptoms include the following: the entrepreneur's feeling that he or she is over-extended and unable to handle growth, problems with communication, coordination and integration, problems with customers and suppliers, and a deteriorating financial performance. During the transition, the organization may face a number of problems such as the entrepreneur's reluctance to let go and the disruptions due to the change in the dominant entrepreneurial culture. Managing transition involves setting organizational policies and rules, delegating more tasks to members of the small firm and changing employees' attitude. Attracting professional managers includes: setting an effective human resource plan and allowing more participation in the decision-making process. Finally, the changing agent must have prestige, power and previous experience to effectively manage the change process.

NOTES

1. A. B. Ibrahim and Joe Kelly, "Leadership Style at the Policy Level," *Journal of General Management* 11, 3, (Spring 1986), pp. 36–45.
2. Charles Hofer and Ram Charan, "The Transition to Professional Management: Mission Impossible?," *The American Journal of Small Business* IX, 1 (Summer 1984), p. 5.
3. R. Charan, C. Hofer and J. Mahon, "From Entrepreneurial to Professional Management: A Set of Guidelines," *Journal of Small Business Management* 18, 1, 1980, pp. 1–10.
4. A. Bakr Ibrahim and Willard Ellis, *Family Business: Text, Readings and Cases,* Kendall/Hunt Publishing Company, 1993.

THE ENTREPRENEUR

Pierre Peladeau—Letting Go

Peirre Peladeau founder of Quebecor Inc., the largest printing company in the world died recently at the age of 70. For years Peladeau has been reluctant to let go of the family business to his two sons Erik and Pierre-Karl. He always felt that neither of his two sons were yet ready to succeed him despite the fact that both sons have been working in the family business for many years.

In 1950 Pierre Peladeau who has graduated with a law degree and a Master in philosophy degree from McGill borrowed $1500 from his mother and bought a small Montreal Weekly newspaper. He continued to buy small weeklies as well as printing companies through out the next two decades. He has always had a good sense of buying small printing or publishing companies at bargain prices and then turning them around into profitable enterprises. By the end of 1997 Peladeau publishing and printing empire generated over $3 billion in revenues.

As an entrepreneur Peladeau possesses many of the qualities necessary for success. He has been labelled a genius, a high achiever and a risk taker. But he was also labelled a tyrant who wouldn't let go of the business to the next generation.

Source: A case study written by Jose Lam (M.B.A.) under the direction of Professor A. B. Ibrahim.

CASES FOR DISCUSSION

_____ **CASE 1** _____

Greenbaum's—The Franchise Alternative

Greenbaum's, as the grocery store arm of Greenbaum Holdings is popularly known, is a chain of stores concentrated in and around an industrial corridor in Canada and the United States. With thirty-eight stores owned and operated by the company, plus an additional five associate stores acquired through the purchase of controlling interest in a smaller chain, Greenbaum's is not a giant on the scale of Kroger, A&P, Loblaws, or Provigo. The chain is, however, large enough to benefit from its scale in much the same fashion, and it enjoys a strong following among consumers within its region. Greenbaum's locations, store facilities, and reputation for quality in meats and produce are clear strengths of the firm, and have made it a potential choice target for takeover and merger proposals. Greenbaum's executives, however, have other ideas. Observing that the market within their region is saturated with their own stores and those of larger competitors, and that there will be little growth and possibly slight decline in demand over the next decade, Greenbaum's management have decided that they will have greater growth potential by investment and acquisition than they could achieve through internal growth. That sentiment was reinforced to no small degree by over a decade of consistent difficulty with the unions representing Greenbaum's store and warehouse employees. The firm, after a succession of collective bargaining agreements which avoided strikes but gave very generous concessions to the employees, finds its retail grocery operations wavering at the brink of unprofitability. Their local personnel costs are simply too great in relation to store revenues, while competition is too stiff to allow significant price increases.

After considering other alternatives, such as merging with one or more other small grocery chains, stock issue, borrowing, or negotiating concessions from the unions, Greenbaum's executives have decided that their most attractive strategic option is to retreat from the front line of the retail grocery business and become a wholesale operator and franchisor. The essentials of their plan are to sell their retail stores to independent entrepreneurs. In the main these would be local investors who would each purchase one or a few stores and operate those as Greenbaum's franchises. The money payable from the sale of retail outlets would then be used to finance other acquisitions. The nature of those acquisitions is at present undecided, but the clear understanding at the head office is that they will be related businesses. The leading contenders are two small grocery chains, which would be "retreaded" as Greenbaum's franchises, and some of Greenbaum's current suppliers. A potentially important byproduct of Greenbaum's strategy is that purchasers of the retail

This case was prepared by Professor Ron Crawford. Revised by Professor A. B. Ibrahim, 1990.

stores would not as franchise operators have any contractual obligation to the unions representing current store employees. Freed from restrictive work rules, and even assuming a level of pay and benefits comparable to unionized chains, the franchise stores would be attractive investments for entrepreneurs. With a strong retail base, Greenbaum's could in turn specialize very profitably in the wholesale and distribution functions, together with providing administrative support for the franchises.

The director of Human Resources at the head office has looked at the franchising strategy with some misgivings. Over three-quarters of Greenbaum's employees are located in the retail stores. While the department would still have an important role to play in working with and for the new owners of the franchise stores, and in ensuring that Greenbaum's reputation for quality, reliability and safety in consumer service is maintained, the members of the human resource staff are justifiably concerned. None of the HR managers have had any experience with franchise retail operations. They recognize that the performance of employees at the store level will be critical to the success of the franchise plan, but they also recognize that they will be servicing a substantially smaller and different work force.

Because of your consulting background in franchised operations, the director of Human Resources at Greenbaum's has asked for your assessment of the problems and priorities which will pertain under the new business arrangement, and for your guidance with respect to the strategy which the department should employ in supporting Greenbaum's franchise initiative.

Kryzowski and Sons Ltd.

Art Kryzowski, one of three sons of an immigrant tradesman, was in his final year of pre-law studies at University of Manitoba in 1941. In more ordinary times he would have looked forward to staying in school, working for admission to the bar, and an eventual comfortable living in a local general practice. His father, a sheetmetal worker by training, had built up a moonlight business repairing and re-selling industrial salvage. By the early 1930s, it had grown into a full-time business, which brokered used machinery to smaller and ethnic businessmen, providing the family with a stable and substantial income. Kryzowski Senior was the personification of the work ethic, pouring countless hours, heart and soul, into running the family business. He dreamed, like so many of his generation, of a company which would become Kryzowski and Sons, and which would allow his children and grandchildren to enjoy the advantages in life that he and Mrs. Kryzowski had missed.

By 1941, Kryzowski Senior's dreams were well on the way to realization. All three sons had been exposed to the business through summer and part-time work. Carl, just finishing high school, was a dismal student and rather easygoing, but had a natural bent for mechanical objects. His good nature and empathic touch with lathes, pumps, and presses made him popular among the shop hands and an obvious candidate for running the production activities of the company. The older brother, Alfred, was the apple of his mother's "eye." Tall, handsome, and outgoing, Alfred frequently accompanied his father on visits to customers. Persuasive and likeable, Alfred was visualized by all concerned as the future sales director of Kryzowski and Sons, although his interests clearly lay more in enjoying the good life than setting sales records. Nominally in his fourth year in business studies at McGill, Alfred was a social lion, active in fraternity life, a dinner-time companion of young men whose fathers ran major corporations, but a "Gentleman's C" scholar only by dint of numerous purchased papers. Art was nearly the opposite of his older brother. Short, stocky, intense, and introverted, Art inherited his father's tendency to be a workaholic. He was regarded by fellow students as somewhat of a greasy grind, but one whose constant efforts were grudgingly respected. Art had comparatively little social life during those years, instead spending most of his spare time helping out in the company office.

Nineteen forty-one was a year of decision for the Kryzowski family. As the war effort moved into high gear, the family business prospered. With new components and virgin materials in short supply, new customers and orders were added. However, the war effort also made its demands upon its manpower. Early in the year, Alfred surprised the family with a dinner-time announcement that he had resigned from the university and enlisted in the R.C.A.F. Three weeks later, Alfred reported for training as a pilot officer, and except for short home furloughs, he was absent until demobilization in July of 1945. From his infrequent letters, it was evident that Alfred cut a dramatic circle in the R.C.A.F.

He flew Wellingtons and later Lancaster bombers on night operations over occupied Europe until late 1944, completing three tours of duty and accumulating several decorations before being posted to an operational training unit in the north of England.

What came through less clearly in his letters was the taste Alfred had acquired for reinforcing his battered nerves with whiskey, which accounted for his failure to advance beyond Flight Leader rank.

Late in 1941, against the protests of the entire family, Carl enlisted in the Navy. Carl's mechanical aptitude was quickly recognized, and he was assigned to a service school for machinists, fitters, and artificers after an initial tour in Corvettes, small anti-submarine crafts. Carl was retained as an instructor by the service school, and passed the remainder of the war as a petty officer. He was able to take most of his furloughs at home, at the cost of many sleepless nights on the train between Halifax and Winnipeg, but was lost as a contributor to the firm for the duration of the conflict. By 1945, Carl was a chief instructor at the technical school and received superlative service evaluations. However, a few stints filling in for the director while the latter was on leave convinced both Carl and his superiors that he would never be an effective administrator.

Nineteen forty-one was also the year in which Kryzowski Senior had his first heart attack. A bull of a man in his mid-50s, Kryzowski rebounded well, but it was a bad portent and forced him to drastically reduce his activities. The brunt of this fell directly on the shoulders of Art Kryzowski. The shop hands were typically older men who had been with the company for years and required little supervision. However, the onus of inspecting, estimating, and haggling on lots and prices, keeping fences mended with established customers, and running the financial side of the business fell increasingly on Art Kryzowski. Despite his ambitions for law school, and accompanied by sub rosa entreaties from Mrs. Kryzowski, Art began to spend mornings, then afternoons and weekends, making calls, visiting suppliers, and trouble-shooting for client firms.

By the Christmas holidays, Art Kryzowski found himself hooked. Every day he spent at the office uncovered new problems and crises which only he had the stamina to unravel. He could count on his father's advice, but all of the footwork and a growing proportion of the key decisions had to be handled alone. In the process, Art also burned bridges behind him. The long hours at the office included many cut classes, late assignments, and a barely passing average for the semester despite dropping one course. When Kryzowski Senior had his second heart attack in February of 1942, Art, who was already hopelessly behind in his coursework at Manitoba, spoke with his faculty advisor and dropped out of school.

Art Kryzowski's youth was all that sustained him through the next three years. With Kryzowski Senior now a partial invalid, although mentally alert, Art not only took over the leadership of the firm, but assumed the equal burden of negotiating every minor change or decision past a suddenly conservative and reluctant Kryzowski Senior. In the months before the end of the war and the return of his brothers, Art learned first-hand the folly of running a firm out of one's hip pocket. Records were disorganized or absent entirely. Scheduling was non-existent. Every supplier and nearly every customer had been demanding and receiving special concessions, and much of the machinery had been jury-rigged so many times that repairs were a nightmare. Art managed. He managed, however, only by putting in still more hours, gradually learning all the peculiarities and wrinkles of the business on a case by case basis, and looking forward to the day his brothers would return and share the responsibility. Having learned the hard way how over-extended and harassed one can become running a business as a one-man band, Art entered into a career which for the most part emulated his father's example.

This is not to say that Art did not make any changes, or that the firm did poorly in his hands. With Mrs. Kryzowski too occupied and distraught caring for her husband, Art found it necessary to hire a full-time bookkeeper and office assistant. He wondered at times if it was the right decision, but it did free him from a lot of routine activities and brought a semblance of order to the financial records. He also engaged a general accountant to handle tax matters and give him periodic financial advice. Art was frankly surprised when he examined the financial statements. The company, despite years of seat-of-the-pants management, was financially healthy. The building, machines, and trucks were owned outright, and there were no outstanding long-term debts. The short-term picture was equally good. The company was paying salaries to himself, both parents, his brothers in absentia at reduced scales, and 18 hourly employees, and was turning a surplus, which his father had been plowing back into inventory. The inventory, in turn, secured any credit necessary to fund new purchases. Nominally valued at $30,000 in 1944, the inventory was a mixed blessing, as many of the items stocked were obsolete and unlikely to sell except as scrap. Looking forward, although little could be done under war-time conditions, the entire physical plant and truck fleet would require replacement within a few years.

The return of Carl and Alfred was initially unremarkable. Alfred was furloughed on terminal leave in July 1945, and Carl in October of the same year. Carl slid unobtrusively into his old activities in the shop, where his knowledge and energy measurably improved output. His old Navy and seaport contacts were extremely useful in obtaining war surplus tools and equipment to modernize the shop and expand the inventory. The shop and warehouse became Carl's personal domain over the years, and on a day-to-day basis he ran them well. Although his title was a more grandiose "vice-president for production," Carl was in fact a glorified foreman, referring any unusual decisions directly to Art Kryzowski.

THE POST-WAR YEARS

The decision to move away from the scrap and salvage business into the provision of new and used pumps and air compressors tended to change the nature of the business. Although the company continued to stock scrap and salvage, the emphasis was on pumps, pipes and hoses. The company became known as the source for used specialized pipe (stainless steel, copper, natural gas, and for hoses for pumping chemicals and corrosive liquids). The pumps sold and re-manufactured by the company were used in the pulp and paper industry, gas transmission, chemicals, and manufacturing. Air compressors provided power for equipment in construction, manufacturing, and assembly work. The importance of pumps and air compressors to the various firms meant that a breakdown required prompt repairs. Often plants or construction sites were shut down for lack of a pump or the failure of an air compressor.

Under the direction of Art Kryzowski, the firm responded to the needs of its customers. Air compressors and large pumps were not only sold and rebuilt, but rented. A 24-hour service department was added. The company prided itself on being able to deliver new or used pumps or air compressors anywhere in the province within 24 hours. The trucking fleet was expanded and increased. As the industries which Kryzowski and Sons served grew after the war, the company prospered along with them.

Art, although he welcomed the reduced workload made possible by Carl's return, was still more hopeful about what Alfred could do for the firm. He looked to his outgoing and imaginative older brother as someone who would be a more active managing partner and who would help to redirect and expand the firm to exploit post-war opportunities. Alfred at least verbally concurred, and agreed to work as rapidly as possible at taking over the entire marketing and customer relations function.

In a business sense, the company did well indeed. The company's reputation for quality repairs and used machines carried over into the new enterprises, often with the same customers. The building was modernized and expanded to include a showroom and a second warehouse. Sales continually grew, and the firm grew with it. Over the next 30 years, the Kryzowskis pursued a conservative and prudent course, building the firm into one of the dominant forces in the regional market. The general economic decline of the late 1970s saw sales peak and then slip, but business remained both comfortable and profitable.

The firm also did well by the Kryzowski family. With the business apparently well in hand, Mr. and Mrs. Kryzowski gradually relaxed their vigilance, slipping by 1950 into unofficial retirement on very healthy executive paycheques. The Kryzowski brothers, as they acquired family responsibilities and their own children grew into their teens, also did well. At the behest of their tax accountant, a real estate subsidiary was formed to rent the Kryzowskis' homes to them, and most of their families were put on the payroll in one or another capacity. It was only when one looked at the internal dynamics of the firm, that any cause for concern might have arisen.

In that initial period of re-organization and expansion after the war, everyone was on unusually good terms. There was so much work to be done that the Kryzowski brothers all worked horrendous hours to keep the growing business together. But Art Kryzowski gradually became aware of a sense of disengagement by Alfred. Alfred dutifully made calls on all of his regular customers and took over the supervision of the one, and then three, young men Alfred and he brought in to keep up with customer relations, direct sales, and running the showroom. However, his initiative in seeking out new clients and trying to broaden offerings gradually trailed off. Alfred spent more and more time in sales lunches with old customers and commensurately less at the office. His conversations with Art increasingly centered on taking more out of the firm. He regularly suggested bringing in bright young professional managers so that he, Art, and Carl could have more time for their families, and seemed to be as concerned with how to set up tax sheltered benefits for family members as with making the company grow. As Art put the situation in a family argument in 1974, Alfred was acting more like a paid employee and less like one of the family team, leaving Art to work ever more hours and make all of the tough, important decisions virtually on his own.

Alfred's version of the story was substantially different. Like Art, he looked back fondly on the rush and bustle of the post-war period, when everyone was too busy to worry about family politics or titles or the like. And in his off-guard moments Alfred would occasionally admit to confidants that he was not going to "kill himself" for the company, like Art. However, Alfred's major objection was the behaviour of Art Kryzowski. In Alfred's terms, Art was treating the company more and more as his personal property, which had to be protected at all costs from mistakes by Alfred or Carl. He insisted that they adopt his viewpoint on all significant decisions, intervened in their deliberations with major customers, and in general acted as though he were the father and they were his teen-aged, impulsive offspring. So if Art wants to run the show, let him. Alfred was making a good living, doing a fair share of the work for what he earned, and if he felt excluded from the corridors of power, he more than compensated by a fuller family and social life.

Carl was largely oblivious to all of this, although the issue occasionally arose in family arguments. He ran his shop and ran it well. And until Art started making mistakes which hurt his shop, he would stick by him.

This process continued for years, never emerging into open confrontation, but never existing far below the surface. Art became the man who dominated the firm, made the key contacts, and met with customers. Customers called Art almost any time of the day or night when a pump failed or an air compressor broke down. During the construction season, customers often demanded immediate service, and Art grew accustomed to staying at the office for extended periods of time.

On July 17, 1980, Art Kryzowski had a heart attack. He was alone in his office, and was not found until the next morning. He was 59 years old.

The death of Art Kryzowski was duly noted in the local obituary column, but it did not cause much of a stir. The company closed for the funeral, and all 30 employees attended the funeral. Everyone knew Art as an intense and likeable workaholic. It was only after the funeral that Carl and Alfred looked at one another helplessly and asked each other, "What do we do with the company?"

Baker Inc.

Markets are changing, competition is becoming more intense and the performance of Baker Inc. has started to slip. It is extremely painful to me to sit and watch Baker Inc.'s profit earning deteriorating. I have put energy, time and more than thirty years into this company. I have asked you to come to this meeting to review the company's situation and to discuss my retirement plan.

So spoke Mr. James D. Parson, President and Chief Executive Officer of Baker Inc. from his executive office on the sixty-second floor of the First Canadian Building. Baker Inc. is a Canadian-owned and managed corporation, manufacturing and selling electrical equipment for industrial and consumer use throughout Canada and the U.S. The company employs over 50 employees and has offices in Toronto and New York.

Baker's historical background would provide any writer with all the ingredients of a corporate drama. Described by a business associate as "a man who felt that he should never quash his instincts with an over-dependency on numbers and facts alone," Mr. James Parson started his business 35 years ago, in 1948, with $10,000 in the bank which he had collected from members of his family, his mother Eva, his brother John, now Vice-President/Human Resources and his brother-in-law George Brown, now Vice-President/Planning. Company sales were $30,000 in 1948 with operating net profit of $2,500; comparable 1989 fiscal year data were $11,210,150 and $3,642,300.

Mr. Parson's retirement plan was not a surprise to many of his top executives. Many problems were obvious in the past three years. Managers have been complaining of Mr. Parson's interference in their work, specifically his relation with their immediate subordinates. Parson still maintains a good relationship with floor level workers and clerks who started early when Baker was still a workshop operation. Many times these people had ignored their immediate supervisors and went directly to James Parson with small problems which had offended their superiors.

There have been problems concerning Parson's style of making decisions. As one manager put it, ". . . his entrepreneurial style was okay 30 years ago when Baker was a small operation." Mr. Parson has recently launched a new product without consulting his top executives and despite the recommendation of his marketing and planning staff that the market is saturated. "Well, the company lost $1,000,000 in this project," commented a senior executive.

Blain's volume became so great that a warehouse was soon needed. And by 1970 the operation was moved from the original 300 to a 1600 square foot drugstore located in a large suburban shopping mall. The increase in sales and turn-over resulted in greater buying power and better gross margins.

Aware of the untapped potential of drugstores as a retail sales business, coupled with the importance of meeting customer's need, Blain, from the start, had directed his efforts towards an efficient merchandising program, a competitive price policy and a competent professional service. He complemented the range of pharmaceutical products with the most current cosmetic, health-care products and household items. And the continued success of this approach resulted in the opening of 20 corporate drugstores from 1970 to 1980.

Each new drugstore received the attention and support needed to ensure both profitability and growth. Rising costs, however, meant that a store launching no longer cost between $50,000 to $75,000 but something closer to $200,000, which necessitated the franchising option.

Although franchising was a viable aid to the growth of the business, it was by no means the ultimate vehicle for growth and expansion. The limitations of the franchise operation rested with the lack of suitable candidates. The only person allowed by law to acquire a drugstore franchise was a licensed pharmacist. Yet, as Blain explained, "Pharmacists are trained to count pills and of the first seven franchises, three were reacquired for not performing to expectations or for deviating from accepted Blain business methods."

Continuing rising costs forced Blain to consider other avenues for growth and he began to acquire existing small pharmacies. Using the original base of business as a nucleus, the small pharmacist was generally moved to a larger location nearby which virtually assured that the drugstore would be profitable within a relatively short period of time. In general, Blain bought out the more experienced, well capitalized pharmacists—"an autonomous pharmacist meant that central management was not required to spend a great deal of time supervising operations." Unfortunately, one drawback which often arose concerned the independence of these pharmacists who had had their own operation and did not feel necessarily bound to abide by Blain's methods and procedures. While some acquisitions were successful, others ended in disputes and lawsuits. "The bottom line in all this," said Blain, "is that I am in a very precarious business—a very high risk group."

FINANCE

The initial financing of Blain Drug Stores Limited in 1967 was from Mr. Blain's very limited personal resources. With time, however, and with the company's continued success, those personal resources increased significantly. It was those resources, coupled with the retained earnings and normal banking arrangements, that financed the expansion and growth which are represented in Exhibit 1. Although there had been some thought at various times of "going public," Mr. Blain never seriously considered it—"there are only two reasons for going public, one, if you need the money, and two, to get more exposure, and I didn't need either of them."

The company had no investment in real estate properties and all locations were leased on a long-term basis. The franchised premises were in turn leased to the franchisee and this provided for annual rentals of up to $1,387,800 per year, with terms expiring some ten years hence. The other long-term assets owned by the Company were mainly equipment and leasehold improvements. The following was a breakdown of the Company's fixed assets as of July 31, 1985.

Leasehold Improvements	$736,700
Machinery and Equipment	15,980
Furniture and Fixtures	1,246,690
Automobiles	12,420
Total	2,011,790
Accumulated Depreciation	873,840
Net	$1,137,950

As of July 31, 1985, the total Long Term Debt of the Company was $497,500, including capital lease obligations of $251,700.

Exhibit 1 indicates the increases and decreases in pre-tax income from 1982 to 1985. It was in light of these figures that Mr. Blain began to look much more critically at some of the operations and organizational structure of his company.

OPERATIONS

By early 1985, the Blain drugstore chain had grown to a network of 34 outlets throughout the western provinces, with plans to increase this number to approximately 40 within a relatively short period of time. Growth was expected to come from conversions and acquisitions of individual stores and smaller chains, and from store openings. Expansion was viewed as a normal business tactic. Mr. Blain believed, "if you do not grow as fast as the market will allow you to, there is always the chance that somebody else will come in and that opportunity will no longer exist."

The Blain organization was mainly a retail chain of drugstores which purchased all the products it distributed from Canadian and foreign manufacturers and brokers. A typical store consisted of a pharmaceutical and a commercial section which, due to legislative restrictions, operated independently from one another. The pharmaceutical section of each store was owned by a pharmacist who was responsible for its management.

All stores carried a wide selection of nationally advertised brand name merchandise, as well as Blain's own private label products. Stores ranged in size from 4,000 to 14,000 sq. ft., averaged around 6,000 sq. ft., and were operated on a self-service basis with the exception of prescription drugs and cosmetics.

The stores were generally located at street level (44%) and in strip malls (38%). The remaining 18% were located in shopping centers. By and large, new stores were located in strip malls or at street levels where the company could enjoy the benefits of 7 days-a-week shopping.

In order to ensure consistency in product quality and pricing, head office was responsible for product selection and pricing. Franchisees ordered directly from the approved list of suppliers while corporate stores were replenished by a coordinator who had responsibility for a group of corporate stores.

Each corporate store was managed by an experienced store manager who was paid partly on a bonus formula. This was a system designed to ensure good control over inventories and encourage optimal performance. It was the company's policy to close any store which did not meet a minimum profitability target.

There were approximately 1,050 non-unionized employees, of which nearly 60% were part-time. The head office staff totalled 50 people.

The Company had over 800 suppliers, none of whom accounted for more than 5% of the purchases. The purchasing department at head office had the responsibility of negotiating, with major suppliers, agreements on behalf of the organization and its franchisees, in order to maximize benefits generated through volume purchases. All inventories were owned by Blain with transfers made to the franchisees as ordered.

FRANCHISING

In 1985, the Blain group of drugstores included 14 franchises whose activities were governed by the Company's Standard Franchise Agreement. The agreement called for the payment of royalties calculated on the basis of sales and was typically for a 10 year term. The franchisees were able to benefit from certain advantages, such as, assistance with store openings, management and operation, and participation in advertising on a large scale. In exchange, the franchisee was required to respect the Blain name in terms of quality, service, merchandising and advertising. Franchisees were supported from Head Office which offered a wide variety of services in the areas of merchandising, expansion, marketing, operation, purchasing, human resources and finance.

Blain's financial philosophy with respect to its franchise operations was to provide a new operator with a franchise banking arrangement which offered a combination of credit and non-credit services. Most commonly this included such features as line of credit, fixed asset financing, installment leasing, and payroll services. Because of Blain's supervision and strong management support, the amounts, terms and rates of the franchising package were more advantageous than would normally be given to an independent business. Blain had established a franchise financing agreement with several institutions to assist its franchisees.

COMPETITION

The retailing of prescriptions and over-the-counter drugs, health and beauty aids and tobacco products was highly competitive. Competition ranged from small and medium sized retailers to regional and national chains. As well, many changes were taking place in the whole industry, not the least of which was the battle between the independents, the discount and the chain stores (see Industry Note). For example, Drug Mart Associates, the Alberta-based buying and advertising group had grown from a small group of community drug stores to a highly-competitive and sophisticated network of stores.

Blain, however, did pride itself in the quality of its services and, in order to retain and improve its position in the marketplace, it provided quality products at competitive prices and targeted specific buying groups through advertising campaigns and programs. For example, a special discount policy was introduced for the Senior Citizens Group.

The Blain group's promotional expenditure averaged 2% of annual sales, with an emphasis on publicity, using mainly circular and radio promotions. Weekly advertising appeared in selected newspapers, a bi-weekly circular was delivered to pre-determined residential areas and a chain-wide circular was delivered six times a year to a wide range of homes.

MANAGEMENT

While Blain had been successful, its founder wondered, in view of the declining profits in particular, whether or not the Company would have performed even better under more professional management. Mr. Blain admitted that he did everything by the seat of his pants and that "six times out of every ten I was right." Blain's entrepreneurial initiative had taken the company along paths that no other pharmacist had dared to venture in the late sixties and seventies. While these accomplishments had been impressive, Blain recalled, "I looked at myself in the mirror one morning and wondered, am I the right person to take this Company much farther? Has the Company outgrown my abilities as an entrepreneur"? Although he felt that return on investment had been good, was it what it might have ben relative to other businesses now in the industry?

In 1985, Blain believed that he had three choices:

1. He could retain control of Blain Drugs; what had worked well in the past might possibly work well again in the future.
2. He could hire several M.B.A.'s, who acting as a team, could help reshape the Company.
3. He could hire an executive vice president to take over most of the decision processes.

Blain recognized that this latter choice could well be the most difficult. He considered himself to be somewhat stubborn and wondered if he could share the control and responsibility with another individual.

In this period of reflection, Blain realized that with any of the three choices, somewhere along the line and to a greater or lesser degree, he would have to start delegating more responsibility. Whatever decision he made was bound to have long term effects on Blain Drugs. Though the Company was not thought to have acute managerial problems, Blain wondered what the best course of action to take might be.

Exhibit 1 Blain Drug Stores Limited (A)
Financial Data
('000)

	Historical			
	1982	**1983**	**1984**	**1985**
Chain Sales (including Franchises)	$23,410	$29,000	$34,880	$40,350
Earnings from Corporate Stores	1,480	2,050	1,780	2,070
Earnings from Franchise Stores	370	500	620	660
Head Office Expenses	950	1,220	1,290	1,720
Pre-Tax Income	$903	$1,340	$1,120	$1,010

	Projections				
	1986	**1987**	**1988**	**1989**	**1990**
Chain Sales (including Franchises)	$45,860	$59,310	$71,690	$85,260	$102,540
Earnings from Corporate Stores	2,420	2,980	3,710	4,520	5,510
Earnings from Franchise Stores	860	1,270	1,510	1,800	2,150
Head Office Expenses	1,950	2,460	3,070	3,480	3,890
Pre-Tax Income	$1,330	$1,780	$2,150	$2,840	$3,770

Note: All financial data have been factored.

Exhibit 2 Blain Drug Stores Limited (A)
Industry Note

There have been many changes in the marketing by pharmaceutical outlets and the following extracts point these out. Not only are there straight marketing differences but there are different regulations covering operations in the respective provinces.

ARTICLES

Drug Merchandising—August, 1989 page 16

Last year, 23% of grocery stores had pharmacies. This is a rapid rise from 1981 when only 7% had pharmacies.

Food/drug combos are growing 28% a year in dollar sales, compared to food stores without a pharmacy growing only 8% a year. There are about 3,500 to 3,800 food/drug combos compared to about 41,000 food stores.

Adding prescription drug sales to food store revenues is not the only advantage of combining food stores and pharmacies: the addition of a pharmacy was also shown to triple sales of health and beauty aids, and helped in promoting the idea of one-stop shopping.

. . . "Many (grocery) retailers don't know that HBA (Health & Beauty Aids) products can offer them several times more net profit per dollar of sales than the average store."

Drug Merchandising—September 1988 page 50

Because of restrictive ownership laws in Quebec, the actual setup of the company (Jean Coutu Group) bears some explanation, says Francois. "It's very confusing but because of the legislation here in Quebec that says you cannot incorporate pharmacies, we can't have corporate stores. While the franchisor may be a public company, all the stores are privately held and are wholly owned by a pharmacist." In this sense, he goes on, Jean Coutu Group's function becomes one of servicing the retail drugstores, "Under our contracts we offer service to the retail stores for a fee, they buy from our warehouse and tap into our advertising as well as our "corporate image."

Drug Merchandising—November 1989, page 12

Because of a new law due to go into effect in Ontario in March that prohibits stores larger than 7,500 sq. ft. from operating on Sunday, Coutu will keep its stores to that size to maintain a seven-day schedule.

Drug Merchandising—July 1988 pages 39, 40

Independent pharmacies continue to be gobbled up by the big guys. For example, Shoppers Drug Mart has cornered 31% of the drugstore market, employs 20,000 people and has 568 stores—and counting.

Competition is heavy for front shop business and the provincial governments are putting a squeeze on dispensing fees. Pharmacies find themselves competing head on with not only the big guys, but also with the grocery chains.

All pharmacies operate on the tripod theory; the first leg is marketing; the second, operations; and the third, finance.

Discount drugstores are strong in the marketing area and advertise deep discount prices. They operate with a minimum of 20,000 sq. ft. and provide limited selection and limited service.

Major chains and franchises are also very strong in the advertising on both TV and print, and are strong in the front shop marketing. They usually range between 5,000 and 10,000 sq. ft., offer a broad selection and have personnel available to provide the necessary service. The finance leg is covered by full-time financial support at head office, who provide monthly financial statements that allow the managers to make effective decisions based on the facts.

The average independent pharmacy has a floor space of 2,500 sq. ft. Stores with a front shop must attract customers with their own mailers and promotions, or engage an independent marketing company to assist. It is, therefore, very difficult for the independents to compete against the big guys with their mass buying, mass advertising, super discount prices, trained personnel and current accurate financial information to manage their operations.

Blain Drug Stores Ltd. (A). Exhibit 2 (Continued)

VII. DRUG STORE UNIVERSE

A. DRUG STORE EXPENDITURES

HIGHLIGHTS—DRUG STORE UNIVERSE— DRUG STORE EXPENDITURES

- Drug store dollar sales increased by ten percent nationally in 1988. This continues the double digit growth rate experienced by the sector since 1981.
- Quebec and Ontario increased their share to 64.3 percent of the national figure (in 1981, the two provinces accounted for 58.4 percent of Canadian drug store dollar sales).
- Drug sales are growing at a faster rate than personal disposable income, therefore, they have increased their importance to 2.1% of P.D.I.
- Total drug has grown at a faster rate than total food thereby drug sales as a percent of food and drug has increased to 18.1 (in 1988) from 11.5 (in 1981).

REGIONAL IMPORTANCE TO TOTAL DRUG STORE SALES DOLLARS 12 MONTHS TO NOVEMBER/DECEMBER

	1981	1982	1983	1984	1985	1986	1987	1988
Maritimes	7.2	7.3	8.0	7.9	8.0	7.7	7.7	7.5
Quebec	21.1	20.9	22.9	24.3	23.4	24.9	24.7	24.4
Ontario	37.3	37.6	37.2	37.3	37.3	37.6	38.6	39.9
Man/Sask	8.1	8.3	7.8	7.2	7.4	6.8	6.4	6.0
Alberta	10.3	10.6	10.9	10.2	10.6	10.2	10.0	9.8
Br. Columbia	16.0	15.3	13.2	13.1	13.3	12.8	12.6	12.4

Source: A. C. Nielsen

DRUG STORE DOLLAR SALES TRENDS, CANADA 12 MONTHS TO NOVEMBER–DECEMBER

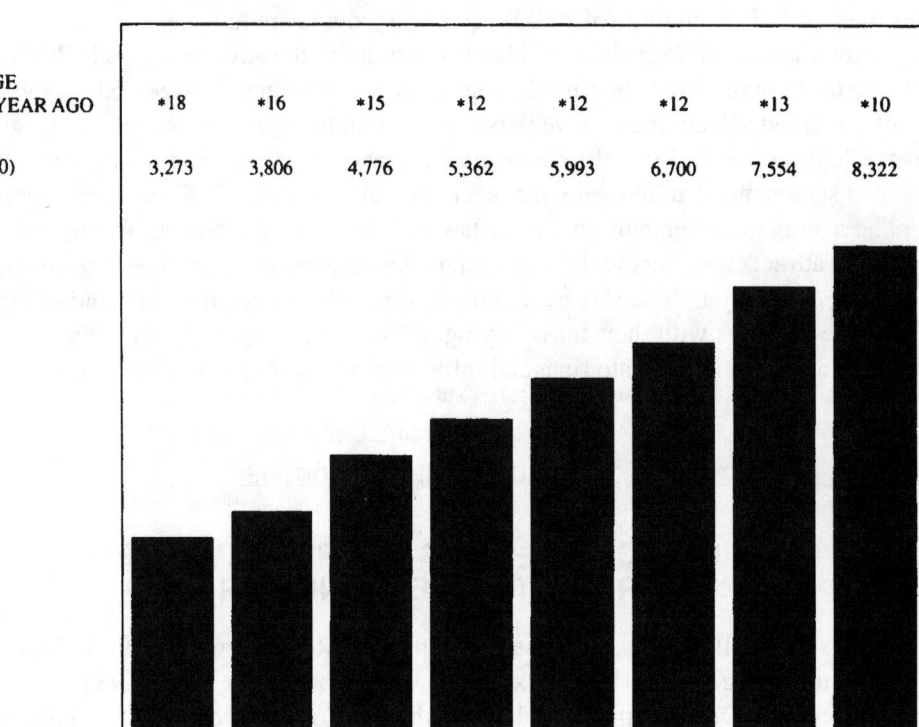

% CHANGE VERSUS YEAR AGO	*18	*16	*15	*12	*12	*12	*13	*10
$(1,000,000)	3,273	3,806	4,776	5,362	5,993	6,700	7,554	8,322
	1981	1982	1983	1984	1985	1986	1987	1988

Source: A. C. Nielsen
*Does not include NFLD, Yukon + NWT

MARKET TRENDS—DOLLAR GROWTH TOTAL FOOD VS TOTAL DRUG—NATIONAL 12 MONTHS TO NOVEMBER–DECEMBER

	Drug	Food	Drug Sales as % Food + Drug
1988	+10	+5	18.1
1987	+13	+6	17.4
1986	+12	+6	16.4
1985	+12	+6	15.7
1984	+12	+6	15.0
1983	+15	+5	14.2
1982	+16	+9	12.2
1981	+18	+14	11.5

*Does Not Include Newfoundland, Yukon & N.W.T.
Source: A. C. Nielsen

DRUG SALES CONCENTRATION—CANADA MARKET SHARE CONTROLLED BY LEADING ORGANIZATIONS

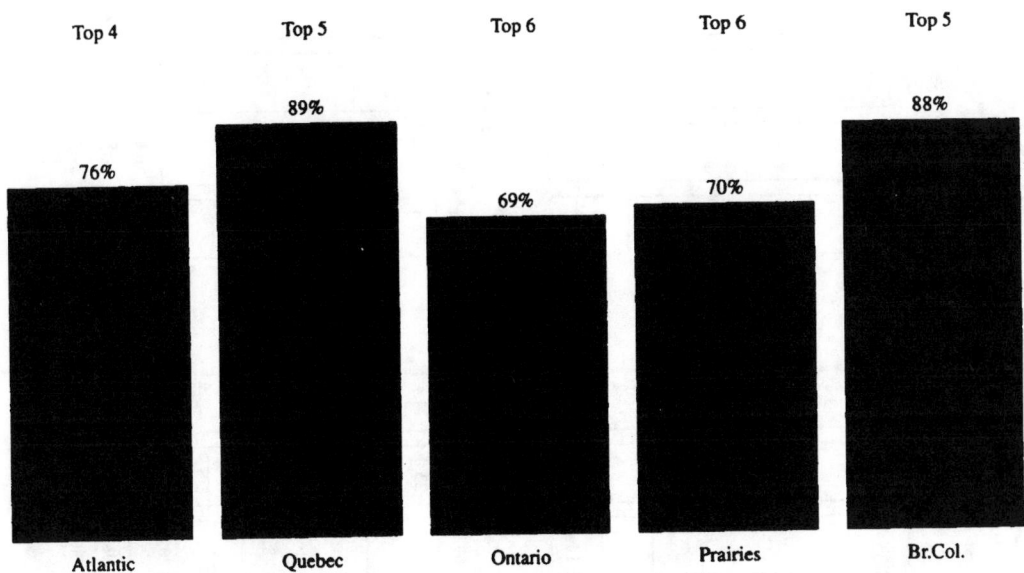

Source: CCTFA Report 1988

HIGHLIGHTS—DRUG STORE UNIVERSE—SALES CONCENTRATION WITHIN THE DRUG TRADE

- While chain stores dominate the food store trade in Canada, large independents are the key retail sector in the drug trade. Shopper's Drug Mart plays a major role in this sector.

SHARE OF ALL—COMMODITY DRUG SPENDING—REGIONAL

MARITIMES

	'85	'86	'87	'88
SUPERMARKETS*	79.4	80.2	81.0	84.0
CHAINS	13.9	14.1	15.5	11.6
LARGE IND.	65.5	66.1	65.5	72.4
MEDIUM IND.	13.4	12.6	12.3	9.3
SMALL IND.	7.2	7.2	6.7	6.7

ONTARIO

	'85	'86	'87	'88
SUPERMARKETS*	80.2	80.3	80.8	82.2
CHAINS	24.2	24.8	27.3	29.6
LARGE IND.	56.0	55.5	53.5	52.6
MEDIUM IND.	13.4	12.5	11.4	10.2
SMALL IND.	6.4	7.2	7.8	7.6

QUEBEC

	'85	'86	'87	'88
SUPERMARKETS*	69.8	71.1	71.4	74.3
CHAINS	23.4	23.5	24.4	21.9
LARGE IND.	46.4	47.6	47.0	52.4
MEDIUM IND.	15.8	14.5	14.6	13.2
SMALL IND.	14.4	14.4	14.0	12.5

BR. COLUMBIA

	'85	'86	'87	'88
SUPERMARKETS*	82.8	83.2	82.8	84.9
CHAINS	37.6	38.2	39.0	37.7
LARGE IND.	45.2	45.0	43.8	47.2
MEDIUM IND.	13.6	10.8	10.6	9.1
SMALL IND.	3.6	6.0	6.6	6.0

MAN./SASK.

	'85	'86	'87	'88
SUPERMARKETS*	62.2	64.7	63.0	64.1
CHAINS	25.7	25.0	24.4	23.9
LARGE IND.	36.5	39.7	38.6	40.2
MEDIUM IND.	23.1	18.8	21.4	21.2
SMALL IND.	14.7	16.5	15.6	14.7

ALBERTA

	'85	'86	'87	'88
SUPERMARKETS*	69.7	69.3	70.9	73.7
CHAINS	20.6	21.2	23.0	24.4
LARGE IND.	49.1	48.1	47.9	49.3
MEDIUM IND.	19.6	20.4	19.0	17.1
SMALL IND.	10.7	10.3	10.1	9.2

*Supermarkets = Chains + Large Independents

NIELSEN DRUG INDEX (NDI) PROJECTED—DRUG STORE DOLLAR SALES (YEAR ENDED NOVEMBER–DECEMBER 1988)

		Total Stores	Chains	Independents
Canada	$ Sales (000)	8,321,929	2,207,396	6,114,533
	% By store type	100.0	26.5	73.5
Maritimes	$ Sales (000)	626,364	72,761	553,603
	% By store type	100.0	11.6	88.4
Quebec	$ Sales (000)	2,031,249	444,658	1,586,591
	% By store type	100.0	21.9	78.1
Ontario	$ Sales (000)	3,324,405	984,928	2,339,477
	% By store type	100.0	29.6	70.4
Man/Sask	$ Sales (000)	500,860	119,529	381,331
	% By store type	100.0	23.9	76.1
Alberta	$ Sales (000)	808,195	197,047	611,148
	% By store type	100.0	24.4	75.6
British	$ Sales (000)	1,030,856	388,473	642,383
Columbia	% By store type	100.0	37.7	62.3

Source: A. C. Nielsen Marketing Research Division

RETAIL CANADIAN DRUG CHAIN STORES BY REGION

	NFLD	Mar.	Que.	Ont.	Man/Sask	Alta	B.C.	Total
Big V				103				103
Bi-Rite					21	1		22
Cumberland (Neiss)			18	4				22
Drug City (Kent)		3		31				34
Drug World				8				8
Herbies (Title)				8				8
Howies (S.D.M.)				9				9
Hy & Zel's				15				15
Jean Coutu (J.C. & St. Onge)			19					19
Lawton's	20	39						59
London Drugs						11	20	31
Metro Drugs					14			14
Pinders					16	5		21

*Key independent organizations include:
Shopper's Drug Mart—312 stores
I.D.A.   —385 stores
Source: A. C. Nielsen Marketing Research Division

NATIONAL DRUG STORE COUNT ESTIMATES AS OF DECEMBER 1, 1986

	National	Maritimes	Quebec	Ontario	Man/Sask	Alberta	Br. Col.
Chains	857	56	126	407	71	92	105
% of total	15.7	14.9	8.7	21.0	13.4	15.7	17.6
Large Indep.	1,487	150	348	566	91	145	187
% of total	27.2	39.9	24.2	29.2	17.2	24.8	31.3
Med. Indep.	1,073	61	276	360	136	146	94
% of Total	19.6	16.2	19.1	18.6	25.7	24.9	15.8
Small Indep.	2,054	109	693	607	231	203	211
% of total	37.5	29.0	48.0	31.2	43.7	34.6	35.3
Total Universe	5,471	376	1,443	1,940	529	586	597
% of National	100%	6.9	26.4	35.5	9.7	10.7	10.9

Source: A. C. Nielsen

HIGHLIGHTS—DRUG STORE UNIVERSE—DRUG SALES (SELECTED PRODUCT GROUPINGS)

- Contrary to combined food categories, the health and beauty aids category has shown some growth (+ 2%) over last year. However, when we compare current growth to recent history, the category's growth rate has reversed it's fast pace and is in decline. This decline has been felt most within the health and hygiene aids category.
- On a national basis, baby care products account for 25% of total health and beauty aid warehouse shipments. They also exhibited the strongest growth rate (+6%).
- The health and beauty aid product classes with the strongest growth rates (12 months – $) are: infant care products (+12%); patent medicines (+11%) and miscellaneous Haba products (+11%).

HEALTH AND BEAUTY AID PRODUCTS WAREHOUSE SHIPMENTS INTO RETAIL FOOD STORES—REGIONAL SUMMARY 52 WEEKS TO JANUARY 16, 1989—DOLLAR BASIS (000'S)

	Oral Hygiene		Baby Care		Hair Care		Patent Med.		Misc. Haba	
	$	% Chg	$	% Chg	$	% Chg	$	% Chg	$	% Chg
National	92.2	+ 3	188.7	+ 6	115.3	+ 4	76.0	+ 1	271.1	− 1
Newfoundland	1.8	+21	1.8	−12	1.8	+22	1.7	+19	4.6	+ 0
Maritimes	5.3	+10	9.3	+14	4.0	+ 7	5.0	+17	16.0	+ 7
Quebec	21.4	+ 5	27.7	− 2	22.9	+ 7	8.7	+ 1	58.8	− 1
Ontario	29.3	− 6	74.6	+ 4	37.3	− 4	18.8	−29	89.7	− 6
Manitoba	5.9	+ 2	15.0	+ 9	9.7	+ 2	6.7	+ 7	18.1	− 6
Saskatchewan	4.8	+20	11.0	+12	6.9	+23	6.5	+23	14.5	+ 7
Alberta	12.6	+ 9	25.3	+14	17.7	+13	16.2	+20	37.0	+ 8
British Columbia	11.1	+ 7	24.1	+ 3	15.1	+ 5	12.6	+28	32.4	+ 2

Source: NWSS (Nielsen Warehouse Shipment Service) Study on Health and Beauty Aids—52 weeks ending January 14, 1989.

CANADA'S 10 FASTEST GROWING DRUG STORE CATEGORIES*
(12 MONTHS ENDING OCTOBER-NOVEMBER 1988)

Category	Outlet Type	Physical Vol. (000) % Change			Retail & Value (000) % Change			Indicated Inflation			Advertising $(000) % Change / $ Ad/$ Sales Ratio		
		1986	1987	1988	1986	1987	1988	1986	1987	1988	1986	1987	1988
1. Incontinent products	Drug	0	8,159	10,584	0	6,616	8,518	—	—	−1	—	1,192	307
		—	—	+30	—	—	+29	—	—		—	+95	−74
2. Diarrhea remedies	Drug	1,053	1,128	1,228	9,390	11,169	14,041	+33	+12	+17	176	187	240
		+0	+7	+9	+33	+19	+26				+3	+6	+28
											.02	.02	.02
3. Diabetic test strips	Drug	368	385	399	10,257	13,178	16,440	+25	+23	+21	0	0	0
		+5	+5	+4	+30	+28	+25				0	0	0
											.00	.00	.00
4. Sugarless gum	F + D	105,361	117,671	136,096	46,633	55,249	68,012	+12	+6	+7	4,150	4,239	4,462
	+ V	+11	+12	+16	+23	+18	+23				+6	+2	+5
											.10	.12	.01
5. Cold caps, tabs, powders	F + D	22,445	25,299	27,618	109,567	137,454	168,757	—	+12	+14	13,193	14,722	17,132
		—	+13	+9	—	+25	+23				+58	+12	+16
											.11	.10	.10
6. Dietary aids	Drug	1,590	1,680	2,007	13,007	13,456	16,146	+3	−3	+0	1,313	658	831
		−9	+6	+20	−6	+3	+20				−28	−50	+26
											.10	−.05	.05
7. Sel. hot/cold kits & compresses	Drug + pharmacy	53	76	87	406	542	648	N/A	−9	+7	0	0	0
		—	+43	+13	—	+34	+20				0	0	0
											.00	.00	.00
8. Lip care products	Drug	5,423	6,279	7,174	7,686	9,699	11,712	+11	+10	+6	138	202	434
		+11	+16	+14	+22	+26	+20				+10	+46	+115
											.01	.01	.02
9. Medical nutritional supplements	Drug	5,898	7,217	7,927	11,389	14,787	17,552	+8	+8	−5	470	0	—
		+20	+22	+10	+28	+30	+19				*	0	—
											.04	.00	.00
10. Hair sprays	F + D	2,051	2,686	2,998	60,229	78,783	92,572	+5	+0	+6	1,671	2,016	2,389
	+ MM	+42	+31	+12	+47	+31	+18				−9	+21	+19
											.03	.03	.03

*Greater Than 200%
** Based on Dollar Growth

CASE 5

Blain Drug Stores Limited (B)

PROFESSIONAL MANAGEMENT

Before joining Blain Drugs, as executive vice president and chief operating officer in 1985, Stuart McMullan had held senior executive positions in a number of industrial and service organizations, some of whom were among the largest in Canada. Lawrence Blain believed that McMullan's proven knowledge of management and marketing would indeed be a strong asset for the Company.

Originally, given the fact that he was new to the Company and the industry when he joined the organization, Mr. McMullan found that he had to spend much of his time on basic operating problems. By 1988 he believed, however, that much of what he had attempted to do had become more or less accepted and operational. He believed that he would now be able to devote more of his time to looking ahead and worrying about longer-term projects. On things in general, he commented,

> "When you reach a certain size, the entrepreneur has a lot of difficulty running the business, because good as he was as an entrepreneur, he's a lousy manager. And as good as I am as a manager, I am a lousy entrepreneur. So the two combined together can take care of both parties and this is what happened here. So I've changed his business, utilized his knowledge of the business and his talent and I've brought to bear my management technique and my knowledge of people. We've got a long way to go—profit is not as it should be, but it's coming."

The addition of a professional manager to the Company was a profound change and not one without its moments of anxiety. Mr. McMullan described his relations with Blain thus:

> "I think for him (Blain) this was probably the most difficult decision he had ever taken. And it is still difficult for him to accept the fact that he built the business and knows it all by heart, piece by piece, and sometimes he's got to accept the decision I'm taking, even where sometimes he doesn't understand the reasoning behind it. Blain's not an expert, he's a pharmacist. If I was in pharmacy, I would be in a hell of a problem. I'm a professional manager, so I know certain things that he doesn't. And it has been very difficult; it's still difficult for him to accept the fact that a lot of companies go bankrupt because the owner, as a matter of pride cannot accept the fact that he just cannot do it and must delegate the responsibility of his business to somebody else. And I can understand that. It's his life. That's why in my role, I have to be firm sometimes, otherwise he would be making all the decisions again and I'd be just a puppet working for him and that's not what he needs. He had that before and got into trouble. But it has not been easy."

In his words, at the time of his joining, Mr. McMullan found:

1. There was no marketing department,
2. The accounting department was in a mess and could not produce regular financial reports,
3. There were no control systems and nobody could tell what the margins were,
4. In purchasing, the Company would follow the suppliers' recommendations and was not getting the best deals,
5. Many of the existing managers were under-qualified and overpaid.

Under his leadership, Mr. McMullan believed that the Company had evolved into a structured organization with key people positioned in the areas of purchasing, finance, human resources, operations and marketing. (Exhibit 1)

The management team in 1988, had an average age of 42 years and industry experience averaging some 11 years.

A group of six key people formed a senior management committee which met on a weekly basis to discuss major issues. The meetings allowed the directors to broaden their view outside their own division and develop a solid knowledge of the Company as a whole.

The Company operated on a decentralized basis where each director was autonomous and responsible for their own day-to-day operations. Being free of any large bureaucratic policies permitted each director to respond quickly to market trends and opportunities. It was management's view that this unique operating approach in the industry allowed the divisional general managers to implement their entrepreneurial abilities toward achieving fiscal goals. The company, as a whole, therefore, combined the strengths and advantages of a large corporation with the qualities of small companies.

More recently, the Company embarked on a program to automate the inventory control, purchase order management and sales analysis system, as a means of improving co-operative advertising and merchandise allowance controls, margins and inventory turnovers. This management information system would also permit electronic communications between all corporate stores and the head office computer, as well as providing the means for continuing development of more sophisticated management controls not only within head office but in the franchisee operations.

Looking to the future, Mr. McMullan described his wishes to "make Blain Drug Stores the most professional, dynamic drugstore chain in Canada." But, in terms of carefully planned long term strategies, Mr. Blain prefers to seek "profitable and sustainable growth so that the Company can withstand competitive or economic threats with its accumulated earnings."

Exhibit 1 Blain Drug Stores Limited (B)

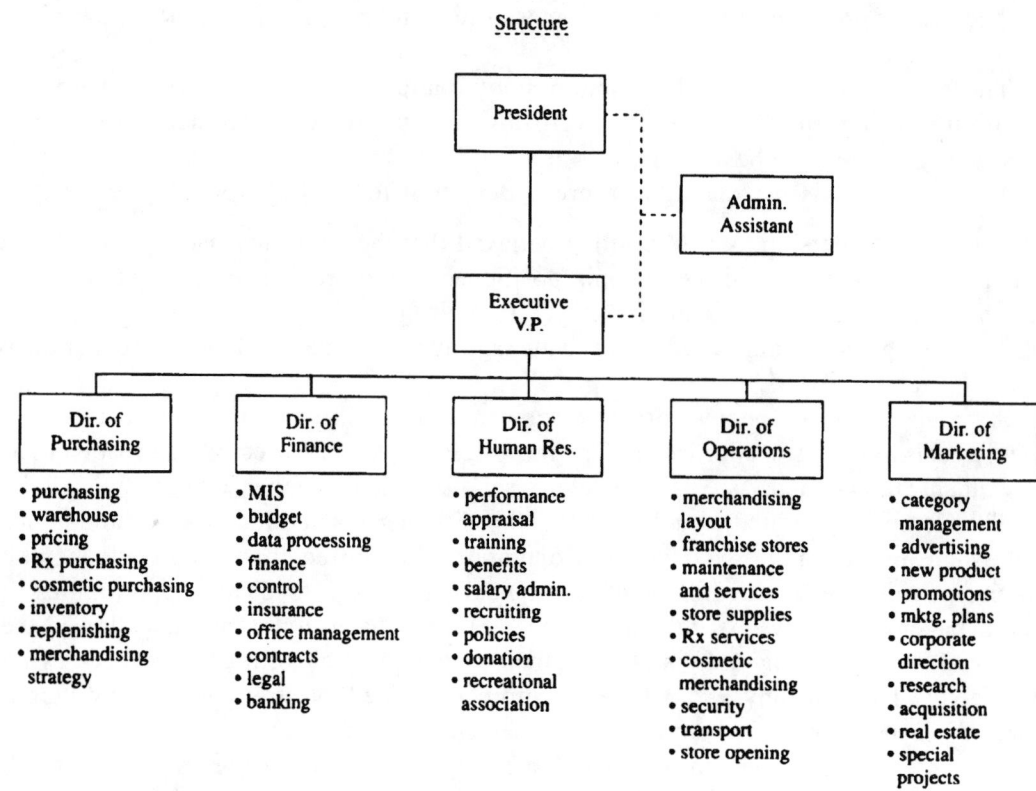

Structure

President

Admin.
Assistant

Executive
V.P.

Dir. of Purchasing	Dir. of Finance	Dir. of Human Res.	Dir. of Operations	Dir. of Marketing
• purchasing • warehouse • pricing • Rx purchasing • cosmetic purchasing • inventory • replenishing • merchandising strategy	• MIS • budget • data processing • finance • control • insurance • office management • contracts • legal • banking	• performance appraisal • training • benefits • salary admin. • recruiting • policies • donation • recreational association	• merchandising layout • franchise stores • maintenance and services • store supplies • Rx services • cosmetic merchandising • security • transport • store opening	• category management • advertising • new product • promotions • mktg. plans • corporate direction • research • acquisition • real estate • special projects

PART FOUR

THE FIELD

△ Research Methodology

△ CHAPTER 21 △
RESEARCH METHODOLOGY

C. Peirce, a great American philosopher said "to satisfy our doubts . . . therefore, it is necessary that a method should be found by which our beliefs may be determined by nothing human, but by some external permanency—by something upon which our thinking has no effect. . . . The method must be such that the ultimate conclusion of every man shall be the same. Such is the method of science."[1]

The field of entrepreneurship and small business is going through a growing stage characterized by confusion, inconsistency and lack of sound empirical and conceptual-type research, and thus could benefit from Peirce's prescription.

IN SEARCH OF A PARADIGM

It goes almost without saying that there is disagreement in the academic community as to the state of entrepreneurship and small business research, basically because there are anomalies which the present paradigm does not address. For Kuhn[2] anomalies, inexplicable by the current paradigm, lead to crisis, to proliferation of competing articulations, explicit discontent, debate over fundamentals, and ultimately that form of scientific revolution we describe as paradigm shift. It is on the verge of this state that research in entrepreneurship and small business finds itself today.

The purpose of this chapter is two-fold. The first is to identify the characteristics and problems associated with research in small business and entrepreneurship. The second purpose is to help students of entrepreneurship and small business understand the fundamental nature of the scientific inquiry. Indeed, sound research enhances our understanding of complex issues such as success, failure and the decision-making process, thus enabling us to construct theories and build paradigms in the field.

WHY HAS THERE BEEN SO LITTLE RESEARCH?

The answer is that the area of entrepreneurship and small business is extremely complicated. There are many variables that are difficult to measure. Take, for example, the construct of failure or the entrepreneurial culture. It also involves many disciplines such as finance, marketing, accounting, organizational behavior, policy/strategy, psychology and sociology.

RESEARCH PROBLEMS IN ENTREPRENEURSHIP AND SMALL BUSINESS

The Interdisciplinary Orientation. Research in entrepreneurship and small business has been enriched over the years by the contribution of researchers from different fields such as psychology, sociology, marketing, management and finance. Indeed, this disciplinary orientation has provided valuable insight to entrepreneurship and small business management from different perspectives. However, each of these disciplines brings its own research methodology, paradigm, as well as its own assumptions and biases. As a result, the field suffers from lack of an integrated research approach that may threaten its development.

 The Case Approach. The second major problem facing research in entrepreneurship and small business is its reliance on the case approach. While the case approach is an excellent pedagogical technique, it has added very little to theory construction, and paradigm building. The case approach assumes that each small business is unique and therefore generalization, an essential assumption in the scientific inquiry, is not applicable. If the field is to develop, there is a need to test empirically, concepts and hypotheses, and ultimately build a conceptual framework to guide researchers and practitioners alike.

THE PRESENT RESEARCH PARADIGM

Research in small business and entrepreneurship can be described in the following typology:

Prescriptive. A large majority of small business research can be described as prescriptive-type writing based on the writer's observation and experience. While this type of writing has enriched the field, it has lacked the scientific approach in terms of data and rigorous method to support different assumptions as it was intended for unsophisticated readers.

Case Studies. A large number of writers have followed a traditional case study approach. In the absence of sufficient theoretical and empirical research, the case approach has helped to enhance our understanding of the field. However, the difficulty with the case approach is that students of entrepreneurship and small business are left without a theoretical and conceptual frame of reference to guide them.

Correlational-Type. Recently a large number of researchers have followed a correlational type approach to give credibility to their work. This approach involves questionnaires and study of documents. Indeed, as research in the field develops, it tends to follow a correlational-type approach.

Experimental-Type. This type of research represents a very small percentage of research in the field, dealing mostly with the psychological make-up of the entrepreneur. This rigorous research approach involves manipulating research variables under a controlled environment.

Let us now examine the scientific inquiry and focus on a number of issues crucial to small business research, including sampling, analysis of data, research design and types of research experiment.

THE SCIENTIFIC INQUIRY

The scientific approach to inquiries starts with doubt and unclear situations from which the researcher tries to formulate assumptions. He begins by surveying the literature and investigating the relevant environment. Once the problem is formulated, the researcher can construct the hypothesis and deduce its implications. The relation between the variables stated in the hypothesis is tested by different methods, be it correlation or experimentation. Finally, the hypothesis is accepted or rejected.

SAMPLING

Small business research, like other disciplines, depends on random sampling to generalize about different problems facing the small business. To learn something about small business failure, for example, we take a few small firms that have failed and study them and reach certain conclusions. It is impossible to imagine studying all small business populations or universes to reach a conclusion concerning failure. Thus random sampling is that method of drawing a portion (sample) of population or universe so that all possible samples of fixed size "n" have the same probability of being selected.[3] A sample of fifty small business owners/managers, drawn at random, is unbiased in the sense that no member of the population has any more chance of being selected than any other members.

The question always raised concerns the sample size. As a rule, the larger the sample size the smaller the error (deviation from population characteristics).

ANALYSIS OF DATA

Analysis of data is simply the sorting, classifying, manipulating and summarizing of research data. The objective of analysis is to try to answer questions formulated earlier. Different types of statistical analysis can be very helpful to researchers in the field including: frequency distribution, graphs, measure of central tendency (mean, median and mode), measures of variability such as the variance and standard deviation, measures of relation such as the product-moment coefficient of correlation (r), and the rank order coefficient of correlation (rho), analysis of variance, profile analysis and multivariate analysis such as multiple regression, factor analysis, discriminant analysis and canonical correlation, and indices such as coefficients of correlation.

While research in the field is still in the early stage and tends to utilize simple statistical techniques, a growing number of researchers in the field are learning to use more rigorous statistical analysis.

RESEARCH DESIGN

Research design is the strategy the researcher is intending to pursue in order to obtain an answer to the research problem. Kerlinger outlined the following criteria for research design: (1) answer to research problems, (2) control of variables, (3) generalizability and (4) validity.[4] Indeed, sound experimental research in entrepreneurship and small business is lagging. There are many unanswered questions in the field. On the other hand, there is much poor ex-post-facto research in the field that should also be avoided and ignored. Unless hypotheses are tested, researchers should be skeptical of ex-post-facto research.

Laboratory Experiment

Laboratory experiment research is accomplished by isolating the research variables under study from the routine activity, thus preventing any independent variables, other than those under study, from influencing the dependent variables. A major disadvantage of the laboratory experiment-type research is artificiality and the lack of external validity. However, it must be understood that the purpose of laboratory experiment research is to test hypothesis and study and manipulate variables under total control. Some research studies on entrepreneurial traits have followed this approach.

Field Experiment

Field experiment research is very similar to laboratory experiment except in two aspects. First, it is a study in the real environment and thus eliminates the artificiality problem. Second, the researcher has less control of the variables, and thus, may face the problem of contamination of independent variables. Many of the early studies on entrepreneurial traits and personality have utilized this approach.

Survey Research

As indicated earlier, survey-type research is the most popular approach in small business research. Survey research is simply a study of a sample from the total population to discover relations among variables. There are different types of data collection in survey research, such as personal interview, telephone interview, mail questionnaire, panel and controlled observation. Telephone and personal interviews are perhaps the most effective types of data collection in small business research. Unlike large organizations, small business owners/managers may feel uncomfortable revealing information about their businesses in writing, and may have difficulty in understanding some of the research questions, and in particular, complex scales and financial performance measures.

THEORY CONSTRUCTION IN ENTREPRENEURSHIP AND SMALL BUSINESS

As Kurt Lewin once noted "nothing is so practical as a good theory." Indeed sound scientific research is the cornerstone for theory building, hence the development of entrepreneurship and small business as a field. To understand theory building, let us discuss a number of issues:

Generalizability and Causality

The scientific inquiry assumes that the phenomena can be generalized. In essence, the assumption of uniqueness of each small business according to the traditional case approach is not necessarily valid.[5] Indeed generalizability of the phenomena under study allows researchers to build theories and paradigms in entrepreneurship and small business.

The scientific inquiry also assumes that causality does exist. Causality is the cornerstone of theory building. For example, a theory in entrepreneurship may assume that causality exists between the entrepreneur and venture success.

Measuring Theoretical Constructs

The field of entrepreneurship and small business is still in the early stage of development in terms of rigorous research. Thus, to test assumptions and build theory, it becomes necessary to establish reliability and validity of the measurement. Reliability of the measurement refers to its consistency. That is, the researcher obtains consistent results with repeated administration. Validity is the ability of the research tool to measure what it is supposed to measure.

Deductive and Inductive Theory

There are two categories of theories—those derived from empirical research (inductive), and those derived from conceptualization (deductive). In building a theory by deduction, a conceptual frame is established or deduced based on certain logical premises. Deductive theories do not lend themselves to testable hypotheses and thus can be described as more philosophical in nature.[6] Inductive theories, on the other hand, are based on empirical research and require cross validation of findings. Inductive theories are crucial in the early stages of the field's growth and development. The distinction between deductive and inductive theory is not a clear cut one. Indeed no theory is totally inductive or totally deductive as can be shown in the following continuum.[7] (See figure 21.1.)

Figure 21.1. Theory building continuum.

RESEARCH DEVELOPMENT STAGES

Research in any field tends to follow a certain pattern of growth. The initial stage tends to follow observation-type research that is loosely controlled and less scientific. That is, we have no reliable or valid measure to confirm the assumption. The second stage tends to

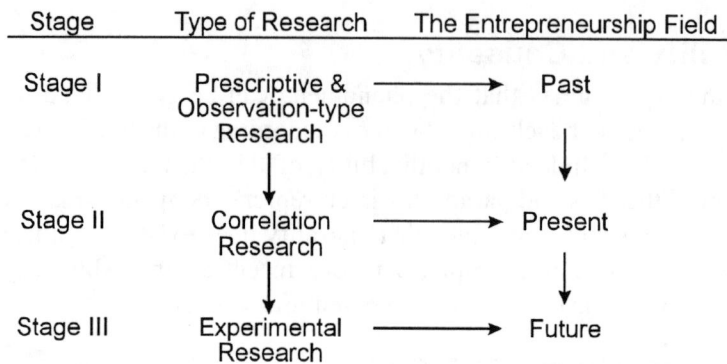

Stage	Type of Research	The Entrepreneurship Field
Stage I	Prescriptive & Observation-type Research	→ Past
Stage II	Correlation Research	→ Present
Stage III	Experimental Research	→ Future

Figure 21.2. Stages of research development in the field.

follow more correlational-type research to lend reliability and validity to the measurement of theoretical construct. The final stage is the experimental-type research where variables are controlled and manipulated. The entrepreneurship and small business field is no exception. The field has moved from the initial development stage to the correlational stage as can be shown in Figure 21.2.

TOWARD A PARADIGM SHIFT IN RESEARCH

If the field is to develop, experimental-type research is needed. The rigor and ability to control and manipulate research variables allow researchers in the field to develop solid guidelines for the entrepreneur and the management of the small business. This type of sound scientific research represents a shift from the early prescriptive writing in the field. Indeed, without experimental-type research, theory constructions and paradigm building would be a difficult task.[8]

RESEARCH FOCUS

Research can enhance our understanding of many issues in the field. The following examples represent a number of issues that can be better understood through research.

- Networking
- Delegation and the entrepreneur

- Managing growth
- The transition from entrepreneurial to professional management
- Franchising as an alternative strategy
- Strategy formulation
- Strategic planning and strategic thinking
- The decision to go public
- Marketing strategy
- Human resource strategy
- The entrepreneur
- Success and failure
- Technology and innovation
- Organizational structure
- Venture creation
- Impact of public policy issues on small business

However, as the field matures, less research effort should be spent on studying the entrepreneur and/or the manager of small business while more should focus on underlying disciplines and relationships.

THE NEED FOR DATA SHARING

The development of the field relies on the concept of data sharing. Because of the difficulties many young researchers face in the data collection stage, data should be made available free to researchers and standards must be set for data sharing by entrepreneurship and small business associations.

SUMMARY

The field of entrepreneurship is going through a growing stage. We have attempted in this chapter to explore and discuss research problems in the field. Research in the field of entrepreneurship and small business can be described as prescriptive, case approach, survey-and empirical-type research. Two major research problems were identified and discussed, the disciplinary orientation and the case approach. Research in the field has been enriched from the contributions of different fields. However, these different approaches have led to a lack of integration. Also, the case approach, while an excellent pedagogical method, has added very little in terms of theory construction and paradigm building in the field. There are many anomalies in the field that need explanation.

NOTES

1.   J. Buchler, ed., *Philosophical Writings of Peirce* (New York: Dover, 1955), Chapter 2.
2.   T. S. Kuhn, *The Structure of Scientific Revolutions* (University of Chicago Press, 1970).
3.   W. Feller, *An Introduction to Probability Theory and Its Applications,* 2nd ed., (New York: Wiley, 1957).
4.   F. Kerlinger, *Foundation of Behavioral Research* (Holt, Rinehart and Winston, 1973).

5. J. B. Miner, *Theories of Organizational Structure and Process* (CBS College Publishing, 1982), pp. 1–9.
6. Ian Mitroff and Richard Mason, "Business Policy and Metaphysics: Some philosophical considerations," *Academy of Management Review* (July 1982).
7. J. B. Miner, *Theories of Organizational Structure and Process,* CBS College Publishing, 1982, pp. 1–19.
8. A. B. Ibrahim, "Methodological Issues in Entrepreneurship and Small Business Research" (ICSB 1986), pp. 34–44.

THE ENTREPRENEUR

Frank Stronach—People Management
Magna International Inc.

The entrepreneurial story of Frank Stronach really began when he immigrated to Canada from Austria in 1954. Trained as a tool and die-maker, Stronach invested what little savings he had and in 1957 opened up his own tool and die shop in a rented garage in Toronto, Ontario, while he was in his mid-20s. Stronach seemed to have found a niche in the market for business grew rapidly in the first two years and he soon employed 30 people. His foreman was apparently cast from a similar entrepreneurial mold because he told Stronach that he wanted to leave and start his own business and the foreman set up the company's second tool and die shop. Whether out of necessity or planned strategy, this was the format followed as the company grew—decentralization with equity participation by its employees.

"If I lose a good person, I'm losing somebody who could be a competitor. I want those people in my camp. That's what business is all about—people management."

For the next 15 years Magna grew almost continuously at an annual rate of 30% or more and by 1985 was opening one new factory every six to eight weeks to keep pace with the demand. Sales for the fiscal year 1989 amounted to $1.92 billion with a net profit of $33.6 million and operating 123 factories.

Some observers attribute its success to Magna's unique "corporate culture" which included a commitment of keeping all Magna plants small, an emphasis on research and development, and rewards for both management and workers through an attractive profit-sharing plan and range of social benefits from day care for employees' children to a recently opened company owned conservation and recreation area.

Under Magna's policy, the profit allocation goes to unalterable segments: 20% to shareholders, 10% to employees, 7% to research and development, 2% to charities and culture, 6% to management (which included 2% for Stonach, amounting to $2 million in 1988), and the remaining 55% reinvested in the company.

Stonach is reported to have said, "We still believe in entrepreneurship, but what we are telling the entrepreneur is, for God's sake, you can't take it all."

Source: *Canadian Business* (May 1988) p. 32; *Financial Post* (July 21, 1989) p. 3.

PART FIVE

READINGS

THE ENTREPRENEURIAL PERSONALITY: A PERSON AT THE CROSSROADS

M. F. R. Kets de Vries

. . . Sometimes I have visions of myself driving through hell, selling sulphur and brimstone, or through heaven peddling refreshments to the roaming souls . . . Brecht, *Mother Courage*

ABSTRACT

This paper reviews the concept of entrepreneurship and empirical studies of entrepreneurial behaviour patterns. In addition, it explores the social, economic and psychodynamic forces influencing entrepreneurship. A conceptualization of the entrepreneurial personality is proposed. Finally, the organizational impact of these entrepreneurial behaviour patterns on work environment and management succession is discussed.

INTRODUCTION

We quickly recognize an element of mythology and legend in the articles about entrepreneurship in such journals as *Fortune* magazine. This journal and others of its kind devote part of each issue to preaching the gospel of enterprise and business leadership. Not surprisingly these themes of individual success and failure are highly popular; they catch the readers' imagination and are empathy-provoking since they awaken the rebellious spirit present in each of us. We see that Prometheus and Odysseus have been replaced by that folk hero of the industrial world, the entrepreneur. He has become the last lone ranger, a bold individualist fighting the odds of the environment. He is that individual who after enduring and overcoming many hardships, trials and business adventures finally seems to have "made it." But frequently there is an epilogue added to these fairy tale endings whereby the "and they lived happily ever after" theme is missing. As in Greek myths success may lead to hubris or excessive pride, and might come to fall. And as we can see in the case of many entrepreneurs success is a very fragile state, easily followed by failure.

Take for example the story of Bernard Cornfeld and Investment Overseas Services.[1] This tale tells us of a displaced person born in Istanbul of Jewish parents. We follow the family's emigration to America. The father, an unsuccessful actor died when our hero was

Reprinted from *The Journal of Management Studies* (February 1977). Used by permission of the publisher.

very young, leaving the mother to take care of the family, having to work extremely long hours. The story continues by describing how Bernard Cornfeld after many difficulties became an investment professional (thus ending his career as a social worker), and began to sell mutual funds overseas (not necessarily to the benefit of its investors) being extremely successful at it. But his fund of funds became like a chain letter game, financial controls were lacking and chaos prevailed in the company. Eventually Cornfeld was deposed leaving the remains of the company wide open to plunder by Robert Vesco.

Another entrepreneurial saga tells the tale of the rise and fall of Charles Steen, from an uranium millionaire to a pauper.[2] When we look at his family history we find a father who squandered all his money on "loose living" and eventually divorced his wife. Charles Steen never saw his father again after this divorce. His mother on her part married a total of nine times. Further study of Charles Steen's personal background reveals that he seemed to have difficulties in holding on to a job. After his last dismissal, unsuccessful in finding a new position, he decided that the only choice left was to strike out on his own. The story continues by describing a period of extreme hardship and poverty finally broken by his uranium find. But his wealth did not last long; excessive spending and poor investments caused his bankruptcy. And now we can find him broke roaming the desert again.

These two stories are spectacular but not uncommon examples of the rise and fall of entrepreneurs. While other stories might be less dramatic and often limited to the successful part of the entrepreneur's endeavour, closer analysis of these various stories reveals that most of these tales of hardship and success contain a number of common, rather familiar themes. We are usually introduced to a person with an unhappy family background, an individual who feels displaced and seems a misfit in his particular environment. We are also faced with a loner, isolated and rather remote from even his closest relatives. This type of person gives the impression of a "reject," a marginal man, a perception certainly not lessened by his often conflicting relationships with family members. The environment is perceived as hostile and turbulent, populated by individuals yearning for control, with the need to structure his activities. We observe an individual who utilizes innovative rebelliousness as an adaptive mode with occasional lapses toward delinquency, ways of demonstrating his ability to break away, to show independence of mind. Due to these reactive ways of dealing with feelings of anger, fear and anxiety, tension remains since "punishment" in the form of failure may follow suit. Failure is expected and success is often only perceived as a prelude to failure. Interrelated with this strange pattern of elation and despair, of successes and failures, we also observe a kind of person who demonstrates a remarkable resilience in the face of setbacks, with the ability to start all over again when disappointments and hardships come his way.

The person we are describing, the entrepreneur or the "creative destructor" to use Schumpeter's[3] terminology, is a highly complex individual, certainly not the simpleton or automaton which many economists would like us to believe he is. The entrepreneur is obviously not that "lightning calculator of pleasures and pains," as Veblen[4] once cynically described him and bears no resemblance to that mythical creature of economic theory, the economic man. On the contrary, we are dealing with an individual often inconsistent and confused about his motives, desires and wishes, a person under a lot of stress who often upsets us by his seemingly "irrational," impulsive activities.

Notwithstanding the multitude of articles written about entrepreneurship and the entrepreneurial organization, the entrepreneur has remained an enigma, his motivations and actions far from clear, a state of affairs aggravated because of contradictory theoretical and research findings. Consequently, the purpose of this article is a review of the concept of entrepreneurship and of empirical studies of entrepreneurial behaviour patterns. Subsequently, social, economic and psychodynamic forces influencing entrepreneurship will be explored. A conceptualization of the entrepreneurial personality will be presented largely based upon interviews and the life histories of a number of entrepreneurs. Finally the implications of these entrepreneurial behaviour patterns for entrepreneurial organizations will be discussed.

ENTREPRENEURIAL ROLES

Economists have always looked at entrepreneurs with a great deal of ambivalence. The often unpredictable, irrational actions of entrepreneurs do not fit the economists' rational, logical schemes; they tend to disturb the implicit harmony of their models. Generally speaking their attitude toward entrepreneurship has been one of "benign neglect." Baumol's exasperated statement that "the theoretical firm is entrepreneurless—the Prince of Denmark has been expunged from the discussion of Hamlet"[5] is not far from the truth. But some economists have shown interest in the entrepreneur. Beginning with Cantillon[6] and Say[7] who stressed respectively the uncertainty bearing and coordinating functions, the entrepreneur has been discussed by various economists.

The term "entrepreneur," derived from the French word *entreprendre,* to undertake,[8] has been defined and redefined by historians, economists and sociologists. Forgetting conceptual niceties, students of entrepreneurship usually define the entrepreneur as that individual instrumental in the conception of the idea of an enterprise and the implementation of these ideas. In this process the entrepreneur fulfils a number of functions which can be summarized as the innovation, the management-coordinating and the risk-taking functions.

The *innovation function* particularly, has been stressed by Schumpeter[9] who stated that ". . . entrepreneurship . . . essentially consists in doing things that are not generally done in the ordinary course of business routine." Schumpeter's entrepreneur is an ideas man and a man of action who possesses the ability to inspire others, and who does not accept the boundaries of structured situations. He is a catalyst of change, able "to carry out new combinations," instrumental in discovering new opportunities, which makes for the uniqueness of the entrepreneurial function. We notice that when a later student of entrepreneurship such as Drucker[10] summarizes the tasks of the entrepreneur as projection (forecasting the future), combination (of major new developments), innovation, and anticipation, he is actually doing nothing else than restating Schumpeter's original propositions.

Less spectacular but essential is *managing-coordinating* which is often regarded as a second function of entrepreneurship, but here the distinction between an entrepreneur and a business executive becomes blurred.[11] Some may even argue that the term manager and entrepreneur are actually mutually exclusive.[12] It raises the question of at what stage of an organization's development the more "bureaucratically inclined" manager is taking over.

As a third function of entrepreneurship *risk-taking* is worth mentioning. After Cantillon this notion has particularly been proposed and developed by Knight[13] who views the entrepreneur as the taker of non-quantifiable uncertainties. But with the division of ownership and management, the use of other than the entrepreneur's personal capital sources, the entrepreneur can be considered more a creator of risk than a taker of it. However, although the entrepreneur does not necessarily bear the financial risk of an operation, he is exposed to a considerable degree of social and psychological risks. More often than not a great decline in prestige and status income is a common phenomenon in the initial phase of entrepreneurship. The "purgatory of entrepreneurship." i.e. the period preceding recognition of one's entrepreneurial abilities, can be a time of extreme hardship during which considerable sociopsychological sacrifices have to be endured. Naturally a certain tolerance for economic risk is necessary but a tolerance for psychosocial risks might be more important.

TESTING ENTREPRENEURIAL BEHAVIOUR PATTERNS

After this brief description of entrepreneurial roles we will turn now to empirical studies of the entrepreneurial personality. Unfortunately, most of these studies have not excelled in conceptual clarity. Not only is there a recurring confusion in definition of differences between entrepreneurs and managers, but, in addition, many of these studies have focused exclusively on specific entrepreneurial sub-groups such as the high technology entrepreneur, or have concentrated on specific personality characteristics which might contribute to successfulness in company performance. Furthermore, the great diversity in test instruments has prevented or at least hampered the possibility of making more general comparisons. But in spite of these seemingly formidable handicaps we might be able to make some generalizations after reviewing a number of these empirical studies.

The major contributor to the empirical study of entrepreneurship has been McClelland as presented in his book *The Achieving Society*.[14] Using Thematic Apperception Tests[15] and specific games of skill he discovered that entrepreneurs scored high on need for achievement (n Ach). He defined this need as the desire to do well in competitive situations where the results of one's effort could be measured objectively. Not only did he find that entrepreneurs are high on n Ach but they also (1) desire to take personal responsibility for decisions, (2) prefer decisions involving a moderate degree of risk, (3) are interested in concrete knowledge of the results of decisions, and (4) dislike repetitive, routine work.

In his most recent study McClelland has shifted the emphasis from achievement to power.[16] He argues that for organizational effectiveness power motivation is required. He concludes that high n Power combined with high self-control (socialized power) as opposed to high n Power and low self-control (personal power) makes for the greatest organizational effectiveness, particularly if n Affiliation is also low. Personal power men (power greater than affiliation, low self-control) characterized by a "conquistador motive pattern" resemble the entrepreneur and represent those individuals who are difficult to organize in any kind of system. Their lack of inhibition or self-control limits their effectiveness as large institution builders in spite of their success in inspiring people in the initial stage of growth of the organization.

T.A.T.s were also used in a wider context (without the emphasis on n Ach and n Power) in the Collins and Moore study *The Enterprising Man*.[17] The major conclusions which Collins and Moore drew from the analysis of T.A.T.s was that entrepreneurs (1) suffer from a lack of problem resolution (to use their words: "It is as though he panics at the idea of success or too much success,"[18]) (2) prefer to have patriarchical relationships with their subordinates, (3) are uncomfortable with authority figures which explains their great need for autonomy, and (4) possess a high degree of anxiety and self-destructiveness.

Schrage[19] was influenced by McClelland's achievement study and the Collins and Moore study when he was looking at the successful R and D entrepreneur and the factors which contribute to successful company performance. His view of the successful R and D entrepreneur was that of a person high on n Ach, low in power motivation and high in awareness of self, market, and employees.

Roberts[20] and Waine and Rubin[21] who were also interested in successful R and D entrepreneurs and company performance, questioned Schrage's findings after discovering discrepancies when the same protocols of Schrage were rescored by the Motivation Research Group at Harvard. They concluded from their own study that the highest performing companies were led by entrepreneurs high on n Ach and moderate on n Power. In addition, they found that entrepreneurs who were high on n Ach and high on n Power performed less well than the sub-groups who demonstrated a moderate level of n Power. If n Ach is an ingredient for success, their findings give some notions about more or less effective entrepreneurial leadership styles. In accordance with McClelland's findings the "right" balance between need for achievement, power and affiliation seems to be an important factor. They felt that a "democratic" style (characterized by a moderate level of n Power combined with high n Ach or a moderate n Ach and a high n Affiliation) makes for more effective and successful performance.

Litzinger[22] compared the motel entrepreneur with the motel manager using as one of his instruments the Gordon "Survey of Interpersonal Values."[23] He found that entrepreneurs are lower in "support" than motel managers, *i.e.* entrepreneurs placed a lower value of being understood, receiving encouragement, and being treated with consideration.

Lynn[24] found—after giving a group of entrepreneurs Eysenck's "Personality Inventory"[25]—that entrepreneurs scored higher on neuroticism (a concept closely linked to anxiety) compared to a group of general managers (a finding which was statistically significant).

Hornaday and Aboud[26] were interested in racial differences among entrepreneurs and compared twenty black and twenty white entrepreneurs using Kuder's "Occupational Interest Survey,"[27] Gordon's "Survey of Interpersonal Values"[28] and a questionnaire composed of three scales from Edward's Personal Preference Scale.[29] In addition, they used data from a similar, earlier study.[30] They found that compared to the population in general, entrepreneurs scored significantly higher on scales reflecting need for achievement, independence, and effectiveness of leadership and low on the scale of need for support. The differences between the black and white subgroups were minor. Furthermore, they felt that the profile they developed of the entrepreneur did not distinguish between a successful one and the individual who made an unsuccessful attempt at entrepreneurship.

Komives[31] studied the values of high technology entrepreneurs. In using Allport-Vernon-Lindsey's "Study of Values"[32] he discovered high aesthetic sense as the most meaningful indicator differentiating entrepreneurs from the general population. Entrepreneurs scored high on theoretical orientation and low on religious values. In using Gordon's "Survey of Personal Values"[33] and Gordon's "Survey of Interpersonal Values"[34] he found that entrepreneurs were high on achievement, leadership orientation and decisiveness but low on goal orientation, need for support, orderliness, conformity and practical mindedness. Moreover, entrepreneurs did not have high scores on economic values.

Litvak and Maule[35] looked at technical entrepreneurs in Canada using a simple questionnaire approach. The responses indicated that entrepreneurs wanted to have their own business because of (1) the challenge, (2) being one's own boss, (3) the freedom to explore new ideas.

Shapero[36] used Rotter's[37] "Internal-External" scale to determine the "locus of control" of entrepreneurs. Entrepreneurs tended to be on the "internal" end of the scale. "Internal" people were defined as individuals who felt that they have some influence on the course of events in their life (as opposed to "external" people who felt dominated by outside forces such as luck or fate). For "internal" people personal destiny comes from within and therefore they tend to be more self-reliant and more in need of independence and autonomy.

The psychological picture which emerges from this brief review is sometimes conflicting and confusing. It appears that particularly high achievement motivation is an important aspect in the entrepreneurial personality, but in addition, autonomy, independence and moderate risk taking are contributing factors. The entrepreneur also emerges as an anxious individual, a nonconformist poorly organized and not a stranger to self-destructive behaviour. Although power motivation is important, the degree of power motivation varies and has an influence on effective leadership style. Entrepreneurs seem to be "inner directed," present themselves as self-reliant, and tend to de-emphasize or neglect interpersonal relations. And finally, entrepreneurs possess a higher than average aesthetic sense which may contribute to their ability to set up "new combinations."

SOME PROPOSITIONS ABOUT ENTREPRENEURIAL TYPES

A further refinement in the study of the entrepreneurial personality particularly as it applies to testing entrepreneurial behaviour patterns might be in place. It is possible that entrepreneurs do not make up a homogeneous group. For example Smith[38] suggested two types of entrepreneurs: the craftsman-entrepreneur and the opportunistic-entrepreneur. He described the craftsman-entrepreneur as an individual narrow in education and training, low in social awareness and involvement, a lack of competence in dealing with the social environment and a limited or circumscribed time orientation. In contrast, the opportunistic-entrepreneur exhibits breadth in education and training, a high social awareness and involvement, a high confidence in dealing with the social environment and an awareness and orientation toward the future. Smith tries to relate these two "ideal" constructed types to type of firm (defined as rigid *versus* adaptive). He then postulates that the craftsman-entrepreneur will tend to build a rigid firm while the opportunistic entrepreneur will create an adaptive firm (rigidity and adaptability depend on customer and product mix, production methods, dispersement of markets and production facilities, and plans for change). A main discriminating factor between these two types seems to be education. To go beyond this simple demographic differential (and establish what the reason for this difference is) a more in-depth analysis of personal history and non-work environment is necessary to see if there are distinctly different personality patterns. Only then are we on more solid ground to explore the possibility of two different types.

Most of the efforts at distinguishing entrepreneurial types have been directed at the spin-off, high technology, R and D or technical entrepreneur.[39] The common background of this "type" of entrepreneur is usually previous work experience in high technology organizations or universities. What characterizes entrepreneurship of this nature most of all is the higher tolerance for formal education (average education a Master of Science degree). In addition, we see the regular use of entrepreneurial teams (a possible indication that interpersonal relations and control are less problematic) for this suggested subgroup.

Although it may very well be that the R and D entrepreneur is distinctly different in personality make-up, insufficient evidence exists at this point and more research is needed. Also the relationship between the opportunistic and R and D entrepreneur is not very clear. The type construction can be questioned. Overlap in types is very likely and the question of other types may be raised.

Naturally, the possibility exists that a new type of entrepreneur is emerging; an individual who is better educated, not as impulsive, less concerned about control and independence and more adaptive in his approach to the environment. If this is a trend in entrepreneurship, its impact on existing large companies (as far as internal entrepreneurship is concerned, creation of new product ventures and new technology divisions in existing companies) could be enormous. Perhaps "internal" entrepreneurship in large bureaucratic organizations is the inevitable response to organizational decay and inertia. Which organizational parameters are important to create a work environment congenial to "internal" entrepreneurship is another issue worth exploring, but will not be dealt with in this paper.

PATTERNS IN ENTREPRENEURSHIP

After this short interlude speculating about possible entrepreneurial types, we will continue this article by reviewing some of the social and economic factors which influence entrepreneurship. Many writers who have studied demographic patterns among entrepreneurs have indicated that entrepreneurs frequently belong to ethnic or religious minority groups.[40] Max Weber's "Protestant Ethic thesis"[41] can be viewed as the starting point in the introduction of hypotheses of this nature. The *Santri* Moslems of Java, the Jains, Parsees, and Sikhs in India, Indians and Chinese in South-East Asia, Lebanese in North Africa, Ibos in Nigeria and the Jews in various parts of the world are only a few illustrations of the role minorities play.

The hypothesis is often put forth that the possession of, and belief in, different value systems from that of the mainstream of society will contribute to the development of unconventional patterns of behaviour—entrepreneurship being one of them. Hagen[42] postulates a cycle of events which culminates in the emergence of the entrepreneurial personality. In a society characterized by traditional values (as reflected in child-rearing practices) status deterioration of a particular segment of the population may cause a psychosocial disequilibrium leading to a situation of withdrawal of status respect and depletion of self-esteem. Anger, anxiety and suppression of traditional values follows eventually, contributing to a state of retreatism for this particular group as reflected in the phenomena of normlessness, shiftlessness and anomie. However, this is an unstable state, and it may trigger off certain personality transformations. The existence of individuals who have gone through this process may be one of the contributing factors to the emergence of creative, innovative entrepreneurial activity. These changes in personality can be explained by the fact that the old patterns of behaviour of social group and family are not respected and acceptable any longer, therefore new innovative modes have to be found to integrate the individual with society. And according to Hagen four types of events can produce this process of status withdrawal: (1) displacement by force (*i.e.* by political upheavals and wars), (2) denigration of valued symbols religion), (3) inconsistency of status symbols with changes of the distribution of economic power, and (4) non-acceptance of expected status of immigrant groups.

We can observe repeatedly how members of minority groups are exposed to discriminatory treatment in one form or another which prevents them from obtaining one of the more established, usually higher status bearing roles in society. As a consequence there is often no other choice open for these groups than doing something new, something which has not been done before.[43] We observe the creation of new roles out of necessity since many existing occupations are closed or barred to these individuals. Immigrants and political refugees who also have to deal with changes in original status position obviously fall into this category. They are another type of minority group suffering from displacement.

Besides the fact that entrepreneurs frequently come from ethnic, religious, or some other form of minority group, there is another pattern which stands out. Many entrepreneurs come from families where the father has been self-employed in one form or another.[44] The vicissitudes of self-employment, its ups and downs, its turmoil and other psychosocial uncertainties have a profound effect on the family situation and will influence career orientation at a later stage. Shakespeare's advice, "better take the ills you have than fly to others that you know not of," seems very appropriate. It appears that in spite of the hardships so often experienced by the father, the son frequently follows his footsteps because, paradoxically enough, familiarity with the fact that obstacles have to be overcome in some way has an assuring quality. Moreover, early exposure to risk may increase one's tolerance to it.

But these conditions do not necessarily make for entrepreneurship. We can only postulate that—given these special background factors—individuals originating from selected segments of society might have a greater disposition for developing entrepreneurial characteristics. We are not describing a causal relationship but probably only a part of a more complex phenomenon which contributes to the emergence of entrepreneurship. Changes in institutional patterns such as the legal system, infrastructure, technology, the political situation and resource availability will be other important dimensions.

As we have pointed out, environmental turbulence appears to be one of the dimensions responsible for the emergence of entrepreneurship. And this relationship is not only applicable to society at large but has some validity for individual industry segments. For example, Peterson and Berger[45] drew attention to the fact that in the popular music recording industry the emergence of entrepreneurship has been directly associated with the degree of turbulence in the industry. But, again we have to be careful not to arrive at simple causal relationships. These various studies point at an environmental turbulence-entrepreneurship loop, but the exact nature of these inter-relationships is far from clear and extremely complex.

ENTREPRENEURIAL FAMILY DYNAMICS[46]

In view of these frequently encountered general background factors of entrepreneurs and the importance of turbulence in the environment it follows that the childhood of many of them is portrayed as a very disturbing experience. Discussions with entrepreneurs are more often than not filled with images of endured hardships.[47] Desertion, death, neglect and poverty are themes which continue to be brought up in conversations with entrepreneurs. And in these conversations facts and fantasies about hardship intertwine and become indistinguishable. This pattern seems to belong to entrepreneurial mythology and the entrepreneurs usually oblige. It is worth realizing that as far as personality dynamics are concerned, the difference between perceived and real hardship is rather slim. For the impact on personality it is perception that counts, even if distorted.

In these "memories of things past" the father appears to be the main villain in the life history of entrepreneurs. He is frequently blamed for deserting, manipulating, or neglecting the family. Death may be interpreted by a child as the ultimate form of desertion or rejection. What these conversations and study of life histories of entrepreneurs indicate is that a remote or absent father makes for a poor role model for the child.[48] The lack of familiarity and unpredictability of a remote father image makes the process of growing up not a very happy or harmonious one. It may leave the child and later the adult troubled by a burdensome psychological inheritance centred around problems of self-esteem, insecurity and lack of confidence. Repressed aggressive wishes towards persons in control are not strange to these individuals and the resulting sense of impotence and helplessness contributes to these feelings of rage, insecurity and low self-esteem.

Given the nature of family dynamics, the absence or remoteness of the father image in the family is often complemented by the mother who assumes part of the father's role. In conversations with entrepreneurs their mothers usually come across as strong, decisive, controlling women who give the family some sense of direction and cohesiveness.

A CONCEPTUAL APPROACH

One way of looking at the family dynamics of entrepreneurs and its role and emerging career orientations is by using a simplified conceptualization of basic personality dimensions. Here, referral is made to the polarities high control-low control, and acceptance-rejection, attitudes expressed by parents toward their children.[49] The way parents relate to these dimensions becomes extremely important for later personality development. The eventual personality make-up of the adult will heavily depend on the way in which these personality dimensions are emphasized and expressed by the parents, and eventually assimilated and internalized by the developing child. Combinations of these personality dimensions lead to four possible configurations for each parent. (Respectively: acceptance and high control, acceptance and low control, rejection and high control, rejection and low control.) Naturally the existence of siblings, the nature and intensity of intersibling rivalry, the competition for parental affection, and the latters' reactions, adds to the complexity of the dynamics of family life.

Consistency in childrearing assumes that parents will take a similar stand toward these personality dimensions. But given each person's unique psychological make-up, this situation will be rare, in spite of the fact that generally accepted childrearing practices encourage parents to make a concerted effort to appear as a "closed front" to their children. It is obvious that the parents of entrepreneurs usually do not fall into the category of consistency in childrearing. At the risk of over-simplification, a possible configuration in the family of the potential entrepreneur (postulating a father who is remote or absent and a mother who is dominant but supportive) gives the impression of the father as low on control and basically rejective (in the child's fantasy world remoteness easily become synonymous with rejection) while the mother will be perceived as high on control and accepting. Naturally, the child's perception of the intensity of each dimension by parent will vary. And we can observe how, in spite of the limited integration of these perceptions by the child (the great dissonance between parental attitudes makes integration of the child's perceptions very difficult), some integration of these images will occur, to be assimilated and internalized by the child. We hypothesize that in the case of the potential entrepreneur a perception of high control and rejection usually becomes the predominant pattern.

The lack of integration of these parental configurations, in addition to each parent's stand on these two personality dimensions leaves the child with a feeling of inconsistency, confusion and frustration. On the one hand the child may submit to the control of the mother mainly with fear, anxiety and a sense of helplessness, while on the other hand the perceived rejection by the father is also resented and leads to aggressive retaliatory fantasies. A state of anger may be the legacy of this particular type of family dynamics, anger which may be directed toward the self or projected to others contributing to a sense of guilt and undermining of self-confidence. In a later state of personality development this tendency toward hostility and anger may injure relationships with peers.

In the case that the predominant attitudes of parents are rejection and high control, the psychologist White (a researcher of longitudinal life histories) comments that:

> . . . When combined with rejection, high control still exerts a pressure for docile compliance but there is now a problem connected with hostility. Rejecting parents offer the child a meagre ration of love in return for his sacrifices of freedom. He submits mainly out of fear, and with resentment. A variety of consequences follow, which are easily understood as different dispositions of the hostility. This may be directed at the self, creating a sense of guilt that eats away at self-confidence and that sometimes plays a part in the development of neurosis. It may injure the relation to other children, promoting either a quarrelsome tendency or, to avoid this, a withdrawal from contact. It may produce half-hearted compliance with authority in which socialized behaviour is performed with sour resignation. It may be displaced to more remote objects such as outgroups seen as enemies of sound values. It may finally come into focus on the parents or on authority in general, producing a belated and often difficult rebellion.[50]

The combination of a dominant, controlling, somewhat nurturing mother and a remote father, perceived as rejecting, can lead to problems in identity formation and career orientation, a process accentuated by the general inadequacy or unacceptability of the prevailing role models. A person with this type of family background may experience difficulties as an adolescent in deciding upon an occupational identity. Consequently he will not be a stranger to rebellious activities as a turnabout from originally half-hearted compliance toward authority figures. His confusion about career choice may not be a temporary one but may persist throughout his life.

THE REACTIVE MODE

Before society at large recognizes his capabilities, the potential entrepreneur enters a period of disorientation, without apparent goals, but also during which he is testing his abilities and ascertaining his strengths. The future entrepreneur drifts from job to job, encounters difficulties in the acceptance of his ideas, in conceptualizing and structuring possible "new combinations." He is perceived by other people as a "deviant," a person out of place, frequently provocative and irritating because of his seemingly irrational, nonconformistic actions and provocative ideas.

Collins, Moore and Unwalla particularly, point out this non-conformistic stand:

. . . the way of the entrepreneur is a long, lonely and difficult road. The men who follow it are by necessity a special breed. They are a breed who cannot do well in the established and clearly defined routes available to the rest of us. The road they can follow is one that is lined with difficulties, which most of us could not even begin to overcome. As a group they do not have the qualities of patience, understanding and charity many of us may admire and wish for in our fellows. This is understandable. In the long and trying way of the entrepreneur such qualities may come to be so much excess baggage. What is necessary to the man who travels this way is great imagination, fortitude, and hardness of purpose.

The men who travel the entrepreneurial way are, taken on balance, not remarkably likeable people. This too is understandable. As any one of them might say in the vernacular of the world of the entrepreneur, "Nice guys don't win." . . .[51]

Non-conformistic rebelliousness becomes the entrepreneur's mode of behaviour, his way of exerting power and control over an environment perceived as dangerous and uncontrollable. The entrepreneur's actions do not derive from inner strength and self-assurance which a secure, consistent family upbringing would have provided. Instead, the confusing and disturbing family interactions forces the entrepreneur to react to situations out of inner insecurity. Optimism and resilience are the manifestations of a denial mechanism originating from a basic depressive conflict and become a form of characterological adjustment. Driving ambition may be viewed as a need to contradict strong feelings of inferiority and helplessness. Hyperactivity becomes a way of covering up passive longings. Passivity changes into activity as a reaction against anxiety.

The future entrepreneur *reacts* against the early demands imposed upon him by his family and immediate environment. If he originally perceives himself as being rejected, he will counteract his helplessness, seize control and do the rejecting himself. But it is behaviour without real conviction, not based on a secure sense of self-esteem and identity. No matter how strong his actions, doubt remains. Feelings of rejection, helplessness, and low self-esteem remain a haunting issue.

The "reactive model" makes for a sense of impulsivity whereby speediness, abruptness and a lack of planning on a longer term basis determines the entrepreneur's actions. It is short-term, operational planning for the purpose of instant gratification which predominates and makes for success in actions. These people seem to be characterized by a low tolerance for frustration and tension and a low attention span, seemingly in pursuit of immediate gains and satisfactions. For the entrepreneur the initial impression, "the hunch," often becomes the final conclusion without a further serious search and deliberation process. There seems to be an absence of concentration, of logical objectivity, judgement and reflectiveness, as if the process of cognition is impaired and does not fulfil its integrative function. A lack of analytical thinking, an absence of active search procedures and self-critical reflections becomes a predominant mode.[52]

THE PARADOX OF SUCCESS

Thus, due to the frustrations and perceived deprivations experienced in the early stages of life, a prominent pattern among entrepreneurs appears to be a sense of impulsivity, a persistent feeling of dissatisfaction, rejection and powerlessness, forces which contribute to an impairment and depreciation of his sense of self-esteem and affect cognitive processes. The entrepreneur is a man under a great deal of stress, continuously badgered by his past, a past which is experienced and re-experienced in fantasies, daydreams and dreams. These dreams and fantasies often have a threatening content due to the recurrence of feelings of anxiety and guilt which mainly revolve around hostile wishes against parental figures or, more generally, all individuals in a position of authority. Distrust and suspicion of everyone in a position of authority forces the entrepreneur to search for non-structured situations where he can assert his control and independence. He is also an individual who tends to deny his hostile wishes and projects these on the outside world. And it is extremely hard, if not impossible for individuals with an entrepreneurial disposition to integrate their personal needs with those of organizations. To design one's own organization, to create and structure organizations centred around themselves—often becomes the only alternative.

The "reactive mode" which characterizes entrepreneurial behaviour makes for an extremely unstable personality make-up. Since prestige, power, and self-confidence are used as reassuring weapons to deal with low self-esteem, inferiority and related feelings of anxiety, any perceived depletion of these outward symbols may be the cause of a psychological disequilibrium and trigger off impulsive reactions. If self-confidence is weak and inner hostility provokes guilt feelings, punishment is expected unconsciously. Any sign of failure means that expected punishment is at hand, any sign of success may be interpreted as an achievement not really deserved, which again indicates that punishment is not far off. Although the entrepreneur fears failure, the "irrational" unconscious notion prevails that punishment is deserved, be it only for hostile wishes against authority figures. Using the same kind of logic, success only means that punishment will follow immediately and therefore causes anxiety about future failures and punishments. Given the existence at an unconscious level of fear of success and fear of failure, combined with impulsivity of action and forgoing thorough deliberation and judgement, it is not surprising that the careers of many entrepreneurs appear to be a remarkable succession of business successes and failures. Actually, because of this psychological process the entrepreneur may feel at his best when he has reached "rock bottom." His feelings of guilt being "paid off," he is "free," unburdened, able to start all over again.

We notice how the entrepreneur emerges as a psychological risk taker subjected to a high degree of psychosocial risks. Due to intrapsychic transformations, original feelings of helplessness, dependency and rejection are replaced by a proactive style in which power, control and autonomy become predominant issues. What used to be an inclination toward submission and passivity becomes an active impulsive mode of behaviour. The entrepreneur may follow what is sometimes described as an "identification with the aggressor" pattern.[53] The role of the passive, helpless victim is replaced by acting the role of the one in control. We have indicated before that the often self-employed father was frequently an undependable and terrifying influence to the entrepreneur in his youth. Now the roles have changed; after having been continuously manipulated at an early age, the entrepreneur will do the manipulation himself (identify with the aggressor) in a compensatory fashion, reliving these actions as a kind of "protective reaction" against first his father and later authority figures in general. We see that the inability to function in structured situations makes it necessary for him to design his own organization where he is in control and at the centre of action. His achievements in setting up enterprises become important tangible symbols of prestige and power and a way of bolstering an easily depleted, insecure sense of self-esteem. But his achievements are not sufficient to ward off a persisting sense of anxiety and other stress indicators. Rejection, dissatisfaction and a sense of failure follow the entrepreneur like an inseparable shadow. (A summary of the various psychological forces working upon the potential entrepreneur is given in Figure 1.)

THE ENTREPRENEURIAL WORK ENVIRONMENT

The preparatory period of entrepreneurship, as we have seen, is accompanied by authority conflicts, failures in organizational socialization, difficulties in adapting to organizational structure and predictable job-hopping behaviour, which has set the stage for the very unique relationship of the entrepreneur with his enterprise. Expectedly, the enterprise becomes the new setting where the entrepreneur's problems in adaptation and conforming to structure are accentuated and dramatized. Naturally, the enterprise itself becomes the tangible symbol to the entrepreneur of his success in "overcoming odds" and assumes a much greater symbolic emotional significance than the reality of the situation may warrant. The enterprise is much more than merely a vehicle for profit maximization; it is not only the entrepreneur's contact with reality but, in addition, demonstrates his ability to create a new reality derived from confused internal images

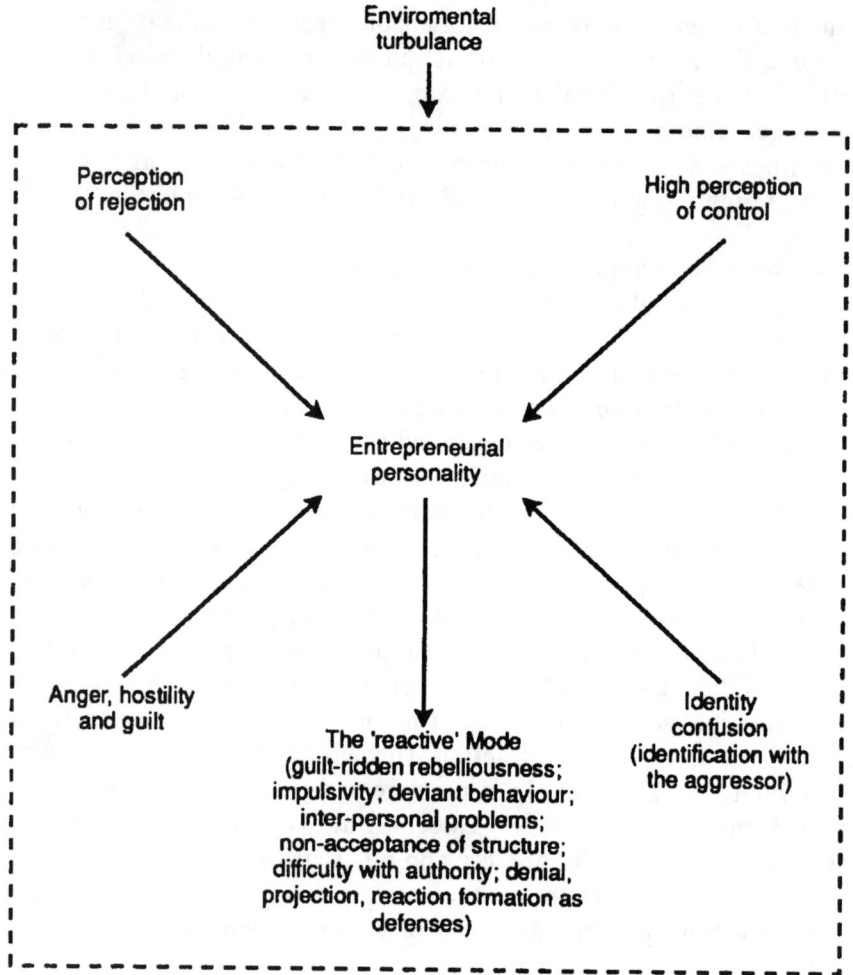

Figure 1. Psychodynamic forces influencing the entrepreneurial personality.

centred around conflict and frustration with authority figures. In a psychodynamic sense—using the defence reaction formation—the enterprise symbolizes the capacity of the entrepreneur in solving and compensating for endured childhood frustrations and hardships by creating an environment where, for a change, he is in control, not dependent on the whims and favours of undependable authority figures—a situation which was so resented in the past. Unlike the manager's relationship with organizations, the level at which an entrepreneur deals with his own organization is therefore far more intense and conflict ridden; this pattern cannot be explained merely by the higher financial risks at stake. While previously avoidance of structure and organizations was his way of coping with life, his own organization becomes the end of the road. For the entrepreneur there seems no other place to go, a development which contributes to the emotional significance of the enterprise.

But this very fact of complete psychological immersion of the entrepreneur—a factor which may have been a key ingredient for the initial success of the enterprise—can lead to serious dysfunctional developments in the future in the case of continued growth of the enterprise. What we frequently encounter in an entrepreneurial organization is an organizational structure and work environment completely dependent and dominated by the entrepreneur. The enterprise is run in a very autocratic, directive way whereby all the decision-making processes centre around the entrepreneur. We are also faced with an individual who refuses to delegate, is impulsive, lacks any interest in conscious, analytical forms of planning, and engages regularly in bold, proactive moves. Bold and proactive moves make for the initial successes and may contribute to the continued success of the enterprise, but due to the absence of a conscious planning effort also carry a high risk component. The entrepreneur makes no distinction between operating, day-to-day decision-making and more long-term strategic moves. The impulsivity of his style, his lack of deliberation and judgement, the importance of "hunches" also makes for a rather limited time horizon. The entrepreneur has no sense of priorities and may spend equal time on the greatest trivia as on major strategic decisions.

Within the organization power depends on the proximity to the entrepreneur, is constantly changing and creates a highly uncertain organizational environment. This state of affairs contributes to a highly politically charged atmosphere where changing coalitions and collusions are the order of the day. The suprastructure is poorly defined, a formal organization chart is outdated by the time it is drawn, or non-existent. It basically resembles a "spider's web" with the entrepreneur in the centre, who is constantly changing loyalties and keeping his subordinates in a state of confusion and dependence. The organization has usually a poorly defined or poorly used control and information system (no sharing of information); there is an absence of standard procedures and rules and a lack of formalization. Instead, we notice the use of subjective, personal criteria for the purpose of measurement and control. Job descriptions and job responsibilities are poorly defined or non-existent. This situation contributes to a high incidence of role conflict and role ambiguity leading to low job satisfaction, low self-confidence, a high degree of job-related tension, a high sense of futility and low confidence in the organization.[54] Withdrawal or avoidance behaviour and a reduction in communication among employees also becomes symptomatic. Information hoarding turns into a common practice and contributes to the general state of disorganization. In addition, given the "spider's web" structure, the number of people reporting to the entrepreneur will be large, adding to a general sense of confusion. (See Table 1 for a summary of the dimensions of the entrepreneurial work environment.)

Table 1. Entrepreneurial work environment.

Leadership style	Autocrative Directive
Decision-making	Centralized Lack of delegation Impulsivity Lack of conscious planning Bold, proactive moves Mixture of operating and strategic decision-making
Time horizon	Short
Power	Proximity to entrepreneur
Organizational environment	High uncertainty Lack of sharing information
Suprastructure	Poorly defined Absence of formal organization chart "Spider's web" structure
Infrastructure	Frequently poorly defined or poorly utilized control and information system Absence of standard procedures and rules No formalized systems (use of subjective, personal criteria) Poor integration of activities Poorly defined job descriptions and job responsibilities (high incidence of role conflict and role ambiguity) Large horizontal span of control

Although the entrepreneur, in the initial stage of development of the enterprise, might have had the ability to inspire his subordinates, the mere fact of growth has complicated this process. His aversion to structure, his preference for personalized relationships and his reluctance to accept constructive criticism makes growth, with its implicit need for a more sophisticated infra- and suprastructure and greater decentralization, increasingly difficult to handle. Hoarding of information, inconsistencies in day-to-day interpretation of company policies, playing of favourites, and refusal or reluctance to let people really know where they stand does not contribute to an efficient and effective organization. And if this pattern becomes predominant and prevails, few capable subordinates will remain in the organization; the ones left will usually be of a mediocre calibre spending a great part of their effort on political infighting. It is the absence of actual responsibility with authority which causes capable people to leave while the yes-man—individuals who do not really challenge the entrepreneur's authority—will stay on.

What we are describing is the potential danger of the entrepreneurial mode; that given the nature of the entrepreneur's conflicts and his peculiar leadership style—useful as these qualities might have been initially—growth may lead to the eventual destruction of the enterprise. If the entrepreneur remains rigid in his attitudes and refuses to formalize the organization and change decision-making patterns. In case of continued growth of the enterprise, the effectiveness of the organization structure and the way of decision-making becomes increasingly insufficient in coping with the complexities of the external environment. The degree of environmental dynamism (change in technology, market behaviour and competitors' reactions) heterogeneity (differences in needs and behaviour of organizational constituents) and hostility (cut-throat competition, resource shortages, etc.) determines how long the entrepreneur will be successful in pursuing his old style.[55] Obviously in a very static industry segment the strain on the organization is not so quickly noticeable. And while the time period may vary before the organizational strains become intolerable, utter disorganization, the increasing necessity of coping with the environment and eventual financial losses will often be the inevitable outcomes of the entrepreneur's leadership style. It is this obsession with control, the unwillingness or inability to "let go," which in the end leaves a rather unpleasant inheritance with the word bankruptcy written all over it. But as we have mentioned before, failure does not come as a surprise; it has been expected by the entrepreneur in a more unconscious sense.

SUCCESSION

Given the rigidity in attitudes, the inability to modify behaviour, abdication and succession is often the only alternative if the continued growth of the enterprise is a major goal, given the self-limiting nature of the entrepreneur's leadership style. But management succession is easier talked about than implemented if we take the emotional investment and symbolic meaning of the enterprise into consideration. Although from a rational point of view it may be better for both enterprise and entrepreneur if the entrepreneur distances himself and starts something new, from an emotional point of view this is not such an easy transition. Many rationalizations to prevent this type of transition are used by the entrepreneur. Usually we will hear the argument that there is no one good enough to take over, a statement with the implicit message that there is no alternative but to stay on, a demonstration of a rather insincere reluctance. The paradox of the situation is that the entrepreneur has created a work environment of high dependency. He has always looked at any potential infringement upon positions of power and control with suspicion, and therefore it is naturally highly unlikely that a capable administrator has risen through the ranks, making his statements about the impossibility of stepping down a self-fulfilling prophecy.

And family members are certainly not excluded but are as suspect, or more so. They also fall into the category of possible intruders threatening the entrepreneur's position of control. As much as family dynamics are acted out in organizations, the presence of family members in these organizations seems only to intensify the eruption of these conflicts.[56] We can observe a confusion of roles between the social system of the family and that of the enterprise. At the base of these conflicts are feelings of rivalry, whereby the conflict-ridden relationship which the entrepreneur possessed toward his parents is transferred toward his son. What we frequently observe is a reenactment of the old "family romance," meaning that the son of the entrepreneur is exposed to the same treatment the entrepreneur felt he once endured. But now it is the entrepreneur who is in the position of authority and control and his son who is dependent on his whims, vulnerable to his erratic and unpredictable behaviour and kept in an infantile position. That the idea of abdication, of stepping down, is resented by the entrepreneur has become obvious, but that succession by his son is even more resented and traumatic has now become less mysterious in view of the reawakening of these old feelings of rivalry with its connotations of frustration and despair.

Edsel Ford's relationship to his father, the first Henry Ford, is a good illustration of the abrasive dimensions these conflicts can reach and the destructiveness of this type of rivalry to the enterprise.[57] Henry Ford's refusal to change strategy, to make alterations to the Model T and his unwillingness to encourage Edsel Ford in his efforts to build an infra- and suprastructure brought the company to the edge of bankruptcy. Under extraordinary pressures changes were eventually made but at an extremely high cost in material resources and manpower. As was the case with the Ford Motor Company, old age or even death seem often the only times when control can be taken away from the entrepreneur. Unfortunately, at that point it might be too late to save the enterprise.

The successful entrepreneur who manages to guide the enterprise through the formative period of development into a stage of growth and maturity tends to follow a path which eventually may lead to his own functional self-elimination. He is a person at the crossroads, an enigma, on one hand highly creative and imaginative but, on the other hand, highly rigid, unwilling to change, incapable of confronting the issue of succession. Christensen[58] after studying over a hundred companies, came to a similar conclusion struck by the frequency in which he encountered a denial of the reality of the succession issue among the entrepreneurs.

Succession becomes identified with loss and losing out and therefore takes the meaning of a taboo. But the issue of succession is inevitable not only for reasons of age but also because of increasing maturation and growth of the company. The entrepreneur is no longer alone, other interest groups such as employees, family members, bankers, customers, suppliers and the government are getting involved. Depending on the strength of the entrepreneur's position they can have some influence on the policies of the enterprise. But change by this type of pressure is usually only of a modest character. A more drastic type of change is needed for continued growth and success of the enterprise apart from changes caused by old age or death. We imply here the attainment of a sense of psychological maturity on the part of the entrepreneur. This means a willingness to assess his personal strengths and weaknesses to master his conflict-ridden behaviour and overcome and surpass the problems of the past. But adaptation to present-day reality and foregoing the legacies of his personal history requires a considerable basis of self-awareness and insight. Important as this psychological state might be for the continued survival of the enterprise for overcoming rigid behaviour and greater flexibility in operating modes, adaptation of this kind is rare and hard to attain. More often than not, separation from the enterprise by the entrepreneur in one form or another turns out to be the only alternative for the purpose of survival. This development highlights the depressive facet of the entrepreneurial dimension. While the entrepreneurial spirit is one of the strong countervailing forces preventing decay and decline of the economy as a whole, in the final deliberation, the entrepreneur pays an extremely high price in an emotional sense in this process of economic growth. ▲

NOTES

1. Raw, Charles, Page, Bruce and Hodgson, Godfrey, *Do You Sincerely Want to be Rich?* New York: The Viking Press, 1971.
2. Becker, W. C., "Consequences of Different Kinds of Parental Discipline," in Hoffman, M. L. and Hoffman, L. W. (Eds.), *Review of Child Development Research,* Vol. 1. New York: Russell Sage Foundation, 1964.
3. Schumpeter, Joseph A., *Theorie der Wirtschaftlichen Entwicklung, e^e Aufl.,* München und Leibzig: Duncker und Humblat, 1931.
4. Veblen, Thorstein, "Why is Economics not an Evolutionary Science?," *The Quarterly Journal of Economics,* Vol. XII, No. 4, 1889, p. 389.
5. Baumol, William J., "Entrepreneurship in Economic Theory," *American Economic Review,* Vol. LVIII, No. 2, 1968, p. 66.
6. Cantillon, Richard, *Essay sur la Nature du Commerce en Général,* Londres et Paris: R. Gyles, 1756.
7. Say, Jean-Baptiste, *Catechism of Political Economy,* London, 1816.
8. Redlich, Fritz, "The Origin of the Concepts of Entrepreneur and Creative Entrepreneur," *Explorations in Entrepreneurial History,* Vol. 1, 1949, pp. 145–66.
9. Schumpeter, Joseph A., "Economic Theory and Entrepreneurial History," in Aitken, Hugh, G. J. (Ed.), *Explorations in Enterprise,* Cambridge, Mass.: Harvard University Press, 1965, p. 51.
10. Drucker, Peter F., "Entrepreneurship in Business Enterprise," *Journal of Business Policy,* Vol. 1, No. 1, 1970.
11. Hartman, Heinz, "Managers and Entrepreneurs: a Useful Distinction," *Administrative Science Quarterly,* Vol. 3, No. 3, 1959, pp. 429–51.
12. Schumpeter states that "we maintain that someone is only then by definition entrepreneur if he 'implements new combinations'—after which he loses this characteristic, when he then continues to manage the founded enterprise systematically." See Schumpeter, J. A., 1931, op. cit., p. 116 (own translation).
13. Knight, Frank H., *Risk, Uncertainty and Profit,* 5th edition, Boston: Houghton-Mifflin, 1940.
14. McClelland, David C., *The Achieving Society,* New York: Van Nostrand, 1961.
15. Murray, Henry A., *Manual for the Thematic Apperception Test,* Cambridge, Mass.: Harvard University Press, 1943.
16. McClelland, David C., *Power: The Inner Experience,* New York: Irvington, 1975.
17. Collins, Orvis F., Moore, David G. and Unwalla, Darab B., *The Enterprising Man,* East Lansing: Bureau of Business and Economic Research, Graduate School of Business Administration, Michigan State University, 1964.
18. Ibid., p. 61.
19. Schrage, Harry, "The R and D Entrepreneur: Profile of Success," *Harvard Business Review,* Vol. 43, No. 6, November/December 1965, pp. 56–69.
20. Roberts, Edward B., "A Basic Study of Innovators: How to Keep and Capitalize on Their Talents," *Research Management,* Vol. XI, No. 4, 1968.
21. Waine, Herbert A. and Rubin, Irwin A., "Motivation of Research and Development Entrepreneurs: Determinants of Company Success," *Journal of Applied Psychology,* Vol. 53, No. 3, 1969, pp. 178–84.
22. Litzinger, William D., "The Motel Entrepreneur and the Motel Manager," *Academy of Management Journal,* Vol. 8, No. 4, 1965.
23. Gordon, Leonard V., *Manual for Survey of Interpersonal Values,* Chicago: Science Research Associates, 1960.
24. Lynn, R., "Personality Characteristics of a Group of Entrepreneurs," *Occupational Psychology,* Vol. 43, 1969, pp. 151–2.
25. Eysenck, H. J., *The Dynamics of Anxiety and Hysteria,* London: Routledge and Kegan Paul, 1957.
26. Hornaday, John A. and Aboud, John, "Characteristics of Successful Entrepreneurs," *Personnel Psychology,* Vol. 24, No. 2, Summer 1971, pp. 141–53.
27. Kuder, Frederic, *Manual for the Kuder Preference Record: Form DD,* Chicago: Science Research Associates, 1970.
28. Gordon, L. V., op. cit.
29. Edwards, Allen L., *Manual for the Edwards' Personal Preference Schedule,* New York: The Psychological Corporation, 1959.
30. Hornaday, John A. and Bunker, Charles S., "The Nature of the Entrepreneur," *Personnel Psychology,* Vol. 23, No. 1, Spring 1970, pp. 47–54.
31. Komives, John L., "A Preliminary Study of the Personal Values of High Technology Entrepreneurs," in Cooper, A. C. and Komives, J. L. (Eds.), *Technical Entrepreneurship: A Symposium,* 1972.
32. Allport, Gordon W. and Lindsey, Gardner, *Assessment of Human Motives,* New York: Holt, Rinehart and Winston, 1964.
33. Gordon, L. V., op. cit.
34. Gordon, Leonard V., *Research Briefs on Survey of Interpersonal Values,* Chicago: Science Research Associates, 1963.

35. Litvak, Isaiah A.,the Maule, Christopher J., "Profiles of Technical Entrepreneurs," *The Business Quarterly,* Summer 1974, pp. 40–9.
36. Shapero, Albert, "The Displaced, Uncomfortable Entrepreneur," *Psychology Today,* November 1975.
37. Rotter, Julian B., "External Control and Internal Control," *Psychology Today,* June 1971.
38. Smith, Norman R., *The Entrepreneur and His Firm: the Relationship Between Type of Man and Type of Company,* East Lansing: Michigan State University, Graduate School of Business Administration, 1967.
39. Roberts, Edward B. and Wainer, Herbert A., "Some Characteristics of Technical Entrepreneurs," *Research Program on the Management of Science and Technology,* Massachusetts Institute of Technology, 1966 pp. 145–66; Roberts, Edward B., 1968, op. cit.; Cooper, Arnold C., "Technical Entrepreneurship: What Do We Know?," *Research* and *Development Management,* Vol. 3, Oxford: Basil Blackwell, 1973, pp. 59–64.
40. Roberts, Edward B. and Wainer, Herbert A., ibid.; Hagen, Everett, *On the Theory of Social Change,* Homewood, Ill.: Dorsey, 1962; Kasdan, Leonard, "Family Structure, Migration and the Entrepreneur," *Comparative Studies in Society and History,* Vol. VII, No. 4, 1965; Kets de Vries, Manfred, F. R., *The Entrepreneur as Catalyst of Economic and Cultural Change,* unpublished Doctoral Dissertation, Harvard University, Graduate School of Business Administration, 1970.
41. Weber, Max, *The Protestant Ethic and the Spirit of Capitalism,* translated by Talcott Parsons, New York: Scribner, 1930.
42. Hagen, Everett, op. cit.
43. The alternative might be the establishment of ghetto areas in case of extreme hostility in the environment with a "normal" distribution of vocations within the ghetto.
44. Newcomer, Mabel, "The Little Businessman: A Study of Business Proprietors in Poughkeepsie, New York," *Business History Review,* Vol. 35, No. 4, 1961; Collins, O. F., Moore, D. G. and Unwalla, D. B., op. cit.; Roberts, Edward B., op. cit.; Litvak, I. A. and Maule, C. J., op. cit; Ket de Vries, M. F. R., op. cit.
45. Peterson, Richard A. and Berger, David G., "Entrepreneurship in Organizations: Evidence from the Popular Music Industry," *Administrative Science Quarterly,* Vol. 16, No. 1, March 1971, pp. 97–106.
46. Forty entrepreneurs were interviewed by the author, individuals who were operating in a wide range of industries. The interviews were of an open-ended nature to have maximum cooperation and a minimum of strain (no psychological tests were used). In addition, thirty life histories of entrepreneurs were studied (autobiographies, biographies and selected articles). Collins, Moore and Unwalla's study *The Enterprising Man* was also very influential in formulating concepts for this article.
47. Collins, O. F., Moore, D. G. and Unwalla, D. B., op. cit.; Collins, Orvis F. and Moore, David G., *The Organization Makers,* New York: Appleton-Century-Crofts, 1970.
48. Collins, O. F., Moore, D. G. and Unwalla, D. B., ibid.; Kets de Vries, M. F. R., op. cit.
49. Becker, W. C., op. cit.; White, Robert W., *The Enterprise of Living,* New York: Holt, Rinehart and Winston, 1972.
50. Ibid., p. 53.
51. Collins, O. F., Moore, D. G. and Unwalla, D. B., op. cit., p. 244.
52. Many of David Shapiro's comments about the "impulsive style" seem very applicable to the entrepreneur. He views as the essential feature of the "impulsive style:" the immediacy of experience and expression of impulse and the immediacy of cognitive response. See Shapiro, David, *Neurotic Styles,* New York: Basic Books, 1965, p. 155.
53. Freud, Anna, *The Ego and the Mechanisms of Defence,* London: Hogarth Press and the Institute of Psycho-Analysis, 1937.
54. Kahn, Robert I., Wolfe, Donald M., Quinn, Robert P. and Snoek, G. Diedrick, *Organizational Stress: Studies in Role Conflict and Ambiguity,* New York: Wiley, 1964.
55. Danny Miller in his doctoral dissertation gives an elaborate description of these dimensions. He uses these dimensions in the formulation of organizational archetypes and the description of their strengths and weaknesses. (See Miller, Danny, *Strategy Making in Context: Ten Empirical Archetypes,* Doctoral Dissertation, McGill University, Faculty of Management, 1976.) For a conceptualization of pathways to success and failure of organizational archetypes including entrepreneurial variations see Miller, Danny, Friesen, Peter and Kets de Vries, Manfred F. R., *The Strategic Audit: and Why Your Organization Might Need It,* McGill University Working Paper, 1976.
56. Levinson, Harry, "Conflicts that Plague Family Businesses," *Harvard Business Review,* Vol. 49, No. 2, March–April 1971, pp. 90–8.
57. Jardim, Anne, *The First Henry Ford: a Study in Personality and Business Leadership,* Cambridge, Mass.: MIT Press, 1970.
58. Christensen, C. Roland, *Management Succession in Small and Growing Enterprises,* Boston: Division of Research, Harvard University, Graduate School of Business Administration, 1953.

THE MEANING OF ENTREPRENEURSHIP

Wayne Long

This paper reviews various definitions of entrepreneurship employed by a number of theoretical economists since Richard Cantillon (circa 1730). Three recurring themes emerge from their definitions, namely that "entrepreneurship" involves: 1) uncertainty and risk, 2) complementary managerial competence, and 3) creative opportunism. The authors argue that modern definitions of entrepreneurship that exclude any of these three fundamental dimensions are basically incomplete.

INTRODUCTION

In a liberal definition of entrepreneurship, even Lenin might qualify as an entrepreneur since he took considerable risk, showed a high degree of independence, and applied to Russian society innovative ideas that led to new organizational forms in many sectors of Soviet life [6, p. 91].

Thus Harwood illustrates the problem of effectively defining the concept of entrepreneurship. Although some researchers are more concerned than others about defining entrepreneurship, many would agree that the problem of how to define entrepreneurship effectively is a problem of notable significance. An effective definition should not necessarily remove all the ambiguity from the concept, but rather ambiguity should be confined to disputable areas where its continuing value is to be provocative. An effective definition of entrepreneurship should include most commonly agreed upon entrepreneurial activities and exclude those activities which most of us would agree are non-entrepreneurial. Thus an effective definition of entrepreneurship would describe Lenin at best as a political entrepreneur, or better still as a social innovator, but not as a prototypic entrepreneur.

Entrepreneurship has meant different things to different people for the last eight hundred years "since *entreprendre* (With the connotation to do something) was in use as early as the twelfth century and in the course of the fifteenth century the corresponding noun developed." The related English terms of adventurer or undertaker (i.e. "Merchant Adventurers") were used from the fifteenth century on [8, pp. 194, 200]. The first formal theoretical use of the concept of entrepreneurship appears in the work of Richard Cantillon around 1730 [4].

Over the last two hundred and fifty years, the concept of entrepreneurship has undergone some systematic development in the hands of a number of economic theorists. Because such formal theorists have been rather precise in their definition of central theoretical concepts,

Reprinted with the permission of the *American Journal of Small Business* (Vol. VIII, No. 2, Fall 1983).

the evolution of the concept within formal economic theories is worthy of study. The purpose of this paper is to review the thematic evolution of the concept of entrepreneurship in a search for major underlying dimensions which delimit the essential nature of the term.

FORMAL THEORIES OF ENTREPRENEURSHIP

Although some analyses of entrepreneurs and entrepreneurship reach back at least as far as the publicans of the Roman Empire [1], formal theories of entrepreneurship had to wait until the latter years of the mercantilist age to find their first expression in the work of Richard Cantillon (circa 1730). It was left to the rich, self-made international banker, Cantillon, to formally define entrepreneurship as self-employment of any and every sort. As long as a person wasn't hired or working for wages then he was an entrepreneur—"the Beggars and even the Robbers are Undertakers" [4, p. 55].

The critical difference between being of the class of entrepreneurs as opposed to the class of hired people was living with the additional uncertainty surrounding self-employment. According to Cantillon, the entrepreneur would buy at certain prices in the present only to sell at uncertain prices in the future. In order to "adjust themselves to risk" entrepreneurs could "proportion themselves in a state to the customers or consumption" [4, p. 53].

During the transitions of the latter part of the eighteenth century, various of the physiocrats following from Quesnay expanded upon the concept of entrepreneurship. As with Cantillon, the physiocrats viewed the entrepreneur as the bearer of uncertainty; yet they went further to conclude that the entrepreneur "must have the capacity of economically combining the appropriate goods and services to the end of his greatest profit." "The entrepreneur bears uncertainty, organizes and supervises production, introduces new methods and new products and searches for new markets." The physiocrat Baudeau further stressed the need for an entrepreneur to be clever and knowledgeable and to be willing "to operate rationally by using the most productive methods" [8, pp. 209–210].

In the early nineteenth century with the industrial revolution now in full swing, the experienced industrialist, J. B. Say, expanded upon the characteristics of successful entrepreneurs. The new era of industry placed new demands on the entrepreneur prior to the advent of the institution of middle management [5]. An "adventurer or master-manufacturer" had need of a number of desirable attributes and talents, according to Say [18, pp. 330–331]:

- he must be able, by the nature of his connections, to procure the loan of capital he may happen himself not to possess.
- he requires such a combination of "moral" qualities of judgement, perseverance and a knowledge of the world, as well as of business.
- he must be able to estimate, with tolerable accuracy, the importance of the specific product, the probable amount of demand and the means of its production.
- at one time, he must employ a great number of hands; at another, buy or order the raw materials, collect labourers, find consumers, and give at all times a rigid

attention to order and economy; in a word, he must possess the art of superintendence and administration.

- he must possess the ready knack of calculation, to compare the charges of production with the probable value of the product when completed and brought to market.

And in an early variation of Murphy's Law, Say concluded:

> In the course of such complex operations there are an abundance of obstacles to be surmounted, of anxieties to be repressed, of misfortunes to be repaired, and of expedients to be devised. Those who are not possessed of a combination of these necessary qualities, are unsuccessful in their under-takings; their concerns soon fall to the ground . . . [18, p. 331].

Although "all branches of industry do not require an equal degree of capacity of knowledge," Say observed that few of his contemporaries had a sufficient combination of the appropriate talents.

At a time when the professional middle manager was a newly evolving phenomenon in the eighteen-nineties, we find Alfred Marshall observing that the activities of undertaking a business are different from the activities of superintendence of a going concern:

> The superintendence of labor is but one side, and often not the most important side of business work; and that the employer who undertakes the whole risks of his business really performs *two entirely distinct services . . . and requires a twofold ability* [16, p. 248].

Echoing J. B. Say, Marshall went on to conclude that people having both sets of abilities may be quite rare:

> The abilities required to make an ideal employer are so great and so numerous that very few persons can exhibit them all in a very high degree . . . and while one employer excels in one set of qualities, another excels in another . . . [16, p. 248].

Yet Marshall was more concerned with describing the holistic requirements of successful business rather than the separateness of the sources from which those talents were to be drawn:

> But in the greater part of the business of the modern world the task . . . has to be broken up and given into the hands of a specialized body of employers, or to use a more general term business men. They "adventure" or "undertake" its risks; they bring together the capital and the labour required for the work; they arrange or "engineer" its general plan and superintend its minor details [16, p. 244].

The entrepreneur may have to grow in his capacities as his business grows yet he must retain "his originality, and versatility and power of initiation, his perseverance, his tact . . . if he is to continue to be successful" [16, p.238]. "A powerful capitalist with a very high order of general business ability . . . (must) rely on (his) own judgement as to what are likely to be the coming relations of demand and supply . . ." [16, p. 245].

By the time we get to Joseph Schumpeter (circa 1910) we know that the professionalization of middle management was well in progress at least in the United States [5, p. 467]. Schumpeter, who has been referred to as the father of modern entrepreneurial thought [3], propounded the view that the entrepreneur was unlike "heads of firms or managers or industrialists who merely may operate an established business" [20, p. 75]. The entrepreneur distinguished himself by "carrying out new combinations" of production forces (i.e., enterprise). The entrepreneur's challenge was to find and use new ideas to jostle the economy out of otherwise repetitive cycles of activities. Schumpeter recognized a range of possible alternative combinations which may initiate entrepreneurial action including: (1) new products or services, (2) new methods of production, (3) new markets, (4) new sources of supply and, (5) new forms of organization [20, p. 75]. As socio-economic innovators entrepreneurs were different from speculators and inventors. They were creators of new business combinations.

> And what have they done: They have not accumulated any kind of goods, they have created no original means of production, but have employed existing means of production differently, more appropriately, more advantageously. They have carried out new combinations! They are the entrepreneurs. And their profit, the surplus to which no liability corresponds, is the entrepreneurial profit [20, p. 132].

Schumpeter recognized that new combinations are introduced via the vehicle of new businesses. Part of the entrepreneurial function was the "founding of new business." However, the founding of a business was a largely undifferentiated concept within the Schumpeterian view of things. Schumpeter noted that "special aptitudes" were required to "obtain the necessary credit" and "set up the organization" [20, p. 133]. Yet he did not elaborate on the skills or processes involved. His emphasis was upon the general creative socio-economic function of "carrying out new combinations" and not upon the specific process by which new organizations were established to carry out these new combinations. Schumpeter went so far as to state that according to his theory the promoter, and not the organization-builder, was his entrepreneurial ideal type:

> The promoter may indeed be, as we say, the purest type of the entrepreneurial genus. He is then the entrepreneur who confines himself most strictly to the characteristic entrepreneurial function, the carrying out of new combinations [20, p. 137].

Knight [12] re-emphasized the importance of judgement and commitment in the face of uncertainty as essential elements in the entrepreneurial process. The entrepreneur, according to Knight, was a man of confidence with the disposition to act courageously upon his own opinions. Knight argued the importance of being involved in the business of organization but only in the abstract sense of performing such managerial functions as "responsible direction" and "control:"

> When uncertainty is present the task of deciding what to do and how to do it takes the ascendancy over that of execution; the internal organization of the productive groups is no longer a matter of indifference or a mechanical detail. Centralization of this deciding and controlling function is imperative . . . [12, p. 268].

But Knight's entrepreneur is more than a high level manager deciding what functions need to be carried out and whom to hire to perform them; Knight's entrepreneur is also an owner—a capitalist entrepreneur.

> Even a man who conducted a business entirely with borrowed and hired labor, but managing himself, would not exemplify pure entrepreneurship . . . (p. 299–300). The entrepreneur must almost of necessity own some property . . . [12, p. 304].

However, the entrepreneur's tendency was neither to build organizations nor to perform organization building functions. Instead, Knight preferred to see the entrepreneur as courageously responding to the pressures of uncertainty while his more timid counterparts were otherwise incapacitated. The entrepreneur would bear the risks of the venture for himself and for others: "securing the owners of productive services against uncertainty and fluctuation in their income." In turn, he would recognize and accept the inevitable uncertainties involved:

> The venture itself may be of the nature of a gamble involving a large proportion of unpredictable factors [12, p. 275].

Although Knight did not write of the entrepreneur as an organization builder, he did recognize the similarity between the requirements of the manager and the entrepreneur. Apparently for Knight they must operate in a similar medium:

> When, however, the managerial function comes to require the exercise for judgement involving "liability of error," and when in consequence the assumption of responsibility for his opinions becomes a condition prerequisite to getting the other members of the group to submit to the manager's direction, the nature of the function is revolutionized; the manager becomes an entrepreneur [12, p. 276].

Penrose outlined a general theory of the growth and development of "enterprising firms possessing or able to attract competent management" [17, p. 33]. For Penrose the concept of a firm is more than the collection of disembodied cost curves familiar in most economic theories. For her a business firm is both an administrative organization and a collection of productive resources whose function is the portioning out of economic resources among various demands for both production and consumption [17, pp. 30, 197]. The management of the firms supplies both entrepreneurial and management services. Not surprisingly, it is the entrepreneurial services which are required for growth and development.

> Entrepreneurial services are those contributions to the operations of a firm which relate to the introduction and acceptance on behalf of the firm of new ideas, particularly with respect to products, location and significant changes in technology, to the acquisition of new managerial personnel, to fundamental changes in the administra-

tive organization of the firm, to the raising of capital, and to making of plans for expansion, including the choice of method of expansion. Entrepreneurial services are contrasted with managerial services, which relate to the execution of entrepreneurial ideas and proposals and to the supervision of existing operations. The same individuals may, and more often than not probably do, provide both types of services to the firm [30, pp. 31–32].

Penrose notes that the entrepreneur is in need of a number of important talents. The entrepreneur should have the imagination and the vision to develop the practical day-to-day innovations needed to keep a firm versatile and opportunistic:

> The Schumpeterian "entrepreneur," though more colourful and identifiable, is too dramatic a personage for our purposes. Schumpeter was interested in economic development and his entrepreneur was an innovator from the point of view of the economy as a whole; we are interested in the growth of firms, and here the entrepreneur is an innovator from the point of view of the firm, not necessarily from the point of view of the economy as a whole [17, p. 36].

Moreover, the entrepreneur should possess fund-raising ingenuity, entrepreneurial ambition and entrepreneurial judgement.

> . . . entrepreneurial judgement involves more than a combination of imagination, "good sense," self-confidence, and other personal qualities. It is closely related to the organization of information-gathering and consulting facilities within the firm . . . [17, p. 41].

Although Penrose is reasonably thorough in her analysis of both the entrepreneurial venture medium and the tools required to develop it, she has most to say about the strategies which entrepreneurs use for development, namely: expansion without merger, the direction of expansion, specialization, diversification, vertical integration, acquisition and merger. Yet throughout her descriptions of these various strategic options runs a common logical thread. Expansion or growth is primarily limited by the availability of managerial (entrepreneurial) services for expansion:

> Under given circumstances, therefore, the maximum amount of expansion will be determined by the relevant managerial services available for expansion in relation to the amount of these services required per dollar of expansion [17, p. 200].

Leibenstein [14] [15] developed a theory of entrepreneurship which likens the entrepreneur even more to a manager than does Knight. Leibenstein argued that businesses were often badly managed, and, as a result, "essentially we visualize one of the concerns of management and entrepreneurship to be the struggle against (inefficiency)" [15, p. 131].

Unlike most other formal theorists Leibenstein identified a number of different entrepreneurial challenges which were important to either organizational efficiency or organization building.[2]

His view of the entrepreneur is that of: a marshaller of inputs (an input completer); an overcomer of obstacles to inputs (a gap filler); and a bearer of uncertainty.[3]

As a bearer of uncertainty, the entrepreneur would be involved in: "(1) cost containing and (2) market sheltering activities—" two sets of activities which are difficult to determine as belonging to either entrepreneurship or management [15, p. 136].

Leibenstein also had more to say about the entrepreneurial medium than either Schumpeter or Knight. Leibenstein described the firm as a system in the sense that it was a time bending, input-transforming entity tending toward entropy over time. Much of what he had to say about entrepreneurship was *de facto* descriptive of the medium within which entrepreneurs work. He stated that his "x-efficiency" or technical proficiency theory for firms and markets can be "connected with the essential tasks of entrepreneurship" [15, p. 133]. Yet given the extent to which Leibenstein was concerned with organization-building, it is surprising that he did not provide a dynamic model of organization through time. Leibenstein's model is static in the sense that the requirements of the organization (and therefore of the entrepreneur) do not vary with the stage of development of the venture organization.

Israel Kirzner [10] [11] developed a complementary notion to the Schumpeterian ideal of the entrepreneur as a disequilibrating economic force. From Kirzner's perspective the entrepreneur functioned primarily as an equilibrating force—smoothing out market imperfections through arbitrage activities.[4]

Kirzner placed somewhat more emphasis on explaining the entrepreneurial process than had Schumpeter, even though his explanation of entrepreneurial activity was limited to venture ideation. According to Kirzner, the entrepreneur is an acutely perceptive individual relying for profit opportunities upon an ability to spot underpriced products or underpriced factors of production in particular markets:

> If I don't know that profit opportunities exist, these opportunities will remain unexplored. Entrepreneurial profit opportunities exist where people do not know what it is that they do not know, and do not know that they do not know it. The entrepreneurial function is to notice what people have overlooked [11, p. 273].

However, once awareness has been attained, the task becomes one for a professional manager. For Kirzner, entrepreneurship begins and ends with opportunities. Kirzner's entrepreneur is an opportunity identifier and definitely not an organization-builder:

> If people know that a gap needs to be filled, and that it is worthwhile to fill, the task is no longer entrepreneurial, it can be handled by competent managers through routine production methods [11, p. 176].

Summary of Important Definitional Attributes

Richard Cantillon (circa 1730)	Entrepreneur defined as a self-employed person. Additional uncertainty accompanies self-employment. Entrepreneurs should proportion their activity to market demands.
Jean-Baptiste Say (circa 1810)	Many managerial talents are required to be a successful entrepreneur. Many obstacles and uncertainties accompany entrepreneurship.
Alfred Marshall (circa 1890)	The abilities to be an entrepreneur are different yet complementary with the abilities to be a manager.
Joseph Schumpeter (circa 1910)	Entrepreneurship is at its essence the finding and promoting of new combinations of productive factors. Entrepreneurship is the prime creative socioeconomic factor.
Frank Knight (circa 1920)	The courage to bear uncertainty is the essential aspect of entrepreneurship. Entrepreneurs are required to perform such fundamental managerial functions as responsible direction and control.
Edith Penrose (circa 1960)	Managerial capacities should be distinguished from entrepreneurial capacities. Identifying and exploiting opportunistic ideas for expansion of smaller enterprises is the essential aspect of entrepreneurship.
Harvey Leibenstein (circa 1970)	Entrepreneurial activity is aimed toward the reduction of organizational inefficiency and to the reversal of organizational entropy.
Israel Kirzner (circa 1975)	The identification of market arbitrage opportunities is the fundamental function of the entrepreneur.

CONCLUSION

Over the last two hundred and fifty years of formal theorizing about entrepreneurship one can recognize three major recurring and inter-related themes in the major theories. In the early part of the eighteenth century, Richard Cantillon recognized the uncertainty associated with entrepreneurial activity. Two hundred years later we find Frank Knight formulating his theory of entrepreneurship upon the same foundation of uncertainty and risk. In the early part of the nineteenth century, Jean-Baptiste Say emphasized the general managerial capacities required for entrepreneurial success. In the first half of the twentieth century, Frank Knight reiterated the need for managerial competence as did Harvey Leibenstein in the latter half of the twentieth century. The third theme—that of creativity and innovation—gained force with Joseph Schumpeter in the early years of the twentieth century although intimations of this theme were to be found in the writings of the physiocrats of the latter part of the eighteenth century and in J. B. Say's notion of the adventurer applying scientific knowledge to industry. Around 1960, Edith Penrose explained organizational growth and development by recourse to a creative opportunistic conception of the entrepreneur. In the Seventies, Leibenstein adapted the Schumpeterian notion of the innovative entrepreneur to the managerial problems of sustaining and enhancing organizational negentropy. Even more recently Israel Kirzner has adapted the concepts

of the creative entrepreneur to the problem of identifying opportunities for market arbitrage activities. In summary, three themes: (1) uncertainty and risk; (2) complementary managerial competence; and (3) creative opportunism, have been interwoven in various combinations and permutations in virtually all formal theories of entrepreneurship.[5]

Modern definitions of entrepreneurship which exclude any of these three fundamental dimensions may lead us along the futile path of rediscovering what we should already know. These dimensions suggest definitional boundaries circumscribing the essential qualities of entrepreneurship. As noted by Bartels [2] a theory should deal with a specific, definable subject and be related to it throughout. "The definition serves as a fundamental hypothesis" [2, p. 5]. A common conceptualization of subject permits research direction and theoretical integration which in turn should ultimately strengthen the practice of entrepreneurship.

Lenin was not an entrepreneur because he was not working within a business medium requiring the type of managerial competences to which Say alludes despite the fact that he was both taking risks and being innovative. ▲

NOTES

1. Note that Knight seemingly contradicts his requirement that the entrepreneur also be an owner in the above statement.
2. Leibenstein does not distinguish organizational efficiency from organizational building. However, presumably the more efficient organizations become, the more they will tend toward an optimal size. The process of creating and developing organizations is unexplored in Leibenstein's writings.
3. Unfortunately Leibenstein's style of writing obfuscates his intended distinction between the concepts of "gap filler" and "input completer." On the surface they appear to be different concepts, yet reading and re-reading Leibenstein's work has not helped to clarify the real differences.
4. Schumpeter recognized but did not develop the idea of an entrepreneur as an exploiter of market imperfections [20, p. 30].
5. Herbert and Link [7] covered much the same ground in their research and concluded that there have been four basic dynamic theory types which reflect differing definitions of entrepreneurship. The theory types are labeled according to the "chief burden" upon the entrepreneur and include: "(1) pure uncertainty; (2) pure innovation; (3) uncertainty bearing and either ability or innovation, and; (4) the perception of adjustment to disequilibria" [7, p. 109].

References

1. Badian, E. *Publicans and Sinners: Private Enterprise in the Service of the Roman Republic.* Ithaca: Cornell University Press, 1972.
2. Bartels, Robert. *Marketing Theory and Metatheory.* Homewood, Illinois: Irwin, 1970.
3. Campbell, R. H. and Wilson, R. G. *Entrepreneurship in Britain 1750–1939.* London: Adam and Charles Black, 1975.
4. Cantillon, Richard. *Essai Sur la Nature du Commerce en General.* London, 1755.
5. Chandler, Alfred D. *The Visible Hand: The Managerial Revolution in American Business.* Cambridge, Mass.: The Belknap Press of Harvard University Press, 1977.
6. Harwood, Edwin. "The Sociology of Entrepreneurship." In C. A. Kent, D. L. Sexton, and K. H. Vesper eds, *Encyclopedia of Entrepreneurship*, N.J.: Prentice-Hall, 1982.
7. Herbert, Robert F. & Link, Albert N. *The Entrepreneur*, New York: Praeger Publishers, 1982.
8. Hoselitz, Bert F. "The Early History of Entrepreneurial Theory," *Explorations in Entrepreneurial History,* 3(4):193–220 (1951).
9. Kirzner, Israel M. *Competition and Entrepreneurship.* Chicago: University of Chicago Press, 1973.
10. Kirzner, Israel M. *Perception, Opportunity and Profit.* Chicago: University of Chicago Press, 1979.

11. Kirzner, Israel M. "The Theory of Entrepreneurship in Economic Growth." In Kent, Sexton, Vesper, eds. *Encyclopedia of Entrepreneurship,* (Englewood Cliffs, N.J.: Prentice-Hall, 1982), pp. 272–276.
12. Knight, Frank H. *The Economic Organization.* New York: Augustus M. Kelley, 1967.
13. Knight, Frank H. *Risk, Uncertainty and Profit.* New York: Kelley & Millman, Inc., 1921.
14. Leibenstein, H. "Entrepreneurship and Development." *American Economic Review,* (May, 1968), pp. 72–83.
15. Leibenstein, H. "The General X-Efficiency Paradigm and the Role of the Entrepreneur." In M. J. Rizzo, ed., *Time, Uncertainty and Disequilibrium,* (Lexington, Mass.: Lexington Books, 1979), pp. 127–139.
16. Marshal, Alfred. *Principles of Economics.* London: MacMillan & Co., Ltd., 8th Ed., 1964.
17. Penrose, Edith. *The Growth of the Firm.* Oxford: Basil Blackwell Publ., 1980.
18. Say, Jean Baptiste. *A Treatise on Political Economy,* Grigg, Elliot & Co., 1847.
19. Schumpeter, Joseph A. "The Creative Response in Economic History." *The Journal of Economic History,* 7(2):149–159 (Nov., 1979).
20. Schumpeter, Joseph A. *The Theory of Economic Development.* Oxford: Oxford University Press, 1974.

THE CONCEPT OF VISION IN THE CONTEXT OF NEW VENTURE CREATION

Alfie Morgan

INTRODUCTION

The concept vision is a central element in the entrepreneurship phenomenon. Entrepreneurs are often viewed as people with "vision." Nevertheless, the concept is yet to be explored empirically in depth. In entrepreneurship literature, the concept is often implied; rarely explored in depth. The main attempts to conceptualize vision are primarily in the literature on leadership theory and strategic management. And these are frameworks that are essentially conceptual and intuitive with little empirical foundation.

This study was designed to develop a concept of entrepreneurial vision that is derived from empirical data. This presentation begins with a review of the literature on "vision" and the conceptual frameworks constructed to represent it. Next, the research design will be described. Then, the results of this research will be presented. The main results here take the form of the conceptual framework itself.

"VISION" IN THE LITERATURE

Interest in the concept "vision" appeared in the literature since the late 1970s and early 1980s. Early writings were in the context of leadership theory (Eden *et al.,* 1979, Maccoby, 1981, Bennis, 1982). Later on, it assumed an important place in strategic management literature (Mintzberg and Waters, 1988, Tregoe *et al.,* 1989, Collins and Porass, 1996, Wilson, 1992, Quigly, 1993, among others).

Definition of "Vision"

Writers in entrepreneurship appear to assume that everyone knows what vision is. Kao (1989), for example, states that the task of the entrepreneur consists of three main things: defining a vision, marshaling resources, and providing leadership. Yet, the term vision was not defined. However, he advances the notion that the entrepreneur leads the enterprise to "a desired future state." Perhaps this "desired future state" can be interpreted as a definition of vision.

Alfie Morgan is professor of Business Strategy and Entrepreneurship at the Faculty of Business Administration, University of Windsor, Windsor, Ontario.

In the fields of leadership theory and strategic management, there are as many definitions as there are authors due to the subjectivity of the construct.

For example, Robert (1983, p. 2) observed that: "Each person that leads an organization, large or small, has a concept or vision of what that organization would look like sometime in the future." Hickman and Silva (1984, p. 151) defined it as ". . . a mental journey from the known to the unknown, creating the future from a montage of current facts, hopes, dreams, dangers, and opportunities." Bennis and Nanus (1985, p. 89), verbalized it as ". . . a mental image of a possible and desirable future state of the organization."

Conceptualizing Vision

Rover (1983) was perhaps the first to identify a number of elements that could serve as a conceptual framework. He uses the term "strategic profile" synonymously with the term "vision." He outlined the components of the strategic profile as follows:

- Time frame
- Driving forces and Business Concept, i.e., forces that will propel the firm in the future such as product, customers, technology, capability, distribution, etc. The choice of a driving force and articulating it then becomes the business concept or purpose of the organization.
- Areas of excellence.
- Product scope.
- Market scope.
- Size and growth guidelines.
- Return and profit guidelines.

Wilson (1992) developed a conceptual framework that includes six elements: (1) "Business Scope"—designates the range and mix of businesses that the company chooses to pursue, (2) "Business Scale"—bounds the desired future size of the company, (3) "Product and Market Focus," (4) "Competitive Focus," i.e., the basis on which the company intends to compete, (5) "Image and Relationships," e.g., relationships with employees and other allies for the firm, and (6) "Organization and Culture," the structure, management systems and operating culture.

TOWARDS AN EMPIRICALLY DERIVED FRAMEWORK FOR VISION

Two main observations provided the motivation for this study:

- The concepts of vision in the literature are purely conceptual. They are constructs developed by the writers to convey what they think vision ought to be. They are not grounded in reality through empirical data from entrepreneurs.
- The lack of consistency among the constructs in the literature begs the question as to what vision really is and what it is made of.

Research Question:

In light of the above, the main research questions for this study were formulated as follows:

- Before they start a new venture, do entrepreneurs "see" a picture of the business firm they intend to build?
- If so, what do they "see?" What are the components of this picture? How do they "hang together" to make up a vision of the intended enterprise?

Research Design

To answer the above research questions, the study proceeded according to the research design outlined below:

1. Types of Data:

   For the purpose of this study, data were determined as the thoughts or the ideas that existed in the entrepreneur's mind in the period prior to starting up the venture. These thoughts are encoded in words. Words are then the data for this study. These words exist in two main forms: oral, i.e., verbalizations by entrepreneurs; and, written, e.g., business plans, notes, and memos.

2. Research Strategy:

   Qualitative research was chosen as the appropriate methodology for conducting this study. Within the methods of qualitative research, grounded theory was chosen as the most instructive as it yields frameworks that are useful in constructing entities such as vision. The approach consists of a systematic set of procedures for developing a theory that is grounded in the data about the phenomenon under study (in this case, vision). "Grounded" means that the theory is inductively derived or discovered from the collected data and provisionally tested and verified from the same set of data (Strauss and Corbin, 1990).

3. Sample:

   Data for this study were collected from a sample of three hundred start-up entrepreneurs. Three data collection strategies were utilized: (1) interviews with entrepreneurs, (2) analysis of case studies focusing on business start-ups, and, (3) actual business plans. First, 150 in-depth unstructured interviews were conducted with entrepreneurs who started a new venture within the preceding three years. The interviews took place between 1993 and 1997. The interviewees were asked to peer deeper into the thoughts that came to their mind when they were contemplating their anticipated venture. They were prompted to look at the details and variety of their thoughts.

   Second, 50 published case studies describing start-up entrepreneurs were analyzed with a view to extracting the ideas that the respective entrepreneurs expressed to case writers. The case studies were gathered from textbooks on entrepreneurship as well as the Harvard case studies collection. Finally, 100 actual business plans that were submitted to investors were examined with the purpose of identifying the ideas that described a new venture.

4. Data Analysis:

According to the grounded theory approach, data are first gathered without the bias of a pre-established theoretical framework. Once collected, data are analyzed in three stages. The first is open coding where categories or concepts are identified by sifting through the data. In the second stage, axial coding, connections are made between categories or concepts according to a paradigm model that can portray how the concepts "hang together." In the third stage, selective coding, a core category is selected, and then related systematically to other categories. Further, such relationships are validated by referring to the original data set and/or by gathering additional data.

FINDINGS

The analysis of the collected data suggests that all the entrepreneurs in the sample had a preconceived notion as to what the enterprise subject of the venture would look like. Every entrepreneur had a mental picture of his or her firm before they formally launch the venture. The content of this mental picture varied with respect to scope and details. Some envisioned the enterprise in greater detail. Others had rough concepts that was augmented later as the venture unfolded.

Grounded theory involves the intensive categorization of ideas and relating the resulting categories to one another into cohesive frameworks. A challenge for the researcher is what ideas to include in a given category. A rule of thumb was established here. For an idea to be considered for a category, it had to be expressed by at least 60% of the subjects. This rule was needed to establish the credibility of an idea as a general trend among the sampled entrepreneurs.

The analysis and categorization of the successful ideas (those expressed by at least 60% of the subjects) yielded thirteen categories. These, in turn, were grouped into two major or core ones. The first core category includes categories that pertained to the business environment in which the enterprise will exist. This was labeled as "vision of the setting." Examples of categories under this heading included ideas regarding an opportunity in the marketplace, a concept of the industry structure (particularly the number of competitors and the pecking order) in which the opportunity existed, and a vision of key success factors. The second major category included categories pertaining to the enterprise itself, its dimensions, and method of doing business. This was labeled "vision of the business." The concept of vision thus appears to be two things in one as shown in Exhibit 1.

Each category is a grouping of a number of sub-categories that were found to be interrelated. Measures of a relationship included the criteria of sequence (what came before what), association (what was done concurrently with what), and dependence (what caused what). Based on these relationships, the sub-categories were related to one another in the

Exhibit 1. Core Categories of Vision Thoughts.

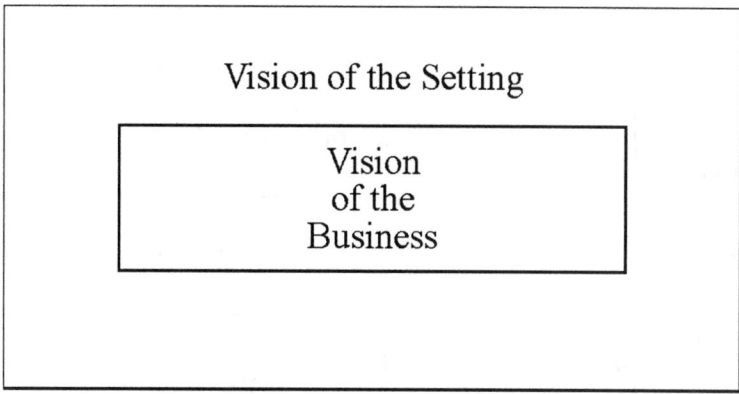

form of mini-frameworks. Two such mini-frameworks are presented in Exhibits 2 and 3 on the following page.

Vision of the Setting

The concepts or sub-categories that appeared in the vision of the setting are shown in Exhibit 2. Each is described briefly below.

Vision of the Broader Environment

The first element in the vision of the setting—a vision of the broader environment within which the enterprise is expected to operate. The entrepreneur is somehow able to imagine or describe in advance what the "broader" environment would be like in the future. This category included perceptions such as conditions of the economy, trends in market demographics, major trends in technology, major trends in social change. Such perceptions were believed to be drivers that create an opportunity arena that attracted the entrepreneur to the venture in the first place.

Vision of the Industry

Nestled with the vision of the broader environment is a "vision of the industry"—a mental picture of the structure of the industry including the key players, basis of competition, the products, the technology, the gaps, etc. The vision of the industry often embodies an opportunity arena that fuels the entrepreneurial dream.

Vision of the Opportunity Arena

The vision of the broader environment and the vision of the industry yield another vision and that is a "vision of an opportunity arena"—the various gaps in the market place that represent opportunities to be pursued. Entrepreneurs, being opportunity driven, are somewhat able to sniff out and map opportunity arenas. An opportunity arena is a range of

Exhibit 2. Vision of the Setting's Mini-framework.

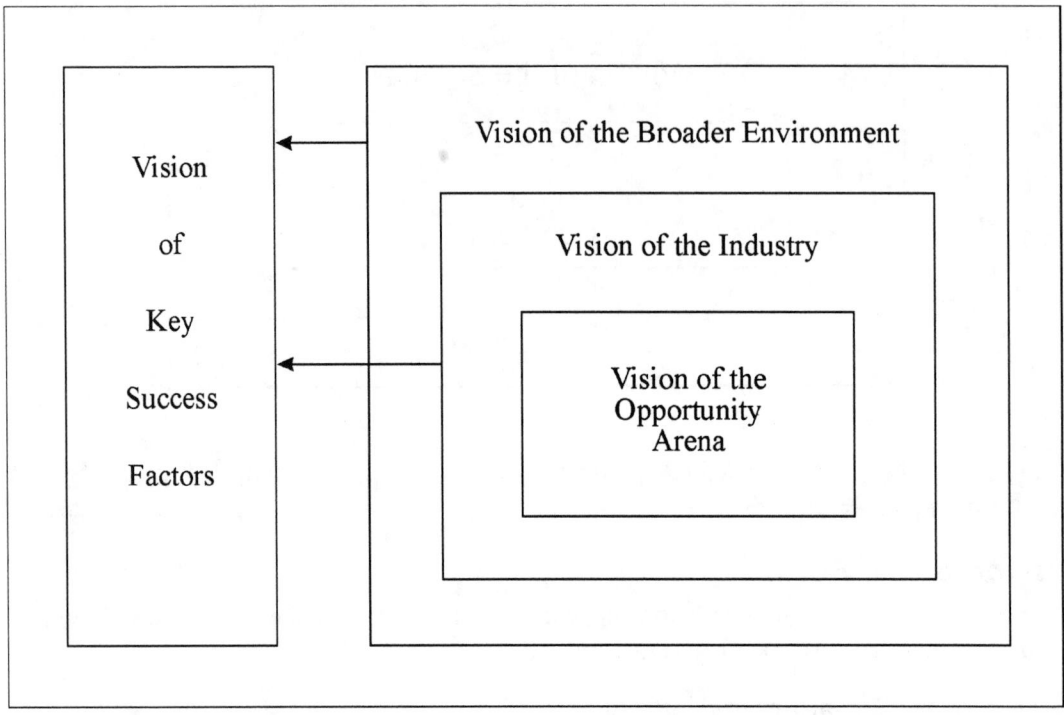

Exhibit 3. Elements of the Vision of the Business.

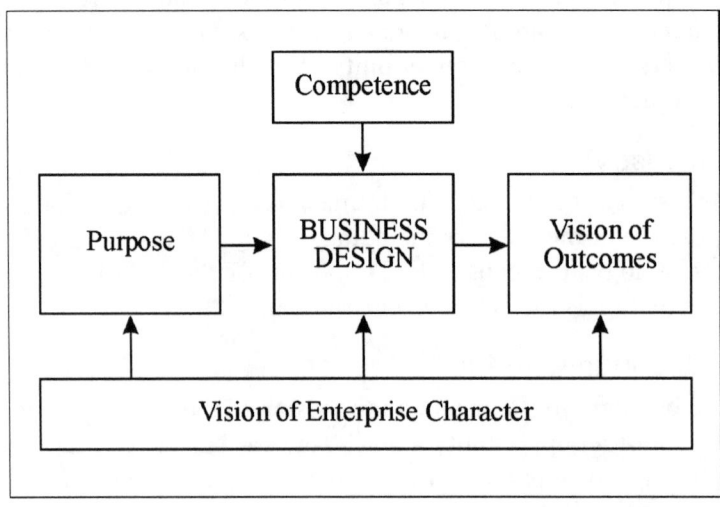

unfilled needs for a market or segment thereof that has the purchasing power to fill this range of needs. For a clothes retailing entrepreneur, the opportunity arena is the full range of needs of those who need to be fashionable. Such an arena includes not only attire and accessories but consulting services in order for the customers to dress for success.

Vision of Success Factors

Concomitant with the visioning of an opportunity arena is the "gut feel" for what it takes to be successful in the envisioned industry. The visionary entrepreneur is often able to identify these critical factors. These, in turn, become part of a set of premises upon which they design their enterprise. A clothes retailing entrepreneur established in advance that having a full line, city center location, and expert service are the key success factors that her venture must possess if she was to make it in that industry. A tool and die entrepreneur considered speed, advanced CAD-CAM, and integration with customers as the key success factors. He thought no one could make it in this industry without possessing these three attributes in abundance.

Vision of the Business

As stated earlier, the vision of the business stems from the vision of the setting. A number of related sub-categories of new venture creation ideas were grouped together into a mini-framework that represents a mental picture of the intended enterprise that is presented in Exhibit 3. These are outlined below.

Concept of Purpose

The concept of purpose is the reason for the firm's existence in the entrepreneur's mind. To the entrepreneur, purpose is where the new venture fits in his or her scheme of things. Thus, for a small business entrepreneur, the purpose might be to create a job or personal wealth. For large scale entrepreneurs, the purpose often involves altering something in the business or industry's environment. When this alteration takes place, it would create an enormous opportunity (in the opportunity arena) for providing sustenance for the firm. The scale of this alteration varies with the ambition of the entrepreneur. It may be as simple as merely exploiting a visible opportunity. It can be as complex as changing the world we live in.

Here are some examples of well known entrepreneurs:

- Steve Job's purpose for Apple Computers was to change the way people compute and perhaps to change the way children learn in school.
- Ray Kroc's purpose for McDonald's was to change the way people eat—to offer standardized meals, at a standardized speed, in a standardized clean environment, at a standardized low price throughout the continent.

The purpose is a strong determinant of the remainder of the vision of the business and its business design.

The Business Design

The business design appears to be the chassis upon which the enterprise will be erected. Every entrepreneur analyzed had a clear idea of a business design. In some cases, the business design was focused on uniqueness (55% of the sample). In the remaining cases, the business design was a replication of an existing business design with minor modifications or improvements.

A business design is a configuration of the activities of the intended enterprise. Such activities can be viewed as a "value stream." A value stream is an end to end collection of activities that deliver value to the customers and to the entrepreneur. The vision of the business design specifies the content of the various activities and how they relate to one another.

Nearly every entrepreneur was deliberately thinking about delivering value to customers that is equal or better than competitors. They thought not only about what value to deliver but also of ways to deliver this value to customers to win customer loyalty and repeat business.

Following are some examples of business designs that became the cornerstone of the vision for some well-known companies:

- Sam Walton's business design for Wal-Mart's business had the following features:
  - ☐ Market and site selection—singling out on second and third tier smaller markets.
  - ☐ Procurement and distribution—a network of suppliers and local distribution networks operating on a just-in-time basis.
  - ☐ Information management—speed and comprehensiveness in capturing and tracking product position on a department by department and store by store basis throughout the continent every working day.
  - ☐ Customer service and employee motivation—the ultimate in customer service delivered by highly motivated employees who operate under a structure that connects customer service with the store's financial performance.
- King and Kelleher's business design for Southwest Airlines can be outlined as follows:
  - ☐ Market segmentation and selection—"cherry picking" of high volume pairs of cities rather than the "hub and spoke" design that all other airlines have.
  - ☐ High asset management and utilization by avoiding the expensive hub and spoke system, one type of aircraft, and a unique approach that emphasizes doing more for less.
  - ☐ No frills—no reservations, no expensive printed tickets, no meals on board, and so on.

Exhibit 4. The Business Design's Mini-Framework.

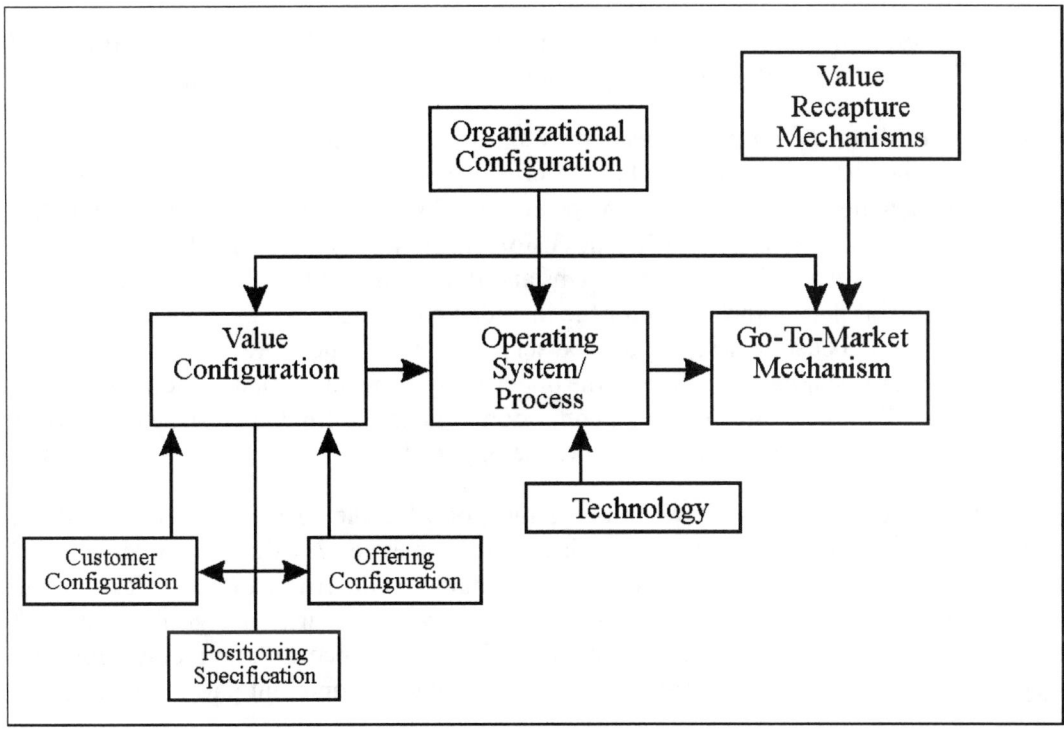

As a further illustration of the concept of business design, consider the case of a trucking firm that does not own trucks. It is designed as a "virtual" trucking company, i.e., it appears as a trucking company but it has no trucks and does not do any trucking. Its business design consists of a large, national network of independent truckers. The company's sales force obtains the orders and its traffic department assigns the various orders to the truckers depending on wherever they are. It tracks them by means of a number of satellite stations that can locate a truck in whatever block of a street that it happens to be in. All trucks are connected to the stations by means of a tracking device installed in the truck. When orders are taken, the nearest truck for the pick up address is located and instructed to make the pick up. Orders are assembled in its warehousing facilities to achieve economies of scale. Trucks delivering freights do not return empty as they are instructed to pick up another load for the return trip. Truckers pick up and deliver. The firm then collects from customers and pays the truckers.

The business design as a core category (for vision of the business) includes nine sub-categories as shown in exhibits 3 and 4. There are six sub-categories in a business, namely, a value configuration, an operating system, technology, organizational configuration, "go-to-market" mechanisms, and value recapture mechanisms. Each will be described below.

Value Configuration. A value configuration consists of three main specifications: customer configuration, offering configuration, and positioning specification.

Customer Configuration. Value is only meaningful to customers. Hence, having a concept of who the customers will be is a crucial part of vision. Furthermore, value is contingent upon the customers' needs and perception. In essence, value is the ratio of output (what the customer gets) to input (what the customer invests—the price paid). Accordingly, the selection of the specific customer groups and the needs that the proposed venture will satisfy is a crucial part of the vision for the intended enterprise.

The envisioned customer segment to be served represent the share of opportunity that the entrepreneur is staking—a subset of the opportunity arena identified in the vision of the setting. It should be remembered that an opportunity is, in the final analysis, customers as they hold the mass of dollars that constitute the opportunity.

Offering Configuration. If value is the ratio of what the customer gets to what the customer pays, the next question is "what" is it the customer gets? The answer: a "container" of satisfactions for the needs in question. This container is the firm's offering. It is *not* the mere product or services. *It is the product or service plus a wide range of enhancing* elements that make up its halo e.g., quality, reliability, assistance with financing, after sale service, image, and the like. Customer perceptions play an important part in determining value.

An offering has a scope, i.e., the range of offering differentiation with respect to the variation among customer segment. A car dealer's offering includes not only a product line of cars comprising several models but also mechanical services. This is often referred to as "product-market scope" and it becomes a major determinant of the intended firm's overall scope. The product market-scope also incorporates the geographic scope of the firm. If the customer groups exist in many locations, the range of locations determines the geographic scope of the firm.

Positioning Specification. The third sub-category in value configuration is the positioning of the offering relative to others in the marketplace. Positioning is the location of the offering on some continua that are determinant of value in the customer's mind. Positioning by itself creates value—perceived value in the eyes of the customer. Consider the perception of positioning terms such as "premium," "upscale," "fastest," "largest," etc.

Operating System/Process. The second sub-category in a business design is the operating system or process that will produce the value stream. Visionaries always think of the operating system as the backbone of the value stream. Fred Smith's vision for Federal Express, singled out the hub (Memphis) and spokes as its operating system. Ray Kroc's vision of McDonald's focused on the operating system that is based on the standardized fast food restaurant (with a specified production process) that we can see today, franchised units, with a network of suppliers.

All entrepreneurs in the sample had a clear vision of the operating system that would underlie their ventures. Even when the venture was perceived as a virtual business, entrepreneurs thought of an operating system or process for conducting the business of the proposed enterprise. A virtual corporation outsources most of its operations and acts as a coordinator of the independent producers who make up its value stream. Its operating system comprises processes that coordinate suppliers' outputs and focus them towards the customer end.

Technology. Technology refers to the know-how that underlies the design of the operating system as well as other parts of the enterprise. In the case of a clothes retailer, technology referred to the specific method(s) of buying clothes and inventory control. For a restaurant, it may be specific method of cooking, e.g., McDonald's versus Burger King in preparing hamburgers. Technology plays a crucial role in engineering the other components of the value stream, e.g., product design. Even if the operations system is not technology based (e.g., a restaurant), information technology still influences the vision of the operating system. In a restaurant, info-tech is utilized in order taking (waiters take orders on an electronic pad that transmits the order to the cook instantly), order processing ("smart" cooking appliances that "know" when the food is ready), and so on.

Go-To-Market Mechanisms. While the operating system and technology produce the offering, another part of business design involves designs for delivering value to the envisioned customer groups at the end of the value stream. Go-to-Market mechanisms appear to be an indispensable part of a firm's vision. They appeared in the thinking of every entrepreneur in the sample. Value exists only when the customer consumes or uses the offering and actually perceives the value in his/her mind. To illustrate, consider the vision of Dell Computers. The centerpiece of Dell's vision for his company was the go-to-market mechanism, which is the mail-order distribution and sale of desktop computer hardware. Ray Kroc, soon after founding McDonald's, resorted to franchising as the main go-to-market mechanism for the firm.

Organizational Configuration. For new venture entrepreneurs, activating the value stream was thought to require organization and an organizational structure. The organization will have to have the kind of configuration or structure that will perform all these major activities in the value stream. Virtual organizations have a different configuration than traditional forms of organization. Along the same lines, there is the matter whether all activities will be centralized in one location or distributed throughout the geographic scope of the firm. Every business plan nowadays includes a section on organizational configuration including the type of people needed, the units of the organization, hierarchy, and the distribution of authority.

Value Recapture Mechanisms. Entrepreneurs always think of ways of getting value for themselves out of the venture. Such thoughts appear to be present long before the venture is launched. Some entrepreneurs (30%) even went further to think of exit value for the venture even before start-up. They perceived exit value to be the appreciation of the venture after having been in operation for a number of years.

The value recapture mechanism is the design for recovering the value for the firm's stakeholders that is contingent on the delivery of value to customers; or simply how will the firm be paid. Consider mail order house businesses. The vision of such firms is based on the principle of being paid in advance—being financed by the customer. Franchisors stress franchise fees and royalties as methods of recovering value from the franchisees.

There are several value recapture mechanisms including payment in advance, payment at the time of purchase, payment after the purchase (the firm financing the customer), barter, leasing, and so on.

Vision of Competence

A critical part of an entrepreneur's vision is a concept of competence—something that would enable his/her firm to perform well and excel over others in the marketplace. Competence here refers to specific skills or ways of doing things that translate into value for the customers while being difficult to copy by competitors.

Vision of competence arises from the interpretation of key success factors and the acquisition of certain skills that allow the venture to possess them. It would seem that Steve Jobs must have envisioned user friendliness as an essential success factor in the desktop computer business. Based on this interpretation, Apple had to have the competence to produce a user-friendly computer. In the case of Dell Computers, it is evident that the competence in mail order selling and sourcing computers cheaply were key parts of Dell's vision for the company. Fred Smith's vision for Federal Express included the competence of doing it all "overnight"—collection, packaging, flying, sorting, and distribution as part of the firm's vision.

Vision of Enterprise Character

Entrepreneurs in the sample tended to structure the intended enterprise in their own image. In a way, they saw it as an extension of their own value system and character. Those that were straightforward people often envisioned their firms being on the up and up always insisting on full disclosure, honesty and transparency.

Vision of Outcomes

Although entrepreneurs were thinking about the dream, they were clear on what the enterprise must accomplish for them personally and for the customers.

Here is a possible list of outcomes that appeared in the visions collected for this study:

- *Financial* outcomes, e.g., levels of profitability and growth, and shareholder value.

- *Strategic* outcomes—envisioning dominance or a strong impenetrable position in the market place.
- *Customer satisfaction* outcomes—defining customer satisfaction as the index of good performance.
- *Human* outcomes—envisioning the firm as a good place to work in, where members of the organization can seek and achieve self-fulfillment.
- *Excellence* outcomes—higher quality, higher rate of innovation for example.

CONCLUSION

The data gathered for this study, suggest that entrepreneurial vision is a "web" of visions—one contingent upon the other. First, there is that of the setting or the habitat in which the venture will operate; and, derived from that is the mental picture of the business enterprise itself, i.e., vision of the business.

The vision of the setting is also a web of visions that include the vision of the broader environment, the industry, an opportunity arena, and key success factors. Born from the vision of the setting is the vision of the enterprise itself which is a web of visions involving purposes, business design, character, and vision of outcomes. ▲

NOTES

1. Bennis, W., and B. Nanus, *Leaders,* New York, NY: Harper and Row, 1985.
2. Collins, J. C., and J. I. Porras, "Building a Visionary Company," *California Management Review*, Winter 1996, pp. 80–100.
3. Eden, C., and S. Jones, D. Sims, and H. Gunton, "Images and Models: The Subjective World of the Policy Maker, *Futures*, February, 1979, pp. 56–62.
4. Hickman, C. and M. Silva, *Creating Excellence: Managing Corporate Culture, Strategy, and Change in the New Age.* New American Library, 1984.
5. Kao, J. J., *Entrepreneurship, Creativity, and Organization: Text, Cases, and Readings.* Englewood Cliffs, NJ: Prentice-Hall, 1989, p. 93, 95, and 96.
6. Langler, "The Vision Trap," *Harvard Business Review,* March–April 1992, pp. 46–55.
7. Maccoby, M., *The Leader,* New York, NY: Simon & Schuster, 1981.
8. Mintzberg, H. and J. A. Waters, "The Mind of the Strategist," in Srivastva, S. *et al.* eds., *The Executive Mind,* San Francisco, CA: Jossey-Bass, 1983.
9. Robert, M., *Strategic Thinking: Charting the Future Direction of Your Organization*, Australia, Decision Sciences International Ltd., 1983, p. 2.
10. Quigly, J. V., *Vision: How Leaders Develop It, Share It, and Sustain It*, New York: McGraw-Hill, 1994.
11. Strauss, A. and J. Corbin, *Basics of Qualitative Research: Grounded Theory Procedures and Techniques,* Newbury Park, CA: Sage Publications, 1990, pp. 23–24.
12. Trogoe, B. B., J. W. Zimmerman, R. A. Smith, and P. M. Tobia, *Vision In Action,* New York, NY: Simon & Schuster, 1989.
13. Wilson, I. "Realizing the Power of Strategic Vision," *Long Range Planning* Vol. 25, no. 5, 1992, pp. 18–28.

STRATEGIC MANAGEMENT: NEW VENTURES AND SMALL BUSINESS

Arnold C. Cooper

This paper examines the factors influencing the formulation and implementation of strategy in new and small firms. Small businesses vary substantially in their resource positions, the goals of their founders and their potential. They also vary in stage of development: thus strategic management is examined separately in the start-up stage, the early-growth stage, and the later-growth stage. Intracorporate entrepreneurship in established firms is also considered. Despite this diversity, small firms create an environment for strategic management in which both the opportunities and constraints are different from those in large organizations.

New and small firms provide a distinctive environment for the formulation and implementation of strategy. This paper, based upon a review of the literature, examines the processes by which strategy is developed in such firms and the nature of the resulting strategies. Because new ventures within established firms have many of the characteristics of new and small businesses, strategic management within this context will also be considered.

Most firms in the United States, the United Kingdom, and other Western countries are small. For instance, about 95 percent of all U.S. firms have fewer than 20 employees.[1] However, the diversity among these small firms is enormous, so that statements which are descriptive of some do not apply to others. They differ in type of founders, in management sophistication, in stage of development, and in performance. Vesper has suggested that small firms might be classified as "mom and pop" companies, stable high-payoff companies, and growth-oriented companies.[2]

By far the majority of small businesses would be classified as mom and pop firms, particularly in retailing and service industries. Many have no hired employees and rely only on the proprietor or members of the family. Their founders often lack formal managerial training, but may have technical skills, such as being able to sell real estate, cut hair, or do automobile repairs. Capital barriers to entry are usually low, management methods intuitive, and profits moderate or low. Start-ups and discontinuances are frequent and the founders often move from blue-collar or clerical jobs to entrepreneurship and back again. Some such places of business need revolving doors, not for the few customers, but for the entrepreneurs who come and go.

Reprinted from *Long Range Planning,* Vol. 14, No. 5, pp. 39–45, 1981. Used by permission of the publisher. This paper is adapted from a chapter in D. Schendel and C. Hofer (Eds.), *Strategic Management: A New View of Business Policy,* Little, Brown & Co., 1979.

Some small retail and service firms and a higher percentage of small manufacturing firms might be classified as stable, high-payoff companies. Their founders often have more formal education and higher expectations than the mom and pop founders. Often they enjoy strong competitive positions deriving from specialized know-how, patents, or a virtual monopoly in a particular local market. Management methods, although informal by large company standards, may be very effective. Without the pressures of growth, the founder may be able to engage in civic activities or achieving a lower golf handicap, while maintaining a high standard of living.

Growth-oriented small firms offer the possibility of high payoff through selling out, through floating public issues of stock, or through controlling a large enterprise. They are started more often by groups, with the founders usually having had managerial experience. Their strategies usually position them in growing markets or involve innovative methods or products which give them clear competitive advantages. However, their growth may impose heavy demands on the founders, in personal commitments and the need to take risks. Capital requirements may bring outside investors and loss of control. Management methods may change to such a degree that the original founders must be replaced.

These classifications are fluid and it is certainly possible for a firm to move from one category to another. However, in general, these types of firms start with different resources, follow different growth paths, and involve different internal environments for the formulation and implementation of strategy.

The context within which strategy is managed also varies by the stage of development of the small firm. In this paper, we shall think of three stages:

1. *the start-up stage,* including the strategic decisions to found a firm and to position it within a particular industry with a particular competitive strategy;
2. *the early-growth stage,* when the initial product-market strategy is being tested and when the president maintains direct contact with all major activities (many firms stabilize at this stage);
3. *the later-growth stage,* often characterized by multiple sites for retail and service businesses and by some diversification for manufacturing firms; organizationally the firm usually has one or more levels of middle-management and some delegation of decision-making.

All of the types of firms just considered pass through the start-up stage and, if they are successful, move on to an early-growth stage. However, only the growth-oriented firms are likely to be found in the later-growth stage.

As a firm grows, at what point is it no longer small? Any answer to this question is somewhat arbitrary, but the focus here, even for firms in the later-growth stage, is upon organizations with less than 500 employees.

STRATEGIC MANAGEMENT IN THE START-UP STAGE

The decision to found a new firm is, in every sense, a strategic decision by the entrepreneur. It involves non-routine decisions to commit major resources to create a particular new business at a particular time and place. The new business then has a strategy (which may or may not have been carefully considered); it provides selected goods or services to particular markets and it emphasizes (whether wisely or not) particular policies to provide a way of competing.

The decision to found a new firm seems to be influenced by three broad factors.[3] They are:

1. the entrepreneur, including the many aspects of his background which affect his motivations, his perceptions, and his skills and knowledge;
2. the organization for which the entrepreneur had previously been working, whose characteristics influence the location and the nature of new firms, as well as the likelihood of spin-offs; and
3. various environmental factors external to the individual and his organization, which make the climate more or less favorable to the starting of a new firm.

Of these factors, the characteristics of the entrepreneur have been most extensively examined. Psychological research suggests that entrepreneurs have a high need for achievement and a belief that they can control their own fate.[4] One group of manufacturing entrepreneurs was characterized as having had poor relations with their fathers, their teachers and their employers. They seemed to be driven to entrepreneurship by their need to avoid being in a subordinate relationship to others.[5] A number of studies have shown that entrepreneurs often come from families where the father or a close relative was in business for himself.[6,7] Some sub-groups of societies have higher rates of entrepreneurship than others; young members of such sub-groups (such as the Chinese in South-East Asia or the Indians in East Africa) are surrounded by "role-models" of entrepreneurship. They may also choose this career path because other career paths are closed to them in the larger society.[8] The thrust of these findings is that some people, by virtue of their family background and early childhood influences, are much more likely to start businesses. However, entrepreneurial inclinations, like musical talent, may or may not be capitalized upon. A number of other factors, discussed below, interact to create a climate more or less favorable to starting a new business.

The typical entrepreneur with technical or managerial training starts his business when he is in his thirties.[9,10] It is then that he has the track record, experience, and savings to make founding feasible, while still having the energy level and willingness to take risks which are necessary. Thus, the conditions which exist when potential technical entrepreneurs are in their thirties, including the organizations they then work for and the environmental climate then extant, determine whether they will be likely to found new businesses. However, evidence on the founders of mom and pop firms suggests a wider range of ages at the time of founding.[11]

A second major factor influencing whether a potential entrepreneur will start a new business is the nature of the organization for which he works. This organization, which might be termed an incubator, seems to play a particularly important role in the founding of high technology firms. It locates the potential founder in a particular geographic area which may or may not have a favorable entrepreneurial climate. (A number of studies have shown that most entrepreneurs start their businesses where they are already living and working; it is the rare founder who moves at the time he is starting a new business.)[12]

The incubator organization also provides the entrepreneur with the experience which leads to particular managerial skills and industry knowledge. Since industries vary widely in the extent to which they offer opportunities for new ventures, this means that the strategy of the incubator organization determines to a great extent whether its employees will ever be in a position to spin off and start their own businesses. Thus an established organization in a mature industry with little growth and heavy capital requirements is unlikely to have many spin-offs. Its employees, no matter how motivated, are not acquiring the technical and market knowledge which can easily be translated into the strategic decision to start a new business.

The policies of potential incubator organizations also appear to determine, to a marked degree, the motivations of the entrepreneur. In brief surveys such as questionnaires, founders tend to report the socially acceptable reasons as to why they became entrepreneurs; these include such factors as the desire for independence and financial gain. However, depth interviews often disclose that the founder was "pushed" from the parent organization by frustration.[3] Studies of spin-off rates from established organizations show that internal factors influence spin-off rates, with internal problems being associated with high rates of spin-off and placid times being associated with low rates.[9] Thus, the extent to which the strategic and operating decisions of the established firm satisfy or frustrate its employees influences whether spin-offs occur.

A complex of factors external to the individual and to the parent organization also appears to influence entrepreneurship. Much of the research in this area is only suggestive, but it seems that climates can change over time and that past entrepreneurship makes future entrepreneurship more likely. The credibility of the act of starting a company appears to depend, in part, upon whether the founder knows of others who have taken this step.[7] Venture capital availability and particularly the existence of well-developed communication channels vary across geographic regions and help to determine the feasibility of entrepreneurship. The presence of experienced entrepreneurs also influences future entrepreneurship; they serve as sources of advice and venture capital and they sometimes do what they know best—start additional new businesses.[3,13] Their companies become excellent incubators for other spin-offs and also offer consulting opportunities for fledgling founders who are seeking income while trying to get started. It seems clear that past entrepreneurship influences the climate for future entrepreneurship. What is not so clear and what deserves additional research is how an area begins to become entrepreneurially active or how an area which has been active becomes less so.

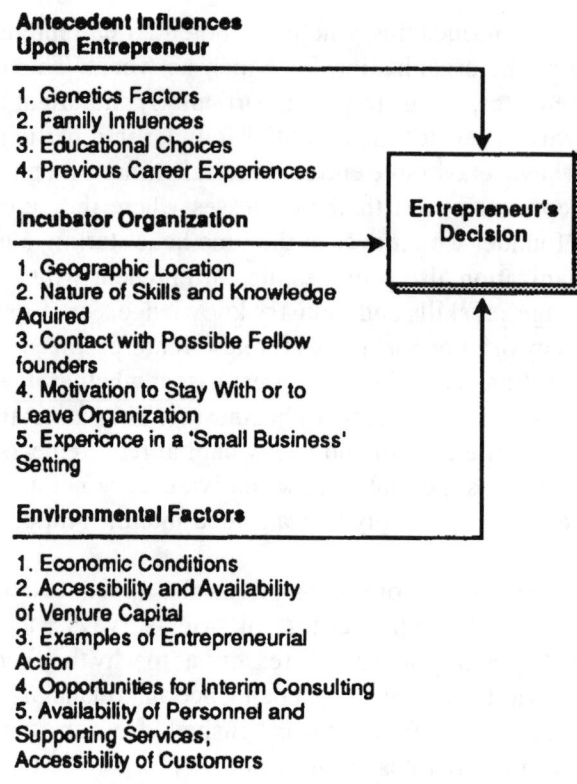

**Antecedent Influences
Upon Entrepreneur**

1. Genetics Factors
2. Family Influences
3. Educational Choices
4. Previous Career Experiences

Incubator Organization

1. Geographic Location
2. Nature of Skills and Knowledge Aquired
3. Contact with Possible Fellow founders
4. Motivation to Stay With or to Leave Organization
5. Experience in a 'Small Business' Setting

Environmental Factors

1. Economic Conditions
2. Accessibility and Availability of Venture Capital
3. Examples of Entrepreneurial Action
4. Opportunities for Interim Consulting
5. Availability of Personnel and Supporting Services; Accessibility of Customers

Entrepreneur's Decision

Figure 1. Influences upon the entrepreneurial decision.

The three broad factors just discussed influence the entrepreneurial decision as summarized in Figure 1.

The Competitive Strategy of the New Firm

The decision to start a new firm is clearly a strategic decision. However, also of interest here is the cluster of decisions which determine the nature of the new business, including the products or services to be offered, the markets to be served, and the policies to be emphasized. What has been learned about the influences upon these decisions in the new firm and about the relationship between particular strategies and performance?

Since the new business draws primarily upon the knowledge and skills of the entrepreneur, one might expect that the product/market choice would be closely tied to the experience gained in the incubator organization. For the most part this is true, although it varies by industry. New companies are closely related to the nature of the business of the parent firms for about 80–85 per cent of high technology firms; for nontechnical manufacturing and service firms, the corresponding percentages are 50–55 per cent.[9,11,14] For new franchises, the percentage is probably very low, since the franchiser supplies the expertise rather than the founder.

Although there has not been much explicit research on how the founder decides upon a business strategy, we can draw some inferences from general descriptions of the process and from case studies. For larger, more professionally-based ventures, and particularly for those seeking venture capital, there typically is a new business plan. Such a plan describes the way in which the proposed firm is to compete and often reflects considerable thought. For that much larger group of new ventures which start without the discipline of seeking outside capital from professional sources, the process of deciding upon a basis of competition seems to be informal and intuitive. It may be based upon an excellent, first-hand "feel" for the market. However, many new service businesses of the mom and pop type seem to be started opportunistically, with the availability of particular facilities or sites being important determinants.[11]

We don't know very much about the relationships between characteristics of founders, the strategies of their firms, and subsequent performance. There has been some research on high technology firms, though, which suggests that successful new firms are more likely to be started by multiple founders, have more initial capital, transfer more technology from the parent organization, are more likely to have a marketing function, show greater concern for personnel matters, and are more likely to have spun-off from large organizations than from small ones.[15,16] With regard to strategy, those new high technology firms whose strategies were related to the parent firms, in markets served and technology utilized, were more likely to be successful. In addition, longitudinal study of 95 new manufacturing firms indicated that those judged to be successful were more likely to have been started by two or more founders and more likely to have founders with both relevant experience and post high school education.[14]

STRATEGIC MANAGEMENT IN THE EARLY GROWTH STAGE

As the new firm becomes established, the founder typically continues to be in direct contact with all activities and decisions. Many businesses of modest potential stabilize at this point, often with no hired employees. Other firms continue to grow, adding employees and sometimes additional management. At this time the founder or founders may delegate operating decisions, but not strategic decisions. Management methods continue to be informal, with few policies and with control exercised primarily through direct contact.

As the new business gets started, it immediately begins to receive "feedback" from the market. Sometimes, the assumptions underlying the new firm's strategy prove to be faulty, and the firm seems likely to run out of cash before reaching the break-even point. It appears that founders often change their strategies at this point. Thus, an electronics component manufacturer switches to sub-contract work or an ice-cream shop becomes a steak-house. The entrepreneur has the opportunity to change quickly at this point; there is no organization to convince and there is little commitment to the status quo. However, much will depend upon how the entrepreneur perceives the environment, whether he perceives it as it really is or as he would like to see it.[17] Founders are sometimes stubborn people with a dream and not really amenable to dispassionate analysis of their plans.

As the new firm becomes established, the extent to which management confronts strategic decisions varies with the kind of firm and the characteristics of its industry. For the mom and pop business in a stable environment, the focus is usually upon operating decisions. Whether the strategy is reexamined and whether opportunities are then pursued appears to depend on the characteristics of management. In experiments conducted in India, owner-managers who had received achievement-motivation training frequently investigated or undertook changes in strategy.[18]

For those businesses which grow to become what we have classified as stable, high payoff firms or growth-oriented firms, there are decisions associated with evolving successful strategies. However, we lack systematic research to indicate whether these firms have high-potential strategies from the time of founding or whether these strategies evolve from the feedback of the market place. One study of 270 manufacturing firms indicated that companies which achieved annual sales of $100,000 or more in sales did so in their first 10 years; old small companies usually didn't grow.[19] The firms in this sample also showed great stability in their strategies, with only one in twelve making substantial product changes in a 9 year period.

There is substantial "wisdom-based" literature analyzing the characteristics of small firms and suggesting the most suitable strategies. Small firms, particularly in the early stages, have limited financial and human resources. They have almost no reputation and little in the way of economies of scale or benefits from experience curves. There is a concentration of risk in one or a few products, markets, and people; there is usually no cushion to absorb the results of bad luck or bad decisions. The capabilities of the new firm are often uneven, reflecting the unbalanced experience of the entrepreneur.

Against these disadvantages, the new firm has no ties to the past; it can innovate, without worrying about the effect on existing sales. This, coupled with the talents and drive of the founding group, is undoubtedly one reason why new and small firms have been such remarkably fertile sources of technical innovation, accounting for major new innovations all out of proportion to their R & D expenditures.[20] (Of course, most small firms are not particularly innovative; it is the growth-oriented small firms which are most likely to have this characteristic.) New firms also have the ability to move quickly; the chain of command is short and decision methods are informal and, if not carefully documented, at least timely. Management often has a first-hand "feel" for the realities of customers and operations, based not upon the abstractions of reports, but upon day-to-day contact. Small firms also can avoid the departmentalization and coordination problems which characterize large, complex organizations. There may be a lack of staff specialists and formalized analysis, but there is the opportunity to focus the attention of the organization upon opportunities. The small organization, with its shared sense of the need to survive, can create a cost consciousness and dedication which are difficult to achieve in large, profitable firms where each individual knows that his contributions are only a small part of the whole. Of course, in all instances these are potential advantages which may or may not be realized, depending upon the competence and commitment of management.

To summarize the advice of most writers, it would be that the small firm should choose a "niche" and avoid direct competition with larger companies. Some would modify this advice to say that direct competition is possible, but that the small firm should concentrate on where it has a competitive advantage or where the large firm is complacent or doing a poor job.[21-23] Thus, large firms tend to concentrate on mass markets, so small firms should concentrate on specialized markets. Large firms tend to be slow to react, so small firms should concentrate on opportunities arising from rapid market change. Large firms tend to be organized to produce in large production runs and to offer standardized service. Small firms can concentrate on short production runs, quick delivery and extra service. Large firms must be concerned about whether raw material supplies, work forces, and manufacturing and personnel policies are suitable for large volume operations. Small companies can use scarce materials, locate in areas with small labor forces, and utilize unique approaches, unconcerned about the implications if these were applied throughout a large corporation. Large firms must be concerned about government regulatory attitudes and their visibility to communities and unions. Small firms have a low profile and can move more quickly and be less concerned about the reactions of such groups. The evidence supporting these recommendations is anecdotal and based upon general observations. Much of it appears to be sound, but there is no systematic research examining the strategies of large number of firms and their performance over time.

The process of strategic planning in small firms has received attention in several articles.[24-27] The small firm environment makes heavy demands upon management for day-to-day operations and there are usually no staff specialists to provide support. Explicit efforts to set aside blocks of time for planning and to shield management from day-to-day pressures may be necessary. Structured approaches to the process of planning have been recommended by several authors. Unlike large organizations the emphasis is not upon deciding how to allocate resources among businesses or upon formal planning as a communication mechanism. The primary focus is upon mechanisms for identifying problems and for "stepping-back" to look at the implications of current strategy. Recognizing the flexibility of small firms, particular emphasis should be placed on short-term planning.[28]

STRATEGIC MANAGEMENT IN THE LATER GROWTH STAGE

Many small businesses stabilize and maintain an environment in which the president is in direct contact with the key activities, possibly with a small management team, each member of which is responsible for a key function. However, growth-oriented small businesses may continue to grow, adding additional levels of management.

The internal environment for management then begins to change, as the sheer volume of activities compels the founder to turn some duties over to others. Typically, the role of the founder changes, with "doing" activities largely delegated and with the job becoming more managerial in character. Many operating decisions may be delegated, although the president continues to be deeply involved in strategic decisions. One of the distinguishing characteristics of the very small firm, the president's direct contact with employees, with products, and customers, begins to change. More formal ways must be developed to keep management informed and to control operations. Policies must be developed and increased formality occurs. Top management must try to develop new skills in managing through others and in developing an organization. Some entrepreneurs are not suited for this kind of managerial task and their shortcomings may prevent the firm from growing successfully or may lead to the entrepreneur's departure.

These changes in the internal environment both aid and hamper effective strategic management. The growth in the organization may give the president more time for planning. The growing firm may have more resources to pursue particular activities and to withstand competitors' challenges. However, growth may cause management to "lose touch;" control of operations may suffer and management's feel for markets, competitors, and organizational capabilities may diminish. Implementation of strategy, which is typically one area where a small firm has a real advantage, becomes more of a problem as the organization grows.

Many growth-oriented small firms seem to be positioned in newly-developing industries. As such, management faces the challenges of adapting strategy to the changing demands of an evolving industry. The strategic implications of industry life cycles become particularly important for these firms.[29] It is widely believed that new industries are characterized by a high rate of new company formation and a high rate of entry by established firms, both small and large. Later, there is often a "shake-out" as the stronger competitors enlarge their market shares. The extent to which small firms survive and prosper as an industry matures appears to vary widely, but the reasons for these differences have not been examined systematically.

Growth-oriented small firms sometimes owe their success to innovative strategies. A number of authors have commented on how the small firm environment is conducive to innovation, with its informal decision processes in which relatively few executives must be convinced, its lack of commitment to the status quo, its low sales requirements to be successful, and its low costs of development.[20,30] However, the small firm may sometimes pioneer and then be faced with severe competition. It is surprising that there has been very little research on the most appropriate strategies for small firms which have been successful in innovation, but then face severe competition in a growing market.

STRATEGIC MANAGEMENT IN INTRACORPORATE VENTURES

A number of writers have suggested that large firms seem to be better at developing existing businesses than at growing new ones.[31-33] The large firm can bring great resources to bear upon new opportunities and can absorb failures. However, performance measurement systems often penalize those divisions and executives who assume risks. New ventures can disrupt existing manufacturing and marketing activities. New ventures often require different kinds of people and facilities and an orientation toward working closely with customers, short production runs, and continually changing technology.[34]

An increasing number of corporations have developed new venture departments to facilitate intracorporate entrepreneurship. Two surveys, both published in 1973, indicated that the number of new venture departments was increasing.[35,36] As might be expected, large firms have adopted formal intracorporate entrepreneurship programs to a greater degree than smaller firms. However, more recent research suggests that many new venture departments are short-lived.[34]

New venture department organizations may range from *ad hoc* task forces with no formal training, to departments with established budgets, to separate legal entities. Typically, these intracorporate entrepreneurial groups study proposed ventures and sometimes proceed to start new businesses—developing, producing, and marketing new products. They usually can call upon the resources of the larger organization, although this sometimes presents problems because of lack of authority over other departments. The performance measurement system may be modified to place less emphasis on short-run profits. If the product is promising or becomes firmly established, it may be transferred to an existing department or become the basis for a new department.

Practices vary in the extent to which new ventures are separate, the timing of when products are transferred to the regular organization, and how venture managers are rewarded. An extreme form of venture management might be termed "sponsored spin-offs" in which, with the parent firm's blessing, a separate new enterprise is created, possibly with the parent company holding some of the equity.[37]

Some of the main issues associated with organizing venture management departments include determining how managers are to be rewarded and how their careers are affected if they return to the main organization. Other issues relate to the extent to which they can call upon resources from the main organization and the degree of delegation—the extent to which they can act as if they were managing their own firms.

Research by Fast indicates that new venture departments usually evolve, becoming operating divisions, staff departments, or new venture departments which differ in size, objectives, and corporate impact from their earlier versions.[34] Sometimes the departments are disbanded. The two major influences upon the evolution of a new venture department appear to be the changing nature of the firm's strategy and its political support within the organization.

In general, these approaches have demonstrated some success, but many companies are experimenting with different ways of creating an environment for intracorporate entrepreneurship.

CONCLUSION

Small businesses differ greatly in their resource positions, the goals of their founders, their stages of development and their potential. Yet, within this diversity, we can note certain common characteristics. These result in an environment for strategic management which creates both constraints and opportunities different from those in large organizations. ▲

References

1. 1967 *Enterprise Statistics, Part 1.* U.S. Government Printing Office, Washington, DC (1972).
2. LaRue Hosmer, Arnold Cooper and Karl Vesper, *The Entrepreneurial Function.* Prentice-Hall, Inc., Englewood Cliffs (1977).
3. Arnold Cooper, *The Founding of Technologically-Based Firms,* The Center for Venture Management, Milwaukee (1971).
4. David McClelland, *The Achieving Society,* C. Van Nostrand, Princeton (1961).
5. Orvis Collins and David Moore, *The Organization Makers,* Appleton-Century-Crofts, New York (1970).
6. Edward Roberts and H. Wainer, Some characteristics of new technical enterprises, *IEEE Transactions on Engineering Management,* EM-18 (3) (1971).
7. Albert Shapero, Entrepreneurship and economic development, *Entrepreneurship and Enterprise Development: A Worldwide Perspective,* Proceedings of Project ISEED, Project ISEED, Ltd. and The Center for Venture Management, Milwaukee (1975).
8. Everett Hagan, The Transition in Columbia, in *Entrepreneurship and Economic Development,* P. Kilby (Ed.), The Free Press, New York (1971).
9. Arnold Cooper, Technical entrepreneurship: what do we know? *R&D Management,* 3 (2), February (1973).
10. Patrick Liles, *New Business Ventures and the Entrepreneur,* Richard D. Irwin, Inc., Homewood (1974).
11. Kurt Mayer and Sidney Goldstein, *The First Two Years: Problems of Small Firm Growth and Survival,* U.S. Government Printing Office, Washington, D.C. (1961).
12. Jeffrey Susbauer, The technical entrepreneurship process in Austin, Texas, in *Technical Entrepreneurship: A Symposium,* A. Cooper and J. Komives (Eds.), The Center for Venture Management, Milwaukee (1972).
13. Lawrence Lamont, What entrepreneurs learn from experience, *Journal of Small Business Management,* July (1972).
14. William Hoad and Peter Rosko, *Management Factors Contributing to the Success or Failure of New Small Manufacturers,* University of Michigan, Ann Arbor (1964).
15. Arnold Cooper and Albert Bruno, Success among high-technology firms, *Business Horizons,* 20 (2), April (1977).
16. Edward Roberts, Influences upon performance of new technical enterprises, in *Technical Entrepreneurship: A Symposium,* A. Cooper and J. Komives (Eds.), The Center for Venture Management, Milwaukee (1972).
17. Harry Schrage, R & D entrepreneur: profile of success, *Harvard Business Review,* 43 (6), November–December (1965).
18. David McClelland, Achievement motivation can be developed, *Harvard Business Review,* 43 (6), November–December (1965).
19. Joseph McGuire, *Factors in the Growth of Manufacturing Firms,* Bureau of Business Research, University of Washington, Seattle (1963).
20. Robert Charpie and others, *Technological Innovation: Its Environment and Management,* U.S. Government Printing Office, Washington, D.C. (1967).
21. Alfred Gross, Meeting the competition of giants, *Harvard Business Review,* 45 (3), May–June (1967).
22. W. Arnold Hosmer, Small manufacturing enterprises, *Harvard Business Review,* 35 (6), November–December (1957).
23. Robert Katz, *Management of the Total Enterprise,* Prentice-Hall, Englewood Cliffs (1970).

24. Frank Gilmore, Formulating strategy in smaller companies, *Harvard Business Review,* 49 (3), May–June (1971).
25. Preston LaBreton, *A Guide for Proper Management Planning for Small Business,* Division of Research, College of Business Administration, Louisiana State University, Baton Rouge (1963).
26. George Steiner, Approaches to long-range planning for small business, *California Management Review,* X (1), Fall (1967).
27. S. C. Wheelwright, Strategic planning in the small business, *Business Horizons,* XIV (4), August (1971).
28. Theodore Cohn and Roy Lindberg, *Survival and Growth: Management Strategies for the Small Firm,* Amacom, New York (1974).
29. Charles Hofer, Toward a contingency theory of business strategy, *Academy of Management Journal,* 18 (4), December (1975).
30. Arnold Cooper, Small companies can pioneer new products, *Harvard Business Review,* 44 (5), September–October (1966).
31. Mark Hanan, Venturing corporations—think small to stay strong, *Harvard Business Review,* 54 (3), May–June, (1976).
32. Richard Hill and James Hlavacek, The venture team: a new concept in marketing organization, *Journal of Marketing,* 36 (3), July (1972).
33. Russell W. Peterson, New venture management in a large company, *Harvard Business Review,* 45 (3), May–June (1967).
34. Norman Fast, The evolution of corporate new venture divisions, unpublished D.B.A. dissertation, Harvard Graduate School of Business Administration, Boston (1977).
35. Jeffrey Susbauer, U.S. industrial intracorporate entrepreneurship practices, *R&D Management,* 3 (3), June (1973).
36. Karl Vesper and Thomas Holmdahl, How venture management fares in innovation companies, *Research Management,* XVI (3), May (1973).
37. Arnold Cooper and Arthur Riggs, Jr., Non-traditional approaches to technology utilization, *Journal of the Society of Research Administrators,* VI (3), Winter (1975).

INTRAPRENEURSHIP IN HI-TECH FIRMS

Louise Kelly

To help cultivate the new breed of employee, many hi-tech companies have implemented a decentralized structure with entrepreneurial profit centers and introduced company-wide cultural change programs. The aim is to produce a new class of entrepreneurs within the business units and establish a network of "learning" organizations equipped to succeed in a knowledge-based industry.

A company within a company is more responsive and flexible, and employees who know their roles in the core process and how to make concrete contributions to the value-added chain are more motivated. In short, the structure is designed to bring the entire organization together as a team and create a spirit of consensus among equal partners.

CHANGE AGENTS

A "change agent" program can be key to intrapreneurial success. Under a change agent program, a small group of high-potential individuals are selected each year to pursue special projects proposed by themselves and to receive special training. The so-called change agents are given a year to work in teams on individual projects, which can range from developing data warehousing strategies to designing new company information systems. The projects can be financed by the individual business units and the corporate headquarters are expected to give a 10-times pay back on the initial investment.

During the course of their one-year project, the change agents are free to attend week long technology-oriented business seminars that are offered by local business schools. They are also encouraged to go to Silicon Valley for a benchmarking tours of companies like Microsoft, Intel, Silicon Graphics, and Netscape. In addition these change agents can work with a consultant who offers project support.

The projects have to be aimed at bolstering a firm's core competencies, which can range from information technology solutions and customer support to reducing costs.

Intrapreneurship is not a faddish management technique, but can be considered a basic of corporate life. It means that people at all levels who have the will to implement good ideas are given the opportunity to develop personally by contributing to the growth of their company.

Take the example of an intrapreneur in a Boston-based hi-tech firm. Sam was one employee who could not wait to leave his company, a manufacturer of laser printers, and do something on his own. He worked in the information processing department, but

Dr. Louise Kelly is an Assistant Professor of Strategy and Entrepreneurship at Northeastern University, Boston.

unknown to his manager, Sam was running a one-man internet access bureau in his spare time. When the manufacturer introduced their intrapreneurship program and discovered Sam, they gave him the opportunity to develop a line of business using the company's name, knowledge of laser printers and worldwide distribution network. Sam's idea was to customize laser printers for the particular needs of an internet based business. The company was astounded that such printers sold for a premium price.

Gifford Pinchott's book "Intrapreneurship" showed how the moribund modern corporation can be brought to life by the injection of entrepreneurial spirit from a few champion employees using "bootlegged" resources and "stolen" company time and working for themselves. Pinchott proposed a system of creating "intracapital" funds and in-company sponsors to promote intrapreneurial efforts. 3M's Art Fry, who is credited with developing "Post-it Notes" on his own initiative, was one of Pinchott's intrapreneurial heroes. Sumatra Goshal of the London Business School and Christopher Bartlett of Harvard have remarked, "Any employee at 3M can propose to start a new business."

Researchers at 3M are encouraged to spend 15% of their time on project work, developing their own ideas. These projects then need a sponsor within the company to integrate the ideas into an effective platform. For example, 3M in U.K. was selling connectors for fiber-optic cables. One of the team members thought of redesigning the product with cables attached as a factory-finished semi-system. The fiber-optic distribution unit met with such success among customers, like cable tv companies, that production had to be put out to a subcontractor—which 3M later bought.

Another example of intrapreneurial success comes from Canon. In the late 1980s a U.K.-based technologist, Hiro Negishi, was looking for new developments to follow the camcorder in Europe. With the audio-visual camcorder, Canon—long known for cameras and reprographics—had taken a small step into the audio field where the U.K. subsidiary had a lot of expertise. Negishi, though a chemist and not a sound engineer who claims that audio is his "hobby," set out to develop a set of speakers that gave out a larger area of quality sound. This would overcome the so-called "hot-spot," that is the deterioration in sound quality which occurs when a listener moves away from a point equidistant from a pair of speakers. Negishi built his prototype at home. The design worked and was patented and the invention was taken up by Negishi's bosses in Japan. It moved Canon decisively into the audio world and now the company's stereo speakers are commercially available.

For Canon the success of "wide imaging stereo" was part serendipity, as there was no formal intrapreneurial system in place. It was more a result of a certain person being in a certain place at a certain time. However, Canon was able to have top management champion a new strategic direction that came from an unexpected, and lower level of the organization. This is a different way of solving the eternal problem of how to harness personal enterprise in a business context, and then make it both productive and continuous. Canon's process was more ad-hoc whereas 3M has a formal system in place. The 3M model has been much admired but seldom imitated. CEOs who are concerned about the level of corporate creativity need to heed these intrapreneurial models and experiences.

The dilemma of a large institution is trying to nurture an atmosphere for entrepreneurial activity while maintaining corporate controls. This can be managed if disciplined reporting systems are balanced with a strong entrepreneurial culture of mutual trust and open communication. There is a reward versus risk ratio that will vary according to the type of company. This will depend on individuals' willingness to take a risk, which will derive from the overall organizational culture. Thus the risk of individual entrepreneuring will relate strongly to support, structure and resources.

A more negative view of entrepreneurship comes from Harold Geneen, ex-chairman of 3M who argues that corporate culture leaves little room for in-house entrepreneurs. Geneen sees large corporations as public trusts from which investors expect 10% annual returns, and that the inherent risks in entrepreneurship threaten the realization of those profits. So, corporate CEOs cannot in good conscience "bet the company" and employees cannot be compensated at the level of owners.

One question that arises is what happens when a company adopts a proposal of one of its innovative managers and the project fails. When this question was put to an executive vice president of Arco, a large U.S. energy company, there was a long silence followed by an admission that it would be hard to promote a manager once his or her project had failed.

The entrepreneurial thrust of an individual can also be destructive to company loyalty. This is that happened when the entrepreneurial team of the MV8000 computer at Data General Corporation, internally dubbed the "Eagle," tried to rescue the company from obsolescence with a new state-of-the-art computer. This innovation was the result of 2 1/2 years of intense work in a basement laboratory by a team of 30 young engineers. As they battled other groups for scarce resources, they began to think they were on a different team. There are reports of how the project leader tried to sneak budgets for the new design concept past the Data General brass.

Despite these criticisms and limitations, a few firms have recognized the importance of providing intrapreneurs with freedom to work on what they like, autonomy, discretionary resources, and an opportunity to fail or succeed. International Business Machines recognized the importance of time control by intrapreneurs almost 35 years ago, when it established the IBM Fellows program. In 1963, IBM named its first eight Fellows, giving them recognition for outstanding technical accomplishments. The designation of Fellow entitle the recipient to five years of total support to begin and support something new.

At 3M employees are encouraged to use the organization's facilities and equipment to test ideas—even during normal working hours. It has been said that at 3M, innovation through entrepreneurship is the "only game in town." 3M does not have a Fellows program like IBM, but it does present "Oscar Awards" to intrapreneurs for their contribution and achievements. Individuals are not paid bonuses but are given discretionary access to corporate resources. They have even considered developing formal career paths for intrapreneurs as an alternative to the normal career ladder. Another proposal at 3M is to develop contracts with intrapreneurs and their teams to specify conditions under which intracapital (internal capital) will be set aside from the profits realized from successful ventures.

In spite of the success stories of IBM, 3M, and Canon and the creative potential of such organizations, most corporations today are not successful in identifying, stimulating, and rewarding creative employees. In a high-technology world innovation is a capital intensive process. The corporation could provide a vital link to accelerating knowledge development. Intrapreneurial incubation centers are the ideal form for the continued flow of innovation that is needed to compete in the modern global economy of increasingly hypercompetition. ▲

HOW MUCH MONEY DOES YOUR NEW VENTURE NEED?

James McNeill Stancill

Every entrepreneur planning a new venture faces the same dilemma: determining how much money is necessary to start the business. More often than not, entrepreneurs estimate on the low side. They may simply not allow for unexpected expenses and lower-than-predicted sales.

It's impossible to know exactly how much a new business will need during its first five years, but it is possible to come up with realistic estimates. These come from the financial forecast: the income statement, the balance sheet, and, most important, the cash flow statement.

This article shows how to calculate the new venture's capital requirements through such financial forecasting. It also shows how financial forecasting provides the basis for determining equity investments.

Thanks to various computer spreadsheet programs, calculations associated with even the most detailed forecasting are fairly simple. What used to require days or weeks now takes only minutes or hours. Such programs enable entrepreneurs to use variables and test scenarios in ways that are impractical with conventional push-the-pencil methods. Such split-second calculating tools should not, of course, blind entrepreneurs to the logic of the numerical estimate and the cash flow model.

BEGINNING THE PROCESS

Simplicity is a virtue in presenting financial statements. Show items in summary form, but reserve all the details for separate schedules or footnotes attached to the financial statements. And make certain the statements conform with generally accepted format practices; creativity is welcome in many areas of business planning but not in financial statements.

For most manufacturing and many other start-ups, the form of the income statement will be like what you see in *Exhibit I*. Each item has a footnote, which is included in "Notes to the financial statements." In these notes, you may refer the reader to another supporting

Author's note: My thanks to Timothy Timmins of Bateman Eichler, Hill Richards, Incorporated for his assistance in the computation of the forecasts used in this article. Partial financial assistance was provided by the Graduate School of Business of the University of Southern California.

Exhibit I. Sample income statement.

Sales[1]	$XXX
Less cost of goods sold[2]	XXX
Gross profit margin	**XXX**
Less general and administrative expenses[3]	XXX
Less selling expenses[4]	XXX
Operating income or loss	**XXX**
Less interest expense	XXX
Income before taxes	**XXX**
Less income taxes[5]	XXX
Net income or loss	**$XXX**

1 The sales forecasts here are based on market research, details of which are provided separately.
2 See the separate cost accounting module for details of how the cost of goods was arrived at (which for the sake of brevity is not shown in this article).
3 See *Exhibit III*.
4 See *Exhibit V*.
5 This includes federal and corporate income taxes.

schedule or you may simply explain the item. Each item has a separate footnote number. Having an explanation for each item is the most important aspect of an effective forecast. By explaining each item, you can defuse disputes about what value an item should have. If much uncertainty exists about an item, you can state in the footnote that the estimate is merely a guess but that the general order of magnitude is probably appropriate.

The financial forecast initially requires three estimates of sales for five years: a most likely, a most pessimistic, and a most optimistic estimate. Express this sales forecast in both number of items sold and dollars to account for factors that might affect the selling price. The sales forecasts should, of course, be accompanied by written justification of the sales estimates so that you can begin to project the required financial statements—first the income statement, then the balance sheet, and finally the cash flow statement.

A pro forma five-year income statement is, of course, only tentative. It is based on the assumption that the proposed output is feasible and that the level of production can be financed.

Before putting together the income statement, the forecaster must project which assets and liabilities will support the forecast sales level. This projection leads to the balance sheet estimate. For most new ventures, the balance sheet form shown in *Exhibit II* is appropriate.

At this preliminary stage, it is important to avoid structuring the balance sheet—and the terms of the financing—by putting in the entire amount of outside investments or loans. Unless the whole proposal is to be syndicated, leave the decision about the allocation of debt and equity to the financiers. Thus the cash account, even if negative, becomes the balancing item on the balance sheet.

Exhibit II. Sample balance sheet.

Assets		Liabilities	
Cash	$XXX	Accounts payable[11]	$XXX
Accounts receivable[6]	XXX	Accrued taxes[5]	XXX
Inventory[7]	XXX	Accrued expenses[12]	XXX
Other assets (prepaids)[8]	XXX	Current portion of long-term debt	XXX
Total current assets	**$XXX**	**Total current liabilities**	**$XXX**
Plant, property, and equipment at cost[9]	$XXX	Long-term equipment loans[13]	$XXX
Less reserve for depreciation[10]	XXX	Equity	XXX
Net plant, property, and equipment	XXX	Retained earnings or loss	XXX
Total assets	**$XXX**	**Total liabilities and capital**	**$XXX**

6 See *Exhibit V* for the aging schedule.
7 For details of the finished-goods inventory, see *Exhibit VII*.
8 For the changes in prepaid assets, see separate schedule (not shown in this article).
9 See separate schedule (not shown in this article).
10 Generally, straight-line depreciation was used for equipment.
11 See separate schedule for details of changes in accounts payable (not shown in this article).
12 See separate schedule for details of changes in accrued expenses (not shown in this article).
13 The face amount of the loans is $140,000, payable in monthly installments of $5,203 for 36 months at an interest rate of 15%.

Most new ventures should do projections for five years—a monthly forecast for the first two or three years and quarterly or yearly projections for the remaining years. The time period each statement covers should be the same. That is, you shouldn't have monthly income statements and quarterly balance sheets for each period.

The monthly forecasts serve two purposes. First, they act as a form of budget, especially for general, administrative, and sales expenses. Second, they show the effect of quarterly tax payments on cash flow. The need to forecast for five years is dictated by the venture capitalist's desire to determine future earnings so as to arrive at a projected value for the business. This value, in turn, largely determines how much equity the venture capitalist will insist on for the capital investment.

GETTING TO COST OF GOODS SOLD

To illustrate the forecasting of capital requirements, I'll use the case of the McDonald Company, which was created to manufacture a water purification unit for maritime and other uses. A colleague and I assumed that the company would start in January of year 1, would not produce any units in the first month, but would then produce 100 units a month in February through April and 300 a month for the next three months. It would then start dropping production in anticipation of seasonally lower sales and make a total of 2,100 units for the first year. The company did enough market research to warrant the sales forecast for the most likely scenario. We assume a selling price of $600 per unit, resulting in sales for year 1 of $1,020,000. We forecast that sales would rise in year 2 to $3 million and in year 3 to $3,780,000 and that the company would grow 25% in years 4 and 5.

After you have made the sales forecast, the next and most important item to estimate is the cost of goods sold. In service and wholesale businesses, making this estimate is not as complicated as in manufacturing. In service and wholesale, pricing and thus sales will probably be a function of labor or costs of materials, and a forecast of sales in units will easily produce a forecast of cost of goods sold.

For a manufacturing venture, simply using a percentage of sales, as you might when the business is reasonably well established, could lead to some serious errors. Unfortunately, the "proper" way is quite laborious and complicated, for it means using a separate forecast model. For the McDonald Company, we did an elaborate cost accounting module for all three scenarios, which turned out to be extraordinarily expensive in terms of time, even though we did it on a computer.

Remembering that the cost of goods sold consists of direct labor, cost of materials, and factory overhead, we handled the cost accounting model in the following way. Starting with a section on volume data, we forecast unit sales. Next, we made a decision on production, which began two months before sales were to commence. (This decision led to an ending inventory total that rose and fell as monthly sales went up and down.) In general, average wage rates and the time needed to assemble a unit were fairly easy to forecast.

Other components of the cost accounting model were raw materials, inventory, work-in-process inventory, finished-goods inventory, total inventory, factory overhead, work-in-process flow in units, and weighted-average cost per unit.

In some cases, estimating cost of goods sold as a percentage of sales, albeit a declining percentage, may be sufficient for the purpose at hand, particularly if you consider all the other variables. For example, after we made the cost accounting model for the McDonald Company, we calculated the cost of goods sold as a percentage of sales. Beginning at 53%, the percentage declined to about 40%. If it were possible to estimate the ratio of cost of goods sold to sales for, say, six-month intervals, the results would be approximately the same as what we got through the modeling. But for the shortcut approach, remember to have the necessary facts on hand to support the assumed percentages, such as efficiency of assembly, declining cost of raw materials because of increasing purchases, and spreading the factory overhead over the growing number of units purchased.

KEY EXPENSES

Estimate the depreciation expenses that are assumed to be included in the cost of goods sold so that this amount can be removed when you are compiling the cash flow statement. (To calculate taxable profit or loss, you must include the depreciation expense in the income statement; you can show it as a separate item.)

General and administrative expense (G&A) is the next income statement item to forecast. Since sales are increasing over the five-year planning horizon and G&A is mostly

Exhibit III. Breakdown of general and administrative expenses for the McDonald Company.

	JAN YEAR 1	FEB YEAR 1	MAR YEAR 1	APR YEAR 1	MAY YEAR 1	JUN YEAR 1	JU YEA
G & A expenses:							
Consultant fees	$ 2,000	$ 2,000	$ 2,000	$ 2,000	$ 2,000	$ 2,000	
Depreciation	400	400	400	400	400	400	
Insurance	200	200	200	200	200	200	2
Legal & acct.	500	500	500	500	500	500	500
Govt. lobbying	3,000	3,000	3,500	500	500	500	500
Office supplies	1,000	1,000	1,000	1,000	1,000	1,000	200
Payroll taxes	840	1,060	1,260	1,260	1,260	1,260	1,
Rent	400	400	400	400	400	400	
Office salaries	1,800	1,800	1,800	1,800	1,800	1,800	
Officer salaries	3,000	3,000	3,000	3,000	3,000	3,000	
Telephone	800	800	800	1,200	1,200	1,200	1,500
Non – sales travel	2,000	2,000	2,000	2,000	1,400	1,400	1,000
Utilities	100	100	100	100	100	100	
Start – up expense	12,000	3,000	8,000	0	0	0	
Bad debts	0	0	0	1,800	5,400	5,400	
	$ 28,040	$19,260	$24,960	$16,160	$19,160	$19,160	

fixed, estimating this item as a percentage of sales is inappropriate. Instead, you must forecast a detailed schedule for all the items. Although the income statement shows only the total G&A expense, a footnote can refer the reader to the detailed schedule of G&A expenses.

The list of items in *Exhibit III* is representative of what might be included. One item deserves special attention: officers' salaries. While entrepreneurs go into business to make lots of money, seeking one's fortune in a struggling new venture is foolish. Even if the entrepreneur is providing all the necessary start-up funds, the wisdom of taking a salary comparable to what might be expected in a more mature company is questionable, to say the least. Investors do not, however, expect the entrepreneur to live on a clerk's salary. Perhaps the best advice is to start off rather low and increase the salary as profits permit. McDonald assumed it would hire a second officer after the first year, so the total was the product of two, and later more, officers' salaries.

McDonald's other G&A expenses included such calculations as payroll taxes, predetermined items like rent and insurance, and items to be negotiated, such as lobbying in the state capital. Some items were mere guesses (nonsales travel and telephone), and some catchall attempts (start-up costs).

Selling expenses can be treated the same as G&A. A company needs to develop a detailed schedule (see *Exhibit* IV for an example) to include the items relevant to the

Exhibit IV. Details of selling expenses for the McDonald Company—most likely case.

	JAN YEAR 1	FEB YEAR 1	MAR YEAR 1	APR YEAR 1	MAY YEAR 1	JUN YEAR 1	JUL YEAR
Selling expenses:							
Advertising	$ 6,000	$ 6,000	$ 8,000	$ 4,000	$ 4,000	$ 4,000	$ 4,000
Travel	3,600	5,800	7,200	7,200	7,200	7,200	7,200
Salaries	3,600	5,800	7,800	7,800	7,800	7,800	7,8
Promo supplies	0	0	10,000	1,000	1,000	1,000	1
Commissons	0	0	0	0	0	0	
	$ 13,200	$17,600	$33,000	$20,000	$20,000	$20,000	$20,

business at hand. For McDonald Company, we included salaries for two salespeople for the first month, three for the second, and four for the fourth month on through the rest of the first year. Travel expenses for the salespersons were estimated to be equal to salaries after the first few months. Interest expense on the equipment loan for the McDonald Company was $2,333 for the first month and declined thereafter as principal was paid.

The only other forecast item on the income statement is taxes. At first, there are no taxes, but even with the tax loss carryforward (forward for 15 years, back for 3), taxes have to be included for the second year. Include state income taxes, if any, and use the percentage to be applied to net profit before tax. Estimating state income taxes is quite simple; the complication comes in forecasting the accrued taxes for the balance sheet. Once the income forecast is complete, you can turn to the balance sheet.

COMPLETING THE BALANCE SHEET

Keep the balance sheet as simple as you did the income statement. The first item on the balance sheet—cash—is the balancing item and is thus not forecast separately. Instead, it results from the computation of the cash flow statement.

Accounts receivable may be forecast in two ways, each yielding different results. The more complicated way is to estimate what percentage of this month's sales the company will collect this month (for the McDonald Company, we assumed 5%), what percentage for the next month (we assumed 50%), and what percentage for the following two months (we assumed 30% and 15%). A separate schedule is necessary (for example, see McDonald's in *Exhibit V*).

The standard way of forecasting accounts receivable is to use a turnover ratio (equal to monthly sales times 12 divided by the turnover figure—for example, 9). Because of the seasonality of sales, you would get dramatically different accounts receivable balances if you applied a constant turnover to each month.

Exhibit V. Details of the calculation of the McDonald Company's accounts receivable balance for each month.

Change in A/R

	Jan Year 1	Feb Year 1	Mar Year 1	Apr Year 1	May Year 1	Jun Year 1	
Beginning A/R	$0	$0	$0	$0	$55,290	$192,060	
Add sales (debits)	0	0	0	58,200	174,600	174,600	← Assumes net of bad debts.
Subtotal	0	0	0	58,200	229,890	366,660	
Collections:							Collections based on the following percentages:
This month's sales	0	0	0	2,910	8,730	8,730	← 5%
1 month ago		0	0	0	29,100	87,300	← 50%
2 months ago			0	0	0	17,460	← 30%
3 months ago				0	0	0	← 15%
Total collections	0	0	0	2,910	37,830	113,490	Representative collection figures assumed for years 4 and 5
Ending A/R	0	0	0	55,290	192,060	253,170	
Change in A/R	$0	$0	$0	55,290	$136,770	$61,110	

Exhibit VI. Turnover at the McDonald Company.

Part A	Turnover of accounts receivable							
	May	Jun	Jul	Aug	Sep	Oct	Nov	Dec
Turnover	39.1%	11.3%	8.5%	5.3%	1.7%	6.8%	12.6%	12.7%

Part B	Turnover of inventory							
	May	Jun	Jul	Aug	Sep	Oct	Nov	Dec
Turnover	3.6%	3.0%	3.7%	3.0%	0.1%	1.0%	1.6%	1.1%

In the first year for McDonald, the turnovers would have been what you see in *Exhibit VI*, Part A.

These turnovers make clear that the first procedure is advisable for monthly cash flow forecasting for a new venture, especially if sales are seasonal.

Inventory presents a more difficult problem than accounts receivable. Because of the pronounced seasonality in production and sales, using a constant turnover for cost of goods sold is not possible. For example, the inventory turnovers for the McDonald Company for the first year were as shown in *Exhibit VI,* Part B.

While the balance sheet shows inventory as one line, three types of inventory are actually on hand at any one time: raw material, work in process, and finished goods. If you are using a cost accounting model, each month will produce these three totals. But because of the complexity of this model, you may wish to estimate (perhaps *guess* is the better term)

Exhibit VII. Calculation of finished-goods inventory for the McDonald Company.

	Jan	Feb	Mar	Apr	May	Jun	Jul	Aug	Sep	Oct	Nov	Dec
Number of units manufactured	0	100	100	100	300	300	300	200	100	200	200	200
Cumulative units manufactured	0	100	200	300	600	900	1,200	1,400	1,500	1,700	1,900	2,100
Less cumulative units sold	0	0	0	100	400	700	1,000	1,200	1,250	1,350	1,500	1,700
Finished-goods inventory	0	100	200	200	200	200	200	200	250	350	400	400

Exhibit VIII. McDonald Company's crudely estimated end-of-month inventory versus actual inventory (in thousands of dollars).

	Jan	Feb	Mar	Apr	May	Jun	Jul	Aug	Sep	Oct	Nov	Dec
Raw material	$198	$100	$154	$150	$140	$132	$120	$110	$132	$120	$110	$330
Work in process	25	25	25	75	75	75	50	25	50	50	50	125
Finished goods	0	32	63	95	158	158	158	126	95	142	173	189
Estimated	$223	$157	$242	$320	$373	$365	$328	$261	$277	$312	$333	$644
Actual	$208	$219	$283	$378	$310	$375	$300	$248	$383	$370	$341	$652

what each of these inventory components will be, total them for each month, and use that number as the amount of inventory for the balance sheet. In the case of McDonald, we estimated unit production for the first year to be as shown in *Exhibit VII*.

By estimating the average cost of each finished unit, you can approximate the finished-goods component of inventory. With an eye to the production schedule, you can estimate how much raw material you will require. By spreading this raw material over the other months, you can get a crude estimate of the raw material component. You estimate work in process by examining the production schedule and assuming an average cost for the units, say, when they are half completed.

Totaling these admittedly crude estimates (as in *Exhibit VIII*) reveals a surprisingly close approximation of the needed inventory level required.

Other assets, which for a new venture include principally prepaid expenses, should be itemized and priced on a separate schedule and the total shown on the balance sheet. Do not show these items as a turnover or a percentage of sales.

Plant, property, and equipment must also be individually budgeted and not shown as a percentage of sales. If the vendor of the equipment or a third party offers financing, show it in the liabilities section of the balance sheet.

For the McDonald Company, the accounts payable amount included all raw material purchases except for the initial one and assumed payment in the following month. These purchases further assumed, of course, that once under way the business could get credit. For other companies, accounts payable might include items in addition to raw material purchases. For the McDonald Company, we put those items in a separate account—accrued expenses (not shown on the sample cash flow statement). For the accounts payable forecast, we simply let the raw materials purchased lag one month.

Accrued expenses for the McDonald Company included prepaid, selling, and G&A expenses less insurance, depreciation, and bad debts. We assumed most of these expenses would be paid in the following month and let them lag one month for balance sheet purposes. Payroll taxes we assumed would be paid quarterly.

Accrued taxes are the result of applying the tax rules to the income statement item for taxes. Taxes are payable on the fifteenth day of the fourth, sixth, ninth, and twelfth months, and estimates can be based on the prior year's taxes or the current year's earnings. (We used the prior year's for McDonald.)

How do you best handle the delicate problem of distinguishing between long-term debt and equity? My preference is to include in long-term debt only what I call bring-along financing—that is, financing that is offered almost as a matter of course on such purchases as equipment. (Real estate, too, might involve such financing, but buying land and buildings at the start of a new venture would be a strange use of precious funds. It's better to rent or lease until the business is well established.)

Structuring the debt-equity ratio of a new venture is quite acceptable if you are underwriting or syndicating the venture yourself. But if you have to go to one or two venture capital sources for the bulk of the financing, you will probably want to leave that decision to your outside investors. (I once lost the financing for a start-up venture when the institution took exception to my "structuring" of the deal. It thought the debt-equity issue was its prerogative and rejected the deal rather than hassle over the matter.) Interest and principal payments will throw off the cash flow forecast, but you can correct this imbalance later.

In this model, the object is to forecast how much money will be needed to capitalize the venture. To avoid anticipating the decision of potential financiers, it's best not to consider how much of this to invest via debt instruments and how much by equity—common or preferred stock. When that decision is made and the capitalization known, the forecast can be revised to include this decision. An overdraft in the cash account can replace the required long-term debt and equity, at least initially.

AT LAST: THE CASH FLOW STATEMENT

Once you have completed the income statement and the balance sheet forecasts, you have the ingredients for the cash flow statement. Essentially a combination of the income statement and the balance sheet, it shows the changes that will occur in the cash balance.

Before considering the items on the cash flow statement, I must point out that for income statement items, the actual dollar amount is shown for the period in question. For example, if net sales for one month were $300,000, the amount would appear on the cash flow statement for that month. (See *Exhibit IX* for a sample cash flow statement.)

Exhibit IX. Sample cash flow statement.

Cash flow statement for the period _____ to _____					
		Month			
Operating cash inflows	+ Net sales	$	$	$	$
	+ Other income				
	− Δ Accounts receivable				
	1 Net operating cash inflows	$	$	$	$
Operating cash outflows	+ Cost of goods sold less depreciation	$	$	$	$
	+ General and administrative expenses				
	+ Selling expenses				
	+ Taxes				
	− Δ Accrued taxes				
	+ Δ Inventory				
	+ Δ Prepaid expenses				
	− Δ Accounts payable				
	2 Total operating cash outflows	$	$	$	$
	3 Net operating cash flow (item 1 less item 2)	$	$	$	$
Priority outflows	+ Interest expenses	$	$	$	$
	+ Current debt repayable				
	+ Lease payments (not included above)				
	4 Total priority outflows	$	$	$	$
Discretionary outflows	+ Capital expenditures	$	$	$	$
	+ Research and development expenses				
	+ Preferred stock dividends				
	+ Common stock dividends				
	5 Total discretionary outflows	$	$	$	$
Financial flows	+ Δ Debt instruments (borrowings)	$	$	$	$
	+ Δ Stock securities (equity)				
	+ Δ Term loans				
	6 Total financial flows	$	$	$	$
Net change in cash and marketable securities accounts	+ Net operating cash flow (item 3)	$	$	$	$

Exhibit IX. (continued)

	– Priority outflows (item 4)				
	– Discretionary outflows (item 5)				
	+ Financial flows (item 6)				
	7 Net change in cash and marketable securities	$	$	$	$
End-of-period cash balance		$	$	$	$

Δ = Period-to period change in total dollar amount.

For balance sheet items, however, it is the period-to-period change that should be included in the cash flow statement, and whether the change is added or subtracted is indicated by the symbol $+\Delta$ or $-\Delta$, which should be read "plus a positive change" or "minus a positive change." Of course, if the change is negative and the symbol is $-\Delta$, then algebraically this would be minus a minus, so the amount should be added.

The cash flow statement has seven parts. The first three deal with the basic operations of the company. Part one, net operating cash inflow, includes sales from the income statement minus a positive change in accounts receivable.

Later, after the venture is reasonably well established, you may want to pledge receivables and/or inventory as collateral for a working capital loan from a bank. In that case, you would add, under $-\Delta$ accounts receivable or $+\Delta$ bank borrowing, the increase or decrease in the loan amount. Including this item in this section, even though it is a financial rather than an operating matter, prevents the net operating cash flow (NOCF) from being negative much of the time.

It's true that if you start out using a receivables-based credit line, you will need less venture capital to start the business. But this type of financing may make it impossible to obtain extra financing later because the company will have no collateral left to offer. It's best instead to leave receivables-based financing as a contingency financing source in case it's really needed.

Even worse would be factoring, which is the sale of the receivable. I first formed this opinion in the course of assisting with the start-up of an ophthalmic laboratory. The entrepreneur's lawyer did his best to convince us that we should sell the receivables to the company for which he was counsel. We resisted, and well we did, for when the venture got into trouble, it was able to use the receivables as another source of capital.

The second part of the cash flow statement, total operating cash outflows, includes cost of goods sold (excluding depreciation), G&A expenses, selling expenses, and taxes from the income statement. Next comes minus a positive change in accrued taxes, plus a positive change in inventory and prepaid expenses, and $-\Delta$ accounts payable. Subtract this second item, total operating cash outflows, from the first, net operating cash inflows, and the result is net operating cash flow. NOCF pinpoints how much cash was generated from the basic operations of the company. This is cash with which to grow the company.

The first use of NOCF is to pay the priority outflows, which consist of interest expense and debt repayment. Here you would also include a large lease payment—say for the premises the company occupies—in lieu of a mortgage payment. (Small lease payments go under cost of goods sold, G&A expense, or selling expense.)

The next section, discretionary outflows, includes a ranking of four discretionary expenditures. For example, in certain businesses—toys, for example—advertising expenses might be as much or more than R&D or capital expenditures in other businesses. Even the sequence can be different. Use whatever sequence fits your business.

If you're planning to buy equipment and have the manufacturer or other third party finance a portion of the price, you would, looking at *Exhibit IX*, record the transaction as follows: you would show the total price of the equipment in the "start" column for capital expenditures, the amount of the note in the start column as a debt instrument in the financial flows section, and periodic payments in their respective time period columns as priority outflow—interest expense and debt repayment.

In the initial financial cash flow forecast for the new venture, I suggest that no entry be made in the financial flows section except the bring-along financing I referred to previously.

The punch line of the cash flow statement is part seven, net change in cash and marketable securities. This is defined as part three (NOCF) minus part four (total priority outflows) minus part five (total discretionary outflows) plus or minus part six (total financial flows). For convenience, the end-of-period cash balance (the same as the balance sheet amount) is shown at the very bottom of the cash flow statement.

Since cash is the balancing item in the financial forecast, part seven would normally be negative for at least the first few months. This information helps answer the question on every entrepreneur's mind.

HOW MUCH CASH IS NEEDED?

The cash flow projection gives a reasonable estimate of the amount of cash needed to start the venture.

If net change in cash is -$57,833 in a month (as it was in February of year 1 for the McDonald Company), the business would have zero dollars at the end of the month if it started that month with $57,833 in its cash (checking) account. Not all monthly changes are negative, but if we algebraically add these changes to net change in cash, a running cash balance emerges for the end of the month.

Exhibit X shows a portion of the most likely scenario for the first two years of the cash flow statement for the McDonald Company. This projected negative cash balance keeps increasing until it reaches a maximum decrease in January of year 2 of -$846,063. From this time on, the cumulative cash balance rises, becomes a positive balance briefly in December of year 2, and falls back to a negative number for several more months until June of year 3, when it becomes positive consistently. This means that the company needs $846,063 in its bank account at the start to finance the most likely scenario of the financial forecast.

But what if the company does not meet these forecasts exactly? Surely it won't!

The solution is to forecast two other scenarios—a most pessimistic and a most optimistic situation. These forecasts are not as much trouble as they may seem, since a number of items are the same for all these scenarios.

While these forecasts are not shown here, we did them for the McDonald Company and noted the largest decrease in the cash balance for each scenario. For the most optimistic scenario, the maximum negative cash balance was $1,052,289 (occurring in April of year 2). For the most pessimistic scenario, the comparable number for the first two years was $859,756 (occurring in April of year 2). It's not really surprising that the most optimistic scenario required more cash than the most pessimistic, as generating more sales meant heightening working capital requirements, especially accounts receivable and inventory.

If you take the larger difference between the maximum negative cash balance for the most likely scenario and either the most optimistic or the most pessimistic situation, you get an estimate of our contingency factor. In this case, the most pessimistic is only $13,693 more than the most likely scenario number, but the difference for the most optimistic projection is $194,846.

Surely, if you listed the capital required as $846,063 plus a contingency reserve of $194,846, your figures would have specious accuracy, which would not speak well for the forecaster. So round off the numbers and state that the business needs capital of $850,000 plus a contingency amount of $200,000, or a total of $1,050,000.

What if the entrepreneurs perceive that their track record will not support a request for the amount needed to finance the venture? They can go back to the income statement and balance sheet and make adjustments that might save money. Perhaps scaling back the sales forecast even more than the most pessimistic estimate might help. A company could save on working capital or buy used machinery instead of new or could subcontract production until the business was healthy. Whatever the alternatives, you can use the same model.

Now a potential venture capitalist might examine these forecasts and say, "Fine, but you don't need all this money now, at the start. Let's put up some of the required capital, and when you need the rest, ask for it."

Such a directive can be the kiss of death for a new venture because when the entrepreneur calls for more money, the venture capitalist can well say, "Sorry, but my funds are tied up right now. You'll have to wait awhile." (This is the response the first start-up venture on which I worked got. As a result, I formed my first law of entrepreneurship: if you want to fly to financial paradise, have enough gas to make the trip, as there are no service stations along the way!)

If the business attempts to raise venture capital once it has started and before it gets to a positive cash flow position (ready for second-stage financing), all it will have to show is a trail of red ink on its financial statements. True, the new business does not need all the required cash on day 1, but the cash should be available when needed.

Exhibit X. Cash flow statement for the McDonald Company.

	Jan Year 1	Feb Year 1	Mar Year 1	Apr Year 1	May Year 1	Jun Year 1
Operating Cash Inflows:						
+ Net sales	$0	$0	$0	$60,000	$180,000	$180,000
− Change in A/R	0	0	0	55,290	136,770	61,110
(1) Net Operating Cash Inflows	0	0	0	4,710	43,230	118,890
Operating Cash Outflows:						
+ COGS (less depreciation)	0	0	0	32,013	94,165	93,227
+ G & A expense (less depreciation)	27,640	18,860	24,560	15,760	18,760	18,760
+ Selling expenses	13,200	17,600	33,000	20,000	20,000	20,000
+ Taxes	0	0	0	0	0	0
− Change in accrued taxes	0	0	0	0	0	0
+ Change in inventory	208,430	10,430	164,430	(5,723)	(67,875)	65,063
+ Change in prepaid expenses	2,200	(200)	(200)	(200)	(200)	(200)
− Change in A/P	43,040	(5,940)	173,000	(176,340)	660	129,480
(2) Net Operating Cash Outflows	208,430	52,630	48,790	238,190	64,190	67,370
(3) Net Operating Cash Flow	(208,430)	(52,630)	(48,790)	(233,480)	(20,960)	51,520
Priority Outflows:						
+ Interest expenses	2,333	2,286	2,237	2,187	2,137	2,086
+ Current debt repayable	2,870	2,917	2,966	3,015	3,066	3,117
(4) Total Priority Outflows	5,203	5,203	5,203	5,202	5,203	5,203
Discretionary Outflows:						
+ Capital expenditures	200,000	0	0	0	0	0
(5) Total Discretionary Outflows	200,000	0	0	0	0	0
Financial Flows:						
+ Debt instruments (borrowings)	140,000	0	0	0	0	0
(6) Total Financial Flows	140,000	0	0	0	0	0
Net Change in Cash and Marketable Securities:						
+ Net operating cash flow (item 3)	(208,430)	(52,630)	(48,790)	(233,480)	(20,960)	51,520
− Priority outflows (item 4)	5,203	5,203	5,203	5,202	5,203	5,203
− Discretionary outflows (item 5)	200,000	0	0	0	0	0
+ Financial flows (item 6)	140,000	0	0	0	0	0
(7) Net Change in Cash and Marketable Securities	($273,633)	($57,833)	($53,993)	($238,682)	($26,163)	$46,317
Projected ending cash balance	($273,633)	($331,466)	($385,459)	($624,141)	($650,304)	($603,987)

*Maximum negative cash balance.

One way to ensure that funds will be available is to arrange with a bank for a letter of credit. Then, if the venture capital source is temporarily short of funds, the bank can advance you the funds based on the venture capitalist's credit.

The process for determining the capital requirements for a new venture really isn't mysterious, only a bit complicated. The key to this determination (and to financial forecasting in general) is the cash flow statement. A two-step financial forecast is advisable, one to summarize the data and two to support the data with details in footnotes and schedules.

Exhibit X. Cash flow statement for the McDonald Company.

Jul Year 1	Aug Year 1	Sep Year 1	Oct Year 1	Nov Year 1	Dec Year 1	Jan Year 2	Feb Year 2	Mar Year 2
$180,000	$120,000	$30,000	$60,000	$90,000	$120,000	$180,000	$300,000	$420,000
17,460	(55,290)	(109,125)	(20,370)	27,645	45,105	74,460	143,085	173,640
162,540	175,290	139,125	80,370	62,355	74,895	105,540	156,915	246,360
93,077	62,498	15,629	31,245	46,845	62,074	92,284	153,179	213,731
19,180	17,380	14,680	15,580	16,480	17,380	29,610	32,010	34,410
20,000	20,000	20,000	20,000	20,000	20,000	41,000	43,400	45,800
0	0	0	0	0	0	9,302	27,426	49,309
0	0	0	0	0	0	9,302	27,426	49,309
(74,717)	(52,068)	134,731	(12,885)	(28,485)	310,076	(50,134)	(111,029)	188,349
(200)	(200)	(200)	(200)	(200)	(200)	2,750	(250)	(250)
(130,320)	1,380	129,240	(130,620)	1,380	327,240	(292,440)	1,960	349,280
187,660	46,230	55,600	184,360	53,260	82,090	407,950	115,350	132,760
(25,120)	129,060	83,525	(103,990)	9,095	(7,195)	(302,410)	41,565	113,600
2,034	1,981	1,928	1,873	1,818	1,761	1,704	1,645	1,586
3,169	3,222	3,275	3,330	3,385	3,442	3,499	3,557	3,617
5,203	5,203	5,203	5,203	5,203	5,203	5,203	5,202	5,203
0	0	0	0	0	0	0	0	0
0	0	0	0	0	0	0	0	0
0	0	0	0	0	0	0	0	0
0	0	0	0	0	0	0	0	0
(25,120)	129,060	83,525	(103,990)	9,095	(7,195)	(302,410)	41,565	113,600
5,203	5,203	5,203	5,203	5,203	5,203	5,203	5,202	5,203
0	0	0	0	0	0	0	0	0
0	0	0	0	0	0	0	0	0
($30,323)	$123,857	$78,322	($109,193)	$3,892	($12,398)	($307,613)	$36,363	$108,397
($634,310)	($510,453)	($432,131)	($541,324)	($537,432)	($549,830)	($857,443)*	($821,080)	($712,683)

The cash flow statement is at the heart of the answer to the question, How much cash is needed to finance the venture? The negative cash balance line on the most likely scenario provides an estimate of the required venture capital. You can calculate the contingency amount of venture capital by comparing the maximum decreases in cash balance for the other two scenarios. ▲

BUSINESS PLANS: TWO MAJOR TYPES

Fred L. Fry and Charles R. Stoner

Increasingly, small business owners are being encouraged to develop business plans for their firms. Many small firms report, however, that effective planning is the most difficult function they have to perform.[1] The time and resources invested in preparing business plans can yield substantial returns. For example, the benefits of planning may include the determination of the unique nature of the business,[2] an objective analysis of the competition,[3] and the development and specification of goals, objectives, and supporting strategies.[4] Even more important, research evidence suggests that planning can facilitate small firm performance and success.[5] Yet the evidence is far from conclusive.[6] It may well be that the process of planning, which involves a careful analysis of the firm and its environment, is just as important as the plan itself.

One problem with discussing plans and planning is distinguishing among the various types of plans.[7] Strategic plans outline the actions necessary to achieve long-range goals. Tactical, or operating plans focus on the short-run, usually one year. Functional plans specify short- to medium-range actions having to do with specific aspects of the business, such as marketing, finance, manufacturing, or personnel. (These tend to differ somewhat from the general "policies" which guide day-to-day action.) Another type of plan is the investment plan, used by small business owners to gain access to financing from banks, the SBA, or venture capitalists.

Planning models have focused largely on the creation and the benefits of operational or working plans. In practice, however, many small business owners devote substantial efforts toward developing financial plans. The financial, or investment plan differs significantly from the preceding types of plans, which are collectively referred to as working plans.[8] The investment plan is designed for the sole purpose of obtaining financing, whereas working plans are designed to guide and control actual business operations. Both types of plans are important, and in many instances the success of one may hinge at least in part on the success of the other.

Small business owners or potential entrepreneurs should be aware of the critical differences between working and investment plans. For example, when a speaker, consultant, government official, or financial advisor suggests that a business plan be developed, the owner may misinterpret what is expected. Further, although the development of any type of plan can be useful, neither type of plan will effectively serve the purpose of the other. This article explores the differences between investment plans and working business plans.

Reprinted with the permission of the *Journal of Small Business Management* (January 1985) pp. 1–6.

Table 1. Differences between working and investment plans.

Factor	Working Plan	Investment Plan
Prepared by	Top management, sometimes with help of consultant or operational managers	Top management, often with help of loan packager, CPA firm, and/or accounting personnel
Prepared for	Top management, middle management, and other employees	Banks, SBA, venture capital firms
Focus	Strategy and operations	Sources and uses of funds
Flavor of plan	Objective, realistic, thorough	Objective, optimistic, crisp
External data needed	Competitor analysis, economic, technological, and social trends	Competitor analysis, technological trends (for hi-tech firms)
Internal data needed	Analysis of strengths as well as weaknesses of current operations, historical trends	Management resources, financial projections. Significance of project, strengths of company and management team
Number of steps	Varies	Varies
Prime ingredients of final plan	Nature of business, objectives, strategies, controls	Nature of the business and market, amount of money needed, sales and earnings forecasts, and makeup of management team
Time to prepare	Substantial—often done over several months while performing other duties	Depends on help from loan packagers—possibly two to four weeks
Desired length	Indefinite—as long as needed	10–15 pages plus documentation, or 1/4 to 1/2 inch thick
Frequency of referral to plan	Periodically, at least quarterly	None, if plan is acceptable
Frequency of revision	Annually	When outside funding is needed or as required by financier
Measure of success	The plan itself, the planning process, achievement of goals	The obtaining of desired funding

DIFFERENCES BETWEEN WORKING AND INVESTMENT PLANS

Table 1 compares working and investment plans on a variety of factors. Keep in mind that one type of plan is not "better" than the other—they merely serve different purposes. One major difference between the working plan and the investment plan lies in the general orientation or focus of each type. The fundamental purpose of the working plan is to provide information and guidance for making operational decisions about the firm. It prescribes objectives, goals, and targets, and it delineates steps to be taken to achieve those goals.

The investment plan has an obvious financial focus. Questions it must answer are: "Why are the funds needed?" "To what use will they be put?" "How many dollars will be required?" "What equity can the owners contribute?" Each question must be answered to the satisfaction of the funding agency. Thus, while the investment plan may include strategic information, its focus is clearly financial.

A second difference between the working plan and the investment plan concerns the individuals involved in the development of the plan. Clearly, both types require CEO involvement. However, the working plan dictates that operating managers and other key employees should be involved, for at least two reasons. First, employee involvement insures more complete input into the plan. Second, employee involvement encourages acceptance of the plan. Typically, such a wide range of inputs is not required for the investment plan. Here, the CEO, the controller, and other financial or accounting personnel will be actively involved, but other personnel are likely to offer minimal contributions, if any.

A third difference between the two plans concerns the individuals or groups who receive the plan. In the case of the working plan, the plan is intended for internal use. Since the plan consists of substantial strategic or operational information, confidentiality is a prime consideration. On the other hand, the investment plan, by nature, must be shown to a variety of outsiders, including bankers, the SBA, or other sources of financing.

The flavor or tone varies considerably between business and investment plans. In both types, objectivity is the key. Yet, in the investment plan, the object is to "sell the plan" to outsiders. Consequently, optimism frequently prevails over realism. This is not to say that investment plans are misleading, only that the company must be presented in its best light by emphasizing the positive. In addition, while thoroughness characterizes the effective working plan, crispness and brevity characterize the investment plan.[9] Investors are hesitant to read, let alone fund, a verbose, padded or highly computerized investment plan.

DATA NEEDED TO PREPARE THE PLANS

The two types of plans have some elements in common, especially with regard to external information needed to prepare the plans, as shown in table 1. In both, external information relating to competitors, technological, and social trends is important. Since much venture capital funding goes to high-tech firms, it is critical that the firm discuss recent and anticipated developments. Similarly, the working plan must include an analysis of the firm's environment, including an industry/competitor analysis and an analysis of the social/technological/political environment (see figure 1).

The primary difference in the two types of plans is the depth of information on competitors, the industry, and the community required by the working plan. Since significant strategic or operational changes may be necessary if these factors change, this information should be continually tracked and updated, thoroughly analyzed, and regularly reviewed. Similarly, changes in the community and its economy or labor force may have a substantial bearing on the firm.

Both plans also require internal data (see figure 1). The investment plan focuses primarily on significant strengths of the firm, the qualifications of the management team, and an in-depth financial analysis. Since it is designed to sell potential investors on the

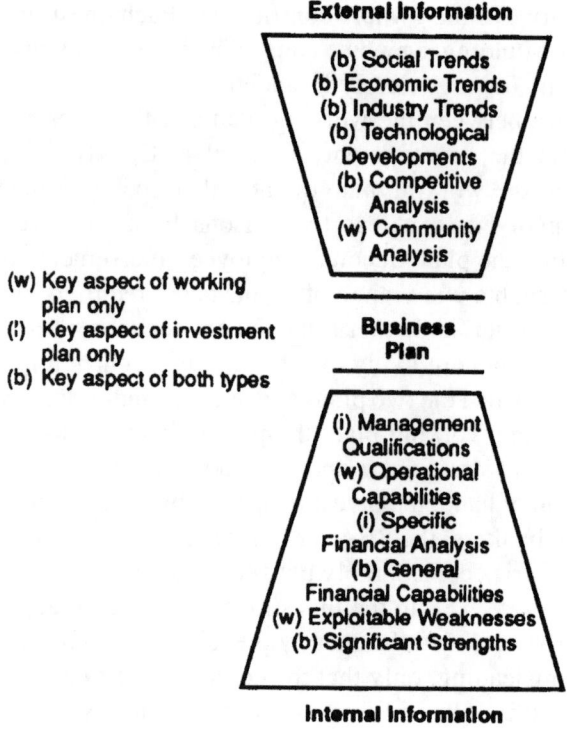

External Information

(b) Social Trends
(b) Economic Trends
(b) Industry Trends
(b) Technological
  Developments
(b) Competitive
  Analysis
(w) Community
  Analysis

(w) Key aspect of working
  plan only
(i) Key aspect of investment
  plan only
(b) Key aspect of both types

**Business
Plan**

(i) Management
  Qualifications
(w) Operational
  Capabilities
(i) Specific
  Financial Analysis
(b) General
  Financial Capabilities
(w) Exploitable Weaknesses
(b) Significant Strengths

Internal Information

Figure 1. Information required for business plan.

firm, it does not dwell on weaknesses of the firm. It does not present operational information in detail unless the funding is for a "high-tech" project. Financiers are interested in a general overview of what will be done, and in knowing that the management team can make it work.

The working plan, on the other hand, explores operational aspects of the firm in detail, and does not ignore or downplay weaknesses of the firm, because these could cause the plan to fail or could be exploited by competitors. Certainly, a financial analysis and overview are important components of the working plan. However, in most instances, a general financial analysis will suffice rather than the in-depth analysis required for the investment plan (see figure 1).

THE FINAL PLAN

The time and effort required to produce a final plan of any kind vary widely. Within the broad category of working plans, strategic plans probably require the most management involvement. Substantial analysis of the competitive environment and internal aspects of the firm are quite time consuming. Functional or operating level plans should require somewhat less time, since they use the strategic plan as a starting point.

The time required to produce a financial or investment plan will vary with (1) the requirements of the financier, and (2) the current state of financial/accounting records in the firm. If the firm's accounting records are accurate and complete, less time will be required than if management or a loan packager must reconstruct the financial history of the firm.

The actual form of working plans is not critical as long as all bases are covered. Planning models appear in nearly all textbooks on strategic planning. Some are simple; others are quite complex.[10] Financial plan models can be obtained from lending institutions. A good example of a financial plan format appears in *Financing Small Business*.[11]

The working plan, since it is intended for internal use, highlights objectives, strategies, and controls—it attempts to uncover the very nature of the firm. It should be remembered that it serves as a tool to motivate management and employees to pull toward common goals. The plan should be referred to often (at least quarterly), and should be updated and revised at least annually. It may be prepared over a period of several months, depending on other demands on the owner's time.

The investment plan is read by outsiders. The final plan includes a brief description of the business and market, the proposed use of the funds, sales and earnings forecasts, and the makeup of the management team.[12] It is a single-use document. In other words, it is prepared for a specific purpose—that of obtaining funding for the project in question. Thus, if the plan is successful, it need not be revised nor referred to later unless required by the financier.

MEASURES OF SUCCESS

Since the reason for creating a financial plan is to obtain financing, the measure of success is clearly the attainment of the needed funds. If funding is secured, the plan was successful. Failure to obtain funding may be due to inadequacies of the plan, but it may also reflect other factors, such as limited availability of funds from financing institutions.

Some may say that the working plan is a success only if the firm achieves the objectives set forth in the plan. It should be kept in mind, however, that the planning process itself has multiple objectives, and that some or all of these may be met. The plan can be considered at least partially successful if the process produces more motivated, loyal employees. The plan is a success if the process develops better-informed managers who can more skillfully adapt to a changing competitive environment. The plan is a success if the objectives or targets become control devices that help to direct activities as well as to set standards against which performance can be measured. The control aspect of a working plan becomes fully apparent only when the plan is put into actual operation. And finally, since the working plan is results oriented, the attainment of the plan's stated objectives is a key measure of the success of the plan. Motivation, loyalty, awareness, and control are all stepping stones to the eventual accomplishment of the working plan's stated objectives.

IMPLICATIONS AND CONCLUSIONS

When small business owner/managers first consider developing a business plan, their orientation and perspective may be limited. If they view business plans as financial plans only, they may be taking a short-sighted view. Both types of plans are important for different reasons. It may be that a firm which has a working plan in operation will have an easier time when it comes to developing an effective and convincing investment plan. By the same token, a firm which lacks a sound financial base is not likely to succeed no matter how good a working plan it adopts.

Financial, or investment plans are constructed to appeal to those who may become stakeholders in the firm through either debt or equity capital. These plans are undertaken mainly to gain funding from an outside source, and only secondarily to improve one's competitive position in the marketplace. But in order to do the latter, it is often necessary to accomplish the former.

Working plans are intended for internal use, and involve a detailed assessment of the environment and the firm's operations in order to set goals for the future. They are periodically updated and revised, and serve as a guide for decision making. In fact, the analysis and detail necessary to structure a comprehensive and meaningful working plan will automatically provide much of the information necessary to prepare the more specialized investment plan. Both types of plans are important for the successful functioning and growth of small firms. ▲

NOTES

1. T. Cohn and R. A. Lindberg, *How Management Is Different in Small Companies* (New York: American Management Association, 1972).
2. R. Moyer, "Strategic Planning for the Small Firm," *Journal of Small Business Management* (July 1982), pp. 8–14; and J. Naor, "How to Make Strategic Planning Work for Small Businesses," *Advanced Management Journal* (Winter 1980), pp. 35–39.
3. W. C. House, "Dynamic Planning for the Smaller Company—A Case History," *Long Range Planning* (June 1979), pp. 38–47.
4. R. Parthasarthy, "Long Range Planning: How to Avoid Recession's Pinch," *Journal of Applied Management* (July/ August 1980), pp. 12–15.
5. R. Kirk and D. W. Schell, "Identifying Small Business Failures and the Development of Turnaround Strategies: A Computer Simulation Approach," *Proceedings: Small Business Institute Directors Association National Conference* (March 1980), pp. 185–195; R. B. Robinson, "Forecasting and Small Business: A Study of the Strategic Planning Process," *Journal of Small Business Management* (July 1979), pp. 19–27; and V. K. Unni, "The Role of Strategic Planning in Small Business," *Long Range Planning* (April 1981), pp. 54–58.
6. For example, see R. B. Robinson, Jr. and J. A. Pearce II, "Research Thrusts in Small Firm Strategic Planning," *Academy of Management Review* (January 1984), pp. 128–137.
7. See, for example, G. A. Steiner, J. B. Miner, and E. R. Gray, *Management Policy and Strategy* (New York: Macmillan, 1982).
8. For an interesting discussion, see J. A. Timmons, "A Business Plan Is More Than a Financing Device:' *Harvard Business Review* (March/April 1980), pp. 28–34.
9. R. Sabin, "What Investors Hate About Business Plans," *Venture* (June 1984), p. 52.

10. For a variety of different strategic planning models see: Arthur A. Thompson and A. J. Strickland, *Strategic Management: Concepts and Cases,* 3rd edition (Plano, Texas: Business Publications, Inc., 1984); Charles Hofer et al., *Strategic Management: A Casebook in Policy and Planning,* 2nd edition (St. Paul, Minnesota: West Publishing Co., 1984); James M. Higgins, *Organizational Policy and Strategic Management: Text and Cases* (Chicago, Illinois: The Dryden Press, 1983); LaRue T. Hosmer, *Strategic Management: Text and Cases on Business Policy* (Englewood Cliffs, New Jersey: Prentice Hall, 1982).

11. *Financing Small Business* (Small Business Reporter Series, Bank of America, 1980).

12. Sabin, "What Investors Hate Most About Business Plans," p. 52.

UNDERSTANDING CASH FLOW:
A SYSTEM DYNAMICS ANALYSIS

Ray Thompson

Working capital management is vitally important to the success of the small business. If sales vary during the year because of seasonality, growth, or uncertainty, then working capital is difficult to control. The firm's current assets and liabilities (in particular, receivables, inventory, and short-term payables) change in response to sales fluctuations. As a result, cash flow may sometimes be inadequate to sustain operations, even though profitability is satisfactory over the whole year.

Improving cash flow management is a major priority for many small businesses. The advent of the microcomputer makes improved planning possible, but there is a related need for modeling approaches which illustrate the realities of small business. One such method, financial simulation using System Dynamics, is described in this article. It has been used by the author to aid cash flow management in firms which suffer from uneven sales. This technique provides a more comprehensive understanding of the causes of working capital changes and suggests what, if anything, can be done to improve the situation.

The second part of this article includes an explanation of the way in which cash flow management problems can affect the small firm. Part three briefly describes the System Dynamics approach and the way in which such models are constructed. In part four, the working capital position of a case study business is analyzed, and the causes of fluctuations in current assets and liabilities are explained.

CASH FLOW MANAGEMENT

A number of analysts have pointed out that the financial "rules of the game" are distinctively different for the small business.[1] The vast majority of small firms are undercapitalized. As a result, they depend on various sorts of short-term financing such as accounts payable, accruals, and lines of credit. Problems arise because these must be liquidated periodically. This, in turn, means that cash must be generated from elsewhere in the business in order to meet these obligations. At a time when sales, inventory, and receivables are in a state of flux, it is difficult for the manager to be sure of an adequate cash flow. In this sense, working capital management is about the *timing* as well as the size of current assets and liabilities.[2]

Problems of liquidity adjustment are especially difficult for the seasonal business. One must bear in mind that rules of thumb such as "cash flow equals after-tax profit plus depreciation" are inadequate guides for financial managers when sales are not uniform due to important differences in the timing of cash flow and profitability.[3] This distinction is especially important for the small firm, because generating sufficient cash to satisfy creditors is essential for short-run survival. Profitability, by contrast, is a much more abstract concept which applies over the long term.

Evidence suggests that many firms are ill-equipped to make the difficult decisions involved in cash flow management. Poor financial control is a major factor contributing to the demise of many small firms.[4] Inadequate financial control and a lack of cash flow and working capital analysis are often associated with financial difficulties. Perhaps the major danger is a belief by some owners that if profits are adequate, cash flow will take care of itself. A related problem is that accountants may emphasize the preparation of financial records at the expense of managerial advice, while owners may believe that financial reporting is carried out chiefly to satisfy the revenue authorities. A number of studies have found common deficiencies in the management of current assets and liabilities. For instance, a survey of 120 small businesses revealed inadequate control of receivables, payables, and inventory as well as cash receipts and disbursements.[5]

What can be done to improve the situation? Experienced analysts can often identify periods when inadequate cash flow is likely to cause difficulties. This sort of expert advice is, however, both expensive and hard to come by.[6]

A computer-assisted approach can be used to gain the same sort of insights that experts provide. The approach described in this article should assist the firm in making decisions about working capital management with a fuller understanding of their likely consequences.

SYSTEM DYNAMICS ANALYSIS

Many methods are available for analyzing and predicting business cash flow. These include cash budgeting, spreadsheets, and other financial models. The case study described here used System Dynamics, a computer simulation package which also provides guidelines for understanding why the firm is behaving the way it does. This facilitates the analysis of alternative financial policies and their effects on the business.

System Dynamics is a way of studying problems caused by a host of factors which are related over time. In the previous section, the way in which fluctuating sales can cause instability in inventory, receivables, and payables was discussed. Such a system is complex and dynamic, meaning that so many things are changing all at once that it is difficult to grasp all of the interrelationships involved.[7] Any computerized financial model can provide quick answers to a host of questions. The particular strength of System Dynamics, however, is that the interactions between different parts of the firm can be examined, enabling us to understand why things happen as they do and how one part of the system is likely to affect other parts. Having gained this understanding, the computer can be used to test different policies to see if the system (firm) can be made to behave more effectively (less cash flow fluctuations, for example). Ways of improving the firm's performance suggested by the model can then be applied by the financial manager.

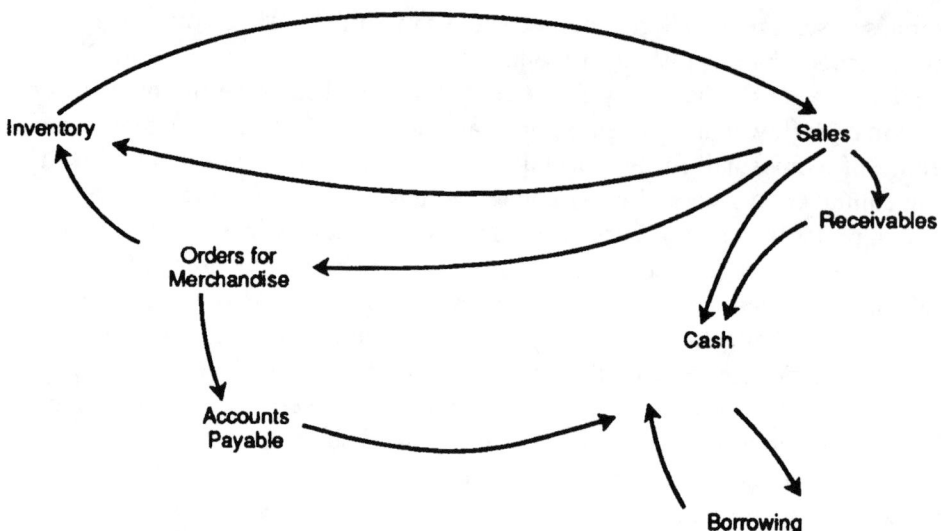

Figure 1. Cash flow.

System Dynamics is designed to deal with those difficult situations where "everything is happening at once." It looks at problems which are caused not by one thing but by the interaction of a number of factors. For example, cash flow behavior is complicated because it increases from current cash sales and from collection of receivables from sales made some time ago. At the same time, cash is being paid out for current operating expenses and to pay off previously incurred payables. Financial managers need to consider the delays involved because it is the *timing* as much as the size of current liabilities which can cause liquidity problems. To illustrate: credit sales only become cash at time of collection; inventory is on the floor for some time before sale and payables incurred in the course of trade will be paid off later. If sales fluctuate, so will all current assets and liabilities. This can bring about liquidity problems.

A System Dynamics model begins by setting out in diagram form the relationships between the variables. (See figure 1.) Each arrow in the diagram suggests the links between the variables; together they provide a picture of the way the system operates. The arrows suggest causes (for instance orders of merchandise cause payables to be incurred). Figure 1 shows the relationships involved in cash flow management for the case study business.

A careful study of figure 1 shows the current asset and liability accounts. Sales are made from current inventories, but unless the business has adequate supplies of merchandise, it is likely to lose out on sales. Orders for merchandise are based on historical, seasonal sales patterns, and after a time these orders show up in inventory. This causes payables to be incurred which must be paid off at a later date. Cash is generated partly from immediate sales and partly from collection of receivables accumulated from prior sales. The firm also borrows from a local bank to enable it to survive periods of negative cash flow. As the figure shows, without sufficient cash the firm must cut back on merchandise orders or restrict the credit it offers to customers. Cutting back inventories or credit are likely to have an adverse impact on future sales.

One can now begin to see why cash flow management is so complex. Not only is everything happening at once; each of the variables is subject to some uncertainty as to future magnitude and timing. Such uncertainties affect all of the other variables in the cash flow equation. The System Dynamics method does not rely merely on making more accurate sales projections. Instead, it accepts that a range of values could apply, and studies what effect each of these might have on the way the firm operates. By tracing the patterns of action and reaction among the working capital accounts through computer simulation, the financial analyst can gain the understanding of system interactions needed to improve financial management.

System Dynamics provides a set of procedures for taking an "influence diagram" like the one shown in figure 1 and turning it into a set of equations which can be run on the computer. This procedure yields time paths for the behavior of variables such as receivables and payables. By studying the way in which these interact, cash flow can be better understood and controlled. A special computer simulation language, DYNAMO, makes these later stages of modeling relatively simple. A major strength of the method lies in its accessibility, which enables the user to make changes in the model easily.

A CASE STUDY

The following, disguised case will serve as an example of cash flow dynamics analysis. Fantastic Fashions sells better ladies' apparel in a medium-sized Pennsylvania town. Sales are heavily concentrated in two periods, early summer and the Christmas season, giving the firm a fluctuating annual sales pattern. Merchandise is ordered through visits to New York fashion houses, which means placing orders many months in advance of demand. When the inventory finally arrives, discounts for prompt payment are large enough that the owner wants to take advantage of them by drawing on a line of credit at a local bank. Eventually, the inventory will be sold, some of it at on-sale prices at the end of the season. Since the business also offers charge accounts to its customers, cash collections can often lag significantly behind.

Building the model for this firm involved working out the relationships between all parts of the system and expressing them in equations with the help of the DYNAMO package. Three sorts of information were incorporated into the model:

1. *Accounting relationships.* These were the familiar formulae for such factors as net income, cash flow, gross profit, etc.
2. *Delays.* These represent the time which elapses between events such as billing and collecting from customers (accounts receivable delay) or between ordering and receiving merchandise (inventory backlog). Each current asset or liability is

a delay and the time lags involved can be estimated through turnover ratios. In System Dynamics, these delays are seen as major causes of problems.

3. *Policies.* These are the "rules" by which the firm is operated, e.g., the way in which the owner has used past sales experience and current inventory levels to describe order quantities. This sort of "soft" information is usually obtained through interviews with those who actually make financial decisions.[8]

RESULTS

Using a System Dynamics model involves interpreting the time paths generated by the model (which represents the real-world system). From a mass of outputs which summarize Fantastic Fashions' operations, three have been chosen for analysis. These represent problems common to many small businesses whose sales fluctuate. Thus, although the model is based on a single business, the conclusions are widely applicable.[9]

The problems illustrated involve differences between profit and cash flow, the way in which the firm's assets and liabilities vary over the operating cycle. These are illustrated in figures 2 through 4 as discussed below.

Many analysts have stressed that profits and cash flow do not necessarily go hand in hand—at least in the short run. This is shown clearly in figure 2, which depicts changes in the firm's cash flow and profits over time. Profits are relatively stable throughout the year, but cash flows fluctuate dramatically. It can be seen that in some periods profitability actually improves while cash flow is worsening. Clearly, cash flows cannot automatically be assumed to be profits plus depreciation. The differences between cash flow and profits are especially significant, because profits fall below zero for only a brief period. By contrast, cash flow is negative for almost as much of the time as it is positive.

Why are cash flow and profit so different? Cash flow depends ultimately on sales and purchases of merchandise, but important time delays occur because of credit. There is a gap between orders for merchandise and payments for them (known as the average payment period). Similarly, there are delays between the time of sale and collection of cash as well as between arrival of inventory and its final sale. These are known as the "average ages" of receivables and inventory. Because of these gaps, the inflows and outflows of cash associated with any item of merchandise will be separated over time.

By contrast, the rules of accounting (in particular, the "matching" principle) measure profits by calculating the cost of inventory sold and subtracting that cost from current revenues. For the small business, cash flow is much more significant than accounting income. That is why small firms need to study cash flow directly rather than relying on inadequate surrogates such as "profits plus depreciation."

To gain further insight into cash flow behavior requires study of the current asset and liability accounts (figure 3). A careful study of the figure explains much about the complex dynamics involved in the operating cycle of a seasonal business. It can be seen that inventory and payables follow roughly similar patterns. This is because merchandise is ordered before sale, thus increasing both inventory and payables.

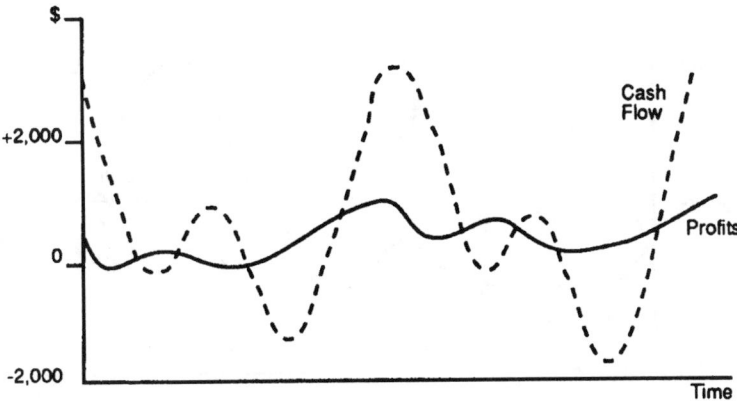

Figure 2. Profits and cash flow.

The turning point for payables is ahead of inventory because payables are paid off after three weeks, but inventory is held for much longer. This fact also explains why cash moves in a pattern nearly opposite to inventories. A rise in inventories caused by merchandise orders will deplete cash when the goods are paid for. Later, inventories will fall as sales pick up and cause the amount of cash to increase, both immediately and after receivables are collected. Thus, understanding the cash flow pattern reveals that orders turn cash into inventory, while sales ultimately turn inventory into cash: since orders for merchandise must precede sales, it follows that cash flow will be negative for a sustained period until receivables are realized.

A final view of the problems seasonality can cause for the small firm is shown in figure 4, which depicts how the firm's need for outside funding changes with the sales pattern. External financing consists of funds borrowed to finance operations, in this case trade credit as well as a line of credit at a local bank. Although sales and external financing needs follow roughly similar patterns, financing need takes precedence over sales since merchandise must be ordered in advance of sale.

As figure 4 shows, financing needs vary much more widely than sales. In some periods the need for external financing is negative, meaning that the firm has *excess* cash for almost half the year. The business could become, on balance, a net *lender* of funds. A temptation could even exist to withdraw this surplus cash from the business for the owner's personal use. Such a withdrawal would be most unwise, however, because the cash would soon be needed again to finance inventory in anticipation of sales.

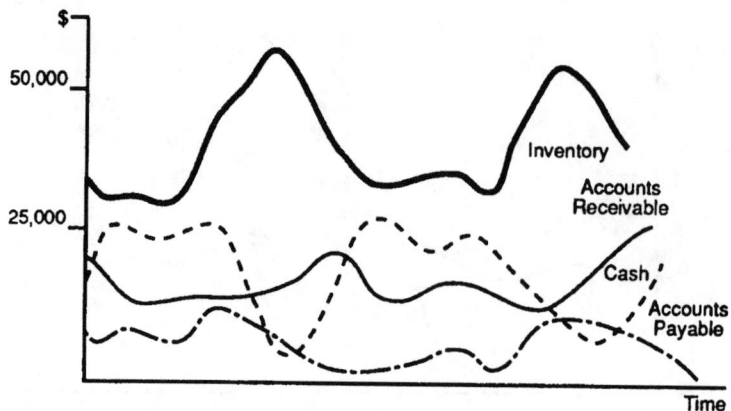

Figure 3. Current account variables.

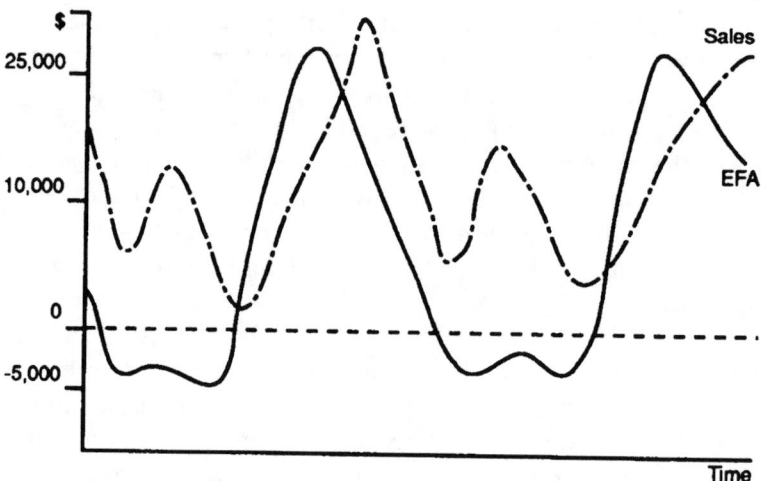

Figure 4. Sales and external financing needs.

CONCLUSION

A summary of the model results illustrates why the financial management of a small business can be so difficult. Cash flows can fluctuate greatly and follow patterns quite different from accounting profits. Inventories, receivables, payables, and cash are complexly related and ever-changing. Moreover, the firm needs large injections of cash at some moments and has surplus funds at others. Add to this the fact that sales are always unpredictable, especially in retailing, and may vary from year to year, and it is clear why the problems involved in financial management can seem very imposing to small business managers, particularly those who experience seasonal fluctuations in demand and sales.

The technique of computer simulation, however, can provide an overview of the complex relationships within the business. The next step is to test alternative scenarios and policies in order to identify those which are likely to improve cash flow management. The kinds of policies to be considered include changing ordering patterns, altering the way payables are financed, using short-term borrowing for different time periods, or some combination of these and other measures. These measures should not aim simply at maximizing sales, but should also consider trade-offs, e.g., between liquidity and reliance on bank financing.

Due to space limitations, the tests and policies developed for the firm in question are not presented here,[10] but they illustrate the complex trade-offs between liquidity, risk, reliance on external financing, and the business's ability to respond adequately to sales fluctuations. Firms need to develop flexible financial strategies which balance these issues and permit rapid responses to unanticipated changes in the environment.

It has been shown that computer modeling enables the manager to gain a much clearer understanding of the causes of cash flow problems. With computer modeling, cash flow can be monitored continuously and in relation to the other current asset and liability accounts, leaving less room for unexpected surprises. The methods described here provide a basis for a more soundly conceived financial management strategy which can reduce threats to firm survival. ▲

NOTES

*The author wishes to acknowledge the support and advice of Ray Shreckengost of RSS Associates, Dr. Herb Myers and Dr. John Clark of Nova University. This paper summarizes the first stages of a research project which uses System Dynamics to improve financial control in small businesses. Further detail and model documentation are available on request.

1. See, for example, J. A. Welsh and J. F. White, "A Small Business Is Not a Little Big Business," *Harvard Business Review* (July–August 1981).
2. J. L. Lyneis developed this approach in "Designing Policies to deal with Limited Financial Resources," *Financial Management* (Spring 1975).
3. A. R. DeThomas explains the interconnections between cash flow and profit using an accounting model in "Ins and Outs of the Flow of Funds," *American Journal of Small Business* (July–September 1982).
4. See entire issue, *Journal of Accountancy* (December 1981).
5. H. N. Weinstein, in the *Journal of Accountancy* (December 1982) suggests that inadequate accounting standards, especially those concerning working capital are major contributory problems to business failures.
6. See, for example, an article on early warning signs of financial difficulty by G. Fox, *Credit and Financial Management* (December 1981).
7. Jay Forrester's *Industrial Dynamics* (1961) and G. P. Richardson and A. L. Pugh's *Introduction to System Dynamics Modelling with DYNAMO* (1981) provide treatments of the major topics. Both are published by M.I.T. Press. An excellent introduction to the method can be found in Nancy Robert's *Introduction to Computer Simulation—A System Dynamics Modelling Approach* (Addison Wesley, 1984).
8. System Dynamics consciously searches out "soft" information and incorporate it into models. Jay Forrester (1961, p. 57) provides a justification for this approach.
9. More complete model documentation is available from the author. Further case studies are currently in preparation.
10. Details are available from the author.

FRANCHISING FROM THE FRANCHISOR AND FRANCHISEE POINTS OF VIEW

Russell M. Knight

Franchising has expanded rapidly in the North American market and around the world during the 1970s and 1980s. Total franchise sales for the United States and Canada in 1984 were estimated to be about $432 billion, about one-third of all retail sales.[1] Over 500,000 franchised business establishments operate in North America, with more than five million jobs in these businesses, and the total is growing daily. An estimate 7,800 franchisors offer franchises in the United States, and over 1,000 Canadian franchisors administer over 2,900 franchise units in Canada.[2]

The Canadian businesses are approximately one-third American controlled, either by means of area franchises, such as McDonald's Restaurants of Canada Ltd., or unit-by-unit franchises directly from the head office in the United States. In turn, Canadian franchisors have franchised over 2,000 units abroad, primarily in the United States.

Only 70 percent of the stores in franchise chains in North America are franchisee operated, with the remaining 30 percent being operated as company-owned stores using hired managers. But company stores are acknowledged to be less profitable, to have lower sales, and to be more expensive to administer than franchised outlets.[3]

However, relatively little research has been done, especially in Canada, on such issues as franchisee motivation, franchise regulation or franchise growth.[4] Most published articles on franchising tend to be of the trade magazine variety or deal with the development of government regulation of franchising, an area in its infancy in Canada.[5] Only Alberta has established formal franchise legislation, while Quebec has included franchising under its Securities Act.[6]

PURPOSE OF THE RESEARCH

A study of franchising was undertaken by the author during the summer of 1982. As part of the study, 148 franchisors and 105 franchisees were surveyed by means of a questionnaire and follow-up interviews with approximately 25 members of each group. In this research, the responses of the franchisee sample are contrasted with those of the franchisors on a variety of franchise-related issues. A previous project compared franchisees and independent entrepreneurs.

Reprinted with the permission of the *Journal of Small Business Management* (July 1986), pp. 8–15.

The purpose of the present study is to examine how franchisees compare with franchisors in their attitudes towards franchising. These issues include personal characteristics, management skills, financing required, support services available in franchised businesses, and controls in the franchise. The follow-up interviews were undertaken in order to meet some of the entrepreneurs personally to discuss the comparison in more detail than was possible in the questionnaire survey. Of the 148 franchisors, two-thirds were based in Canada and one-third in the United States. All of the franchisees were Canadian.

SAMPLE SELECTION

The selection of the franchisee sample was as random as possible, using franchisees in a variety of well-known franchises across Canada. In addition, franchisors were asked for a copy of their franchisee list, and questionnaires were sent to a random sample from the lists provided. Nearly 500 franchisee questionnaires were mailed, and nearly 100 were returned unopened because of address changes, new owners, etc. Usable responses were obtained from 105 franchisees, for a net response rate of approximately 25 percent from those who received a questionnaire. The franchisors (148) were chosen from a directory of franchises,[7] and the response rate was about 20 percent. They were chosen from a variety of industries, although they were not necessarily responses from the same firms for both franchisor and franchisee.

Any bias, therefore, is likely to be attributable to nonresponse bias. The difficulty rests in estimating whether the more successful, larger firms with fewer complaints responded, or vice versa.

The average length of the term of franchise agreements was 12 years for both groups, with the average franchise fee being $20,000 and the average capital investment being $115,000 for both groups. The average franchisor reporting had 28 company-owned stores and 132 franchised stores, and two-thirds of them felt that franchised outlets had both higher sales and profits than company-owned stores. Most franchisors (88 percent) also felt that the company-owned stores were more expensive to administer than franchises. Half had franchises in other countries, the majority of them in the United States. Those in other countries were usually operated by the parent company directly or as an area franchise. Most franchisors (85 percent) franchised on a unit-by-unit basis, while 62 percent franchised on a territory basis. The average franchisor started franchising in 1967 in the United States and in 1972 in Canada.

Franchisees most often reported that their franchises were about 10 years old, with 15 percent of franchisees having more than one unit. Sixty-five percent of franchisees had also considered starting an independent business, while 11 percent had previous experience in franchising, usually in the same type of business. Most (98 percent) were actively involved in the daily operation of their franchise, while 67 percent employed other full-time management people, and 12 percent employed other family members. The 2 percent not directly involved in daily operation had another full-time job. Gross sales by franchise ranged from under $100,000 (11 percent) to over $1 million (23 percent), while profits ranged from a loss for 19 percent to over 8 percent of sales for 35 percent of the sample. Table 1 summarizes the royalty and advertising fee responses.

Table 1. Royalty and advertising fees for franchises.

Royalty Range (as % of Sales)	% Franchisees Reporting	% Franchisors Reporting
None	15	8
0–3%	12	13
3–6%	37	57
6–9%	28	18
More than 9%	8	4

Advertising Fee Range (as % of Sales)	% Franchisees Reporting	% Franchisors Reporting
None	9	17
0–2%	46	35
2–4%	24	9
More than 4%	19	1
Negotiated	—	38

Table 2. Personal franchisee characteristics required for success.

	Franchisee %			Franchisor %		
	Very Important	Important	Not Very Important	Very Important	Important	Not Very Important
Previous Management Experience in Same Industry	0	20	80	2	14	84
Previous Experience in Own Business	12	46	42	16	47	37
Management Ability*	84	15	1	66	31	3
Desire to Succeed	90	10	0	93	7	0
Willingness to Work Hard	92	8	0	93	6	1
Creativity*	26	56	18	12	44	44
Strong People Skills	63	32	5	64	34	2
Financial Backing	71	27	2	67	27	6
Support from Family	52	28	20	46	32	22

*Indicates significant difference in responses at the .05 level.

RESULTS OF THE SURVEY

Franchisees and franchisors were asked to identify the personal characteristics required as success factors for franchisees. The results in table 2 show they agree on the relative importance of these factors, with differences only in rating management ability and creativity.

Table 3. Advantages of franchising.

	Franchisees' Agreement %	Franchisors' Agreement %
You can make more money in a franchise than in an independent operation.	51	47
A franchise is less risky than an independent business.*	78	88
A franchise offers greater job satisfaction than salaried employment.*	95	82
A franchise offers more independence than salaried employment.*	92	83
A franchise offers a proven business formula.*	83	99
A franchise offers the benefit of a known trade name.	96	99
You can develop a franchise more quickly than an independent business.	92	86

*Indicates significant difference in responses at the .05 level.

Table 4. Initial services provided by franchisor and franchisee and degree of satisfaction with each.

Service	Franchisee Response				Franchisor Response			
	% Providing	Degree of Satisfaction			% Providing	Degree of Satisfaction		
		High	Med.	Low		High	Med.	Low
Lease Negotiation*	66	42	38	20	77	67	29	4
Market Survey*	64	33	41	26	79	58	39	3
Site Selection*	72	48	39	13	85	76	21	3
Store Design and Leasehold Improvement	74	52	34	14	87	81	17	2
Management Training Programs*	85	36	42	22	94	70	24	6
Operating Manuals*	89	45	38	17	93	64	31	5
Recognized Trademark	98	74	22	4	99	84	16	0
Franchise Financing	36	42	31	27	32	52	20	28
Equipment Package*	59	43	46	11	76	66	31	3

*Indicates significant difference in responses at the .05 level.

Table 3 illustrates the close agreement between both groups concerning the advantages of franchising. In general, franchisees were slightly less enthusiastic about the merits of franchising.

Franchise Services and Disclosure

Services provided by franchisors; and the degree of franchise satisfaction are illustrated in tables 4 and 5. Franchisees reported a much lower degree of satisfaction with initial and ongoing services than franchisors believed they experienced.

The next area explored was the sources of information recommended by franchisors and used by franchisees before they signed a franchise agreement. In general, franchisees did not consult as many outside sources as franchisors claimed to recommend. Both groups reported lawyers, existing franchisees, accountants, and bankers as the most important sources, in that order. Franchise consultants were usually perceived as salespeople for various franchises, and were regarded as the least useful of all sources reported.

Table 5. Ongoing services provided by franchisor and franchisee and degree of satisfaction with each.

Service	Franchisee Response				Franchisor Response			
	% Providing	Degree of Satisfaction			% Providing	Degree of Satisfaction		
		High	Med.	Low		High	Med.	Low
Centralized Purchasing	61	52	28	20	74	53	34	13
Advertising and Promotion	93	35	41	24	97	50	34	13
Bookkeeping*	31	24	44	32	34	37	48	15
Regular Operating Assistance	64	26	40	34	97	58	40	2
Availability for Advice*	94	44	34	22	100	77	22	1
Marketing Research*	58	25	39	36	65	44	42	14
Information Bulletins	84	41	44	15	82	52	40	8
Refresher Courses	58	31	48	21	59	46	40	14
Inventory Control*	37	42	33	25	57	55	36	19

*Indicates significant difference in responses at the .05 level.

Table 6. Issues covered by franchise agreement.

Issue	Percent Franchisors Reporting	Percent Franchisees Reporting
Purchase of Supplies	85	77
Approved Suppliers*	76	67
Quality Control*	90	74
Territory Restrictions	87	73
Non-competition Clause	76	63
Buy-Back Agreement	58	53
Renewal Clause	79	80
Termination Clause	98	96
Franchisee's Right to Open Competing Business	80	85

*Indicates significant difference in responses at the .05 level.

Table 6 summarizes the issues covered by the franchise agreement. Both groups generally replied that the franchise could be sold only to a franchisor-approved buyer.

Franchisors stated that their reason for buying back franchises was usually (62 percent) to resell poorly operated franchises or to eliminate weak franchises (57 percent). Terminations usually (98 percent) indicated franchisee default of the agreement or substandard franchisee performance (69 percent).

Government Regulations

Table 7 lists areas which should be covered by any forthcoming government regulation of franchises in Canada, as reported by both franchisors and franchisees. Even franchisees are averse to any kind of regulation, other than disclosure by the franchisor. Overall, both sides appear to believe that government should stay out of the franchise picture.

Table 7. Areas where government regulation is needed in Canada.

Issue	Percent Franchisees Reporting	Percent Franchisors Reporting
Length of Term	27	19
Renewals	39	34
Terminations	52	46
Disclosure*	70	84
Tying Purchase Arrangements*	32	48
Suppliers	22	27
Territory Restrictions*	38	26
Dual Distribution Systems	28	27
No Regulation Needed	60	68

*Indicates significant difference in responses at the .05 level.

Franchise Problem Areas

Common problems listed by franchisees include lack of franchisor support (37 percent), fees (20 percent), advertising (14 percent), and purchasing (10 percent). Suggestions for improvement included better communications with the franchisor (17 percent) and franchise associations (10 percent). In fact, 24 percent of the responding franchisees currently belong to a franchise association, while 69 percent of them meet informally with other franchisees to discuss mutual areas of concern. A separate paper on the subject of franchise associations is available from the author.

Problems cited by franchisors included shortage of capital and the general economic climate (61 percent of respondents). Problems experienced by franchisors with franchisees include a shortage of suitable applicants (44 percent of franchisors), a shortage of suitable locations (reported by 36 percent), and difficulties with maintaining standards, with fees, and with advertising policies. Most franchisors suggest, however, that most new franchisees readily adopt all suggestions and policies of the franchisor. However, once franchisees become more experienced, it appears that they feel their success is due to their own efforts. They begin to question the fees being paid to the franchisor and the standards and policies of the franchisor.

The franchisors suggest that improved controls and better communications are the solution in such situations. Other suggestions included lower interest rates, improving the management skills of potential franchisees, and lower overall investment costs for franchises.

CONCLUSIONS AND RECOMMENDATIONS

Both franchisees and franchisors were quite cooperative in providing information for the survey, stating that an evaluation of franchising was long overdue. In general, both sides felt that franchising was very successful and had a bright future. However, both groups saw problems.

One issue raised by both groups was the increase in the number of illegitimate operators on the franchise scene—those who merely defraud new franchisees without providing anything for the money, thus creating a poor image of franchising in general. For this reason, both sides felt that certain government disclosure regulations were necessary to control the "con artists and frauds" operating today. At the same time, however, both franchisees and franchisors felt that good initial advice, especially from lawyers and existing franchisees, could protect prospective franchisees.[8]

Some franchisors have instituted advisory councils of franchisees as sounding boards for new ideas and to serve as an ideal communication medium with franchisees. In the United States, franchisee associations are quite common, but they have just emerged as a familiar concept in Canada.

American franchisees tend to have been in existence for at least a decade longer than those in Canada. They are thus more experienced in dealing with problems. For example, when a franchise comes up for renewal, the franchisor usually charges higher rates than the franchisee originally paid, and franchisees may resist paying the higher fees. Franchisees may feel they are receiving too little assistance from the franchisor to justify paying the old rates, much less the new, higher rates. The older American franchises have dealt with this problem, and many offer renewal at the old rates to overcome this problem.

Based on the results of this survey, it appears that prospective franchisees should discuss the franchise, especially the franchising agreement, with both existing franchisees and a lawyer experienced in franchise agreements before signing. Conversations with a banker experienced in franchising may also help to smooth the way for financing the franchise. Many franchisors can recommend a particular bank, and the major banks now have franchise financing specialists who are familiar with franchise terms and particular franchises. In addition, both franchisors and franchisees suggest that prospective franchisees should compare similar franchises before signing an agreement.

Existing franchises cite certain problems in dealing with franchisors. These are often handled much more easily through a franchise association, where the franchisee is dealing from a position of strength, with the support of other franchisees with a similar problem. Franchise associations are seen as a way to protect franchisees from abuses. In fact, most franchisors are beginning to favor franchisee associations of various kinds, from advisory councils to compulsory membership associations for all their franchisees. A minority of franchisors treat these associations as "franchise unions," but most believe they are an ideal self-regulatory mechanism. When these associations bring problems to the attention of franchisors, they know it is a problem with more than one or two rebellious franchisees, and are usually willing to discuss the problem with association members.

Franchisors can also benefit from franchisee associations, which often serve as an advisory council. For example, many franchisee associations have handled the problem of new product introductions by having a sample of franchises hold a trial introduction or market test of the product. Many franchisee associations have suggested that the franchisor conduct such test markets in company-owned stores.

In conclusion, the future for franchising in North America looks bright, as new concepts continue to be introduced in a franchise format, and new ways of administering franchises are developed. Studies such as this one, which reveal the problems with franchising for both owners and franchisees, enable both sides to take appropriate actions to improve franchise operations. ▲

NOTES

1. *Franchise Annual* (St. Catherines, Ontario: Info Press, Inc., 1985).
2. *Franchising—An Information Source* (Drie: Government of Canada, 1984).
3. R. N. Knight. "The Independence of the Franchise Entrepreneur," *Journal of Small Business Management* (April, 1984).
4. P. Berlinski and S. Pavlista. "Franchise Entrepreneurs," *Restaurant Business* (October, 1976).
5. F. Zaid. "Franchising in Canada: Considerations," (Toronto: Osler, Hoskin, and Harcourt, 1980).
6. R. M. Knight. "The Role of Franchise Associations," *Canadian Journal of Administrative Sciences* (Toronto, June 1986).
7. *Franchise Annual,* 1982.
8. Lowell E. Stockstill. "Multilevel Franchise or Pyramid Scheme?" *Journal of Small Business Management* (October 1985), pp. 54–58.

PERSONNEL PRACTICES IN SMALLER FIRMS: A SURVEY AND RECOMMENDATIONS

Glenn M. McEvoy

An interview survey of 54 businesses with between 25 and 250 employees was carried out in an effort to discover the strengths and weaknesses of current personnel practices in smaller firms. Most firms seemed to do reasonably well in terms of written personnel policies, providing praise and recognition for employees, and in carrying out informal job analyses. Areas needing improvement were human resource planning, job descriptions, performance evaluation, motivation and satisfaction of employees, creative recruitment and selection methods, pension planning, and upgrading the overall knowledge about personnel by those responsible for the human resource function. Recommendations for cost effective ways of addressing these shortcomings are made.

INTRODUCTION

Recently, there has been a surge of interest in the personnel management function as it relates to smaller businesses. This interest comes both from the personnel field and the small business community, as demonstrated by recent journals devoting entire issues to the topic [13] [14]. In part, this interest may be accounted for by the new vigor that the personnel field in general has been experiencing due to rising employee concern for "quality of work life" and increasing legal constraints and directions from various governmental agencies. However, a more significant reason for this surge of interest may be that it complements and parallels the renewed attention to small businesses and the reasons for their successes and failures. The startling statistics regarding the high incidence of small business failures have appeared with dogged regularity in the popular press. Surveys into the reasons for these failures invariably discover that personnel-related problems are near the top of the list. A recent Roper Organization poll of small businesses revealed their number one problem to be "finding competent workers then motivating them to perform" (cited in [17]).

There is, therefore, little doubt that the effective management of human resources is a key element in the success of smaller businesses. Most articles written on this topic are designed to give advice to the small business practitioner or student on "how to do it better." Yet there is a notable absence of articles describing "how it is currently being done." Surely,

Reprinted with the permission of the *American Journal of Small Business* (Vol. VIII, No. 2, Fall 1983).

before one makes recommendations to small business people on how to improve the personnel function, one ought to have some notion of the strengths and weaknesses of current practice in the field. The survey research reported in this paper provides a start in this direction.

METHODOLOGY

All of the 141 businesses with between 25 and 250 employees within a single zip code near a major metropolitan area in the Midwest were asked if they would be willing to submit to an interview to survey their current personnel practices. Firms agreeing to participate numbered 54 (a 38% response rate). Thirty-eight percent of the participating firms had 101–250 employees while 62% employed 25–100. The average size was 83 employees. One-third of the firms were unionized. Most (78%) of the participating firms were either in retail, construction, or manufacturing, with minor representation from wholesale, restaurant, financial, and automobile sectors. Data were gathered utilizing a 36-item questionnaire that was filled out by an interviewer during a 30 minute interview with the person responsible for the personnel management function at each firm.

RESULTS AND RECOMMENDATIONS

The results of this survey are reported under headings pertaining to the various functions of human resource management. Recommendations for improvement are made where appropriate. These recommendations are made with the limited financial and human resources of small businesses in mind.

Human Resource Policies and Planning

Organizationally, 37% of the firms sampled had separate personnel departments. The average size of these departments was four people, but the most frequent size was one. Firms indicated that they had added separate personnel departments to their organization structure when their size reached an average of 86 employees. For those firms without a separate personnel department, the most common position to have the personnel responsibilities rest with was the "office manager."

A surprisingly large 77% of all firms maintained written personnel policies in the areas of wages, benefits, promotions, layoffs, training, safety, etc., though the areas of coverage varied significantly from firm to firm. It is the author's opinion that any firm with greater than 25 employees needs to have written personnel policies to protect itself in this emotionally charged and increasingly litigious arena. A simple set of personnel policies is not difficult to write, and guidelines are available in various sources [4] [15].

Over one-third of all respondents did not maintain written job descriptions for most jobs. While this is a serious and easily rectified omission, the impact of the lack of job descriptions seemed to be ameliorated by the fact that over half of those firms not having job descriptions indicated that they did perform a job analysis before recruiting new employees. This would be a minimum requirement for meeting Equal Employment Opportunity (EEO) legislation. Very little advanced planning was done for recruitment or promotion of employees. Seventy-three percent of all firms planned less than a month in advance for recruitment, and 58% planned less than a month in advance for promotion.

Persons responsible for the personnel function kept their knowledge current in the field by reading primarily general publications such as the *Wall Street Journal* or *Business Week*. Only about one-third read personnel journals or periodicals. This would seem to be a reasonably simple, inexpensive, and efficient way to improve the level of personnel management knowledge in smaller firms.

Performance Appraisal

It was interesting to find that fully 71% of these small firms reported having a formal performance evaluation system (the national average for all companies is 95% [5]), with evaluations occurring usually once a year. By far the most frequently cited technique of performance evaluation was the use of "objective measures of productivity." This is an interesting contrast to larger organizations where the tendency is to use trait rating scales because so few jobs have a measurable output directly under the control of the employee. Maybe this speaks to one of the strengths of smaller businesses—larger, less specialized jobs for employees from which flow identifiable, measurable outputs. The ability to measure performance objectively in smaller businesses may also help account for the fact that fully 88% of the firms felt that their performance evaluation process worked well— again in a significant contrast to larger firms where the satisfaction rate with the performance appraisal process is closer to 10% [2].

Two items from the questionnaire produced less encouraging responses related to performance appraisal. Forty-two percent of the firms surveyed indicated that performance review meetings were used simultaneously to provide feedback to improve performance (development) *and* to discuss compensation matters (evaluation). Research shows that when both of these items are discussed in the same meeting, compensation matters predominate in the minds of the employees to such an extent that little effort is made to concentrate on the developmental aspect of the performance review [10]. Clearly, there is a need for small business managers to make sure the evaluative and developmental aspects of performance appraisal reviews are handled separately.

The second interesting finding from the survey indicative of a need for some attention was that not a single firm utilized the critical incidents method [3, pp. 85–86] of performance evaluation. This non-quantitative technique, involving the supervisor's keeping a written record of behaviors indicative of clearly superior or clearly substandard performance ("critical incidents"), is ideal for small businesses with few employees in similar jobs. In situations where objective measures of performance are not available and where the costs of developing unique appraisal forms are prohibitive, the critical incidents technique is probably the best alternative (it certainly is a superb tool for satisfying the developmental needs of the performance appraisal process). Furthermore, critical incidents recorded over time can form the basis for the development of unique performance rating instruments (e.g., Behaviorally Anchored Rating Scales [3, pp. 91–93]) should the number of people performing similar jobs increase enough to warrant such development at some future time.

Recruitment, Selection, and Training

Small firms rely heavily on local newspaper advertising and walk-ins in the recruitment of new employees. These two accounted for 63% of the most frequently used methods for filling job openings. Much less use was made of employment agencies, personal contacts, professional associations, or high schools and colleges. Recalling the Roper poll cited earlier where "finding competent workers" was a major problem [17, p. 1], one cannot help but speculate that much of this problem is related to the lack of creativity in recruitment strategies. Walk-ins and those responding to newspaper ads may not be the most qualified or motivated group of applicants. Small firms should consider more use of the other methods mentioned above. An additional alternative with high promise may be to contact nearby high schools or colleges to see if they have "Co-operative Education" programs (most do) which place students in part-time or temporary full-time jobs while in school. During the student's Co-op Education placement, the firm gets work done at little or no cost and, more importantly, gets a trial run with a student who is a potential full-time employee after graduation.

Approaches to selection of employees were equally traditional. The application blank and interview accounted for 85% of the most frequently used techniques. Not surprisingly, 87% of the firms sampled had not really followed up to check the validity of their selection techniques by seeing if they were able to predict good from poor performers in advance. While small firms do not hire in large enough numbers to allow for formal validation studies, it would be an easy task to keep selection records and periodically review them to see which interviewers or which biographical data points (e.g., number of years of relevant experience, high school diploma, number of years on most recent job, etc.) seemed to be the best predictors of future job performance.

Interestingly, work samples and probation periods were the selection method of choice for only four firms. The advantages of these techniques are that they have high content validity (thus, they are likely to be acceptable to equal employment opportunity authorities) and they can be simple and inexpensive to use. Work samples, in general, are vastly underutilized. Designing typing tests for typists, repair jobs for mechanics, or simulated sales situations for salespeople is not a difficult or expensive task. And utilizing a probationary period may be the best approach to use when little relevant predictive data can be gathered prior to hiring. This would be the case when, for example, the firm wanted to hire someone who couldn't initially do the job but who they believed was trainable. The ability to use this approach is, of course, dependent upon having good performance evaluation techniques because the decision to retain or separate at the end of the probationary period would have to be based on performance data. As was reported earlier, the small business people sampled did not seem to see the availability of such performance data as a problem. The bigger issue may be whether small business managers are capable (i.e., have the skills and can devote the time) of doing the on-the-job training (OJT) required to use probationary periods.

OJT was the clear training technique of choice cited by those firms sampled (84%). Only a very small number of firms had formalized training programs of their own or utilized those of trade associations, colleges and universities, or other outside groups. Recalling once again the words of the Roper poll cited earlier—that the biggest problem for small business is "finding competent workers then motivating them to perform" [17, p. 1]—one cannot help but wonder how many firms experiencing employee performance problems are incorrectly assuming that these are motivation problems when, in fact, they are training shortcomings.

Motivation and Satisfaction

Employee satisfaction was not measured directly, but 70% of the respondents believed that their work force was highly satisfied. Unfortunately, the turnover statistics provided did not seem to support this belief. Respondents said that, on the average, the percentage of employees remaining with the firm for one, two, and five years was 63%, 47%, and 38% respectively. These figures indicate a turnover rate in the first two years (37% and 53%) that is significantly higher than the national average of 23% per year [16, p. 119]. To the extent that turnover is an expression of job dissatisfaction—and there is good reason to believe that it is—these figures lead one to think that employee satisfaction is not as high as the respondents indicated. On the bright side, however, having 38% of employees last longer than 5 years may indicate that at least some workers attracted to smaller businesses may be very satisfied with their jobs.

An interesting finding from the study was the heavy reliance on "extrinsics" as motivation techniques. The three most frequently used motivation strategies were reinforcement and recognition for a job well done (42%), pay raises (18%), and job security (15%). While there is reasonably strong evidence that reinforcement using either praise or money can result in higher job performance, there is little reason to believe that job security (or any other employee benefit) can be an effective motivator because the reward is not contingent on the employee's achieving high levels of performance [8].

While money was the second ranking motivation technique, the fact that respondents indicated that employee pay was directly related to productivity only 8% of the time leads one to wonder if it is not, in fact, under-utilized. The usual reasons for not using pay as a motivator are administrative complexity and inability to measure performance objectively. As indicated earlier, survey respondents said that objective measures of productivity were frequently used. If that is so, then it would seem that the opportunity for using pay as a motivator would be constrained only by the ability of the owner or manager to develop a simple pay incentive plan that is readily understood and easily administered. Variations of piece rate, commission, bonus, or profit-sharing plans (see, for example, [9]) deserve high consideration by small business owners and may go a long way toward alleviating the problem of poor motivation found in the Roper poll cited earlier.

The other side of the motivation question involves "intrinsics"—the use of the work itself or the design of the work—to provide motivation and/or satisfaction for employees. Challenging jobs and goal setting were mentioned as key motivation strategies by only 3 and 5 firms, respectively. These areas may provide the greatest opportunity for improving employee motivation at little or no cost to the employer. It would seem that the flexibility inherent in small businesses would lend itself readily to designing and modifying jobs in such a way as to provide a challenging work environment. Interested readers may want to pursue additional materials that discuss in detail the process of job redesign to enhance employee satisfaction and motivation [6].

The clearest oversight in the motivation area is not utilizing to a much greater extent the process of goal setting. While Management-by-Objectives (MBO) has been the subject of much criticism recently, there is no escaping the well-proven finding that employees with goals are more productive than employees *without* goals [12]. The clarification of expectations and the establishment of objectives for all employees is so basic to the process of management that one can hardly say a firm is being managed at all without clear emphasis on goals. Goal setting facilitates the performance evaluation process and is likely to pay for itself many times over in clarifying misunderstandings and job expectations early before they become problems at a later point in time.

Wages and Benefits

Not surprisingly, informality pervades the pay policies and structures of small firms. Only 28% of the firms indicated that they did any formal salary survey of the relevant labor market to assure that their pay policies were competitive. And only one-three firms indicated that they used any formal job evaluation system to assure that their pay structures were internally equitable. This area may become increasingly troublesome for small business as the issues of equal pay and comparable worth grow as concerns in the 1980s. All organizations will be under increasing pressure to insure that their pay policies are nondiscriminatory. A simple job evaluation system, either developed internally (see, for example, [7]) or obtained through a trade association, will be a minimum requirement for employers in this regard.

The types of benefits offered most frequently by small businesses centered around vacations, holidays, rest breaks, and life and health insurance. Pensions came further down the list. Contrary to national statistics [1], none of the survey firms indicated that they had discontinued their pension plans since the passage in 1974 of the Pension Reform Act (Employee Retirement Income Security Act) involving additional funding and reporting requirements. Interestingly, only 30% of the firms sampled were familiar with Simplified Employee Pension (SEP) plans authorized by the Revenue Act of 1978, and only 5% of the firms used them. This seems to be a significant oversight for many small businesses because a SEP plan is no more difficult to set up than an Individual

Retirement Account (IRA)—it is, in fact, an IRA—and is simpler for a firm to administer than other retirement plans.

Seven of the 54 firms in the sample operated on a four-day work week basis. Eight offered flexible working hours ("flextime"). These two "benefits" probably deserve more attention from small business. For more firms, at least, these two non-traditional working hour formats might prove to be practical approaches to attracting and retaining a more qualified workforce.

Governmental Relations

Seventy-five percent of the firms said that their facilities had been inspected by a representative of the Occupational Safety and Health Administration (OSHA). Contrary to much that appears in the popular press, however, most firms felt that the OSHA inspector exhibited a high degree of professionalism and that they received fair treatment from OSHA.

A much smaller percentage (17%) of firms had had dealings with one or more equal employment opportunity (EEO) agencies. These agencies got slightly lower ratings on professionalism and fairness of treatment than OSHA, but still the sampled firms did not seem to be overly negative in their feelings toward the EEO agencies.

CONCLUSION

Some items in the survey were designed to assess how the interviewees felt about various personnel practices of their firms. For the most part, they expressed a very positive outlook on these practices. They felt that job interviews were handled professionally and that applicants were given realistic information about both the positive and negative aspects of the job for which they were applying. Respondents felt that their firms were careful in the evaluation of training needs and the monitoring of performance after an individual had been trained. They were generally positive about the level of motivation and satisfaction of their workforce, and, overall, fully 65% agreed with the statement that "our firm approaches personnel management in a systematic, planned, well thought-out manner."

While the survey produced a few results consistent with this upbeat conclusion, for the most part we must conclude that personnel practices in smaller firms need significant modernization and improvement. Small firms do not hire many people with personnel backgrounds, and those involved in personnel do not keep current with the most recent techniques in human resources management. While businesses will hire specialists in marketing, accounting, finance, and production very early in their life cycle, personnel continues to be overlooked until much later in the firm's existence. This seems to be a holdover from earlier times when personnel was so simple that "anyone could do it." That situation no longer exists today.

It has been suggested [11] that a good way for small firms to get the specialized knowledge they need in personnel without a large investment is to hire a consultant on a "permanent part-time" basis. Thus, for example, one day a week the consultant would function as the personnel manager for a given firm. It is important that this be a long-term relationship so that the individual involved can learn the specific problems of the firm he or she is operating and can be around to be accountable for the results of specific programs that are initiated.

This sort of arrangement would help the small firm keep its personnel practices current. The "permanent part-time" personnel manager could help the firm evaluate some of the specific ideas noted in this paper—development of job descriptions and written personnel policies, use of critical incidents in performance appraisal, Co-operative Education hiring, use of work samples and probation periods in selection, development of simple incentive pay schemes, redesign of jobs to make them more satisfying and to include clear statements of objectives, exploration of SEP and other benefit options—to see if they are feasible and advisable for that particular firm.

The message here is that an organization doesn't have to be large to benefit from the most current knowledge in human resource management. Some very creative approaches to personnel can be taken if the firm's management at least is aware of the possibilities. Employing a personnel specialist on a "permanent part-time" basis may be an economical way of increasing this awareness. ▲

REFERENCES

1. Chilton, Kenneth W. and Murray L. Weidenbaum. "Small-Business Performance in the Regulated Economy." Public Policy Discussion Series, National Federation of Independent Business, 1981.
2. Colby, John D. and Ronald L. Wallace. "Performance Appraisal: Help or Hinderance to Employee Productivity?" *The Personnel Administrator,* October, 1975, 37–39.
3. Cummings, L. L. and Donald P. Schwab. *Performance in Organizations: Determinants and Appraisal.* Glenview, Illinois: Scott, Foresman and Company, 1973.
4. Ellman, Edgar S. "How to Write a Personnel Manual." *INC.*, October, 1981, 69–72.
5. Gorlin, Harriet. "Personnel Practices: Recruitment, Placement, Training, Communication." The Conference Board, 1981.
6. Hackman, J. Richard and Greg R. Oldham. *Work Redesign.* Reading, Massachusetts: Addison-Wesley Publishing Company, 1980.
7. Henderson, Richard I. *Compensation Management.* Reston, Virginia: Reston Publishing Company, Inc., 1979.
8. Lawler, Edward E. *Motivation in Work Organizations.* Monterey, California: Brooks/Cole Publishing Company, 1973.
9. Lawler, Edward E. *Pay and Organization Development.* Reading, Massachusetts: Addison-Wesley Publishing Company, 1981.
10. Meyer, Herbert H., Emanuel Kay, and John R. P. French, Jr. "Split Roles in Performance Appraisal." *Harvard Business Review,* January–February, 1965, 123–129.
11. Miner, John B. "Personnel Strategies in the Small Business Organization." *Journal of Small Business Management,* July, 1973, 13–16.
12. Mitchell, Terence R. "Organizational Behavior." *Annual Review of Psychology,* 1979, 243–281.
13. "Personnel and Smaller Companies." *Personnel Administrator,* April, 1981.
14. "Personnel Problems." *Journal of Small Business Management,* July 1973.
15. Smith, Terry W. "Developing a Policy Manual." *Personnel Journal,* June, 1982, 446–449.
16. Walker, James W. *Human Resource Planning.* New York: McGraw-Hill Book Company, 1980.
17. *Wall Street Journal,* March 20, 1980, p. 1.

COST ACCOUNTING FOR THE SMALL BUSINESS

Richard F. DeMong and David B. Croll

Few companies see the need for a cost accounting system until their business has grown substantially in size of financial needs. By law, all businesses keep tax records of their revenues, expenses and payroll. Financial accounting is usually considered when demands are made for additional money. Banks generally require that financial statements be prepared before they will lend. These financial statements may or may not be audited. If the company issues stock and trades it across state lines, the SEC requires annually audited financial statements. In contrast to tax and financial accounting, cost accounting addresses itself exclusively to internal managerial needs of the business, and therefore it comes almost as an afterthought. These needs can be put off while the more pressing problems of starting and operating a business, meeting the legal requirements of the government, and providing new funds to the business are met.

Cost accounting systems are designed to aid the manager in the important tasks of planning and controlling the use of the company's assets whether they be in the form of inventory, equipment, labor or cash. Thus, within the cost accounting system we find budgets, actual or standard costs and break-even analysis.

Just because a business has not yet established a cost accounting system does not mean that it does not desperately need cost accounting. Its lack of a cost system may simply mean that no one externally is requiring it to provide cost data. It is only after having lacked the needed information to set prices, to decide when or if to enter a new variation of business or to control costs, that the business falters. It then becomes obvious that there was a desperate need for cost data years earlier. This need could manifest itself in the overextension of the business into losing enterprises as well as the inability of the business operation to function without the owner constantly present.

BENEFITS OF COST ACCOUNTING SYSTEMS

Cost accounting provides a number of benefits for the company that can afford the time that it takes to install a system. The primary benefit of a cost accounting system is controlled and reduced expenses. Costs can often be reduced by systematically reviewing them. A cost accounting system is designed to establish, then monitor review procedures to eliminate unnecessary expenses often caused by inattention and neglect.

Reprinted with the permission of the *American Journal of Small Business* (Vol. V, No. 4, Spring 1981).

A cost accounting system is dynamic rather than static. Cost relationships do not remain fixed. Sound decisions to purchase a truck and make unlimited mileage-no-charge deliveries may have been correct when fuel was cheap and very wrong now that fuel is expensive. Small purchases of supplies only as needed may well have been correct while the business was small but not correct now that it has grown. Acceptance of small jobs producing a thin profit may have been necessary when any profit was good but now may be sapping required resources that should be spent on higher profit items. These are examples of costs and cost decisions that could be easily monitored by cost accounting systems.

Capital expenditures, purchases of equipment or plant facilities should be made on a cost justified basis. Cost accounting systems develop the data necessary for a thorough cost benefit analysis. This can be done by measuring the labor and marginal savings produced by the installation of new equipment and by comparing that amount to the cost of the item. Without a systematic approach to capital expenditures, the major purchases of the business are often based more on whim than on intelligent business decisions.

Inventory costs can be controlled by keeping past as well as present records of the cost of inventory purchases as well as the costs of holding inventory. With this information, the manager can set inventory levels to best minimize the costs of purchases.

Cost accounting also benefits budgeting. In order to correctly budget, it is necessary to forecast future sales in such depth that a meaningful budget can be formed. This not only produces a good budget but should, by stressing planning and expected performance, free that owner/manager from day-to-day control so that he or she can leave for short periods of time. To an owner/manager who has never felt secure enough to take a vacation, this benefit in itself may justify installing a cost system.

DISADVANTAGES

The major disadvantage of a cost system is the total expense of the system in time and money. A cost system no matter how simple or complex requires that the owner/manager spend time on its output to warrant the time spent in gathering the data. All systems necessitate the defining of terms. Unless terms are fully understood, which is a time-consuming endeavor, the system soon starts producing information that is just not usable. The system has the added expense of data collection. The more complex the system, the greater the cost in time and money to keep it running.

Setting up the system is an additional cost. Any competent bookkeeper should be able to maintain a system but it will take someone with expertise to set it up, to determine the desired level of the system, and to train the bookkeeper. There is also the additional cost in both time and effort of assuring the employees that this is not just a system geared to find fault with their work; it is designed to enable the manager to efficiently and effectively operate the firm. Without a proper explanation of their purpose, control systems have in the past met with varying resistance from employees. Without cooperative employees to put the proper time and effort into the budget, there will not be an authentic budget from which comparisons can be made.

Given the benefits of the cost accounting system, the expenses are usually outweighed by the rewards of the system. This involvement of the owner-manager in this process should enhance his or her ability to effectively manage the firm. The budgets, standard costs and breakeven analyses enable the manager to make intelligent decisions based on the facts and not on perceived impressions of the company. Further, the cost accounting data enables the manager to base an intelligent plan on the facts of his company's current situation.

FEASIBILITY OF A COST SYSTEM FOR A MEDIUM OR SMALL BUSINESS SYSTEM

Is a cost system feasible for a medium or small size company? Definitely yes, but it should be proportionate to the needs of the company. Accounting systems can get so large that the business spends more time on data gathering than on using the data gathered. A well-designed accounting system should, then, collect just the necessary information.

A fairly simple system would merely categorize data so it could be arranged to give historic information on the product mix, past pricing and past job costs for control purposes. The data needed for product mix decisions are cost accumulated by product, revenues by product and common costs (overhead costs) matched with the cause of their expenditure. With this data, it is relatively easy to present the revenues and costs by product. Consequently, decisions about which products to emphasize and which to drop, what areas to spend time in and what areas to ignore become very easy to make. Since costs can be categorized by product, the owner/manager will be able to make correct pricing decisions once he determines which costs are variable and which are fixed. Even if the product is in a competitive market where others set the price, this collection of data by product should enable the owner/manager to determine if he should produce and sell that product at all.

With records of costs accumulated on past products, it should be easy to project labor, material and overhead costs for any new job. True, the estimates won't be exact but they should be close enough. If the new costs come in close to the projected costs, then little management time needs to be spent in this area. If, however, they are far off from projected costs, then they should be investigated. Perhaps, the projections were off. Perhaps, the costs are too high and more control of labor and material expenditure is in order. Which projection was incorrect and why can be ascertained by comparing the actual costs to the projected costs.

The nature of the work determines how costs are accumulated. There are two standard forms of cost accumulation: process and job order. If the nature of the work follows a series of individual jobs as it does in a job shop, then cost is accumulated by assigning a job number to each job and accumulating all costs under that number. If the nature of the work follows a single repetitive task or a series of mutually exclusive tasks, then costs are accumulated per unit by taking all costs and dividing them by the number of completed and partially completed units. Both methods take some planning. Once set in motion, they are simple to maintain.

Standard cost is a control tool that takes considerable time and money to set up and therefore may be feasible only for the medium and large firms. Standard cost necessitates setting standards for labor, material and overhead for all items produced. Then the costs of production at various intervals are compared to the authorized standards. Since labor traditionally is reviewed daily or weekly and material and overhead is reviewed weekly or monthly, a standard cost system gives early warning of any variance from the budget. For the medium to large business with thin profit margins, a standard cost system is essential in order to give early warning of rising costs.

Budgeting is a cost accounting tool that can vary greatly in the degree of its implementation. Simple budgeting should be done by all businesses. Time should be taken in advance of expenditure to decide on what and where to spend cash. Depending on the needs of the business, this budgeting can become quite sophisticated allowing most major cash decisions to be made well in advance of the pressure period when the item is needed and clear thinking is hard. The size and sophistication of the budget system should grow with the needs of the business.

HOW DO YOU SET UP A COST SYSTEM?

Depending on the needs of the business, there are three general groups of firms that provide, for a fee, assistance in establishing a cost system. For a small, simple system, the accountant/CPA that already assists the business can do an adequate job. He or she normally is the individual that first sees the need for more financial information, and he or she already understands the particular business and can set up a simple cost accumulation and review system. The disadvantage of using your CPA is that CPA's are trained in financial accounting, not cost accounting. Although he or she may know one particular business in an industry, he or she probably does not know many businesses in the same industry and has seldom, if ever, established any type of cost system.

If a slightly more complex cost system is needed, many industry associations make arrangements with consultants to provide a cost system that fits their specific industry. Such an arrangement does not cost nearly as much as a personalized cost system; it also allows the system to meet the needs of a variety of problems including those unanticipated by a specific business, and it provides for a sharing of solutions to problems faced by an individual company. The disadvantage of an association shared consultant is that this consultant narrowly specializes in one industry.

If you need a complex cost system, a group of national consulting firms can provide this expertise. The advantage, of course, with a large national firm is that it will bring to any individual business the broad industrial expertise that it has acquired. The disadvantages are that the firm may never have worked in this particular industry, and its charges tend to be quite high.

A SIMPLE BUDGETING EXAMPLE

To illustrate a simple budgeting system, a hypothetical company named Meriwether Company will be analyzed. The Meriwether Company needs a cash budget to determine if it must borrow money in the near future and a pro forma income statement and balance sheet to determine if it will make a profit and be able to stay in business. As of December 30, 1979 certain information is known by Meriwether:

Current assets & cash	$ 12,000
Inventory	63,000
Accounts receivable	10,000
Fixed Assets—Net	100,000
Current liabilities	————

Past sales for the month of December 1979 were $40,000, a forecast of the next four months sales are as follows:

January 1980	48,000
February	60,000
March	80,000
April	36,000

Past history of the Meriwether Company shows that 75% of all sales are for cash and 25% are on accounts receivable and, traditionally, are all collected within 30 days of sale. Gross profits average 30% of sales and all purchase discounts are treated on the income statement as "other income" by this company.

Salaries average 15% of sales, rent 5%, all other expenses, excluding depreciation, 48%. Depreciation expense is $750 per month. All expenses are paid in the month incurred.

There is a basic inventory of $30,000. The policy of the company is to purchase, each month, additional inventory in the amount necessary to provide for the following month's sales. Purchase terms are 2% discount if paid within the first 10 days; otherwise, the total bill must be paid by the 30th day (2/10 net 30). All discounts are taken and purchases are paid for in the month of purchase. Two capital expenditures are planned: $600 in January and $400 in February. The company feels it must always keep $8,000 cash on hand. If it must borrow, it feels it must do so at the beginning of the month in $1,000 dollar amounts and pay off as much as it can at the end of the month since interest is 12%.

Schedule A. Estimated Monthly Dollar Receipts.

Item	Dec.	Jan.	Feb.	March
Total Sales	40,000	48,000	60,000	80,000
Credit Sales	10,000	12,000	15,000	20,000
	30,000	36,000	45,000	60,000
Receipts:				
Cash Sale		36,000	45,000	60,000
Collection on Accts. Rec.		10,000	12,000	15,000
Total		46,000	57,000	75,000

The example is designed to determine, in advance, the balance sheet, income statement and the cash flow including short-term cash needs for the next three months. With this advanced knowledge, favorable loan arrangements can be established with a local bank. In addition, the owner/manager will be able to project the firm's profitability, its financial position, and expected cash flows over the upcoming period.

To determine the firm's cash flow and profitability, the owner first estimates the monthly dollar receipts as Schedule A illustrates. This is done by estimating the firm's sales and the speed with which the customers have in the past paid their bills, adjusted for any change in credit policy. For Meriwether, 25% of the dollar amount is paid in the month after the sale; the rest is paid in cash. Thus, the January cash receipts include 75% of the estimated January sales volume of $48,000 or $36,000 in cash plus 25% of December's sales of $40,000 or $10,000 in cash for a total of $46,000 cash receipts in January. This procedure is followed for each of the upcoming months.

A similar methodological approach is taken in Schedules B and C to estimate the cash disbursements. These are totaled in Schedule D and added to the cash receipts in Schedule E.

Given the company's policy of keeping $8,000 on hand for emergencies even if the firm has to borrow, Schedule F identifies the amounts that must be borrowed, the time period that the loan will be outstanding, and the months that the loan can be repaid. Meriwether will have to borrow $4,000 in January and $12,000 in February. The firm will easily be able to repay the loans in March and will have cash beyond their immediate needs. These funds can be put in a savings account, a money market fund or Treasury bills to return interest until they are needed. The need for cash can be determined by expanding the cash flows to 12 months, thus ascertaining what motivators are needed on the short-term investments.

The projected or pro forma financial statement can be analyzed to determine the future health of the Company. Again, this information is extremely helpful in convincing the banker that you are a good risk and that you will have the resources available to repay the loan.

Schedule B. Estimated Monthly Cash Disbursements of Purchases.

Item	Jan.	Feb.	March	Total
Purchases[1]	42,000	56,000	25,200	123,200
Less 2% Cash Discount	840	1,120	504	2,464
Disbursements	41,160	54,880	24,696	120,736

[1] 70% of Next Months Sales.

Schedule C. Estimated Monthly Cash Disbursements for Operating Expenses.

Item	Jan.	Feb.	March	Total
Salaries	7,200	9,000	12,000	28,200
Rent	2,400	3,000	4,000	9,400
Other Expenses	1,920	2,400	3,200	7,520
Total	11,520	14,400	19,200	45,120

Schedule D. Estimated Total Monthly Disbursements.

Item	Jan.	Feb.	March	Total
Purchases	41,160	54,880	24,696	120,736
Operating Expenses	11,520	14,400	19,200	45,120
Fixtures	600	400	—	1,000
Total	53,280	69,680	43,896	166,856

Schedule E. Estimated Cash Receipts and Disbursements.

Item	Jan.	Feb.	March	Total
Receipts	46,000	57,000	75,000	178,000
Disbursements	53,280	69,680	43,896	166,856
Net Cash Increase			31,104	11,144
Net Cash Decrease	7,280	12,680		

Schedule F. Financing Required by.

Item	Jan.	Feb.	March	Total
Operating Cash	12,000	8,720	8,040	12,000
Net Cash Increase			31,104	11,144
Net Cash Decrease	7,280	12,680		
Cash Position Before Financing	4,720	(3,960)	39,144	23,144
Financing Required	4,000	12,000		16,000
Interest Expense			360	360
Financing Retired			16,000	16,000
Closing Balance	8,720	8,040	22,784	22,784

Interest Computation

$ 4,000 12% for 3 months =	120
$12,000 12% for 2 months =	240
Interest Expense	360

Meriwether Company

Pro forma Income Statement for the Quarter Ending March 31, 1980

Sales		$188,000
Cost of Goods Sold		131,600
Gross Margin		$ 56,400
Selling and Administrative Expense		
Sales and Wages (Sch. C)	$28,200	
Rent (Sch. C)	9,400	
Other Expenses (Sch. C)	7,520	
Depreciation (750 × 3)	2,250	$ 47,370
Net Operating Income		$ 9,030
Deduct Interest Expense		360
		$ 8,670
Purchase Discounts		2,464
Net Profit		$ 11,134

Meriwether Company

Pro forma Balance Sheet
March 31, 1980

Assets		
Cash	$22,784	
Accounts Receivable	20,000	
Inventory	55,200	
Fixtures	1,000	
Other	97,750	$196,734
Liabilities and Stockholders Equity		
Liabilities	$ —	
Equity	196,734	$196,734

CONCLUSIONS

Although most small businesses start without a cost accounting system, its usefulness becomes quickly apparent to the owner/managers. A well-designed cost accounting system with its budgets, standard costs and break-even analyses will enable managers to make better decisions. A cost accounting system may also be required for certain government contracts.

All firms within the same industry will not require the same things from a cost accounting system. The larger firms will need a sophisticated system to enable them to make frequent decisions on the prices and costs of their products. A smaller firm may only need a basic budget and some standard cost figures for their more infrequent pricing and cost decisions. In any case, all firms should have basic cost accounting systems with budgets and standard costs which can be used for planning and control. This or any system should be easy to use, understand, and maintain. In addition, it should be flexible and cost effective. ▲

References

Horngren, Charles T., *Cost Accounting: A Managerial Emphasis,* 4th edition. Englewood Cliffs, NJ: (Prentice-Hall, Inc.), 1977.

GOING PUBLIC: INFORMATION FOR SMALL BUSINESSES

James M. Johnson and Robert E. Miller

Much has been written about new corporate stock offerings over the past decade. However, most of the attention has focused upon investor issues such as rates of return,[1] hot and cold markets,[2] underwriter prestige,[3] and the like. But what of the business which wishes to raise capital in the new issues market? Such a business is more interested in knowing how a new issue can be sold, how much can be raised, and what (if any) options are available to maximize corporate objectives.

Accordingly, the purpose of this article is to examine new public equity offerings from the standpoint of the issuer. Methods, characteristics, and options related to public offerings are presented. The methods section describes the various forms of best efforts offerings and underwritten offerings. Characteristics of new offerings are summarized from a study of all equity issues sold in the U.S. from 1979 through 1982. Finally, discussions with investment bankers were conducted in order to present a description of how offering methods are matched to businesses.

METHODS OF GOING PUBLIC

A business may make an offering of common stock in several ways: the offering may be made by the business itself (direct) or via an investment banker; it may be public or private; and it may be made to new or existing shareholders. Until or unless a business evolves to the point that the original owners wish to sell all or part of their equity in a business, direct and private offerings are highly desirable. Direct private offerings permit the issuer to avoid considerable expense, information disclosure, and time delays.

However one of the major reasons for making a public offering is to satisfy a capital need which cannot be fulfilled by a private offering. To effect a private offering, a business must comply with state blue sky laws and meet the registration exemption criteria set forth by the Securities and Exchange Commission (SEC). If, for example, a business needs equity financing in excess of $1.5 million (the ceiling to qualify for an SEC Regulation A issue), or it cannot sell sufficient equity to a group of thirty-five or fewer "sophisticated investors" (a typical state blue sky restriction), it may be compelled to offer an issue to the public in one of several ways.

Reprinted with the permission of the *Journal of Small Business Management* (October 1985), pp. 38–44.

A business which offers its shares to the general public for the first time is making what is termed an "initial public offering," or IPO. IPOs tend to be marketed by one or more investment banking firms, since these firms have the required expertise, the channels of distribution to sell the product, the licensing to sell securities, and the customer base. The specific role of the investment banker, however, can be quite different from issue to issue.

Underwritten Offerings

The two basic ways by which investment bankers handle the sale of an IPO are on an underwritten or best efforts basis. If the investment banker handles an issue on an underwritten basis, the offering company quite literally sells the issue to the investment banker. Successful remarketing of the issue to the public (at a price which preserves the banker's profit, or spread) is the exclusive problem of the banker, which is referred to as underwriting risk. In an underwriting, the banker is acting as a principal for his or her own account, much as a wholesaler does who buys products from a manufacturer and then resells at retail, at what is hoped will be a favorable spread.

Best Efforts Offerings

In a best efforts offering, the investment banker does not buy the issue outright from the offering company, but rather obligates his firm to use due diligence in attempting to sell the shares of the offeror. A best efforts basis means that the investment banker is acting as an agent for the offeror, rather than as a principal. If the issue is not sold, however, the banker has no financial obligation to the offeror to purchase shares. Thus, the main distinction between underwriting and best efforts is that in the former case the offering company is by definition guaranteed a sale of its securities, while under best efforts, the underwriting risk shifts from the underwriter to the offeror.

There are three major types of best efforts offerings: straight best efforts, mini/maxi best efforts, and best efforts-all-or-none. The three types differ in the threshold number of shares which must be sold in order for the financing to be "successful," or upheld. In a straight best efforts offering, any and all shares sold remain sold—regardless of the number or the percentage of the available shares sold. The investment banker is entitled to earn a commission on all shares sold, and also may be entitled to recover certain expenses as well.

In a mini/maxi offering, a minimum and maximum number of shares are stipulated as available for sale during a specified period. In order for the sale to be successful, the specified minimum number of shares must be sold. During the sale period, proceeds from share sales are placed in an escrow account. If and when the minimum number of shares are sold, the sale is binding and the offeror receives the proceeds minus banker commissions and expenses. In the event that the minimum number of shares is not sold during the agreed upon period, the issue is "pulled," escrow funds are returned to investors, and the banker receives reimbursement for certain expenses only—no commissions are earned.

The best efforts-all-or-none type offering amounts to a mini/maxi issue in which the minimum number of shares necessary for a successful issue equals the maximum number of shares which may be sold. That is, all of the shares offered for sale must be sold.

CHARACTERISTICS OF INITIAL PUBLIC OFFERINGS

To develop a better understanding of the characteristics of IPOs, the authors compiled data on all pure equity offerings made in the United States during the years 1979 thorough 1982 (excluding Regulation A issues, which are not true public offerings). Table 1 offers a summary of specific IPO characteristics. For both best efforts and underwritten issues, the data have been broken down in several ways. First, average statistics are reported for each dimension (share price, number of shares offered, and total offering size) and for each group (best efforts and underwritten issues). Second, minimum and maximum values are given for price per share, total shares offered, and total size. Third, the data have been split between offerings at less than $1, and $1 or more. Finally, all 969 issues are aggregated at the bottom of the table.[4]

An examination of the data summarized in table 1 permits several noteworthy observations. It can be seen, for example, that offering prices of best efforts issues tend to be relatively low—the highest price offered in the period examined was $15; the average was a mere $1.45. When best efforts penny stocks (under $1) are compared with best efforts non-penny stocks, the offering price per share is found to be positively related to issue size, but negatively related to the number of shares offered. Thus, as the size of a financing grows, offering price tends to increase, while the number of shares offered tends to decrease. When the underlying data are analyzed, the same relationship holds.

Very few underwritten issues are offered at less than $1 per share—a mere 2 percent of all underwritings (see table 1). In addition, the average price offered ($8.74) is fully six times that of the average best efforts issue. Underwritten issues also exhibit the same price/share/offering size relationships as noted for best efforts issues: offering prices tend to be disproportionately higher for larger financings; total shares offered, therefore, are considerably lower.

Although penny stocks account for over half of all best efforts offerings, very few penny stocks are underwritten. Within each group (best efforts and underwritten issues), the total offering size of penny stock financings is substantially smaller than that of non-penny stock offerings. Best efforts penny stock financings are roughly half the size of non-penny stock best efforts financings, and underwritten penny stock offerings are about one-third the size of non-penny stock underwritten issues (in terms of total size of the financing). Thus, penny stock offerings are associated with relatively small financings.

When the total offering size of penny stocks is evaluated on the basis of best efforts vs. underwritten, it is seen that best efforts financings are about two-thirds the size of the underwritten penny stock issues. On the other hand, there is a much greater disparity between non-penny stock best efforts and non-penny underwritten issues: best efforts non-penny stock financings are only about forty percent of the total offering size of non-penny stock underwritten issues. This indicates that penny stock financings are relatively small in general, regardless of whether the issue is underwritten or sold best efforts.

Table 1. IPOs: 1979–1982.

Issue Type	Offering Price Per Share		All
	Less than $1	$1 or more	
Best Efforts			
Average Data			
Price per share	$ .18	$ 2.88	$ 1.45
Shares offered	18,368,236	2,026,185	10,653,693
Total offering size	$ 1,894,064	$ 3,759,081	$ 2,774,477
Number of issues	189	169	358
Minimums			
Price per share	$ .01	$ 1.00	
Shares offered	479,600	65,000	
Total offering size	$ 100,000	$ 360,000	
Maximums			
Price per share	$ .75	$ 15.00	
Shares offered	300,000,000	14,500,000	
Total offering size	$ 6,000,000	$58,500,000	
Underwritten			
Average Data			
Price per share	$ .38	$ 8.97	$ 8.74
Shares offered	11,754,881	1,139,014	1,417,007
Total offering size	$ 2,855,038	$ 9,169,329	$ 9,004,466
Number of issues	16	595	611
Minimums			
Price per share	$ .10	$ 1.00	
Shares offered	3,300,000	100,000	
Total offering size	$ 1,500,000	$ 750,000	
Maximums			
Price per share	$ .75	$ 40.00	
Shares offered	25,000,000	10,000,000	
Total offering size	$ 5,000,000	$ 120,174,195	
All Offerings			
Average Data			
Price per share			$ 6.05
Shares offered			4,829,529
Total offering size			$ 6,702,778
Number of issues			969

Overall, the data in table 1 reveal that the average underwritten issue raised $9 million, whereas the average best efforts issue raised only $2.8 million. In general, best efforts issues tend to be about one-third the size of underwritten offerings. In terms of total funds raised, the disparity between best efforts and underwritten issues is even greater. Underwritten issues raised $6.5 billion during the four-year period studied, whereas best efforts issues raised $1 billion; i.e., best efforts issues raised only 18 percent of the amount raised in underwritten issues. Best efforts issues tend to be priced quite low—$1.45 per share, compared to $8.74 per share for those underwritten. Best efforts issues also tend to offer a substantially greater number of shares than underwritten issues: an average of 10.7 million for the former, as compares to 1.4 million for the latter.

MATCHING THE OFFERING TYPE TO A BUSINESS

In theory, most businesses engaging in an IPO should prefer an underwritten offering over best efforts. An underwriting amounts to a securities sale by the offering company to an investment banker or bankers and thus insures that the financing will be successful in terms of both price per share and total financing secured. Remarketing the securities issue to the investing public becomes a challenge for the banker. Whether or not the issue is successfully resold, the underwriting risk is borne (and presumably compensated for in the spread) by the banker.

In a best efforts financing, however, the offeror is not guaranteed a successful sale. Best efforts IPOs effectively transfer underwriting risk from the banker to the offering business. Why, then, would any business prefer to engage in a best efforts financing? The answer is that none is likely to prefer best efforts, but there are two major reasons why the method is employed.

Perhaps the most important point to make with respect to IPO types is that the issuer has little discretion in the matter. Offering type—best efforts or underwritten—is generally dictated by the investment banking community. Whether a business has the ability to be underwritten in an IPO depends primarily upon two factors: marketability and size. The first factor, marketability, depends on the investment banker's perception as to the market's willingness to invest in the offering business. Whether a prospective offeror can "pass" the marketability "test" is determined by the financial strength of the issuer, its market power, growth potential, ability to protect a proprietary product or service, and whether it is in an "interesting" industry. Some of these factors are obvious; some are more subtle. In any event, even if a business passes the marketability test, this does not assure that it can be underwritten. The business must also meet the size indicative of the total offering size criterion: small issues are generally sold on a best efforts basis, whereas larger issues are generally underwritten.

At first glance, there appears to be no logical connection between the if-then relationship of size and offering type. Why would a high marketability business need to use best efforts financing if its needs are relatively modest—say, $2 million? The answer may be found by examining the structure of the investment banking industry.

Investment bankers may be grouped into two major categories: national and regional/local "houses."[5] National houses tend to market IPOs almost exclusively on an underwritten basis. Their philosophy is that if a business meets their marketability test they will buy (underwrite) it; if it does not, they would prefer not to handle the issue at all. If, however, an issue passes their marketability test but is judged too small, they will frequently refer the prospective issuer to a regional/local house.

If the offeror is dealing with a regional/local house, there is a high likelihood that the regional banker will propose to handle the issue on a best efforts basis. This will typically be the case, even for highly marketable offerors, due to the relatively modest capitalization of many regional houses. In essence, small high-quality issues tend to be sold on a best efforts basis due to the inability of many regional houses to finance an underwritten issue (referred to as capital impairment).

It is worth noting that of the two main criteria employed by national houses—marketability and size—the former is far more important. This is supported by the data in table 1, which indicate that national houses will handle smaller issues from time to time. Their willingness to underwrite smaller offerings, however, will depend largely upon the amount of financing the offeror is expected to need during the next several years. For example, if a high quality offeror needs to raise $2 million now and does not anticipate future financings, it will likely be referred to a regional house. However, if the $2 million is envisioned to be the first of several rounds of financing, a national house may well accommodate the issuer, with the expectation of future business.

Issuers which meet both marketability and size criteria, then, may be underwritten by a national investment house. If the issuer falls short on either dimension, it may be necessary either to deal with a regional house or to abandon the financing. If the issuer negotiates with a regional house, it must recognize the strong likelihood that the issue will be handled on a best efforts basis. The type of best efforts offering which will be made will depend upon the bargaining power of the issuer, which in turn depends upon its marketability. A highly marketable offeror should be able to have an issue handled on a best efforts all-or-none basis. Although there is no guarantee that the issue will be sold, the investment banker shows confidence in the marketability of the issue by tying the bank's compensation to a "sellout" in this type of a best efforts sale. Since bankers do not desire to expend effort without pay, an offer to sell an issue on an all-or-nothing basis is a de facto assurance of a successful sale. In short, an all-or-nothing, best efforts offering is a regional banker's equivalent to an underwriting by a national house.

If an offeror's marketability rating is respectable but not outstanding, a regional banker may offer to handle the issue on a mini/maxi basis. In this case the banker may have reservations about the possibility of selling the entire issue. If the offeror's perceived marketability is low, the banker may offer to sell what he or she can, or may not wish to handle the issue at all.

Thus, the type of IPO made by a business is not ordinarily its choice, but rather the result of an investment banker's assessment of the company's marketability, the offering size, and the potential for future business with the bank.

SUMMARY

Descriptions are given in this article of the types of IPOs a business may use to raise capital along with a statistical breakdown of IPOs made in the U.S. over a recent four-year period. In addition, based on conversations with investment bankers, a description of how businesses are matched with a specific offering type is presented.

Of the two major types of IPOs, underwritten issues tend to be considerably larger than best efforts issues, and are the preferred offering arrangements for issuers. However, issuers usually have little choice as to the type of IPO the bank will handle for them. Underwritten issues tend to be handled by national houses, whereas best efforts offerings tend to be handled by regional houses.

Marketability and size of the offering are the two main criteria applied by bankers which determine how an issue will be offered. Of the two criteria, marketability is by far the most important in determining whether an issue can be underwritten, or on what type of a best efforts basis it will be offered. Again, whether a business engages in an underwritten or best efforts offering is usually not a business choice, but the result of banker assessments of the company's marketability. ▲

NOTES

1. The landmark study of returns from investment in IPOs is attributable to Roger Ibbotson, "Price Performance of Common Stock New Issues," *Journal of Financial Economics* (1975), pp. 235–272. For a thorough review article regarding returns on IPO investments, the reader is referred to Brian Neuberger and Chris La Chapelle's article, "Unseasoned New Issue Price Performance on Three Tiers: 1975–1980," *Financial Management* (Autumn 1980), pp. 23–28.
2. See Roger Ibbotson and Jeffrey Jaffe, "'Hot Issue' Markets," *Journal of Finance* (September 1975), pp. 1027–1042.
3. The major work on underwriter prestige and underwriter hierarchies is that of Samuel Hayes, "Investment Banking: Power Structure in Flux," *Harvard Business Review* (March–April 1971), pp. 136–152. See also Neuberger and La Chapelle, "Unseasoned New Issue Price Performance."
4. In all cases shown in table 1, the total offering size does not equal price per share multiplied by total shares offered. This is as it should be, since each dimension (price per share, number of shares, and total offering size) is averaged separately.
5. See Hayes, "Investment Banking."

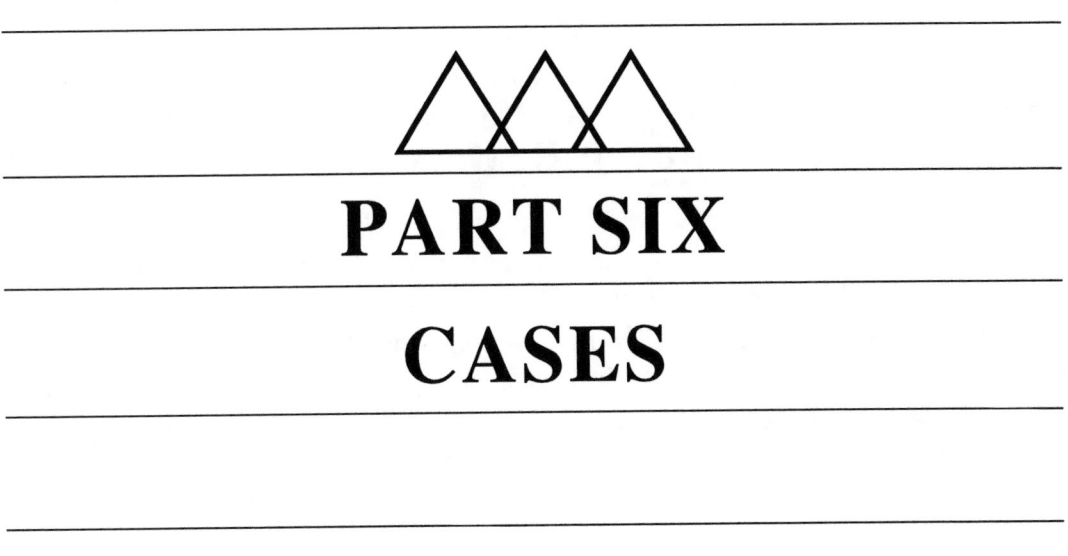

PART SIX

CASES

Steven B. Belkin

Wake up, Steven! It must be some mistake, but American Express is calling and says it's important. It's something about your credit rating.

His wife's voice roused Steven Belkin from a fitful sleep. A cascade of problems swept through his mind as Joan handed him the telephone:

This must be about my $15,000 overdue credit card bill. Joan hasn't realized I'm in quite so deep . . . she's going to be a bit shaken by this. I can see I'd better reassure her when I get off the phone . . . but to tell the truth, if I don't find investors soon, I'm really in trouble.

It was 11:30 the night of December 5, 1973. Steven Belkin had charged many of his expenses while trying to set up a new group travel business. Finding investors was proving much more difficult than he had anticipated, and he had had to let his bill slip for a couple of months. Steven was going to have to find a new financing strategy fast to keep The Travel Group from being a one-way ticket to disaster.

BACKGROUND

Steven Belkin, age 26, had lived in Grand Rapids, Michigan, as a youth. There he had his earliest business experiences. When he was 12, his grandfather had given him some salvaged automatic letter openers. Steven decided to set up a raffle with $1 tickets and the letter openers as the prize. He enjoyed selling the tickets and felt wonderful telling the purchasers who had won. Another time he sold light bulbs door-to-door. Taking the idea from a school fund-raising project, he made it a summer job for his own profit. Steven's parents were of modest means, and financial pressures were a source of family discord. Steven resolved that his own excellence and success would provide family happiness.

Several people advised Steven that the way to success was to couple engineering with business school. After graduating from high school where he had been captain of his basketball and tennis teams, Steven received an industrial engineering degree from Cornell. He concentrated on obtaining good grades at Cornell and also was active in student government and other school activities to improve his chances for admittance to graduate school. After graduation in 1969, Steven entered the M.B.A. program at Harvard. Steven recalled an interview he had set up:

I tried to figure out how best to improve my odds to get in. I came down and had an interview and talked to different people. I don't know if it helped—they say it doesn't, but I don't know. I always took the attitude to absolutely give everything you have. Then if you don't make it, at least you have given all you've got.

Steven saw life as a series of plateaus. At Cornell, grades had been important to reach the next level. Having reached business school, Steven now wanted to concentrate on learning about different kinds of business and on getting to know his classmates. Steven recalled:

I felt I needed to get there faster than the usual course. It wasn't okay for me to get there in the regular process, riding someone else's wave. I needed to get ready to jump on my own wave. In order to do that, to speed up the process, I needed to have more experience and contacts than my years. You get that extra knowledge from the experiences of others. And the families and friends of your classmates are a wealth of contacts.

Steven and another student obtained the resume concession at Harvard Business School, which not only helped with expenses but also gave him a chance to meet all members of his class.

Innovative Management

During the summer between the first and second years of the M.B.A. program, Steven decided he wanted to do consulting for small businesses. He asked friends and professors for leads, with little success. However, he did find that four graduating students were starting a new consulting company in that area which they would name Innovative Management (IM). Actually, one student had some possible business sources and had found a financial backer who would provide $50,000 for working capital. That student had asked the others to join for a salary and 5 percent portions of equity. Steven joined in the same fashion and the group quickly got underway. Steven described their start-up:

We would go to bankers and individual venture capitalists who had made loans or investments in companies that weren't doing as well as they had hoped. We offered to go in and analyze the situation and either suggest that they write off the situation or propose a plan to improve the company. Then we would actually go in and implement our suggestions.

The bankers and private investors we approached often didn't have the time or the ability to do this type of analysis. So they would go to the head of a company in trouble and point out that things weren't going very well, then suggest that the company employ us for the study as a condition of providing more funds. The companies would pay our fees which usually were $4,000 to $5,000.

Initially, we would approach a new source of projects and offer to do the first job at no cost. After we showed what we could do, they would usually give us additional assignments.

Our customers were companies with annual sales from $2 million to $10 million. Most were fairly new entities. Usually we could provide a needed control system, a marketing strategy—an entire business plan. Although the owners usually were under considerable pressure to let us in, they often were very stimulated by what we did. They knew they had problems and they didn't have the luxury of our education. After we gave our report to the financial backer, we also gave it to the company. Often we could provide our recommendation in only three or four days.

By the end of the summer, we were so successful that we began hiring additional business school graduates. I continued to manage several others during my second year of school.

In addition to running the resume service and continuing his consulting business, Steven did a survey of interest in small business among students in the top 10 business schools as his second year project.

My purpose was to show that there was a strong interest among these students in new ventures and starting your own company even though most schools were not teaching that. The survey confirmed this, and I used the data to write some articles that we used to publicize our consulting firm. For example, we had stories in the *Boston Globe* and the SBANE [Small Business Association of New England] paper.

People are always fascinated about people who do surveys and who have statistics. It makes you an instant expert to have a survey! It bought us new contacts and more credibility.

Looking back, Steven commented that he had done too much during the second year:

I was incredibly busy. I cut a lot of classes. But the income was tempting, and I was just ready to get the second year over with. But you are always going to have work, yet you only have the second year of business school once. I missed an awful lot. I didn't realize then that the cases contained so much practical experience—I felt they were "text booky." I just didn't absorb that they really reflected day-to-day problems.

During the last half of the second year, Steven explored the job market, interviewing primarily with consulting firms. Although none of the firms caught his fancy, Steven thought the process was worthwhile:

It was a terrific educational experience to be able to talk to these high caliber people in the different companies where they were trying to sell you and tell you all about their companies. But I guess I was a bit spoiled after already having my teeth in it, giving suggestions to people and seeing them implement them the next week. The big companies seemed a little academic—nothing, really, compared to what I was doing.

Steven remained with Innovative Management when he graduated in June 1971. A year later, however, the company was sold and Steven decided to leave. Steven explained:

We grew from 5 people to 22 in that first two years. Then one of the individual venture capitalists who had given us some work wanted to buy the company. The other four founders wanted to sell, but I thought that we would lose our objectivity as an affiliated consultant. I wasn't very happy about it, so I left the firm.

Group Touring Associates

Having decided to leave Innovative Management, Steven Belkin reviewed his situation. Financially, he had limited resources. Steven had been earning almost twice the $12,000 typical starting salary of his class. Joan, whom he had married just after graduation, worked as a teacher for a smaller salary. Steven had received $15,000 for his interest in the consulting company but also still owed several school loans that were not yet due for payment. Their net worth was about $10,000. Steven had no special ideas for starting a different business and was not attracted to seeking a job with a larger company. It appeared to him that he should continue small business consulting on his own.

The sale of IM took place at the end of the summer of 1972. Before Steven embarked on an independent course, however, he was approached by Frank Rodgers, the original investor in Innovative Management. Rodgers had been squeezed out of that investment when the company was sold. Rodgers said he would like Steven to work for him helping other companies in which Rodgers had investments and Steven agreed.

Steven found he had a special attraction for a group travel company that was one of Rodgers' first assignments. This company, Group Touring Associates (GTA), developed tours that were sold to various groups by mail using their membership lists. GTA had been started by Robert Goode in 1966 with the backing of Rodgers and a few other private investors. Rodgers had invested $200,000 to date; the others, another $200,000.

Sales had grown to $1.8 million over the past year, but GTA had yet to make a profit. Losses had been increasing from $50,000 four years ago to over $250,000 last year. Robert Goode had convinced his investors to continue their backing by pointing to the rising sales. He contended that the front-end marketing costs of mailings and of setting up the trips would cause him to show losses as he grew. On the other hand, the unearned customer deposits made prior to the trips provided much of the cash needed for the growing operation. Rodgers agreed that some losses might have been necessary as the company got its start, but now was alarmed by the continuing deficits. Rodgers felt that the deposit cash flow was disguising more fundamental problems and wanted Steven to help the situation.

After a brief analysis of the business, Steven felt GTA had excellent potential and that it could be built profitably with better management. He accepted an offer to join the company and became GTA's executive vice president:

> Looking back at my other consulting clients, there wasn't one business that I wanted to do. I had done one project for another tour operator, but they marketed through travel agents and student groups. The combination of group travel with direct mail made this very fascinating to me—this was the business for me. Okay, I needed solid experience in this one. This was a good opportunity, and I could earn a piece of the action.

A year later, Steven could point with pride to sales that had grown 50 percent and to a profit of over $150,000. Steven credited the turnaround to basic planning and well-managed execution:

> There was little organization when I came: no business plan, budgets, or anything like that. What I did was to clearly define our product and focus our operational and

selling efforts. All within a budget and a plan. Before, the salespeople would try to find what trips various groups might be thinking about and come back and try to put one together. I introduced the strategy of defining the trips with the greatest general demand, then putting the trips together, and having the salespeople fill them up.

This strategy let us buy better, put together better promotional material and better control our costs. I was very sensitive to the fact that we were in the direct mail business rather than just the group travel business. We had to provide better value for the travel dollar and promote it well by mail.

At the end of his first year as executive vice president, Steven reopened discussion about his future role in GTA with Robert Goode. He had initially accepted a salary of $22,000 with the understanding that they would renegotiate his position after Steven had proven himself. Now Steven felt he should receive a $30,000 salary and also be given 10 percent of the company. Robert would not agree. Steven recalled:

Robert and I went back and forth quite a bit. GTA was finally making money, and I felt I deserved part ownership. Robert wouldn't go over $25,000 in salary and wanted to wait another year for the equity.

As we reached an impasse, Frank Rodgers arranged several more meetings between us. However, now that the company was profitable, Goode no longer needed more equity, and Rodgers didn't have enough power to force Goode to agree to my demands. I think Robert also felt that he had run the company for six years and, now that I had gotten GTA over the hurdle, he wanted to be the boss again.

I tried very hard to reach an agreement; I wanted to stay. I felt that if I could be earning the $30,000 and have 10 percent of a profitable, growing company, I would be on my way to being successful. I was really running the show; I felt I was going to make money; I was fulfilling my entrepreneurial goals.

CONSIDERING AN INDEPENDENT COURSE

As Robert Goode's position hardened, Steven began to consider leaving GTA to start his own group travel packager. Looking at the industry structure made him feel this segment was a good opportunity. Potential air travelers could arrange pleasure trips directly on their own, choose ground packages offered by "tour wholesalers" such as American Express, or select complete air/ground packages such as those organized by GTA using chartered airlines. Traits of these choices are shown in Table 1.

Although the group air charter industry had only developed over the last 10 years after the introduction of jet air service, this mode of touring had already become a popular travel alternative. Steven felt the key attractions were lower cost, professional tour management and the comfort and peace of mind of the sponsoring organizations' endorsements.

The lower costs were the direct result of the use of chartered aircraft—the group tour organizer guaranteed to pay for all seats and took the risk of filling the flight. Many travelers were willing to accept the fixed schedules of charters to take advantage of the lower prices. The offer of complete tour packages with professional tour guides was convenient, espe-

Table 1. Comparison of Pleasure Travel Options.

	Direct Selection by Traveler	Use of "Tour Wholesaler"	Charter Tours
Air travel	Via scheduled airline	Via scheduled airline	Chartered airplane
Land arrangements	Individual plans and arranges directly with provider or through retail travel agents	Provided by tour wholesaler	Provided by group travel wholesaler
Flexibility	Complete	Travel timing flexible Only selected destinations and accommodations	Fixed departure and return schedules Only selected destinations and accommodations
Usual cost	Highest price	Sold as service; cost often same as direct	30 percent to 40 percent lower
Sold by	Individual carriers, hotels, etc.; retail travel agents	Retail travel agents	Group-sponsored direct mail, some retail travel agents
Other limitations			Must be member of "affinity group"

cially for travelers unfamiliar with the desired destination. Also, each traveler was a member of a group that sponsored the tour and could feel that his or her own representative would make sure the tour was a good trip and that the group would receive everything for which they had paid. This was particularly important in 1973 because there had been some recent publicity about tours that had been stranded or given inferior accommodations or service.

Steven saw these advantages as clear distinctions between group charter companies and tour wholesalers that used scheduled air carriers. The tour wholesalers also marketed primarily through retail travel agents whereas charter tours were normally sold using direct mail.

Looking at competition, Steven knew there were 10 major group tour operators in the United States. GTA ranked about seventh in that list. Where GTA provided tours for about 8,000 people per year, the largest U.S. operators moved about 50,000 customers yearly. As he viewed the market, he felt there was certainly room for one more:

In the United States, there were regulations that you had to belong to an organization to go on a group trip. These had been eliminated about six years ago in Europe. With that, some of the group tour operators did more business than some of the scheduled carriers. The largest European companies running group charters were moving over a million people per year each. These regulations were relaxing in the United States, so I felt there would be great opportunities.

Steven received encouragement from Alan Lewis, GTA's most productive salesman. During Steven's negotiations with Robert Goode, Steven had described his growing frustration to Lewis. When Steven mentioned that he would be happy for Alan to join him if he left, Alan suggested that Steven should go out on his own whether or not Goode agreed to his demands. Alan would like to join him and was anxious to get an ownership position himself.

Steven's discussions with Goode made no further progress, so Steven resigned and left in early September 1973. Alan Lewis also resigned, and the two of them began to develop The Travel Group, their own group travel business.

THE TRAVEL GROUP

Steven's idea for The Travel Group (TTG) was to duplicate the strategy that had been successful for Group Touring Associates. They would start with limited tour offerings to the most popular destinations, then expand as their reputation grew. They would use five sales representatives to call on groups across the United States to develop sponsors for direct mail promotions. They would carefully control their customer service and tour operations to minimize costs and gain customer satisfaction.

The tours they would offer were complex logistical tasks with large financial commitments. Running a tour meant chartering an entire plane, which would accommodate up to 200 passengers. The company would also have to commit to blocks of hotel rooms and meals and provide ground transportation and other assorted support services. Once the package was planned, promotional material had to be written, printed and distributed. Then inquiries had to be answered and reservations made.

To run the company, Steven would be president and major shareholder. He would be responsible for raising the capital they would need, for negotiating the trip arrangements, and for setting up the internal operations. Alan Lewis would be executive vice president. He would hire and manage the sales force, cover key clients personally and work with sponsoring groups to fill the tours. Steven described their deal:

> I had planned to give five key salespeople 5 percent of the company each. Alan convinced me to give him the entire 25 percent, and he would give away whatever was necessary to hire the others. Thus we became partners, but I would have a minimum of 51 percent ownership, Alan up to 25 percent, and the remainder would be for me or the investors. He ended up keeping all 25 percent after hiring four other excellent salespeople. Equity for our financial backers would come out of my share.

Steven and Alan immediately swung into action. Steven concentrated first on creating a business plan, while Alan began his search for salespeople and selling efforts for an initial tour he and Steven had outlined. By October 1, 1973, the business plan was finished, and Steven prepared to raise $250,000:

> Developing the plan was fairly straightforward. We knew the basic charter travel destinations and seasons. We planned to run one airplane a week in season during the

first year, two planes a week the second, and build each year. It was important to run "back to back" tours as much as possible so that the chartered plane could take one tour and return with the prior week's group. I added cost projections and made cash flow assumptions to give an overall financial plan.

The plan showed an accumulated deficit of $155,000 for the five months before our first tour. Then I expected profits and tour deposits to provide cash for growth. I felt I should raise $250,000 for a safe cushion to fund that deficit with room for unexpected costs, delays, or errors.

The business plan for The Travel Group is shown in Exhibit 1. Steven intended this document to be a simple, easy to follow business plan rather than a formal investment memorandum. He explained his reasoning:

> Most people make business plans so complicated that people understand nothing and get scared by them. If you repeat things two or three times, then they say, "Oh, yes. I understand that." They think they understand what they are investing in. If you keep giving them more and more inputs and ideas, they just can't absorb it.
>
> When people finish reading my verbal description, they understand what I have said. That does not mean they understand the business. But they have understood what I said, so therefore they think they understand the business.

Financing Strategy

Steven and Alan had direct experience in the operational tasks confronting them. Finding the needed financing was less familiar. However, several of Steven's earlier IM consulting assignments had involved raising money for smaller companies. Steven described IM's role:

> Some situations we investigated needed more equity along with the strategic and management changes we might suggest. If asked to implement our plan, we would agree to raise the money along with providing an executive vice president to bolster management and increase the company's credibility to investors. In return, we would receive part of the equity.
>
> We tried to keep this from being threatening to the president. Rather, we worked to convince the president that we'd be adding some new skills and helping to make the company valuable. Not like we were after the president's job.
>
> We'd approach individual venture capitalists for investments of $25,000 to $50,000 each. Our total needs were usually $100,000 to $200,000. The Rodgers family was very well connected, and we had developed other contacts in the course of our projects.
>
> Pricing was rather arbitrary. The company probably didn't have earnings, and we were selling the future. There was no scientific approach. We tried to show that the investors would double their money in a three-year period, then double it again to a value four times their original investment by the end of year five.
>
> Structurally, these investments sometimes ended up as a combination of debt and equity. This might be a loan with stock warrants. If all went well, they'd get most of their money back in a year or so and keep an equity ride with the warrants. The investors were very interested in not losing—not making mistakes, and less worried about how to get their equity out. That was less well structured—something down the road.

With this limited fund-raising experience, Steven developed a financing strategy. First, he assessed the situation from an investor's point of view. TTG had a large upside. Few start-ups could show the rapid sales growth Steven had projected. There were good margins that gave an excellent profit potential and unusually attractive cash flows. The management team had strong credentials. Steven's education was a plus, and both he and Alan had been successful running a similar company. They would also be using an experienced sales force. The group travel market in the United States had much less penetration than in Europe and should grow rapidly. Finally, there was little sophisticated competition in this industry, so their management skills would give them an extra advantage.

To demonstrate long-term potential, Steven could also show evidence that a group tour operator could be attractive as a public stock offering. One large U.S. tour operator had gone public in 1967 at a price of $10 per share. Within two years, the price had risen as high as $93 per share. The shares were currently trading for about $8, but this was primarily the result of that company's poor results in diversifying into restaurants, cruise ships and hotels.

Steven decided that this set of characteristics made TTG a good deal for institutional venture capital groups. He would attempt to raise the $250,000 in five units of $50,000. He hoped that two or three investors would subscribe to the entire total. Steven felt this was a better alternative than going to wealthy individual investors for smaller units.

> I thought the larger shots would be easier. I had the right background and credentials and a good business plan. I was sophisticated enough to present it to institutional investors. I felt this was a good package to offer, that they would buy me and would buy the business plan.

As insurance, Steven would also present the plan to a few individual investors, but his main thrust would be the institutional groups.

For leads, Steven turned to the "hit" list he had been developing since he had been in business school:

> I kept a notebook of people I met who might be good contacts. I'd put in notes on meetings and phone calls, addresses, correspondence. Some were filed in various institutional categories—others were just alphabetical.
>
> I put the people I would approach in priority by relationships. I wasn't going to ask people directly to invest. Rather, I would ask for their help: "What should I do to raise money?" I didn't want to put them on the defensive—once you ask them if they'd invest they have to protect themselves. This way, they could talk to me totally straight and really give me advice. If they were interested, then they would say they'd like to look at my plan further. Either way, they'd often recommend someone else to see.

Prospects, 5: Investors, 0

Steven had contacts with five well-known institutional venture capital companies. He approached each, describing his idea and asking advice. Out of these five, two were interested enough to ask to consider his plan. After being initially encouraged by this interest, Steven soon began to feel that none of these firms was likely to invest. He described the problem areas he encountered:

> First, I was confronted with the developing fuel crisis. There were headlines in the newspapers saying airlines were cancelling charter flights. Only needed scheduled flights would be flying. There I was telling people I was starting a new charter company just as TWA was grounding all of its charters!
>
> I had to explain that I could buy space on regular flights if necessary, but that the *charter airlines* would continue to run. The charter airlines were separate airlines encouraged by the government so that additional aircraft would be available in a national emergency. They only flew charters and were not cancelling their flights. I also argued that if flights were rationed, my old relationships with the airlines and the professionalism we would be bringing in would give us preference in charter assignments.
>
> I felt I was making some of the venture capital companies comfortable about the fuel problem, but I also found them reluctant to invest because there were no hard assets to "lend" against. They'd say, "There's nothing there! You aren't buying any machinery; all the money's going for working capital. There's no product line, no proprietary technology."
>
> I believe they were thinking that if it didn't work, with hard assets they could still minimize their losses somehow and get something out of it. I got the feeling they were just more liberal bankers, which was different from my earlier concept of venture capitalists.

Approaching Wealthy Individuals

Scheduling appointments and follow-up visits with the venture capital companies took most of October with some discussions continuing into November. At the same time, Steven also was calling on wealthy acquaintances in a more casual way:

> I'd say, "You know I'm raising money on Wall Street, but this might be something you'd be interested in. I'd like to get your input. Do you have any suggestions?" I'd mostly ask for advice and references to other venture capitalists or investment bankers.

As it became evident that the venture capital companies were not showing great enthusiasm, Steven more seriously pursued wealthy individuals:

> I primarily approached other successful business executives who either still ran their own businesses or had sold their businesses in the last few years. I thought that a $50,000 investment would be easy for them. It was a lot tougher than I thought.
>
> By November, I was letting everyone know I was trying to start this company. I was using every contact I could to get referrals to wealthy investors.

Out of all of his contacts, Steven developed two serious leads. One investor who was also a friend indicated he might provide $20,000. The other wanted Steven to come back when he had raised most of the remainder of the offering. Steven had expected wealthy individuals to be excited by the opportunity he saw in TTG. Now he found that wealthy individuals were going to be more difficult to attract as investors than he had anticipated.

Offer of a Bank Loan

Steven's discussions with the wealthy individual who knew him did lead to an unexpected offer of debt financing. Steven explained:

> I didn't think any part of my deal was bankable at all. I clearly felt that all equity money would be required. Yet the one wealthy individual who was my friend said he did think the idea had merit and that he would introduce me to his bank. He gave me a very strong personal endorsement and to my surprise, his banker said he would match every dollar of equity I raised with one dollar of debt!
>
> Once this bank opened my eyes, I approached several downtown banks to see what they would do. They wouldn't have any part of a loan—there were no assets to lend against.
>
> The bank willing to give me a credit line was located outside of the main metropolitan area. They were more aggressive to compete, but they also saw TTG as a good cash flow generator and needed the deposits.

The loan offer opened welcome new possibilities to Steven. Now if he could raise as little as $125,000 in equity, the total of $250,000 would be available to him. However, the use of the debt line would greatly increase his own exposure because the bank would be lending against his personal guarantee. He was not anxious to do this himself, and the idea was frightening to Joan:

> I was signing a $125,000 note, but my net worth was less than $10,000. Sure. I decided it didn't make any difference—if things went bad, I couldn't pay it anyway, so why worry about it? I would be more concerned about signing a $25,000 note because I conceivably could pay that.
>
> But they also required Joan to sign it, and this was very, very stressful for her. It was overwhelming and very upsetting. We talked about it, and I said it was the same way for me too. But if it's $125,000 or it's a million, it doesn't make any difference right now.

The note Steven and Joan Belkin signed was a contingent line of credit at 2 percent over the prime lending rate. The credit line would equal the amount of TTG's equity up to a maximum of $125,000. Steven could draw on the line at his discretion. However, both he and Joan were very anxious not to use this credit so that they would not actually incur the personal liability of their guarantee.

Growing Pressures

Signing the credit line agreement and the slow progress in raising the needed equity were not the only sources of the pressures Steven felt building. There was also the hectic pace of beginning TTG operations.

If TTG was to run its first tour during the late winter season, the package must be put together and ready for sale by the beginning of January. To do this, Steven and Alan had been continually working to develop their first trip and get their sales effort underway since October. By October 15, they had hired a secretary who had worked with them at GTA and set up operations in Steven's apartment. By the end of October, they had added another secretary and the first additional salesman. Steven described what it was like:

We just assumed we would get the money and that we had to make it work. So we had to get the sales.

Joan was teaching, so she went off to work at seven o'clock and came home about 3:30. She had been very, very helpful in putting together the business plan, but she's a very organized person and had her own work to do. When all the people were in the apartment, that started getting to her. Not only would there be no privacy and no quiet to plan her classes and grade papers, but sometimes we'd raid the refrigerator for lunch, and she'd find that what she had planned for supper had disappeared. We would often work past seven o'clock talking to the West Coast. She could go into a bedroom by herself, but in that small two bedroom apartment, it was more of a prison than a refuge.

On November 15, we rented a 10' by 20' office that had been the rental office in my apartment building so things were a bit better, but we still used my apartment. We were sharing desks and had no place to have meetings with potential backers or sales contacts. I always met people at the airport, said I was just leaving on a flight, then waited until they had gone before going back to our office.

Steve Belkin and Alan Lewis were funding the office expenses and salaries for the other employees from their own pockets. So far they had invested almost $10,000 in cash. In addition, each of them was charging every possible expense on their personal American Express credit cards. Since both of them were traveling around the United States and Europe to talk to group sales prospects, interview sales representative candidates, and set up the first tour, they had accumulated outstanding charges of about $15,000 each. They had both been heavy users of their credit cards before, which gave them high credit limits. They had made no payments since September and were starting to get overdue reminder letters, which emphasized they were about to lose their hard-earned credit.

As business paused for the Thanksgiving holiday, Steven wasn't quite sure how much he should be thankful. There was little progress finding equity investors, and Steven's bills and responsibilities grew.

He felt he had to provide others emotional support just when he was the least sure of what he might have done to his own position:

I was having to play Mr. Completely-in-Control: "Everything is great. We're going to get our money." The only one who was really starting to worry was Alan. He was the only one I really talked to. He hadn't had much exposure to raising money. I was starting to let him know I was getting nervous, and he didn't know how to read that. "What does it mean when Steve's nervous?"

I'd also gone far enough that everyone knew I was doing this. It's not like I could have a quiet failure. I'd gone to close friends and family for contacts—the ones I'd worked so hard to impress. I'd always been Mr. Successful: "Here's Steve. He went to Harvard, was captain of his tennis team and basketball team, and always got good grades. He had his own consulting firm." Now Mr. Successful was starting his own company, and Mr. Successful was in trouble.

WHAT NOW?

By the first week of December, Steven knew he had only a few weeks left before TTG would start to unravel. Finding money was the key:

> I felt I really had to switch gears here. I had to scrape it together. Initially I wanted to do it the business school way. Now, I had to become a street fighter. I might have to go out and beg, and it would be very difficult for me to go to people and say, "I need your help."
>
> I only had a little time. Should I put more emphasis on the venture capital route and really try to close one of those? Should I continue with the wealthy investors? Or should I go to friends and relatives and try to piece it together in fives and tens? Because I had so little time left, I really felt the main options I should consider were to find one venture capitalist for $250,000 or go to friends for small amounts.

In deciding on his last ditch strategy, Steven also contemplated whether he should change his offering to be more attractive. Pricing had never been explicitly discussed with the institutional venture firms. When talking to wealthy individuals, Steven was offering to sell 250,000 shares at $1 per share. He and Alan would be issued 750,000. What ways of repricing or restructuring the deal would help him to raise his equity fast?

"This is not exactly how I thought it would be," Steven thought to himself as he struggled to find a creative solution that December evening. "This is a good opportunity. Why haven't I been successful raising the money yet? I wonder if it was a mistake to resign so quickly? Well, here I am. Maybe I'll think of something tomorrow." It seemed that he had just drifted away, when the phone rang.

Exhibit 1. TTG Business Plan-October 1, 1973.

> [The entire narrative of the business plan is reproduced below. Title pages have been removed and the layout has been condensed. Only selected financial exhibits are included.]

I. The Introduction

The Travel Group is being formed to meet the tremendous need for low cost group travel. People now have more leisure time than ever before, and they are becoming aware that group vacations are available at prices almost everyone can afford. A week in Europe or the Caribbean for $199 per person is an affordable price for most people.

The group travel industry is less than 10 years old. The market penetration for this new industry has barely begun. There are unlimited groups available. Alumni organizations, professional associations, religious groups, fraternal organizations, employee associations, unions, corporations, women's clubs, etc. The Travel Group will be concentrating on "prime groups." These are organizations that are known to be extremely responsive to group travel (e.g., Shriners, medical associations, bar associations, teacher associations).

The Travel Group will provide "deluxe" group tours. The attitude of management is to send "prime groups" during "prime season." Hotel accommodations will be at deluxe hotels (e.g., Hilton, Sheraton, Hyatt) and air transportation will be via scheduled carriers (e.g., United, Braniff, American) when possible.

The Travel Group will be classified as a "back-to-back wholesaler" in the travel industry. The corporation will market its group tours to travel agents throughout the United States. This should comprise less than 10 percent of the sales during the first two years, but eventually should produce 25 percent of the sales volume.

The primary source of sales for The Travel Group will be through direct sales. The corporation will have their own sales force, and each salesman will be assigned a different territory.

During the first year of operations, The Travel Group projects the movement of only 6,861 passengers. The four salesmen that management will offer positions currently move more than 18,000 passengers per year. Thus, the first year projection of less than 7,000 passengers is quite conservative. Management has also allowed six months before the departure of the first flight. This will provide the sales force with more than sufficient time to sell the first back-to-back charters to Hawaii.

Sales of *$2,766,397* are projected during this first year and a profit of *$169,223*.

The second year of operations, 1975, should produce sales of $8,059,589 with a profit before tax of $832,636. In five years, 1978, The Travel Group should achieve a sales volume of $18,241,542 and a before tax profit of $2,150,121.

There is a tremendous positive cash flow in the group charter business. This allows for rapid expansion without additional financing. The potential of The Travel Group is open-ended, but management will expand cautiously.

II. The Industry

The back-to-back group charter business is in the early stages of growth. The industry is less than 10 years old. The management in the industry is quite unsophisticated. Financial and management controls are lacking. The market penetration of group charters has barely begun. Few companies have creative and organized marketing programs.

The main regulatory organization in the industry is the Civil Aeronautics Board (CAB). The trend in the past two years has been for more and more "low cost group travel." The CAB is oriented toward making travel available at a cost affordable for the mass public. This is very favorable for firms like The Travel Group, and, thus, governmental regulation should be beneficial to the company.

The United States is several years behind Europe in low cost vacations. In 1972 group vacation charters provided more revenue to the European airlines than the regularly scheduled flights.

In the United States, the same growth pattern is developing. In the past four years, charters on the North Atlantic have grown at the rate of 58 percent per year. In 1972 charter flights accounted for 30 percent of all passengers flown on the North Atlantic.

It is easy to understand this tremendous growth in the group charter business by simply looking at the money saved by a typical vacationer.

Assume an individual would like to travel to Hawaii for one week. He departs on a weekend, flies coach class and all accommodations are deluxe:

	Regular Rate	Group Charter Rate	Savings
Air fare	$510	$225	$285
Hotel	140	84	56
Dinners	56	40	16
Transfers	20	10	10
Tour operator's fee	0	113	−113
Total cost	$726	$472	+$254

Thus, an individual can save 35 percent, or $254, during a one week visit to Hawaii.

III. The Company

The Travel Group will be selling deluxe back-to-back group charters. *Back-to-back* means that, for a set period of time, groups will be sent *every* week to a particular destination. The aircraft, which takes one group to the destination, will pick up the group that is ending their vacation. This allows substantial savings on air fare. There is also tremendous buying power at the hotels because rooms are utilized every week.

These cost advantages will allow The Travel Group to sell vacations to destinations all over the world at savings of 35 percent or more (see Industry section).

The Travel Group will have salesmen assigned to different territories in certain sections of the country. These salesmen will call on prime traveling groups. They will be selling deluxe packages, principally during prime season. The "sell" is usually easy because the organization has nothing to lose and much to gain. The Travel Group will pay for the mailing of a brochure describing the vacation to all the members of the organization. For each reservation the group produces, the organization will be given about $15. Thus, if a group fills a 150-seat airplane, the organization will receive $2,250 (150 × $15) and will have provided vacations for its members at substantial savings.

Groups that will be approached by the sales force include Shriners, Masons, medical associations, bar associations, Elks, Moose, alumni associations, teacher associations, unions, employee groups and Knights of Columbus. There is an unlimited number of groups. Management will develop a mailing list of all the prime groups in the country to provide additional direction for the sales force.

The cash flow in the business is very favorable. Deposits from passengers are often received more than 90 days in advance. Final payments from passengers are due 45 days before departure. Payments to the airlines occur 30 days before departure, and hotel bills are not paid until 30 days after departure. Thus, the majority of receipts are in-house 45 days in advance of departure while disbursements occur 15 to 90 days after the initial receipts are in.

IV. The Competition

The group travel industry is in its early stages of growth. The industry is less than 10 years old, and there is only a limited number of group tour operators. Sophisticated and experienced management is scarce in the industry. The few back-to-back group travel companies, which do exist, have had substantial sales growth in the past three years. In the last eighteen months, there have been several new companies started that have been running back-to-back charters. One of these companies had sales of close to $8 million during its first year and before tax profits of over $500,000.

Competition in the industry has not developed to the point of pricing of the same packages. Sales growth is achieved by contacting the proper groups and then appropriately following up these leads.

Back-to-back operators always concentrate on a few destinations. With the vast number of destinations, there is limited competition among tour operators in providing packages to the same place. For instance, one of the new tour operators is just specializing in running trips to Greece, while another has programs just to the Orient.

Currently the East Coast is the only section of the country that has become familiar, to some extent, with group charters. Amazingly, 60 percent of all charter flights are out of New York. The South, Midwest and Central States have barely been touched.

Less than five back-to-back tour operators have a national sales force. The Travel Group's national sales force will be comprised of experienced travel salesmen who are currently working in different territories throughout the United States for other tour operators.

V. The Management

There are two key departments in the group charter business. One is sales, and the other is operations. By providing a well-organized business plan and by making equity available, The Travel Group has attracted some of the most qualified people in the industry.

Mr. Steven B. Belkin will be president. He will be responsible for directing the operations of the company. Mr. Belkin is thoroughly familiar with the day-to-day operations as well as the overall business planning of a back-to-back tour operator.

He is a graduate of Cornell University and Harvard Business School. He was one of five founders of Innovative Management, a small business consulting firm in the Boston area. Some of his consulting projects included the development and implementation of a marketing program for a ski charter travel firm, running a chain of sporting goods stores with sales of over $6 million, and serving as president of a film school and production company. When Mr. Belkin left and sold his interest in this consulting firm, it had grown to 22 full-time consultants.

For more than a year, Mr. Belkin has been devoting full time to a travel group charter firm which was in severe financial difficulties. With the development and implementation of a new business plan, creation of a national sales force and tighter management and financial controls, this firm has now been turned around. The year before Mr. Belkin's involvement, the firm had sales of approximately $1 million with a loss of over $250,000. This year the company has already reported a respectable profit for the first six months and has more than doubled the previous year's sales.

The sales force that is available is comprised of some of the best salesmen in the industry. Each man has thorough familiarity and personal contacts with the prime groups in the different sections of the country.

The sales team will have a minimum of six months before the first back to back charter will start. This should provide more than sufficient time to sell the program. During the first year of operations, the sales force needs to move only 6,861 passengers. This year the four salesmen being considered moved more than 18,000 passengers. Thus, the first year programs should be sold fairly easily, and this will allow the sales team to start concentrating on the second year programs well in advance.

VI. The Financials

[Some exhibits omitted.]

A. TRIP COST ANALYSIS
    Exhibit I   Hawaii
    Exhibit II   San Juan
    Exhibit III   Ad hoc
    Exhibit IV   Acapulco
    Exhibit V   Spain

B. PROFIT AND LOSS STATEMENTS 1974 and 1975
    Exhibit VI   Pro Forma Profit and Loss Statement (1974 and 1975)
    Exhibit VII   Plane and Passenger Projections (First Year 1974)
    Exhibit VIII   Monthly Pro Forma Profit and Loss Statement (First Year 1974)
    Exhibit IX   General and Administrative Expenses
    Exhibit X   Plane and Passenger Projections (Second Year 1975)
    Exhibit XI   Monthly Pro Forma Profit and Loss Statement (Second Year 1975)

C. CASH FLOW ANALYSIS
    Exhibit XII   Cash Flow Assumptions
    Exhibit XIII   Monthly Cash Flow Projections (First Year 1974)
    Exhibit XIV   Monthly Cash Flow Projections (Second Year 1975)

D. FIVE YEAR PROJECTIONS
    Exhibit XV   Pro Forma Profit and Loss Statements (1974–1978)

A great deal of time and effort has been devoted to the preparation of the following financial exhibits. Management will use them for budgeting as well as for projections.

The Trip Cost Analysis section clearly outlines the revenues and expenses associated with each trip on both a per passenger and per airplane basis. The air fare, hotel, meals, transfers, mailing, giveaways and load factor are all expenses that have been determined by historical statistics and actual experience.

The Profit and Loss Statements for the first two years have been prepared on a month-to-month basis. Management has determined the number of planes and passengers that can be accommodated each month to a particular destination. During the first year of operation, no passengers are projected to be moved until June. There is a good possibility that ad hoc programs will be sold before this time, so sales and profit could be greater than projected.

The Cash Flows have been prepared for the first two years on a month-to-month basis. The cash flow assumptions are very important, and management feels the assumptions made are conservative.

The five-year, pro-forma profit and loss statement illustrates the potential of this new and growing business. The Travel Group hopes to have sales of over $18 million within five years and profits before tax of over $2 million.

Exhibit I
Cost analysis per passenger Hawaii.

Selling Price	$429 + 10% =	$471.90
Direct Costs: Air	$225	
Hotel	84	
Meals	40	
Transfers	10	−359.00
Gross profit before acquisition costs		$112.90
Acquisition costs:		
Mailing costs 10¢ brochure		
+Nonprofit mailer		
(.50% return rate)	$20.00	
Giveaways ($20/reservation)	20.00	
Load factor (90%)	20.00	-60.00
Gross profit		$52.90

Hawaii Trip Analysis per Plane		
Total sales	= $471.90 X 135 passengers	= $63,706
Cost of sales	= $419.00 X 135 passengers	= $56,565
Total profit	= $ 52.90 X 135 passengers	= $ 7,141
Options: $10 net/passenger	= $1,350/plane	
(Options include additional profit on such items as bus tours, which are arranged through the charter operator.)		

Exhibit VI
The Travel Group, Inc.
Pro forma profit and loss statement (1974 and 1975).

	1974	1975
Sales	$2,766,397	$8,059,589
Cost of sales	2,345,594	6,870,953
Gross profit	$ 420,803	$1,188,636
General and administrative	251,580	356,000
Profit (before tax)	$ 169,223	$ 832,636
Earnings per share	$ .17	$ .83
Value/share (10 multiple)	$1.70	$8.33
Number of planes	44	128
Number of passengers	6,861	22,183

Exhibit VII.
The Travel Group, Inc.
Plane and passenger projections first year of operation (1974).

	Jan.	Feb.	March	April	May	June	July	Aug.	Sept.	Oct.	Nov.	Dec.	Total
Hawaii													
Passengers						750	600	750	600	600	750	600	4,650
Planes						5	4	5	4	4	5	4	31
San Juan													
Passengers											895	716	1,611
Planes											5	4	9
Ad Hoc													
Passengers						150	150	150	150				600
Planes						1	1	1	1				4
Total													
Passengers	0	0	0	0	0	900	750	900	750	600	1,645	1,316	6,861
Total Planes	0	0	0	0	0	6	5	6	5	4	10	8	44

Exhibit VIII.
The Travel Group, Inc.
Pro forma profit and loss statement first year of operation (1974).

	Jan.	Feb.	March	April	May	June	July	Aug.	Sept.	Oct.	Nov.	Dec.	Total
Sales													
Hawaii (150-seat plane) (31 planes) (4,650 passengers)						318,530	254,824	318,530	254,824	254,824	318,530	254,824	
Hawaii options (net)						7,500	6,000	7,500	6,000	6,000	7,500	6,000	
San Juan (179 seat plane) (9 planes) (1,611 passengers)											263,120	210,496	
San Juan options (net)											4,475	3,580	
Ad hoc programs (4 planes) (600 passengers)						65,835	65,835	65,835	65,835				
Total Sales 44 planes 6,861 passengers						391,865	326,659	391,865	326,659	260,824	593,625	474,900	2,766,397
Cost of Sales													
Hawaii						276,070	220,856	276,070	220,856	220,856	276,070	220,856	
San Juan											219,200	175,360	
Ad hoc programs						59,850	59,850	59,850	59,850				
Total Cost of Sales						335,920	280,706	335,920	280,706	220,856	495,270	396,216	2,345,594
General and administrative costs	15,000	15,000	18,000	18,000	22,716	22,716	22,716	22,716	22,716	24,000	24,000	24,000	251,580
Net profit (before tax)													$ 169,223

Exhibit XII
Cash flow assumptions.

A. Receipts

1. Deposits and final payments are only received 15 days before the date of the trip (very conservative since final payments are due 45 days before departure, and deposits are often received 90 days in advance).

2. Net Operational Tour Receipts are received the week of the trip.

B. Disbursements

1. Airlines are paid 30 days in advance.

2. Hotels are paid 30 days after the trip (requires letter of credit and cash deposits).

3. Meals and transfers are paid 30 days after the trip.

4. Acquisition costs are paid 30 days in advance.

5. Ad hoc program payments require $10,000 deposit 30 days before departure and the balance paid the week before departure.

6. General and administrative expenses are assumed to be paid/disbursements during the month they are expensed. (Conservative since telephone and travel and entertainment expenses are usually not disbursed until a minimum of 30 days after being expensed. These two expense categories are approximately 20% of G + A expenses.)

Exhibit XIII.
The Travel Group, Inc.
Cash flow projections first year of operation (1974).

	Jan.	Feb.	March	April	May	June	July	Aug.	Sept.	Oct.	Nov.	Dec.
Receipts												
Hawaii					159,265	286,677	286,677	286,677	254,824	286,677	286,677	254,824
Hawaii options (net)					7,500	7,500	6,000	7,500	6,000	6,000	7,500	6,000
San Juan										131,560	236,808	210,496
San Juan options (net)											4,475	3,580
Ad hoc programs					32,918	65,835	65,835	65,835	32,918			118,504
Total Receipts	—	—	—	—	192,183	360,012	358,512	360,012	293,742	424,237	535,460	593,404
Disbursements												
Hawaii					192,375	153,900	282,825	226,260	244,350	264,735	226,260	244,350
San Juan										100,000	80,000	199,200
Ad hoc					10,000	59,850	69,850	59,850	49,850			92,880
General + administrative	70,608	15,000	18,000	18,000	22,716	22,716	22,716	22,716	22,716	24,000	24,000	24,000
Total Disbursements	70,608	15,000	18,000	18,000	225,091	236,466	365,391	308,825	316,916	388,735	330,260	560,430
Monthly Cash Surplus (Deficit)	(70,608)	(15,000)	(18,000)	(18,000)	(32,908)	123,546	(6,879)	51,186	(23,174)	35,502	205,200	32,974
Beginning Cash Balance	—	(70,608)	(85,608)	(103,608)	(121,608)	(154,516)	(30,970)	(37,849)	13,337	(9,837)	25,665	230,865
Ending Cash Balance	(70,608)	(85,608)	(103,608)	(121,608)	(154,516)	(30,970)	(37,849)	13,337	(9,837)	25,665	230,865	263,839

Exhibit XIV.
The Travel Group, Inc.
Cash flow projections second year of operation (1975).

	Jan.	Feb.	March	April	May	June	July	Aug.	Sept.	Oct.	Nov.	Dec.
Receipts												
Hawaii	254,824	286,677	286,677	254,824	254,824	286,677	286,677	286,677	286,677	286,677	286,677	382,236
Hawaii options (net)	6,000	6,000	7,500	6,000	6,000	6,000	7,500	6,000	7,500	6,000	7,600	6,000
San Juan	210,496	236,808	236,808	157,872	52,624					105,248	210,496	315,744
San Juan options (net)	3,580	3,580	4,475	3,580	1,790						3,580	3,580
Acapulco	237,008	266,634	266,634	177,756	59,252					118,504	237,008	355,512
Acapulco options (net)	5,400	5,400	6,750	5,400	2,700						5,400	5,400
Spain					148,006	333,014	333,014	333,014	333,014	148,006		
Spain options (net)						4,500	5,625	4,500	5,625	4,500		
Total Receipts	717,308	805,099	808,844	605,432	525,196	630,191	632,816	630,191	632,816	668,935	750,661	1,068,472
Disbursements												
Hawaii	226,260	264,735	226,260	244,350	226,260	264,735	226,260	282,825	226,260	282,825	226,260	398,250
San Juan	175,360	195,360	175,360	159,200	95,360	47,680				80,000	80,000	255,360
Acapulco	92,880	234,900	211,680	194,940	118,800	59,400				92,880	92,880	304,560
Spain					174,600	218,250	252,900	316,125	252,900	97,875	78,300	
General and administrative	28,000	28,000	28,000	28,000	28,000	30,000	30,000	30,000	30,000	32,000	32,000	32,000
Total Disbursements	522,500	722,995	641,300	626,490	643,020	620,065	509,160	628,950	509,160	585,580	509,440	990,170
Monthly Cash Surplus/(Deficit)	194,808	82,104	167,544	(21,058)	(117,824)	10,126	123,656	1,241	123,656	83,355	241,221	78,302
Beginning Cash Balance	263,839	458,647	540,751	708,295	687,237	569,413	579,539	703,195	704,436	828,092	911,447	1,152,668
Ending Cash Balance	458,647	540,751	708,295	687,237	569,413	579,539	703,195	704,436	828,092	911,447	1,152,668	1,230,970

Exhibit XV
The Travel Group, Inc.
Pro forma profit and loss (1974–1978).

	1974	1975	1976	1977	1978
Sales	$2,766,397	$8,059,589	$12,029,894	$15,124,878	$18,241,542
Cost of sales	$2,345,594	$6,870,953	$10,305,490	$12,910,496	$15,481,421
Gross profit	420,803	1,188,636	1,724,404	2,214,382	2,760,121
General and administrative	251,580	356,000	480,000	540,000	610,000
Profit (before tax)	$ 169,223	$ 832,636	$ 1,244,404	$ 1,674,382	$ 2,150,121
Earnings per share	$.17	$.83	$1.24	$1.67	$2.15
Value/share (10 price/ earnings)	$1.70	$8.33	$12.44	$16.74	$21.50
Number of planes	44	128	192	240	288
Number of passengers	6,861	22,183	33,275	41,595	49,915

CASE 2
REAL Shlugar, Inc.

Encouraged by recent trends in the toy industry, combined with a positive response to her hand-made stuffed bunny rabbits, Karen Rothman felt that now was the time to act. Although technological toys were selling well pre-Christmas 1986, the plush, "back-to-the-basics" stuffed animals, such as Wrinkles and Pound Puppies, were experiencing trebling sales volume.

In her last year as an M.B.A. student at Concordia University, Karen realized her schedule would be restricted, and consequently wanted to allow sufficient time to prepare for operations. She hoped to have her product on the market for an original run Christmas '87 and, if successful, a second one for Easter '88.

BACKGROUND

Karen Rothman grew up in Montreal, the third of four children. Her parents bought a country house when she was four years old, before the birth of her younger sister:

> I vividly remember when my mother gave birth to my sister. When I visited them in the hospital, I noticed the most beautiful white fluffy bunny rabbit, with pink ears, a pink tail and pink eyes. My mother let me have her and I named her Sugar, which quickly became Shlugar. My mother also allowed us to pack our own bags for the country. The rare weekends I forgot to pack Shlugar were very traumatic. She was REAL to me. Being without Shlugar was akin to being without a member of my family.

While studying for her B.A. in psychology, Karen was required to do a research paper on infant-inanimate object attachment:

> Two things happened—All my feelings for Shlugar, were rekindled, and I *had* to fix her up. She was threadbare, and her foam stuffing had virtually disintegrated from years of washing and loving. I searched high and low to find the right material. Secondly, I came across a passage in *The Velveteen Rabbit* (See Exhibit 1).

Having grown up in a creative atmosphere, Karen fixed up the original Shlugar, and, using her as a pattern, sewed another one.

Karen got married and began her M.B.A. in 1984. At that time, her friends were getting married, and even having children. When her closest friend had a baby girl, she sewed her a Shlugar.

This case was prepared by Karen Rothman under the direction of Professor A. B. Ibrahim as a basis for class discussion rather than to illustrate either effective or ineffective handling of an administrative situation.

The response was phenomenal. I got pictures of the baby hugging the bunny, and reports that she wouldn't go anywhere without her. My friend kept telling me to go into business. Then my husband required knee surgery, and the blue Shlugar I sewed was a huge hit at the hospital. Not only did babies love them, but adults kept asking me to make Shlugars—for them! They are absolutely irresistible.

The opportunity to act on this creative outlet was presented to Karen in her Small Business and Entrepreneurship class.

THE PRODUCT

REAL Shlugars are huggable, lovable stuffed bunny rabbits. They are made from fun-fur, a polyester material, and stuffed with 100% pure polyester fibre. They are hypo-allergenic, machine washable and dryable. The eyes and nose are hand embroidered so that cautious parents need not worry about curious children eating buttons.

Each Shlugar has been hand made, thus attaining the obvious differences inevitable in creative craftsmanship. They are usually made up of two colors—a basic body color with contrasting tail and underside of the ear. The only limit on color depends upon the availability of the material and embroidery skeins.

At the retail level, material costs $9.00/metre, with four rabbits possible per metre. The embroidery floss is 69¢/skein, with five rabbits/skein. Assembly by hand takes two hours per Shlugar, and clearly is not viable at this rate.

At the wholesale level, material costs $3.00/metre, but a minimum of 800 metres/colour must be ordered. A pattern designer has been consulted to adapt the "hand-sewn" pattern to a machine pattern, thereby decreasing the costs due to a decrease in assembly time (See Exhibit 2).

THE MARKET

Although suitable for children and adults alike, REAL Shlugars may be easier to successfully market if a specific niche could be found. Many consumer toy-buying guides and market-study articles find that the baby-boomers and Yuppies are buying plush animals—for themselves!

The Quebec market has some inherent advantages and disadvantages. The language issue may be resolved with bilingual packaging, and REAL Shlugars may be R.E.A.L. Shlugars, and thus a "non-English—non-French" word. Similarly, the Quebec market has traditionally been accepting of concepts similar to Shlugar. Lastly, living in Quebec's major metropolis, Karen is familiar with potential distributors and will be able to supervise operations closely.

FINANCING

Karen will set up a corporation in January 1987. With cash rolled over from another family owned corporation, Karen will be able to finance this venture without debt.

> I am aware of government loans for entrepreneurs, for small businesses and for women entrepreneurs in small business. My husband and I talked about it, and we'd prefer to do this "no debt." I don't plan on losing money, but if it does fail, and I don't think it will, the tax loss wouldn't hurt me that much.

Pro forma Financial Statements can be found in Exhibit 3.

UNRESOLVED ISSUES

Acknowledging an existing opportunity, and a generous time frame, Karen Rothman must deal with certain issues to see if the opportunity is viable.

Production

It is evident that hand-sewing the Shlugars would be too time consuming, and piecework would still be very costly. However, since Montreal has a very active garment trade, it would be possible to subcontract the work out to a factory. With production runs for each season, it would be possible to slip in between the run for Summer '88 (which is done Fall '87), and if Christmas is successful, then a second run can be manufactured in time for Easter 1988. Karen felt 1000 Shlugars would be a good initial investment for a test market.

A contractor has quoted production costs which would include pattern cutting, sewing and overhead.

The initial production run of 1000 will be undertaken to minimize costs, with the option of selling material and stuffing back at 40% of cost to recoup losses if necessary.

A second production run of 8000 would take advantage of cost minimization through economies of scale and usage of materials. The second run will also coincide with Easter which is traditionally represented by bunny rabbits.

Table 1. Production/Contractor Costs.

Quantity	Cost per Unit	Cost
1–1,000	$3.00 per	$ 3,000
1,001–2,000	2.75	2,750
2,001–4,000	2.25	4,500
4,001–6,000	2.00	4,000
6,001–8,000	1.75	3,500
		$17,750
	$17,750–8000 units $2.22 per unit.	

After the 9000 Shlugars have been produced, Karen feels it would be time to review and assess the situation before committing further.

I would have to see if it's been successful and, if so, would I distribute nationally? internationally? expand operations? I guess I can only wait and see. . . .

Material

A recent estimate from a knitting mill revealed that a minimum of 800 metres of material per colour must be purchased, unless there is some "on the floor."

Even if I wanted to manufacture only three colours—white, blue, pink—that would be 2400 metres or 9600 bunnies. I originally did not want to produce that many, and it would also raise my material costs to $7200.

The mill would buy back the unused material and stuffing at 40% of cost if the first run is not successful.

Legal Considerations

A patent lawyer should be contacted. As well, there are legal considerations regarding the labelling of goods in compliance with the Upholstered and Stuffed Articles Act.

Packaging

Both Karen and her husband felt that packaging was the crucial marketing issue of Shlugar.

We feel that proper packaging could make Shlugar appealing to different ages and sectors in the market, and therefore not restrict us to only children—or only adults.

A box, with airholes—"so Shlugar does not suffocate"—and a window so that the product can be seen was devised. The box would be lined with a product similar to Easter grass—"for Shlugar's comfort and consumer appeal." The box would be marked "Fragile—REAL Shlugar." There is also the possibility of obtaining *The Velveteen Rabbit,* in full or an excerpt, from Avon books.

Although the fancy packaging will increase the cost, and therefore the price of Shlugar, Karen felt it was an important selling tactic:

I need something to distinguish my Shlugar from all other stuffed animals. A lot of market research has come out lately indicating that people are willing to spend a lot more on unique toys—so they shouldn't mind spending it on Shlugars.

In order to professionalize the packaging, Karen consulted a graphic design and a packaging manufacturer. The prices for packaging can be found in Table 2.

Karen decided to package and store the first 1000, at a cost of $1.00 per Shlugar, plus the cost of paying someone minimum wage to do it. The re-order of 8000 will be done by the manufacturer at a cost of $.75 per Shlugar.

Table 2. Packaging Costs.

Straw and Box (1st 1000)	$1.25 per Shlugar
Packaging and storage by Producer (re-order of 8000)	.75 per Shlugar
Straw and Box	$1.00 per Shlugar
Packaging and Storage by Karen and Distributor (re-order of 8000)	.60 per Shlugar

Distribution

Karen contacted a distributor/wholesaler who has good contacts in the toy industry, is a good seller, and has the proper facilities for the packaging and delivery of the Shlugars. The distributor also possesses good coordination skills, and Karen is confident he will be able to successfully manage storage and facilities.

It would also be possible to use some of Karen's contacts, as she knows a family who owns a chain of toy stores.

> I won't go behind my distributor's back. I would only introduce them. I also don't want to sell on a consignment basis. I want people to like Shlugar so much they'll know she'll sell well. Also, if you sell on consignment you can risk getting your product back due to poor sales effort.

Price

A price breakdown can be found in Exhibit 4, with Shlugar being sold to retailers for $9.00, who can sell them for up to $18.00 quite easily.

They are not as profitable if made by hand. First, it would not be possible to make it in large quantities, which would increase the cost of material. Time considerations would also increase cost, which would result in prohibitive costs to the consumer.

> When I buy material retail, and put in the two hours to produce a Shlugar, the cost to me is approximately $3.00 without my time, and my time is definitely worth more than $4.00/hour! I think the secret to success is to keep the production costs down to approximately $5.00–$6.00 per Shlugar.

If a knitting mill can't be found to produce the material at a lower minimum volume, it would also be possible for Shlugar to grow, with the only difference in cost being the larger amount of required material and stuffing, which is minimal. However, the price to retailers can increase substantially since there is much "more" visually.

Partnership

With selling the finished good a recognized weak spot, Karen has considered offering the distributor a partnership in the venture.

> Offering him 20% of the equity will truly establish his commitment to the idea, and will strengthen my concept due to his knowledge of the sales market. He is willing to put up $6000, and has agreed not to have any input as to the design of the bunnies. Offering him a partnership also justifies the 40¢ sales commission he will be paid. This way, he'll also earn 20% of the profits.

What Next?

Karen was not sure what to do next:

> I realize I have to get in touch with patent lawyers and more knitting mills. I want to be able to have more direction when I approach this venture. I'm also planning on working full time when I graduate, so this is an "aside" as opposed to a career, unless it really takes off. As yet, I'm unsure of my long-term strategy.
>
> I'm afraid that "mini" mass production of Shlugar will take away the home-made, hand sewn charm, although I will insist that the face be hand-embroidered in a factory. That will keep the irresistible charm of the concept; after all, you're no bunny till some bunny loves you!

Exhibit 1.

The Velveteen Rabbit or How Toys Become Real, was written by Margery Williams, and the New York Times Book Review called it "a treasure for rabbit lovers regardless of age." It is published by Avon Books. The relevant excerpt follows:

What is REAL? asked the Rabbit one day. Does it mean having things that buzz inside you and a stick-out handle?

Real isn't how you are made, said the Skin Horse. It's a thing that happens to you. When a child loves you for a long, long time, not just to play with, but REALLY loves you, then you become Real. It doesn't happen all at once. You become. It takes a long time. Generally, by the time you are Real, most of your hair has been loved off, and your eyes drop out, and you get loose in the joints and very shabby. But these things don't matter at all, because once you are Real you can't be ugly, except to people who don't understand. Once you are Real, you can't become unreal again. It lasts for always.

Exhibit 2. Assembly Time Comparison: Hand vs Machine Sewing.

	Hand	Machine
	(min.)	(min.)
Ears	20	2.0
Head	12	.5
Attach Ears to Head	10	1.0
Embroider Face	15	5.0
Tail	3	.5
Back—includes Tail to Back	5	1.0
Head to Neck and Body	10	1.0
Bottom to Body	45	4.0
Total	120 mins. = 2 hours	15.0 mins.

Note: Pattern cutting time not included as it will be equal for both.

Exhibit 3. REAL Shlugar Inc.

Initial Investment Required:

Material 3 rolls	$ 7,200.00
Stuffing	3,600.00
Embroidery	100.00
Patent fees	1,000.00
Graphic design	1,500.00
Pattern development	200.00
Legal	500.00
Accounting	500.00
Office supplies	500.00
	$15,100.00

Overhead Items to Be Amortized Over 9000 Unit Production Run

Patent fees	$1,000.00
Graphic design	1,500.00
Pattern development	200.00
Legal fees	500.00
Audit fees	500.00
Office supplies	500.00
	$4,200.00

$4,200.00/9000 Units = .47 per Unit

Note: Although according to GAAP these items should be amortized over their useful life, for investment analysis they will be expensed over the first two production runs.

Pro Forma Income Statement

	1000 Units	8000 Units
Sales $9.00 per	$9,000.00	$72,000.00
Cost (see Exhibit 4)	6,050.00	40,160.00
Gross Profit	$2,950.00	$31,840.00
Expenses (.47 per)	470.00	3,760.00
Profit before tax	$2,480.00	$28,080.00

Exhibit 4. REAL Shlugar Inc.

	1000 Units	**8000 Units**
Cost per Bunny		
Material/Embroidery	0.80	0.80
Stuffing	0.40	0.40
Sewing	3.00	2.22
Packaging	1.00	0.75
Handling	0.25	0.25
Shipping	0.20	0.20
Sales Commission	0.40	0.40
Total	6.05	5.02

AL-CO

"Think about it" said the man from Canon as he gave Alain Langlois his business card. Langlois watched the recruiter walk to the next display booth.

It is the first week of May 1992. Langlois is a student at the Teccart Institute, Quebec's premier electronics junior college. Along with all members of the graduating class of '92, he is presenting his final year project at Teccart's annual technology exhibition, a choice hunting ground for corporate recruiters. Representatives from GE Canada, Pratt & Whitney, Siemens, Xerox, Bombardier and many other firms are present.

Langlois's project, a user friendly alarm control box, has generated much interest, and one job offer. The Canon representative wants to hire him as an instructor for Canon's technical support & services centre in Montreal. There he would teach maintenance technicians from across the province employed by Canon's authorized dealers how to repair and service Canon's product line. The salary and working conditions are very attractive.

If he accepts the job, Langlois knows he will have to cancel plans to start his own company, to be called AL-CO. He must choose. Will he go for a safe, steady job, or will he roll the entrepreneurial dice. If so, does his venture plan need any adjustment?

The man from Canon wants an answer within a week.

LANGLOIS

Alain Langlois is a born tinkerer. As a youth, instead of playing with electronic toys and games, he would dismantle them. On a slow weekend, he would deconstruct and then reassemble his motorcycle, or he would construct radio sets out of scavenged parts. Back—issues of *Popular Mechanics* and *Omni* littered his room, and at the annual high school science fair, he was a presence that even students 2–3 years more senior had to reckon with.

Langlois's last summer job, in 1991, had been with ADT Inc, Quebec's largest security central. Tens of thousands of homes' and businesses' alarm systems were electronically monitored by ADT. Langlois served as a repairman for these alarm systems.

An idea for a product formed in his mind when an elderly lady, an ADT client, asked him why alarm systems were so hard to operate. For Langlois, this was the sound of opportunity knocking.

This case was prepared by Didier Pomerleau, M.B.A., and Sylvia Kovats, M.B.A., under the direction of Professor A. B. Ibrahim as a basis for class discussion rather than to illustrate effective or ineffective handling of an administrative situation, 1993.

Another product idea occurred to him as he was dismantling his older personal computer for parts.

The combination of these two ideas form the basis of AL-CO.

THE BUSINESS CONCEPT

AL-CO is in the consumer electronics business. Its two projects at present are a Math Co-Processor Emulator Board and a User Friendly Alarm System Control Box. Other products can be added as they are designed and developed by Alain Langlois.

THE PRODUCTS

Math Co-Processor Emulator Board

The Math Co-Processor Emulator Board is a substitute product for the standard math co-processor integrated circuit used in IBM-compatible personal computers which, until recently, was manufactured exclusively by Intel and which sold for $400 to $600 retail. In the past few months, competitors have entered the market with math co-processors which sell in the range of $110 to $275 retail.

The function of a math co-processor is to increase computer speed by performing the mathematical calculations and floating point arithmetic while the CPU (central processing unit) handles other aspects of the program. The AL-CO math co-processor emulator board contains a ROM chip with built-in software which performs the same function as the standard math co-processor, although slightly more slowly, since it uses the computer's CPU, rather than having its own. Given the high price of the standard math co-processor, there exists a window of opportunity for a product which offers:

1. Low price: sells for under $100 retail (AL-CO would get $40 per unit, wholesale).
2. Easy installation into one of the computer's expansion slots by the customer and "portability" to another computer should the customer upgrade to another computer.

User Friendly Alarm System Control Box

The User Friendly Alarm System Control Box, which will possibly be named the "Bon-sécur," is designed for residences or small businesses and has four or five programmable "zones." Each zone is a function or task that the alarm system can do independently of the other zones. The first zone is usually a 24 hour fire alarm/panic switch, while the others can be burglar alarms connected to various types of sensors and can be turned on and off by the user.

As with other systems presently available, the control box can set off various types of alarms in the home or business, and/or can dial a central company which constantly monitors all its subscribers' alarm systems. When the central receives a call, it immediately telephones the customer to see if there is some sort of false alarm, and if there is no answer, it calls the police.

The AL-CO Control Box is distinguished from other products in that it has a liquid crystal display (LCD) screen which provides instructions and helps the user to program the system, using a key-pad. All but the most expensive control boxes ($1500 and up) presently available have no screen and the user must read a long instruction manual to find out how to enter the commands.

Bonsécur offers two advantages:

1. Ease of programming by the customer. This will appeal to those customers who want a user friendly alarm system.
2. Lower price than other models with LCD screens.

PATENTS

The Alarm System Control Box is not patentable, because it is not defined by Canada Industry, Trade and Commerce as an invention but as an improvement over existing devices.

The Math Co-Processor Emulator Board, however, is patentable at a cost of $450. The patent is valid for 17 years.

PROTOTYPES

Functioning prototypes (including maintenance manuals for users and technical manuals for repairmen) of the Emulator Card and the Alarm System were completed by April 1992, as a required assignment at Teccart. The assignment was to design and develop one or two electronics products that are of professional quality.

THE MARKET

Math Co-Processor Emulator Board

The potential market for the Math Co-Processor Emulator Board consists of all owners of IBM compatible personal computers (XT or AT-286) who would like to speed the calculation time of software such as Quattro or AUTOCAD, and who do not want to pay a high price. Since this product cannot function in other computers, such as the MAC or MIN-IVAX, the market size is dependent on the number of XT and AT-286 personal computer owners. The XT and AT-286 presently form the largest category of personal computers being sold to individuals, businesses and schools. The total number of XTs and AT-286s worldwide was estimated by *Byte* at 30 million in March 1991.

XTs are no longer being produced at all, since with the decrease in prices, the more powerful AT has become the standard. Production of the AT-286 is ending. The abundance of clones, competing on price, has transformed the AT into a commodity. The market for the low priced AT continues to exist alongside the newer and more powerful, but more expensive, personal computers (such as laptops and workstations). Newer computers, such as the 386 and 486 personal computers have built in math co-processors. The lifespan of the Math Co-Processor Emulator Board, therefore, is limited by the lifespan of an aging, but enormous, pool of earlier model personal computers.

Two M.B.A. students, acquaintances of Langlois, conducted a small preliminary market survey (see appendix A) to get an indication of potential Montreal customers for both the AL-CO math co-processor emulator board and the AL-CO alarm system control box. The sample was quite small (56 respondents) and was skewed toward the younger age groups, since most of the respondents were students. However, it is useful as a feasibility study and can be followed by a larger and more complete survey:

- 64% of the respondents own an XT or AT personal computer.
- 25% of the owners of XT or AT computers already have standard math co-processors installed.
- 83% of XT or AT owners who do not already have a math co-processor expressed an interest in buying the AL-CO math co-processor emulator board by checking a price range at which they would be willing to buy the unit.

User Friendly Alarm Control Box

The alarm system market exists because of fear—usually fear of fire or theft. The Solicitor General's Report says that there are 106,000 illegal break-ins in Quebec each year. In the U.S., sales of security devices such as locks and alarms has been rising at the rate of 15% per year. With crime rates increasing (there is a burglary every 10 seconds in the U.S.), alarm systems could be a growth industry for the foreseeable future. In the U.S., it has been shown by *Consumer Report Magazine* that a home with a burglar alarm system is only one-sixth as likely to be broken into as a home without an alarm. Informal conversations with Montreal police officers from several precincts and with ADT personnnel suggest that Canadian trends follow U.S. trends.

Langlois's survey gave the following results for the questions concerning the alarm system control box.

- 44% of the respondents do not have an alarm system of any kind in their home. If sales of alarms in Canada are growing at or near the U.S. rate of 15% per year, there is still enormous growth potential.
- Both owners and non-owners ranked "Reliability" as the most important feature of an alarm system. The AL-CO system is competitive with the best alarm systems on the market in terms of reliability.
- Owners of alarm systems were divided between "Availability of Service" and "Ease of Set-Up and Programming" as the second most important feature, whereas non-owners were split between "Low Price" and "Ease of Set-Up and Programming." Since the AL-CO system is characterized by ease of set-up and programming and low price compared to other "user friendly" systems, Langlois feels that this is an indication that AL-CO can meet a customer need with this product.

THE INDUSTRY

The Math Co-Processor Emulator Board

The industry is characterized by cut-throat price competititon made possible by the ease with which products are "cloned." Copies are different enough from the original so as not to violate patents, but will do exactly the same job, often with improvements. Substitute products quickly become available for any new product. (The Math Co-Processor Emulator Board is one of these substitute products.)

The Alarm Systems Industry

Since the AL-CO alarm system control box can be used with fire alarms, burglar alarms, or both, we will discuss both types of alarms. Fire alarms can be simple smoke detectors, which retail for under $50 and sound a horn when they detect smoke particles in the air. These alarms are competitors for the AL-CO alarm systems only for customers who just want a horn to wake them up in case of fire. Similarly, inexpensive burglar alarms provide surveillance for small areas and sound an alarm at the site only. An example of an intermediate-priced programmable alarm system is in appendix B. The price of the control box alone is $578.95. This model, by Radio Shack, does not have an LCD screen, but recognizes the problem of difficult set-up and operation by offering a "Talking owner's manual" tape. This may be considered an improvement. AL-CO's LCD screen, which prompts the owner to input commands, is a better solution to the problem. The cost of alarm system control boxes has increased from $150 in 1987 to $350 for a comparable box in 1992. This increase in price outpaces both inflation and technological improvements in the product, which indicates that demand has outpaced production capability. It is a seller's market.

Government/legal requirements in Montreal and in a growing number of cities include city bylaws requiring all dwellings to have fire alarms.

The alarm systems industry is dominated by major players: ADT, Honeywell, Radio Shack, Black and Decker, and Asian imports. These companies have large advertising budgets and influence over distributors.

MARKETING PLAN AND STRATEGY

The Math Co-Processor Emulator Board

As a low-priced substitute for an expensive product (the standard math co-processor), the AL-CO Math Co-Processor Emulator Board will target owners of AT and XT personal computers who do not already own a standard math co-processor. Distribution will be through stores that sell computers, related equipment and software, such as Tyfu, the Université de Montreal and Concordia University computer cooperatives. Advertising at first will be through in-store displays. Later, if sales warrant, advertisements could be placed in computer magazines, such as *Byte* and *PC Sources*, which are regularly read by computer "hackers," and which would assist in market expansion to the U.S. Pricing would be cost-plus basis, as there is no market as yet (and hence no market price) for Math Co-Processor Emulator Boards. Production costs $22.95 per unit, and $17.05 will be added to cover fixed costs and allow for a profit, bringing the wholesale price to $40.00.

The Alarm System Control Box

The special benefit that differentiates this product is its user friendly feature, which comes from its LCD screen and programming which prompts the user to input commands. The target market will be the growing number of people who want to protect their house, apartment or business from fire and theft, who would like to have a programmable alarm system and who would like to be able to program their alarm system easily. This market would be willing to pay a little more for the user friendly feature than for a comparable alarm system which would require them to read a programming instruction book and learn to program an alarm box.

Langlois spoke with the purchasing agent for Addison Electronics, a larger consumer electronics distributor/manufacturer, about the possiblity of Addison buying the AL-CO Control box to sell to its customers. Before the prototype was even fully completed Addison was interested in buying 100 units per month. The control boxes would be packaged and sold under the Addison house brand, as part of complete alarm systems, and would be warranted and serviced by Addison. AL-CO would supply the technical and user manuals. If Addison can sell more than 250 units per month, it would be willing to produce the control box itself. This idea is unacceptable to Langlois because AL-CO would lose control of the unpatentable design.

Pricing: AL-CO can produce the Alarm System Control Box for $136 per unit. Addison is willing to purchase the AL-CO Alarm Control Box at $275 per unit, to be retailed from $400 to $700. The AL-CO system is superior to the "no-frills" units offered by Addison.

Distribution would be through:

1. Retailers of consumer electronic equipment, such as Addison Electronics, and possibly later, Sears and/or Consumer Distribution.
2. Alarm system central companies like ADT. The central would buy the units directly from AL-CO and install them for new customers and as a replacements for old equipment when it breaks down.

Promotion would be through Addison's catalogue, as well as point-of-purchase advertising, which would stress the fact that this product performs like the high-end control boxes, but at only a slightly higher price than the low-end models. Direct sales by AL-CO would be used to offer the product to the alarm central companies.

A short-term objective is to get the control box approved by U.L.C. (Underwriters' laboratories). This will help to build credibility for the product with potential customers.

THE PRODUCTION PLAN

Production Capacity

Production would be on a craft-shop basis. No mass production techniques would be used. Mass production, with its high fixed costs, would be uneconomical at low volumes. If future sales require expanded production, it would be possible to contract out production work to an assembly line type of producer.

Contracting out production of the emulator board is simple. The few large producers contacted were not interested, due to their own production schedules, retooling implications and the lack of credit record of AL-CO. Scores of independent craft shops like AL-CO operate in Montreal; many are owned by acquaintances of Langlois and his fellow alumni of Teccart. These shops would be willing to produce "spec jobs" for AL-CO.

Langlois can produce ten Math Co-Processor Emulators a day (one every forty minutes). With an assistant requiring only the expertise typical of a freshman at a technical college or having expertise in soldering circuitry, twenty units can be produced in a day (one every twenty minutes).

Alternatively, Langlois can produce five alarm systems in a day, or ten with an assistant with some basic introductory knowledge of electronics.

Langlois and his associates project sales of 10 Math Co-Processor Emulators per month.

For the Alarm System Control Box, projected sales are of 100 units per month in the first year, based on the number Addison Electronics is willing to buy. In the second year, Langlois & associates believe they could continue to sell 100 units per month to Addison, and an additional 20 units to other customers, and even more if ADT agrees to distribute AL-CO's box to its networks.

Supplies

All of the hardware parts for both the Emulator card and the Alarm System are readily available at specialized retailers throughout Montreal, such as Active Electronics. To obtain discounts, large quantities will be ordered from the distributors, requiring orders to be made one month before expected delivery. In situations of understocking for unforeseen high production levels, parts can be bought in a matter of hours from the retailers.

Facilities

Production will occur in a spare room in Langlois's apartment that has been converted into a workshop. Production will be clean and quiet, and will occur in the daytime. As a Teccart student, Langlois already owns the equipment he will need on a day-to-day basis, and the infrequently used equipment (such as calibration tools) can be borrowed from friends or from Teccart.

Quality control will be performed by Langlois, who will verify every unit produced.

Inventory will be reordered as it nears one month's worth of supplies, given that delivery time is between two weeks and a month.

SELECTION OF LOCATION

AL-CO will be located in Montreal because of:

- Easy access to Teccart's resources (shops, students/workers, technical library, teachers/ advisors)
- Easy access to electronic retailers
- Langlois's industry contacts in Montreal
- Availability of supplies from local sources
- Langlois's and his fiancée's preference to live in Montreal.

HUMAN RESOURCE PLAN

Langlois has recruited two acquaintances from Teccart's freshman class who will assist him with production. They are Steve L'Écuyer, who will help with the Alarm System, and Yvon Savoie, who will help with the Co-Processor Emulator. Each will be paid $8.00 per hour and will receive all necessary training from Langlois. Langlois will also be paid $8.00/hr for his production work, in addition to his salary.

[handwritten annotations: "← ASST", "$8/hr", "LD $8/hr salary"]

THE MANAGEMENT TEAM AND ORGANIZATIONAL STRUCTURE

The management team for both the Math Co-Processor Emulator and the Alarm System is the same.

- Langlois will be the owner-manager of the ventures and will have final decision making authority in all aspects of the business. He will concentrate his efforts, however, in production, technical development and personnel.
- To assist Langlois, Didier Pomerleau, an M.B.A. student, will be assistant manager on a part time basis and will focus on finance, accounting and law. Both Langlois and Pomerleau will work on Marketing, which is critical to the venture's *[handwritten: & KSF]* success. The two have known each other for almost 20 years and have cooperated on previous projects. Each is comfortable with the other's "style."
- Sylvia Kovats, also an M.B.A. student, will act in a consulting capacity, as well as contributing through her contacts in the computer industry.

AL-CO ORGANIZATIONAL CHART

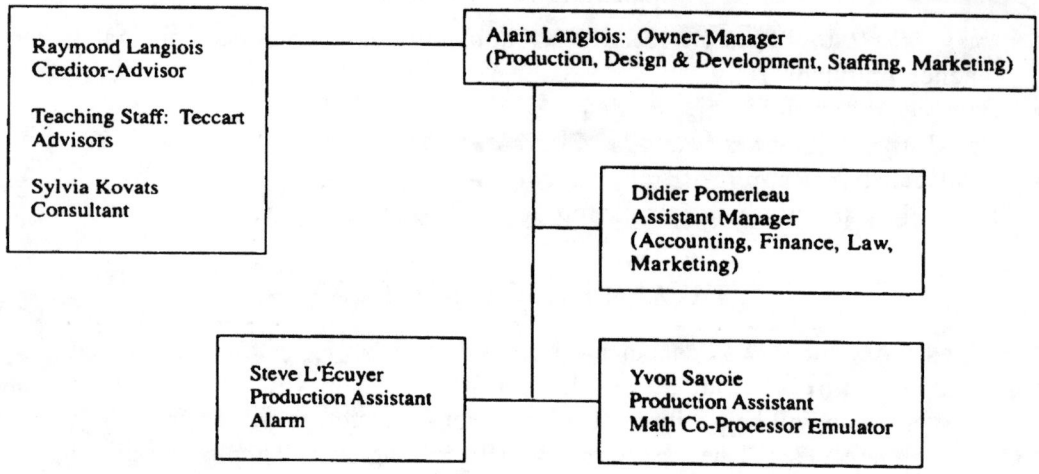

THE LEGAL FORM OF THE ORGANIZATION

AL-CO will be a Quebec incorporated business.

THE DEAL STRUCTURE

Since bank financing is usually not available for small business start-ups, financing will be through loans from family and friends of Alain Langlois as follows:

Raymond Langlois	$10,000 at 12%	To be invested at month 0
Richard Langlois	5,000 at 12%	To be invested at month 2
Alain Langlois	1,000 at 0%	To be invested at month 3
Didier Pomerleau	2,000 at 0%	To be invested at month 3
Sylvia Kovats	2,500 at 0%	To be invested at month 3
Total Financing	$20,500	

All loans are to be paid back by the end of year 1.

The funds invested at 0% interest will be priority debt, that is, they will be paid first should the company be unable to meet its obligations.

Ownership will be	Mr. Langlois:	85%
	Mr. Pomerleau:	7 1/2%
	Ms. Kovats:	7 1/2%

RISK ASSESSMENT

The recent entry of new competitors for the standard math co-processor board has pushed retail prices down from $400–$600 to $110–$275 per unit. This erodes AL-CO's competitive advantage, as consumers may be less interested in paying $40 + retail markup for what is essentially a substitute for the real co-processor.

Langlois is not worried. The math co-processor makes up only a small portion of AL-CO's projected sales and if it fails, there is always the alarm system control box. One of the reasons for offering two different products is to diversify risk. —D 2 products.

Consumer electronics in general, however, is a highly competitive sector, characterized by fast change, rapid product obsolescence and continuous product improvement. Successful innovations are quickly absorbed and imitated, often by large multinational firms with considerable resources in production, marketing and distribution. Again, Langlois is not concerned. Large competitors keep their prices high to cover huge overheads, or if they are cost efficient, to maintain high rates of return. They will not "kill the goose" by marking down the price of their high end alarm systems so as to match AL-CO, unless AL-CO becomes a threat to their market shares. Langlois does not intend to grow that much.

Nevertheless, if AL-CO is successful, it may find its window of opportunity to be short lived. This prospect does not faze Langlois. He is not interested in founding a corporate empire, nor does "being his own boss" inordinately attract him as a lifestyle. "I just want to make some money," says Langlois. "If we go in, and then we go out a couple of years later, I'll be satisfied, as long as we come out with a neat pile of cash. By then there will be new products to create (and more money to develop them), with new opportunities to be seized. In this business, I won't get bored." ENTREP

LOVES what does PASSION

THE FINANCIAL PLAN

Assumptions:

- Supplies paid c.o.d.
- Wages payable and accounts receivable settled within 30 days.
- No sales for the first three months of operation

UNIT VARIABLE COST: MATH CO-PROCESSOR EMULATOR BOARD

MATERIAL:	UNIT COST:
ROM Chip (EPROM 64 K memory X 8 bits, 120 nanosecond, 8 megahertz)	$ 5.60
Printed Circuit Board (PCB) Blank (double side)	2.00
Buffers, circuit components, hardware	10.00
TOTAL UNIT MATERIALS COST	$17.60
Labour (40 minutes per card. $8.00 per hour)	5.35
TOTAL UNIT VARIABLE COST	$22.95

UNIT VARIABLE COST: ALARM SYSTEM CONTROL BOX

MATERIAL:	COST:
LCD Screen	$12.00
Power Transformer	10.00
CPU for microcontroller	40.00
Circuit components	40.00
Keyboard	10.00
Chassis	15.00
Small hardware	1.00
Tech manual (printing subcontracted)	4.00
Maintenance manual (printing subcontracted)	1.00
TOTAL MATERIALS COST PER UNIT	$120.00
Labour: 2 hours @ $8.00/hr.	16.00
TOTAL UNIT VARIABLE COST	$136.00

AL-CO PRO FORMA INCOME STATEMENT
FOR THE FIRST TWO YEARS OF OPERATION
JUNE 1–MAY 31

		1992–93	1993–94
Sales: Alarm		$247,500	$396,000
Emulator		3,600	4,800
Total Sales		251,100	400,800
Cost of Goods Sold:			
Materials:	Alarm	108,000	172,800
	Emulator	1,584	2,112
Labour:	Alarm	14,400	23,040
	Emulator	482	642
Total COGS		124,466	198,594
Contribution Margin:	Alarm	125,100	200,160
	Emulator	1,534	2,046
Patent for Emulator		450	0
Common Costs (Overhead):			
Interest		1,800	0
Registration Cost		20	0
Rent (One room in Langlois's Apt.)		450	600
Administrative:			
Salary:	Langlois	8,000	10,000
	Pomerleau	2,000	5,000
Selling Expenses		2,000	2,500
Miscellaneous Expenses		2,000	2,500
Incorporation Costs (includes initial set up & annual reporting costs)		1,000	1,000
Net Income Before Tax		$108,914	$180,606
Tax @ 10% (Tax incentive for new businesses)		10,892	18,060
Net Income		$98,022	$162,546
Dividends		$50,000	$100,000

AL-CO PRO FORMA BALANCE SHEET
FOR THE FIRST TWO YEARS OF OPERATION

	June 1, 1992	June 1, 1993	June 1, 1994
Assets:			
Cash	$ 9,000	$43,384	$95,020
Inventory		15,220	17,620
Incorporation cost	1,000		
Total Assets	$10,000	$58,604	$112,640
Liabilities:			
Loan from R. Langlois	$10,000		
Owner's Equity:	0	$58,604	$112,640
Total Liabilities & Owners' Equity	$10,000	$58,604	$112,640

BREAK-EVEN ANALYSIS

Let A = Number of Alarms produced in the first year
Let E = Number of Emulators produced in the first year

Profit = revenues − variable expenses − fixed costs
Profit = (275A + 40E) − (136.00A + 22.95E) − 17,720
Profit = 139A + 17.05E − 17, 720 = 0 for break-even

If E = 0, A = 128 units per year need to be sold to break even. This is well within the realm of possibility, since projected sales are of 900 units in the first year.

If A = 0, E = 1040 units per year need to be sold to break even. This is much less likely. AL-CO projects sales of 90 emulators in the first year. It will concentrate its production efforts on the Alarm System Control Box, with the Math Co-Processor Emulator as something of a sideline.

→ Small portion

Alternative
→ make only alarms

AL-CO PRO FORMA MONTHLY CASH FLOW STATEMENT
FOR THE FIRST TWO YEARS OF OPERATION

Month	1	2	3	4	5	6
Opening Balance		8,230	12,930	2,960	16,779	30,598
From Investors	100,000	5,000	5,500			
Sales				27,900	27,900	27,900
Materials			15,220	12,176	12,176	12,176
Labour				1,655	1,655	1,655
Rent						150
Incorporation cost	1,000					
Salaries						
Patent	450					
Selling Expense	200	200	150	150	150	150
Registration	20					
Misc.	100	100	100	100	100	100
Debt Repayment						
Interest						
Tax						
Dividends						
Closing Balance	8,230	12,930	2,960	16,779	30,598	44,267

AL-CO PRO FORMA MONTHLY CASH FLOW STATEMENT
CONTINUED

Month	7	8	9	10	11	12
Opening Balance	44,267	52,986	66,708	80,327	93,946	107,515
From investors						
Sales	27,900	27,900	27,900	27,900	27,900	27,900
Materials	12,176	12,176	12,176	12,176	12,176	12,176
Labour	1,655	1,655	1,655	1,655	1,655	1,655
Rent						300
Incorporation Cost						
Salaries	5,000					5,000
Patent						
Selling Expense	150	150	150	150	200	200
Registration cost						
Misc	200	200	300	300	300	400
Debt Repayment						20,500
Interest						1,800
Tax						
Dividends						50,000
Closing Balance	52,986	66,708	80,327	93,946	107,515	43,384

AL-CO PRO FORMA MONTHLY CASH FLOW STATEMENT
CONTINUED

Month	13	14	15	16	17	18
Opening Balance	43,384	59,783	64,290	80,689	97,088	113,487
From investors						
Sales	33,400	33,400	33,400	33,400	33,400	33,400
Materials	14,576	14,576	14,576	14,576	14,576	14,576
Labour	1,975	1,975	1,975	1,975	1,975	1,975
Rent	50	50	50	50	50	50
Incorporation cost		1,000				
Salaries						7,500
Patent						
Selling Expense	200	200	200	200	200	200
Registration cost						
Misc	200	200	200	200	200	200
Debt Repayment						
Interest						
Tax		10,892				
Dividends						
Closing Balance	59,783	64,290	80,689	97,088	113,487	122,386

AL-CO PRO FORMA MONTHLY CASH FLOW STATEMENT
CONTINUED

Month	19	20	21	22	23	24
Opening Balance	122,386	138,785	155,184	171,583	187,982	204,281
From Investors						
Sales	33,400	33,400	33,400	33,400	33,400	33,400
Materials	14,576	14,576	14,576	14,576	14,576	14,576
Labour	1,975	1,975	1,975	1,975	1,975	1,975
Rent	50	50	50	50	50	50
Incorporation cost						
Salaries						7,500
Patent						
Selling Expense	200	200	200	200	250	250
Registration Cost						
Misc	200	200	200	200	250	250
Debt Repayment						
Interest						
Tax						18,060
Dividends						100,000
Closing Balance	138,785	155,184	171,583	187,982	204,281	95,020

APPENDIX A
ELECTRONIC PRODUCTS QUESTIONNAIRE

We are two Concordia M.B.A. students who are making this survey as part of a course assignment. We would very much appreciate your taking a few minutes to fill out this questionnaire. All responses are anonymous: we are not trying to sell you a product. Thank you in advance for your help.

Does your household own an alarm system (fire, burglar, or other)? Yes [_] No[_]

If you do not have an alarm system, is the reason because: too expensive [_] too hard to operate [_] other _____

If you were shopping for an alarm system, in what order would the following features be important? (Please put 1 beside the most important feature, 2 beside the second most important feature, etc.)

low price [_] ease of set-up & programming [_] reliability [_] brand name [_] availability of service [_] recommendation from salesperson [_]

How much would you be willing to pay for a computerized alarm system that:
- can be set to detect smoke as well as someone trying to break into your home, and
- has an LCD screen that gives instructions and prompts to make it easy to program?

Under $200 [_] $201 to $300 [_] $301 to $400 [_] $401 to $500 [_] $501 to $600 [_] $601 to $700 [_] $701 to $800 [_] $801 to $900 [_] $901 to $1000 [_] Over $1000 [_]

Definitely would not buy [_]

Your age range: Under 20 [_] 21 to 30 [_] 31 to 40 [_]

41 to 50 [_] 51 to 60 [_] Over 60 [_]

Your income range: Under $10,000/yr [_] $10,000 to $30,000 [_] $30,000 to $50,000 [_] $50,000 to $70,000[_] Over $70,000 [_]

Please answer the next section if you own an IBM-compatible computer or are considering buying one:

Is your computer equipped with a Math Co-Processor? Yes [_] No [_] Don't know [_]

If your computer does not have a Math Co-Processor, how much would you be willing to pay for a Math Co-Processor emulator board that:
- would fit into one of your computer's expansion slots and
- would speed mathematical calculations significantly (although slightly less than a standard Math Co-Processor)

Under $50 [_] $51 to 100 [_] $101 to $150 [_] $151 to $200 [_] $201 to $250 [_] $251 to $300 [_]

Definitely would not buy [_]

Thank you for completing our questionnaire.

Massachusetts Microwave Corporation (MMC)

Massachusetts Microwave Company (MMC) is a privately owned American corporation. The founders, Russell Johnson and George Guest, established the corporation in 1989 to provide consulting and custom design services to the North American microwave communications industry. Their area of expertise is the application of state-of-the-art high precision printed circuit technology to microwave subsystems.

The corporation is based in the high technology area of Boston, Massachusetts, close to government agencies and many microwave companies.

COMPANY OBJECTIVES AND STRATEGY

MMC intends to take advantage of a growing microwave market and a shortage of available engineering expertise to establish a profitable microwave consulting, subsystem design and manufacturing company based on its proficiency in the application of precision printed circuit technology. In order to compete effectively against its large competitors, MMC will develop the ability to rapidly develop and test subsystems.

The founders have adopted a conservative growth strategy for the company. They will avoid the need for a large amount of seed capital by initially concentrating on consultation work within the microwave design and development market. This approach will also permit the owners to assess market opportunities and improve their contacts within the microwave industry. Based on this experience, MMC intends to develop and manufacture microwave components.

Much of MMC's initial work is expected to come from customers of Bollweevil Technologies Inc. (BTI). Both founders of MMC are former employees of this company. Many of BTI's customers were left in the lurch when BTI went bankrupt. Since the owners of MMC were working on many of these unfinished projects, they are very familiar with them and will, therefore, have a competitive advantage in obtaining contracts to complete the work.

This case was prepared by Andrew Crowly, revised by Russell Buche and Peter Tsias under the direction of Professor A. B. Ibrahim as a basis for class discussion, rather than to illustrate either effective or ineffective handling of an administrative situation. This is a disguised case, based upon an actual company. Adjustments in location and facts have been made to assure anonymity.

MANAGEMENT AND PERSONNEL

The company will be managed by the founders, Russell Johnson and George Guest (see Exhibits 1 and 2 for the Curriculum Vitae of these individuals). In order to compensate for their lack of managerial experience, the owners will employ professional accounting and legal services whenever necessary. Legal assistance will be particularly important (and costly) in the initial stages in order to draft the contracts. Attempting to enter into the first few contracts without expert legal advice could result in extremely damaging mistakes.

The founders expect no hiring difficulties due to growth in the foreseeable future. Their personal contacts will provide a ready labour pool for the next several years.

In the first year, most of the design work not performed by the founders will be accomplished by part-time workers. These are people already known to the founders and will work in the evenings and on weekends. This will keep the overhead low while allowing the founders to evaluate in detail the professional capabilities of these part-time workers.

FACILITIES

The facilities needed to start a consulting firm in this industry are modest. These will consist of an office equipped with furniture, a micro-computer with engineering, project management and accounting software and a small manufacturing area (see a detailed list with approximate prices in Exhibit 3).

Microwave test equipment will be rented from the federal government's Communications Research Center (CRC). As more work is undertaken, critical test equipment can be leased or purchased, as appropriate.

MANUFACTURING

MMC will promote the capability to produce prototypes as part of its strategy of providing quick turn-around design service. These facilities will consist of an etching section to fabricate precision printed circuit boards (PCBs) and a prototype assembly area.

Larger scale manufacturing will be limited to key technologies or specialized skills unique to MMC, since there are many suppliers of electronic components and assemblies which can be subcontracted to perform most manufacturing tasks.

FUTURE PRODUCTS

Product development will be financed through a combination of internal funding, bank loans and governmental assistance. MMC views consulting as an excellent method of scanning the market in order to assist in determining the direction of future development. Presently, the most promising product appears to be the low cost millimetric wave filters. However, the market for these components has not yet been fully evaluated.

MMC plans to begin providing prototype production services and will design a suitable product for small scale production and distribution. The first product is expected to be an extension of design work carried out for customers as a result of proposals made to government.

A list of tasks to be undertaken in the first two years is shown in Exhibit 4, with more attention given to Year One.

INDUSTRY DESCRIPTION

The microwave industry is composed mainly of two market segments: telecommunications and military systems. Both sectors are enjoying real growth of between six and ten percent per annum.

The increased demand for telecommunications services is driven by computer-generated data transmission, fax machines and the continually growing number of telephones. The frequency spectrum is already congested as cellular telephones, police radios, CB radios and military communications all compete for the available band width. The only solution to this overcrowding is to move to higher frequencies into the microwave band. This is the dominant trend in telecommunications, military communications and electronic warfare today.

The move to higher frequencies has left many companies without the engineering expertise to develop or modify products. One of the key factors in developing new systems is the ability to rapidly prototype and test circuits and subsystems, particularly using Computer Aided Design (CAD) models. Therefore, if a company requires a microwave subsystem, it will subcontract the design and manufacture because of the specialized expertise required.

Microwave designs are often implemented incorrectly because of a limited understanding of critical manufacturing processes. This is an area in which MMC excels. It has specialized in designing and producing complex microwave and millimetric products.

There is a trend in the high technology industry away from specialized design departments in large companies since they tend to produce less innovative work than smaller companies. It is often very difficult for a designer to be innovative in a large company if he/she is stifled by mountains of forms, protocol and other bureaucracy, production problems and restrictive job descriptions. Furthermore, design specialists are often not fully utilized since demand for their services is project-based or cyclical. Many large companies have, therefore, realized that it is often uneconomical to employ full-time design specialists and have moved to hiring contractors or consultants.

INDUSTRY TRENDS

There are several trends in the microwave industry which will influence the long-term viability of MMC:

1. Monolithic Microwave Integrated Circuits (MMICs) are likely to have a similar positive effect on the microwave industry as integrated circuits have had on the electronics industry; and

2. The main driving forces in the microwave industry to date have been the requirements of the military and industrial telecommunications users. However, microwave systems are now moving into the consumer marketplace with the development of mobile satellite communications for automobiles and other vehicles and satellite navigation systems for use on pleasure boats. Consumers are expected to take advantage of this new technology in rapidly increasing numbers over the next five years.

These trends will have a negative impact on most small companies due to the high level of capital investment needed to manufacture MMIC circuits and mass production techniques necessary in the commercial market are forcing small companies to vertically integrate. Still, the founders expect these trends to have a positive net effect on the performance of MMC since more and more companies and individuals will be using microwave components and will thus need experts to advise them and develop subsystems; the trends will provide significantly expanded market opportunities.

COMPETITION

MMC will experience very little direct competition since few firms offer turn-key design services. However, the market is restricted in other ways:

1. Large companies usually have in-house design departments and do not use outside consultants, particularly in the defense industry where security and confidentiality are important considerations;
2. Small companies often do not have the financial capability to hire consultants; and
3. Employees within microwave design groups (be they large or small) often perceive the use of outside consultants as a threat to their jobs.

The main advantage a small consulting firm can offer is rapid results. Since the ability to get designs to market quickly is now recognized as a critical success factor in the microwave industry, MMC will specialize in rapid design and development services.

GOVERNMENT

MMC intends to take full advantage of government assistance for high-technology firms. Two federal programs have been identified to date: the Industrial Research Assistance Program and the Department of Supply and Services Unsolicited Proposal Program. Applications will be made to any other governmental assistance programs, as appropriate.

Through his contacts at the CRC, George Guest will develop proposals suitable for the CRC's unsolicited proposal program, as well as monitoring the direction of CRC developments in telecommunications technology. Close contact with the CRC is important since MMC intends to rent their microwave test equipment in order to test circuit and subsystem designs.

MARKET SUMMARY

The microwave industry is fragmented into highly specialized niches. As a result, there is little direct competition and the barriers to entry are knowledge-based rather than capital-based. There are several large, vertically integrated companies, but no dominant industry leader. Many small companies are leaders in differentiated technological niches.

Most microwave subsystems are custom designed with very close liaison between customers and suppliers.

Both small and large system manufacturing companies rarely employ full-time micro-wave specialists since between most designs their services are not required. However, companies find that the costs associated with finding and hiring part-time or temporary specialists can be prohibitive. Many manufacturing companies that have microwave design departments are questioning this investment.

There are also other disadvantages which are forcing manufacturers to reexamine their designing functions. These companies are organized with the usual rigid structures and controls. This environment is usually not conducive to the effective, flexible and creative design and development of prototypes.

Thus, many manufacturers have discovered that an attractive alternative to in-house design departments is the use of a consultant.

TARGET MARKET

The target market can be divided into two segments:

1. MMC will target PCB manufacturers who need expertise in order to expand into the manufacturing of microwave substrates. There are only a few PCB companies in the New England area. These have already been identified and negotiations are presently underway with Mitec Electronics. Other companies who have expressed an interest are OEM Precision Printed Circuits and APREL Inc.
2. MMC will also target companies in the telecommunications and defense industries which require design consultants due to the job-shop nature of projects, a shortage of microwave designers and/or a demand for the specialized expertise of MMC. The majority of these companies have been identified. Contacts within many of these firms were established while the founders were working for BTI.

MARKETING PROGRAM

Russell Johnson, as Chief Engineer at BTI, was in constant contact with customers. This enabled him to understand problems faced by the customers and develop personal contacts. These individuals will be sent a company profile which will include a description of MMC's capabilities (see Exhibit 6). This will be followed up with a telephone call and, if applicable, a visit to the company.

As a result of its previous experience with these companies, MMC has information regarding current projects and design requirements. Therefore, the covering letter, phone call and in-house presentation can be directed towards the customer's specific requirements.

MMC considers the most promising short-term opportunity to be providing consulting services to the PCB manufacturers intending to expand capabilities into the growing microwave market. Substrate manufacturers see the expansion into producing microwave circuits as an opportunity to add to their present product line without large capital outlays. They do not, however, have the required expertise. Several companies have approached MMC expressing an interest in developing or improving their microwave substrate manufacturing capabilities. A relationship with OEM Precision Printed Circuits has already been established.

Due to the industrial nature of the industry, the regional target market, and a limited advertising budget, the principle marketing strategy will be to rely on word of mouth and direct marketing to key members of the microwave community. This will be reinforced by writing technical articles and obtaining other available free publicity (as well as limited paid advertising) in trade journals such as *Microwave Journal, Microwave Systems News, RF Design*, etc.

PRICING POLICY

Separate pricing policies will be necessary for various types of consulting and development functions:

1. For the consulting work, the pricing will depend on the type of work undertaken. For general microwave design functions, the principle competition will come from internal design departments. Large companies have a total cost of approximately $350 to $400 per engineering person day. Smaller companies can have total costs as low as $300. MMC will, therefore, charge an initial rate of $300 plus non labour expenses.
2. If the consulting service requires specialized expertise, such as the application of high precision PCBs, the daily rate will approach $500. However, most of these contracts will be individually negotiated due to the custom nature of this type of design work.
3. For larger development contracts, the objective will be to use milestone payments wherever possible in order to ensure a continuous cash flow.

FINANCIAL DATA

MMC considers its financial projections to be conservative and even a little pessimistic. For example, no income is assumed during the first three months of operation, even though several promising leads have already been established. It is also assumed that no development contracts will be started during the first year due to initial inertia resulting from governmental and corporate bureaucracy and extended proposal assessment periods.

A loan of $20,000 will be needed to augment the $8,000 equity injected by the founders. It will take the form of a personal loan secured by the founders' private assets.

A detailed monthly cash flow for the first 12 month period, with appropriate assumptions, is provided in Exhibit 5. Also described are the assumptions, the expected start-up costs, a projected income statement for the first nine months of operation, and a pro-forma balance sheet for the end of the first year. Positive cash flow is expected in the sixth month. The capital purchases projected for after month six are optional and will depend on the contracts received, since they are intended to establish the assembly facility.

Consulting fees are assumed to be an average of $300 per day. Revenues are conservatively assumed to reach a maximum of only 50% utilization of available labour.

While it is true that consulting services rarely provide as consistent an income as is indicated in the financial statements, the projected net income of $40,000 over 12 months is considered realistic.

RISK FACTORS

The principle uncertainty is related to successfully publicizing the services provided by MMC so as to generate sufficient income to cover expenses once the seed capital is exhausted. The emphasis for the first quarter will be marketing and establishing a customer base for the company. MMC expects little or no income during this period. The founders expect that, once MMC's services are known in the microwave industrial community, the company will generate sufficient income from the demand for microwave design services so as to sustain future endeavors.

LIST OF ABBREVIATIONS

MMC. Massachusetts Microwave Corporation.

BTI. Bollweevil Technologies Inc.

CRC. Communications Research Center.

PCB. Printed Circuit Boards.

CAD. Computer Aided Design.

MMIC. Monolithic Microwave Integrated Circuits.

Exhibit 1. Russell Johnson.

University Education

M.A.Sc. 1984–1988, MIT, Department of Electrical Engineering (completed part-time).

Thesis: "The Design and Realization of a 20 GHz FET Amplifier Using a Combination of Finline and Microstrip." The study consisted of the design, fabrication and subsequent measurements of a 20 GHz low noise FET amplifier. The circuit made use of a combination of finline and microstrip circuitry on a single substrate. In addition, a theoretical investigation into the effect of metalization thickness on various electrical parameters of finline was carried out.

Courses: Microwave Engineering, Telecommunications Engineering, Image Processing, etc.

B.A.Sc. 1979–84, MIT, Electrical Engineering.

Publications and Patents

A description of numerous articles published in trade journals, several lectures presented at technical conferences, as well as two patents pending is available upon request.

Teaching Experience

MIT, 1984–86, Laboratory Demonstrator for the following fourth year courses: Microwave Devices, Robotics, and Real Time Programming.

Computer Skills

UNIX, VMS and MSDOS operating systems

FORTRAN, BASIC and ASSEMBLY languages

TOUCHTONE, SUPERCOMPACT and AUTOCAD computer automated design packages.

Work Experience

May 1988. Presently negotiating consulting contract with General Electric Aerospace Department, Utica, New York. This contract is to carry out work which had been initiated with Bollweevil Technologies Inc. and not completed prior to the company's collapse.

May 1986–May 1988. Bollweevil Technologies Inc. Chief Engineer. Responsibilities included marketing, project management, microwave and millimeter wave circuit design, as well as the development of new circuit fabrication technologies. Specifically, circuits designed include mixers, amplifiers, filters and power dividers using E-plane as well as microstrip and stripline techniques. This work experience was extremely valuable to me in that I learned a great deal about microwave printed circuit fabrication (primarily on soft substrates) as well as circuit design. Unfortunately, this company went bankrupt in May 1988 due to low cash problems.

May 1983–September 1983. U.S. Research Council. Performed measurements on cryogenically cooled low noise GaAs FET amplifiers. I also designed a hermetically sealed ohm 50 coax air line to be incorporated into a cryogenic test station.

Exhibit 2. George Guest.

Education

M.A.Sc., 1982, MIT.

Thesis Title: "Numerical Analysis of IN-VIVO Dielectric Sensors."

Area of Concentration: Microwave and antenna theory, numerical methods, optimization theory and dielectric spectroscopy.

B.A.Sc. (Electrical Engineering), California State Polytechnic University, 1979.

B.Sc. (General Biology), University of North Carolina at Chapel Hill, North Carolina, 1977.

Academic Awards and Scholarships

NRC Scholarship (graduate studies), 1979–81.

Graduated 1st in class, summa cum laude (undergraduate studies), 1979.

IBM Award for engineering studies, 1979.

Dean's Honour List and Scholarship, 1978 and 1979.

Professional Seminars

Dielectric Resonators, October 21–31, 1986, University of Florida, Miami, Florida.

Modern Antennas, February 22–26, 1988, Texas Instruments, Dallas, Texas.

Experience

August, 1987–May, 1988: Microwave Design Engineer, Bollweevil Technologies Inc.
Duties:
- design of microwave and millimeter-wave passive and active components (E-plane filters and Gunn oscillators) and microstrip antennas;
- proposal writing.

1981–1987: Microwave Design Engineer, U.S. Research Council.
Duties:
- design and development of microwave components for satellite communications earth-terminals including mixers, modulators, frequency multipliers and oscillators up to frequencies of 30 GHz in various media such as microstrip, waveguide and finline;
- procurement and development of computer-aided design software;
- supervision of technician and graduate students;
- monitoring industrial and university research contracts.

1984: Sessional Lecturer, MIT, Department of Engineering.
Duties:
- taught 4th-year level course in antenna theory.

1978–1981: Teaching and Laboratory Assistant, MIT, Department of Engineering.
Duties:

- laboratory demonstrator for 3rd and 4th year level control theory courses dealing with analog computers and electromechanical servos;
- laboratory assistant performing dielectric measurements on soils and biological materials and field pattern measurements on cancer diathermy applicators.

Publications and Patents

A description of numerous articles published in trade journals, two lectures presented at technical conferences as well as one patent pending is available upon request.

Exhibit 3. Capital Expenditures.

Computer Aided Design Station	
Engineering Computer (With plotter and printer)	$8,000
Microwave Design Software ("CADEC")	5,250
Office Equipment	
Office furniture (desk chairs, etc.)	600
Photocopier	1,600
Assembly Equipment	
Solder Station	500
Milling/ Drilling machine	2,000
Assorted hand tools	500
Supplies	
Office supplies (Business cards, stationery, etc.)	500
Assembly supplies (Semiconductors, substrates, etc.)	2,000
TOTAL	$20,950

Exhibit 4. Schedule of Tasks.

First Year

First Quarter

1 Rent office, have telephone connected, etc.
2 Purchase computer, software and office furniture.
3 Develop a list of potential clients.
4 Send 3 company profile and capabilities, with covering letter.
5 Follow up 4 with phone call.
6 Follow up 5 with company visit.
7 Follow up 6 with proposal.
8 Reestablish contacts at CRC.

Second Quarter
1 Continue marketing plan.
2 Fulfill consulting contract(s) obtained in first quarter.
3 Research proposal for DSS unsolicited proposal program.

Third Quarter
1 Continue marketing plan.
2 Fulfill consulting contract(s) from second quarter.
3 Write proposal for DSS unsolicited proposal program.
4 Submit proposal to DSS.

Fourth Quarter
1 Continue marketing plan.
2 Fulfill consulting contract(s) from third quarter.
3 Review pricing and marketing plan.
4 Develop plan to produce components.
5 Evaluate funding requirements for 4.

Second Year

First Half
1 Start work on unsolicited proposal.
2 Start prototyping facility.
3 Start prototyping contracts.
4 Hire one engineer.

Second Half
1 Purchase test equipment.
2 Start short production runs.
3 Hire technician/assembler.

Exhibit 5. Massachusetts Microwave Corporation Monthly Cash Flow Projection.

						MONTH							
	1	2	3	4	5	6	7	8	9	10	11	12	TOTAL
Cash Receipts													
Consulting Fees	—	—	—	2000	3000	4000	4000	5000	5000	5000	6000	6000	40000
Equity	8000												8000
Loans (New Venture)	20000												20000
TOTAL	28000	—	—	2000	3000	4000	4000	5000	5000	5000	6000	6000	68000
Cash Disbursement													
Equipment purchases	6000	6000	1000					500		1000	2000	1600	18100
Rental expenses	120	120	120	120	120	120	120	120	120	120	120	120	1440
Accountants' fees	150	150	150	150	150	150	150	150	150	150	150	150	1800
Insurance	100	100	100	100	100	100	100	100	100	100	100	100	1200
Office supplies	170	30	30	30	30	30	30	30	30	30	30	30	500
Telephone	150	150	150	150	150	150	150	150	150	150	150	150	1800
Loan repayments	210	210	210	210	210	210	210	210	210	210	210	210	2520
Personal Drawings	3000	3000	3000	3000	3000	3000	3000	3000	3000	3000	3000	3000	36000
TOTAL	9900	9760	4760	3820	3820	3820	3820	4320	3820	4820	5820	5420	63360
Net Cash													
Monthly surplus	18100					180	180	680	1680	180	180	580	
Monthly deficit		(9760)	(4760)	(1820)	(820)								
Cumulative (to date)	18100	8340	3580	1760	940	1120	1300	1980	3660	3840	4020	4600	

Monthly Cash Flow Assumptions

1. Price-large companies have total cost of between $350 and $400 per engineering person day; smaller companies can go as low as $300. Therefore, a rate of $300 plus expenses is assumed as an initial price for design services. Based on this price, an income of $6000 per month represents 20 mandays, which is only 50% capacity, assuming a five-day week.

2. There is no income expected during the first three months. Efforts will be concentrated on marketing and writing proposals. Most companies will take this time to evaluate our proposals.

3. The computer and software is assumed to be a fixed cost and will be needed from the beginning to write proposals and to send letters to prospective customers. It is also assumed that the computer cannot be leased because the company is new and has no credit history. The tools for the assembly area a the photocopier will be purchased as deemed necessary by the type of work contracted.

4. An extra $5000 line of credit is to be negotiated, with a lending institution to cover any large projects which may be contracted. This would cover the expenses of components and fabrication of prototypes if this type of work is required.

Exhibit 5. (continued)

Start-Up Expenses and First Three Months of Operation

Equipment purchased		$18,100
Operating expenses (three months of operation):		
Rent	$360	
Accountant's fees	450	
Insurance	300	
Office supplies	230	
Telephone	450	
Loan repayment	630	
Personal drawings	9,000	
Total		$11,420
Total start-up expenses		$29,520

Projected Income Statement (9 Months)

Fees		$40,000
Operating expenses		
Rent	$1,080	
Accountant's fees	1,350	
Insurance	900	
Office supplies	270	
Telephone	1,350	
Loan repayment	1,890	
Personal drawings	27,000	
Total		$33,840
Operating Income		$ 6,160

Projected Balance Sheet at the End of First Year

Assets		
Cash		$ 4,600
Total current assets		$ 4,600
Equipment	$18,100	
Less depreciation	$(3,020)	
Total fixed assets		$15,080
Total assets		$19,680
Liabilities		
Current liabilities	none	
Long-term loan	$20,000	
Total liabilities		$20,000
Founders' equity		($ 320)
Total liabilities and equity		$19,680

Exhibit 6. Massachusetts Company Profile.

Massachusetts Microwave Corporation is a U.S. owned private corporation. It was established to provide a consulting and custom design service to the North American microwave industry and government. In addition, the corporation is developing a line of microwave and millimetre-wave components utilizing the latest developments in high precision printed circuit technology. The company's personnel has had extensive experience in the design of active and passive microwave and millimetre-wave components and subsystems and has been directly responsible for major developments in the field of planar microwave circuit fabrication. This experience, combined with an array of state-of-the-art computer-aided-design (CAD) software allows the company to meet the customers' most demanding needs.

Areas of Expertise

- Design and fabrication of filters, mixers, modulators, switches and detectors using E-plane (finline) and microstrip technology.
- Design and fabrication of multipliers, amplifiers and oscillators using microstrip technology.
- Design and fabrication of a full line of passive components including phased array corporate feed networks, couplers and power dividers.
- Design and fabrication of printed antenna elements.

Facilities

- Access to a full line of microwave and millimetre-wave test equipment.
- Facilities for high-resolution microwave printed-circuit fabrication.
- State-of-the-art commercial and proprietary CAD software.

Recommended Readings

*1. Microwave Communications. *Communications News,* 25: 24–34, O'88.
*2. User study: More Corporations Turned on by Microwave gear. S. J. Lowe Graph. *Data Communications,* 17: 76 Ap'88.
3. Microwaves Cook up Big Phone Savings. J. Bienkowski. *Bankers Monthly* 106: 73 Ap'89.
4. Short Haul Microwave—A Versatile Solution. B. Jennings, *Telecommunications,* 22: 47–48, Je'88.
5. European Firms Increase Efforts to Develop Millimeter Wave Radars. P. J. Klass, *Aviat. Week Space Technology.* 129: 153+ S'88.
6. Design Considerations for Monolithic Microwave Circuits. R. A. Pucel. *IEEE Trans. Microwave Theory Tech.,* pt. I, vol. MTT-29. pp. 513–534, June 1981.

CASE 5

Heather Evans

It was May 10, 1983, and Heather Evans's graduation from Harvard Business School was less than a month away. Although she had just taken the last of her final exams that morning, Heather's thoughts could not have been further from school as she boarded the Eastern Shuttle and headed back to New York. The trip was a familiar one, for Heather had been commuting between school and Manhattan in an attempt to get her dress company off the ground.

Many of the elements of the business were falling into place, but the securing of $250,000 in financing remained elusive. Her business plan had been in the hands of potential investors for over a month now, and her financing group was simply not coming together. Her contact at Arden & Co., a New York investment firm and hoped-for lead investor, was not even returning her phone calls. A number of small, private investors had been stringing along for some weeks, but whenever Heather tried to go that next step and negotiate specific financing terms with any one of them, the rest of the group seemed to move further away. Heather expressed her frustration:

> I was really counting on Arden & Co. to be my lead investor; this would lend both credibility to the deal and give me *one* party to negotiate terms with. Then I could go to these private investors, point to the deal I'd struck with Arden and say, "These are the terms—make a decision."
>
> Now, if I give each of these investors what they want, I'll end up giving the company away. But I do need the money, and fast. In order to get out a holiday (winter) line, I need to start placing orders for fabric in the next month. All this, in addition to the rent and salaries I'm committed to.
>
> I don't know whether I should stick with the private investors I have and somehow try to hammer out a deal; or really work on getting a venture firm as a lead investor—maybe there is still a chance of bringing Arden & Co. around. Maybe I should try to get less money, or move back my timetable and wait for spring to introduce a line.

HEATHER EVANS

Heather Evans graduated from Harvard College in 1979, having earned her bachelor's degree in philosophy in three years. A Phi Beta Kappa graduate, Heather had been a working model throughout her college career, appearing in such publications as *Mademoiselle*, *Seventeen*, and *GQ*.(See Exhibit 1.)

Heather applied to the Harvard Business School during her senior year, and was accepted with a two-year deferred admit to the class entering in 1981. She accepted a position with Morgan Stanley as a financial analyst. Heather explained the origin of her interest in a business career:

My father is an attorney with a Wall Street firm, and many of my parents' friends were "deal-makers" who had gone to the Business School. I thought that I would like that kind of work and the lifestyle that went along with it. In addition, my career as a model gave me a taste of running my own business—the independence, the travel, the people—and I loved it. I knew, though, that I would need a good solid background to gain the skills and credibility necessary for success.

I thought that working for an investment bank like Morgan Stanley would give me the technical and financial training that I would need during my career.

Heather left Morgan Stanley and began her two years at HBS with her basic orientation unchanged:

I was still focused primarily on a deal-making, venture-capital type of career. I had always been interested in the fashion business and thought that I might, at some point, financially back a designer. I decided to work on Seventh Avenue for the summer and got a job as the assistant to Jackie Hayman, president of a woman's clothing company.

Heather saw the business and financial side of the business as well as the design and marketing aspects:

I was convinced and confident that I could run a business like this. That summer was actually the first time I believed that business school education had much value at all. I was able to understand the business very well, and my education and experience allowed me to grasp the fundamental issues quickly.

Heather returned to HBS in September, committed to starting her own venture in the garment industry.

THE EVOLUTION OF HEATHER EVANS INCORPORATED

Heather began by defining the concept of the company and its product line. Based on her experience in investment banking and at business school, Heather was convinced that the current mode of business dress for women—primarily suits—was, in fact, ill-suited to the demands and desires of businesswomen. Heather conceived a line of dresses in natural and wear-worthy fabrics that would better meet these women's needs (see business plan for full description).

In September, she began working with Robert Vin, an assistant designer in New York, in an attempt to transfer her concepts to finished design sketches and patterns. By November, it was clear to Heather that this arrangement was not going to work out; she decided that she would be both the chief designer and operating manager of her firm. Although it

Low NEED FOR CONFORMITY

was an extremely untraditional approach to a start-up in the garment business, Heather reasoned that it would make more sense for her:

> First, I didn't get along that well with Robert on a personal level. More important, though, I found myself doubting both his design sense and my own ability to judge someone else's design sense. Fundamentally, I had more trust in myself and my abilities as a designer.

Thus was Heather Evans Incorporated born.

Heather spent November and December flying between Boston and New York and developing, in further detail, her concept of the business. By December, Heather had put together a plan of action, which she submitted for approval as a field study (see Exhibit 2). After her first-semester exams ended, Heather moved to New York. She scheduled all of her classes on Monday and Tuesday and planned to spend the rest of her time in New York getting the key elements of her business in place.

Staff

Heather decided that the first person she needed was an assistant designer. "I wanted someone who had the technical training and experience in design that I lacked. I needed someone who knew more about design than I did, but who didn't mind working for me as an assistant."

Heather interviewed several individuals and in early February offered the position to Belinda Hughes, who had served as an assistant designer with two major firms. Heather began paying Belinda (out of her own pocket) to do freelance work based on detailed discussions with Heather about the content of the line, with the promise that full-time employment would begin in April or May.

Heather also began looking for a pattern-maker; someone who could transform a sample dress into specifications and a design for production.

Heather asked several industry acquaintances, and a vice president at Marjori (a major fashion manufacturer) recommended Barbara Tarpe. Heather called Barbara and the two hit it off. During their meeting, Barbara indicated that she would like an equity position in the company. Heather thought that Barbara could make a significant contribution and that her request was reasonable. Heather genuinely liked Barbara and thought that she would make a good partner.

One week later, before proceeding further, Heather decided to call another friend in the industry who might know Barbara.

> Martin is an old friend, and I trust his judgement; he told me that Barbara was a terrible liar and had no real talent. I looked back at my original notes after our meeting: "Very good rapport with Barbara. She seems *HONEST*. Feel she can run entire inside of business." I didn't hire Barbara and was shocked at how wrong I could be about someone. I had always felt comfortable trusting my own judgement.

Office and Showroom Space

Heather spent countless afternoons scouring New York's garment district (around Seventh Avenue from 42nd to 34th Streets) for potential showroom, office and working space. Showroom space is very important, because store buyers visit here during the buying season to make their decisions.

> I decided that I needed about 1,500 square feet of space for an office, sample and pattern-making space and a showroom. For $7 or $8 per square foot, I could get space in buildings which were somewhat off the main center of the district and which housed other relatively "unknown" designers. For $20–$25 per foot, I could be in a building that was more centrally located and that housed better-known firms.

By late February, Heather had decided to lease 1,500 square feet of space in a building at $10 per foot, for $1,500 per month.

Although the building was in a less desirable location, and would get less traffic from buyers than more expensive buildings, Heather reasoned that she should attempt to conserve as much cash as possible. Heather sent a deposit on this space and would begin paying rent May 1.

A month later, an acquaintance in the garment business called and offered Heather space in 550 Seventh Avenue—the most prestigious building in the garment center, housing such designers as Ralph Lauren, Oscar de la Renta, and many other famous names. Heather would have her own office space and would share the showroom space with another designer (who sold a line of clothing that would not compete directly with Heather's). Heather accepted his offer on the spot, even though she would have to start paying rent as of March 15, and the rent was $2,000, substantially more than the other building, and there was less space.

Financing

In the fall, Heather had begun talking informally with potential investors—friends at school and former colleagues in the investment banking and garment industry. She was hesitant, however, to do more than this until she had a business plan and a proposed deal.

Then in February, a friend and recent Business School graduate called to suggest that the two get together for a drink.

> Anne Snelling and I had both worked for Morgan Stanley and then gone on to the Business School. She had graduated one year earlier than I and gone to work for Arden & Co. (a private investment bank). I assumed that our meeting would be social, but Anne was soon putting on the hard-sell for Arden, convincing me that they should do the whole deal. I was quite surprised and pleased. Arden had an excellent reputation, and their financing would be a "stamp of approval" on the deal.

Heather and Anne met once or twice during January and February, and Anne asked Heather to accompany her to Vail for a week of skiing over spring break the first week in March. Heather reasoned that it would be a wise move to go.

I didn't really feel comfortable taking off for a week—I had an incredible amount to do. Yet, I was anxious for Arden's participation, so off to Vail I went. I was unsure whether Anne intended our week to be business or pleasure, but I brought along all of my papers and was prepared to negotiate a deal.

Once we got there, Anne said she wanted to talk about the deal, but was constantly on the phone pursuing other business. I came back to New York feeling pretty discouraged; we had never had a chance to really discuss my business.

Heather called Anne that next week and voiced her concern: time was running out, and Heather still had no clear idea where Arden or Anne stood on the issue.

Anne suggested that we get together for dinner that evening and tie things up—I was relieved. But when I walked into the restaurant, Anne was sitting there with her sister, Susan, and Susan's fiance. She apologized—they had just flown into the city, and Anne had asked them to join us. I was livid.

At this point, Heather realized that the financing was not going to come as easily as she had hoped, and she began pushing some of her other potential investors to get a sense of their interest. She raced to finish the business plan (see Exhibit 3) and sent this out to Arden & Co. and 15 individual investors during the first week in April.

DOWN TO THE WIRE

During the month of April, the pace of Heather's efforts accelerated and the business began eating up more cash. Belinda's part-time salary was now running about $1,000 per month; rent was running $2,000 per month. Finally, Heather had begun shopping the fabric market and would soon have to order and pay for $3,000 worth of sample fabric.

Heather had already invested about $10,000 of her own funds in the business, and her remaining resources were dwindling quickly. Because of the timing of the cycles in the garment industry (see Exhibit 4) Heather would have a great many more expenses before any cash came back into the business; most significantly, she would have to pay for the fabric for the entire holiday line—about $40,000 worth.

Yet Heather was having a difficult time bringing the investor group together. Anne Snelling was not returning her phone calls, and the private investors were interested, but had made no firm commitments. Heather's major problem was trying to negotiate with all of these potential investors individually; without a lead investor, there was no one party to negotiate the terms of a deal with.

The process of raising funds was hampered by Heather's extremely busy schedule. Besides talking to retailers, working on designs and getting settled in her new office space, Heather was still going to school during this time, and exams were coming up. Heather commented on the strain:

The spring semester was a rough one; trying to get my company started really took its toll. I had always considered myself a responsible student. I prepared about a half-dozen cases the entire semester and only made it to half my classes. I felt bad about it, but I knew I had to do it to get my business going.

FINANCING OPTIONS

Heather had several options available, but knew that she did not have sufficient time to pursue them all.

Arden & Co.

Heather held out some hope that Arden was still interested in the deal. Perhaps if she really pushed for a commitment, Arden would come through.

Venture Capital Firms

Heather had spoken with one or two firms that had indicated some interest. She knew that starting fresh with people who were unfamiliar with the company, as well as dealing with the bureaucratic decision-making process, would take a great deal of time. In addition, Heather suspected that they might drive a harder bargain than private investors, but at this point she welcomed the opportunity to negotiate with anyone just to get an idea of what valuation to put on the company.

Helen Neil Fashions, Inc.

Heather had approached another small venture capital firm which had Helen Neil Fashions, Inc. in its portfolio of companies. Helen Neil herself was a proven designer, and the company had established a base of relationships with manufacturers and retailers. The company, however, lacked any real operating management. This venture firm had indicated an interest in financing Heather if she would ally herself with Helen Neil and essentially embark on a joint venture. This idea had not yet been broached with Helen Neil, however, and Heather knew that any deal was dependent on the approval of Helen and her company's management.

Private Investors

Heather had a pool of 20 or so private individuals who seemed interested in investing in the company. The problem here was the amount of time it took to negotiate with each of these people individually, and their diverse desires for the terms of the investment. Heather was unsure how to structure the deal to satisfy the divergent interests of these individuals whom she was fairly sure would invest under any reasonable set of terms. She had spoken to a small sample of these investors (see Exhibit 5) to get their point of view, but was hesitant to speak to any more investors before she could present them with a deal.

HEATHER'S REQUIREMENTS

Heather had given some thought to the different aspects of the deal and had decided that the following terms were important to her:

- Control of the company: Heather felt that she should be able to control over 50 percent of the equity, as well as have a majority of the voting control of the company.
- License of the name *Heather Evans:* Heather felt that she had already expended considerable effort in building up her own name, and that if she left the company, she should have the right to use it.
- Ability to remain private: Heather did not want to be in a position where her investors could force her to become a public company. Liz Claiborne, a successful women's clothing company, had recently gone public, and potential investors were naturally excited by the returns inherent in a public offering. (See Exhibit 6 for excerpts from the Liz Claiborne prospectus.) Heather knew that she had to offer her investors some means of exit and getting a return on their investment.

With exams finally over, Heather could concentrate her full energies on pulling together her financial backing and getting the business off the ground.

Exhibit 1. Heather Evans modeling one of her designs.

Exhibit 2. Field Study Plan.

The purpose of this project is to develop a business plan and a strategy for approaching investors for a women's designer clothing manufacturing company, which I will form upon graduation from HBS. This company will offer high price, high quality dress and jacket combinations to executive women, ages 27 to 45.

The business plan will include:

I. A marketing plan, including an analysis of the relevant market, how I will position my product (in terms of price and image) and a retailing and promotion strategy.
II. A description of the organization, including people and physical plant.
III. Pro forma financial statements, based on sales projections from I, and operating costs from II.
IV. A financing proposal.

The attached time schedule outlines the process of putting together this plan. You will note that I have allotted substantial time to drafting and redrafting the plan, relative to research. This is because I have already spent a lot of time gathering information and find that I now need to organize that information in order to see what is missing. I will, however, spend the first half of January meeting with department store buyers to refine my retailing strategy, which I recognize is weak.

The final product for my Independent Research Report (IRR) will be the business plan actually presented to investors and a broader strategic document describing how the plan fits into my investor strategy.

Field Study Project Schedule Week of:

December 13, 1982	— Settle issue of adviser for IRR.
	— Gather examples of business plans.
December 20	— Complete survey of existing market research and financial information on comparable companies. (Sources: Fairchild Publications' library; 10-Ks ordered from companies.)
December 27	— Vacation
January 3, 1983	— Prepare preliminary outline of plan.
	— Review outline with adviser.
	— Set up meetings with buyers from Filene's, Nieman's, Macy's, Bergdorf, Saks, Bloomingdales, Nordstrom and others.
January 10 and 17	— Prepare first draft of plan Parts I and II.
	— Meet with buyers.
January 24 and 31	— Talk with various industry contacts to fill information "holes," especially regarding Part II of plan (e.g., salary levels for various employees, equipment needs and costs, and optimal showroom and design studio locations).

February 7	— Prepare second draft of plan, including detailed pro formas (Part III).
	— Begin interviewing candidates for design assistant, sales/PR director and business manager positions. (These individuals should be named in the plan.)
February 14	— Review second draft with adviser.
	— Present plan to CPA for review.
	— Prepare list of potential investors and consider order of approach.
	— Select law firm.
February 21 and 28	— Select and recruit key employees.
	— Revise plan, Parts I-III.
	— Present revised plan to lawyer.
	— Explore financial structure alternatives with lawyer, adviser and others.
March 7	— Draft Part IV of plan.
	— Determine preferred investor group profile and strategy for approaching investors.
	— Select factor and discuss terms, to the extent appropriate at that point.
March 14, 21, 28	— Vacation.
April 4 and 11	— Meet informally with key investors.
	— Finalize plan.
April 18	— Distribute plan to potential investors.

Exhibit 3. Heather Evans Incorporated business plan, April 7, 1983 *(Confidential).*

TABLE OF CONTENTS

Exhibit 3. (continued)

HEATHER EVANS INCORPORATED BUSINESS PLAN
I. SUMMARY

COMPANY
: HEATHER EVANS INCORPORATED, incorporated in New York on March 9, 1983, and located in New York City.

BUSINESS
: The Company will design, contract for the manufacture of and market a line of clothing for professional women.

MANAGEMENT
: *Heather H. Evans, President and Designer*

Ms. Evans will graduate from Harvard Business School in June 1983. She has worked as assistant to the president of Catherine Hipp, a designer clothing firm; as a financial analyst at Morgan Stanley, an investment bank; and as a photographic model, with Ford Models.

Belinda Hughes, Assistant Designer

Most recently, Ms. Hughes was head designer at Creations by Aria. For two years before that, after her graduation from Parsons School of Design, she worked as Mr. Kasper's assistant at Kasper for J. L. Sports.

CONCEPT
: The Company will offer a "designer" line to fit the lifestyle of professional women. Based on her experience in investment banking and at business school, Ms. Evans has conceived a style of clothing, based primarily on dresses, which better fits the lifestyle and demands of businesswomen than the suits and other looks currently offered to them by existing clothing manufacturers.

STATUS
: The Company has already begun designing its holiday line, obtained showroom and studio space in a prestigious designer building, reserved production capacity in a high-quality factory, and arranged for credit with an apparel industry factor.

In order to present its first line for the Holiday 1983 season, the Company must be assured financing prior to May 1983. The Company is seeking $250,000 to cover start-up expenses, to fund development of its first line, and to provide initial working capital. Thereafter, the Compnay anticipates that it will generate sufficient cash from operations, which, together with normal industry factoring, will fund growth internally.

Legal Counsel:
: Kaye, Scholer, Fierman, Hays & Handler

Accountants:
: Rashba & Pokart

Bank:
: Citibank

Exhibit 3. (continued)

II. CONCEPT

HEATHER EVANS INCORPORATED aims to become a substantial apparel company. Its success formula is a combination of powerful elements:

- a new look,
- for an unmet and quickly growing market,
- promoted and sold by a unique individual, Heather H. Evans,
- within a professionally managed and controlled organization.

Ms. Evans recognized the need for a *new look* for professional women when she shopped for clothes to wear to her job at an investment bank. She found few clothes that fit the functional demands of her work, while having some "style." Since then, she has spoken with hundreds of professional women who voice the same complaint. They work in an environment that strictly defines what is considered appropriate; "Seventh Avenue" does not understand these women.

The HEATHER EVANS "look" will be based on dresses, worn with untailored or softly tailored jackets, with:

- A clean and elegant silhouette.
- Distinctiveness through cut and line, without frills, excessive detail, or sexual suggestiveness.
- Undistracting colors, in solids or subtle patterns (e.g., Glen plaid or pinstripe).
- Comfortable fit.
- Travel-worthy fabrics in all-natural fibers, such as silk-wool blends.
- Quality construction.

Dresses and jackets will be priced and sold separately, along with coordinated skirts and tops, as a *complete* line:

- To permit the customer to coordinate an entire workplace wardrobe from the line.
- To position the line in "sportswear" departments of department stores, which are more updated and better displayed than "dress" departments.
- To avoid resistance to the high price tag of a combined outfit, from a customer who usually buys sportswear pieces.

Each collection will include 30 to 70 pieces, depending on the season, which is comparable to other complete designer sportswear lines. The Company will sell five collections: for the holiday, early spring, spring, transition and fall seasons. These are the regular "sportswear" market periods.

Unlike most designer collections, which include many kinds of clothes for different activities and different times of day, the HEATHER EVANS collection will include only clothes appropriate for the conservative workplace. This focus is critical in establishing the

Exhibit 3. (continued)

confidence of upper-strata professional women in the "look" for officewear. Later, the Company can introduce other lines (e.g., leisurewear) under the HEATHER EVANS name, in order to benefit from its reputation and customer franchise.

HEATHER EVANS clothes will be sold through better department and specialty stores. The line will be marketed as "designer" clothing, but will be priced at the upper end of the "bridge" category, which is the next lower price category. The bridge category was born and grew dramatically with such lines as Liz Claiborne and Evan Picone, which targeted the flood of women into the workplace over the past decade; HEATHER EVANS will capitalize on the second stage of this demographic trend, as women become accepted in large numbers in better-paid, professional and managerial roles. Positioning the line at the top of the bridge category:

- Will place the line in stores next to other lines currently bought by the target customer (e.g., Tahari, Harve Bernard, Nipon Collectibles).
- Responds to growing price resistance among customers, but
- Permits the Company to create a quality garment.
- Develops the HEATHER EVANS label for future licensing potential.

Heather H. Evans

Ms. Evans is uniquely qualified to develop and sell a new style of clothing for conservative businesswomen. As a former investment banker and a graduate of Harvard Business School,

- She has lived the lifestyle of these women, and knows their needs.
- She understands the limits of appropriateness within a formal office environment, which Seventh Avenue designers, who have tried to capture this customer, clearly do not.
- She can gain the confidence of the target customer through identification of her own background with their own lives.

Moreover, as a former model, Ms. Evans has experience at projecting herself through the media and can attract publicity as a designer/personality. She will actively seek to publicize the Company in business media, as well as fashion media, to reach the target customer. She is currently working on stories about the Company with writers from *Vogue* and *Savvy*. (Ms. Evans's resume is included as Appendix A.)

III. MARKET

HEATHER EVANS will initially position its products as designer clothing for the "formal" professional woman to wear to the office. Later, the Company can serve a virtually unlimited number of markets based on its reputation for quality and taste, as established through its original line of clothing.

Exhibit 3. (continued)

Professional Women's Clothing

Target Market

HEATHER EVANS will target the upper end of a subsegment of the working women's clothing market, identified as "formal professional" women in a 1980 market study by Celanese.

These women are an extremely attractive market because they are:

- a large, fast-growing group,
- with high disposable incomes,
- who are concentrated in metropolitan areas,
- where they buy at a select group of better department and specialty stores,
- with relative insensitivity to price,
- attention to quality,
- apparel brand loyalty,
- and *still-developing tastes and preferences in professional clothing.*

Celanese found the formal professional segment to be a well-defined purchasing group: it "includes accountants, lawyers, sales managers, executives and administrators who work in highly structured and formal environments. They can be characterized by a strict dress code and overriding concern with presenting a professional image. Members of this group wish to convey occupational status at work and in nonwork activities and can be considered investment dressers."

- 4.3 million women fall within this group.
- They spend $5 billion per year on clothes.
- They represent the fastest growing segment of the working women's clothing market, with real growth forecast at 8–10 percent per year.

HEATHER EVANS will target the upper end of this group, whose concerns about quality and appropriateness are highest, commensurate with their level of income and responsibility.

The following statistics suggest that the upper end of the market is growing even faster than the formal professional market as a whole:

- In 1980, 793,000 women made over $25,000 per year.
- 147,000 women made over *$50,000* per year, up *22 percent* from the previous year.

Thus, HEATHER EVANS will target the new ranks of established executive and professional women. Whereas Liz Claiborne and others capitalized on the initial entry of women into the work force in the 70s, HEATHER EVANS will capitalize on their acceptance in positions of responsibility in the 80s.

Exhibit 3. (continued)

Style Trends

Formal professional women are a ripe market for a well-conceived new clothing label because their tastes and habits in officewear are evolving, but they have few options among existing clothes.

Women in the upper end of the market, HEATHER EVANS's target, are still wearing mostly classic or modified tailored suits, with a blouse and neck ornament. The lower end shows movement toward softer looks and, particularly, dresses. Ms. Evans believes that this trend toward more varied looks will also be seen in the upper end of the market. However, the existing untailored bridge lines, dress lines and designer sportswear lines are inappropriately styled for that segment.

Manufacturers have recently seen the demand for suits flatten, as interest in dresses has renewed. Responding to this trend, Liz Claiborne and Albert Nipon both opened dress divisions aimed at executive women, priced in the "better" range. The president of Liz Claiborne Dresses voiced the expectations of many in the industry when she told *Women's Wear Daily* that, unlike the 70s when working women wore mostly tailored sportswear for fear of standing out, "in the 80s I think they're going to be a lot more adventuresome in what they wear." As evidence, the dress division of Liz Claiborne hit around $10 million in wholesale sales in less than a year, approximately 10 percent of the entire company's sales.

These examples illustrate the receptivity of the working women's market to new styles and designers. However, the offerings of these companies and others are inappropriate for the more conservative elements. HEATHER EVANS intends to fill this gap.

Competition

The "designer" fashion market is a relatively easy one to enter, because—

- *Competition is fragmented.* For example, although there are no comprehensive trade statistics available, it is worth noting that Liz Claiborne, which is one of the two largest companies in the market, can claim less than 3 percent of the market, with $155 million in latest 12 months sales.
- *Channels welcome new products.* Department store buyers are responsible for identifying and promoting new, promising lines, so that customers perceive the buyer's store as a fashion leader. In particular, major department store chains are seeking new lines in the bridge price range, in which HEATHER EVANS will position its products. They foresee this price category becoming increasingly important.

Retailers are encountering consumer price resistance, which suggests that the designer-priced sportswear market has matured: the continual "trading-up" by customers in the 70s has ended. In response, manufacturers are generally lowering prices, both within existing lines and by introducing new lines in lower price categories. Many designer companies will target the bridge market, where customers are value-conscious, but have disposable income.

Exhibit 3. (continued)

The Company anticipates that the opportunities created by renewed interest in this area will favor the Company's strategy and outweigh the threat of other new entrants and competition.

Designer Products Market

Once it has established a franchise in the expensive businesswear market, HEATHER EVANS can expand into any of several immediately related markets:

- Accessories (e.g., belts, shoes, scarves) in a similar price category to coordinate with the original clothing line.
- Leisure clothing in the same price range for the same customer as the original line.
- Lower-priced office-wear for a different, wider customer group (i.e., the rest of the 4.3 million formal professional women).

Finally, numerous tertiary markets exist for a well-managed designer name. For example, Bill Blass has licensed his name for chocolates, while Ralph Lauren has licensed his for a full line of home furnishings.

In the past, these designers have developed their names in the couture or designer sportswear levels; however, the extraordinary success of Norma Kamali, whose clothes retail for $30 to $100, demonstrates that a "designer" name can be made in any price range.

Thus, the Company can serve a virtually unlimited number of markets based on its reputation for taste and quality, as established through its original line of clothing. In Calvin Klein's case, his name is used on products with combined retail sales of $1 billion.

Licensing

Designers profit enormously from licensing agreements, through which they attach their names to products in return for a 5–10 percent royalty. These products are manufactured and marketed—and often designed—by the licensee. For example,

- Pierre Cardin reaps over $50 million a year in royalties on $1 billion of wholesale sales on 540 licenses, with minimal related expenses.
- The top 10 designers collect over $200 million in royalties between them each year.

Long-Run View

The designer label has replaced the better department store label as the arbiter of taste and quality for the American consumer. After some designers (most notably Cardin) licensed their names indiscriminately in the name-craze of the mid-70s, consumers became more evaluative about the value of a given designer's name, but they continue to purchase according to that name.

This shift has been disastrous for department stores, which have lost their business to discounters, which carry the same designer names for less with comparable service, and to specialty stores, which offer superior service at comparable prices. Although this shake-up in the retail industry will have repercussions for designers, it is unlikely to reverse a now well-entrenched phenomenon.

Exhibit 3. (continued)

IV. MANAGEMENT AND OPERATIONS

Organization and People

Design

The design group is the core of the Company: it creates five new product lines each year, on which the eventual success of the Company will depend. It is important to recognize that sales of the line will depend as much on existing specifications of fit, construction, fabrics and coordination of pieces within the line as on the design sketches themselves; these are all parts of the design function.

The design process for each line takes approximately nine months, so that several lines are being worked on in various stages at any time. For each line, the design function is to—

- Plan the line; determine the number of styles, colors and fabric groups, on the basis of overall line balance, ranges of buyer climates and tastes, and other marketing factors.
- Define the theme and tone of the line.
- Choose and order specific fabrics and other supplies, after surveying the market for these products.
- Create and select sketches.
- Cut, drape and sew samples. Perfect fit of samples.
- Select final samples for the collection.
- Prepare patterns for production and communicate with normal industry contract manufacturers.

Ms. Evans will spend 40 percent of her time on design and production functions. She will oversee the entire process, with emphasis on *planning* and defining the theme of each line, and *selecting* fabrics, sketches and final samples.

Ms. Hughes and Ms. Evans will work as a team on all design-related tasks. Ms. Hughes has significant expertise in the creative and technical aspects of fashion design. She is experienced in creating specific styles from a general concept for a line. Her vocabulary of stylistic detail, production feasibility and textile characteristics complement Ms. Evans's market-driven design direction. (Ms. Hughes's background is described in Appendix B.)

Ms. Hughes has already been retained by Ms. Evans on a free-lance basis and is designing a Holiday line. It is expected that Ms. Hughes will join the company on a full-time basis shortly after funding is received.

The Company plans to hire a design assistant in June. The design assistant will make sample patterns, cut the samples and oversee the sample makers. She will work with an outside pattern maker on production patterns and with the factory to assure that the final product meets the specifications of the sample garments.

The Company plans to hire one sample maker in June and another in September 1983.

Exhibit 3. (continued)

Production

The production function manages the process from the sample through the shipment of the final garment to the stores. The concerns of the production staff are quality, timely delivery and cost. During the first two years, Ms. Evans and the design assistant will oversee production as part of their design responsibilities.

Following normal industry practice, the Company will subcontract all manufacturing, including the grading and marketing of its patterns, cutting of its piece goods and sewing of its garments, to independent suppliers. Initially, all its suppliers will be located in New York City and other locations in the northeastern United States. There is capacity available in suitable shops in this area, where management can carefully monitor the quality and timing of production. As production volume increases, the Company may consider manufacturing in Hong Kong, Taiwan or elsewhere, where manufacturing costs for quality workmanship may be lower.

Malcolm Wong, a contractor located at 226 West 37th Street, has agreed to reserve time to produce production patterns and sew the Company's entire first collection. Mr. Wong's factory is a high-quality, non-union shop, with 20 operators. Ms. Evans may use other contractors for all or part of the line, if these contractors offer a more favorable price.

The Company has arranged for its shipping to be done through Fernando Sanchez, as part of its rental arrangement with that firm (see Facilities and Equipment). Fernando Sanchez will provide space, shipping personnel and shipping supplies. After July 1984, the Company expects to add one shipping employee of its own.

Sales and Promotion

Sales are made during "market weeks" which last approximately three weeks for each of the five seasons, spread through the year. Store buyers write orders based on the sample line, which they view in the Company's showroom or in one of several regional marketplaces. The Company plans to join the New York Fashion Council, Inc. and has tentatively arranged through this group to reserve space in the key regional market shows.

Ms. Evans will spend 40 percent of her time in sales and promotion.

Initially, Ms. Evans will handle all department store sales and some specialty store sales, in the showroom and in "trunk shows" to the Dallas and L.A. markets. Ms. Evans's personal attention is important in this stage to communicate the philosophy of the line, to use her Harvard Business School contacts in department store managements, and to save money.

The Company plans to retain an established, independent representative to sell the line to specialty stores in the Northeast (except New York City). Ms. Evans is currently negotiating with a well-known representative for several designer lines, with whom she has worked previously. The representative will show the line to his customers in the Company's showroom.

Exhibit 3. (continued)

Once critical customer relationships have become established and sales volume warrants, Ms. Evans will hire full-time, experienced showroom personnel and, possibly, retain additional independent sales representatives. Ms. Evans will then direct her efforts to more promotional activities and to managing the sales personnel.

Ms. Evans will also carry out an active campaign of nonsales promotion. She will communicate with customer fashion directors, concerning use of samples in cooperative advertising and scheduling personal in-store appearances, and with newspaper and magazine editors to encourage editorial coverage. She will also oversee production of promotional materials to announce the opening of each collection.

Control

Financial and production control will occupy 20 percent of Ms. Evans's time. These functions are critical to, but often neglected in, apparel manufacturing companies. In particular, fabric purchasing and production decisions must be made so as to maximize sales, yet minimize inventory at the end of the season when it becomes obsolete. Ms. Evans's experience in financial analysis and her business school training are valuable assets in the control function.

The Company plans to hire a part-time bookkeeper during its first months of operation. In July 1984 or thereafter, the Company will retain a full-time office manager.

Facilities and Equipment

The Company has arranged for showroom and design studio space in the 550 Seventh Avenue building. This is one of the most prestigious buildings in the garment district, with such other tenants as Bill Blass, Halston, Ralph Lauren and Oscar de la Renta.

HEATHER EVANS's showroom will be within the showroom of Fernando Sanchez, a new and successful high-priced, designer line. Ms. Evans feels that the exposure of the HEATHER EVANS line alongside the Sanchez line and within the 550 Seventh Avenue building will be very beneficial for the Company. The Company's line does not compete with the Sanchez line and will often be bought by different buyers from a given store.

The Company's design studio and office space will be adjacent to the Fernando Sanchez showroom, with its own entrance. The Company will be provided with shipping space at another location, 226 West 37 Street, as part of its arrangement with Fernando Sanchez. These facilities should be adequate for the first two years of operation.

V. FINANCIALS

The Company anticipates raising $250,000 in equity capital. This level of capitalization is adequate, together with normal industry factoring, to develop and to grow a substantial apparel company, without additional equity financing. This is a business plan and is not intended, of itself, to be an offering of stock or debt.

Exhibit 3. (continued)

Industry Financial Characteristics

High fashion apparel manufacturing offers high returns on capital within a short time frame to those companies whose clothing becomes *"fashion."*

- Margins run 40 to 60 percent.
- Operating costs after cost of goods sold and sales commissions (approximately 10 percent of sales) are relatively fixed. Basically, the cost of designing a line is the same at $1 million in sales as at $20 million.
- Investment in working capital is low: with 60-day terms from fabric suppliers and receivables factoring, cash received from shipment of finished goods can be applied to the cost of those same goods.
- Investment in fixed assets is limited to equipping and remodeling showroom, studio and shipping space. All manufacturing is subcontracted.
- After an initial introductory period of one to two years, acceptance of a line may proceed extremely rapidly, with annual sales growth rates of 100 to 500 percent not unusual.

Whether a line does become "fashion" and to what extent depends on a number of variables that cannot be tested or foreseen until the clothing is presented to the fashion press and the consumers. These variables include the appeal of the specific styles and fit of the line, general fashion trends and specific competitive styles offered at the time the line is presented, and media interest in the line. Thus, investors are rewarded for putting at risk the cost of developing, producing and marketing a line of clothing during an initial introductory period.

Sales Projections

The Company has prepared sales projections for the first two years of operation, as presented in Exhibit 1. These projections are based on typical order sizes for new lines in the Company's price range and reasonable rates of trial by stores, taking into account supplier credit limits.

For reasons mentioned above, having to do with the nature of fashion, the Company cannot meaningfully forecast sales growth beyond the introductory period.

Financial Statements

Projected financial statements for the company's first and second years of operation are included as Exhibits II and III, respectively. These forecast net income of $167,173 on sales of $1,712,500 in the second year.

A detailed list of assumptions for the forecasted financial statements is included as Exhibit IV. These estimates were developed by Ms. Evans, based on the experience of comparable companies, and discussed in detail with Rashba & Pokart, certified public accountants, who have extensive experience with apparel industry clients.

Heather Evans Incorporated Business Plan-Exhibit 3. (continued)

Exhibit I. Heather Evans Incorporated.

Sales Projections

| | Season | Market Period | Shipping Period | Specialty Store | | | Department Store | | | Total |
				Number of Orders	Avg. Order Size ($000)	Sales Volume ($000)	Number of Orders	Avg. Order Size ($000)	Sales Volume ($000)	($000)
Year 1	Holiday	August	October-November	38	$2	$75	9	$8	$75	$150
	Early spring	September	December-January	50	1	50	12	4	50	100
	Spring	October	February-April	50	3	150	12	12	150	300
	Transition	February	May-June	58	1	57.5	14	4	57.5	165
	Total									$ 715
Year 2	Fall	March	July-September	62	3.5	217.5	15	14	217.5	435
	Holiday	August	October-November	60	2	120	15	8	120	240
	Early spring	September	December-January	75	1	75	19	4	75	150
	Spring	October	February-April	94	4	375	23	16	375	750
	Transition	February	May-June	80	1	80	20	4	80	160
	Total									$1,735

Exhibit 3. (continued)

Exhibit II. Heather Evans Incorporated.

Projected Statement of Income
Year Ended May 31, 1984

	Total	June	July	Aug.	Sept.	Oct.	Nov.	Dec.	Jan.	Feb.	Mar.	April	May
Total Sales	607500	0	0	0	0	75000	75000	50000	50000	100000	100000	100000	57500
Less: Discounts	48600	0	0	0	0	6000	6000	4000	4000	8000	8000	8000	4600
Net Sales	558900	0	0	0	0	69000	69000	46000	46000	92000	92000	92000	52900
Cost of Goods Sold Inventory-Beginning	0	0	0	0	24375	61875	53750	41250	57500	82500	82500	68688	48750
Piece Goods & Trimmings	257438	0	0	24375	24375	16250	16250	32500	32500	32500	18688	20000	40000
Contracting Costs	116313	0	0	0	13125	13125	8750	8750	17500	17500	17500	10063	10000
Total	373750	0	0	24375	61875	91250	78750	82500	107500	132500	118688	98750	98750
Less: Inventory—Ending	70000	0	0	24375	61875	53750	41250	57500	82500	82500	68688	48750	70000
Cost of Goods Sold	303750	0	0	0	0	37500	37500	25000	25000	50000	50000	50000	28750
Gross Profit	255150	0	0	0	0	31500	31500	21000	21000	42000	42000	42000	24150
Operating Expenses:													
Production	149100	11300	11300	11300	12800	12800	12800	12800	12800	12800	12800	12800	12800
Selling and Shipping	53513	1000	1000	1700	1000	8825	5125	3750	3750	6500	10200	6500	4163
General and Administrative	120369	9727	9727	9727	10132	10132	10132	10132	10132	10132	10132	10132	10132
Factor's Charges	24300	0	0	0	0	3000	3000	2000	2000	4000	4000	4000	2300
Total Operating Expenses	347282	22027	22027	22727	23932	34757	31057	28682	28682	33432	37132	33432	29395
Net Income (-Loss)	-92132	-22027	-22027	-22727	-23932	-3257	443	-7682	-7682	8558	4868	8568	-5245

See accompanying Summary of Significant Projection Assumptions and Summary of Significant Accounting Policies.
Preliminary Draft. For discussion purposes only; all exhibits are tentative and subject to change.

Exhibit 3. (continued)

Exhibit II.

Projected Schedule of Operating Expenses
Year Ended May 31, 1984

	Total	June	July	Aug.	Sept.	Oct.	Nov.	Dec.	Jan.	Feb.	Mar.	April	May
Production Expenses:													
Designer's Salary	30000	2500	2500	2500	2500	2500	2500	2500	2500	2500	2500	2500	2500
Assistant Designer and Samplehand's Salaries	55500	3500	3500	3500	5000	5000	5000	5000	5000	5000	5000	5000	5000
Pattern Maker Salary	39600	3300	3300	3300	3300	3300	3300	3300	3300	3300	3300	3300	3300
Design Room Supplies	24000	2000	2000	2000	2000	2000	2000	2000	2000	2000	2000	2000	2000
Total	149100	11300	11300	11300	12800	12800	12800	12800	12800	12800	12800	12800	12800
Selling and Shipping:													
Salesmen's Commissions	30375	0	0	0	0	3750	3750	2500	2500	5000	5000	5000	2875
Travel and Entertainment	20100	1000	1000	1700	1000	4700	1000	1000	1000	1000	4700	1000	1000
Freight Out	3038	0	0	0	0	375	375	250	250	500	500	500	288
Total	53513	1000	1000	1700	1000	8825	5125	3750	3750	6500	10200	6500	4163
General and Administrative:													
Rent	24000	2000	2000	2000	2000	2000	2000	2000	2000	2000	2000	2000	2000
Office Salary	9600	800	800	800	800	800	800	800	800	800	800	800	800
Telephone	8400	700	700	700	700	700	700	700	700	700	700	700	700
Stationery and Office	12000	1000	1000	1000	1000	1000	1000	1000	1000	1000	1000	1000	1000
Legal and Audit	12000	1000	1000	1000	1000	1000	1000	1000	1000	1000	1000	1000	1000
Dues and Subscriptions	3600	300	300	300	300	300	300	300	300	300	300	300	300
Depreciation and Amortization	2700	225	225	225	225	225	225	225	225	225	225	225	225
Insurance	7200	600	600	600	600	600	600	600	600	600	600	600	600
Business and Payroll Taxes	13470	1010	1010	1010	1160	1160	1160	1160	1160	1160	1160	1160	1160
Utilities	4500	375	375	375	375	375	375	375	375	375	375	375	375
Employee Benefits	22899	1717	1717	1717	1972	1972	1972	1972	1972	1972	1972	1972	1972
Total	120369	9727	9727	9727	10132	10132	10132	10132	10132	10132	10132	10132	10132

See accompanying Summary of Significant Projection Assumptions and Summary of Significant Accounting Policies.
Preliminary Draft. For discussion purposes only; all exhibits are tentative and subject to change.

Exhibit 3. (continued)

Exhibit II.

Forecasted Balance Sheets
June 1983 through May 1984

Assets	June	July	Aug.	Sept.	Oct.	Nov.	Dec.	Jan.	Feb.	Mar.	April	May
Current Assets:												
Cash and Due from Factor	203398	181596	159094	122262	119230	124273	116816	100609	109402	114495	130726	125769
Merchandise Inventories	0	0	24375	61875	53750	41250	57500	82500	82500	68688	48750	70000
Total Current Assets	203398	181596	183469	184137	172980	165523	174316	183109	191902	183183	179476	195769
Fixed Assets—Net	17775	17550	17325	17100	16875	16650	16425	16200	15975	15750	15525	15300
Other Assets	6800	6800	6800	6800	6800	6800	6800	6800	6800	6800	6800	6800
Total Assets	227973	205946	207594	208037	196655	188973	197541	206109	214677	205733	201801	217869
Liabilities and Stockholders' Equity												
Current Liabilities:												
Accounts Payable	0	0	24375	48750	40625	32500	48750	65000	65000	51188	38688	60000
Stockholders' Equity	227973	205946	183219	159287	156030	156473	148791	141109	149677	154545	163113	157869
Total Liabilities and Stockholders' Equity	227973	205946	207594	208037	196655	188973	197541	206109	214677	205733	201801	217869

See accompanying Summary of Significant Projection Assumptions and Summary of Significant Accounting Policies.
Preliminary Draft. For discussion purposes only; all exhibits are tentative and subject to change.

Exhibit 3. (continued)

Exhibit II.

Projected Statements of Cash Flow
Year Ended May 31, 1984

	Total	June	July	Aug.	Sept.	Oct.	Nov.	Dec.	Jan.	Feb.	Mar.	April	May
Cash and Due from Factor—Beginning	0	0	203398	181596	159094	122262	119230	124273	116816	100609	109402	114495	130726
Receipts:													
Initial Capitalization	250000	250000	0	0	0	0	0	0	0	0	0	0	0
Net Sales	558900	0	0	0	0	69000	69000	46000	46000	92000	92000	92000	52900
Total	808900	250000	203398	181596	159094	191262	188230	170273	162816	192609	201402	206495	183626
Cash Disbursements:													
Accounts Payable—Piece Goods & Trimmings	197438	0	0	0	0	24375	24375	16250	16250	32500	32500	32500	18688
Contractors Payable	116313	0	0	0	13125	13125	8750	8750	17500	17500	17500	10063	10000
Operating Expenses—Net	344582	21802	21802	22502	23707	34532	30832	28457	28457	33207	36907	33207	29170
Security Deposits	6800	6800	0	0	0	0	0	0	0	0	0	0	0
Purchase of Fixed Assets	18000	18000	0	0	0	0	0	0	0	0	0	0	0
Total	683132	46602	21802	22502	36832	72032	63957	53457	62207	83207	86907	75770	57857
Cash and Due from Factor—Ending	125769	203398	181596	159094	122262	119230	124273	116816	100609	109402	114495	130726	125769

See accompanying Summary of Significant Projection Assumptions and Summary of Significant Accounting Policies. Preliminary Draft. For discussion purposes only; all exhibits are tentative and subject to change.

Exhibit 3. (continued)

Exhibit III. Heather Evans Incorporated.

Projected Statement of Income
Year Ended May 31, 1985

	Total	June	July	Aug.	Sept.	Oct.	Nov.	Dec.	Jan.	Feb.	Mar.	April	May
Total Sales	1712500	57500	145000	145000	145000	120000	120000	75000	75000	250000	250000	250000	80000
Less: Discounts	137000	4600	11600	11600	11600	9600	9600	6000	6000	20000	20000	20000	6400
Net Sales	1575500	52900	133400	133400	133400	110400	110400	69000	69000	230000	230000	230000	73600
Cost of Goods Sold:													
Inventory—Beginning	70000	70000	113750	113750	105625	93125	78500	56000	112875	200375	200375	145125	81250
Piece Goods & Trimmings	585000	47125	47125	39000	39000	24375	24375	81250	81250	81250	26000	47125	47125
Contracting Costs	299625	25375	25375	25375	21000	21000	13125	13125	43750	43750	43750	14000	10000
Total	954625	142500	186250	178125	165625	138500	116000	150375	237875	325375	270125	206250	138375
Less: Inventory—Ending	98375	113750	113750	105625	93125	78500	56000	112875	200375	200375	145125	81250	98375
Cost of Goods Sold	856250	28750	72500	72500	72500	60000	60000	37500	37500	125000	125000	125000	40000
Gross Profit	719250	24150	60900	60900	60900	50400	50400	31500	31500	105000	105000	105000	33600
Operating Expenses:													
Production	153600	12800	12800	12800	12800	12800	12800	12800	12800	12800	12800	12800	12800
Selling and Shipping	114288	4163	8975	9675	8975	11300	7600	5125	5125	14750	18450	14750	5400
General and Administrative	149524	10132	12672	12672	12672	12672	12672	12672	12672	12672	12672	12672	12672
Factor's Charges	63020	2116	5336	5336	5336	4416	4416	2760	2760	9200	9200	9200	2944
Total Operating Expenses	480432	29211	39783	40483	39783	41188	37488	33357	33357	49422	53122	49422	33816
Income Before Provision for Income Taxes	238819	-5061	21117	20417	21117	9212	12912	-1857	-1857	55578	51878	55578	-216
Provision for Income Taxes	71646	-1518	6335	6125	6335	2764	3874	-557	-557	16673	15563	16673	-65
Net Income—(Loss)	167173	-3542	14782	14292	14782	6448	9038	-1300	-1300	38905	36315	38905	-151

See accompanying Summary of Significant Projection Assumptions and Summary of Significant Accounting Policies.
Preliminary Draft. For discussion purposes only; all exhibits are tentative and subject to change.

Exhibit 3. (continued)

Exhibit III.

Projected Schedule of Operating Expenses
Year Ended May 31, 1985

	Total	June	July	Aug.	Sept.	Oct.	Nov.	Dec.	Jan.	Feb.	Mar.	April	May
Production Expenses:													
Designer's Salary	30000	2500	2500	2500	2500	2500	2500	2500	2500	2500	2500	2500	2500
Assistant Designer and Samplehands's Salaries	60000	5000	5000	5000	5000	5000	5000	5000	5000	5000	5000	5000	5000
Pattern Maker Salary	39600	3300	3300	3300	3300	3300	3300	3300	3300	3300	3300	3300	3300
Design Room Supplies	24000	2000	2000	2000	2000	2000	2000	2000	2000	2000	2000	2000	2000
Total	153600	12800	12800	12800	12800	12800	12800	12800	12800	12800	12800	12800	12800
Selling and Shipping:													
Salesmen's Commissions	85625	2875	7250	7250	7250	6000	6000	3750	3750	12500	12500	12500	4000
Travel and Entertainment	20100	1000	1000	1700	1000	4700	1000	1000	1000	1000	4700	1000	1000
Freight Out	8563	288	725	725	725	600	600	375	375	1250	1250	1250	400
Total	114288	4163	8975	9675	8975	11300	7600	5125	5125	14750	18450	14750	5400
General and Administrative:													
Rent	24000	2000	2000	2000	2000	2000	2000	2000	2000	2000	2000	2000	2000
Office Salary	31600	800	2800	2800	2800	2800	2800	2800	2800	2800	2800	2800	2800
Telephone	8400	700	700	700	700	700	700	700	700	700	700	700	700
Stationery and Office	12000	1000	1000	1000	1000	1000	1000	1000	1000	1000	1000	1000	1000
Legal and Audit	12000	1000	1000	1000	1000	1000	1000	1000	1000	1000	1000	1000	1000
Dues and Subscriptions	3600	300	300	300	300	300	300	300	300	300	300	300	300
Depreciation and Amortization	2700	225	225	225	225	225	225	225	225	225	225	225	225
Insurance	7200	600	600	600	600	600	600	600	600	600	600	600	600
Business and Payroll Taxes	16120	1160	1360	1360	1360	1360	1360	1360	1360	1360	1360	1360	1360
Utilities	4500	375	375	375	375	375	375	375	375	375	375	375	375
Employee Benefits	27404	1972	2312	2312	2312	2312	2312	2312	2312	2312	2312	2312	2312
Total	149524	10132	12672	12672	12672	12672	12672	12672	12672	12672	12672	12672	12672

See accompanying Summary of Significant Projection Assumptions and Summary of Significant Accounting Policies. Preliminary Draft. For discussion purposes only; all exhibits are tentative and subject to change.

Exhibit 3. (continued)

Exhibit III.

Forecasted Balance Sheets
June 1984 through May 1985

	1984							1985				
Assets	June	July	Aug.	Sept.	Oct.	Nov.	Dec.	Jan.	Feb.	Mar.	April	May
Current Assets:												
Cash and Due from Factor	104309	132776	153418	179135	188572	209584	207952	175695	231498	283601	369154	373163
Merchandise Inventories	113750	113750	105625	93125	78500	56000	112875	200375	200375	145125	81250	98375
Total Current Assets	218059	246526	259043	272260	267072	265584	320827	376070	431873	428726	450404	471538
Fixed Assets—Net	15075	14850	14625	14400	14175	13950	13725	13500	13275	13050	12825	12600
Other Assets	6800	6800	6800	6800	6800	6800	6800	6800	6800	6800	6800	6800
Total Assets	239934	268176	280468	293460	288047	286334	341352	396370	451948	448576	470029	490938
Liabilities and Stockholders' Equity												
Current Liabilities:												
Accounts Payable	87125	94250	86125	78000	63375	48750	105625	162500	162500	107250	73125	94250
Income Taxes Payable	-1518	4817	10942	17277	20041	23914	23357	22800	39474	53037	71710	71646
Total Current Liabilities	85607	99067	97067	95277	83416	72664	128982	185300	201974	162287	144835	165896
Stockholders' Equity	154327	169109	183400	198182	204631	213669	212369	211069	249974	286289	325193	325042
Total Liabilities and Stockholders' Equity	239934	268176	280468	293460	288047	286334	341352	396370	451948	448576	470029	490938

See accompanying Summary of Significant Projection Assumptions and Summary of Significant Accounting Policies.
Preliminary Draft. For discussion purposes only; all exhibits are tentative and subject to change.

Exhibit 3. (continued)

Exhibit III.

Projected Statements of Cash Flow
Year Ended May 31, 1985

	Total	June	July	Aug.	Sept.	Oct.	Nov.	Dec.	Jan.	Feb.	Mar.	April	May
Cash and Due from Factor—Beginning	125769	125769	104309	132776	153418	179135	188572	209584	207952	175695	231498	283601	369154
Receipts:													
Net Sales	1575500	52900	133400	133400	133400	110400	110400	69000	69000	230000	230000	230000	73600
Total	1701269	178669	237709	266176	286818	289535	298972	278584	276952	405695	461498	513601	442754
Cash Disbursements:													
Accounts Payable—Piece Goods & Trimmings	550750	20000	40000	47125	47125	39000	39000	24375	24375	81250	81250	81250	26000
Contractors Payable	299625	25375	25375	25375	21000	21000	13125	13125	43750	43750	43750	14000	10000
Operating Expenses—Net	477732	28986	39558	40258	39558	40963	37263	33132	33132	49197	52897	49197	33591
Total	1328107	74361	104933	112758	107683	100963	89388	70632	101257	174197	177897	144447	69591
Cash and Due from Factor—Ending	373163	104309	132776	153418	179135	188572	209584	207952	175695	231498	283601	369154	373163

See accompanying Summary of Significant Projection Assumptions and Summary of Significant Accounting Policies. Preliminary Draft. For discussion purposes only; all exhibits are tentative and subject to change.

Exhibit 3. (continued)

Exhibit IV. Assumptions for Pro Forma Financial Statements.

Income Statement
1. Sales: See Exhibit I, Sales Projections
2. Discount: 8 percent (assume discount taken on all sales)
3. Cost of goods sold:
   —Inventory—see Balance Sheet below
   —Piece goods and trimmings—65 percent of COGS
   —Contracting costs—35 percent of COGS
4. Gross profit: 50 percent of gross sales (42 percent of net sales)
5. Operating expenses—see below
6. Factor's charge—4 percent net of sales (actual charges will be commission equal to a fixed percentage of sales plus interest charge for advances against uncollected receivables)

Operating Expenses
1. Production expenses
   —Salaries
      Designer—$2,500 per month, starting June 1983
      Assistant designer—$2,000 per month, starting June 1983
      Samplehands—$1,000 each per month, starting June 1983, another starting September 1983
      Pattern maker—$3,300 per month, starting June 1983
2. Selling and shipping
   —Salesmen's commission—10 percent on all specialty store sales, based on standard independent representative commission rate
      —Travel and entertainment—
      General travel and entertainment—$1,000 per month
      Announcements—$700 each holiday, spring and fall market period
      Trunk shows—$3,000 each spring and fall market period
   —Freight out—0.5 percent of sales
3. General and administrative
   —Rent—$2,000 per month
   —Office salary—
      Part-time bookkeeper—2 days per week, at $100 per day, starting June 1983
      Office manager—$2,000 per month
   —Telephone—$700 per month
   —Stationery and office—$1,000 per month
   —Legal and audit—$1,000 per month

—Dues and subscriptions—$300 per month

—Depreciation and amortization—$225 per month, based on $18,000 invest-ment in equipment, furniture and lease improvements, depreciated on a straight-line basis over an average life of 7 years.

—Insurance—$600 per month

—Business and payroll taxes—10 percent of full-time payroll

—Employee benefits—18 percent of full-time payroll

Balance Sheets

1. Cash and due from factor—includes 100 percent of invoices for goods shipped in each month
2. Merchandise inventories—includes piece goods and trim received 60 days in advance of sale; finished goods shipped within month
3. Fixed assets—net—depreciated straight-line over 7-year average life, from $18,000 base, as follows:

Sample room equipment	$7,000
Office and showroom furnishing	6,000
Remodelling	5,000
	$18,000

4. Other assets—includes lease deposit of $6,000 (3 months) and telephone deposit of $800
5. Accounts payable—includes piece goods and trimming payable within 60 days; contractors paid within 30 days; all other expenses assumed paid within month
6. Stockholders' equity—$250,000 initial capital

APPENDIXES

Appendix A. Resume of HEATHER H. EVANS.

Education

1981–1983

HARVARD GRADUATE SCHOOL OF BUSINESS ADMINISTRATION
Candidate for the degree of Master of Business Administration in June 1983. Awarded First Year Honors (top 15 percent of class).

Resident Business Tutor, South House, Harvard College: supervised pre-business program and oversaw student activities in residential unit of 350 undergraduate students. Instructor, Economics Department, Harvard College: designed and taught full-credit undergraduate course in managerial economics and decision analysis.

1976–1979
HARVARD COLLEGE
Bachelor of Arts degree, *cum laude*. Philosophy major. Phi Beta Kappa. Dean's list all semesters. Completed undergraduate course requirements in three years.

Publisher and Executive Committee member, *The Harvard Advocate* magazine. Vice Chairman, South House Committee.

Work Experience

Summer 1982

JACKIE HAYMAN, INC.
Assistant to President. Aided president of young firm that manufactures designer clothing under Catherine Hipp label. Involved in all areas of business, including sales, public relations, working capital management, credit, design, production and shipping.

1979–1981
MORGAN STANLEY & CO. INCORPORATED
Financial Analyst.
Mergers and Acquisitions: Identified possible acquisition targets, recommended prices for those companies and formulated strategies to locate buyers. Analyzed financial and market data to determine the target's long-range earning potential and the effect of the acquisition on the buyer.

Corporate Finance: Supervised preparation of debt financings for 10 clients. Negotiated terms of security documents and coordinated the activities of teams inside and outside Morgan Stanley.

1975–1979
FASHION MODEL
Managed own career as a fashion model. Represented by Ford Models, Inc., New York, N.Y.; The Model's Group, Boston, Mass.; and L'Agence Pauline, Paris, France. Credits include: *Mademoiselle, Seventeen, GQ, LeMonde, Boston,* and *The Boston Globe.*

Summer 1978
RESOURCE PLANNING ASSOCIATES
Research Associate. Planned and executed study that led RPA to add antitrust economic support work to its services. Worked on projects in oil price forecasting and U.S. mineral reliance.

Personal Background
Attended the Spence School, New York, N.Y. and Lycée Montaigne, Paris, France. Speaks fluent French and conversational Greek.

Appendix B. Background of Belinda Hughes

Belinda Hughes received her Bachelor of Fine Arts Degree in fashion design from Parsons School of Design in May 1981. After graduation, she worked as Assistant Designer to Kasper at Kasper for J. L. Sports. She designed pants, blouses and jackets for the Kasper line and prepared sketches and maintained records of fabrication and styles for the company's Japanese licensee. In May 1982, Ms. Hughes became head designer for Creations by Aria, a moderate-price dress house. She covered layout of the dressy dress line, from selection of fabrics to preparation of dresses, and oversaw the sample room staff. Recently, Ms. Hughes has been working as a freelance designer for several lines, including Choo-Chee, Elan Shoe Corp., Roslyn Harte, and College Town, for which she has designed collections ranging from shoes to loungewear.

Ms. Hughes's design talent has been recognized by many academic and industry awards, including: Recognition in Design Citation from Levis (1979), scholarship award from St. John's University (1979), scholarship award from the Switzer Foundation (1980), ILGWU Design Merit Award (1980), ILGWU Design Creativity Award (1981).

Exhibit 4. Timing of cycles in the garment industry.

	March	April	May	June	July	August	September	October
Holiday line	Order sample fabrics	Sketch and design line		Make samples and order production quantities of fabric		Market weeks- take orders	Contract out cutting and sewing	Deliver garments to stores
Early spring line			Early spring line begins					
Spring line				Spring cycle begins				
Transition line							Transition line begins	
Fall line	Fall line finishes up							

Exhibit 5. Heather Evans's notes on preliminary discussions with potential private investors.

1. *David Ellis,* attorney, family friend (excerpt from April 28, 1983, letter):

From an investor's point of view, one would expect at least a 50 percent equity share, and probably substantially more although in nonvoting stock. The investors' stock would be convertible into voting (and indeed, control) stock in case certain minimum standards of solvency and cash flow and performance weren't met. Additional stock would be made available to management if certain performance goals were exceeded. Thus management might start with 25 percent, plus an option on a second 25 percent if the company proves to be a world-beater.

That of course may sound too complicated; but if it's to be an arm's-length *minimally* attractive proposal, I think you have to offer investors at least 50 percent or 60 percent, albeit in nonvoting shares.

If it were a proposal such as that, I would be thinking in terms of a $20,000 or $25,000 participation for myself (i.e., an investment).

But if you can get 70 percent for yourself, with only 30 percent to investors—*take it!* If that's the way it goes, I would want to make a gesture of support and encouragement— thus a $5,000 unit.

2. *Paul Hood,* classmate, HBS:

—Says he is interested in investing for three reasons:
- Heather Evans: trusts intelligence, dedication, design sense, and business judgement.
- Concept: gut feel that there is a market need, has spoken with women in business about idea.
- Upside: mentioned Liz Claiborne deal.

—Key needs in a deal:
- *No* limit to upside via forced call on equity.
- Wants company to own "Heather Evans" name rather than licensing; if Heather Evans can walk after business established, this limits upside.

—Willing to invest $25,000 to $40,000.

3. *Herbert Greene,* president, Greene Textiles:

—I felt that Greene was a good contact with potential fabric, textile suppliers.

—Name (especially if on board) adds credibility on Seventh Avenue/Garment Business.

—Was in on Liz Claiborne deal, made *very* big dollars.

—Wants in deal terms:
- Right to force registration/issue in public market in five to seven years.
- Low limit on my salary with incentive compensation.
- Investors get board control until minimum performance criteria met.

—Willing to invest $35,000–$55,000.

4. *John Merrill,* old friend, HBS classmate:

—Wants company to own name: says if company does very well, main value created will be in name, company should own this.

—Liquidation protection (i.e., if company goes bust, investors get what's left before I get anything).

—Three- to five-year employment contract with three-year noncompete clause at termination of employment contract.

—Right to sell equity, pro rata, on same terms as Heather Evans in any offering.

Exhibit 6. Liz Claiborne Prospectus—Excerpts.

---

liz claiborne, inc.

Common Stock
(Par Value $1 Per Share)

Of the shares of Common Stock offered hereby, 345,000 shares are being sold by the Company and 805,000 shares are being sold by certain stockholders. The Company will not receive any proceeds from the sale of shares by the Selling Stockholders. See "Principal and Selling Stockholders."

Prior to this offering there has been no public market for the Company's Common Stock. See "Underwriting" for information relating to the method of determining the initial public offering price.

THESE SECURITIES HAVE NOT BEEN APPROVED OR DISAPPROVED BY THE SECURITIES AND EXCHANGE COMMISSION NOR HAS THE COMMISSION PASSED UPON THE ACCURACY OR ADEQUACY OF THIS PROSPECTUS. ANY REPRESENTATION TO THE CONTRARY IS A CRIMINAL OFFENSE.

	Price to Public	Underwriting Discounts (1)	Proceeds to the Company (2)	Proceeds to the Selling Stockholders (2) (3)
Per Share	$19.00	$1.28	$17.72	$17.72
Total	$21,850,000	$1,472,000	$6,113,400	$14,264,600

1. See "Underwriting" for a description of indemnification and insurance arrangements among the Underwriters, the Company and the Selling Stockholders.
2. Before deducting expenses estimated at $356,201 payable by the Company and $168,369 payable by the Selling Stockholders.
3. The Selling Stockholders have granted the Underwriters an option to purchase up to an additional 115,000 shares to cover over-allotments. If all such shares are purchased, the total Price to Public, Underwriting Discounts and Proceeds to the Selling Stockholders will be increased by $2,185,000, $147,200 and $2,037,800, respectively.

The Common Stock is being offered subject to prior sale, when, as and if delivered to and accepted by the several Underwriters and subject to approval of certain legal matters by counsel and to certain other conditions. It is expected that certificates for the shares of Common Stock offered hereby will be available on or about June 16, 1981. The Underwriters reserve the right to withdraw, cancel or modify such offer and to reject orders in whole or in part.

Merrill Lynch White Weld Capital Markets Group
Merrill Lynch, Pierce, Fenner & Smith Incorporated

June 9, 1981

PROSPECTUS SUMMARY

The following information is qualified in its entirety by reference to the detailed information and financial statements (including the Notes thereto) appearing elsewhere in the Prospectus.

Liz Claiborne, Inc.

Liz Claiborne, Inc. (the "Company") designs, contracts for the manufacture of and markets an extensive range of women's clothing under the LIZ CLAIBORNE and LIZ trademarks. Since the Company's founding in 1976, it has concentrated on identifying and furnishing the wardrobe requirements of the business and professional woman. Although the Company's products are conceived and marketed as "designer" apparel, they are priced to sell in the "better sportswear" range. The Company's products are sold to over 900 customers operating over 3,000 department and specialty stores throughout the United States. Products are manufactured pursuant to the Company's specifications by independent suppliers in the United States and abroad. See "Business."

The Offering

Common Stock to be sold by:	
Company	345,000 shares
Selling Stockholders	805,000 shares (1)
Common Stock to be outstanding after the offering	3,479,560 shares
Estimated net proceeds to the Company	$5,757,199
Use of net proceeds by the Company	To reduce indebtedness and for certain capital expenditures. See "Use of Proceeds."
Dividends	None. See "Dividend Policy."
Proposed NASDAQ Symbol	LIZC

(1) Assumes the Underwriters' 115,000 share over-allotment option is not exercised.

Selected Consolidated Financial Data
(in thousands of dollars except per share amounts)

	Jan 19, 1976 (Inc.) through Dec. 31, 1976	Fiscal Year Ended				Three Months Ended	
		Dec. 31, 1977	Dec. 31, 1978	Dec. 29, 1979	Dec. 27, 1980	March 29, 1980	March 28, 1981
Net Sales	$2,060	$7,396	$23,279	$47,630	$79,492	$20,747	$26,523
Net income	50	342	1,189	3,497	6,220	1,953	2,687
Earnings per common share (1)	$.02	$.12	$.38	$1.12	$1.98	$.62	$.86

	March 28, 1981 (unaudited)	
	Actual	As adjusted (2)
Working capital	$11,854	$16,307
Total assets	27,918	32,613
Long-term debt, including current portion	63	—
Short-term debt	3,884	2,884
Stockholders' equity	13,589	19,346

(1) Adjusted to reflect the issuance of 65 shares of the Company's Common Stock for each share of its predecessor company's common stock pursuant to a merger effected on April 21, 1981. See Notes 1 and 5 of Notes to Consolidated Financial Statements.

(2) Adjusted to reflect the sale of the shares offered by the Company hereby and the anticipated use of the net proceeds therefrom as well as the repayment of long-term debt in April, 1981. See "Use of Proceeds" and "Capitalization."

See "Dilution" and "Shares Eligible for Future Sale" with respect to the availability of shares for sale after this offering and the immediate dilution in net tangible book value per share to be incurred by the public investors.

IN CONNECTION WITH THIS OFFERING, THE UNDERWRITERS MAY OVER-ALLOT OR EFFECT TRANSACTIONS WHICH STABILIZE OR MAINTAIN THE MARKET PRICE OF THE COMMON STOCK OF THE COMPANY AT A LEVEL ABOVE THAT WHICH MIGHT OTHERWISE PREVAIL IN THE OPEN MARKET. SUCH STABILIZING, IF COMMENCED, MAY BE DISCONTINUED AT ANY TIME.

SELECTED FINANCIAL DATA

The following tables set forth information regarding the Company's operating results and financial position and are qualified in their entirety by the more detailed Consolidated Financial Statements included elsewhere in the Prospectus.

Selected Income Statement Data

	Jan 19, 1976 (inc.) through Dec. 31, 1976	Fiscal Year Ended				Three Months Ended	
		Dec. 1, 1977 (unaudited)	Dec. 31, 1978	Dec. 29, 1979	Dec. 27, 1980	March 29, 1980	March 28, 1981
Net sales	$2,060,118	$7,395,898	$23,279,304	$47,630,227	$79,492,035	$20,747,500	$26,523,023
Net income	49,862	342,489	1,188,857	3,496,575	6,219,592	1,952,998	2,686,670
Earnings per common share (1)	$.02	$.12	$.38	$1.12	$1.98	$.62	$.86
Dividends declared per common share (1)(2)	—	$.007	$.023	$.046	$.077	—	—

Selected Balance Sheet Data

	Dec. 31, 1976	Dec. 31, 1977	Dec. 31, 1978	Dec. 29, 1979	Dec. 27, 1980	March 28, 1981 (unaudited)
Working capital	$246,471	$ 454,196	$1,179,071	$ 4,456,954	$ 9,302,745	$11,854,311
Total assets	674,806	1,901,492	5,144,142	10,786,982	19,281,718	27,918,402
Long-term debt, including current portion (3)	170,000	173,333	173,333	134,815	77,037	62,593
Short-term debt (4)	—	—	—	—	—	3,883,676
Advances from factor (4)	330,696	666,077	2,782,863	—	3,546,098	—
Stockholders' equity	135,029	455,128	1,571,649	4,923,551	10,902,023	13,588,693

(1) Adjusted to reflect the issuance of 65 shares of the Company's Common Stock for each share of its predecessor company's common stock pursuant to a merger effected on April 21,1981. See Notes 1 and 5 of Notes to Consolidated Financial Statements.

(2) The Company has no present plan to continue to pay dividends. See "Dividend Policy."

(3) The Company repaid its long-term debt in April, 1981.

(4) Factoring advances were replaced by a line of credit in March, 1981. See notes 2 and 10 of Notes to Consolidated Financial Statements.

BUSINESS

Introduction and Background

The Company designs, contracts for the manufacture of and markets an extensive range of women's clothing under the LIZ CLAIBORNE and LIZ trademarks. Organized in 1976 by its present management, the Company has concentrated primarily on identifying and furnishing the wardrobe requirements of the working woman, providing apparel appropriate in a business or professional environment as well as apparel suitable for leisure wear. The Company offers its customers a broad selection of related separates (referred to in the apparel industry as *sportswear*) consisting of blouses, skirts, jackets, sweaters, and tailored pants, as well as more casual apparel such as jeans, knit tops, and shirts. The Company believes that the increasing number of business and professional women has contributed both to the Company's own growth and to the growth of the market for women's "sportswear" in general.

LIZ CLAIBORNE products are conceived and marketed as "designer" apparel, employing a consistent approach to design and quality, which is intended to develop and maintain consumer recognition and loyalty across product lines and from season to season. The Company defines its clothing as "updated," combining traditional or classic design with contemporary fashion influences. While the Company maintains a "designer" image, its products are priced in the "better sportswear" range, which is generally less expensive than many designer lines. Although no comprehensive trade statistics are available, the Company believes, based on its knowledge of the market and such trade information as is available, that measured by sales of women's "better sportswear," it is the second largest producer of such merchandise in the United States.

In 1980, LIZ CLAIBORNE products were sold to over 900 customers operating over 3,000 department and specialty stores throughout the United States. Measured by their purchases of LIZ CLAIBORNE apparel, the Company's largest customers during 1980 included Saks Fifth Avenue, Lord & Taylor, Bamberger's, J. L. Hudson, Bloomingdale's and Macy's—New York. A great many retail outlets that carry the Company's products maintain separate LIZ CLAIBORNE areas in which a range of the Company's products are sold. Approximately 25 percent of the Company's 1980 sales was made to the Company's 10 largest customers; approximately 71 percent of 1980 sales was made to the Company's 100 largest customers. Certain of these customers are under common ownership. For example, 16 different department store customers owned by Federated Department Stores, Inc. (which include Bloomingdale's, Abraham & Straus, and Burdine's) accounted for approximately 12 percent of the Company's 1980 sales. The Company believes that each of these department store customers makes its own decisions regarding purchases of the Company's products.

Although the Company expects that sales to its 100 largest customers will continue to account for a majority of its sales, increasing emphasis is being placed on sales to local specialty stores and direct-mail catalog companies. The Company began licensing its trademarks in 1978 and presently receives royalties under arrangements with three licensees that sell various products under the LIZ CLAIBORNE and LIZ trademarks.

The Company's products are designed by its own staff and are manufactured in accordance with its specifications by independent suppliers in the United States and abroad. Domestically produced merchandise accounted for approximately 55 percent of the Company's sales during 1980; the remaining approximately 45 percent consisted of merchandise produced abroad, almost entirely in the Far East. Company personnel in the United States and abroad regularly monitor production at facilities that manufacture its products.

PRINCIPAL AND SELLING STOCKHOLDERS

The following table sets forth certain information, as of March 28, 1981, with respect to the number of shares of Common Stock owned, to be offered for sale, and to be beneficially owned after this offering, by all persons who were known by the Company to own beneficially more than 5 percent of the then outstanding Common Stock, all Selling Stockholders, each of the Directors of the Company, and the Company's officers and Directors, as a group:

Name and Address	Ownership of Common Stock prior to Offering (1)		Shares to be Sold (2)	Ownership of Common Stock after Offering (1)(2)	
	Number of Shares	Percent	Shares to be Sold (2)	Number of Shares	Percent
Elisabeth Claiborne Ortenberg (3) 1441 Broadway New York, NY	523,640	16.71	134,478	389,162	11.18
Arthur Ortenberg (3) 1441 Broadway New York, NY	523,640	16.71	134,478	389,162	11.18
Leonard Boxer 4 Emerson Lane Secaucus, NJ	523,640	16.71	134,478	389,162	11.18
Jerome A. Chazen 1441 Broadway New York, NY	523,640	16.71	134,478	389,162	11.18
J. James Gordon	65,000	2.07	16,693	48,307	1.39
Joseph Gaumont 200 E. 57th Street New York, NY	227,500	7.26	58,425	169,075	4.86
Charness Family Investments Ltd. (4) 2 St. Clair Avenue, East Toronto, Canada	162,500	5.18	41,733	120,767	3.47
Catway Investments Ltd. (4)	97,500	3.11	25,040	72,460	2.08
Albert Fink Milton (5)	97,500	3.11	25,040	72,460	2.08
Elizabeth Fenner Milton (5)	65,000	2.07	16,693	48,307	1.39
Albert Fenner Milton, Custodian, F/B/O Elizabeth Hunt Milton under the Uniform Gifts to Minors Act (5)	9,750	0.31	8,346	1,404	0.04
Jerome Gold	65,000	2.07	16,693	48,307	1.39
Martin J. Tandler	65,000	2.07	16,693	48,307	1.39
Jacob Rosenbaum (6)	40,625	1.30	10,433	30,192	0.87
Belle Rosenbaum (6)	40,625	1.30	10,433	30,192	0.87
Theodore Brodie (7)	40,625	1.30	10,433	30,192	0.87
Simmi Brodie (7)	40,625	1.30	10,433	30,192	0.87
All officers and directors as a group (7 persons)	2,159,560	68.90	554,605	1,604,956	46.13

(1) All shares listed are owned of record and, to the Company's knowledge, beneficially.

(2) Assumes the Underwriters' 115,000 share over-allotment option is not exercised. Percentage is based on total shares to be outstanding after this offering.

(3) Arthur Ortenberg and Elisabeth Claiborne Ortenberg are husband and wife; each disclaims beneficial ownership of all shares owned by the other.

The Original Shower Dry

EXECUTIVE SUMMARY

Product: THE ORIGINAL SHOWER DRY is a unique, new consumer choice.

Concept: This product works like a shower door and is priced competitively with shower curtains. It is practical, aesthetic, and easy to use.

Design: Through the application of value engineering, Dean has developed a simple, cost efficient design.

Status: The design components and product prototype were completed in March 1993. The U.S. patent was secured in September 1992. The Canadian patent was secured in December 1992. Trademark applications have been filed. Presently, Dean is seeking a major bathroom accessories manufacturer and distributor as a licensing partner for THE ORIGINAL SHOWER DRY.

PRODUCT CONCEPT

THE ORIGINAL SHOWER DRY is a unique, new product with characteristics that could potentially revolutionize a segment of the shower curtain industry. The innovation has distinct product positioning and could be strategically offered as a competitive alternative to all standard curtains. The most important of these product characteristics are as follows:

- A practical, easy to use alternative to standard curtains.
- An aesthetic, functional evolution of the standard curtain.
- The effective design has appeal for a large target market.

Dean recognized a need, and subsequently developed his product after it became necessary to discard a wall to wall bathroom carpet in his home simply because the carpet corners near the tub ends were mildewed. SHOWER DRY is Dean's solution to the water leakage problems he and many others experience with their standard shower curtains. Dean's product is designed to provide consumers with the same closure advantages as a shower door, within the price range of a shower curtain.

This case was prepared by D. Beamish, M.B.A., under the direction of Professor A. B. Ibrahim, professor of Management at Concordia University, Montreal, as a basis for class discussion, rather than to illustrate either effective or ineffective handling of an administrative situation

There is no direct competition for this product. As it stands, consumers currently purchase a shower curtain or a shower door to meet their shower closure needs. THE ORIGINAL SHOWER DRY offers a sensible choice because the consumer has the opportunity to get shower door protection at shower curtain prices.

Dean Dyckow will enter into a licensing agreement with a major bathroom accessories company who will produce, distribute, and sell THE ORIGINAL SHOWER DRY. Further details may be found in the "Deal Structure" section of this document.

PRODUCT DESIGN

Dean has displayed the use of distinctive competence in the product design concept through the application of value engineering. This approach allowed Dean to perfect the product in a simple, cost efficient way.

The superiority of the design rests in the fastening and sealing arrangement which is accomplished in one motion. This proves to enhance the overall aesthetic appeal of SHOWER DRY.

Dean has undertaken all necessary research and development for the product in conjunction with two McGill professors, and a team of McGill University engineering students. The design components are complete. The simplicity of the product will prove to be one of the major contributors to its success. The appendix contains contains a visual representation of the concept.

THE ENTREPRENEUR

Dean Dyckow is a Canadian entrepreneur. He is a personable individual, with strong communication skills. Dean's sales and small business experience, combined with the ability to network, delegate and encourage teamwork have served him well in his efforts to design and develop his invention. This, in addition to his entrepreneurial spirit and deep commitment will lead Dean Dyckow to successfully bring THE ORIGINAL SHOWER DRY to market.

TRADEMARKS AND PATENTS

Trademark applications have been filed and the product is presently know as THE ORIGINAL SHOWER DRY. The name is marketable, however, this does not supersede a willingness to accept a licensee's discretion with regard to name.

Dean's product is patented in both the United States (#5,148,580: Sept. 22, 1992) and Canada (#2020320: July 3, 1992). Please refer to Appendix I and II.

There exist more than 20 other patents attempting to solve the same problems as Dean's patent does. This fact is further evidence of the need for this type of product concept. These other inventions tend to be cumbersome, unaesthetic or difficult to use, as they lack the simplicity and sleekness of Dean's innovative product. Most have never made it to market.

MARKET

In the U.S.A. retail sales for the shower curtain industry were $376 million in 1991, up $12 million from 1990. The number one supplier of shower curtains is Hygiene Industries, with annual sales of $100 million. Springs Industries is the number two supplier. The retail industry is divided among three major groups. Department stores held a 17% market share in 1991, mass merchant chains such as K-Mart, Wal-Mart, Woolworth and others shared 48% of the market, and specialty stores, catalogues and others made up the remaining 35%.

The purchase cycle in the shower curtain industry has an average range of one to three years. Because the industry has reached maturity, product differentiation is important to the consumer purchase decision. Accessorizing has helped to revitalize shower curtain sales in recent years. Matching shower curtains, rugs, and other bathroom accessories known as coordinates has become very popular. It has become an important factor in today's market, particularly for retailers, as it results in more sales and higher average ticket purchases.

Upscale designer looks and juvenile collections with coordinates are also popular. New pvc materials are emerging to compete with the texture and look of cloth curtains at a much lower price. DPC (double polished clear) shower curtain lines are increasingly popular. Cloth shower curtains of cotton/polyester, teflon-treated polyester, and nylon maintain the high-end of the price range.

Price or new product innovation is what provides leading companies a competitive advantage in this market. It is well known that in many industries large firms turn to inventors and entrepreneurs for product innovations. Dean Dyckow's SHOWER DRY offers an opportunity for a leading firm in the bathroom accessories industry to gain market share with the product early in its life cycle.

The potential market in North America for THE ORIGINAL SHOWER DRY can be categorized as follows:

Consumer Target Market

- 100.8 million households

Commercial Target Market Segments

- 40,525 hotels
- 14,070 motels

The consumer target market is characterized by consumers who adhere to the following consumer profile.

Consumer Profile

- Inhabit dwellings with standard 3-wall tub enclosures
- Single and double income households
- Shower curtain buyers
- Value conscious
- Price sensitive
-  Concerned with product aesthetics

The hotel/motel industry represents an additional, significant market for SHOWER DRY. This is particularly true, based on the fact that the consumer buying motives for the product apply to both consumers and commercial clients. Please see the "Marketing" section of this document for a list of consumer buying motives.

Market research for SHOWER DRY was conducted primarily in the province of Quebec. This research involved a search for existing, similar product concepts. In addition, an investigation ascertained the consumer target market and the potential retailers' views of the product.

Market Research Methods

Product Search

A search of retail outlets for similar product concepts was conducted in Quebec, Ontario, and the States of New York and Vermont.

Surveys

Group A: Consumer Target Market

Random sample of 500 participants.

I. Personal interviews were conducted with 450 respondents.
II. Telephone interviews were conducted with 50 respondents.

Group B: Potential Retailers

Selected sample of 30 small and medium sized firms, and 6 major Canadian department stores.

I. An individual buyer survey was presented to 30 small and medium sized firms on issues of product potential.
II. The product concept was introduced to 6 major Canadian department store buyers and their reaction-responses were noted.

At a retail level, the search revealed that there exists no rival product concepts in the Canadian and New England marketplace. Results from the surveys indicate that approximately 80% of potential consumers surveyed expressed an interest in purchasing this product. That is, only 16% of those respondents from Group A declined any form of interest in purchasing the product at some point. Although one could not expect an 80% market share, survey results indicate that a viable market does exist for THE ORIGINAL SHOWER DRY.

Results from potential retailers were equally encouraging. Twenty-three of the twenty-five respondents from Group B-I expressed an interest to either partake in this venture or see the product when it was ready for distribution. Buyers from the 6 major Canadian department stores were intrigued by the product concept and provided useful recommendations regarding the product's market potential.

LOCATION

Given the potential of THE ORIGINAL SHOWER DRY it would be most beneficial to launch this new product in the United States. American consumers tend to be less conservative than Canadian consumers. Generally, they are more willing to try new products. For this reason, Dean seeks a licensing partner in the U.S.

PRODUCTION

As mentioned under the "Design" section of this document, the product research, development, and design components are complete. U.S. and Canadian patents are secured, and trademark applications have been filed.

The product is made from common, inexpensive materials and employs current manufacturing methods. Candidate materials for the production of THE ORIGINAL SHOWER DRY include:

Candidate Materials

- Steel strips
- Magnetic discs
- Polyvinyl chloride
- Rust-proofing agent
- Rubber base adhesive
- Acrylic adhesive
- Polypropylene
- UPV

Manufacturing Methods

- Extrusion
- Assembly

The following presents an estimated cost structure, based on the design component costs for the product.

Estimated Material Cost		
Component Parts	**Costs Per Unit**	
L-Extrusion	$0.01/ft. × 4 ft. =	$0.04
Steel Strip	$0.07/4 ft. =	0.07
Acrylic Adhesive	$0.06/ft. × 4 ft. =	0.24
Magnetic Discs	$0.05 ea. × 14 =	0.70
Corner Piece	$0.08/ft × 6 in. =	0.04
Rustproff Coating	$0.07/strip (.005″) =	0.08
Total Materials Cost Per Unit:		$1.16

The above are variable material costs, excluding the shower curtain. Full production costs are calculable based on the quality of shower curtain, and the context of the interested licensee.

MARKETING

There are approximately 10 major competitors in Canada and the U.S. bathroom accessories industry. SHOWER DRY's licensee will have an opportunity to lead an evolution in the industry. The competitive advantage this innovative new product will provide over rivals in a mature market is significant. As such, this competitive edge depends on the licensee's use of effective marketing. It would be advantageous if the innovation is offered as a complement to the existing product line. The licensee could readily do this since the innovation is fully compatible with present distribution networks.

The key to the competitive advantage is contingent on the distinct features of the innovation itself. SHOWER DRY is in a class of its own. If licensed, this innovative product would not be available to competitors. Product positioning is ideal as the innovation provides shower door protection at shower curtain prices.

It is a marketable product, with a number of consumer buying motives inherent to it. Besides being a practical, easy to use alternative to standard curtains, with an aesthetic, functional and effective design, the following consumer buying motives also apply.

Consumer Buying Motives

- Contemporary appeal
- Prevents costly water damage
- Prevents messy, time consuming clean-ups
- The curtain no longer billows inward when showering
- Hand held shower heads may be freely used without spraying outside the curtain
- Reduces the use of environmentally harmful cleaners
- Perfected product in its simplest form
- Competitively priced with standard shower curtains

Price will be a primary factor in the purchase decision for this product. Ideally, the licensee's objective would be to provide the consumer with a good quality, durable product that is not overpriced. Through use of a comparable to standard shower curtain pricing strategy the licensee could expect to make increased profits with the volume sold. Given the potential for this product and the fact that there is little or no competition, there is room to attract a considerable market share.

The following are some suggested methods in which SHOWER DRY may be packaged, promoted, and advertised.

- Packaging
  - Long and narrow, perhaps cylindrical to provide unequalled distinction.
  - Attractive carton in eye opening colours that would first draw the consumer's attention and then have a powerful silent salesman affect.

- Promotion
  - Display the product apart from other shower curtains.
  - Use a miniature shower enclosure with a reinforced mini SHOWER DRY to demonstrate its effectiveness to consumers.

- Advertising
  - "Why shower curtain when you can SHOWER DRY?"

DEAL STRUCTURE

The following proposition is meant to serve as a jumping-off point for the negotiation of a licensing agreement. The objective is to clarify the offering to the prospective licensee and identify the licensor's expectations. It does not necessarily represent an exact definition of the final licensing agreement to be negotiated between the two parties.

The Offering

SHOWER DRY is a patented product concept, registered in both Canada and the United States. Respectively, the patent numbers are #2020320 and #5,148,580. In addition, SHOWER DRY is a completed design concept. Value engineering has been applied to the research and development of the innovation, resulting in a perfected product in its simplest, most cost efficient form. Under a satisfactory licensing agreement Dean is prepared to offer exclusive production, marketing and distribution rights for the product in return for reasonable compensation.

Proposed Compensation

As the licensor of SHOWER DRY, Dean Dyckow seeks compensation for the exclusive right to produce, market and distribute his invention in the form of a fee that will be expected upon signing the licensing agreement. In addition, royalty on sales will be forthcoming, based on a percentage of invoice pricing not including any taxes, sales, excise or GST. Starting in year two of the agreement there will be a minimum royalty which will gradually increase for 3–4 years and then level off and remain constant over the balance of the term of the agreement.

Appendix I. The Canadian Patent

Consumer and
Corporate Affairs Canada

Patent Office

Consommation et
Affaires commerciales Canada

Bureau des brevets

| Canadian Patent | 2020320 | Brevet canadien |

Date on which the application was granted and issued	1992/12/01	Date à laquelle la demande a été accordée et délivrée
Filing date of the application	1990/07/03	Date du dépôt de la demande
Date on which the application was open to public	1992/01/04	Date à laquelle la demande est devenue accessible au public

To Whom It May Concern

The Commissioner of Patents has received a petition requesting the grant of a patent for a new and useful invention. The requirements of the Patent Act have been complied with. The title and a description of that invention are contained in the specification, a copy of which is attached to and forms an essential part of this document.

The present patent grants to its owner and to the legal representatives of its owner, for a term which expires twenty years from the filing date of the application in Canada, the exclusive right, privilege and liberty of making, constructing and using the invention and selling it to others to be used, subject to adjudication in respect thereof before any court of competent jurisdiction.

To maintain this patent in effect, annual maintenance fees must be paid. If these fees are not paid, the patent rights will be lost.

À qui de droit,

Le Commissaire des brevets a reçu une demande de délivrance de brevet visant une invention nouvelle et utile. Les exigences de la Loi sur les brevets sont respectées. Le titre et la description de l'invention figurent dans le mémoire descriptif, dont une copie est annexée au présent document et en constitue une partie essentielle.

Le présent brevet confère à son titulaire et aux représentants légaux du titulaire, pour une période expirant vingt ans après la date du dépôt de la demande au Canada, le droit, la faculté et le privilège exclusifs de fabriquer, de construire et d'exploiter l'invention ainsi que de le vendre pour fin d'exploitation, sous réserve d'un jugement rendu à cet égard par un tribunal de juridiction compétente.

Des frais annuels de maintien doivent être payés pour que le brevet demeure valide. En cas de non paiement, les droits qui se rattachent au brevet seront perdus.

Commissioner of Patents
Commissaire des brevets

Canada

7530-21-936-3256 (11-92) 4

Appendix I. (continued)

Consommation
et Corporations Canada

Bureau des brevets

Ottawa Canada
K1A 0C9

Consumer and
Corporate Affairs Canada

Patent Office

(11) (C) **2,020,320**

(22) 1990/07/03

(43) 1992/01/04

(45) 1992/12/01

(52) 160-21
C.L. CR. 4-46

(51) INTL.CL.^{5} A47K-3/22

(19)(CA) **CANADIAN PATENT** (12)

(54) Shower Curtain Sealing and Fastening Arrangement

(72) Dyckow, Dean W. , Canada

(73) Same as inventor

(57) 11 Claims

Canada

Appendix II. The U.S. Patent

US005148580A

United States Patent [19]

Dyckow

[11]	Patent Number:	**5,148,580**
[45]	Date of Patent:	Sep. 22, 1992

[54] **SHOWER CURTAIN SEALING AND FASTENING ARRANGEMENT**

[76] Inventor: **Dean W. Dyckow**, 4876 St. Urbain, Montreal, Quebec, Canada, H2T 2W2

[21] Appl. No.: 723,592

[22] Filed: Jul. 1, 1991

[30] **Foreign Application Priority Data**

Jul. 3, 1990 [CA] Canada 2020320

[51] Int. Cl.⁵ A44B 21/00; A47K 3/22
[52] U.S. Cl. 24/303; 24/462; 160/349.2; 4/608
[58] Field of Search .... 24/303, 304, 306, 442, 24/460, 461, 462, 72.5; 160/349.1, 349.2, DIG. 6; 4/558, 608

[56] **References Cited**

U.S. PATENT DOCUMENTS

2,303,502	12/1942	Rous	4/608
2,319,292	5/1943	Boggs	160/349.1
2,554,106	5/1951	Hedrick	
2,608,250	8/1952	Hoy	
2,771,945	11/1956	V	
3,102,314	9/1963	Algener	24/303
3,205,547	9/1965	Rieske	
3,282,328	11/1966	Mushro et al.	
3,386,106	6/1968	Clemens	4/608
3,639,919	2/1972	White	
3,808,610	5/1974	Mortensen	160/349.1
3,855,642	12/1974	Blitch	160/349.2
3,879,806	4/1975	Armstrong	
3,895,399	7/1975	Giarrante	4/608
3,934,686	1/1976	Simmons	
4,070,735	1/1978	Canaday	160/349.2
4,077,072	3/1978	Dezura	160/349.1
4,088,174	5/1978	Edwards	
4,197,616	4/1980	Panuski	
4,333,187	6/1982	Schuler	
4,361,915	12/1982	Siewert	
4,759,087	7/1988	Beilinger	24/462
4,944,050	7/1990	Shames et al.	160/349.2

FOREIGN PATENT DOCUMENTS

960956	1/1975	Canada
997670	9/1976	Canada

Primary Examiner—Victor N. Sakran
Attorney, Agent, or Firm—ROBIC

[57]   ABSTRACT

A kit for use to fasten the outer surface of a shower curtain to an adjacent wall in the shower closure. A sealing protrusion extends from the wall adjacent the fasteners so that, when the outer surface of the curtain is fastened to the wall, the edge of the curtain abuts the protrusion.

15 Claims, 5 Drawing Sheets

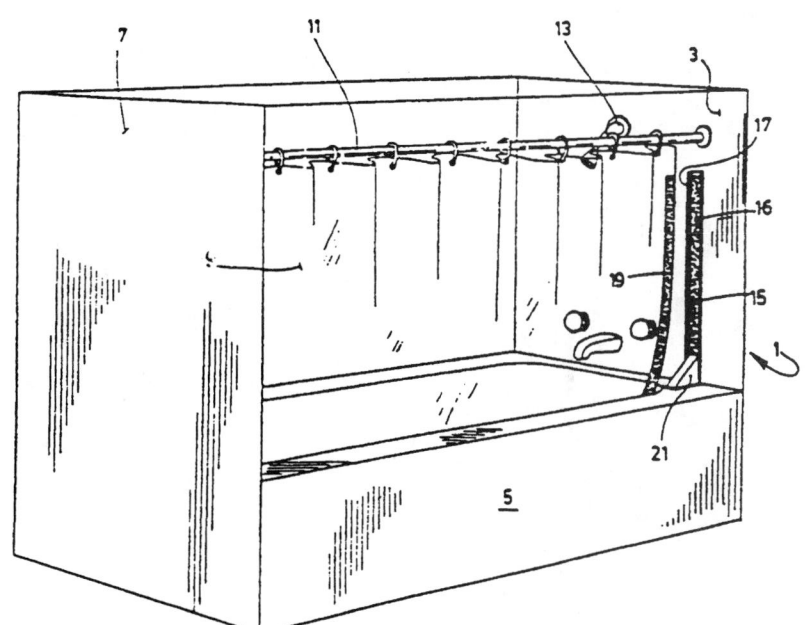

Appendix II. (continued)

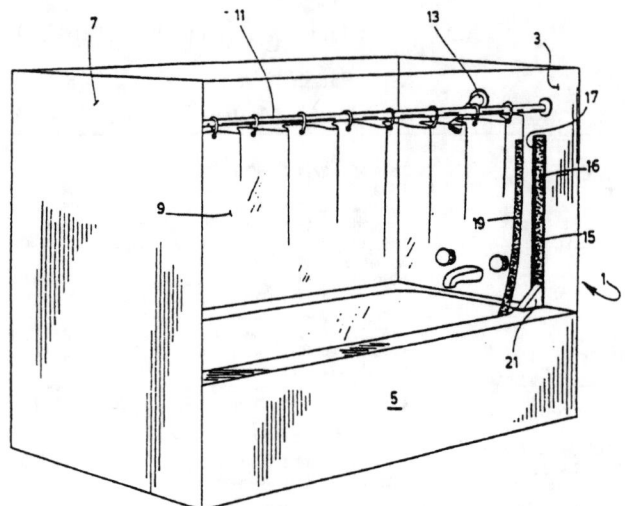

Figure 1.

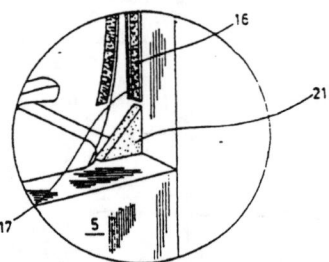

Figure 1a.

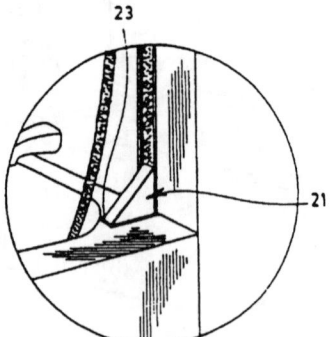

Figure 1c.

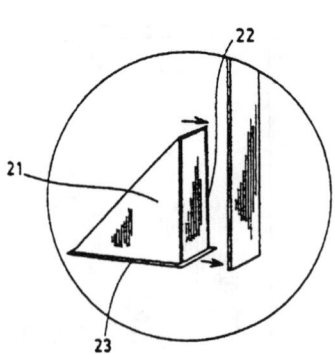

Figure 1b.

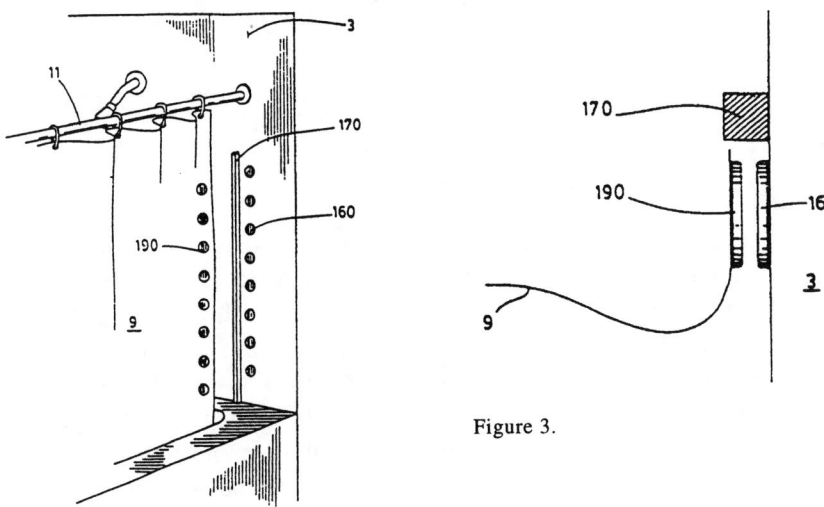

Figure 2.

Figure 3.

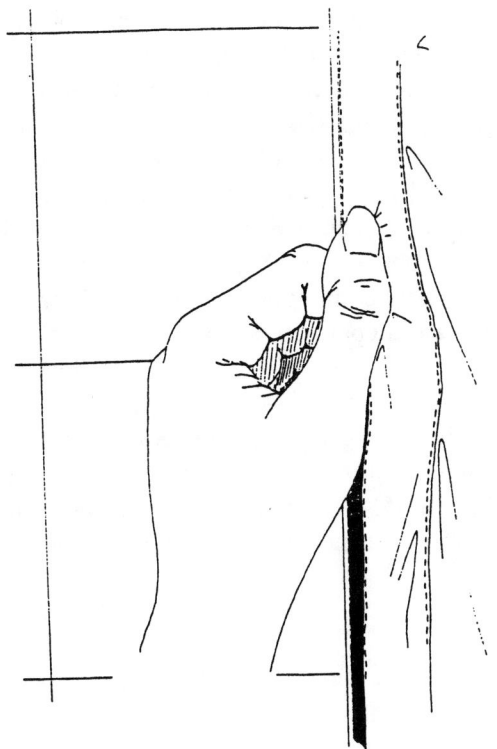

Figure 6.

CASE 7
Chipco

In mid-April 1982, Chips Klein was trying to determine what to do with The Eye Maker™ 3-way mirror she had invented almost two years ago. Since October 1980, when she had formed her company Chipco, Chips had been doing everything she could think of to get her mirror off the ground and into the marketplace. During the first six months of 1981 Chips had tried unsuccessfully to interest a large Canadian-based cosmetics company in licensing her invention. She had also failed to generate any significant sales of the product as evidenced by her 1980–1981 sales volume of $1585 (see Exhibit 1). In fact, almost all of her sales that year were attributable to Ostrich Eggs, hand-woven wool rugs, and ivory jewelry which she imported and sold from her native South Africa in order to help finance her mirror efforts.

During the second half of 1981 Klein had hired a commission sales representative which resulted in a significant improvement in her sales picture. Between November 1981 and March 1981 Chipco sold almost 4000 of the 5000 units produced in its first production run. However, Chips realized that this sales volume, while encouraging, did not accurately reflect her mirror's popularity insofar as they had not received a single reorder from any customer during the entire 4-month period. For reasons that puzzled her, the mirrors just were not being bought by the final consumer. This fact, coupled with the relatively negative evaluation report she had recently received from the Canadian Industrial Innovation Centre/ Waterloo about her proposed Eye Maker "Compact" model, made her wonder whether or not she should continue to commit both her time and her family's limited financial resources to this project. If she did continue, she knew she might have to develop a new marketing approach for her Eye Maker Table model, as well as decide whether or not to proceed with the development of the Compact. Any changes would require a significant further investment of funds which up to now she had generated internally from savings or product sales. As she contemplated her choices, she remembered how many times over the past two years she had been told that 95% of all new products end in failure. Chips had rarely failed in anything she had ever done and wondered what she needed to do to revive her mirror before her funds ran out.

PERSONAL BACKGROUND

Chips was born in South Africa in 1947. Her father, Abe, had been a top sales representative for one of the country's leading pharmaceutical wholesalers, while her mother Thea had been a concert pianist and music director. During the first five years of her life Chips had undergone three serious facial operations to correct certain birth defects. At the age of 6, with her mother's encouragement, she began to dance, and later became a well-known flamenco dancer throughout South Africa and Spain. Her professional dancing name was Chiquita Albeniz, but her friends called her Chips, after a popular South African snack called Chipita Chips.

Early on, Chips realized her dancing career would be shortlived and so enrolled in a cosmetics school to study the anatomy and biology of skin care.

For the next 10 years Chips worked for a variety of cosmetic companies including Revlon, Coty, and Lancome, where she either sold cosmetics or did makeup demonstrations. She always found these one-on-one demonstrations exciting, giving her the hands-on opportunity to maximize her customer's facial features. She continued working and dancing right through the birth of her two children in the early 1970s. In 1973 tragedy struck Chips' family when her only brother died at the age of 29 after a long illness, during much of which she cared for him in her home.

THE IDEA

It was during these years of dancing and doing cosmetic retailing that her idea for a new type of cosmetic mirror germinated. As a Flamenco dancer, Chips had always insisted on perfect makeup. Much of the time she was forced to apply this makeup in a cramped dressing room where she "just about had to stand on her head to make sure her makeup and false eyelashes were applied properly." As well, during cosmetic "makeovers" Chips realized how much easier it was doing someone else's makeup rather than her own. "When I had somebody sitting down and I was looking at them and doing their makeup, I was doing their eyes from the top and I would say, look down, and I could see their whole eyelids and I could do the shadowing and contouring. Then I'd say to them to look up for me and I could do the underlining and so on. But when I was doing my own makeup I couldn't do that. So it was logical to develop a product that allowed me to see myself the same way a makeup artist would see me."

In 1972, while seated at her Dolly Vardon makeup table the idea for a 3-way cosmetics mirror struck. Chips wondered whether, by using the 3-mirror concept of her dressing table, one could perhaps create a mirror that would allow a woman to see her entire upper lid, lower lid, or eye straight on, without any physical contortions. "You know, women were willing to spend vast sums of money on cosmetics but when it came to application, they would bend over the bathroom sink and peer into a traditional flat mirror."

Aided by her husband Paul, Chips built a single prototype out of cardboard, chewing gum, modelling clay, glue and glass which she and some of her dance colleagues used quite successfully to apply their makeup. However, in 1975 Chips and her family emigrated to Canada to escape South Africa's political turmoil and her idea for the 3-way mirror was put on hold. "Life in Canada was very exciting and a real challenge. You see, in South Africa it was common for most people to have nannies who looked after the day-to-day household chores. In Canada I had to learn everything from scratch; simple things like how often you clean the bathroom. Luckily, I had always been energetic. You know, I was always firmly convinced that the world was categorized into two parts: the doers and the nodders. I was always the one at committee meetings who stuck up her hand and said 'I'll do it.'"

By 1980, after five years in Canada, Chips was looking for something to fill her time. "Once the kids were in school full days I decided the time had come to get a job, either back in cosmetics or dancing, or something. Finally Paul and I decided 'The Mirror' would be it. I would go at it full time and really see if I could start a business. We would live on Paul's salary as a sales engineer and devote almost $10,000 savings towards the venture."

THE COSMETICS MARKET

"The cosmetic industry is like no other market in the whole world. These are a group of people unto their own, with their own jargon, and you have to learn how to deal with them; what works, what doesn't." The Canadian cosmetics market in 1981 totalled well in excess of a billion dollars in sales annually. The market had been growing quite rapidly over the past few years as more and more women joined the workforce giving them more discretionary income to spend on products like cosmetics. On average, Canadian women spent hundreds of dollars a year on cosmetics in their desire to beautify themselves. According to Chips "cosmetic manufacturers sold dreams. Women hoped and prayed that by using this or that makeup they would somehow change their appearance to that of their favourite movie star."

Most cosmetic companies tended to supply their own application accessories along with the product for buyer convenience and additional profit. For instance, eye shadow came with its own applicator, blush with its own brush, rouge and powders with their own puffs and mirrors. While there was a separate cosmetic accessories market for brushes, bags, sponges, mirrors, etc. it was very small compared to the sales volume of the actual cosmetics. As Chips explained, most manufacturers and retailers tended to ignore accessories for the most part, putting their effort into the sale of their much more profitable cosmetics products. "It was heartbreaking when you walked into a decent store and saw all these cosmetics counters and there was this teeny-weeny accessories counter somewhere in the background and you had to fight your way to it."

As far as mirrors themselves were concerned, there was a whole range of different sizes and shapes on the market, each with different functional, material, and price range features.

The most common type was the non-portable standard household mirror usually found in bathrooms or bedrooms. Furthermore, in addition to the portable mirrors supplied by the cosmetics companies themselves, there was a wide range of small plastic models, usually made in the far East and retailing for under $5.00. The more expensive boudoir metallized mirrors retailed in the $35–$45 price range while the relatively "high-tech" mirrors with lighting and/or magnification could run anywhere from $50 to $200 depending on their size, function, and design. Total estimated Canadian sales of all types of makeup mirrors in 1981 equalled almost two million units.

The cosmetics industry was dominated by major international companies, many of them based in the United States, France, England, or Japan, where most of the new product development and introductions took place. In the direct sales cosmetic market, Avon door-to-door, and Mary Kay via its house parties, dominated. In the more traditional retail store sector there were many well known firms such as Revlon, Estee Lauder, Lancome, Shiseido (Japanese), Innoxa, Coty, Max Factor, and Yardley. Most of these companies sold their upscale, higher priced lines to the better department stores like Eatons, Simpsons, and the Bay under separate brand names (i.e. Clinique, Orlane, Charles of the Ritz) and their downscale mass appeal "pegboard" lines to the lower end department stores as well as to the drugstore chains like Shoppers Drug Mart. For example, Revlon would sell its Ultima II line exclusively to fine department stores and boutiques, and its Moondrops line to drugstores. While there were some cosmetic firms that focussed on a single market segment, this two-pronged approach to cosmetics marketing was quite common and necessitated individualized images, promotions, packaging, and distribution programs. Chips commented that in many cases there was actually very little functional difference in the contents of the cosmetics sold to the high and low ends of the market.

Another recent entry in Canadian cosmetics retailing were companies like Merle Norman, who sold their own cosmetics through a chain of Merle Norman franchised outlets typically located in major shopping malls. These outlets, besides selling cosmetics and accessories, did complete facial makeovers for their clients, as well as colour consulting which was another growing trend as women became more interested in a personalized cosmetics approach that was right for them. In addition, the industry was trending towards the development of quick and easily applied cosmetics designed for the growing number of women who didn't want to spend a lot of time applying them.

The cosmetics industry followed a seasonal pattern geared to four key annual events: Valentines Day, Mothers Day, Back-to-School, and Christmas. Historically, between sixty and seventy-five percent of annual cosmetic gift sales fell in the last three months of the year. For this reason most new fragrances or cosmetics lines were launched in the fall prior to Christmas when store traffic was increasing. Besides sales seasonality, the cosmetics market had a product seasonality in terms of Winter, Spring, Summer, and Fall lines, each of which promoted different colour ranges and textures. In this respect, cosmetics often were sold on a promotion basis similar to many fashion items like handbags, and apparel, in that companies were developing new lines 6–9 months ahead of the season. In fact, product change in the industry had accelerated over the past few years as competition intensified, and manufacturers fought for customer loyalty and market share. Age variations also played a significant part in cosmetics marketing as entire lines of products were developed specifically for the teenage, young adult, or older woman sector of the market (i.e. Cover Girl). Finally, it was estimated that there was a steady non-promotional year-round demand for staple products like eyeliner and mascara that amounted to perhaps 20% of the overall cosmetic market.

GETTING STARTED

From her experience in the cosmetic industry Chips felt that the best product approach for her mirror would be to first develop the small folding Compact model for the handbag market. Chips felt that women typically carried one and sometimes 2 mirrors in their purse for makeup purposes, so gaining even a fraction of the Canadian market could be profitable. Therefore in early 1980 Chips began visiting numerous local plastics manufacturers trying to describe her Compact mirror idea to them so they could tell her whether it was possible and how much it would cost to manufacture some proper prototypes that she could show to potential customers. However, without detailed drawings these attempts were unsuccessful and Paul and Chips once again constructed their own samples, this time substituting duo-tangs and double-sided tape instead of chewing gum for the mirror hinges. Chips then took her sample to a large cosmetic manufacturer where it promptly fell apart on the desk in the middle of a meeting. Realizing that a home-made sample was neither professional nor left a good first impression Chips once again went to various plastics producers to see about prototype manufacturing, this time armed with drafting sketches of the mirror Paul had done. However, time after time she was told the same story; that because of the complicated hinged construction of the mirror, tooling, production, and assembly costs would make low volume manufacture of the Compact model totally unfeasible. Therefore, after discussions with her husband Paul, Chips decided to redirect her efforts into developing a simplified table model in order to get established and then return to the hinged Compact design later on.

For the next couple of months, Chips spent considerable time visiting local metal and plastic fabricators, showing them Paul's drawings and learning as much as she could about plastics processing methods. She found these visits extremely interesting especially the plant tours which she invariably asked for. Slowly, Chips began to absorb the terminology and uses of plastics in terms of design (thicknesses, angles, dimensional tolerances, finish), materials (styrene, A.B.S., polypropylene), fabrication techniques (extrusion, injection moulding, rotational moulding, vacuum forming), and moulds (wood, epoxy, aluminum, gated, fluted, offsets, undercuts, etc.).

As a result of these investigations Chips settled on vacuum forming as the most economical short run process to use and ordered through Paul's company 60 plastic frames at a cost of $5.00 each without the glass, to be made from wooden tooling. These

60 units were delivered on November 24, 1980, shortly after Chips and Paul had formed a general partnership under the company name of Chipco. The partnership, which was registered at a cost of about $10.00, was for the purpose of "obtaining goods and importing and exporting goods for retail and wholesale distribution." This reference to importing and exporting in the business description was done purposely in order that Chips could begin to sell various South African luxury products to generate cash flow. At that time Paul and Chips felt a partnership arrangement was preferable since they had always done things together as a team. As well, Paul had an established credit rating that Chips could use and the $800 to $1000 cost of incorporation they felt was well beyond their financial means. Chips also coined the Trademark "The Eye Maker" for their future product line and ordered some business cards and stationery in a buff colour with brown printing.

In January 1981, after purchasing $50.00 worth of cut mirror from a supplier in Toronto, Chips and her family assembled the first 60 units. These prototypes had white frames which was the cheapest stock colour the plastics fabricator could supply. Assembly of the mirrors proved quite time consuming due to the poor dimensional tolerances obtained from vacuum forming. As well, the mirrors were left unpackaged since making custom boxes would have been too costly for Chipco. Nevertheless, while Chips herself admitted the product didn't look perfect, it did function properly and for under $1000 she now had something tangible that wouldn't fall apart to show the marketplace. Finally, Chips made an educated guess at a target retailing selling price of $10.00 for her mirror, based on looking at other mirror products in the stores, talking to people, and combining this input with a "gut" feel as to what the market would pay for her product. She realized that $10.00 retail translated into a wholesale selling price of about $5.00 out of which she would have to cover all her costs plus make a satisfactory profit. She hoped that on a volume basis this would be possible although at this point she had no firm fix on what her actual production costs would be to back up these pricing estimates.

MARKETING THE PRODUCT

Having worked previously for some of the large cosmetic companies in South Aftica, many of whom had Canadian subsidiaries, Chips decided to approach companies such as Revlon, Avon, and Mary Kay, to try and persuade them to either buy her mirrors or preferably to assume the development, manufacture, and marketing of The Eye Maker in return for a negotiated licensing fee. Working out of a friend's home in Toronto in order to minimize long distance charges, Chips began combing through the Toronto and Montreal yellow pages phoning every cosmetics company she felt could help her.

However, for reasons she couldn't understand Chips was not very successful with this approach. Revlon wasn't at all interested and Avon, who expressed some initial interest and had asked for a sample mirror, sat on her product for months. This rejection by Avon was especially disheartening for Chips.

Many of the hundreds of phone calls she made resulted either in total rejection or a request for brochures which she didn't have. When she did succeed in showing a company buyer her product they usually liked the concept but invariably made comments such as, "it looks chintzy," "its too expensive," "we sell cosmetics not accessories," "what does your packaging look like," "who else are you selling to," and "what's your track record so far." After a few months of these experiences it became obvious to Chips that no one was willing to be the first to risk money on her mirror.

As a result of this negative feedback Chips began to alter her sales tactics somewhat. First, she approached a local box manufacturer and purchased some white boxes to put her mirrors into. As well, at the suggestion of Paul, who wrote her a "canned" phone script to use, Chips began to deemphasize the "selling" of her product. She began asking buyers if they would spend a few minutes with her to give her their expert opinion about a unique product she had developed but was not sure what to do with. This approach was not only less threatening for Chips, who was totally new at making cold calls and discussing business, but it was also flattering to the buyer. As well, Chips began to strike up acquaintances with the various phone receptionists she spoke to. "When a receptionist asked for my name I always responded Chips, like chocolate, and Klein, as in Calvin. They would in turn tell me their first name and from then on whenever I called we knew each other immediately."

Using this revised approach Chips got to see a number of companies including a large distributor of male contraceptives in Toronto. While unable to use the product directly, he was enthusiastic about it and exposed Chips for the first time to the marketing concept of Premium or Incentive selling which his company and others in the cosmetics and pharmaceutical industries often used to help sell their main products.

One very large cosmetics wholesaler became very interested in Chips' mirror after an initial meeting with the buyer. "The woman was so excited about the product. She was at that time looking for something new to develop and I happened to walk in with my little mirror at the right time. She took one look at the product and did a back somersault. She and I were going to the moon with my mirror. She asked all kinds of questions regarding F.O.B. points, quantity discounts, terms of payment, promotion, and of course I didn't have any answers. So I wrote them all down and promised to get back to her." However, at a subsequent meeting with top management Chips was unsuccessful in her attempt to negotiate a distributorship agreement. While discouraged by yet another setback, Chips felt that they may have been fortunate in a way. "Paul told me later that not only had I given away our house at the meeting but the two kids as well and that we probably would have ended up losing 25¢ on every unit we made."

FINDING AN AGENT

Realizing that working with a distributor was too costly, Chips concentrated her efforts on contacting manufacturers' representatives, preferably selling related items on a commissioned basis to the same retail channels. Working once again with the yellow pages, Chips contacted numerous agents, most of whom sold totally unrelated lines, since there was no breakdown of representatives by product in the phone book. Finally, Chips had a breakthrough when she contacted Fred Becker Sales, a one-man rep company that appeared quite interested in the product. Mr. Becker was semi-retired but had spent 40 years in business, first as a toy manufacturer and subsequently as an agent, selling products such as plastic pails, laundry baskets, hair nets, bobby pins, cook pots, and baking tins to companies such as Pro Hardware, D. H. Howden, Home Hardware, Towers and Woolco.

As soon as he saw the mirror and how it worked Mr. Becker became very enthused. It appeared to be a unique product and at a target retail price of under $10.00 he felt The Eye Maker could be a real moneymaker that could be sold all year round. His initial enthusiasm was confirmed over the next few weeks as Mr. Becker showed the mirror and how it worked to a number of women he knew, all of whom fell in love with it. As Mr. Becker explained, "I got lots of Wows from the ladies once they realized what the mirror could do. Invariably they'd say what a great idea." Only one lady, who operated an exclusive facial care and cosmetics salon in downtown Toronto rejected the product as being too cheap and "tinny" for her clientele. Based on this informal market survey and the fact that he and Mrs. Klein seemed to work well together, an exclusive sales agreement was drafted that made Mr. Becker the sole representative for The Eye Maker throughout Canada with possible extension to the United States as well (see Exhibit 2).

Immediately Mr. Becker went to work promoting The Eye Maker. He began approaching individual drug stores in Toronto, speaking with store managers trying to interest them in spending some of their discretionary budget on stocking perhaps a dozen mirrors in their cosmetics department. He also approached a number of department stores and was able to convince Towers to order an initial 35 dozen mirrors, the largest order Chipco had ever received. By August Mr. Becker had visited enough potential customers to become convinced that Chips should go ahead and manufacture a run of 5000 mirrors, the minimum amount she had told him it was worthwhile setting up to make. During June of 1981 Chips obtained a legal opinion from a firm of Patent and Trademark attorneys as to the advisability of filing for patent protection on her mirror. Chips was constantly concerned about the possibility of an unscrupulous cosmetic company or plastics fabricator stealing her idea and using their larger financial resources to bring the product to market before her. Patent law turned out to be quite complicated. The granting of patents was an expensive process, costing between $3000–$6000 per product patent per country. Consequently, rather than a patent, Chips opted for the drafting of a short non-disclosure agreement (see Exhibit 3) which was drawn up by her lawyer. Chips would in future insist that this agreement be signed by any company interested in seeing her mirror, which she hoped would offer her some protection should an attempt be made to copy her idea.

SOURCING AND PRODUCTION

With Fred Becker responsible for the sales and marketing function, Chips, during the months of July and August, began to concentrate her efforts on finding sources of supply for the components required to make her mirror. These components included a 2-piece plastic frame, 3 pieces of glass, a vinyl covered wire stand, and packaging (see Exhibit 4). "I began to look at different kinds of plastic, different grades and thicknesses, comparing both their structural and appearance characteristics: for example, whether I could use a thinner grade or go to a thicker gauge and what the increase in cost would be." For the frames Chips received quotes from 4 or 5 different vacuum forming fabricators based on 3 volume options: 1000, 3000, and 5000 units. She found a significant range of prices between these suppliers for the same specifications. Normally, Chips would disregard the lowest and highest price quotes and choose one that fell somewhere in the midrange. Besides price, Chips worked hard at negotiating with suppliers to extend her normal payment terms rather than cash with order or on delivery that new companies are typically subjected to. "I remember having such a fight with a guy who was going to make me some labels. He said, 'I want your money up front.' I replied, 'what do you mean you want your money up front? What if the labels you make for me are faulty?' He replied, 'You come in off the street, I've never heard of you and you want us to make 5000 labels and you don't want to pay ahead of time.' So I picked up my briefcase and left. And do you know what? I eventually found a fellow who was more than happy to make me rolls and rolls of labels and send me an invoice."

In addition to prices and terms Chips considered personal supplier rapport to be quite important. "You know, often I was treated as a silly little female who they were going to take for a ride." Ultimately, after reviewing the quotations on the plastic frames she chose a supplier and asked for some prototypes to be made to verify the design and structural features of the part. Instead of the pure white colour she had used for her previous frames Chips decided to go to an off-white which she thought would be more fashionable. For cost reasons, she had also decided to utilize a 4-cavity epoxy mould that would be textured in order to allow the use of a slightly lower grade, less expensive type of raw material. The first prototype frames that came off the new mould were not satisfactory. "What a shock I had when I saw the first frames. The sides were wavy and wouldn't glue together properly and there were many imperfections in the finish. When I complained, the production manager threw up his hands and exclaimed that there was nothing he could do about this shoddy workmanship given the unreliability of today's younger generation. At which point I told him, 'Fine, then when I receive your bill I will forget to pay it and when you call I will tell you there is nothing that can be done about my shoddy workmanship!' I think he grasped my point." The mould was modified at no charge and acceptable prototypes were run.

Regarding assembly of the mirror, she planned to have her plastics supplier glue the front and back halves of the frame together and insert the wire stand. However, she still needed to find a facility where the 3 pieces of glass could be economically assembled and the completed product packaged and shipped. She realized that with 5000 units to produce, a job of this magnitude could not be handled by her family and friends as she had done previously. Therefore, Chips began talking with people and visiting various non-profit organizations such as ARC industries and Torchlight, to see if they would be interested. Finally, one of her contacts mentioned approaching the prison system, which often operated small workshops as rehabilitation centres for their inmates. Chips followed up on this suggestion and after a series of meetings with the Vanier Centre for Women, chose this facility to be the assembly and shipping point for her product. Her idea would be to have her component suppliers ship directly to Vanier where the remainder of the production process would take place. Chips realized there were risks involved with choosing Vanier for assembling her product. She would have to hire and train all her operators and supply everything that would be needed by them to operate including gloves, glue, etc. She also knew she would personally have to ensure the quality of the final product as well as deal with any problems of theft or malicious breakage of the components. However, Vanier offered her such a cost advantage over other facilities that she was willing to incur these risks which she felt she could manage.

Regarding boxes, Chips would need individual packages as well as shipping cartons each of which would hold 12 units. The product packaging she decided would be brown and beige with a diecut front panel covered with a clear acetate film to allow the customer easy viewing of the mirror. "You see, I could not afford package photography so I hoped that looking through the acetate they would be able to see exactly how the mirror worked and say to themselves, 'I've got to have one of these!'" In addition to the visual impact, Chips planned to put detailed user instructions on both side panels of the box in French and English (see Exhibit 5).

THE MEETING

In late August, Chips met at home with Paul and Fred Becker to decide whether or not to proceed with the manufacture of the first 5,000 units. Both Fred and Paul encouraged Chips to proceed almost immediately in order to take advantage of the Christmas season, as well as deliver on time their first 35 dozen mirrors that Fred had taken from Towers. However Chips resisted. While Fred was positive he could sell enough units to recoup the $15,000–$20,000 outlay required to produce these units, currently he had only about 500 units as confirmed orders. What if Fred didn't come through and her family incurred a major loss of funds, much more than the $3000 she had spent on the venture thus far. Beyond these financial considerations, Chips also worried about her own personal resources and whether they were equal to the task. She had never run a company before and knew that to do so would require a major commitment of her time which meant denying her husband and children some of the care she had given them in the past. Nevertheless after a few hours of discussion Chips decided, with the prodding of Fred and Paul, to proceed with her production and sales plans for The Eye Maker.

PRE-STARTUP SEPTEMBER–OCTOBER 1981

During the month of September Chips drew up formal purchase orders for all the components required to build the mirror. Exhibit 9 lists the major orders placed including prices, delivery dates, payment terms as well as when these orders were actually paid for. Chips asked all her suppliers to target delivery for about the 20th of October but in some cases set partial shipment dates to accommodate suppliers' production schedules as well as her own. She was counting on about 2 weeks for the assembly of her initial orders which were due the second week of November.

Besides ordering supplies, Chips began investigating various gluing technologies for attaching the glass to the frames. Restricted to the use of non-solvent based adhesives by prison regulations Chips finally settled on a hot melt glue applied with an industrial glue gun. She also spent considerable time selecting and training the individuals who would assemble her product. Using recommendations from the prison staff Chips interviewed several candidates. As a general guideline she decided to select only women who had been charged with fraud (as opposed to any type of violent criminal behaviour) as well as women who were close to the end of their two year term. Each assembler would be paid a specific piece work rate which worked out to 15¢ per unit with an additional 10¢ going to the prison to cover its overhead and administrative costs.

In terms of training Chips wrote and distributed to each of her assemblers a comprehensive instruction manual that covered routines to be followed for the inspection of incoming materials, assembly of the mirrors and labels to the frames, as well as packaging, shipping, and glue gun maintenance (see Exhibit 7). "In the beginning I would show them how to do the assembly but after a few weeks most of them had worked out little shortcuts that made them much faster than me. They found for example, that when they pressed the glass into the plastic it was hot from the glue and their thumbs would get sore from the heat, from pressing so hard. So I bought them cotton gloves but these didn't work very well because they were too thin and got caught in the glue. So one of the women crocheted little thumb protectors that worked beautifully."

During this preproduction period Chips also obtained her Provincial Sales Tax number exempting her from the 7% tax on purchased materials and an exclusive Canadian Grocery Product Code (C.G.P.C.) number that would be printed in code or symbol form on her packaging to properly identify her product in the stores. Chipco's payment terms would be 2% 20, Net 30 days to try and induce customers to pay their bills as soon as possible after invoicing.

As the 20th of October approached, a last minute delivery problem with the wire stands occurred that threatened to scuttle Chips' delivery schedule. Realizing that they had underquoted the price for these wire stands, the supplier was purposely delaying production in the hope that Chipco would eventually cancel the order and go elsewhere. Chips decided to personally confront the president of the company with her problem and after a short meeting was assured of delivery of her stands by the next day at the originally quoted price. Apologizing to Chips for the delay the president explained to Chips that it was little companies like hers that had made his a large company.

STARTUP AND PRODUCTION NOVEMBER '81–MARCH '82

On the 9th of November Chipco's first order of 420 mirrors was ready for shipment to Towers. However, Chips ran into a serious problem while on her way to Toronto to deliver this order. "Every time I put on my brakes, the boxes moved backwards and forwards and there was a tinkling sound. Each time I turned a corner, I heard 'tinkle tinkle tinkle.' Eventually, I stopped the car, got out, shook one of the boxes, and when I opened it, I discovered that the glass part of the mirror had fallen off its base. So I headed right back to the factory. We opened all the boxes and found more than half the mirrors had the glass just hanging by threads of glue. Absolute disaster. I got on the phone to the mirror people, the glue people, and the plastics supplier, and everyone came right down to look at the problem. After much discussion we realized that the method of applying the glue was incorrect. We were gluing the glass to the plastic, but we should have been gluing the plastic and pressing the glass on it. We all worked overtime to reglue those mirrors, so that we could meet the delivery date. I also started doing a drop test that used to drive my people crazy. There was a concrete floor at the prison and I would walk down the rows of workers and knock a mirror on to the floor. The glass sometimes shattered, but it wouldn't come unglued. After that I became known affectionately to my girls as the Dragon Lady."

In addition to the glue problem, Chips also encountered significant tearing of the acetate window during shipment which resulted in a number of customer returns. As well, some of the glass she received was substandard due to bubbly edges, smoky clarity, or improper size and had to be reworked or replaced by the supplier. Despite these difficulties, after the initial startup Chipco was able for the most part to supply quality mirrors to its customers on schedule, which gave Chips a certain sense of satisfaction.

SALES

Throughout the fall of 1981, Mr. Becker spent considerable time selling The Eye Maker through any significant retail outlet he could find including a large beauty supply wholesaler (1500 units), Simpson's (500 units) (Exhibit 8) and Drug City (120 units). Another 870 units were sold to a large Toronto contact lens producer as well as a prominent opthalmologist who gave a free mirror to his patients with each purchase of a pair of contact lenses. Chips had stumbled into the contact lens market by accident after a visit to the University of Waterloo optometry department in search of a possible means to magnify her mirror.

A single sample mirror was sold to Amway while a further 6 dozen went to a small chain of Toronto cosmetics stores. Surprisingly, a small boutique in one of Toronto's fashionable shopping areas was able to move almost 100 units before Christmas, mainly to their male clients who were looking for a unique gift for their wives or girlfriends.

CHIPS' CONCERNS—APRIL '82

Assessing the performance of Chipco during the past six months, Chips was plagued with mixed feelings. While pleased to have sold almost 4000 units at the full wholesale price, she was concerned about a number of disturbing facts. First, she noticed that sales of the mirror had drastically dropped after the New Year as indicated below. Secondly, almost none of her customers had placed a reorder for the mirror after receiving the first shipment because the mirrors simply were not moving, even after they had been marked down substantially. On the positive side, however, none of their customers had complained about the quality or functionality of the mirror.

	Sales	
	Units	Dollars
October	0	0
November	1705	7735
December	826	3760
January	545	2465
February	571	2600
March	334	1520
	3981	18080

Thirdly, in early March, Chips had received a product evaluation report from the Canadian Industrial Innovation Centre in Waterloo (see Exhibit 9). Chips had commissioned this report at a cost of $150 to investigate the technical and market feasibility of her original Eye Maker Compact. While applauding the uniqueness and function of her mirror the report stressed that "The actual market is a serious concern. A cursory survey of potential users indicated that few people carried a make-up mirror or even considered one necessary. . . . In light of our observations we are hesitant to predict commercial success for your proposal. . . . In fact, our opinion at this point is that you will be unlikely to recover your initial development investment because the market is well served already and not very active. . . . Consequently, we are recommending that you do not begin to invest heavily in the idea without crucially studying the market." In addition, Chips was quite concerned with the report's view that legal protection would probably not be worth the expense because of the "obvious nature of the idea." If this were true, Chips wondered how long she would be able to protect her idea from a larger and more financially stable competitor.

Reviewing all of these factors in her mind, Chips realized she was at a turning point with her mirror. While her income statement for the past four months (see Exhibit 10) indicated she had just about broken even, she wasn't sure she had sufficient financial resources to continue to operate effectively in the competitive cosmetic industry. Whether and/or how to proceed further with her venture would have to be decided quickly in order to take advantage of the fast approaching fall season.

Exhibit 1. Chipco Balance Sheet as at September 30, 1981.

Assets			
Inventory			$12,085

Liabilities			
Accounts Payable			$ 5,777

Partners' Equity			
	P. Klein	C. Klein	Total
Balance October 1, 1980	$ —	$ —	$ —
Capital contributions	4,655	4,654	9,309
Net loss	< 8,001>	5,000	< 3,001>
Balance September 30, 1981	<$3,346>	$9,654	$ 6,308
			$12,085

Chipco Financial Statements (Unaudited—See Notice to Reader) for the year ended September 30, 1981.

Sales	$1,585
Cost of Sales	
Inventory at beginning of year	—
Purchases	13,127
Freight and duty	997
	14,124
Less: Inventory at end of year	12,085
	2,039
Gross Profit <Loss>	< 454>
Expenses (business portion only)	
Mortgage interest	586
Maintenance fees	103
Municipal tax	99
Utilities	86
Automobile and travel	423
Telephone long distance	249
Entertainment and promotion	240
Professional fees	282
Office and stationery	295
Advertising	47
Capital Cost Allowance	137
	2,547
Net Income <Loss>	<$ 3,001>
Partnership Income <Loss> Allocated	
C. Klein	5,000
P. Klein	< 8,001>
	<$ 3,001>

Exhibit 2.

AGREEMENT

BETWEEN:

, hereafter referred to as C,

AND

FRED BECKER, and/or FRED BECKER SALES

, hereafter referred to as B.

C, by signing this letter, appoints B as its exclusive Canadian sales agent for the "EYE MAKER" and any other related make-up mirror related products. B will work at a commission rate as outlined below and will not be entitled to any expenses unless specifically agreed to in writing by C. B will bear his own selling expenses but it is understood when it comes to trade shows, advertising of any kind, that C is expected to bear the costs of such expenditures after both parties have consulted regarding merits of same, and C has approved the costs.

B is committed, while earning commissions from C, not to carry any line of mirrors or beauty aids and products that would conflict in the slightest degree with the mirror products distributed by C. B may use the titles such as Director of Marketing, National Accounts Executive and/or General Sales Manager.

B will appoint the necessary sales force across Canada, supervise same and make payments to respective sales organizations out of the commissions received by B. The actual correspondence will be handled by C at head office but B will be available for consultation and advice where same should be necessary in connection to correspondence relating to salesmen and customers. If for any reason C has any objections whatsoever to any representative or sales organization appointed by B, C has the right to request cancellation of such representative within a time frame of ninety days from their request.

If anything unlawful were to occur in the conduct of business by B's appointees or by B himself, such a cancellation of terminating arrangements can be made effective immediately.

It is understood that any representative appointed by B will have to abide by the guidelines and instructions and price schedule specified by C. If any deviations are required they must be approved by C beforehand. Likewise if C requires a change in commission structure when for instance, quoting a particularly low price, this too should be discussed and stated beforehand.

B is to receive copies of all invoices and correspondence as same are being sent out by C. Commissions are payable by the fifteenth of each month following shipment for the goods shipped the previous month.

Exhibit 2 (continued)

Commission rate is ten percent (10%) on all shipments in Canada. If orders between the date of this agreement and the end of the year amount to 1200 units there would be a bonus commission of two percent (2%) due to B. For each additional 1200 pieces, B will be credited with an extra two percent (2%) up to a maximum of five percent (5%), this to apply on legitimate credit approved orders received by C and to be shipped by C before December 31st, 1981. These extra commission percentage points are due to B, (even if C's production prevents proper shipment), provided the total quantities of orders produced meet the aforementioned standards. Also it is understood that this bonus commission in each case is applicable on dollar-one in each instance. So if legitimate orders before the end of 1981 total 2400 mirrors, the commission rate would be fifteen percent (15%) on the invoice amount of all 2400 mirrors shipped.

If B produces between *now and December 31st, 1981, orders totalling at least 2500 mirrors to be shipped before the end of 1981,* then this arrangement is automatically renewed for the year of 1981. In order to obtain the five percent (5%) bonus commission for 1982, B would have to produce orders for 10,000 mirrors by June 30th, 1982 and to qualify for the bonus for the next 6 months, additional orders of 15,000 mirrors would have to be produced. When we speak of mirrors we are talking strictly of the "EYE MAKER" and any other products to be sold at that time will automatically qualify at the fifteen percent (15%) commission rate.

If a sales volume based again on orders received by B, for at least $125,000.00 is obtained in 1982, these arrangements are automatically renewed for 1983 with an option for the year 1984, which should be discussed in December, 1982 in the light of circumstances prevailing at that time.

B would like to have the opportunity and the chance of first refusal in connection with possible sales to U.S.A. Any arrangements regarding that territory and possibly other export sales to be spelled out separately from these Canadian arrangements.

In the event of B's death, this Arrangement is null and void at that time, with the exception that B's estate will receive regular commission of orders on hand at that time. Furthermore, a commission of five percent (5%) will be due to B's estate on all orders received for a period of six months after B's death.

SIGNED, this   day of   , 1981.

_____

_____

Exhibit 3. Note: This agreement is a sample only and may not be suitable for your particular situation.

SAMPLE CONFIDENTIALITY AGREEMENT

This Agreement made this   day of   , 198   .

WHEREAS   ("The Owner")

has information in relation to a "   ", all of which information is confidential;

AND WHEREAS the undersigned ("the Disclosees") wish to receive such information for the purpose of evaluating its commercial potential on behalf of ("the Company");

AND WHEREAS the Owner has particularly disclosed and is prepared to further disclose the information in confidence under the terms and conditions which follow;

NOW THEREFORE in consideration of the premises and of the disclosure of the information and One Dollar and other good and valuable consideration the receipt and adequacy of which the parties hereby acknowledge, the Disclosees hereby agree as follows:

The Disclosees agree to keep confidential all of the subject information received from the Owner until such time as the information has become public knowledge in a manner not in breach of this Agreement. Specifically, the Disclosees agree not to make any disclosure of the information to any persons other than employees of the Company who need to know the information for the present purposes, and only on receiving the agreement of said employees to be bound by the terms of this Agreement. The Disclosees further agree not to make any unauthorized use of the information.

For the purposes of this Agreement, all information transmitted by the Owner to the Disclosees shall be considered to be proprietary and confidential, unless the information has become public knowledge in a manner not in breach of this Agreement, or unless the Disclosees can demonstrate to the satisfaction of the Owner that the specific information was already in their possession or in the Company's possession at the time of the disclosure by the Owner.

IN WITNESS WHEREOF the Disclosees have hereunder executed this Agreement as of the date first above written.

SIGNED, this   day of   , 1981.

_____

_____

Exhibit 4.

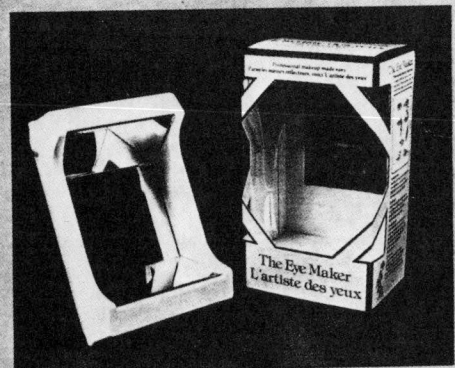

Exhibit 5.

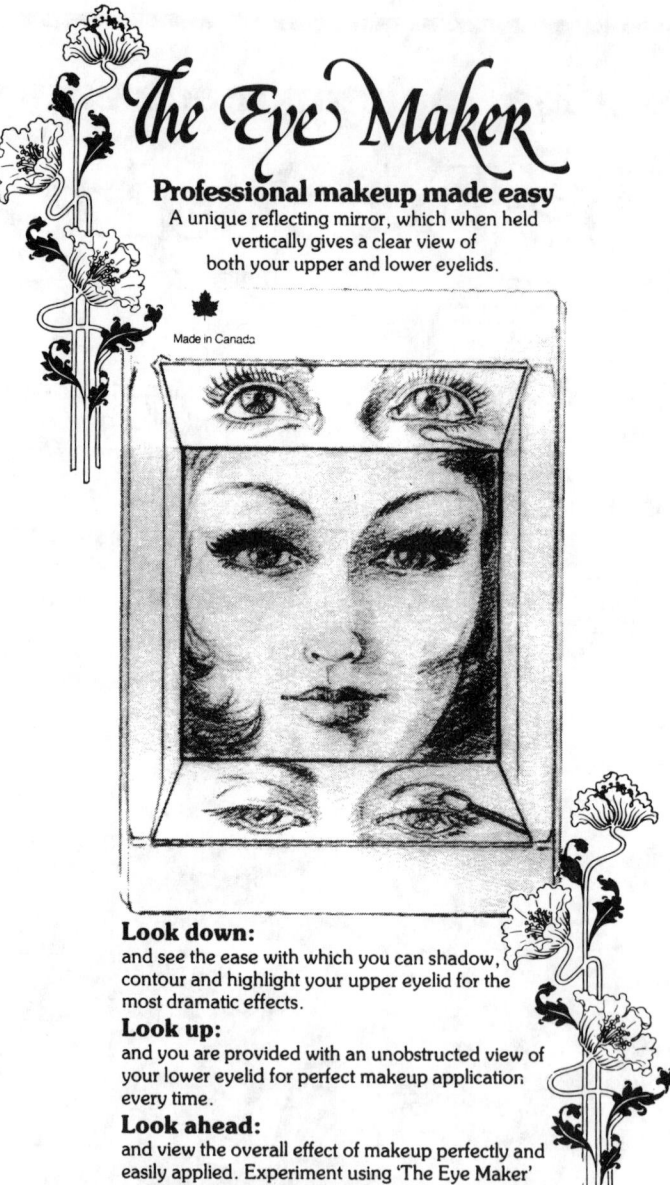

The Eye Maker

Professional makeup made easy

A unique reflecting mirror, which when held
vertically gives a clear view of
both your upper and lower eyelids.

Made in Canada

Look down:
and see the ease with which you can shadow,
contour and highlight your upper eyelid for the
most dramatic effects.

Look up:
and you are provided with an unobstructed view of
your lower eyelid for perfect makeup application
every time.

Look ahead:
and view the overall effect of makeup perfectly and
easily applied. Experiment using 'The Eye Maker'
and you too can achieve a professional appearance.

Contains:
a multi-angle stand, which doubles as a handle or a
hanger. 'The Eye Maker' can be used hand-held, or
mounted on the wall or on the adjustable stand.

A   Chipco   PRODUCT

Exhibit 6. List of key supply costs September '81–March '82.

	Invoice Date	Payment Terms	Date of Invoice Payment	Quantity Ordered	Quoted Cost/Unit
September/81					
4-cavity Epoxy Tool	8th	$600 dep. bal. COD	same	1	$935 total
Polystyrene Material for Frames	25th	COD	Oct. 1	3585 lbs.	$1.25/lb. + F.S.T.
October/81					
Wire Stand	14th	$175 Dept. Bal. Net. 30 days	Dec. 15	5100 units	$.14 ea.
Mirror Sets:					
(2 pc. - 2 1/4 × 3 7/8)	15th	Net 30	Dec. 1	2000 units	$30/100
(1 pc. - 3 1/2 × 4)	21st	Net 30	Dec. 1	3020 units	$30/100
Film Charges					
Re: Packaging	15th	Net 30	Dec. 1	1	$335 total
Individual Boxes	29th	Net 30	Dec. 1	5350 units	$471/M
(5 1/16 × 3 1/2 × 8 7/16)					+ $140 setup
Bulk Cartons (15 5/8 × 14 5/8 × 8 9/16)	30th	Net 30	Dec. 1	471 units	$.79 ea.
Plastic Frames	22nd	2% 10 Net 30	Nov. 6	1200 units	$.89 ea. + F.S.T.
	29th	2% 10 Net 30	Nov. 6	1324 units	$.89 ea. + F.S.T.
Glue Sticks	16th	COD	Same	1 carton	$110 total
Glue Sticks & Applicator Gun	20th	COD	Same	1 carton	$185 total
November/81					
Mirror Assembly	9th	Cash	Same	1500 units	$.25 ea.
	30th	Cash	Dec. 11	1024 units	$.25 ea.
Sales Commissions	30th	20th of following month	Dec. 16	—	$970 total
Plastic Frames	30th	2% 10 Net 30	Dec. 9	2490 units	$.70 ea. + F.S.T.
December/81					
Glue Gun	3rd	Net 30	Jan. 7/82	1	$75 total
Glue Sticks	17th	Net 30	Feb. 2/82	1 carton	$110 total
Sales Commissions	31st	20th of following month	Jan. 2/82	—	$470 total

Exhibit 6. (continued).

	Invoice Date	Payment Terms	Date of Invoice Payment	Quantity Ordered	Cost/ Unit
January/82					
Promotion Flyers	25th	Net 30	Feb. 26	1000	$215 total
Sales Commissions	31st	20th of following month	Mar. 1	—	$310 total
February/82					
Industrial Design	4th	Net 30	Feb. 26	—	$300 total
Labels (The Eye Maker)	12th	$80 Dep. Bal. Net 30	Feb. 26	2000 units	$60/M
Promotion Flyers	17th	Net 30	Apr. 5	2500 units	$305 total
Sales Commissions	28th	20th of following month	Mar. 16	—	$325 total
March					
Frame Assembly	5th	Net 30	Apr. 5	1459	$.25 ea.
Glass Mirrors Reworked	15th	Net 30	Apr. 30	742 rework 320 new	$195 total
Sales Commissions	31st	20th of following month	June 28	—	$190 total
Miscellaneous Costs *October '81–March '82*					
Printing (cards, price lists, catalogue sheets, invoices, etc.)					$170
Express Freight (in & out)		Net 7 days			$ 65

1. F.S.T. is 9% Federal Sales Tax
2. Chipco was exempt from 7% Provincial Sales Tax

Exhibit 7. Chipco "The Eye Maker" instruction manual.

1.	BASES
1.1	General visual check for obvious flaws such as scratches, holes, drips, incomplete glueing, etc.
1.2	Ensure that the handle is attached and functions properly.
2.	MIRRORS
2.1	General visual check for obvious flaws such as cracks, scratches, blotches, smokiness, etc.

Note: It is best to check the mirrors before assembly, as once they are glued in, they are impossible to remove without damaging them or the bases.

3.	ASSEMBLY OF MIRRORS TO BASE
3.1	Bring glue gun up to temperature.
3.2	Apply 2 blobs of glue to side mirror site on plastic base, one site at a time. Each blob is to be approximately the size of a nickel and should be placed 1–11/4″ in from the edges. The centre mirror requires 4 blobs of glue.
3.3	Press mirror into place within 8 seconds of applying glue. Leave to cool at least 2 hours before cleaning the mirror.
3.4	In the case of the side mirrors, ensure that the arrissed (sanded) edge is placed in the upright position.
3.5	For side mirrors, use material, flannel side to plastic, to "shoe-horn" the mirror into the base.
3.6	Press mirror in and down to ensure that it goes into the "groove."
3.7	In the case of all mirrors, check that they are correctly positioned and that no glue has squeezed out. If glue is showing, either reduce the amount applied slightly, or move it further in from the edge.
3.8	Clean mirrors with dry, paper cloth.
4.	LABELS
4.1	Check for clarity of letters.
4.2	Apply one per mirror to the outer, curved surface of the base.
5.	UNIT BOX ASSEMBLY
5.1	General visual check for obvious flaws such as poorly glued seams, incorrect ink colours, rips, scratches, etc.
5.2	Fold flaps and tuck in bottom end.
5.3	Insert assembled mirror and hold for inspection.
6.	MASTER CARTON
6.1	Fold, tuck and tape bottom end.
6.2	Insert 12 assembled and inspected unit boxes.
6.3	Seal, number and date stamp cartons.
7.	GLUE GUN
7.1	Ensure that glue gun is unplugged when not in use.
7.2	At end of day, clean off the glue gun to prevent glue backing up.

Note: As a guide to good production, "When in doubt, leave out." Also, always look at the product as if you were going to buy it.

Exhibit 8. Simpsons Christmas Flyer, December, 1981.

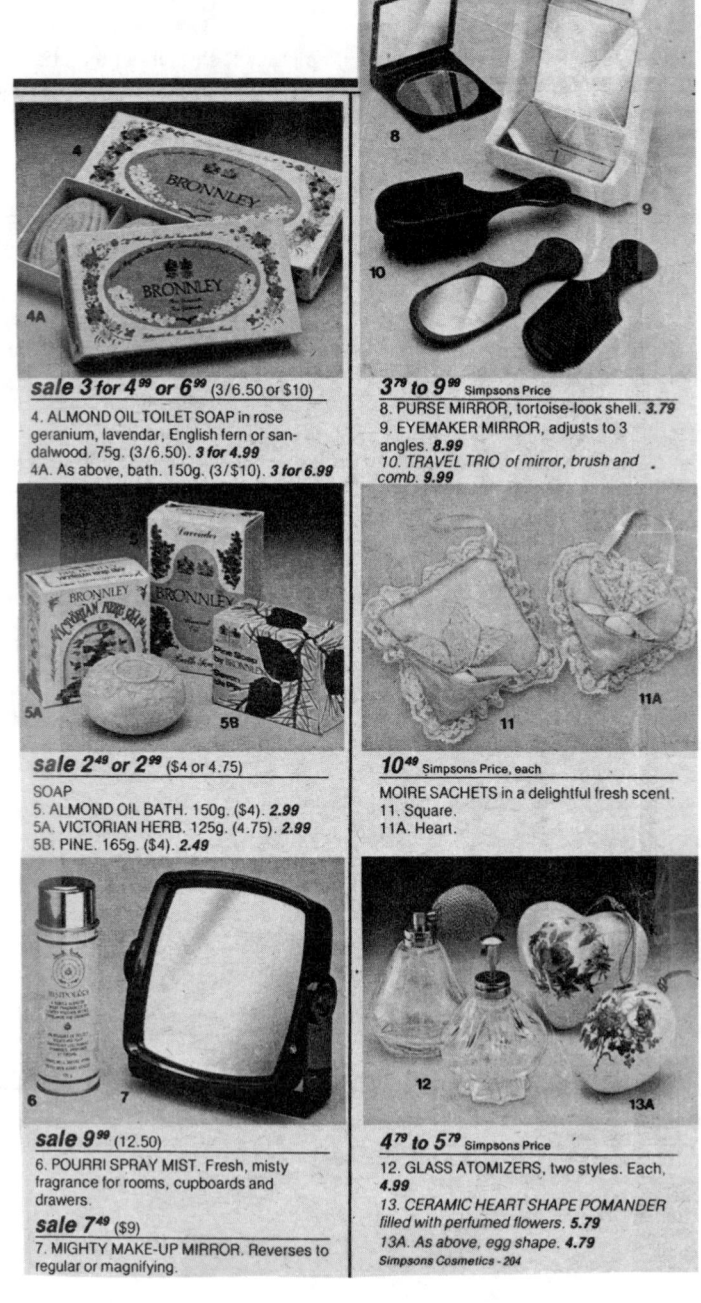

sale 3 for 4⁹⁹ or 6⁹⁹ (3/6.50 or $10)

4. ALMOND OIL TOILET SOAP in rose geranium, lavendar, English fern or sandalwood. 75g. (3/6.50). *3 for 4.99*
4A. As above, bath. 150g. (3/$10). *3 for 6.99*

sale 2⁴⁹ or 2⁹⁹ ($4 or 4.75)

SOAP
5. ALMOND OIL BATH. 150g. ($4). *2.99*
5A. VICTORIAN HERB. 125g. (4.75). *2.99*
5B. PINE. 165g. ($4). *2.49*

sale 9⁹⁹ (12.50)

6. POURRI SPRAY MIST. Fresh, misty fragrance for rooms, cupboards and drawers.

sale 7⁴⁹ ($9)

7. MIGHTY MAKE-UP MIRROR. Reverses to regular or magnifying.

3⁷⁹ to 9⁹⁹ Simpsons Price

8. PURSE MIRROR, tortoise-look shell. *3.79*
9. EYEMAKER MIRROR, adjusts to 3 angles. *8.99*
10. *TRAVEL TRIO of mirror, brush and comb. 9.99*

10⁴⁹ Simpsons Price, each

MOIRE SACHETS in a delightful fresh scent.
11. Square.
11A. Heart.

4⁷⁹ to 5⁷⁹ Simpsons Price

12. GLASS ATOMIZERS, two styles. Each, *4.99*
13. CERAMIC HEART SHAPE POMANDER filled with perfumed flowers. *5.79*
13A. As above, egg shape. *4.79*
Simpsons Cosmetics - 204

Exhibit 9. Inventor's assistance program office interpretation "The Eye Maker Model 2" (Pocket Eyemaker) KLE8201 16.

We have completed our preliminary assessment of your innovation, the "Eye Maker Model 2." To become commercially viable any new proposal must possess certain favourable characteristics, among them numbering; uniqueness or novelty, technical feasibility, manufacturing feasibility, safety and legality, a strong market position and a price befitting the function. After this initial analysis only a few of the points appear unfavourable and even these may not be irrevocably so.

Technically the "Eye Maker Model 2" is simple to produce, as you have indicated. We concur with the choice of injection moulding of the pieces. Die and tooling costs are a significant investment in this process so to minimize costs we recommend that the two folding covers are identical. Likewise the entire unit should snap together to reduce the assembly costs. Double sided foam backed adhesive tape could be a suitable adhesive system for the mirrors. Although pin hinges and other adhesives may spawn a more durable product we do not envision such abuse, in the open position, to warrant the added cost.

The final design should be as aesthetically pleasing as possible. Providing stops to align the covers in the correct attitude is merely a part of the moulding process. The actual angles can be easily arrived at with basic sketches and some experimentation. We feel that the entire unit should be designed by an industrial engineer who has experience in making consumer products "attractive." Although many professional designers are available, an economical, albeit slower, route may be to approach a community college teaching industrial design courses to see if a student would do the work as a project. Particularly for a simple device as the "Eye Maker Model 2," the lack of experience may not be a serious detriment. An attractive product will be a key in the sales volume.

The actual market is a serious concern. A cursory survey of potential users indicated that few people carried a make-up mirror or even considered one necessary. This sampling was by no means a formal Market Study but may be indicative of the nature of the general market. If a person went out to purchase a compact mirror they would be inclined to do so because of the attractiveness of the case and the selling price. We doubt that a customer would pay significantly more for your proposal because of the claimed functional features. If you can produce a price competitive product, however, and the point-of-purchase promotion (Catalogue sheets, easel displays, packaging and so forth) is attractive and eye-catching, a portion of the market may be captured. We do not envision getting a large market share, however.

One possible way to broach the market would be to sell the unit to a cosmetics distributor as a sales giveaway. In this case the mirror would be given as a "free gift" for a certain dollar value purchase. Even this may be a difficult approach because the gift is usually a product from the distributor's line. It is probably an avenue worth investigating, however.

Exhibit 9. (continued)

Legal protection for the product is probably not worth the expense. The idea does not appear patentable because of its obvious nature and an Industrial Design, for which it would qualify, will do nothing to protect the function. Any design change in the case would permit a competitor to enter the market. Although not overly expensive the actual worth of the protection must be assessed before spending the money.

In light of our observations we are hesitant to predict commercial success for your proposal. In fact, our opinion at this point is that you will be unlikely to recover your initial development investments because the market is well served already and not very active. Consequently we are recommending that you do not begin to invest heavily in the idea without crucially studying the market. A fairly reliable method to gauge potential sales, price and so forth is to carry out a market survey (Appendix B). If the results are favourable you would cut your losses by discontinuing the project. A positive market survey should also help in getting equitable distribution agreements.

The distributor, of course, is important. We note that you have located one and assume that you have carefully selected them for their cosmetics product line. If you proceed with the project you should not be hesitant in changing distributors if you feel you are not sufficiently represented. Establishing potential alternate distribution routes, even if you are now satisfied, is always a useful exercise to keep you abreast of prices, new competition and better ways of selling.

We regret that we could not be more optimistic in this report but our market reservations are sincere. If you continue with the project we recommend the route we have outlined. We hope that this report will not be discouraging but will aid in this and your future endeavours.

Exhibit 10.

Income Statement

November 1981 to March 1982

Gross Sales	$18,235.22
Discounts & Allowances	753.80
Net Sales	17,481.42
Direct Cost of Goods Sold (4000 Units)	12,892.00
Gross Profit	4,489.42
Gross Profit (Percent)	25.16
Expenses	
Commissions	1,931.36
Advertising	453.78
Subscriptions	258.79
Stationery	47.31
Transport	67.54
Tooling	933.04
Other	500.00
Total	$4,191.84
Net Profit	$ 397.60

Télécité Inc.

It was 7:00 am on March 10, 1994, and Marshall Moreyne, President and CEO of Télécité, was already at his desk in his office in Pointe-Claire, Québec. For the past two months, the financial resources of the company had been foremost on his mind. In 1992, the company had shifted its focus and resources from research and development to manufacturing and installing electronic display panels for subway cars. However, the sales of advertisement time slots had been below his expectations, and the Montréal Urban Community Transit Corporation (MUCTC) had recently informed him that the negotiation for the contract to install LED display panels in the Green line may not start until other renovation work was completed in mid-1997. On the bright side, the reviews of the product, the Visual Communication Network that he had developed over the past five years, were very positive. His thoughts then turned to the road ahead, and specifically to the strategic direction that was required to pursue growth.

COMPANY HISTORY

Marshall Moreyne has always considered himself an entrepreneur. The 40-year old Montréal native studied Mechanical Engineering at Concordia University; in 1977, he decided to pursue business studies by enrolling part-time in the M.B.A. program at McGill University. For the next two years, he studied at night while working full-time for Northern Telecom. In 1979, he quit his job to do the M.B.A. program full-time. Meanwhile, Marshall and a classmate, Frank Ruffolo, set up a computer-software business; but the venture did not last long, as they were unable to attract enough clients to keep the business viable.

After graduating in 1980, Marshall left Montréal to work at Booz-Allen & Hamilton's management consulting office in Britain, but five years later he was back in Montréal scouting for business opportunities in high technology. One of the products that caught his attention was the old-fashioned electronic display panels. These Light-Emitting-Diode (LED) electronic signs were simple in nature and acted as "flasher boards" that would display text in red colour.

This case was prepared by Jose Lam, M.B.A., and Linda Rizzetto, DIA, under the direction of Dr. A. B. Ibrahim as a basis for class discussion rather than to illustrate effective or ineffective handling of an administrative situation. Certain information and financial figures in the case have been disguised to maintain and respect confidentiality. The authors wish to thank and gratefully appreciate the time and kind collaboration of Messrs. Marshall Moreyne and John Iwanic of Télécité Inc.

This case was supported by a research grant from the Certified General Accountants Association of Canada (CGA).

© Dr. A. B. Ibrahim, 1996.

Marshall thought that the functionality of these LED display panels could be improved by adding other colours, graphics and animation and by using these new features in a network to generate advertisement revenue. He discussed these ideas with his friend, Frank, and decided to pursue the business concept further. One possibility was to adapt and manufacture these electronic display panels for advertising purposes that could be set up in buses, subway cars, shopping malls and/or airports.

In 1986, Marshall set up Télécité Inc. as a privately-owned management consultancy and communications company, with the objectives of offering and maintaining the highest standards of excellence in its products, services and professional conduct. The vision of the company was to establish itself as an innovator in the field of worldwide communications. This would be achieved by committing the company's mission towards applied research and development conducted to refine electronic high technology in its application to mass transit systems.

FINANCING RESEARCH AND DEVELOPMENT (R&D)

Marshall's first step was to approach Frank, who has an electrical engineering background as well, to evaluate if this technology could work in real-time in the subway. Next he tried to persuade the MUCTC of the merits of his proposed LED display panels. Although the reception by the MUCTC was enthusiastic, Marshall could not get a financial commitment from it. In 1987, a business plan was developed to raise funds to support R&D. The federal government (Transport Canada) contributed $60,000 for a feasibility study. In addition, Marshall asked the Canadian National Institute for the Blind (CNIB) and the Canadian Hearing Society (CHS) to participate in the review committee of this project in order to ensure that the needs of the visually- and hearing-impaired were met.

The feasibility study evaluated the new proposed electronic display panels (named Visual Communication Network) as a product which could enhance the safety of the visually-impaired, hearing-impaired and the elderly travelling in the subway. The main advantage of the Visual Communication Network (VCN) was that emergency messages could be flashed in the display panels almost immediately, thus providing timely information to subway passengers.

Notwithstanding the positive recommendations of the feasibility study, Marshall was now faced with the task of selling the idea and raising needed money to develop a pilot VCN display panel. Marshall approached private investors who evaluated the project and concluded that the project's potential revenues were still not solid.

Nonetheless, Télécité started the development of a prototype to be used in the pilot study. A committee, made up of members from MUCTC, Transport Canada, Transport Québec, CNIB and CHS, was set up to oversee the project. In addition, Frank joined Télécité full-time, and two other engineers were hired full-time, one to handle hardware development and the other to handle the software development of the VCN system network.

Meanwhile, Marshall had also started to approach governmental transport agencies, banks, and private investors for additional funds. However, one key step was to persuade the MUCTC of the merits of the VCN as a medium that could be used not only to improve safety, but also to enhance the trip of the subway passengers by providing information about bus stops, news, weather reports and sports and cultural events. At first, the MUCTC was reluctant to participate in such a pilot study because it was concerned about potential disruptions of, or damage to the subway's electrical systems. However, after months of negotiations, the MUCTC agreed to a six-month pilot study once the prototype had been developed.

One advantage of the VCN technology is that in addition to the safety advantages, the sharper images and text displayed also provided a new medium for a captive audience. This opened an opportunity to sell and show advertisement in the display panels.

In 1989, Marshall started to approach large companies. The idea was to get companies to become sponsors of the pilot study by purchasing advertisement time blocks during the testing of the pilot. After several months, Marshall received commitment of $650,000 from several major advertisers, including Eaton's, Kraft General Foods, Videotron, CJAD, Johnson & Johnson, Gillette, Molson, Bell Canada, Air Canada and others.

Marshall's hard work over the past year had finally started to pay off. In 1990, further financing for R&D came from the federal and provincial Transport Departments ($350,000).

THE MUCTC CONTRACT

In the spring of 1991, the VCN prototype was finally developed. The six-month pilot study called for Télécité to install its VCN panels in a single train of the Orange line of the Montréal subway. After the success of the pilot study, Télécité negotiated and signed a 20-year contract in December 1991 with the MUCTC to install and operate the VCN display panels in all the cars of the Montréal subway.

The terms of the contract first applied to three of the four Metro lines, namely the Orange, Blue and Yellow lines. Télécité would own the display panels for the first 12 years (from 1992 to 2003). After that, the MUCTC would own the panels, but Télécité would receive half the advertising-sales profits for a further eight years (to 2011).

Work on the 423 cars of those three lines would wrap up in May 1994, while work on the fourth, 333-car Green line would commence in mid-1997 and continue to the end of 1998. The 20-year term of the Green line contract would be delayed accordingly (to 2009 and 2017).

THE VISUAL COMMUNICATION NETWORK

Marshall's original idea was to redesign the old-fashioned LED display panels. These electronic panels were essentially "flasher boards" which could display static text or a moving message. Marshall wanted to improve the looks and functionality of the panels. For example, instead of just the standard red colour, he wanted his panels to display other colours, as well as graphic animation. In addition, the VCN would be integrated to an advanced information system network, which would not only control the information content to be displayed, but also add pre-recorded digitized vocal messages.

The final version of the VCN combined an automatic stop announcement and emergency communication system with state-of-the-art media creation and display technology, which enhanced and provided the ultimate in real-time transit LED display information delivery systems.

The VCN's technology utilized Customer Information Screens (CIS) that were designed to meet the *Americans with Disabilities Act* (ADA) regulations. The dimensions of these displays were 192 mm by 960 mm, and the screens, which utilized the latest high intensity flat view LED matrix, had a resolution of 160 dots by 32 dots. Each LED matrix consisted of a 16 by 16 LED array in a 96 mm square construction, with a dot size of 5 mm and a dot pitch of 6 mm. Each dot was capable of displaying red, green, black and yellow colours.

In contrast to the older technology which used individual discrete LEDs, the LED arrays used for the VCN screens were cast in one solid 96 mm square matrix using flat top cavities for each LED dot. This resulted in a display screen with unparalleled luminosity, visibility and readability. This enhanced visual messaging capabilities and capacities substantially, thus providing the visually-impaired and the elderly accessibility to timely information on safety and system status.

The size of the display and the super wide angle of 165 degrees offered other benefits in that a reduced number of displays would be needed to be installed as more people had visual access to the information displayed on the screens (refer to Exhibit 1).

Furthermore, the use of high definition and colour display technology resulted in a new expressive and creative medium. The benefits were the unique display driver and controller processor board, designed for the VCN by Frank and his team of engineers, which allowed the creation of flicker-free full animation sequences along with a mixture of text and graphics (refer to Exhibit 2).

The on-board processor also allowed sprite animation and program sequencing. At the VCN control centre, messages created by VCNet® software could be programmed or targeted by subway station location, time of day, day of the week and/or by calendar date. The program was also designed so that emergency messages would have top priority and could override other messages. Maintenance and diagnostic feedback of the system was also controlled at the VCN control centre. The Transit control centre could relay emergency information, through a modem, to the VCN control centre immediately. In turn, these messages were transmitted via FM, VHF, or UHF radio signals to radio cables in the subway tunnels (refer to Exhibit 3).

The automatic station stop system consisted of passive radio frequency (RF) that reflected location identification tags mounted between the rails. Télécité developed patented technology which scanned these location ID tags to determine the location of the train. Once the location data is received by the on-board reading equipment, the location ID information triggers the station stop announcement, a visual message synchronized with a pre-recorded, digitized voice announcement that has been stored in the display memory. In addition, the LED display panels were also synchronized to display relevant information about the coming subway stop and about bus connections.

THE MARKET AND INDUSTRY

Public Transit Authorities

In 1992, there were approximately 300 major urban transit systems in the world. Of these transit systems, 81 also operated a subway. There are 15 subways in North America, of which the largest are located in New York City, Mexico City, Chicago, Montréal, Toronto and Washington. In Europe there are 35 subways; the largest are located in London, Moscow, Paris, Berlin and Madrid. In Asia, the largest subways are located in Tokyo, Osaka, Hong Kong and South Korea. It is estimated that there are approximately 49,000 subway cars in operation in the world. The market size of subway cars is approximately 16,700 (North America), 22,500 (Europe), 7,800 (Asia) and 2,000 (others).

Tables 1 and 2 provide subway and bus fleet summaries of the Montréal Urban Community Transit Corporation (MUCTC), the London Regional Transport (LT), the Paris Transport Authority (RATP), the New York Metropolitan Transit Authority (MTA), the Toronto Transit Commission (TTC) and the Mexico Coordinacion General de Transporte (CGT).

Table 1. Summary of Some Major Subways and Light-rail Trains in the World.

City	Number of lines	Number of cars	Number of stations	Passenger-journeys* in million (year)	Manufacturer(s)
Montréal Metro	4	756	65	208 ('90)	Bombardier
London Underground	11	3,918	272	815 ('88) 765 ('89) 775 ('90)	Various
Paris RATP	15	3,472	368	1,235 ('88) 1,225 ('89) 1,228 ('90)	GEC-Alsthom, ANF-Industrie
Paris RER (regional)	4	1,328	160	317 ('88) 326 ('89) 359 ('90)	GEC-Alsthom
New York MTA	26	6,108	469	1,074 ('88) 1,073 ('89) 1,028 ('90)	Kawasaki, St. Louis Car, Bombardier, Westinghouse- Amrail
NY—Staten Island	1	64	22	6 ('88) 6 ('89) 6 ('90)	St. Louis Car
NY—New Jersey PATH	4	342	13	57 ('88) 56 ('89) 56 ('90)	St. Louis Car, Hawker-Siddeley, Kawasaki, Works Car

NY commuter lines (New Jersey, Long Island and Connecticut)	3	2,750	430	179 ('89) 173 ('90) 170 ('91)	Various
Toronto TTC	2	622	60	177 ('89) 180 ('90) 270 ('91)	Hawker-Siddeley UTDC/Can-Car Rail
Toronto Tramway	10	265	not available	56 ('88) 57 ('89) 75 ('90)	UTDC, Hawker-Siddeley, Can-Car, Swiss Industrial
Mexico City STE	9	2,424	135	1,543 ('89) 1,448 ('90) 1,444 ('91)	Alsthom, Bombardier, CNCF-Concarril

*Passenger-journeys refer to linked trips within the subway every weekday.

Table 2. Summary of the Bus Fleet of Some of the Major Transit Authorities.

City	Number of buses	Passenger-journeys* in million (year)	Manufacturer(s)
Montréal MUCTC	1,709	394 ('88) 389 ('89) 386 ('90)	GM, Nova Bus
London LT	5,040	1,015 ('88) 948 ('89) 872 ('90)	MCW Metrobus, Leyland Titan, Routemasters
Paris RATP	4,012	807 ('88) 837 ('89) 814 ('90)	Saviem/Renault
New York MTA	3,659	153 ('88) 154 ('89) 150 ('90)	GMC
Toronto TTC	1,777	198 ('80) 203 ('90) 349 ('91)	GM, OBI
Mexico Ruta 100	6,595	1,971 ('85) 2,117 ('86)	Various

*Passenger-journeys refer to bus and subway linked trips every weekday.

Urban Transport Vehicles Manufacturers and Suppliers

The urban transport manufacturing industry is highly fragmented. There are many companies that manufacture whole transit systems, subway and light-rail vehicles, traction equipment, buses, trolley buses, vehicle and maintenance equipment, as well as a large number of suppliers of, and consulting companies for, electrical systems, signal and communication equipment, traffic control systems, revenue collection equipment, and so on.

In the subway and light-rail industry, there are only a handful of large companies operating worldwide; for example, Bombardier/UTDC, ABB, Hitachi/Kawasaki, GEC-Alsthom, and Siemens, which can provide a full range of products and services. Other manufacturers are Concarril (Mexico), ANF-Industrie (France), Daewoo and Hyundai (Korea), Nippon Sharyo and Tokyu Car (Japan), Breda, Fiat and Sofer (Italy), CAF (Spain), AEG-Westinghouse and Morris-Knudson (USA).

In addition, there are about 20 manufacturers which specialize on new technology and/or innovative transit systems. Some of these companies are ALRT (Canada), Newtran and Portliner (Japan), Magnetbhan (Germany), Briway and Maglev (U.K.), SK and VAL (France) and Aeromovel, Aerobus and Astroglide (USA).

Suppliers of electrical and electronic equipment include ABB, AEG Westinghouse, Hitachi, Mitsubishi, Toshiba, GEC-Alsthom, Hawker Siddeley and Siemens among others.

The bus manufacturing industry is even more fragmented. There are over 200 large manufacturers of buses around the world. For example, some of the major manufacturers are Mercedes Benz, Volkswagen, Renault, Daihatsu, Mazda, Nissan, Toyota, Daewoo, Hyundai and Volvo. In North America, intra-city buses are manufactured by Nova Bus, Orion, New Flyer, Flexible and GM among others. Inter-city and tourist/charter buses are manufactured by Bluebird, Prevost, Connaisseur and MCI among others.

Trends

Public transit authorities are similar around the world. These are organizations that are financed by operations (passenger fares) and government subsidies. The economic recession of the early 1990s has negatively impacted the operation of Canadian public transit authorities, as provincial governments were forced to reduce transit subsidies. Transit authorities had to become more efficient, effective and productive to counteract these decreasing subsidies. Expense reduction was accomplished by a variety of means, including operational improvements, changes in the collective agreements with the workers, and additional rehabilitation to extend service life of vehicles. Transit authorities also had to find ways and means to increase their ridership to increase revenues.

In 1990, the American Congress passed the *Americans with Disabilities Act* (ADA) that forced the country's 35 largest transit authorities to improve, rehabilitate and make the facilities more accessible to the elderly, the disabled or anyone with any sort of impairment, including those who have visual or auditory disabilities, or those who are wheelchair-bound. This act also requires that by the year 2000, the 35 largest transit authorities in the United States install display panels in station platforms of subway stations, and eventually inside the subway cars as well.

In addition to the industry factors above, a marketing trend that has emerged in North America during the 1980s is the concept of micromarketing. Micromarketing is essentially an extension of target marketing which capitalizes on flexibility to develop marketing strategies and publicity to reach fragmented consumer markets, for example, working women, the elderly, young teenagers and so on. Finding and being able to target such micromarkets, especially if captive, can result in increased advertising and product sales.

PRODUCTION

Production of the display panels posed other challenges to Marshall. The main one is that in-house production brought along a new set of operational problems. First, the company did not have experience in manufacturing. Marshall and his team essentially had acted as researchers and consultants. Second, the company did not currently have the funds to set up a high-tech electronics manufacturing and assembly facility. Third, the MUCTC was not willing to pay for the display panels, especially since their operational budgets had been cut over the previous two years.

In order to raise the funds required to manufacture the display panels, Marshall pursued not only the same companies who had originally purchased advertisement time for the six-month pilot study, but also new companies and not-for-profit organizations.

Télécité's main strengths lay in R&D and marketing of the products. Therefore, after evaluating their strategic options, Télécité decided to subcontract the majority of sub-assembly manufacturing to other companies. The printed circuit boards, LED blocks, aluminum extrusions and other electrical and mechanical components were either manufactured by subcontractors, or sourced from a variety of Original Equipment Manufacturers (OEM) in the Montréal region, as well as overseas (Japan, Taiwan, Indonesia, Ireland and the U.S.). The final assembly of the display panels and quality control was done in-house.

All production and manufacturing activities were the responsibility of the newly-hired vice-president of Manufacturing, Angelo Guercioni, a production engineer with experience at Northern Telecom. As well, another engineer was added to the team to oversee quality control and maintenance. To ensure that Télécité's product would be of the highest quality, the company instituted a policy that all suppliers and sub-contractors were to be ISO 9000 certified.

Frank's primary function as vice-president engineering was critical since he was responsible for ensuring that the VCN's system and software were compatible and fully integrated with the MUCTC's system network. In addition, the graphic designers and a recently-hired advertising salesperson also reported to Frank. In addition to the above, Frank had the added responsibility of further product, technology and software R&D. Frank conducted much of this R&D personally, especially with regard to the operating software, while he supervised the R&D efforts of his two engineers.

MARKETING AND SALES

After the prototypes had been developed and tested on the Orange line of the Montréal subway, Télécité and the MUCTC commissioned several surveys and focus groups which demonstrated that the VCN display panels were a hit with the passengers. Most riders mentioned that the messages and the animation provided entertainment and enjoyment to their ride. "We use animation and we have seen so many occasions when people start laughing while they're watching," said Marshall. "Before the display panels were installed, the Metro was a morbid place."

In 1991, Télécité sold just over one million dollars in advertising (including the original $650,000 commitment from 1989). The company also performed some consulting activities. These consulting activities were side projects, mostly engineering, electrical, and computer information system analysis, that were done for private clients. Often these clients were the same companies that had purchased advertising time blocks on the VCN system.

In early 1992, after the success of the test pilot, Marshall spent about 65% of his time in sales and public relations activities. He started to visit and meet with officials of other transit authorities, notably the Toronto Transit Commission. In addition, he spent a large amount of time trying to sell repeat advertisement slots to Montréal-based companies. A characteristic of the advertising industry is that most sales take place in September when the advertisement season starts for fall and winter advertising campaigns.

His efforts paid off, and in 1993 Télécité had sales of $4.5 million. For the first six months of 1994, sales increased to over $3 million.

In order to free up more time for Marshall, Télécité hired a salesperson in the winter of 1993 to sell repeat advertising time blocks to companies and to seek new advertising clients. However, Marshall was still the main salesperson of the VCN system and display panels.

Selling to transit authorities requires special skills and lots of patience. Industrial marketing to transit authorities depends not only on the clear benefits of the product, but also on quality, service, experience and reputation. In addition, providing information about the product or service requires submitting detailed technical proposals, often to consultants or engineers at the transit authorities, followed by presentations to the board members of the transit authority. Exhibit 4 shows a sample of technical literature for transit authorities' engineers.

In the transit industry, the process from an initial visit to a detailed response to a "Request For Bid," and finally to a contract award could often take three to five years. On average it would take one to two years to work on a bid, and once a bid is awarded, it could take between one to three years to deliver and install the product. As each transit authority has different equipment, different ridership profiles, and different passenger information needs, each potential new project pursued would require a degree of custom engineering for the VCN system to be supplied. On average about 30% of the system capital cost would consist of custom engineering work.

Télécité's VCN had an inherent appeal to advertisers because of its combined state-of-the-art public information system. The VCN's uniqueness had the potential to tap into an emerging micromarketing trend. In addition, no potential audience is more captive than passengers riding a bus, subway or commuter train. Exhibit 5 shows the advertising benefits of the VCN over printed advertising in the subway cars. Advertising posters and other printed advertising and/or safety information were the only competing products in subways cars.

Télécité faced fragmented competition from manufacturers of the old-fashioned monochrome LED flasher board panels, as well as from manufacturers of systems for highway information and manufacturers of large-scale scoreboard-type of displays. However, none of these competitors undertook the extensive R&D efforts to design and produce a product that would offer a minimum of 15 years operational life required in a harsh, dusty, wet and vibration-filled transit environment. Marshall felt that there was a window of opportunity to push and lead the market with the VCN technology.

HUMAN RESOURCES AND ORGANIZATIONAL STRUCTURE

From the outset Télécité adopted a functional organizational structure which was well suited to its single product line. Exhibit 6 outlines Télécité's organizational structure which was built around two functional areas: engineering and manufacturing.

The management team of Télécité consisted of Marshall and two senior vice-presidents: Frank and Angelo, who were responsible for engineering and manufacturing respectively. Within the management team, responsibility was divided primarily by function. However, over time, Marshall had taken on many of the tasks not assigned by a formal function. Therefore, in addition to strategic decisions, Marshall also oversaw all operations in the company, ensured financial control and did most of the marketing/sales contact work.

Télécité had a lean staff of sixteen employees working at its headquarters in Pointe-Claire. This staff consisted of five engineers, two computer programmers, two software developers, three graphic designers, one salesperson, one accountant, one secretary and one receptionist. Nonetheless, Marshall wondered whether the current organizational structure was appropriate for the potential growth he foresaw for Télécité. As the company grew in size, it became more difficult to separate the production activities from the advertisement revenue-generating activities. He also felt that Télécité still needed more human resources in production, marketing and advertising design in order to pursue other markets.

FINANCE

Exhibits 7 and 8 provide a summary of the financial statements for Télécité.

Additional financing in 1991, to commercialize the prototype, came from the federal Transport Department and from the newly-created St. James Financial Corporation, providing nearly $1 million in long-term debt. Of the $1 million in advertising sales in 1991, approximately half was spent on manufacturing and installing display panels. The remaining revenue was invested in R&D and product extensions and applied to advertising production and operating costs.

In 1992, venture capitalists provided a further $8 million in equity. From 1991 to mid-1994, total assets grew from $1.9 million to $10.9 million, largely because Télécité owned the VCN panels. Each complete nine-car train cost approximately $200,000 to equip with the VCN system—two VCN display panels per car (one master, one slave) plus a control unit for each three-car "triplet."

STRATEGIC DIRECTIONS FOR THE FUTURE

Marshall's vision was to make Télécité a truly world-renowned company. It had been a long struggle since that day almost eight years ago when Marshall had come up with the idea of redesigning the old LED electronic display panels. In the process, Télécité has become a truly innovative company, moving from a management consulting business into both a manufacturing and a communications media company. Not only did Télécité develop a unique communications network for subways, but it also created a new advertising medium, one where advertisers had access to a large captive audience. In addition to providing safety communication to the visually- and hearing-impaired passengers, the VCN also provided entertainment to the Metro users.

After the successful completion of the pilot in late 1991, Télécité had outfitted almost all the cars on the MUCTC's Orange, Blue and Yellow lines of the Montréal Metro. Marshall expected that by the end of May 1994, the last of the 423 cars of the first three lines would be outfitted, while the installation of the VCN panels for the 333 cars of the remaining Green line was expected to run from mid-1997 to the end of 1998. Thus Marshall faced the problem that the production and manufacturing team would be idled for the next two and a half years.

Meanwhile, Marshall thought that Télécité could continue generating sales of advertising slots in Montréal. However, Marshall's advertisement sales projections had fallen short. His objective in 1991 was to sell $5 million for 1992 and $7 million for 1993 Nonetheless, Marshall was confident that revenues would increase by 15% per year over the next three years as a result of increased sales in advertisement time slots.

At this point, Télécité had several options for growth. For example, Télécité could target other subway systems in the world. One problem was that most subways had cars with slightly different physical sizes, and different electrical/electronic systems, thus necessitating custom engineering for each different transit job. In addition, passenger information needs and the need to meet government regulations differed among transit authorities.

In fact, since last year, Marshall had contacted a few officials of the Toronto Transit Commission, who became interested in the VCN display panels after evaluating the 1991 pilot study in Montréal. However, the transit officials were reluctant to pay for the full cost of the LED display panels.

Alternatively, a potential market was to develop a VCN system for the London Underground. While living in London, Marshall had frequently used the London Underground to commute from home to work, and thought that because of its size and large ridership, it could offer excellent opportunities for sales of the VCN system. One disadvantage, though, was that many of the cars were old, and had been supplied by a variety of manufacturers.

Another interesting idea that Marshall had been considering was to franchise the media capabilities of the VCN technology. In December of 1992, Marshall had been contacted by three communications companies in Paris which were interested in licensing the systems technology from Télécité, and in manufacturing the VCN display panels in France in order to equip the Paris Metro and the RER. Because the VCN system in the Montréal Metro was fully functional in French, there were only a few adaptations required in the physical dimensions of the display panels and in the electrical system.

As an innovator, Marshall thought that yet another direction might be to develop VCN display panels for buses. However, this would be quite a technological challenge because it would require extensive research and development to come up with a system that would work on buses, operating on a non-fixed route basis. Frank had estimated that about $2 million would be required to develop a prototype.

Another market opportunity would be to develop LED display panels for station platforms. It was expected that in early 1994 transit authorities in the U.S. would start to implement the ADA passed in 1990. He had recently read a report where NYCTA had allocated U.S. $1 billion for station renovations and rehabilitation, which included platform display panels to communicate system information and safety and security messages. All work on these station rehabilitations needed to be completed by the year 2000. Again minor adaptations would be required in the physical size of the display panels in order to conform with ADA requirements, and a prototype could be developed at a cost of about $1 million.

Given that Télécité was still a small company, Marshall wondered whether these were the best options for growth.

Exhibit 1

Exhibit 2

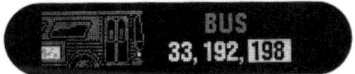

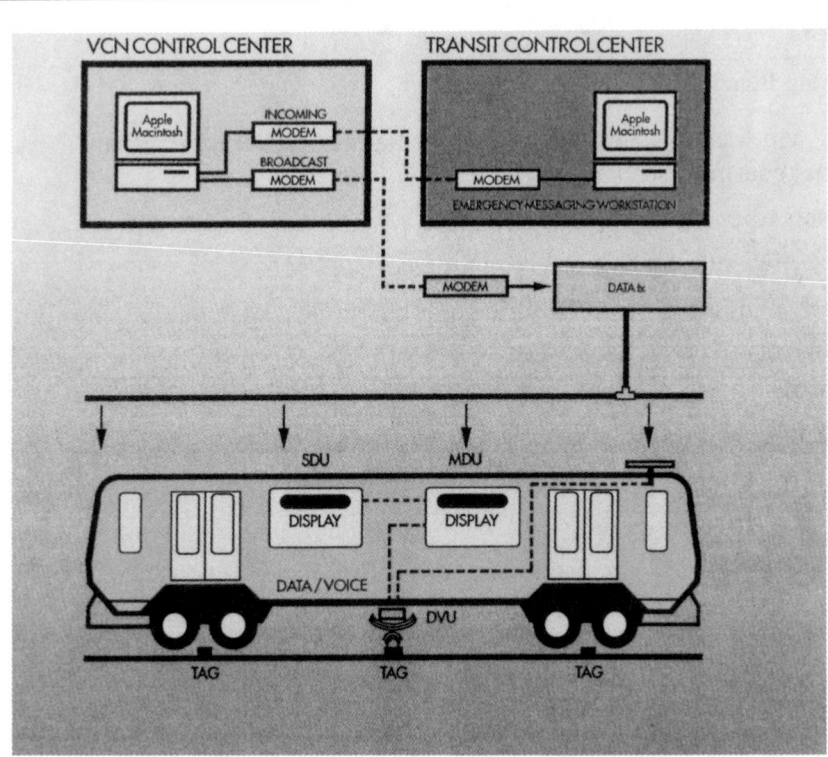

Exhibit 3

Exhibit 4

Technical Literature

- Variable Message High Intensity Bright (red and multi-colour) LED Display Panels for use on-board subway/metro, commuter and other railway vehicles.
- Variable Message High Intensity Bright (red and multi-colour) LED Display Panels for use indoors on subway/metro, commuter line, railway and other platform locations.
- Variable Message High Intensity Super Bright (red and multi-colour) LED Display Panels for use outdoors on subway/metro, commuter line, railway and other platform locations.
- Development of Communications Interfacing Software for seamless data, voice, and visual links in passenger information networks.
- Development and enhancement of Télécité Inc.'s proprietary Visual Communication Network (VCNet®) software to be used in conjunction with, and operation of, the variable message display panels.
- Management and communications consultancy services to users, and potential users, of real-time and pre-programmed message generation and delivery.

Exhibit 5

Advertising Benefits of the VCN

VCN is a powerful new advertising media with several important advantages over traditional consumer media:

- Mass audiences in closed, receptive environment
- Very low comparative cost per thousand (CPM)
- Micro-marketing flexibility through quick message change potential
- High advertising awareness and credibility closely linked to meaningful public information
- Potential to link messages closely to point of sale
- Creative interest and attraction of variable and colourful graphics

---

Exhibit 6. Télécité Inc. Organizational Chart

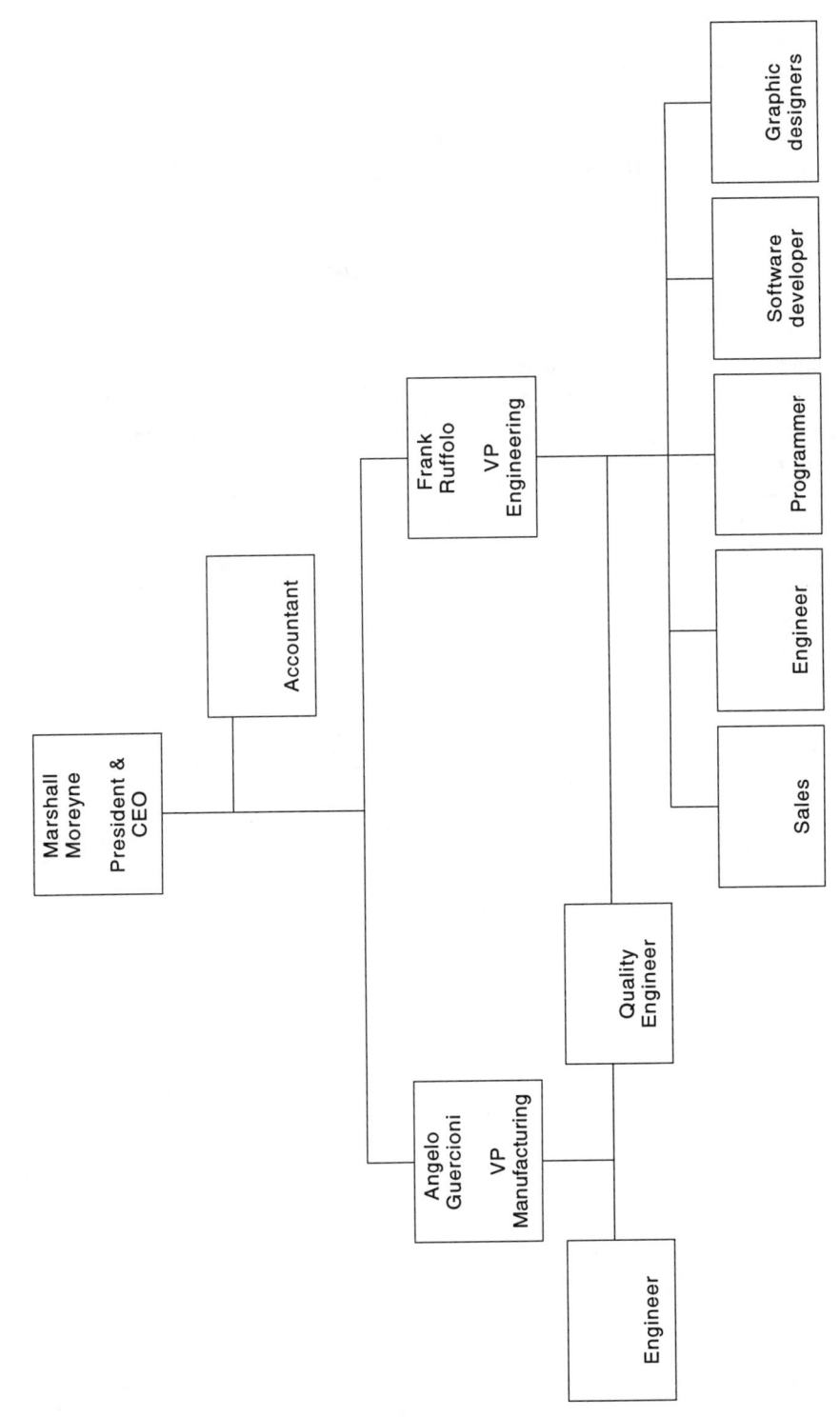

Exhibit 7

Télécité Inc. Income Statement
(in thousands of dollars) year ended August 31

	1994 First Six Months	1993	1992	1991
Advertising sales	$3,028	$4,504	$2,872	$1,009
Cost of sales	1,602	2,821	1,694	627
Gross profit	**1,426**	**1,683**	**1,178**	**382**
Maintenance expense	94	166	157	117
Sales and promotion expenses	165	256	192	96
Administrative expense	188	322	194	92
Amortization expense	495	323	141	74
Interest expense	46	47	46	56
R&D expenses	77	150	136	57
Income before tax	361	419	312	(110)
Income tax	15	30	27	0
Net income (Net loss)	**$ 346**	**$ 389**	**$ 285**	**($ 110)**

Exhibit 8

Télécité Inc. Balance Sheet
(in thousands of dollars) at August 31

	28 February 1994	1993	1992	1991
Assets				
Current assets				
Cash and cash equivalents	$ 1,831	$ 2,842	$ 5,228	$307
Accounts receivable	819	778	487	452
Inventory	128	93	115	53
Total current assets	2,778	3,713	5,830	812
Capital assets				
Equipment	675	662	623	611
Display panels	8,119	6,865	3,850	519
Less accumulated amortization	(711)	(507)	(193)	(74)
Net capital assets	8,083	7,020	4,280	1,056
Total assets	$10,861	$10,733	$10,110	$1,868
Liabilities				
Current liabilities				
Accounts payable	$347	$404	$106	$103
Current portion of long-term debt	49	61	64	66
Total current liabilities	396	465	170	169
Long-term liabilities				
Long-term debt	721	770	831	895
Shareholders' Equity				
Share capital	8,721	8,721	8,721	721
Retained earnings	1,023	777	388	83
Total liabilities and shareholders' equity	$10,861	$10,733	$10,110	$1,868

Case 9

McAuslan Brewing Co.

INTRODUCTION

It was November 28, 1994 and Peter McAuslan, President of McAuslan Brewing Co., still had a big smile on his face. Several days ago, McAuslan's beers won four medals at the World Beer Championship held in Chicago. St. Ambroise Oatmeal Stout (platinum medal), Griffon Extra Pale Ale (silver medal), and Griffon Brown Ale (silver medal) were each rated in the top two of their categories in the world. The other beer, St. Ambroise Pale Ale, came third with a bronze medal.

Peter then glanced at the most recent financial report and wondered whether this was the best time to seek more sales growth. The brewery had been operating at near capacity for the past two years, but foremost in Peter's mind was the ability of McAuslan to cope with competition and the changes that were taking place not only in the microbrewery industry, but also in the brewery industry overall.

According to Peter, beer sales for 1995 were expected to be higher than for the same period in 1994. Even though domestic beer consumption in Québec had slowly declined since the mid-1980s, he felt that sales of McAuslan beers could grow by another 30%.

ST. AMBROISE STREET

During the 1980s, consumer behaviour towards alcoholic beverages was changing. Consumers were drinking less beer, but on the other hand, were demanding more choices and better tasting beer. Peter was also one of those consumers who was tired of drinking the typical beer brewed by any of the big three Canadian breweries, that is, Molson, Labatt and Carling O'Keefe. He found that the taste of those beers was not only bland, but also indistinguishable from each other. As a beer connoisseur, Peter preferred to drink microbrews which offered a more distinctive taste. In addition, microbrews, unlike the national beers, were brewed without any additives or preservatives.

Peter McAuslan considers himself an entrepreneur. In 1987 Peter and his wife, Ellen Bounsall, gave up their jobs as administrators at Dawson College in Montréal and sold their house to raise money to start a microbrewery. In 1988, construction of the brewery started

This case was written by Jose Lam (M.B.A.) and Ludo Segers (M.B.A.) under the direction of Professor A. B. Ibrahim as a basis for class discussion rather than to illustrate effective or ineffective handling of an administrative situation. Certain information and financial figures in the case have been disguised in order to maintain and respect confidentiality.
This case was supported by a research grant from the Certified General Accountants Association of Canada (CGA). © Dr. A. B. Ibrahim, 1997.

in the St. Henri district of Montréal. Ellen, who has a background in biology, became assistant brewmaster to British brewmaster Allan Pugsley, who was hired on a short-term contract to develop the recipe for the company's first beer.

In January of 1989, McAuslan began brewing operations and launched St. Ambroise Pale Ale, a draft beer named after the street where the brewery is located. "We'd go to sleep with the hissing sounds of the brewery and I'd think that's the independence of your own business, right?" says Peter.

Peter became the company's first salesman. He started by giving free samples of the beer to pubs in the Montréal area. Beer drinkers welcomed this new microbrew which tasted like an imported ale but at a cheaper price.

THE BREWERY INDUSTRY

The Brewing Process

The making of beer dates back to the beginnings of civilization. In ancient Egypt, beer was an important part of daily life, enjoyed by slaves and Pharaohs alike. Brewmasters, who were mostly women, were highly respected in those times. The art of brewing was continued, over 1000 years ago, by monks in Europe. They mixed barley malt, hops, yeast, water and other ingredients to produce a brew with an alcohol content of up to 10%. Essentially, very little has changed since those times. Beer brewed today still uses the same natural ingredients and beer recipes remain closely guarded secrets. Often, it can take up to two years for a brewmaster to perfect a beer recipe.

Beer can be packaged and sold to customers as draft beer in kegs, as bottled beer or as canned beer. Non-pasteurized beer has a shelf life of about 5–6 months. Large breweries add preservatives to extend the shelf life to about one year.

The Canadian Beer Industry

In Canada, the brewery industry is highly regulated. These regulations cover production, distribution, sale and consumption. Although the market for alcoholic beverages falls under provincial jurisdiction, the federal government levies taxes on production (Federal Excise Tax), importation (Importation of Intoxicating Liquors Act) and sales (Goods and Services Tax).

The combined federal and provincial tax on beer for home consumption represents about 53% of the price, the highest in the world. For example, in Québec, the average base price of a case of 24 beer bottles (341 ml) is $14.30. The price to retailers after excise taxes (applied by volume) is $19.54 and the final retail price to consumers, after markup and consumer taxes, comes to $22.73. In 1992, $3.1 billion were generated as tax revenues for the federal and provincial governments.

Moreover, every province has its own regulations that restrict not only the number of commercial breweries that can operate, but also the import of beer from other provinces. For example, there is a 90% tariff applied to beers brewed in other provinces. In order for a brewery to bypass this tariff, it would need to set up a brewery in the province.

Inter-provincial trade barriers are the major impediment for breweries who wish to seek geographic expansion in Canada. As well, there are restrictions in the sale and distribution of beer. In certain provinces, domestic beer can only be purchased from government-operated stores, while in other provinces, beer can be purchased in supermarkets, convenience stores and/or privately-owned liquor stores.

In Ontario, the distribution and retailing of beer is controlled by Molson and Labatt through the Brewer's Warehousing Co. This restrictive practice favours the two large breweries by centralizing their distribution and reducing their costs. Beer from other provinces will incur an extra distribution cost because the beer is first shipped to the Liquor Control Board of Ontario (LCBO), and then from there it is shipped to Brewers Retail stores or LCBO stores. In addition, Ontario also applies an environmental levy that favours domestic bottled beer over imported canned beer.

In Québec, there are also restrictive practices which prevent competition from outside the province. First, a brewery from outside the province must get a distributor's permit and set up a distribution company in Québec. Second, beer produced outside the province must be shipped to a Québec Liquor Board warehouse where it is tested; once approved, the beer can then be shipped to a distributor and sold to retailers. Recent discussions between the federal government and the provinces have proposed that Canadian beer from outside Québec be shipped directly to distributors in order to cut the cost of shipping to the Québec Liquor Board testing warehouse. Third, regulations also require that beer sold in convenience stores must be in refillable containers.

Other restrictions are applied to pricing and alcohol content as well. Minimum pricing ensures that any price difference between a domestic beer and a foreign beer is kept to a minimum. This restriction prevents foreign competitors from gaining substantial market share.

In order to bypass government regulations, a type of franchising practice has evolved, where one brewery contracts a brewery in another province (or state) to brew and package its beer, while the "franchiser" maintains control over marketing, sales and distribution. For example, Molson now brews Miller beer targeted to the Canadian market for Miller Brewing Co. Many of the smaller breweries in the United States also have adopted this practice as a way to sell their microbrews in other states.

Although the beer industry was originally exempted from the Canada-U.S. Free Trade Agreement, the provinces have been under pressure from the federal government, the United States and the General Agreement on Tariffs and Trade (GATT) to open the beer market.

In August 1993, an agreement was reached between Canada and the United States to end the "beer war" between the U.S. and Ontario. The agreement called for a lifting of punitive levies on beer exports to each respective (provincial) market, a reduction of $1–2 per case of 24 (depending on alcohol content), maintenance of environmental levies and greater distribution accessibility for American breweries. Also, Canadian provinces reached an agreement to remove interprovincial beer trade barriers effective in the summer of 1995.

The beer industry has been primarily a local or regional industry. In the last 80 years, technological advances in the use of additives and preservatives, efficient production, operations and distribution have changed the face of the industry.

Between 1920 and 1960, the Canadian beer industry underwent a process of rationalization through mergers and acquisitions, leading to an industry dominated by the "Big Three" (Carling O'Keefe, Molson and Labatt). Further rationalization took place in 1989 as a result of the merger between Carling O'Keefe and Molson. By 1992, there were 26 brewing plants operated by Molson and Labatt, down from the 41 plants operated by the "Big Three" in 1978.

This rationalization towards bigger and more efficient plants has been even more dramatic in the United States, partly became of the absence of interstate trade barriers. For example, Anheuser-Busch, the largest brewer in the world, not only produces five times the Canadian annual consumption of beer, but it also has one plant that can produce 75% of all Canadian beer consumption.

The drive towards cost reductions in the beer industry is primarily noticeable in the United States. Although studies indicate that the minimum efficient scale lies in the 2–3 million hectolitres range, American breweries have capacities in the 10–20 million hectolitres range. There are several factors that favour American breweries, notably lower transportation costs, lower wages, lower taxes, the use of cans rather than bottles, higher market densities and greater population densities. In addition, the large American breweries normally produce a small number of beer brands. This in turn maximizes the benefits of volume production and reduces the costs associated with advertising and marketing.

The Canadian Beer Market

The two largest breweries in Canada are Molson and Labatt. Both of them employed about 9,500 people in 1993, down from 11,400 in 1990. In Québec, it is estimated that the industry creates over 20,000 direct and indirect jobs, excluding hospitality jobs.

The brewery industry generates revenues in other industries; for example, advertising companies, media companies, entertainment and cultural companies, hotels, restaurants and others. Combined advertising expenditures for Molson and Labatt were almost $100 million in 1992. Domestic purchases of barley, malt, bottles, cans, cartons, labels and other materials were $730 million.

Estimated consumer expenditure on beer in Canada was $8.91 billion (1990), $9.43 billion (1991). $9.60 billion (1992), and $9.55 billion (1993). In 1993, consumer expenditure on beer was $3.56 billion in Ontario, $2.54 billion in Québec, and $1.23 billion in British Columbia (B.C.). Between 1990 and 1993, sales in Ontario and Québec declined by about 1%, while in B.C. they rose by 1.4%. It is expected that the Canadian beer market will grow 1–2% per year over the next three years. Beer sales fluctuate according to the season. Over 50% of sales take place in the summer months.

Imports held about 3% of the total market, down from 4% in 1989. Imported beer comes primarily from the U.S. In 1993, American beer accounted for about 50% of the total import market, down from 70% in 1989. The other major exporters of beer to Canada are the U.K.,

Germany, Mexico and the Netherlands. Exports of Canadian beer are mainly to the U.S., where it held 28% of the import segment in 1993, up from 21.5% in 1987.

Molson and Labatt dominate the Canadian market with a combined 93% market share. Both Labatt and Molson have lost market shares to regional breweries such as Moosehead (New Brunswick), Oland (Nova Scotia), Pacific Western Brewing (B.C.), Lakeport Brewing Corp. (Ontario) and others. These regional breweries and microbreweries hold about 4% market share. Each percentage point represents about $90 million in sales. Exhibit 1 lists the top Canadian breweries and their production capacity.

The American Beer Market

The American beer market was worth about $45 billion in 1992, up from $40 billion in 1988. Between 1983 and 1993, consumption of beer increased from 216 million hectolitres to 223 million hectolitres. Consumption of imported beer increased from 7.4 million hectolitres in 1983 to 11.0 million in 1987 and 1988. Consumption of imported beer declined between 1989 to 1992, but has gone up again to 10.8 million hectolitres in 1993. The beer market is dominated by Anheuser-Busch with a 46.9% market share in 1993. Exhibit 2 lists the top American breweries and their production capacity.

The American beer market can be segmented into several categories: premium (Budweiser, Coors), light, popular (discount or low quality), malt liquor (high alcohol content), super-premium (competes against imports), dry and imports. As a percent of total beer sales, premium beer sales in the U.S. have steadily declined from 44.8% in 1989 to 32.6% in 1993. In contrast, sales of light beer have steadily increased from 30.7% in 1989 to 40.6% in 1993. Sales of popular beer have fluctuated between 17.4% in 1989, down to 15.4% in 1991, and up to 19.2% in 1993.

Trends

The beer industry in North America has been experiencing a flat and declining market for the past two decades as a result of changes in social attitudes and demographics. In the 1970s, increased consumer awareness about health and fitness, social pressure to consume alcohol in moderation, and stricter enforcement of drinking and driving laws have affected industry growth (Exhibit 3). Since 1985, per capita consumption of beer has fallen about 3%, while wine consumption and hard liquor consumption are down 23% and 21%, respectively.

Canadian consumption of beer since the late 1980s has declined to the consumption levels seen in the early 1970s. In 1993, per capita consumption of beer in Canada was about 71 litres, down from 82.5 litres in 1987.

Furthermore, consumer behaviour towards beer has changed in other ways as well. For example, consumers are drinking fewer alcoholic beverages in bars and restaurants (on-premise) and more at home (off-premise). In 1993, off-premise sales accounted for about 71% versus 29% for on-premise sales.

A notable difference between American and Canadian breweries is that Canadian breweries had always offered more beer brands to consumers than their American counterparts. The reason is that Canadian breweries grew by taking over smaller regional breweries. Because consumers get used to the taste of their local beers, the large breweries continued to offer beer with local flavours. In contrast, in the American market, large breweries take full advantage of economies of scale to concentrate on the production of a few beer brands.

Consumer surveys show that young people (18–24) drink on average 12 bottles of beer per week. For this segment, image is the most critical consideration and peer pressure and emotion drive their choices. They also drink very little light beer, and approximately half of the drinking occurs in bars.

The next segment of drinkers are those aged between 25–34. These consumers drink on average about 9 bottles of beer per week. They tend to drink more at home and are more interested in unique tastes, quality, value and sophistication.

The largest segment belongs to the ageing baby boomers (older than 34). This segment accounts for about 40% of beer consumption. The baby boomers drink about 6 bottles of beer per week, mostly at home, and are more rational in their drinking behaviours. They are also becoming less brand loyal and are the biggest drinkers of discount beer and light beer.

The Microbrewery Industry

The difference between a brewery and a microbrewery is based on production. In Canada, a microbrewery is defined as an independent operation that produces less than 75,000 hectolitres per year (a hectolitre is 100 litres and represents about 12 cases of 24 bottles). A regional brewery produces more than 75,000 hectolitres per year, while a national brewery has, in addition, brewery facilities across the country.

In the United States, the definitions vary. A microbrewery produces less than 17,600 hectolitres per year. A regional brewery produces between 15,000 and 500,000 hectolitres and a large brewery produces more than 500,000 hectolitres per year.

The microbrewery industry originated in the 1970s as a result of changes in technology that allowed for small-batch brewing. This in turn created opportunities for pubs to brew beer on their own premises. Changes in regulations in the U.S. (late 1970s) and Canada (early 1980s) allowed people to brew beer at home, pubs to brew beer on their premises and microbreweries to distribute and sell their beer to consumers.

These microbreweries were started mainly by entrepreneurs who saw an opportunity to offer something different to consumers. Most of these entrepreneurs invested on average $1 million to start the microbrewery. The failure rate of microbreweries is 1 in 2 in Canada and 1 in 8 in the United States. In Canada, labour represents about 51% of the cost. Primary ingredients account for 9% of the cost, while energy, maintenance, storage, inventory and other materials account for 40%. The more expensive production methods of the microbreweries result in a beer that is priced higher than regular beers.

In an industry saturated with mature beer brands, microbrews have carved out a niche market. In general, microbrews appeal to young, affluent, well educated and above average drinkers. Although the price is higher than regular beer, microbrews also appeal to the young with limited income.

A 1994 survey found that the following groups have tried a microbrew: 25% of young people (18–24); 28% of Generation X'ers (24–35); 27% of young baby boomers (35–44); and 20% of baby boomers (older than 45).

Microbrew drinkers are also more serious about beer. They drink beer more for the full, rich taste than for alcoholic content. Some microbrew drinkers are beer enthusiasts who will drink only microbrews. The microbrew movement has also started to project an image of family and community sense. In the United States, beer festivals that celebrate seasonal beers and microbrews are becoming annual attractions in many states. The atmosphere in these events is casual and always fun.

In the U.S., the growth of microbreweries (and regional breweries) in the late 1980s and early 1990s has been spectacular. In 1993 there were about 400 microbreweries, up from about 40 in the early 1980s. These represent the fastest growing (average of 40% a year for the past ten years) and the most profitable segment of the industry. In 1993, the microbrewery industry had a 1.3% share of the market and total sales were about $1.5 billion. Growth in sales has been at the expense of the large breweries and imported beer.

In Canada, the number of microbreweries grew from 4 in 1984 to 33 in 1989. As of 1993, there are 28 microbreweries operating in Canada. During the same period of time, conventional breweries declined from 38 in 1984 to 25 in 1993. The microbrewery industry accounted for about 0.5% of the Canadian beer market in 1989; by 1993, the market share had risen to about 2%. Exhibit 4 lists the top Canadian microbreweries, their beer sales volume, and their market shares.

After flat sales in 1992, Canadian sales of microbrews in 1993 increased by 26% from 1992; and it is expected that 1994 sales will be up by another 25%. Many microbreweries have been increasing production capacity in order to keep up with demand. Some former microbreweries, such as Sleeman, Lakeport and Pacific Brewing have now joined the ranks of regional breweries.

Microbreweries have also grown geographically by reaching franchising agreements with microbreweries in other provinces or states. Boston Beer Co., brewer of the Samuel Adams brand and one of the largest American microbreweries, has successfully used this strategy to expand in 60% of the U.S. The company contracts other breweries to make and distribute the beer while Boston Beer concentrates on the marketing.

A potential disadvantage of contracting other breweries to make the beer is that local consumers may not want to drink a microbrew that is available nationally, while other consumers may not want to drink a microbrew from another state when they know that the beer is brewed in their own state.

The packaging and marketing of the beer are also important elements that can increase sales. For example, sales at Upper Canada Brewing went up 40% when the beer label was redesigned from a simple design to a sophisticated one. While in the early years of operation microbreweries were targeting mainly young, university-educated and adventurous people, the advertising focus lately has been towards older consumers, travellers and drinkers disenchanted with the offerings from the big breweries. Typically, a consumer in a bar or restaurant would start with a microbrew as the first drink and then switch to regular beers, which are perceived to be less heavy.

Since microbreweries do not have the big advertising budgets of the big breweries, they mainly concentrate their advertising on extolling the benefits of image, unique taste, quality and the natural qualities of microbrews. Although competition amongst microbreweries is fierce in terms of distribution and gaining important shelf space in retail stores, there is nevertheless cooperation amongst microbreweries.

Microbreweries from Alberta and B.C. have grown through increased exports to the western states market, where the beer culture is strong. Other microbreweries have grown by increasing their product line; for example, adding an ale or a lager to complement their other brands, producing seasonal beers, or expanding their current line by adding dark, pale, or draft beer.

Even though microbreweries only hold about 2% of the market, the large breweries have taken notice and have launched an offensive to take advantage of the growth seen in this beer segment. In the U.S., the strategies of the large breweries include taking over or investing in microbreweries, quietly starting their own microbrewery, or developing brands that resemble microbrews. In 1993, Molson launched the "Signature Series" brand of premium beers (without additives and preservatives) aimed at sophisticated drinkers. The advertising budget for their first beer, La Rousse, was estimated to be over $1 million.

Molson and Labatt also have a powerful control of the distribution channels and have used this advantage to keep the microbreweries in check. Rather than relying on and paying the high cost to use the distribution channels of the "Big Two," many microbreweries have opted for developing their own small distribution channels.

Another tactic used by the "Big Two" in Canada has been to push a standard beer bottle for the industry. This is not directly aimed at the Canadian microbreweries, but rather is a defensive move against the American breweries; nevertheless, this initiative would incur more costs for microbreweries should they not follow the industry standard.

Several other initiatives undertaken by the "Big Two" to defend against the entry of discount American beer also affect the microbrewery industry. For example, Labatt has succeeded in using a strategy of innovation to the extent that, in 1993, 25% of its beer sales were from new brands, such as Labatt Ice and Genuine Draft. In contrast, Molson has used a strategy of building and reinforcing brand loyalty. Both breweries have also developed discount beers, as well as strong beers (alcohol content over 6%).

The Québec Beer Market

In 1993, the province of Québec was ranked fifth in Canada in terms of per capita consumption of beer (after Yukon, North West Territories, B.C. and Ontario). Québecers prefer to drink wine over beer. Per capita consumption of wine in Québec was the third highest in Canada.

In terms of market size, the Québec beer market was worth about $2.5 billion in 1993. Zero growth or a slight decline is expected for 1994 and 1995. Molson and Labatt control

98% of the market. In 1993, microbreweries held about 1.5% of the market share, and it is expected to go up to 3% by 1995. Combined sales of the top five microbreweries were estimated to be about $14 million in 1992, up 40% from 1990.

In Québec, the first microbreweries started operations in 1988. There are presently six microbreweries: McAuslan, Brasal, Les Brasseurs GMT, Les Brasseurs du Nord, Unibroue and Portneuvoise.

Unibroue

Unibroue recently became the largest microbrewer in Québec. In 1993, the company took over a small microbrewer of lager beer, Massawippi, located in Lennoxville, Québec. In addition, the company invested close to $5 million to consolidate its brewery and packaging centre into a new plant with a production capacity of 35,000 to 40,000 hectolitres.

In 1993, Unibroue had consolidated sales of $4.8 million, up from $1.6 million in 1992. Sales in 1994 are projected to be $8.5 million which would confirm the company's position as the leader in the Québec microbrewery market. The company's brands, which were unknown in 1991, have now reached over 50% awareness in its target market. The company brews four beers: Blanche de Chambly, La Maudite, La Fin du Monde and Massawippi.

A famous Québec rock singer, Robert Charlebois, is a minority shareholder of the company. He has added not only some notoriety to the company, but he has also become the company's biggest spokesperson. Mr. Charlebois was recently nominated for President of the French Brewers' Association, a group of 17 breweries in France.

Unibroue's strategy in Québec is to expand distribution of its beers to other regions of Québec and New Brunswick. Unibroue and the other four large microbreweries have reached an agreement to jointly distribute their beers in the northern part of Québec (Lac St. Jean and Saguenay), where there is a large population of craft beer and wine enthusiasts. Furthermore, the company has reached agreement with an American distributor to sell its beers in Florida and Massachusetts, as well as with a French distributor to sell in France and eventually in other European countries. The management is committed to maintaining an European image for its beers and is constantly searching for new European beer recipes.

Les Brasseurs du Nord

Les Brasseurs du Nord is now the second largest microbrewer in Québec. Over the past year, it increased capacity from 18,000 to 20,000 hectolitres. In the summer of 1994, the company invested about $2 million to relocate to a new, larger plant with a current capacity of 23,000 hectolitres and ability to further expand.

In November of 1994, the company launched a fourth ale, Boréale Forte (a strong beer), to complement the other three brands: Boréale Rousse (a red ale), Boréale Blonde (an amber), and Boréale Noire (dark). In 1993, Les Brasseurs du Nord had a market share of approximately 4.2% and sales of $5.5 million (compared to $192,000 in 1989).

The company's strategy is to increase production capacity, efficiency and productivity. It presently employs 27 people. In addition, the company would like to develop new brands and consolidate its position in Québec by increasing the number of points of sale. The company distributes its beers to more than 1,200 convenience stores and supermarkets, as well as some 250 bars.

Brasal-Brasserie Allemande

Brasal has a production capacity of 20,000 hectolitres. It was the second microbrewer in Québec to package beers in bottles (after McAuslan). The product, a German lager, is brewed according to the Bavarian Purity Law and is targeted as a gourmet, premium beer that is sold at a higher price than domestic beer, but a lower price than imported beer. Beers are distributed to liquor stores and upscale grocery stores, restaurants and bars.

Brasal's strategy is to focus on quality and taste, while pursuing growth in Ontario, the U.S. and possibly even Europe. From the start, Brasal was the first brewery with automated production capabilities. Sales in 1993 were estimated to be around $4 million, up from $2.5 million in 1990. The company has four beer brands: Hopps Brau, Brasal Light, Brasal Special and Brasal Bock.

Les Brasseurs GMT

GMT has also recently doubled its capacity from 11,000 hectolitres to 22,000 hectolitres. GMT's first beer was Belle Gueule, which is very popular amongst young French people. This beer also attracts the well educated, intellectual crowd. The strength of this beer has been its taste and sophisticated label. GMT's beers are distributed in convenience stores, supermarkets and bars.

In 1993, GMT launched a draft beer, La Tremblay, which is mainly targeted to a wider French market segment. GMT's strategy has been to focus on the Québec market. Once again the company is evaluating the feasibility of relocating to a larger and more modern plant in order to increase efficiency and productivity. The goal of management is to concentrate on quality and to become the microbrewery leader in terms of sales within the next three years. In addition to the lagers, GMT is planning to launch a double fermentation ale to add to its product line.

Smaller Microbreweries

There are another three smaller microbreweries located in the northern part of Québec, of which La Portneuvoise is the largest. This microbrewery, located near Québec City, was listed as the fifth largest in Québec in 1990; however, the company ran into financial difficulties because of poor beer quality and trying to expand too quickly. La Portneuvoise restarted operations in 1992 and has been trying to rebuild its market and image. The company's beer, a dark ale, is being targeted to craft beer enthusiasts. Distribution of this beer is still limited.

La Brasseur de l'Anse and Brasseries Beauce Broue are two smaller microbreweries with a limited market and distribution.

In addition to these microbreweries, there are also about 10 brewpubs. Brewpubs can brew beer on their premises, and can only sell this beer on the pub's premises.

McAuslan Brewing

McAuslan was one of the first microbreweries to operate in Québec. The company's first beer, St. Ambroise Pale Ale, became a success with the younger, well educated crowd. The sophisticated label projected an image of quality, adventure and uniqueness. Its taste and flavour is reminiscent of traditional English style ales.

In 1990, McAuslan was the leader amongst Québec microbreweries. St. Ambroise Pale Ale was also the first bottled microbrew in Québec. In 1991, the company launched another three beers to complement the first beer: St. Ambroise Oatmeal Stout (a rich dark beer), Griffon Brown Ale and Griffon Extra Pale Ale (Exhibit 5). "It isn't really our goal to rival Molson. We are a niche product. Our goal is to produce beer that's good, beer that's different," says Peter McAuslan.

Management

During the company's first three years, there was no formal organizational chart, as Peter and Ellen were basically responsible for almost all the functions in the company. As the operations of the brewery became more complex, Peter created a flat organizational chart in 1991 (Exhibit 6). As the President of the company since the start, Peter has been responsible for marketing, public relations, regulatory affairs and business development.

The next most important position in the company, production, is the responsibility of the brewmaster, Ellen. Under her leadership, McAuslan has concentrated on producing quality beer and St. Ambroise beers are now recognized as some of the best in the world. She oversees brewing production, quality control, research and development, packaging and shipping.

Two other managers report to Peter: Gary Yee, the financial officer, is responsible for personnel policies, financial management, sales forecast and accounting; Susanne Dion is the company's controller.

There is no formal human resources department. Each department is responsible for hiring new employees as it sees fit. It is up to each department head to set the salaries and compensation policies, train the employees and provide feedback. Moreover, top management believes in empowering the employees by encouraging them to participate and contribute to the overall goals of the company.

Peter feels that it is important to create a family atmosphere amongst the 29 employees and he is proud that, after nearly six years in business, McAuslan has remained a family-oriented business. However, as the company expanded in the past, it became more difficult to maintain this informal culture. In addition, he wondered whether the present organizational structure was adequate for future growth.

Production

Production capacity has also increased from 9,600 hectolitres (1990) to 14,000 (1991), and 20,000 (1992). For the past two years, the brewery has been operating at capacity, with two shifts Monday–Friday and one shift on Saturday.

Production capacity is limited by the size of the plant and the volume of the fermentation tanks. The company still occupies the original building which is 17,000 square feet, but with the option of expanding to 38,000 square feet.

Over the past two years, McAuslan has further invested close to $500,000 in new equipment to facilitate the brewing, fermentation and refrigeration process as well as to improve quality. Additional investment was used to improve packaging and bottling operations.

According to Peter, the objective is to create a flexible workforce that can react to fast changes. Nonetheless, Peter feels that further improvement is required to control operating expenses.

In contrast to the large breweries, McAuslan's employees, except for the truck drivers, are non-unionized. The company would not be able to compete if it had to pay the higher wages that a brewery employee receives at Molson or Labatt. Although turnover of production employees is low, McAuslan can count on a large pool of brewery workers which were laid off by the big breweries.

Marketing

Marketing has been one of the major strengths of McAuslan. The company has targeted its advertising mainly to university students, professionals and intellectuals. Over the past three years, McAuslan led the other microbreweries in terms of using traditional advertising media, such as radio and print, to promote its beers.

For Peter, it is important that McAuslan maintain an image of a local brewery that cares about the community. With that in mind, the company sponsors public events, such as the Montréal World Film Festival and the Montréal Chamber Orchestra. In addition, it participates and supports a wide variety of social and charity events.

In terms of microbrewery market shares, McAuslan was ranked first in Québec in 1991 and 1992 (Exhibit 4). In 1993, McAuslan ranked a close second to Les Brasseurs du Nord. McAuslan used a strategy of gradually gaining market share in the Montréal and Québec market. Although the Québec microbrewery market is shared almost equally by the six main microbrewers, growth in sales is still possible from market penetration, market and product expansion and geographical expansion. In 1993, McAuslan started to market its beers in the Vermont, Upper New York and New Jersey areas. However, export sales are still low, at about 1% of total sales. McAuslan's goal is to increase U.S. export sales to 10% in the next five years.

In September 1993, McAuslan signed a reciprocal agreement with Upper Canada Brewing of Ontario. The agreement called for McAuslan to brew Upper Canada beer and distribute it in the Québec market, while Upper Canada Brewing would do the same for McAuslan beer in Ontario.

Also at the beginning of the year, Mont Tremblant, a popular ski resort area north of Montréal, asked McAuslan if it would design and brew a private label beer that would only be sold in the resort area. This beer would only be brewed on contract for Mont Tremblant who kept all the rights to the beer.

Although contract brewing could bring extra revenues, Peter was unsure about the advantages and disadvantages of providing contract brewing to other breweries or organizations and/or about using contract brewing to expand geographically. Revenues from the Mont Tremblant contract accounted for less than 2% of total sales.

Distribution

Peter still has fond memories of the first two years of operation when he was practically on the road all the time, trying to persuade convenience store owners and pub owners to buy his beer. At that time, he had another salesman, Michael Ryan, to help him. They slowly developed a distribution channel that covered some 500 convenience stores and supermarkets by 1990. McAuslan beer is now widely distributed in Montréal and Québec city convenience stores, supermarkets and pubs. Furthermore, over the past two years, McAuslan has targeted pubs throughout the province as a prime objective. McAuslan draft beer is now the only microbrew draft commonly found in a large percentage of pubs and taverns.

Financial Statements

The company is largely controlled by Peter McAuslan and a number of smaller shareholders. Total assets of the company have increased from about $2.08 million in 1991 to $3.09 million in 1994 (unaudited). From the beginning, McAuslan's main objective was to become a profitable business. Exhibits 7 and 8 summarize the financial statements for the last four years. Sales revenues in 1994 were estimated at $4.45 million, up from $3.78 million in 1993.

After the company invested in newer equipment and production processes, Peter's objective was to control administrative expenses which he felt were above microbrewery industry standards. For the past year, McAuslan carefully looked at ways to become more efficient and productive. Now, looking at the latest financial statements, Peter became also concerned about sales expenses which he thought were quite high. At the beginning, it was easy to control sales and distribution expenses because there was only one hired salesperson. Over the past two years, McAuslan has hired another three salespersons who report to him and one telemarketer who reports to Michael Ryan. However, given Peter's time constraints, he has not been able to properly train these new salespeople.

One of Gary Yee's objectives has been the use of financial software to better forecast sales. Beer consumption tends to be seasonal with a large part of the sales taking place in the summer. A hot summer can increase sales considerably. The Christmas season also tends to generate a fair amount of sales, although not as extensive as in the summer. In an effort to provide better services to customers, McAuslan started to offer better credit terms, especially to the bigger, more established customers.

Future Directions

Peter's thoughts returned to the paperwork on his desk. Next week, December 7, the brewery was going to celebrate, as it has done for the past five years, St. Ambroise Day—the patron saint of beer lovers all over the world. But apart from heavenly advice, Peter sensed that McAuslan required a new strategic direction if McAuslan were to remain not only profitable, but also a leader in the microbrewery business.

Exhibit 1

Top Canadian Breweries
1993 Production Capacity
(in Thousands of Hectolitres)

	Location	Production Capacity
Molson	Canada	10,500
Labatt	Canada	9,600
Moosehead Breweries	New Brunswick	1,200
Oland Breweries	Nova Scotia	620
Pacific Western Brewing	B.C.	400
Lakeport Brewing	Ontario	330
Sleeman Brewing	Ontario	235
Great Western Brewing	Saskatchewan	205
Northern Breweries	Ontario	150
Drummond Brewing	Alberta	150
Norther Breweries	Ontario	95
Brick Brewing*	Ontario	87

*Brick Brewing has jumped from a capacity of 42,000 hectolitres to 87,000 hectolitres in the past year.

Exhibit 2

Top American Breweries
1993 Market Share (%) & Production Capacity
(in Millions of Hectolitres)

	Market Share (%)	Production Capacity
Anheuser-Busch	46.9	115.6
Miller	23.7	57.5
Adolf Coors	10.7	31.7
Stroh	6.9	16.5
Heileman	4.8	10.7
Pabst	3.8	12.3
Genesee	1.2	4.7
Falstaff	0.6	1.4
Latrobe	0.6	1.4
Pittsburg Brewing	0.5	1.0

Exhibit 3

Advertisement from the Canadian Brewers' Association

Please drink responsibly.

Exhibit 4.

Top Canadian Microbreweries Beer Sales Volume & Market Share (%)[1]
(in thousands of Hectolitres)

Rank 1993	Rank 1992	Rank 1991	Company	1993 Sales	1993 %	1992 Sales	1992 %	1991 Sales	1991 %
1	1	1[2]	Algonquin Brewing (Ontario)	65.0	19.7	45.0	18.2	45.0	16.9
2	2	2	Brick Brewing (Ontario)	45.0	13.6	42.0	17.0	42.0	15.8
3	3	3	Upper Canada Brewing (Ontario)	35.0	10.6	25.0	10.1	25.0	9.4
—	—	4[3]	Pacific Brewing (B.C.)	—	—	—	—	17.2	6.5
4	5	5	Granville Island (B.C.)	16.5	5.0	14.0	5.7	14.0	5.3
5	6	6	Vancouver Island (B.C.)	15.0	4.5	13.0	5.3	13.0	4.9
6	8	8	Big Rock (Alberta)	15.0	4.5	10.0	4.0	10.0	3.8
7	10	10	Les Brasseurs du Nord (Québec)	14.0	4.2	8.4	3.4	8.4	3.2
8	7	7	Creemore Springs (Ontario)	14.0	4.2	11.5	4.7	11.5	4.3
9	9	9	McAuslan Brewing (Québec)	13.8	4.2	9.6	3.9	9.6	3.6
10	12	12	Shaftesbury Brewing (B.C.)	11.0	3.3	7.0	2.8	7.0	2.6
11	—	—	Les Brasseurs GMT (Québec)	11.0	3.3	—	—	—	—
12	13	13	Niagra Falls Brewing (Ontario)	10.0	3.0	6.0	2.4	6.0	2.3
13	11	11	Brasal Brasserie (Québec)	9.1	2.8	8.0	3.2	8.0	3.0
14	11	11	Conners Brewery (Ontario)	8.0	2.4	8.0	3.2	8.0	3.0
15	13	13	Wellington County (Ontario)	8.0	2.4	6.0	2.4	6.0	2.3
16	—	—	Whistler (B.C.)	7.0	2.1	—	—	—	—
17	14	14	Hart Breweries (Ontario)	2.4	0.7	3.6	1.5	5.0	1.9
			Other	30.0	9.1	30.0	12.1	30.0	11.3
			Total Market	329.8	100.0	247.1	100.0	265.7	100.0

1. Unibroue completed its mergers in 1993; its constituent parts fall into "Other" in this table.
2. Algonquin increased production capacity from 16,000 hectolitres in 1990.
3. Pacific Brewing is now treated as a regional brewery.

Exhibit 5

Product Advertisement

ST-AMBROISE Oatmeal Stout

Full bodied dark and rich, slightly sweet with subtle accents of mocha, sure to lease the discerning palate.

GRIFFON Extra Pale Ale

Blond, golden hued and a hinting of malted barley: a great tasting Québecois ale!

GRIFFON Brown Ale

Flavorful and distinctive, with a creamy texture, a malty aroma and mahogany color.

ST-AMBROISE Pale Ale

Deep amber-red, hoppy and fruity from its bouquet to its long clean finish, recognized by experts as being the best beer brewed in Canada.

Exhibit 6. Organization Chart

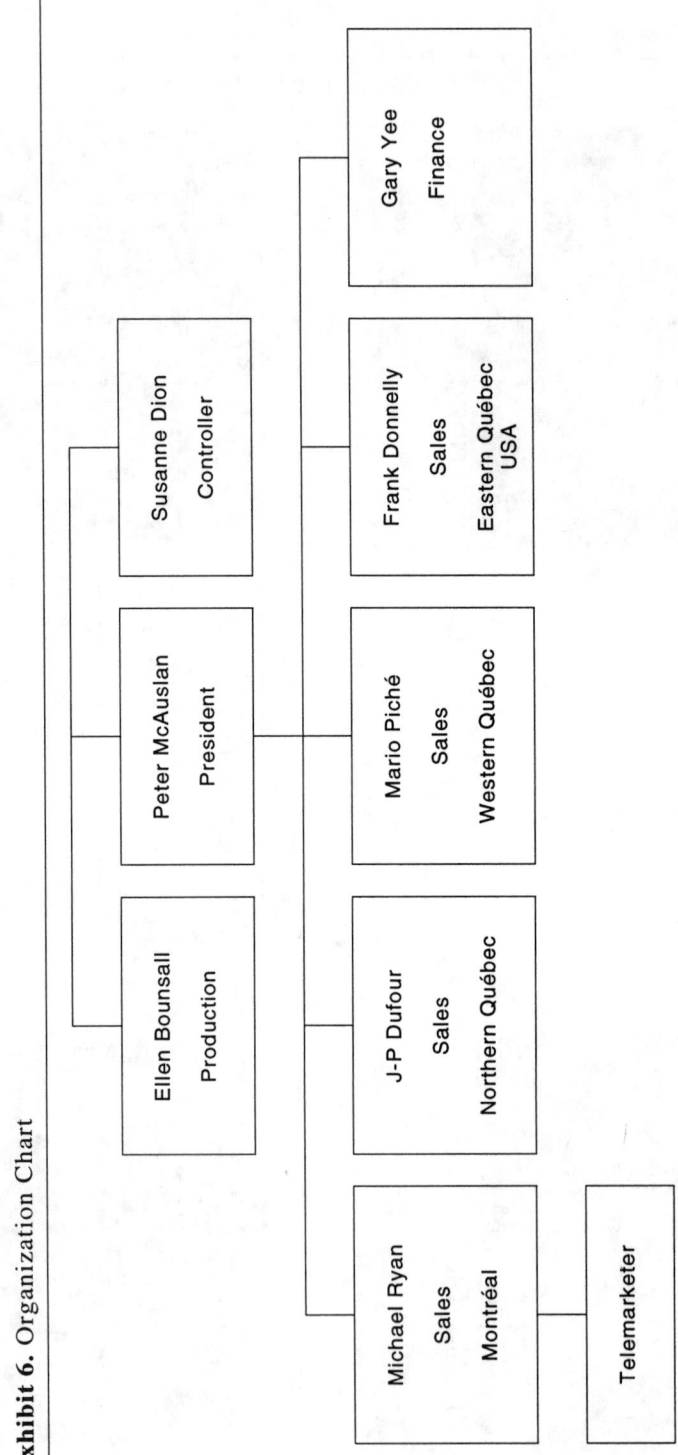

Exhibit 7

Balance Sheet at October 31
(in 000's)

	1991	1992	1993	1994
				Unaudited
Assets				
Cash	$362	$326	$265	$ 204
Receivables	115	106	129	348
Inventories	188	193	238	341
Prepaid expenses	35	24	16	59
Total current assets	700	649	648	952
Property	75	75	75	75
Plant	445	468	515	520
Equipment	1,007	1,256	1,988	2,006
Accumulated amortization	(146)	(178)	(259)	(461)
Total assets	$2,081	$2,270	$2,967	$3,092
Liabilities				
Accounts payable	$26	$59	$112	$149
Bank indebtedness	21	32	187	224
Taxes	16	21	56	50
Current long-term debt	16	57	86	83
Total current liabilities	79	169	441	506
Long-term debt	701	641	892	809
Total liabilities	780	810	1,333	1,315
Shareholders' Equity				
Common stock	800	800	800	800
Retained earnings	501	660	834	977
Total shareholder's equity	1,301	1,460	1,634	1,777
Total liabilities and shareholders' equity	$2,081	$2,270	$2,967	$3,092

Exhibit 8

Income Statement years ended October 31
(in 000's)

	1991	1992	1993	1994
				Unaudited
Sales	$2,098	$2,452	$3,788	$4,453
Cost of goods sold	831	1,098	1,679	2,055
Sales and promotion	287	541	904	1,155
Administrative	207	422	645	712
Interest	40	39	133	128
Amortization	52	81	125	178
Research & development	14	33	42	12
Income before tax	$ 667	$ 238	$ 260	$ 213
Net income after tax	$ 447	$ 159	$ 174	$ 143

Case 10

Velan Valve

At the age of 79, A. K. Velan, President and CEO of Velan Inc. has shown no signs of slowing down. He was recently named "Entrepreneur of the Year" by *Canadian Business Magazine* for 1996. He has added this title to a long list of other awards for outstanding business performance. However, at some point in time A. K. realizes that the reins of the family business will have to be relinquished to one of his three sons who are all Executive Vice Presidents within the company.

COMPANY BACKGROUND

A. K. Velan fled his native Czechoslovakia in 1949 when the Communist government took power. He came to Canada armed with his engineering know-how and a belief in the strength of innovation. To him, Canada was a land of opportunity and freedom. He felt that this was a country in which he could obtain success with his ideas. In 1950, A. K. started his business in Montréal based on his development and patent of a device that would eliminate condensation from steam piping, the bimetallic steam trap. The company was incorporated in 1952 under the name of Velan Inc.

In the early years A. K. struggled to make his business a success. He was on the road a great deal of the time trying to sell his product. When he wasn't selling he was at the drawing board trying to improve his product and to develop others. He worked from his home (garage) making prototypes of his inventions, tested them and modified them. His first big break came when the U.S. Navy ordered the Velan bimetallic steam trap for seven of their new destroyers. These were challenging times as A. K. struggled to keep production up to the flow of incoming orders. He can remember the late nights in his garage working with his wife to pack the steam traps destined for the U.S. Navy.

But A. K. thrived on his new found success and greeted the challenges with great enthusiasm. He was not afraid of hard work but rather enjoyed seeing the success of his inventions. He began developing new types of valves, many of which were patented. With the onset of his new innovations, his business became too big for his house so he moved it to a manufacturing plant.

In the late 1950s, A. K. saw a window of opportunity developing with the birth of nuclear power. He began developing valves to be used specifically in the nuclear power

This case was written by Ingrid Sinclair (M.B.A.) under the direction of Professor A. B. Ibrahim as a basis for class discussion rather than to illustrate effective or ineffective handling of an administrative situation. This case is based on public information from the company's prospectus and other publicly available information. This case was supported by a grant from the Certified General Accountants Association of Canada (CGA).
© Dr. A. B. Ibrahim, 1997.

industry. His products were used by the U.S. Navy and NATO for ships, nuclear submarines and aircraft carriers. Newly established nuclear power plants were also using his products. A. K.'s company now offered a product line of forged steel gate, globe and check valves in addition to steam traps. These products were sold mainly in North America. By 1957, Velan Inc. had established sales organizations in Western Europe, the Middle East and Asia.

A. K. pioneered many valve technology innovations which went on to become industry standards. As the nuclear power industry matured, technical bodies began developing manufacturing standards required for equipment used in this industry. In 1971, Velan Inc. was one of the first valve manufacturers to receive the American Society of Mechanical Engineers (ASME) "N" stamp certification. This stamp authorized Velan to supply nuclear Class 1, 2 and 3 valves to nuclear power plants.

Under the direction of A. K., Velan Inc. continued to grow and prosper. By 1972, Velan had two manufacturing plants in Montréal and one in the U.K. Velan also owned an assembling plant in Plattsburg, New York. In addition, A. K.'s three sons were now also working for the company. A. K. was never content with his current level of success, but rather strove to continue growing. His ultimate goal was to be the largest valve manufacturer in the world. To this end, Velan continued its international expansion. Due to its nuclear technical expertise, in 1974 Velan entered into a 50/50 joint venture with a French company to supply valves to the growing nuclear power program.

Velan Inc. continued to grow and expand its product line such that it purchased another manufacturing facility in Granby, Québec in 1976. Then in order to increase its market presence in the United States, Velan built a manufacturing plant in Williston, Vermont in 1978. As the company continued to grow, there came a point where it needed an influx of capital to purchase new manufacturing equipment. This caused Velan to sell 50% of its interest to the German company Deutsche Babcock in 1979. The Velan family retained control of the day-to-day operations of the company.

In the 1980s, foreign competition in the valve industry became more intense and Velan saw its profit margins and domestic market share decreasing. Rather than moving its manufacturing overseas, Velan Inc. expanded further domestically. In 1984 Velan built an additional manufacturing plant in Montréal to increase its manufacturing capacity and accommodate a growing product line. During the remainder of the eighties, Velan Inc. concentrated on its foreign exposure. In 1988, Velan acquired a manufacturing plant in Korea and increased its interest in a Portuguese plant from 50% to 88%. In 1990, Velan entered into joint venture contracts with manufacturers in France and Taiwan, recognizing the importance in both Europe and Asia.

The early nineties began with an emphasis on Total Quality Management and ISO certification. Velan was not to be left behind. In fact, Velan's four North American manufacturing plants were the first in the North American valve industry to be certified to ISO 9001. The Velan plants in the U.K., Portugal, Taiwan and Korea were ISO 9002 certified.

Velan Inc. started as a small business operated by its founder, A. K. Velan and grew to a multinational corporation with eight manufacturing plants in six countries and over 1,100 employees.

THE VALVE INDUSTRY

Valves are important devices that are used in piping systems in every type of process industry. Valves can be used for on/off service or for controlling a process flow. There are many types of valves available such as gate, globe, butterfly or check. The type of valve utilized depends on the service it is used for and whether the process is liquid, gas, solid or slurry based.

According to industry data, annual global sales of industrial valves were U.S. $1.7 billion in 1995. This amount is projected to grow by an average of 3.3% annually. Industrialized nations such as the United States are the most significant market for valves. Thus while the major market is currently the United States, it is expected that the greatest growth in demand for industrial valves will be from the Far East, South America, and Eastern Europe because of the development of resource-based processes and power generation industries. Any developing country with a growing infrastructure will have an expanding market for valves. The percentage of world valve production end users have been estimated by industry data as follows:

End User Market as a Percentage of World Valve Production

	1994 (%)	1995 (%)	1996 (%)
Chemical Processing	17.3	17.4	17.4
Water Treatment	17.2	17.6	17.7
Power Generation	12.4	12.5	12.5
Petroleum Production	12.4	11.5	11.2
Petroleum Refining	10.6	10.6	10.5
Oil and Gas Distribution	8.0	7.8	7.8
Pulp and Paper	7.0	7.0	6.9
Food and Beverage	2.3	2.3	2.5
Iron and Steel	2.0	1.9	1.9
Other	10.8	11.4	11.6

There are hundreds of valve manufacturers around the world. The companies may carry a broad product line of valves, as Velan does, or they may specialize in a certain product line. The companies may also manufacture complementary industrial products such as pumps, flanges and fittings. The manufacturers may have their own marketing and sales departments or they may rely to some extent on distributors and sales agents. Currently, the majority of industrial valve production takes place in North America, Western Europe and Japan. These countries are recognized as the areas which produce the highest quality products and hence the most expensive. Production of valves in other areas than the Triad countries are generally recognized as being less competitive due to their low product quality.

The industrial valve market can be divided into two main sections: commodity valves and engineered valves. An engineered valve is built for a specific purpose.

The scope of rivalry among valve manufacturers is extensive. Manufacturers can be large global companies or small niche market companies. The commodity valve market is highly price sensitive. To successfully compete in this area, manufacturers must be very cost effective. This has been achieved through low-cost of labor in developing countries and increased productivity through automation. Triad companies have been establishing production sites in developing countries or have been buying components from suppliers based in low-cost countries to remain competitive. Automation can also reduce costs by cutting labor costs and reducing waste while increasing quality.

The engineered part of the market is less affected by competition from low labor cost countries. It is generally the Triad companies that have the engineering know-how to produce engineered valves. Companies in developing countries have not yet developed this capability. In order to be successful in this segment, the manufacturer must constantly remain innovative. Technology innovation means finding new materials or new designs to make valves more efficient, reliable, cost effective, safe and maintainable. Innovation also means establishing a relationship with their large customers and working together to design a valve that meets the customers' technological challenges.

The industry demand for valves is cyclical due to the dependence on capital investment of processing industries whose budgets are governed by general economic conditions. The sales generated through general maintenance and servicing are less cyclical than those generated by capital investments. In the chemical and petrochemical industries, it has been estimated that 50% of worldwide sales were for maintenance and servicing. There are also industry specific factors that affect the demand for valves such as environmental guidelines and demand for alternate energy utilization.

Developed countries have mature markets but do require replacement valves for operating facilities. Operating facilities generate a constant flow of valve sales revenue through general maintenance replacement and service repair. This demand is stable and less cyclical because once a valve reaches its end of life, replacement cannot be postponed. The growth of replacement valves is also being affected by stricter environmental guidelines. Some valves have had to be changed before the end of their useful life due to fugitive emissions or leakage. Buyers in this market are less price sensitive than in the new-use market. In the replacement market the end-users are experienced plant operators and are thus more sophisticated buyers. Replacement valve buyers are more concerned with ease of use, reliability, safety, ease of maintenance, although price competitiveness is still important. The valve replacement market currently represents one-third of the world's sales and is growing faster than the overall market. Replacement buyers will also tend to deal with the valve manufacturers that they have prior experience with, since they will be familiar with the product and its level of quality/reliability.

	Forecast Growth in Valve Shipments By End-User Market 1994–2000
Chemical Processing	0.035
Water Treatment	0.04
Power Generation	0.034
Petroleum Production	0.007
Petroleum Refining	0.028
Gas Distribution	0.024
Pulp and Paper	0.005
Food and Beverage	0.052
Iron and Steel	0.031
Other	0.051

Source: Elsevier Advanced Technology

The market demand is growing the most in developing countries where infrastructures are also being developed. The customers in this segment are generally the large engineering firms who are often hired to build turnkey projects. These buyers are more price sensitive since the contracts are normally obtained through a bidding process. They will buy the cheapest product that meets the pre-established standards.

Developing countries are experiencing rapid growth and thus there is a great need for plastics, energy, chemicals, steel, etc. This need may translate to companies setting up projects to meet the needs of developing countries. Southeast Asia, the former Eastern bloc countries and South America are expecting to have the greatest growth in capital investment projects.

The trends in the industry include worldwide sourcing and price competitiveness. Worldwide sourcing involves manufacturers buying components from countries that have lower manufacturing costs. Valve end users are now expecting superior quality and reliability for valves at a lower price. To respond to the price sensitivity, valve manufacturer have to concentrate on reducing costs.

Many valve end users are now instituting preferred supplier status. Such companies will have a list of suppliers that have met all their criteria of quality, reliability and price competitiveness. When the company wishes to purchase a valve they will tender bids only to the suppliers on the list. Manufacturers should also have a broad product line to be included on the list. Improving technology is also another important trend in valve manufacturing. Innovation is the key. Valve manufacturers must strive to enhance the durability, performance, environmental soundness and overall quality of valves mainly through improved engineering designs and increased quality testing.

As manufacturers work to reduce costs, increase technological advancements and maintain preferred supplier status, many companies have used consolidation through mergers and acquisitions to remain competitive. There has also been a trend towards relaxing trade regulations. Under the NAFTA agreement, valves and parts meeting minimum North American content requirements can be sold without duty between Canada and the United States. The duty rates under GATT for valves and valve parts entering North America continue to be reduced.

VELAN'S POSITION IN THE INDUSTRY

Velan is the largest steel valve manufacturer in North America and the second largest in the world. The largest steel valve manufacturer in the world is KITZ of Japan. Velan offers a broad range of valves to its customers throughout the world in many industries such as power generation, oil and gas, petrochemical, chemical, pulp and paper, and shipbuilding. The valves can be made from carbon, alloy or stainless steel in sizes varying from 0.5 inch diameter to 48 inches in diameter. The company specializes in the manufacture of valves for high pressure and temperature applications which must adhere to high quality standards. The company has the ability to construct prototype valves and "made to order" valves, due to in-house engineering, research and design. This sets Velan apart from other manufacturers since many of their competitors do not have the facilities nor the technology to offer this type of service. Since Velan sells a huge array of different products, its competitors vary from product line to product line.

Velan sells its products in 50 different countries around the world. Sales are achieved through many channels such as direct sales, authorized distributors, and sales agents. The company supports all sales efforts with its customer service department. In addition, annual sales conferences are held for distributors to enhance their knowledge of Velan's products. Currently the distribution network is composed of 68 distributors with 195 branches in the Unites States, 7 distributors with 28 branches in Canada, and more than 40 distributors and agents overseas.

The goal of the company is to continue to be a world leader in the manufacture, design and marketing of its steel industrial valves. Velan implements several strategies to achieve its corporate goal. A key strategy of the company has been to offer a broad line of products. The company is still focusing on expanding its products either through in-house manufacturing or through acquisitions of complementary manufacturers. This is a competitive advantage for Velan as the industry trend has been for end users to deal with a short list of preferred suppliers. Velan has been put on the preferred supplier list for such companies as Bechtel and Dow Chemical. An example of an engineering company's recommended vendor list can be found in Exhibit 1. Velan manufactures highly engineered valves as well as commodity valves, thus the company has a large number of competitors. Generally there is less competition in the highly engineered valves than commodity valves. Velan has placed more focus on the manufacture of highly engineered valves and generally these valves have the highest profit margins.

The Valve Manufacturers Association (VMA) is an association for valve manufacturers that are incorporated in the U.S. or Canada. The association has over 100 members that account for approximately 85% of the total industrial valve shipments out of the U.S. The American valve industry, in turn, supplies 40% of the worldwide valve demand. Many of these manufacturers have facilities overseas in addition to their North American facilities. As Velan, most have broad product lines. The manufacturers differ in the types of valves offered, the fabrication material (that is, valves could be made of iron, steel, plastic, brass, etc.) and engineering capabilities, to name a few. These manufacturers all fabricate the same type of valve but will differ to some extent on sizes, uses and material. This illustrates the level of competition and fragmentation of the industrial valve market.

Velan continues to place emphasis on product innovation. The company has had a long history of pioneering valve technologies which have eventually become industry standards. The company conducts research and design to improve and develop valves which are high quality, reliable, safe, long lasting and easy to use. The company has a respected reputation among end-users and is known for its high quality. Focus on quality in valve production has been further enhanced through ISO 9000 certification and investing in state of the art manufacturing facilities.

The market for steel industrial valves is highly fragmented due to the different types of technology needed by different industries. For instance, the valves used in nuclear power generation would not be the same as that used in a water treatment plant. Velan is very aware of this fragmentation, which is why it strives for global sales and distribution of its products. The company has felt it important to continue to develop markets in other countries to ensure continued growth. The most recent expansion has been in the Chinese market where Velan has hired distribution agents. The company's focus in China to date is to develop a position in the power generation steel valve market. The company is also looking to expand into the Indian power generation market. The company's international market development section is continually searching for new market opportunities.

Velan has over 500 customers where no single customer accounts for more than 10% of the company's sales. These customers can be end users, architect/engineering firms, contractors or distributors. Examples of some of Velan's customers in different industry segments include:

Power

- Florida Power & Light
- Taiwan Power
- Ontario Hydro

Chemical

- BASF
- Bayer
- Union Carbide

Pulp and Paper

- MacMillan Bloedel
- Scott Paper
- Mead

Oil and Gas

- British Petroleum
- Petro Canada
- Kuwait Petrochemical

Shipbuilding

- Bath Iron Works
- Ingalls
- Brooklyn Navy Yard

Engineering Firms

- Fluor Daniel
- Foster Wheeler
- ABB Lummus

Other

- General Electric
- M&M Mars
- Procter & Gamble

Velan has been successful in getting and keeping customers through a broad range of industries. Even though price competition has been heightened, Velan believes that companies still place a great deal of emphasis on valve performance, quality, customer service, engineering know-how and a reputation for meeting project deadlines. Velan does not generally compete based on price competitiveness except for its commodity valve product line.

HUMAN RESOURCES AND ORGANIZATIONAL STRUCTURE

Velan Inc. prides itself on being a family business run by family members. Over 50% of Velan's employees have been with the company for over twenty years. Velan also tries to provide opportunities for other immigrants to North America. For hundreds of immigrants to Canada, Velan has been able to offer them their all important first job. The management of the company is composed of family members as well as employees that have worked their way up through the ranks. Velan is a streamlined organization with a dynamic and loyal workforce. The company has a very personal management style and acknowledges the importance of their employees.

A. K. Velan founded the company in 1950. He is the president and the Chief Executive Officer of the company. His three sons grew up in the company. His eldest son, Ivan, began working at Velan in 1970 after obtaining an M.B.A. from the University of Michigan. He started at Velan in the position of Sales Administrator then moved onto Marketing Manager. Currently he is the Executive Vice-President North American Sales, Quality Assurance and MIS. A. K.'s middle son, Peter, joined the company in 1968 after graduating from McGill with a bachelor in mechanical engineering. He was then promoted to Plant Manager. Currently, Peter is the Executive Vice-President of Engineering and Production. The youngest son, Thomas, joined the company in 1974. Tom has a bachelor degree in commerce with honours in economics from McGill. Tom began his career as an order administrator then became Director of Export Sales. Currently, Tom is Executive Vice-President of Export Sales and Overseas Operations. Extended family also hold positions at the company from grandchildren to spouses of grandchildren. A. K.'s sons have acquired extensive knowledge of the company and are generally recognized as very capable managers. An organizational chart of the upper management can be found in Exhibit 2.

The remainder of the upper management of the company consist of eight vice presidents who are not Velan family members. The titles of the positions are as follows: Vice-President of Total Process Improvement, Vice-President of Engineering Quarter-Turn Valves, Vice-President of Engineering Multi-Turn Valves, Vice-President Quality Assurance and Quality Control Engineer, Vice-President of U.S. Sales, Vice-President Finance, Vice-President Marketing and Vice-President of International Sales. The management personnel have an average of over 25 years of experience with the company.

Velan and its subsidiaries have close to 1,100 employees. More than 70% of these employees are located in Canada, 20% are in the United States and the remainder are overseas. Of the companies that Velan has 50% ownership (those located in France. Taiwan and the United States) there are 230 employees. The production workers in the Québec plants and the Vermont plant are unionized. In the last five years, the company has not had any major work stoppages through strikes or labor disputes. The corporate structure is illustrated in Exhibit 3.

The corporate control of all Velan's facilities is maintained at headquarters in Montréal. The organizational structure of the company is generally controlled by product line, yet each geographical division will have a certain amount of independence. The European facilities (Portugal, U.K. and France) support the European market through marketing and selling their products. The French plant specializes in supporting the nuclear industry whereas the Portugal plant manufactures commodity valves. The Korean and Taiwanese facilities also concentrate on manufacturing commodity valves. The joint venture with the American company, Q.A. Products, services the niche market of high pressure valves for the replacement market and "fast track orders." The remainder of Velan's North American manufacturing facilities have dual capacity to provide both commodity and specialty/engineered valves. The plants are generally differentiated by product line but there are crossover capabilities between them. See Exhibit 4 for details on the facilities.

Global strategy is directed from the headquarters in Montréal. Major worldwide projects are quoted from Montréal. Upper management is actively involved in the sales efforts of large projects ($1 million plus). The corporate engineering facilities are also located in Montréal. Coordination and communication between the geographical facilities are done when required, otherwise the facilities are independent to a point. The facilities are free to operate as they see fit on the day-to-day basis but they must follow the corporate strategy set from headquarters. Corporate directives could include meeting product quotas and ensuring broad product line deliveries for large orders. Corporate strategy is assisted by the marketing and sales group at headquarters and the field representatives located around the world.

Velan has a number of incentive plans for their employees. Production personnel receive incentives for achieving production deadlines and delivery dates. Other than production personnel, a formalized incentive plan is not in place. For North American operations, the company has an RRSP program where they meet the employee's contributions up to specified limits. The employee benefits plan is comparable to companies of comparable size. Executives have an incentive plan where they are eligible to receive options to purchase shares.

Velan invests in training programs to improve the skills of their employees. The greatest of which is the firm belief in Total Quality Management. The company also conducts quarterly training programs regarding the different products offered by the company. Exhibit 5 outlines Velan's total quality program.

FINANCIAL STATEMENTS

Velan Incorporated has shown a profit throughout its history and has been growing steadily from the beginning. From 1992 to 1996, Velan's consolidated sales have grown from $163 million to $233 million. Net income from this period has grown from $12.4 million to $28.1 million during this time period. The financial statements are included in Exhibits 6 through 9.

The 1995 fiscal profit margin for Velan's U.S. operations was 12.1% which more than doubles the industry average margin as reported by the Valve Manufacturers Association of America.

The company went public in the Fall of 1996 as Deutsche Babcock wanted to sell its interest in the company. The shares are traded on the Toronto Stock Exchange. The initial public offering was at $16/share. In February of 1991 the shares have been trading at $24/share.

The company continues to look for new growth opportunities either through expansion or acquisition. In February 1997, the company acquired the Securamax unit of Derlan

Manufacturing Inc. of Toronto for $4.8 million. The unit manufactures specialty service metal seated ball valves which complement Velan's existing general service metal ball product line. The company continues to spend capital for new manufacturing technologies and upgrading its existing facilities. This investment ensures that state of the art technology is used to manufacture quality valves and enables the manufacturing facilities to be retrofitted to allow for increased production.

TO THE FUTURE

At 79 years old, A. K. Velan continues to lead his company and push for its continued growth. A. K. enjoys pursuing new markets and recently took part in the Team Canada trip to Asia. His grandchildren have called him the "Energizer Bunny" who keeps going and going. This is a good description of A. K., as he has shown no signs, nor willingness, of slowing down. The dream to be the largest manufacturer in the world is getting to be a reality as growth of the company continues. A. K. still enjoys the thrill of achieving that all elusive sale. He propagates the active, participatory, hands-on management of the company. A. K. has an entrepreneurial flair that is impossible to replace. A succession plan does exist, but its contents are not known publicly.

Exhibit 1

Example of Typical "Acceptable Valve Manufacturers List" for an Engineering Company

Small Forged Steel Gate, Globe and Check Valves
Forged Steel and Low Alloy Steel, 1/2″ to 2″ Sizes:

Anvil	United States
Bonney Forge	United States
DSI	Italy
Hancock	United States
Hitachi	Japan
Newco	Korea
RP&C	United States
Rockwell	United States
Shoritsu	Japan
Smith	Hong Kong/Singapore
Velan	Canada/United States
Vogt	United States
Yonecki	Japan

Cast Carbon Steel Gate, Globe and Check Valves 2″ and Larger:

Hitachi	Japan
Kinka	Japan
KITZ	Japan
Nibco	United States
Newco (150-300#)	Taiwan
Newco (600#+)	Italy
OIC	Korea
Pacific	United States
Powell	United States
Raimondi	Italy
Rockwell	Italy
RP&C	Italy
Stockham	Korea
Takamisawa	Japan
Triangle	U.K.
Velan	Canada
Walworth	Mexico
Wheatley (check only)	U.S.
Yonecki	Japan

Exhibit 1 (continued)

Ball Valves—High Temperature—Metal or Graphite Seated
Carbon Steel, Stainless Steel and Alloys

Argus	Germany
MC Canna	USA
Mogas	USA
Neles-Jamesbury	USA/Finland
Orbit	USA
TK	USA/Scotland
Valvtech	USA
Valvtron	USA
Velan	USA/Canada
Worcester	USA

Butterfly Valves—Utility Services
Class 150 or Less—Air and Water

Allis Chalmers	USA
Amri	USA/France
Center Line	USA
Dezurik	USA
Keystone	USA
Norris/O'Bannon	USA
Pratt, Henry	USA

Exhibit 2. Organizational Structure of Velan Inc. Upper Management

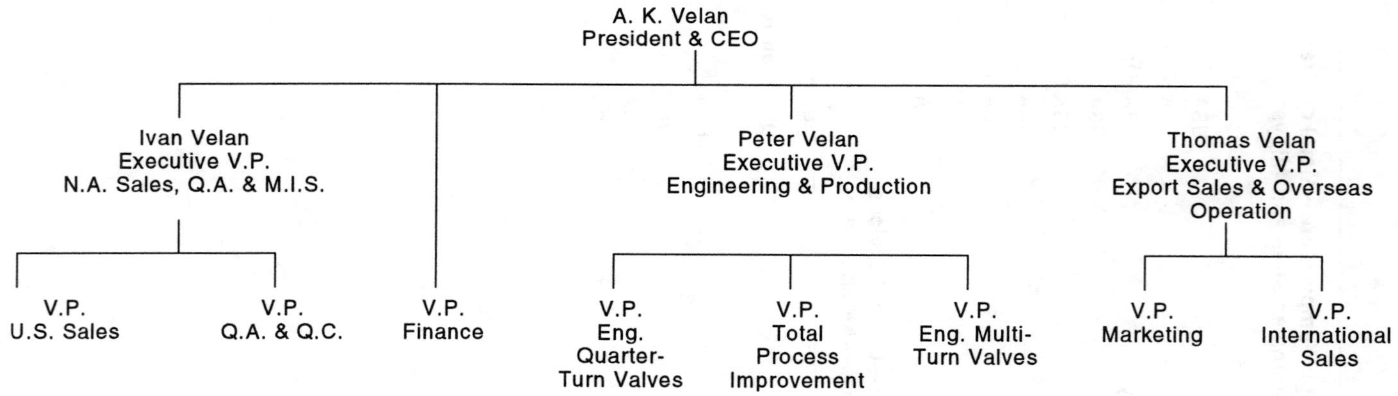

A. K. Velan
President & CEO

Ivan Velan
Executive V.P.
N.A. Sales, Q.A. & M.I.S.

V.P.
U.S. Sales

V.P.
Q.A. & Q.C.

V.P.
Finance

Peter Velan
Executive V.P.
Engineering & Production

V.P.
Eng.
Quarter-
Turn Valves

V.P.
Total
Process
Improvement

V.P.
Eng. Multi-
Turn Valves

Thomas Velan
Executive V.P.
Export Sales & Overseas
Operation

V.P.
Marketing

V.P.
International
Sales

Exhibit 3. Corporate Structure of Velan Inc.

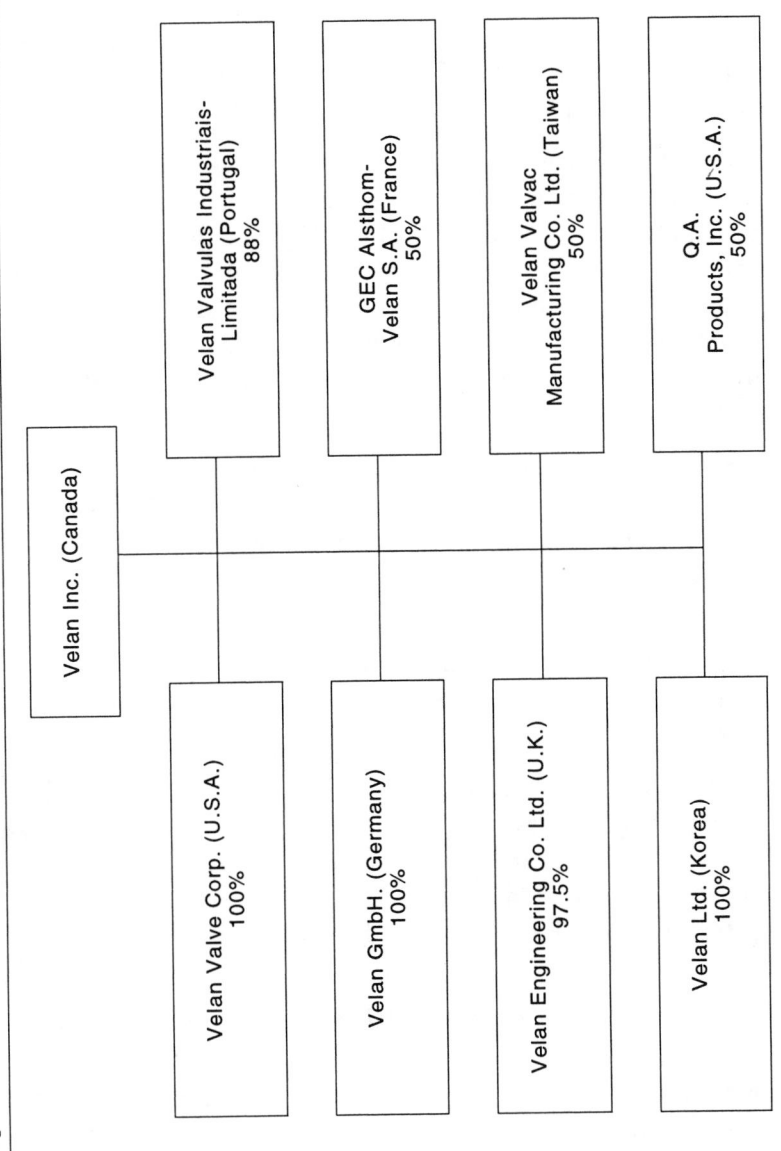

Velan Inc. (Canada)

Velan Valvulas Industriais-Limitada (Portugal)
88%

GEC Alsthom-Velan S.A. (France)
50%

Velan Valvac Manufacturing Co. Ltd. (Taiwan)
50%

Q.A. Products, Inc. (U.S.A.)
50%

Velan Valve Corp. (U.S.A.)
100%

Velan GmbH. (Germany)
100%

Velan Engineering Co. Ltd. (U.K.)
97.5%

Velan Ltd. (Korea)
100%

Exhibit 4

Velan's Manufacturing Facilities

1. *PLANT 1, Montréal, Québec:*
   Concentrates on the mass production of small (1/2" to 2") multi-turn industrial valves. Plant 1 is certified to ISO 9001 and has received nuclear production authorization ("N" stamp) from the American Society of Mechanical Engineers.

2. *PLANT 2/7, Montréal, Québec:*
   Manufactures large (up to 48") multi-turn and quarter-turn valves for high performance applications and is low volume highly engineered valve type manufacturing operation. Plant 2 is certified to ISO 9001 and has the American Society of Mechanical Engineers "N" stamp certification. A new addition to Plant 2, designated Plant 7 (scheduled to commence production in the spring of 1997), will be dedicated to the production of metal seated butterfly valves and specialty ball valves.

3. *PLANT 3, Williston, Vermont:*
   Manufactures cast and forged gate, globe and check valves in sizes up to 24". It is certified to ISO 9001, has the American Society of Mechanical Engineers "N" stamp certification and the American Petroleum Institute's 6D certification.

4. *PLANT 4/6, Granby, Québec:*
   Manufactures gate, bellows seal and cryogenic valves as well as ball valves up to 12" The Granby Plant is certified to ISO 9001 and to the American Petroleum Institute's 6D certification.

5. *GEC ALSTHOM—VELAN S.A., Lyon, France:*
   Velan's 50/50 joint venture with GEC Alsthom in France operates a large facility specializing in the manufacture of nuclear valves and cryogenic butterfly valves. It also services 58 Electrite de France nuclear power plants. The Lyon facility is certified to ISO 9001. Part of the product line is manufactured under license from Velan.

6. *VELAN-VALVULAS INDUSTRIAIS LIMITADA, Lisbon, Portugal: (Commodity Values)*
   The Lisbon facility manufactures cast steel valves up to 12". Its sales are targeted primarily at the European, Asian and South American markets. This facility is certified to ISO 9002.

7. *VELAN LTD., Ansan City, Korea: (Commodity Values)*
   The Korean facility manufactures cast steel valves and ball valve components sold to other Velan facilities. This facility is certified to ISO 9002.

8. *VELAN VALVAC MANUFACTURING CO. LTD., Taichung, Taiwan: (Commodity Values)*
   This 50/50 joint venture manufactures ball valves up to 2″ in size, as well as components. This facility is certified to ISO 9002. To increase competitiveness and capacity, a specialized foundry has been built by Velan Valvac and a joint venture partner to supply quality precision castings.

9. *VELAN ENGINEERING CO. LTD., Leicester, U.K.:*
   This facility manufactures bonnetless valves and modifies other Velan products to suit customer requirements. This facility is certified to ISO 9002.

10. *Q.A. PRODUCTS, INC., Oakland, California:*
    This 50/50 joint venture manufactures valves in special materials for difficult applications, utilizing a specialized process which yields high quality defect-free castings. This facility has the ability to ship these specialized valves with short lead times.

11. *SECURAMAX UNIT of Derlan Manufacturing Inc., Toronto, Ontario:*
    Recent 100% acquisition (January 1997) by Velan Inc. The unit makes metal seated ball valves.

Exhibit 5

Velan's Total Quality Program

To supplement the traditional quality assurances and quality control programs, Velan created and implemented in 1990 a Total Quality Management (TQM) Program. The goal of the TQM program is to achieve continuous improvement of all the Company's valves and services to a level which exceeds the expectations of customers.

The following five quality control systems have been implemented to meet the overall product quality goals:

1. *WORLD CLASS VALVE DESIGN*

   All valves are designed to comply with industry specifications and special customer requirements. Velan incorporated exclusive design features in many product lines. The design process is undertaken with input from procurement and production personnel to ensure superiority of design at a competitive price.

2. *QUALITY ASSURANCE*

   Every step from procurement through production and testing complies with written procedures documented in the Company's quality assurance manuals.

3. *QUALITY CONTROL*

   Designated quality control personnel are responsible for monitoring all processes from receipt of material to matching, assembly, testing and packaging.

4. *PRESSURE TESTING*

   Each valve is pressure tested in accordance with industry standards and special customer requirements in order to maintain consistency in the reliability and quality of each valve.

5. *IMPROVEMENT TEAMS*

   Teams are established at point of manufacture to improve quality at source, process control and workmanship and to encourage employee responsibility for quality.

Excerpt from Velan's Prospectus, p. 16

Exhibit 6

Velan Inc.
CONSOLIDATED BALANCE SHEETS
as at May 31, 1996 and 1995
(in thousands of dollars)

ASSETS	1996	1995
Current Assets		
Cash	3,984	6,098
Short-term investments—at cost	23,535	24,920
Accounts receivable	60,211	56,650
Inventories	80,715	62,516
Deposits and prepaid expenses	1,079	1,606
	169,524	151,790
Capital assets	30,957	26,717
Other assets	1,338	646
	201,819	179,153

LIABILITIES	1996	1995
Current liabilities		
Bank loans and advances	11,885	3,817
Accounts payable & accrued liabilities	23,573	28,515
Income and withholding taxes payable	5,441	5,998
Customers' deposits	7,314	9,033
Provision for performance guarantees	8,172	9,032
Current portion of long-term debt	2,838	88
Deferred income taxes	211	283
	59,434	56,766
Long-term debt	2,127	4,102
Other long-term liabilities	1,572	1,500
Deferred income taxes	1,809	1,482
Non-controlling	391	256
	65,333	64,106

SHAREHOLDERS' EQUITY	1996	1995
Capital stock	18,441	13,441
Contributed surplus	1,204	1,204
Retained earnings	113,726	95,617
Foreign ex. translations adjustment	3,115	4,785
	136,486	115,047
	201,819	179,153

Exhibit 7

Velan Inc.

CONSOLIDATED STATEMENTS OF RETAINED EARNINGS

(in thousands of dollars)

	Years ended May 31,				
	1996	**1995**	**1994**	**1993**	**1992**
Balance—Beginning of year	95,617	79,108	69,010	54,693	47,330
Net earnings for the year	28,109	21,509	17,098	20,317	12,363
	123,726	100,617	86,108	75,010	59,693
Dividends—					
Class A shares	8,960	3,960	6,120	5,440	4,760
Series A first preferred shares	1,040	1,040	880	560	240
	10,000	5,000	7,000	6,000	5,000
Balance—End of year	113,726	95,617	79,108	69,010	54,693

Exhibit 8

Velan Inc.

CONSOLIDATED STATEMENTS OF EARNINGS

(in thousands of dollars)

	Years ended May 31,				
	1996	**1995**	**1994**	**1993**	**1992**
Sales	232,589	198,608	174,759	181,794	162,854
Cost of sales	155,239	138,360	120,473	124,515	118,738
Gross profit	77,350	60,248	54,286	57,279	44,116
Expenses (other income)					
Engineering, selling, general & administrative & research	29,197	23,960	21,185	23,179	20,439
Interest—					
Long-term debt	301	150	164	442	562
Other	633	376	620	656	1,510
Amortization	4,894	5,367	4,764	4,360	4,292
Other expenses (income)	(954)	(1,374)	3,552	(122)	(48)
Foreign exchange loss (gain) on consolidation	297	(330)	(1,905)	(1,073)	(863)
	34,368	28,149	28,380	27,442	25,892
Earnings before income taxes & non-controlling interest	42,982	32,099	25,906	29,837	18,224
Provision for (recovery of) income taxes					
Current	14,486	10,521	8,319	9,702	6,032
Deferred	255	(50)	393	(114)	(194)
	14,741	10,471	8,712	9,588	5,838
Earnings before non-controlling interest	28,241	21,628	17,194	20,249	12,386
Non-controlling interest	(132)	(119)	(96)	68	(23)
Net earnings for the year	28,109	21,509	17,098	20,317	12,363

Exhibit 9

Velan Inc.

CONSOLIDATED STATEMENTS OF CHANGES IN FINANCIAL POSITION

(in thousands of dollars)

	Years ended May 31,				
	1996	**1995**	**1994**	**1993**	**1992**
Cash provided from (used for):					
Operations					
Net earnings for the year	28,109	21,509	17,098	20,317	12,363
Items not affecting cash—					
Amortization	4,894	5,367	4,764	4,360	4,292
Deferred income taxes	255	(50)	393	(114)	(194)
Non-controlling interest	132	119	96	(68)	23
Loss (gain) on disposal of capital assets	(13)	546	(9)	65	113
Increase in long-term liability	72	326	686	125	159
Unrealized foreign exchange loss (gain) on long-term debt	(93)	160	200	162	350
	33,356	27,977	23,228	24,847	17,106
Net change in non-cash working capital items	(29,294)	(12,113)	(7,518)	9,101	(8,809)
Change in foreign exchange translation adjustments	(1,670)	2,936	1,098	3	655
	2,392	18,800	16,808	33,951	8,952
Investment					
Additions to capital assets	(9,042)	(5,954)	(6,658)	(5,453)	(7,633)
Proceeds on disposal of capital assets	86	126	45	145	297
Increase in other assets	(108)	(207)	(85)	(18)	(36)
Acquisition of 50%-owned company	(678)	—	—	—	—
	(9,742)	(6,035)	(6,697)	(5,326)	(7,372)
Financing					
Proceeds from issue of Series A first preferred shares	5,000	—	2,000	4,000	4,000
Increase in long-term debt	799	720	—	320	903
Repayment of long-term debt	(19)	(875)	(788)	(5,733)	(771)
Change in non-controlling interest in translation adjustment	3	32	(53)	17	11
Dividends	(10,000)	(5,000)	(7,000)	(6,000)	(5,000)
	(4,217)	(5,123)	(5,841)	(7,396)	(857)
Net increase (decrease) in cash	(11,567)	7,642	4,270	21,229	723
Cash—Beginning of year	27,201	19,559	15,289	(5,940)	(6,663)
Cash—End of year	15,634	27,201	19,559	15,289	(5,940)

Cash represents cash and short-term investments less bank loans and advances.

Vista Windows Inc.

Early on Friday morning April 1, 1994, as he drove to his office in the Palisades Industrial Park, John King wondered how productive the morning's management meeting would be. For some weeks now he and the company's department heads had been trying to develop a strategy that would pull VISTA out of its current sales slump. Until four years ago the company had placed little emphasis on strategic planning—VISTA's products were in such demand that the company could hardly keep up with sales. In 1989 VISTA had expanded its operations by moving into larger premises and offering installation services. Recently, however, the recession in the Canadian economy had curbed construction activities; consequently, demand for architectural aluminum products had fallen dramatically. As president and owner of VISTA, John was concerned about the company's ability to continue growing in an increasingly competitive environment, while positioning itself well within the industry for the coming years.

COMPANY HISTORY

VISTA Windows Inc. was formed in 1976 through the merger of two small companies, Viterie Jean and Viewthrough Inc., each of which manufactured window and door frames predominantly for residential buildings. Finding themselves unable to bid successfully for larger commercial contracts, the two competitors decided to join forces. With the combined technological expertise and greater financial resources, VISTA quickly became one of the main players in the Quebec market for residential frames. Despite its reputation for quality and service, VISTA was nevertheless unable to make inroads into the non-residential market until the mid-eighties. Their first major commercial contract, however, created a snowball effect. Following its participation in the renovation of Montreal's largest and most prestigious shopping complex, VISTA was invited to bid on virtually all of the major construction projects in the province. The gains achieved in the commercial market enabled the company to grow at double digit rates throughout the mid to late eighties. In order to compensate for its reduced presence in the residential market, VISTA began to offer installation service (i.e. installing the glass and frame) as well. This strategic move was

This case was prepared by Dominique Balas, M.B.A. under the direction of Dr. A. B. Ibrahim, Professor of Management at Concordia University, Montreal, as a basis for class discussion, rather than to illustrate either effective or ineffective handling of an administrative situation. This case was supported by a research grant from IBM Corporation, and the Certified General Accountants Association of Canada (CGA).
© Copyright A. B. Ibrahim, 1994.

based on management's desire to reduce their dependence on the commercial/institutional market and be involved in more stages of the construction process.

The decision was one of the first that John King had made in his new capacity as president of VISTA. John, a lawyer by training, had become disillusioned with corporate law after 15 years of practice and had decided to accept his father's offer of taking over the management of the company. As owner of Viewthrough Inc., Ray King had been one of the founders of VISTA. Despite John's lack of experience in the architectural aluminum industry, Ray was adamant that his son become involved in the business. It had always been his dream that the business remain under family control.

INDUSTRY CHARACTERISTICS

The Quebec market for architectural aluminum products can be divided into distinct segments: residential and commercial/institutional; and within the latter group, custom design and standard design. In 1993 the *residential* segment accounted for 58% of industry sales. Of all the segments, it is by far the most competitive with more than 30 manufacturers vying for market share. As the building boom of the early eighties tapered off, competition intensified, forcing companies to slash profit margins and invest heavily in new technologies. As a result, the capital requirements for residential frame manufacturers now exceed those of commercial/institutional manufacturers. By late 1993, however, the increasing number of housing starts signalled an end to the prolonged recession, renewing optimism about the future profitability in this market. The majority of residential manufacturers produce standard-sized windows. A minority fabricate frames according to customer specifications. These are generally for homes in the high end of the housing market. Sales of residential frames are made through small contracting companies or larger housing development firms.

The Quebec *commercial/institutional* market is dominated by a small number of medium-sized companies. While they all manufacture standard-sized frames, only four or five actively compete for the largest custom-design projects (such as a 50-storey office building). The labour, skill, and production capacity required for such projects have effectively narrowed down the competition to the largest manufacturers. For most of these projects—90% of which are either in Montreal or Quebec City—bids are submitted both by Quebec companies and firms from outside the province. The general tendency, however, is to award contracts to local manufacturers. By the same token, Quebec companies have more difficulty bidding successfully for projects outside the province, since the same pattern of "protectionism" prevails elsewhere. The super projects, as they are called in the industry, represent over a year's worth of production and can amount to $25 million of aluminum curtain walls, window and door frames. Contracts are awarded primarily on quality and durability considerations; price is generally of secondary importance.

Until recently, with the same four or five companies consistently bidding for the same contracts, this segment of the industry was characterized by friendly competition. While never officially agreed upon, the manufacturers tended to respect a minimum price level in preparing their bids. This practice, combined with a sufficient number of construction projects, allowed the average profit margin for this segment of the industry to remain at approximately 5%. Although influenced by the same economic conditions as the residential market, the commercial/institutional segment has been less severely affected by the recession. Profit margins on custom design projects dropped to a low of 1.5% in 1990 as compared to the net losses in the residential segment. Since then, average industry profit margins have hovered around 3%. The lower profitability of super projects is partially due to the increased cost consciousness within the industry. Organizations commissioning new buildings are now demanding the same level of quality and durability at a lower cost.

Manufacturers in the commercial/institutional market bid on custom-design projects through one of two channels. Either they arrange to have their products specified by the architectural firm responsible for the design or they join forces with a glass jobber. (Within the construction process glass jobbers are responsible for fitting the glass purchased from glass fabricators and distributors into the frame and installing the final window or door into the building.) Some architects prefer the latter method since the entire window (frame and glass) is provided by one party, which reduces their own coordination requirements. Once architects are satisfied with the quality of a manufacturer's products, they tend to be very loyal and specify the same company in most of their design work. A proven track record is of crucial concern to architects, since their reputation is harmed by specified products that fail to meet durability and quality standards over time.

For small-scale construction and renovation projects, less expensive standard-sized door and window frames are generally used. Manufacturers in this market carry an inventory of frames in various colours, styles, and grades of quality, which are shipped on demand to the customer. Orders originate directly from the contractor or construction company; few manufacturers are "specked-in" by an architect. The decision to buy from one manufacturer rather than another is predominantly based on price considerations. While quality is important—as most manufacturers offer the same range of products—brand name is not as significant. Discount pricing is a commonly employed competitive practice within the industry. Gross margins are lower and manufacturers spend considerable sums on trade advertising to set themselves apart. Overall, the competition for market share is substantially stiffer than in the custom-design segment. Companies specializing only in standard frames possess a distinct advantage over those that also manufacture special order frames. Manufacturers in this second category frequently run out of stock of standard frames while working on custom-design products.

PRODUCTION

By 1990, VISTA manufactured architectural aluminum products principally for commercial and institutional buildings. In 1993 residential sales accounted for only 10% of VISTA's revenue (Exhibit 1). Originally, the founders had intended to serve both market segments; but the success of VISTA's curtain walls meant that an increasing percentage of sales was generated in the commercial/institutional market—more specifically in the custom-design market. The changing taste—to sleek and modern exteriors—in commercial and institutional design included a heavy emphasis on aluminum curtain walls (in Montreal the exterior of both the prestigious Maison Alcan and IBM tower are covered with aluminum curtain walls). VISTA is virtually the only company in Quebec that has mastered the craft of making flawless curtain walls.

Manufacturing of all custom-design and standard products takes place at the company's factory in the Palisades Industrial Park just east of Montreal. The move to these new premises raised VISTA's production capacity from $21 million to $30 million. At the time the decision was made to purchase the new building, John was confident that VISTA would reach such a sales level in the not-too-distant future. The process of forming and shaping the aluminum extrusions is labour-intensive and requires a considerable amount of space to house both the sheets of aluminum and the finished products. On average, one third of the square footage is needed for finished goods and raw materials inventory. This space requirement can grow substantially during periods when VISTA processes curtain walls for special construction projects. In order to create space, the production manager has often let inventory levels of standard frames fall below the 10% to 15% level required to adequately service customers. Raw materials are purchased from aluminum manufacturers at going market rates. At times—although this occurs infrequently—VISTA is able to obtain a small price reduction for volume purchases.

In 1989, recognizing an opportunity to become involved in more aspects of the construction process and to accelerate the company's growth, John King decided to expand VISTA's product mix to include the installation of finished windows and doors (frame and glass). Previously, VISTA had sold its frames to glass jobbers; these former customers are now its competitors. Providing the installation service meant that VISTA had to carry additional raw materials inventory (glass) and hire 15 workers trained in the cutting, treating, and installation of glass (these workers are not part of the factory union). The first few years of providing installations had been rough. The plant was not equipped to handle the storage of large quantities of fragile glass. To John it seemed that the unionized workers, angered at the presence of non-unionized workers, almost went out of their way to drop and break sheets of glass. Furthermore, as a result of customer complaints VISTA frequently had to re-install windows and doors that had not been sealed properly.

Glass jobbers were equally opposed to VISTA's entering their market. They constituted a strong, tightly-knit group within the glass industry. Many had increased their presence in the market and gained economies of scale in production by merging with or acquiring glass manufacturers; the six largest glass jobbers accounted for 86% of the market. Glass jobbers were willing to cut prices in order to protect market share. In 1993 industry sales amounted to $257. million with gross margin rate of 18.5%.

HUMAN RESOURCES AND ORGANIZATIONAL STRUCTURE

VISTA's management team consists of John King, the three department heads (production, finance and design), and the most senior sales representative (see Exhibit 2 for organizational chart). The group meets weekly to discuss operating issues or problems of concern. John, however, interacts on a daily, sometimes hourly, basis with each of his immediate subordinates. He likes to be informed of all current matters and decisions being made within the organization. With only three people reporting directly to him, John has often commented that the organizational structure is ideal for such frequent interaction. The only change to the structure in the past 14 years was the elimination of the position of general manager. John King assumed the responsibilities of both founders (President and General Manager) on his arrival at the company. Very few members of the original management team still remain from the early days of VISTA's operation. In fact, despite salaries that are above industry average, turnover within management has been alarmingly high. This is especially true of the production department. Guy Lavoie is the fourth production manager to be hired in six years.

Employee loyalty within the design department is considerably stronger. Within this division five design engineers work on a full-time basis developing designs predominantly for special construction projects. The standard-sized window and door frames are adjusted only sporadically to reflect changing tastes and trends within the industry. The designers work in a separate area of the building under the supervision of the design director Monique Chester. John King personally hired each of the designers from the best Canadian universities. John was often heard boasting that he liked to surround himself with the "best and the brightest." This had, on numerous occasions, caused some conflict with the director of human resources, Gail Richards. Although Gail was responsible for the recruitment and hiring of all personnel, John, without Gail's knowledge, often approached talented designers at competing companies about employment at VISTA.

VISTA employs 250 unionized workers in its plant. Currently, management-labour relations are amicable but considerable tension has strained them in the past. Through persistent efforts on the part of John King and union representative Peter Shaw, a cooperative spirit was finally achieved in the late eighties. As part of its reconciliation with the union, VISTA agreed to increase workers' benefits and paid sick days. Although these measures raised overhead rates considerably, VISTA's management team believed it to be the only alternative available to fend off recruitment efforts by the National Union. The National is considered by industry insiders to be substantially less flexible and less favourably inclined towards management. VISTA's production manager, Guy Lavoie, had noticed on several occasions that representatives from the National union had invited VISTA's employees to their meetings.

MARKETING AND SALES

For the first 14 years, VISTA engaged in very few advertising and promotional activities. In the residential market the company had relied primarily on word-of-mouth promotion and good business relations with numerous contractors, established during the time that VISTA was still Viterie Jean and Viewthrough Inc. The company's difficulty in entering the commercial/institutional market was largely the result of the founder's reluctance to advertise.

Viterie Jean and Viewthrough Inc. had both been very successful in the residential market without the use of costly advertising or promotion. The founders were confident that they could replicate this success using the same sales strategy in the commercial/institutional market—and to a large extent they were able to do so. Through a contractor, a close business friend who had successfully made the transition from the residential to commercial market, VISTA obtained its first commercial contracts. The company's technical expertise and skill in crafting architectural aluminum products quickly earned VISTA a reputation for high quality and durability. During this period, promotional efforts consisted of a sales catalogue and brochure depicting the various construction projects to which VISTA had supplied either frames or curtain walls. Yet even this effort had been in response to pressure from construction companies who wanted to be provided with promotional material.

In 1990, when John King replaced the original founders as President and CEO, the company adopted a slightly more aggressive sales strategy. VISTA's brochure was updated to give it a more sophisticated and polished look. VISTA's sales representatives also began to attend trade shows. But since VISTA's products and services were in sufficient demand, John felt it was unnecessary to augment the sales effort any further. The three in-house sales representatives worked closely with the design engineers to develop bids for construction projects. Attention to the custom-design market occurred at the expense of the standard frame market. The sales representatives frequently complained (and still complain) that all they could do about these products was to process the orders that were either faxed or phoned in. They were sure that, given more time and resources, the export portion of VISTA's sales could be expanded. About 27% of the orders for standard frames originated from other provinces, in particular, Ontario and the Maritimes. In the past VISTA's bids for super projects were often solicited from the architects. Increasingly, however, VISTA was finding out about planned construction projects through competitors and industry "talk." As price became a more important consideration, architects liked to compare the bids of as many qualified manufacturers as possible.

One of the advantages VISTA sought in providing full installation services was to differentiate itself from its competitors. Consequently, VISTA's sales representative had been emphasizing the company's new service to its customers. In doing so, John and the sales representatives were confident that they could continue charging a price premium for their frames. None of the other competitors consistently offered such a service. Some had done so for specific projects but the trend was to leave this part of the process to glass jobbers.

FINANCES

When John took over VISTA in 1988, the company benefited from a solid financial position. Ray King and Yves Turcotte were cautious business men who did not enjoy unnecessary financial risk. Consequently they had financed VISTA's growth predominantly through available capital (retained earnings and personal investments) and with a minimum of outside debt. A strict credit policy kept receivables below the standard industry terms of 45 days. Similarly, VISTA followed a policy of paying suppliers within the established terms. By the mid-eighties, exceptional growth made it more difficult to finance internally and collect receivables on time. In 1989 John took out a long-term loan to finance the acquisition of land and building at the Palisades Industrial Park. The proceeds from the company's old building paid for part of the acquisition but additional funds were needed (see Exhibits 3 & 4 for financial statements). John was certain that with the larger premises the company would be in a better position to meet the aggressive growth objectives he had established for VISTA. John saw himself as the CEO of one of Quebec's larger companies by the end of the decade.

All of VISTA's financial and accounting matters are handled by the company's controller. Scott Ember had been an associate of John's at Drucker & Drucker law offices and he joined VISTA in 1991 (Scott Ember is a tax attorney by training). Since his arrival at the company Scott had implemented a management information system to strengthen and control activities in marketing, production and finance. Although the system was also meant to update the company's accounting system, Scott lacked the support staff to implement further changes.

DECISIONS ABOUT THE FUTURE

By 1994, VISTA had reached a crucial point in its life cycle. John recognized that the transition and growth from being a small manufacturer in the residential market to becoming one of the largest manufacturers in the commercial/institutional market was due both to hard work and "being in the right place at the right time." While VISTA was not in an immediate crisis situation, the time had come to address key strategic and operating issues to avoid finding itself in such a position. The main concern of VISTA's management team was which market to serve. John wondered whether VISTA should pull out of the residential market completely and devote all of the company's resources to the commercial/institutional market. Even within this latter product category, he was unsure how to balance custom-design, standard frames, and service installations. John hoped that these issues would finally be resolved this morning thus enabling the management team to outline a concrete strategy plan for VISTA.

Exhibit 1. Sales/Gross Margin by Product Line (in 000's).

	1990	1991	1992	1993
Residential	$3,259	$3,858	$3,004	$2,682
Percent of Total Revenue	16.00%	15.40%	11.00%	10.45%
Gross Margin	$196	$212	$210	$177
Percent Gross Margin	6.00%	5.50%	7.00%	6.60%
Commercial				
Standard Frames	$6,416	$7,892	$8,738	$7,701
Percent of Total Revenue	31.50%	31.50%	32.00%	30.00%
Gross Margin	$1,636	$1,933	$2,185	$1,848
Percent Gross Margin	25.50%	24.50%	25.00%	24.00%
Custom-Design	$10,082	$11,549	$11,469	$9,895
Percent of Total Revenue	49.50%	46.10%	42.00%	38.55%
Gross Margin	$4,134	$4,389	$3,785	$2,969
Percent Gross Margin	41.00%	38.00%	33.00%	30.00%
Service	$611	$1,754	$4,096	$5,390
Percent of Total Revenue	3.00%	7.00%	15.00%	21.00%
Gross Margin	($9)	$35	$123	$270
Percent Gross Margin	−1.50%	2.00%	3.00%	5.00%
Total	$20,368	$25,053	$27,308	$25,669
Percent of Total Revenue	100.00%	100.00%	100.00%	100.00%
Gross Margin	$5,956	$6,570	$6,303	$5,263
Percent Gross Margin	29.24%	26.22%	23.08%	20.50%

Exhibit 2. Organizational Chart 1993 Vista Windows Inc.

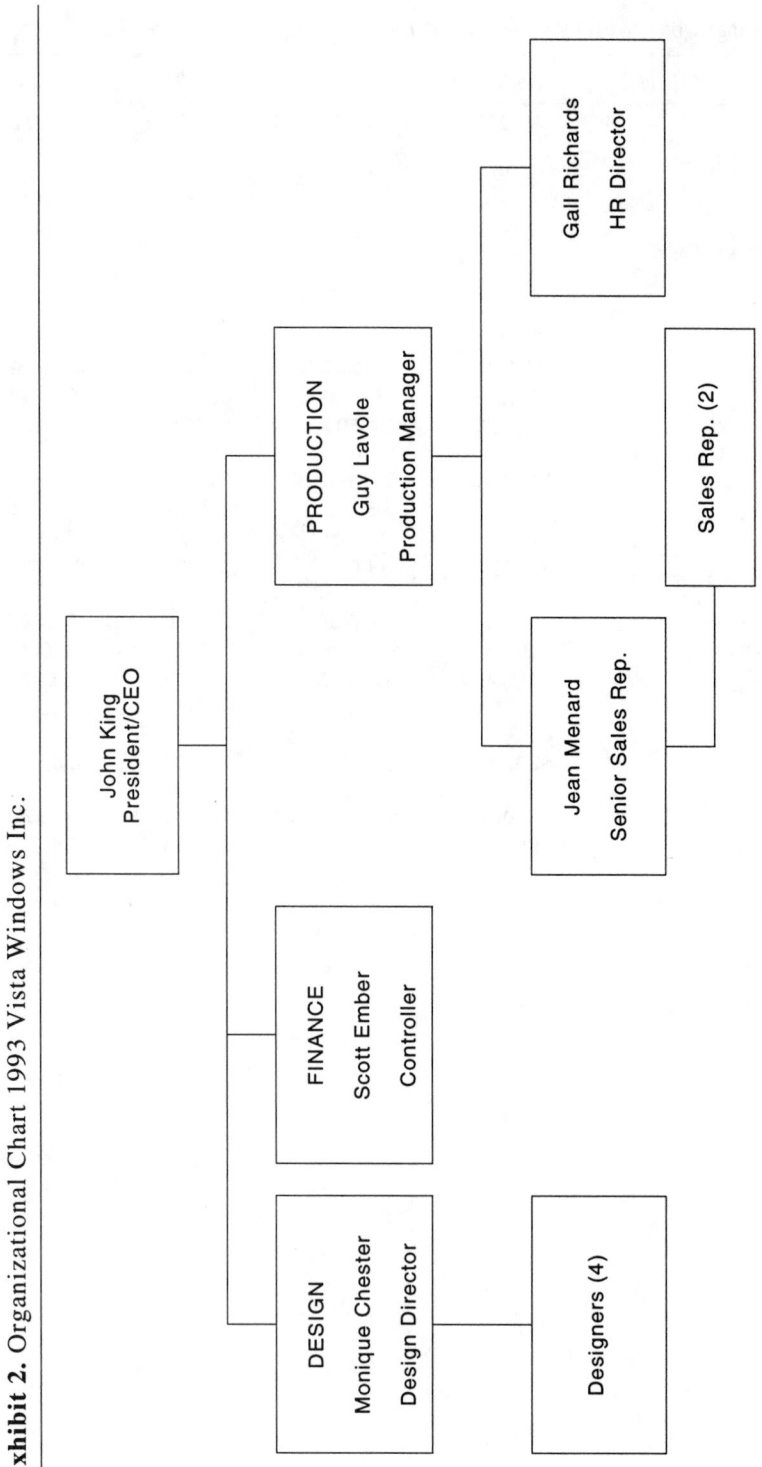

Exhibit 3. Vista Windows Inc. Operating Performance 1991–1993 (in 000s).

	1991	1992	1993
Sales	25,053	27,308	25,669
Cost of Sales	18,483	21,005	20,406
Gross Margin	6,570	6,303	5,263
Selling & Administrative	3,608	3,605	3,594
Shipping Expenses	529	528	623
Advertising	75	109	128
Depreciation	75	73	75
Interest Expense	275	315	374
Income before Tax	2,008	1,672	469
Income Tax	442	368	103
Net Income	$1,566	$1,304	$366

Exhibit 4. Vista Windows Inc. Balance Sheet 1991–1993 (in 000s).

Assets	1991	1992	1993
Current Assets			
Cash	501	410	257
Account Receivable	4,890	5,281	5,545
Inventory			
Raw Materials	1,894	2,310	2,002
Finished Goods	1,613	2,605	3,132
Pre-Paid Expenses	489	512	356
Miscellaneous	285	102	180
Total Current Assets	9,672	11,220	11,472
Property, Plant & Equipment at Cost			
Land	900	1,000	1,000
Building & Improvements	5,237	4,975	4,906
Furniture, Fixture & Equipment	1,576	1,543	1,467
	7,713	7,518	7,373
less: accumulated depreciation	1,989	2,098	2,173
	5,724	5,420	5,200
Total Assets	$15,396	$16,640	$16,672
Liabilities & Owner's Equity			
Current Liabilities			
Accounts Payable	4,570	4,389	4,670
Accrued Expenses	1,769	2,651	2,132
Total Current Liabilities	6,339	7,040	6,802
Long-term Debt	3,670	4,201	4,987
Total Liabilities	10,009	11,241	11,789
Stockholder's Equity	3,550	3,550	3,550
Retained Earnings	1,837	1,849	1,333
Total Liabilities & Shareholder's Equity	$15,396	$16,640	$16,672

CASE 12

Quebecor Inc.

It was a cool morning on November 12, 1993 and as Beethoven's third movement of the Fifth Symphony played in the background, Mr. Pierre Peladeau, President and CEO of Quebecor Inc., took some time off to reflect upon the performance of the company. Quebecor, which is in the communications business, had achieved new financial milestones for the fiscal year ended December 31, 1992. As a result, shareholders had seen dividend increases in the last quarter of 1992 and the first quarter of 1993.

This was an exceptional performance, more so given that the entire printing industry was struggling in general. He also felt happy because Quebecor had started on the path towards becoming a global company through the acquisition of a printing company in France. "You know, Pierre, we are changing the face of printing," said to him by a business colleague in Paris, still resonated in his mind.

However, his thoughts now were turned more towards the future, specifically on how Quebecor should meet the challenges of the next decade. The business environment in the printing and publishing industry was changing dramatically. There were new technologies available not only in the printing industry, but also in the information field. The printing industry in North America was contracting into fewer players; and there were new concerns that could affect the industry, such as environmental issues, the proliferation of digital technology, and the arrival of the information superhighway.

Also, the company was involved in a labour-management confrontation with the workers at the daily tabloid "*Le Journal de Montreal*" over salary freezes and job cuts that needed to be made in order to modernize the operations of the paper as well as to increase competitiveness. As a result, management had to impose a lockout on the striking employees.

In addition, Pierre was already 68 years old and he had wanted to retire at 70. But he felt that neither of his two sons, Erik nor Pierre-Karl, were yet ready to succeed him. Of course, as a very successful entrepreneur who has been in business for more than four decades, he was a bit reluctant to let go of his company, especially at this time.

This case was written by Jose Lam, M.B.A. under the direction of Professor A. B. Ibrahim as a basis for class discussion rather than to illustrate effective or ineffective handling of an administrative situation. This case was supported by a research grant from Shell Corporation and The Certified General Accountants Association of Canada (CGA). © Dr. A. B. Ibrahim, 1995.

HISTORY

In 1950, Pierre Peladeau, who had graduated with a law degree and a Masters in philosophy degree from McGill University, borrowed $1,500 from his mother and bought a small Montreal weekly newspaper. He continued to buy small weeklies as well as printing companies throughout the next two decades. He has always had a good sense of buying small printing or publishing companies at bargain prices and then turning them around into profitable enterprises. By the end of 1992, Peladeau's publishing and printing empire generated $2.5 billion in revenue.

As an entrepreneur, Peladeau possesses many of the qualities necessary for success. He has been labelled as a genius, a workaholic and a tyrant. He is also a very outspoken person and at times highly controversial. Nonetheless, he is admired and respected by friends and feared by enemies.

Quebecor, which was incorporated in 1965, became a public company in 1972. During the 1960s and 1970s, the company focused its strategy on expanding the Quebec market. In the late 1970s, the company expanding into the Ontario market by buying printing plants, as well as small companies in the communications field such as music publishing and photo finishing. In 1979, Quebecor Group Inc. was created and all subsidiaries became divisions of this new company.

In the early 1980s, Quebecor continued its diversification strategy by acquiring a small share in First Choice Canadian Communications Corporation, a Pay-TV enterprise. Meanwhile, the company continued to expand into other markets such as Manitoba and British Columbia and to diversify into other product lines such as photographic paper, books, telephone directories, retail catalogues, and larger commercial newspapers. In 1985, Quebecor America Inc. (later renamed Quebecor Printing USA Holdings), a wholly owned subsidiary, was formed to acquire a publishing company in New Jersey and to explore other markets in the U.S.

In the mid-1980s, Mr. Peladeau met and became friends with Robert Maxwell, the British publishing magnate. In 1987, Peladeau and Maxwell joined forces and acquired 55% share in Donohue Inc., a company in the forestry and pulp and paper sector. The year 1987 was a turning point for Quebecor, as the company continued to acquire more publishing and printing companies in Canada and the U.S. Although small radio stations and advertising agencies were also added to Quebecor's business portfolio the company was mainly concentrating its resources on the core business of printing, by continuing to use a dual strategy of geographic and product expansion.

By 1988 Quebecor was ranked the number one printer in Canada and had started to explore international markets. The acquisition of BCE Publitech in 1988, the largest transaction in Canadian history, added banknotes to the company's repertoire of printing products. In late 1989, Quebecor made news again by purchasing from Maxwell fourteen Graphic Holding Enterprises printing facilities in the U.S., the largest acquisition in printing history. This move afforded Quebecor the economies of scale necessary to compete in the tough U.S. market and signalled Quebecor's intentions to become a major player in the American printing market.

During the early 1990s, Quebecor continued its predator strategy by buying up more companies in the printing, publishing and distribution business. The company restructured itself into three subsidiaries: Quebecor Group Inc., Quebecor Printing Inc., and Mircor Inc. (the majority shareholder of Donohue Inc.,). Exhibit 1 provides a simplified organization chart for Quebecor. The rest of the case will focus on Quebecor printing and the printing industry.

QUEBECOR PRINTING INC.: WE PRINT NORTH AMERICA

Mission: Quebecor Printing Inc. is a customer-driven printer, determined to be a leader in each of its market segments. The company is committed to optimizing the contribution of people, technology and other resources to meet and exceed customer expectations.

Quebecor Printing, a diversified commercial printer, has made a strategic commitment towards print as a medium of communication. The management's vision is for Quebecor Printing to lead the printing industry into the 21st century.

Quebecor Printing is the flagship company of Quebecor Inc. It was formed in late 1989 and became a public company in 1992. It operates 65 printing facilities with over 400 presses in Canada, United States and Mexico and employs about 12,000 people. Quebecor Printing is now considered the largest commercial printer in Canada and the second largest in North America.

In 1992, Quebecor Printing purchased Graficas Monte Alban of Mexico, a large publisher of Spanish books serving the large Latin American market. This was a strategic acquisition done in anticipation to the signing of the North American Free Trade Agreement (NAFTA). This vision to become a global player in the printing industry signalled a major strategic move. In July 1993, the company announced its intention to buy 70% interest in Groupe Fecomme, which operates three printing plants in France. This news came after the company had failed in its bid to acquire a printing plant in the Southwest of France that was owned by Maxwell Communication Corp. PLC (Britain).

Geographic expansion was not only limited to France; in August of 1993, Quebecor Printing signed a shareholders' agreement to set-up a joint-venture with Tej Bhandu Group, a directory publisher in New Delhi (India). Tej Quebecor Printing would publish all the telephone directories for India's major cities, such as Bombay, Madras, New Delhi and others.

For Mr. Peladeau, acquiring other printers was the best way to expand his business. Strategic acquisitions allowed Quebecor to enter niche markets or to expand operations geographically, without investing large amounts of capital to start printing facilities from the beginning. Also, he felt that Quebecor could do a better management job that leverages the resources found in a large company. This in turn would result in better services for customers, who were becoming more demanding in an increasingly more complex industry.

Financial Performance

Quebecor Printing contributed $1.44 billion to Quebecor's $2.53 billion in consolidated sales revenue in 1992. Exhibit 2 shows the financial statements for 1990–1992. Profit margin for the company has grown from 9.5% in 1988 to 14% in 1992. Net income in 1992 was $54.5 million compared to $33.2 million in 1991 and $21.6 million in 1990. In addition to the increase in operating profit margins, sales revenues have steadily increased at a time when the entire printing industry in North America was shrinking. Annual sales in 1988 were $405 million compared to the $1.44 billion mark achieved in 1992. About 62% of the revenues and operating profit were generated in the United States.

At the beginning of 1993, Quebecor Printing had approximately $235 million of unused long-term revolving bank credits available. During the spring and summer, the company utilized this available credit to finance the acquisitions of Haughton Graphics Inc. (Toronto), Photo engravers and Electrotypers Ltd. (Toronto), and three printing facilities from Arcata Corporation (U.S.).

Photo Engravers and Electrotypers Ltd. (renamed Quebecor Printing PE&E) is a large printer of catalogues (such as the Sears catalogue) and advertising supplements and is probably the only rotogravure printer remaining in Canada. On the other hand, the acquisition of Arcata's printing facilities, with the option to buy the remaining publishing facilities in the next three years, would strategically position Quebecor Printing as the second largest manufacturer of books in North America. It is estimated that by the end of 1993, Quebecor Printing would still have about $75 million of unused long-term revolving bank credit available.

Cash flow derived from operations has also been increasing steadily. In 1992, the figure was $156.2 million compared to $118.2 million in 1991 and $94.5 million in 1990. Some of this cash flow is used to finance business acquisitions (for example, $71 million was used in 1992); however, a large percentage has been reserved for capital expenditures. For example, in 1992 capital expenditures were $62.1 million, up from $59.8 million in 1991 and 1990 respectively. It is expected that for 1993 capital expenditures will be about $85 million.

The Organization

The impressive financial results achieved over the past three years can be attributed to the management team of Mr. Jean Neveu, Chairman and CEO, and Mr. Charles G. Cavell, President and Chief Operating Officer (COO) of Quebecor Printing. To strengthen this team, Erik Peladeau (Peladeau's son) was promoted to Senior Vice-President and assistant to the President in December 1992.

Growth and opportunity are the two keywords that describe the shaping of Quebecor Printing. The company has grown, just as its parent company did, through strategic acquisitions and has taken advantage of the opportunities available in different niche markets to mould the company into a whole that is stronger than the sum of its parts. Exhibit 3 summarizes the vision and strategic plan developed by top management in 1989.

The company's objective so far has been to become the market leader in multiple niches, rather than being number one in the industry. Through acquisitions the company has diversified into the broadest product line of any printer in North America. It offers gravure, web offset and sheetfed printing capacity.

The type of products include the printing of inserts, circulars, magazines, catalogues, books, directories, cheques, bonds, banknotes, annual reports, direct-mail promotions, newspapers and custom-made items from calendars to posters. In addition to products, the company also provides services ranging from mailing and distribution to typesetting and prepress.

As of the end of 1992, the printing of inserts and circulars made up 34.8% of the company's total sales revenues. The printing of magazines, catalogues and books contributed 25.8%, 10.8%, and 6.3%, respectively, of the total revenues. Also, the printing of cheques, bonds and banknotes represented 6.2% of revenues, while specialty products contributed a share of 5.5%. Although the company started as a printer of newspapers, the contribution to revenues from this business sector accounts for only 1.3%. Related services contributed 2.7% of revenues.

In becoming a market driven organization, Quebecor Printing also seeks to develop strong, long-term relationships with suppliers and customers. For example, the company has secured long-term contracts (in excess of five years) with such clients as Sears, L. L. Bean, Parade (widest read magazine found in Sunday newspapers in the U.S.), Time Inc., Time Canada Ltd., Reader's Digest (Canada), Tele-Direct (Publications) Inc., B. C. Tel, and others (see Exhibit 4 for a list of major clients and circulation figures). According to Mr. Peladeau, the key to succeed in the printing industry is the ability to provide and deliver superior service at the lowest prices.

Technology and People

In an effort to keep up with modern technology, Quebecor Printing has been investing in new printing and manufacturing machinery that can improve productivity and add value to its products. However, despite the advantages of the new technology, the company often faces resistance to change from its employees.

For example, the printing of the *Journal de Montreal*, the largest French daily in North America is a sample case. The paper still relies on labour-intensive practices, such as cutting and pasting columns on the master pages, while other newspapers, such as the *Globe & Mail*, utilize computers to set-up and lay-out the pages, as well as satellite transmission to print issues across the country. As a result, the introduction of new technology and the need to streamline operations in order to remain competitive has created labour-management problems that threaten the good working relationship that has existed between management and labour.

Notwithstanding the labour problems, Quebecor Printing is committed to investing in employee training. There has been a move to empower employees with more responsibilities and to promote a spirit of innovation and entrepreneurship among the employees. The goal is to have a workforce that can adapt to new technologies, market demands, and changes in the environment.

In 1992, Quebecor Printing established two strategic services: Quebecor Imaging Services (QIS), to research, develop and implement new state-of-the-art electronic prepress and desktop publishing technology; and Quebecor Destination Services (QDS) to integrate customer delivery services with the company's mail analysis system in order to provide a more cost effective and faster shipping and delivery of products.

THE PRINTING INDUSTRY

Economic and Consumer Trends

As of 1992, the commercial printing industry in North America is estimated to be worth about US$55 billion, down from the estimated US$64 billion in 1991. R. R. Donnelley & Sons is the industry leader with an estimated market share of about 7.6%. Quebecor Printing is a distant second with an estimated market share of about 2.6%.

The printing industry enjoyed good growth during the 1980s. The growth rate of the industry was 3.6% compared to the 3% average growth of GNP in the 1980s. It is expected that for the 1990s the real growth rate for the printing industry will be about 2.8%, while economic growth will average about 2.5%.

In terms of industry output, 1993 will be relatively flat, while a small increase of 1.2% is predicted for 1994. In addition, employment in the industry will grow by about 24,000 jobs in 1994, to an average of 1.53 million people. It is also expected that paper costs will go up in 1994 and that operating costs will also increase. In an effort to cut costs, large printers have started to shift operations and manufacturing from the big cities to the rural areas.

The North American printing industry, which is highly fragmented, has been consolidating into fewer and larger players. It is estimated that there are over 40,000 printers in North America. Medium- and small-sized printers, unable to compete, have gone into bankruptcy or have been bought by the larger printers. It is expected that this trend of mergers and acquisitions will continue in the future. Exhibit 5 lists the top ten commercial printers in North America, in terms of revenue generated. In Canada, the top five printers control about 35% of the commercial printing market; while in the United States, the top ten printers control about 19% of the market.

The economic recession of the early 1990s has also affected the entire industry as well. Most printers are operating below capacity as clients reduce their orders for printed material. As competition intensifies, printers will need to vertically integrate operations by offering other services such as prepress and postpress functions, as well as distribution and management services. Other printers will be forced to develop partnerships and joint-ventures in order to survive.

Institutional, industrial and retail customers are not only demanding better quality products at the cheapest prices, but are also asking for faster delivery and distribution of the products. Technology will play a major role in influencing future customers, as well as their expectations. For instance, one major trend in the consumer market is the move towards "personalization" of direct mail; that is, magazines or catalogues which not only carry the name and address of the person, but also reflect his/her buying habits and lifestyles. This customization can be done via satellite transmission, flexible printing and selective binding of large volumes of an issue that can have a different mix of editorial, articles and advertising. Selective binding also represents a more focused, more personalized and more effective communication tool that is better targeted to the end reader.

In addition, printers will have to focus their attention towards better customer satisfaction and customer needs. The ability to develop long-term close working relationships with customers will be a key criterion. In order to achieve this, printers will need to not only modernize operations, but also ensure that it has a well-trained flexible workforce that can adapt to sudden changes in the business environment.

According to market reports, it is predicted that for 1994 the printing of financial and legal products will continue to grow, while books will remain about the same as in 1993. Another trend observed is the continuing decline in newspaper circulation and the increase in periodical circulation. Increased competition will also start from on-line magazines and publications that are sent to businesses and homes via the digital information superhighway. Other new products in the market are information packaged in CD-ROM or available through multimedia, on-line information services and databases, or cable television.

Historically, commercial printers were locally based. The commercial printing industry has been typically characterized by regional geographic scope. These markets are segmented into North America, South America, Europe and Asia. With the recent trend towards globalization, the commercial printing industry in the future may likely serve one single (global) market made up of many niches, segmented according to customers' needs.

Technological Trends

In general, the printing industry is being shaped by not only economies of scale in production and distribution, but also advances in electronic and digital technology. This industry, which used to be primarily characterized as highly labour intensive, is now becoming more capital intensive.

From a technological perspective, not much has changed in the printing industry since Gutenberg invented the movable printing press in the year 1440. The printing of books required three main elements: paper, water and ink. Typesetting was done by hand, typically cut and paste the master pages. In the early years of printing, designs were done by hand and transferred onto printing plates. Later, with the invention of film photography, pictures were developed and transferred to master plates.

Advances in information technology in the last twenty years (that is, desktop publishing, electronic and digital presses, multimedia and the information superhighway) are radically changing the structure of the printing industry. For example, high-speed data communication networks in combination with telecommunications and satellite systems enable the transmission of large volumes of files to simultaneous printers in multiple locations. The advantage of this type of technology is that it allows printers to incorporate both economies of scale and economies of scope in their operations.

The proliferation of automated presses has cut down the number of workers required in sheet-fed printing and manufacturing, while at the same time increasing productivity. Selective binding equipment enables printers to print different versions of a catalogue or magazine in a single bindery run.

Time-consuming tasks that had to be done manually during the prepress stages can now be done faster and better through desktop publishing. Computer-aided art and design is changing the relationship between printers and graphic artists, as commercial printers try to adapt to the new digital imaging printing technologies. For example, the invention of the digital scanner will lead the way into colour electronic prepress systems. In addition, new ink-jet imaging technology enables printers to print customized and personalized messages on the magazines, catalogues or advertising material.

Another new technology that may change the commercial printing market is computer-to-plate (CTP) prepress that can be applied to the printing of high quality colour catalogues, magazines and brochures. For the moment, the disadvantage of this technology is that capital investments are required to install the systems and there is uncertainty as to whether this is the right technology. Furthermore, printers are not sure whether direct-to-plate or direct-to-press will become the key technology of the future in the printing business.

The greatest challenge facing the printing industry may be in dealing with the arrival of the information superhighway. The impact of this threat has not been fully assessed, given that most printers and customers still do not understand the technology. Nonetheless, this new technology will create not only new forms of competition, but also new opportunities. Information will flow and reach businesses and homes directly, thus bypassing the traditional printed products. For example, in France telephone directories can be accessed on-line and there are projects underway to provide electronic books to libraries on-line or via electronic mail (e-mail).

It is predicted that major structural changes will occur in the printing industry, as printers redefine their business by including alternative outputs such as desktop publishing, fax publishing, on demand-printing, CD-ROM and internet services. However, there will still be a need for printed products in the future. In fact, the demand for more electronic communications products has created a derived demand for more printed products such as catalogues, manuals and packaging materials.

Environmental Concerns

The environmental or "green" movement has had an impact on the evolution of this industry. The popularity of recycling newspapers and magazines has forced printers to search for environmentally-friendly ink that will not interfere with recycling processes. For example, in the United States, the Environmental Protection Agency (EPA) has tried, unsuccessfully, to bring forth new regulations that would have forced newspaper printers to search for alternatives to oil-based inks and reduce the use of petroleum-based solvents.

Gravure printers are concerned that they may be legislated out of business, because the petroleum-based ink used in the printing process creates environmental hazards. However, there are new technologies coming into the market which would partially reduce environmental pollution. One is the development of waterless printing which reduces the use of chemicals.

Also, the developed countries seem to be moving towards a "paperless" society, as evidenced by regulatory developments in Germany to restrict and reduce the volume of printed materials. The big environmental issues of the 1990s point towards reducing reusing and recycling materials.

Competition

There are a number of major players in the printing industry (see Exhibit 5). Quebecor Printing's main competitors are:

R. R. Donnelley & Sons Co.

The industry and world leader is R. R. Donnelley & Sons Co., which had revenues of $4.1 billion in 1992. This company has been actively acquiring small and medium sized competitors. The company has over 32,000 employees worldwide and 140 plants in the U.S. and abroad (Western and Eastern Europe, Pacific Rim and Far East). The company considers itself to be in the business of delivering information from publishers to consumers.

The main product lines are books, magazines, mail production, catalogues, computer documentation, directories and financial documentation. R. R. Donnelley & Sons is strong in the printing of financial documents. According to Jonathan Ward, President of R. R. Donnelley Financial, "Our plan from the beginning was either to be the industry leader or to get out of the business . . . It's what we do in all the markets we serve."

"The future of the printing industry is not on paper," says Mr. John R. Walter, CEO of the company. Since the early 1990s, the company has invested heavily in new technologies; for example, satellite networks that can print a stock offering simultaneously in different parts of the world, or a whole service division that can package catalogues on computer disks. Also, the company is betting that a new technological process called computer-to-plate (CTP) will be the dominant technology in commercial printing. The advantages of this new technology are that it not only lays a digital architecture foundation for future commercial printing, but it also creates the potential to transfer this technology to other systems throughout the company. By doing so, Walter hopes that R. R. Donnelley & Sons will continue to lead the industry through technological innovations.

Under the direction of Mr. Walter, R. R. Donnelley & Sons has not only maintained, but also increased market share in the ink-and-paper businesses. Nonetheless, since he took over the company in 1989, Walter has redefined the corporate mission of the company, shifting it from the core printing business into flexible electronic media such as multimedia, trade publishing and database management (the company has started to print certain catalogues and other products in CD-ROM). In addition, R. R. Donnelley & Sons is expanding globally through international ventures in Europe (U.K., Ireland, Scotland, Spain, France), Latin America (Mexico) and Asia (Singapore, Hong Kong).

Banta Corp.

In a span of three years, from 1989 to 1992, Banta Corp. jumped from being the 14th largest commercial printer in North America to the number three position. This company had sales revenue of $637 million in 1992. It operates at least 21 plants in the U.S. and has over 4,000 employees. Product lines include magazines, books, catalogues, direct mail, and labels.

Wallace Computer Services Inc.

Wallace Computer Services Inc. is mainly involved in business forms, labels, office products and commercial printing. It has about 26 plants and a workforce of 2,600 employees. In 1992, it reported $511 million in sales revenues. It ranks number 4 in North America.

Groupe Trans-Continental Inc. (GTC)

GTC is Quebecor's closest competitor in Canada, in terms of sales revenue. The company is involved in the printing, publishing and distribution business. Consolidated revenues in 1992 were $544.6 million, of which $469.4 million were generated from commercial printing. Also, there has been a move to expand the company through acquisitions in different geographic markets and product lines.

Maclean Hunter Ltd.

Maclean Hunter is only the third Canadian company to be listed in the top ten in North America. Maclean Hunter, with a workforce of over 12,000 employees, describes itself as a communications company that is involved in the publication and commercial printing of magazines and newspapers, and in broadcasting cable television and radio. In 1992, the company had revenues of $1.6 billion; however, revenues were mainly generated from cable T.V. and broadcasting operations.

Maclean Hunter has acquired the business forms printing operations from Southam Inc. Other product lines include publishing and printing of medical information. It only has printing plants across Canada. The strategic objective of Maclean Hunter is to develop a global publishing network and to focus more on electronic publishing.

The company, however, may be taken over by Rogers Communications Inc., a diversified Canadian high technology company involved in the fields of cable television, video rental and mobile telecommunications. This acquisition may set a precedent because Rogers Communications would probably become the first telecommunications company to move into the printing business.

STRATEGIC ISSUES

As the last notes of Beethoven's Fifth Symphony ended, Mr. Peladeau thought that there were too many issues to deal with. He wanted Quebecor Printing to continue to grow into the next century. He and other top executives felt that there was no need to redefine the business vision and that the printing industry was a sunrise industry, full of new opportunities and challenges. The printing industry in general was still highly fragmented and Quebecor Printing could continue expanding into new geographic areas, such as California, the Southwest of the United States, Europe and/or the Pacific Rim.

At the same time, product expansion into new electronic and digital products would also be an attractive choice. Lately, there has been too much talk about the so-called information superhighway, but not too many people knew what it was all about. Nonetheless, the top management at Quebecor Printing believes that the information superhighway is and will remain paved with ink and paper.

The issues of technology are inevitably linked to people, too. Quebecor has done a good job in terms of managing the workforce and instilling a spirit of innovation and entrepreneurship among its employees. In addition, the company believes that training of employees is essential in moulding a flexible workforce. On the other hand, the good relationship that has existed between labour and management may be put to a test, as workers at *Le Journal de Montreal* threaten to escalate the confrontation in response to management's goal to trim the "fat" from the organization.

Within the printing industry, Mr. Peladeau's philosophy has always been to focus on the customers' needs, rather than on what the competitors have been doing. Nevertheless, the possible acquisition of MacLean Hunter by Rogers Communications posed different concerns. Rogers Communications was not in the business of printing but rather in the business of telecommunications. But then again, it seemed that Quebecor had been preparing itself all along to move into the arena of international media and communications.

Exhibit 1. Quebecor Inc. Organization Chart

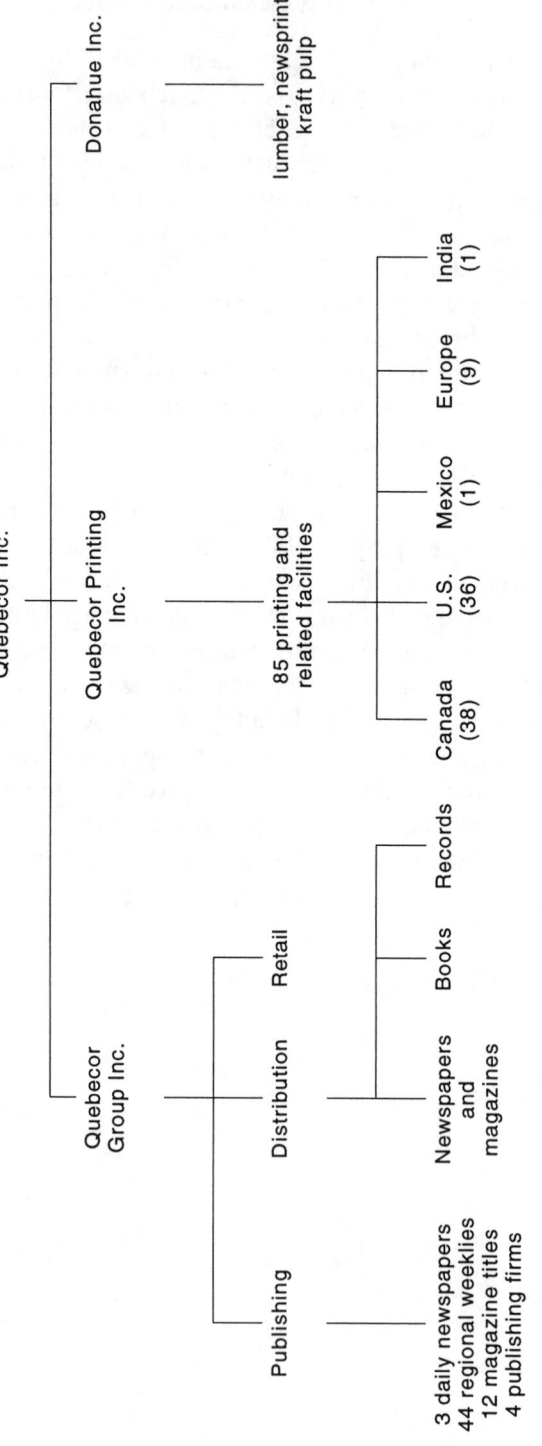

Exhibit 2. Quebecor Printing Financial Statements.

Balance Sheet

Assets (000's)

Fiscal Year ending:	December 31, 1992	December 31, 1991	December 31, 1990
Receivables	201,344	200,676	194,153
Inventories	82,814	77,627	85,019
Prepaid expenses	6,261	7,780	7,836
Other current assets	0	0	10,520
Total current assets	290,419	286,083	297,528
Gross fixed assets	975,030	872,356	819,369
Accumulated depreciation	(203,258)	(143,259)	(88,557)
Net fixed assests	771,772	729,097	730,812
Miscellaneous assests	157,321	161,990	163,686
Total assets	1,219,512	1,177,170	1,192,026

Liabilities (000's)

Fiscal year ending:	December 31, 1992	December 31, 1991	December 31, 1990
Accounts payable	184,522	162,060	146,980
Income taxes payable	8,306	6,898	4,033
Dividends payable	3,848	0	0
Current portion of long-term debt	4,807	5,080	5,730
Notes payable	0	13,929	3,135
Other current liabilities	2,425	1,255	0
Total current liabilities	203,908	189,222	159,878
Long-term debt—Net	360,515	573,728	655,999
Deferred taxes	129,707	111,544	100,400
Minority (Liabilities)	9,816	9,448	15,203
Other long-term liabilities	38,121	49,413	43,875
Total liabilities	742,067	933,355	975,355

Equity (000's)

Fiscal year ending:	December 31, 1992	December 31, 1991	December 31, 1990
Common stock	315,636	108,735	103,314
Preferred stock	0	4,621	10,269
Contributed surplus	88,737	88,737	88,737
Foreign translation adjustment	(8,690)	(5,279)	(5,393)
Retained earnings	81,762	47,001	19,744
Shareholder's equity	477,445	243,815	216,671
Total liabilities and equity	1,219,512	1,177,170	1,192,026

Exhibit 2. Continued

Income Statements (000's)			
Fiscal year ending:	December 31, 1992	December 31, 1991	December 31, 1990
Sales; revenues; interest income	1,444,426	1,386,852	1,264,937
Operating expenses	1,235,324	1,200,863	1,102,621
Operating income	209,102	185,989	162,316
Depreciation and amortization	73,657	66,613	54,258
Long-term interest	31,118	53,040	62,084
Short-term interest	4,929	3,070	1,890
Amortization of debt issue	2,689	1,450	2,072
Capitalized interest	(698)	(2,917)	(3,101)
Total interest expense	38,038	54,643	62,945
Income before tax	97,407	64,733	45,113
Income taxes	41,527	29,938	21,309
Deferred taxes	23,112	15,282	14,802
Minority interest (Income)	1,389	1,572	2,161
Net income after tax	54,491	33,223	21,643
Net income	54,491	33,223	21,643
Preferred dividend requirements	251	545	0
Common dividends declared	11,999	5,421	6,443

Exhibit 3. Strategic Plan.

- Prepare for a free trading North America by strengthening our base in Canada and expanding our geographic range across the U.S. and Mexico;

- Build a diverse product line within our core business of printing to provide greater stability of earnings;

- Be one of the major suppliers in every market we serve, to ensure market strength and competitiveness;

- Be a low-cost supplier in all our key markets by optimizing the benefits of our economies of scale, asset utilization, specialization and technology transfer, and;

- Above all, be a customer-driven company that meets and exceeds customer expectations.

Exhibit 4. Circulation Numbers of Major Publications.

Name of Publication	Weekday	Saturday	Average
Journal de Montreal	294,000	327,000	
Le Devoir	28,000	35,000	
Clin D'Oeil			72,000
TV Guide (Canada)			838,000
TV Guide (U.S.)			14,614,000
Reader's Digest (Canada)			1,639,000
Reader's Digest (U.S.)			16,256,000
Time (Canada)			364,000
Time (U.S.)			4,335,000
People			3,453,000
Sports Illustrated (Canada)			145,000
Sports Illustrated (U.S.)			3,608,000
Travel & Leisure			1,006,000
Marvel Comics			13,174,000
DC Comics			1,482,000

Crawford, Michael (1993). Prey for the Paper Tiger. *Canadian Business*, 66:11, November, page 23.

Exhibit 5. North American Commercial Printers.

Company	Printing Revenues (U.S. Millions) 1992
1. R. R. Donnelley & Sons Co. (Illinois)	4,193.1
2. Quebecor Printing Inc. (Quebec)	1,444.4
3. Banta Corp. (Wisconsin)	637.4
4. Wallace Computer Services Inc. (Illinois)	511.5
5. Quad/Graphics Inc. (Wisconsin)	500.0
6. Trans-Continental Printing Inc. (Quebec)	469.4
7. Taylor Corp. (Minnesota)	460.0
8. Maclean Hunter Ltd. (Ontario)	320.0
9. Graphic Industries Inc. (Georgia)	316.9
10. American Signature (New York)	300.0

Crawford, Michael (1993). Prey for the Paper Tiger. *Canadian Business*, 66:11, November, page 24.

Fun Wheels Inc.

Nicole Rhodes watched her grandchildren test-drive their new tricycles in her large living room. She had just given each of them the latest model of tricycles from her company and, as usual, the tricycles were a tremendous success. But slowly her mind began to wander to the problems her company, Fun Wheels Inc., was facing. Sales in 1988 had shown an improvement from the previous three years, but profitability had not kept pace. In 1985 the company had undergone a dramatic change in operation by manufacturing rather than merely importing wheeled toys. But manufacturing had brought about a new set of problems for the company. Nicole knew that she and her management team would have to address these problems if Fun Wheels was to improve its profitability, protect its market position from the increased competition, and adapt to the changing market environment.

COMPANY HISTORY

Nicole Rhodes, a mechanical engineer, formed Fun Wheels Inc. in 1980 after accepting her employer's generous early retirement package for senior executives. Having worked at Alcan for over 25 years, Nicole was ready for a change of life-style and was eager to become self-employed. The last of her four children had graduated from university in the spring of 1979, leaving Nicole free to pursue her own interests. Although she had dreamt of starting her own business for many years, Nicole had decided to wait until all of her children were financially independent. In her last years at Alcan Nicole had, nevertheless, been thinking of ideas that would enable her to build and develop a profitable business. Because she knew that the demands of self-employment were rigorous—both in terms of time and energy—she only considered product ideas which appealed and interested her personally.

The idea for Fun Wheels Inc. developed out of her experience with the tricycles and scooters her children had played with when they were younger. During the early part of her career at Alcan, Nicole and her family had been posted in West Germany. It was here that Nicole, through her children, first became familiar with Welle Go-Carts. In Europe, Welle was the market leader of high quality wheeled toys for children between the ages of three to thirteen. The company's go-carts, scooters, tricycles and bicycles were highly recognized for their durability, design and educational value. Most of Welle's manufacturing took place

This case was prepared by D. Balas, M.B.A., under the direction of Dr. A. B. Ibrahim, Professor of Management at Concordia University, Montreal, as a basis for class discussion, rather than to illustrate either effective or ineffective handling of an administrative situation. This case was supported by a grant from the Certified General Accountants Association of Canada (CGA). © Copyright A. B. Ibrahim, 1994.

in West Germany. It exported its toys to other European countries through agents and distributors.

When the Rhodes family returned to Canada in 1976, Nicole noticed that wheeled toys of comparable quality were unavailable in North America. While her own children had outgrown Welle's go-carts, Nicole was still interested in the educational and developmental value of quality wheeled toys. She was confident that a market niche for such toys existed in Canada. In the fall of 1980 Nicole visited the Welle head office in Frankfurt, West Germany, and returned home as their exclusive Canadian distributer.

INDUSTRY CHARACTERISTICS

Structure

The Canadian toy industry is segmented into five main categories: wheeled toys and doll carriages; dolls, dolls' clothing and parts; various skill games, puzzles, construction toys and stuffed toys; video and electronic games (Exhibits 1 and 2). It is a highly concentrated industry both in terms of sales and geographic location. A handful of large companies, offering a broad range of toys, dominate the market: 60% of sales in 1988 were made by 10% of firms. Medium sized companies accounted for 30% of sales while the remaining sales were made by small, privately owned and family-operated companies. Seventy-five percent of Canadian toy manufacturers fall within this latter group of small companies.

In general, small firms specialize in the production of a few toys, such as dolls or games, for niche markets. The presence of small entrepreneurial firms has lead to a higher level of market fragmentation than would be suggested by the concentration and dominance of the larger firms. Capital requirements for manufacturing toys are low—it costs only about $20,000 to produce a line of dolls or plush animals—thus encouraging cottage industry within this sector of the economy. Furthermore, many creative entrepreneurs (for example, Trivial Pursuit) contract manufacturing to other firms. In recent years a substantial proportion of manufacturing has moved to lower-cost producing nations such as China and Taiwan. This shift has lead to a decline in employment within the toy industry and is displacing Canadian manufacturing—assembly, packaging and distribution are becoming more common activities. Companies that manufacture bulky toys such as wheeled toys (as compared to smaller toys such as board and video games), have been less affected by competition from foreign manufacturers. Video and electronic game manufacturers, on the other hand, face an 83% import rate for their products.

Of the 96 companies operating in the industry in 1988, 49 were located in Ontario while 24 were located in Quebec. Since the early 80s, the Canadian toy industry has been subject to consolidation and increased foreign ownership. By 1988, U.S. manufacturers controlled virtually 60% of the toy companies in Canada. Nearly 80% of exports of Canadian toys are destined for the U.S. market. Canadian subsidiaries of U.S. firms are frequently assigned the production of toys and to eliminate apparent contradiction in many respects the Canadian industry is merely a branch-plant sector of U.S. manufacturers, producing toys and games according to U.S. specifications. Canada possesses no competencies or inherent attributes that enable it to be truly competitive on a global scale. In contrast, the U.S., either by ownership or controlling interest, is the international market leader. Through extensive distribution networks, economies of scale and sophisticated advertising campaigns it has staked its place in an increasingly global market.

Marketing

In many respects the toy industry is similar to the fashion industry. Both face extremely seasonal sales patterns and sell products whose demand is based on fads and current tastes of customers. While companies in the fashion industry have two or more seasons to generate sales, companies in the toy industry only have one—the Christmas season. Approximately 65% of all toys are sold in the fourth quarter of the year. The toys most affected by seasonality are *promotional* toys—toys whose success is almost exclusively based on a fad. Manufacturers must stimulate early demand for such toys through extensive promotion and costly advertising campaigns. Television advertising, directed at children, is a crucial part of successfully marketing a promotional toy. The extremely short life span of promotional toys leaves manufacturers only one to two years to recover costs and earn a profit from such a toy. Manufacturers begin preparing, by attending trade shows and soliciting orders from retailers, for the Christmas season in the previous spring. Toys that are not on the shelves of retailers by October have essentially missed the most crucial selling season.

Even if a new toy is able to stand out from the plethora of new offerings, and make it to the retail level, there is still no guarantee of its success. What makes a toy a "hit" and what makes it a "miss" remains a mystery to most toy manufacturers. Because of the high failure rate (80%) of new toys, manufacturers are extremely vulnerable to both inventory risk and copy-catters. On the one hand, it is not uncommon for a toy manufacturer to face enormous inventory build-up because demand for its product never materialized, or because demand "died" considerably faster than anticipated. On the other hand, one of the biggest fears in the industry is to miss sales because demand has been underestimated. Once a sale is missed, it is often lost for good. The lack of brand loyalty among consumers makes duplication of successful product concepts a common practice in the toy industry. Children are fascinated by the toy itself—not by who makes the toy. By flooding the market with the same product concept, copy-catters accelerate the speed at which children tire of a new toy. Unlike many consumer goods, toys rarely lead to a repeat purchase by a given customer—that is, parents will rarely buy their child the same toy twice. Thus, toy manufacturers and retailers must continuously add new toys to their product line to maintain sales levels.

Classic toys are somewhat insulated from the problems plaguing promotional toys. Classics, as they are called in the industry, are the staples of a manufacturer's product line. The Barbie doll is an example of a classic toy that has successfully weathered the fads and trends of the industry for over 50 years. The stability and predictability of the sales of classics serves to reduce a toy company's erratic sales pattern and to stabilize its cash flow. Many companies have been saved from bankruptcy by their portfolio of classic toys. Because of their educational value and/or ability to capture a child's attention for a longer period of time, classic toys can be priced slightly higher than promotional toys. Brand loyalty, particularly for preschool level toys, is considerably stronger in this category. Advertising of classic toys is targeted at adults.

The wheeled toy segment of the Canadian toy industry includes all go-carts, scooters, tricycles and bicycles for children under the age of 13. Bicycles for older children are considered part of the sporting goods industry. Most of the firms manufacturing wheeled toys have traditionally competed in the lower-quality segment (Exhibit 3). But since the mid-to late 80s, changing consumer tastes have shifted competition to the higher-quality segment. Consumers are demonstrating a stronger preference for wheeled toys that can withstand the wear and tear of active children. This change in demand can be attributed both to the tremendous popularity of sturdy mountain bikes, and to a broader trend within the overall toy market. In recent years, the increase in the number of single parent or dual-career households has meant that, while disposable income levels have increased, "family time" has decreased. Consequently, parents are looking to toys to aid in their child's development rather than just to entertain them.

Until 1985, Fun Wheels was the only company to market quality wheeled toys. But in that year Breining expanded its product line to include quality wheeled toys; by 1988 these accounted for 68% of the company's production. Breining had been acquired by a large U.S. toy manufacturer that follows a strategy of being the market leader in each segment in which it competes. To that end, the new management at Breining expanded the capacity of its plant and introduced more sophisticated production methods. Breining's goal was to hold the largest market share in the wheeled toy segment by 1993.

PRODUCTION

For the first year of Fun Wheels' existence, the Rhodes' garage served as the base of operations. Nicole's youngest son, Mark, was the company shipper and delivery person; Nicole was responsible for all other functions. Fun Wheels imported and distributed four classes of wheeled toys: go-carts, scooters, tricycles and bicycles. Each of these products was, and still is, available in two to four sizes and in three colours (red, orange and yellow). By mid-1983 demand for Fun Wheels' toys lead Nicole to lease warehousing and office space in the industrial park just east of Montreal. Although this move raised fixed expenses substantially, the company could no longer operate out of the Rhodes' home.

At this time, several factors also lead Nicole to re-evaluate the viability of importing toys. First, the stronger Deutsch Mark—as compared with the Canadian Dollar—had increased the cost of goods sold. Second, the transportation expenses for the bulky wheeled toys was disproportionately high. Third, the Canadian tariff structure covering the toy industry discouraged assembly of toys in Canada. Essentially, because of irregularities in the tariff schedule, it is less expensive to import assembled toys than to import the un-assembled parts for the same toy. Exorbitant transportation costs, however, made it impossible for Fun Wheels to receive its toys in completed form. Consequently, in late

1984, with a renegotiated license contract from Welle Go-Cart, of West Germany, Nicole decided that Fun Wheels would manufacture the toys in Canada.

By March 1985, Fun Wheels owned a manufacturing plant with production capacity of $33 million. Since the sale of Fun Wheels' toys alone was insufficient to reach such a level, the company also began to manufacture bicycles for the Anderson Toy Company, the Canadian subsidiary of the large U.S. multinational Howard Inc. Modifications were required to adapt the manufacturing process to the production of Anderson bicycles, but these were paid for by Anderson. In return, Fun Wheels signed a contract to manufacture Anderson bicycles until 1992 (Refer to Exhibit 4). While the agreement allowed annual manufacturing levels to be determined jointly by both companies, a sales level of $7 million was set as a fixed minimum. Under the terms of the agreement Fun Wheels was obliged to pay a $750,000 fine if it chose to terminate the contract prior to its expiration. Manufacturing for Anderson Toys enabled Fun Wheels not only to achieve efficiencies in production, but also to take advantage of volume discounts offered by suppliers. In order to contain its premium prices, savings in production cost are crucial to Fun Wheels. In the past Canadian suppliers to the industry had not offered interesting saving opportunities for manufacturers. But more recently—as they witnessed the shrinking of their own market—suppliers were becoming more flexible in terms of credit policy and discounts. They were still not able, however, to match the price points of Asian suppliers. Fun Wheels sources predominantly from Canadian manufacturers; but wheels and seats are imported from Germany.

Anderson bicycles are targeted at children 13 years of age and older and, therefore, do not compete with Fun Wheels' own products. Between 1985 and 1987, manufacturing Anderson bicycles had little impact on the production of Fun Wheels toys. But in late 1987 both internal capacity constraints and external pressure from Anderson began to make this arrangement less beneficial for Fun Wheels. In early 1988 Fun Wheels was unable to accept orders for its own products because it lacked the production capacity. The production department, headed by Richard Tremblay, is further sub-divided into two divisions: Anderson and Fun Wheels. Each of these is supervised by a different manager who is solely responsible for scheduling workers, production runs, and purchasing requirements (refer to Exhibit 7 for organizational chart). Raw materials and workers are moved from one division to the other only in exceptional circumstances. Nicole had denied Richard Tremblay's request to switch part of the company's production process from Anderson to Fun Wheels toys. She did not want to further erode the company's already strained relationship with Anderson Toys.

Managers at Anderson, under pressure from the U.S. head office, had become increasingly demanding about cost reductions. With more and more Canadian manufacturing being replaced by Asian manufacturing, Nicole had concerns about finding her company in the same precarious position as many other Canadian manufacturers. Anderson guaranteed a minimum sales level, and its management had recently indicated the intention of increasing the size of its contract with Fun Wheels if Fun Wheels could meet certain price/cost conditions. Manufacturing under contract for Anderson could be very profitable since Fun

Wheels was not obliged to engage in any sales, advertising or distribution activities for the products. Competition in the quality wheeled toy segment is intensifying as both Canadian and foreign toy manufacturers devote a growing amount of attention to this segment. In the short term Fun Wheels is still insulated from foreign imports by high import tariffs (Canadian tariffs are higher than U.S., European and Japanese ones). But, as a result of the Canada-U.S. Free Trade Agreement over the next ten years, protective tariffs will be eliminated, thereby potentially threatening Fun Wheels' viability.

MARKETING

Marketing at Fun Wheels Inc. is the responsibility of Nicole's son. Mark Rhodes has been working at Fun Wheels, in various capacities, since the company's inception. Initially it was only part-time and during the summers, but in 1984 he became a full-time employee. Nicole had begun to worry about the issue of succession and she was relieved when one of her children finally decided to join the business. For most of 1984 Mark worked in an administrative capacity. But he quickly found his duties tedious and asked Nicole to assign him the position of Marketing Manager. Mark convinced Nicole that his degree in cinematography gave him the ability to develop creative and innovative advertising and promotional campaigns. Nicole conceded because she felt the time had come to develop and use a more aggressive promotional strategy. Until then the company had relied almost exclusively on direct selling. The only print advertising used by Fun Wheels were sales brochures provided by Welle Go-Carts in West Germany.

Fun Wheels' initial marketing and sales activities had been directed at traditional toy retailers. Nicole had used the same strategy employed by Welle Go-Cart. It soon became apparent, however, that Canadian market characteristics were different from European ones. Canadian parents, accustomed to more "gimmicky" and "faddy" American toys, resisted the high price tag associated with Fun Wheels' products. In contrast European customers were willing to pay a premium for well-designed and educational toys. Furthermore, while the Welle name was highly recognized in Europe, it was not familiar to most North American parents.

In 1984, following the advice of one of the company's sales representatives, Jean Claude Bustros, Nicole changed her company's sales strategy. Fun Wheels began to target institutional customers such as kindergartens, elementary schools and physiotherapy departments of clinics and hospitals for children. Because these institutions were more concerned with quality than price, the new strategy was considerably more successful. Fun Wheels' expanded sales force met directly with school principals and physiotherapists, explaining and demonstrating to them the educational and developmental benefits of the company's products. The endorsement of schools gave Fun Wheels the market recognition it needed—without costly promotional expenditures. Parents saw how much their children enjoyed these scooters, tricycles and bicycles, were impressed by the toy's durability, and soon began inquiring about the possibility of buying one of the toys for their own home. In response Fun Wheels decided to give the retail market one more try. This time, however, it marketed its toys through up-scale sporting goods stores. These stores carried fewer product lines, devoted more space to each line and specialized in better quality merchandise than did large retail chains such as Toys'R'Us. Fun Wheels' sales increased dramatically as a result of their expanded distribution network.

Fun Wheels adhered to this strategy until Mark Rhodes became Marketing Manager in mid-1985. Mark was confident that an extensive advertising campaign would accelerate the company's growth even further. Mark envied the success of many American toy companies, which, according to him, could be directly attributed to the sophisticated and sleek television advertising promoting their products. During 1987 and 1988 Fun Wheels advertised periodically on various local television stations during Saturday morning cartoon shows. The commercials, developed by Mark, promoted the scooters, tricycles and bicycles as the "ultimate speed machines." As part of his new marketing strategy, Mark had laid-off close to a quarter of the company's sales force, eliminated most print advertising in magazines (Good Housekeeping and Parenthood) and hired account representatives—all with the objective of entering the retail toy market. Jean Claude Bustros, the company's sales director, adamantly opposed this move. The sales force had worked hard to build a strong customer network among institutional buyers, and was just beginning to benefit from the company's entry into the sporting goods distribution network-.

HUMAN RESOURCES AND ORGANIZATIONAL STRUCTURE

Fun Wheels' organizational structure is built around five main functional areas: administration; production; marketing; sales; and finance and accounting. Each constitutes a separate department and is treated as an independent profit centre—as opposed to a cost centre. Essentially, all divisions are charged for the services they receive from other departments. Managers receive a fixed salary, but are also eligible for bonuses depending on the profitability of their departments. With this dual reward system, managers at Fun Wheels earn higher salaries than their counterparts at other Canadian manufacturing firms. The department managers report directly to Nicole, who, as President and CEO, oversees all of the company's activities. Departmental budgets are prepared by Nicole and assigned to the respective departments at the beginning of the year.

The administration department is responsible for daily operations including human resources and purchasing. It is headed by Carlo Sanchez; a family friend of the Rhodes and a 30% shareholder of Fun Wheels. Carlo had been an accountant at Alcan and had, like Nicole, taken advantage of the company's early retirement package. The design of both Fun Wheels' organizational structure and reporting relationships was one of his first contributions to the company. In order to obtain a structure that closely resembled the one in place at Alcan, Carlo had created departments along functional line. Over the years Nicole and he have clashed on several administrative issues. Fun Wheels had, for example, missed the 1984 Toronto toy fair because according to Carlo "the company was rushing into things." Nicole subsequently heard that a competitor (Breining) who did attend the fair had secured a large order from the Mississauga Public School Board. Despite their differences, Nicole, remembering his outstanding performance at Alcan, considered him to be a very capable businessman and, therefore, frequently conceded to his wishes.

Fun Wheels employs 321 workers in its manufacturing plant and 43 employees in various administrative and support functions. Relations with the plant workers have always been, and continue to be, amicable. In fact, recruitment efforts by the local union have had virtually no success at Fun Wheels. Many of the employees who joined Fun Wheels were former employees of other Canadian toy manufacturers—manufacturers who had either reduced the size of their operations or even declared bankruptcy. Essentially, the labour market in this segment has enabled Fun Wheels to adhere to a low cost hiring practice (that is, hire lowest cost workers) and pay workers less than union dictated rates. As a result of this policy (initiated in 1986) Fun Wheels employs a disproportionately high number of older workers, since they attach less importance to being unionized than do younger workers. Carlo defended this policy by noting that the high levels of absenteeism and longer vacations were more than compensated for by lower wage rates.

Credit policy, accounts receivable, accounts payable and issues relating to financing are among the duties of the finance department. Both the administration and the finance department are involved in establishing credit terms with suppliers and customers. In terms of the company's marketing activities, Jean Claude Bustros (Sales Director) supervises the sales force, while Mark Rhodes (Marketing Manager) is responsible for all other marketing functions. Jean Claude had threatened to resign in reaction to Mark's dismissal of several sales representatives. Although Nicole questioned the wisdom of Mark's decision, she was reluctant to interfere. She was eager for Mark to learn all aspects of the business, with the objective of him eventually taking over management of Fun Wheels.

FINANCES

A large part of the initial capital required to finance Fun Wheels' operations had come from Nicole's personal savings. During the years that the company was only importing toys, fixed operating costs had been minimal. Virtually all costs were variable—inventory risk and foreign exchange risk were Fun Wheels' greatest concerns. In order to become a manufacturer, Nicole had taken on additional external debt (long-term loan at 7.5% interest rate) thereby enabling Carlo Sanchez, in exchange for equity, to become a significant shareholder. Since 1985, several additional investors were given the opportunity to buy Fun Wheels shares.

Nicole and Carlo had set a financial objective of performing better than industry average in terms of controlling cost of goods sold (industry average gross margin is 27%) and inventory management. The very volatile and seasonal nature of the toy industry demands that a company be watchful of its inventory turnover and accounts receivable. With an average inventory turnover of four times per year and an average collection period of 53 days, the toy industry is considerably less "liquid" than many other consumer industries. To Nicole it seemed that in spite of a healthy growth rate, Fun Wheels was facing greater financial difficulties than ever before (Exhibits 5 and 6).

DECISIONS ABOUT THE FUTURE

Nicole knew that, as her company was heading into its ninth year of operation, several issues would have to be resolved if Fun Wheels was to remain viable in the future. While Fun Wheels had grown to be one of the largest competitors in the wheeled toy industry, other, more recent, entrants to the industry had been alarmingly successful at capturing market share. Several issues concerned Nicole. First, she was uncertain about which product line—Anderson or Fun Wheels—would better enable the company to remain competitive in the longer term. Second, decreased profitability was becoming a pressing concern for Fun Wheels. Nicole was certain that the operational efficiency of the company had to be improved; but she was not certain where to begin.

Exhibit 1. Canadian Toy Industry Industry Statistics.

	1986	1987	1988
Number of companies	100	84	96
Number of employees	2,829	2,531	2,033
Sales ($ millions)			
Exports	56	53	48
Domestic	200	157	162
Total Canadian Production	256	211	210
Imports	372	455	506
Total Canadian Market	$572	$612	$668

Exhibit 2. Canadian Toy Industry Sales by Category ($ millions).

	1986	1987	1988
Dolls & Accessories	109	95	116
Games & Stuffed Toys*	202	194	189
Video & Electronic Games	88	135	177
Wheeled Toys	119	135	140
Doll Carriages	55	53	47
Total	$573	$612	$669

*Includes skill & action games, puzzles, construction toys and stuffed toys

Exhibit 3. Wheeled Toys Market Share of Canadian Production (in $000).

	1986	1987	1988
Toys In Motion Inc.	$48,227	$50,273	$51,491
	45.00%	42.89%	40.30%
Breining	$10,074	$19,129	$32,326
	9.40%	16.32%	25.30%
Fun Wheels Inc.	$16,504	$21,802	$25,937
	15.40%	18.60%	20.30%
Nicholson	$26,900	$20,383	$11,244
	25.10%	17.39%	8.80%
Others	$5,466	$5,626	$6,772
	5.10%	4.80%	5.30%
TOTAL	$107,172	$117,213	$127,769

Exhibit 4. Fun Wheels Inc. Sales/Gross Margin by Product Line (in $000)

	1986	1987	1988
ANDERSON BICYCLES			
Revenue	$8,500	$7,000	$7,000
Percent of Total Revenue	33.99%	24.30%	21.25%
Gross Margin	$1,814	$1,313	$1,187
Percent Gross Margin	21.34%	18.76%	16.95%
FUN WHEELS			
Revenue	$16,504	$21,802	$25,937
Percent of Total Revenue	66.01%	75.70%	78.75%
Gross Margin	$6,859	$8,263	$8,728
Percent Gross Margin	41.56%	37.90%	33.65%
TOTAL COMPANY SALES	$25,004	$28,802	$32,937

Exhibit 5. Fun Wheels Inc. Operating Performance 1986–1988 (in $000).

	1986	1987	1988
Sales	25,004	28,802	32,937
Cost of Sales	16,331	19,226	23,023
Gross Margin	8,673	9,576	9,914
Administrative Expenses	2,235	2,540	2,628
Advertising	1,100	2,802	4,022
Sales & Promotion	1,950	2,100	2,273
Depreciation	440	518	494
interest Expense	500	570	294
Income before Tax	2,447	1,045	204
Income Tax	538	230	4
Net Income	$1,909	$815	$199

Exhibit 6. Fun Wheels Inc. Balance Sheet 1986–1988 (in $000).

Assets	1986	1987	1988
Current Assets			
Cash	965	879	432
Accounts Receivable	3,987	5,136	6,341
Inventory	4,322	6,591	9,342
Pre-Paid Expenses	789	764	861
Miscellaneous	281	198	201
Total Current Assets	10,344	13,568	17,177
Property, Plant & Equipment at Cost			
Building & Improvements	6,712	6,712	6,712
Furniture, Fixture & Equipment	1,432	1,601	1,734
	8,144	8,313	8,446
less: accumulated depreciation	978	1,496	1,990
	7,166	6,817	6,456
Total Assets	$17,510	$20,385	$23,633
Liabilities & Owner's Equity			
Current Liabilities			
Accounts Payable	4,982	4,561	5,385
Accrued Expenses	2,003	2,263	5,143
Total Current Liabilities	6,985	6,824	10,528
Long-term Debt	6,321	6,432	4,808
Total Liabilities	13,306	13,256	15,336
Stockholders' Equity	4,204	7,129	8,297
Total Liabilities & Shareholder's Equity	$17,510	$20,385	$23,633

Exhibit 7. Organizational Chart 1988 Fun Wheels Inc.

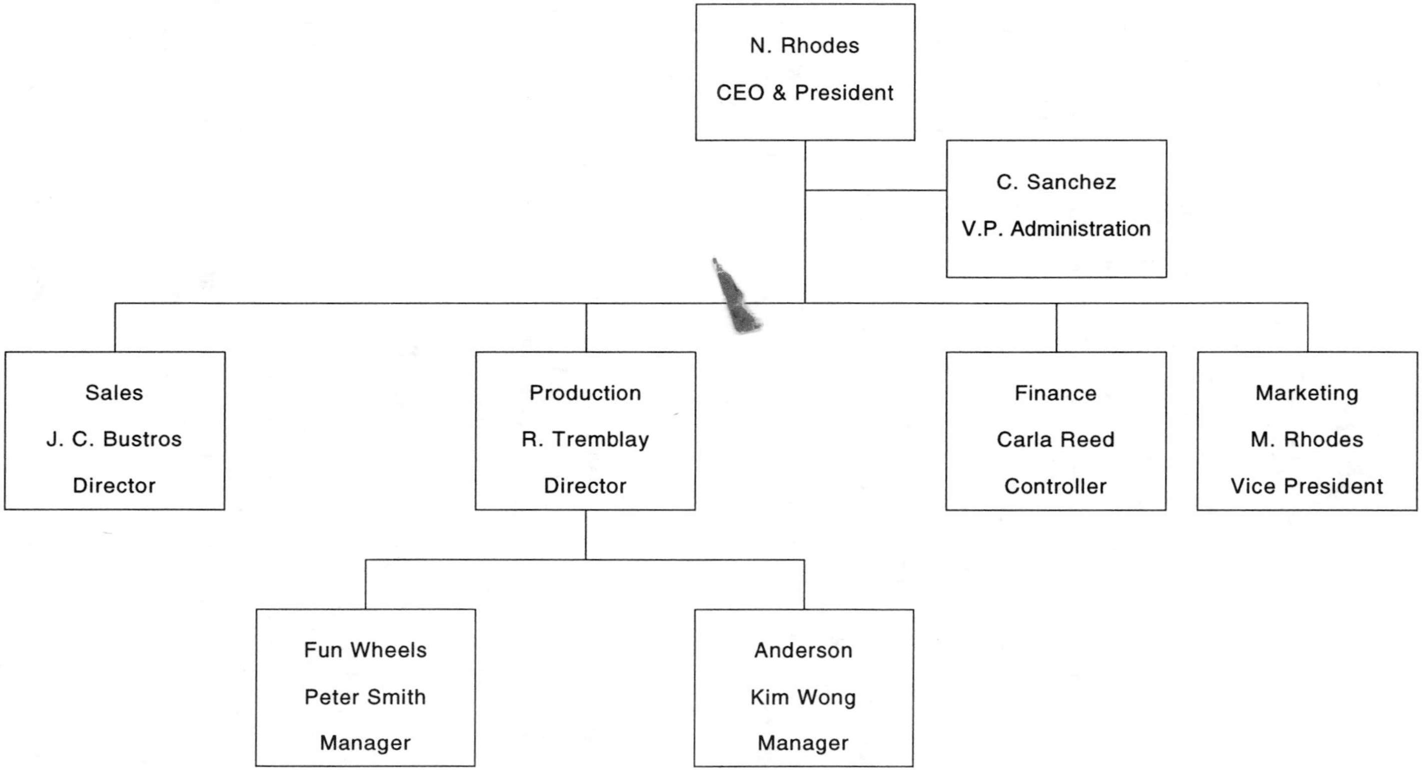

N. Rhodes
CEO & President

C. Sanchez
V.P. Administration

Marketing
M. Rhodes
Vice President

Finance
Carla Reed
Controller

Sales
J. C. Bustros
Director

Production
R. Tremblay
Director

Fun Wheels
Peter Smith
Manager

Anderson
Kim Wong
Manager

CASE 14

The Body Shop

As Margot Franssen, President of The Body Shop Canada (a franchisee of The Body Shop International PLC) sat sipping her caffeine-loaded coffee, she reflected on the Monday morning meeting which had just ended. Although she had a lot on her mind, her door was, as always, open. She prided herself on the open-door policy she had created throughout the organization and actually looked forward to the variety of ideas and opinions she knew would be coming through that door over the course of the day; she knew the meeting's discussion would be on everyone's mind.

During the meeting Margot's assistant Diana had given her a hard time over her reference "on national TV, of all places" to The Body Shop as "the Mother Teresa of cosmetics." But that's the way Margot liked it. Her hand-selected core team was made up of young, talented, enthusiastic, hard-working and, most importantly, open and honest women that were not afraid to give her a piece of their mind. No, Diana's comments did not concern her; she nurtured and encouraged such openness. What did concern her, and the others at the meeting, was the effect their growth was having on the public, their employees/franchisees and the structure of the organization.

With no plans to hold back their growth, Margot realized they would need to plan and prepare if they were to avoid some of the managerial and production problems that the International operation was experiencing due to their phenomenal growth. She would need to consider how company-wide communications and standards could most effectively be maintained. And how best to deal with the back-orders, "copy-cats" and disgruntled customers that seemed to be popping up more and more.

THE PRODUCT

The Body Shop is a United Kingdom (U.K.)-based franchise operation which sells "naturally inspired" skin preparations and a large range of body products. The products range from bath and body lotions to cleansers, toners, oils, creams, treatments and specialty items such as cosmetics, perfumes and aromatherapy oils (Exhibit 1—The Products). They can be purchased individually or packaged in brightly coloured gift bags and baskets. Although pre-made gift baskets are available in a variety of motif colours, customers are free to select

This case was prepared by Ronda Fisher under the direction of Prof. F. Westley and Prof. W. H. Ellis, McGill University, as a basis for class discussion rather than to illustrate either effective or ineffective handling of an administrative situation. Copyright © Professor Ellis and Professor Westley, 1990. All rights reserved.

their own products and have them gift-packaged in the store. On average, each store in Canada sells between 12,000 and 15,000 gift packages a year.

HISTORY OF THE BODY SHOP INTERNATIONAL

The first Body Shop was opened in 1976 in Brighton, England by Anita Roddick. The impetus for the venture had come when her husband, Gordon Roddick, expressed a yearning to trek on horseback from Buenos Aires to New York. Although Anita was "all for it," the 33-year-old mother realized she would need some way to support herself and their two young daughters while Gordon was away on his adventure.

At the age of 23, Anita had worked a year for the United Nations' International Labour Organization in Geneva in the department concerned with women's rights in Third World countries. Following that, she had travelled through the South Pacific, India and North Africa and had learned that "there are ways of cleaning and polishing the body that don't have to come out of a tube or a jar." She, therefore, planned to open a shop that would sell the naturally inspired skin preparations she had encountered during her Third World travels.

After securing a £4000 ($8000) bank loan, Anita went about locating a supplier of the natural ingredients she would need, such as cocoa butter, aloe vera, jojoba oil, sweet almond oil and oat protein (the five basic ingredients found in many of The Body Shop's skin care preparations). The large pharmaceutical manufacturers were of no help—they had never heard of the items and were used to dealing in large volume orders. Anita then found an herbalist, Mark Constantine (who still makes 50% of all the products), in the yellow pages and subsequently discovered he not only had the ingredients but made cosmetics as well. When he explained that no one bought the cosmetics because "they're so ugly," Anita knew she had found the right person. She then chose the name The Body Shop "in a joking reference to American garages" and paid an art student £25 to design the logo the company still uses.

The first Body Shop was opened in March 1976, jammed between two funeral parlours on a small side street. In fact, it was through the parlours' objection to the name and her lack of funds that Anita began to realize the power of free publicity. She contacted the local newspaper outlining the parlours' objections and the betting houses' 16:1 odds that "the young housewife would be closed within three months." The resulting publicity attracted more customers than Anita could keep up with. By 1990, the Company had over 450 shops in 37 countries (150 in the U.K.), sold over 350 products and had never paid for any advertising. Although it has been said that "not advertising is like winking in the dark—you know what you're up to but no one else does," The Body Shop has managed to attract editorial coverage both in print and television that, had it been paid advertising, would have cost up to 2 million pounds a year. And their answer to that is "the best ad is a good product, a good shop, a good company. In fact, being good is good business."

The Roddicks (Gordon returned in 1977 and assumed financial responsibility for the business) experienced rapid growth in the number of products, shops and countries that they served by establishing a franchise system. Because they did not have the capital to expand the operations themselves, they entered into franchise agreements with individuals who shared their aims and ideals. The first U.K. franchise was opened in 1977, and the first international shop was opened in Belgium in 1978.

In 1984, The Body International went public with a flotation on the unlisted securities market. On their first day shares doubled, within a year they were worth eight times issue price and by 1990 were trading at over 25 times issue. The share prices reflected the explosive growth in reveneues and profits that the company experienced during the 1980s, oftentimes doubling from their previous year (Exhibit 2—BSI Financials).

The Roddicks—or more precisely The Body Shop International, PLC—today consider themselves manufacturers and wholesalers, although they maintain 34 company-owned stores in the U.K. The majority of products are manufactured in the U.K. In addition to the company's 320,000 sq. ft. of warehouse and production space, there are licensed suppliers who manufacture some of the products under Anita's strict ethical and environmental guidelines. As for the corporate stores, their purpose is for test marketing. All merchandising posters, window displays and product launches are coordinated by The Body Shop International. Various ideas are, therefore, tried out in the corporate stores before they are sent world-wide.

DISTINGUISHING FEATURES

There are many identifiable characteristics that make The Body Shops, worldwide, stand out. The products are available in a variety of sizes and are plainly packaged. Listed ingredients and product testers are provided for every item. The bottles are returnable for refilling or recycling. As well, the shops are painted green and contain suggestion boxes prominently displayed. Although many of these features started with very logical and practical beginnings—Anita had no money—they have turned into an integral part of the corporate culture and philosophy.

- Only 15 products were originally available. They were, therefore, offered in 5 sizes to add variety and to allow the customer, for the first time, the opportunity to buy cosmetics in the same way as groceries—as much or as little as one wanted.
- The preparations were packaged in cheap plastic bottles with hand-written labels to minimize costs. As well, Anita did not believe the hype and waste generated from most cosmetic packaging was necessary nor good for the environment.
- Detailed information about the ingredients and how they work were displayed with each product in order to explain to the customer why the product inside looked so different from anything they may have seen or bought before. This information, coupled with the product testers, has encouraged non-exploitative selling and self-service shopping. Customers are not pressured, by either advertising or forceful sales staff, into buying something they do not really need or want.

- Because Anita had a limited number of bottles and the products sold so quickly from the start, customers were told they could bring the bottles back for a re-fill and discount. Due to regulatory restrictions, a refill service is not available in North America, although customers are encouraged to return their bottles for recycling and a discount.
- Although the colour green is now synonymous with the environmental movement, Anita originally painted the walls green because that was the only colour that would hide the damp patches that were so prevalent in the first shop.
- Anita's rule of thumb in market research has been to avoid paying for it by doing it yourself. The suggestion boxes in each store, shop visits and organized meetings with managers, franchisees and suppliers are, therefore, Anita's way of keeping in and up with the marketplace—"to me, hiring a Market Researcher, seems like driving a car by looking through the rear view mirror."

As Anita explains "all these were brilliant accidents because we had no money—but I think the real genius came when we had the money but did not change things, only made the business better." And it has been this philosophy of constantly striving to improve that drives The Body Shop to ever greater success.

When asked why The Body Shop has been so successful, Ms. Roddick's reply is,

"The Body Shop really is an idea whose time has come. In the 70s we sold to people already aware of the benefits of natural materials, the danger of over-packaging and the need for the environment. These people were a minority then: we were probably three years ahead of the main market. Now the public is much more educated and concerned about these things."

And The Body Shop believes it has made a contribution to that education.

Another distinguishing feature of The Body Shop is that, for the most part, shops are owned, run and staffed by women. Anita puts an emphasis on feminist principles and believes gut feelings and instincts are important in the decision-making process.

PHILOSOPHY

The Company has a moral and philosophical background of ecological and social responsibility. Their mission statement claims that "we will be the most honest cosmetic company in the world." And they have managed to expand and succeed without in any way diluting their original premise which is: a) to promote health rather than glamour, b) to sell cosmetics with a minimum of hype and packaging, c) to use naturally-based and close-to-source ingredients whenever possible, d) not to test ingredients or final products on animals, e) to respect the environment and f) to use retail as an educational tool.

a. Health not glamour

> "The cosmetic industry is exploitive, controlled by men who for years have created needs that don't exist to make women unhappy with what they have." (Anita Roddick)

Instead of talking about beauty, The Body Shop talks about health, self-empowerment and well being. Employees are continually trained, not on how to make a sale, but on the nature and uses of the products, so they can best meet the needs of the customer. Anita makes no pretence about what skin care can and cannot do:

> "You can clean, polish and protect the skin and hair, that is all. I have never met a cosmetic scientist who is 50 years old but looked 20 or even 10 years younger. There is no product that can take away the lines from the face for the simple reason that there is no product that can remove stress, grief, laughter or sorrow."

b. No hype or excess packaging

Although this is consistent with their philosophy of honesty and low environmental impact, it also represents a sound business practice. As Charles Revson, founder of Revlon, said "in the factory we make cosmetics, in the store we sell hope." The cosmetics industry makes its money through packaging and advertising which represent 85% of the costs. The advantage for The Body Shop is that, in the absence of advertising and fancy packaging outlays, they are able to keep production costs low. This means that new products and lines can be cheaply and easily introduced. With new products continually being researched, tested and introduced, The Body Shop is able to keep one step ahead of their competition. Anita is forever travelling to Third World countries "looking into ancient customs, products and ingredients that can help The Body Shop and help create industry in economically deprived areas. It is this marriage of traditional wisdom and knowledge of raw ingredients with modern scientific research that makes The Body Shop products unique and effective."

c. Trade not aid

By purchasing, at First World prices, products and ingredients that are close-to-source, The Body Shop has created trade and employment in Third World countries. They have helped set up projects (such as the making of wooden foot-massage rollers in Boys Town, India and soap making in Easterhouse, Scotland where unemployment reaches 56%) to further create trade in economically deprived areas. As well, by making it lucrative to grow the ingredients, The Body Shop has found a way to do their share to protect endangered environments and cultures, such as the tropical rainforests.

d. Against animal testing

All the ingredients and products are guaranteed free from testing on animals—"it is unacceptable that animals suffer for the questionable ideals of vanity or fashion." Instead, The Body Shop uses and supports alternative methods of testing. It relies on natural or naturally-derived ingredients that have been tried and tested over many years of human use (which ensures their efficacy and safety) and new products are tested on human volunteers.

As well, all suppliers to The Body Shop must sign a declaration that their ingredients have not been tested on animals in the past five years (the standard amount of time that records are maintained).

e. Environmental Awareness

This includes concern and responsibility for society and the environment on a global as well as local level. There is an unwritten rule that every Body Shop in the world must take on a community project, and that means sending staff, every week, into food banks, handicapped centres or old age homes on company time.

> "It is not enough to vote a chunk of money to charity, what is important is to involve people in giving, in sharing, in helping." This is indicative of The Body Shop's commitment to "put something back into society and the community from which we derive our profits." (Margot Franssen)

All the products are biodegradable, are bottled with a minimal amount of packaging, and are manufactured with state of the art technology to minimize the environmental impact (in terms of energy consumed and waste generated). As well, the Company (including all franchisees in all countries) recycles waste and uses recycled paper wherever possible. They use only natural plant ingredients that are easily renewable and are not scarce. Synthetic ingredients are, however, used as acceptable alternatives to those "natural" materials that would otherwise be derived from threatened environments or from threatened species (such as spermaceti or musk from whales). The Body Shop has also run joint campaigns with such organizations as Friends of the Earth, Amnesty International and the World Wildlife Fund. These campaigns have helped raise hundreds of thousands of dollars and have increased awareness of such issues as acid rain, the ozone layer, the slaughtering of whales and the destruction of the rainforests. The shops have been used to:

> "provoke discussion and mobilise customers to clamour for greater concern and provision for care for the environment by asking such questions as 'Why does a tree have measurable value when it is chopped down and sold but not while it is giving us oxygen?'" (Anita Roddick)

f. Education

Every Body Shop, world-wide, is used as an arena of education for social and environmental issues. Employees and customers alike are kept informed through window displays, free informational leaflets, information boards, in-store videos, newsletters and staff training (Exhibit 3—Examples of Leaflet Covers).

> "The Body Shop believes information is power. Grassroots changes in environmental practice will only take place when enough people see it is crucial. We keep our customers—some half million per week—constantly informed about the causes we support and the actions we are taking and, where appropriate, information about following suit." (U.K. Environmental Projects Co-Ordinator)

"Not all our customers are necessarily into our issues and bottle recycling, some just like our products. So we use our shops as a vehicle to show people that there is a different way and even if they don't shop that way now, if they come back enough times and pick up enough leaflets, then they will get the message" (Betty-Ann Franssen, Canadian Franchise Partner).

"Our shops successfully combine the warmth and friendliness of the old cornerstore with informative and effective presentation, providing what today's consumer wants. The new customer wants honest information, not only about the product but about the company as well." (Anita Roddick)

By educating its staff and customers, The Body Shop has established credibility—everyone knows what the company's values and business practices are—and that creates loyalty. Staff and customers, therefore, actively promote the company, its products and philosophy, and this fuels growth. As one Canadian employee explained,

"I thought I had found Utopia being able to sell products that I totally believed in. It was so easy to sell and it felt good to educate people about the cosmetics industry. And coming from an educational angle meant you didn't have to pressure. You could actually generate excitement based on the information you were giving."

The philosophy *is* Anita—it reflects her personal feelings and beliefs. So when she incorporated that philosophy into her company, she was there to act as the role model, to bring her enthusiasm, sincerity, energy and passion. And as Descarte once said, "The passions are the only advocates which always persuade. The simplest man with passion will be more persuasive than the most eloquent without." Anita nurtures that passion in her employees and franchisees, so that they too can pass on the message—"the company is the message and the message is values."

This philosophy has attracted employees and franchisees who feel a deep sense of personal commitment to the Company.

"All of us work here because our ethics are like the company's. We all have a real passion for these issues. It makes you feel proud to work here." (a Canadian Assistant Manager)

"Innovation, awareness, honesty and above all a caring attitude towards people and the environment are the factors which make The Body Shop a unique way of life for all of us." (a Franchisee in Aberdeen)

In Canada, many of the employees, from head office to manufacturing to the shops themselves, explained, "I had always believed in the ideas but never acted on them as strongly as I do now that I have been working here." And with such commitment the maintenance of the philosophy seems ensured.

THE ULTIMATE GOAL

The Body Shop believes that, "profit is a lubricant to make things happen in the market place to create more jobs, and its ultimate aim is to be the legitimate agent for social change."

"We cannot go into the '90s thinking that business is merely a machine for grinding out profits. Profit is not our main objective. We are certainly not against making a profit. But I also want to sleep at night and know that I'm building a future for my child. In order to do that, we must operate on the principle of sustainable development. We must conduct ourselves in a holistic fashion." (Margot Franssen)

Over the years, as greater amounts of revenue were generated and compounded, the company has been able to concentrate on, organize and expand its environmental and social responsibilities. And that has meant spreading the wealth and challenging the multinational corporations to follow suit—"All a successful company is is a rich neighbour, it should be extending its arms out to other neighbours." The Body Shop declares that it will be a force for social change.

"No decision is ever made without first considering its social and environmental implications. Although it makes our life at The Body Shop far more difficult and troublesome, it is infinitely richer in every sense. It's that constant search for a better way, a more ethical way, that gives my company its morale and sense of purpose and its enormous sense of fun.

"We are trying to show that you can run a business different from the way most businesses are run: That you can share your prosperity with your employees and can empower them without being in fear of them. That you can rewrite the book on third world trade and global responsibility, on the role of educating the company, customers and shareholders. That core values don't have to be increasing affluence but can be community, caring for the environment, creating, growing things and personal development.

"We communicate with passion and passion persuades; we print, preach, teach, educate and inform. Our employees dream of noble purposes not by selling a moisture cream but by working on community projects, campaigning on environmental and social issues and by being in the company of those who need their help. Do you really imagine any employee after being told explicitly that this company has no responsibility to them or anyone else, no responsibility to the community or the environment in so far as to maximize profits, do you think they would be loyal and committed or willing to go to extraordinary lengths to solve its problems? I wouldn't.

"We have never once stopped believing that you have to earn the permission of the market place. Newman Marcus said 'Profit is not the objective of my business, it is providing a product and a service that's good enough that people will pay a profit for providing it.' We worship the customer; as Mahatma Ghandi said 'A customer is the most important visitor on our premises. He is not dependent on us, we are dependent on him. He is not an interruption on our work, he is the purpose of it. We are not doing him a favour by serving him, he is doing us a favour by giving us the opportunity to do so.'" It is that commitment to values, sound management and customer service that makes The Body Shop what it is. And as Margot's assistant explains "it is not because we are an envrionmental company that we have taken off, it is because we have proven commitment to all aspects of our company, including philosophy, policies, people and product." (Anita Roddick)

CANADIAN HISTORY

In order to present the Canadian Body Shop history, one must appreciate the history of Margot Franssen, the feisty young feminist who brought The Body Shop to Canada.

At the age of 18, Margot left her home in Alberta to work in Toronto. She worked for some time at McLeod, Young, Weir as a secretary but was compelled to quit when they would not pay for her to take the securities course—"they claimed that women could never pass the course anyway." She then worked for Alfred Bunting and Co. while studying for her license. Upon completing the course, with excellence, she was once again compelled to quit when her promotion did not materialize—"I knew I was too good a secretary for them to lose."

Eventually, Margot registered as a mature student in York University's Business Programme. After two weeks of falling asleep during lectures, she switched into philosophy and realized she had found her niche.

In her final year of studies, at the age of 27, Margot received a U.K. Body Shop gift-basket and fell in love with "the non-gimmicky approach." With the financial backing of the man she was living with (Hall Tingley) and with the intention of copying the concept, Margot flew to England and visisted the seven existing shops. Although she knew nothing about cosmetics or retailing, she realized there was more going on than simply a great product—"there was an energy, in the look of the shop and in the employees, that just seeped out of everywhere and I knew that I could never duplicate it."

Arrangements were made to meet Anita and the two women immediately hit it off. Margot was invited to the Roddick's home for dinner where, after many hours of talking, Gordon asked what it was exactly that she wanted. "It just popped out that I wanted the franchise rights for all of Canada or nothing"-it was, and still is, an agreement based on a drunken, 3:00 A.M. handshake.

When Margot returned to Canada, she met with a lawyer "who almost blew the deal. He couldn't appreciate that everything was based on trust." So she fired him and hired a female lawyer and a female accountant, which marked the Canadian continuation of The Body Shop as a "very womanly company which operates on the principles of nurturing, caring and developing others. In fact, the men in the Body Shop are considered honourary females." (Margot Franssen).

It was the second international franchise agreement that the Roddicks had entered into. That was in December 1979 and by March 1980, Margot had recruited her 19-year-old sister, Betty-Ann, to help open the first Canadian store which was located in a small basement shop on a trendy downtown avenue in Toronto, Ontario. Since that first shop, where they painted, sanded the shelves and laid the floors themselves, the sisters have gone on to develop a network of some 77 franchise and company owned stores across Canada with retail sales exceeding $50 million (Exhibit 4—Body Shop Canada Sales Figures).

FRANCHISING

The first Canadian franchise was opened in October 1980 by two women in their early twenties. Between them, however, they had many years of retail experience. When they initially approached Margot, she wondered why these "high fashion retail queens" were interested in her "crunchy granola store, with its loose herbs, soap that had to be cut by hand, Indian wallets and hand-written labels." But she also knew that in order to expand she would need to franchise.

At that time, there was no formal franchise selection process—"we didn't know what we were doing." Instead, like Anita before her, Margot relied on her gut feelings and instincts. It was, therefore, decided that the women would look for a shop location and would pay a franchise fee of $5000 (a sum which Margot chose based on her needs at the time). When they managed to find a sub-lease in the Toronto Eaton Centre, Canada's largest shopping mall at the time, Margot knew she had chosen wisely—"although the philosophy and good product spreads its own reputation, you also need the right people, staff and location." The shop was an immediate success.

By 1990, there were 61 Canadian franchises. The Franchise Programme, including location and franchisee selection, had evolved into a relatively standardized procedure; "after 10 years, I think we have the right franchise selection system and it is something that we have done totally on our own with no direction from the U.K.—often we just couldn't wait for their information to arrive." (Betty-Ann Franssen).

With its 10 years of success, The Body Shop no longer had difficulty in securing prominent mall locations. Their corporate lawyer of 6 years left his position with a downtown law firm to join The Body Shop full-time—"it just got to the point where I was spending 50% of my billable time but 100% of my thinking on The Body Shop, and I realized my heart was here but my body was downtown." He can now be found in bicycle shorts as he works on establishing and dealing with all the necessary documentation, leases and agreements. As he explains, "when I came on in 1989, the Franchise Programme was adhoc. I have since set it up so that we all understand how it works and what the process is. As well, the construction of the stores has now been standardized for consistency."

The Franchise Selection Process now includes an offbeat questionnaire (Exhibit 5—The Franchise Application), a personality assessment and a series of interviews that eventually terminate in a meeting with the Franssens and Tingley. As Betty-Ann explains, "to do the things that we do, we have to first make money; so we don't want franchisees who just want to hug a tree nor do we want those who just want to count their money at the end of the day—you have to have a bit of both." But she goes on to say, "for the most part, we have managed to get tremendous people. I think that if you don't believe in the philosophy you will want to get out within a year because you will be so tired of us."

Margot is quick to point out that "we are not in the business of selling franchises but rather in making our business better." For this reason, once franchisees are selected, it is not odd for the Franssens and Tingley "to hold locations for people until they are ready to take them." And this extends to those existing franchisees who are interested and deemed capable of opening a 2nd or 3rd store. An organization has thus been created where more than 90% of the franchisees are women and most are under 30 years old.

Under the franchise agreement (Exhibit 6—The Franchise Agreement), the franchisee has the right to do business under The Body Shop trademark, but they are required to follow certain guidelines. They must purchase the complete line of Body Shop products from the franchisor (The Body Shop Canada), must maintain shop standards and must operate the business and be present in the store at least 40 hours per week. This last requirement is to ensure that only committed individuals, who will maintain the high standards, are granted a shop. In return, the franchisor provides advice and assistance with respect to building the shop, provides all necessary training in product knowledge and the actual mechanics of operating the business, and maintains an adequate inventory to meet franchisee requirements.

EVOLUTION

In many respects, the Canadian and U.K. operations have evolved concurrently. During the early 1980s there was limited direction from the U.K. and as the first Canadian franchisee explained,

> "there was probably more emotion than thought in the company—everyone was there because their heart was in it, the thought was secondary. The U.K. direction was very limited. There were no manuals or documentation with regards to merchandising. The manuals, standards and procedures that you see today were all a function of growth that took place concurrent with the U.K."

For example, a Canadian developed training manual became the prototype for all The Body Shop franchises around the world.

With time, the company streamlined its look;

> "in the early days we had so many sundries. The stores were filled with stuff and it was a lot messier and looser. Now we are much more focused in terms of the products and appropriate sundries that we carry." (Canadian Trainer)

The company's social and environmental awareness is another area that evolved. Both Margot and Betty-Ann explained,

> "at first, we were just concerned with survival, we didn't have time to think about anything else. Then we started spreading out and people started to know of us. It wasn't until we were settled with a customer base and were training staff that we could take a breather and think about where we could go and what we could do. That was around '83–'84 and that is when the environmental stuff all started. We got involved with groups and people, learned off them and put those practices into place

and they became our ideals. The green part was just a natural evolution of our ethical approach. We were used to educating our staff and customer about the raw ingredients, so it was just a natural evolution to start educating them about social and environmental issues."

"Body Shop product window displays are organized by the U.K. and are changed every 3 weeks. But 4 window slots a year are now devoted to issues and causes of National interest. England knows exactly what we are doing but they understand that countries are individual. So we pick issues that are of concern to Canadians and educate it the way we see fit. For instance, we are the only country that does fund-raisers with the selling of t-shirts and calendars (in the U.K. they do more petitions). But, I'm really afraid of shoving things down people's throats. I want to educate without them having to always buy something. So, we switch between educational and fund-raising windows." (Betty-Ann Franssen)

Most recently, The Body Shop Canada combined efforts with Amnesty International, raised $100,000+ for the World Wildlife Federation in a three week period, and in the same amount of time, raised $30,000 for Friends of the Earth along with 20,000 signatures on a petition asking the Federal Environment Minister to curtail the use of chlorofluorocarbons.

INDEPENDENCE

The Body Shop Canada has evolved into a relatively independent business with a distinct culture and organization of its own. Although Canada must purchase all Body Shop products and merchandising supplies (such as window displays and product posters) from the U.K., it is free to arrange its own sundry purchases, incidental packaging, environmental campaigns and training (with U.K. approval). And Margot has made those arrangements as Canadian and as close to philosophy as possible. For instance, instead of buying Taiwanese fancy gift baskets, in 1990 it was arranged for the Canadian needs to be fulfilled by the New Brunswick Micmac indians (which would have a profound affect on the Micmac unemployment rate of 96%). As well, the Franssens recently introduced an environmentally friendly Body Shop canvas bag, and instead of going with a large manufacturer, production was delayed until a young Canadian was found who wanted to start their own business.

Margot has also given England a lot of ideas about business and how to deal with employees and their development.

"For example, we have a Service Awards Programme to reward our long-term corporate employees; we give a Body Shop watch for one year, a Body Shop gold ring for three years, and a Rolex watch for five years of service. We also have the Bravo Programme (Exhibit 7) that recognizes employees who go above and beyond the call of duty. And Academy Awards for such things as lifetime achievement which we present at our 'all-company' functions. I think all these programs are what develop and drive the spirit and the spirit comes from the comradery. And we have been rewarded with a very low turnover rate, which is virtually unheard of in retail." (Margot Franssen)

As the network of stores grew (Exhibit 8—List of Shops), Margot and Betty-Ann often found themselves overwhelmed with the amount of work required to maintain their own shops while handling the head office duties (which, among other things, included using their basement as a make-shift warehouse). As Betty-Ann explains, "back then nobody knew about retail and we were just trying to keep our head above water. We did everything from building the shop interiors, to filling the bottles, to training and working in each of the shops." Although it meant a lot of work, it also meant a closeness and comradery were established amongst everyone; the Franssens knew and had a rapport with all the franchisees and shop employees, and vice versa. And it was this closeness and rapport that led to the development of the company culture.

CULTURE

Margot's assistant, Diana, seemed to summarize the culture the best when she described how she appeared in a suit for her job interview but quickly realized they were much more casual, "because my parents were their good friends, I knew the lifestyle Margot and Quig lived at home and at the cottage but I never realized that they were that way in their company."

The culture is definitely very casual, very open, family-oriented and womanly. Rather than stuffy three-piece suits, the norm is more jeans, bicycle shorts and cotton skirts. People feel free and are encouraged to give their opinions. There is a definite comradery and team spirit, especially amongst the corporate staff who, for the most part, represent the longer-service employees. And because 95% of the company is female, women's issues and intuition also play a prominent role. One needs only to speak with the employees to get a feel for the culture and a feel for their commitment to the company:

> "For me the attraction is the fact that Margot actually listens to and appreciates my opinion. And I think the amount of input that most people have ensures that a lot of problems are avoided."
>
> "When I started in 1984, it did not take long to get a sense of that family atmosphere. Margot and Quig (Margot's husband) were very much around the stores then. They would drop in and get sandwiches and coffee for the shop staff. And I remember how they let one of their employees live with them awhile until she got settled."
>
> "Interviewing with Margot and Quig is like meeting family. They are good at getting the right people and in developing and giving trust. I remember when I first started they gave me a key within my first month. They trust and treat their employees as an equal and that is why the loyalty factor is so high. The open communication is also part of it; you know you can give negative feedback and you won't be penalized."
>
> "What other company would think about putting in a day care centre even though there are only 3 or 4 people who currently have kids (but we are looking into the future) or wants to offer really flex or reduced hours to women who have children and who want to go back to school."
>
> "In many ways I think we helped make the culture. We're a bunch of women and that's the most interesting thing of all. I love being able to tell the truth and to give

my opinions—I would have problems playing boardroom games in other organizations."

"I could never work for a typical corporation now because I have been brainwashed by The Body Shop. I work really well with women and find them a lot more open and honest, we don't let feelings get in the way."

"It makes us all feel good when we can have an impact. The windows, the training of the staff, the back-up literature, the ability of the staff to say 'hold on and I will ask our environmental department that question' and the fact that we liaise with environmental groups is what makes me unable to work anywhere else."

ORGANIZATION

Exhibit 9 presents "The Body Shop Starship" which outlines the corporate organization. In keeping with its family-oriented culture, there are no organizational charts with a hierarchy or lines of command. Margot is the President of The Body Shop Canada which includes, over and above the shops, a Head Office, Training School and Retail Operation (Exhibit 10—Descriptions of Operations). As well, there is a processing operation—Quig Manufacturing—which is set-up as a separate enterprise from The Body Shop Canada.

Each operation is located in Toronto and is housed in a separate building within the same small Industrial complex, with the exception of Retail Operations which is located in the downtown core "close to many of the Toronto Body Shops." The executives are, however, currently considering moving the operations north of the city where a single building could be purchased to house all the various departments under one roof.

> "Now that we are in separate locations a lot of information can get lost. So communication and the Monday morning meeting with all the departments is all the more important." (Corporate Merchandiser)
>
> "Part of the motivation for moving is also to provide many of our employees with the opportunity to afford a house and lifestyle that living in the city makes impossible." (Margot Franssen)

QUIG MANUFACTURING

In 1983, Quig Tingley, Margot's husband, joined the Company—"I had been a successful trader at McLeod Young Weir Ltd. for 13 years but wasn't having fun any more." Initially, Quig was just "delighted to leave the world of three-piece suits behind to take over responsibility for the company's financial affairs," but eventually that goal turned to opening Quig Manufacturing, the only Body Shop manufacturing operation outside of the U.K.—"because of the U.K.'s rapid growth, they were often unable to keep up with product demand. One solution was (and still is) to try to make as many products internally as possible."

Quig Manufacturing was originally started as a bottling facility, to bottle the finished products that arrived from the U.K. in large barrels. By 1990, however, it had grown to include a microbiological lab (to test all batch and on-line samples), a cold-mixing operation (to produce shampoos and bubble bath) and most recently, a hot-mixing operation (to produce creams and lotions). As well, Quig coordinates all warehousing and distribution in their 25,000 sq. ft. building.

In manufacturing, all but one of the raw ingredients are sourced from local, Canadian suppliers (as are all the packaging components). The one missing ingredient, Product X, is purchased from The Body Shop U.K. and for this reason, no royalties are collected on the 20-odd products that Quig currently manufactures. And to ensure that the high standards set in the U.K. are maintained in Canada, all products produced are triple tested (by the Quig lab, an independent lab and the U.K. lab).

The idea has been to maintain the retail price at a constant level, while reducing the costs of product through higher volume purchasing made feasible by expansion through the franchise system. Quig anticipates that they will be able to further reduce their costs in this manner as well as through beginning to manufacture more of the products domestically rather than importing them from the U.K.

Although the Quig operation has provided Canada with greater autonomy and revenue (Exhibit 4—Quig Sales Figures), the continued rapid expansion of both the U.K. and Canadian operations (in terms of new shops and sales per store increasing some 40% per year) has, in some cases, compounded the back-order problems.

> "The U.K. supply of finished goods and ingredients needed in manufacturing is often unreliable. By the time we receive a back-order list, 2 more orders have gone through the system. This creates an avalanche effect—we run out, so then the stores run out, they increase their order, which means we must increase our back-order which, ultimately, puts even more pressure on the U.K. The back-order problem is then compounded by an internal system that lacks responsiveness; we don't have a Management Information System, so we rely on faulty data with which to forecast our inventory and order needs. We usually under-forecast by 30–40% and this puts a further strain on the whole system." (Quig Warehouse Manager)

STRUCTURE

The company's evolution has led to the semi-structured organization of today. But as Margot explains,

> "I am concerned with becoming too bureaucratic. I think the lack of hierarchy and the fact that everyone is willing to do everything has allowed our phenomenal growth to occur. But, there is now pressure from those who want change and feel we must become more structured in order to continue growing."

The fear is that structure will stifle the innovation and adaptability.

> "There is none of this network of approvals that we have to go through before a decision can be made. We don't just sit on ideas and suggestions. If it is mentioned and it sounds good and fits with our philosophy, we will jump on it and start organizing it, no matter who's idea it is." (Margot's Assistant)

"Sure, sometimes we jump too quickly. We have $100,000 of silk flowers sitting in our warehouse that we don't know what to do with. And we were the first to organize biodestructable bags but then had to deal with the negative coverage when it turned out they were not completely biodegradable—but we can only do as much as time and current technology permits. It is always easier in hind sight. But it is through making mistakes that we learn." (Merchandising Director)

Perhaps the most striking characteristic is the absence of any job descriptions. As Margot explains, "we want problem-solvers not employees and titles inhibit this." Betty-Ann further explains,

"There are no job descriptions because positions are always changing. We don't just hire people for the sake of hiring—I feel people should work to their maximum. We are constantly thinking of how to utilize people and that is why anyone's job may change at any time."
"We keep a small staff and try to get everyone, including the warehouse staff, thinking with the same mentality as middle management." (Quig Tingley)

Some employees did, however, raise some concerns associated with this lack of structure:

"Because we are growing so much, job descriptions change and that can be difficult when franchisees call in to speak to someone who is no longer doing that job. But I think what we lack in continuity we make up for in flexibility."
"With everybody doing everything, there are times when we get exhausted. But the system is flexible enough to allow us to take some time off when it is needed; there are enough good, trained people to fill in."
"You have to constantly snatch and schedule in personal time otherwise The Body Shop will take over. But you can't not be available—all of us have to be there for each other."
"There are a lot of workaholics in this company. We all work long hours with a minimal personal life outside of work. I wonder if this is really building a strong management team or they are slowly burning-out the core people."

Consistent with their willingness to jump on ideas, is the companies willingness to provide everyone with the opportunity to develop to the best of their ability. Margot credits their success to their unique methods of staff training which include "providing the stimulation one needs to realize one's full potential."

EMPLOYEE DEVELOPMENT

By looking at the evolution of the long-service, core people, one can better appreciate how the culture and structure are involved in the employee development. The core people can best be described as the long-service women, who have been with the Franssens from the early Canadian beginnings.

For the most part, the women who would eventually make-up the core team were fresh out of high school and started as sales staff in the fledgling corporate stores. Although many intended their employment to be temporary, before they knew it, The Body Shop had become a way of life.

"When I started in '83, there was this feeling that what we were doing was very important. There was a lot of young and entrepreneurial energy and a high level of involvement. Back then there were 6 stores and Margot was my supervisor, so even though I was in Vancouver you always had a global picture. In those days you met and worked with Margot right away." (Corporate Operations)

"By my second week I had worked with Margot and I had bought all the skin and body products. It just escalated from there. I just loved everything about the Body Shop."

Generally, the women were promoted to shop management within the first 6 months of their employment. This provided the Franssens the opportunity to deal with their head office and franchise duties. It gave them the time to visit, advise and ensure consistency amongst the growing number of franchise and corporate stores.

With time, the Franssens drew on the womens' shop management experience. The number of stores had grown beyond the two women's direct involvement. The natural development was, therefore, to get their shop managers involved in trouble-shooting, and organizing and overseeing new shop openings. They often teamed-up and travelled to the respective corporate and franchise shops. And the more they travelled, the more they learned and the more focused they became. For example, one employee explained,

"My talent is not endurance but rather quick shots in the arm. Margot recognized it and so I have focused on shop openings and trouble-shooting. But it is also the open lines of communication where I can feel comfortable telling Margot that I don't or do like something."

"Margot has been very wise in picking her key people and keeping them very happy. She is very perceptive in recognizing and nurturing people's talents and strengths. She is also great at layering people and setting up teams. So, as long as you have the passion and enthusiasm to do something wonderful and to the absolute best of your ability, then you are able to grow." (Merchandising Director)

"These jobs did not exist before, we just grew into them. I basically wrote the job description myself although it never actually went down on paper. I would just see what had to be done and would do it. People are respected on their merit and you know when someone is contributing to the company." (Retail Director)

"Margot knows we are making decisions for the good of her company because we don't just say it's Margot's company, we feel just as much akin to it as she does. After all, we've put almost as much time into it as Margot has. (Corporate Merchandiser)

"Decision making is basically put back on my shoulders. I will often ask for advice when I'm not sure but ultimately the decision rests with me if it's within my realm." (Corporate Merchandiser)

RECENT CONCERNS

By 1990, however, the personal contact with the Franssens was no longer possible. Most of their previous responsibilities had been transferred to the core team and/or the core team's assistants. Although they were still involved in the ultimate business decisions, their day to day duties had taken them out of the stores and into new areas of involvement. The majority of Margot's time was spent making public appearances and acting as corporate spokesperson, while Betty-Ann was busy overseeing retail operations and acting as liaison with the environmental groups.

> "I love speaking out and shaking things up. I love my missionary role of spreading the word as much as I love getting my hands dirty working in the stores. But, at the same time, I am not prepared to give up my family (Quig and our two year old son); we take the month of July off to go up to our cottage—with no business contact—in order to keep our own family culture." (Margot Franssen)
>
> "We used to know everyone that worked for us, now I find myself signing payroll cheques for employees I've never met. I am scared of growth. If you talk to anyone who has been around awhile they will tell you that the company is not what it used to be. Back then we all socialized together and talked a lot more." (Betty-Ann)

As well, some of their key employees were starting to show signs of fatigue and/or concern:

> "It is pretty scary that now I have to commit myself to Monday morning meetings (that I can't always make) in order to keep up to date and on top of things. I now have to take control of budgets and make sure that everybody is doing what they are supposed to be doing. I said to Betty-Ann that the ideal situation for me at this point in time would be to just give up what I'm doing now to get back into a store for 6 months to get back in touch with it—and that is exactly what I am going to do once I get everyone trained."
>
> "We now have 16 corporate stores and I don't know why they are so hard to run—I used to have no problems. Due to our rapid growth we've had to hire a lot of outside managers and I don't think they can get used to our high standards and high volumes on low ticket items. Coming from other retail operations, they're not used to our high involvement and open communication. They don't know how to shout for help and, therefore, rarely survive with us."
>
> "We are hearing the stores complain that they don't see Margot enough. Although it is no longer Margot doing the store visits, we try to deal with them or get our assistants to deal with them the same way we were dealt with by her. Given that it is not the exact same training we received and given the sheer volume of people we are now dealing with, it is a huge task to try to keep things as intimate."
>
> "The major problem for her has been going, almost over night, from being hands-on in the stores working one-on-one with the franchisees and managers to being forced into a director position that is so foreign for me that it is hard to adapt. I feel that I am losing control because I am no longer the one always doing it. The workload and people just keep doubling. I've gone from someone who managed a store, to someone who had a small supervisory position to 'OK, here is the country, go with it' and it's scary. We can't get out to our stores as quickly or as personally as we used to."

"I don't think I am ready to do what they want me to do. I think if they brought in a more seasoned professional they would achieve a lot more with fewer mistakes."

"Sure, sometimes there doesn't seem to be enough of me to go around, but it just means I have to hire and train someone so there is enough of me to go around."

"You have to be an adaptive type person, one who is able to work amidst a sea of confusion in order to work here."

COMMUNICATION

Communication was another area of concern:

"It is easy to say this is what we want, but it is really hard to incorporate that into 1,000 employees across Canada. Not everyone is a good trainer, so it is sometimes hard ensuring that the message goes across to everyone. Also, how do we maintain the standards and quality of staff and keep the corporate philosophy going when we are dealing with so many people. Communication starts to get hard because it has to go through so many channels (i.e. from the U.K. to us to the franchises to the staff) and the more channels the more diluted it gets." (Betty-Ann Franssen)

"The network of communication has to be developed. We are used to being small, where you tell someone something and then everybody knows, but now we realize there is more than just talking that we have to do." (Comptroller)

"Stores out west talk about the long distance feeling. They don't feel as connected and I think this is something we will always be battling with. To combat this problem we have fax machines in every store, weekly memos and newsletters that are consolidated by Betty-Ann, who ensures there is no conflicting information included." (Corporate Merchandiser)

THE PUBLIC

"Now we are big enough that we are not just covered in a local paper but are run nationally. And the communications and support systems have gotten so much better that the merchandising in Vancouver is very close to that in Toronto." (Corporate Operations)

The greater media and public awareness had, however, also brought greater expectations of perfection. In the past, their obscurity had afforded them the luxury of trying new innovations, of admitting and learning from their mistakes—"We make most of our mistakes trying to be right." But the public no longer seemed so patient.

"We have to deal with people saying we are not doing enough, why haven't we gone all the way, people forgetting that we are retailers first. For example, people complained about the sparkles and non-reusable decorations in our gift baskets, so we got rid of them. Now we must find an alternative to wrapping our t-shirts in plastic (which we started for cleanliness) because people are complaining. People say we use too much plastic but we can only do as much as the present technology allows. It is those customers who read a lot and are aware of the many points of view, that seem to pick up on all the good that we have done in such a short amount of time and with limited resources. Our biggest problem is with people who are ill informed, who have decided to jump on a band wagon and criticize us because we are not perfect. We get caught making mistakes because we make them in the public forum but I wish I could phone those people who attack us and tell them that they have missed the point—that it is OK to make mistakes and to learn from them." (Margot's Assistant)

COMPETITION

As their public profile increased, so too did their competition. By 1990, some of the larger cosmetic and retail companies had started to sell their own lines of natural products. For example, The Bay had come out with the Body Lines. But the real concern was with the small imitators, some of whom were producing packaging and logos similar to The Body Shop's. The problem was two-fold. Not only were they copying the wrong things—"unfortunately, no one seems to be copying our good points, like our philosophy and culture," but it appeared that some were even trying to sabotage The Body Shop reputation. This had forced both the U.K. and Canada to deal with legal matters and infringement rights.

To a certain extent, however, the Franssens were feeling relatively secure in their position.

"We fought for 8 years to get the prime locations. Now we are well located and we're improving them all the time. Therefore, any competition will be fighting an up hill battle." (Quig Tingley)

They were quick to point out, however, that they would have to deal with complacency.

"It's getting harder to keep ahead. We see that our last year's Christmas is what everyone else is doing this year in packaging. Without realizing it we've become a leader so we have to stay fresh because if we miss one year they've caught up to us. As well, we have to ensure that excellence in display, execution and customer service are upheld. The store owner has total control over that and if they let that slip, they're the same as the competition coming in." (Quig Tingley)

THE FUTURE

By 1990, none of the markets in which The Body Shop operates had yet reached saturation point. It was believed that the U.K. alone could easily support another 200 outlets. On a worldwide scale the potential seemed virtually limitless as the concept evidently crossed national frontiers with ease. Yet, the disadvantages of rapid growth were starting to take their toll.

Canada had recently received the franchise rights to seven northern states. They would, therefore, need to consider if the time was right to enter the U.S. market. And if so, how should they best deal with the recent concerns that had arisen due to their phenomenal growth.

Exhibit 1.

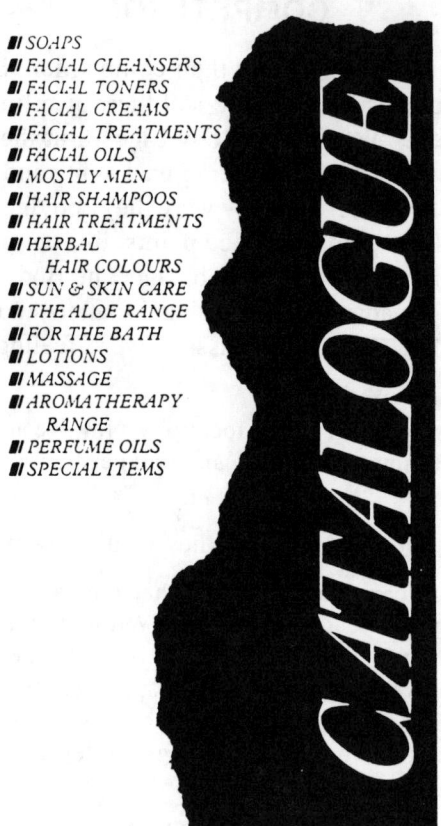

- SOAPS
- FACIAL CLEANSERS
- FACIAL TONERS
- FACIAL CREAMS
- FACIAL TREATMENTS
- FACIAL OILS
- MOSTLY MEN
- HAIR SHAMPOOS
- HAIR TREATMENTS
- HERBAL
  HAIR COLOURS
- SUN & SKIN CARE
- THE ALOE RANGE
- FOR THE BATH
- LOTIONS
- MASSAGE
- AROMATHERAPY
  RANGE
- PERFUME OILS
- SPECIAL ITEMS

NOT TESTED ON ANIMALS.

 SAVE AND RECYCLE

Exhibit 2. Body Shop International PLC
Financial Information
(Years ending 30 September)
(L'000)

	1983	1984	1985	1986	1987	1988	1989
Revenues—UK	1,839	3,953	7,391	13,560	21,255		
—Overseas	304	957	1,971	3,834	7,221		
Total	$2,143	$4,910	$9,362	$17,394	$28,476		
Cost of Sales				(9,452)	(14,645)		
Distribution Costs				(969)	(1,434)		
Administrative Costs				(3,557)	(6,415)		
Rent/Bank Interest Receiv.				79	80		
Interest Payable				(44)	(64)		
Profit Before Tax	$ 202	$1,044	$1,929	$ 3,451	$ 5,998	$9,300	$20,400
Average Number of Shares in Issue ('000)	19,520	19,750	20,000	20,000	20,099	N/A	42,629
# of Shops—UK	38	45	66	77	93	110	139
—Overseas	52	83	102	155	186	250	318

Note: As of Nov. 1990, there are 164 UK shops and approximately 400 Overseas shops

Exhibit 3.

ISSUES

Animal Testing and Cosmetics

C R U E L
U N N E C E S S A R Y
R E J E C T E D B Y
T H E B O D Y S H O P

WASTE COSTS THE EARTH

WE PRODUCE ONE TON OF WASTE
PER HOUSEHOLD PER YEAR

FRIENDS OF THE EARTH
THE BODY SHOP
HELPING THE EARTH
FIGHT BACK

Exhibit 4. The Body Shop Canada
Total Sales Figures

	CORPORATE STORES		FRANCHISE STORES		TOTAL
	NO.	SALES	NO.	SALES	
1987	15	$5,151,798	37	$10,980,863	$16,132,661
1988	19	$7,601,608	46	$20,607,080	$28,208,688
1989	16	$11,408,273	56	$34,110,129	$45,518,402

Quig Manufacturing Limited
Total Sales Figures

JULY 1/87 to JUNE 30/88	$8,687,074
JULY 1/88 to JUNE 30/89	$16,188,220
JULY 1/89 to JUNE 30/90	$27,500,941

Exhibit 5. Franchise Application Form.

A. Please complete this form in your own handwriting.
B. Unlike most application forms, in the interest of forests everywhere, our eyesight, and the postman's back . . . please do not attach additional sheets of paper!

PERSONAL DETAILS

Name _____

Address _____   Telephone Number:

_____   Day _____

_____   Night _____

Age _____

Occupation _____

Spouse's Occupation _____

Children (Number and Ages) _____

Are you a Canadian resident?   Yes _____ No _____

Please list the geographical area(s) in which you would like to operate.

_____

Would you be prepared to move?   Yes _____ No _____

EMPLOYMENT HISTORY

Please give a brief summary including dates and salary levels, and state the number of jobs you have had over the last 10 years.

EDUCATION

This can include qualifications attained at the University of Life.

PRINTED ON RECYCLED PAPER

FINANCE

Please give a summary of your financial position and any other business interests that you may have. Please outline how you intend to finance your franchise.

ASSETS		LIABILITIES	
Cash in Bank	_____	Money Owed	_____
Savings	_____	Owing on home	_____
Shares and Bonds	_____	Owing on other property	_____
Value of home	_____	Owing on vehicles	_____
Value of any other property	_____	Other Liabilities	_____
(do not include household furnishings)			
Value of own business, if any other assets	_____		

Describe any additional security you may have to support a bank loan.

_____

Have you or your spouse ever been declared bankrupt?

Yes _____ No _____

What are your total monthly expenses (include such items as mortgage or rent, taxes, etc.)

$ _____

HEALTH

Have you ever suffered from any serious illness?

      Yes   No

If so, please give details.

_____

_____

_____

ADDITIONAL INFORMATION

What do you do when you are not working?

_____

What are the good things about your present occupation?

_____

_____

_____

What have you done to feel proud of?

_____

_____

_____

. . . and not proud of?

_____

_____

_____

 PRINTED ON RECYCLED PAPER

If you could change the World, what are the five things you would put at the top of the list, and are realistically capable of implementation over the next decade?

1. _____

2. _____

3. _____

4. _____

5. _____

Favourite quotation and source?

_____

_____

_____

What car do you drive?

_____

What car would you like to drive?

_____

What was the last: _____

Book you read   _____

Film you saw   _____

Concert you went to   _____

Play you saw   _____

PRINTED ON RECYCLED PAPER

What newspapers/magazines do you read?

_____

What's the best thing you've seen on T.V.?

_____

Who is your hero (living) ?

_____

Who is your heroine (living) ?

_____

What would you like to be?

_____

Favourite menu

_____

_____

Who do you hate most?

_____

What natural gift would you like to have?

_____

Who said "never dilute your image"?

_____

PRINTED ON RECYCLED PAPER

Who said "A customer is the most important visitor on our premises. He is not dependent on us. We are dependent on him. He is not an outsider on our business. He is part of it. We are not doing him a favour by serving him. He is doing us a favour by giving us the opportunity to do so."

_____

How would you like to die?

_____

_____

Which countries have you visited and what did you like/dislike about them?

_____

_____

_____

What characteristics are important in a business?

_____

_____

_____

How would you describe your present state of mind?

_____

_____

Please return the completed form to the franchise department:

The Body Shop
15 Prince Andrew Place
Don Mills, Ontario
M3C 2H2

 PRINTED ON RECYCLED PAPER

Exhibit 6. The Franchise Agreement.

While the actual franchise agreement is a rather long and tedious document, seemingly designed for lawyers, the following should provide a precis of its intent, thrust and salient points.

- the franchisee has the right to do business under The Body Shop trademark for a predetermined period of time.
- the lease on the premises will be held in the franchisor's name and sub-let to the franchisee.
- the franchisee will submit, on a regular basis, all relevant financial data pertaining to the business.
- the franchisee must operate the business and be present in the store at lease 40 hours per week.
- the franchisee shall not reveal any such privileged information for its own benefit without prior consent of the franchisor.

Duties of the Franchisor:

- to provide advice and assistance with respect to building the shop.
- to provide to the franchisee all necessary training in product knowledge and the actual mechanics of operating the business.
- to maintain an adequate inventory to meet franchise requirements.

Purchase of Products:

The Franchisee must purchase the complete line of Body Shop products from the franchisor. With the exception of the first shipment (which is on a C.O.D. basis), shipments will be paid on a "30 day ex-warehouse" basis.

The Franchisee may purchase accessory products from outside suppliers, however, these products and suppliers must be approved by the franchisor. This to ensure that products distributed through Body Shops conform to our standards.

Maintenance of Shop Standards:

The shops must be maintained in a manner that meets both local legal standards as well as our high standards. All people working in the shop will meet those standards of knowledge, presentation and attitude as set by the franchisor.

Promotion:

The franchisee will remit 1 1/2–2% of gross sales to the franchisor, on a quarterly basis, for promotion and publicity purposes.

Service Fee:

The franchisee will remit to the franchisor a fee (presently $200 per month) to cover administration expenses incurred for servicing the franchisee.

Royalties:

The franchisor does not currently charge royalty fees.

COSTS INCURRED IN OPENING A BODY SHOP FRANCHISE

This is a breakdown of the costs in opening a Body Shop store. While there is some variation in overall costs, these variations usually occur in two areas: costs of building the actual shop, and the amount of inventory a shop opens with.

While the costs will vary somewhat, a prospective shop owner must be prepared to invest a substantial amount of both capital and time. While it has proven to be a very rewarding investment in the past, we cannot guarantee that all of this time and money will result in success.

We can guarantee that we will do everything in our power to help every shop in our system in every way.

Costs:	Minimum		Maximum
Franchise Fee	$ 15,000	—	$ 15,000
Shop Fixturing	100,000	—	120,000*
Opening Inventory	90,000	—	110,000*
Design Fee	5,000	—	5,000
Public Relations	0	—	3,000
Legal Documentation Fees	3,000	—	3,000
First and Last Month's Rent	5,000	—	6,000
Training Accommodation Costs	0	—	4,000
Site Selection	6,000	—	6,000
Management Assessment Test	900	—	900
	$224,900	—	$272,900

*Due to the size of the store and expected sales volumes, these items may be increased by as much as 10%. Also, provincial sales tax on shop fixtures will be payable. The first $60,000 of opening inventory must be paid for on a C.O.D. basis (thereafter, essentially all shipments will be made on a 30 day ex-warehouse basis).

SALES POTENTIAL

Our current sales figures are roughly equal to those attained in the U.K. in 1986. Currently the 91 U.K. stores average £8,000 per week, or annual sales per store in Canadian dollars of $900,000.

The U.K. retail pricing structure is significantly lower than Canadian due to the fact that we face shipping costs, duty and additional warehouse costs in Canada. It is unlikely that we shall ever be able to match their retail prices.

However, the Canadian consumer has significantly more disposable income than his/her U.K. counterpart which offsets much of the pricing differential.

We feel that the U.K. sales figures are a reasonable target of our potential over the next 3–4 years. Certainly our history of sales which has tracked those of early U.K. sales suggests that these goals, while aggressive, are not out of reach. Our current store average sales are approximately $660,000.

SALES EXPECTATIONS

Unfortunately, there are no sales guarantees. However, we have consistently maintained the top sales per square foot ratings in those malls where we have shops. Gross sales vary with each location, however, we generally manage to do 2–3 times the average sales of the malls in which we are situated. Also, curiously, the higher the average sales of the mall, the relatively better we do.

Reasonable sales expectation: new shop (600–800 square feet) first year:

Sales	$475,000	
Cost of Sales	247,000	
Rent	42,000	
Salary	65,000	(inc. $24,000 to owner)
Common Area Charges	9,600	
Publicity and Advertising	9,500	(required Mall Advertising)
Insurance	1,200	
Business Taxes	1,200	
Telephone	900	
Travel	1,500	
Service Charges	2,400	
	$ 94,700	(before Government's bite)

These figures represent a rational first year's sales expectation for a shop in a good trading environment. They do not include principal and interest payments or depreciation and amortization on leasehold improvements. Principal and interest payments on any loans are not included as this will vary with the individual owner.

We, the franchisor, demand a minimum of one half of total investment to be backed by the owner's free liquid capital. The chartered banks will generally initially lend against a Body Shop franchise 80% leasehold improvements and 50% against inventories.

We have been very fortunate in the past that new body shop franchises have earned profits from the outset of trading. However, prudence dictates that the investor have adequate capital resources to withstand any reasonable problems associated with slow initial sales, should this eventuality occur. Thus, as confident as we are in our business, we want all shops to be conservatively capitalized.

A new shop can reasonably anticipate a 30% increase in trade in its second year of operation. The rent figure will increase proportionally, however, other costs should increase at the rate of inflation.

On average, the shops sell over $1,200 p.s.f. against an average of $275 p.s.f. of the malls we are located in. Rental paid currently averages about $70 p.s.f. (8% of sales).

Cost of sales average about 51% of retail sales including shipping. Our philosophy has been to maintain our retail price at a constant level, while reducing our costs of product through higher volume purchasing made feasible by our expansion through the franchise system. We anticipate that we will be able to further reduce our costs in this manner as well as through beginning to manufacture more of our products domestically rather than importing them from the U.K.

Exhibit 7. The Body Shop !Bravo! Program.

Performance Reviews come once every six months, and although it's nice to know how you have been doing, somehow it's not enough. Wouldn't it be nice to be recognized on the spot for doing something right, something great or something just plain nice? Wouldn't it be wonderful if everyone knew what you did and that the recognition came from your peers, the people at home office or your manager?

Introducing The Body Shop !Bravo! Program—designed to let you get that extra special boost and to get the appreciation that you deserve, when you deserve it. Here is how this exciting and wonderful program works . . .

We would like to reward you for those extra special things that you do. Not just for being a good employee—that is expected—but for caring enough to go the extra yard. Since we can't always be there to see your stellar performance we thought it would be a great idea if these deeds could be brought to our attention by your teammates. All they have to do is fax in and let us know what you did. You will then be sent a special letter of congratulations, a small token of our appreciation and Bravo points toward the performance rewards.

Here is the breakdown of how many points you get rewarded for what deed:
1 point is issued for a JOB WELL DONE
    —this could include a truly great sale or act of customer care.
2 points are issued for THANK GOD FOR YOU
    —this could include taking extra time to tidy the stock room or organize your work area without telling anyone or being asked.
3 points are issued for ABOVE AND BEYOND THE CALL OF DUTY
    —this could include staying late in order to clean up a disaster such as a flood or break-in and not telling a soul about it.

4 points are issued for EXCEPTIONAL WORK

—this could include preparing a training schedule for your new teammates or taking over a function of your team in a brilliant way.

5 points are issued for OUTSTANDING ABILITY

—this could include taking over the running of your store or department in the absence of the manager or department head and keeping everything ticking against all odds.

We want to reward specific tasks and not general good work so be specific when relating the deed to us. We will decide upon the points that the specific task is worth. It is important that we decide on the points so as to ensure that it is the same across the country. Never write in your recommendation, fax it in always so that we may immediately recognize the outstanding person and their deed.

Once you have started to accumulate points the real fun begins and you can begin to decide what to do with them. Refer to the performance Rewards Chart and carefully study the awards available. Once you have reached five points you will have to decide if you wish to cash them in for cash, product, a prize or KEEP SAVING for a bigger award. Once you have cashed your points in you begin again at zero.

The only rules are:

1. You may only claim these awards while you are a Body Shop or Quig Manufacturing employee.
2. Your reward is specifically for your good performance and points can not be pooled together with other employees.
3. If your employment is terminated you may only use your points towards a cash award. Product and prizes are not available in this case.
4. Have fun and don't forget to watch for great performances.

THE BODY SHOP PERFORMANCE REWARDS CHART

You may claim the rewards below when you have saved up the specified number of points they are worth. Points can be cashed in throughout the year or accumulated for higher prizes.

You may choose either cash or Body Shop product (using your employee discount for added value) or one of the prizes listed in the category of your choice.

POINTS	CASH	PRODUCT	PRIZES
5	$20.00	$25.00	—Protect an acre of Rainforest
			—Classic Books Gift Cert. ($25.00)
			—Mag. Subscript. Your Choice ($25.00)
			—Nylon Stocking Gift Cert. ($25.00)
			—Gourmet Food Basket ($25.00)

10	$50.00	$55.00	—Day Off With Pay
			—Popcorn Popper with Corn
			—Body Shop Umbrella
			—Foot Massager Bath
			—Maid Service for a Day

15    $80.00 $90.00

—Day at the Spa
—Record Gift Cert. ($90.00)
—Collegiate Sport Gift Cert. ($90.00)
—Vaurnet Sun Glasses
—Tickets to Rock Concert—for two

20    $110.00 $130.00

—Sterling Silver Pic. Frame
—Shopping Spree/Lunch
—Personalized Horoscope
—Hot Air Balloon Trip
—Long Distance Vouchers ($130.00)

25    $150.00 $175.00

—Telephone Answering Machine
—35mm Camera
—Rent a Hot Car for the Weekend
—Picnic Basket, Cutlery, Linens
—Casablanca Ceiling Fan

30    $190.00 $225.00

—Community College Course
—Compact Waterproof Binoculars
—His and Her Handknit Sweaters
—Three Piece Luggage Set
—Waterproof Sports Walkman

35    $240.00 $280.00

—Exercise Rowing Machine
—Microwave Oven
—Electric Typewriter
—Monthly Flowers for a Year
—Season's Theatre Subscription

40    $290.00 $340.00

—Astronomical Telescope
—University Course
—Duvet with Cover
—Provincial Health Ins.—1 year
—Hotel Weekend with Breakfast

45	$350.00	$405.00	—1 Ounce of Pure Gold —CD Player —Mountain Bike —Futon —Rail Pass and Weekend Accom.
50	$410.00	$475.00	—Antique Pine Blanket Box —Colour TV —2 "Think and Talk" Berlitz Courses —Membership to a Gym —Gourmet Kitchen Appliances
55	$480.00	$550.00	—Metro Pass for One Year —$550.00 Gas Coupons —Video Recorder —Series of 13 Body Massages —Weekend for Two at a Resort
60	$550.00	$630.00	—Body Shop Int'l Stock Cert. —Pure Bred Puppy or Kitten —Air Canada Pass Worth $630.00 —Gold Birthstone Ring —Free Rent for a Month

Exhibit 8. Number of Shops by Year.

Year	Corporate	Franchise	Total
1980	1	1	2
1981	1	2	3
1982	5	3	8
1983	7	6	13
1984	12	8	20
1985	13	11	24
1986	14	17	31
1987	15	38	53
1988	19	47	66
1989	16	56	72
1990	16	61	77

Exhibit 9. Starship Body Shop.

COMMANDERS

BETTY-ANN FRANSSEN	MARGOT FRANSSEN	QUIG TINGLEY
"Top Gun"	"Navigator"	"Strategic Flight Commander"

FIRST OFFICERS

ACCOUNTANT	FRANCHISE SYSTEMS
"Control Tower"	"Flight Operations"

FLIGHT LIEUTENANTS

Warehouse Manager	Production Managers	
Manuf. & Q.C. Manager	Corporate Operations	Merchandising Director
Training Director	Quig Operations Manager	

FLIGHT CREW

Corporate Stores Liaison	Corporate Stock Control	Corporate Merchandiser
Corporate Administration	Receptionist	Franchise Area Manager
Franchise Operations Assistant	Payroll	Franchise Liaison
Merchandising Assistant	Communications/P.R.	Training Assistant
P.R. Administration Assistant	Order Entry	Warehouse Liaison
Retail Operations Receptionist	Order Entry	Assistant Accountant

Exhibit 10. Description of Operations.

HEAD OFFICE

The Head Office is in charge of all accounting, public relations and franchise operations.

> "People feel that things are being done and head office is always willing to listen and that accounts for a lot. For instance, they have organized an Advisory Board made up of elected franchisees who meet with them to talk about problems, situations and possible solutions. Head office then compiles and distributes that information to all the franchises." (Advisory Board Member)

TRAINING SCHOOL

In March 1990, the Canadian Training School was opened with its own small conference room, fully equipped salon, and completely stocked and merchandised shop. It is here that new employees and franchisees formally learn about the corporate philosophy, human anatomy and company products. And, where necessary, shop management and operation. They are encouraged to work with the products and experiment with merchandising ideas first hand.

The training is generally scheduled 4 times a year and ranges from a 2 day induction course for new head office and warehouse employees, to an 8 week training programme for the new franchisees (see the Training Courses Available on the next page). As one employee explained, "what you learn is of benefit for your whole life. It taught me about a healthy way of living. It was so good I would have paid to take it."

Although they usually try to coordinate new store openings with the training schedule, this is often not possible. As one franchisee who owns 3 stores explained,

> "We do most of our own training because it is very hard to schedule with the head office training. They don't necessarily offer the training when you need it. So I take the Train the Trainer course at head office and keep in contact with them because they are the information source and then I do with it what I feel is necessary for my needs."

RETAIL OPERATIONS

The bulk of Retail Operations work revolves around the franchise and corporate store image, and compliance with and consistency of set standards. They are in charge of all store openings, product merchandising and window displays. As well, they deal with the suppliers and liaise with the environmental groups and coordinate all the issue windows, campaigns and pamphlets.

Compliance on environmental policies, display windows and community work, is enforced by four announced inspection visits and one surprise visit annually.

"Everything we do comes from our gut feelings about what is right for the consumer and how we like to be treated when we're shopping," says Margot. And it's an approach that seems to work. Nationally, per store sales increases have averaged 38% for each of the last 5 years. Sales average $800 to $1400 per sq. foot, almost three times the national average for stores in shopping malls.

Salaries in retail are traditionally low, and The Body Shop is no exception. But as Quig explained, "we have enough young people around to keep us on track. Everyone is involved and they are too young to have a vested interest just in money." Unlike many retailers, however, The Body Shop pays salary and store bonus as opposed to commission—"we don't want to pit one sales person against another. We want them motivated by the store's total sales."

In total, there are 75 employees on the payroll, not including the corporate store managers and staff. Quig manufacturing accounts for 49 employees (16 in production, 19 in warehousing and 14 in the office). The remainder are divided between the Head Office (where there is a staff of 12), and Retail and Training (where there are 14 employed). In each corporate store there is, on average, 4 to 6 full-time sales staff (including the manager and her assistant), 2 part-time sales staff and 2 part-time stock girls. As well, in preparation for the Christmas rush, 4–5 part-time gift-makers are usually hired. The average shop consists of 800 sq. ft. of store and 400 sq. ft. of inventory space.

SOME OF THE TRAINING COURSES AVAILABLE

Pre-Training Meeting (new franchises)

Corporate Induction (2 days)

Administrative Training (2 days)

Customer Sensitivity (2 days)

Public Relations Training

Meeting Key Home Office Personnel

Training Techniques (3 days)

Merchandising and Display (4 days)

Aromatherapy

Body Product Basics

Problem Skin

Herbal Hair

Colourings (2 days)

Franchise Shop Visit

Review Meetings

In-Store Assignments (2 to 10 days)

Tender Touch Car Wash Ltd.

As Mr. Paul Ursini, aged 35 and second generation owner of the family business, sat down to read the consultant's report he could not help but reflect over the history that had brought Tender Touch to its current situation. Although it was still strong financially, Tender Touch's profits were beginning to fall. But this was not the first time that the full service car wash had experienced a need for change. In the 7 years since Paul had taken over his father's business, he had implemented at least two major phases of change. It would, however, be the first time that major construction was considered.

A consultant had been hired to assess the viability (in terms of market, size and costs) of constructing a coin-operated car wash adjacent to the existing business. As Paul suspected, the consultant felt that Tender Touch was in a good position to expand both in terms of the physical building and the target market. The report made reference to the feasibility of constructing a 10 bay coin-operated car wash on the adjacent vacant property which, like the current Tender Touch location, was debt free and owned by the Ursini family.

BACKGROUND

Tender Touch Car Wash Ltd. was originally opened in 1959 by John Ursini, who took pride in his wash and always said "a clean car rides better and lasts longer." It was a full service car wash (interior and exterior) that was completely labour intensive. Originally, twenty-four men hand-washed as the cars passed by on an assembly line conveyor. This number was, however, eventually decreased to an average of fourteen employees (including a cashier and a manager) as new equipment replaced some of the labour (Exhibit 1).

Located in the west end of Toronto, in the borough of Etobicoke, Tender Touch was situated on a main artery which provided it with exposure to plenty of traffic. In the early 1970s, the area of Etobicoke began to boom. Its proximity to the downtown core attracted many families which, in turn, attracted a variety of businesses. Among the businesses established were numerous car dealerships which presented an opportunity for Tender Touch. In order to improve the salability of their cars, particularly the used cars, the dealers liked to have the cars completely cleaned. This often involved an exterior buff wax (simonize) and an interior shampoo. To hire someone to do it on their own property

This case was prepared by Robert Ursini, Leslie Becker and Ronda Fisher under the direction of Prof. W. H. Ellis, McGill University, as a basis for class discussion rather than to illustrate either effective or ineffective handling of an administrative situation. Copyright © Professor W. H. Ellis, 1990. All rights reserved.

occupied both space and time, but those were two things that Tender Touch could supply. To test out the viability of the business, John offered this service at a reasonable rate of one of the dealerships. After four months and word of mouth, other dealerships began to follow. As a result, Tender Touch added on a simonize room in order to service this market effectively and efficiently. This allowed Tender Touch to establish itself with the dealerships in the area which, eventually, lead to contracts to wash the employees' cars as well.

Also in the early 1970s, newly developed equipment was purchased and installed. High pressured water, rotating brushes and a dryer were used to rinse, clean and dry the cars. Fresh water was used, unlike some washes that recycled their dirty water back into the wash, because John Ursini always felt that "people were willing to pay a little extra for a truly clean car." Soon after, equipment was installed so that the "wax option" could be offered.

During this period, John's son Paul had been sporadically involved in the business. In the late 1970s, however, Paul became increasingly interested, and soon managed the day to day operations of the business under John's watchful eye. This proved to be invaluable training in light of John's untimely passing in the early 1980s, after which full ownership of the car wash fell into Paul's hands. The ownership of the land was left to the Ursini brothers; it was therefore agreed that Paul would lease the property from this partnership.

RECENT HISTORY

By the time Paul took over, the business had become quite stagnant. He felt Tender Touch had lost its edge over its competitors and that a change was needed. He therefore decided to convert the wash to a new Soft Cloth System. The new system would limit the number of fine scratches that appeared due to extended use of the old brushes. Tender Touch would be the first wash to introduce such a system in the Metropolitan Toronto area and Paul felt this would give them the edge they were looking for. The cost of the system was relatively high, but it was quickly justified by the immediate and positive reaction received from the old and new customers. Old customers felt it showed that Tender Touch really did care about their cars, while new customers, who previously would never use automated car washes due to the scratch factor, were attracted for the first time.

Another goal Paul set for himself was to create an image at Tender Touch of cleanliness and order. He purchased new shirts for the employees and had them printed with a Tender Touch bubbles logo on the front and the expression "A clean car rides better and lasts longer" on the back. As well, he organized the printing of information pamphlets, price lists and small plastic bags (Exhibit 2). This gave the business a professional look which, in turn, gave the customers a feeling of confidence when they handed their car over to the staff.

The second major phase of change Paul implemented was in 1986 when he leased, for $50,000 per year, an existing six bay coin-operated (coin-op) car wash that was situated near the full-serve location. For the two years that the coin-op was in operation, a net income of approximately $40,000 per year was generated. Although Paul wished to continue the operation, the lease was not renewed in 1988. The owner of the coin-op, Ryder Truck, chose to reclaim the land in order to expand their parking capacity. They, therefore, tore down the facilities, thus removing the only coin-op within a 10 mile radius. Given the established market for this operation, Paul felt that a new coin-op in the area could be both a viable and low-risk venture. He, therefore, considered hiring a consultant to assess this viability.

THE INDUSTRY

The car wash industry in Toronto is very seasonal. Winters are the busiest time due to the presence of salt and sand on the roads. Summers, on the other hand, are slow due to the fact that cars tend to stay cleaner longer and people are more likely to clean their cars themselves.

Traditionally, the most critical problems faced by the car wash industry were: the high wages and availability (or lack thereof) of quality labour; the high cost of equipment and maintenance; competition from the gas stations; and the need for improving customer appeal with promotions and advertising.

In general, the industry experiences a high turnover rate due to the long hours (10 hours per day), instability (workers are often sent home due to lack of work on rainy days) and monotony the job entails. At Tender Touch, however, labour problems have been minimal. Paul's father, John, nurtured respect and loyalty from his workers by providing fair and stable positions; he was able to attract long-term employees by offering relatively high wages with full benefit plans for those who stayed for a year. He also offered full-pay on slow days in order to provide greater stability for these family men. The turnover rate had, therefore, been very low; so by the time Paul took over, most of the employees had been with the company for many years and were prepared to stay for many more. The employees' experience and reliability had the added bonus of ensuring that the expensive equipment was well maintained which, in turn, minimized breakdowns and customer frustrations.

Gasoline stations were fast becoming the greatest threat to the industry. They had the capital and the space to invest in the automated equipment and the construction of the buildings. As well, they were in a position to use the washes as an incentive to drivers to buy their gasoline; the prices for their washes were low as they made their money on the gasoline sales. Fortunately, Tender Touch had been able to minimize this threat through a deal they had worked out with the Petro-Canada service station located directly beside them. For years, when a customer filled up at the station, Petro-Canada provided them with money off coupons for use at the Tender Touch car wash. Petro-Canada paid Tender Touch an annual lump sum which was negotiated at the beginning of each year. This deal had the added advantage of providing Tender Touch with a form of promotion and advertising.

FINANCIALS

Historically, Tender Touch's profits have been consistent. As the last three years' income statements indicate, operating earnings have been around the $220,000 mark (Exhibit 3).

There is relatively little in the accounts receivable (Exhibit 4), as most customers pay with cash or credit card. Although the dealerships are invoiced, they usually pay on a weekly basis. The proximity of and the good relations with the dealerships have made for easy collection of receivables. It is rare to have a receivable outstanding for more than one month.

CONSULTANT'S RECOMMENDATIONS

The consultant recognized the need to address the stagnating sales and to add to the existing business. It appears that both these needs could be addressed by expanding into the coin-operated car wash business.

In addition to owning the land where Tender Touch was located, the Ursinis also owned the adjacent vacant lot. In the past, the vacant lot had been leased out to other businesses, including a truck rental agency and used-car dealership, who used the property as a parking lot. It had, however, been sitting empty for five years. The recommendation was, therefore, to lease the adjacent property from the Ursini partnership in order to build a ten bay coin-operated car wash. A steady flow of income could, therefore, be generated from both the property and the coin-op business.

The vacant property was zoned as second class industrial land which meant that only 10% of it could be used as office space and the rest as warehouse. Construction of the coin-op would, therefore, be permitted.

THE TENDER TOUCH COIN-OP

The recommended coin-op would have ten bays or stalls. Each stall would have one high pressure wand, one foam brush, and a set of mat holders. The floors would also be heated for customer convenience in the winter. The high pressure wand would be used to rinse, wash and wax the car. The foam brush would be used to wash the car and would also allow the washers' hands to remain dry. All of these would be controlled, one at a time, by a switch located with the money deposit slot. A covered vacuuming area would also be built to allow the customers to vacuum the interiors of their cars in any type of weather. A designated dry-off area would also be provided.

FINANCING

The total cost of the proposal was estimated to be $580,000 (see Exhibit 5). The property that the coin-op would be built on was valued at approximately $800,000. It was therefore felt that the property could sustain the full loan in the form of a first mortgage; banks generally provide 100% financing for car washes because their simple construction and low maintenance ensure low costs per square foot and high returns relative to other industrial endeavours. The Cash Flow Statement (Exhibit 6) indicated that a $600,000 loan would be sufficient to cover the construction and start-up costs.

Based on Paul's previous coin-op experience, the projected annual revenue and operating costs were $120,000/30% of sales ($36,000), respectively. It was felt , however, that the earnings from the full-serve could, however, help offset any cash flow or financial problems which could arise.

The Pro-Forma Financial Statements (Exhibits 7 and 8) indicated that the coin-op would have a significant impact on Tender Touch's income and balance sheet.

IMPLEMENTATION

The estimated duration of construction from the time the ground was broken to the time the wash was up and running was approximately three months. A fall opening would therefore be preferred in order to allow Paul to prepare for the busier winter months; a winter operation would mean the cash flow coming into the business would be at one of its highest points and would get the coin-op off to a good start.

The loan would need to be attained at commencement of construction as builders progress bill (i.e., partial payments would have to be made as work was completed).

Before construction could begin, there would be many things to take care of, such as the Site Plan Approval, the Application for a Business License and the Notice for the Erection of a Sign. Also Engineering Certificates would need to be attained along with a Surveyor's Certificate.

Construction would start with the excavation and removal of fill. The footings would then be set and the sewers and drains put in place. Next would come the masonry or erection of walls, along with the placement of the structural steel. Roofing would be the last step to finish off the physical building. The internal aspects would then be looked after, such as electrical, plumbing and heating. The final concrete would be laid at the same time as the equipment. The final touches would then be added such as caulking, painting, insulation, asphalting and landscaping.

TARGET MARKET

In the past Tender Touch had serviced a specific portion of the car wash consumer market. This segment was made up of mature (over 35 years old) men and women who were financially secure and willing to pay more for the convenience of a full service wash.

Tender Touch had, however, overlooked a large portion of the car wash consumer market; their relatively high prices, a minimum cost of $7.50 for a full service car wash, had typically eliminated many potential customers. The coin-op car wash would therefore target and attract the younger adults of the market as well as the car enthusiasts. The young adults, with their limited disposable income, did not consider a clean car to be a priority.

The significantly lower costs of the coin-op would, however, make them more likely candidates.

The car enthusiasts would also be attracted to wash their cars at the new coin-op. Found in various age brackets and income levels, the appeal for them would be the scratchlessness and the fact that you "do-it-yourself." They took great pride in their cars and definitely considered a spotless car to be of importance. Fearful of scratching or other damage to their cars, they avoided full service car washes, opting to wash their cars themselves. At a coin-op, however, it would be possible to wash the car without the fear of scratching.

The young adults and car enthusiasts were a large proportion of the market that Tender Touch had alienated in the past, yet, as past experience indicated, there was a market for a coin-op at Tender Touch.

ADVANTAGES OF THE PROPOSAL

Given the proximity of the existing full service car wash, it was felt that the limited amount of care and maintenance needed to run the coin-op could be absorbed by Tender Touch. Paul or his general manager would be available to attend to any immediate problem that might arise. The cost of running the coin-op would therefore be kept minimal. The location would also ensure that customers received the help they required when a machine malfunctioned.

The coin-operated car wash would also complement the full service car wash already in existence. In addition to expanding their customer base, the coin-op would turn Tender Touch from a full service car wash into a complete car care centre, ready to provide the entire car wash market with the cleaning method of their choice.

Labour concerns were another area that would be addressed by a coin-op system. With the available labour supply decreasing, it was felt that the "labour pinch" would translate into an increase in wages and a decrease in productivity, and eventually an increase in service charges to the customer. The coin-operated, "do-it-yourself" car wash would, therefore, avoid such problems because additional labour would not need to be hired.

The consultant also felt the proposal of a coin-op made sense in terms of management and experience. Paul had years of experience in the car wash industry; he had seven years of direct experience in the full-serve wash and, more relevant to the proposal, two years of coin-op experience. He was familiar with the equipment, as were some of his employees. He could, therefore, avoid both the added costs of calling a repair man and the loss of business due to an "out of order" sign if there were a problem or breakdown in the machinery. Paul was also familiar with the car wash customer; he knew what they wanted and how to provide it.

THE COMPETITION

Competition in the exterior car wash market was, however, becoming fierce. Gas stations were beginning to build washes into their sites simply to attract customers to buy their gas; the price of their washes were, therefore, kept to a minimum and could directly undercut independent car wash operators. In the past, Tender Touch had targeted the upper-middle class customer, pushing service that the other exterior-only washes could not offer. With the construction of the coin-op, however, Tender Touch would be competing directly with the other exterior car washes.

There were a few coin-ops located beyond the ten mile radius that could be considered competition, but they were also viewed as potential opportunities. Although they were in operation, they were typically older, run down sites with outdated equipment and a high rate of equipment malfunction. Most of the owners were older (over 55) and no longer worked the business as diligently as they had in the past. There was, therefore, the possibility that Tender Touch could expand their coin-op market share in the future should these owners decide to retire or sell their respective site(s).

In contrast to these older sites, Tender Touch's coin-op would be equipped with updated machinery and accessories that were unavailable before. The site would be aesthetically more pleasing and would be continually maintained in order to minimize equipment malfunction. Although these differences would require the charging of a higher price ($1.25 to $1.50 for Tender Touch versus a $1.00 at the older sites) it was believed that people would be willing to pay for the superior service offered.

THE FUTURE

After considering all the advantages associated with the consultant's recommendations, Paul still questioned whether he was prepared to take on the added responsibility and increased competition associated with the coin-op. Although the six bay coin-op he had operated before managed to make a small profit, he wondered whether he was financially in a position to take on the significant increase in overhead that the proposal would require. As well, he was concerned about his future labour supply; although, in the past, he had been blessed with a low turnover rate, he did not know how long these highly experienced employees would be around in the future.

Exhibit 1. Organizational Chart.

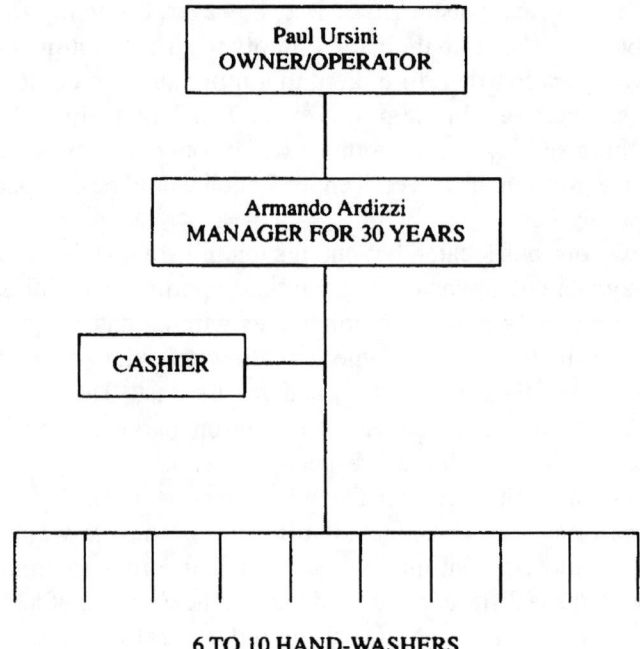

6 TO 10 HAND-WASHERS

Exhibit 2.

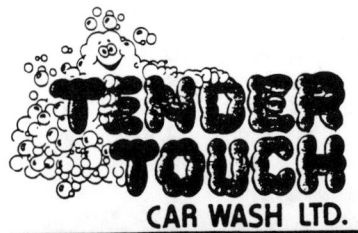

Automotive

Detail Centre

Simonizing high speed polish & hand waxing

    small car .... $ 85.00

    medium car.. $ 95.00

    large car $105.00

    vans, trucks, RV & boats .... by estimate

Overspray removal .... by estimate

Interior shampoo & deodarize

    small car .... $ 75.00

    medium car.. $ 85.00

    large car .... $ 95.00

    station wagon, vans, trucks, RV & boats .... by estimate

Engine cleaning	$ 30.00
with paint	$ 50.00
Mag & Spoke wheel treatment	$ 29.95
Armoral Interior & Exterior	$ 34.95
Armoral Interior	$ 19.95
Armoral Exterior	$ 19.95
Vinyl roof Detail, shampoo & dressing	$ 24.95
Headliner (Subject to Inspection)	$ 19.95
Scotchguarding	$ 39.95
Handwash & Interior Clean	$ 25.00 & up

ABOVE PRICES MAY VARY DUE TO SIZE OR CONDITION OF VEHICLE
TAX EXTRA

Shell, Visa, Mastercard, American Express Honoured.
Open 5 Days: Mon.–Fri. 8 a.m.–6 p.m.

"At Tender Touch the difference is professionalism"

Tender Touch Car Wash
2141 Dundas St. E.
Mississauga L4X 1M3
625-1982

Exhibit 3. Tender Touch Car Wash Limited Income Statements for the Years Ended
December 31, +

	19X3	19X2	19X1
REVENUE			
Car Washes	$559,520	$519,958	$481,948
Simonizes and Shampoos	144,118	159,799	162,544
Waxes	46,507	29,887	24,872
Accessories and Sundry	21,790	27,438	13,913
	$771,935	$737,082	$683,277
DIRECT COSTS			
Business Taxes	2,756	2658	2,462
Canada Pension	6,412	5,231	4,570
Damage to Customers' Cars	3,678	620	2,447
Employee Benefits	7,594	5,982	7,265
Hydro and Gas	23,666	23,937	21,910
Insurance	7,977	7,782	6,956
Maintenance: Equipment	14,447	18,885	8,336
Building and Premises	6,321	8,928	4,478
Purchases—Accessories	19,852	24,958	12,578
Realty Taxes	9,192	8,864	8,209
Soap and Chemicals	20,010	17,807	18,637
Shop Supplies	12,552	8,001	15,525
Unemployment Insurance	10,902	9,389	10,566
Wages and Commissions	358,489	318,743	286,168
Workmen's Compensation	10,394	9,872	7,671
Water	17,188	13,330	11,502
Depreciation: Wash Equipment	25,386	30,180	33,368
Leasehold Costs	2,604	0	2,609
	$559,420	$515,167	$465,257
OPERATING EARNINGS	$212,515	$221,915	$218,020
ADMINISTRATION COSTS			
Accounting	7,825	7,500	7,300
Advertising & Bus. Promotion	20,210	22,908	22,838
Bad Debts	0	153	700
Bank Charges & Interest	17,141	21,903	28,262
Cam & Trucks	28,729	24,353	10,762
Management Salaries	36,020	34,100	37,340
Office—General & Legal	11,422	13,079	13,427
Office Rent	2,250	1,875	1,258
Office Salaries	28,803	21,475	25,354
Telephone	3,701	6,529	5,856
Total Administration Costs	$156,101	$153,875	$153,095
NET PROFIT BEFORE TAXES	$ 56,414	$ 68,040	$ 64,925

Exhibit 4. Tender Touch Car Wash Limited Balance Sheet for the Years Ended December 31, +

	19X3	19X2	19X1
ASSETS			
Current			
Cash	$45,000	$45,000	$45,000
Accounts Receivable	54,715	50,250	39,998
Inventory	5,800	5,200	6,310
Prepaid	5,618	8,800	8,270
Loans Receivable	72,864	90,020	110,810
Total Current Assets	$183,997	$199,270	$210,388
Fixed Assets			
Land	500,000	500,000	500,000
Coin-op (leased)	0	26,756	26,756
Building (full serve)	295,000	295,000	295,000
Wash Equipment	230,450	226,940	215,755
Leasehold Improvements	0	26,087	9,087
Accumulated Depreciation	(129,795)	(114,285)	(83,588)
Total Fixed Assets	$ 895,655	$ 960,498	$ 963,010
Total Assets	$1,079,652	$1,159,768	$1,173,398
LIABILITIES			
Current			
Bank Indebtedness	11,678	8,755	4,887
Bank Loans	97,200	175,120	203,000
Accounts Payable	29,065	30,558	22,918
Payroll Liabilities	10,436	7,928	7,610
Income Tax Payable	2,068	9,740	18,458
Unredeemed Car Wash Coupons	23,014	0	11,500
Loans Payable—Shareholders	9,677	19,527	0
Total Current Liabilities	$183,138	$251,628	$268,373
Long Term Liabilities			
Bank Loans	0	0	0
Total Liabilities	$183,138	$251,628	$268,373
SHAREHOLDERS EQUITY			
Capital Stock			
Authorized—Preferred = 18,750			
—Common = 4,000			
Issued = 100 Common Shares	100	100	100
Retained Earnings	896,414	908,040	904,925
Total Shareholders Equity	$ 896,514	$ 908,140	$ 905,025
Total Liab. & Shareholders Equity	$1,079,652	$1,159,768	$1,173,398

Exhibit 5. Estimated Costs of Coin-op Construction

Set-up, shack, surveyor	$3,500
Disposal boxes	3,000
Excavate, remove fill, back fill, compaction sand	8,800
Footings re-bars, concrete, forms	14,500
Masonry—block brick	64,000
Kalamein door frames and doors	1,900
Hardware—locks, handles, nails . . .	5,000
Structural steel	50,000
Misc. iron—angles, lintels . . .	9,650
Metal roof deck	16,000
Roofing—4 ply, built up, flashing	18,000
Cant strips, fascia 500'	3,500
Canopy roof	12,000
Metal siding on canopy	25,000
Aluminum windows and doors	14,000
Concrete	50,000
Concrete finishing	6,000
Sewers—drains, tanks . . .	21,250
Floor reinforcing—mesh, re-bars	5,200
Electrical	50,000
Plumbing	20,000
Heating, A/C, ducts	10,000
Equipment, vacuums . . .	100,000
Signage, pylons, bases . . .	10,000
Drywall, acoustics	5,000
Caulking	3,000
Painting	2,500
Insulation—vapour barrier	1,700
Flooring—carpet, tile, wood	5,000
Asphalt paving	30,000
Landscaping, curbs	8,000
Engineering certificates	3,500
TOTAL COST	$580,000

Exhibit 6. Tender Touch Car Wash Limited (with Coin-op) Cashflow Statement by Month for the Year X4

	June	July	Aug.	Sept.	Oct.	Nov.
Cash in Bank	$650,000	$573,289	$302,578	$59,867	$46,656	$44,845
Sales	0	0	0	5,000	7,000	9,000
Operating Costs	0	0	0	1,500	2,100	2,700
Operating Profit	0	0	0	3,500	4,900	6,300
Construction	70,000	264,000	236,000	10,000	0	0
E.B.I.T.	(70,000)	(264,000)	(236,000)	(6,500)	4,900	6,300
Loan Payments	6,711	6,711	6,711	6,711	6,711	6,711
Cash Inflow (Outflow)	(76,711)	(270,711)	(242,711)	(13,211)	(1,811)	(411)
Net Cash in Bank	$573,289	$302,578	$59,867	$46,656	$44,845	$44,434

	Dec.	Jan.	Feb.	Mar.	Apr.	May	Total
Cash in Bank	$44,434	$44,723	$45,712	$46,701	$47,690	$48,679	$650,000
Sales	10,000	11,000	11,000	11,000	11,000	10,000	85,000
Operating Costs	3,000	3,300	3,300	3,300	3,300	3,000	25,500
Operating Profit	7,000	7,700	7,700	7,700	7,700	7,000	59,500
Construction	0	0	0	0	0	0	580,000
E.B.I.T.	7,000	7,700	7,700	7,700	7,700	7,000	(520,500)
Loan Payments	6,711	6,711	6,711	6,711	6,711	6,711	80,532
Cash Inflow (Outflow)	289	989	989	989	989	289	(601,032)
Net Cash in Bank	$44,723	$45,712	$46,701	$47,690	$48,679	$48,968	$48,968

Exhibit 7. Tender Touch Car Wash Limited Pro Forma Income Statements for the Year Ended December 31,

	19X6	19X5	19X4
REVENUE			
Coin-op	$120,000	$110,000	$40,000
Car Washes	680,000	640,000	600,000
Simonizes and Shampoos	160,000	155,000	150,000
Waxes	47,000	47,000	47,000
Accessories and Sundry	21,000	21,000	21,000
	$1,028,000	$973,000	$858,000
DIRECT COSTS			
Business Taxes	3,000	2,900	2,800
Canada Pension	8,000	7,500	7,000
Damage to Customers Cars	3,000	3,000	3,000
Employee Benefits	7,500	7,500	7,500
Hydro and Gas	24,400	24,200	24,000
Insurance	8,000	8,000	8,000
Maintenance: Equipment	15,000	15,000	15,000
Building and Premise	7,000	7,000	7,000
Purchases-Accessories	20,000	20,000	20,000
Realty Taxes	10,500	10,000	9,500
Soap and Chemicals	23,000	22,000	21,000
Shop Supplies	13,000	13,000	13,000
Unemployment Insurance	11,000	11,000	11,000
Wages and Commissions	450,000	430,000	390,000
Workmen's Compensation	11,400	11,100	10,800
Water	22,000	21,000	20,000
Depreciation: Wash Equipment	17,000	19,000	22,000
Leasehold Costs	2,000	2,000	2,000
	$655,800	$634,200	$593,600
OPERATING EARNINGS	$372,200	$338,800	$264,400
ADMINISTRATION COSTS			
Accounting	8,600	8,300	8,000
Advertising & Bus. Promotion	23,000	23,000	24,000
Bad Debts	200	200	200
Bank Charges & Interest	85,000	90,000	95,000
Cars & Trucks	34,000	32,000	30,000
Management Salaries	39,000	38,000	37,000
Office—General & Legal	12,000	12,000	12,000
Office Rent	2,250	2,250	2,250
Office Salaries	34,000	32,000	30,000
Telephone	4,000	4,000	4,000
Total Administration Costs	$242,050	$241,750	$242,450
NET PROFIT BEFORE TAXES	$130,150	$97,050	$21,950

Exhibit 8. Tender Touch Car Wash Limited Pro Forma Balance Sheet For the Year Ended December 31,

	19X6	19X5	19X4
ASSETS			
Current			
Cash	$45,000	$45,000	$45,000
Accounts Receivable	67,350	60,950	55,000
Inventory	6,900	6,700	6,500
Prepaid	7,000	6,500	6,000
Loans Receivable	15,000	32,000	52,000
Total Current Assets	$141,250	$151,150	$164,500
Fixed Assets			
Land	500,000	500,000	500,000
Building (full serve)	295,000	295,000	295,000
Building (coin-op)	580,000	580,000	580,000
Wash Equipment	245,000	240,000	235,000
Accumulated Depreciation	(175,000)	(160,000)	(145,000)
Total Fixed Assets	$1,445,000	$1,455,000	$1,465,000
Total Assets	$1,586,250	$1,606,150	$1,629,500
LIABILITIES			
Current			
Bank Indebtedness	19,000	17,000	15,000
Bank Loans	50,000	55,000	85,450
Accounts Payable	30,000	30,000	30,000
Payroll Liabilities	11,000	11,000	11,000
Income Tax Payable	4,000	4,000	4,000
Unredeemed Car Wash Coupons	22,000	22,000	22,000
Loans Payable—Shareholders	0	0	0
Total Current Liabilities	$136,000	$139,000	$167,456
Long Term Liabilities			
Bank Loans	480,000	530,000	
Total Liabilities	$616,000	$669,000	$767,450
SHAREHOLDERS EQUITY			
Capital Stock			
Authorized—Preferred = 18,750			
Common = 4,000			
Issued = 100 Common Shares	100	100	100
Retained Earnings	970,150	937,050	861,950
Total Shareholders Equity	$970,250	$937,150	$862,050
Total Liab. & Shareholders Equity	$1,586,250	$1,606,150	$1,629,500

CASE 16

Applied CAD Knowledge, Inc.
A: The "Boom/Splat" Syndrome

Something is seriously wrong with this planet. Look at us. I'm working a hundred and twenty hours a week or more, and not catching up. I've got these two friends— both recently divorced, like me—who aren't working at all: they're living off their girl friends, and loving it. One of them is basking in Hawaii. But here I am, busting my ass and giving my customers problems anyhow.

Some guys go on television and say, "Send money now," and people *do*. I ask my best customer to send $30,000, and he goes bankrupt instead. What's wrong with this picture?

Jeff Stevens, president and 90 percent owner of Applied CAD Knowledge, Inc., was reporting on current sales and production levels to the two business school professors who comprised his Board of Directors. It was late August of 1987, and the three men sat in a booth at Bogie's restaurant. The waitress, Patty, was accustomed to these monthly meetings; she offered another round of Lite beer. "Make mine cyanide," said Stevens. "On the rocks, please."

Applied CAD, a small service bureau which designed electronic circuit boards, was experiencing the highest sales levels in its three-year history. June sales had reached $50,000—leaving a backlog of $90,000; July shipments had set a record at $58,000; August would be nearly as high. The problem facing Stevens through the summer of 1987 was a shortage of good designers to work as part-time freelancers. The surge in business saw Stevens sitting at the computer consoles himself, doing design work on second and third shifts, six or seven days a week. After eight weeks of this schedule, the strain was showing. One director asked about the longer-range sales picture, and Stevens summed it up:

There's nothing on the books at all for late Fall, and not much likely. Every major customer we have is in "busy phase" right now. When these designs are finished, it will be another four to six months before their next generation of product revisions. In the meantime, everybody is burned out. All I'm hoping for right now is a front porch, a rocking chair, a lobotomy and a drool cup.

This case was prepared by John A. Seeger, Bentley College, and Raymond M. Kinnunen, Northeastern University, as a basis for class discussion. Distributed by the North American Case Research Association. All rights reserved to the authors and the North American Case Research Association. Permission to use the case should be obtained from the authors and the North American Case Research Association. This case has accompanying videotapes of Jeff Stevens in a question and answer session in front of an executive M.B.A. class that can be purchased from Northeastern University, College of Business Administration, Boston, MA 02115. Copyright © 1990 by John A. Seeger and Raymond M. Kinnunen, reprinted with permission.

THE ELECTRONICS INDUSTRY AND CIRCUIT BOARD DESIGN

The United States electronics industry in 1987 was a sprawling giant, some of whose sectors were growing while others remained in a protracted slump. In 1986, total industry size was variously estimated as $100 billion to $182 billion.

A basic part of nearly every electronic product was the printed circuit board (PCB) to which a variety of electronic components were attached. These components ranged from old-fashioned resistors and capacitors to transistors and the most modern integrated circuit chips. All components needed some sort of platform to sit on, and some way to make connection with other components.

In the 1930s and '40s, circuit boards were made from thin, non-conducting fibreboard with metal pins and sockets attached. Assembly operators wound the wire leads of the circuit's resistors, capacitors, etc. around the proper pins and soldered them in place. By the 1960s, this technology had become highly automated. Numerically-controlled machines positioned the components and connected the pins to one another with wires. By the 1980s both the pins and the wires had disappeared, replaced by electrically conductive lines which were "printed" or plated onto (or under) the surface of the board itself. Wire leads from electrical components are inserted through small holes in the board and soldered on the underside. (Figure 1 shows specimen PCBs.)

The increasing complexity of electronic circuits presented a problem for PCB technology. When connections were made with wires, assemblers simply attached one end, routed the wire over the top of everything between the two pins involved, and attached the other end where it belonged. With printed circuits, however, designers are constrained to two dimensions on a flat board; they must route the line between two pins without touching any other lines. Furthermore, efficient design calls for the components to be tightly packed together, grouped by function. Designers frequently find situations where they cannot lay out a trace from one point to another without interfering with other traces.

"Multilayer" PCBs (see Figure 2) ease this problem by providing "upstairs" layers on the board, allowing the designer to "go over the top." Multilayer boards contain at least three layers of traces, and sometimes more than twenty layers. Skilled designers seek to minimize the number of layers required for a given circuit, in order to reduce manufacturing costs: multilayer PCBs are far more expensive to manufacture.

Board design was made more complicated by increasing density of components, by sensitivity of components to heat (some threw off large amounts of heat, while others would go haywire if their operating temperature was disturbed) and by radio-frequency interference (some components generated static, while others might "hear" the noise and try to process it). The layout of components on the board had tremendous impact on how well the finished product worked, as well as on its manufacturing cost.

In 1983, according to *Electronic Business* magazine, multilayer boards had sales of $900 million, or 25 per cent of the PCB market. By 1993, multilayer boards were forecast to reach sales of $5.6 billion, or 41 per cent market share. Exhibit 1 shows PCB sales and projections by type of board.

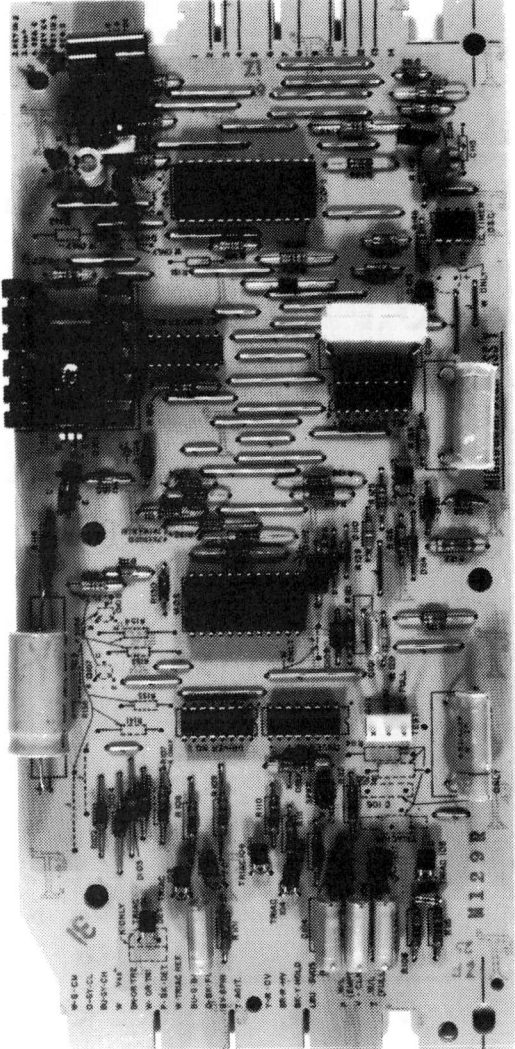
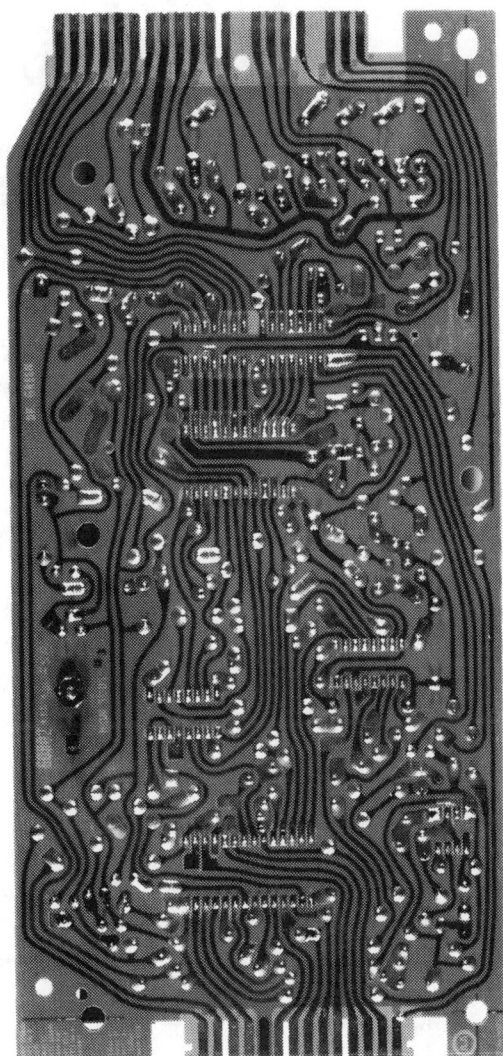

Figure 1a. Top and bottom views of a fully-assembled circuit board, taken from a Kenmore washing machine. Electronic components are visible in the top view (left); their soldered connections are visible in the bottom view (right). Shown one-half actual size.

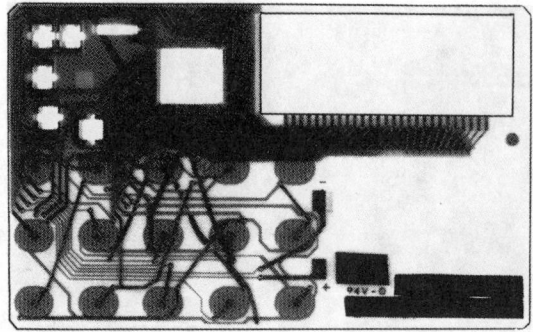

Figure 1b. Circuit board for a ten-key hand calculator. This board is made of transparent plastic; both the top and bottom levels of traces are apparent.

Frost and Sullivan, Inc., a New York market research firm, estimated (in "The Printed Circuit Board Market in the U.S.," July 1986, quoted by permission) that the total U.S. PCB market reached $3.7 billion in sales in 1985, a decrease of 12 per cent from 1984's production. PCBs were projected to grow to a likely $6.5 billion by 1990 and to $10.8 billion in 1995. Multi-layer PCBs were expected to be the fastest-growing type, averaging 15.7 per cent per year annual growth. A little over half the market was served in 1985 by independent PCB fabricators, as opposed to captive suppliers, Frost & Sullivan said.

TRENDS IN CIRCUIT BOARD DESIGN EQUIPMENT

Originally (and still, for simple circuits), an engineer or technician worked from a "schematic" drawing of the circuit, which showed how the various components were connected. On a large layout table, the PCB designer manually drew in the components and linked them with black tape (or ink), to produce a "photo master" film which was in turn used to manufacture the circuit board. As circuits became more complex, the manual process bogged down.

By the mid 1970s, computer-aided design (CAD) vendors began to offer computer systems specifically for PCB designing. Racal-Redac, Inc., a British firm, was the first to offer a system which permitted PCB designers to interact with the computer, trying various routings of traces to see how they looked on the graphic display. This approach, based on the moderate-price DEC PDP-11, competed well against established CAD systems such as those made by Gerber Scientific or Computervision, whose equipment was priced in the $500,000 class and still lacked interactive design capability.

By 1982, prices for PCB design systems had fallen below $100,000. New CAD equipment makers entered the field with automated routing or documentation features which carried substantial advantages over the established Redac software. Calay and Cadnetix, as examples, introduced strong entries—neither being compatible with the Redac

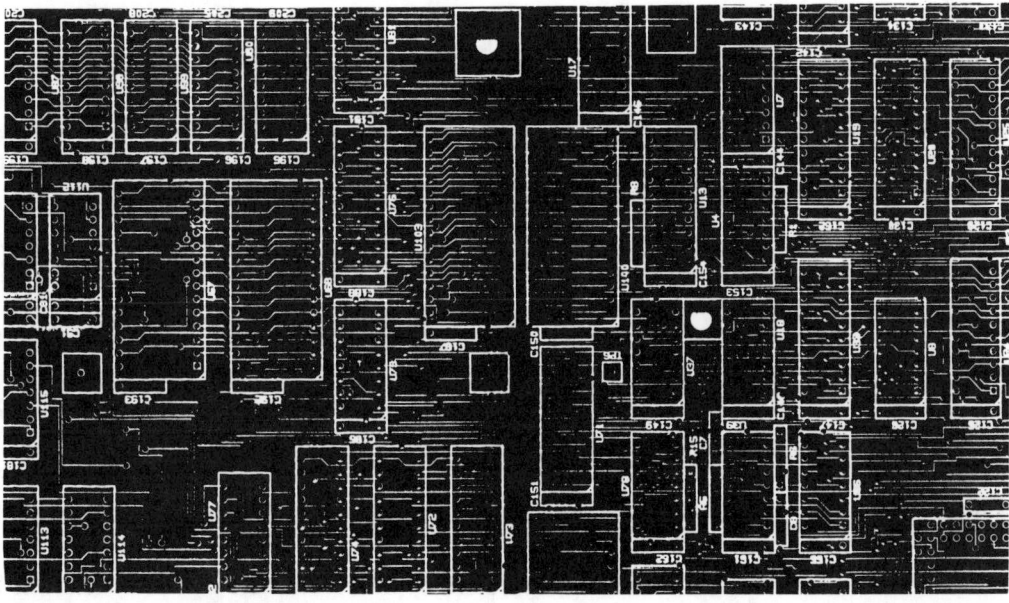

Figure 2. Sections of the top surface (above) and the bottom surface (below) of a four-level circuit board designed by Applied CAD Knowledge for the maker of a communications controller. The entire board measures $10\frac{1}{2} \times 15$ inches.

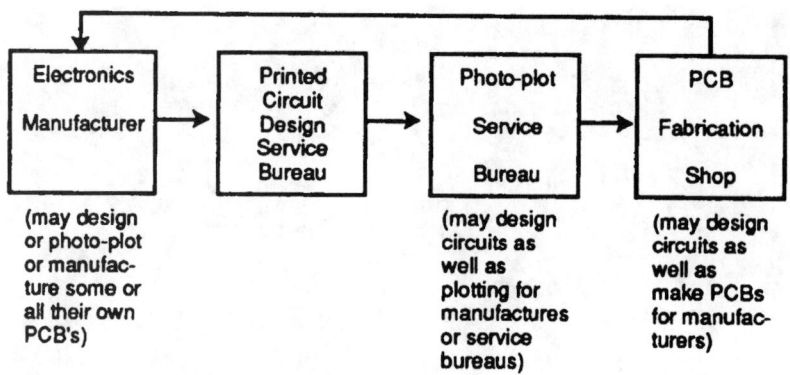

Figure 3. Work flow between firms in production of printed circuit boards.

or SciCards or Telesis equipment already in the field. Racal-Redac Ltd. had perhaps taken the greatest strides to tailor its software to run on a variety of computers. Said Ian Orrock, chief executive of Redac's CAD division in England, "We're all going to end up being software houses."

Another important feature of the new CAD equipment was ease of use; the older systems might require months of learning time before a designer became proficient.

SERVICE BUREAU OPERATIONS

In the late 70s, with high equipment costs and low availability of trained designers, only the largest electronics firms designed and produced their own PCBs. Service bureaus took advantage of the market opportunity, acting as the primary design resource for smaller clients and as peak load designers for firms with in-house capacity. These small service firms specialized in design, working for electronics companies in the same way an architect works for real estate developers. (Figure 3 shows the relationship between firms in the PCB production process.)

When the design phase of a job was finished, the computer tape or disk containing the final output would be carried to a photoplotting service bureau for creation of the precision film needed for manufacturing. The equipment for photoplotting was far more complex and expensive than the computer systems needed for design. Only a few design shops in the New England area had their own photoplotting capability; they performed this work for other service bureaus and for electronics firms' in-house design departments as well as for their own design clients.

The actual production of PCBs might be done by the electronics company itself or by a fabrication shop which specialized in the work. The New England area was home to some 80 to 100 fab shops, many of which offered design as well as manufacturing services. A few large firms (Hadco at $125 million in sales) were equipped to service very large orders—100,000 or more boards of a design—but most fab shops fell in the $1 to $2 million size range, with an average order size of 25 to 30 relatively small boards. One such fabricator estimated its average low-tech PCB was priced at $22 each, with a setup charge of $150. For the most difficult boards, in small quantities with rigid testing requirements, Applied CAD's customers might pay as much as $1,000 each for fabrication.

As electronics firms purchased and began to use the newer CAD systems, they wanted service bureaus to be equipped with similar or compatible machines. A firm with its own Telesis equipment, for example, would favor Telesis-equipped service bureaus for its overload work. Service bureaus felt the pressure to acquire the most up-to-date hardware and software available, in order to qualify as bidders.

When a service bureau invested in CAD equipment, the sheer size of the investment created pressure to use the equipment intensively. Multi-shift operations were common, but the supply of designers to staff them was severely limited. Typically, a service bureau did not hire permanent staff for all three shifts: the work load was too unpredictable. Service bureaus generally hired moonlighting designers from established electronics firms to staff their second and third shifts.

Printed circuit board design requires a peculiar combination of human skills, primarily in spatial geometry, circuit insight, memory and persistence. A talented designer—perhaps capable of completing a complex design in three weeks of console time—might be several times more productive than a "journeyman." In the early 1980s, talented designers willing to work odd shifts were earning over $100,000 per year; few of them had college educations.

Most customers requested separate quotations for each board; often, customers asked for bids from several service bureaus. Design clients always ran on tight schedules, Jeff Stevens observed, wanting their work to be delivered "yesterday":

> Circuit board design is usually one of the last steps before a new product goes into production. Our design time may be the customer's time-to-market. It's natural for them to be in a hurry.

For the design of a large, complex, four-layered PCB a client might pay between $10,000 to $15,000. Such a project might require five to six man-weeks of labor input (two-thirds of which might be designer's time); it might involve extensive communication between Applied CAD and a wide variety of the client's technical personnel, and it would often require the designer to work through the night at various project stages to make deadlines. Much of the time would be spent sorting out and coordinating conflicting information and directions from different technical people in the client company. Stevens noted,

> Even our clients themselves won't always know completely what they want. When we take their directions to their logical conclusions, problems often occur. Then we have to show them what developed. You spend a lot of time on the phone with clients, sometimes at 3 A.M. Often, I make decisions for the client, so the work can go ahead; later, I have to convince the client the decision was right.

Clients were inclined to stay with their existing service bureaus, unless they were severely burned. Good relationships between service staff and engineering personnel helped minimize communication errors, and availability of the data base from the original job allowed for revisions or modifications at much lower cost. Design reliability remained a key attribute of a service bureau's reputation, since whole product lines (or engineers' jobs) might depend on the PCB design's working properly, and on its prompt delivery:

> We had one job, in the old days, where a satellite was literally sitting on the launch pad, waiting for a corrected module design. The engineers had discovered a design flaw. They flew into town with the specs, and then took turns sitting behind the designer at the scope, or sitting beside their hotel room telephone, waiting to answer any questions that might come up. In this business, you have to deliver.

FUTURE TRENDS IN PCB DESIGN

By the end of 1986, a number of vendors had developed PCB design packages to run on personal computers—primarily the IBM XT or AT machines. These software systems, some including automatic routing, were priced as low as a few hundred dollars or as high as $13,000, and varied widely in their features and capabilities. In-house design capability thus became practical for most electronics firms, although many lacked the PCB expertise that still marked the better service bureaus. Freelance designers, too, could now acquire their own equipment. Exhibit 2 compares the features and prices of 24 such software packages.

In the 1980s, as the cost of entering the service bureau business dropped, many new firms appeared. Jeff Stevens observed, "When I started at Redac in 1978, there were three service bureaus in New England. By 1983 there were maybe a dozen. Now there might be seventy-five, and it could reach 100 in another year." In 1987, several competing service bureaus in the area were owned by former employees of Racal-Redac, where Jeff himself had learned the business. Exhibit 3 lists the major competitors in the Northeastern United States in 1986. The small firms in this listing were design specialists like Applied CAD, Stevens noted; the larger firms all supplied finished boards to their customers.

For the longer run, some industry analysts speculated that constant advances in miniaturizing electronic circuits might permit semiconductor technology to reduce certain whole PCBs (such as those developed for computer memory) into a single integrated circuit chip.

APPLIED CAD KNOWLEDGE, INC.: HISTORY

Jeff Stevens had learned the rudiments of circuit board design in his first job after high school graduation, as a technician in a five-person product development laboratory. Here, in 1975, one of his duties was to prepare enlarged prints of circuits, using black tape on white mylar. In another, concurrent job as a technician in an electronics manufacturing firm, he learned how the circuits themselves worked.

In 1977, Stevens left his two technician jobs for an entry-level design position with Racal-Redac in Littleton, Massachusetts. Redac operated a service bureau to complement its sales of DEC hardware and British software. As a pioneer in the field, Redac at the time boasted a near-monopoly in powerful systems dedicated to PCB design. Jeff Stevens, in a training rotation, joined Redac's service bureau as a data-entry technician.

> We had three computer systems—about 20 people altogether. A system then cost about $200,000 and a lot of companies didn't have enough design work to justify buying one.
>
>   In data entry, you prepare code to represent all the terminals and components on the board. I refused to code the first job they gave me, and nearly got fired. Finally I convinced them that the job *shouldn't* be coded: the turkey who engineered it had the diodes in backward, and the circuit wasn't going to work. About a week later, they put me in charge of data entry, supervising the guy who had wanted to fire me.

Stevens became a designer, then a lead designer, then operations manager of the service bureau. Under his leadership, the operation dramatically improved its reputation for quality and on-time delivery, as well as its financial performance:

> When I took over in October of 1981, monthly sales were $50,000 and monthly expenses were $110,000. In six months we turned it around: monthly sales were $110,000 and expenses were $50,000. There was a tremendous amount of dead wood. We had a big bonfire with it, and went from 26 people to 16. In some ways, it was a brutal campaign, I guess.

In June 1983, Stevens left Racal-Redac to work as a consulting designer, helping electronics firms with their CAD decisions as well as doing freelance design work. He had developed design and management expertise and established a reputation in industry circles which he could now broker directly to clients who were familiar with his previous work.

In December 1983, Jeff established Applied CAD while still working from his home in Pepperell, Massachusetts. By purchasing used computer equipment and installing it himself in his living room, Stevens was able to hold his initial investment to $35,000; the largest cost element was $28,000 for the software purchased from his former employer. (Financial data on Applied CAD's latest three years of operation are shown in Exhibit 4.)

> The equipment pretty well filled up the living room, and through the summer I couldn't run it during the daytime: we didn't have enough electricity to cool it down. Winter solved that problem, though; the PDP-11 heated the house.

Jeff had sought the help of a business school professor who lived in Littleton, to negotiate the purchase of software from his former employer. This professor and another, also from a well-known Boston area school, purchased small stock interests as Applied CAD was incorporated and became members of the Board of Directors. By the Fall of 1985, the Board met monthly for three to four hours, usually during the first week of the month. At most meetings the Board first discussed the previous month's sales and current levels of cash, accounts receivable, backlog and payables. (Exhibit 5 shows the data recorded in these talks.) Other typical agenda items ranged from the purchase of new equipment and/ or software, to marketing, to personnel problems and bank relationships.

In late 1984, Applied CAD leased a 1,000 square foot office suite on the ground floor of a new building near the Merrimack River in Tyngsboro, Mass. Jeff Stevens designed the interior space to hold a central computer room (with special air conditioning), a darkened "console room" for the actual design work, and a large front office. By January of 1985, the computing equipment was installed and operating. The console room was furnished with two Recaro ergonometric chairs (at $1,100 each) for the designers' use; the front office held a large receptionist's desk and a sparse collection of work tables, file cabinets and spare hardware.

HARDWARE AND SOFTWARE

After moving into his new quarters, Jeff Stevens located another PDP-11/34 computer— this one for sale at $7,000. Adding it to his shop required purchase of another Redac software package, but the added capacity was needed. Other, competing CAD systems were now available, but the decision to stick with Redac seemed straightforward to Jeff:

> Redac systems had several advantages. They were specifically dedicated to PCB design work and they had software that was brutally efficient. They were familiar to most of the freelance designers in the area. Wide acceptance of Redac's software makes it easier to get overflow work from companies who demanded compatibility with their own equipment. Not to mention that I know this gear backward and forward, and could keep several machines busy at once.

The Redac software was originally developed in 1972, which made it very old by industry standards. Jeff pointed out, however, that because machines were slower in 1972 and had much less memory, their software *had* to be extremely efficient. Having used this software for a long time, he said, "I've been able to make process modifications to improve its efficiency, and I know all its intricacies." Jeff had developed some proprietary software for PCB design work which he believed kept him at the cutting edge of the competition. At times, he wondered about the possibilities of licensing his proprietary software to other PCB design firms. He concluded, however, that the small market for this type of software product would probably not justify the necessary marketing and additional product development costs.

In addition to the original equipment purchased by Jeff in 1983, the company purchased a VAX Model 11/751 and a Calay Version 03 in December of 1985 at a cost of approximately $170,000. (See Exhibit 6 for the cash flow statements prepared for the bank to obtain a loan). The VAX was intended to be used as a communications and networking device and for developing new software. The Calay was a dedicated hardware system that included an automatic router which could completely design certain less complex boards without an operator. On more complex boards it could complete a major percentage of the board, leaving a designer to do the remainder. Jeff and the Board felt that this automatic routing capability might open a new market for the company for less complex boards. They also felt that the manufacturer of the Calay, as well as the Calay user group, would supply new customer leads. Some of these expectations had been met.

In September of 1986, a software upgrade to the Calay was purchased for approximately $28,000. Although bank financing was available, Jeff decided to pay cash for this purchase, to avoid raising his monthly fixed expenses. The new purchases gave Applied CAD enough machine capacity to support some $2 million in annual sales.

The VAX, however, was not being fully used as originally intended—to allow hands-off automation of the firm's varied pieces of computing equipment, as well as providing batch data processing capacity. In its ultimate form, the VAX might actually operate the older, more cumbersome systems. It would be able to juggle dozens of design tasks between work stations and autorouters, queuing and evaluating each job and calling for human intervention when needed. One director, visualizing robots sitting in Applied CAD's Recaro chairs, called this the "Robo-Router plan." To carry it out would require an additional investment of approximately $15,000 in hardware and another $10 to $20,000 in programming, along with a significant amount of Jeff's time. The investment would result in very substantial cost reductions and reduced dependence on freelance designers, but it would only pay for itself under high volume conditions.

APPLIED CAD'S ORGANIZATION

Jeff oversaw all operations in his company, did all the high level marketing/sales contact work with clients, and did much of the technical design work as well. Another full-time designer was hired in May of 1985 but had to be terminated in September of 1986 due to persistent personal problems. Steve Jones, Jeff's data manager and former assistant at Redac, became a full-time employee in January 1986. Among other duties, Steve covered the telephone, coordinated technical work done by freelance contractors in Jeff's absence, and performed various administrative duties. Steve had a B.S. in Engineering and, before Redac, had worked for other PCB electronics companies. In April of 1987 Jeff hired John Macnamara, a former subcontract designer, on a full-time, salaried basis.

In May of 1987 Jeff also hired a part-time person to keep the books, write checks and handle other office related matters. For her first three months, she focused on straightening out the books and tax-related items. She was also trying to find time to set up an accounting package on the personal computer. The package had been purchased in August of 1986 (at the request of Board members), for the purpose of generating accurate monthly statements. Since the company's founding, the Board had been asking for accurate end-of-month data on sales, accounts receivable, cash balance, backlog and accounts payable. They also wanted monthly financial statements, although Stevens himself saw little point in them:

cash flow projections served his immediate needs. The accounting package was chosen by one of the Board members, based partly on its broad capabilities. For example, it could assist in invoicing and aging receivables.

Jeff had other capable designers "on call"—available for freelance project work when the company needed them. Depending upon the market, there were time periods when Jeff could obtain the services of several contractors to meet peak work loads. In general, design contractors worked on a negotiated fixed-fee basis for completing a specific portion of a design project. In July of 1987, however, (after sales in June reached approximately $50 thousand and the backlog reached $90 thousand) Jeff found it hard to attract contract designers with free time. The backlog consisted of about 15 boards ranging in price from $800 to $15,000. The electronics industry had turned upward and in busy times everyone was busy. Consequently, freelance designers were committed to their own customers or employers who were also busy. Jeff attempted to fill the production gap by working as a third-shift designer.

At most of its meetings, the Board of Directors spent considerable time discussing the current business climate and the future sales outlook. This usually led to a discussion of hiring someone to take over the marketing and sales function. It was generally agreed that such a person could not only contribute to the company's growth in sales but also free up a considerable amount of Jeff's time that could be devoted to design and operational matters. When Applied CAD was busy, however, Jeff had very little time to devote to finding, hiring and working with such a person. Even if one were hired, a salesperson would require Jeff's time for introductions to the present customers and for responding to questions about new sales potentials.

When Applied CAD was *not* busy, Jeff's concern over the reliability of future cash flows made him hesitant to make the major salary commitment that a marketing professional would require. He was aware of the contrary pressures: "I can't get out of the 'boom-splat' syndrome," he said.

To Jeff, the "splat" came when backlogs and cash balances fell. The winter of 1987, for example, had felt to him like hitting a wall. (See Exhibit 5 for monthly totals of sales, backlogs, etc., as estimated by Jeff at monthly Board meetings.)

CURRENT BUSINESS OPTIONS

In August of 1987, Jeff was contemplating the current business climate, his accomplishments with Applied CAD over the past three years, and where the company was headed. His major objective—agreed with the Board—was growth. Jeff had discussed many times with his Board the needs for a marketing person and a promotional brochure for the company. He hoped to attract someone with top management credentials, who could work with him as a peer. On occasion, he had talked with marketing people about the job, but most of these prospective employees lacked the level of skills and PCB experience Jeff hoped to acquire. He had also talked with commercial artists about design of a brochure. Jeff and his Board felt that a "first class" brochure would cost between $5 and $10 thousand.

Marketing in the PCB business, especially among companies with sales of under $1 million, was characterized as informal. Very few companies had full-time people devoted to the marketing task; in most cases it was the owner-president who handled marketing and sales. Most small companies had their own list of faithful customers and new customers tended to come by word of mouth. In the under $1 million segment it was not uncommon for a company when extremely overloaded with work to farm out a board to a competitor. Also, certain other services, such as photoplotting, were done by shops that also did design work. Consequently, there was considerable communication among the competitors; the players seemed to know who got what jobs.

The marketing job at a company like Applied CAD would consist mainly of coordinating the advertising and a sales brochure, calling on present customers and attempting to find new customers. Such a person needed a working knowledge of PCB design which required experience in the industry. People with these qualifications normally made a $40–50,000 base salary plus commissions; frequently their total compensation exceeded $100,000 per year. Of major concern to Jeff were Applied CAD's erratic history of sales and cash balances, and the difficulty of predicting sales volume any further than two months in advance. He balked at taking on responsibility for an executive-level salary, lacking confidence in the future. "This would probably be somebody with kids to feed or send to college," Jeff said. "How could I pay them, in slow times?"

Still, marketing appeared to be the function most critical to achieving the growth rates Jeff Stevens and his Board hoped for. It was key, also, in meeting the major potential threat posed by the recent availability of inexpensive software which could enable personal computers (PCs) to design printed circuit boards (see Exhibit 2). Jeff had heard that some of that new software could perform almost as well as the more expensive equipment used by Applied CAD. He wondered how the advent of low-cost software might be turned into an opportunity, not a threat.

Four possible responses had occurred to Jeff and his Board: Applied CAD could ignore the PC software, adopt it, distribute it, or sell its own software to the PC users. Ignoring the new technology might work in the short run, since the complex boards designed by Applied CAD would not be the first affected; in the long run, however, failure to keep up with technology would leave more and more jobs subject to low-cost competition.

By adopting the new software for his next equipment expansion, Applied CAD could take a proactive stance. Jeff could buy a system or two to see how good they were, and hire people to work on the new systems on a freelance basis. Of course, he would need a flow of jobs to experiment with. A variation of this alternative was to sit back and wait while ready to move quickly if he saw something developing.

A third alternative, acting as a distributor for the PC software, would give Applied CAD a product to sell to prospects who insisted on doing their own design. This could establish relationships with people who might later need overload capacity.

Fourth, Applied CAD could proceed with development of its proprietary software, creating a product to sell to PC users. Jeff estimated that his Automated Design Review System could save both time and grief for other designers. In some tasks, it could cut the required design time in half. In all jobs, the capability to check the finished design against the original input automatically and completely could improve quality. ADRS already existed in rough form; it was one of the elements which would make up the "Robo-Router" system, if that were implemented.

Many of these options seemed to require significant marketing skills—strengths— where the company was presently weak. The technical questions could be answered, if Jeff had the time to work on them. But the marketing questions called for a person with extensive industry experience, broad contacts, a creative imagination and the ability to make things happen.

Amid all the other problems facing him as owner of a small business, Jeff was trying to figure out how to shape his business for the long-range future, and how to attract the kind of person he could work with to assure growth—and survival. He looked across the table at Bogie's restaurant, caught the eye of one director, and yawned. Tonight, after this meeting, he hoped to finish the design of a particularly complicated board. His best customer was desperate for this job.

Exhibit 1. Sales and projections for PCBs by type of board.

PCB Type	1983			1993	
	Sales in $ Millions	Market Share	Annual Growth Rate	Sales in $ Millions	Market Share
Multilayer	$ 900	25%	20%	$5,600	41%
Double-sided	2,000	56	13%	6,700	49
Flexible	353	10	10%	916	7
Single-sided	307	9	4%	454	3
	$3,560	100%		$13,670	100%

*Source: *Electronic Business* Feb. 1, 1985 p. 87.

Exhibit 2. Low cost PC board design software available, spring 1987.

TABLE 1—REPRESENTATIVE LOW-COST PC-BOARD LAYOUT PACKAGES

COMPANY	PRODUCT	BASE PRICE	REQUIRED HARDWARE	OPERATING SYSTEM	AUTO-ROUTER	AUTO-ROUTER PRICE	AUTO-PLACEMENT	COMPATIBLE NET LISTS	MAXIMUM NUMBER OF COLORS	MAXIMUM NUMBER OF TRACES	MAXIMUM NUMBER OF COMPONENTS	MAXIMUM NUMBER OF LAYERS	PACKAGING TECHNOLOGIES
ABACUS SOFTWARE	PCBOARD DESIGNER	$195	ADAR 520ST OR 1040ST	GEM	•				2	1100 LINES	250	2	SMD
ACCEL TECHNOLOGIES	TANGO-PCB	$495	IBM PC/XT OR PC/AT	MS-DOS	•			ACCEL OMATION, ORCAD	16	28,000 LINES	1000	9	SMD
APTOS SYSTEMS	CRITERION II	$4000	ARTIST 1 CARD AND IBM PC/XT OR PC/AT	MS-DOS		$5000	•	APTOS, FUTURENET, P-CAD	16	2000 NETS	1000	50	SMD, ECL, ANALOG
AUTOMATED IMAGES	PERSONAL 570	$8000	IBM PC/XT OR PC/AT	MS-DOS				APPLICON, FUTURENET, ORCAD	16			16	SMD, HYBRID
B&C MICROSYSTEMS	PCBDE	$395	IBM PC/XT OR PC/AT	MS-DOS (AND THE AUTOCAD DRAFTING PACKAGE)				B&C	16				
CAD SOFTWARE	PADS-PCB	$975	IBM PC/XT OR PC/AT	MS-DOS	•	$750	•	FUTURENET	16	4511 NETS	784	30	SMD, FINE-LINE
CASE TECHNOLOGY	VANGUARD PCB	$4250	IBM PC/RT, SUN-3, OR DEC MICROVAX	MS-DOS, UNIX, OR VMS	•	$5500	•	CASE	16	2000 NETS	1000	256	SMD
DAISY SYSTEMS	PERSONAL BOARDMASTER	$8000	IBM PC/RT OR DAISY PL388	DMX				DAISY	7	14,000 LINES	14,000	256	SMD
DASOFT DESIGN	PROJECT-PCB	$950	IBM PC/XT OR PC/AT	MS-DOS	•		•	DASOFT	6			4	FINE-LINE
DESIGN COMPUTATION	DRAFTSMAN-EE	$1147	IBM PC/XT OR PC/AT	MS-DOS	•	$2450			16	4000 NETS	300	20	SMD, ANALOG
DOUGLAS ELECTRONICS	DOUGLAS CADCAM	$395	APPLE MACINTOSH	MACINTOSH					2				SMD, CONSTANT-IMPEDANCE
ELECTRONIC DESIGN TOOLS	PROCAD	$2495	IBM PC/XT OR PC/AT AND 68000 COPROCESSOR	MS-DOS	•	$2495	•	ELECTRONIC DESIGN TOOLS	16	10,000 NETS	3000	56	SMD, CONSTANT-IMPEDANCE
ELECTRONIC INDUSTRIAL EQUIPMENT	EXECUTIVE CAD	$11,000	IBM PC/XT OR PC/AT	MS-DOS	•		•	ELECTRONIC INDUSTRIAL EQUIPMENT	16			4	SMD, ECL
FUTURENET	DASH-PCB	$13,000	IBM PC/AT AND 32032 COPROCESSOR	UNIX	•			FUTURENET	4			10	FINE-LINE
HEWLETT-PACKARD	EGS	$7000	HP 9000	HP-UX	•			HP	15			255	HYBRID
KONTRON	KAD-286	$10,400	IBM PC/AT	MS-DOS	•	$6000		KONTRON	64	5300 LINES	3200	256	ECL, SMD, HYBRID
PERSONAL CAD SYSTEMS	PCB-1	$5000	IBM PC/XT OR PC/AT	MS-DOS	•		•	P-CAD, FUTURENET	16	1000 NETS	300	50	SMD
RACAL-REDAC	REDBOARD	$12,000	IBM PC/XT OR PC/AT	MS-DOS	•	$2000	•	RACAL-REDAC	16	1900 NETS	511	16	SMD
SEETRAX (IN US, CIRCUITS AND SYSTEMS)	RANGER	$5000	IBM PORT	MS-DOS	•		•	SEETRAX	16	10,000 LINES	1400	18	SMD
SOFTCIRCUITS	PCILOPLUS	$1024	COMMODORE AMIGA 1000	AMIGADOS	•				16				
VAMP	McCAD	$395	APPLE MACINTOSH	MACINTOSH	•	$995	•	VAMP	2	32,000 LINES	32,000	6	SMD, METRIC
VISIONICS	EE DESIGNER II	$1875	IBM PC/XT OR PC/AT	MS-DOS	•	$1475	•		16		900	26	SMD
WINTEK	SMARTWORK	$895	IBM PC/XT OR PC/AT	MS-DOS	•			WINTEK	3			6	SMD
ZIEGLER INSTRUMENTS (IN US, CADDY)	CADDY ELECTRONIC SYSTEM	$2495	IBM PC/XT OR PC/AT	MS-DOS	•	$2500		ZIEGLER	16			128	ANALOG

Exhibit 3. PC Design Service Bureaus in New England.

Design Houses by Sales Volume	
0–1 MILLION DOLLARS / YEAR	**2–5 MILLION DOLLARS / YEAR**
Abington Labs.	Tek-Art Associates
Berkshire Design	Stratco Reprographix
CAD Tec	Altek Company
Cadtronix, Ltd.	Eastern Electronics Manufacturing Corporation
Computer Aided Circuits, Inc.	Datacube, Inc.
Dataline PCB Corporation	Owl Electronic Laboratories
Design Services	
Energraphics	**5–10 MILLION DOLLARS / YEAR**
Graphics Technology Corporation	
Herbertons, Inc.	Triad Engineering Company
HET Printed Circuit Design	Photronic Labs, Inc.
High Tech CAD Service Company	
Jette Fabrication	**10+ MILLION DOLLARS YEAR**
LSI Engineering	
P C Design Company	Algorex Corporation
PAC-Lab, Inc.	ASI Automated Systems, Inc.
Packaging for Electronics	Augat Interconnection Group
PC Design Services	Racal-Redac Service Bureau
Point Design, Inc.	Synermation Inc.
Power Processing, Inc.	
Product Development Company	
Qualitron Corporation	
Quality Circuit Design, Inc.	
Research Labs, Inc.	
Scientific Calculations, Inc.	
Tracor Electro-Assembly Inc.	
Winter Design	
1–2 MILLION DOLLARS / YEAR	
Automated Images, Inc.	
Automated Design, Inc.	
CAD Services, Inc.	
Antal Associates	
Multiwire of New England	
Teccon	
Tech Systems & Design	
Kenex, Inc.	
Alternate Circuit Design Technology	
Photofabrication Technology, Inc.	

Source: Adapted from Beacon Technology, "New England Printed Circuit Directory."

Exhibit 4. Financial Statements of Applied CAD Knowledge, Inc.

Balance Sheet

	1985	1986	1987
Assets			
Current assets			
Cash	$128,568	$ 14,148	$ 33,074
Accounts receivable, trade	18,865	15,375	14,250
Prepaid taxes and other current assets	4,853	1,200	5,074
Total current assets	152,286	30,723	52,398
Property and equipment	174,079	190,079	203,079
Less accumulated depreciation	48,697	86,357	124,062
Total Property and Equipment	125,382	103,722	79,017
Total Assets	$277,668	$134,445	$131,415
Liabilities and Stockholders' Equity			
Current liabilities:			
Accounts payable, trade	$127,685	$9,025	$21,823
Current maturities of long-term debt	13,300		
Income taxes payable	4,008		2,303
Other current liabilities	5,000	5,373	70
Total current liabilities	149,993	14,398	24,196
Long-term debt, less current maturities	41,121	83,247	53,663
Stockholders' equity:			
Common stock, no par value; authorized 15,000 shares, issued and outstanding 1,000 shares	25,000	25,000	25,000
Retained earnings	61,554	11,800	28,556
Total stockholders' equity	86,554	36,800	53,556
Total Liabilities and Stockholders' Equity	$277,668	$134,445	$131,415

Statement of Income and Retained Earnings

	1985	1986	1987
Net Revenues	$328,262	$232,540	$346,627
Cost of revenue:			
Salaries, wages, and outside services	134,686	116,835	209,998
Research and development	14,154	7,551	13,731
Software costs	65,131	18,864	
Total cost of revenue	$213,971	$143,250	$223,729
Gross profit	114,291	89,290	122,898
Selling, general, and administrative expenses	72,320	143,051	77,732
Operating profit	41,971	(53,761)	45,166
Bad debt expense			(28,660)
Interest income (expense), net	2,331	3,176	(10,103)
Income before income taxes	44,302	(50,185)	6,403
Income taxes	4,508	0	0
Net income	39,794	(50,185)	6,403
Retained earnings, beginning of year	21,760	62,385	22,154
Retained earnings, end of year	$61,554	$11,800	$28,557

Exhibit 5. Monthly Sales and Month-End Receivables, Backlogs, Cash Levels. (All in $000's).

	A/R	Sales	Backlog	Cash
January 1986	$18	$20	$20	$98
February	*	10	*	*
March	18	10	12	62
April	18	10	20	28
May	24	20	26	26
June	*	10	*	*
July	14	25	*	18
August	70	50	30	15
September	90	40	*	8
October	50	30	*	26
November	19	5	10	17
December	24	10	18	14
January 1987	13	3	*	7
February	40	21	*	8
March	35	28	22	6
April	32	22	37	11
May	25	22	50	5
June	50	50	90	10
July	90	58	30	10

*information not available

Exhibit 6. Applied CAD Knowledge, Inc. Cash Flow Projections as of December 16, 1985.

	Dec 1985	Jan 1986	Feb 1986	March 1986	April 1986	May 1986	June 1986	July 1986	Aug 1986	Sept 1986	Oct 1986	Nov 1986	Dec 1986	Total $(000's)
Sales	25	30	30	30	30	30	30	30	30	30	30	30	30	360
Expenses[6]	20	24	29.5	29.5	29.5	29.5	29.5	29.5	29.5	29.5	29.5	29.5	29.5	348.5
Profit	.5	.6	.5	.5	.5	.5	.5	.5	.5	.5	.5	.5	.5	11.5
Opening cash	141	148	102	102.5	88	88.5	89	89.5	90	90.5	91	91	91.5	
Receivables	37	17	30	30	30	30	30	30	30	30	30	30	30	
Disbursements[5]	50	24[1]	29.5[3]	29.5	29.5	29.5	29.5	29.5	29.5	29.5	29.5	29.5	29.5	
Taxes[4]		29[2]		15										
Closing cash	148	102	102.5	88	88.5	89	89.5	90	90.5	91	91	91.5	92	

1. Includes loan payment of 4K/mth
2. 25% of equipment costing 156K
3. Includes new employees at 66K/yr
4. Taxes based on the following assumptions: 1985 Profit of 150K; 50K software expense on new equipment; 20K depreciation on new equipment; 10K misc. expenses; investment tax credit of 15K
5. Figures do not include depreciation which would only influence total profit
6. Expenses include rent, heat, light, power, salaries, contract work, telephone, etc. This level of expenses will support sales double those projected.

Applied CAD Knowledge, Inc. (B)

In September of 1987, as the summer rush slowed, Jeff Stevens began to talk seriously with Jerry King, Regional Sales Manager of Calay Systems, Inc., about the marketing problems of Applied CAD Knowledge, Inc. Stevens wanted someone to become in effect a co-owner and officer of the small firm. King had been a principal in his own service bureau in the very early days of automated PCB design, and retained friendships and contacts with high level personnel in many electronics firms. (Exhibit 1 shows King's resume.)

After a month of conversations and negotiations, including a meeting with the Board of Directors, the two men reached tentative agreement on employment terms which would give King a 3% commission on all company sales, a car allowance, and a base salary of $40,000 per year. Since the marketing person would be influential in pricing many jobs, it was important to preserve his regard for profitability; King was offered a stock interest in Applied CAD, contingent on the bottom line at the end of 1988. With a handshake of agreement, Stevens set out to reduce the terms to an employment contract letter.

The following night, Jerry King called Stevens to express his regret that he would be unable to accept the Marketing VP position, after all: he had just received an offer from AT&T, to set up Australian operations for a new venture. It was simply too good an offer to refuse, King said. A dejected Jeff Stevens reported the development at the next Board meeting; "We're back to square one," he said. "And the next ' splat' is just about to arrive."

Applied CAD's monthly sales dropped to half their mid-1987 level, and the backlog dropped to near zero. On December 8, however, Jerry King called Jeff to say he had just decided against Australia, and would like to apply again for the Marketing Vice President position, if it was still open. Jeff agreed, and the next day Jerry presented to Jeff and the Board a plan for reaching $1 million in sales in 1988, and for growing by $1 million per year in the following two years. (This plan is partially reproduced in Exhibit 2.) Concerned with the timing of cash flows, one of the directors asked how long it would take to generate enough new sales to cover their added marketing expenses. King responded, "If I couldn't provide more than enough sales to cover my pay, I wouldn't take the job."

Although not officially joining Applied CAD until January 4, Jerry spent the rest of December in joint calling, with Jeff, on customers where Calay and Applied CAD shared some interests. In these first weeks, the "chemistry" Jeff Stevens had hoped for became

This case was prepared by Raymond M. Kinnunen, Northeastern University, and John A. Seeger, Bentley College, as a basis for class discussion. Distributed by the North American Case Research Association. All rights reserved to the authors and the North American Case Research Association. Permission to use the case should be obtained from the authors and the North American Case Research Association. Copyright © 1990 by Raymond M. Kinnunen and John A. Seeger.

readily apparent. The two men's skills complemented each other well: this would be a highly effective team, Stevens felt.

As 1988 began, King and Stevens continued to work closely together. Since Applied CAD's office layout did not provide the privacy needed for telephone prospecting, Jerry worked out of his home, joining Jeff several times per week on joint sales calls. At the January 8 meeting of the Board of Directors, the two men presented detailed sales projections for the first quarter and broader estimates for the entire year (see Exhibit 3). One account alone—California PrinCo—held the promise of some $250,000 in sales over the next four months. An old and steady customer of Applied CAD, PrinCo was nearing a decision on a major expansion in their use of circuit boards.

January sales totalled only $6,000 but many prospects seemed close to signing for large orders. At the February 19 Board meeting, Jeff and Jerry predicted sales of $100,000 per month for February and March; it appeared a 1988 sales goal of $1,000,000 might still be reachable. (Exhibit 4 shows monthly sales and backlogs through January, 1988.)

Exhibit 1. Resume of Jerry King.

Married
Four Children
Excellent Health

Education

FAIRLEIGH DICKENSON UNIVERSITY, Madison, New Jersey
Major: Business Administration

U.S. NAVY, Electronics "A" School, Pearl Harbor, Hawaii

CONTINUING EDUCATION, including numerous seminars and workshops in Corporate Finance, Power Base Selling, Territory Time Management, The Art of Negotiating, Computer Graphics in Electronics, Sales Management and Marketing Techniques.

Experience

GENERAL BUSINESS MANAGEMENT: Establishing policies and procedures for high volume cost efficient business operations, planning promotions for new business development, hiring, training and supervising personnel, including management level, designing and conducting management, sales, marketing and CAD/CAM training seminars internationally.

TECHNICAL BACKGROUND: Twenty one years of direct Printed Circuit Design, Fabrication and Electronics CAD/CAM marketing experience. Helped to create detailed business plans for three start-up companies including a high volume printed circuit design service bureau and raised five million dollars in venture capital used to purchase state-of-the-art CAD/CAM systems and other related equipment. Managed the development and marketing of a PCB Design Automation turn-key system which was sold exclusively to Calma/GE in 1977 and integrated with their GDSI TRI-DESIGN system. Very strong market knowledge in Computer Aided Engineering (CAE), Computer Aided Design (CAD), Computer Aided Test (CAT), and Computer Aided Manufacturing (CAM).

Accomplishments

Particularly effective in areas of personnel management, motivation and training, thereby increasing sales volume production flow, productivity and employee morale. Significant career accomplishments in customer relations, marketing and sales leadership and management.

Employment History:

1986–Present Calay Systems Incorporated, Waltham, Massachusetts
 SENIOR ACCOUNT MANAGER.
Responsible for a direct territory consisting of Northern Massachusetts, Vermont, New Hampshire, Maine and Quebec.

1985–1986   Automated Systems Incorporated, Nashua, N.H.
 EASTERN REGIONAL SALES MANAGER.
Responsible for regional design and fabrication service sales with a regional quota in excess of $5 million.

1981–1985   Engineering Automation Systems, Inc., San Jose, California.
 WESTERN REGIONAL SALES MANAGER.
Responsible for new Printed Circuit Design CAD/CAM system. Set up regional office, hired and trained sales and support staff of twelve people. Western regional sales were in excess of fifty percent of the company's business.
September 1984 PROMOTED TO NATIONAL SALES MANAGER.

1978–1981   Computervision Corporation, Bedford, Massachusetts
 NATIONAL PRODUCT SALES MANAGER.
Responsible for all electronic CAD/CAM system sales and related products. Provided direct sales management and training to the national field sales team, conducted sales training internationally, assisted in developing competitive strategy, technical support and new product development. Reported to the Vice President of North American Division.

 March 1980 PROMOTED TO MANAGER, CORPORATE DEMONSTRATION and BENCHMARK CENTER.

Managed team of 38 people who performed all corporate level demonstrations and benchmarks. Supported field offices with technical information and people worldwide. Reported to the Vice President of Marketing Operations. THIS WAS A KEY MANAGEMENT POSITION FOR THE COMPANY.

1966–1978   King Systems, Inc., San Diego, California (A Printed Circuit Design CAD/CAM and NC Drilling Service Bureau.) FOUNDER, PRESIDENT, CHAIRMAN and MAJOR STOCKHOLDER.

Served as Chief Executive Officer in charge of all aspects of the operation. Primary activities in sales management, direct field sales and customer relations. Responsible for financial administration, production operations and personnel administration. Assessed future needs and created business planning for increasing market share, facilities capability and penetrating new market opportunity. Developed a new concept in contract services for blanket sales to large government and commercial prime contractors.

Exhibit 2. Excerpts from Jerry King's Dec. 9, 1987, Board Presentation.

INTRODUCTION

The plan is a detailed road map for taking Applied CAD Knowledge, Incorporated (ACK) from the current sales volume to more than three million annual sales volume over the next three years. It identifies target markets, competitive environment, and sales tactics which will be used for achieving the sales projections during the plan period from January 1st 1988 through December 31st 1990. The projections show a monthly breakdown for 1988 and a yearly number for 1989 and 1990. The monthly projections were created on Lotus and provide for projected, forecasted and actual sales bookings for each month. As each month passes the actual numbers are entered and a goal status report is generated as part of the end of month reporting. At the end of each quarter a new quarter will be added so that there will always be four consecutive quarters of monthly projections.

The aggressive growth which is outlined will require significant expansion of facilities, personnel and equipment in order to maintain consistent QUALITY and ON TIME deliveries and insure REPEAT BUSINESS from established customers. It is required that the management and the Board of Directors of ACK provide the necessary production controls and capital/operating budgets to support expansion commensurate with sales volume increases over the term of the plan.

The PCB design service market can be divided into three major segments. Each of these segments will include companies who design and manufacture electronic equipment for Commercial, Industrial, Aerospace and Military vertical market areas.

Major Accounts & Government Sub-Contractors (MA)

Major Accounts are Fortune 1000 companies. They present a significant opportunity for multiple board contracts and blanket purchase agreements. Any one company could fill ACK's capacity.

Primary Accounts (PA)

Primary accounts are companies who have been doing business for more than three years (not a start-up) and typically do between 5–500 million in annual sales. These companies represent the most consistent level of business. The type of contracts available from this market segment are usually on the level of one to four board designs per month. Typically, each board of project has to be sold separately at the project engineering level.

Venture Start-up Accounts (VA)

Venture start-up companies usually are operating on stringent budgets. They typically have no internal CAD capability and therefore must rely on outside service. The business potential for this market segment is very significant. This market represents a high risk and therefore is avoided by the major competitors leaving more opportunity for the smaller operation. It is not unusual to obtain sole source product level contracts from companies in this market.

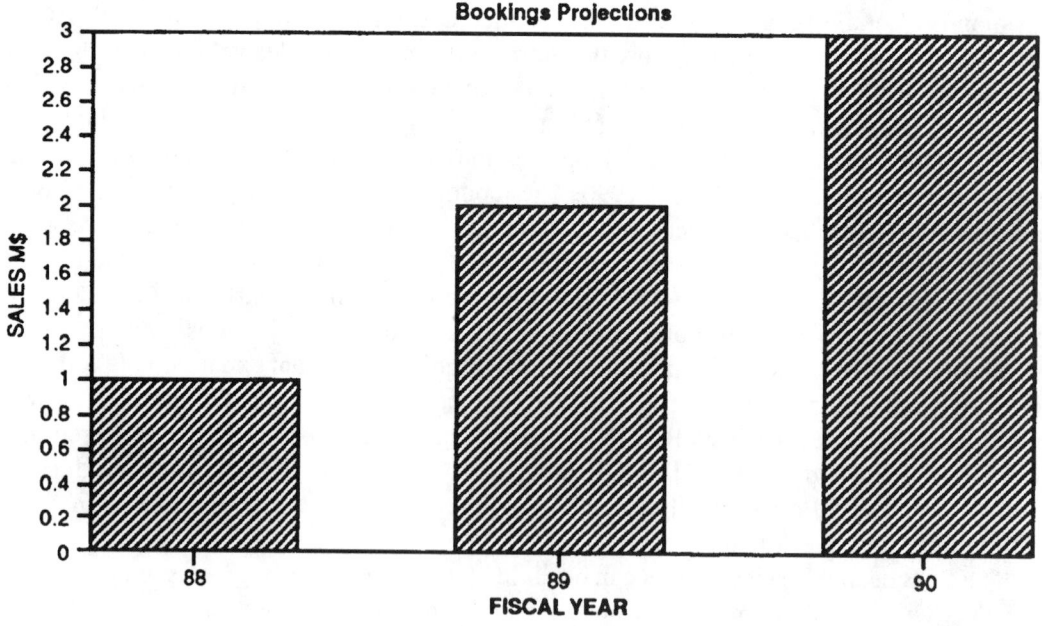

PBC DESIGN MARKET
Source Frost & Sullivan Oct. 85

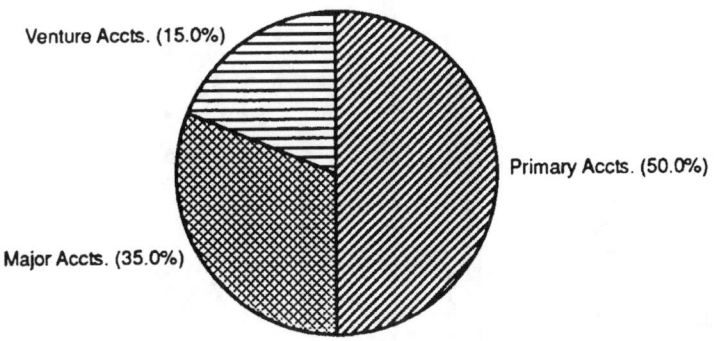

Exhibit 3. Sales Projections Presented to the Board, January 8, 1988.

Forecast Q1 1988: Sales by Customer

Account Name	Jan 50%	90%	Feb 50%	90%	Mar 50%	90%	Total 50%	Total 90%	Grand Total
Customer A	0.0	20.0	0.0	8.0	20.0	0.0	20.0	28.0	48.0
Prospct I	0.0	7.0	0.0	0.0	0.0	0.0	0.0	7.0	7.0
Prospct II	5.0	0.0	2.0	0.0	2.0	0.0	9.0	0.0	9.0
Customer B	0.0	0.0	12.0	0.0	0.0	0.0	12.0	0.0	12.0
Customer C	12.0	0.0	0.0	0.0	0.0	0.0	12.0	0.0	12.0
Customer D	0.0	0.0	12.0	0.0	0.0	0.0	12.0	0.0	12.0
Customer E	0.0	30.0	0.0	0.0	20.0	0.0	20.0	30.0	50.0
Prospct III	0.0	0.0	15.0	0.0	20.0	0.0	35.0	0.0	35.0
Prospct IV	0.0	0.0	15.0	0.0	20.0	0.0	35.0	0.0	35.0
Prospct V	0.0	6.5	0.0	0.8	0.0	3.8	0.0	11.1	11.1
Customer F	0.0	0.0	0.0	7.0	0.0	0.0	0.0	7.0	7.0
Total	17.0	63.5	56.0	15.8	82.0	3.8	155.0	83.1	238.1

Forecast FY 1988: Bookings by Product Type

	Service	Software	Total	Accum. Total
January	33	15	48	48
February	48	5	53	101
March	53	15	68	169
Quarter 1	124	35	169	
April	60	5	65	234
May	68	15	83	317
June	75	5	80	397
Quarter 2	203	25	228	
July	80	15	95	492
August	85		85	577
September	88	15	103	680
Quarter 3	253	30	283	
October	90	8	98	778
November	95	15	110	888
December	98	15	113	1001
Quarter 4	283	38	321	

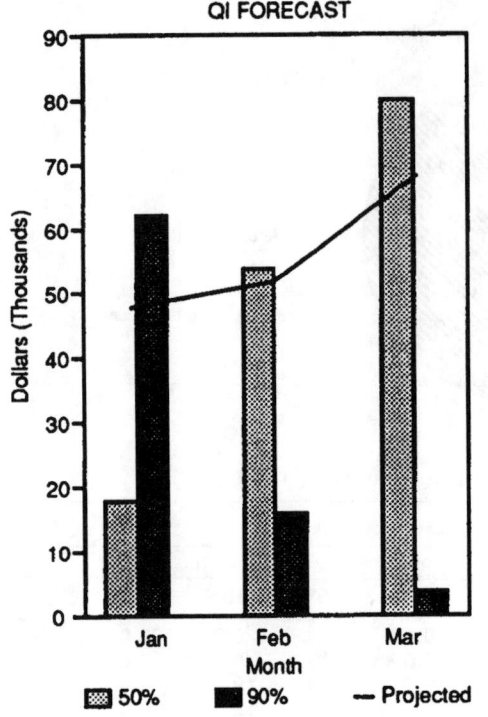

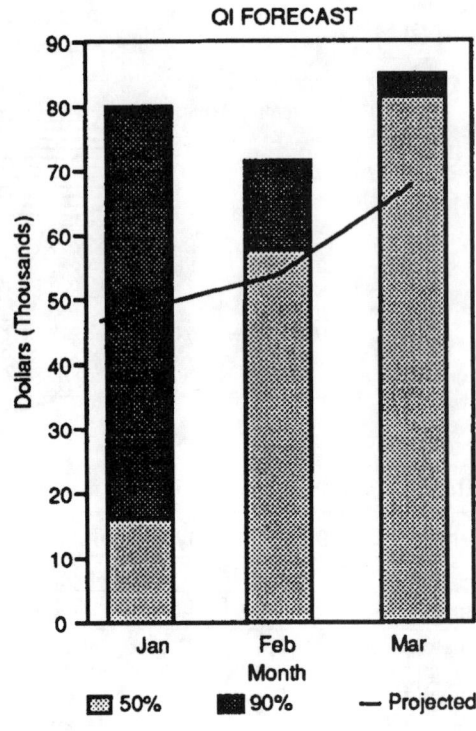

Exhibit 4. Monthly Sales and Month-End Receivables, Backlogs, Cash Levels (All in $000's).

	A/R	Sales	Backlog	Cash
January 1986	18	20	20	98
February	*	10	*	*
March	18	10	12	62
April	18	10	20	28
May	24	20	26	26
June	*	10	*	*
July	14	25	*	18
August	70	50	30	15
September	90	40	*	8
October	50	30	*	26
November	19	5	10	17
December	24	10	18	14
January 1987	13	3	*	7
February	40	21	*	8
March	35	28	22	6
April	32	22	37	11
May	25	22	50	5
June	50	50	90	10
July	90	58	30	10
August	*	25	*	10
September	34	25	50	21
October	62	48	9	8
November	50	24	*	*
December	14	34	9	33
January 1988	8	6	*	19

*information not available

ABC Ltd. (Revised)

In early 1980, Mr. A. Simon, president of ABC Ltd., a small company located in Montreal, talked about the problems of his firm and its future direction. Of particular concern was defining the nature of ABC's business and developing a product-market strategy.

THE HISTORY OF ABC

ABC was incorporated in late 1970 by Mr. A. Ross, a self-employed engineer; Mr. B. Carter, a sales representative for G-Enterprises; and Mr. A. Simon, also self-employed in research and development subcontracting. The company was formed to produce load stabilizers, a product designed to reduce electricity costs during periods of high usage. This new type of load stabilizer competed with the mechanical load stabilizers then in existence. In 1970, ABC produced the first electronic load stabilizer in Canada.

The electronic load stabilizer was supported by the provincial hydroelectric company (Hydro Quebec) and users. The market need for this product can be illustrated by a short description of the problems it was designed to solve.

In the 1960s, electric energy was cheap and abundant in the Province of Quebec. Companies often installed larger-capacity electric motors than required in order to reduce capital replacement costs. Although the initial cost was higher, longer life and less wear provided smaller total life cost. Sawmills, especially, found it cheaper to use electric energy for their heating and power needs. Hydro Quebec responded by supplying service to sawmills even when they were isolated. In building the service lines, the capacity of the line would be designed for the peak usage of the sawmill. Although the peak usage would occur infrequently, any smaller service line would burn out. Companies were encouraged by discounts to become totally electric. Faced with variations in demand in users and finding its returns reduced by heavy capital investment and discounts, Hydro Quebec introduced a tariff schedule which billed peak electrical usage at a substantially higher rate than regular demand.

The concept of a load stabilizer to smooth out electrical power usage became obvious. A load stabilizer would cut off nonessential energy demand in the plant when peaks became apparent. Firms which were totally electrically dependent found that paybacks from load stabilizers were very short.

The application of load stabilizers was particularly desirable in firms which had or were installing concrete wire mesh heating systems. The stabilizer would provide electricity for heat at times other than when the plant was producing or the sawmill was operating.

The major competitor of ABC was G-Enterprises, which had developed a mechanical unit. G-Enterprises also sold wire mesh heating systems. Since it was to the mutual advantage of Hydro Quebec and other power companies to have a load stabilizer installed on new construction sites, an electric company representative and a salesman for G-Enterprises would visit a new construction site together. The electric company representative would promote a 100 percent electrical system. A G-Enterprises representative would illustrate the feasibility of a total electrical system by using their products. Favours were often exchanged between representatives.

ABC Ltd. evolved from the association of Carter, working with Simon, and Ross, who was then going under the name of Ross and Associates, Engineering Consultants. Ross learned of the development in the field of load stabilizers from a friend in the electric company. His major interest was in the field of wire mesh heating. Ross became friendly with Carter, a representative for G-Enterprises. The arrangement initially was that Carter sold the load stabilizer and wire mesh heating systems of his company, and Ross performed the engineering services required for installation of the products. Together, they could give the customer a complete package, including installation.

The size and bulkiness of the electromechanical load stabilizer produced by G-Enterprises presented certain difficulties. Carter and Ross subsequently proposed to G-Enterprises that the electromechanical unit be converted to solid-state electronics. The idea was rejected on the grounds that the company had made a substantial investment in electro-mechanical technology, there was no effective competitor and the unit worked well.

Carter and Ross began to pursue the possibility of the development of an electronic load stabilizer with Simon, a self-employed engineer in research and development. Simon believed that the unit could be developed for $40,000. Simon agreed to invest $20,000 and Ross, $20,000. Carter agreed to invest $20,000 at a later date. The development took one year, and by August 1970, the first prototype was ready. ABC was incorporated by Ross, Carter and Simon in the summer of 1970.

The unit was approved by the Canadian Standards Association in the fall of 1970, and the first sale was made to a sheet metal firm. The product was not patented because the partners feared other companies would copy the product. In January 1971, the partners decided to devote the majority of their time to the new business. G-Enterprises within a few years abandoned the load stabilizer field and moved into laser technology.

THE EARLY YEARS, 1972–1973

The partners operated the company from a rented office, where the units were also assembled. Mr. C. E. Sen, a salesman, was hired away from G-Enterprises. Carter and Sen built sales upon their previous contacts, which were made while working for G-Enterprises. Electronic load stabilizers and wire mesh heating systems were the only products offered by ABC Ltd. Sales increased rapidly, and by August 1971, a technician was added to the staff. Simon gave up his research and development activities and devoted himself full-time to ABC Ltd.

One of the problem areas which surfaced and which would recur in the future related to installation of the units. An electrician was now required to connect the load stabilizer. Also, an entirely new main panel board and a control switch were required which had to be incorporated in a cubicle and installed together.

Sales in 1971 amounted to $214,000. Mr. Sen was made a partner, with an ownership of 10 percent.

The partners decided to pay no dividends but to use all their funds for research and development. They also assumed that they could, by innovation, build a solid firm and perhaps sell out at an attractive capital gain. Their expectations about a sellout were not unrealistic. Westinghouse approached them about a buyout, but the terms were not attractive.

THE DEVELOPMENT OF NEW PRODUCTS

In 1972, ABC developed its second product—a pool heater. The development of the pool heater and the firm's entry into the consumer market was partly accidental. Carter and his neighbour had installed swimming pools in their back yards. Heating the pool became a necessity because of the cool summer nights. Carter's neighbour began to investigate the purchase of a pool heater and found that because he heated with electricity, the addition of an electric pool heater required expensive modifications to his present electrical system. Carter shared the identical problem. Carter took the problem to Simon, who found that by applying the electronic load control mechanism to a pool heater, a unit could be operated without expensive changes in the house's present electrical systems. Two units were produced and installed—one in Carter's pool and the other in the neighbour's pool. The results were excellent.

ABC began to produce pool heaters and to market them through electricians. The results were very poor. Although the electricians were impressed with the units, they were more anxious to sell units which were already on the market, since they required expensive changes to the existing house electrical systems at a price between $1,000 and $2,000. The cost of installation of an ABC heater was $50–$100.

ABC conducted a market survey and concluded that the proper channel was through pool retailers such as Val-Mar, Dauphin and so on. Pool dealers had found that the expensive heating units were obstacles to sales. The retailers of pools found that the low-cost ABC unit solved some of the sales problems.

ABC first produced a 10 kw unit, made of stainless steel. Pool dealers soon began to suggest other models since the 10 kw was too large for smaller pools and too small for big pools. By 1973, ABC began to produce four models—P-5; P-10; P-15; P-20. The company began to have problems with inventories of the various models.

During visits to sawmill operators, Ross, who had retained his consulting business, sold ABC products and also a new hydraulic water jet system for debarking logs. Mill operators shared with Ross their problems in keeping track of inventory and transformation costs. Ross shared these concerns with Simon, who proposed that an analog computer, sensors and the use of microprocessors would solve the mill owners' problems. Work was begun on a working model called the MS-1000, and the first unit was completed in 1973. Four units were produced. Problems resulted from dust in the mills which clogged the sensor. Servicing costs were high because of the location of the mills. At the end of 1973, ABC discovered that a Swedish firm also produced similar units at substantially lower costs.

The MS-1000 cost approximately $200,000 to develop. Only one additional unit was sold in 1974. The product was discontinued in 1974, although servicing costs would continue for several years.

In 1973, Hydro Quebec moved from a position of active marketing of electricity to a passive marketing position. A punitive tariff schedule began to be strictly applied. ABC decided to concentrate on the energy conservation sector.

At the same time, the decision to discontinue the MS-1000 left development costs unpaid. In view of the switch in Hydro Quebec's concern for energy conservation, the company decided to make use of its microprocessors, which had represented the major cost of the development of the MS-1000. Hydro Quebec had decided to apply the penalty tariffication to KVARs. (KVARs measure the wastage when volts and amps are out of phase.) Hydro firms install two meters in a plant—one is for watts (volts × amps), the other is for KVARs. Some industries had an operator control the flow of electricity to eliminate KVARs. ABC decided to enter this market with its microprocessors and to develop an automatic power factor.

In 1974, the first global oil crisis was making itself felt. In view of the escalating costs of oil, many residential oil users were switching to electricity. ABC entered the market with an H-15 air duct heater. The technology was to attach a load stabilizer to an electric heating element which was installed in the air duct system of the existing oil furnace. After a market survey, they decided that the market could absorb at least 1,000 units annually. ABC immediately produced 500 units. The units were promoted through electricians. Four hundred units were sold, and the market disappeared. From 1974 to 1979, ABC would hold an inventory of 100 units, with no market for the product.

In 1975, ABC saw an opportunity to enter the U.S. market by bidding on a project for a proposed energy control system through Niagara-Mohawk. Although ABC believed they would have the lowest bid and were encouraged to bid on the project, they lost the bid. They believed the reason was their Canadian identity. The lack of sales of the power factor, the cost of bidding on the Niagara-Mohawk (New York State Power Company) study, and the lack of sales of the electric heaters made the company short of cash. Although the company believed entry into the U.S. market required the formation of a U.S. subsidiary, no action was taken.

In 1976, the company received a contract from the Regie des Installations Olympiques, who were having trouble with the ice on the cables at the Olympic stadium in Montreal.

The cash generated from the R.I.O. permitted ABC to build a new plant. A site was chosen in Laval, Quebec, and in mid-1976, the company moved into a new plant.

THE POWER FACTOR

The power factor to automatically regulate KVARs was fully developed by mid-1976. The major problem was marketing. Users did not understand KVARs, the penalty rate, nor the system. It took an average of three days to make a sales presentation. Sixty thousand dollars worth of the power factors were sold in 1976. Consequently, the company decided to push this aspect of their business.

The market for the power factor increased dramatically when Hydro Quebec announced that effective January 1, 1979, efficiency ratings of 95 percent would be required to avoid penalty rates. In 1977, sales reached $350,000. The company anticipated that other companies such as IBM, Honeywell and Johnson Controls would enter the Canadian market. Honeywell had developed a similar product earlier and was marketing it in the United States as a "total energy management system." Johnson Controls were also in the business. ABC added a sales agent in Vancouver for the power factor and other products in 1977.

The power factor designed to regulate KVARs was combined with the microprocessors and sensing systems to create a total energy management system labelled the 10-series. The total energy system permitted the automatic control of lights, heat and power utilization of elevators, escalators, doors and so forth. The system also provided warnings about open doors, over-utilization of electricity and so on.

In early 1978, the company received a major boost for its 10-series total energy system when it was awarded a contract for a post office. A large food chain purchased one of their energy control systems. Sales were extended to the Western market, where a distributor was instrumental in selling $200,000 of power factors to major British Columbia lumber operators.

By late 1978, ABC Ltd. operated three assembly plants (5,400 square feet, 1,000 square feet and 2,500 square feet). A 3,200 square-feet expansion was planned for the 5,400 square-feet plant. These plants were under the supervision of a production manager, who along with a sales manager and a vice president, were the three senior executives reporting to the president.

THE YEAR 1979

In 1979, the company began to face different types of problems. The plant was unable to handle incoming orders, and backlogs developed. The air duct heaters (50 in stock in early 1979) which had been sitting on the shelf since 1975 were sold out in June. Orders for this product increased in September and again in December. The president was unsure of the source of the demand and tried to estimate how many more to produce.

Mr. Ross sold his engineering firm and joined ABC on a full-time basis. A 10-series model was sold to a major real estate investment company. The company began to push the

10-series through promotions at trade fairs and advertising in trade journals. The sales manager, Mr. Sen, expressed the new orientation of the company. "Now we are shifting our efforts from the power factor, our present breadwinner, to the 10-series. We feel it's the product of the future."

However, Mr. Simon recognized that ABC still had many different kinds of problems and pondered which was the wisest direction to go. He noted that:

In our type of business, complexity can kill your market. People either don't understand or just don't care. In the future, we will have to change. Our products will have to come from the market. Take the pool heaters—we are in the business just by luck. We had the load stabilizers, and they wouldn't sell. There was a conflict of interest with the electricians. We attached the load stabilizers to a pool heater, and our promotion has been to the pool dealers, not the electricians. Now, we're in the pool heater market. Just luck.

Take the air duct heaters. How do you find clients? It seemed like the perfect product. For five years, we couldn't sell a single one. Now, all of a sudden, orders are pouring in. How come? We're not sure. Do we produce, do we stock? Seventy percent of heating systems are oil/air in Quebec. There's potential, but when?

You know we are a small firm. Sometimes it's good, sometimes it's bad. Large firms are slow to react. They've got so much paperwork. When I developed the paging device,[1] I think I had more paperwork to prepare for them than I spent time developing the thing. Paperwork costs are astronomical for them. On the other hand, we might have only a tenth or less of the expense there. But we suffer in another area: back-up.

Being small has another drawback. It's hard to get in the door. People don't trust us.

You know, large companies can invest in pure R&D; that's fine. But they lack a "feeling." Companies such as the food chain like us. We have the technical ability. They don't. They're sales only. So they know that since we are small, we'll take care of them. But then if we were back at $250,000 (sales), no, they wouldn't want us.

The big companies usually come to us when they have a problem. We are sort of a last resort. You know, large companies like Alcan, for example, have set specifications (rules) for purchasing. We've got to try to change those specifications; it's costly. I understand. They don't want to take the risk on small guys like us. But that's hard on us.

The pool-heater market is great. It's the right size for us, and it's too small to attract the big guys. We try to look for markets that are highly variable and technical with few buyers. We use the strategy: buy Canadian, buy Quebec—and it works.

We are better than Honeywell technologywise. We are faster, less costly and more advanced. They said it. But then the risk is greater with ABC. We're small.

We are trying the bigger jobs. We underprice the big companies. They burn themselves out on technical jobs.

We are successful locally. We have got opportunities to go across Canada. But how do you train salesmen? Then there is service. I must answer all the technical questions. We are looking for standard products to go national. We have got to change from R&D innovation to marketing innovation. Our products are the best in the world, but they don't sell. We are getting too diversified, and that's dangerous. We will stay with buildings, and we will quote high on the other jobs.

Take the new government complex, for example. It's a three-to-six-man-month proposal. We can bid 40 percent lower than the competition. But then they will think that we are jokers and not serious. They are probably including us in there just because they need a third bid. And you know that, on the government jobs, we must absorb the consulting costs.

We have got to get to know the marketing side. We are concentrating on shaping up our present products. We are already too diversified. We are not looking for new products right now. Nobody is sure in this field, not even us.

We're too weak on the marketing side. We must look up customers. Maybe rental of our products is a solution?

There are many new products in energy conservation. Evaluation of them is hard. What are the proper ones? Firms (R&D-wise) are in front of the market. That's where you get burned. Especially small firms.

Appendix 1. Extracts from the financial statements of ABC Ltd.

ABC LTD. Balance Sheet Data (in thousands)										
	1970	1971	1972	1973	1974	1975	1976	1977	1978	1979
Assets										
Current assets:										
Cash	$3	$5	—	—	$10	$11	$13	—	—	$5
Accounts receivable (net)	—	77	$75	$84	166	104	238	$258	$375	300
Inventory (cost)	1	16	68	103	85	161	199	253	277	460
Other	—	—	—	1	—	4	4	6	14	2
Total current assets	4	98	143	188	261	280	454	517	666	767
Fixed assets	—	3	3	3	4	8	164	171	180	205
Other	—	—	—	—	—	—	1	2	4	7
Total assets	$4	$101	$146	$191	$265	$288	$619	$690	$850	$979
Liabilities and Equity										
Current liabilities:										
Accounts payable accrued		$29	$24	$28	$46	$69	$115	$128	$185	$166
Overdraft and bank loan		22	62	77	97	60	148	222	318	340
Other	$1	7	2	10	8	19	33	18	20	47
Total current liabilities	1	58	88	115	151	148	296	368	523	553
Long-term debt		18	33	39	35	34	157	156	154	157
Other							4	2	3	5
Total liabilities	1	76	121	154	186	182	457	526	680	715
Equity										
Capital stock					10	10	10	10	10	10
Retained earnings	3	25	25	37	69	96	152	154	160	254
Total equity	3	25	25	37	79	106	162	164	170	264
Total liabilities and equity	$4	$101	$146	$191	$265	$288	$619	$690	$850	$979

Appendix 2. Sales Summary (dollars in thousands).

Year	Pool Heater	Service	Air Duct Heater	Load Stabilizers	Trellis*	Power Factors	10-Series	Total
Sales:								
1979	$398	$22	$59	$133	$96	$1,086	$108	$1,902
1978	284	16	10	118	171	584	44	1,227
1977	305		20	146	166	249	140	1,026
1976	210			280	140	70		700
Sales by percentage ($):								
1979	21%	1%	3%	7%	5%	57%	6%	100%
1978	23	1	1	9	14	47	5	100
1977	30		2	14	16	24	14	100
1976	30			40	20	10		100
Sales by territory:		Quebec	Canada			USA	Total	
1979		$1,148	$702			$52	$1,902	
1978		976	129			48	1,155	

*Part of a load stabilizing system.

NOTES

1. A separate product, unrelated to those previously discussed.

Unican Security Systems Ltd. (A)

The annual general meeting of the shareholders of Unican Security Systems Ltd., held in Montreal, Canada on December 11, 1986 had drawn to a close and now Mr. Aaron M. Fish, (54), chairman, president and chief executive officer could immediately turn his thoughts to heading down to North Carolina to escape the wintery blasts of a Quebec winter. That is not to say that he didn't have a few other things on his mind but he had been able to report to the shareholders that for FY 1986 sales had reached approximately $80.2 million with net income some $3.6 million compared with about $25 million and $500,000 respectively, ten years previously. (Financial statements, Exhibits 1, 2, 3, 4). Looking ahead, Mr. Fish told the shareholders that "there will always be a demand for our products because when the economy goes up, people have more to lock up; when the economy goes down, they need to protect what they have—we can't lose."

The Company had been through a series of mergers, acquisitions and divestitures as well as having made concerted efforts in product development. The most crucial of the latter, at the moment, was that of the electronic hotel lock which would represent the beginning of a new stage in the design of an overall corporate structure and strategy of the corporation. This development would not only lead the organization into new growing markets, giving it an opportunity to develop further as a service business on an international scale, but require it to confront the task of building the complete organization to handle this venture. Not only that, but the whole program of transition and succession had a place in Mr. Fish's thoughts.

BACKGROUND

Mr. Fish's apprenticeship started at the age of nine, working in his father's one-man locksmith shop. At the age of thirteen, he was the number two man at "General Repair Shop" on St. Lawrence Boulevard (The Main) in the heart of Montreal's immigrant district. From here he would peddle his bicycle from locksmith shop to locksmith shop selling key blanks and related supplies.

Four years later, at the age of seventeen, he left high school to go into business on his own, forming Canadian Key and Lock Supply. With an initial capital of $20.00 and a line of credit from his uncle, who was in the wholesale locksmith supply business in Toronto,

This case was prepared by Professor Willard H. Ellis, McGill University, as a basis for classroom discussion. It is based, in part, on an M.B.A. report submitted by Brian Brenie and Group of McGill University. Copyright © 1987 by W. H. Ellis.

Ontario (some 335 miles to the west), he continued selling key blanks and locks to local shops. Realizing that he could not cover his territory adequately on a bicycle, he bought a "broken-down taxi" and for the next three years (until 1951) worked from his home. His first major expansion was to a rented garage. In 1953, Mr. Fish got married, bought his own home and set up business in the basement with his bride handling the bookkeeping.

The first inside employee was hired in 1954 while Mr. Fish continued to do the outside selling, and three years later, a second man was added to the inside staff.

Recognizing the importance of keeping in touch with developments in the industry, Mr. Fish attended locksmith conventions and training courses throughout Canada and the United States, "learning all I could about locks and security systems." He had built up good relationships with personnel in the Canadian government and in the locks and locking devices industry.

Confident that business in the security field was in for rapid growth, partially due to the increase in crime, he believed that self-service discount stores would be selling large volumes of deadlocks, night latches and door knobs. With three employees, Mr. Fish began blister and skin packaging imported hardware for mass distribution.

This immediately required a move from the home basement and subsequently in 1962, another move to their own 20,000 square foot building. Meeting in 1962 with the then coordinator of security and industrial defence at Bell Canada, the problems that were involved in the security access and control of this major corporation were made known, specifically for a mechanical keyless access control system.

By the end of the next year, a working hand model of a mechanical, combination changeable, pushbutton lock with electrical supervision had been developed. Patents were taken out with the guidance of Mr. Ira Jones in Milwaukee, described by Mr. Fish as "the best patent attorney for locks." By 1964, with the first order for 50 pushbutton locks confirmed by Bell Canada, the business began to expand, leading to the formation of Security Hardware Company and an influx of new capital. There were four original shareholders, including Mr. and Mrs. Fish who, in turn, invited seven friends to invest a total of $35,000.

Introductions to people in the industry and expansion led Mr. Fish to areas of security in both Canada and the United States. At this point also, production began on the "Unican" lock. By late 1964, Unican Systems Limited was incorporated, utilizing the $35,000 cash raised previously, the assets of Security Hardware Company and the patents. The Company charter called for the development and manufacture of a keyless security system for industrial, commercial and residential use. The lock had five pushbuttons, and a capacity for over 1,000 different combinations. "Resetting in less than a minute" was the theme used in the advertising material. The lock was first exhibited at a convention in Philadelphia for the American Society for Industrial Security.

In 1966, the man from Bell, John Marrett, joined Unican as Vice-President of Sales to help market and create a distribution network in the United States. His efforts resulted in Unican being awarded contracts with the United States government, Cape Canaveral, Lockheed Missile Center and Bell Laboratories.

According to Mr. Fish, the leaders of the mechanical locking industry looked with mild interest at the fast growing group of entrepreneurs who were quickly developing and marketing a vast array of electronic devices to augment the mechanical devices commonly known to the industry. However, he added, many of the new businesses created to serve the growing markets for security products were neither properly financed nor did they put sufficient emphasis on educating the installer and user of the new products. This led, in his opinion, to a great quantity of products being sold to the public which did not really meet the needs of the user; and furthermore, proper service facilities did not exist which would insure reliable use from the installed system.

In the meantime, Unican set about to build a business around a product, but development and early production costs depleted resources at a rapid rate requiring an ever increasing supply of funds since, with a relatively small volume, the cost of marketing each lock far outstripped the profit it brought in. Nevertheless, Mr. Fish commented that, "Growth opportunities came fast and frequently, with not always enough time to thoroughly investigate these opportunities. Fortunately for all of us, the big ones turned out successfully; and some, if not all, of the little ones were either absorbed or liquidated."

MERGERS, ACQUISITIONS AND DIVESTITURES

In considering the matter of acquisitions, Mr. Fish commented that:

> The most important thing in looking at each situation, and I get a lot of phone calls, is that I have two criteria. Do I have the marketing and/or do I have the manufacturing capability for that product? If I lack both of them, I tell the man "Thank you, good bye, we're not into it." If I have one of them, I will look into it. Today we are concentrating absolutely in the areas that we are strong in and that is furniture hardware, OEM components, consumer hardware which includes home security products and replacement key blanks and padlocks and things of that nature, packaged goods replacement and access controls, of which we have the mechanical pushbutton lock. That was the basis of the Company and even though we are continuing in that direction, there are three new products coming up now and we are into the electronic access controls. That's our business and we are not going out of those businesses.

Management had decided on a three pronged strategy direction—1) to search aggressively for acquisition opportunities of manufacturing facilities, 2) to respond to the increasing demand for electromechanical security devices, and, longer-range 3) to effect a market entry into the United States. (Exhibit 6—Management and Corporate Structure.)

Recognizing the need for additional facilities and experienced personnel and also the necessity to diversify its product line, *Capitol Industries Ltd.* and *Richmond Machine Tool & Die Casting Co. Ltd.* were acquired in 1969. These provided an integrated manufacturing capability that had been lacking previously, together with personnel with many years experience in the design and production of hardware items. It also meant growth in sales from $180,000 to $3.8 million and a staff of from six to a work force of over 350.

Capitol Industries supplied approximately 75% of the Canadian furniture hardware market (zinc-cast handles, drawer pulls, self-closing hinges, and locks) and exported also to the U.S. As well as a broad range of specialty items for the furniture and cabinet industries, for builders, wholesalers and retailers, Capitol produced a large volume and variety of custom zinc die castings. Technically, the company had the ability to take a project from initial conception to finished product, through design, prototype models, engineering, tooling, production casting, assembly, finishing and electroplating or painting. It also designed and produced dies, jigs and special tooling.

Richmond Die Casting Co. Ltd., incorporated in 1944, was manufacturing die-casting machines and specialty dies and had recruited over the years a large and highly-skilled staff of engineers and tool designers.

In its more recent years it had concentrated its efforts in the very specialized field of aluminum die-casting with much of its work being custom for some major Canadian companies including I.B.M., General Electric, Black & Decker and Bombardier Ltd.

The purchase price for both companies was a total of $555,000 in cash and 56,260 common shares valued at $8 per share.

During 1969 and 1970, to provide Canada-wide distribution through chain stores, mass merchandisers, building supply dealers and standard hardware retailers and to market and merchandise Capitol products, Unican purchased the outstanding shares of **Home Hardware Manufacturing Corp.** for $80,000 cash and 20,000 common shares at $4 per share. The company, which in 1972 became an integral part of Capitol, was equipped with modern packaging facilities, including blister and skin-pack machinery. Point-of-purchase displays and support advertising were created to attract the home decorator and handyman.

Unican was able then to offer a comprehensive range of home decorative hardware products throughout North America for both the Original Equipment Manufacturer (OEM) and replacement markets.

The Company's first move into the United States came on May 6, 1968 with the incorporation of **Unican Security Systems Corp.** In June 1971 Unican acquired 65% of the outstanding shares of **Simplex Security Systems Inc.** of Collinsville, Conn. The company owned the patents for and supplied the central control chamber around which the Unican keyless security locks were designed. It also produced a medium-priced line of push-button locks for the commercial and residential markets and for college dormitories in the United States.

In January 1972 after almost two years of negotiation, Unican finalized its acquisition of **Ilco Corp.** of Fitchburg, Mass. which was founded in 1834 as the Nashun Lock Company. This move made the Company one of the largest and broadest based manufacturers and distributors of builders and replacement security products including key-cutting machines in North America. At that time, Ilco Corp. was the world's largest single-source supplier of keys and key-cutting machines; a major supplier of builders' door hardware, replacement and auxiliary locks as well as for original equipment manufacturers in the United States.

Later in 1972, Unican acquired the assets and business of **Dynation Corporation** of Little Falls, N.J., manufacturers of heavy-duty, high-security cable locks and padlocks. Distributing the Dyna Lok line through the Ilco network provided Unican with a comprehensive one-source listing of locks and security products. The manufacturing functions of Dynation have since been integrated into other plants and all assembly operations transferred to the Rocky Mount plant in North Carolina.

Subsequently in 1974, a 154,000 sq. ft. plant was built in Rocky Mount to increase output to meet the growing demands for Unican products.

Also in 1974 **Unican Electrochemical Products Limited,** Montreal, was incorporated to handle developments in that field. However, when the operation did not turn out to be profitable it was dropped in 1977.

By 1973, Unican was able to turn part of its attention to the potential market overseas, starting with Britain where a reciprocal arrangement was made with **N.T. Locks,** giving Ilco exclusive marketing rights in the United States for a modern line of hydraulic door closers under the Unican/Briton label. On the other side of the Atlantic, N.T. Locks assembled and marketed an Ilco line of cylindrical lock sets.

In Europe, **Ilcorp,** established in Geneva, Switzerland, sold and distributed selected Unican products with special emphasis being placed on the marketing of Ilco key-cutting machines. An arrangement with Cransnianski-France S.A. of Grenoble, a manufacturer and distributor throughout the European Common Market of KIS steel blanks and keycutting equipment, resulted in the formation of two subsidiary companies:

Unikis Limited—incorporated in 1973, developed a line of colour-coded, plastic-headed key blanks and started manufacturing. Marketing was done through the Ilco/Unican organization.

Unikis Japan Co. Ltd.—was established in Osaka in 1980, to distribute cabinet hardware, key-duplicating equipment and replacement keys manufactured in Montreal, the U.S. and Grenoble.

Complying with a directive from the Board of Directors that "management activities should be streamlined and concentrated both as to location of facilities and product line in those areas where our experience and expertise give us maximum advantage in the marketplace" the Richmond Machine Tool & Die Casting Company Limited was sold back to one of its original owners for $700,000. In 1980, an agreement was signed with the Minister of Light Industry in China, exchanging technology and tooling capability for padlocks. This lead to the formation of Ilco Unican in Hong Kong. In the same year, Unican acquired all of the outstanding shares of Quebec Bolt and Screw Limited and Beejay Industrial Supplies Limited, wholesalers of industrial supplies and La Visserie Soviq Limitee, a manufacturer of screws in Quebec. The company became **Soviq, Inc.** formed as a joint venture between Unican and Rona Hardware group. Soviq supplied the fasteners for Unican's industrial use and Rona's retail trade.

The **Sagar Corporation** was acquired in 1982 as a quick step into the manufacture of milling cutters used on the key duplicating machines. Unican acquired **Dominion Lock**

Company Limited in 1985. The company manufactured key blanks, key duplicating equipment, builders' and furniture locks and post office boxes.

Three months after the purchase of Dominion Lock, Unican purchased **Dominion Lock Australia** (July 1985) which meant the first overseas manufacturing and distribution subsidiary.

In June 1986, Ilco Unican acquired **Taylor Lock Co.** of Philadelphia. Founded in 1912, Taylor employed 126 people in the manufacture and distribution of key blanks, key duplicating machines and auxiliary door hardware. This latest addition was designed to broaden Unican's distribution base, while increasing manufacturing efficiency. The Taylor line complemented similar products manufactured in Rocky Mount in North Carolina and the Dominion Lock Division in Montreal. It further broadened the product range of key blanks, key duplicating machines and locksmith supplies, expanded the customer base, increasing group sales for the fiscal year ending June 1987 by approximately $8 million.

PRODUCTS AND PRODUCTION

The Unican group of companies compete in three broadly defined industries:

1. *Furniture Hardware* in a range of designs aimed at both the consumer and Original Equipment Manufacturers (OEM),
2. *Security Hardware* including locksets, auxiliary locks, cam-locks, mechanical keyless locks, padlocks, electronic locks, and other security devices and
3. *Locksmith Supplies* consisting of key blanks, key duplicating machines and other tools.

All three of these industries can be characterized as mature. Very few of the products in the groups are complex or require a complex production process. All are experiencing low growth rate and a resultant increase in competition for market share. (See Exhibit 7 for details of Unican's product line.)

Furniture Hardware

Over 90% of Unican's furniture hardware output is sold to Original Equipment Manufacturers (OEM) and the Company is reported to dominate the Canadian market with an estimated 80%–90% share and an increasing share, believed to be 12%, of the U.S. market.

The competitive environment in the industry is defined by slow growth and a large number of firms competing for market share. Sales of OEM hardware are tied to furniture sales and the simple nature of the product makes switching costs low.

Price is important but differentiation among suppliers is based on product quality and level of service. Product quality is defined by the type of materials used, quality of style and consistency of colours. While this is a standard feature of North American products, it is often lacking in low-cost imported hardware.

Service depends not only upon the ability to deliver to the OEM customer, but also the capacity to quickly produce new designs requested by furniture makers. The ability to design a range of decorative styles for potential customers is an important advantage and is aided by the hardware producer's proximity to the furniture makers. In this respect, the low cost import manufacturers are at a disadvantage.

Import competition comes not only from imported hardware but from imported furniture. Since the furniture hardware industry depends on furniture sales, it will depend to a large extent on the health of North American furniture makers. In the U.S., furniture imports in 1984 amounted to $2 billion, a 40% increase over 1983. This would suggest that import manufacturers were making some inroads into the market. However, 17% of the imports originated in Canada and therefore came with Canadian furniture hardware. In addition, some importers of furniture from low-cost countries add the hardware once it is in the U.S. market.

There are few substitutes for decorative hardware. Some producers use plastic or wooden handles while some furniture makers' designs do not require hardware. Zinc remains the most common material for furniture hardware production.

Security Hardware

The products in this category range from a simple deadbolt lock to complex electronic security systems. The majority of this industry is comprised of relatively simple products made by several North American firms. Slow growth in the lower end of the industry has led manufacturers to compete more strenuously for market share and to pay more attention to the upper-end of the market.

Import competition among the least complex security products has caused some North American producers to reconsider their position in this market. Some have ceased to produce products vulnerable to import competition and have instead turned to importing.

Industry sources believe that a large part of the future growth in the security industry will come from electronic access control systems. While many of these systems use impressive technology, there is very little of this technology which is patentable. Entrance barriers here will come from restricted access to distribution channels and low market knowledge.

Several companies now produce keyless electronic locks using magnetic stripes or optic technology. Other more advanced systems include finger-print readers and voice-activated access controls.

Locksmith Supplies

This industry includes key blanks, key duplicating machines and other peripheral supplies. The customers in this market segment include original installation and replacement key blank purchasers. Key blanks, being an undifferentiated commodity, compete mainly on price, with the most efficient producer capturing the largest market share. The trend in recent years has been for lock manufacturers to buy keys for the locks they produce, from large volume key producers rather than making them in-house. Slow growth in the North American markets would dictate that the major thrust would remain towards cost reduction and that any growth would have to be achieved internationally.

CORPORATE STRATEGY

As a basic premise, Mr. Fish would describe the Company's strategy simply as "You Position your company to be first in what you are doing on an international level or you go out of business."

With this in mind, the four components of the Company's strategy have been categorized as:

1. *Global Enterprise*—a belief that the world must be the market for a company to be successful with the realization that all the Company's products are basic and mature. Therefore, growth must come from taking advantage of opportunities in foreign markets.
2. *First in Meeting Market Needs*—a conscious striving to make the market needs a reality.
3. *First in Quality*—an aim to serve the high quality segment of their respective markets.
4. *First in Cost Effectiveness*—Realizing the mature nature of their products, management has been relentless in being cost effective.

These four strategies have been implemented in a number of ways.

Global Enterprises

The result of these activities has been to expand Unican's markets across Canada, the United States and into some thirty countries around the world. The relative significance of this strategy becomes apparent from the geographical sales distribution data which show the United States accounting for approximately 73%, Canada 22% and Overseas 5% in 1986. (Exhibit 8.)

The Company's penetration of the North American market has been essentially through horizontal integration and it now feels that it is in a position to market its products internationally with its success depending upon how well it remains first in its respective divisions.

First in Meeting Market Needs

It was Mr. Fish's opinion that many of his larger competitors do not have the grass roots experience that he has in the locksmith trade to give them an adequate appreciation of security problems and adds that even in the more advanced electronic lock, it was he who wrote the specifications before any design work was done. Also, being "market-driven" Unican served both the domestic and foreign markets from the most appropriate location. For example, in the furniture OEM market, while other American producers were geographically situated to respond quickly to design needs of furniture manufacturers, Unican was located in Montreal, thus in a position to effectively serve the domestic and foreign markets. To be close to the American OEM furniture market, centered in North Carolina, Unican has a design office at High Point, N.C. in the heart of the U.S. furniture market. This office monitors customer needs and with customer input helped Unican design five to seven new decorative hardware styles per week. It was estimated that of these styles, approximately 150 prove to have been sufficiently popular to be mass produced each year.

The time between design and production of customer samples can be as short as one week. After an order is placed, six weeks are required to make a die, produce the order, finish the pieces and deliver them to a customer. This rapid response, in addition to maintaining a "lean" management staff, the Company feels it has an action orientation which results in superior customer service and a steadily increasing market share.

The Company has also developed a broad range of push-button locks in order to further serve its markets. It was the Company's first product and the Unican and Simplex 1000 and 2000 series are produced for commercial applications, the Simplex lock for light-duty, the 3000 series for narrow style doors, such as aluminum store fronts, and a residential access control. For high security needs, a 10-button, 1 million combination access control lock is being developed.

First In Quality

While a market driven strategy means staying close to the customer and responding rapidly to his needs, being first in quality to Mr. Fish means the conscious decision to produce for the high quality end of each market served. "Make the best product possible, at the best price possible, to do the job."

In the decorative hardware business, quality has been an apparent major advantage over imported products. OEM customers in particular have demanded consistency in colour tone and finish in the components added to their products. "Satisfying these requirements has helped Unican maintain a strong position in the North American market."

This strategy has been employed also with regard to the push-button locks and, Unican feels, with the same relative results. In the electronic hotel lock, which is currently the focal point for product development, Unican is of the opinion that it has developed the best electronic system available. The product has been under study for over five years and the system is now being evaluated by pilot installations in several of Canada's largest hotel chains.

The Company believes that the development of an electronic hotel lock will lead to an infinite number of possibilities such as hotel employee control, payroll, automatic check-in and check-out facilities, control of charges within a hotel and management information.

In some lines, Unican has not been able to compete with low cost producers, such as residential locksets, with the result that it withdrew from these markets. This policy is in keeping with its strategy of being identified only with high quality products and withdrawing from those where a quality product cannot be produced competitively.

First in Cost Effectiveness

This strategy recognizes the potential for change in the external environment such as pressure from imports, inflationary tendencies in resource prices, global economic conditions and the general volatility of all factors influencing the firm's competitive position. The components which have had an integral effect on this strategy may be described thus:

a. *Integration*—The vertical integration of suppliers of components or materials commenced in 1971 with Simplex, the supplier of the locking chamber for the mechanical push-button lock; in 1982, Soviq Inc. was established to supply screws and other fasteners and Sagar, a producer of cutting wheels for key duplicating machines was acquired in the same year. In 1986 the brass conversion mill in Rocky Mount N.C. started producing substantial quantities of brass for key blanks. Aside from its modern production capabilities, the mill will operate only at night, thereby saving $30,000–$40,000 per month on electricity charges alone. The net effect will be brass conversion at 71% of the current price for brass, reportedly making Unican the "world's most efficient maker of key blanks."

b. *Brass Conversion Mill*—In 1974 Unican produced 3 million brass keys per month. In 1986, 19 million will be produced with the short-term goal of increasing this to 30 million per month. Each pound of blank keys requires two pounds of brass and the cost to Unican of each pound of brass was $0.98. Of this $0.50 was metal value, and $0.48 was the value of the conversion to key stock. The brass conversion mill which started operations in June 1986 at Rocky Mount, N.C. will lower Unican's cost of converting two pounds of brass to one pound of key stock from $0.96 to $0.56.

  According to Mr. Fish, "Integrating backward to convert brass was an opportunity to solidify Unican's position as the leader in making brass key blanks in the world's most efficient conversion mill."

RESEARCH AND DEVELOPMENT

Referring back to the Company's earlier attempts at R & D, Mr. Fish commented that he would always go back and emphasize that each time the Company tried something out of "our main thrust, out of keys, locks and the regular hardware, we lost money. We had a research department here for ten years in zinc air batteries—high technology batteries. We were successful. We made batteries for the General Motors electric car. We made a wonderful battery for hearing aids which worked on air effectively. Air was a catalyst—with six times the output of a mercury battery. Better voltage stabilization, but we lost money and we closed it down because it was not really our main thrust."

  Excerpts from the Annual Report (1986) show the following highlights relative to current activity in Research and Development:

- Research and Development expenditures have grown from $204,205 or 1/2% of sales in 1981/82 to $1,445,701 or 1.8% of sales in 1985/86.

HUMAN RESOURCES

In dealing with the human resources of the Company, Mr. Fish commented:

> We built up the business with pride of product. This is something that too many chief executives have lost track of, especially conglomerates. They are sitting on top looking at numbers. They are not looking at the product. They are losing touch with their employees, they are losing touch with their customers and it's a numbers game, rather than a product game, which if all goes well, will create good numbers for you. I emphasize to our shareholders that this is primarily an employee oriented company. We do what is good for the employees. We do what is good for our customers. The result of the two is generally good for the shareholders. That is the way we work. Without happy employees, it doesn't work. We now have 1,300 people in four major locations and no unions. The key to that is good supervisors who are close to the people. Unless you have good supervisors, that will never fly. You have to be sensitive to the people's needs. Not necessarily money. It could be a clean toilet, it could be the availability of sanitary napkins for the women, or to relate to their needs. When there is extra work available, give them the overtime. Let them make those extra dollars. My philosophy is to give one man a full loaf of bread rather than two people halves. And of course, I am the guy that says if we are going to lay off or if we are going to hire. When I see big business coming in, before we hire people, we give overtime, a lot of overtime. Now, if the drop is back, you drop back on the overtime. You don't bring in a bunch of clowns. But the people who are here, they know it. They know that the boss is thinking about them and giving them that overtime and the extra dollars. And that goes a long way. We also build and drop inventory to keep employment stable. What we would like to reach is a no layoff company. It is difficult but we are working towards it. As for compensation, that has to be such that your top and middle management just will never leave.

Mr. Fish added that everybody was on incentive and that the incentive for top management was structured on a corporate basis, based on return on investment. The moment that a bigger return than is normal is attained or expected or that guidelines provided for, were exceeded—the board of directors (Exhibit 9) sets the guidelines—then there is a pool for everybody from the president all the way through to the purchasing agent and the personnel director.

> Too many people forget the personnel director. In fact, he is one of your most important people. In our case, the personnel director is close to the people and he is in charge of safety. So there is a pool and everybody gets a percentage of the pool, which is approved by the board, in relationship to his salary. So, if I have the biggest salary, I get the biggest piece but that is in tune with my responsibilities.

Mr. Fish indicated that it took him some ten years of "real work" to create the incentive program, where he said that in any one year, the incentive could go as high as 50% of the salary for the year. "Now that is a felt incentive—as a matter of interest, last year we paid out 43%. This year I think it will be 50%."

Mr. Fish explained the operation of the incentive plan thus:

The employee signs a letter that if he is terminated for any reason whatsoever, he automatically is discounted from the incentive program. If you make $50,000 and this year the rate was 50%, your incentive bonus would be $25,000. You get $12,500 immediately and you get the other $12,500 over a period of five years, without interest. This is done for two reasons. A guy makes $50,000, gets a bonus of $25,000, his cost of living suddenly goes to $75,000. Now, if next year his salary went from $50,000 to $52,000 and he only gets 10%, he is in trouble. He will have spent at the rate of $75,000! By giving him half the incentive and half on a pay-out, when we look at a five-year program—and we are now 3–4 years into the program—everybody's salary has been very even and going up.

Once we had a bit of a downer in 1982, there were no incentives, but the guy didn't get smashed. Between a raise and some incentives owing from previous periods plus a small or no incentive, even in the third year, you have had three good years. If you get no incentive in the fourth year, between your raise, your total income is still quite comfortable. Whereas, if you have received these incentives and suddenly you are missing $30,000 at the end of the year, you are in deep trouble. Plus the money is in the bank. We have people here now with $50,000 in the bank. They quit, they lose it. He knows that if he doesn't perform, he is going to get terminated. Everybody is rated because not everybody has the same formula. We have corporate involvement. If you are low, you go down to 80% of corporate involvement. If you are the president of a division or a manager of a division, or myself, we are 100% corporate involvement. I devised a plan which I thought was fair. I kept bouncing the idea off people in meetings and there was a great deal of resistance with them saying, "Why should you hold back my money"? My reply was very simple. "It is not your money. And if you like, you can still participate but for you—you don't want me to hold your money—therefore for you, your maximum incentive can only be 25% of salary"—which is still a felt incentive. He would say, "Oh, no!" I said, "Then I am going to hold up the other 25% or 50%, so take your choice. Either you go in with a maximum of 50%, you get half now and half later, or you go in with a maximum of 25%. You get it all now and you have nothing later."

Mr. Fish continued on the subject of incentives saying that they are the only thing that works.

You have got to have the carrot out there. I think that the thing that a chief executive needs today, in every business, are two major tools—a long needle to give it to the next group below you, and a five year vision of where the industry is going.

The only unions we ever had was when we had bought them with a company and got rid of them. People only need unions if you don't treat them right. You treat them right and they don't want to pay a union for nothing. The best example is that Dominion Lock had an in-house organization with an outside organizer. Eight weeks after we took over they voluntarily disbanded the whole thing and said "We don't need it with you guys." So unions were there because management was insensitive to people's needs and that goes back historically to the sweat shop. We have to worry about their money, we have to worry about their welfare, we have to worry about their security, about safety, about the way they are treated, about the way you talk to them—the whole thing is a big package. You cannot make them feel like animals. When we get a union, believe me, it is very costly, because they have to show performance and the only way that they show performance is on your back and eventually if you are a world class performer, you are going to be knocked out of the box. It is different than construction. If you want to put up a building on one point, it is a one shot deal and you are finished. A manufacturer making a product every day, competing in a world market, is not finished because somebody else comes in with a low cost labour. What is significant today, and we have all to watch, is the so-called countries with low labour and they are very low by our standards. Those people are putting in the most modern equipment so they have the advantage of low labour, good output and good quality because of the new equipment. Keep up with it or watch out.

Another example of union activity came back in September 1974 with the acquisition of the Ilco Corporation in Fitchburg, Mass. In writing in the company publication "Our first 20 years," Mr. Fish stated that with the ink hardly dry on the acquisition, the International Union of Electrical workers, representing 600 bargaining unit workers, made it clear that they intended to take charge. If Ilco was to survive, the plant had to be modernized, facilities upgraded and costs controlled. The union insisted on staying with entrenched, inefficient methods. The Fitchburg plants were antiquated and dumping pollutants into the nearby river. After a four-and-a-half month strike, the company settled but production was phased out of Fitchburg and some of the operations moved to Rocky Mount, N.C.

FINANCE

The initial financing in 1949 of what was to subsequently become Unican Security Systems Ltd., consisted of $20.00 personal capital of Mr. Fish plus a line of credit from a wholesale supplier uncle, together with a basic key inventory of $100.00. Going from this "Start-up," the present Company was incorporated on November 13, 1964, to include assets of $35,000 in cash raised from a group of seven investors of Security Hardware, and that Company's assets and patents.

Growing demands continued to put pressure on finances and relationships with the bank so much so that by 1966 the Company's current liabilities of $125,000 were then three times greater than its consolidated net worth. In the words of Mr. Fish, "We were at the wall . . . go public or go bankrupt." In reviewing the circumstances of that period, Mr. Fish commented: By December (1966) we had stretched our financial resources to the limit. Fortunately 1967 and 1968 were good times for entrepreneurs and venture capitalists. Paper was being printed for every conceivable idea and here we were with a good idea but no money. Working with a Montreal brokerage firm, the Company went public in 1967 raising $240,000 of cash in return for 120,000 common shares representing 20% of the Company. The actual prospectus was dated March 4, 1968. "For the first time in many years, the bank was off my back," was the gleeful remark by Mr. Fish.

Unican shares were soon trading at $8.00 and the Company took advantage of this receptivity and finalized a second offering of 120,000 shares on the last day of 1968, acquiring almost $1 million to assist in the financing of its development and growth. Mr. Fish discussed his concept of a small company going public, which Unican certainly was at the time.

"After we went public, we ended up buying out all of the original investors in Home Hardware, all of the investors who were then Capitol Industries and supplying us with components for the lock, and we suddenly went from about 13 to 250 employees and from $180,000 to $2.5 million in sales. But the ability to do that was the result of going public and access to outside funds. I am a great believer in going public. I believe that it puts discipline into your thinking, which does not otherwise occur. It should but it doesn't. You have a board of directors, you have outsiders that you answer to and have input. You have financial discipline which most small companies don't have and you have to recall that we went public with only $180,000 in gross sales. But already the financial disciplines came in because we needed audited statements that little companies don't spend money on and they end up looking back and saying, 'Oh, my God, what happened?' when it is too late. So the discipline of going public is just a great vehicle."

Two more acquisitions were completed in 1971 and 1972. First Mr. David Creedon, Manager of Simplex Systems Inc., the manufacturer of the locking chamber used in the Unican pushbutton lock, was given 48 hours in which to purchase the Division or it would be sold to others. Within 24 hours, Mr. Fish and Mr. Creedon put together an Offer to Purchase all of the assets of Simplex, winding up with Unican holding 65% and Mr. Creedon the remaining 35%. Simplex now is reputed to be the largest manufacturer of mechanical, combination changeable pushbutton locks in the world.

In the same year, Ilco Corporation, based in Fitchburg, Mass. was "in trouble." The leading manufacturer of replacement keys, key duplicating machines and locksmith supplies, with divisions which manufactured builder's hardware and automotive locks, 1300 employees and $13 million in annual sales. "Ilco's battered management spent more time selling the Company than running it. I envisioned a quick turn around to profitability but the plan was radical," commented Mr. Fish.

In doing so, Mr. Fish was able to restructure Ilco's debt, obtain forgiveness of other debt while Unican invested approximately $1 million as equity plus $700,000 in loans. Further refinancing and equity injection brought Ilco out of its net worth deficit position and some working capital. Unican had now become a company of some 1700 employees with over $200 million in sales. Within weeks of acquisition the Ilco group was operating above break-even after the five years of continuous losses.

Financing of the Ilco Corporation in 1972 was arranged with a group of lending institutions in the United States amongst whom were First National Bank of Boston, Massachusetts Business Development Corporation and the Worchester County National Bank. Unican was able to go to the market again and on October 19, 1972, sold 250,000 common shares at $4.25 each to a group of private investors.

Unican acquired 03.3% of Ilco's common shares and 71.4% of the preferred shares for a total of $1,125,018 (U.S.) and a subordinated note for $782,000. The three years that followed saw a period of recession, labour unrest, acquisitions, start-up costs at the new plant in Rocky Mount, N.C., the cumulative effect of which by June 1975, wiped out 50% of Unican's consolidated net worth and all of its working capital.

"The banks were crawling all over me," remarked Mr. Fish. The First National Bank of Boston was the first to call its loan of $2.6 million, "the action was on my desk. I took calls from all suppliers, buying time and closing deals. Everyone got a little money each week. Only one supplier, Anaconda Brass, bailed out. Cominco, our largest Canadian supplier and the life-blood of our business, was most supportive. It extended our line of credit and gave us endless support," recalled Mr. Fish.

In 1979 the floating of a $5.5 million debenture was crucial in enabling the Company to cope with the high interest rates that followed in 1980 and 1981 and was a factor in allowing the Company to pay its first dividend of 0.05 cents per share, on February 26, 1981. That year, profits eliminated tax loss credits from previous years and "the Banks Stopped Calling."

In 1982, Unican acquired all of the outstanding shares of *Sagar Inc.,* Rocky Mount, N.C., for approximately $801,000. Sagar manufactured cutters which were used on the key-cutting machines.

In the 1980s, Dominion Lock had found itself in financial difficulties and accepted a loan from Simpson Hardware, the American parent of Taylor Lock. Ostensibly, Simpson saw this as an opportunity to acquire DL, and with its term-loan secured the right to some management in DL. A short time later, more capital was required to bring DL back to profitability, necessitating an extension of the demand loan to some $1.5 million. In late 1984, Simpson called the demand loan forcing DL into receivership. When unsecured creditors of DL forced the DL into bankruptcy, Unican was able to get an injunction stopping Simpson from liquidating it. Subsequently, Unican contested in court Simpson's right to effectively assume control of the firm for the price of its loans, arguing that Unican was offering a price for DL which was greater than its liquidated value. Unican won its case, paying $6.2 million and assumed $2 million in long-term debt, in 1985.

Aside from the potential for substantial gain in domestic market share, Unican knew that the purchase would also strengthen its distribution network in some foreign markets, give a broader product line from which to choose profitable items, and incorporate the expertise of some DL personnel. In addition, Unican was in need of more production capacity and DL had a modern 150,000 sq. ft. facility in Montreal, valued on its books at $2 million.

The Taylor Lock Company of Philadelphia was acquired in June 1986 for a cash consideration of over $3.3 million, and repayment of almost $1.6 million of inter-company debt to the previous owners.

The effect of the various acquisitions on this Company's sales over the years, rising to $80.3 million in 1986, is shown in Exhibit 5.

In 1986, Unican class A shares ranged between $9 3/4 to $20 3/8 and the class B between $8 1/2 and $10 1/2 per share. A stock split of common shares was approved at the Special Shareholders meeting held October 30, 1986. The objective of the stock split and the creation of convertible preferred was to create an additional "float" in the market while enabling the Company to raise new capital without seriously diluting the voting power of the existing shareholders. The use of the convertible shares was for the purpose of purchasing the 35% of Simplex Security Systems, Inc., which Unican did not presently own.

The impact of these transactions is shown graphically in Exhibit 4, with net worth rising to $21.7 million, working capital to $17.8 million and pre-tax profit to $6.8 million respectively for the fiscal year 1986.

A VIEW TOWARD THE FUTURE

In commenting about the future direction of the Company, Mr. Fish expressed his views as follows:

There is another thing that you have to look at very, very carefully—business is opportunities. If you don't jump when the time is there to do it, you will generally miss it. Opportunities never come when you want them and you are never ready for them. They come when they happen and if you sense it and you see it is there, jump. Try to do your acquisitions or your opportunities on a scale that if you blow it, it is not going to blow the company. It may be a little strain, and that you should be ready for, but won't destroy the company. When you are starting up, every risk can destroy the company and you would never have a start-up. But once you mature and start that working capital and look at the thing and say, "look, can I risk 25% of my working capital and X% of my net worth"—then go and gamble. If you lose it, you'll lose it for a few years and get the fat back on your bones. But don't gamble so much that you are going to blow the whole thing. So, where do we go from here? We have to keep three or four things in mind. The Company has a good base. When I say good base, we have a very solid day-to-day product. It's bread and butter. You need it to serve an industry, to serve your customer and your consumer. But, that's a dangerous position to be in and I just sent a memo off to every one of our managers saying, "Because we are doing well, don't become complacent because in five years we will be out of business."

We are looking at each one of our major businesses and we are trying to make each business, each product range, either it is unique and we are making it better and expanding the range of products in its uniqueness. Example: pushbutton locks, mechanical, changeable pushbutton locks . . . we have turned out some 550 locks a day—two models. We are bringing out three more models. We are expanding the range. A lower cost model for residential use; another model in-between, but we are now developing what we call a "high-in lock." Now let me give you price points. Our price points today are wholesale—$56 and $125. We expect the residential model wholesale will be something in the order of $40 and the high-in to be about $175 to $200, but the high-in will be the very heavy-duty model. It will have things which will allow handicapped people to open the door and instead of a thousand possible combinations it should have a million possible combinations.

So we have a range and also we are becoming more efficient in turning out these locks. But because we are doing well doesn't mean we are sitting back on a product. We are spending more than a million dollars a year in R & D.

With regard to key blanks, at the beginning of 1984 we were running at the rate of 8 to 9 million a month in brass. We are planning in 1986 to be at 30 million. But just to make a key blank doesn't mean you are going to be successful because a lot of people, who are good tool makers, can start making key blanks. We are putting in the brass conversion mill as a result because metal is four-fifths the cost of making a key. We will be the most efficient producer of key blanks from the metal or virgin metal point to the finished product. And we are investing $4 to $5 million to be the most efficient converter of virgin to stripped brass in the world. We are at the forefront of technology and we hired two metallurgists, engineers, and we put them to work. (Production started in June 1986.) The inspiration for these developments?—Mine all the way! I'm the guy that said, "Look, I can't compete with the little guy in the small shop where he is the tool maker, the designer, the production man and his wife is the bookkeeper and the order taker. Well, what can I do that the little guy cannot do? I could have a huge investment in converting to metal. He can't." And this goes back to Bernard Baruch. If you read his book, he said, if you are going to do business, do it with the big guys. Don't get into the little items that every little guy on the corner can do and compete with you. And that's what it is. We are now in the metal business. There isn't one key blank maker in the world that can afford to put in what we did. When I first conceived the idea, we were using 300,000 to 500,000 pounds of metal per month. At a million we are running a very efficient operation, and of course, with our new capacity, we will be up to three million. That is the second part of our business.

The third part of our business is key duplicating machines. We amalgamated all the lines of Dominion Lock and Ilco, put in good engineering and we are putting in a CAD/CAM system. I am the guy who insisted on switching all machines to metric. These are being made in the United States, where metric is a dirty word. I explained to our people that by making a metric machine, two things happen. First of all, they are going to have to buy all the parts from us in the U.S. They can't even get a screw in the hardware store. But more important, we can now make deals with companies throughout the world—sell them the basic parts which are very expensive to tool up in their precise machines, and there may be six machines of that nature. When you go into a Third World country, let him buy the parts on a local basis. He can buy a shaft, a screw, a motor, a belt, a switch . . . they don't need all of the safeties that we need. I am the supplier of the parts, my volume will go up. It took my knowledge of the world market and leadership to say, "Hey, here is the way we are going to do it." The other thing that we have done is develop a centre in Montreal where we have the most modern CAD/CAMs that we can—three dimensional with turning and contour capability. What they have now is CAD/CAMs with standard geometric shape, really contour because when you do a French Provincial or a Mediterranean handle, there is no standard geometric shape. There are all kinds of curls within curls and contours. We are starting to train people. We now have a designer and a model maker and sandbox. And then they make tooling. We can have the designer work on a TV screen. The plotter will give him a shape, the tape output will be put on a computer controlled milling machine and in the morning we are going to have components to make dies and tools and moulds. In 1986, we will have appropriated one and a half million dollars to CAD/CAMs and C&C equipment so that we can really go from the design stage into a mould making stage very quickly and have the machines work all night because of the C&C equipment . . . even if there is one person around, four machines can operate fine. So we are into that and it is a very big stage of development for the Company.

We will also have to expand our engineering in terms of being the best dye casters and the best millers. We just have to know all the modern technologies in working with metal.

By having a metallurgist on our staff and having our own foundry . . . one of the things I put into this brass conversion—we had an induction furnace which melts 22,000 pounds of metal at one shot. I also bought one that has 3,000 pound capacity and they said, "Look, you guys, the industry is traditionally being affected by the big brass mill, which makes 60% copper and 40% zinc, with a little junk in between and that is what we have to work with. Maybe it would be better to have 53% copper but they aren't interested in the volume of key blanks. A million pounds a month to a big brass mill is nothing. There are mills in the U.S. that do a million pounds a day. So what we are going to do now is that we put on a complete laboratory, spectograph, all of the tensile testing equipment, metallurgists, small furnaces, and then we will develop alloys for our industry. Again, the small guys can't compete with us. We are going to be a world class Company and we will be the most efficient at what we do of anybody in the world. That's what we are going to spend our money on."

We will, over the next two years, and with no acquisitions in mind—although an acquisition could come down the pike—get ready, financially. We are just going to put fat on our bones and get ready for something big, because, and this is very important, we are living in an era where it is in fact cheaper to buy companies than develop your own. They have the space in store, it's cheaper to buy space and product than try to knock him out. So that's one of the next steps.

Of course, building management has been a problem but each one of our guys can run his own division and they really work well together. If something happens to me, there is at least one who will be able to step in. You are not going to have the dynamic push and it is a new deal. It is a manager. Right now, it is an entrepreneur who is the biggest shareholder and every time we spend a dollar, it comes right out of my pocket. I feel a little different than a manager. But I instil in them the saving of the pennies, watching the paper clips, flying economy class or Super Saver. In fact, one whole division was turned around by watching the pennies. I proved it to the manager. He is probably our best manager today. We are bringing in a new director. That gives us a broader outlook to be able to attract more people. As we grow, we will have to put up new factories, new buildings and develop new people to operate them.

Exhibit 1. Unican Security Systems Limited (A) Consolidated Balance Sheds as at June 30 ($000.).

Assets	1967	1970	1971	1972	1973	1974	1975
Current							
Cash	—	9	24	280	172	39	—
Accounts Receivable	15	914	1,179	4,114	3,930	5,237	4,006
Inventories	26	557	762	5,666	7,304	9,325	7,843
Prepaid Expenses	—	126	164	123	187	204	172
Total Current Assets	41	1,606	2,129	10,183	11,593	14,805	12,021
Restricted funds for plant construction	—	—	—	—	5	564	451
Investments and Advances	—	37	37	—	95	63	127
Fixed	30	1,753	1,987	4,215	5,340	7,719	7,587
Goodwill	—	—	—	—	—	—	—
Deferred expenses/foreign exchange	132	—	—	68	327	151	83
Patents and franchised rights	52	60	102	106	119	141	152
Excess of costs over book value of acquiring shares of subsidiary companies	—	674	674	—	238	190	141
Total Assets	255	4,130	4,929	14,572	17,717	23,633	20,562

Exhibit 2. Unican Security Systems Limited (A) Consolidated Balance Sheets as at June 30 ($000.).

Liabilities	1967	1970	1971	1972	1973	1974	1975
Current							
Bank indebtedness	72	726	897	3,754	3,844	6,302	5,870
Accounts payable and accrued liabilities	27	876	933	3,698	4,112	4,544	5,517
Income taxes payable	—	14	58	—	—	—	—
Current portion of long-term debt	26	55	98	297	473	554	546
Total Current Liabilities	125	1,671	1,986	7,749	8,429	11,400	11,933
Long term debt	3	1,004	1,104	2,527	2,461	4,516	4,275
Deferred income taxes	—	40	109	167	405	672	532
Minority interest	—	—	12	637	494	470	53
Contingency and commitments							
Shareholders' Equity							
Capital stock	127	1,883	2,068	3,954	5,482	5,485	5,485
Excess of appraised value of fixed assets over cost	—	—	—	—	—	—	—
Contributed surplus	—	—	12	23	35	61	73
Retained earnings	—	(468)	(364)	(485)	411	1,205	(1,590)
Less cost of common shares in treasury	—	—	—	—	—	176	199
Total Shareholders' Equity	127	1,415	1,716	3,492	5,928	6,575	3,769
Total Liabilities and Shareholders' Equity	255	4,130	4,929	14,572	17,717	23,633	20,562

Exhibit 1. (continued)

1976	1977	1978	1979	1980	1981	1982	1983	1984	1985	1986
—	82	100	299	404	825	981	611	569	465	1,357
4,781	4,076	4,337	5,015	6,805	8,205	7,776	8,569	10,183	12,266	14,266
6,714	6,459	8,877	10,656	12,967	13,299	13,761	13,352	15,411	19,795	26,602
165	110	201	207	277	245	535	386	486	303	401
11,660	10,727	13,515	16,177	10,453	22,574	23,053	22,918	26,649	32,829	42,626
340	227	113	—	—	—	—	—	—	2,370	—
137	166	194	200	126	105	106	438	567	528	752
7,392	6,531	6,436	6,528	8,778	9,041	9,646	9,771	10,904	19,596	25,268
—	—	—	—	169	133	244	178	112	57	22
19	65	21	—	—	—	—	—	260	475	542
149	140	127	103	90	77	65	54	47	—	—
94	—	—	—	—	—	—	—	—	—	—
19,791	17,856	20,406	23,008	29,616	31,930	33,114	33,359	38,539	55,855	69,210

Exhibit 2. (continued)

1976	1977	1978	1979	1980	1981	1982	1983	1984	1985	1986
5,323	5,102	4,631	3,173	3,923	4,766	5,079	4,450	3,327	6,205	9,972
5,000	3,848	5,213	5,065	6,289	6,133	6,280	6,308	7,163	8,775	12,540
—	—	121	242	363	603	246	382	938	404	233
637	513	459	669	664	500	494	489	991	1,728	2,082
10,960	9,463	10,424	9,149	11,239	12,002	12,099	11,629	12,419	17,112	24,828
3,617	2,794	3,130	5,173	6,654	6,314	6,048	5,681	8,210	17,034	18,536
803	725	729	683	481	994	1,062	1,549	1,494	2,300	2,675
74	100	143	169	223	317	437	542	721	1,004	1,477
5,485	5,485	5,485	5,485	5,999	5,999	6,439	5,999	5,558	5,319	5,319
—	—	—	—	684	669	654	639	624	609	594
131	131	131	131	131	131	131	131	131	131	131
(1,117)	(680)	411	2,224	4,346	5,885	6,389	7,264	9,402	12,346	15,650
162	162	47	6	132	372	145	75	20	—	—
4,337	4,774	5,980	7,834	11,019	12,303	13,468	13,958	15,695	18,405	21,694
19,791	17,856	20,406	23,008	29,616	31,930	33,114	33,359	38,539	55,855	69,210

Exhibit 3. Unican Security Systems Limited (A) Consolidated Statement of Income and Retained Earnings for the year ended June 30 ($000).

	1970	1971	1972	1973	1974	1975
Sales	4,801	5,418	16,105	24,820	29,361	25,242
Cost of sales and expenses except for the undernoted:	4,586	4,853	14,593	22,411	26,239	25,561
Depreciation of fixed assets	117	192	378	650	832	1,016
Amortization of other assets	4	4	10	—	48	196
Interest on long-term debt	47	72	141	503	892	452
Other interest	—	48	192	—	—	817
Equity on net earnings [loss] of investor companies	—	—	—	—	—	40
Research and development, net of government assistance	56	104	66	167	203	228
	4,810	5,273	15,380	23,771	28,214	28,310
Earnings before income taxes and minority interest	(9)	145	725	1,049	1,147	(3,068)
Provision for income taxes:						
Current	26	—	9	13	35	20
Deferred	56	88	308	478	514	(140)
	82	88	317	491	549	(120)
Earnings before minority interest	(91)	57	408	558	598	(2,948)
minority interest	—	—	(22)	(31)	(23)	393
Extraordinary items	33	18	202	417	219	(127)
Net earnings	(58)	75	588	944	794	(2,682)
Earnings per share	—	0.08	0.50	0.57	0.44	(0.85)

Exhibit 3. (continued)

1976	1977	1978	1979	1980	1981	1982	1983	1984	1985	1986
28,238	24,801	28,314	34,158	38,332	43,512	42,145	45,023	53,852	64,649	80,257
24,892	22,734	24,716	29,448	33,063	37,386	37,497	39,362	45,242	53,446	66,951
1,087	1,062	1,156	1,233	1,370	1,558	1,681	1,800	2,108	2,400	2,950
177	178	181	131	29	50	80	78	104	123	109
418	333	316	617	830	825	770	733	695	1,098	1,836
620	565	590	443	508	807	917	626	666	501	551
18	23	18	(8)	(16)	(5)	—	81	72	76	(108)
216	137	46	190	151	204	204	234	449	995	1,204
27,428	25,032	27,023	32,054	35,935	40,825	41,149	42,914	49,336	58,636	73,493
810	(231)	1,291	2,104	2,398	2,687	996	2,109	4,516	6,013	6,764
178	116	724	987	722	994	267	514	1,879	1,601	2,275
271	78	4	(46)	287	—	—	487	(55)	806	375
449	194	728	941	1,009	994	267	1,001	1,824	2,407	2,650
361	(425)	563	1,163	1,389	1,693	729	1,108	2,692	3,606	4,114
(21)	(28)	(25)	(39)	(53)	(71)	(94)	(129)	(190)	(305)	(502)
134	890	573	689	879	—	—	—	—	—	—
474	437	1,091	1,813	2,215	1,622	635	979	2,502	3,301	3,612
0.27	0.25	0.62	1.00	1.17	0.83	0.34	0.54	1.39	0.98	1.07

Exhibit 4. Unican Security Systems Ltd. (A).

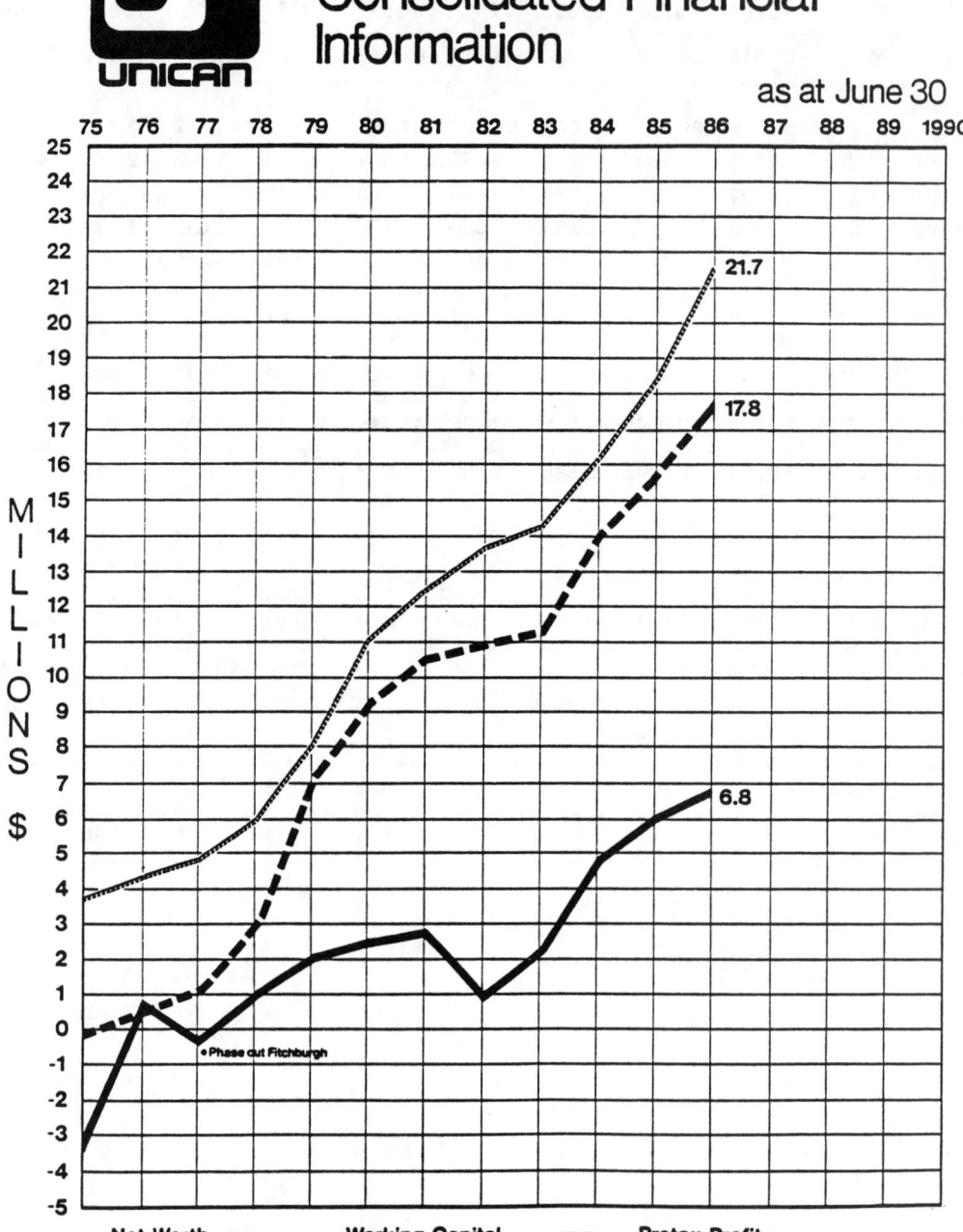

Consolidated Financial Information

as at June 30

Exhibit 5. Unican Security Systems Ltd. (A).

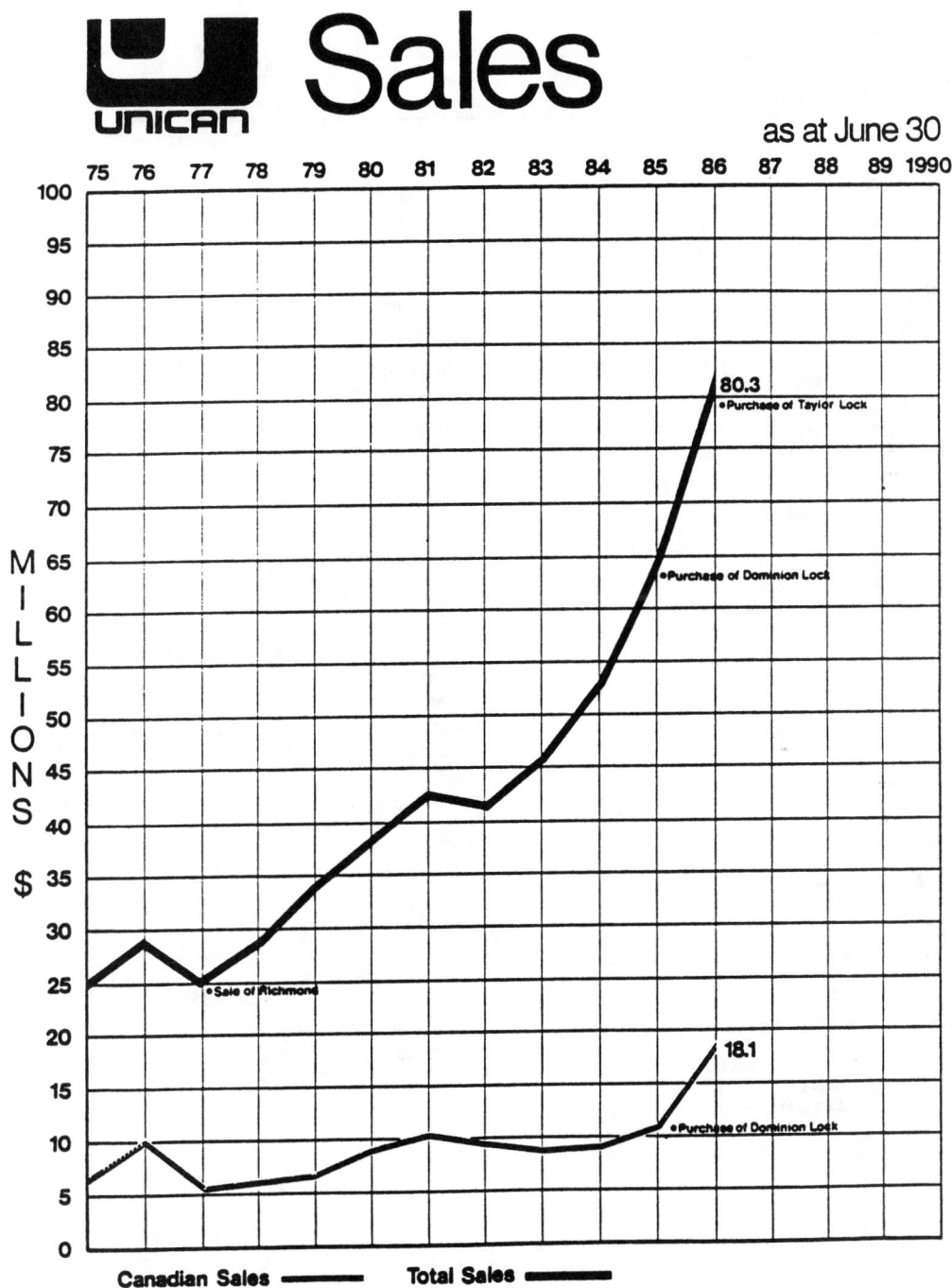

Sales

as at June 30

Canadian Sales ————   Total Sales ══════

Exhibit 6. Unican Security Systems Ltd. (A) Management and Corporate Structure.

UNICAN SECURITY SYSTEMS LTD.
5795 de Gaspé Ave.
Montreal, Que., Canada H2S 2X3
Tel.: (514) 273-0451 Telex: 05-24651
Facsimile: (514) 273-3521

Subsidiaries

ILCO UNICAN INC.
Capitol Division
Henry Marco, Group Vice-President
Montreal, Que., Canada H2S 2X3
Tel.: (514) 273-0451 Telex: 05-24651
Facsimile: (514) 273-3521

Dominion Lock Division
Stan Mazoff, Group Vice-President
Montreal, Que., Canada H4P 2G7
Tel.: (514) 735-5411 Telex: 05-827733
Facsimile: (514) 735-8707

ILCO UNICAN CORP.
ILCO UNICAN INTERNATIONAL
CORP.
Robert L. D'Amato
Vice-President (Manufacturing)
Don Wright
Vice-President (Marketing)

Rocky Mount, N.C., U.S.A. 27801
Tel.: (919) 446-3321 Telex: 579476
Facsimile: (919) 446-4702

Plattsburgh, N.Y., U.S.A. 12901
Tel.: (518) 563-6616 Telex: 05-24651

SIMPLEX SECURITY SYSTEMS, INC.
David Creedon, President
Collinsville, Conn., U.S.A. 06022
Tel.: (203) 693-8391
Facsimile: (203) 693-4705

ILCO UNICAN, S.A.
Al Durisch, Vice-President
Geneva, 3, Switzerland
Tel.: (41) 22-36-9920 Telex: 289879
Facsimile: (41) (22-21-79-70) 36-9920

ILCO UNICAN (H. K.) LTD.
Edmond Pang, Director
Kowloon, Hong Kong
Tel.: (0) 284-247 Telex: 39078

DOMINION LOCK AUSTRALIA
(PTY) LTD.
David Cohen, Managing Director
Sydney, Australia NSW
Tel.: 2-460-4544 Telex: 177182

SOVIQ INC.
Janis Terauds, President
Pointe-aux-Trembles,
Que., Canada H1B 5L8
Tel.: (514) 645-1608

TAYLOR LOCK CO.
2034 W. Lippincott St.
Philadelphia, PA, U.S.A. 19132
Tel.: (215) 223-7766 Telex: 831787
Facsimile: (215) 223-0340

Affiliates

UNIKIS JAPAN CO. LTD.
Takashi Mori, President
Minami-Ku, Osaka, Japan
Tel.: (06) 244-0385
Cable: UNIKISJAPAN
Facsimile: (81) 6-251-4045

METL-STIK LIMITED
Robert Dumsday, Managing Director
Corby, Northants, England
Tel.: (0) 536-61524 Telex: 342116

General Information

Auditors
Richter, Usher & Vineberg
1 Westmount Square
Montreal, Que., Canada H3Z 2Z9

Counsel
Heenan Blaikie
1001 de Maisonneuve Blvd. W.
Suite 1400
Montreal, Que., Canada H3A 3C8

Meadows, Johnson, Spinks
225 South Franklin St.
Rocky Mount, N.C., U.S.A. 27801

Exhibit 6. (continued)

Stock Exchanges
Toronto Stock Exchange
Montreal Exchange
Symbol UCS

Register—Transfer Agents
Royal Trust Company
Montreal and Toronto

Bankers
Bank of Montreal
119 St. James Street W.
Montreal, Que., Canada H2Y 1L6

Branch Bank & Trust Company
Station Square
Rocky Mount, N.C., U.S.A. 27802

Rhode Island Hospital Trust
National Bank
One Hospital Trust Plaza
Providence, Rhode Island
U.S.A. 02903

Banque Nationale de Paris
BNP Tower
Montreal, Quebec
Canada H3A 2W8

Central Building,
Queen's Road, Central Hong Kong

1 Quai du Mont-Blanc
CH-1211 Geneva, Switzerland

12 Castlereagh Street
Sydney, Australia NSW

Directors

Aaron M. Fish
Chairman of the Board

Solomon I. Belzberg, B. Sc., P. Eng.
Consultant, Ilco Unican Inc.

Peter M. Blaikie, Q.C. *
Partner: Heenan Blaikie

Ira Milton Jones
Patent Attorney

Stewart Maclellan
President and CEO
Dominion Automotive Industries

David Stendel, C.A. *
Partner: Stendel, Fruchter

Gerald D. Sutton *
President, C.E.D. Ltd.

Jack L. Switzer, B. Sc., P. Eng.
President, Richmond Die Casting Ltd.

Alexander G. Lester
Honorary Director
Retired Executive Vice-President
Bell Canada

Members of the Audit Committee

Corporate Officers

Aaron M. Fish
Chairman of the Board and President

Henry Marco
Group Vice-President

Stanley S. Mazoff
Group Vice-President

Eddy Rosenberg, C.A.
Vice-President, Finance

David Stendel, C.A.
Secretary

Janis Terauds
Group Vice-President

Exhibit 7. Unican Security Systems Ltd. (A) Products and production.

Exhibit 8. Unican Security Systems Ltd. (A) Geographical sales distribution.

Location							
	1980	1981	1982	1983	1984	1985	1986
	%	%	%	%	%	%	%
U.S.A.	75	73	75	77	79	80	73
Quebec and Atlantic Canada	13	14	13	11	10	8	11
Ontario and Western Canada	9	9	8	9	8	9	11
Overseas	3	4	4	3	3	3	5
	100	100	100	100	100	100	100

Source: Company reports

Exhibit 9. Unican Security Systems Ltd. (A) October 1986.

BOARD OF DIRECTORS

Aaron M. Fish

Solomon I. Belzberg

Peter M. Blaikie

Ira Milton Jones

David Stendel

Gerald D. Sutton

Jack L. Switzer

Alexander G. Lester
Honorary Director

Stewart Maclellan

CASE 20

Unican Security Systems Ltd. (B)

At the annual general meeting of shareholders of Unican Security Systems Ltd., held in Montreal, Canada on December 11, 1986, Mr. Aaron M. Fish, Chairman, President and Chief Executive Officer, reported that for FY 1986, consolidated sales had reached approximately $80.2 million with net income $3.6 million compared with $64.6 million and $3.3 million respectively for the FY 1985. (Financial statements, Exhibits 1, 2, 3, 4, 5.)

Mr. Fish pointed out that the company had spent a lot of time, effort and money on the research and development of the electronic hotel lock. While the company did have an extensive line of products available for the security industry as a whole, it was Mr. Fish's opinion that the electronic hotel lock was only a wedge into a much wider area of growth leading to a vast potential market in complex electronic, computer designed and related systems. These could cover not only the security aspects as it is generally perceived, but a whole range of activities such as accounting, inventory, food, front desk and anything that involved controlled mechanisms and procedures. (Details of the company's history and developments are in Case A).

ELECTRONIC HOTEL LOCK

Electronic locks are systems which use a microprocessor to recognize entry codes which in turn activate a lock. Although the system has many a problem, Mr. Fish believed there was an industry trend towards electronic systems, and Unican had the potential to take advantage of the same technology.

These security systems replaced the traditional brass key with a plastic card which could carry an entrance code able to open a mortise lock. Several systems were already on the market, some since the mid-1970s. Unican used its knowledge of the security needs of hotels along with the flaws it had found in competing systems to develop its own product.

For the hotel industry, the appeal of electronic locks is two-fold. With the high incidence of theft and violent crimes, and the attendant increase in liability premiums, hotels were anxious to increase their level of security. Since card activated locks eliminate the need for keys, they also eliminate the security problems which arise from lost or stolen room and master keys. Electronic locks not only provide the ability to change entry codes

This case was prepared by Professor Willard H. Ellis, McGill University, as a basis for classroom discussion. It is based, in part, on an M.B.A. report submitted by Brian Brenie and Group of McGill University. Copyright © 1987 by W. H. Ellis.

rapidly, but also allow the hotels to audit entry in cases of theft. These features effectively eliminate the problems of security caused by personnel, former guests or thieves with duplicate keys.

The second appeal of electronic locks is their low cost. To maintain the security of key-activated locks, it is necessary to frequently re-key locks and cut new keys. To re-key a hotel lock once can cost as much as $50. A blank key for a hotel lock costs from $1 to $2. An electronic lock by comparison need never be re-keyed and replacement cards cost as little as six cents. In terms of repairs, both key-activated and electronic systems use the same mortise lock. Experience to date suggests that the electronic components of the card access system require very little maintenance. Although the electronic systems may be more than twice the purchase price of key-activated locks, over the lifetime of the products, electronic systems will be the least expensive.

Unican's electronic hotel lock was developed from the design flaws and deficiencies observed in competitors' systems. The improvements to the Unican product included a redesigned reader for fewer mis-reads, and a clutch mechanism to disengage the handle, thereby preventing forced activation of the mortise lock. Mr. Fish noted that one competitor's system could be opened by a tap with a rubber mallet, while another could be opened by introducing any card into the reader several times in rapid succession, causing the reader to "peak" and open.

Unican management believed that entering the industry later than other competitors allowed it to learn from the mistakes of others. In addition, Unican believed that it had an advantage over larger firms in that it was centralized and generally proactive, with an ability to more aggressively take advantage of new opportunities. On the other hand, the small size of the firm did not give it the capital to invest heavily in research and development. Furthermore, the Company faces a formidable challenge in building the kind of organization required to market the electronic hotel lock on a large scale.

Its current strategy for the product is to offer it on a full-service lease basis at a premium in order to exploit the weaknesses of other products and carve out a place for itself in the servicing of its product.

The Electronic Hotel Lock Market

Virtually all of the major chain hotels are committed to installing electronic hotel locks. Most chains are specifying electronic locks for all new hotels and recommending them for retrofit as required. It is possible that smaller and lower-quality hotels and motels will also become markets for electronic locks. With the cost of liability insurance, especially in the United States, all hotels may be forced to increase security to reduce violent crimes on their premises and to reduce insurance premiums.

Typically, individual properties, either corporate or franchise hotels, buy from the chain's central supply division, although they also have the option to buy directly from a distributor or manufacturer. These central supply divisions will often test a number of locks and recommend only those which meet quality standards. The unit management makes its choice from the list of approved suppliers. Even unit management in corporate hotels have significant input into the purchase decision. While manufacturers must first have their product approved by a chain's central supply, suppliers must also direct a marketing effort at the individual hotels.

It would appear that leading electronic locks are enjoying a high degree of acceptability in the hotel industry. Incidence of thefts are reported to have dropped sharply since the installation of electronic locks and hotel operators appear to be almost unanimous in their endorsement of the products from a cost point of view. Users of the leading systems have suggested that, based on their limited experience with these products, they may easily be expected to last indefinitely with relatively little cost in replacement parts.

Security Systems Inc. of Troy, Michigan, maker of Saflok electronic locks offers a four year renewable warranty after its initial one year warranty. For $1.25 per lock per month, Saflok will replace any worn or defective part on their system and provide an annual inspection and repair to all locks. Saflok, in effect, is projecting that each lock will require less than $15 per year in new parts. The fact that Saflok's warranty provides only parts may be a recognition of the hotel's fixed cost of repairs.

There is therefore a large but a very competitive and maybe diminishing market potential for electronic hotel lock sales in North America, and it would appear that at least the leading producers of electronic hotel locks have been generally successful in meeting market needs in terms of security. Furthermore, cost of service of some locks appears to be relatively low and, given their level of security, effectively imposes a ceiling on the premium which may be commanded for products which require less service.

Some questions that have been raised regarding the production: Do the improvements in Unican's hotel lock contribute to meeting a widespread market need? How aggressively and on what basis will Unican have to compete to be successful in this industry?

Competition for Hotel Electronic Locks

Hotels have been installing electronic hotel locks since the early 1970s. Prior to this, locks were usually hard-wired systems which were not easily adapted to existing hotels. Uniqey, a Hong Kong based firm, was one of the first to produce a stand-alone unit, in 1978.

Some 17 companies other than Unican have entered, or are about to begin producing electronic hotel locks. Most of these firms, like Unican, have come from the security hardware industry. The leaders to date are believed to be *Yaletronics* from *Scovill Inc.'s* Yale Group and Saflok, from Security Systems Inc. of Troy, Michigan. Each of these manufacturers has modified its system since the introduction of its respective products and each has sold at least 50,000 units.

Security Systems Inc. introduced the Saflok 1 about 1983, continued to develop the Saflok 2 and 3 and now markets the Saflok 4. With each new innovation, Security Systems Inc. offered its customers of previous systems the chance to purchase the improved models at cost. Since all four models used the same housing and mortise lock, the improvements were relatively cheap. Saflok apparently does not plan a fifth model, indicating that perhaps it has reached a level of security which satisfies its customers' needs, certainly for the time being. Instead, it has begun, as has Yale, to consider the needs of the small hotel market.

The trend in the industry seems to be towards integration of security systems with other systems in the hotel using the same technology. There may be distinct possibilities in the future that with the advent of other computerized systems that guests may be able to check in and out by themselves, stopping only at the front desk for the key.

It is readily apparent from the above that there is a great deal of activity within the industry and some of the significant factors may be:

1. The technological change and the number of new competitors taking advantage of relatively low entry barriers, means that no technology will remain unique for long. Good ideas will be copied quickly or improved upon as new applications are found.
2. Based on the current trend in sales and the apparent acceptability of electronic hotel locks, the market for these products may become saturated quickly. With the long life expectancy of these products, a replacement market may never develop. Instead, the industry focus may move to producing parts or designing improvements compatible with existing products, as Saflok has done.
3 . Research and development will be important as the technology and applications change. Whether a firm chooses to apply the technology to other needs in the hotel, adapt it to other markets, or develop more sophisticated systems, it is clear that a large amount of funds will have to be committed to product development. The specific avenue to take in the light of several large competitors could well be difficult and expensive.

Thus, in a rapidly changing, high technology industry in which barriers to entry are relatively low there is a constant risk that other producers may develop new locks or improve old ones as well as develop further uses in computerized applications which equal or surpass any that are currently available.

In presenting its version of the electronic hotel lock, Unican's marketing strategy was thought to face at least three major considerations:

1. Should the lock be offered on a lease basis?
2. Should it be priced at a premium? and
3. When should it be offered and on what scale?

1. Full-Service Lease

In a rapidly changing environment, hotels may react favorably to the opportunity to lease locks, which would give them the opportunity to up-date technology. By maintaining and up-dating the systems, Unican would gain control over its reputation for quality and also secure a portion of the total market revenue for servicing its products, which might go otherwise to outside service companies.

If Unican was to profit from the lease and the service of its own products, it would have to develop an organization capable of giving fast, effective service to the hotels. Typically, hotels maintain an in-house maintenance staff which, among other things, maintains the hotel's locks. The large amount of relatively minor service needed for locks and the need to have service done quickly, makes reliance on outside service scarcely feasible. To compete with the hotel's own service capability, Unican would have to establish an extremely efficient network of service representatives.

One of its main competitors, Saflok, sells its lock outright with a one-year full service warranty and the option to purchase a renewable parts warranty. This would relieve the company of financing costs and allow them to generate revenues from the sale of parts. The full service warranty would allow Unican to correct any problems related to installation and training of hotel personnel and continued presence over the life of the extended warranty, would leave the company in a good position to discover and exploit any possibilities for other applications of the magnetic stripe technology which might develop.

Exhibit 1. Unican Security Systems Limited (B) Consolidated Balance Sheets as at June 30 ($000.).

Assets	1967	1970	1971	1972	1973	1974	1975
Current							
Cash	—	9	24	280	172	39	—
Accounts Receivable	15	914	1,179	4,114	3,930	5,237	4,006
Inventories	26	557	762	5,666	7,304	9,325	7,843
Prepaid Expenses	—	126	164	123	187	204	172
Total Current Assets	41	1,606	2,129	10,183	11,593	14,805	12,021
Restricted funds for plant construction	—	—	—	—	5	564	451
Investments and Advances	—	37	37	—	95	63	127
Fixed	30	1,753	1,987	4,215	5,340	7,719	7,587
Goodwill	—	—	—	—	—	—	—
Deterred expenses/foreign exchange	132	—	—	68	327	151	83
Patents and franchised rights	52	60	102	106	119	141	152
Excess of costs over book value of acquiring shares of subsidiary companies	—	674	674	—	238	190	141
Total Assets	255	4,130	4,929	14,572	17,717	23,633	20,562

2. Pricing

Current thinking in Unican is that it should ask a premium for its lock based on the superiority of its product and the risk it will bear in offering a full-service lease.

3. Expansion of the North American Market

The hotel lock industry appears to have become crowded and many competitors are rapidly improving and aggressively marketing their products. The net effect of this has been a rapid penetration of the hotel market in North America with uncertain prospects for a replacement market.

Exhibit 1. (continued)

1976	1977	1978	1979	1980	1981	1982	1983	1984	1985	1986
—	82	100	299	404	825	981	611	569	465	1,357
4,781	4,076	4,337	5,015	6,805	8,205	7,776	8,569	10,183	12,266	14,266
6,714	6,459	8,877	10,656	12,967	13,299	13,761	13,352	15,411	19,795	26,602
165	110	201	207	277	245	535	386	486	303	401
11,660	10,727	13,515	16,177	20,453	22,574	23,053	22,918	26,649	32,829	42,626
										—
340	227	113	—	—	—	—	—	—	2,370	
137	166	194	200	126	105	106	438	567	528	752
7,392	6,531	6,436	6,528	8,778	9,041	9,646	9,771	10,904	19,596	25,268
—	—	—	—	169	133	244	178	112	57	22
19	65	21	—	—	—	—	—	260	475	542
149	140	127	103	90	77	65	54	47	—	—
94	—	—	—	—	—	—	—	—	—	—
19,791	17,856	20,406	23,008	29,616	31,930	33,114	33,359	38,539	55,855	69,210

Exhibit 2. Unican Security Systems Limited (B) Consolidated Balance Sheets as at June 30 ($000.) (continued from Exhibit 1).

Liabilities	1967	1970	1971	1972	1973	1974	1975
Current							
Bank indebtedness	72	726	897	3,754	3,844	6,302	5,870
Accounts payable and accrued liabilities	27	876	933	3,698	4,112	4,544	5,517
Income taxes payable	—	14	58	—	—	—	—
Current portion of long-term debt	26	55	98	297	473	554	546
Total Current Liabilities	125	1,671	1,986	7,749	8,429	11,400	11,933
Long term debt	3	1,004	1,104	2,527	2,461	4,516	4,275
Deferred income taxes	—	40	109	167	405	672	532
Minority interest	—	—	12	637	494	470	53
Contingency and commitments	—	—	—	—	—	—	—
Shareholders' Equity							
Capital stock	127	1,883	2,068	3,954	5,482	5,485	5,485
Excess of appraised value of fixed assets over cost	—	—	—	—	—	—	—
Contributed surplus	—	—	12	23	35	61	73
Retained earnings	—	(468)	(364)	(485)	411	1,205	(1,590)
Less cost of common shares in treasury	—	—	—	—	—	176	199
Total Shareholders' Equity	127	1,415	1,716	3,492	5,928	6,575	3,769
Total Liabilities and Shareholders' Equity	255	4,130	4,929	14,572	17,717	23,633	20,562

Exhibit 2. (continued)

1976	1977	1978	1979	1980	1981	1982	1983	1984	1985	1986
5,323	5,102	4,631	3,173	3,923	4,766	5,079	4,450	3,327	6,205	9,972
5,000	3,848	5,213	5,065	6,289	6,133	6,280	6,308	7,163	8,775	12,540
—	—	121	242	363	603	246	382	938	404	233
637	513	459	669	664	500	494	489	991	1,728	2,082
10,960	9,463	10,424	9,149	11,239	12,002	12,099	11,629	12,419	17,112	24,828
3,617	2,794	3,130	5,173	6,654	6,314	6,048	5,681	8,210	17,034	18,536
803	725	729	683	481	994	1,062	1,549	1,494	2,300	2,675
74	100	143	169	223	317	437	542	721	1,004	1,477
5,485	5,485	5,485	5,485	5,999	5,999	6,439	5,999	5,558	5,319	5,319
—	—	—	—	684	669	654	639	624	609	594
131	131	131	131	131	131	131	131	131	131	131
(1,117)	(680)	411	2,224	4,346	5,885	6,389	7,264	9,402	12,346	15,650
162	162	47	6	132	372	145	75	20	—	—
4,337	4,774	5,980	7,834	11,019	12,303	13,468	13,958	15,695	18,405	21,694
19,791	17,856	20,406	23,008	29,616	31,930	33,114	33,359	38,539	55,855	69,210

Exhibit 3. Unican Security Systems Limited (B) Consolidated Statement of Income and Retained Earnings for the year ended June 30 ($000).

	1970	1971	1972	1973	1974	1975
Sales	4,801	5,418	16,105	24,820	29,361	25,242
Cost of sales and expenses except for the undernoted:	4,586	4,853	14,593	22,411	26,239	25,561
Depreciation of fixed assets	117	192	378	650	832	1,016
Amortization of other assets	4	4	10	—	48	196
Interest on long-term debt	47	72	141	503	892	452
Other interest	—	48	192	—	—	817
Equity on net earnings [loss] of investor companies	—	—	—	—	—	40
Research and development, net of government assistance	56	104	66	167	203	228
	4,810	5,273	15,380	23,771	28,214	28,310
Earnings before income taxes and minority interest	(9)	145	725	1,049	1,147	(3,068)
Provision for income taxes:						
Current	26	—	9	13	35	20
Deferred	56	88	308	478	514	(140)
	82	88	317	491	549	(120)
Earnings before minority interest	(91)	57	408	558	598	(2,948)
Minority interest	—	—	(22)	(31)	(23)	393
Extraordinary items	33	18	202	417	219	(127)
Net earnings	(58)	75	588	944	794	(2,682)
Earnings per share	—	0.08	0.50	0.57	0.44	(0.85)

Exhibit 3. (continued)

1976	1977	1978	1979	1980	1981	1982	1983	1984	1985	1986
28,238	24,801	28,314	34,158	38,332	43,512	42,145	45,023	53,852	64,649	80,257
24,892	22,734	24,716	29,448	33,063	37,386	37,497	39,362	45,242	53,446	66,951
1,087	1,062	1,156	1,233	1,370	1,558	1,681	1,800	2,108	2,400	2,950
177	178	181	131	29	50	80	78	104	123	109
418	333	316	617	830	825	770	733	695	1,098	1,836
620	565	590	443	508	807	917	626	666	501	551
18	23	18	(8)	(16)	(5)	—	81	72	76	(108)
216	137	46	190	151	204	204	234	449	995	1,204
27,428	25,032	27,023	32,054	35,935	40,825	41,149	42,914	49,336	58,636	73,493
810	(231)	1,291	2,104	2,398	2,687	996	2,109	4,516	6,013	6,764
178	116	724	987	722	994	267	514	1,879	1,601	2,275
271	78	4	(46)	287	—	—	487	(55)	806	375
449	194	728	941	1,009	994	267	1,001	1,824	2,407	2,650
361	(425)	563	1,163	1,389	1,693	729	1,108	2,692	3,606	4,114
(21)	(28)	(25)	(39)	(53)	(71)	(94)	(129)	(190)	(305)	(502)
134	890	573	689	879	—	—	—	—	—	—
474	437	1,091	1,813	2,215	1,622	635	979	2,502	3,301	3,612
0.27	0.25	0.62	1.00	1.17	0.83	0.34	0.54	1.39	0.98	1.07

Exhibit 4. Unican Security Systems Ltd. (B).

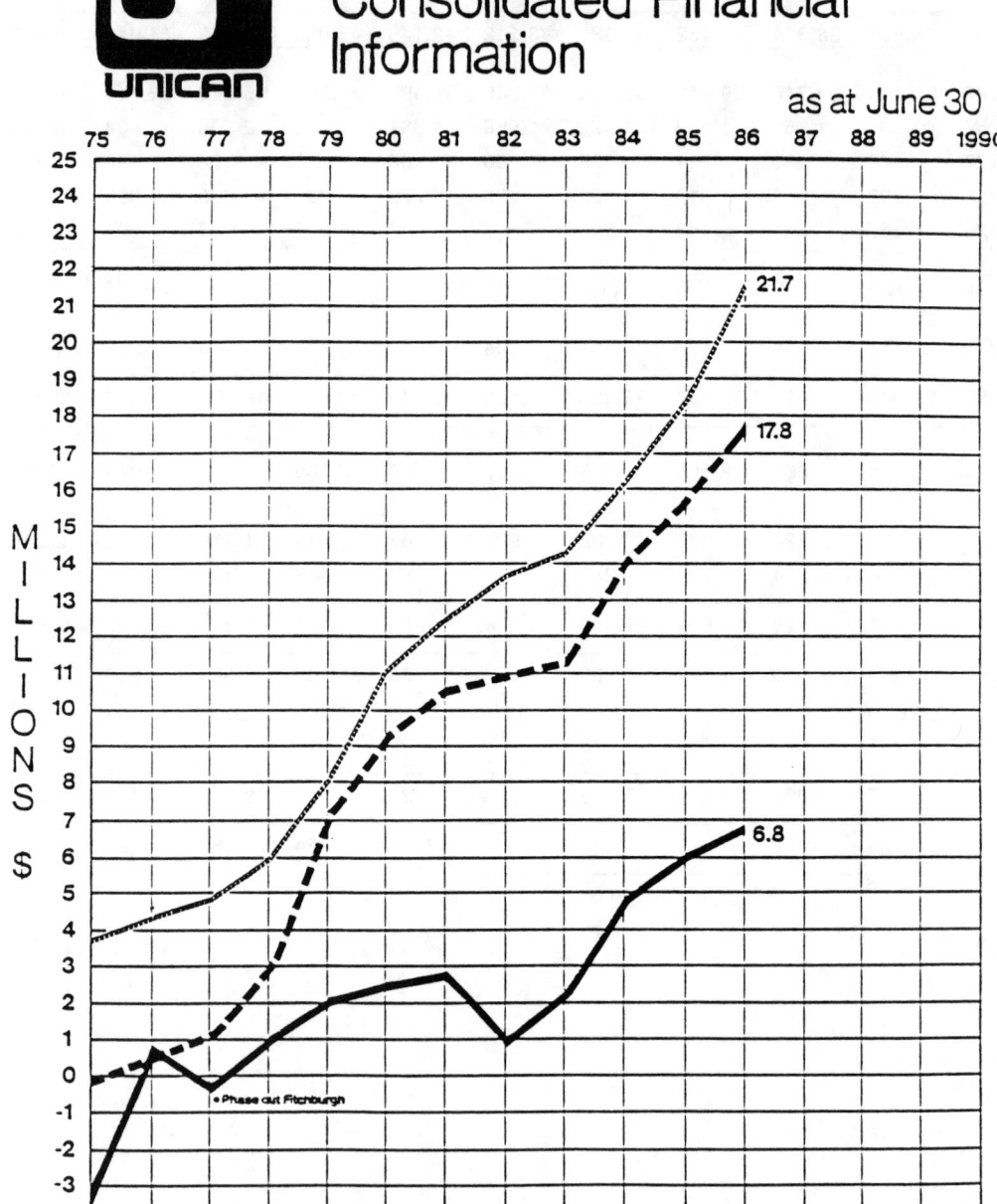

Consolidated Financial Information

as at June 30

Exhibit 5. Unican Security Systems Ltd. (B).

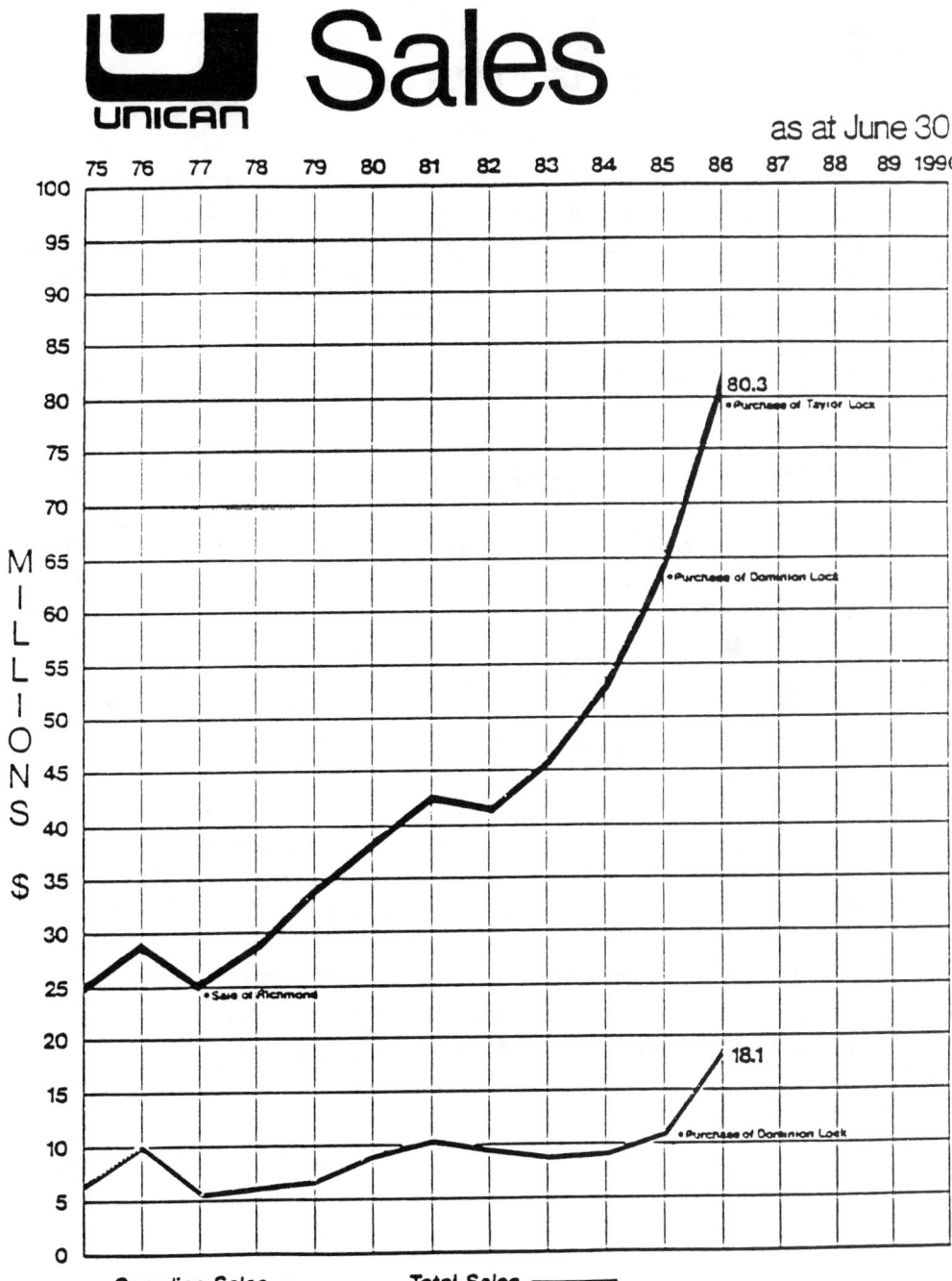

CASE 21

Laval Structures Ltd.

On April 3, 1977, the bankers to Laval Structures Ltd., a Quebec-based home builder, called a meeting with the partners in Laval Structures—Jean and Pierre Montreaux. At this meeting, executives from Roy-Nat, the primary lending company, expressed their dissatisfaction with the company's performance. They wanted to know why the numerous problems had occurred and what was going to be done about the current crisis. More to the point, they announced that Roy-Nat intended to call its loans in two weeks' time unless the explanation and recovery plan were satisfactory. With this news, the Montreauxs hurriedly left the meeting.

BACKGROUND

Laval Structures Ltd. commenced operations under Jean and Pierre Montreaux, owners and managers of two small companies in Laval, Quebec. The two businesses which they operated were Montreaux and Frere Construction Co., which built small houses under contract and on speculation, and Montreaux Engineering Lumber, which sold building materials and prefabricated chalets and houses. In 1959 they expanded through the purchase of a sand and gravel pit on 130 acres of land located in the area. A new company, Montreaux Gravel Pit Ltd., was formed to develop the gravel and sand business.

In 1962 they decided to expand the gravel pit operations through the purchase of new equipment for sifting and loading sand and gravel. As part of this expansion they sought and secured a loan for $150,000 from Roy-Nat. The lending company was impressed with the purity of the reserves (estimated at 1 million yards) and the integrity and good credit rating of the owners. The balance sheet of Montreaux Gravel Pit upon which they secured the loan is shown in Table 1.

The sales of Montreaux Gravel Pit Ltd. are found in Table 2. The first year of profitability for the company was in 1966 when it earned $5,000. By using the profits from their other companies, they established a reputation for prompt loan payments and good financial management.

Table 1. Montreaux Gravel Pit Ltd. Balance Sheet November 30, 1962 (in thousands).

Assets		Liabilities	
Current assets:		Current liabilities:	
Cash	$ 4	Current	$ 24
Receivables	28	Bank loan	30
Inventory	20	Notes and liens	55
Prepaid expense	2	Total current liabilities	109
Total current assets	54		
Fixed assets:		Other liabilities:	
Land	18	First mortgage	135
Sand pit	133	Liens	78
Machinery	150	Notes (long term)	14
Rolling Stock	29	Total other liabilities	227
Total fixed assets	330	Net worth	48
Total assets	$384	Total liabilities and net worth	$384

Table 2. Sales of Montreaux Gravel Pit Ltd. (dollars in thousands).

Year	Sales
1960	$70
1961	192
1962	209
1963	205
1964	233
1965	259
1966	305

Table 3. Sales of Montreaux Engineering Lumber (dollars in thousands).

Year	Sales	Profits
1963	$715	$3
1964	808	5
1965	1,096	20
1966	1,741	40

Table 4. Sales and profits of Montreaux Businesses (dollars in thousands).

Year	Sales	Profits
1963	$1,866	$22
1964	2,651	(31)
1965	3,142	(8)
1966	Not available	47

The two other businesses of the partners were conducted through limited partnerships. Montreaux Engineering Lumber was the more profitable and expanding component of the business. The sales and profits of this business are shown in Table 3.

On a combined basis for all the various companies and businesses, Jean and Pierre Montreaux reported sales and profits as shown in Table 4.

The businesses were short of working capital as a result of the necessity of expanding their facilities and equipment. The cousins were, however, anxious to grow and expand. This desire for growth led them into three directions:

1. In 1967 through Montreaux Gravel Pit Ltd., they again sought additional loans from Roy-Nat. Funds were provided which brought their outstanding loans to the original figure of $150,000. Up to 1967, loan payments had been made on schedule.
2. The Montreaux Engineering Lumber Co. began to add other prefabricated components to their line of houses and chalets—premanufactured trusses and walls. The company had built facilities in the early years for the manufacture of houses and chalets. The workshop, with the new products, varied in employment from 75 to 150 people. In 1966 the company sold 100 prefabricated houses. The houses represented only one third of sales, while the trusses and prefabricated wall units represented two thirds of sales.

    The original chalet model line was expanded by the addition of two standardized houses. One size was 24 feet by 36 feet, and the other was 24 feet by 50 feet. Prices varied between $8,000 and $11,000. The houses were erected by local contractors, who built foundations and installed wiring, plumbing and heating.
3. Montreaux Gravel Pit Ltd. planned to become the financing agent for an International Village to be erected to accommodate visitors to Montreal's Expo '67. Although this project was not funded, the company sold its components to build Place d'Afrique at Expo '67 and a 350-room motel.

LAVAL STRUCTURES LTD.

The companies of the cousins were operated in various legal forms. Montreaux Gravel Pit was a limited company, while the other companies were partnerships. Several of the minority partners held various parts of the company through liens and mortgages. When one of the silent partners died, his estate demanded payment of the value of its interests. In order to solve these and other financing problems, in 1968 the various companies were reorganized under the name Laval Structures Ltd. In this new company Jean Montreaux held 54 percent of the shares and Pierre held 44 percent. The remaining fraction was used to settle the claims and interests of the various minority partners. Roy-Nat was approached to assist in financing the new company and increased its loan commitment to $235,000. The combined sales and profits of Laval Structures Ltd. are found in Table 5.

By 1968 the company had established itself as a leading producer of prefabricated housing and components. It was estimated that it held 80 percent of the Quebec market. Its only competitor was Alcan. The housing section of the business, which had an excellent reputation as a producer of quality components, represented 70 percent of the total sales of the corporation.

Table 5. Combined sales and profits of Laval Structures Ltd. (dollars in thousands).

Year	Sales	Profits
1967	$3,758	$95
1968	3,976	25
1969	4,803	3
1970	4,806	35

Table 6. New dwelling starts by province (population centres of 10,000 or over).

Year	Atlantic Provinces	Quebec	Ontario	Prairies
1970	5,326	40,041	66,497	21,893
1971	7,359	42,116	78,476	32,249
1972	9,483	47,109	91,114	31,416
1973	11,963	49,169	92,211	29,510
1974	9,970	39,374	71,519	24,959
1975	11,748	43,141	67,644	32,744
1976	10,882	53,491	71,301	44,513

Source: Canadian Housing Statistics, 1979, Statistical Services Division, Canada Mortgage and Housing Corporation, Ottawa, March 1980, p. 5.

Expansion and Growth

The major growth of the company began in 1970. In 1971 it formed a joint venture to build 600 homes in a community south of Montreal. This joint venture was planned to last for four years (until 1975). The venture proved very profitable and assured a steady market of about 150 homes annually. Another 200 houses were sold to a mining company. In order to meet the demand, the company began a move to shift work. The demand for houses was seasonal, and often houses could be transported and erected only during the summer months in northern areas. Nonetheless, the market for prefabricated units appeared very promising. The company, however, was unable to make substantial inroads in Montreal, where almost 62 percent of the people lived in rental quarters, but its products were sold in the suburbs.

Laval Structures foresaw a rising demand for their products. The period 1970–71 was one of increases in the number of housing starts, as shown in Table 6.

In anticipation of increased sales and markets, the plant at Laval was expanded. In 1971 the company was capable of producing 25 houses per week. In 1972 the facilities were expanded further to increase the capability to 40 units per week. A construction company was formed to work in northern Quebec, erecting the prefabricated units. This latter company purchased lots, developed subdivisions, and performed the total installation for the customer.

By 1972 Laval Structures Ltd. offered 22 different models of chalets and houses which ranged in price from $7,500 to $9,000 (F.O.B. Laval). The balance sheet of the company for December 31, 1971, is contained in Table 7.

Table 7. Laval Structures Ltd. Balance Sheet as of December 31, 1971 (in thousands).

Assets		Liabilities	
Current assets:		Current liabilities:	
Cash	$57	Bank loans	$ 865
Accounts receivable	1,731	Accounts payable	1,066
Inventory	763	Tax payable	87
Prepaid expenses	12	Other	109
Total current assets	2,563	Total current liabilities	2,127
Fixed assets:			
Land and buildings	578	Long-term liabilities:	
Reserve	(175)	Long-term debt to shareholders	402
Machinery and equipment	424	Other	222
Reserves	(270)	Total long-term liabilities	624
Vehicles	367	Deferred taxes	29
Reserves	(153)		
Furniture and quarry	39	Net worth:	
Reserves	(24)	Shareholders' equity	610
Total	1,408	Total liabilities and shareholders' equity	$3,390
Less: Reserves	(622)		
Total fixed assets	786		
Other assets:			
Mortgage receivable	6		
C/V life insurance	10		
Finance charges	25		
Total other assets	41		
Total assets	$3,390		

The Management at Laval Structures

The two cousins who had started Laval Structures Ltd. occupied senior-level positions in the company and continued the same management style they had used in the earlier years. Management responsibilities were shared, while the day-to-day operations were carried on by a minority shareholder in the company. A plant manager oversaw the operations of the assembly area. The success which they enjoyed permitted the owners extended southern vacations and substantially improved their lifestyles. Financial statements were prepared on an annual basis, orders were filled as they were received, and the downturn in orders was accompanied by variations in plant employment.

In 1974 Roy-Nat encouraged the owners to restructure the company. A sales manager was hired along with a controller and a production manager. However, the first appointee to the position of production manager was fired after only a few months. The lending group encouraged the company to prepare pro forma budgets and monthly financial reports, instead of the previous annual ones. The minority shareholder, who had been the effective manager of the operations, purchased the northern Quebec construction company and left Laval.

Following this brief attempt to restructure the company, the cousins resumed their past habits. There was to be no director of production or finance and no formal organization structure. They based their operational decisions and their sales efforts on their desire to grow and expand, and their familiarity with the market—even though they had no cash controls, cost records, nor market analyses.

Table 8. New dwelling starts by province by type (population centres of 10,000 and over).

Year	Atlantic Provinces	Quebec	Ontario	Prairies
	Single Detached			
1970	2,110	11,096	13,978	7,720
1971	2,953	13,173	21,996	11,562
1972	4,926	19,414	27,818	15,173
1973	5,964	19,172	27,921	16,905
1974	5,376	20,664	22,577	16,947
1975	6,103	22,012	23,854	19,100
1976	5,463	23,219	22,617	19,641
	Apartment and Other			
1970	2,449	23,765	40,428	9,438
1971	3,129	25,972	42,544	15,439
1972	3,104	24,150	46,855	12,274
1973	4,523	27,164	45,436	10,086
1974	3,243	16,698	33,988	4,994
1975	3,704	18,729	23,664	7,999
1976	4,179	27,549	23,387	14,063
	Semidetached, Duplex, and Row			
1970	767	5,180	12,091	4,735
1971	1,277	2,971	13,936	5,248
1972	1,453	3,545	16,441	3,969
1973	1,476	2,833	18,854	2,519
1974	1,351	2,012	14,950	3,018
1975	1,941	2,400	20,126	5,645
1976	1,240	2,781	25,297	10,809

Source: Canadian Housing Statistics, 1979, p. 11.

Laval Structures Ltd. expanded its sales efforts from Quebec into the Maritimes and the United States. The company noted with pride that its buildings were approved in all 50 states. Structural units for motels, apartments and schools were added to the product line. Sales of housing units (single-family houses) for the years 1972–1975 were as follows: 1972—1,100 units; 1973—1,435 units; 1974—1,203 units; 1975—1,076 units.

The breakdowns of dwelling starts by province and metropolitan area are found in Tables 8 and 9. Table 10 illustrates the dwelling unit type and tenure by 1976 census metropolitan areas.

The desire for further expansion led the company into the Ontario market in 1974 through the purchase of a bankrupt construction company in Kingston. The company, along with its assets and liabilities, was purchased for $1. The cousins considered this a bargain, since no initial capital investment was required. A manufacturing operation was established under a general manager. During the first year of operations the company sold 50 houses and secured a contract for an additional 200 houses. Although the company had expected to sell 500 houses and had built the plant for this level of sales, the Ontario market did not meet their expectations. In 1975 the construction company, along with the facilities for the manufacturing of homes, was sold for a loss of $1,005,000. The company felt that the general manager had not performed adequately, and he was fired. See Appendices 1 and 2 for 1973–75 financial statements.

Table 9. Dwelling starts by metropolitan area.

Area	1970	1971	1972	1973	1974	1975	1976
Calgary	6,740	8,801	7,047	6,981	6,487	7,872	11,360
Chicoutimi-Jonquiere	860	791	1,425	1,581	1,463	1,261	964
Edmonton	6,330	11,286	9,500	7,384	5,362	8,647	12,370
Halifax	2,343	2,551	2,540	4,181	3,095	2,708	3,499
Hamilton	4,545	5,408	8,321	8,708	5,968	6,720	5,490
Kitchener	3,075	3,905	5,349	5,054	4,085	3,380	3,926
London	2,738	5,192	5,444	3,872	3,311	3,783	3,318
Montreal	23,017	22,285	24,731	30,700	24,758	26,702	37,531
Oshawa	1,302	1,571	1,832	1,821	1,589	2,376	3,500
Ottawa-Hull	11,345	11,141	14,887	15,511	9,709	7,156	7,059
Ottawa	8,204	8,603	10,808	11,951	7,327	4,122	5,117
Hull	3,141	2,538	4,079	3,560	2,382	3,034	1,942
Quebec	6,421	8,274	8,420	4,648	3,209	4,884	5,427
Regina	418	1,307	1,304	1,366	2,271	2,982	3,070
St. Catharines-Niagara	1,810	2,814	4,219	3,937	3,233	3,195	4,167
Saint John	498	1,048	1,608	1,085	1,139	2,283	1,732
St. John's	679	1,222	1,307	1,705	1,876	2,151	1,386
Saskatoon	259	498	877	1,342	1,232	2,486	2,965
Sudbury	1,961	3,761	1,685	933	449	922	1,058
Thunder Bay	722	515	1,139	1,355	874	919	1,491
Toronto	32,423	35,209	38,695	37,697	29,580	26,457	26,555
Vancouver	13,437	15,553	16,210	17,334	14,452	13,315	16,702
Victoria	2,559	3,102	4,192	4,013	2,630	3,980	4,439
Windsor	1,956	2,214	2,983	2,033	2,602	1,643	2,002
Winnipeg	6,661	7,726	9,134	7,698	5,628	5,294	6,718
Total	132,099	156,174	172,849	170,939	135,002	141,116	166,729

Source: Canadian Housing Statistics, 1979, p. 6.

By 1975 the construction process had become formalized and highly structured. Houses were built in halves and joined together in the field. Although the houses looked like two trailers, when joined they made an attractive small house. The company had devoted a great deal of their capital to improvements in the facilities and buildings. In 1973 the company spent $247,000; in 1974, $72,000; and in 1975, $478,000. By early 1975 the plant represented a moderate-sized factory with five separate buildings. The plant operated 16 hours per day, 5 days per week in the summer. In winter, production and employment dropped about 50 percent. At capacity, the plant employed 700 people. The major assemby work was conducted in a 65,720-square-foot building. A preassembly building of 21,415 square feet prepared components for the production line. The other buildings were used for a welding shop, storage and offices.

The company relied upon agents in the field to sell the houses, secure lots, erect the buildings and install the needed wiring, plumbing and heating. Ninety agents, who were often local contractors or building supply companies and were price-sensitive to the market demands, operated in Quebec.

Table 10.

Metropolitan Area	All Dwellings	Dwelling Type (Percent)				Tenure (Percent)	
		Single Detached	Semidetached and Duplex	Row Housing	Apartment and Other	Owner Occupied	Rental
Calgary	155,155	58.5%	11.3%	4.9%	25.3%	58.4%	41.6%
Chicoutimi-Jonquiere	33,850	47.8	25.2	1.7	25.4	60.9	39.1
Edmonton	179,635	55.9	6.9	6.2	31.1	55.6	44.4
Halifax	81,845	48.1	12.7	3.6	35.6	55.7	44.3
Hamilton	172,515	58.8	7.1	4.9	29.1	63.8	36.2
Kitchener	87,880	53.8	10.8	5.4	30.0	60.4	39.6
London	91,770	56.1	8.1	5.8	29.9	57.8	42.2
Montreal	924,635	24.2	7.7	2.2	66.0	38.2	61.8
Oshawa	41,445	60.2	12.2	3.9	23.7	67.7	32.3
Ottawa-Hull	225,105	41.8	12.3	9.0	36.9	51.5	48.5
Quebec	164,600	36.5	12.4	2.0	49.1	46.2	53.8
Regina	49,790	66.9	5.2	2.7	25.2	65.3	34.7
St. Catharines-Niagara	97,395	69.7	9.5	2.3	18.5	72.2	27.8
Saint John	34,065	43.4	15.7	3.0	37.9	55.3	44.7
St. John's	36,800	50.2	23.2	11.5	15.1	68.5	31.5
Saskatoon	44,800	63.2	10.7	2.6	23.5	63.3	36.4
Sudbury	45,710	57.1	13.3	3.5	26.1	61.6	38.4
Thunder Bay	37,270	70.4	10.0	1.9	17.7	72.0	28.0
Toronto	909,530	39.8	13.3	4.9	42.0	55.8	44.2
Vancouver	407,560	56.9	5.8	2.5	34.8	59.4	40.6
Victoria	81,005	58.0	5.7	2.5	33.8	60.9	39.1
Windsor	80,190	67.0	8.6	3.7	20.6	69.6	30.4
Winnipeg	197,305	58.5	7.1	2.6	31.8	59.0	41.0
Canada	7,166,095	55.7%	9.4%	3.0%	31.8%	61.8%	38.2%

Source: Canadian Housing Statistics 1979, p. 98.

The 1976–1977 Crisis

The company's sales were concentrated almost 80 percent in Quebec and 10 percent each in Ontario and the Maritime provinces. There were 25 models of homes which sold for an average price of $15,000. Since the company began operations in 1968, several other competitors had entered the field. One company was located in Quebec City, and a competitor near Montreal produced similar products. Each of these competitors was small and had not enjoyed the growth of Laval Structures. The competitors were also considered inferior in the size of their plants and facilities as well as in their variety of offerings. These companies concentrated in the house-building area and did not produce components for schools, motels and apartment buildings. The major competitor was Atco.

In 1975 the company secured a contract for 155 furnished houses as part of the James Bay Hydro Project. The joint venture in the town south of Montreal was also coming to a close.

Since 1974 the company had tried to sell its products abroad to take advantage of the rising demand for housing in Saudi Arabia and countries in South America. The cousins had made several trips abroad in search of these sales, and in late 1975 the company sold 50 houses for a new housing project in Libya and 100 houses to a South American government. The Libyan contract was expanded in early 1976 by an additional 70 houses.

In late 1975 the company was short of working capital. It requested and received a loan of $600,000 from Roy-Nat, of which $300,000 was for the plant which was built in 1975 and the remainder for the financing of contracts it had received from abroad. On the basis of its foreign contracts and expected sales in Quebec, the company prepared pro forma financial statements for 1976 which are found in Appendices 3 and 4. The order of $2.8 million from Libya and the $1.2 million order for South America are included in these figures.

Before the formal year-end financial statements were available for 1976, the company again approached its lending sources. Roy-Nat increased its commitment to $1 million. A chartered bank was approached and made a working capital loan to finance the order. This loan from the chartered bank would ultimately reach $4 million. (See Appendix 5.)

In the early months of 1977 the formal statements for Laval Structures became available. Sales of houses had totalled 694, rather than the 1,650 projected. In the first five months of 1977 the company shipped 183 houses and had total orders for 195 (including the foreign contracts).

Laval Structures manufactured 100 houses for the Libyan order, crated them for shipment and transported the houses to the Port of Montreal for shipment in the spring of 1977. The Libyan buyers refused to honour the order and refused acceptance. The South American order was not completed.

In early 1977 the company's working capital was in serious condition. In the first three months the company lost $770,000. Roy-Nat investigated the financial affairs of the company and discovered that it had more than $1 million in accounts payable that were over 45 days old and had total bank loans and accounts payable of $7,181,623. With this knowledge, Roy-Nat called the meeting for April 3.

Appendix 1. Laval Structures Ltd. Income Statements for the years ending December 31, 1973–1975 (in thousands).

	1973	1974	1975
Sales	$19,300	$19,300	$21,800
Cost of goods sold	17,700	17,400	19,800
Gross profit	1,600	1,900	2,000
Cost of transport and erection	204	275	390
Operating income	1,396	1,625	1,610
Income from joint venture	195	71	954
Total income	1,591	1,696	2,564
Expenses:			
Sales	306	462	330
Administration	738	887	1,142
Finance	170	181	374
Loss or gain on sale of assets	15	2	(2)
Total expenses	1,229	1,532	1,844
Gross profit	362	164	720
Taxes current	96	115	384
Tax credit	(2)	46	(62)
Net income	$ 264	$ 95	$ 274

Appendix 2. Laval Structures Ltd. Balance Sheet as of December 31, 1973–1975 (in thousands).

	1973	1974	1975
Assets			
Current assets:			
Cash	$22	$21	$ 385
Accounts receivable	2,200	1,200	2,250
Notes receivable	25	10	50
Joint venture equity	101	103	284
Inventories	2,500	1,850	3,300
Advances to affiliated companies	323	935	—
Prepaid expenses	142	92	9
Prepaid taxes	92	—	—
Total current assets	5,405	4,211	6,278
Investments	16	16	6
Fixed assets:			
Land and buildings	1,775	1,825	1,400
Reserve (depreciation)	(650)	(800)	—
Total fixed assets	1,125	1,025	1,400
Other assets	30	17	284
Total assets	$6,576	$5,269	$7,968
Liabilities			
Liabilities:			
Loans	$1,700	$1,700	$ 830
Cheques outstanding	—	177	1,038
Accounts payable	2,900	1,000	3,300
Deposits	—	80	77
Tax payable	197	106	103
Deferred income tax	58	126	476
Current due on notes	151	205	235
Total liabilities	5,006	3,394	6,059
Due directors	88	74	64
Long-term debt	677	1,064	927
Shareholders' equity	805	737	918
Total liabilities and shareholders' equity	$6,576	$5,269	$7,968

Appendix 3. Laval Structures Ltd. Pro forma Balance Sheet for the year ending December 31, 1976.

Assets

Current assets:	
Cash	$ 463,728
Accounts receivable	2,085,000
Notes receivable	—
Joint venture equity	307,000
Inventories	2,236,250
Prepaid expenses	
Total current assets	5,091,978
Other assets:	
Investments	400,000
Other	70,441
Fixed assets	1,700,000
Total assets	$7,262,419

Liabilities

Liabilities:	
Loans	
Outstanding cheques	$ 200,000
Accounts payable	1,430,000
Deposits	75,000
Income tax payable	1,046,478
Deferred income taxes	425,000
Current due notes	237,704
Total liabilities	3,414,182
Due directors	63,921
Long-term debt	1,120,422
Shareholders' equity and retained earnings	2,663,894
Total liabilities and shareholders' equity	$7,262,419

Appendix 4. Laval Structures Ltd. Pro forma Income Statement for 12 months ending December 31, 1976.

Sales	$25,550,000
Cost of sales	22,310,000
Gross profit	3,240,000
Net cost of transportation and erection	24,000
Operating income	3,216,000
Income from joint venture	900,000
Total income	4,116,000
Expenses:	
Selling	305,044
Administration	1,036,799
Financial	362,802
Profit (loss) on sale of fixed assets	295,355
Total expenses	2,000,000
Income before taxes	2,116,000
Income taxes	996,000
Net Income	$ 1,120,000

Appendix 5. Laval Structures Ltd. Balance Sheet for 11 months ending November 30, 1976 (in thousands).

Assets		Liabilities	
Current assets:		Current liabilities:	
Cash	$27	Bank loans and cheques outstanding	$ 4,038
Accounts receivable	4,468	Deposits for loans	835
Deposits	835	Accounts payable	2,471
Advances to affiliated companies	463	Deposits—houses	60
Joint venture	65	Current debts—long term	234
Inventory	2,645	Taxes payable	614
Other	231	Total current liabilities	8,252
Prepaid expense	53	Other liabilities:	
Taxes receivable	21	Long term debt	1,370
Total current assets	8,808	Other	93
Other assets:		Shareholders' loans	52
Equity in affiliates	766	Taxes	54
Cash value—life insurance	2	Total other liabilities	1,569
Total other assets	768	Capital account:	
Total current assets and other assets	9,576	Shareholders' equity	1,545
Fixed assets	2,801	Total liabilities and shareholders' equity	$11,366
Reserve	(1,011)		
	1,790		
Total assets	$11,366		

Laval Structures Ltd. Income Statement for 11 months ending November 30, 1976 (in thousands).

Sales	$16,730
Cost of goods sold	12,020
Fabrication and erection	2,710
Gross profit	2,000
Cost of sales:	
Sales	220
Administration	1,252
Finance	508
Total cost of sales	1,980
Gross profit on operations	20
Gain on sale of assets	15
Profit before taxes	$ 35

Mike's Submarine Sandwiches Limited

As we see it, we may now be approaching saturation in the Quebec market. We may have to start to look at another metropolitan area as a base from which to spread out and repeat what we have done in the province of Quebec, rather than spread out helter-skelter with single stores.

These were the words of Mr. Lars Muller, president of Mike's Submarine Sandwiches, a rapidly growing fast-food chain which specialized in submarine sandwiches and pizzas. Mike's Submarine had grown primarily in the Montreal vicinity in the province of Quebec, and in early 1978 the management of Mike's were investigating three alternative metropolitan areas for future growth. They had tentatively concluded that the most favourable location for expansion was Boston, Massachusetts, and were about to consider the various details involved in such a move.

THE ORIGINS OF MIKE'S SUBMARINE

Mike's Submarine Sandwiches Limited was established in Montreal in March 1967 by the Marano brothers, who had seen a similar concept operating in the United States. Later that year the company was incorporated under federal charter as Mike's Submarine Sandwiches Limited.

The company's products—submarine sandwiches and pizzas—won immediate favour, and the brothers proceeded to open additional outlets. The four brothers, Antonio, Michael, Dominico and Aldo, divided the responsibilities amongst themselves, including those for store operations, new sites and construction, and the franchising of outlets which began in 1969.

In the latter part of 1969 Mike's was brought to the attention of Mr. Austin C. Beutel and his associates as an investment possibility. Beutel explained: "My group was interested in investments in smaller companies as developing enterprises, turnarounds and emerging companies, and Mike's fitted the criteria for investment, so we proceeded."

Commenting on the earlier days of the restaurant operation, Muller stated that the investment people were impressed with the Maranos' ability to "punch things through" and their willingness to work 24 hours a day if necessary.

This case is based on two cases prepared by Professor W. H. Ellis of McGill University. Copyright © 1978 by W. H. Ellis. Edited by Mark C. Baetz, 1986.

Muller commented further:

The Maranos went and opened up stores but really were better small business managers than corporate managers. For all of the good things that they did, they really never understood the basic principles of finance. They looked at the till and the bank balance, and everything looked rosy. When the creditors or the tax man came in, they were in trouble. Two weeks afterwards, if sales were good, they were flush again. You can't finance that way, and you can't build a company that way.

Antonio (Tony) resigned from the company's management in 1972 and acquired C. Segatore Bakery Company Limited. He subsequently supplied bread and other food products to Mike's and many of its franchises. During fiscal year 1976 purchases by Mike's from Segatore Bakery amounted to nearly $125,000.

Two years after Tony's resignation, Michael Marano, who had become the chief operating officer of the company, and his brother Dominico, an employee, both resigned.

Following these resignations, Mr. Michael Hockenstein was appointed president of Mike's on October 1, 1973, with the responsibility of overseeing all the company's operations. Hockenstein was a chartered accountant by training who had previously operated a small computer service company and had worked for eight months as an analyst for Mr. Beutel.

The last of the Marano brothers, Aldo, served as second in charge to Mr. Hockenstein until February 1975 when he resigned to acquire a franchise. Three months later, Hockenstein himself resigned and was replaced in May 1975 by Mr. Lars Muller as president of Mike's Submarine Sandwiches Limited.

MANAGEMENT AND ORGANIZATION STRUCTURE

Mr. Muller became president of Mike's at the age of 35. He had embarked upon a university career but "just got fed up with it" and joined an investment house because "it seemed like a nice place to work and I had read somewhere that the closer you are to the money, the easier it is to make it." Muller's activities in the securities business and involvement in corporate finance led to his association with Beutel. On becoming president of Mike's, Muller was also appointed secretary-treasurer of its parent company, Restaurant Holdings of Canada Limited (see Exhibit 1 for organization structure).

Mike's supervisory staff consisted of Mr. Peter Deros, vice president, and Mr. Steve Deklaras, operations manager, who worked directly with the franchisees to maintain the company's quality standards and overall image.

Deros joined Mike's in February 1975 at the age of 27. He had had 10 years' experience in the fast-food industry, and his functions were described as being concerned with the selection of the franchisees, problems related to the start-ups of the stores, and "working deals." His responsibilities also included quality control and supplies. "I want him out there helping to get the stores opened," stated Muller.

Exhibit 1. Mike's Submarine Sandwiches Limited (Organization Chart, June 1977).

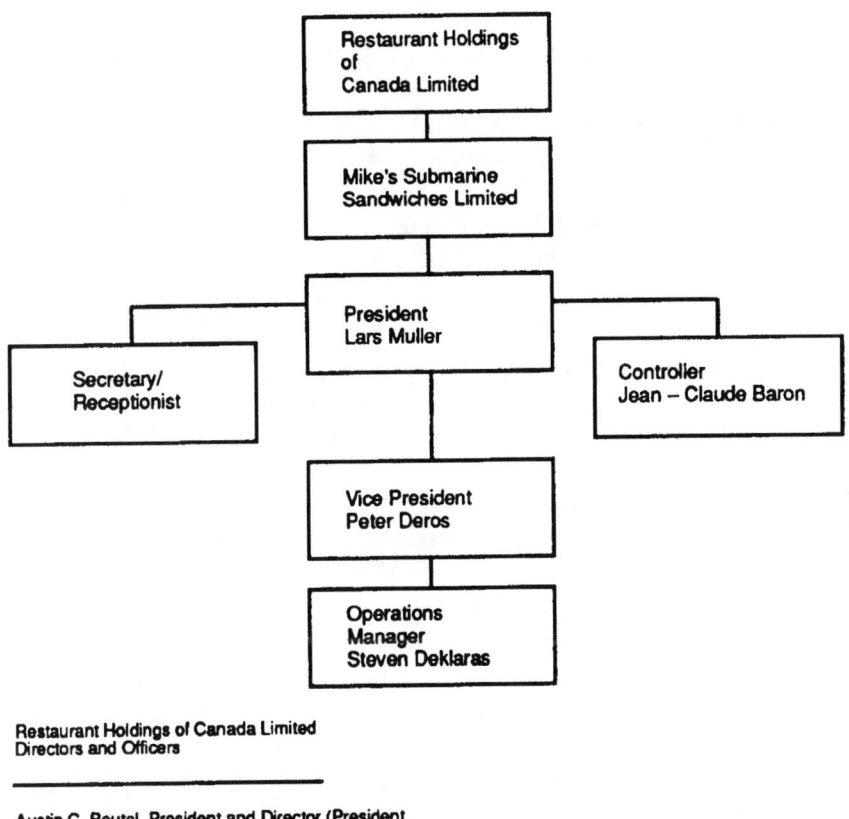

Restaurant Holdings of Canada Limited
Directors and Officers

Austin C. Beutel, President and Director (President,
Beutel Goodman & Co. Ltd.)l

Ken Hitzig, Director (Vice President, Aetna Factors Corp. Ltd.).
Jean M. Beck, Director (President, Prefac Concrete Co. Ltd.).
Antonio Marano, Director (President, C. Segatore Bakery Co. Ltd.).
Lars Muller, Secretary – Treasurer and Director (President, Mike's
Submarine Sandwiches Ltd.).

Deklaras, 26, who joined Mike's a short time after Deros, was the "franchisee's services man," working closely with Deros at the operational level. His duties were described as the day-to-day contact with the franchisees, "everything from money problems to moral support, spending 95 percent of his day on the road." The service aspect was considered by management to be a critical facet of franchising relationships, "requiring a salesman-type background," which Deklaras had had. "He gets the things done and he does them nicely," was the view expressed by Muller.

The remaining head office staff consisted of a controller-accountant and a bookkeeper-typist who worked directly with Muller. Muller himself estimated that he spent about 50 percent of this time on the control aspect of Mike's, with the remainder being spent "in the field or on site selection."

The members of the board of directors of Mike's Submarine Sandwiches Limited were all representatives of the parent company, Restaurant Holdings of Canada Limited, which in turn held all of Mike's stock.

Beutel, as president of the parent company, described his role relative to Mike's as "one largely of liaison with Lars Muller, representing the financial interest. The other directors and I are consulted on advertising strategy, growth strategy, and general business policies. In this latter area, I do spend a lot of time, but the day-to-day operations, control and details are left to Mr. Muller."

As an overall comment on Mike's organization, Muller commented: "As a policy, I want to be about one man short at all times. That means everybody is going to have to stretch a little."

COMPANY STRATEGY AND OBJECTIVES

Mike's Submarine Sandwiches Limited was conceived by Beutel and his associates as being in the business of establishing, franchising, financing, and to a lesser degree, operating fast-food establishments specializing in submarine sandwiches and pizzas. While the company was founded initially as a restaurant operation, it quickly began to franchise stores, and over the years the ratio of franchised to company-owned and operated stores had increased substantially (see Table 1).

The majority of stores (21 out of 28 in mid-1977) were located in the greater Montreal area, with four being in the Quebec City area and two in Eastern Ontario. All locations were leased for varying periods of time, except for a location owned by the parent company. Also, with two exceptions, the leases were in the name of Mike's, while in one other instance, the franchisee was the property owner. Elaborating further on the basic concepts of Mike's, Beutel made the following comments dealing with various facets of the operation:

> We decided that the proper concept, given our limited resources of manpower and finances, was the franchise route, and so we proceeded not only to franchise out the restaurants we had but kept in mind that every future restaurant would be built for the purpose of franchising out.
>
> Really, you might say that we are in the financing business more than we are in the submarine business or food business.
>
> Our basic strategy is to maximize the return to the investor group. This means that we are trying to build a chain of restaurants by acquiring a strong consumer franchise within a geographic area which is continually expanding. Someone will come along and be prepared to buy the whole damn thing from us at a price that will reflect considerable goodwill for the market niche that we have built for ourselves.

Table 1. Stores in operation.

	Company Owned	Franchised	Total
October 1971	4	7	11
December 1972	6	3	9
December 1973	8	3	11
December 1974	3	10	13
December 1975	2	16	18
December 1976	4	21	25
June 1977	2	26	28
December 1977 (estimated)	2	31	33

We have tried to build the chain as rapidly as possible and focus all our resources, people and money on the name and concept of Mike's as we know it, to become the dominant factor in our narrowly defined product line in a given market area because that is when you are in a position to be a leader.

It is basically a marketing game from the point of view of the public, and you are best off in a marketing game as we see it to have as much saturation and exposure as possible within a given market area. You then have the best economies of scale in advertising and promotion costs.

We made a pretty clear decision when Mr. Muller came in (after fumbling for a number of months) to focus on the Mike's concept and build the Mike's operation with the limited resources of people and money we had. We were not going to try to acquire a number of diverse operations under the same parent company—not even acquire a number of different restaurant operations—but just focus on the very narrow concept of submarines and pizzas under Mike's name.

The role of management today is to select sites, build and equip the restaurant, find a franchisee, make the deal with the franchisee, and supervise him to make sure that the standards of quality are maintained and that he is reporting properly—that is, presenting the right thing to the customer, doing that repeatedly, and paying us the agreed share.

We train the people, we supervise them and we inspect, but really the money that the company is going to make is based on its sources of revenues, that is, franchise payments for the stores and royalties on sales.

The success of the operation will be a function of the success of the individual franchisees. But really we make our money as a finance and royalty company.

FINANCING AND CORPORATE PERFORMANCE

New Venture Equities Ltd., a venture capital affiliate of Beutel Goodman and Company Limited and others had initially advanced Mike's $150,000 in 1969, on a term basis, repayable in three to five years, for which they received, in partial consideration, 50 percent of the equity of Mike's. Representatives of New Venture Equities were elected to the board of the company.

On May 14, 1972, Rawhide Resources Limited, the name by which Restaurant Holdings of Canada Limited was then known, acquired all of the issued and outstanding shares of Mike's Submarine Sandwiches Limited for 1 million shares of its common stock then valued at $45,000.

At the time of the transaction, Mike's had a deficiency of net assets amounting to $95,000 so that the purchase consideration exceeded the net assets acquired by $140,000. In the 33 weeks remaining in 1972 Mike's had sales of $669,000 and net earnings of $20,900. During the year 1973 sales virtually doubled to $1,371,000, with net earnings of nearly $38,000 derived from the operations of 10 stores.

While the year 1973 saw rapid price increases in ingredients and escalating wage costs, the management of Mike's believed the return on investment and the commitment of funds in the establishment of new locations under Mike's banner were extremely attractive. Accordingly, the company pursued a program of expansion focused on the greater Montreal area and adjacent territory.

By the end of 1975 there were 18 stores in operation of which all but two were franchised. This year saw the conversion to and emphasis on franchised rather than company-operated locations. The immediate effect of this policy change was that corporate sales volume declined but was replaced by increased franchise sales and fees.

The direction of Mike's management activities became centered on securing new locations, providing leasehold improvements and equipment, enlisting franchisees and supervising the franchise operations. Management was now of the opinion that the most serious limitation to growth was the availability of capital funds to invest in equipment and leasehold improvements and to finance the franchisee receivables.

The average cost per outlet in 1976 was estimated at about $50,000, depending on such factors as location, size and existing facilities. At this time, it was believed that $250,000 would provide the company with sufficient funds for five or six outlets. These funds, together with down payments received and excess cash flow over repayments to the bank, would provide the company with sufficient funds to open up 8 to 10 stores per annum on an ongoing basis. To this end, an arrangement was made for revolving bank credit, first for $250,000 and later increased to $400,000 in April 1977.

The bank credit line was limited to 75 percent of the next 36 months of franchise payments receivable and was secured by such receivables, by the real estate owned by the company, and by a floating charge on all the company's assets. The franchise payments receivable consisted of the payments owed to the company by franchisees and were created contractually at the time a franchise was sold. Typically, the franchisee made an agreed-upon down payment, and the balance was payable monthly over five years in 60 even installments, principal and interest blended. Restaurant Holdings, as owner of 100 percent of Mike's shares, guaranteed the bank debt. The financial performance of Mike's from 1972 to 1977 is presented in Exhibits 2 and 3.

Exhibit 2. Restaurant Holdings of Canada Limited Consolidated Statement of Earnings and Retained Earnings for the years ended December 31.

	1977	1976	1975	1974	1973
Total restaurant sales					
(memorandum only—unaudited)	$6,655,000	$4,574,000	$2,598,131	$1,934,990	$1,370,790
Revenues:					
Company restaurant sales	504,555	530,396	687,663	1,054,520	844,819
Franchise sales and fees	716,801	399,094	230,083	118,347	167,149
Other	50,964	55,528	24,636	4,590	3,754
Total revenues	1,272,320	985,018	942,382	1,177,457	1,015,722
Costs and expenses:					
Company restaurants	440,684	460,253	636,716	1,114,398	932,268
Administrative and other	460,171	273,076	192,347	—	—
Interest on long-term debt	15,865	15,000	13,406	6,249	14,125
Depreciation and amortization	143,837	97,687	46,975	47,244	31,454
Total costs and expenses	1,060,557	846,016	889,444	1,167,891	977,847
Earnings before income taxes					
and extraordinary item	211,763	139,002	52,938	9,566	37,875
Provision for income taxes—current	35,323	16,425	17,504	5,252	20,784
—deferred	62,109	48,439	10,764	—	—
Total provision for income taxes	97,432	64,864	28,268	5,252	20,784
Earnings before extraordinary item	114,331	74,138	24,670	4,314	17,091
Extraordinary item	—	7,219	10,623	5,252	20,784
Net earnings	$114,331	$81,357	$35,293	$9,566	$37,875
Earnings per share:					
Before extraordinary item	$0.315	$0.214	$0.088	$ 0.017	$ 0.0879
Extraordinary item	—	0.021	0.037	0.021	0.1010
Net earnings per share	$ 0.315	$ 0.235	$ 0.125	$ 0.038	$ 0.1889
Source of funds:					
Provided from operations:					
Earnings before extraordinary					
item	$114,331	$74,138	$24,670	$4,314	$37,875
Charges not requiring cash outlay	—	—	—	—	—
Depreciation and amortization	143,837	97,687	46,975	47,244	31,454
Deferred income taxes	52,217	48,439	10,764	—	—
Total from operations	310,385	220,264	82,409	51,558	69,329
From other sources:					
Recovery of income taxes on					
application of losses of prior					
years	—	7,219	17,504	5,252	—
Increase in long-term debt	50,000	—	—	—	—
Exercise of employee stock options	18,250	11,000	—	—	—
Issue of shares in exchange for					
convertible debt of the subsidiary					
company-contra	—	—	100,000	—	—
Issue of long-term debt	—	—	150,000	—	—
Other	—	—	—	750	2,440
Total sources of funds	378,635	238,483	349,913	57,560	71,769
Use of funds:					
Addition to fixed assets	$680,277	$349,100	$333,931	$142,571	$28,977
Conversion of long-term debt of					
subsidiary-contra	—	—	100,000	—	—
Increase in deposits	3,458	10,595	4,922	2,773	45
Total use of funds	683,735	359,695	438,853	145,344	29,022

Exhibit 2. (continued)

	1977	1976	1975	1974	1973
Increase in working capital deficiency	305,100	121,212	88,940	87,784	(42,747)
Working capital deficiency at beginning of year	366,181	244,969	156,029	68,245	110,992
Working capital deficiency at end of year	671,281	366,181	244,969	156,029	68,245
Retained earnings (deficit) at beginning of year	21,199	(60,158)	(95,451)	(105,017)	(142,892)
Net earnings for the year	114,331	81,357	35,293	9,566	37,875
Retained earnings (deficit) at end of year	$135,530	$21,199	$(60,158)	$(95,451)	$(105,017)

Exhibit 3. Restaurant Holdings of Canada Limited Consolidated Balance Sheet for the years ended December 31.

	1977	1976	1975	1974	1973
Assets					
Current assets:					
Cash	$5,842	$485	$132	$ 37,752	$80,933
Accounts receivable	40,920	13,928	19,898	19,919	13,201
Inventories at the lower of cost or net realizable value	3,286	5,829	4,521	26,247	21,175
Prepaid expenses	34,011	18,915	12,239	8,449	11,416
Total current assets	84,059	39,157	36,790	92,367	126,725
Fixed assets	1,325,388	788,948	537,535	250,579	155,252
Balances receivable on sale of franchises—contra	1,231,580	585,727	414,946	115,934	4,462
Intangible asset arising from acquisition of subsidiary	171,952	171,952	171,952	171,952	171,952
Other assets	24,340	20,188	9,593	11,552	11,885
Total assets	$2,837,319	$1,605,972	$1,170,816	$ 642,384	$ 470,276
Liabilities					
Current liabilities:					
Bank advances	$ 479,183	$163,253	$46,477	$34,785	$34,014
Accounts payable and accrued liabilities	246,278	240,517	235,282	213,611	160,956
Income taxes payable	20,689	1,568	—	—	—
Deferred income taxes	9,190	—	—	—	—
Total current liabilities	755,340	405,338	281,759	248,396	194,970
Long-term debt	200,000	150,000	150,000	100,000	102,356
Unearned income on sale of franchises contra	1,231,580	585,727	414,946	115,934	4,462
Deferred income taxes	112,122	59,203	10,764	—	—
Total liabilities	2,299,042	1,200,268	857,451	464,330	301,788
Shareholders' Equity					
Capital stock:					
Authorized—991,540 shares without par value					
Issued—353,540 shares (1975— 342,540)	402,747	348,505	373,505	273,505	273,505
Retained earnings (deficit)	135,530	21,199	(60,158)	95,451)	(105,017)
Total liabilities and shareholders' equity	$2,837,319	$1,605,972	$1,170,816	$642,384	$470,276

COMPETITION

"Everybody in the whole fast-food industry is our competitor," explained Muller. There were approximatey 89 fast-food franchise operators reported to be in Canada in February 1977. Trade sources believed that McDonald's Restaurants of Canada Limited would continue to set the pace in hamburger houses and fast foods. Scott's Restaurants Company Limited, the largest operator of Kentucky Fried Chicken outlets, reportedly dominated the take-out chicken business. Foodex Systems Limited (Ponderosa) was expected to hold its lead in budget steak houses for the family restaurant sector.

In 1977 in the metropolitan Montreal area alone, McDonald's had 23 outlets; Kentucky Fried Chicken, 51; Harvey's, 22; and Mr. Submarine, probably more closely competitive with Mike's, 4. There was no indication that any of these particular companies was content to remain with those numbers. For example, in 1977 the executive vice president for marketing at McDonald's stated: "A very important part of our growth now is going to be taking business away from competitors." Nevertheless, other fast-food companies were entering the market (Big Daddy's, Pizza Hut).

Competition for good suburban sites was also more intense, with prices rising appreciably. One company chain reported that its first stores in 1953 cost only $15,800 for land and building. By 1977 prices were rising that much in a single year.

There was quite a variation in the installation costs facing the various firms in the fast-food industry. Store-front chain family restaurants cost $90,000 to $120,000 to build and equip. Drive-ins with eating facilities were said to cost $240,000 to $260,000 and upwards. The big chains such as McDonald's faced installation costs of $500,000 to $1 million, with companies like Harvey's coming in at about $150,000 to $180,000. Mike's needed to spend up to $150,000, whereas Pizza Hut's installation costs were over $200,000.

The annual store volumes of firms such as Pizza Hut were under their construction costs, but Mike's store volumes were close to double the construction costs. According to Muller: "These numbers give us the leeway to gain new contracts."

PHYSICAL PLANT

There was no standard design for Mike's stores although the logo on the exterior and the interior decor of all stores was intended to provide a similarity for the company's outlets.

In 1977 six of the locations had drive-in and parking facilities, whereas the majority, particularly in the downtown or urban areas, were located in leased buildings that provided ready access for walk-in traffic.

The stores ranged in seating capacity from the smallest at 24 persons to the largest which was able to seat 130 persons. They all featured Mike's red-orange colour combinations on walls, counters and printed matter, including menus, and all served the same standard product at the same prices. All of the stores had sit-down facilities and, with the exception of two, offered delivery of the company's product at approximately a 10 percent differential.

The lack of parking facilities was thought by a franchisee to be a serious inhibitor to his particular sales growth:

> I know that customers will circle around once looking for a place to park, and if they can't find one, I have lost a sale. Hopefully they will come back another time, but I can't be sure.

SITE SELECTION

In general, downtown locations with high traffic flow were favoured by some operators. However, the advantages of high exposure had to be weighed against five-day business activity and high site costs downtown, as opposed to seven days in the suburbs and something in between for intermediate locations in semi-industrial and semi-residential areas.

In discussing site selection, Muller noted: "The only thing that I want to see is concentration—as many people within a mile or a mile and a half as we can get. In Montreal that is about 100,000. One of my favourite ways to determine the feasibility of a site is just to sit on the curb and count the people going by—it is really that simple."

A mixture of commercial and residential populace was another criterion considered in the selection of new Mike's sites. With such a location the store would be able to obtain two meals per day instead of one. In the downtown area, they get lunch and the evening meal. The heavy industrial areas were a source of "massive" lunches and no evening meals, whereas in the residential area few lunches tended to be served, but the evening meals were large.

A further comment was made by Beutel on the company's site selection policy:

> Because we started in Montreal and are now a dominant factor there, maybe it will support more stores per given population than other areas where others may be established and aren't waiting for us. It is a matter of clawing your way in where there is service already and then, as the years go on and the product has become more accepted, we may find, as McDonald's and others have found, that an area that may have started on a 1:100,000 basis, can now support 1:50,000.

The company had extended its store operations to Cornwall and Kingston, 80 and 190 miles to the west, and to the Quebec City area, 160 miles to the east, with other stores opened or opening in the more northerly region of Quebec. Speaking of Quebec City, Beutel remarked, "Quebec City is just so large, and our fourth store will be opening there next month and that will be it. We may look for a fifth and possibly a sixth but no more."

Mike's management was reluctant to spread their sites too far afield:

> If you are going to take an isolated trading area where there is no spillover from a big city and the maximum it can support is one store, you will find that the economies of scale in terms of procurement and advertising promotion are against you. You will have another store, but it will be marginal, tough to service and expensive to supervise.

FRANCHISE OPERATIONS

Under Muller's direction, franchise sales and store openings had moved ahead aggressively so that by the end of 1977 there were two company-owned and 31 franchised stores for a total of 33.

Franchisees who had been in operation prior to 1975 felt that there had been a definite lack of guidance and direction from head office but that it had been remedied by the appointment of Muller. Muller, in turn, believed that the organization had to be just as concerned about the profitable performance of the franchisee's operations as it was for those owned by the company.

Franchises were awarded on the basis of the availability of a suitable franchisee, both in terms of financial resources and managerial competence. The franchise agreement provided for a level of performance for which failure to comply could result in the loss of the franchise privilege.

Mike's main attention was now focused on seeking out suitable locations, arranging for leasehold improvements and equipment for the outlets and seeking franchisees to take over the operations. In addition, the company supervised quality and housekeeping standards, assisted franchisees with their operational problems, provided menus and, wherever possible, arranged for supplies through a designated commissary arrangement which afforded the company a nominal advertising allowance.

The company did not sell or lease real estate, fixtures or equipment to its franchisees. The franchise agreement conveyed the right to use these fixed assets and to exploit the company's name and goodwill.

Franchisees purchased their own food and supplies. However, to enable Mike's and its franchisees to obtain the most advantageous prices and, at the same time, assist in the preservation of uniformity and quality, Mike's arranged contracts with a number of major suppliers and encouraged its franchisees to participate.

Despite this assistance (and similar to the experiences of many other companies in the fast-food industry), not all of Mike's units had been as successful as had been anticipated when they were opened. By mid-1977 a total of four stores had been closed, basically due to poor site locations and/or lack of attention on the part of the franchisee. Management now believed there would be considerably less opportunity for a repetition of similar situations where either the company had to take a store back or the franchisee would have to cease operations.

In discussing the control of the operation, Beutel remarked:

Each Friday I have the sales figures for each store for the week ending the previous Sunday. Our year is divided into 13 four-week periods, and we budget on that basis. By looking through, I know how each store has done relative to the same week last year, how it is doing relative to budget. What I frequently do is look at the stores that are out of kilter. Most of our stores have been doing better than forecasted, but where there is a negative variance, I ask questions. It could be because there is a particular depressing factor in the area or any number of reasons. One of the suspicions is that you have a lousy manager there and he is scaring customers away.

Although franchisees had been interested in acquiring more than one outlet and had made this view known to management. Beutel said that from his experience, "in the few times we have tried it, it just hasn't worked. We have found that our successful franchisees, and most of them are successful, are those who own and operate a single store. The guy's own money is on the line, and the best operation follows when he is working in the store full-time."

FRANCHISEE SELECTION

"Management, and this includes our franchisees, is the single greatest recurring problem we have," reported Beutel in discussing this aspect of the company's operations. This problem was by no means unique to Mike's and was a theme repeated time and again by many operators in the fast-food industry. Many of the large chains had extensive training programs, ranging from the nearly $10 million spent by McDonald's through its Hamburger University, Elk Grove, Illinois, down to the small operator who relied on the selection of friends and relatives who had little or no experience in the business. However, one report stated, "Entrepreneurial spirit is starting to give way to professional management techniques."

In Mike's experience, the franchisee most likely to succeed "tended to be an eager fellow who was anxious to make money, generally had a fairly limited education, in most cases was an immigrant, and was not afraid to work very hard for long hours and to get his hands dirty."

Most of the franchisees were people who had worked in Mike's stores as chefs and cooks or were relatives or good friends of the existing franchisees.

Expanding on Mike's franchisee selection policy Beutel commented:

We went the franchise route because the incentive is built into the franchisee. He has put up his own bucks and because of the leverage of the business, he can make a much bigger buck on his own. He tends to make his own decisions right on the spot rather than waiting for head office to make them. You have delegated out the responsibility automatically by virtually making him his own boss. The big decision occurs when one guy comes up and he has the $15,000 and another guy has a lot of valuable experience but doesn't have the $15,000. Sometimes you make a mistake and sometimes you are pleasantly surprised. But in our experience we know within a fairly short time period whether we have selected correctly or not.

FRANCHISE FINANCING

The company was prepared to franchise a store at the time of its opening for a down payment usually between $5,000 to $15,000 and a total price which exceeded the cost to the company of the equipment and leasehold improvements by approximately $5,000 to $10,000. Part of this excess over cost was spent in preopening expenses, promotional efforts at the time of opening and occasional head office assistance. The balance of the franchise sale carried varying interest rates ranging from 8 percent to 12 percent per annum and payable in equal monthly installments varying from 48 months to 60 months and occasionally longer.

The major function of the company was the creation of restaurant locations and equipping and improving them so as to increase the number of franchised outlets which in turn would enlarge the base on which the company collected its 7 percent royalty payments.

All leasehold improvements and equipment were purchased either for cash or on a short-term unsecured credit basis from suppliers.

The growth and profitability of Mike's was the direct function of sales at the consumer level, and since these were a function of the number of outlets, the company's objective was to continue opening stores and franchising them. This activity required outside financing as the total cost of equipping a store substantially exceeded the down payment received.

Commenting on the franchisee financing aspects of the operation, Beutel stated:

> Because of the acceptance of our products and because our stores have been gaining momentum rapidly, we have changed our numbers. Our fee structure is quite frankly geared to what the market will bear. It has changed a fair amount in the past two years. Part of that reflects inflation and part reflects our ability to command a premium.
>
> We normally look for anywhere between $10,000 and $20,000 down. On the other hand, if it is a man that we know and have a lot of confidence in, we might be prepared to take $5,000 down, $5,000 in three months, and $5,000 in six months in addition to the regular schedule of payments. The most we have ever received as a down payment was $20,000.

MARKETING

"We are serving a product that is almost tailor-made for our market," reported Muller in discussing Mike's market and promotional approach. Basically, this market was believed to be composed essentially of industrial and office workers, ethnic groups and, on the whole, the 18- to 40-year age group.

"We are creating a product that we are selling, but the product we are creating is stores. We own the proprietary rights to the concept that we have and to the name. What we really sell to the franchisee is the right to exploit our name, our menu and to benefit from the services that head office provides by way of advertising, identification, supervision, quality format and so on," reported Beutel.

Mike's marketing strategy was to open up stores and establish a primary position in its market. Muller, in commenting on the company's progress to date, said, "I don't know if 50 percent sales growth is an achievable objective, but it is looking good so far."

Beginning in 1977 there were two issues uppermost in the minds of Mike's management with regard to its market development: (1) the saturation of Quebec and (2) what to do, if anything, toward expanding into another major market area.

So far as the existing market in Quebec was concerned, an examination of the sales of each outlet, week by week, year by year, indicated that store sales had built rapidly to a given plateau and thereafter had grown slowly in line with certain population factors, growing acceptability of the products and inflation. In terms of number of stores, Muller believed that Quebec would be saturated at about 45 stores. Nevertheless, the increase in the number of stores in recent years had not cut into the sales of the existing outlets. As far as the company could determine, the fluctuations in an individual outlet, apart from seasonal factors, were the result of the particular manager's or franchisee's skills. In other words, certain stores had displayed declining trends at various periods of time, and when the manager or franchisee had been replaced, the trend had been reversed.

The impact of more outlets seemed to afford the company the opportunity for increasing exposure. This, in turn, led to increased popularity and acceptability and a larger base for advertising and promotional efforts. With this in mind, management set aside a budget of approximately 1.5 percent of sales for advertising and promotion but, since 1975, had been spending nearly 2 percent annually. By comparison, McDonald's was reported to set aside 4.5 percent of all store revenues for advertising, promotion and charitable projects. In 1976 the company spent $50,000 on radio spots, in the print media and for the production of the company's menus.

Television was used for the first time in 1977, when the budget was increased to $125,000. In addition to the other promotional media used previously, a theme song was developed—"We are trying to create an image."

Other merchandising material such as T-shirts and stickers were made available for franchisee use as well as part of the company's overall campaign.

THE FUTURE

In 1977 comments on the future of the fast-food industry were sprinkled with conclusions such as "Either for convenience or sheer pleasure, the forecast is that many Canadians will soon be eating two meals out of three away from home." Similar trends had also been forecast for the United States with three out of four being suggested as indicative of the future in that country.

While the eating-out market was expected to continue a growth pattern, the sailing was not expected to be quite as smooth as it had been in the past. (See the Appendix.) Amongst the reasons frequently cited were the escalation of costs and overexpansion, particularly in certain segments of the industry and in certain areas of both Canada and the United States. Furthermore, as competition became more intense, the marketing role was expected to become a more important function as firms struggled to capture not only increasing primary demand but more and more market share from each other.

Fully cognizant of the many problems facing the future not only of the industry in general but of Mike's Submarine Sandwiches in particular, Beutel summarized his thinking about the company's future moves:

> We have a small but dynamic head office group whose focus has been on selecting locations and opening stores, finding the franchisees for them and so on. We have pretty well saturated the Quebec market area where we started.
>
> We could say we have done a job here, sit back, and with a minimum of supervision and effort clip the coupons by collecting the fees and returning the money to the shareholders. Or we could say we want to go to another major metropolitan area or major marketing area. For the first store in that new area, there would be no exposure and there would be all the front-end expenses of starting, and the second time around is always more expensive than the first time.

ALTERNATIVE MARKETS FOR FUTURE GROWTH

The rule of thumb which guided Mike's Submarine market and site selection was the ratio of approximately one site per 100,000 population, preferably in relatively concentrated clusters. A new market would have to be a major centre, with local sources of supply for ingredients as well as advertising media, which could support a sufficient number of stores to justify administrative personnel and serve as a base for further outward expansion.

For instance, Quebec City could support four or five stores but not a permanent regional office nor become a base for further outlets. Therefore, using Montreal as the centre, a series of concentric circles were drawn with a maximum radius of 300 miles, representing about one hour's flying time from the focal point. Three major markets fitting the rule-of-thumb criteria became readily apparent: (1) Toronto, Ontario, (2) the Albany-Schenectady area, and (3) Boston, Massachusetts. Each location was then evaluated as follows:

(1) Toronto, Ontario

The Greater Toronto area had a population of just over 2.2 million, making it the largest metropolitan centre in Canada. The city had been experiencing rapid growth for several years and had a diversified and growing ethnic population. It would be relatively easy to arrange for supplies and promotional activity, and banking arrangements would be an extension of existing credits. However, the number of fast-food outlets appeared to be approaching saturation, and store rentals had escalated in recent years. It would also be difficult to obtain desirable locations. Furthermore, in the sale of submarine sandwiches there was one dominant supplier, Mr. Submarine, whose base was Toronto, with over 150 outlets throughout the city and a substantial advertising budget.

(2) Albany-Schenectady, New York

The major attraction to this area is that it fell well within the prescribed radius limit from Montreal, although airline connections were not as frequent and travelling time would actually be increased over the other two prospective locations. Furthermore, while the area could serve as a base for expansion eastward into populated New England, westward to upstate New York cities, and southward toward New York and New Jersey, the metropolitan region itself did not seem to possess the necessary vitality and appeal. Finally, there were a number of Mike's Submarine shops, independently owned and now completely unrelated, that would have created an identity problem. Thus, the "uncomfortable" feel and competitive situation in this area persuaded the company to consider the one other market possibility.

(3) Boston, Massachusetts

Studies of this area showed that the northeast part of the United States, particularly Massachusetts, had a lower concentration of fast-food shops relative to population than most of the other market areas under consideration. Boston was the home of the "Hero Sandwich," and there were a lot of such shops, hence a basic familiarity with the submarine concept. There was no dominant supplier in contrast with the situation in Toronto. Another feature that seemed to be attractive about Boston was the relatively dense population not only in the metropolitan area itself but along the corridor toward New York City. Even if New York City itself was by-passed, Mike's believed that there would be considerable potential in moving gradually into adjacent areas that would easily support the 1:100,000 ratio mentioned previously.

The Boston market was not without its drawbacks. Boston had quite different population concentrations compared with Montreal and was considerably more spread out. Some sections of downtown Boston tended to become virtually vacant in the evenings, and that was hardly conducive to maximum utilization of a fast-food outlet, even with a concentrated populace. The traffic patterns were vastly different to those in Montreal so that additional studies would be required in order to define desirable locations. There appeared to be a higher proportion of the greater Boston population living in single-family dwellings than was the situation in Montreal resulting in a much more scattered pattern.

While Boston was an appealing place to live, Mike's would have to establish completely new banking connections as its Canadian arrangements could not include the security of foreign-based assets. Further, the decline of the Canadian dollar made for difficulty in currency transactions and foreign exchange complications. Finally, Mike's would have to arrange for new suppliers of everything from equipment to ingredients to services and deal with a completely different set of rules, not only locally but nationally.

THE NEXT MOVE

After reviewing the advantages and disadvantages of each location, Beutel and Muller concluded that Boston was the preferable location. Beutel described the next move:

> We went down to Boston and were introduced to people in the real estate business by friends whose opinions we respected. We toured the areas and, granted that we had a bias that we were ready to be impressed, we came away with a favourable feeling that we should proceed.

APPENDIX: THE FAST-FOOD INDUSTRY

The fast-food franchise operator in Canada, based on recent trade information, had shown a "sizzling" growth rate in recent years, even more dynamic than that of the United States.

Fast-Food Franchise Operations

	Canada		Percent Increase in Canada	Percent Increase in the United States
	1974	**1976**		
Number of units	1,952	2,606	33.5%	20%
Total sales	$449 million	$764 million	69.8	32
Average sales/ unit	$230,000	$293,000	27.4	10

Source: *Food Service and Hospitality,* February 1977.

The average sales per unit in Canada in 1976 was higher than the $275,000 U.S. average. Comparative data in share of market by menu type showed significant variations from the U.S. pattern.

Fast-Food Menu Operation, 1976

Major Menu	Percent in Canada	Percent in United States
Hamburgers, franks and roast beef	43%	54%
Steak	5	15
Chicken	40	13
Pizza	7	8
Seafoods	1.5	3
Other (pancakes, sandwiches, ice cream)	16	10

Source: *Food Service and Hospitality,* February 1977.

The main reasons cited for the growth of the franchised operators in foodservice and lodging sectors were:

1. Franchise operations were usually controlled by professionals skilled in all operating areas. These skills were made available to every franchisee and substantially improved their operating efficiency and effectiveness.
2. Efficiency in marketing and "brand" recognition attracted new and repeat customers while reducing unit promotion and advertising costs as a percentage of sales.
3. Development costs of establishing and operating units were spread over a larger base, both in number of locations and number of customer transactions. Improved profits and lower consumer prices were, therefore, possible.
4. Ability of multiunit operators to buy in larger quantities meant lower unit prices, better uniformity in products or services provided and greater efficiency in staffing and operations.
5. The franchise operator was less vulnerable if a local market condition reduced sales or profitability in one or several units. Single unit operators could be very vulnerable to local conditions.
6. Franchisors have taken increasing advantage of technology, particularly the availability of new, improved equipment and more efficient methods of operation.
7. Better financing and banking was available under the umbrella of a franchise group, whether or not franchisors were directly involved in the financing through funding or guarantees. Improved confidence on the part of the funds supplier meant more funds were available, often at a lower rate.

Applied Management Systems, Inc.

It had been another busy day as Messrs. Clark, Sargent and Finlay sat in their office reflecting upon the events of the past few days. Their young company, Applied Management Systems, was finally beginning to stabilize its business somewhat but the company lacked an organized sense of direction. Two new products had recently been completed and now the question was how to get those products to the appropriate markets, what exactly were the markets for the products, and what the future direction of the company should be.

COMPANY HISTORY

Applied Management Systems is based in Worcester, Massachusetts, and was founded in 1981 as an outgrowth of another company which Paul Clark and Charles Sargent had founded a couple of years earlier. Clark's and Sargent's prior company, DAPA, primarily did small computer programming jobs and computer consulting work. One of DAPA's most successful programs was a golf handicap system which was used by several area country clubs. DAPA was strictly a part-time operation that provided supplemental income for Clark and Sargent. At the time, both Clark and Sargent were employed at Worcester Quality Foods where Clark was the controller and Sargent was in charge of data processing. After performing several programming jobs for various parties, Clark and Sargent felt that there was an ample market need for custom developed software that was designed to function with the growing microcomputer market. Together with Bob Finlay, a former co-worker from Worcester Quality Foods, they decided to go into business for themselves, founding Applied Management Systems in January 1982.

Paul Clark—Clark's background is in accounting and finance. Paul received his accounting degree from a reputable school in the Boston area and has taken several courses toward his M.B.A. Clark has served as the assistant controller for a Fortune 500 company and as controller of Worcester Quality Foods which grew from $12 million to $120 million during the time Paul was employed. In addition to his financial skills, Clark has also had experience with corporate planning.

Bob Finlay—Finlay's background has been in the financial area also. Prior to joining AMS, Finlay was employed by a local university where he served as manager of accounting operations, supervising a staff of seven officeworkers. Bob has also served as the manager

Prepared by David Kahl and Professor William Naumes of Clark University and Professor Margaret Naumes, of Assumption College. This case material is designed as the basis for class discussion, not to demonstrate either effective or ineffective management. All rights reserved to the case authors.

of a small computer supply and panel manufacturer and as the accounting/office manager at Worcester Quality Foods. Bob has his associates degree in accounting, a bachelor's degree in management technology and has also completed a specialized, brief, intensive sequence of courses in computer programming.

Charles Sargent—Sargent's background has been in computers since he received his engineering degree from Boston University. Sargent has worked with the IBM 360-20, the Prime 300 and the Prime 550. Sargent has served as chief programmer, systems analyst and manager of data systems during his prior work experience. He has written an entire on-line order entry system, accounts receivable, accounts payable and total accounting system during his employment at Worcester Quality Foods.

BACKGROUND ON THE INDUSTRY

By pooling the talents of the three founders, AMS intended to capitalize on the growing microcomputer market by developing custom software designed to work with the most popular types of microcomputers. Prior to widespread acceptance of the micro in a business setting, large organizations such as banks and insurance companies relied upon minicomputers and mainframe computers to do all their information processing. While the micro was not designed to replace the mainframes or minicomputers in every area, there are many areas where a micro can reduce many time-consuming functions such as word processing and spreadsheet analysis. In addition, micros can also supplement the data generated by larger computers. An executive who may want to see a report prepared in a certain manner may not be able to get the changes he wants from a larger computer system. Larger systems usually require programming staffs to run the system and modify existing data output. However, with the flexibility of a microcomputer, an executive can frequently generate the information he wants quickly and without the involvement of programmers.

During the latter part of the 1970s and early 1980s, a number of significant technology breakthroughs were made which allowed the microcomputers to perform functions similar to those performed by their minicomputer predecessors at a significantly reduced cost. Today, the capabilities found in a $7,000 microcomputer are not significantly different from the capabilities found in a $40,000 minicomputer of just a couple of years ago. The resultant price/performance capabilities found in the microcomputer open a whole new field of potential uses.

PRODUCT HISTORY

In early 1982, AMS got its first big programming job. A local bank was having discussions with a nearby microcomputer hardware retailer regarding the use of microcomputers. During these discussions, the hardware vendor quickly realized that the needs of the bank were beyond the capabilities of the standard software. In order to complete the sale, the hardware vendor contacted AMS to see if it might be interested in developing the appropriate software to meet the bank's needs. After several meetings, the bank awarded the software contract to AMS and the company had its first big break. The bank project involved developing a portfolio and investment record-keeping system, an accounts payable system, a budgeting system, and a complete general ledger system. As a result of this contract, a complete investment portfolio analysis module was developed and was ready to market at the time of the case.

ORGANIZATIONAL STRUCTURE

Paul Clark is the president of AMS with Finlay and Sargent both serving as vice-presidents. The ownership of the company is divided equally among the three partners. The responsibilities of the three owners are as follows:

- Paul Clark—New Product Design, Marketing Evaluation, Sales, Customer Service, Financial Adviser, Customer/Vendor Negotiations
- Robert Finlay—Business Systems Analysis, Customer Training, Sales, Financial Adviser, Internal Accounting and Reporting
- Charles Sargent—Manager of Data Processing, Products Development, Systems Design, Applications Development, Utilities Program Development

DAY-TO-DAY OPERATIONS

After a specific project has been accepted, the flow of operations is as follows: Finlay and/or Clark would go to the customer's site and gather specific information regarding a particular business application. Clark or Finlay would return to AMS's office where the information would be given to Charles Sargent. At that time, Sargent would begin developing the appropriate software to fit the application. Occasionally, Sargent would have to go to the customer's site personally to gather data when programming information could not be gathered by either Finlay or Clark due to specific training which Finlay and Clark do not have. Once the program had been written, Finlay would install it at the customer's office and provide the necessary training.

During the development project at the local bank, Finlay and Clark would often get trapped into answering questions and providing training on systems which AMS did not provide. As Paul Clark noted;

> "We provided only a part of the total system at the bank. However, because we were constantly in and out of there, the staff at the bank would often grab one of us to help them with a problem that wasn't related to our system." "We need to have more control over an installation. It's crazy for us to spend our time training users on systems that we don't provide. We have to either deny the users this type of assistance or gain control over the entire system. That includes the hardware as well as all the software. We have already proven our competence with the software, and Charlie and Bob are both capable of servicing the hardware on minor repairs." "We can always

determine the source of a problem. We can determine whether or not we can fix the problem and then take the necessary steps to resolve the situation."

PRODUCT/SOFTWARE DEVELOPMENT

AMS's philosophy regarding product development can be summarized in the following statement by Paul Clark: "We typically accept projects where we feel the end product is generally resellable. Products developed for the specific use of only one client typically are not resellable and therefore have no future value. We try to take on all assignments that will generate a good end product. We retain the right to package and sell the software to other customers.

"We recognize the fact that many executives don't want to learn how to run a computer. All they want to do is get the information out of the system in a relatively easy and timely manner, without having to learn how to program the system or how it works. Executives are too busy with their own operations. Taking the time to learn how to set up the program is a luxury most can't afford."

At the time of the case, AMS had an inventory of three completed projects which were ready for resale. The three products were the Investment Portfolio Analysis Module (IPAM), the Seminar and Meeting Reservation System (SMRS) and the Visicalc Pro-Forma Model (VPFM).

IPAM. The IPAM module had been developed initially during a project for a local college. The program had been written so that the college could keep track of its endowment portfolio. Later, the same module was modified and refined to become part of the total system for the local bank. Now the product was finished and was ready to be marketed.

Since the IPAM had been the first module installed at the bank, it received a great deal of attention. It also received very favorable reviews from its users. Some additional outside interest was generated for the IPAM module as Mr. Clark demonstrated the product's capabilities to a couple of other area banks. However, by the time of the case, no additional sales of the product had been made.

An outside hardware manufacturing firm also expressed interest in the IPAM module, and negotiations had taken place between Clark and the hardware manufacturing firm. IPAM was designed to meet the needs of organizations that must manage investment portfolios. Target organizations include banks (both commercial and savings), credit unions, insurance companies, educational institutions' endowment funds, etc.

SMRS. The seminar and meeting reservation system had been the pet project of the one other staff programmer at AMS. The other programmer, Dave, was an extremely bright and competent programmer who was also very creative. The SMRS program was selected because of an apparent void in the market which Clark had noticed. At the time of the case, the SMRS product was finished, yet there had been no sales. The SMRS was designed to meet the needs of organizations which organize and hold seminars for various groups.

VPFM. The Visicalc Pro-Forma Model utilizes the very popular Visicalc software package and incorporates a special template designed for pro-forma forecasting. This product resulted from a request by the controller at the bank for which the IPAM model had been developed. After initially thinking that such a model could not be built and then spending a great deal of time developing the model, AMS produced a very sophisticated modeling system. The model was designed for financial institutions where pro-forma calculations are necessary. The model output includes interest rate assumptions, securities and investment projections, mortgage loan projections, deposit flow projections and balance sheet and profit and loss statements.

"The first few projects undertaken by AMS were designed to be long-run investments of time and money," explains Paul Clark. "We know that our products, just like any others in this industry, are labor intensive. We plan to recoup our initial investment through future product sales. We feel our product is good and is capable of generating enough demand to produce cash inflows sufficient to fund future development projects we have planned. We intend to finish our financial system and be one of the first vendors to offer a complete information processing system designed specifically for banking institutions which run on microcomputers."

Because of AMS's philosophy on long-run profits, the pricing of their initial products had been very inexpensive. Software prices for comparable minicomputer based systems were five to six times more expensive. AMS's service and support costs were also much less costly than the fees charged by minicomputer software companies. In addition, because AMS's products ran strictly on Apple III microcomputers, the hardware costs were also greatly reduced. It was this tremendous cost advantage which allowed AMS to gain much of its early development work.

Both the SMRS and the IPAM modules are designed to run on a "stand alone" basis on the Apple III computer equipped with a hard disk storage device. Each module costs $2,500. A total hardware and software system would cost under $10,000 for either module.

MARKETING

At the time of the case, very little formal marketing had been done by AMS. Paul Clark had had some preliminary discussions with a couple of local banks and a major hardware vendor, yet no final commitments had been made. All of the organizations to which Paul Clark had shown the IPAM module were extremely impressed with its performance, simplicity and price.

In addition to direct sales methods by Clark himself, AMS had begun discussions with an individual located in New York who would act as a sales representative for AMS. The individual was extremely well known in the financial community. He had been the president of an important organization for mutual savings banks and had developed a time-sharing model for use by savings banks a few years earlier. In addition to being well respected within the financial community, Clark felt that the contacts this individual had would be a great asset. This person would initially work with the IPAM module and would begin his efforts in the New York area.

CUSTOMER INDUSTRIES

AMS plans to focus its products and its marketing efforts at two primary target industries: banks and educational institutions. These two target industries were selected because of the development work at the local bank and the backgrounds of Clark and Finlay, and because of the perceived market potential.

The IPAM and the VPFM packages were designed to handle the needs of financial institutions where portfolio management and pro-forma modeling functions are required. These products are directly applicable to other banks including savings banks, commercial banks, savings and loan institutions and mutual savings banks.

Clark and Finlay's work experience has been in the financial field. Both have a detailed understanding of finance and accounting and know the types of information a financial person needs to perform his/her functions.

In general, both banks and educational institutions are slow to adopt new developments in the information-processing field. Due to the nature and the volume of information that these two industries process, there is a tremendous market potential for the use of micro-computers and appropriate software to manage specific functions.

COMPETITION

Presently, there are only a few companies which compete directly with AMS in the microcomputer field. Most of the products developed for micros are not industry specific and can be run by a variety of organizations in many settings. As Paul Clark states, "Presently, our competition comes from software companies whose products run on minicomputers. They sell their systems for $20,000 to $30,000 when we sell ours for $10,000; and ours does just as much. The difference is in the hardware technology between the minicomputer and the microcomputer."

"In the future, software companies that have developed their products for minis will have to switch their machines to micros and totally rewrite their software. This is where we have the jump. By the time these companies finally rewrite their programs, we hope to have installed a significant user base to sustain our momentum. These minicomputer companies have big marketing and sales forces who will be a real threat once they have a competitive product behind them. We just have to get our products developed and installed in time to stay in the running."

GEOGRAPHIC MARKETS

AMS has targeted the geographic market for its products to be two main areas: the area within a one-hour driving time from Worcester, and the greater New York City area. These two markets were selected based on sales force coverage, support capabilities and concentrations of financial and educational institutions.

Exhibit I. A.M.S. Inc. Balance Sheet January 31, 1983.

Assets		Liabilities	
Cash	−5,311.83	Accounts Payable	1,092.82
Investments	5,919.25	Notes Payable	3,000.00
Notes Receivable	0.00	Fed. Tax Liabilities	945.76
Accts. Receivable—Net	12,641.35	State Tax Liabilities	442.31
Inventory	3,336.40	Total Current Liabilities	5,480.89
Prepaid Supplies	2,948.54	Notes Payable—Long Term	22,300.00
Total	19,533.71	Total Liabilities	27,780.89
Fixed Assets		Equity	
Office Equipment	1,910.75	Capital Stock	300.00
Data Processing Eq.	16,104.00	Retained Earnings	3,800.58
Less: Accumulated Depreciation	−4,598.70	Current Period Profit and Loss	2,968.29
Net Fixed Assets	13,416.05	Total Equity	7,068.87
Deposits	1,900.00		
Total Assets	34,849.76	Total Liabilities and Equity	34,849.76

Exhibit II. A.M.S. Inc. Profit and Loss Statement January 31, 1983 (4 mos.).

Sales—Net		72,279.35
Purchases		19,936.35
Freight In		22.31
Gross Profit		52,320.69
Salaries	22,716.25	
Rent	2,575.00	
Supplies	4,185.19	
Casual labor	6,727.82	
Telephone	1,721.72	
Postage	328.92	
Interest	2,746.50	
Advertising	307.72	
Professional Services	1,163.91	
Depreciation	4,598.70	
Insurance	636.72	
Travel and Entertainment	638.80	
Payroll Tax Expense	146.46	
Dues and Subscriptions	107.95	
Miscellaneous	750.74	
Total Operating Expenses		49,352.40
Pretax Income		2,968.29
Federal Taxes		
Net Income after taxes		

Exhibit III. A.M.S. Inc. Projected Statement of Earnings January 1983–December 1983.

	Jan. 83	Feb. 83	Mar. 83	Apr. 83	May 83	Jun. 83	Jul. 83	Aug. 83	Sep. 83	Oct. 83	Nov. 83	Dec. 83	Total
Revenue	30,533	20,911	17,154	24,500	25,725	27,011	31,063	35,722	41,081	47,243	54,329	62,479	417,751
Cost of Goods Sold													
Purchases	18,500	1,079	7,899	10,699	11,234	11,796	13,565	15,600	17,940	20,631	23,726	27,284	179,953
Freight	0	0	0	535	562	590	678	780	897	1,032	1,186	1,364	7,624
Total Cost of Goods Sold	18,500	1,079	7,899	11,234	11,796	12,386	14,243	16,380	18,837	21,662	24,912	28,649	187,577
Gross Profit	12,033	19,832	9,255	13,266	13,929	14,626	16,819	19,342	22,244	25,500	29,417	33,830	230,174
Officers' Salaries	3,600	7,200	7,200	7,200	1,000	1,000	1,000	1,000	1,000	1,000	1,000	1,000	105,200
Wages	0	350	1,190	3,200	3,200	4,000	3,200	3,200	4,000	3,200	3,200	4,000	32,740
Payroll Taxes	241	505	562	342	342	428	342	342	428	342	342	428	4,646
Rent	285	456	456	456	700	700	700	700	700	700	700	700	7,253
Advertising	0	503	384	1,000	10,000	10,000	3,500	2,500	2,500	2,500	2,500	2,500	37,687
Depreciation	475	475	475	475	570	570	570	570	570	570	570	570	6,460
Insurance	360	302	636	200	200	200	200	200	200	200	200	200	3,098
Travel	183	235	521	250	250	250	250	250	250	250	250	250	3,189
Telephone	264	206	235	150	150	150	150	150	150	150	150	150	2,055
Postage	34	68	15	50	75	75	100	100	100	100	100	100	917
Professional Services	3,789	1,718	600	500	500	500	500	500	500	500	500	500	10,607
Legal	0	0	270	125	125	125	125	125	125	125	125	125	1,395
Supplies	102	386	180	75	75	75	75	75	75	75	75	75	1,343
Benefits	0	0	0	1,100	1,100	1,100	1,100	1,100	1,100	1,100	1,100	1,100	9,900
Membership Fees	0	0	0	25	25	25	25	25	25	25	25	25	225
Miscellaneous	0	0	0	100	100	100	100	100	100	100	100	100	900
Total G & A	9,333	12,404	12,724	15,248	27,412	28,298	20,937	19,937	20,823	19,937	19,937	20,823	227,815
Net Income Before Interest & Taxes	2,700	7,428	−3,469	−1,983	−13,483	−13,672	−4,118	−595	1,421	5,643	9,480	13,007	2,359
Interest Expense	54	—	34	415	649	774	852	875	883	901	845	760	7,042
Net Income After Interest Expense	2,646	7,428	−3,503	−2,398	−14,132	−14,446	−4,970	−1,470	538	4,742	8,635	12,247	−4,683

Exhibit IV. A.M.S. Inc. Projected Statement of Earnings January 1984–December 1984.

	Jan. 84	Feb. 84	Mar. 84	Apr. 84	May 84	Jun. 84	July 84	Aug. 84	Sept. 84	Oct. 84	Nov. 84	Dec. 84	Total
Revenue	67,080	69,763	72,554	75,456	78,474	81,613	84,878	88,273	91,804	95,476	99,295	103,267	1,007,931
Cost of Goods Sold													
Purchases	29,294	30,466	31,684	32,952	34,270	35,640	37,066	38,549	40,091	41,694	43,362	45,097	440,163
Freight	586	609	634	659	685	713	741	771	802	834	867	902	8,803
Total Cost of Goods Sold	29,880	31,075	32,318	33,611	34,955	36,353	37,807	39,320	40,892	42,528	44,229	45,998	448,966
Gross Profit	37,200	38,688	40,236	41,845	43,519	45,260	47,070	48,953	50,911	52,948	55,066	57,268	558,965
Officers' Salaries	10,150	10,150	12,700	10,150	10,150	12,700	10,150	10,150	12,700	10,150	10,150	12,700	132,000
Wages	5,200	5,200	5,200	5,200	5,200	5,200	5,200	5,200	5,200	5,200	5,200	5,200	62,400
Payroll Taxes	1,397	1,397	1,629	1,397	1,397	1,629	1,397	1,397	1,629	1,397	1,397	1,629	17,690
Rent	1,200	1,200	1,200	1,200	1,200	1,200	1,200	1,200	1,200	1,200	1,200	1,200	14,400
Advertising	3,500	3,500	3,500	3,500	3,500	3,500	3,500	3,500	3,500	3,500	3,500	3,500	42,000
Depreciation	570	570	570	570	700	700	700	700	700	700	700	700	7,000
Insurance	300	300	300	300	300	300	300	300	300	300	300	300	3,600
Travel	350	350	350	350	350	350	350	350	350	350	350	350	4,200
Telephone	350	350	350	350	350	350	350	350	350	350	350	350	4,200
Postage	200	200	200	200	200	200	200	200	200	200	200	200	2,400
Legal	150	150	150	150	150	150	150	150	150	150	150	150	1,800
Supplies	250	250	250	250	250	250	250	250	250	250	250	250	3,000
Benefit	1,300	1,300	1,300	1,300	1,300	1,300	1,300	1,300	1,300	1,300	1,300	1,300	15,600
Membership Fees	75	75	75	75	75	75	75	75	75	75	75	75	900
Miscellaneous	150	150	150	150	150	150	150	150	150	150	150	150	1,800
Total G & A	25,142	25,142	27,924	25,142	25,272	28,054	25,272	25,272	28,054	25,272	25,272	28,054	312,990
Net Income Before Interest & Taxes	12,058	13,546	12,312	12,312	18,247	17,206	21,798	23,681	22,857	27,676	29,794	29,214	245,975
Interest Expense	653	413	558	361	449	205	310	50	105	-140	-104	-402	2,458
Net Income After Interest Expense	11,405	13,133	11,754	11,951	17,798	17,001	21,488	23,631	22,752	27,816	29,898	29,616	243,517

Exhibit V. A.M.S. Inc. Projected Statement of Condition March 1983–December 1983.

	Mar. Act.	Apr.	May	June	Jul.	Aug.	Sep.	Oct.	Nov.	Dec.
Assets										
Cash	1,919	2,000	2,000	2,000	2,000	2,000	2,000	2,000	2,000	2,000
Investments	5,000	5,000	0	0	0	0	0	0	0	0
Receivables	11,032	10,000	22,050	23,153	24,310	27,957	32,150	36,973	42,519	48,815
Inventory	4,045	7,350	7,718	8,103	9,319	10,717	12,324	14,173	16,272	18,744
Other Assets	2,397	500	500	500	500	500	500	500	500	500
Total Current Assets	24,393	24,850	32,268	33,756	36,129	41,173	46,974	53,646	61,290	70,059
Property Equipment—Net	12,837	12,623	17,329	17,040	16,756	16,477	16,203	15,933	15,667	15,406
Total Assets	37,230	37,473	49,597	50,796	52,885	57,651	63,177	69,578	76,957	85,465
Liabilities										
Notes Payable—Current	3,000	3,000	3,000	3,000	3,000	3,000	3,000	3,000	3,000	3,000
Accounts Payable	0	5,678	5,962	6,260	7,199	8,279	9,521	10,949	12,570	14,480
Taxes Due	3,090	1,500	3,000	4,500	1,500	3,000	4,500	1,500	3,000	4,500
Other Current Liabilities	417	500	500	500	500	500	500	500	500	500
Total Current Liabilities	6,507	10,678	12,462	14,260	12,199	14,779	17,521	15,949	19,070	22,480
Long-Term Debt	12,000	11,750	11,500	11,250	11,000	10,750	10,500	10,250	10,000	9,750
Long-Term Financing	22,000	20,720	45,442	59,539	68,909	72,815	75,311	78,792	74,665	67,766
Deferred Income										
Other Liabilities	10,000	10,000	10,000	10,000	10,000	10,000	10,000	10,000	10,000	10,000
Total Liabilities	50,507	53,148	79,404	95,049	102,108	108,344	113,332	114,991	113,735	109,996
Stockholders' Equity										
Capital Stock	300	300	300	300	300	300	300	300	300	300
Retained Earnings	−13,577	−15,975	−30,107	−44,553	−49,523	−50,993	−50,455	−45,173	−37,078	−24,831
Total Equity	−13,277	−15,675	−29,807	−44,253	−49,223	−50,693	−50,155	−45,413	−36,778	−24,531
Total Liabilities and Stockholders' Equity	37,230	37,473	49,597	50,796	52,885	57,651	63,177	69,578	76,957	85,465

Exhibit VI. A.M.S. Inc. Statement of Sources and Uses of Cash April 1983–December 1983.

Sources	Apr. 83	May 83	Jun. 83	Jul. 83	Aug. 83	Sep. 83	Oct. 83	Nov. 83	Dec. 83	Total
Operating Income	-2,398	-14,132	-14,446	-4,970	-1,470	538	4,742	8,635	12,247	-11,254
Depreciation	475	570	570	570	570	570	570	570	570	5,035
Provided from Operations	-1,923	-13,562	-13,876	-4,400	-900	1,108	5,312	9,205	12,817	-6,219
Decrease (Increase) Inventory	-3,305	-368	-385	-1,216	-1,398	-1,607	-1,849	-2,099	-2,472	-14,699
Increase (Decrease) Payables	5,678	284	298	939	1,080	1,242	1,428	1,621	1,910	14,480
Increase (Decrease) Accrued Expenses	0	0	0	0	0	0	0	0	0	0
Increase (Decrease) S.T. Notes	-250	-250	-250	-250	-250	-250	-250	-250	-250	-2,250
Increase (Decrease) Other Liabilities	-1,507	1,500	1,500	-3,000	1,500	1,500	-3,000	1,500	1,500	1,493
Working Capital Sources	616	1,166	1,163	-3,527	932	885	-3,671	772	688	-976
Total Sources	-1,307	-12,396	-12,713	-7,927	32	1,993	1,641	9,977	13,505	-7,195
Applications (Uses)										
Increase (Decrease) Receivables	-1,032	12,050	1,103	1,157	3,647	4,193	4,823	5,546	6,296	37,783
Increase (Decrease) Unbilled Costs	0	0	0	0	0	0	0	0	0	0
Increase (Decrease) Other Assets	-2,030	-294	-289	-284	-279	-274	-270	-266	-261	-4,247
Total Applications	-3,062	11,756	814	873	3,368	3,919	4,553	5,280	6,035	33,536
Increase (Decrease) in Cash	1,755	-24,152	-13,527	-8,800	-3,336	-1,926	-2,912	4,697	7,470	-40,731
Net Balance Sheet Flow/Operations	1,755	-24,152	-13,527	-8,800	-3,336	-1,926	-2,912	4,697	7,470	-40,731

Exhibit VII. A.M.S. Inc. Projected Statement of Condition January 1984–December 1984.

	Jan.	Feb.	Mar.	Apr.	May	June	July	Aug.	Sep.	Oct.	Nov.	Dec.
Assets												
Cash	2,000	2,000	2,000	2,000	2,000	2,000	2,000	2,000	2,000	2,000	2,000	2,000
Investments	0	0	0	0	0	0	9,113	31,626	52,130	73,560	101,930	129,932
Receivables	56,231	60,372	62,787	65,299	67,910	70,627	73,452	76,390	79,446	82,624	85,928	89,366
Inventory	20,124	20,379	21,766	22,637	23,542	24,484	25,463	26,482	27,541	28,643	29,789	30,710
Other Assets	500	500	500	500	500	500	500	500	500	500	500	500
Total Current Assets	78,855	83,801	87,053	90,435	93,953	97,611	110,528	136,998	162,617	187,326	220,147	252,508
Property and Equip—Net	20,066	19,731	19,402	19,079	18,761	18,448	18,141	17,839	17,541	17,249	16,961	16,679
Total Assets	98,921	102,982	106,455	109,514	112,714	116,059	128,669	154,837	180,158	204,575	237,108	269,186
Liabilities												
Notes Payable—Current	3,000	3,000	3,000	3,000	3,000	3,000	3,000	3,000	3,000	3,000	3,000	3,000
Accounts Payable	15,546	16,718	16,814	17,487	18,186	18,914	19,670	20,457	21,276	22,127	23,012	23,724
Taxes Due	2,000	4,000	6,000	2,000	4,000	6,000	2,000	4,000	6,000	2,000	4,000	6,000
Other Current Liabilities	10,000	10,000	10,000	10,000	10,000	10,000	10,000	10,000	10,000	10,000	10,000	10,000
Total Current Liabilities	21,546	33,168	26,814	23,487	26,186	28,914	25,670	28,457	31,276	28,127	31,012	33,724
Long-Term Debt	14,500	14,250	14,000	13,750	13,500	13,250	13,000	12,750	12,500	12,250	12,000	11,750
Long-Term Finances	66,001	54,007	43,880	38,565	21,518	5,384	0	0	0	0	0	0
Other Liabilities	1,000	1,000	1,000	10,000	10,000	10,000	10,000	10,000	10,000	10,000	10,000	10,000
Total Liabilities	112,047	102,425	94,694	85,802	71,204	57,548	48,670	51,207	53,776	50,377	53,012	55,474
Stockholders' Equity												
Capital Stock	300	300	300	300	300	300	300	300	300	300	300	300
Retained Earnings	-13,426	-293	11,461	23,412	41,210	58,211	79,699	103,330	126,082	153,898	183,796	213,412
Total Equity	-13,126	7	11,761	23,712	41,510	58,511	79,999	103,630	126,382	154,198	184,096	213,712
Total Liabilities and Stockholders' Equity	98,921	102,982	106,455	109,514	112,714	116,059	128,669	154,837	180,158	204,575	237,108	269,186

Exhibit VIII. A.M.S. Inc. Projected Statement of Cash Flows January 1984–December 1984.

Sources	Jan. 84	Feb. 84	Mar. 84	Apr. 84	May 84	Jun. 84	Jul. 84	Aug. 84	Sep. 84	Oct. 84	Nov. 84	Dec. 84	Total
Operating Income	11,405	13,133	11,754	11,951	17,798	17,001	21,488	23,631	22,752	27,816	29,898	29,618	238,243
Depreciation	570	570	570	570	700	700	700	700	700	700	700	700	7,880
Provided from Operations	11,975	13,703	12,324	12,521	18,498	17,701	22,188	24,331	23,452	28,516	30,598	30,316	246,123
Decrease (increase) Inventory	-1,380	-805	-837	-871	-905	-942	-979	-1,019	-1,059	-1,102	-1,146	-921	-11,966
Increase (Decrease) Payables	1,066	622	646	673	699	728	756	787	819	851	885	712	9,244
Increase (Decrease) Accrued Expenses													
Increase (Decrease) S.T. Note	-250	-250	-250	-250	-250	-250	-250	-250	-250	-250	-250	-250	-3,000
Increase (Decrease) Other Liabilities	3,000	2,000	2,000	-4,000	2,000	2,000	-4,000	2,000	2,000	-4,000	2,000	2,000	7,000
Working Capital Sources	2,436	1,567	1,559	-4,448	1,844	1,536	-4,473	1,518	1,510	-4,501	1,489	1,541	1,278
Total Sources	14,411	15,270	13,883	8,073	20,042	19,237	17,715	25,849	24,962	24,015	32,087	31,857	247,401
Applications (Uses)													
Increase (Decrease) Receivables	7,416	4,141	2,415	2,512	2,611	2,717	2,825	2,938	3,056	3,178	3,304	3,438	40,551
Increase (Decrease) Unbilled Cost													
Increase (Decrease) Other Assets	4,660	-335	-329	-323	-318	-313	-307	-302	-298	-292	-288	-282	1,273
Total Applications	12,076	3,806	2,086	2,189	2,293	2,404	2,518	2,636	2,758	2,886	3,016	3,156	41,824
Increase (Decrease) in Cash	2,335	11,464	11,797	5,884	17,749	16,833	15,197	23,213	22,204	21,129	29,071	28,701	205,577
Net Balance Sheet Flow/Operations	2,335	11,464	11,797	5,884	17,749	16,833	15,197	23,213	22,204	21,129	29,071	28,701	205,577

Sales Force Coverage. Currently AMS is negotiating with a New York based sales representative to provide market coverage in the New York and New Jersey area. The area within a one-hour driving radius from Worcester will be covered by AMS directly. In the future, AMS hopes to bring its products to a national market.

Support Capabilities. As part of the purchase of a system from AMS, training and support are included in the package. Because support is such an important part of an effective system installation, only those areas which can be supported directly by AMS or a sales representative will be considered as target markets.

Concentration of Financial and Educational Institutions. The majority of target financial and educational institutions that AMS's products are aimed for are located within a one-hour driving time from Worcester or are located in the greater New York City area. The major cities that are accessible within an hour driving time from Worcester include Boston, Springfield, Providence and Hartford.

FINANCIALS

AMS was founded with a limited investment from each of the partners with no additional outside venture capital. The initial funding was spent on purchasing hardware for their own development work, establishing an office and providing a limited amount of working capital. Currently, each of the founders receives only a modest salary.

According to Clark, "The next few months are extremely important for AMS. At this point, there have only been a limited number of product sales. The bank project provided us with a needed source of cash inflow; however, that project is nearing completion and we must concentrate our efforts on generating future cash inflows." Based on some preliminary projections made by Paul Clark, AMS would like to obtain a $100,000 line of credit with a local bank in order to stabilize the business. According to Clark, "We would put the money toward software development, marketing, the purchase of additional hardware and the hiring of another programmer. Currently, Bob and I can generate more business than Charlie can handle by himself. We need at least one other advanced programmer and another junior programmer to do the routine stuff."

CASE 24

The Best Pizza in Town! Honest

As he neared age 60, James R. Eure began to reflect over his career and business involvement of the past ten years. In those brief years he had built a substantial financial empire in the pizza business—one any entrepreneur would be proud of. Building the empire, though, had had its costs as Eure had devoted long, hard hours in establishing the business. He wondered if maybe he shouldn't try to "enjoy life" a little more. He looked at the construction delays on his new pizza restaurants and considered the impact the energy crisis would have on the eating habits of Americans. Eure thought again about his naturally pessimistic nature.

As he reflected upon the direction he ought to take, Eure thought about the earning capacity of the business and the volume it was doing. Perhaps, he thought, he should look for a quality buyer—someone whom he thought would continue the business as it was intended to be. Should he decide to sell, he wondered about the asking price he should attempt to establish for the business. Then his mind flashed back to how it all got started.

"I guess I was born an entrepreneur," said James R. Eure, describing how he came to go into the pizza business. A product of the depression, Eure recounted how, even at an early age, he displayed signs of being a potential entrepreneur.

> During the depression, I would grow peanuts off the farm and sell them for five cents per bag, which was pretty good money in those days. When I graduated from high school in 1936, it was in the midst of the depression and there was little hope of going to school that year.
>
> My brother and I borrowed $75 and rented what had been an old drug store in this little drying up town in West Texas where we were living. With just $75 we put in what we called a confectionery—a little soda fountain, a little ice cream and school supplies, hamburgers and some drugs and sundry items.
>
> But, typically I suppose, I didn't know what I wanted to be so I drifted from that to selling magazines and taking my pay in chickens (which I had to catch myself).

After bouncing around awhile, Eure decided to go into the Air Force. He spent twenty-five years in the service and retired with the rank of Lt. Colonel in 1964. His career in the Air Force was spent as a communications electronics officer.

The research and written case information were presented at a Case Research Symposium and were evaluated by the Case Research Association's Editorial Board. This case was prepared by Ed D. Roach and Jack D. Eure, Jr. of Southwest Texas State University as a basis for class discussion. All rights reserved to the authors and the Case Research Association. Permission to use the case should be obtained from the Case Research Association.

HISTORY AND DEVELOPMENT

When Eure retired from the Air Force, by his own account, he did not have anything specific in mind. He was, however, determined that he would not let occupation determine where he would live. He wound up in Stephenville, Texas (population 7,000 with a small college), about 60 miles southwest of Ft. Worth. He and his wife built a new home with their own hands. Then he decided to think about going into the restaurant business.

> I knew that it was the one sure way for me to make some money. I knew that you can make money in any service business if you give good service. There is always a shortage of good things.

James R. Eure managed to scrape up enough money to open a "hole in the wall" in Stephenville. Before that time, no one had even tried to sell pizza there. Eure indicated that at the time it was generally believed that pizza could succeed only in larger cities. In addition to pizza, the restaurant served charburgers and submarine sandwiches. Eure called his new business venture the "Yucca Hut."

> The charburgers were a whole lot better than the pizza because I knew how to make a good hamburger. I didn't know the first thing about pizza. I figured that by the time I got opened I would learn how to make pizza. Sure enough I didn't learn. The cheese companies, the tomato companies, etc. would give you all sorts of recipes to make pizzas. None of them worked and none of them were good.

Despite his failure to invent "the perfect pizza" by opening day, Eure indicated that the people in this small town were so hungry for something besides chicken-fried steaks and Dairy Queen hamburgers that they "mobbed" him the first day. In fact, the response was so unexpectedly large that he had run completely out of food before 6:00.

> As bad as the pizza was, they even liked that. We had no idea of the people that were going to mob us. We weren't stocked, manned or equipped. We had good intentions and that's about all. So we actually shut down. We put up a sign on the reader board saying "Oops, we goofed!! We will reopen in a few days." This was my first experience and worst.

After this rather unexpected start in business, Eure set about to deal with the surprising level of demand. While on a trip to Dallas to look for a used walk-in cooler, he met a person who was to change the course of his business. This individual was in the pizza business, and Eure noted that he "had some sharp looking methods." Eure asked him to help him learn the pizza business. For a modest contract, essentially based on 2 percent of sales in two years, this pizza entrepreneur agreed to share some of his secrets with Eure and to furnish the spices to mix the pizza sauce. He showed Eure how he did everything except the spices.

"Yucca Hut" apparently was a tongue-twister for the people of Stephenville and after a few months, everyone had more or less changed the name to "Pizza Place." In the meantime, Eure had purchased the property next door with the anticipation of building a restaurant large enough to accommodate the ever-increasing demand for his pizza, charburgers and submarine sandwiches. He closed his restaurant on the last day of school and began preparation for building and moving to the property next door. With this restaurant, Eure started on a long journey of growth and innovation in the pizza business which was to change his life drastically.

THE PIZZA PLACE AND ATMOSPHERICS

By Eure's assessment, the Pizza Place was pretty innovative for the town and the time.

> That was my first venture into split-level dining and to my little privacy booths and to the showing of old movies. I found that people loved to go up and down steps. They seemed to go first to the available seating which was hardest to get to. I also found that people like lots of privacy. People are territorial. The more that a customer can stake out his territory and say "This is mine," the more comfortable he will be. So it's not so much privacy as the satisfying of the territorial urge.

Eure observed that the little privacy booths came to be one of his most important gimmicks. Eure believes that gimmicks are very, very important.

> You have to create a gimmick to create good advertising. You have something that generates your own advertising by making people talk about you. You have something different and they will go and say, "You should go to that place; they even have this." So you try to put something that is different in each one.

For the size of the town, Eure believed the Pizza Place to be very successful. However, in 1968, because of school problems of his handicapped son, he leased the business and moved to Austin, Texas.

FROM PIZZA PLACE TO MR. GATTI'S

After a brief and unsuccessful attempt at selling real estate, Eure decided that he would "back his ears and get back into the kitchen making pizza." So he picked a spot in Austin.

> I don't know why I picked it except that the rent was cheap. It was a location which many of my subsequent locations have been—dismal failures—but these are the locations you can get on your own terms. It was originally to be a U-Totem Store [a chain of small, convenience stores] and it was a different design. U-Totem had a 15-year lease for $300 per month and a Seven-Eleven had already opened around the corner. There was an informal arrangement between Seven-Eleven and U-Totem that they wouldn't get that close to each other. Anyway, U-Totem never opened the store, and I got it cheap.

Eure indicated that he knew immediately that the new pizza operation would be a success, but it was not an immediate, raging success. Within six months, however, traffic was very heavy. Too many people were coming in, in Eure's opinion, for the size of the restaurant. Therefore he started looking for a second location, more in the thought of an overflow to take some pressure off the first rather than to put in a second restaurant to "make lots of money." Number two was opened one year after the first Austin "Pizza Place." It was in a shopping center store front. The location had just failed as a pizza operation. About this time, Eure began to see, according to his accounts, the potential for growth and expansion. He was, however, determined to do it very cautiously and to do it only out of cash flow.

Only a year after the opening of Number 2, additional space was leased to double the seating capacity of this unit. Sales grew from first-month sales of $6,800 to better than $15,000 per month sales within a relatively short time span. Number 3 was soon opened opposite the main gate of the Air Force base located on the outskirts of Austin. It was housed in a building which had seen a succession of failures in its five-year life. Its immediate success prompted negotiations for a larger facility.

> Before Number 1 had been open a year we had three places opened. In opening Number 3 I discovered how easy it was to open a pizza restaurant. If you have a central commissary, you can put in an oven and some tables and chairs and some refrigerators. Then you send some people that you have taught how to put some pizzas together. You control the quality in the commissary.

Number 4 was opened 16 months after Number 1 opened. It also contained the first complete commissary, supplying other stores with preportioned and "idiot-proofed" supplies [see later for a discussion of the commissary concept]. Its sales increased steadily from a first-month of $7,000+ to a volume in excess of $24,000 per month.

Number 5 opened in August of 1971 in a large regional shopping center in Austin. Eure believes this to have been the first pizza operation in a shopping mall. Several of the better known chains now have mall locations. Eure noted that this store not only enjoyed a steady increase in sales but provided much publicity and recognition for other outlets. It quickly reached a volume of $20,000 per month in sales and was highly profitable.

Cautious expansion was continued in Austin. In addition, in September of 1972, San Marcos Number 1 [San Marcos is a small city of around 20,000 population located 28 miles south of Austin] was opened. Second month sales were $11,000 or approximately $10 per square foot.

Writing in 1973, James R. Eure observed that

> . . . this business has easily survived the transition from "Mom and Pop" operation. After taking accelerated depreciation and every permissible write-off for tax purposes, our net profit is thirteen percent. Our salaries and wages are equal to or above the industry average; salary and bonuses of the two top executives this year will total $84,000.

MR. GATTI'S

Eure indicated that the name "Pizza Place" was getting more and more confusing.

> I would call up somebody and say, "I'm 'so and so' with the Pizza Place." They would say, "Which one? The one over on Guadalupe." "No," I'd say, "We don't have one on Guadalupe. That's Shakey's." "The one on so and so?" "No. That's Pizza Inn."

So many people thought "pizza is pizza," and maybe some still do. That's one reason why we decided to change our name. I wanted to leave pizza completely out of the name. I wanted the name to be "Mr Gatti's," comma, and then in smaller print, "Pizza, etc." I was convinced the vagueness of the name "The Pizza Place" would hamper future expansion.

Eure explained that the name "Mr. Gatti's" was decided upon after reviewing names submitted by employees in a contest to rename "The Pizza Place." "Gatti" is the maiden name of Eure's wife.

MANAGEMENT AND ORGANIZATION

Upon reaching the decision to go into business in Austin, Eure decided to ask relatives to enter a partnership with him. His sister and his nephew agreed to a partnership arrangement. They remained a partnership until January 1971 when a Subchapter S corporation was formed by the original partners. At the same time, Jonathan D. Wilson[*], who had been accountant and operations manager, was permitted to buy stock equivalent to one-seventh ownership. The original three partners retained the remaining stock (two-sevenths each).

Four locations were in operation before the first full-time employee was hired. Eure used nothing but students and other part-time workers.

Nobody had any responsibility. I did all the scheduling and all the hiring. I didn't have a single person other than my wife who had any responsibility for the stores when they were not there. In other words, they came in and worked and then they went home.

As things began to get more and more complex with the addition of other locations, Eure decided that what he needed was someone whose main job would be to figure what the stores needed each morning and figure up how much the commissary should make that day to get ready for the various locations. From the product delivered to them this person should be able to calculate how much money should be in each restaurant.

We had Number 4 opened and this young man who had just graduated from the University of Texas with a degree in finance went to work for us. He had worked his way through college working at Shakey's. Prior to going to college he had been a naval pilot. He was a whiz at mathematics and accounting. He knew quite a bit about computers. He was very good for the business.

We were a good combination. He never questioned philosophies and policies. If he didn't think that everything I wanted to do was the greatest he did not let on. He backed me 100 percent in everything.

Eure began to give more and more decision-making authority to Wilson, although at first it was very difficult to part with the authority.

He had been given 95 percent of the decision making. But it took a long time for him to get to that level. Buying was the hardest thing for me to turn loose of. I wanted to

* Name disguised.

buy everything. If we needed a pound of nails, I wanted to buy them. I soon found that I couldn't do all these things, and I gradually turned bigger and bigger things over to other people once I gained confidence in them.

The second full-time employee hired had the responsibility of going around and collecting the money and making the deposits. Then as the number of restaurants increased, stronger and stronger people were hired to work in the headquarters office. Eure desired that one headquarters person should be held responsible for about four stores.

Eure recognized himself to be a stern taskmaster, a perfectionist. He indicated that one of his faults was to initially not have enough confidence in people.

> I'm too much of a perfectionist. I don't give people enough credit for being able to do the job initially. Once they prove themselves to me then I'm inclined to give them too much leeway. I know I'm a very difficult person to work for. However, I'm very good to my people. I pay them well. On the other hand, I've given lots of thought as to why, the way I pay people, I can't get the same kind of longevity and loyalty and dedication that [some people get].

Knowing that people find him difficult to work for, Eure indicated that he tried to isolate himself two or three steps from employees. He said, "I put one trusted person who can put up with me between me and the employees."

STRATEGIC DEVELOPMENT

Eure described his business as a well-above average pizza restaurant. Mr. Gatti's never did advertise cheap prices. Their prices, according to Eure, were known to be a little higher than the competition. As an above-average pizza restaurant, Mr. Gatti's sought to cater to a sophisticated, mature crowd.

> Steak and Ale and that type of restaurant is our competition. The better restaurants, the ones catering to a lively crowd, are our competition.

Eure indicated that he never was afraid of taking on the likes of Pizza Hut, Pizza Inn or Shakey's. He gave the following account as to why.

> I once knew a fellow who had a little hamburger joint. I had a friend who owned the property and he asked me to go by and visit with this fellow and kind of evaluate his operation. So I did. The significant thing that came out of the conversation was that he was going to turn out a good product, but he was in no way going to attempt to be as good as McDonald's.
>
> I think that the big boys are sitting ducks for any single, quality operator. I mean you are not going to hurt them but you can operate all around them. You must take advantage of them because you are a single owner-operated enterprise, and you should be able to do so much better in quality, size and product.
>
> So I don't think the little operator needs to fear the big boys if he knows this and applies it.

PRICE AND QUALITY

Gatti's, under Eure's direction, did not price according to competition. The best ingredients were figured into the product; the products were then priced to keep food costs around 20 to 25 per cent. No resistance to the company's pricing policies has been encountered according to Eure.

> At times we've had to raise the prices to maintain food costs and we have not hesitated one minute to do so. I did have a price-raising strategy. I leapfrogged prices. That is, I would never raise prices across the board. There were always some products that were dragging heels, some that were under-priced anyway. So those would go and become over-priced. I would leave some things alone. For example, one time I'd raise the price of small and leave the large and medium alone. Next time I would raise the medium and leave the small and large alone.

PRODUCT MIX

Eure stressed the philosophy of "keeping it simple" and doing what you do well. His strategy was not to try to satisfy everyone. The theme was to do what you do well and leave the rest up to somebody else. In the first Austin location, he started out with pizza only. He then added the submarine sandwich. However, he indicated that the submarine sandwich was not added until the pizza was established.

> I haven't really developed a new product since Stephenville that succeeded. We have never sold a dessert because we have not come up with anything that would not take away from our efforts to sell pizza.
>   When Shakey's a few years ago first came out with their big announcement that they were going to serve fried chicken and mojo potatoes I laughed and said that was wonderful. I said that if they can't make pizza they sure can make pizza and chicken. And I was right in thinking that it would make their pizza worse, their service worse, and their business worse. People who think they have got to grab whatever somebody wants to eat think they are missing out if they're not there to satisfy them. We want our customers to go somewhere else to eat chicken.

ADVERTISING AND PROMOTION

In the early phases of operation, Mr. Gatti's was so small that the only promotion was through "Welcome Wagon." After four locations opened, one-inch, one-column ads simply stating "Mr. Gatti's—South Congress" were run in the paper. These ads got larger as the number of stores grew. Seldom, however, was anything run in the newspaper except the logo and the name. The radio spots were kept as short as possible, never more than 30 seconds. Many of the spots were for 20 seconds. Eure indicated that he wanted the customers to be so happy that they weren't "bugged for a whole minute" that they were left with a good feeling toward Mr. Gatti's. In other words, Eure said, "Give our name and what we do and then we're gone."

Promotion coupons that we handed out never used a discount or "you buy one get one free" theme. The promotion coupons were always no strings attached. This was in keeping with the quality image which Mr. Gatti's tried to promote. "When we gave away beer, we would say 'come in for a free Michelob.'" That may cost us only one cent more.

OPERATIONS

James R. Eure expressed "a terrible fear of deterioration of products." This led him to develop two concepts which became a trademark of his operations. These two concepts were the "commissary principle" and "idiot-proofing" as he labeled it. Essentially this meant doing the important part of the food preparation in the back of the restaurant. Then the people who were to put the pizza together in the rush at night would have everything laid out for them. Eure observed that the important steps are cooking the sauce, mixing the dough and even chopping the onions.

Eure found that he could get stable, permanent-type help from people who were looking for daytime work. Then, he relied on students and part-time help to put the pizzas together and cook them at night.

As noted previously, Eure did all of the hiring, interviewing and scheduling for all the stores in the early history of Mr. Gatti's. At the stage where he had four restaurants, he bought a little pick-up and put a cooler on the back of it to haul the groceries. It was while doing this that Eure says that he "perfected the method of restocking the stores."

> The concept was to sell out. Theoretically, it meant they were not supposed to have a scrap of food left. But in practice they would have some left. The more perishable the item was the more often it was required that they run out of it. That was one of the biggest battles—overcoming the fear of running out of something. One of the most important things is running out of something often. If something has only a two-day shelf life and you are afraid of running out of it, you are going to be selling about 90 percent of the time a product which is on the tail-end of its shelf-life and is deteriorating. If you have enough before you run out, you have too much and today when you like to be serving a nice, fresh product you are still serving yesterday's leftovers.

Another thing which Eure believed had made his operation profitable was the fact that he had no losses on products. He required that stock would be maintained at a level that they would run out of one size of pizza crust in a store every night. The attempt was made to schedule the "run-out" just after the rush hour. Eure scheduled his salads to run out at some point during the supper rush. He maintains that no one was offended if they ran out of salads.

The commissary principle and "idiot-proofing" allowed Eure to manage his operations in such a way that the people in the stores had nothing to do with how much merchandise was brought to a particular restaurant. The employees in a restaurant had nothing to do with scheduling, etc. Therefore, Eure alleges, "there was nothing to manage."

Whoever got there first was the manager. Usually someone had already been there and put the stuff in the refrigerator for him before he got there.

Eventually, we started the commissary at three or four in the morning and we had restocking procedures laid out. With brief calculations, we would know how much to start producing to build the stores back up to a Monday, Tuesday, etc. stock level. It really worked quite well. It made each store identical. You could go into any one of them and get exactly the same quality food.

Eure's operations manager "knew computers." For a long time prior to the hiring of Wilson, Eure had been interested in computers and in "teaching a computer how to stock and control his restaurants." The type of control he ultimately was able to achieve he attributes to the use of computers and to Wilson's knowledge of how to use them.

FINANCE

Consolidated balance sheets and income statements are shown for Mr. Gatti's (Exhibits I and II).

Exhibit I. Consolidated Balance Sheets.

Financial Statement	1969	1970	1971	1972	1973	1974
Assets						
Current Assets						
Cash	$ 2,620	$7,395	$ 13,713	$ 28,253	$ 52,760	$ 39,879
Accounts Receivable	—	1,342	2,532	3,346	5,637	26,823
Inventories	951	8,471	12,385	14,251	37,734	106,003
Other Current Assets	—	—	23,392	4,639	25,507	24,288
Total Current Assets	3,571	17,208	52,022	50,489	96,131	196,993
Loans to Shareholders	—	—	—	—	5,000	9,609
Building and Other Fixed						
Deprec. Assets	12,199	68,196	129,349	331,791	586,828	732,370
Land	—	—	2,000	12,958	32,317	32,317
Other Assets	2,370	6,173	5,244	8,112	—	10,314
Total Assets	$18,140	$91,577	$188,615	$403,350	$745,783	$976,603
Liabilities and Capital						
Current Liabilities						
Accounts Payable	—	$25,551	$27,183	$ 65,658	$ 97,064	$354,362
Notes Payable in less than 1 Year	—	25,424	17,545	17,655	48,651	41,775
Other Current Liabilities			27,078	44,175	81,250	92,502
Total Current Liabilities	—	50,975	71,806	127,488	226,965	488,639
Notes Payable in more than 1 Year				73,986	125,275	179,471
Partner's Capital	$18,140	40,602	—	—	—	—
Capital Stock	—	—	64,890	64,890	69,890	66,640
Paid-in or Capital Surplus	—	—	22,730	22,730	48,840	37,270
Retained Earnings Unapprop.	—	—	(1,094)	(3,294)	44,457	73,443
Shareholders' Undistributed Taxable						
Income Previously Taxed	—	—	30,283	117,550	230,356	131,140
Total Liabilities & Shareholders' Equity	$18,140	$91,577	$188,615	$403,350	$745,783	$976,603

Exhibit II. Consolidated Profit and Loss Statements.

Financial Statement	1969	1970	1971	1972	1973	1974
Net Sales	$70,871	$313,981	$479,426	$1,050,791	$1,772,123	$2,952,548
Cost of Sales	20,166	92,240	124,760	271,644	480,201	805,077
Gross Profit	50,615	221,741	354,666	779,147	1,291,922	2,147,471
Total Expenses	39,405	193,371	302,641	658,982	1,119,581	1,875,042
Taxable Income	$11,210	$ 28,370	$ 52,025	$129,165	$ 172,341	$ 272,429

GROWING PAINS AND OTHER PROBLEMS

Reflecting upon the strains that almost any business experiences that has been successful enough to grow, James R. Eure rather philosophically observed:

> I know many businesses have been a booming success as a single operation and they make good money and have decided to expand. They didn't take into consideration that they and their families were doing a large share of the work. They often use the family automobile and their personal tools to fix things and they're able to do all the repairs. They use their garage for their warehouse. They do their own bookkeeping, etc. When they start growing suddenly they have to hire someone to do their maintenance and they have to buy a set of tools and a truck and rent a warehouse. They suddenly stop working and start spending. Labor and capital become strained.

In the specific case of Mr. Gatti's, Eure noted that he ultimately got up to eighteen stores. The pressures and the work resulting from such a large number of stores made Eure wonder about the desirability of continued expansion when he was already making more money than he "really wanted to spend." He remarked, however, how it was difficult to stop once the venture is started and some talent is attracted by the expansion.

> You are committed from then on. You can't stop because the minute you stop everybody will abandon ship. So I had this pressure of "You got to keep rolling." We had passed the "one-at-a-time, we conceive one, build it, finish it and open it" stage. At one time we had four big ones going, and this was at the time the recession [of 1973] hit. We had construction delays and we had other problems.

Among those "other problems" was the loss of Eure's key man, Jonathan Wilson. Along toward the latter part of his tenure with Mr. Gatti's, Wilson, according to Eure, began wanting to inject himself into advertising, design, etc. These were areas in which Eure felt himself particularly qualified in the case of Mr. Gatti's and even more that Wilson lacked proven expertise in.

> He came back from a restaurant show once with a whole bunch of propaganda. He wanted us to hand out buttons to everyone saying "Pizza Makes Me Passionate." Also, he wanted to hand out balloons for the kids. I said, "Jonathan, we are not Shakey's; we are not Pizza Hut. This is an important thing. A business has to decide who it is,

who are you, and constantly—everything you do—to work toward that image. We worked to be a quality place and we deliberately avoided gimmicks and give aways, promotions and the like such as balloons and things to encourage kids to come in."

When Wilson left he took two or three of Eure's top people with him. By the time Wilson decided to leave, Eure had got almost completely out of operations. He was leaving the "nuts and bolts" up to Wilson and concentrating upon the strategy and policy side of the business.

At this stage, Eure began to search for a replacement for Wilson. He ran ads in paid publications such as the *Wall Street Journal*. He got numerous applications from all over the country. He read through the piles of resumes and sorted out those which appeared to have any promise at all.

I'd get on the phone and talk to them. I'd go to Denver and then swing over to New York City and talk to them. . . . I'm a great pessimist. People who are looking for jobs—you don't want to hire them.

Eure indeed knew that it was hard to find good people. As he again thought of the construction delays, energy crisis, his advancing age and naturally pessimistic nature, maybe it was time to sell the business. But that would bring a whole new set of problems.

CASE 25

Kolapore, Inc.

In January 1986 Mr. Adriaan Demmers, president and sole employee of Kolapore, Inc., a firm based in Guelph, Ontario, specializing in the importation, processing and sale of high-quality souvenir spoons, was becoming increasingly frustrated with the pace at which his business was developing. Over a two-year period, Demmers had taken his idea of importing souvenir spoons from Holland to Canada to annual sales of nearly $30,000. He believed the potential existed for well over $100,000 in Canadian sales plus exports to the United States. This success to date had been a strain, however, on Demmers's limited financial resources and had not provided any compensation for the long hours invested. Demmers was beginning to question if he was ever going to have the major breakthrough which he had always believed was "just around the corner."

Recently, Demmers had accepted a full-time position with another firm in an unrelated business. While Demmers realized that he could continue to operate Kolapore, Inc., on a part-time basis, he wondered if he should "face reality" and simply fold up the business or try to sell it. Alternately, Demmers could not occasionally help wondering if he should be devoting himself full-time to Kolapore.

BACKGROUND

In February/March 1984 Demmers conducted a feasibility study of starting a business to market souvenir spoons. His idea was to offer a high-quality product depicting landmarks, historic buildings and other unique symbols of the area in which the spoons were to be sold.

There were numerous spoons on the market, but most tended to be for Canada or Ontario rather than local sites of interest and were generally poorly made and not visually appealing. There were few quality spoons, and the ones that did exist were priced in the $15–$40 range.

Sources of spoons were examined and quotations were received from firms in Canada, the United States and the Netherlands (Holland). The search process for a country from which to source the spoons was a limited one and was settled quickly, thanks to Demmers's Dutch heritage, the existence of a well-recognized group of silversmiths in Schoonhoven, plus a particular company which already had over 40 Canadian-specific dies and lower prices.

This case was prepared by Professor Paul W. Beamish, School of Business Administration, University of Western Ontario. Copyright © 1986 by Paul W. Beamish.

Demmers felt the key factors for success were good quality product, using designs of local landmarks and an eye-catching display. He felt displays should be located in a prominent position in retail stores because souvenir spoons are often bought on impulse.

As part of his feasibility study, Demmers conducted a market analysis (including customer and retailer surveys), a competitive analysis (both manufacturers and distributors) and developed an import plan, marketing plan and financial projections (including projected breakeven and cash flows). Excerpts from this study follow.

1. Market Analysis

The market for souvenir spoons consists of several overlapping groups—primarily tourists and the gift market. There are also groups interested in spoons for more specialized purposes such as church groups, service clubs, associations and others. These are very specialized and for special occasions.

A random telephone survey conducted in March 1984 of 50 people in Guelph revealed that 78 percent owned souvenir spoons. Forty-six percent of those people had purchased the spoons themselves, while 54 percent had received them as gifts. In total, almost 25 percent of the people in the sample collected souvenir spoons or had a rack on which to hang them. Retailers indicated that sales occurred primarily during the summer months and at Christmas time. Twelve retail outlets were visited to obtain information regarding quality, sales and prices. Background on a selection of these retailers is summarized in Appendix 1.

There was a high awareness of souvenir spoons in the market, but the product quality was generally at the low end of the market. For example, rough edges on the bowls were common, and the crests on the spoons were often crooked. In fact, one manufacturer's spoon had a picture of Kitchener City Hall which was out of focus and off-center. (Terms concerning souvenir spoons are explained in Appendix 2.)

A limited variety of spoons was often available, and few of the spoons were of local points of interest even though these were the spoons that were most in demand. One retailer noted that of a total of 140 spoons sold in 1983, 106 were one variety, a spoon with a relief design in plastic of a Conestoga wagon. This was the only unique spoon Demmers found in the area "other than the cheap picture spoons."

There was no advertising for souvenir spoons due to the nature of the product and the lack of identification with a particular brand.

Souvenir spoons appeared to be a low priority in many producing companies, with little marketing effort made to push the products. Even the packaging was of poor quality; often, boxes were not supplied for gift wrapping.

The sale of spoons was viewed as seasonal by some retailers. Point-of-purchase displays were removed once the summer rush was over in many instances.

Spoons were not prominently displayed in most stores, yet they are largely an impulse item. In several stores they were kept in drawers and only taken out when requested.

2. Competitive Analysis

Souvenir spoons essentially serve two customer functions: as gifts or commemoratives. They can be used as gifts for family, friends or special occasions such as Christmas. They can also serve as a commemorative token of having visited somewhere or for a special anniversary (for example, The Province of Ontario's 200th anniversary). They can be either functional (used for coffee or teaspoons) or may be used for decorative purposes (hung in a spoon rack or put in a cabinet).

Competition comes from all other gift items and all other souvenir items in approximately the same price range.

Demmers identified 11 companies that distributed souvenir spoons in the Southwestern Ontario area and gathered what data he could—much of it anecdotal—on each. This process had provided encouragement for Demmers to proceed. Background on these suppliers is summarized in Appendix 3.

Southwestern Ontario contained a number of large urban areas including Toronto (over 2 million people), Hamilton/Burlington, Kitchener/Waterloo and London with over 300,000 people in each, plus many smaller cities such as Guelph. Guelph was located roughly in the centre of the triangle formed by Toronto, Waterloo and Burlington and was within an hour's drive of each.

3. Importing

To import goods into Canada on a regular basis in amounts over $800, an importer number was required. This was available from Revenue Canada, Customs and Excise. Requirements for customs were an advise notice from the shipper and a customs invoice. These were available in office supply stores. A customs tariff number and commodity code were also required to complete the customs B3 form.

Souvenir spoons of either sterling silver or silver plate were listed in the customs tariff under number 42902-1. The Netherlands has Most Favoured Nation status, so the duty was 20.3 percent. On top of the cost of the merchandise (excluding transportation and insurance but including duty), there was a further 10 percent excise tax and 10 percent federal sales tax.

A customs broker could be hired to look after the clearing of goods through customs. Rates were approximately $41 plus $3.60 for every thousand dollars of value, duty included.

Insurance on a shipment of less than $10,000 costs a fixed fee of about $150 with insurance brokers. This can be reduced if insurance is taken on a yearly basis, based on the expected value of imports over the year. Freight forwarders charge approximately $2.00 per kilo regardless of the total weight of the shipment.

The importing can be easily handled without help on small shipments such as spoons. The product can be sent by airmail and insured with the post office. It can also be sent to a small city like Guelph rather than Toronto, and this avoids the busy Toronto customs office and possible delays of several days. The customs office in Guelph can easily clear the goods the same day they arrive.

Product

The proposed souvenir spoons would be a high-quality product with detailed dies made to give them a relief design far superior to any competitive spoons (except for those retailing in the $30 range). These spoons are available in silver plate and alpacca which makes them similar to jewellery.

Designs would be of specific points of interest. In the Kitchener-Waterloo area, for example, possible subjects would include the Seagram Museum, Schneider House, Doon Pioneer Village, university crests and city crests. Kitchener-Waterloo would be printed under the picture, also in relief in the metal, along with the title of the particular picture.

4. Marketing Plan

See Figure 1.

Price Points

$2.25 — Metropolitan Supplies—nickel-plated.

$4.50–$6.00 — Breadner Manufacturing—rhodium-plated and silver-plated.
Candis Enterprises.
Gazelle Importers.

$7.00–$8.00 — Oneida or Commemorative—simple designs with engraved insignia.
Appear to be made of a silver alloy.

$10.00–$14.00 — Proposed price range for retail.
—Quality comparable to $30.00 spoons, but silver content is lower.
—Detailed designs of local landmarks.
—Variety of 6–10 spoons in each market.

$30.00 and up — Breadner
—Sterling silver.
—Fine workmanship.
—Very limited variety of designs.

Place

Because souvenir spoons are purchased on impulse, locations with high traffic are essential. Jewellery stores and gift stores in malls and tourist areas are probably most suitable in this respect.

Due to the price range proposed and the quality of the merchandise, the quality and image of the store has to be appropriate. This would eliminate discount jewellery stores and cheap souvenir shops for the aforementioned reasons. Secondly, it would not please higher-end retailers if the same spoons were sold for less in the same area and would likely restrict distribution in the appropriate channels.

Jewellery stores are perceived by many people as selling expensive, luxury items that are not part of one's everyday needs. For this reason it would be helpful for these stores to have a window display.

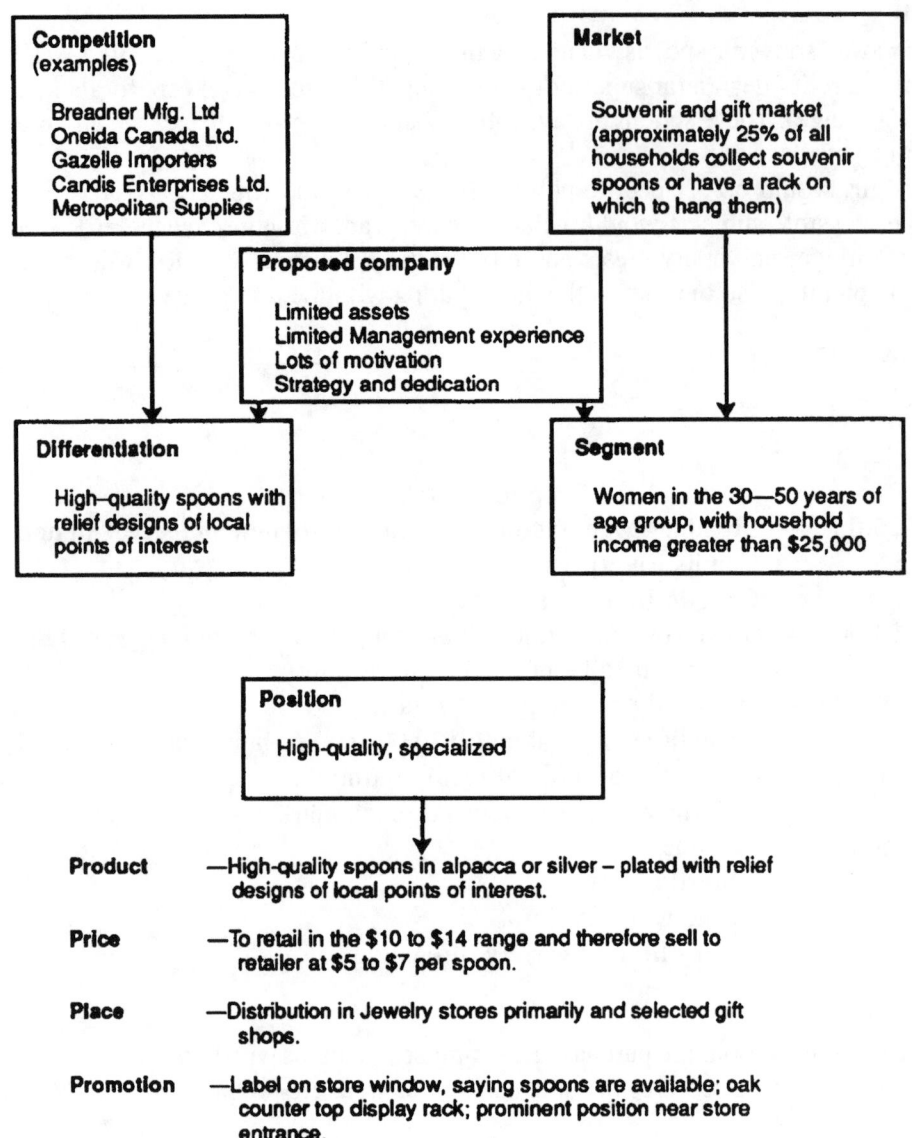

Figure 1.

Promotion

Each retail location will carry a minimum product line of six varieties of spoons: one with a Canadian theme, one with a provincial theme, and at least four spoons with designs of local landmarks or points of interest.

Table 1. Forecast variable costs and margins of spoons.

	Alpacca	Silver Plate
Quote by Dutch manufacturer (Zilverfabriek) (in guilders) 1 guilder = $.43 Cdn.	2.20 guilders	3.10 guilders
Factory cost in $Cdn.	$0.95	$1.33
Duty @ 20.3 percent	.19	.27
Cost, duty included	$1.14	$1.60
Federal sales tax @ 9 percent	.10	.14
Federal excise tax @ 10 percent	.11	.16
Freight and insurance	.10	.10
Cost	$1.45	$2.00
Contribution margin	$2.05 to $3.55	$1.50 to $3.00
Cost to retailer	3.50 to 5.00	3.50 to 5.00
Retailer markup	3.50 to 5.00	3.50 to 5.00
Retail price	7.00 to 10.00*	7.00 to 10.00

*These prices are lower than originally forecast due to Demmers's recognition that a $10 to $14 retail price was too high.

The packaging will be suitable for gift wrapping, so will likely consist of a small box with a clear plastic cover.

Each retail location will have an oak countertop display rack. There will be a relatively high cost to the displays initially, but they will attract attention and convey the quality of the spoons. Different sizes can be made depending on the number of spoons for a particular market.

Because souvenir spoons are primarily an impulse purchase, location in the store is important and should be near the entrance or have a window display. This is something which can be controlled only by persuading the retailer that this would increase the turnover and consequently his profits.

5. Finance

Contribution margin per spoon has been calculated using the most conservative numbers and at a wholesale price of $3.50. Typically, retailers would mark prices up by 100 percent (see Table 1). The contribution margins worked out to $2.05 on alpacca spoons and $1.50 on silver-plated spoons.

The breakeven, assuming costs of $25,250 per year and a contribution margin of $2.05, would be sales volume of 12,317 spoons with sales value of $43,110 (see Table 2). Assuming the spoons would be introduced in the Toronto market and distribution obtained in 100 retail locations, this means sales of 124 spoons per store.

Upon graduating from a university business school in April 1984, Demmers planned to devote his efforts to Kolapore. He felt that while there could be a short-term financial drain, his cash balance would be positive at the end of the second month of operation (see Table 3).

Table 2. Forecast breakeven.

Distribution costs (transportation)	$ 4,000
Rent expense (work from home)	—
Salary	15,000
Office supply costs (including telephone)	1,000
Inventory costs	1,000
Merchandising expenses (displays and boxes)	3,000
Investment in dies (10 @ $125 each)	1,250
Total fixed costs	$25,250
$25,250/$1.50 = 16,833 spoons	
$25,250/$2.05 = 12,317 spoons	
$25,250/$3.00 = 8,416 spoons	

Table 3. Forecast cash flow, May–August 1984.

	May	June	July	August
Cash	$3,000	$(750)	$1,000	$7,500
Disbursements:				
Moulds	1,250	—	—	—
Purchases	—	7,250	—	7,250
Promotion expenses	2,000	1,000	—	—
Car expenses	500	500	500	500
Total disbursements	3,750	8,750	500	7,750
Net cash	(750)	(9,500)	500	(250)
Receipts:				
Accounts receivable	—	10,500	7,000	10,500
Cash balance (to be borrowed)	$(750)	$ 1,000	$7,500	$10,250
Terms n/30.				

SUBSEQUENT EVENTS

Soon after graduating in April, it became clear to Demmers that Kolapore was not going to realize forecast sales of $28,000 by September 1984. Due to delays in getting shipments from Holland and difficulty in obtaining distribution in Canada, sales were only $1,830 over the summer. A number of assumptions in the original feasibility study (as described in the first section) had proven incorrect:

1. The number of dies ultimately required (each of which costs $125) was not going to be 10 but closer to 50.
2. The federal sales tax rate had increased to 10 percent from 9 percent.
3. Duty was payable on the dies themselves as well as on the spoons at the rate of 20.3 percent excise tax plus federal sales tax.
4. Delivery time for new dies was closer to six months than the forecast 10–12 weeks (the artist had been ill for several months). Several orders were cancelled during this period as a result.
5. Packaging costs per spoon were closer to 32 cents per unit than the estimated 10 cents.
6. Distribution had been difficult because the large chain stores which dominated the market all had established suppliers.

Table 4. Actual cash flow, 1984.

	May	June	July	August
Cash	$2,600	$1,000	$ 950	$ 530
Disbursements:				
Purchases	1,000	550	870	1,460
Expenses	1,000	80	300	300
Total disbursements	2,000	630	1,170	1,760
Net cash	600	370	(220)	(1,230)
Receipts:				
Accounts receivable	400	580	750	1,100
Cash balance	$1,000	$950	530	$ (130)

7. The target market was not nearly as upscale as originally envisioned. Although Kolapore's spoons were readily identifiable as being of superior quality, most customers would only pay a maximum of $7–$8 retail for any spoon. Demmers had estimated the total Canadian souvenir spoon market at about $1.5 million annually. Within that, a very small portion was for sterling silver (where Demmers could not compete), about $450,000 was at the $7 retail price point where Demmers was selling (some of his competitors were promoting similar or poorer-quality spoons at the same price), with the balance of the market reserved for lower-priced/lower-quality spoons.

The goal of 100 stores by September 1984 was still a long way off.

Demmers had also discovered that the chain stores plan all their buying from 6 to 12 months in advance. Because many of the spoons he had designed did not arrive until September 1984, this meant that he had missed much of the tourist season (and nearly all of the Christmas market).

On the positive side, the Dutch guilder had depreciated relative to the Canadian dollar. In September 1984 it cost Canadian $0.39 for 1 guilder rather than $0.43 as forecast. In addition, delivery times for spoons from existing dies required three to four weeks rather than the expected four to six weeks, and the cost of display cases was only about $16.00 each. These were made of plastic rather than the originally envisioned oak.

Although Kolapore was showing a negative cash balance at the end of August 1984 (see Table 4), sales began to improve in September (see Table 5), growing to nearly $16,000 by the end of the first full year of operation (see Tables 6 and 7 for financial statements). A financial loss of $1,800 was incurred for the first year of operation, and this took no account of the countless hours Demmers had invested. Since the business was not yet self-supporting, in September 1984 Demmers had begun to look for other sources of income.

Between September 1984 and January 1986 Demmers worked for five months in a fibreglass factory, acquired a house in Guelph in which he was able to live and to rent out rooms, sold Bruce Trail calendars on a commission basis, worked at organizing and selling several ski tours (which did not take place) and opened an ice-cream store in a regional resort area (Wasaga Beach). Due to a low volume of traffic, this latter venture in the summer of 1985 resulted in an $8,000 loss. In the fall of 1985 Demmers accepted a position as production manager for a weekly newspaper in Guelph.

Table 5. Actual sales, 1984–1985.

May	$ 400
June	580
July	750
August	1,100
September	2,600
October	2,540
November	1,500
December	1,400
January–March	4,923

Table 6. Kolapore Inc. Balance sheet as at March 31, 1985 (Unaudited—See Notice to Reader).

Assets

Current assets:	
Cash	$1,708
Accounts receivable	1,763
Inventory	2,873
Total current assets	6,344
Incorporation expense	466
Total assets	$6,810

Liabilities

Current liabilities:	
Accounts payable and accruals	$ 268
Due to shareholder (note 2)	8,342
Total liabilities	8,610

Shareholders' Equity

Retained earnings (deficit)	(1,800)
Total liabilities and shareholders' equity	$6,810

Notice to reader: These financial statements have been compiled solely for tax purposes. I have not audited, reviewed or otherwise attempted to verify their accuracy or completeness.

Guelph, Ontario   Chartered Accountant
May 2, 1985

By this time, Demmers was selling direct to retailers in 20 towns and cities in Ontario and through five chains: Simpson's and United Cigar Stores and, to a much smaller extent, Eaton's, Birks and Best Wishes. Other chains such as The Bay, Sears and Woolco had been approached but so far without success. Demmers was hoping to find the time so that he could approach the buyers at K mart, Zeller's, Consumer's Distributing, Robinson's, Woodwards and others.

Kolapore spoons were sold in Simpson's stores from Windsor, Ontario, to Halifax, Nova Scotia and in 18 United Cigar Store locations in southern Ontario. Four months after Demmers's first delivery to the chain outlets in the summer of 1985, about half the stores were sold out of Kolapore spoons. Neither chain would reorder stock part way through the year.

Table 7. Kolapore Inc. Statement of income year ended March 31, 1985 (Unaudited—See Notice to Reader).

Sales	$15,793
Cost of sales:	
Inventory at beginning of year	—
Purchases	8,453
Duty and freight	2,288
Dies	3,034
	13,775
Less: Inventory at end of year	2,873
Cost of sales	10,902
Gross profit	4,891
Expenses:	
Office	657
Samples	582
Auto expenses	1,137
Car allowance	3,900
Bank interest and charges	139
Advertising	26
Accounting	250
Total expenses	6,691
Net profit (loss) for the year	$(1,800)

Notes: 1.   Significant accounting policies:

KOLAPORE INC. is a company incorporated under the laws of Ontario on April 6, 1984, and is primarily engaged in the importing and selling of souvenir spoons. The accounting policies are in accordance with generally accepted accounting principles.

Inventory is valued at lower of cost or net realizable value.

Incorporation expense is not amortized.

2.   Due to shareholder is noninterest bearing and payable on demand.

To sell direct in some of the smaller cities, Demmers's practice had been to drive or walk through the main shopping areas, stopping at jewellery stores or other likely retail outlets. If he was unable to meet with the store owner, he would usually leave a sample and a letter with some information (see Exhibit 1 for a copy of the letter). Demmers's experience had been that unless he personally met with the right person—which sometimes took three or more visits—no sales would occur. When he was able to meet with the owner, his success rate was over 70 percent. To sell direct in larger centres such as Toronto (where he had 40 customers), Demmers had focused his efforts on hotel gift shops. Having established these customers, he could now visit all 40 customers in Toronto personally in two to three days.

By year-end, Demmers had access to a pool of 89 Canadian-specific dies. Demmers's supplier in Holland had 46 dies in stock which another Canadian from Western Canada had had designed. Spoons based on these dies were no longer being sold anywhere as far as Demmers could tell.

Exhibit 1. Kolapore, Inc., letter of introduction.

Kolapore, Inc.
P.O. Box 361
Guelph, Ontario
N1H 6K5

Dear

    Kolapore, Inc., would like to offer you the opportunity to have your own design on a spoon made up in metal relief, for example, a logo, code of arms, crest, building or whatever you would like.

    There is always a large market for souvenir spoons of unique design and high quality. Kolapore Collection Spoons fit this category extremely well and are priced very competitively.

    The spoons are available in silver plate at $3.50 per spoon. This price includes a gift box, federal sales tax and shipping.

    The minimum order is 100 spoons to get a new design made up, and there is also a one-time die charge of $125.00 to help off set the cost of making the new die. Delivery time is approximately three months if a die has to be made up; subsequent orders will take four to six weeks.

    The dies for Kolapore Collection Spoons are made by master craftsmen in Schoonhoven, Holland, the silversmith capital of the world. The spoons themselves are made in Canada. As a result, the quality of the spoons is exceptional and recognized by the consumer at a glance.

    I trust that this is sufficient information. I look forward to hearing from you. If you have any questions or concerns, please don't hesitate to contact me. Thank you for your time and consideration.

Sincerely,

Adriaan Demmers
President

For the most part Demmers, was selling spoons based on his own designs. (For those spoons which Demmers had had designed, he had exclusive rights in Canada). In less than two years he had 43 more dies made up (see Exhibit 2 for a complete list). In some cases Demmers had asked a particular company/group to pay the cost of the dies; in others, such as for universities, he had built the die cost into his price for the first shipment; while in others he had simply gone ahead on his own with the hope that he could achieve sufficient sales to justify the investment.

There was a wide variability in the sales level associated with each spoon. Sales from his best-seller—the Toronto skyline (which depicted major buildings and the CN Tower)—were about 1,000 spoons a year. Demmers's second best selling spoon in Toronto was 300 units of Casa Loma. (For a list of some of the major tourist sites in Toronto, see Exhibit 3). This spoon had quickly sold out on site in 10 days. (However the buyer had been unwilling to order more part way through the year). Spoons with other Toronto designs were selling less than 50 units a year.

Table 8. Kolapore Inc. Statement of income eight months* ending November 30, 1985 (Unaudited).

Sales	$21,000
Cost of sales:	
Inventory at beginning of year	2,873
Purchases	12,000
Duty and freight	3,500
Dies	1,950
	20,323
Less: Inventory at end of year	5,000
Cost of sales	15,323
Gross profit	5,677
Expenses	6,500
Net profit (loss) for the year to date	$ (823)

*Annual sales expected to be $30,000.

By December 1985 inventories had increased and Kolapore, Inc., was still showing a small loss (see Table 8). Any gains from changes in the rate of import duty on spoons (20.3 percent in 1984 to 18.4 percent in 1986) had been negated by changes in federal sales tax (9 percent in 1984 to 11 percent in 1986) and exchange rates. The fluctuating Dutch guilder was at a two-year high relative to the Canadian dollar. From a March 1984 value of Cdn. $0.43, the guilder had declined to $0.36 in February 1985 and climbed to $0.50 by December 1985. Partially due to these exchange fluctuations, during the past eight months Demmers had also arranged for the spoons to be silver plated at a cost of 40 cents each in Ontario. This had resulted in a saving of 15 cents a spoon (which varied with the exchange rate). More significantly, because many spoons were purchased as souvenirs of Canada, by adding sufficient value by silver plating in Canada, the imported product no longer had to be legally stamped, "Made in Holland." In fact, the packaging could now be marked "Made in Canada." Demmers was quite optimistic regarding the implications of this change because a number of potential store buyers had rejected his line because it did not say "Made in Canada." Demmers's supplier was upset, however, with the change.

Exhibit 2. Kolapore collection spoons—designs available.

Canada
Deer
Elk
Caribou
Cougar
Mountain goat
Moose
Bighorn sheep
Grizzly bear
Salmon
Coast Indian
Indian
Coat of arms
Mountie
Maple leaf
Province of Ontario
✓ Trillium
✓ Windsor, Ambassador Bridge
✓ Sarnia, Bluewater Bridge
✓ Chatham, St. Joseph's Church
✓ London, Storybook Gardens
✓ Woodstock, Old Town Hall
✓ Stratford, swan
✓ Kitchener, Schneider Haus
✓ Waterloo, The Seagram Museum
✓ Waterloo County, Mennonite horse and buggy
✓ Elora, Mill Street
✓ Guelph, Church of our Lady
✓ Guelph, Credit Union
✓ Guelph, St. Joseph's Hospital
✓ Kitchener-Waterloo, Oktoberfest
✓ Hamilton, Dundurn Castle
✓ St. Catharines, Old Court House
✓ Niagara Falls, Falls, Brock Monument and Maid of the Mist
✓ Acton, Leathertown (hide with buildings)
✓ Toronto, skyline
✓ Toronto, City Hall
✓ Toronto, St. Lawrence Hall
✓ Toronto, Casa Loma
✓ Kingston, City Hall
✓ Ottawa, Parliament buildings
✓ Collingwood, Town Hall
✓ Owen Sound, City crest
University and community college crests/coats of arms
✓ Wilfrid Laurier
✓ Waterloo
✓ Carleton

✓ Guelph
✓ York
✓ Western
✓ Windsor
✓ McMaster
✓ Brock
✓ Fanshawe
✓ Humber
Province of Quebec
Montreal, skyline
Montreal, Olympic Stadium
Province of Nova Scotia
Bluenose (schooner)
Yukon Territory
Coat of arms
Gold panner
Province of British Columbia
Coat of arms
Prince George
Victoria, Parliament buildings
Victoria, lamp post
Victoria, Empress Hotel
Nanaimo, Bastion
Dogwood (flower)
Totem pole
Kermode Terrace
Smithers
Northlander Rogers Pass, bear
Northlander Rogers Pass, house
Kelowna, The Ogopogo
Okanagan, The Ogopogo
Vancouver, Grouse Mountain/skyride/chalet
Vancouver, Grouse Mountain skyride
Vancouver, Grouse Mountain skyride/cabin
Vancouver, Cleveland Dam
Vancouver, The Lions
Vancouver, The Lions Gate Bridge
Province of Alberta
Banff, Mount Norquay
Banff, Mount Rundle
Banff, Banff Springs Hotel
Calgary, bronco rider
Edmonton, Klondike Mike
Wild Rose (flower)
Oil derrick
Jasper
Jasper sky tram

Note: Check mark denotes those made up on Demmers's initiative.

Exhibit 3. Some major tourist sites in Toronto.

1. Metro Zoo
2. CN Tower
3. Casa Loma
4. Royal Ontario Museum (ROM)
5. Black Creek Pioneer Village
6. Art Gallery of Ontario (AGO)
7. Canada's Wonderland
8. Ontario Place
9. The Ontario Science Centre

Meanwhile, the feedback he was receiving from many of his customers was positive—in most cases they were selling more of his spoons than any other brand. Some customers, in fact, had enquired about other products. Since he had so far not experienced any competitive reactions to his spoons, Demmers was thinking of investigating the possibility of adding ashtrays, letter openers, key chains, lapel pins and bottle openers to the product line in 1986—if he stayed in business. Each one of these products could have a crest attached to it. These crests would be the same as those used on the spoons and would thus utilize the dies to a greater extent. The landed costs per metal crest from the same supplier would be 85 cents. Demmers contemplated attaching these crests himself onto products supplied by Canadian manufacturers. However, initial investigations had revealed no obvious economical second product line.

Demmers also planned to phase out alpacca imports—all products would now be silver plated. In fact, Demmers was also wondering if he should acquire the equipment and materials in order to do this silver plating and polishing himself.

With no lack of ideas, many of the original frustrations nonetheless remained. The buyers at major chains such as Eaton's and Simpson's had changed once again, and because they did not use an automatic reorder system, new appointments had to be arranged. This was as difficult as ever. Also, Demmers still had not been able to draw anything from the firm for his efforts. These factors, coupled with his lack of cash and the demands of his new full-time position, had left Demmers uncertain as to what he should do next. With the spring buying season approaching—when Demmers would normally visit potential buyers—he realized that his decision regarding the future of Kolapore could not be postponed much longer.

APPENDIX 1. SURVEY OF SPOONS CARRIED BY LOCAL RETAILERS IN GUELPH AND KITCHENER-WATERLOO REGION

- A Taste of Europe—Delicatessen & Gift Store—Guelph Eaton Centre
  - A selection of spoons from Holland with Dutch designs.
  - One with the Canadian coat of arms which looked good.
  - Rhodium-plated spoons—$5.98 per spoon.
  - Well displayed at front of store.
- Eaton's—Guelph Eaton Centre
  - Breadner spoons with maple leaf or Canadian flag and "Guelph" stamped in the bowl.
  - Rhodium-plated—$4.98.
  - No display and hard to find.
- Pequenot Jewellers—Wyndham Street, Guelph
  - Carry Candis spoons, which look cheap and do not sell very well.
  - $4.98.
  - Poorly displayed.
- Smith & Son, Jewellers—Wyndham Street, Guelph
  - Do not carry souvenir spoons because they are not in line with the store's image. They often get requests for them.
- Franks Jewellers—King Street, Waterloo
  - Carry Breadner spoons with the Waterloo coat of arms.
  - Rhodium-plated spoons—$4.50 per spoon.
  - Not on display but kept in drawer.
  - Sell less than 12 per year.
- Copper Creek—Waterloo Square Mall, Waterloo
  - Candis spoons—$5.00 each
- Birks—King Centre, Kitchener
  - Carry Oneida and Breadner spoons.
  - Rhodium-plated spoons for $5.98.
  - Oneida spoons were $8.95 and looked like a silver alloy.
  - Sterling silver Breadner spoons for $31.95.
  - Displayed in a spoon rack, looked good.
  - Birks regency spoons with crest of each province, $12.50.
- Eaton's—Market Square, Kitchener
  - Breadner spoons, two types for Canada only.
  - Rhodium-plated—$4.98 each.
- Young's Jewellers—King Street, Kitchener
  - Rhodium-plated Breadner spoons, $4.50 each.

- Walters Jewellers
  - Against chain policy to carry souvenir spoons because of poor quality and low turnover.
- Peoples Jewellers
  - Do not carry souvenir spoons.
- Engels Gift Shop—King Street, Kitchener
  - Carry Breadner, Oneida, Gazelle, and Metropolitan.
  - Altogether about 20 varieties.
  - Well displayed near entrance of store; prices range from $2.25 for Metropolitan spoons to $7.98 for Oneida spoons.
  - Saleslady said they sell hundreds every year, mostly in the summer.

APPENDIX 2. TERMS CONCERNING SOUVENIR SPOONS

Crest
—Emblem, either metal, plastic or enamel, that is affixed to a standard spoon.

Picture spoon
—Spoon with a picture under plastic which is heat moulded to the spoon.

Relief design
—Spoon with an engraving or picture which is moulded into the metal of the spoon.

Enamel
—Opaque substance similar to glass in composition.

Plated
—Thin layer of metal put on by electrolysis.

Rhodium-plated
—Shiny "jeweller's metal" which does not tarnish (no silver content).

Silver-plated
—Silver covering on another metal (such as steel).

Sterling silver
—Alloy of 92.5 percent silver and 8.5 percent copper, nickel and zinc.

Alpacca
—Alloy of 82 percent copper and 18 percent nickel.

APPENDIX 3. SOUVENIR SPOON SUPPLIERS

Breadner Manufacturing Ltd. Breadner appears to have national market distribution and includes two major retailers, Birks and Eaton's. According to some of the store managers interviewed, their sales of souvenir spoons in each location was low. Several retailers also expressed dissatisfaction with the Breadner line because of the slow turnover. Typically, there was a basic design for the spoon which did not change except for a different crest glued on for the different locale.

Breadner has been in the jewellery business since 1900 and has a plant in Hull, Quebec. They manufacture to order various types of pins, medals and advertising specialties but advised Demmers that in general they use their entire output of souvenir spoons for their own sales.

They have many varieties of spoons in their catalogue and an established distribution system across the country. Demmers recognized the possibility that they could upgrade their selection in a short time span to compete directly with his intended selection of spoons.

Typical retail prices for Breadner spoons were $4.50 and up, the cost to the retailer being $2.25 and up. Breadner's high-end sterling silver spoons were available at Birks, for $31.95, with the cost to Birks estimated at about $15.00 per spoon. Both rhodium-plated and silver-plated spoons were available, but rhodium-plated was more common. Silver-plated spoons were not carried.

Candis Enterprises Ltd. Candis is located in Willowdale, Ontario. This company has good distribution in gift shops (for example, the 650-outlet United Cigar Store Chain) and in some jewellery stores. They have a line of rhodium-plated spoons marketed under the MaR-VEL name and silver-plated spoons under the Candis name.

Their strategy appears to be one of putting out a large variety of spoons for each place in which they sell. However, the quality seems to be toward the low end: many of the spoons have rough edges on the bowls and there is no detail in the dies.

Wholesale cost ranges from $2.00 per spoon for a rhodium-plated picture spoon to $3.25 for a silver-plated spoon with a five-colour ceramic crest.

Metropolitan Supplies Ltd. Metropolitan Supplies is located in Toronto and distributes its goods across Canada primarily to gift shops and souvenir shops in tourist areas. This company deals with all sorts of souvenirs and novelty items. They have a large selection of spoons, each of which can be crested to suit the buyer. The quality of the spoons is at the low end. Prices range from $0.55 per spoon (wholesale) for iron and nickel-plated spoons to $2.00 per spoon for silver-plated spoons.

Gazelle Importers and Distributors. Gazelle Importers and Distributors is located in Grimsby, Ontario. They previously imported spoons from Holland but later manufactured in Ontario. Their spoons are sold under the Gazelle name. They retail for $5.95 and, therefore, presumably cost the retailer about $3.00. Spoons have designs for Ontario and Canada but nothing local. Quality seems about the same as Breadner's less-expensive line.

Oneida Canada Ltd. Oneida is located in Niagara Falls, Ontario, and is a division of Oneida Ltd. in the United States. The Niagara Falls plant manufactures stainless steel and silverplate flatware. Their product is distributed in several jewellery stores including Birks and gift shops. The quality is better than any other spoons except for Breadner's sterling spoons. Prices are also somewhat higher with a retail price of $7.98, giving a probable cost to the retailer of about $4.00 per spoon. There is little variety. All spoons come in one design with a different engraving in the top of the spoon.

Commemorative Spoons. This firm is located in Ottawa and sells spoons in the $6.95–$8.95 range. They have three basic designs (supplied by Oneida). They have large accounts with Simpson's and Cara and frequently deal with clubs for whom they make up special spoons for fund-raising.

Hunnisett and Edmunds. This is a distribution company which specializes in selling to card shops and variety stores. They use a somewhat unique packaging system—selling via fly-top displays of 12 spoons.

Parsons-Steiner. This firm is located in Toronto. The quality of the product is low. Retail prices range from $1.99 to $5.98. Spoons tend to be picture spoons, and the least-expensive ones appear to be made of cast iron with a decal attached.

Boma. This company is located in Vancouver, British Columbia. The quality is very good. Spoons are made out of pewter with designs of such things as totem poles. Retail prices range from $10 to $20.

Aalco Souvenirs. Located in Vancouver, this company carries over 300 "three-dimensional" models of spoons. They are made in Canada and are nickel plated with a white gold flash. Aalco's products are distributed across Canada. They also carry other souvenir items such as bells, bottle openers, key chains, lapel pins and charms. Prices for spoons range from $2.50 to $3.00 each.

Souvenir Canada. Located in Downsview, Ontario, and operating throughout Canada and the United States, this company carries spoons with plastic decals, key chains, bottle openers, bells, lapel pins, mugs, plates, glasses, clothing and special promotional items. They have been in business for about 10 years and use standardized spoons with crests attached. Retail price per spoon is $3.00.

Canadian Casting Company Limited

In July 1980 Peter Johnston, 45, president of the Canadian Casting Company Limited (CCC), Ancaster, Ontario, was deeply involved with a review of his current operations and plans for expanding the company's facilities and personnel. CCC had grown rapidly in the four years since he had taken it over, for the second time, so that now all aspects seemed to be "bursting at the seams."

Canadian Casting Company, as its name implies, was engaged in the casting of a wide variety of intricate parts, requiring a high degree of precision and quality for an equally diverse number of industries. Johnston regained control of the company in 1976. Sales for the fiscal year ending on March 31, 1980, had risen to over $2.8 million with a net profit of approximately $334,000. (See Tables 1 to 4.)

THE CASTING PROCESS

Investment casting, the process utilized by CCC, was also known as the "lost-wax" process or "precision" casting. The concept was said to have been developed initially in China some 4,000 to 5,000 years ago, and trade literature described it thus:

> The term *investment* refers to a cloak, or special covering, in this case, a refractory mold, surrounding a refractory-covered wax pattern. In this process, a wax pattern must be made for every casting and gating system; that is, the pattern is expendable.

A number of variants of the process existed, but they had the following points in common: (See the appendix for further explanation.)

- Disposable or expendable patterns are used.
- Molding is done with a fluid aggregate or slurry.
- The aggregate is hardened in contact with the pattern, providing precise reproduction of the pattern.
- The aggregate is bonded with an inorganic ceramic binder.
- The mold is heated to drive off all wax.
- Pouring is performed with the mold preheated to a controlled temperature in order to pour thin sections that would not otherwise fill out.

This case was prepared by Professor W. H. Ellis of McGill University. All names have been disguised. Copyright © 1981 by W. H. Ellis. Edited by Mark C. Baetz, 1986.

COMPANY BACKGROUND

Following his graduation as an electrical engineer from a well-known Canadian university, Johnston joined a large firm specializing in electronics. "Electronics were my life at the time," remarked Johnston, who added that having seen a radio at an earlier age, "by the time I was 11, I started working night and day studying it." By 1971 Johnston had risen to the position of chief engineer of the company's communications division. Johnston described his situation as follows:

> At that point, I had studied on my own, had my engineering degree, and had worked on electronics all my life. Having achieved the position of chief engineer, I said, "Where do I go from here at the age of 36?" My main goal all through life was to do some kind of innovation, to do experiments, and if I wanted to do that in the future, I had to have a foundation that I could control, that I could utilize, like having the people, the facilities, and the resources. I said, "This is where my electronics career ends. There isn't much further I can go in this company."

The electronics firm had a division that made investment castings but had been operating at a loss of about $250,000 annually for five or six years. The company had decided to cease the casting operation and to dispose of it. Johnston described subsequent events as follows: "Just at that time, I started thinking of my own career. I had heard about the investment casting plant, so I thought I would take a chance on it and subsequently made arrangements for its purchase in November 1971."

PRODUCTION

Coming from an electronics background, investment casting was indeed a "foreign field" to Johnston. However, with an engineering degree and a desire to innovate, Johnston "went in there and worked on the process, first in department number one, then number two and so on until I understood the whole process. I did everything in the whole plant."

CCC faced a difficult introductory period of approximately eight months with "no orders and seven people to pay." Finally, after approximately eight months of calling on former customers, orders started to come in. By August 1972, some 10 months after taking over CCC from the electronics parent, Johnston had received "so many orders, I didn't know what to do with them—about $300,000 worth without the money to produce them." The situation was alleviated somewhat when orders and production increased rapidly. By mid-1975 CCC purchased a machine shop and machined castings and custom-produced parts for aircraft. By that time, there were 85 employees.

In discussing the production process, Johnston stated that precision investment casting has been around for 4,000 or 5,000 years but had not been controlled until recently by scientific means:

> Having been in the electronics business, being used to the progress in technology, I may be able to push more than other people in the industry. I am going to find a better

way of doing it. So this is one of the reasons CCC is keeping ahead of others in production. We would like to mechanize the processes a bit more and obtain more consistency.

Pursuing production and his product philosophy further, it was Johnston's view that the day of simple products was gone and it was necessary to go with high technology products. For example, he argued:

> If you go out and make a pair of shoes for people, which everybody can do, then the chance of survival is very, very small. Besides, there are developing countries that can take over at any time they want to. Look at textiles; there is no way that you can compete. Within the Western Hemisphere, we have to stay with high technology to be able to survive and be profitable. The first thing you should say when you look at a product is "Can we survive with it?"

To emphasize this point further, Johnston added that he looked at precision casting products and believed there was a definite market for them. "I can survive knowing that this kind of process cannot be replaced in the near future. There are no replacements, even now, and I don't see any in the immediate future. Therefore, there is an excellent chance for CCC."

FINANCING

"Of course, I didn't have the money in 1971 to buy the investment castings operation," remarked Johnston in talking about the financial aspects of CCC, "but I looked for a partner and found one in the person of Lester Greenfield. Together, with all my savings, we bought it with a very small amount of cash."

The initial financing of CCC consisted of $5,000 from Johnston's personal savings and an equal amount from Greenfield. With this pool of $10,000, they negotiated a price of $160,000 for the plant, the balance payable over a period of 10 years.

A $20,000 line of credit was negotiated with the banks but disappeared very quickly with no production underway. Even with orders to $300,000 and receivables at $60,000, the banking fraternity was reluctant to provide any additional backing. Finally, one bank agreed to give CCC 75 percent of the value of the accounts receivable on the basis of a personal guarantee to be equally signed by both Johnston and Greenfield. When Greenfield refused to sign, the bank's retort to Johnston was, "If your partner has no confidence, why should we lend you the money?"

Faced with this critical situation, Johnston's only recourse was to friends, who ultimately contributed a total of $120,000, all on the basis of Johnston's personal guarantee. With this backing, together with a continued growth in orders and accounts receivable, a commercial bank finally agreed to lend CCC up to the value of 60 percent of the receivables. However, increased orders created a corresponding demand for inventory, which in turn required more cash than Johnston had raised through personal loans and regular commercial banking facilities. The Federal Business Development Bank (FBDB), which had previously refused to provide funding, was approached again and this time, in mid-1975, saw the way clear to grant additional financing, with sales of the company reaching $1.2 million. In fact, by 1976 the FBDB approached Johnston to invest 30 percent, but Johnston said he was not interested.

A CHANGE OF OWNERSHIP

In early 1976 Greenfield concluded he would like to change his role from being a passive, silent partner to one of running CCC and said to Johnston, "Let me take over; you run the production part, and I will look after management."

Johnston pointed out that the business and customers were built upon a close relationship which required comprehensive technical knowledge beyond the pure casting technology. He commented to Greenfield, "To run a business like ours is not a matter of mass producing the components. Pure administration alone is not really the normal way of operating this business. For example, you can't sit down and do time studies; these are all jobbers—each part is different." Following further discussion, a meeting of the board of directors was held at which time Johnston was out-voted by the combination of Mr. and Mrs. Greenfield, both of whom were directors. Johnston was promptly told to step aside as president of the company.

The dialogue that ensued went along these lines: "Fine, I'm fired," said Johnston. "I am going to leave the company, but let's make a decision right now at this meeting. We are going to have a sell-out agreement set here and now. You have the option. You can buy me out or sell it to me, at whatever price you come up with. I don't care." Greenfield replied, "We'll have a buy-out agreement, and I will buy you out. I will give you $75,000 cash in 90 days, and I'll buy you out." Johnston answered, "Right! I'll take it, and I'll leave the company, but with one stipulation. I am free to do whatever I want to do."

The stipulation was received with something less than enthusiasm by Greenfield. A compromise was finally reached granting Johnston's decree but on the added condition that Johnston guarantee the $220,000 in loans outstanding at the time. Johnston believed that he had no choice.

Johnston commented on the situation that developed over the ensuing six months:

In a very short time, by the beginning of 1977, Greenfield and the company were in deep financial trouble. I found out why. Once I left, my partner didn't really know the processes and yet insisted on controlling everything. He took a stopwatch, went inside and started timing everybody, and insisted that everyone work faster. He insisted on it because he thought that if the current production methods could make so much money for the company, by pushing the workers a little bit more, he could increase the output correspondingly. Well, the operators disagreed. They disliked someone standing behind them and timing them. He didn't go through the foremen, the supervisors, or the production managers. He went directly down to the production level and said, "You can go faster than that." The workers replied, "Sure we can go faster, but it may not be good." "Do it anyway!" The workers did as they were told with the result that the rejection rate soared to 85 percent compared with the normal rate of 12 percent. Greenfield, himself, would put the castings in the box, even if they were of doubtful quality.

After about six months of this, Greenfield asked the accountant to contact me, to see if I would buy the company back. Following a third refusal, we agreed to terms and arranged a joint meeting with a lawyer and an accountant to complete the transaction.

On arriving at the meeting, Greenfield announced that he was not going to sell and turned around and walked out. By August 1977 the bank took over and liquidated the company.

In the six-month interval after leaving the company, Johnston had started to build up a related casting business. By the time the liquidation proceedings had been completed on CCC, Johnston's new operation was underway, serving different customers and markets. Now Johnston was able to merge the two functions and again took over CCC's complete facilities. When word of CCC's demise reached many long-standing customers, "They flocked to my office—from Florida, Hughes Aircraft in Tucson, Lockheed, Pratt and Whitney, Boeing—they all came in here. They sat here and said, 'Now, Peter, what are you going to do? We need castings!'"

It is the custom in the investment casting industry that the customer retains ownership of the tools required for the production of the specific products it orders. With the liquidation under Greenfield, customers had to obtain a release from the creditors in order to transfer the material to Johnston's new operation. Customers then came to Johnston saying, "Peter, we need the castings now. Can you get them fast?"

Johnston explained subsequent events as follows:

They sat here for weeks until we could get the process started again. We worked here day and night, trying to get things done. We had a hard time in that period because these big customers cannot stop their production. Often they might have as many as 5,000 people waiting on a production or assembly line for one small casting piece.

Companies like Boeing are so big and yet they couldn't do much about it. Whenever they can, they take a tool to somebody else in the States, but a lot of them cannot do this type of casting. We finally got it going. For four and a half years, I worked 16 hours a day, day in and day out, but we got the volume up to about $1.2 million in our first year.

MANAGEMENT PHILOSOPHY

In reflecting on his corporate experience to date, Johnston described some of his management philosophies in the following way:

I have found out one thing that perhaps management people haven't thought much about, and that is the internal atmosphere you try to generate in your company. This is all the responsibility of the president since nobody else can set it. If I want a certain atmosphere in the company, I'll make sure I set it up myself.

In Johnston's view, one of the most important ways that a certain atmosphere was set was in the way managers dealt with people. Johnston explained his approach to people as follows:

> In a small company, it is possible to know everybody and care about what they are doing. If I saw something not being done correctly, I would pick up the casting, call the individual aside, and say, "You can do better than that. I will show you how to do it." I would then demonstrate the correct procedure to the employee and repeat it until the employee attained perfection. They knew that I didn't crucify them. They were learning something. If you do enough of this, people will respect you and care about their work. Once a person makes a mistake, they know it. All I say is "That's a mistake, and now let's do it properly."

It was Johnston's philosophy never to "put a person down," and he insisted that all his managers followed a similar philosophy. Teamwork was also regarded highly. "People have to work together, and I insist on it in the company," he commented.

Although the managers in CCC had their titles and clearly defined responsibilities, this did not preclude Johnston from imparting to them, "Every job in the company is your job. If I am shorthanded in here, you come and help me; if you are shorthanded, then I go on the line. Every problem is yours. Once you have that atmosphere, the people know it is crucial that we have to work together as a team. More than that, they all know each other's job well enough that they can step in if anything happens."

Through the medium of regular formal and informal meetings, attempts were made to guarantee that this "teamwork atmosphere" prevailed and moved down the line to the direct labour, ensuring that they were happy with the company. This, in Johnston's view, avoided a lot of problems, including union problems. "You treat people like human beings. We make a point of never pushing people around. If one does 10 pieces a day and another does 2, we leave the latter alone, knowing that these are their individual speeds. We want it that way because in this business quality is everything, not the speed of production."

In addition to creating the team atmosphere, bonuses were awarded every six months, "depending on the whole company's performance, not the individual—the whole company's. At the end of every six months, I worked out the figures, sales against the number of employees, and determined what the bonus would be."

Johnston recognized that this was easy to do with 100 to 120 employees and expressed the opinion that some other criteria would have to be developed when CCC became substantially larger. At this point in time, "It works out fine, maybe one of the reasons being that all the people know and trust me."

As an illustration of the team atmosphere that was apparent in the early stages of the company's operation and continued throughout, Johnston recalled the production of the first castings. "Because customers were waiting for their orders, we had worked into the evening, and at 9:00 P.M., we poured the first casting. The production manager said, 'Fine, now let's stop and call it a day.' The men got cleaned up and walked into my office where I was still working, carrying two bottles of whiskey. I didn't know it, but they had had these bottles hiding inside for a week, waiting for this particular moment. We drank until midnight. So they do sort of care for the company."

A LOOK TO THE FUTURE

In keeping with his product philosophy, Johnston believed that there was virtually no end to the demand for CCC's investment precision castings. With expected improvements in technology, Johnston was forecasting nearly $6 million by 1983 and expected sales up to $30 million to $40 million a year before too many years passed by.

Part of the reason for Johnston's optimism for increased sales was the lack of competition. In Canada, a total of 10 companies were reported to be engaged in CCC's type of "lost-wax" process, compared to 235 in the United States. Johnston further assessed the competition in the following way:

> There aren't that many good companies who can produce premium quality products. So, really, the competition is not that great. For example, there are parts that we make now that can only be produced by six companies in the world, not just in North America.
>
> When you get that kind of technology, people will buy from you, and they push you to produce it. That is the kind of industry we are in and the kind of company we operate. But you have to keep up with recent developments. You have to have new ideas. You have to produce technology that other people don't have so that you are always in the forefront. If you stay in the top 10, you are O.K. In fact, I would like to stay in the first 2 if I can, but that takes time. It's not too bad though. After starting production again in 1977, we were able to get into the top 10.

In addition to the expansion of the casting part of the business, Johnston was considering that the next area of development might be machining. "Certain castings have to be machined before being used. Right now, the customer asks us to do it, but we don't have the means."

In looking to the future, Johnston was also concerned about the plant's physical location should continued expansion take place, particularly outside Canada. CCC sales were currently in the United States, the United Kingdom, Germany and France, with contacts in Hong Kong, Israel and Spain—"whoever deals in aeroplanes or electronic equipment."

Not the least of Johnston's concerns about the future growth of CCC was the role he should play. "I worry about that a lot. Although I have 10 management people under me running the company [see Exhibit 1], I have yet to find one who can run the whole show. Finding people is very difficult. I am looking for good people all the time. I'll be glad to take every day off and let somebody run the show for me."

Table 1. Canadian Casting Company Limited Balance Sheet at March 31.

	1980	1979	1978	1977 (5 Months Ending March 31)
Assets				
Current assets:				
Accounts receivable	$ 646,209	$406,205	$260,469	$11,654
Loans receivable	4,505	13,871	—	1,313
Inventories	760,997	383,595	228,643	39,740
Prepaid expenses	14,619	25,671	14,082	—
Rent deposit/subscriptions receivable	—	—	—	4,500
Total current assets	1,426,330	829,342	503,194	57,207
Fixed Assets	1,736,355	458,633	344,037	230,081
Other	5,186	7,527	9,869	13,469
Total assets	$3,167,851	$1,295,502	$857,100	$300,757
Liabilities				
Current liabilities:				
Bank indebtedness	$ 557,435	$ 254,539	$162,712	$ 87,735
Accounts payable and accrued charges	409,567	219,832	155,733	41,134
Income taxes payable	40,172	4,620	14,840	—
Long-term debt due within one year	81,692	61,130	21,250	6,250
Deferred income taxes	3,163	6,900	—	—
Total current liabilities	1,092,029	547,021	354,535	135,119
Long-term debt	1,225,221	316,792	284,152	159,560
Deferred income taxes	135,927	51,780	30,138	127
Total liabilities	2,453,177	915,593	668,825	294,806
Shareholders' Equity				
Capital stock	5,500	5,500	5,500	5,500
Retained earnings	709,174	374,409	182,775	451
Total shareholders' equity	714,674	379,909	188,275	5,951
Total liabilities and shareholders' equity	$3,167,851	$1,295,502	$857,100	$300,757

Table 2. Canadian Casting Company Limited Statement of Earnings and Retained Earnings for the years ended March 31.

	1980	1979	1978	1977 (5 Months Ending March 31)
Sales	$2,824,637	$1,980,304	$1,280,843	$11,668
Cost of goods sold (schedule) inventory, end of period	1,989,162	1,482,677	833,163	5,614
Gross profit	835,475	497,627	447,680	6,054
Expenses				
Advertising and sales promotion	25,997	16,151	16,075	683
Amortization—deferred expenses	2,342	2,342	3,600	220
Amortization—leasehold improvements	—	—	—	298
Automobile	15,294	11,597	13,427	—
Bad debts (recovery)	(1,453)	10,442	2,000	—
Commissions	88,142	59,973	25,026	—
Delivery and freight out	5,494	12,226	5,297	—
Depreciation—automobile	1,808	2,584	—	—
Depreciation—machinery and equipment	—	—	—	1,550
Depreciation—office furniture and equipment	2,987	2,243	1,342	75
Directors' fees	—	700	12,500	—
Donations	50	500	100	—
Dues and subscriptions	1,695	617	379	—
Equipment rental	—	—	10,362	—
Factory expense	—	—	—	175
Interest and bank charges	27,481	9,937	20,437	—
Interest on long-term debt	52,609	20,040	14,757	—
Loss on disposal of fixed asset	—	832	—	—
Management fees	2,890	3,175	39,652	—
Office salaries	113,002	74,076	21,845	—
Office supplies and postage	8,827	7,588	4,097	—
Professional fees	21,661	22,212	11,838	1,000
Rent	—	—	—	1,123
Sales discounts	11,278	10,704	6,472	—
Telephone	10,471	8,301	7,675	—
Travel	7,710	3,265	3,624	352
Total expenses	398,285	279,505	220,505	5,476
Earnings from operations	437,190	218,122	227,175	578
Other earnings				
Rental income	18,238	—	—	—
Earnings before income taxes	455,428	218,122	227,175	578
Income taxes	120,663	26,488	44,851	127
Net earnings	334,765	191,634	182,324	451
Retained earnings, beginning of year	374,409	182,775	451	—
Retained earnings, end of year	$709,174	$374,409	$182,775	$451

Table 3. Canadian Casting Company Limited Statement of Changes in Financial Position for the years ended March 31.

	1980	1979	1978	1977 (5 Months Ending March 31)
Source of working capital				
From operations:				
Net earnings	$ 334,765	$191,634	$182,324	$451
Items not requiring an outlay of working capital:				
Depreciation	134,238	61,318	42,056	1,625
Deferred income taxes	84,147	21,642	30,011	127
Amortization—deferred expenses	2,342	2,342	3,600	—
Amortization of leasehold improvements	—	—	—	298
Loss on disposal of fixed asset	—	832	—	—
	555,492	277,768	257,991	2,501
Increase in long-term debt	908,429	32,640	124,592	—
Issue of common shares	—	—	—	5,500
Loan payable—shareholder	—	—	—	115,810
Loan payable	—	—	—	43,750
Sale of fixed asset	—	1,285	—	—
	1,463,921	311,693	382,583	167,561
Use of working capital				
Additions to fixed assets	1,411,941	178,031	156,012	—
Purchase of fixed assets	—	—	—	232,004
Purchase of other assets	—	—	—	13,469
Increase in working capital	51,980	133,662	226,571	(77,912)
Working capital, beginning of year	282,321	148,659	(77,912)	—
Working capital, end of year	$ 334,301	$282,321	$148,659	$(77,912)
Represented by:				
Current assets	$1,426,330	$829,342	$503,194	$ 57,207
Current liabilities	1,092,029	547,021	354,535	135,119
Working capital	$ 334,301	$282,321	$148,659	$(77,912)

Table 4. Canadian Casting Company Limited Schedule for the years ended March 31.

	1980	1979	1978
Cost of goods sold			
Raw materials:			
Inventory, beginning of year	$232,105	$102,972	$ 25,598
Purchases	533,327	435,598	286,746
Freight and duty	15,132	19,197	7,954
	780,564	557,767	320,298
Inventory, end of year	481,544	232,105	102,972
	299,020	325,662	217,326
Direct costs:			
Direct labour	803,938	594,918	404,589
Payroll levies	85,345	57,923	37,016
Contract labour	62,691	49,074	16,210
Tools and dies	525,413	261,271	138,082
	1,477,387	963,186	595,897
Manufacturing expenses:			
Amortization—leasehold improvements	5,579	5,077	4,535
Amortization—jigs and fixtures	4,650	4,650	4,650
Depreciation—machinery and equipment	72,312	46,764	31,529
Depreciation—building	46,902	—	—
Electricity and heating	79,493	66,432	33,094
Insurance	4,042	8,989	1,338
Plant maintenance and repairs	22,933	20,011	2,998
Production costs	—	—	5,889
Rent	37,371	26,744	15,933
Shop supplies	45,270	23,753	13,474
Taxes	22,166	17,228	18,029
	340,718	219,648	131,469
	2,117,125	1,508,496	944,692
Work in process			
Inventory, beginning of year	118,411	113,875	14,142
	2,235,536	1,622,371	958,834
Inventory, end of year	227,428	118,411	113,875
Cost of goods manufactured	2,008,108	1,503,960	844,959
Finished goods			
Inventory, beginning of year	33,079	11,796	—
	2,041,187	1,515,756	844,959
Inventory, end of year	52,025	33,079	11,796
Cost of goods sold	$1,989,162	$1,482,677	$833,163

Exhibit 1. Organization chart (1980).

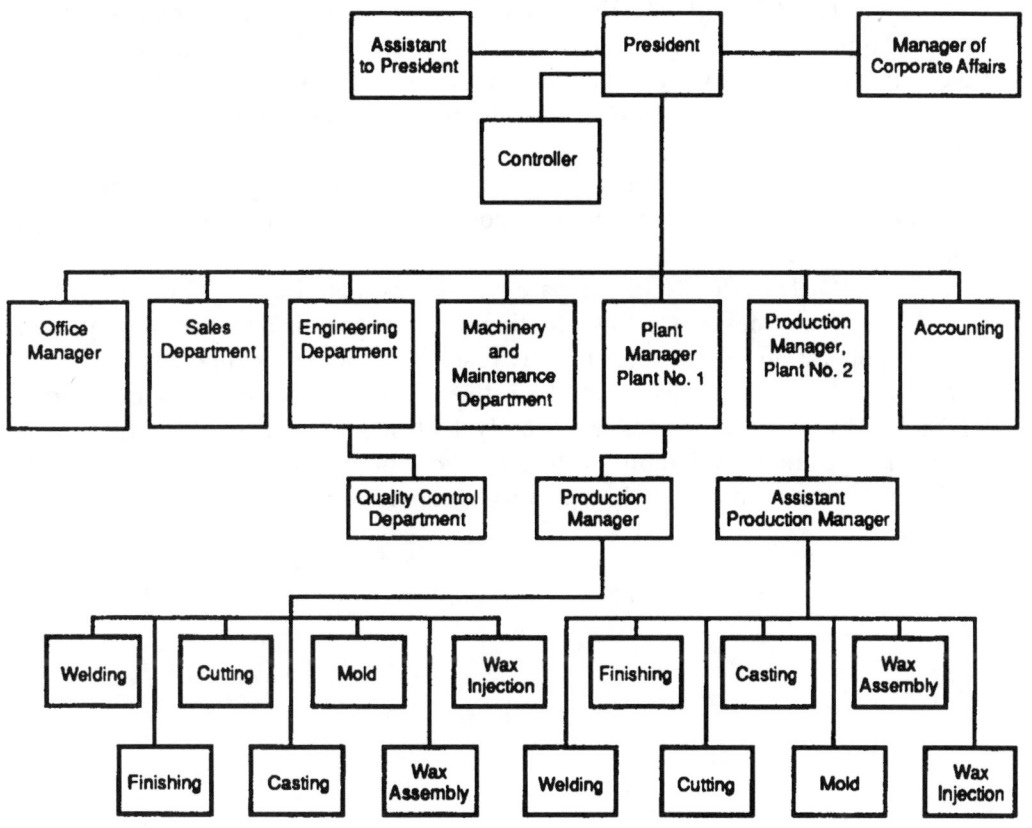

APPENDIX

With many years of experience in manufacturing precision investment castings, Canadian Casting Co. is able to meet the most demanding requirements, to transform designs into actual components and to meet tight delivery dates. The Foundry produces castings in ferrous and nonferrous castable alloys by the lost wax method of investment castings. This method produces castings of a high level of precision, complexity and quality and can save many costly machining operations.

Meticulous quality control and the most modern equipment ensure close conformity with drawings and specifications and a high degree of consistency between the individual castings. Careful selection of raw materials and the use of a well proven investment shell process in addition to our own process patents, produce castings of excellent definition, surface finish and metallurgical quality.

FACTS YOU SHOULD KNOW ABOUT CASTINGS

PRECISION INVESTMENT CASTINGS require one wax pattern for each casting to be made. For this a die (tooling) is required. This is followed by mold making, removal of the wax pattern from the mold cavity and, finally, filling of the mold cavity with metal. The casting is produced by breaking the mold apart and cutting it away from its gating arrangement.

SAND CASTINGS are less precise as a general rule, and require a great deal of machining so that the final component cost is high, usually with one additional disadvantage of lower quality.

PERMANENT MOLD CASTINGS compare with Investment Castings in quality. However, the process does not allow for the same precision and complexity. More machining operations are needed, usually resulting in a higher final cost.

DIE CASTINGS are mass-produced and Investment Castings normally cannot compete with them. However, die prices are usually 10 times greater, so that the price per casting may go up considerably on limited runs. In such cases, properly designed Investment Castings can offer a high quality product at a competitive, and even lower, price.

Investment Casting Process

How it works...

1. WAX INJECTION

2. WAX PATTERN REMOVAL

3. WAX ASSEMBLY

4. SLURRY DIP

5. SHELL MOLDING

6. DEWAX

7. PRE HEAT MOLD

8. POURING OF METAL

9. SHELL REMOVAL

10. GATE REMOVAL

11. CASTING

CASE 27

Marketing Direct Inc.

Upon his return to work on March 13, 1995, following a holiday in the south with his young family, Desmond Lacey, president and founder of Marketing Direct, is wondering how to go about implementing plans for a new company direction. He is concerned that slower sales over the past couple of years are an indication that the company is nearing market saturation with its current product line and that the days of company dependence on a single supplier are drawing to a close. In July 1994, another wholesale supplier had approached Lacey with the request that Marketing Direct consider becoming a distributor for Chateau Argent, one of Quebec's largest jewellery manufacturers. Following a three month test of the product from October through December of 1994 by the Montreal branch office, Lacey was convinced that the product was a good seller. The major difficulty that he noted during this trial period was that having salespeople market two very different products proved to negatively effect their motivation.

This test raises concerns for Lacey that product diversification may entail more than simply choosing the right supplier. Nevertheless, he must determine whether or not to incorporate this new product into a company that, for the past four years, has exclusively been marketing artwork framed and supplied by Columbia Frame & Images 2000 (Columbia). To date, the quality of both the prints of artwork by Renoir, Monet and other artists and the framing of these prints supplied by Columbia has been key to the success of Marketing Direct. If product diversification is now in order, a strategy must be devised to facilitate the addition of the new line.

As a young and progressive entrepreneur, Lacey is open to the potential benefits change might bring. He is reluctant, however, to do anything to disturb the winning formula of Marketing Direct's current company structure and de-motivate the sales force. Branch managers have voiced an increasing number of complaints that dissatisfaction with the incentive system is on the rise, and for Lacey, this raises concerns about future financial and management control. He feels that the recession in the Canadian economy has had little impact on sales activity for the company. As president and founder of Marketing Direct, Lacey wants to enhance profit potential with a strategic product mix that will carry company growth forward.

This case was prepared by D. Beamish, M.B.A., under the direction of Dr. A. B. Ibrahim, Professor of Management at Concordia University, Montreal, as a basis for class discussion, rather than to illustrate either effective or ineffective handling of an administrative situation. This case was supported by a research grant from IBM Corporation and the Certified General Accountants' Association of Canada (CGA). © Dr. A. B. Ibrahim, 1996.

COMPANY HISTORY

Shortly after graduating from Harvard Business School in 1990, Desmond Lacey moved to Montreal and founded his company, Marketing Direct Inc. With the help of a wealthy and enthusiastic silent partner and a solid partnership agreement with the supplier, Columbia Frame & Images 2000, Marketing Direct grew at breakneck speed. Just over four years later, the company boasts six branch offices located in Montreal, Toronto, Calgary, Vancouver, Tampa (Florida) and Houston (Texas). Each of these locations averages up to $1 million gross sales annually, marketing quality artwork directly to the general public at prices 60% below retail.

Despite the risk usually associated with dependence on a single supplier, Marketing Direct's relationship with Columbia is cemented in the knowledge that it has become the predominate distribution channel for the Quebec manufacturer. With monthly sales in each Marketing Direct branch office often topping 1,500 units, the direct marketing company has become a much more important channel for the manufacturer than Zellers, Club Price and The Bay combined. This is not to mention the access Marketing Direct provides its supplier to the American consumer. Due to the volume of sales by the Tampa branch office, for example, four nearby art stores were put out of business within the branch's first ten months of operation. That was, however, in 1992. Today, Lacey wishes to devise a strategy that will prevent his company from one day becoming an obsolete channel for the manufacturer.

The Quebec-based Columbia Frames & Images 2000 has grown to rely on a breadth of distribution from Marketing Direct that it cannot get from its other retail customers. Through word-of-mouth and a growing reputation, the success of this relationship between supplier and distributor has attracted the recent offer from Chateau Argent, a company that has its headquarters in the same industrial park as Marketing Direct. The jewellery manufacturer is willing to provide its product entirely on consignment to Marketing Direct in order to establish a relationship with the distributor similar to the one Columbia has enjoyed for the past four years.

This offer from Chateau Argent was unsolicited by Lacey. Prior to the offer, he had not been considering diversifying Marketing Direct's product line to include jewellery, but now that the opportunity has arisen, he is considering it. After all, he has been experimenting recently with new types of artwork (such as prints by modern artists and signed and numbered prints by contemporary artists), frames have replaced laminates, and product sizes are now larger. These changes have been in response to the changing tastes of consumers, as well as to the need to switch to a new product once market saturation is achieved. After three years of selling the small laminated black and white photo prints, for example, in a city the size of Montreal, there is very little remaining market potential for the product. Maintaining an effective product mix requires some research and a lot of input from the sales staff. The offer from Chateau Argent has Lacey wondering if he may be running out of artwork product/price variations that appeal to consumers.

Another key factor in the continued success of Marketing Direct is the people recruited, their training and the support they receive as they are promoted to running their own branch offices. The vulnerability of Marketing Direct to errors in assessing the capability of personnel became especially clear when, in 1992, the Tampa branch began losing money. Declining profits in the Tampa branch office at that time were directly related to the branch manager's poor performance.

The problem was addressed by dismissing the branch manager in question and sending a relief management team from Toronto to Florida for six months to stabilize the Tampa branch office. Early in 1993, the current branch manager, Stan Miller, was established there, and the Tampa branch was back on its feet earning profits as it had been prior to the trouble. Fortunately for Marketing Direct the problem was addressed expediently and effectively. Now more than ever, Lacey keeps his finger on the pulse of each of the branch offices, helping to ensure the company's continued success. As Marketing Direct continues to expand, however, he worries that his ability to do this may become increasingly diluted. Such worries are aggravated by the many complaints he has been receiving from branch managers about the difficulties they face motivating and maintaining their sales force. Their requests for new and better incentives to address their problems makes Lacey wonder if the Tampa incident is a foreshadowing of things to come.

INDUSTRY CHARACTERISTICS

The market for framed images and artwork is highly competitive, characterized by a large number of sellers, each of whom offers almost identical products. It is easy to enter and exit the industry, and market price is determined by competitive forces. Retailers include large department store chains such as Zellers and The Bay, a great number of small family-owned operations, and a few medium-size family-owned or partnership firms with five to ten locations within a single metropolitan area. Apart from the large chains, retailers tend to be locally based, with a concentration ratio of approximately three shops for every 100,000 people. Manufacturers and importers also tend to be numerous, with approximately two suppliers for each retail operation. In this industry, small to medium-size family-owned or partnership manufacturing operations tend to be supplying small to medium-size family-owned or partnership retailers. The larger of the manufacturers are able to secure contracts as suppliers to the retail chains, but within these relationships, bargaining power remains with the retailer. Following the retail boom of the eighties and with the onset of recessionary times, competition intensified, particularly for the manufacturers who faced ever increasing costs and price competition from importers.

In Montreal, most of the smaller privately-owned retail operators average well below $250,000 in net annual sales. Their medium-size counterparts are not considerably larger and net, on average, just over $300,000 annually. Together, these firms account for over 50% of annul industry sales, with the major department store chains accounting for the balance. Retailers tend to sell their products from a store-front outlet in which consumers can view a display of the various products they offer or custom-order frames for their artwork. There are few, if any, direct competitors to Marketing Direct in any of the centres in which it is presently located. However, competition in general is quite fierce. The turnover of retail operators tends to be relatively high, with the rate of failure increasing as recessionary effects in the Canadian economy deepen. Artwork is considered a luxury item and as such is one of the first items to be eliminated from the average consumer's list of expenditures in the face of dwindling purchasing power.

Regardless of their size, most manufacturers provide custom designs to meet retailers' needs. They may provide frames only for a private art gallery or a series of frames and prints for a frame and picture-print shop. In addition, manufacturers offer retailers standard designs of frames and frame-print combos with a choice of frame colours and sizes. It is with this standard line of product that manufacturers face the steepest price competition from import dealers. Because of the nature of the industry and the small size of most manufacturing operations, owners tend to be owner-operators involved in the hands-on details of filling custom design orders.

COMPANY STRUCTURE

The six Marketing Direct branch office managers were promoted through the ranks of the company from the direct marketing sales staff. Following training and experience in the field of direct marketing, managerial candidates moved on to train new sales staff. Potential management candidates eventually gained valuable management experience leading road trips in preparation for the opening of a branch office in their chosen location. Desmond Lacey is well aware that the success of Marketing Direct depends on the calibre of people hired, trained and retained in the management ranks of the company.

Marketing Direct, like many other direct marketing companies such as Avon or Amway follows a sales pyramid structure, with commissions and incentives built in to all levels of the organization. As president and founder, Lacey built up the Montreal branch office first. He began in 1990 by selling the artwork provided on consignment by Columbia directly to the consumer. On any given day, this involved choosing an area in the city and literally going out and selling from door to door. With samples of his product in tow, he would enter every commercial location within a five block radius, be it an office, restaurant, bar, fire station or school. His customers were the people who worked in these locations. He encouraged them to buy on impulse the quality artwork that he offered them at 50 to 60% off retail prices. Today, Lacey is no longer directly involved in selling, but the business of Marketing Direct remains the same, and every branch office manager starts out the same way as Lacey did.

Early on, the exponential profit growth experienced by Marketing Direct was proof enough to secure the involvement of Lacey's silent partner, who provided the capital required for expansion. In June 1991, Clara West opened the Toronto branch office of Marketing Direct. She did this following a market test in the area. This early market test took the form of a three-week road trip to the city in which she managed her team of sales people. The road trip has remained a management readiness test and continues to be used by the company as a training tool. Although branch managers rely on the company for branch start-up costs, each branch becomes an autonomous sales unit relatively quickly. Branch managers enjoy profit-sharing arrangement with Marketing Direct based on a 10 to 15% of gross sales. In addition, branch managers earn a $0.50 override fee on each unit sold by each member of their sales team, as well as a $1,000 bonus for every $100,000 of gross sales that may emerge from their sales team.

In 1992, three new branch offices were launched. Marketing Direct opened its first American operation in Tampa, Florida with an individual from Clara's sales team in Toronto. By January 1993, this individual was replaced by Stan Miller, a Tampa, Florida native recruited to the branch office sales team shortly after operations were established in 1992. Around the same time that the Tampa operations began, Yves Leblanc, a member of the Montreal sales team, became manager of the new Vancouver branch office. Near the end of that same year, Yves' leading assistant manager, Shelley Burns, opened a branch office in her former home town of Calgary.

Marketing Direct's most recent Houston branch office was opened in 1994 by another American from Stan's sales team. The Houston branch office manager, Susan Riley, is well known throughout the company for holding the undisputed title for a record month of sales as assistant manager. It is unusual for assistant managers to hold such a title since much of their effort is spent training and motivating new sales staff to eventually work in their own future branch office. Marketing Direct's organizational chart is presented in Exhibit 1.

MARKETING AND SALES

The direct marketing environment is not unlike the "wild west" of early American history. It is characterized by a wealth of opportunity for those brave sellers willing to go out and try to sell in the market as they find it. The enormous international success of companies such as Avon, Grolier and Amway is indicative of potential profit available by marketing directly to the consumer.

Although direct marketers compete on price, they offer the consumer comparable products. In fact, as is the case with Marketing Direct, consumers are often offered the same product available to them through retail outlets at a 50 to 80% price reduction. Due to the nature of the business and the resulting significantly lower overhead, direct marketing companies are able to enjoy a considerable proportion of profit from the 300 to 500% mark-up over cost of goods from the manufacturer.

A common theme among direct marketers is, "everybody wins." In their view, the consumer, the direct marketer and the manufacturer all win. A second common theme is, "take control of the sale." In the retail environment, the customer is said to be in control of the sale because of the physical relationship between buyer and seller. Within the context of a retail outlet, the customer is mobile and the seller stationary. For the direct marketer, control of the sale is gained through a reversal of the sales environment; the customer is stationary, and the seller is mobile. When combined with the law of averages, which holds that the greater the number of consumers solicited, the greater the number of actual sales, the potential advantage of the direct marketing strategy becomes obvious.

A key ingredient to the success of a direct marketing firm is the sales team. Therefore, issues such as training and turnover are critical. At Marketing Direct, sales people see up to one hundred customers a day and must deal with 90% rejection. Turnover for new employees is 75 to 85% in the first two weeks. This gives some indication of just how much of the direct marketing firm's efforts are spent recruiting, training and motivating sales people. At Marketing Direct, these issues are particularly pressing for the branch managers, who spend at least 40% of their time recruiting new salespeople. Many believe that much of their problems could be alleviated with a more attractive incentive system. Of equal importance to the successful direct marketing formula is a quality product that can be readily adapted to the rapidly changing tastes of consumers. It is the strength of the combination of these two elements on which a direct marketing firm pins its success.

Lacey bases company sales success on three key elements. These include what he calls "the ten steps to success," "the law of averages" and "the five steps to a sale." As outlined in Exhibit 5, the principles that make up these three elements underpin the training program for the company and are repeated daily in morning sales meetings. Newly hired staff are sent out on their own for their first two days with the company. They are then provided with a week of training with an assistant manager. After six weeks of successful sales, they are promoted to assistant manager. As assistant managers, individuals become potential candidates for branch manager and are expected to train, manage and motivate their trainees as well as continue to sell. After six months to a year of successfully fulfilling these responsibilities and leading at least one road trip as a test for branch manager readiness, assistant managers may be offered the opportunity, with complete financial support from Marketing Direct, to open a branch office in one of two locations of their choice.

FINANCES

Although over the past two years sales growth has started to level off, since it was founded in 1990, the company has enjoyed a solid record of strong financial growth. Financial risk has been kept to minimum despite rapid expansion. Marketing Direct's growth has been financed primarily through retained earnings and personal investments by Lacey and his silent partner, with next to no debt. A cash only policy directly complements the sales strategy of impulse buying and makes receivables a non-issue. Because of the congenial nature of the relationship with the supplier, the established terms for payment are easily renegotiated and altered to better suit Marketing Direct's changing needs. The company owns no land or buildings, and each of the branch offices is under lease. The bulk of inventory is kept in the individual sales representatives' vehicles, so weekly inventory checks are required at each branch to maintain inventory control system.

Financial and accounting matters for Marketing Direct are handled out of the Montreal head office by the company's controller, Sandra Groning, a CGA, and her permanent staff of two assistants. Following rapid company expansion in 1992, Lacey has been thinking about implementing a management information system to better address issues concerning the control of sales transactions and accounting activities for the company. Exhibits 2, 3 and 4 summarize the company's financial position.

LOOKING TO THE FUTURE

Moving into its fifth year of operation, Lacey feels that Marketing Direct is in a solid position to address key strategic issues. Questions of whether or not to diversify the company's product line and if so, how, are pressing. Heavy reliance on one supplier and a narrow product line could eventually bring sales growth to a standstill. Yet concerns of incorporating changes that would lead to further company growth without upsetting the existing balance within the company structure are at the forefront of Lacey's thoughts. Questions of how to better motivate and maintain the sales force seem always to be on the minds of Lacey's branch managers. Also, doubts about his ability to maintain management and financial control with the current systems have nagged Lacey ever since the Tampa branch incident. He hopes to address the most pressing of these issues by drawing up a written plan of action to be presented to his partner for approval within the next few weeks.

Exhibit 1. Marketing Direct Inc. Key Organizational Personnel—1995

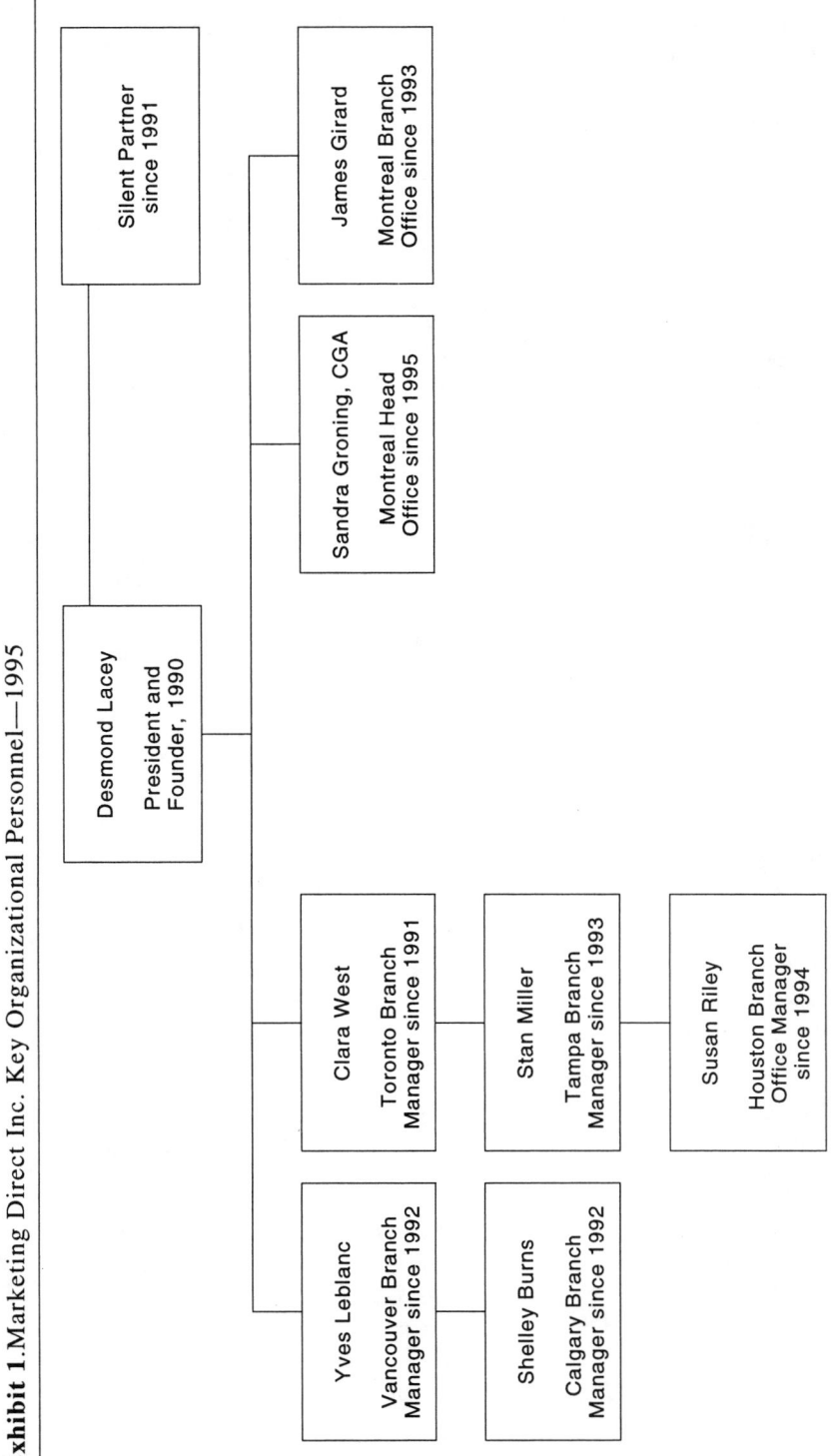

Exhibit 2. Marketing Direct Inc. Revenue & Gross Margin Percentages by Product Line 1991–1994 (in $000's).

	1991	1992	1993	1994
Laminates	836	2,948	1,032	—
% Total Revenue	100%	100%	26%	—
B&W's Small Size	290	1,133	540	—
% Total Revenue	34.7%	38.4%	13.6%	—
Gross Margin	79	340	221	—
% Gross Margin	27.2%	30%	41%	—
Classic's Standard Size	546	1,815	492	—
% Total Revenue	65.3%	61.6%	12.4%	—
Gross Margin	278	873	183	—
% Gross Margin	51%	48.1%	37.2%	—
Glass & Frame Prints	—	—	2,938	5,785
% Total Revenue	—	—	74%	100%
Classic Standard Size	—	—	1,429	665
% Total Revenue	—	—	36%	11.5%
Gross Margin	—	—	529	60
% Gross Margin	—	—	37%	9%
Modern Standard Size	—	—	1,509	2,036
% Total Revenue	—	—	38%	35.2%
Gross Margin	—	—	604	556
% Gross Margin	—	—	40%	27.3%
Foils Large Size	—	—	—	1,921
% Total Revenue	—	—	—	33.2%
Gross Margin	—	—	—	480
% Gross Margin	—	—	—	25%
Wildlife Stills Large Size	—	—	—	1,163
% Total Revenue	—	—	—	20.1%
Gross Margin	—	—	—	198
% Gross Margin	—	—	—	17%
Total Revenue	836	2,948	3,970	5,785
% Total Revenue	100%	100%	100%	100%
Gross Margin	357	1,213	1,537	1,294
% Gross Margin	42.7%	41.1%	38.7%	22.4%

Exhibit 3. Marketing Direct Inc. Income Statements years ending 1992–1994 (in 000's).

	1992	1993	1994
Sales	$2,948	$3,970	$5,785
Cost of sales and commissions	1,735	2,433	4,491
Gross margin and overrides	1,213	1,537	1,294
Administration	531	476	694
Loss on inventory	105	318	378
Amortization	22	21	25
Income before taxes	555	722	197
Income taxes	128	166	40
Net income	$ 427	$ 556	$ 157

Exhibit 4. Marketing Direct Inc. Balance Sheet 1992–1994 (in 000's).

Assets	1992	1993	1994
Current assets			
Cash	$270	$978	$1,056
Marketable securities	1,137	2,348	2,641
Inventory	308	1,236	1,715
	1,715	4,562	5,412
Capital assets			
Furniture and fixtures	181	181	223
Less: Accumulated amortization	(29)	(50)	(75)
Investments	1,489	3,809	3,225
	1,641	3,940	3,373
Total Assets	$3,356	$8,502	$8,785
Liabilities and Shareholders' Equity			
Current liabilities			
Accounts payable	578	1,545	2,414
Accrued expenses	215	1,517	1,233
	793	3,062	3,647
Long-term debt	163	1,236	1,052
	956	4,298	4,699
Share capital	2,322	4,121	4,034
Retained earnings	78	83	52
	2,400	4,204	4,086
Total Liabilities and Shareholders' Equity	$3,356	$8,502	$8,785

Exhibit 5. Marketing Direct Inc. Desmond Lacey's Three Key Elements To Sales Success.

Ten Steps to Success

1. Be on time.
2. Be prepared.
3. Have a positive attitude.
4. Take control of the sale.
5. Work a full eight hours.
6. Work your territory thoroughly.
7. Rehash.
8. Make five sales pitches after 5:00 p.m.
9. Show your clients your product, let them touch it.
10. Recruit your own sales team.

Law of Averages

Nine out of every ten people one attempts to sell to will not buy. Therefore, the more people you see in a day, the more you sell.

Five Steps to a Sale

1.	Introduction	• (3) seconds
		• Hello, listen.
		• Excuse me, but . . .
		• Remember to smile. Look people in the eye. Be enthusiastic.
2.	Story	• Don't complicate your story, be clear.
		• Go straight to the point, don't waste time.
3.	Demonstration	• Put the product in the client's hands.
		• Don't waste time with those who won't buy.
		• Emphasize that it is a good deal.
4.	Close	• (Get the money in your hands as quickly as possible.)
		• Key questions
		—Which do you prefer?
		—My employer allows discounts on large quantities.
		—Is this for you? Your office? A gift?
5.	Rehash	• Continue your story, try to schedule a return visit, keep the sale going until your client says NO!

REFERENCES

Barnes, L.B. and Hershen, S.A. "Transferring Power in the Family Business." *Harvard Business Review,* July–August 1976, pp. 105–114.

Birley, S. "The Role of Networking in the Entrepreneurial Process." *Journal of Business Venturing 1,* 1985, pp. 107–117.

Blau, P. M. and Schoenherr, R. A. *The Structure of Organizations.* New York: Basic Books, 1971.

Buchler, J. *Philosophical Writings of Peirce.* New York: Dover, 1955.

Burns, T. and Stalker, G. *The Management of Innovation.* London: Tavistock Publications Ltd., 1961.

Chaganti, R. "Small Business Strategies in Different Industry Growth Environments." *Journal of Small Business Management,* July 1987, pp. 52–59.

Charan, R., Hofer, C. and Mahon, J. "From Entrepreneurial to Professional Management: A Set of Guidelines," *Journal of Small Business Management,* Vol. 18, No. 1, 1980, pp. 1–10.

Churchill, N. and Lewis, V. "The Five Stages of Small Business Growth." *Harvard Business Review,* Vol. 61, No. 3, May–June 1983, pp. 30–50.

Clark, B., Davis, C. and Harnish, V. "Do Courses in Entrepreneurship Aid in New Venture Creation?" *Journal of Small Business Management,* Vol. 22, 1984, pp. 26–31.

Cooper, A., Gary, W and Woo, C. "Strategies of High Performing New and Small Firms: A Re-examination of the Niche Concept." *Journal of Business Venturing,* January 1986, pp. 247–260.

Crawford, R. and Ibrahim, A. B. "A Strategic Planning Model for Small Business." *Journal of Small Business and Entrepreneurship,* Vol. 3, No. 1, Summer 1985, pp. 45–52.

Davig, W "Business in Smaller Manufacturing Firms." *Journal of Small Business Management,* January 1986, pp. 39–47.

Dean, D., Mihalasky, J., Ostrander, S. and Schroeder, L. *Executive ESP.* Englewood Cliffs, N.J.: Prentice-Hall, 1974.

Drucker, P. F. *Management: Tasks, Responsibilities, Practices.* New York: Harper & Row Publishers, 1973.

Emery, E. and Trist, E. "The Casual Texture of Organizational Environment." *Human Relations,* Vol. 18, February 1965, pp. 21–32.

Feller, W. *An Introduction to Probability Theory and Its Applications.* 2nd ed. New York: Wiley, 1957.

Gatewood, R. and Field, H. S. "A Personal Selection Program for Small Business." *Journal of Small Business Management,* Vol, 25, No. 2, October 1987, pp. 16–24.

Greenfield, W. M. *Developing New Ventures.* New York: Harper & Row Publishers, 1989.

Henderson, B. D. "On Corporate Strategy." in R. B. Lamb. (ed.) *Competitive Strategic Management.* Englewood Cliffs, N.J.: Prentice-Hall, 1984, pp. 1–34.

Hisrich, R.D. and Peters, M. *Entrepreneurship: Starting, Developing and Managing a New Enterprise.* 3rd ed. Irwin, 1995.

Hofer, C. and Charan, R. "The Transition to Professional Management: Mission Impossible?" *The American Journal of Small Business,* Vol. IX, No. 1, Summer 1984, pp. 1–14.

Hofer, C. and Sandberg, W. "Improving New Venture Performance: Some Guidelines for Success." *American Journal of Small Business,* Vol. 12, No. 1, Summer 1987, pp. 11–25.

Hofer, C. W. and Schendel, D. *Strategy Formulation: Analytical Concepts.* St. Paul, MN: West Publishing, 1978.

Hornaday, J. and Aboud, J. "Characteristics of Successful Entrepreneurs." *Personnel Psychology,* Vol. 24, 1971, pp. 141–153.

Hughes, E. "Responding to Changes in Process Technology: Strategies for the Small Business." *Journal of Small Business Management,* January 1984, pp. 9–15.

Ibrahim, A. B. & Ellis, W. *Family Business Management: Concepts and Practice.* Iowa: Kendall/Hunt Publishing Company, 1994.

Ibrahim, A. B. "Is Franchising the Answer to Small Business Failure Rate? An Empirical Study." *Journal of Small Business and Entrepreneurship,* Vol. 3, No. 2, 1986, pp. 48–54.

Ibrahim, A. B. and Argheyd, K. *Strategic Management.* McGraw/Hill, 1992.

Ibrahim, A. B. "Strategy Formulation in Small Business: A Conceptual Framework." *Journal of Small Business and Entrepreneurship,* Vol. 9, No. 4, 1992.

Ibrahim, A. B. "Strategy Types and Small Firms' Performance: An Empirical Investigation." *Journal of Small Business Strategy,* Vol. 5, No. 1, 1993.

Ibrahim, A. B. "International Strategic Directions for Canadian Entrepreneurs." *Export Digest,* December 1988, pp. 3–4.

Ibrahim, A. B. and Ellis, W. H. "An Empirical Investigation of Causes of Failure in Small Business and Strategies to Reduce It." *Journal of Small Business and Entrepreneurship,* Vol. 4, No. 4, Spring 1987, pp. 18–24.

Ibrahim, A. B. and Goodwin, J. R. "Perceived Causes of Success in Small Business." *American Journal of Small Business,* Vol. 11, No. 2, 1986, pp. 41–50.

Ibrahim, A. B. and Kelly, J. "Leadership Style at the Policy Level." *Journal of General Management,* Vol. 11, No. 3, Spring 1986, pp. 36–45.

Kao, R. *Entrepreneurship and Enterprise Development.* Toronto: Holt, Rinehart and Winston of Canada Limited, 1989.

Katz, D. and Kahn, R. L. *Social Psychology of Organizations.* 2nd ed. New York: Wiley, 1978.

Kaynak, E., Ghauri, P. and Olofsson-Bredenlöw, T. "Export Behavior of Small Swedish Firms." *Journal of Small Business Management,* April 1987, pp. 26–32.

Kelly, J. *Organizational Behavior: Its Data, First Principles and Applications.* 3rd ed. Homewood, Illinois, Richard D. Irwin, Inc., 1980.

Kelly, J. and Ibrahim, A. B. "A Critique of Executive Behavior—Its Facts, Fictions, Paradigms." *Business Horizons,* January–February, 1991.

Kerlinger, F. *Foundation of Behavioral Research.* Holt, Rinehart and Winston, Inc., 1973.

Kets de Vries, M. "The Entrepreneurial Personality: A Person at the Cross Roads." *Journal of Management Studies,* Vol. XIV, 1977, pp. 34–57.

Kotler, P. *Marketing.* Englewood Cliffs, N.J.: Prentice-Hall Inc., 1987.

Kourilsky, M. "The Kinder-Economy: A Case Study of Kindergarten Pupils Acquisition of Economic Concepts." *The Elementary School Journal,* Vol. 3, 1977, pp. 39–50.

Kroeger, C. V. "Managerial Development in Small Firms." *California Management Review,* Vol. 17, No. 1, 1976, pp. 41–47.

Kuhn, T. S. *The Structure of Scientific Revolutions.* Chicago: The University of Chicago Press, 1970.

Lawrence, P. and Lorsch, J. *Organization and Environment: Managing Differentiation and Integration.* Boston: Harvard Business School, Division of Research, 1967.

Legnic-Hall, C. "Innovation and Competitive Advantage: What We Know and What We Need to Learn." *Journal of Management,* Vol. 18, 1992, pp. 399–427.

Levitt, T. "Marketing Success Through Differentiation of Anything." *Harvard Business Review,* February 1980.

MacMillan, I. C. "Criteria Used by Venture Capitalists to Evaluate New Venture Proposals." *Journal of Business Venturing,* Vol. 1, 1985, pp. 119–128.

McClelland, D. "Characteristics of Successful Entrepreneurs." *The Journal of Creative Behavior,* Vol. 21, No. 3, 1987, pp. 219–233.

Miles, R. and Snow, C. *Organizational Structure and Process.* New York: McGraw-Hill, 1978.

Miner, J. B. *Theories of Organizational Structure and Process.* New York: CBS College Publishing, 1982.

Mintzberg, H. *Structuring of Organizations.* Englewood Cliffs, N.J.: Prentice-Hall, 1979.

Mintzberg, H. "Structure in 5's: A Synthesis of the Research on Organization Design." *Management Science,* March 1980.

Mintzberg, H. and Waters, J. "Tracking Strategy in an Entrepreneurial Firm." *Academy of Management Journal,* Vol. 25, No. 3, 1982, pp. 465–499.

Mitroff, I. and Mason, R. "Business Policy and Metaphysics: Some Philosophical Considerations." *Academy of Management Review,* July 1982.

Montagne, R. V., Kuratko, D. F. and Scarcella, J. H. "Perception of Entrepreneurial Success Characteristics." *American Journal of Small Business,* Winter 1986, pp. 25–32.

Namiki, N. "Export Strategy for Small Business." *Journal of Small Business Management,* April 1988, pp. 32–37.

Peterson, R. *Encouraging Entrepreneurship Internationally,* Dubuque, Iowa: Kendall/Hunt Publishing Company, 1988.

Peterson, R. and Ainslie, K. *Understanding Entrepreneurship.* Dubuque, Iowa: Kendall/Hunt Publishing Company, 1988.

Pinchot 3rd, G. *Intrapreneuring.* New York: Harper & Row, 1985.

Porter, M. E. "How Competitive Forces Shape Strategy." *Harvard Business Review,* Vol. 57, No. 2, March–April 1979, pp. 141–147.

Porter, M. E. *Competitive Strategy: Techniques for Analyzing Industries and Competitors.* New York: Free Press, 1980.

Porter, M. E. "From Competitive Advantage to Corporate Strategy." *Harvard Business Review,* May–June 1989, pp. 43–59.

Prahalad, C. and Hamel, G. "The Core Competence of the Corporation," *Harvard Business Review,* May–June 1990, pp. 79–91.

Pratt, S. E. *Guide to Venture Capital Sources.* 6th ed. Prentice-Hall, 1982.

Rich, S. R. and Gumpert, D. E. "How to Write a Winning Business Plan." *Harvard Business Review,* May–June 1985, pp. 156–166.

Rugman, A. and Verbeke, A. "Does Competitive Strategy Work for Small Business?" *Journal of Small Business and Entrepreneurship,* Vol. 5, No. 3, 1988, pp. 45–49.

Rumelt, R. "Evaluation of Strategy: Theory and Models," in Dan Schendel and Charles Hofer (ed.). *Strategic Management: A New View of Business Policy and Planning.* Boston: Little Brown, 1979.

Ryans, C. C. *Managing the Small Business.* Englewood Cliffs, N.J.: Prentice-Hall, 1989.

Said, K. and Hughey, K. "Managerial Problems of the Small Firm." *Journal of Small Business Management,* January 1977, pp. 37–43.

Sandberg, W. and Hofer, C. "Improving New Venture Performance: The Role of Strategy, Industry Structure and the Entrepreneur." *Journal of Business Venturing,* May 1987, pp. 5–28.

Scarborough, N. and Zimmerer, T. *Effective Small Business Management.* 2nd ed. Ohio: Merrill Publishing Co., 1988.

Scheré, J. "Tolerance of Ambiguity as a Discriminating Variable Between Entrepreneurs and Managers." *Academy of Management Proceedings, 1982.*

Seely, R. and Iglarsh, H. "International Marketing in the Context of the Small Business." *American Journal of Small Business,* Vol. VI, October–December 1981, pp. 33–37.

Sexton, D. L. and Bowman, N. "Determining Entrepreneurial Potential of Students: Comparative Psychological Characteristics Analysis." *Academy of Management Proceedings, Dallas,* 1983, pp. 408–412.

Sexton, D. and Van Auken, P. "Prevalence of Strategic Planning in Small Business." *Journal of Small Business Management,* 20, 1982, pp. 20–26.

Stancill, J. M. "LBOS for Smaller Companies." *Harvard Business Review,* January–February 1988, pp. 18–44.

Stevenson, H., Roberts, M. and Grousbeck, H. *New Business Ventures and the Entrepreneur.* 3rd ed. Homewood, IL: Irwin, 1989.

Stevenson, H. H. and Gumpert, D. E. "The Heart of Entrepreneurship." *Harvard Business Review,* March–April 1985, pp. 85–94.

Stoner, C. R. "Distinctive Competence and Competitive Advantage." *Journal of Small Business Management,* April 1987, pp. 33–39.

Vesper, K. *New Venture Strategies.* Englewood Cliffs, N.J.: Prentice-Hall, 1990.

Watkin, D. "Toward a Competitive Advantage: A Focus Strategy for Small Retailers." *Journal of Small Business Management,* January 1986, pp. 9–15.

Woodward, H. N. "Management Strategies for Small Companies," in David Gumpert (ed.). *Growing Concerns—Building and Managing the Smaller Business.* Harvard Business Review Executive Book Series. John Wiley & Sons, 1984, pp. 131–141.

Woodward, J. *Industrial Organization: Theory and Practice.* London: Oxford University Press, 1965.

NAME INDEX

SUBJECT INDEX